A Guide to the Major Trusts

1999/2000 Edition

Volume 1
The Top 300 Trusts

Luke FitzHerbert
Dominic Addison
and
Faisel Rahman

DIRECTORY OF SOCIAL CHANGE

A GUIDE TO THE MAJOR TRUSTS
Volume 1 © 1999
1999/2000 Edition

Luke FitzHerbert, Dominic Addison and Faisel Rahman
with additional material on the Sainsbury Family
Charitable Trusts by Susan Forrester

Published by
The Directory of Social Change
24 Stephenson Way
London NW1 2DP
Tel: 0171 209 5151, fax: 0171 209 5049
e-mail: info@d-s-c.demon.co.uk
from whom further copies and a full publications list are available.

The Directory of Social Change is a Registered Charity no. 800517

First published 1986
Second edition 1989
Third edition 1991
Fourth edition 1993
Fifth edition 1995
Sixth edition 1997
Seventh edition 1999

Copyright © The Directory of Social Change 1999

British Library Cataloguing in Publication Data

A catalogue record for this book is available from the British Library

Cover design by Kate Bass
Designed and typeset by Midlands Book Typesetting Company
Printed and bound by Page Bros. Norwich

Other Directory of Social Change departments in London:

Courses and Conferences tel: 0171 209 4949
Charity Centre tel: 0171 209 1015
Charityfair tel: 0171 209 1015
Research tel: 0171 209 4422

Directory of Social Change Northern Office:

3rd Floor, Federation House, Hope Street, Liverpool L1 9BW
Courses and Conferences tel: 0151 708 0117
Research tel: 0151 708 0136

Contents

Introduction

This, the seventh edition of the Guide to the Major Trusts, has been one of the most interesting to write and edit. This was, first, because of the SORP, the new regulations for charity reports and accounts, (described, insofar as they are special to grant making charities, in the box on page 8 below). Many trusts are now publishing more and better information about their work. For example, for the first time we are able to offer readers a comprehensive account of the remarkably extensive and interesting grants made by the fourteen large foundations of the Sainsbury family. Secondly, trusts have begun experimenting with new grant making approaches and techniques. Thirdly, there are signs of rising concern about the geographical unfairness of much trust funding – London and the South East getting most of the money and everywhere else going without a reasonable share.

New funding approaches

The last two years have seen developments in funding approaches beyond the now conventional 'three year' project funding that has become a straitjacket (not long ago, it was a daring advance). The 'core funding' approach of the Baring Foundation, the tightly targeted work of the Karten Charitable Trust, the dramatically different approach of the Lloyds/TSB Foundation for Scotland, the competitive bidding element of the work of the Cleveland Community Foundation or the 'special funding programmes' of the City Parochial Foundation are examples of this.

The Sainsbury Family Charitable Trusts

One result of the SORP is that full (and often overdue) information is now available for this amazing group of trusts. Not only do they approve nearly £60 million in grants a year, the way in which they do so is impressively different to that of almost all the other foundations described in this book; and the collective input from so many members of one family is unprecedented. The research for this book has been carried out by Susan Forrester who has taken a particular interest in this subject. Besides an entry for each individual trust, there is an entry for the group as a whole under the title 'The Sainsbury Family Charitable Trusts'.

Geographical fairness

For many years edition after edition of this book has complained about the unfairness of the distribution of grants from many so-called 'national' trusts. Time after time, we have found a hugely disproportionate amount of the money being spent in London and the Home Counties (and that is after excluding London-based national charities). Some progress is being made. Henry Smith's Charity, for example, a major target in this respect, has managed to get part of the way towards a proper distribution. However the big influence for improvement has been the National Lottery Charities Board. It set fixed regional budgets based on population and weighted for measured disadvantage (and within regions, it seeks to achieve the same). Its exact example has already been followed by the mighty Lloyds/TSB Foundation for England and Wales (which will probably be giving away £30 million a year during the currency of this book).

Many more trusts are now reporting their geographical distribution, which is at least a recognition of the issue. However few have realised the necessity of expressing this not as regional totals but as values per head, as the population of the regions varies greatly. Trusts not having the figures to hand can contact this editor. In some cases we have done those calculations ourselves and printed the result in the entry concerned.

Overall, there will be a big step forward during 1999 when the Association of Charitable Foundations will be publishing the first full analysis of where trust funding actually goes. This will give proper support to what has only been superficially apparent up till now.

Which Trusts are in this Guide?

Three hundred of the top grant-making trusts in the UK that have grant making capacity of at least £250,000 are described. Smaller trusts will be found in the companion A Guide to Major Trusts, Volume 2, or in the DSC's regional trust guides. All can be found together in the DSC's CD-ROM Trusts Guide.

Not included are

- Company charitable trusts, dependant on annual allocations from, and operated by, the company. For full details see The Guide to UK Company Giving, also published by the Directory of Social Change.

- 'Single issue' grant makers ie, those which support one clearly defined and limited cause, such as Help the Hospices or the Mental Health Foundation;

- Trusts which only fund overseas activities (see The Third World Directory, also published by DSC);

- Grant makers funded from the public purse (even though they may have charitable status). Examples include the Arts Councils and regional arts boards, English Heritage and the Countryside Commission, or Community Relations Councils. However information about the National Lottery Charities Board has been included as an exception.

The tax blow to trust funding

The removal of Advance Corporation Tax credit from these charities will mean that, over the next few years, the income and therefore the grant making capacity of these trusts will be between 10% and 20% lower than would otherwise have been the case – a probable loss to charities of something over £100 million a year. It is a pity that the trust sector did not enjoy enough public recognition and respect to make such an attack politically difficult.

Accounting for trust activities

Nearly a third of the trusts described in this book ignored their obligation to supply copies of their Reports and Accounts on request. Some attempted to extract an exorbitant charge for this of up to £60. Less than a quarter are meeting the full requirements of the SORP (as set out in the box on page 8). Many provide no information about their policies to potential applicants, complaining the while about the number of applications that they receive as a consequence. Some still believe that by saying they will 'consider all applications on their merits' they escape the need to explain where they consider merit to lie.

The influence of the National Lottery Charities Board

Many of the developments reprinted in this book are influenced by the work of the National Lottery Charities Board (which has a brief entry itself). The NLCB's £300 million a year of grants, about £200 million of it for two or three year 'projects', has encouraged other trusts to look at alternatives to this form of funding. Its publicly announced regional budgets, based on a combination of population and need, set a precedent for fair grant making that it is hard for other 'national' funders to ignore.

Contact with applicant charities

Many charities have long felt that the best value for trust grants was obtained by those that accompanied their grants with a high level of personal interest and support. We were impressed to see the Tudor Trust reporting over 450 face to face meetings by trustees and staff with potential or actual applicants; we saw efforts in the same direction reported by the Lloyds/TSB Foundations and we noted with the pleasure the decision of the Esmée Fairbairn Foundation to increase the resources dedicated to establishing personal contact with more of the organisations that it funds. There are more trusts, like Lankelly, that meet with all applicants whose requests are being seriously considered.

Can charity accounts be copyright?

As this book was going to press, we were informed by a well known firm of solicitors, Farrers, that they had copyrighted the accounts of one of their clients described in this book, the Mulberry Trust, and that it would therefore be illegal for us to reproduce material from them. Farrers also said that this procedure has the agreement of the Charity Commission.

How to use this guide

The trusts are listed alphabetically.

At the front of the book a list of trusts ranked by funding size also gives their main areas of interest. We recommend new fund raisers start with this listing and tick those boxes which *might* be relevant to you – starting with the biggest.

When you have ticked enough to be getting on with, read each of these entries carefully before deciding to apply. Very often their interest in your field will be limited and precise, and may demand an application specifically tailored to their requirements – or, indeed, no application at all.

Remember to cover all parts of the guide, do not just do A to K. It is surprising but true that trusts near the end of the alphabet receive fewer applications.

It is particularly important to show awareness of all available information, to acquire up to date guidelines where possible, and to target your applications with respect to the needs of the each trust. Inappropriate and ill-considered approaches, especially those that show that you have not read their published guidelines, antagonise trusts and damage your organisation's reputation.

This edition includes a chart to help with your applications. It shows, for some 130 trusts, the months when trustee meetings are held, and when applications need to be submitted.

For those new to raising money from trusts, the box herewith containing advice from the Association of Charitable Foundations is strongly recommended as a starting point.

Classification

In Volume 2 of this book we will provide a summary 'subject' and 'geographical' classification (and this is also available on the DSC's CD-ROM Trusts Guide).

However most trusts in this book do not have clear policies that they adhere to with any rigidity. Those policies that do exist may be of quite different kinds. A trust may seek out projects which help children in need; or ones that have low overhead costs; or ones that are imaginative, and so on almost indefinitely.

Classifications can only list like with like and in the case of trust policies this is often impossible.

Serious applicants, we believe, do best if they go to the most promising entries in this book and try to establish links between what the trust seems to be interested in and what their organisation is trying to do. If we could find a way of reducing it to a mechanical process we would, but we can't. Trusts want partners in whose work they too can take both pride and satisfaction. This is usually a personal rather than technical process, particularly if there is a substantial sum of money involved.

Notes on the entries

Total grant-aid and financial year

The most up to date available information is given. In a few cases the financial information in the main text is for preceding year/s. This is the result of 'last minute' amendments by the trust unaccompanied by additional information, or too late for inclusion.

The main areas of funding

These categories have been chosen by the editors from an analysis of the trusts' funding. They are indicative rather than definitive, and useful in a preliminary trawl through the guide. They are no substitute to a close reading of each entry.

The correspondent

The lead person nominated by the trust. (Often they are solicitors or accountants handling trust affairs). Other useful administrative contacts may also be given under the 'Applications' or within the main body of text.

Beneficial area

The area/s within which the trust is permitted to fund are given. When a trust with a UK- wide remit shows an interest in a particular locality this is noted. Whilst this information usually comes from the trust itself, it may also arise from a pattern of grant making seen by the editors.

Information available

Published reports, application guidelines or other leaflets available directly from the trust are noted.

The basic information source about a trust is its annual report and accounts. These should be available from the trust, but often they are not. A copy should always be on the public file at the Charity Commission. We give the dates for the most recent accounts available at the time of our research, and note the extent to which they meet the requirements laid down.

The main body of the entry

A summary usually prefaces the text.

Trusts' policy notes and applicant guidelines, where these exist, are normally reprinted in full.

More trusts now analyse their own funding in their annual reports and this material also will usually be quoted in full. For the majority, though, any analysis has been carried out by the editors based on grant lists accompanying the accounts.

Where appropriate, there may also be independent comment by the editors on aspects of the work of the trust being described.

Exclusions and Applications

These reproduce, where possible, the trusts' own information or comments.

Comment and criticism

This book continues to be both a guide for potential applicants and also an independent and sometimes critical commentary on the work of these charities. Our comments anger some trusts, not usually on the grounds that they are inaccurate, but because we are felt to be interfering in private business. We disagree, on the grounds that charitable trusts are registered charities and, as such are public institutions, not private ones. And because of the sheer size of the trust sector, their activities concern everyone with an interest in the voluntary sector as a whole.

Some trusts seem to believe that just because a course of action (such as the payment of trustees, where this is allowed by the trust deed) is legal it is therefore also beyond criticism. For the record, we have come across nothing that would lead us to call the police. However there is quite a lot which we believe calls for the attention of the Charity Commission in its role as the promoter of good practice.

Failing to supply accounts on request

All charities are required to supply on request a copy of their most recent accounts (though they may make a reasonable charge for the copying and postage costs). We wrote, with a reply paid envelope, to almost 350 trusts in the Spring of 1998 asking for this. The following are just some of the more than 100 from whom they were not forthcoming:

The Eranda (Rothschild) Foundation
The Gosling Foundation
The Djanogly Foundation
The Wolfson Family Charitable Trust
The Kalms Foundation
The Jacob Rothschild Charitable Trust
The Beaverbrook Foundation

Do trusts earn their tax reliefs?

Looking at the trust sector as a whole, we think it fair to ask whether the charitable trusts described in this book justify the large tax reliefs they receive (and which have to be paid for by the tax-paying public)?

We believe that most of them do, including, perhaps, all of the very large ones. Some are deeply impressive organisations whose work it has been a privilege to describe. However there are plenty of others whose activities, as described by themselves, create less confidence that they are earning the public support that they get.

The following, from the entry for the Dunhill Medical Foundation, is exceptional:

'The administration of the trust, as described in its annual report for 1996/97, is startling. Among other things, the Senior Trustee is paid over £100,000 to act as the Administrator of the trust, two thirds of the high investment management fees are paid to a company of which another trustee is a Director, and the total cost of administration is £6,000 for each new grant or fellowship awarded.'

Readers, however, will come across other cases where we note high and unexplained administrative costs; levels of payment for investment advice that seem quite out of line; the payment of trustees for unexplained reasons and sometimes at very high levels; cases where substantial sums are paid to 'connected persons' for services rendered, without any explanation of why this is necessary.

Good trust reports

While the most striking result of the introduction of the SORP requirements, spelt out in the box herewith, has been to highlight the delinquents that have failed to meet its stipulations, it has also led to more positive results. This book now contains numerous examples of excellent reports from a far larger number of trusts than ever before. Apart from longstanding examples of excellence, such as the Gulbenkian Foundation or the Milly Apthorp Trusts, interesting reports are reprinted in the entries, among others, for the following (some of which may surprise and please readers of earlier editions of this book):

The Lord Ashdown Charitable Trust
The Wates Foundation
The Eveson Foundation

The Barnwood House Trust
The Headley Trust (Sainsbury)
Mrs D Rope Charitable Settlement
The Pilgrim Trust
The Esmée Fairbairn Charitable Trust
The Goldsmith's Company's Charities
The Linbury Trust (Sainsbury)

Costs that are high and unexplained

The variation in administrative costs is not easily explained. Expressed as either a proportion of grants (our basic measure), or as proportion of income or as a cost per grant, there are huge differences between trusts whose reported activities are closely similar.

Many trusts, including some large ones, have negligible costs; the trustees do the work for free. Others, who appear to simply process and read written applications, and have simple investments, can spend less than 2% of the value of grants. Other excellent trusts, such as the City Parochial Foundation spend much more (14%) because they do much more. Their expert staff, active policies, personal involvement and support for

---

The SORP (Statement of Recommended Practice for Charity Accounts)

Since 1995 the SORP has set out the recommended form for the annual reports and accounts for all charities, grant making trusts included. The Charity Commissioners, it said, 'expect the accounts of charities to comply fully'. For financial years ending from March 1996 the SORP has been more than recommended; parts of it are now backed by statutory Regulation, specifically including the requirement to provide 'such particulars of any grant made by the charity to another institution of which the SORP requires disclosure ...'.

The SORP calls for three things that are particularly relevant to the entries in this book:

- the disclosure of all material grants: All grants of £1,000 or more 'should be regarded as material and should be disclosed', though disclosure 'unless contained in a separate publication should be limited to the 50 largest grants or such other number as may be considered necessary to convey a proper understanding of the charity's grant making activities'.

If disclosure of a particular grant would damage either the grant maker or the recipient, there is sensible provision for withholding 'details of the grant concerned'.

- material grants should be 'appropriately analysed and explained'. Some trusts do this on a grant by grant basis; others do it by grouping and categorising their grants; some do both.

- there should be a narrative annual report containing, among other things, 'a review of the development, activities and achievements of the charity during the year' and enabling the reader to judge its effectiveness and to appreciate 'the general progress of the charity' and 'important events affecting the charity or the areas in which it works, and how the charity has responded to them'.

Some trusts just ignore these requirements; a box herewith lists some whose publicly filed accounts do not contain any list of the grants made. For many, there is simply no attempt at analysis or explanation. And often there is no attempt at a narrative report of the kind described.

Other trusts are wriggling (usually through their solicitors) to escape some or all of these provisions.

First, some are using the sensible provision for withholding details of a particular grant as an excuse for keeping secret all their grants. Baron Davenport's Charity Trust in Birmingham, supporting almshouses and children's organisations, has used this provision as a reason to ask the Charity Commission to withhold details of all its grants from the public file; and the Commission agreed to do so.

Secondly, some are saying that the requirement that grants should be 'analysed and explained' is met by a simple listing of the recipients and the amounts they got, with no further analysis or explanation at all. We have another box showing some of the trusts where only a bare list of this kind is available.

Thirdly, there are some who argue that their only policy is to make grants, and that by saying so they have met the requirements for the annual report set out above. However making grants is not in itself a charitable activity, only a means to such activity, and the report should be about the charitable work these grants are intended to support. Again we list in the box herewith some of the larger trusts from whom there is no such report.

applicants, and constant search for the most effective possible use of their money, all fully reported each year, is necessarily expensive. But the Dulverton Trust, for example, reports few such activities, yet it still reports administrative costs that are 12% of the value of its grants. It is not unusual.

Some other trusts that we record as having costs that are both high and unexplained are listed below. In each case it is possible that there are activities that fully justify the unusual expenditure involved, but they are not sufficiently reported by the trusts, as they should be.

The Constance Green Foundation
The Dunhill Medical Trust
The Drapers' Charitable Fund
W O Street Charitable Foundation
The Hedley Foundation
The Beaverbrook Foundation

Investment management charges

We are concerned that large sums of trust money are being ill spent on buying investment advice. It is apparent that many trusts are able to get such advice for as little as 0.15% a year of the value of their investments. Yet other foundations pay far more. Dunhill, for example, argues that its 0.35% is reasonable 'by City standards'. This may be so, but we do not think it is reasonable by charity standards, and, if general, would represent a drain of £50 million a year from trusts instead of about £20 million.

Nuffield, for example, paid 0.11% on £203 million to out-perform the WM charity index. Both the Tudor Trust and the Rowntree Foundation, with investments of more than twice the value, actually paid substantially less than Dunhill. The fact that much of Dunhill's fees were paid to a company associated with one of its own trustees is a separate matter.

Failure to disclose grants

As noted above, trusts are now expected to disclose, at the very least, their fifty largest grants (if these are for £1,000 or more). Without this information, their activities and policies cannot even be deduced. Among those not doing so were the following:

Baron Davenport's Charity Trust
The Fishmongers' Company's Charitable Trust
The Gosling Foundation
David and Frederick Barclay Foundation
The Elton John Aids Foundation
Sir James Colyer-Fergusson's Charitable Trust
The Mulberry Trust

Allchurches Trust

Payment of trustees

We support the notion that charity trustees should not benefit from their trusts and believe that it is possible to find trustees, of the highest quality, who will not require payment for the interesting and charitable job of giving away someone else's money. This is the situation for the great majority of the trusts in this book. Some of the exceptions were as follows:

Lord Barnby's Foundation
Mr and Mrs Pye Charitable Settlement
The Dunhill Medical Trust
The Constance Green Foundation

Nor is it desirable, we believe, for a charity to purchases services from the companies or partnerships of their trustees. The custom of some legally qualified trustees charging for their services is hallowed by long custom, but it is undesirable and should be discontinued. Trusts reporting such payments to connected organisations include:

The Constance Green Foundation
The Dunhill Medical Trust
Mr & Mrs Pye's Charitable Settlement
Benesco Charity

No narrative report

As described in the 'SORP' section above, trusts are required, like all other charities, to file a narrative report on their policies and achievements every year, and also to 'analyse and explain' their grants. Among the trusts whose reports fell far short of this were the following:

The Rayne Foundation
Sir John Eastwood Foundation
van Geest Foundation
The Alan Sugar Foundation
The Laura Ashley Foundation
Sir James Colyer-Fergusson's Charitable Trust
Help the Aged
The Bernard Sunley Charitable Foundation

Applying To A Charitable Trust Or Foundation

The following note has been written and published by the **Association for Charitable Foundations**, to which we are grateful for permission for its reproduction here.

There are about 8,800 grant-making trusts and foundations in the UK. They give in total about £1.25 billion per year to charitable causes. To this might be added £320 million given by the National Lottery Charities Board and £280 million by a dozen large operating charities which make grants in the course of their work (eg Cancer Research, Oxfam), making £1.85 billion in all.

Total grant-giving to the voluntary sector by trusts is about the same as that of central or Local Government (apart from government grants to housing associations and employment schemes), and larger than that of the corporate sector. The figures are, however, notoriously difficult to analyse, and are complicated by the 'contract culture', so comparisons can be misleading. For example, although government gives little aid to voluntary organisations in the educational field, its total spending on education is about £31 billion, whereas trust spending is about one-hundredth of this: £320 million. Similar comparisons emerge in social welfare. This is why trusts fight shy of long-term funding of services, especially services which could reasonably be part of State provision. In particular fields however, trust funding can be significant, eg research in medicine and housing.

Trusts can only preserve their distinctive role by doing special things. They therefore like to concentrate their funding on:

- new methods of tackling problems;
- disadvantaged and minority groups that have trouble using ordinary services, or which are inadequately served by them;
- responses to new or newly discovered needs and problems;
- work which is hard to finance through conventional fund-raising;
- one-off purchases or projects, including research;
- short and medium term work which is likely to bring long term benefit and/or to attract long term funding from elsewhere.

Core funding is not ruled out for work which falls into one or more of these categories.

Trusts vary enormously in their policies, styles of working, and administrative capacities. So three golden rules are:

1. Do your homework beforehand;
2. Prepare your application carefully;
3. Leave plenty of time.

Selecting trusts

Use the various directories to locate trusts which may be able to help - and to rule out those which will not be interested. Draw up a short list of possible trusts. You list should include:

- trusts which operate in your geographical area. Look especially for any trusts which can only fund in your area or which express a preference for it. Don't approach a trust which cannot fund in your area, nor ask for funding for a national project from a trust which is limited to a particular locality. A trust which funds nationally may be interested in a local project if it particularly matches the trust's interests and/or is of national significance; i.e. it would make a grant because of the pioneering nature of the project's work rather than because of the needs of the area. Only the very largest national trusts (the top 50 or so) are able to fund local projects more widely than this.

- trusts which are interested in your field of work and the sort of people who will benefit from it. If a trust says that it makes grants only in a particular field or to benefit a particular age group, it means it. Likewise, if a trust says that it does not fund general appeals or that projects of a particular type are excluded, don't try and persuade it that you are the exception;

- trusts which make (and have sufficient funds to make) grants of the size you need. Don't ask for a small trust for too much (or a large one for too little).

Many trusts publish information leaflets for applicants. (The same information is often reproduced in various directories.) Write off for these details if necessary, and use them to refine your short list, which will usually be quite short - perhaps only three or four trusts, and probably not more than twenty. Where a trust's information says that it has an application form, obtain this before proceeding any further; don't waste time drafting a letter until you have completed the form. Most trusts however do not use an application form.

If you can't find any trusts that seem likely to be interested, think again about how to present your work. Can you describe it in a different way, emphasising different (and preferably unusual) aspects that may attract different groups of funders? If the amount you need is too large, can you sub-divide the proposal into smaller projects?

Writing your application

Remember to include the following points:

- The purpose of the work to be funded- who it will help and how, what is distinctive about it, what will be achieved if a grant is given (and perhaps what will not be achieved if the grant is not given);

- A budget for the project. Work out your needs carefully. Don't economise on essentials, such as training or unavoidable overhead costs;

- Ask for a specific sum of money. If necessary, say that you are seeking a contribution of £X towards a budget of £Y, and that you hope to raise the remainder from other sources which you specify. Do not simply say that you are a very worthwhile organisation and desperately need funds.

- Your name, address, and phone number - oh yes, people do forget!

Make the application long enough to describe what you want properly, but short enough to be easy to take in the first reading - usually no more than two pages for your main letter.

Don't overload the application with attachments. A trust which is seriously interested will ask for information it hasn't got.

You should, however, always include your most recent annual report and accounts. (If your accounts show apparently large reserves, attach a note explaining why you hold them and why they cannot be used to fund the project for which you are seeking funds. If you cannot explain the size of your reserves, consider spending them instead of applying for grants!)

If your organisation does not have charitable status, explain why the work funded is charitable, and if possible name a registered charity that will take responsibility on your behalf (providing written confirmation from that charity). You must identify such a charity when applying to a trust that has a policy of only funding registered charities.

Connecting with trusts

Apply well before you need the money. Trusts generally make decisions through trustees' meetings which take place every two or three months. Some meet only two or three times a year. While a few trusts have a small grants programme where a fast response can be given, most are unable to deal quickly with even the very best applications.

Trusts generally have quite a limited administration capacity. Although the largest trusts are quite substantial organisations, only the top 300 or so employ any staff at all. The vast majority of trusts are run on a part-time or voluntary basis, and are themselves very small organisations. Don't try and expect too much of them. The sheer volume of applications means that most trusts do not normally acknowledge applications, and many are unable to reply to applicants who are ultimately unsuccessful. If you want to be sure of an acknowledgement, send a reply-paid postcard addressed to yourself.

Many trusts visit at least the larger applications they are considering and if you receive a visit it is usually a sign that you have got over the first hurdle. Try to establish what the funder wishes to see and who he or she wishes to meet. It is useful to identify how long the funder can spend with you. Are they hoping to see your project in action as well as discuss the organisation's work? Are they interested in the whole organisation or just this particular project? The answers to these questions will help you decide which of you should be there.

What trusts look for

Trust usually make visits in order to assess the need for the project and the extent at which the applicants have come up with a good solution. They will also be looking for reassurance that the applicants have the ability to deliver what they promise. This is your chance to bring the project to life so try to ensure that the person meeting the funder both knows about the project and is enthusiastic about it.

While some trusts will want to visit you, others will deal with your application entirely by letter. Some will be willing to discuss the application (or a prospective application) over the phone, while others will not. (If a trust's entry does not include a phone number, this means that calls are unwelcome. It will not help to trace the number through Directory Enquiries.)

If you happen to know a trustee of a trust, tell him or her that you are applying. but in general it won't help you to approach trustees direct; deal with a trust through its designated secretary or correspondent.

Remember that trusts may get more applications than they can fund. A typical trust, if there is such a thing, may be able to fund only one in four of the eligible applications received, and half or more enquiries it receives may be ineligible. So if you don't succeed, it may not reflect on the quality of your application. The reasons that applications are ineligible are that they are outside the trust's stated guidelines, or lack obvious details such as a return address.

A continuing relationship?

If you are lucky enough to receive a grant, ensure first of all that you acknowledge receipt of the cheque and thank the funder – it is surprising how many applicants do not do this. Thereafter try to keep in touch in whatever way the funder suggests. If the funder wants frequent reports then make sure you supply them but if the funder only wants a report once a year do not bombard them with information in between times.

Do let your funder know if there are problems. It is far better to be alerted at an early stage to any difficulties- when a funder may be able to help, for example, by varying the times at which the grant is paid, or helping you to identify other funders who might be able to make up a short fall or offering advice if similar problems occurred in other organisations. Don't wait until there is a real crisis before letting the funder know what is happening.

On the positive side, if you receive any particular significant good news, such as increased funding, good publicity or the achievement of a particular objective, do let your funders know. Finally it is worth checking, perhaps six months before your current funding runs out whether that particular funder is willing to consider further applications!

Dates for your diary

☒ = the usual month of trustees'/grant allocation meetings

ⓐ = the last month for receipt of applications, where this is specified

Note that ample time must be left for applications to be processed in advance of meetings. Some trusts have separate deadlines for their different programmes.

	Jan	Feb	Mar	Apr	May	Jun	Jul	Aug	Sep	Oct	Nov	Dec
29th May 1961 Charitable Trust		x			x			x			x	
Architectural Heritage Fund		a	x		a	x		a	x		a	x
Baily Thomas Charitable Fund					a	x				a	x	x
Baring Foundation	x	x		x	x		x		x	x		x
Barnby's Foundation		x					x				x	
BBC Children in Need Appeal	x		xa				x			x	a	
Beaverbrook Foundation					x						x	
Bedford Charity	x		a	x		a	x		a	x		a
Bilton Charity Ltd			x			x			x			x
Burdens Charitable Foundation	a		x	a		x	a		x	a		x
Cadbury Charitable Trust					x						x	
Cadbury Trust Cadbury Fund	a		x		a		x		a		x	
Campden Charities	x	x	x	x	x	x	x		x	x	x	x
Carnegie United Kingdom Trust	a		x	a		x			a		x	
Cass's Foundation			x			x			x			x
Charities Aid Foundation		x	a		x		a	x	xa		x	a
Charity Know How	a		x	a		x	a		x	a		x
Childwick Trust				a	x				a	x		
Church Urban Fund	xa		xa	x	xa				xa		x	x
City Parochial Foundation	xa		xa				x	a		x	a	
Cleveland Community Foundation			x	a			x	a			x	a
Clothworkers' Foundation and other Trusts	x	a	x	a	x	a	x	a	a	x	x	a
Cloudesley's Charity		x		a	x				x	a	x	

12

	Jan	Feb	Mar	Apr	May	Jun	Jul	Aug	Sep	Oct	Nov	Dec
Coates Charitable Trust	x					a	x					a
Colt Foundation					x						x	
Colyer-Fergusson's Charitable Trust		a	x		a	x		a	x		a	x
Cook Trust	a		x					a		x		
Daiwa Anglo-Japanese Foundation		a	x		a	x		a	x		a	x
Davies Charity				a	x					a	x	
Diana, Princess of Wales Memorial Fund				xuk		xint		a			xuk	
Dulverton Trust	x				x		x			x		
Dunhill Medical Trust			x		x				x		x	
Englefield Charitable Trust						x						x
Equitable Charitable Trust	X	X	X	X	X	X	X	X	X	X	X	X
Eveson Charitable Trust	xa		x		a		x	a		x	a	
Fairbairn Charitable Trust		x	a		ax		x	a			xa	
Fishmongers' Company's Charitable Trust		a	x		a	x		a	x			
Fraser Foundation	x		a	x		a	x		a	x		a
Frazer Trust			x						x			
Gannochy Trust	X	X	X	X	X	X	X		X	X	X	X
Getty Charitable Trust			x			x			x			x
Gibson Charitable Trust			a		x							
Grand Charity of Freemasons	x			x		a	x			x		
Great Britain Sasakawa Foundation			a		x				a		x	
Green Foundation	a		x		a	x			a		x	
Greggs Trust			a		x				a		x	
Gulbenkian Foundation		x		x			x				x	
Hamlyn Foundation		xa		xa		x		a		x		a
Hampton Fuel Allotment Charity	a	x	a	x	a	x	a	x	a	x	a	x
Higgs Charity	x	a	x	a	x	a	x	a	x	a	x	a
Historic Churches Preservation Trust			x		x						x	
Hodge Foundation	Jx	Fx	Mx	Apr	Mx	Jx	Jx	Ax	Sx	Ox	Nx	Dx
Housing Associations Charitable Trust (HACT)		xa		xa		x	a		x	xa		xa

13

	Jan	Feb	Mar	Apr	May	Jun	Jul	Aug	Sep	Oct	Nov	Dec
James Bristol Foundation	a	x		a	x		a	x		a	x	
James Charitable Foundation		x	a		x	a		x	a		x	a
James Pantyfedwen Foundation			x		x		x		x			x
Jeffreys Road Fund	x		a	x	a	x	a	x		a	x	a
Jurgens Charitable Trust			a	x	x			a	x	x		
Karten Charitable Trust								a				
Kershaw Trust									a		x	
King George's Fund for Sailors			x				x					x
King's Fund		x		x			x		x		x	
Kleinwort Benson Charitable Trust		a	x		a	x		a	x		a	x
Knott Trust	a	x			a	x				a	x	
Laing Biblical Scholarship Trust	x	x	x	x	x	x	x	x	x	x	x	x
Laing Trust	x	x	x	x	x	x	x	x	x	x	x	x
Lambeth Endowed Charities	a		x	a		x		a		x	a	x
Lane Foundation		x		a		x		a		x		a
Lankelly Foundation	x			x			x			x		
Levy Charitable Foundation		x			x						x	
Lloyds TSB Foundation for Northern Ireland		a	x		a	x		a	x		a	x
Lloyds TSB Foundation for Scotland		x	a		x	a		x	a		x	a
Lord's Taverners	a	x		a	x				a	x		
Mackintosh Foundation				x							x	
MacRobert Trusts			x			a				ax		
Marshall's Charity	ax			ax			ax			ax		
Martin Trust				a		x				a		x
Medlock Charitable Trust			x			x			x			x
Milton Keynes Community Trust		x			x				x		x	
Moore Foundation	x		a	x		a	x		a	x		a
National Art Collections Fund	x	x	x	x	x	x	x		x	x	x	x
Needham Cooper Charitable Trust			x					x				
Norwich Town Close Estate Charity	a	x	a	x	a	x	a	x	a	x		a

	Jan	Feb	Mar	Apr	May	Jun	Jul	Aug	Sep	Oct	Nov	Dec
Nuffield Foundation		x		x			x			x		
Nuffield Trust	a		x		a		x		a		x	
P F Charitable Trust	x	x	x	x	x	x	x	x	x	x	x	x
Pilgrim Trust	x	a		x	a		x	a		x	a	
Pilkington Charities Fund			x							x		
Polden-Puckham Charitable Foundation	a		x					a		x		
Porter Foundation			x				x				x	
Pye's Charitable Settlement		a	x		a	x		a	x		a	x
Queen Mary's Roehampton Trust				a	x				a		x	
Rank Benevolent Trust	a			x			a			x		
Rank Foundation	a		x	a		x	a		x	a		x
Reckitt Charity				a	x					a	x	
Robertson Trust	x	a	x	a	x	a	x	a	x	a	x	a
Rose Foundation					x							
Rowan Trust	x						x					
Rowntree Charitable Trust	a		x	a		x	a		x	a	x	
Rowntree Foundation			xa			xa			xa			xa
Rowntree Reform Trust Limited		a	x		a	x		a	x		a	x
Saddlers' Company Charitable Fund	x			a			x				a	
Save & Prosper Educational Trust		a	x	a	x	a	x		a	x	a	x
Scott Charitable Trust		a	x			a	x		a	x		
Scott Charitable Trust	x			a	x			a	x	a	x	a
Sheepdrove Trust			x						x			
Sherman Charitable Trust	x	x	x	x	x	x	x		x	x	x	
Smith Charity	a		x	a		x	a		x	a		x
Souter Foundation	x		x	x		x			x	x	x	
Southover Manor General Education Trust		x		x		x		x		x		x
Spitalfields Market Community Trust	x	x	x	x	x	x	x		x	x	x	
Stewart Trust		x		a		x		a		x		a
Sunley Charitable Foundation	x			a	x				a	x		a

● **Dates for your diary**

	Jan	Feb	Mar	Apr	May	Jun	Jul	Aug	Sep	Oct	Nov	Dec
Sutton Coldfield Municipal Charities	x	x	x		x	x	x		x	x	x	
Talbot Village Trust		a		x				a		x		
Triangle Trust		x				x			x		x	
Trust for London	a		x	a		x			x	a		x
Turner Trust				x				x		x		x
Ulverscroft Foundation	x		a	x		a	x		a	x		a
Warburg's Voluntary Settlement	a	x				a	x		a	x		
Waterhouse Charitable Trust	a											
Welton Foundation	a	x				a	x		a	x		
Westminster Foundation		x			x				x		x	
Westminster Foundation for Democracy	x	a		x	a		x	a		x	a	
Will Charitable Trust	a		x					a		x		
Wolfson Family Charitable Trust			a			x			a			x
Wolfson Foundation			a			x			a			x

	Grants	Trust	Main grant areas	Page no.
❑	£285,000,000	**National Lottery Charities Board**	Those at greatest disadvantage in society	*Page 258*
❑	£227,000,000	**Wellcome Trust**	Biomedical research, history of medicine, public understanding of science	*Page 362*
❑	(£58,000,000)	**Sainsbury Family Charitable Trusts**	See separate entries for each trust	*Page 309*
❑	£39,999,000	**Sport and the Arts**	Sport, the arts	*Page 324*
❑	£28,591,000	**Gatsby Charitable Foundation**	Technical education, mental/other health, economic and social research, children/young people, welfare, development in Africa, plant science, arts, general.	*Page 138*
❑	£22,717,000	**Tudor Trust**	Social welfare, general	*Page 345*
❑	£22,430,000	**Weston Foundation**	Arts, education, health, general	*Page 365*
❑	£21,000,000	**Smith Charity**	Social welfare, disability, health, medical research	*Page 317*
❑	£18,336,000	**Wolfson Foundation**	Hospitals and university medical departments, health	*Page 373*
❑	£17,711,000	**BBC Children in Need Appeal**	Child welfare	*Page 57*
❑	£17,000,000	**PPP Healthcare Medical Trust**	Healthcare	*Page 282*
❑	£15,240,000	**Leverhulme Trust**	Research and education	*Page 222*
❑	£12,821,000	**Linbury Trust**	Major capital projects, chronic fatigue syndrome, arts/art education, drug abuse, education	*Page 228*
❑	£11,589,000	**Fairbairn Charitable Trust**	Social welfare, arts and heritage, education, environment, social and economic research	*Page 129*
❑	£10,100,000	**Bridge House Estates Trust Fund**	Welfare in London	*Page 64*
❑	£10,000,000	**Help the Aged**	Day centres, hospices, general, for the elderly	*Page 178*
❑	£9,036,000	**Lloyds TSB Foundation for England and Wales**	Social and community needs, education and training	*Page 231*
❑	£8,000,000	**Northern Rock Foundation**	People with disabilities and their carers	*Page 263*
❑	£7,844,000	**Comic Relief**	Community based UK charities, Africa	*Page 105*
❑	£7,530,000	**Rank Foundation**	Christian communication, youth, education, general	*Page 285*
❑	£6,770,000	**Rowntree Foundation**	Research and development in social policy	*Page 300*
❑	£6,465,000	**Northern Ireland Voluntary Trust**	Social welfare	*Page 261*
❑	£6,399,000	**Nuffield Foundation**	Education, child protection, family law and justice, access to justice, mental health, ageing.	*Page 266*
❑	£5,124,000	**City Parochial Foundation**	Social welfare in London	*Page 94*
❑	£5,078,000	**Variety Club Children's Charity**	Children's charities, 'Sunshine Coaches'	*Page 356*
❑	£4,980,000	**Moores Foundation**	The arts, particularly opera, social welfare	*Page 256*
❑	£4,909,000	**Shetland Islands Council Charitable Trust**	General, in Shetland	*Page 316*
❑	£4,569,000	**Robertson Trust**	General, mainly in Scotland	*Page 291*
❑	£4,500,000	**Diana, Princess of Wales Memorial Fund**	Welfare, especially of children (1999 only)	*Page 114*

17

● The major trusts ranked by grant total

	Grants	Trust	Main grant areas	Page no.
❑	£4,473,000	**Parthenon Trust**	Medical research, emergency relief, Third World, social welfare, education, disabled	*Page 273*
❑	£4,428,000	**Monument Trust**	Health & community care, HIV/AIDS, environment, arts, social development, general	*Page 251*
❑	£4,337,000	**Action Research**	Medical research into disabling diseases	*Page 29*
❑	£4,182,000	**J W Laing Trust**	Christian evangelism, general	*Page 210*
❑	£4,102,000	**Thorn Charitable Trust**	Medical research, medicine, humanitarian purposes	*Page 338*
❑	£3,900,000	**Allchurches Trust Ltd**	Churches, general	*Page 32*
❑	£3,825,000	**Ellerman Foundation**	Community development, social welfare, medical research and care, disability arts, conservation	*Page 123*
❑	£3,663,000	**Sobell Foundation**	Jewish charities, health and welfare	*Page 321*
❑	£3,650,000	**Dunhill Medical Trust**	Medical research, integrated care and accommodation for the elderly	*Page 120*
❑	£3,631,000	**Rowntree Charitable Trust**	Poverty, economic and racial justice, handling conflict, Ireland, South Africa, democratic process and the abuse of power, corporate responsibility	*Page 295*
❑	£3,365,000	**Rank Benevolent Trust**	The Methodist Church, Christian-based social work	*Page 284*
❑	£3,202,000	**Clothworkers' Foundation and other Trusts**	Clothworking, general	*Page 99*
❑	£3,179,000	**Wolfson Charitable Trust**	Medical research, health, education, Jewish charities, general	*Page 371*
❑	£3,135,000	**Headley Trust**	Arts, environment, education, health and social care, medicine, overseas development	*Page 175*
❑	£3,125,000	**29th May 1961 Charitable Trust**	Social welfare, general	*Page 29*
❑	£3,120,000	**Baring Foundation**	Strengthening the voluntary sector, arts in education and in the community, international	*Page 42*
❑	£3,091,000	**Gannochy Trust**	General	*Page 137*
❑	£3,020,000	**Lankelly Foundation**	Social welfare, disability	*Page 216*
❑	£3,000,000	**Westminster Foundation for Democracy**	Strengthening democracy overseas	*Page 364*
❑	£3,000,000	**Childwick Trust**	Education in South Africa, health, medical research	*Page 89*
❑	£3,000,000	**Equitable Charitable Trust**	Education of disabled/disadvantaged children	*Page 126*
❑	£3,000,000	**Jerwood Foundation**	Education, arts, general	*Page 192*
❑	£2,928,000	**Cripps Foundation**	Education, healthcare and churches in Northamptonshire, Cambridge University	*Page 111*
❑	£2,910,000	**King George's Fund for Sailors**	The welfare of seafarers	*Page 198*
❑	£2,900,000	**Benesco Charity Limited**	See below	*Page 62*
❑	£2,884,000	**Wolfson Family Charitable Trust**	Jewish charities, medicine, arts, education	*Page 372*
❑	£2,881,000	**Architectural Heritage Fund**	Loans for building preservation, grants for feasibility studies	*Page 34*

	Grants	Trust	Main grant areas	Page no.
❏	£2,881,000	**Clore Foundation**	Jewish charities, arts/museums, education, children, general	*Page 98*
❏	£2,806,000	**Hamlyn Foundation**	Arts, education, overseas, publishing	*Page 168*
❏	£2,772,000	**Sunley Charitable Foundation**	General	*Page 333*
❏	£2,713,000	**Church Urban Fund**	Welfare, Christian development in disadvantaged urban areas	*Page 91*
❏	£2,704,000	**Dulverton Trust**	Youth and education, general welfare, conservation, Christian religion	*Page 118*
❏	£2,696,000	**Kleinwort Charitable Trust**	Health, environment/conservation, overseas, general	*Page 205*
❏	£2,640,000	**Glencore Foundation for Education & Welfare**	Education, welfare, Jewish charities	*Page 148*
❏	£2,618,000	**Lloyds TSB Foundation for Scotland**	Social welfare, education and training, medical research	*Page 238*
❏	£2,567,000	**Ashdown Charitable Trust**	Inter faith and racial harmony, Jewish education, community development	*Page 37*
❏	£2,500,000	**Mayfair Charities Ltd**	Orthodox Judaism	*Page 248*
❏	£2,468,000	**Baily Thomas Charitable Fund**	Mental illness, mental disability	*Page 40*
❏	£2,463,000	**Cadbury Trust, and the Barrow Cadbury Fund**	Civil rights, community democracy, disability, gender, penal affairs, racial justice	*Page 69*
❏	£2,411,000	**Maurice Laing Foundation**	Medicine (including complementary medicine), welfare (especially of the young), general	*Page 212*
❏	£2,407,000	**National Art Collections Fund**	Acquisition of works of art by museums and galleries	*Page 257*
❏	£2,378,000	**Pilgrim Trust**	Social welfare, art and learning, preservation	*Page 276*
❏	£2,345,000	**Jerusalem Trust**	The promotion of Christianity	*Page 191*
❏	£2,300,000	**Arbib Foundation**	General	*Page 34*
❏	£2,222,000	**Drapers' Charitable Fund**	General	*Page 116*
❏	£2,131,000	**Duffield Foundation**	Children, the arts	*Page 117*
❏	£2,126,000	**George Balint Charitable Trust**	Jewish charities, general	*Page 40*
❏	£2,095,000	**Peacock Charitable Trust**	Medical research, disability, general	*Page 275*
❏	£2,085,000	**Rufford Foundation**	Conservation, environment, general	*Page 307*
❏	£2,083,000	**Cadbury Charitable Trust**	Religion, general	*Page 72*
❏	£2,058,000	**Eveson Charitable Trust**	Health, Welfare.	*Page 128*
❏	£2,024,000	**Gulbenkian Foundation**	Education, arts, welfare	*Page 160*
❏	£2,000,000	**Trusthouse Charitable Foundation**	General	*Page 344*
❏	£1,844,000	**King's Fund**	Health and health care	*Page 199*
❏	£1,843,000	**Whittington's Charity**	Social welfare	*Page 369*
❏	£1,730,000	**Rayne Foundation**	Higher education, medicine, social welfare, the arts, general	*Page 289*

The major trusts ranked by grant total

Grants	Trust	Main grant areas	Page no.
□ £1,608,000	**Rothschild GAM Charitable Trust**	Heritage	*Page 294*
□ £1,601,000	**Kendall Leukaemia Fund**	Research into leukaemia	*Page 197*
□ £1,589,000	**Sherman Charitable Trust**	Jewish charities, arts	*Page 316*
□ £1,567,000	**Getty Charitable Trust**	Social welfare, conservation	*Page 144*
□ £1,556,000	**Tedworth Trust**	Parenting, family welfare, child development, environment	*Page 337*
□ £1,487,000	**Sackler Foundation**	Probably art, science, medical research	*Page 308*
□ £1,471,000	**Will Charitable Trust**	Environment/conservation, cancer care, blindness, mental handicap	*Page 369*
□ £1,460,000	**Eranda Foundation**	The arts, general	*Page 127*
□ £1,445,000	**Lyon's Charity**	Children and young people in North and West London	*Page 242*
□ £1,385,000	**Fraser Foundation**	General	*Page 136*
□ £1,370,000	**Prince's Trust**	Disadvantaged young people	*Page 282*
□ £1,361,000	**Lord's Taverners**	Minibuses for people with disabilities, cricket	*Page 240*
□ £1,350,000	**Tyne & Wear Foundation**	Social welfare, general	*Page 351*
□ £1,337,000	**Hodge Foundation**	Medicine, education, religion, mainly in Wales	*Page 181*
□ £1,333,000	**Wates Foundation**	Social welfare	*Page 358*
□ £1,266,000	**Goldsmiths' Company's Charities**	General, London charities, the precious metals craft	*Page 149*
□ £1,241,000	**Hayward Foundation**	Welfare, medical research, elderly, special needs, general	*Page 173*
□ £1,240,000	**CHK Charities Limited**	General	*Page 91*
□ £1,222,000	**Glass-House Trust**	Parenting, family welfare, child development	*Page 147*
□ £1,212,000	**Kinross Charitable Trust**	Mental health	*Page 203*
□ £1,205,000	**Alchemy Foundation**	Health and welfare	*Page 31*
□ £1,200,000	**Manifold Trust**	Historic buildings, environmental conservation	*Page 245*
□ £1,195,000	**P F Charitable Trust**	General	*Page 272*
□ £1,174,000	**Kirby Laing Foundation**	General	*Page 211*
□ £1,171,000	**Knott Trust**	General, in the North-East	*Page 206*
□ £1,162,000	**Medlock Charitable Trust**	Education, general	*Page 249*
□ £1,156,000	**Barclay Foundation**	Medical research, welfare	*Page 41*
□ £1,155,000	**Mackintosh Foundation**	Performing arts, education, young people, the homeless, AIDS, S E Asian refugees, general	*Page 243*
□ £1,130,000	**Lloyds TSB Foundation for Northern Ireland**	Social and community need, education and training, scientific and medical research	*Page 237*
□ £1,126,000	**Carnegie United Kingdom Trust**	Community service, arts, heritage	*Page 80*
□ £1,122,000	**Achisomoch Aid Company**	Jewish religious charities	*Page 29*

20

	Grants	Trust	Main grant areas	Page no.
❏	£1,104,000	**Barnwood House Trust**	Disability charities in Gloucestershire, medical research	*Page 55*
❏	£1,102,000	**Mercers' Charitable Foundation**	Independent schools, education, general	*Page 249*
❏	£1,084,000	**Westminster Foundation**	General	*Page 364*
❏	£1,083,000	**Grand Charity of Freemasons**	Health, education and welfare	*Page 152*
❏	£1,055,000	**Laing Biblical Scholarship Trust**	Christian evangelism	*Page 211*
❏	£1,049,000	**Jones 1986 Charitable Trust**	General, especially in Nottinghamshire	*Page 195*
❏	£1,045,000	**Woodward Trust**	The arts (particularly opera), children, disability, welfare, general	*Page 377*
❏	£1,042,000	**Hampton Fuel Allotment Charity**	General, in Twickenham and Richmond	*Page 171*
❏	£1,037,000	**Levy Charitable Foundation**	Young people, health, medical research, Jewish charities	*Page 227*
❏	£1,032,000	**Sebba Charitable Trust**	Jewish charities in Israel and Britain	*Page 314*
❏	£1,028,000	**Paul Balint Charitable Trust**	Jewish charities, medicine, children and general	*Page 40*
❏	£1,018,000	**Scott Charitable Trust**	Disadvantaged people	*Page 313*
❏	£1,000,000	**Hilda Laing Charitable Trust**	Christianity, poverty	*Page 210*
❏	£1,009,000	**James Bristol Foundation**	Education, general in Bristol	*Page 189*
❏	£1,001,000	**Save & Prosper Educational Trust**	Education	*Page 312*
❏	£1,000,000	**Leathersellers' Company Charitable Fund**	General. See below.	*Page 219*
❏	£982,000	**Campden Charities**	Welfare and education in Kensington, London	*Page 75*
❏	£971,000	**Housing Associations Charitable Trust (HACT)**	Housing and related social need	*Page 183*
❏	£966,000	**Sutton Coldfield Municipal Charities**	Relief of need, education and general in Sutton Coldfield	*Page 335*
❏	£955,000	**Spitalfields Market Community Trust**	Education, employment, welfare in Tower Hamlets	*Page 323*
❏	£951,000	**Karten Charitable Trust**	Technology centres for disabled people, post-graduate scholarships	*Page 196*
❏	£927,000	**Zochonis Charitable Trust**	General, especially Greater Manchester	*Page 378*
❏	£924,000	**Artemis Charitable Trust**	Psychotherapy, parent education, and related activities	*Page 35*
❏	£915,000	**Wills 1965 Charitable Trust**	General, environment	*Page 370*
❏	£899,000	**Hedley Foundation Ltd**	Health, welfare.	*Page 177*
❏	£863,000	**Henry Moore Foundation**	Art, particularly sculpture	*Page 253*
❏	£863,000	**Trust for London**	Small community-based organisations in London	*Page 342*
❏	£846,000	**Livanos Charitable Trust**	Medical research, hospitals, general	*Page 231*
❏	£840,000	**Moores Family Charity Foundation**	General, especially in Merseyside	*Page 254*
❏	£839,000	**MacRobert Trusts**	General, mainly in Scotland	*Page 244*

● The major trusts ranked by grant total

	Grants	Trust	Main grant areas	Page no.
❑	£819,000	**Cymerman Trust Ltd**	Jewish Orthodox education, other Jewish organisations	Page 112
❑	£805,000	**Cass's Foundation**	Education in inner London	Page 83
❑	£802,000	**Peabody Community Fund**	Social welfare in London	Page 273
❑	£799,000	**Steel Charitable Trust**	Social welfare, health, medical research, general	Page 329
❑	£796,000	**Bilton Charity Ltd**	Young, old or disabled people, medicine	Page 62
❑	£792,000	**Moores Foundation**	Social welfare in Merseyside and Northern Ireland	Page 255
❑	£775,000	**Capital Radio - Help A London Child**	Children in London	Page 77
❑	£769,000	**Welton Foundation**	Hospitals, medical research, general	Page 363
❑	£764,000	**Bedford Charity**	Education, welfare and recreation in and around Bedford	Page 61
❑	£761,000	**Souter Foundation**	Christianity, third world, social welfare	Page 322
❑	£761,000	**E B M Charitable Trust**	Children and young people, animals, general	Page 122
❑	£759,000	**Lord Leverhulme's Charitable Trust**	Education, general	Page 227
❑	£750,000	**Rowntree Reform Trust Limited**	Innovative and reforming work, ineligible for charitable status.	Page 305
❑	£750,000	**Gloucestershire Environmental Trust Company**	Environmental improvements	Page 149
❑	£741,000	**Marshall's Charity**	Parsonage and church improvements	Page 246
❑	£728,000	**Andrew Balint Charitable Trust**	Jewish charities, welfare	Page 41
❑	£722,000	**Leigh Charitable Trust**	Israel, Jewish charities, general	Page 221`
❑	£718,000	**Beatrice Laing Trust**	General	Page 209
❑	£711,000	**van Geest Foundation**	Medical research and welfare	Page 354
❑	£711,000	**Sugar Foundation**	Jewish charities, general	Page 332
❑	£711,000	**Leeds Hospital Fund Charitable Trust**	Hospitals in Yorkshire, charities in Leeds	Page 220
❑	£709,000	**Nuffield Trust**	Research and policy studies in health	Page 271
❑	£702,000	**Stewart Trust**	Medical, social and religious research	Page 329
❑	£701,000	**Cripplegate Foundation**	Social welfare in Cripplegate/Islington, London	Page 109
❑	£700,000	**Gosling Foundation Ltd**	Naval charities, general	Page 152
❑	£700,000	**Cloudesley's Charity**	Medicine, welfare, churches,	Page 101
❑	£700,000	**Sutton Trust**	Education	Page 336
❑	£699,000	**Richmond Parish Lands Charity**	General, in Richmond	Page 290
❑	£696,000	**Allen Charitable Trust**	General	Page 32
❑	£683,000	**Laing's Charitable Trust**	General	Page 208
❑	£677,000	**Lolev Charitable Trust**	see below	Page 240
❑	£673,000	**Warburg's Voluntary Settlement**	Medicine and education	Page 357

	Grants	Trust	Main grant areas	Page no.
❑	£659,000	**Rose Foundation**	General	Page 293
❑	£641,000	**John Aids Foundation**	HIV/AIDS welfare and research	Page 194
❑	£638,000	**Caritas**	Heritage, Jewish charities, general	Page 78
❑	£635,000	**Ashden Trust**	Environment, homelessness, urban rejuvenation, community arts, general	Page 36
❑	£632,000	**Colyer-Fergusson's Charitable Trust**	Church buildings, general, in Kent and Suffolk	Page 104
❑	£615,000	**Queen Mary's Roehampton Trust**	War disabled ex-service people and their dependents	Page 284
❑	£603,000	**Staples Trust**	Overseas development, environment, women's issues, general	Page 328
❑	£599,000	**Djanogly Foundation**	General, Jewish charities	Page 116
❑	£594,000	**Marshall Charitable Trust**	General	Page 246
❑	£585,000	**Lewis Family Charitable Trust**	General, Jewish charities	Page 228
❑	£580,000	**Apthorp Charitable Trust**	Health, old people and youth in North-West London	Page 33
❑	£576,000	**Charities Aid Foundation**	Charity management and finance	Page 84
❑	£572,000	**Gavron Charitable Trust**	Arts, policy research, disability, general	Page 143
❑	£563,000	**Cook Trust**	Rural environment, conservation techniques, general	Page 108
❑	£556,000	**Great Britain Sasakawa Foundation**	Links between Great Britain and Japan	Page 153
❑	£546,000	**Tompkins Foundation**	Health, welfare	Page 340
❑	£542,000	**Lane Foundation**	Disadvantaged minorities, unpopular causes	Page 213
❑	£536,000	**Cadbury Charitable Trust**	Society of Friends, churches in the West Midlands, health, social welfare	Page 73
❑	£535,000	**Davenport's Charity Trust**	Children, almshouses/residential homes, in the Midlands	Page 113
❑	£534,000	**Fishmongers' Company's Charitable Trust**	Relief of hardship and disability, education	Page 135
❑	£527,000	**Newman Foundation**	Medical research and equipment	Page 261
❑	£526,000	**Network Foundation**	Environment, human rights, peace, arts	Page 260
❑	£526,000	**Entindale Ltd**	Orthodox Jewish charities	Page 126
❑	£525,000	**Harris Charitable Trust**	General	Page 173
❑	£521,000	**Hayward Trust**	Welfare, health	Page 174
❑	£512,000	**Underwood Trust**	General	Page 354
❑	£506,000	**Carlton Television Trust**	Young people	Page 78
❑	£505,000	**Rowan Trust**	Third world development, social welfare	Page 294
❑	£504,000	**Weinstock Fund**	Jewish charities, arts, medical and social	Page 361
❑	£500,000	**Charity Association Manchester Ltd**	Jewish charities	Page 86

● The major trusts ranked by grant total

	Grants	Trust	Main grant areas	Page no.
❑	£500,000	Lambeth Endowed Charities	Education, general social needs in Lambeth.	Page 213
❑	£499,000	Greggs Trust	Alleviation of poverty and social deprivation	Page 157
❑	£497,000	Beckwith Charitable Trust	General	Page 61
❑	£494,000	Sherburn House Charity	Residential care, welfare in the North East	Page 315
❑	£490,000	Stobart Newlands Charitable Trust	Christian causes	Page 331
❑	£488,000	Gibson Charitable Trust	Churches, hospitals, medical research, general	Page 146
❑	£487,000	Linder Foundation	Health, welfare	Page 230
❑	£484,000	Reckitt Charity	Society of Friends, general	Page 289
❑	£481,000	Isle of Anglesey Charitable Trust	General in Anglesey	Page 187
❑	£475,000	Historic Churches Preservation Trust	Historic churches	Page 181
❑	£468,000	Leech Charity	Health and welfare in the North East	Page 219
❑	£466,000	R & L Sainsbury Charitable Trust	Education in the arts, general	Page 309
❑	£465,000	Leverhulme Trade Charities Trust	Charities benefiting commercial travellers, grocers or chemists	Page 221
❑	£461,000	Forrester Trust	Disability	Page 136
❑	£460,000	A & L Sainsbury Charitable Fund	Civil and minority rights, general	Page 309
❑	£456,000	Porter Foundation	Jewish charities, general	Page 281
❑	£453,000	Rubens Charitable Foundation	Mainly Jewish causes	Page 306
❑	£450,000	Pilkington Charities Fund	General	Page 280
❑	£450,000	Jeffreys Road Fund	Road and transport research and education	Page 190
❑	£447,000	James Charitable Foundation	Education, general, in Bristol	Page 188
❑	£447,000	Elkington Charitable Trust	Social welfare, general	Page 123
❑	£444,000	Kaufman Charitable Trust	Jewish charities	Page 197
❑	£440,000	Rope Third Charitable Settlement	Religion, education, relief of poverty, general	Page 292
❑	£438,000	Green Foundation	Medicine, health, social welfare, general	Page 157
❑	£434,000	Palumbo Charitable Foundation	Education, relief of poverty, conservation, general	Page 273
❑	£431,000	Colt Foundation	Occupational and environmental health research	Page 104
❑	£430,000	Triangle Trust	General	Page 342
❑	£426,000	Street Charitable Foundation	Education, disability, young people, welfare	Page 331
❑	£421,000	Joffe Charitable Trust	Overseas causes	Page 194
❑	£418,000	Dahl Foundation	Haematology, neurology, literacy	Page 112
❑	£417,000	Trades House of Glasgow	Social welfare, general	Page 341
❑	£415,000	Charity Know How	Central and Eastern Europe and the former Soviet Union	Page 87

	Grants	Trust	Main grant areas	Page no.
❑	£412,000	**Hilden Charitable Fund**	Minorities, third world, penal, homelessness, general.	*Page 179*
❑	£412,000	**Blagrave Charitable Trust**	Disabled sports people, youth, medical research, elderly	*Page 63*
❑	£399,000	**Al Fayed Charitable Foundation**	Community, children, health and general	*Page 31*
❑	£396,000	**Rubin Foundation**	Jewish charities, general	*Page 306*
❑	£395,000	**Van Leer Foundation**	Childhood development	*Page 355*
❑	£392,000	**Southover Manor General Education Trust**	Education, youth	*Page 323*
❑	£386,000	**Eastwood Foundation**	Social welfare, health, in Nottinghamshire	*Page 122*
❑	£383,000	**Samuel Charitable Trust**	General	*Page 312*
❑	£382,000	**Higgs Charity**	Child welfare, general	*Page 179*
❑	£381,000	**Metropolitan Hospital-Sunday Fund**	Sick and disabled people in London	*Page 250*
❑	£380,000	**Cohen Foundation**	Music and the arts, Jewish charities, general	*Page 103*
❑	£380,000	**Burton Charitable Trust**	Health, Jewish charities, welfare and general	*Page 69*
❑	£377,000	**Burdens Charitable Foundation**	General	*Page 68*
❑	£377,000	**Cleveland Community Foundation**	General, in Cleveland	*Page 98*
❑	£371,000	**Whiteley Charitable Trust**	Art, environment, general	*Page 368*
❑	£371,000	**Talbot Village Trust**	General	*Page 337*
❑	£368,000	**Pye's Charitable Settlement**	Environment, mental health, general	*Page 283*
❑	£364,000	**Peel Trust**	Medical research, health, general	*Page 275*
❑	£361,000	**Kirkham Foundation Ltd**	Ex-services, general	*Page 205*
❑	£357,000	**Kershaw Trust**	Medical research, education, general.	*Page 198*
❑	£356,000	**Frazer Trust**	General	*Page 136*
❑	£353,000	**Colchester Catalyst Charity**	Health in north east Essex	*Page 103*
❑	£350,000	**Woods Charitable Foundation**	Young people, education, disability, health	*Page 376*
❑	£348,000	**Clover Trust**	Elderly, young people	*Page 102*
❑	£344,000	**Adint Charitable Trust**	Children, medical research, disabled	*Page 30*
❑	£330,000	**Corob Charitable Trust**	Jewish charities, art, general	*Page 109*
❑	£328,000	**Pilkington Trust**	General, see below	*Page 280*
❑	£327,000	**Sykes Trust**	General	*Page 337*
❑	£322,000	**Turner Trust**	General	*Page 351*
❑	£321,000	**James Pantyfedwen Foundation**	Religion, education, general, in Wales	*Page 189*
❑	£321,000	**Grocers' Charity**	General, independent schools	*Page 159*

The major trusts ranked by grant total

	Grants	Trust	Main grant areas	Page no.
❑	£313,000	**Solev Co Ltd**	Jewish charities	*Page 322*
❑	£307,000	**Ulverscroft Foundation**	Sick and visually impaired people, ophthalmic research	*Page 353*
❑	£305,000	**Barnabas Trust**	Evangelical Christianity	*Page 54*
❑	£304,000	**Jurgens Charitable Trust**	Welfare, general	*Page 195*
❑	£301,000	**Gibson Charitable Trust**	General	*Page 147*
❑	£300,000	**Garrick Club Charitable Trust**	Prabably arts, children in London	*Page 138*
❑	£300,000	**Ashley Foundation**	Education, general	*Page 38*
❑	£300,000	**Kreitman Foundation**	Jewish charities, the arts, general	*Page 208*
❑	£298,000	**Kreitman Foundation**	Jewish charities, arts	*Page 208*
❑	£297,000	**Saddlers' Company Charitable Fund**	General	*Page 308*
❑	£296,000	**Winham Foundation**	The welfare of elderly people	*Page 371*
❑	£295,000	**Summerfield Charitable Trust**	The arts, the elderly, the needy and general, mainly in the Gloucestershire area	*Page 332*
❑	£295,000	**HSA Charitable Trust**	Health care	*Page 186*
❑	£294,000	**Sheepdrove Trust**	General in North Lambeth, environment, education and care for the elderly	*Page 315*
❑	£293,000	**Polden-Puckham Charitable Foundation**	Peace and security, ecological issues, social change	*Page 280*
❑	£291,000	**Kalms Foundation**	Jewish charities, general	*Page 196*
❑	£291,000	**Chippenham Borough Lands Charity**	General in Chippenham	*Page 90*
❑	£291,000	**Waterhouse Charitable Trust**	Health, social welfare and countryside preservation	*Page 358*
❑	£290,000	**Burton Charitable Trust**	Jewish charities, social welfare, education, the arts, especially in Yorkshire	*Page 68*
❑	£284,000	**Englefield Charitable Trust**	General, in Berkshire	*Page 126*
❑	£284,000	**Mulberry Trust**	General	*Page 257*
❑	£284,000	**Norwich Town Close Estate Charity**	Education in and near Norwich	*Page 265*
❑	£280,000	**Dunard Fund**	Not known	*Page 120*
❑	£276,000	**Posnansky Charitable Trust**	Jewish charities , health, welfare	*Page 281*
❑	£274,000	**Greater Bristol Foundation**	Social welfare, health	*Page 155*
❑	£273,000	**Duchy of Lancaster Benevolent Fund**	Welfare, churches, general	*Page 117*
❑	£271,000	**Milton Keynes Community Trust**	Welfare, arts	*Page 250*
❑	£270,000	**Needham Cooper Charitable Trust**	Medical, general	*Page 260*
❑	£269,000	**Barnby's Foundation**	General	*Page 54*
❑	£268,000	**Kobler Trust**	Arts, Jewish charities	*Page 207*

	Grants	Trust	Main grant areas	Page no.
❑	£267,000	**Hampstead Wells and Campden Trust**	Welfare in Hampstead	Page 171
❑	£264,000	**J J Charitable Trust**	Environment, literacy, general	Page 187
❑	£263,000	**Davies Charity**	Not known	Page 114
❑	£261,000	**John Coates Charitable Trust**	Health, community, environment, arts	Page 102
❑	£260,000	**Elman Charitable Trust**	Jewish charities	Page 125
❑	£256,000	**Stein Charitable Trust**	Jewish causes	Page 329
❑	£254,000	**Scott Charitable Trust**	Welfare, church restoration, village halls, general	Page 314
❑	£252,000	**Martin Trust**	General, especially in Yorkshire	Page 247
❑	£251,000	**Daiwa Anglo-Japanese Foundation**	Anglo-Japanese relations	Page 113
❑	£247,000	**Kleinwort Benson Charitable Trust**	General	Page 205
❑	£243,000	**Crook Foundation**	Education, general, in Bristol	Page 111
❑	£243,000	**Handley Charitable Trust**	General, in Northumberland and Tyneside	Page 172
❑	£224,000	**Clark Charitable Trust**	Nursing - palliative care in the community	Page 98
❑	£342,000	**William Harding's Charity**	Education, welfare in Aylesbury	Page 172
❑	£218,000	**Horne Foundation**	Education, arts, youth, in or near Northampton	Page 183
❑	£207,000	**Chase Charity**	Social welfare, heritage, the arts	Page 87
❑	£200,000	**Beaverbrook Foundation**	General	Page 60
❑	£184,000	**Moore Foundation**	General, mostly in Yorkshire	Page 254
❑	£183,000	**Thompson Family Charitable Trust**	General	Page 338
❑	£134,000	**Clydepride Ltd**	Jewish charities, general	Page 102
❑	£122,000	**Dinwoodie Settlement**	Postgraduate medical education and research	Page 115
❑	£65,000	**Judge Charitable Foundation**	General	Page 195

The 29th May 1961 Charitable Trust

£3,125,000 (1997/98)

Social welfare, general

c/o Macfarlanes, 10 Norwich Street, London EC4A 1BD
Tel: 0171-831 9222

Correspondent The Secretary

Trustees V E Treves; J H Cattell; P Varney; A J Mead.

Beneficial area UK, with a perhaps diminishing preference for the Warwickshire/Birmingham/Coventry area.

Information available Report and accounts available. Grants list but no narrative.

General The trusts gives grants for both capital and revenues costs. Three types of grants are given: 'one-off' (usually for capital costs), 'recurring', or 'spread over two to three years'. Most of the grants are made in the UK, with a preference for the Midlands. Grants went mainly to arts, leisure and youth; education and training; health and social welfare organisations. Most of the organisations have been supported in previous years.

In 1997/98 the trust had an income of £3.3 million, generated from assets of £84 million. Grant giving totalled £3.1 million in 356 awards, making an average of about £9,000. This was sub-divided as follows:

Arts, leisure and youth	£1,078,000	34%
Health	£555,000	18%
Social welfare	£617,000	20%
Education and training	£340,000	11%
Homelessness and housing	£338,000	11%
Offenders	£128,000	4%
Conservation and preservation	£69,000	2%

A breakdown of grant giving by area shows that one third of the money now goes to national charities, and that 40% of remaining grant giving is concentrated in the Midlands, including at least 35 grants in the Birmingham, Warwickshire and Coventry.

Midlands	£1,259,000	40%
London and the South	£696,000	22%
North	£31,000	1%
N. Ireland	£12,000	1%
National	£1,064,000	34%
International	£63,000	2%

Examples of the larger grants given include those to the University of Warwick (£307,000); Coventry and Warwickshire Awards Trust (£200,000); National Portrait Gallery (£125,000); NSPCC (£110,000) and the London Federation of Clubs for Young People (£100,000).

Large grants also went to Prince's Youth Business Trust (£75,000); Coventry Day Care Fund for the Mentally Handicapped (£65,000); British Association of Cancer United Patients (£52,000) and grants of £50,000 each to the Abbeyfield Society, Birmingham St Mary's Hospice, Crisis, Sadlers Wells Trust and St Basil's Centre Ltd.

Nearly 240 grants were for less than £10,000. Examples of beneficiaries include Greater London Fund for the Blind (£7,500); Refugee Council (£5,000); National Council for One Parent Families (£8,000); Farms for City Children (£5,000); Book Aid International (£4,000); Prisoner Advice Service (£3,000); Warwickshire Wildlife Trust (£2,000); and Birmingham Young Volunteers Adventure Camp (£1,000).

Unfortunately the trust does not explain what work its grants were for. However the trust notes its future commitments as of 1997, in figures implying that just under half the grant giving was for at least two years:

1999	£857,000
1999	£397,000
2000	£58,000

Exclusions Grants only to registered charities

No grants to individuals.

Applications To the secretary in writing. Applicants must enclose a copy of their most recent accounts. Trustees meet in February, May, August and November.

Achisomoch Aid Company

£1,122,000 (1997/98)

Jewish religious charities

26 Hoop Lane, London, NW11 8BU
Tel: 0181-455 7132

Correspondent I M Katz, Secretary

Trustees I M Katz; D C Chontow.

Beneficial area Unrestricted.

Information available Partial accounts and grant list supplied for this entry.

General The trust seeks to advance religion in accordance with the Jewish faith.

In 1997/98 income derived mainly from donations to the charity, there being no permanent endowment.

Almost 500 grants were made to Jewish charities, mostly for hundreds rather than thousands of pounds, and many for smaller sums still – Beth Hayaled, £59 or I Kohn Char, £55.

The largest single grant was to another grant maker, itself featured in this book, the Lolev Charitable Trust (£103,338). The other major awards were to Marbeh Torah Trust (£63,490), WSRT (£29,781), Achiezer (£32,033), Gateshead Talmudical College (£33,002) and the Jewish Secondary Schools Mov. (£21,224).

Action Research

£4,377,000 (1996/97)

Medical research into disabling diseases

Vincent House, North Parade, Horsham, W Sussex RH12 2DP
Tel: 01403-210406; Fax: 01403 210541

Correspondent Dr Tracy Swinfield, Head of Research Administration.

Trustees Chairman Sir Greville Spratt; Patrick Brenan (Treasurer); Peter Batten; J Claughton; Professor David Delpy; Mrs Helen Earle; Lady Martin Fitzalan Howard; Colin Hunsley; Mrs Karen Jankel; Mrs Petronella Keeling; Dr Colin Kennedy; Ian McNeil; Professor A S McNeish; Terence Mansfield; Lord Rea of Eskdale; Prof Mary Ritter; Anthony Wieler.

Beneficial area UK.

Information available Guidelines for applicants, annual review and accounts available from the charity.

Summary Two types of grants are available:

Project Grants:

For up to three years duration, in support of one precisely formulated line of research. Support covers salary costs, consumable and items of equipment essential for carrying out the work. There is no upper limit, but awards average around £75,000. Up to 90% of the funding is in this category.

Grants are normally made to holders of an established post in a university or institution. However research workers who require their own personal support from a project grant, and who have made a substantial intellectual contribution to the grant proposal, may be named as co-applicants with an established member of academic staff as the principal applicant.

Research Training Fellowship:

These are for up to three years duration for the training of young medical and non-medical graduates in research techniques and methodology in areas of interest to the charity. These grants are about 10% of total funding, and on average five fellowships are awarded each year.

General This trust is both a fund raiser and a grant giver. Established in 1952 it explains its remit as follows: 'with the exception of cancer, cardiovascular and HIV/AIDS research, we support a broad spectrum of research with the objective of:

- preventing disease and disability, regardless of cause or age group
- alleviating physical disability.

'Please note that our emphasis is on clinical research or research at the clinical/basic interface.

'Within these criteria we also support the research and development of equipment and technologies to improve diagnosis, therapy and assistive technology including orthoses, prostheses and aids to daily living.

'Please note that we do not provide grants purely for higher education, grants for medical/dental electives or grants to other charities.'

The charity categorised its 1997 grant making as follows:

Pregnancy and the Unborn Child (12%): Many of these grants are concerned with the causes of premature labour

Babies (16%): Looking at the first year of life particularly newborn babies and the consequences of prematurity.

Children (35%): From toddlers to teenagers, including preventative measures such as vaccinations.

Adults (25%): All these grants are concerned with the diseases and disabilities which occur in adulthood.

The Elderly (12%): Research to help find treatments for conditions that particularly affect the elderly such as incontinence and osteoporosis.

In 1996/97 total income amounted to £4.62 million, made up mainly from donations and fundraising activities. Expenditure on fundraising and publicity was very high at £1.7 million, or 47% of the £3.6 million raised (though even this was an improvement on the remarkable 57% of the previous year).

The grant total for 1996/97 was £4,053,000 in 55 grants. Action Research received 288 applications, making the success rate roughly 20%. About £3.6 million went in project grants for medical research, and £422,000 went as grants for research training fellowships. Grants ranged in size from £3,000 to over £300,000. Average grant size was about £70,000.

Examples of the larger programmes supported included:

Brain Cooling to Avoid Damage in Newborn Babies, University College London (£324,000 for a programme grant over three years to study mild hypothermia for neural rescue therapy in term and preterm newborn infants exposed to hypoxia-ischemia);

Urine collection device, Brunel University (£92,000 over 18 months).

Kidney Failure from Haemolytic Uraemic Syndrome, University of Newcastle and Royal Victoria Infirmary (£104,000 over three years for an investigation of the role of factor H in familial and sporadic cases of this syndrome)

Brain Scanning in Epilepsy, Institute of Neurology in conjunction with Hammersmith Hospital (£101,000 over two years for functional imaging investigations of refractory partial epilepsy);

Pain Reduction Following Nerve Injury, University of Liverpool (£92,000 over three years to study the functional consequences of the alterations in the spinal innervation by sensory axons that occurs following nerve injury).

Exclusions Cancer, cardiovascular and HIV/AIDS research.

Applications To the correspondent.

The Adint Charitable Trust

£344,000 (1996/97)

Children, medical research, disabled

BDO Stoy Hayward, 8 Baker Street, London W1M 1DA
Tel: 0171-486 5888

Correspondent Alfred Davis

Trustees Anthony J Edwards; Mrs Margaret Edwards; D R Oram; Alfred A Davis.

Beneficial area UK.

Information available Report and accounts on file at the Charity Commission.

General The trust gives to organisations concerned with children, medicine and health. Grants range in size from tens of thousands of pounds to a few hundred. Many organisations have recieved payments for a number of years

In 1996/97 income of £271,000 was generated from assets of £7.8 million. Grant giving of £344,000 was awarded in 58 grants, making the average about £6,000. The largest grant has gone yearly to HCBA (£42,500 in 1996/97 and £37,500 in 1995/96) and the smallest to Imperial Cancer Research (£250). Most grants were given to national organisations, and spread between children, medical and health charities.

Other large grants went to Cash for Kids (£17,500) and Milton Keynes Community Trust (£14,000). Ten grants were for £10,000: Childline Charitable Trust; CRISIS; Hearing Research Unit; Help the Hospices; I CAN; KIDS; MERU; National Benevolent Fund for the Aged; Radio Lollipop for Children in Hospital and Starlight.

Exclusions Grants can be made to registered charities only and in no circumstances to individuals.

Applications To the correspondent, in writing only. There is no particular form in which applications are required; each applicant should make its own case in the way it considers best.

Thee trust notes that they *cannot* enter into correspondence.

The Al Fayed Charitable Foundation

£399,000 (to institutions 1997)

Community, children, health and general

87-135 Brompton Road, Knightsbridge, London, SW1X 7XL
Tel: 0171 225 6673, Fax: 0171 225 6872

Correspondent Belinda White

Trustees M Al-Fayed; A Fayed; S Fayed.

Beneficial area UK.

Information available Reports and accounts on file at the Charity Commission.

General Set up to support the charity giving of Mr. Al-Fayed and his Harrods company, this charity gives to both individuals and institutions.

The foundation is reported to be set to receive a £7 million cash injection from the sale of Mohammed Al Fayed's collection of royal memorabilia from the Paris home of Edward and Mrs Simpson. The sale is expected to triple the available grant-making income.

Interesting items on sale include two items relating to the 1936 abdication; a George III mahogany library table, where King Edward VIII signed the Instrument of Abdication; and a 78 rpm recording of the famous abdication broadcast.

The foundation has also recently bought the Princess of Wales' former school, West Heath, which went bankrupt. The foundation plans to turn it into a home for the Beth Marie Centre for educating abused children.

Income, coming almost entirely from a covenant with Harrods Holdings Plc, amounted to £646,000 for 1997, with assets of only a few thousand pounds of cash-in-bank. This funded total grant giving of £616,000; £217,000 to individuals, and £399,000 to institutions in 22 grants.

Grants varied in size, with the foundation giving a small number of large donations; average grants were about £9,000. The largest grant went to The Kam Centre for Meningitis (£82,000).

Grants were given to community, children and health organisations such as Zoe's Place, Baby Hospice (£40,000); People's Trust (£28,000); St. Michaels Hospice (£25,000); Samaritans (£25,000); Tommy's Campaign (£19,000); and Charlton Park Schools (£9,400).

Examples of other grants given include those to the Christian Democrats (£45,000), Red Cross International (£39,000), Islamic Cultural Centre (£10,000), and English National Ballet Enterprises (£3,000).

Applications In writing to the correspondent.

The Alchemy Foundation

£1,205,000 (1996/97)

Health and welfare

Trevereux Manor, Limpsfield Chart, Oxted, Surrey RH8 0TL

Correspondent Richard Stilgoe

Trustees Richard Stilgoe; Annabel Stilgoe; Rev. Donald Reeves; Dr Michael Smith; Esther Rantzen; Alex Armitage; Andrew Murison; Holly Stilgoe; Jack Stilgoe; Richard Stilgoe; Rufus Stilgoe.

Beneficial area UK and overseas.

Information available Report and accounts with list of grants of £2,000 or over.

Summary Several hundred donations are made a year, many to institutions giving direct help to individuals. Main beneficiaries are charities working with children, the disabled, and for the prevention/relief of famine. Grants for outside organisations vary from under £2,000 up to £100,000 (typically £2,000-£5,000).

General The foundation was established as the 'Starlight Foundation' in 1985 by Richard and Annabel Stilgoe. Two years later its name was changed to the Alchemy Foundation to avoid confusion with an American charity, recently arrived in the UK, also called Starlight. The major sources of income are the royalties from the musicals Starlight Express and The Phantom of the Opera which Mr Stilgoe has assigned to the foundation.

The foundation is a good example of a personal, rather than an institutional

grant-maker – the trustees (particularly the settlors) contribute a substantial amount of their time on a voluntary basis; an effort which no doubt helped to keep the management and administration costs down to £155 in 1996/97 and which goes far towards excusing the fact that the accounts do not meet the new SORP requirements. A major allocation is made annually to a sister organisation, the Orpheus Trust that shares the same trustees and whose work supports music projects for disabled people.

In 1996/97 the foundation made 522 awards from an income of £1,560,000. Donations to the Orpheus Trust amounted to £544,000 – 37% of the sum value of grants, while a further £625,000 was allocated to institutions and £36,000 to individuals.

The foundation's objects are to make grants for:

- General charitable purposes, especially to help
    - i) persons (in particular babies and children) suffering from mental or physical illness or disability
    - ii) relief of famine;
- Mental and spiritual welfare of the elderly and dying;
- Medical research;
- The Orpheus Trust.

The foundation does not analyse donations by category and the only way of knowing which causes are actually benefiting is through study of the bare names in the grants list. This list shows only the largest grants – about 70, which together account for 67% of charitable expenditure. The largest awards were those to the Orpheus Trust, which included a gift of North Park Farm (valued at £375,000) and other donations totalling £169,000. Aside from these the most substantial awards were to WaterAid (£100,000), Save the Children (£50,000), Oxfam (£30,000), the Osteopathic Centre for Children (£20,000) and Bridget's Home for the Disabled, Cambridge (£18,000). All other gifts were for £10,000 or less with most of the remaining funds disbursed in donations of less than £2,000 (unlisted in the accounts).

The general category consists mostly of grants to community, penal, housing and arts projects. Examples of these are the awards to Camphill Community of Ireland (£8,000), Howard League for Penal Reform (£5,000), Capital Housing Project (£3,000) and Street Symphony Development Project (£5,000).

An approximate breakdown of grants by category is as follows:

Orpheus Trust	*£544,000*	*37%*
Famine	*£134,000*	*9%*
Children	*£92,000*	*6%*
General	*£71,000*	*5%*
Disabled	*£47,000*	*3%*
Elderly	*£11,000*	*1%*
Medical research	*£nil*	*0%*
Unknown	*£569,000*	*39%*

Applications In writing to the correspondent, although applicants should know that the foundation felt that a wide spread of applicants was already being addressed without the additional load that inclusion in this Guide might produce.

Allchurches Trust Ltd

£3,900,000 (planned for 1997)

Churches, general

Beaufort House, Brunswick Road, Gloucester GL1 1JZ
Tel: 01452-528533

Correspondent R W Clayton, Secretary

Trustees C A McLintock (Chairman); Viscount Churchill; M R Cornwall-Jones; Rt Rev D G Snelgrove; B V Day; W H Yates; Mrs S Homersham.

Beneficial area UK.

Information available Report and accounts. For reasons that are not referred to in the report, the charity has not provided the usual list of grants.

General This trust is formed 'to promote the Christian religion and contribute to the funds of charitable institutions'. It is the parent of the wholly owned Ecclesiastical Insurance Group plc whose commercial operations generate its income – an impressive example of bringing commerce to the aid of charity.

Perhaps because of this structure, the charity's annual report is concerned primarily with its commercial activities and there is only the following about its apparently very large charitable activities (though conversations with the charity's helpful staff suggest that references below to 'the Church' refer largely to the Anglican Church).

These editors are uncomfortable with a charity neither reporting its grants in the usual way, nor explaining in its annual report why it is not doing so.

In general terms the trustees make charitable grants to the Church and the Christian community.

'Grants will normally be made to appeals in support of Churches, Church establishments, religious charities, charities preserving UK heritage, theological colleges, schools promoting Christian religion, charities sponsored or recommended by the Church, the local community and those concerned with the welfare of the disadvantaged and disabled.

'Grants will normally be made in the form of single payments.'

This information can no longer be confirmed or illustrated by reference to the actual grants made. The last list of grants was publicly filed at the Charity Commission in 1990. At that time the trust gave most of its support to Anglican churches and church institutions in the UK.

There was also a £100,000 programme of small grants, about a hundred of them a year and mostly of amounts from a few hundred to a couple of thousand pounds, to other charities in the health and welfare fields. Recent correspondence with the trust has confirmed that this programme is still being continued.

Exclusions The trustees do not make grants to charities with political associations. They do not generally make grants to national charities, or appeals from individuals.

Applications 'Applications should be submitted to the correspondent, detailing charity number, the objectives of the charity, the appeal target, how the funds are to be utilised, funds raised to date and previous support received from the trust. If available, the application should be accompanied by supporting literature and annual report.'

Trustees meet quarterly.

The H B Allen Charitable Trust

£696,000 (1997)

General

Bolinge Hill Farm, Buriton, Petersfield, Hants GU31 4NN
Tel: 01730-265031

Correspondent P B Shone

Trustees H B Allen; P B Shone.

Beneficial area UK.

Information available No accounts were on file at the Charity Commission in Autumn 1998 since those for 1994/95, though we have been informed that they have been routinely filed each year. Balance sheet and grants lists supplied for use in this entry.

Summary Grants, usually between £5,000 and £25,000, to a wide range of charities, national and local, but including apparent special interests in:

- nautical charities, both welfare and environmental
- child welfare
- hospices
- third world development
- homelessness

There are few or no grants for the arts, or for education, other than for those with disabilities.

General The grants list for 1997 shows 47 grants, all but two for amounts between £5,000 and £25,000; all are in round figures, suggesting that they may be contributions to the general work of the charities involved, rather than grants to pay for individually costed projects.

Most of the larger grants, and therefore probably most of the money, are for organisations also supported in the previous year. The smaller grants are more widely spread.

The major grants were as follows (with those supported in the previous year asterisked):

Royal Naval Museum	*£100,000*
*Portsmouth area Hospice**	*£50,000*
Church and Community Trust	*£25,000*
*Great Ormond Street Hospital**	*£25,000*
*St Mungo Association**	*£25,000*
*Crisis**	*£25,000*
*The Children's Society**	*£25,000*
*Cancer Relief Macmillan**	*£25,000*
*Intermediate Technology**	*£25,000*
YMCA Tavool Trust	*£25,000*
Calvert Trust (Keswick)	*£25,000*

The trust says that St Mungo's and Crisis have been supported for some time.

Other grants with watery connections included those to The Hebridean Trust (£20,000), Mounts Bay Lugger Association (£10,000), Scottish Sea Bird Centre (£10,000), St Wyllow Church, Near Fowey (£20,000), and the Missions to Seamen (£5,000).

The interest in children showed itself further with support for The Children's Trust (£16,000), Oxford Home Start (£5,000) and the Children Say Charity (£5,000). There were two further grants for hospices, beyond that to The Rowans in Portsmouth, listed above.

Grants for work overseas included those to Intermediate Technology (£25,000) and Tools for Self Reliance (£5,000).

Exclusions No grants to individuals, or to organisations which are not registered charities.

Applications In writing to the correspondent. Trustees aim to meet in March, June, September and December, but applications can be sent at any time though probably not in November or December. "The trustees receive almost 1,000 appeals each year. In view of this large number, it is not their practice to acknowledge appeals, and generally they prefer not to enter into correspondence with applicants other than those to whom grants are being made or from whom further information is required."

The Milly Apthorp Charitable Trust

£580,000 (1996/97)

Health, old people and youth in North-West London

c/o BDO Stoy Hayward,
8 Baker Street, London W1M 1DA
Tel: 0171-486 5888

Correspondent The Secretary

Trustees John D Apthorp; Lawrence S Fenton.

Beneficial area North-West London, mainly the London Borough of Barnet.

Information available
Exceptionally full reports and accounts on file at the Charity Commission, or available from the trust for £5.

Summary Most grants are made through three specific programmes run for the trust by the London Borough of Barnet, with a fourth general grants programme whose grants may stray over the boundaries of that borough.

General The trust was established in 1982 by its namesake, who died in 1989 leaving a large bequest to the trust. Milly Apthorp's wealth, and therefore the trust's, derives from the Bejam food business. Grants are made for projects which 'enrich the lives of the community', particularly the young and/or disabled. The trust carries out this mission with considerable enthusiasm and care which is reflected in its voluminous

annual report and accounts and the employment of a research worker to 'make visits to establish how well the funds provided are being used'.

In 1996/97, the trust's £9 million of investments generated the high income of £622,000. Nearly 600 donations were made to organisations and individuals within four grant programmes. Most funds are disbursed by three programmes with designated funds administered by the London Borough of Barnet: the Administered Fund; Apthorp Adventure Fund; and the Holiday Fund. The fourth programme of direct grants are made from an unrestricted general income fund. The report and accounts contain around ten pages of narrative reviewing the projects assisted, programme by programme. These are too long to reproduce here, but are summarised below.

The largest award in the year was made towards the building costs of the London Borough of Barnet Art Gallery, (£50,000 – the second instalment of a five year £250,000 grant). Other substantial donations were to the Howard League Project in Secondary Schools, £15,000 (£10,000 in 1997/98); Barnet Music Education Services £10,000 (£10,000) and; £11,000 to Barnet Hospital Art Projects towards landscaping of courtyards.

Apthorp Adventure Fund The object of the fund is to give 'opportunities for personal development and social education to adolescents'. A total of £37,000 was distributed in grants benefiting 277 individuals to 'enjoy

adventurous expeditions and character building activities'.

Holiday Fund The mission of this fund is to enable 'physically handicapped people and/or their carers and families to go on holiday'. In 1996/97, £33,000 was disbursed to help 55 families go on respite holidays.

General Income Fund In 1996/97 grants totalled £65,000 (£113,000 in 1995/96) but as much as £289,000 has been disbursed from the fund in previous years (1993/94). Of this money, £33,000 was in the form of forgone rent for RELATE and Samaritans offices and a further £25,000 was donated to the Rainbow Youth Centre (Dollis Valley Project) towards adapting a building for youth work. The Youth Hostels Association received £5,000 as the third instalment of a five year £25,000 award sponsoring subsidised breaks.

In past years the general fund's major projects have included £100,000 to the Mount Moat Residential Centre for youth opportunity activities and £70,000 to Clitterhouse Youth Community Centre.

This admirable trust is exemplary in the way it has found its own mechanisms for meeting its objectives, and for the care with which they are monitored.

Exclusions The trust states that grants are normally only given to registered charities and that trustees do their own research into areas of interest; 'unsolicited appeals are not welcome and no reply is given to unsuccessful applicants.'

The Milly Apthorp Charitable Trust

Grant allocations in 1996/97 (1995/96 figures in brackets):

Administered Fund	265 grants,	£439,000	(246	£324,000)
Young people	97 grants	£167,000	(81	£58,000)
– character building activities	18 grants	£56,000	(17	£78,000)
– job training	62 grants	£46,000	(48	£59,000)
– medical/combating drugs	2 grants	£22,000	(2	£25,000)
– sport	15 grants	£43,000	(14	£13,000)
Sports	9 grants	£24,000	(8	£9,000)
– disabled	4 grants	£7,000	(6	£6,000)
– general	5 grants	£17,000	(2	£3,000)
Illness/disability				
– facilities	81 grants	£138,000	(70	£117,000)
Elderly	22 grants	£28,000	(19	£24,000)
– homes	7 grants	£20,000	(10	£18,000)
– care	15 grants	£8,000	(9	£6,000)
General community benefit	56 grants	£82,000	(68	£115,000)

Applications No applications to the Milly Apthorp Trust are invited. Trustees meet in March, June, September and December.

Organisations in the area of the London Borough of Barnet can apply for the three funds administered by the borough. Applicants 'must be a registered charity or other non-profit making body which provides a service for residents of the Borough and its environs and will normally be based in the Barnet area.

'Grants may be awarded for either capital or revenue projects, which are designed to extend existing levels of provision or to develop new services, and which demonstrate a clearly defined benefit to local people. Awards will not generally be made to support existing activities alone. Projects will be monitored and close attention paid to how the grant awarded is meeting its objectives.

National charities are not eligible to apply but autonomous local branches of national charities may do so. Applications must be submitted in the approved format and accompanied by latest audited accounts, plus constitution of rules and most recent annual report if one is produced. Projects should not normally exceed three years, and at the end of the funding period should be self financing or have an alternative source of funding available'. For fuller details and an application form, contact the Grants Unit, Chief Executive's Dept., London Borough of Barnet, Town Hall, Hendon NW4 4BG (081-202 8282 ext. 2092).

The Arbib Foundation

£2,300,000 (but see below, 1997/98)

Human and animal welfare, medical research

The Old Rectory, 17 Thameside, Henley-on-Thames, Oxon RG9 1LH
Tel: 01491-417 000

Correspondent Linda Sanderson

Trustees M Arbib; A H E Arbib; Hon J S Kirkwood.

Beneficial area Unrestricted, but with a special interest in the Henley area.

Information available Accounts and report, including grants list, on file at the Charity Commission.

General The Arbib foundation supports the philanthropy of Mr. Arbib, the owner of the very successful Perpetual company which deals in personal equity plans.

Income for 1997/98 totalled £1.2 million, made up almost entirely from donations to the foundation. Grants of about £2.3 million were made.

The charity has supported a wide range of general causes including medical, community and social work, and animal welfare, but most large grants are to organisations with which the foundation has an established connection. New beneficiaries are usually local charities in the Henley area.

The trust's objectives specify, among other things, that 'the foundation's aim is to support the establishment of a museum in the Thames Valley for the education of the general public in the history, geography and ecology of the Thames Valley and the River Thames'. Consequently the majority of the grant total has been directed towards this museum (£1.8 million of the grant total to the River and Rowing Museum in Henley). The museum has been completed, to excellent architectural reviews, and opened in Summer 1998, though further grants for its on-going development are possible.

Grants range in size from as little as £500 to as much as £100,000. However, the average appears to be between £2,000 and £5,000. Examples of some of the larger grants in 1997/98 include:

Animal welfare: Animal Health Trust (£100,000), Thames Salmon Trust (£20,000), Tuskforce Wild at Heart (£15,000), Wildlife Trust (£10,000) and the Tiger Trust (£2,500).

Medical research: Institute of Cancer Research (£75,000) and the Leukaemia Research fund (£5,000).

Social and community work: Barbados Children's Trust (£25,000), Help the Hospices (P£20,000), Almshouse Association (£20,000), Wiltshire Community Fund (£5,000) and NSPCC (£4,000).

Applications To the correspondent.

The Architectural Heritage Fund

£2,881,000 (for new loan offers, 1997/98)

Loans for building preservation, grants for feasibility studies

Clareville House, 26-27 Oxendon Street, London SW1Y 4EL
Tel: 0171-925 0199; Fax: 0171-930 0295

Correspondent Hilary Weir

Council of Management
Sir John James, Chairman; David Adams; Colin Amery; Nicholas Baring; William Cadell; Robert Clow; Malcolm Crowder; Sir Brian Jenkins; Jane Sharman; Roy Worskett; Dr Roger Wools.

Beneficial area UK.

Information available Extremely thorough and informative annual report and accounts (in return for donation sufficient to cover costs); detailed application forms; book on forming a buildings preservation trust; directory of funding sources for historic buildings in England and Wales; information sheets.

Summary The fund makes low interest loans and gives advice and information to encourage and assist the preservation and rehabilitation of old buildings by preservation trusts and other charities. Loans supplement funds which groups raise themselves. Grants are also made for feasibility studies on potential projects and to assist with administrative costs of projects.

General The Architectural Heritage Fund (AHF), an independent charity, was established in 1976 to encourage and support the work of organisations dedicated to the preservation and renewal of buildings of architectural and historic significance which have failed to find a viable re-use on the open market.

The AHF is controlled by a Council of Management, half of whom are appointed by the Department for Culture, Media and Sport. The AHF's principal source of working capital over the years has been Government grants supplemented by donations from companies, charitable trusts and individuals.

By the end of the 1997/98 year the fund had contracted loans worth £5.7 million and £3.8 million was on offer in loans for a further 30 projects. In the year the fund received 38 applications for loans amounting to £6.5 million. From these, 33 loan offers amounting to £4.6 million were approved. Fourteen new loans totalling £2.7 million were contracted within the year. The largest was £567,000 to Cockburn Conservation Trust to repair and convert a granary in Leith, Edinburgh, into flats and offices.

Four other building preservation trusts received loans of £300,000 or more, three in England (for an 18th century terrace in Wolverhampton, an old market complex in Hove, and a group of houses in Bury St Edmunds, two of which date back to the 17th century) and one in Northern Ireland (for a former Roman Catholic school building in Belfast).

Almost £96,000 was awarded in grants for 32 feasibility studies in 1997/98, £6,000 more than the 28 grants disbursed in the previous year. Only one of the new loans contracted in 1997/98 was for a project investigated with the aid of one of the fund's grants, but some other buildings studied have subsequently been repaired for re-use by third parties and many are the subject of potential projects by the Building Preservation Trusts concerned. Three grants were in excess of the normal maximum of £5,000 but only one was for the 'exceptional' maximum of £7,500.

Two project administration grants were offered in 1997/98 and £17,000 disbursed from previous and new offers. Two loans associated with such grants were contracted.

The fund operates the following programmes:

Loans

Loans are available to Building Preservation Trusts and other organisations with charitable status for repair projects that involve a change in the use and/or the ownership of historic buildings (normally through their acquisition by the borrower). Only buildings which enjoy the statutory protection of being listed, scheduled or in a conservation area are eligible. Loans are usually for a period of up to two years and for up to 75% of the estimated cost of a qualifying project, subject to a ceiling of £500,000 per loan. (For projects by borrowers that are not Building Preservation Trusts, the AHF will lend up to 50% of the estimated cost and up to £250,000.) Every borrower must provide adequate security. The AHF charges simple interest at 5% for the agreed loan period.

Feasibility Study grants and

Project Administration grants

The AHF makes grants for feasibility studies on historic buildings that Building Preservation Trusts hope to acquire for repair, and grants to enable some Building Preservation Trusts to pay a part-time administrator. Details of the AHF's requirements, terms and conditions are set out in guidance which accompanies the application forms.

The AHF has always restricted its feasibility study grants to Building Preservation Trusts, and for projects which the applicant itself intends to undertake if feasibility is confirmed. The maximum grant is £7,500 (project administration grants are fixed at £3,000), but the AHF expects most studies to cost much less than this.

Other forms of assistance

The AHF gives advice on setting up a BPT and carrying out a project. It organises conferences and seminars, either on its own or with the UK Association of Building Preservation Trusts (APT) to which the AHF provides financial and practical support. AHF publications include 'How to rescue a ruin by setting up a local buildings preservation trust' and 'Funds for Historic Buildings in England and Wales – a Directory of Sources'.

Exclusions Applications from private individuals and non-charitable organisations. Applications for projects not involving a change of ownership or of use, or for a building not on a statutory list or in a conservation area.

Applications Detailed notes for applicants for loans and feasibility studies are supplied with the application forms.

Applicants must provide evidence of charitable status, a description and photographs of the property, architect's drawings and specifications, details of estimated income and expenditure, and either a qualified professional's written estimate of the property's resale value or the name of a repayment guarantor. The AHF budgets for an average commitment of over £1.25 million each quarter in new loan offers. Offers normally remain open for a period of six months.

The AHF's Council of Management meets quarterly to consider loan and grant applications. Please telephone to ascertain dates of meetings and of grant deadlines. If you have any queries, or would like to discuss your project before submitting a formal application, please contact the AHF.

The Artemis

Charitable Trust

£924,000 (1994)

Psychotherapy, parent education, and related activities

Brook House, Quay Meadow, Bosham, West Sussex PD18 8LY

Correspondent Richard Evans

Trustees Richard Evans, Joyce Gai Evans.

Beneficial area UK.

Information available Full accounts, but without a narrative report, are on file at the Charity Commission.

Summary About 15 grants are made a year ranging from £500 to £240,000. A few, large donations account for the vast majority of the money given. Recipients are usually developing organisations providing counselling or psychotherapy services. At least a third of grants are repeated from the previous year and these account for around 90% of total grant expenditure.

General The trust was set up in 1985 by Richard and Gai Evans, the current trustees. Their unchanged policy has been to make 'grants to aid the provision of counselling, psychotherapy, parenting, human relationship training and related activities'. Its capital base has been slowly and steadily decreasing – where it totalled £4.8 million in 1991, at the end of 1997 this figure was down to £3.5 million. This is not due to unlucky investments but because: 'It is the policy of trustees to make grants on the basis of the current needs of grantees, utilising both the capital and income of the trust, and not to restrict grants to the level of income from year to year'.

In 1997, 13 awards were made, the smallest for £500 and the largest for £197,00. Six of these, amounting to £424,000 or 98% of charitable expenditure, were repeated from 1996. However, only one was supported as far back as 1992 – the National Association for Staff Support (which receives around £35,000 annually). The largest grants went to Counselling in Primary Care Trust (£197,000, £230,000 in 1996), PIPPIN (£111,000 in 1997 and 1996) and Parent Network (£60,000, repeated from 1996). New recipients included the British Trust for Conservation Volunteers and Chichester Counselling Services (£1,000 each).

The trust is unusual in its policy of

giving sustained support to a few new initiatives in their early years of development – its example could be usefully followed by some other trusts.

Applications The trust can only give grants to registered charities. 'We cannot entertain applications either from individuals or from organisations which are not registered charities. Applicants should also be aware that most of the trust's funds are committed to a number of major on-going projects and that spare funds available to meet new applications are very limited.'

The Ashden Trust

£635,000 (approved, 1996/97)

Environment, homelessness, urban rejuvenation, community arts, general

See entry for the 'Sainsbury Family Charitable Trusts'
Tel: 0171-410 0330

Correspondent Michael Pattison, Director

Trustees Mrs S Butler-Sloss, R Butler-Sloss, Miss J S Portrait.

Beneficial area UK and overseas.

Information available The trust provides a full report and accounts. Its principal officers in 1996/97 included the Director, Paul Spokes, Finance Director and Miss J Shepherd, Executive.

Summary: This trust is one of the Sainsbury Family Charitable Trusts which share a joint administration. It tackles issues of environmental policy in the UK – transport, pollution, energy efficiency, etc, and key social welfare problems such as homelessness and drug abuse. Overseas ventures (primarily renewable energy projects) that promise to be self-sustaining, both technologically and financially, are supported. In addition those small scale arts activities its supports have social/ environmental aims.

Grant approvals have nearly doubled between 1994/95 and 1996/97.

General Sarah Sainsbury is the settlor of this trust. Its asset value was over £13 million in April 1997 and nearly half of its investments, at market value, were

held in J Sainsbury plc. The trust received another £1 million from the settlor during the year which was included as expendable endowment.

Environmental Projects – UK

'The trust continues to initiate and support work on issues of transport policy, pollution, energy efficiency and renewable energy technology. It has made grants for projects which seek to demonstrate alternative transport schemes and for accessible and objective research to inform both transport policy makers and the general public. The trust has undertaken a number of projects in partnership with the statutory and non-statutory sectors. In 1997 the trust has given particular attention to two studies about company cars, one highlighting best practice in fleet management and another examining company car taxation and how the current system can distort driver behaviour. These reports were officially launched in June 1997.'

In 1996/97 six of its nine projects were concerned with transport policy. The largest allocation, a third of the total given in this category, was made to Company Car Taxation Research (£44,309). Another project was jointly funded with the Department of Transport, Company Car Best Practice (£15,500). IT Power received £30,000 for monitoring and dissemination work on a project to demonstrate solar hot water systems for social housing in the UK.

In the previous year the largest transport allocation was to the Transport 2000 Trust for a part time co-ordinator to develop partnerships between statutory and non-statutory bodies, to encourages alternatives to car use (£45,000 over 3 years).

Environmental Projects – Overseas

'The trust continues to support community based renewable energy projects which aim to help people to help themselves in an environmentally sustainable way. These projects often combine solar, biogas, micro-hydro technologies with income generation and agricultural activities. The trust is particularly interested in piloting technology for potential wide dissemination. Increasing attention is being given to helping develop the renewable energy infrastructure in East African countries where the trust is most active. In 1997 projects have included the development of low-cost technology, training for engineers and setting up credit mechanisms.'

In 1996/97 Energy Alternatives Africa (EAA) in Kenya received two allocations – £25,000 for a revolving loan fund to support income generation in the micro-enterprise sector, using solar power and £15,000 towards a domestic solar energy project for low income households in rural Kenya. Other loan funds supported were East West Environment Ltd, environmental solutions to water and energy supply for a pilot ecotourism project in south Albania (£15,000) and Tropical Whole Foods/Fruits of the Nile, Uganda to a revolving loan fund for small, rural dried fruit producers to use solar powered drying equipment.

Homelessness

'Grants are made to organisations which help people to secure permanent accommodation and to regain economic independence. The trust is interested in the relief of homelessness through the provision of healthcare for people whose circumstances might exclude them, temporarily, from mainstream services. In 1997 the trust has also supported two

The Ashden Trust

	1996/97 No of grants			1995/96 No of grants		
Environment UK	£133,000	9	21%	£155,000	9	32%
Environment – Overseas	£145,000	12	23%	£127,000	8	26%
Homelessness	£134,000	10	21%	£42,000	2	8%
Urban Rejuvenation	£152,000	12	24%	£119,000	5	24%
Community Arts	£55,000	13	9%	£26,000	5	5%
General	£16,000	7	2%	£19,000	8	4%
Total	**£635,000**	**63**	**100%**	**£487,000**	**37**	**100%**

projects seeking to address the problems encountered by those with mental health problems among the homeless agencies in Bristol.'

In 1996/97 Bristol Cyrenians were given support to employ a training and employment development worker and to explore the potential for offering these services to other homeless agencies in Bristol (£25,000). Other beneficiaries included Crisis (at Christmas) to expand its mental health outreach co-ordinated in partnership with a mental health organisation and up to eight local authorities or local health authorities (£20,000) and to Synergy, to support individuals trying to establish projects of social or environmental benefit (£16,000 over 2 years).

Urban rejuvenation

'Funding in this category is aimed at schemes which help people to develop skills, improve self-esteem and increase employment prospects in areas of urban deprivation. This also includes projects concerning drug misuse and offending.'

The grants in 1996/97 under this banner included Turning Point: Drugslink Hammersmith towards the cost of a new drugs education worker in schools plus some outreach work (£45,000 over 3 years), Knowsley Compact for an employment worker on local estates (£42,000 over 2 years), DEMOS for a pilot project on recycling and employment creation (£20,000 over 2 years), and the Women's Education Centre, Sunderland towards its core costs (£15,000 over 3 years).

Community arts

'The trust continues to support a number of grass-roots arts activities, and in particular those groups for which relatively modest grants can have considerable impact. Support focuses on a small number of organisations, ranging from special needs to inner city groups. The trust continues to develop an interest in drama initiatives which seek to inform their audiences about environmental issues.

Two environmental drama projects have been initiated in 1997, one seeking to establish comparative information on environmental drama companies throughout the UK and another working with the University of Greenwich to develop environmental drama in primary schools.'

Most grants were between £1,000 and £5,000. The three exceptions were Channel Arts Association towards a National Youth Arts Festival (£17,505), the Kaleidoscope Project for a part time

arts worker at its community drugs project (£9,300) and Youth Power 2000 to support projects put forward by young people in five local authorities in the North west (£6,900).

General

In 1996/97 the category included emergency appeals and human rights activities.

Exclusions No grants direct to individuals.

Applications The trust met eight times in 1996/97 (five times in the preceding year). 'Unsolicited applications are rarely successful.' See the entry 'Sainsbury Family Charitable Trusts', for address and application procedure.

The Lord Ashdown Charitable Trust

£2,567,000 (1996/97)

Inter faith and racial harmony; Jewish education; community development

c/o Clive Marks FCA, 44a New Cavendish Street, London W1M 7LG
Tel: 0171-486 4663;
Fax 0171 224 3942.

Correspondent C M Marks

Trustees C M Marks; G F Renwick; J M Silver; Dr R Stone.

Beneficial area UK.

Information available Excellent report and accounts.

Summary This impressive foundation, whose future funds are already very heavily committed, has two main areas of work, and is adding a third: it gives extensive support to Jewish education and to a range of community development and welfare activities. To these is being added an increased commitment to interfaith and racial harmony.

Unfortunately for many readers of this book, the trust says – and its level of future commitments supports the statement – 'that the trustees are no longer likely to respond to unsolicited applications'.

General The trust describes its work in its 1996/97 Annual Report, most of which is reprinted below. However, this entry first picks out three particularly interesting topics.

Future policies

In future 'the trustees will be concentrating principally on four areas:

- Inter-faith and racial harmony
- Jewish education
- Sustaining a number of existing beneficiaries
- Grass roots community development.'

The charity has long supported work for inter-faith and inter-race harmony, but it has not had the priority seen above (and

---

The Lord Ashdown Charitable Trust

The 1997 grants and forward commitments for 1998/1999

	1997	1998/99 commitments
Arts	£72,000	£30,000
Children/youth	£151,000	£200,000
Community	£1,345,000	£650,000
Education	£526,000	£2,000,000
Hospice and aged	£59,000	£150,000
Interfaith/race	£9,000	£400,000
Mental health	£30,000	£5,000
Medical	£61,000	£140,000
Preventative medicine	£135,000	£60,000
Students	£30,000	£25,000
Grants for less than £250	£29,000	£–
Grants for consultancy	£–	£160,000
Research and advice to donees	£120,000	£60,000
Total	**£2,567,000**	**£3,880,000**

reflected in the forward funding commitments seen in the table below). While there are a number of other trusts active in the inter-race field, the inter-faith field seems to be relatively underfunded (unlike ecumenical work within Christianity) and so this initiative is most welcome.

Support for charities

The trust offers more than money to many of the charities it supports. 'The trust funds a small number of specialist consultants to advise charities on their internal structure, budgeting, staff training, as well as future planning and efficiency.' A somewhat similar approach is noted and welcomed in the entry for Lloyds TSB Foundation for Scotland. Further, 'the trustees work closely with many of the organisations funded. They frequently attend meetings and events, together with on-site visits.' While this may be the case with many other trusts described in this book, it is seldom reported – the Tudor Trust is another rare example where this is done.

Small grants

'Up to £50,000 is reserved for small donations (of £250 or below), which help towards funding projects such as those dealing with deprived children's holiday schemes, disabled students, equipment for people with disabilities and families in need. 135 applications were successful.' This programme fills a gap below the Small Grants Scheme from the lottery, with its £500 minimum.

The charity also, by funding some individuals in need or distress, has rejected the relatively easy option of simply saying 'No grants for individuals' and has faced up to the apparently inevitable consequence; it received no less than 7,500 applications in 1996/97.

Level of expenditure

The charity had 'income' of only £723,000 in 1996/97. However, unlike most trusts in this book, its level of grant seems to be based on the more appropriate measure of the 'total return' on its investments; this includes unrealised capital gains as well as dividends and interest, and is often a much larger figure. To do otherwise is, over time, effectively to accumulate rather than put to use a charity's resources.

Annual report 1996/97
Principal aims and activities

'The principal aims of the trust are to support a wide range of registered charities and to encompass many areas of the community, particularly those involved in improving inter-faith and inter-race relations, as well as funding projects for the homeless and other disadvantaged sectors.

'With regard to education, emphasis will be given to the learning and teaching of Jewish history, as well as the training of rabbis, teachers, lay leaders and counsellors.

'In the year under review £285,000 was allocated to both hospices and preventative medicine.

'Up to £50,000 is reserved for small donations (of £250 or below), which help towards funding projects such as those dealing with deprived children's holiday schemes, disabled students, equipment for people with disabilities and families in need. 135 applications were successful. In addition it should be noted that during the year many applications between £250 and £5,000 were also researched; our researchers allocating up to two working days each week for this aspect of the trust's work.

'At present ... the trust ... receives approximately 7,500 applications a year, out of which, for 1997, there there were 358 grants (4.8%) over £250 and 135 grants (1.8%) of £250 and under. This, regrettably means a disappointingly large number of applications will inevitably be unsuccessful. Over 95% of the applications for grants over £250 are rejected. This position will not improve for the foreseeable future.

Review of activities

'The trustees work closely with many of the organisations funded. They frequently attend meetings and events, together with on-site visits. Monitoring is carried out by a small research team. This has enabled the trust to continue to support only the most efficient and effective charities, giving them confidence for on-going support.'

Grants in 1996/97

Grant making is summarised in the table herewith. Only the fifty largest grants are listed; which takes the list down to the £10,000 level and covers about half the charity's awards by value. The list gives both the name of the recipient and a note of the purpose of the grant.

The ten largest awards were as follows:

Charta Mede Trust (£40,000 for anti-discrimination work)

Centre for Advanced Professional Educators (£39,000 towards a general appeal)

Templar Trust (£38,000 for Christian/Jewish media work)

Jewish Association for Business Ethics (£37,000 for work on role models in commerce)

Jewish Child's Day (£36,000 for Chernobyl victims)

The 1990 Trust (£36,000 for education on a black vote project)

Bayswater Homeless Families (£36,000)

The Mangrove Trust (£35,000 for Afro-Caribbean community development)

Jewish Memorial Council (£31,000 for religious education with small communities in the UK)

National Alliance for Schizophrenia and Depression (£30,000 for research)

Exclusions The trust does not, except in exceptional cases, fund the mainstream arts, large well-established national charities, exploration or adventure projects, purely academic research (although it does assist in medical research with practical objectives); nor does it give grants to enable students to study overseas, support elective periods of medical students, or assist with fees at private schools.

Applications Individual applicants must live in the UK and must provide proof of need.

Organisations must provide the most recent audited accounts, a registered charity number and, most important, a cash flow for the next twelve months.

All applications should have a stamped addressed envelope attached. It is also important that the actual request for funds must be concise and preferably summarised on one side of A4 paper.

Due to the commitment of nearly all the funds available, the trustees are no longer likely to respond to unsolicited applications.

The Laura Ashley Foundation

£300,000 (to organisations, 1997/98)

Education, general

3 Cromwell Place, London SW7 2JE
Tel: 0171-581 4662

Correspondent Mrs Annabel Thompson

Trustees Sir Bernard Ashley; Jane Ashley; Martyn Gowar;

Professor Susan Golombok;
Geraint Talfan Davies.

Beneficial area England and Wales (for organisations); UK (for individuals)

Information available Report and accounts with grants list but no narrative analysis of grant-making; guidelines; information sheets for individuals.

Summary Grants are made mainly to education organisations in the South of England, but there is also an interest in Wales where a broader range of causes are supported. New guidelines (as of April 1998) state that the foundation is 'unable to process group applications from Ireland or Scotland'. Awards are in the range of £100 to £20,000 (average £5,000) and may be repeated. A number of individuals are also supported in their educational endeavours.

General 1998 was the twelfth anniversary of the foundation which was set up and endowed by Laura and Bernard Ashley and their family with the purpose of making grants in support of 'individuals and group projects, in a wide range of educational and creative fields'.

In the year ending September 1997, the foundation's investments in Laura Ashley holdings took a £7.2 million tumble and this was only partially offset by gains in other investments of £1.6 million. By the end of this disastrous financial year the foundations assets had fallen by 30% to a total of £13.8 million (£19.8 million in 1996). This savagely illustrates the risk of running an undiversified investment portfolio. Although the trustees of family foundations sometimes have an understandable attachment to the company they founded, the long term may reveal such loyalty to be a misplaced virtue. Despite this setback, investment income remained stable at £552,000 – a fall of only £3,000 from the previous year.

Grants to individuals accounted for 18% of charitable expenditure (down from 38% in the previous year) – but this entry concentrates on the £391,000 in grants to organisations. Only one grant was over £20,000 (£24,000 repeat award to the University of Northumbria, the purposes of which are not known). A further nine donations of under £20,000 and over £10,000 amounted to £128,000 (27% of the sum of grants to organisations). The remaining grants were mostly at the smaller end of the £100 to £10,000 range.

Although a variety of charities can be seen in the grants list, practically all are involved in educational projects. The location of the beneficiaries was also varied but with a predominance of Southern or London based organisations. However, this might simply be due to a correspondingly high number of applications from the South. Examples of such typical grants include those to Farms for City Children (£14,000); Brixton College (£1,500) Bournemouth College of Art (£640); Goldsmiths College (£2,700); and Westminster College (£1,800). Other less typical awards were to the Somali Mental Health Project (£500), the Newcastle Society for the Blind (£6,000) and St Warwicks' Church (£5,000).

The guidelines state:

Group projects – for England. Group projects which may be funded – from £1,500 to £10,000 – should have an educational bias (for those aged 25 to 60 years) – special attention will be given to projects offering a second chance.

Group projects – for Wales. Because of the Ashley family interest in Wales and continuing commitment the foundation is interested in more broadly ranging applications for social and community arts projects for all ages and the exclusions do not apply to Wales.

For the foreseeable future we are unable to process group applications from Ireland or Scotland.'

Exclusions No grants will be made to organisations outside Wales for:

buildings; trips or study abroad; home study; mother tongue; childcare; degree courses; alternative medicine; counselling; career guidance; drug related projects; making tapes/videos; publications; buses; conferences; residential; exhibitions.

Grants are not given to post-graduates for:

study abroad; counselling; art and dance therapy; MBA; career guidance; dance; drama; correspondence.

Applications

Applications from organisations

In writing to the correspondent (see below) along with a copy of your latest accounts and annual report (if you have one).

Please read the format carefully and follow the instructions as requested below.

- Adjust to suit your proposal but answer all questions.
- Set out answers 1-7 on one side of A4 only on your headed paper.
- Your application form will be read by the trustees – therefore if it is not set out in an easy to follow format it will not be included for the next trustees' meeting.
- Two trustees meetings are held each year: early March, and early October – applications should reach the office 4 weeks prior to the meetings.

1) Give brief description on the overall work of your organisation (6 lines).
2) Have you ever received funding from the Laura Ashley Foundation? Brief description and the amount granted – is the project continuing?
3) Give brief description of the project for which you are applying for funding in the format it took last year (6 lines).
4) If the project was running last year – how many students participated, what was their average age, what was the length of the course (hours per week and weeks per year) and what are these students doing now.
5) Give brief outline of the project for which you seek funding (6 lines).
6) What will be taught – how many students per course – how many hours per week and weeks per year is the course – how many courses per year.
7) What funding is requested and for what exact purpose (4-6 lines).
On a separate page – financial and staff details for this project:
7a. breakdown of budget for this project;
7b. funds sought and received from other sources (amount and organisations);
7c. number of staff involved – their titles – who funds these posts;
7d. number of students involved – per course.

The Trustees meet twice a year.

Applications from individuals

Post graduate study: Students should write with details to the foundation to receive an information sheet. Grants are made to students aged 25 to 60 who have been resident in the UK for at least ten years and on courses which reflect the Ashley family interests.

Further education: Students should write to the foundation with details. Individuals studying A level, BTech, horticulture, design, craft, vocational courses may apply for funds towards tuition fees or high travel costs. Students should be aged 25 to 60 years (discretion may be made for exceptional younger students).

The Baily Thomas Charitable Fund

£2,468,000 (1996/97)

Mental illness, mental disability

Ernst & Young, 400 Capability Green, Luton LU1 3LU
Tel: 01582-643125

Correspondent Mr G R Mean

Trustees: Charles J T Nangle; Richard F Chadburn; Professor Michael G Gelder; Michael R Macfadyen.

Beneficial area UK, with a special interest in Nottingham and surrounds.

Information available Report and accounts listing largest 50 grants only and without narrative analysis.

Summary An unknown number of grants are made to organisations said to be working in the fields of disability/ illness care or research. Most of these are probably specifically involved with mental health. The largest grant possible is around £270,000. Beneficiaries are usually national charities or based in and around London or Nottingham.

General The fund was established in 1970 with the aim of supporting 'charitable purposes or charitable institutions connected with the prevention, treatment or relief of mental or other form of illness'.

In the year ending October 1997 assets totalled £66 million and income was over £15 million (including a settlement of £12.7 million). Administration costs absorbed only £91,000 or 4 pence for every pound donated. As the accounts list only the top 50 grants (accounting for 58% of charitable expenditure) this entry can only explore these. They varied between £10,000 and £265,000 (average £36,000) and nearly all were repeated in the preceding year (sometimes for a different sum).

Five grants of £100,000 or more accounted for 29% of the total value of donations, 6 awards between £50,000 and £75,000 for 14% and 23 of over £10,000 and under £50,000 for 18%. Often the amount paid to organisations was larger than the amount initially awarded but the fund does not explain why this is.

Moreover, the fund does not state the purpose for which grants were made and it does not categorise grants by the cause benefited. However, from studying the grants list it appears that these large recipients are indeed of the sort described by the guidelines:

'The Baily Thomas Charitable Fund is a registered charity which was established to aid both the research into the causes of mental disability and illness and the care and relief of those affected by making grants to voluntary organisations working within these fields.

'Applications will only be considered from voluntary organisations which are registered charities or are associated with a registered charity.

'Advocacy projects: applications will only be considered from projects based within a 75 mile radius of Nottingham.

'Applications for research grants will only be considered from established research workers and will be subject to the normal professional peer review procedures.'

The largest grants of 1996/97 went to the Mental Health Foundation – Children and Young People Initiative (£265,000 paid and a further £200,000 awarded); National Autistic Society (£250,000 paid, £200,000 awarded); Great Ormond St Hospital Children's Charity (£127,000 a year for two years); Martha Trust (£100,000 a year for two years) and; Shaftesbury Society (£100,000 a year for two years).

Exclusions Not normally awarded to individuals.

Applications Application Forms are available from the correspondent. Annual report and accounts must be sent. Trustees' meetings are usually held in June and November/December each year and applications should be submitted not later than 1 May or 1 October for consideration at the next meeting.

Paul Balint Charitable Trust

£1,028,000 (1996/97)

Jewish charities, medicine, children and general

c/o 26 Church Crescent, London N20 0JP

Correspondent The Secretary

Trustees Dr Andrew Balint; Dr Gabriel Balint-Kurti; Paul Balint; Marc Balint.

Beneficial area UK and overseas.

Information available Accounts on file at the Charity Commission, but without a narrative report.

General The trust gives most of its money to Jewish charities with the remainder given to a variety of social and medical organisations.

From assets of £3.3 million in 1996/97, the trust generated an income of £183,000. Prolific grant giving of £1.03 million, resulting in a deficit of about £860,000, was covered by payments from the trust's capital.

A total of 100 grants were made. Although only 35 grants were made to Jewish charities, they amount to 90% of total grant giving. The main bulk of the grants (about 72% of the grant total) went in seven awards: Nightingale House (£300,000); Jewish Care (£120,000); Jewish National Fund (£108,000); Jewish Philanthropic Association (£97,000); Institute of Advanced Education in Jaffa (£83,000); World Jewish Relief (£19,000); and Shaare Zadek Medical Centre. All of these organisations received substantial grants in previous years.

The remaining grants were mostly around £2,000 to £3,000 and went to a variety of children's and medical organisations. Examples of the larger ones included Chabads Children Of Chernobyl (£61,000), QEH Children's Fund (£5,000), Children with AIDS (£3,000); Norwood Children (£2,000); Marie Curie Cancer Care (£2,000), Fight for Sight (£10,000) and the British Retinitis Pigmentosa Society (£2,000).

Exclusions No grants for religious purposes or to individuals.

Applications To the correspondent in writing.

The George Balint Charitable Trust

£2,126,000 (1996/97)

Jewish charities, general

Suite A, 4-6 Canfield Place, London NW6 3BT
Tel: 0171-624 2098

Correspondent G Balint

Trustees G Balint; A Balint; Dr A Balint.

Beneficial area UK and overseas.

Information available Accounts are on file at the Charity Commission, but without the required analysis or explanation of grants.

General In 1996/97 the trust had assets of £4.25 million, which generated the high income of £625,000. Grants far exceeded income, as in previous years, at £2.13 million. This trust has similar grant giving policies to the Paul Balint and Andrew Balint Charities (see separate entries)

About 227 grants were made in 1996/97, with most of them going to Jewish charities. About half the grant total went to nine charities that all also received donations in the previous years: Beizit Lepletof (£205,000); Galil Education Centre (£123,000); Jewish Care (£150,000); Schlafids Trust (£100,000); British Erunah (£150,000); Jewish National Fund Israel (£108,000); Ohel Sarah (£50,000); Yohav Study Centre (£50,000); and World Jewish Relief (£27,000).

Other substantial grants included those to Friends of the Sick (£50,000) and Chabads Children of Chernobyl (£61,000).

The remaining money was spread between a variety of health, children and welfare organisations, with grants rarely more then £5,000.

Exclusions No grants to individuals, including students.

Applications In writing to the correspondent.

The Andrew Balint Charitable Trust

£728,000 (1996/97)

Jewish charities, welfare

Suite A, 4-6 Canfield Place, London NW6 3BT
Tel: 0171-624 2098

Correspondent A Balint

Trustees A Balint; Mrs A Balint; Dr G G Balint-Kurti.

Beneficial area UK and overseas.

Information available Accounts are on file at the Charity Commission but without a narrative report.

General In 1996/97 the trust had an income of £258,000 generated from assets of about £4 million. A total of 141 grants were made to a variety of mainly Jewish charities, though there was an interesting and substantial award for Quaker Social Action. There were a large number of small grants and a small number of large grants; six grants accounted for 70% of the total and ninety-nine were for less than £1,000.

The six largest grants were to: Jewish Care (£150,000); Jewish Philanthropic Association (£120,000); Jewish National Fund Israel (£108,000); BIA Quaker Social Action (£61,000); Institute of Advanced Education in Jaffa (£41,000); and the Shaare Zadek Medical Centre (£30,000). The rest of the money was given to a wide variety number of welfare and children's organisation.

This trust shares some of its grant giving interests with the other Balint Trusts (see adjacent entries).

Exclusions Personal problems, education and travel.

Applications In writing, but the correspondent stated 'funds are fully over-committed for the near future'.

David and Frederick Barclay Foundation

£1,156,000 (1997)

Medical research, welfare

20 St James's Street, London SW1A 1ES
Tel: 0171-915 0915

Correspondent Lord Peyton, Chairman

Trustees Lord Peyton of Yeovil, Chairman; David Barclay; Frederick Barclay; Lord McAlpine.

Beneficial area UK.

Information available Report and accounts, now without a grants list but with a good description of some selected grants.

Summary Grants to organisations vary from a few hundred pounds to £100,000. A limited number of small grants are made to individuals.

General The foundation was established in 1989 by David and Frederick Barclay whose continuing donations are used to make grants of around £1 million a year. In 1997 there were 60 grants of £1.000 or more.

The foundation's report and accounts for 1996/97 do not contain a grants list, although there is a narrative exploration of the 13 'more substantial donations' (which does not show the amounts awarded). Therefore it is not clear where the bulk of support is going, nor whether the 13 gifts analysed give a fair and accurate impression of the trust's support.

The Chairman's statement for 1997 was as follows:

'The value of the fund on 1st January was £367,000 (1996 £425,000).

'Donations received during the year amounted to £1,135,000. In the eight years of the foundation's life a total of some £9 million has been distributed.

'While charities naturally welcome promises of continued support over a number of years, this has serious disadvantages for donors; flexibility and freedom of manoeuvre are seriously diminished. For that reason, I have avoided anything in the nature of a firm commitment and have simply told those who have expectations that they must make do with hopes, rather than promises.

Our more substantial donations this year have been:

'*Anna Douglas-Pennant Charitable Trust.* Continued research into cystic fibrosis by Professor John Warner at Southampton General Hospital.

'*Bromley by Bow Centre.* In the twelve years in which Andrew Mawson has run the centre, he has achieved little short of miraculous progress; he has made it into something of a pathfinder and an example to others of how best to solve the myriad problems which beset underprivileged areas.

'Andrew Mawson arrived in Bromley by Bow, one of Britain's most depressed districts, in 1984, as the newly appointed minister at a United Reformed Church, which was on its last legs. The once cold and leaking church has been refurbished and opened out to serve as a nursery, toy library, crèche, art gallery and a church. The adjacent hall is thriving with activity ranging from a large community care programme to a set of artists' workshops for local people.

'The centre is the base for a literacy project for 300 local Bengali families. The 870 staff, volunteers and centre members usually eat in a self-financing cafe attached to the building. A health centre, which is the first in Britain to be owned by its patients, has just been opened by the Health Minister Tessa Jowell, after an investment of more than £1.5 million in a stylishly designed building. This project is described by the new Government in the Green Paper "Our Healthier Nation", as a pathfinder project with national significance.

'The Royal and Sun Alliance insurance group is financing a £300,000 three year project to create new ways of diverting young people away from crime.

Nat West Bank has awarded the centre £220,000 for a three year scheme to promote young local entrepreneurs. The adjacent three acre park in which the health centre has been built has been redesigned, incorporating a series of sculptures, a garden and a play area. Seventeen homes with care and support have been built on the perimeter of the park for homeless people and a plan for an enterprise centre is now being developed.

'Out of nothing has emerged a thriving centre running 125 activities and used by some 2,000 people each week. It combines health and welfare with work and enterprise, serving young and old, working with local and central government, the private and voluntary sectors and the church.

'*Cardiovascular Research, St Thomas' Hospital.* The foundation has provided funds to go towards equipping a dedicated microscope laboratory, a thermal cylinder and microcentrifuge to separate cellular components for determination of the levels of protein produced by the gene of interest in heart tissues and cells.

'*Harefield Hospital Research and Development Appeal:* To keep Harefield at the forefront of research and treatment and to safeguard employment of young key researchers.

'*Imperial College School of Medicine, St Mary's.* The five year programme has contributed to significant progress which has been made in inducing the re-growth of nerve fibres after spinal cord injury; a few years ago this was thought to be impossible. This does give some hope of a major step forwards eventually becoming possible.

'*NSPCC Justice for Children Appeal.*
'*RAFT/Phoenix.* A collaborative project of research into improving the healing of nerves where they have been severed in an accident. Recent results have shown that the dual approach to treating nerve severance is often more effective than the current method of using nerve grafts and has considerable potential for closing

quite large gaps between the nerve ends. Healing will be much less traumatic for patients, require fewer hospital resources and will avoid the need to remove healthy nerves from donor sites. Other important discoveries about the growth and behaviour of nerves have been made in the course of this project. The foundation's support has enabled the Phoenix Appeal to employ a dedicated scientist for three years and has led to important new knowledge which will benefit many thousands of people in the future.

'*Rose Road Association.* Develops and provides services, information and support for children and young adults who have profound and multiple disabilities.

'*Royal National Theatre.* Contribution towards the cost of a lift for disabled people.

'*Thrombosis Research Institute*

(a) Research into the development of novel anti-thrombotic therapies based on highly specific synthetic inhibitors of thrombin, an enzyme which plays a crucial role in the development of a blood clot. Over 200 novel compounds have been synthesised, a lead compound has already been investigated in detail and shown to be highly effective and safe in various models and is currently in clinical phase II studies.

(b) Work on the development of a simple blood test, which can be used for detecting high risk individuals who are likely to suffer a fatal heart attack or stroke.

(c) Beatrice Research Centre. A large scale study has been undertaken involving 850 volunteers, the aim of which has been to assess whether the adoption of a lower body temperature over a period of time results in reduced levels of markers of cardiovascular disease and chronic fatigue syndrome. Very exciting results have been obtained and this has formed the basis of eight papers published to date.

'*University College,* London. Research aimed at developing a new clinical test which will be used to help in the management of patients with Graves' Disease. The first phase of the work has been completed and the molecular biology been started.

'*Winged Fellowship.* Contribution for funds for redevelopment of a holiday centre for disabled people.

'The tide of requests for help from individuals and from charities, large and small, national and local has continued

to grow. Since resources are, in the nature of things, always limited, one is faced constantly with the painful task of rejecting appeals made on behalf of deserving causes. David and Frederick Barclay have by their generosity placed many people in their debt. I am very conscious of the immense demands made upon them and most grateful to them for the sympathetic way in which they have responded when, like Oliver Twist, I have asked for more.'

Applications In writing to the chairman.

The Baring Foundation

£3,120,000 (1997)

Strengthening the voluntary sector, arts in education and in the community, international

60 London Wall, London EC2M 5TQ
Tel: 0171-767 1348; Fax: 0171-767 7121

Correspondent Toby Johns, Director

Trustees Nicholas Baring, Chairman; Lord Ashburton; Tessa Baring; R D Broadley; Lord Howick; Janet Lewis-Jones; Lady Lloyd; Sir Crispin Tickell; Martin Findlay; Anthony Loehnis; J R Peers.

Beneficial area UK, with a special interest in the London, Merseyside and Tyne and Wear and Cleveland areas; also UK charities working with NGO partners in developing countries. See below and under 'Applications' for more details.

Information available Exemplary annual report and guidelines for individual programmes are available from the foundation.

SUMMARY

Forced by the collapse of Barings Bank, its main source of funds, to reconsider its activities, the foundation has developed eight exceptionally interesting and innovative programmes, under three headings, to replace its former rather generalised giving.

A key and most unusual activity, under each heading, is the giving of grants for core costs of up to £25,000 a year for up to three years. This is a most welcome alternative the now almost universal orthodoxy of 'project funding'. This aspect of the foundation's work is not advertised 'as it seems likely that the foundation' administration would be overwhelmed if these grants were open to general application. ... The selection ... follows an extended period of consultation and information gathering'.

This system of allocation, done in a systematic fashion and on a substantial scale, is in itself a novelty. The written application, itself quite a recent innovation, rules almost all the grant making described in this book.

A second theme running through most of the programmes is a desire to encourage co-operation and mutual support between different voluntary organisations.

There are excellent and detailed descriptions of the programmes guidelines, reprinted below, followed at the end of the entry by equally specific 'Guidelines' for applicants to each programme, as they stood in September 1998.

Applicants should note that there is little or no provision for general grants in the fields concerned – grants are for specific programmes or sub-programmes – and that there are often very specific criteria by which applications and organisations will be assessed.

The new programmes are as follows (with the number and value of the grants in 1997):

Strengthening the Voluntary Sector 210 grants		£1,641,000
Arts in education and the community 115 grants		£638,000
International 14 grants		£138,000

There were 1,705 applications, of which 1,384 were eligible, and there were 339 grants in all.

Strengthening the voluntary sector (£1.6 million in 1997).

'The foundation wishes to support the growth of a vigorous, effective and creative voluntary sector, and of smaller organisations in particular. The programme is intended to assist the strengthening and the further development of the sector across the the whole range of activities in which voluntary, charitable and community based organisations are engaged. Grants are not normally made for more than £30,000, and most are expected to be for much less. They are available to national organisations and to local organisations in Merseyside, the North East and, in some cases, in London.

'There are four funds within this programme:

- Core Costs (£893,000 in 1997), underpinning the central running costs of selected organisations (see above).
- Organisational Skills and Effectiveness (£495,000 in 1997), seeking to improve the effectiveness of organisations, both internally and in relation to other voluntary organisations
- Knowledge and Skills Exchange (£54,000 in 1997), providing opportunities for interaction between organisations with common interests
- Mergers and Joint Structures (£199,000 in 1997), responding to the need for organisations to think about major structural change.

Arts in education and the community

- Core costs fund (5 grants totalling £375,000 agreed in 1997)
- Small Projects Fund: £160,000 a year. The foundation is interested in supporting a wide range of different types of activity across all art forms and in all parts of the UK. Grants from £500 to £5,000.
- Knowledge and Skills Exchange Fund: £90,000 a year. The foundation wishes to support high quality work by artists and arts organisations in educational and community settings. The fund is to enable people in the field to learn from each other through the exchange of knowledge, skills and ideas. Grants from £500 to a usual maximum of £3,000.

International Grants Programme

'£138,000 in 1997, but budgeted to grow to £625,000 a year . Support for activities that will enhance the effectiveness of the voluntary and community sector, especially in sub-Saharan Africa and Latin America – in particular through the sharing and transfer of expertise, knowledge and skills within those regions and between them and other parts of the world.'

'Grants not normally made for more than £15,000, and most are expected to be for much less.

In November 1998 the foundation announced the appointment of Toby Johns as its new Director. Previously working at the Rural Development Commission, he has a civil service background.

GENERAL

This long entry is arranged as follows. After an introductory section, there is a detailed description of each of the three programme areas taken in turn, from the excellent 1997 Report on Activities. This is followed by the contents of the detailed Information Sheets published by the foundation.

The foundation is independent of ING Barings bank, though still housed in its offices. Despite the collapse of the bank, which was wholly owned by the foundation (following its previous collapse and rescue at the end of the last century), the foundation still had an endowment worth £60 million at the end of 1997. This generated an investment income of £2.5 million. There was further income bringing the total to over £3.3 million. Given the extensive grant programmes described below, the grant making costs of the foundation were modest, at £189,000 or less than 6% of income.

The staff of the foundation was as follows in the Autumn of 1998:

Director:	Toby Johns
Administration Officer:	Mrs B. Allerhand
Administration Officer:	Miss Z.A. Kaye
Administration Officer:	Mrs T. Skelhorn
Information Officer:	Anne Murray.

Advisers

Lucy Ball (Mergers and joint structures)Emma Crewe (International) Julia Unwin (Strengthening the voluntary sector) Phyllida Shaw (Arts)

The Chairman's Introduction to the 1997 Report on Activities reads in part as follows:

'... it was an extremely busy year for the Director, the staff and the advisers. The programmes set in place in and since 1996 are all functioning and result in a very heavy workload. These programmes were formally set up to run till the end of 1999 and while we believe that they are hitting the targets we set, it will only be possible to come up with a fully considered judgement when they have been running for a somewhat longer period.

'... a major change has come about through the recruitment of our Director, David Carrington, to run the PPP Healthcare Trust (See separate entry. Ed). We are greatly in his debt ... .

The rest of this entry, apart from some concluding remarks, is taken entirely from the foundation's Report and Activities (David Carrington's last for this foundation), and Guidelines. Quotation marks have been omitted in the interest of clarity.

Aims and priorities

The starting point for all the foundation's grant making activity is a belief in the importance to the whole community of having an active, well informed and ably led voluntary sector, nationally and locally. The voluntary sector is extraordinarily diverse; it contains community associations and self-help groups, national cultural institutions and universities, as well as charities in the traditional sense. All the organisations within it, however, whether or not they employ staff, have volunteers as trustees or management committee members - volunteers who have come together to provide a service to others, to highlight a need or injustice or to generate new resources or activities within their particular shared community. The foundation concentrates its efforts on helping strengthen those organisations' capacity and confidence.

Distinct grant programmes have had to be developed to be appropriate to the particular circumstances of arts organisations and of voluntary organisations that work internationally, but, for all of its work, the foundation aims to use charitable grants to support voluntary organisations in ways that will enhance their ability to respond effectively to changes in funding or government policy, to identify and tackle new opportunities or challenges with skill and confidence, and to manage their affairs in ways that ensure their charitable purposes are efficiently and competently fulfilled.

Though each grants programme has special priorities, they all contain three features:

- core costs grants to underpin over three years the central running costs of a selected group of voluntary organisations
- the exchange of practical knowledge and skills between people involved as staff or volunteers in running organisations
- one or more defined funds for which organisations can apply for grants

Core costs

60% of the foundation's grants budget is committed to supporting the central core running costs of selected voluntary organisations. By the end of 1999, 64 organisations will have been provided with core costs grants. The first 18 were awarded during 1997. Each grant is made for three years for up to £25,000 a year (subject to review at the end of each year). The specific purpose of each grant is not formally restricted, but all recipient organisations designate the grants to support one or more of their central functions.

The thinking behind the decision of the

foundation's Council to allocate more than half of their grants to the underpinning of organisations' core costs stems from their analysis of the impact on the role of grant giving trusts of recent changes to the funding of voluntary and community organisations. An increasing amount of the funding of such organisations is now tied to specific projects or is restricted in purpose. Though such systems of funding have strengths, they can leave unfunded the leadership and creative core of an organisation and constrain its ability to plan ahead and to develop new policies and ideas. Charitable organisations that have limited opportunities to raise money from the general public are particularly vulnerable to the effect of these changes as are 'infrastructure' organisations - voluntary organisations providing information, training or other support services to other voluntary or community organisations. These sorts of organisations have been a particular priority for the foundation.

A secondary objective of the core costs grants programme is to provide the foundation with close links over a period of years to a range of organisations working across the charitable sector, enabling the foundation itself to be kept well informed about developments and issues within each organisation's particular area of activity.

The availability of the core costs grants is not advertised as it seems likely that the foundation's administration would be overwhelmed if these grants were open to general application. The selection by the foundation's Council members of the organisations to be offered core costs grants follows an extended period of consultation and information gathering.

As 1997 was the first year of this part of the foundation's programme, it is as yet too early to judge if the core costs grant system is realising the foundation's hopes. Preliminary evaluation, however, has proved positive, the recipient organisations reporting that the grants have enabled them to strengthen and to develop their work and internal operations in ways that would not otherwise have been possible. Further comment on the experience of the initial grants can be found later in the report in the sections on the individual programmes.

The remainder of this report describes and comments on each grants programme in turn. Each of the foundation's specialist advisers has contributed to the sections on the parts of the programmes with which they have been involved, Julia Unwin on

Strengthening the Voluntary Sector, Phyllida Shaw on the Arts and Emma Crewe on International grants.

STRENGTHENING THE VOLUNTARY SECTOR

Introduction

4 grants programmes: 453 eligible applications, 210 grants, £1.64 m agreed.

The voluntary sector faces significant change. This has always been the case but the last few years have witnessed changes in both the policy and the funding environments that have posed many major challenges to the charitable sector and its methods of operation. It is in this context that the Baring Foundation has decided to commit its largest grants programme to 'Strengthening the Voluntary Sector'.

The previously clear distinctions between the responsibilities of the state and of charities have been eroded, with three important consequences. Firstly, services provided by local authorities or health authorities are increasingly managed within the charitable sector. Secondly, it is widely accepted that the effective regeneration of run down rural and urban areas requires the involvement of strong community organisations. Thirdly, the Government increasingly looks to the voluntary sector for help and advice in policy formulation. While these changes are largely welcomed, they present a challenge to many existing voluntary organisations: how to engage more effectively with the statutory sector, while preserving the independence of the voluntary sector.

All this is taking place in a tight, and changing, funding climate. Although total statutory funding of the voluntary sector has increased, the use of funding is more rigidly prescribed. There is a growing emphasis on achieving targets and a reluctance to offer open-ended funding. At the same time there has been a growth in new funding sources. The national lottery, in particular, has changed the fund raising landscape. While voluntary organisations have benefited from new resources, there remains a need for smaller grant making trusts to take a lead in supporting strategic activities aimed at protecting the independence of the sector and promoting development.

Within the Strengthening the Voluntary Sector Programme, the Baring Foundation has identified four areas where it can make a positive impact, and has established a fund to support each one. These funds are:

1. Core Costs, underpinning the central

running costs of selected organisations

2. Organisational Skills and Effectiveness, seeking to improve the effectiveness of organisations, both internally and in relation to other voluntary organisations

3. Knowledge and Skills Exchange, providing opportunities for interaction between organisations with common interests

4. Mergers and Joint Structures, responding to the need for organisations to think about major structural change.

The priorities underlying each of these funds, together with the progress of each in 1997, are provided in the following sections.

Core costs grants

13 grants offered, £892,500 agreed.

Priorities

In 1997, the foundation awarded core costs grants to 13 organisations within the Strengthening the Voluntary Sector grants programme. The selected organisations reflected the broad sweep of the foundation's interests, including education and health, conservation and the environment as well as community development and social services. The traditional geographic priorities of the foundation were also maintained, seven of the grants going to national voluntary organisations and two each to organisations working in London, Merseyside and the North East of England. Several are membership organisations with a well established self-help ethos; others are 'infrastructure' organisations providing support, training and other services to local and community organisations; several act as advocates for groups of people currently or previously in institutional or other forms of statutory care.

The foundation targeted organisations that were small enough to find it extremely difficult to finance their own core costs through other activity, but avoided those that were so small that the contribution would be greater than 10% of the total turnover. Voluntary organisations that already had significant unrestricted revenue, for example from legacies or general public donations, were not chosen. Nor were organisations that were primarily dependent upon income earned from contracts with statutory bodies; it is the view of the foundation that contract prices should include the real core costs of the organisation that are attributable to the contracted service.

Evaluation

This programme has been evaluated by visiting every organisation that received a grant in 1997. The findings confirmed the Council members' confidence that they had been right to support core costs since all the recipients argued that either their survival or their development would have been in jeopardy without this source of unrestricted funding. Most of the organisations had used the grant to underpin the salary cost of a senior staff member. Others had invested in development work to strengthen the organisation's own capacity or the network which it supported, some because they were facing unusual demands or opportunities for growth.

Benefits were clearly accrued. Many recipients reported that the change of government in May 1997 had resulted in particularly high demands for their policy work and core funding was critical in enabling a positive engagement in the policy debate with the government. For two of the organisations, the funding had enabled them to develop their own earning potential and to explore the scope for self-sufficiency. A further two organisations reported that the funding was crucial in maintaining their work during a year when obtaining funds had been exceptionally difficult.

By 1999, the foundation will have supported the core costs of 36 organisations within this part of its grants programme. In doing so, it hopes to have a significant impact in strengthening organisations that it believes are important to the development of a diverse and creative voluntary sector. By continuing to monitor the effectiveness of core cost funding, it hopes to influence other funders to consider also the value of supporting 'those parts of an organisation that no one else wants to fund'.

Organisational skills and effectiveness

452 applications, 394 eligible applications, 80 grants, £494,954 agreed.

Priorities

The largest block of the foundation's funds that is open to direct applications is intended to support the further growth and enhancement of 'a vigorous, effective and creative voluntary sector, and of smaller organisations in particular'. Open to applications from national voluntary organisations across the UK and from community and other volunteer managed organisations in London, Merseyside and the North East of England, the grants programme attracted 394 eligible applications in

1997. 80 grants (20% of those that were eligible) were agreed, totalling £494,954. The grants ranged in size from £750 to £30,000, the average being £6,187.

The guidance sent out by the foundation to prospective applicant organisations stated that the foundation 'will not normally make single grants of more than £12,000 and expects most to be for much less'. Despite this, 156 of the 394 applications (40%) were for £12,000 or more. Only 5 organisations received grant offers of more than £12,000 and, of the successful applications, 85% received grants of less than £10,000.

Distribution by type of organisation

The funds are available to organisations across the whole spectrum of voluntary sector activity. This breadth of scope was reflected in both applicants and grant recipients, which included advice services and helplines, advocacy and campaigning organisations, community groups and neighbourhood development projects, self help groups, domiciliary and day-care services, arts organisations, projects for homeless people, and organisations providing infrastructure services to other organisations (information, training and representation). The applicant and recipient organisations can be divided into seven categories according to their primary interest, as shown in Chart 2. This indicates that the majority of both applications and grants related to organisations involved in either community development or the provision of social care services.

Applications and grants by category of organisation (approximate figures)

	Applications	Grants
Social care	47%	41%
Community development	30%	40%
Culture/arts	7%	10%
Health	9%	2%
Environment	4%	4%
Education	3%	3%
Housing	2%	2%

Not only was the success rate of organisations in the community development sector higher than in the others, but the successful applications included the highest proportion (58%) of grants of over £10,000. This difference reflected the foundation's preference for supporting initiatives intended to increase organisational leadership skills and knowledge rather than measures designed only to improve or extend specific service provision. This is further reflected in the high proportion (69%) of successful applications where the funded activity aimed to assist several organisations or whole networks rather than solely the applicant organisation.

Activities funded

The majority of grants were made for some aspect of organisations' training needs or for consultancies or to help pay either for a feasibility study or towards initial start up costs, as indicated in the chart (approximate figures)

Training	39
Feasibility studies	14
Consultancies	12
Start-up costs	9
Other	6

Of the training activities that were supported, 15% were focused specifically on user involvement, 10% on staff only, 8% on volunteers and 36% on committee members/trustees.

Geographical spread

In deciding to restrict access to these funds to organisations that were either based in three specific regions or worked throughout at least one country in the UK, the foundation has maintained the geographic priorities it had established a decade previously. The geographical breakdown of the organisations making applications and receiving grants in 1997 is as follows:

	Applications	Grants	
National	155	38	£265,000
London	160	30	£159,000
Merseyside	32	5	£33,000
North East	47	7	£37,000

National organisations include those that work throughout the UK or at least one country within it. Of the latter, organisations working only in Northern Ireland, Scotland and Wales formed a small but important sub-set of the total:

	Applications	Grants
Northern Ireland	7	1
Scotland	19	1
Wales	7	3

The amounts of money distributed at national and regional levels were roughly in line with the numbers of applications received and the number of grants offered.

Grants to promote strategic thinking

The foundation has been keen to improve the quality and depth of information about the work of voluntary organisations - in comparison with other sectors within the economy, the voluntary sector has, too often in the past, relied on anecdotal, out of date or insufficiently rigorous information about its role. A number of the foundation's grants in 1997 were intended to help

tackle this. These included the help given to the National Council for Voluntary Organisations (NCVO) to set up Third Sector Foresight and to involve small organisations in its study of changing attitudes to charity, and also the grant to the Welsh Council for Voluntary Action (WCVA) to gather (at a time of major change in the structure of local government in Wales) up to date information about the work of voluntary organisations. During the year, too, work progressed on studies to which the foundation made grants in 1996 and which will be published in 1998, including the study on the employment role of the voluntary sector, being prepared as part of the RSA's Redefining Work Project, and the research at the Centre of the Child and Society at Glasgow University into the involvement of voluntary organisations in the local planning of childcare services.

The foundation also supported a number of voluntary sector initiatives exploring how best to respond to the increasing regionalisation of central government's funding and decision making systems. The grants to the Council for the Protection of Rural England (CPRE), to Liverpool Council of Social Services (for the Northwest Partnership Task Force on Social Inclusion) and to Community Matters (for the Community Sector Coalition's Conference) are examples of this policy interest.

Two reports that had been commissioned by the foundation were published during 1997, both intended to assist the work of grant making charities. Lending Money: The issues for grant-making trusts by Julia Unwin and Computers in Grant-making by Jacqueline Rae were published and distributed for the foundation by the Association of Charitable foundations (ACF). ACF also published Local Funding: The impact of the National Lottery Charities Board, a study co-funded by the Baring Foundation and Charities Aid Foundation (CAF).

Knowledge and Skills Exchange

88 grants, £54,446 agreed.

Priorities

The Knowledge and Skills Exchange Programme reflects the foundation's enthusiasm about the practical value that people who are involved in voluntary and community organisations can gain from sharing experience at first hand with each other - by visits and meetings, by having work demonstrated in a seminar or on a video, by organising opportunities for mentoring by or the shadowing of experienced practitioners.

Committee members and trustees, staff and volunteers - all can contribute to such activities and have their own work enhanced; such links, once made, can also be of continuing and long term benefit.

Distribution of grants

In setting up this pilot programme, the foundation worked in partnership with eight organisations, each of which has its own network of voluntary or community organisations. The eight organisations involved in the pilot scheme were BASSAC, Community Matters, Contact a Family, Development Trusts Association, DIAL UK, MIND Cymru, Scottish Council for Voluntary Organisations and Sia.

Each organisation publicised the availability of the grants within their own sector, helped interested organisations to identify possibly useful partners and assisted with advice about budgeting. A total of 88 grants were made, ranging in size from £30 to £2,300, the average being £484. Each grant created a link between at least two organisations, and over 250 organisations became involved in exchanges of knowledge and skills during 1997.

The grants supported a wide range of activities, including:

37% to investigate a scheme before implementing it29% to discuss key issues with a similar organisation13% To convene a meeting or collaboration between several groups

At the end of the pilot, representatives of the eight organisations attended a meeting at the foundation to review the scheme. It was clear from the joint assessment that the scheme was providing valued learning opportunities that would not otherwise have taken place. As a result, each organisation has agreed to develop the scheme further over a two year period, also taking on a direct responsibility for the payment and monitoring of the grants. The total budget for 1998 is £80,000 of which the partner organisations' administrative 'fees' total 10%.

Mergers and joint structures

59 applications, 29 grants, £198,980 agreed.

Priorities

The Baring Foundation's commitment to strengthening and supporting the voluntary sector has included an interest in the shape and structure of the organisations themselves. There are considerable pressures for change at the moment. The need to demonstrate efficiency and to offer cost effective services has led many organisations to consider the ways in which they operate. At the same time, concern about duplication of activities has made many charities consider their structural relationships with organisations working in the same field.

There have always been mergers within the voluntary sector. However, the Baring Foundation was concerned that there may be barriers preventing proper investigation of structural change, particularly by smaller organisations. In 1996 the foundation launched a pilot grants programme to support voluntary organisations that were considering such change. This resource was intended to make possible an open exploration of the issues, and – because it was not tied to a major funding source – to allow voluntary organisations to reflect on their positions, without having to make definitive commitments. In establishing this specialist fund, the foundation did not wish to be seen as supporting or encouraging mergers. The intention of the fund was to allow organisations to consider their options, for example through the services of a consultant, or by freeing time for senior staff to engage in strategic thinking.

24 grants were agreed during the pilot phase and, at the end of 1996, the foundation decided to continue with the fund for a further three years and to extend the eligibility from the initially limited number of areas to the whole of the UK .

Distribution of grants

A total of 59 applications were received in 1997, of which 29 were approved for funding. The total value of grants made within this programme was just under £200,000. Applications were received from across the UK. 10 grants were offered to national organisations, and 19 to organisations working within specific regions or localities. Proposals were not supported if they were simply about greater collaboration, rather than a more structured change, or if the organisation held sufficient unrestricted reserves to finance the work internally.

The approved grants were used to fund various activities relating both to the investigation of a proposed merger or joint structure and the implementation of an agreed plan to merge. Most grants were used to fund consultancies as is shown in the table herewith.

Grants offered covered a range of the interest areas of the foundation. The table indicates that the majority of grants helped to fund organisations within the

social care and personal services category, but voluntary housing organisations and community organisations also featured prominently:

	No.of grants	Value
Community and economic development	6	£42,000
Education and training	1	£6,500
Health	1	£12,000
Housing	7	£41,000
Social care and personal services	14	£97,000

The Strengthening the Voluntary Sector programme has an explicit brief to support smaller organisations. In line with this aim, grants made to support mergers and joint structures were focused on organisations at the lower end of the income range: 18 organisations (62% of recipients) had annual incomes of less than £250,000, and all but 8 of the grants were awarded to organisations with a total annual income of under £500,000. (But the average income of charities is much less than £5,000 a year, so these are only small in some relative sense. Ed)

Evaluation

The evaluation of the grants made in 1996, the pilot phase of the fund, highlighted a number of specific spurs to considering merger. The availability of significant capital grants from the National Lottery, for example, has provided an important incentive for some voluntary organisations to consider their relationships with others. There were also examples of voluntary organisations which had been rescued from collapse by merging with a stronger organisation, to the continuing benefit of those whom the charity was set up to help.

The review of the fund recognised concerns that some mergers have been encouraged, perhaps too actively, by an organisation's major funder. However, it also suggested that, among all those concerned with the future of an individual charity, small grant making trusts, as minority funders, may be in a position to suggest examining options for structural change. A discussion paper produced by the foundation raised this issue within the wider grant making sector and stimulated considerable interest.

ARTS IN EDUCATION AND THE COMMUNITY

3 new grants programmes: 752 eligible applications, 115 grants, £638,395 agreed.

Introduction

The foundation's funding for the Arts in Education and in the Community is

designed to achieve two things: the recognition and encouragement of good practice and the provision of opportunities to participate in the arts. While grants are modest in amount, the first year of the programme has confirmed that these aims are being achieved. The Programme comprises three funds: the Core Costs Fund, the Small Projects Fund, the Knowledge and Skills Exchange Fund. The Core Costs Fund is open only to those invited by the foundation to apply. The remaining two funds are open to application from arts organisations working throughout the UK and across all art forms.

Core costs fund

5 grants, £375,000 agreed.

Priorities

The Core Costs Fund was created to further the achievements of arts organisations with an excellent reputation for their work in educational and/or community settings. The foundation recognises that many such organisations operate within tight financial margins and that education and community activity may be particularly vulnerable to reductions in funding. The aim of the Core Costs grant is therefore to underpin, for three years, the creative and managerial costs that cannot be met in other ways. Each grant is for a maximum of £75,000 and is paid in three equal annual instalments. Five grants were made in 1997, and a further five will be made in both 1998 and 1999. These grants will be distributed throughout the UK.

Grants

The grants awarded in 1997 were to the Artists' Agency, Sunderland, the Whitechapel Art Gallery and Shape London and the Lemon Tree, Aberdeen and Scottish Dance Theatre, Dundee. Initial monitoring of how these organisations have used the grants suggested that the injection of £25,000 and the knowledge that the money is secure for two further years has proved to be a stabilising influence. The grants are providing the leadership of the organisations with freedom to think, to research and to experiment and to build upon their achievements of previous years, and to strengthen their ability to work more effectively. Specifically, grants are being used to underpin the salary of key personnel and to develop new initiatives. This is exemplified by the approach of the Artists' Agency. The Agency specialises in working with individuals and communities who have had little previous experience of, or contact with, art. Its programmes of artist-in-residence schemes and of national and international exchanges aim to enable practising artists from all disciplines to explore the social role of art. The Agency regularly advises others who work or wish to work in this field. The Artists' Agency is using the grant to reduce the administrative responsibilities of the Agency's two Co-Directors and to create a new post of Development Manager, to extend the Agency's work with artists in residence to a number of targeted communities, to share the Agency's good practice with others and to raise more funds for this work.

Small projects fund

832 applications, 592 eligible applications, 64 grants, £178,146 agreed.

Aims and priorities

The Small Projects Fund is designed to support small-scale arts events and projects in educational or community settings. It is available to arts organisations based anywhere in the UK, but only for projects budgeted at less than £20,000.

The Small Projects Fund welcomes applications that:

- include more than one art form
- feature partnerships between arts organisations, educational institutions and community groups
- aim to increase access to the arts in locations where access is limited
- provide a new creative experience for participants
- promote interaction between different cultural forms
- serve as a development stage of a larger project.

Grants were awarded to a diverse range of activities including £3,000 to Art Discovery in Orkney for a series of arts workshops linking Neolithic sites with the practice of contemporary artists; £2,450 to Bristol Poetry Slam for twelve all-day performance poetry workshops in secondary schools and £3,500 to Sound It Out, a community music organisation in Birmingham, for a 12-month series of music workshops for people who are housebound and their carers.

The majority (66%) of the 64 grants made from the Small Projects Fund were for projects in which the participants worked together leading up to a performance, an exhibition or some other form of public event.

Knowledge and Skills Exchange Fund

189 applications, 160 eligible applications, 46 grants, £85,249 agreed.

Aims and Priorities

The Knowledge and Skills Exchange Fund is a response to the fact that artists and arts managers working in educational or community settings have too few opportunities to learn from each other.

The aim of the fund is to support activity which increases knowledge and skills in this field and raises standards of practice. Activities supported can include:

- exchanges between arts groups within the UK or with groups abroad
- the development of new contacts in the UK or abroad
- mentoring initiatives
- the organisation of seminars or conferences
- the production of guidelines and case studies
- the exchange of knowledge and skills through new technologies.

46 grants were awarded in 1997; all but two were for £3,000 or less and the average grant was for under £2,000. Grants made included £3,000 to Common Ground Sign Dance Theatre for the British leg of a three-way exchange between integrated performing arts companies, from Liverpool, Amsterdam and Barcelona and £1,750 to ENGAGE (the National Association for Gallery Education) towards the cost of a conference promoting exchange between gallery educators and curators.

The majority of the grants went to exchange visits or mentoring schemes (31%), conferences or seminars (22%) or the production of guidance materials (19%).

Beneficiaries

The foundation has not set targets prescribing who should benefit from the Arts in Education and in the Community Programme, believing that everyone should have access. However the focus of applications is monitored: 51% of grants funded work with children and/or young people; 16% of grants benefited people with disabilities; and 9% of grants were awarded to organisations run by or for members of ethnic minority communities.

Geographical spread

The geographical location of applicant organisations is monitored by country and, within England, by Regional Arts Board area. The location is where the organisation is based, not where the activity will take place. The number of applicant organisations in London is, therefore, disproportionately high as such a large number of national arts organisations are based there. 87% of the eligible applicant organisations were based in England. London produced

29% of all eligible applications, followed by the Yorkshire and Humberside region with 10%.49 eligible application

INTERNATIONAL GRANTS PROGRAMME

14 grants, £138,416 agreed.

After consultation with development specialists, the foundation launched a separate international grants scheme towards the end of 1997. The international programme corresponds to the objectives of the foundation's national (UK) Strengthening the Voluntary Sector programme by supporting comparable activities in sub-Saharan Africa and Latin America.

Aid to governments in sub-Saharan Africa and Latin America has declined during the 1990s while poverty and inequality have steadily increased. For this reason and because governments are transferring aspects of development and welfare to the private, voluntary and community sectors, the work of local non-governmental organisations (NGOs) and community-based organisations (CBOs) is growing in importance.

UK NGOs have better access to European charitable funds, but to ensure a longer-term, sustainable reduction of poverty, it is African and Latin American NGOs/CBOs, rather than their expatriate partners, that must be ultimately responsible for the delivery of services. Since the foundation does not have the capacity to form direct partnerships with Latin American or African NGOs, grants have been made only to UK charities or similar voluntary organisations that contribute to the development of the voluntary sector in Africa and Latin America.

Aims and Priorities

The new grants programme aims to help African and Latin American organisations to develop their capacity in three ways:

- by improving co-ordination between agencies so that they can learn from each other, exchange information about on-going work, avoid duplication and, where possible, collaborate. This might involve, for instance, organising meetings between NGOs and CBOs to plan new work in particular areas, or to establish new systems of information exchange.
- by increasing the efficiency and influence of several NGOs or CBOs so that they can more effectively address the interests of disadvantaged groups and encourage other

organisations to adopt good policies and practices. Examples of this might be the arranging of visits to be undertaken by African or Latin American trainers, or the representation of NGO/CBO staff at a key conference to advocate on behalf of disadvantaged groups.

- by enabling greater participation and control by intended beneficiaries in the planning, management and evaluation of development work. This might be achieved, for example, through the production of a manual on participatory approaches, or meetings between representatives of disadvantaged groups and policy-makers to discuss the plans for a new initiative.

Any UK charity seeking to benefit people who are living in poverty and marginalised from decision-making can apply to the International grants programme. Since women, girls and displaced people tend to be particularly disadvantaged, work that improves their social, economic or political position has been given priority. Applicants have been encouraged to apply for work that might normally be difficult to fund, such as feasibility studies or activities where the exact outcomes are not easily predicted. Conversely, projects that rely heavily on UK expertise in the longer-term or require high levels of capital investment are not likely to be considered.

The foundation has decided to fund development work rather than welfare. Emergency or relief work has been excluded, so grants have not been given for work taking less than six months to plan. Work that has already been completed, or will have started while the application is being assessed, is also ineligible. Funding for the continuation or replication of an activity can only be considered if further innovation is involved.

While the beneficiaries of the international programme reside in Africa and Latin America, the foundation acknowledges that the people involved in the voluntary sector in those, and other, regions have skills that can be useful to British voluntary organisations. In the national Strengthening the Voluntary Sector grants programme, experts from Africa, Asia or Latin America can be funded to come to the UK to help enhance skills and knowledge of two or more voluntary or community organisations in this country.

International Grants Activity in 1997

In a full year, the budget for the

International grants programme is £625,000 - this includes the resources needed for five core costs grants as well as the funds with which to respond to eligible grant applications. The programme was not operational for all of 1997 and the first core costs grants will begin in 1998, but fourteen grants, totalling £138,416, were made during 1997 to UK organisations working overseas.

The largest grant, of £50,000 to Charity Know How, was not made as part of the new International programme but was the extension, over a further two years but at a reduced level, of the foundation's support for, and involvement in, the joint funding scheme set up in 1991 by UK grant giving trusts, the Government and the Charities Aid Foundation to support the development of voluntary and community organisations in Eastern and Central Europe and the former Soviet Union.

Excluding the grant to Charity Know How, grants were awarded to a range of different activities, as shown below:

Grants awarded, by type of project

Type of activity	No. of grants	Value
Business plan	2	£15,000
Conference	1	£1,250
Consultancy	1	£4,280
Exchange scheme	1	£4,700
Feasibility study	3	£27,704
Start-up funding	2	£4,200
Training	3	£31,282

The largest grant in the new programme, £14,000 to SOS SAHEL International UK, was for a feasibility study to investigate the possibilities for making links between pastoralist groups, NGOs, and government representatives, in West and East Africa. The purpose of the links will be for groups and organisations to support each other in solving problems faced by pastoralists in the Sahel.

The geographical distribution of the grants is summarised below. As this programme aims to improve collaboration and co-ordination, some grants have been given to organisations working on projects based in several regions, one of which must be sub-Saharan Africa or Latin America. These grants are listed under 'multiple regions':

	No. of grants	Value
Latin America	3	£21,700
Sub-Saharan Africa	6	£41,766
Multiple regions	4	£24,950

The foundation relies on UK recipients and their partners to monitor the progress

and impact of their work. In addition, plans have been made for gathering feedback from successful and unsuccessful applicants, as well as those who have not applied for a grant, on the foundation's international policy, information for applicants, and assessment and grant management procedures. The initial collation of this monitoring information will take place during 1998, enabling the foundation to assess the impact of the programme and apply the lessons learnt to its subsequent development.

GUIDELINES FOR APPLICANTS

Strengthening the voluntary sector

Mergers and joint structures

The Baring Foundation has established a special fund to help organisations in the voluntary sector which wish to combine their work with others, either through a merger or within a formal joint structure. The foundation recognises that there are many pressures on voluntary organisations to review their own structures and their formal relationships with others: a wish to reduce costs, to reduce duplication, and to improve the quality of services. The foundation invites applications from voluntary organisations anywhere in the UK which are considering a merger or other formal joint structure and wish to explore the possibility further, as well as from organisations which have decided on the steps they need to take and need help in implementation.

This special fund is part of the Baring Foundation's main grants programme: Strengthening the Voluntary Sector. The foundation has had a long commitment to supporting the growth of a vigorous, effective and creative voluntary sector, and of small organisations in particular. The grants programme is intended to assist the further development of the sector across the whole range of activities in which voluntary, charitable and community based organisations are engaged.

Confidentiality

The Baring Foundation has always publicised details of the grants that it has made. It recognises, however, that organisations considering a merger or other joint structure may not want publicity. The foundation will treat any application for assistance from this fund as confidential and will not, therefore, name in its Annual Report or other publicity the organisations to which grants are made within this part of its programme except with the agreement of the organisation concerned.

Fundable activity
- the cost of consultants to assess the feasibility of a merger or formal joint structure
- the cost of releasing a member of staff to investigate a merger or formal joint structure
- the legal, or other professional costs associated with a merger

The foundation does not expect the grants made from this special fund to be large; it anticipates they will be between £2,000 and £10,000.

Exclusions
- initiatives that are intended to lead to better co-ordination or collaboration between organisations - but have no implications for the creation of new formal structures. (Such initiatives may be eligible for support within the foundation's main grants programme).
- the foundation's other main exclusions will apply; for details see the leaflet about the main grants programme, available on request from the foundation

Who can apply?
- local and regional organisations anywhere in the UK
- national voluntary organisations, including organisations that work in only one country within the UK as well as UK wide organisations
- UK charities working with partner organisations and community groups in developing countries

An application can be made jointly by all the organisations involved in a specific proposal or by just one - in the latter case, the foundation will need to know that the other organisations support the request; if several organisations apply jointly, one will have to take on the role and responsibilities of grant recipient.

In providing this special fund, the foundation is aware that there may at times be inappropriate pressure on small organisations to merge and welcomes applications from organisations that do not want to merge, but do wish to devise some formal joint structure that protects their independence while sharing some costs and/or functions.

In assessing applications, the foundation will need to consider the extent to which the work of each of the organisations involved will be enhanced. It will also want to examine whether some or all of the proposed work can be funded from the organisation's own reserves.

How to apply
All applicants must complete the datasheet (available from the foundation) and send it to the foundation together with:

- a brief description of the current work and experience of the applicant organisation including details of staffing, organisational structure and use of volunteers. An outline of the work of the other organisations involved in the proposed new structure should also be included.
- an outline description (not exceeding 2 pages) of:– what is proposed and will be achieved with the grant– the need that will be tackled and how it was assessed– how long the activity will take to be completed– who will carry out the work and who will benefit– how the proposed activity will be documented and evaluated (a condition of any grant will be that a final report is made available to the foundation)– why the proposed activity cannot be funded from elsewhere and what, if any, funding might be attracted from elsewhere if the initiative is successful
- the detailed brief, if funding is requested to pay for a consultancy
- a detailed budget for the activity for which the grant is requested
- the income/expenditure projection of the applicant organisation for the current year
- the organisation's most recent audited accounts or financial report required by the Charities Act (if the year covered by these accounts ended more than 12 months previously, an income/expenditure report for the most recent complete financial year must also be included)
- (the organisation's most recent annual report, if one is published, and those of the other organisations involved in the proposed new structure.

This grants programme has no deadlines; applications can be sent to the foundation at any time. All will be acknowledged within two weeks of receipt. The foundation's staff or advisers may need to telephone or visit the applicant organisation. A decision will usually be made within two months and the applicant will be notified of the outcome by letter.

Applications will only be considered if all the supporting information listed above and the completed datasheet (available from the office above) are sent to the foundation.

Strengthening the voluntary sector
The Baring Foundation has had a long commitment to supporting the growth of a vigorous, effective and creative voluntary sector, and of smaller organisations in particular. The foundation's main grants programme is intended to build on this experience and to assist the strengthening and the further development of the sector across the whole range of activities in which voluntary, charitable and community based organisations are engaged.

Who can apply?
- national voluntary organisations, including organisations that work only in Wales or Scotland or Northern Ireland or England as well as UK wide organisations (the foundation will favour smaller organisations which have limited resources available to fund additional activities)
- voluntary organisations in London which work in several London boroughs or across the whole of London; organisations working in only one borough will only be eligible to apply if they provide services to other voluntary organisations throughout the borough
- community and other voluntary organisations in the Merseyside region (including Skelmersdale and Halton) and the North East of England (the former counties of Cleveland and Tyne & Wear plus, in Northumberland and County Durham, primarily the former coalfield areas)

The Baring Foundation will give priority to organisations and activities that are considered to be difficult to fund or are unlikely to attract public support. The foundation values and will support infrastructure or second tier organisations within the voluntary sector that exist to assist and strengthen the work of other voluntary and community organisations; the foundation is especially concerned to assist organisations that are supporting refugees.

Who is not eligible to apply?
- local or regional voluntary organisations in areas other than London, Merseyside or the North East of England
- local authorities or other statutory agencies
- individuals

Fundable activity
Examples of the activities which could be supported by the foundation within this grants programme are:
- training initiatives from which several organisations in an area or with a shared specialist concern will benefit

- feasibility studies or the initial development work on new activities intended to enhance the work of two or more organisations
- the preparation of practical guidance on good practice
- visits to the UK (arranged by a UK voluntary organisation) by people with expertise from Africa, Asia or Latin America to help enhance the skills and knowledge of two or more voluntary organisations in this country
- initiatives intended to lead to better co-ordination or collaboration between organisations
- consultancies designed to improve an organisation's effectiveness and efficiency or its operational systems
- releasing key staff for short periods to concentrate on strategic matters or planning
- initiatives intended to lead to active participation in the development or management of a project by those who are intended to benefit

The funded activity could concern the whole of an organisation's work or be concentrated on specific functions e.g. the skills of its management, its ability to communicate effectively, its use of information technology or the way it supports its staff and volunteers.

Exclusions

The foundation will not support within this grants programme:

- The purchase, conversion or refurbishment of buildings
- Appeals or charities set up to support statutory organisations
- Office equipment or IT hardware
- Vehicles
- Medical research or equipment
- Animal Welfare Charities
- Grant maintained, private or LEA schools or PTAs
- Bursaries or Scholarships
- Expeditions
- Religious activity
- Individuals
- Work that has already been completed or will have started while the application is being considered
- General fundraising appeals

The foundation also will not usually support:

- The continued funding of activity that is already taking place
- The repeat of an activity that took place in a previous year
- The increase in the scale of an existing service

The foundation will not normally make single grants of more than £12,000 and expects most to be for much less. It also expects most funded activities to be completed within 12 months but will consider requests to support work that will last for two or three years if a case is made that the objective of the proposed activity will take longer than a year to be completed.

How to apply

All applicants must complete the datasheet (available from the foundation)and send it to the foundation together with:

- a brief description of the current work and experience of the applicant organisation including details of staffing, organisational structure and use of volunteers
- an outline description (not exceeding 2 pages) of:
  - what is proposed and will be achieved with the grant
  - the need that will be tackled and how it was assessed
  - how long the activity will take to be completed
  - who will carry out the work and who will benefit
  - why your organisation is equipped to carry out the work
  - how the proposed activity will be documented and evaluated (a condition of any grant will be that a final report is made available to the foundation)
- why the proposed activity cannot be funded from elsewhere and what, if any, funding might be attracted from elsewhere if the initiative is successful
- the detailed brief, if funding is requested to pay for a consultancy
- a detailed budget for the activity for which the grant is requested
- the income/expenditure projection of the organisation for the current year
- the organisation's most recent audited accounts or financial report required by the Charities Act (if the year covered by these accounts ended more than 12 months previously, an income/expenditure report for the most recent complete financial year must also be included)
- the organisation's most recent annual report, if one is published

This grants programme has no deadlines; applications can be sent to the foundation at any time. All will be acknowledged within two weeks of receipt. The foundation's staff or advisers may need to telephone or visit the applicant organisation. A decision may take up to six months and the applicant will be notified of the outcome by letter.

Applications will only be considered if all the supporting information listed above and the completed datasheet are sent to the foundation.

Arts and education in the community
Knowledge and Skills Exchange Fund

The Baring Foundation wishes to support high quality work by artists and arts organisations in educational and community settings.

It has established this fund to enable artists and arts managers working (paid or unpaid) in the field to learn from each other through the exchange of knowledge, skills and ideas, with a view to strengthening arts in education or arts in the community.

How much is available?

The total amount available for distribution from this fund is £90,000 per year. Most grants made by the foundation will be worth between £500 and £3,000. Exceptionally, a larger grant may be made.

Who can apply?

Only constituted, not-for-profit arts organisations, anywhere in the UK, are eligible to apply to this fund.

Who is not eligible to apply?

Individuals, local authority departments/ projects and school arts projects that are not independently constituted are not eligible to apply to this fund.

Fundable activity

The foundation is looking for applications that will result in the sharing of knowledge and skills among artists and arts managers who work in educational or community settings. The element of exchange is important, as is the extent of the likely impact of the proposed activity or initiative on standards and the quality of practice. Examples might include:

- mentoring initiatives or the opportunity to shadow an experienced practitioner
- exchanges between small, UK-based groups within the UK or with others abroad
- the development of new contacts in another part of the UK, or abroad
- the organisation of seminars, conferences or workshops (please see Exclusions overleaf)
- the production of guidelines, documentation, case studies, etc. (A dissemination plan must form part of the proposal)
- information exchange through new technologies

Please note: the foundation will not pay the salaries of those taking part in an exchange or visit, or the cost of covering their post during their absence.

Exclusions

The foundation will not support:

- vocational training or courses of academic study
- course, conference or seminar attendance fees
- the cost of equipment including the lease or purchase of computer or other hardware related to new technologies
- research trips specifically to develop a creative product, e.g. an exhibition, play, film, composition etc.
- the continuation of an existing link with a colleague or colleagues elsewhere in the UK or abroad
- one-way exchanges from overseas to the UK
- activity related to the preparation of a Lottery bid
- work that will have begun before the date (see below) when the application will be considered by the foundation.

How to apply

Application should be made by completing the application form and sending it to the Baring Foundation together with supporting materials as listed on the last page of the form.

Deadlines

Applications for £3,000 or less will be considered throughout the year but a decision may take up to 3 months.

Applications for more than £3,000 will be considered at Committee meetings in January, May and September and must reach the foundation by 30 October (for consideration at the Committee meeting in the following January), by 26 February (for consideration in May) and by 30 June (for consideration in September).

Projects that will have begun before the date when the application will be considered by the foundation will not be eligible.

Evaluation

The Baring foundation will expect to monitor the impact of all grants. For grants of more than £3,000, it may appoint a representative to monitor and evaluate the use made of the grant. For grants of £3,000 or less, recipients will be asked to complete a report form.

A list of grants already made from this fund is available on request from the foundation.

Arts: Small Projects Fund

The Baring Foundation wishes to make a number of small grants towards the costs of small-scale arts events and projects in education or the community. The foundation is interested in supporting a wide range of different types of activity across all art forms and in all parts of the UK through this Small Projects Fund.

How much is available?

The total amount available for distribution from the Fund is £160,000 per year. The foundation will make grants worth a minimum of £500 and maximum of £5,000.

Who can apply?

Only constituted, not-for-profit arts organisations, anywhere in the UK, with a proposal for a small-scale arts project or event in education or the community are eligible to apply.

The organisation applying may be of any size, but the total budget of the initiative or project for which it seeks funding must not exceed £20,000. The proposed activity can be for people of any age.

Who is not eligible to apply?

Individuals, local authority departments/projects and school arts projects that are not independently constituted are not eligible to apply to this fund.

Fundable activity

The foundation is particularly interested to support work that involves one or more of the following elements:

- more than one art form
- partnerships between arts organisations and educational institutions or community groups
- collaborations between different cultural forms
- a new creative experience for participants
- increased access to the arts in locations where access is limited
- a pilot project or development work for any of the above, or for a larger-scale project

An organisation may only make one application to this fund within a twelve month period.

Exclusions

This Fund may not be used to support:

- projects taking place outside the UK
- a continuation of an organisation's normal programme
- a repeat of an activity that has taken place within the past two years
- the running costs of an existing activity or organisation
- projects that will have begun before the date (see below) when the application will be considered by the foundation
- activity related to the preparation of a Lottery bid
- the cost of equipment including the lease or purchase of computer or other hardware related to new technologies
- general fundraising appeals

How to apply

Applications should be made by completing the enclosed application form and sending it to the Baring Foundation together with supporting materials as listed on the last page of the form.

Deadlines

Applications will be considered at Committee meetings in January, May and September. Applications must reach the foundation by 30 October (for consideration at the Committee meeting in the following January), by 26 February (for consideration in May) and by 30 June (for consideration in September).

Projects that will have begun before the date when the application will be considered by the foundation will not be eligible.

Evaluation

On completion of the activity for which this grant is made, the recipient will be asked to complete a simple form assessing the impact of the grant.

A list of grants already made from this fund is available on request from the foundation.

International grants programme

The Baring Foundation has always been committed to assisting communities internationally to apply accessible and affordable technical expertise and resources to the provision of clean water, food, shelter and sustainable livelihoods. In this aspect of its grant making, the foundation has supported UK based charities that work in other countries in partnership with community organisations and NGOs and has given particular priority to initiatives that are intended to strengthen the further development of vigorous and resilient community based organisations and self help groups.

For its new international grants programme, the Baring Foundation has decided to concentrate its support on activities that will enhance the effectiveness of the voluntary and community sector, especially in sub-

Saharan Africa and Latin America - in particular through the sharing and transfer of expertise, knowledge and skills within those regions and between them and other parts of the world.

Who can apply?

Registered charities or similar voluntary organisations within the UK that:

- rely on close working partnerships with organisations or groups in Sub-Saharan Africa or Latin America. Partners might be non-government organisations (NGOs) or community based organisations (CBOs)

and

- seek to benefit disadvantaged or marginalised people, in particular women or displaced people

The foundation will also consider applications from UK organisations that work internationally for grants from its Mergers and Joint Structures programme and, within its main Strengthening the Voluntary Sector programme, for grants to bring to the UK people with expertise from Africa, Asia or Latin America.

Fundable activity

The foundation will give priority to activities that are intended to:

- achieve better co-ordination and collaboration between agencie
- improve the efficiency and influence of several NGOs or community based organisations
- lead to more control and decision-making in the development and management of initiatives by those intended to benefit.

Examples of the kind of activities that could be supported, or partly supported, within this grants programme are:

- a series of meetings between pastoralists in an East African country to share advice about how to establish and run community based organisations effectively
- a workshop held by an inter-NGO Shelter Forum in West Africa with community-based organisations to exchange and develop advocacy skills
- the preparation of a training manual about gender and credit with community development workers in four Central American countries
- a consultancy visit by a Peruvian agriculturist to advise Bolivian NGOs on how to carry out feasibility studies so that the demands of potential beneficiaries are central to planning
- a visit by energy specialists from Africa and South America to the UK to inform key policy and decision makers about the priorities of

community and self help groups in their regions.

Exclusions

The foundation will not support within this grants programme:

- Individuals
- Expeditions
- Bursaries or scholarships
- Medical research or equipment
- Animal welfare charities
- Vehicles
- The purchase, conversion or refurbishment of buildings
- Religious activity
- Work that has already been completed or will have started while the application is being considered
- Emergency or relief work
- General fundraising appeals

The foundation also will not usually support:

- The continued funding of activity that is already taking place or will be repeated, unless it leads to further innovation
- Activity designed to support exclusively the work of governmental organisations

Applications

The foundation will not normally make single grants of more than £15,000 and expects most to be for less. It also expects most funded activities to be completed within 12 months but will consider requests to support work that will last for two or three years if a case is made that the objective of the proposed activity will take longer than a year to be completed.

The assessment of applications and applicant organisations

When applications are being assessed, the foundation will be looking for evidence that:

- the planned activities will respond in practical ways to specific problems and opportunities that have been identified by partner organisations and community-based group
- the capacity-building and training activities have clearly defined objectives and will be linked to work that directly benefits disadvantaged women and men
- the recruitment methods for selecting participants and the plans for follow-up activities are designed to ensure that the newly acquired skills and knowledge will be applied in practice
- close partnerships with other partner NGOs and/or community-based organisations are being or will be developed

- the planned activities contain strategies for ensuring that several organisations learn new skills and knowledge
- the impact of the activities will be cost-effective in social and/or economic terms
- there will be positive impact on women and girls
- there are mechanisms for establishing, or handing over, control of the activities to partner organisations or community based groups

In addition, the applicant organisation will need to demonstrate that they have:

- appropriate and effective management structures and systems
- the ability to plan, monitor, and evaluate regularly and participatively, and report to donors
- an understanding of, and strategies to respond to, potentially changing local, national and international contexts
- appropriate ways of co-operating with other development agencies, including long-term commitments to key partners
- a track record of considering the potential effects of their work on the environment and avoiding harmful impacts
- experience of, or willingness to learn about, capacity-strengthening work
- a commitment to equal opportunities including positive action to ensure that more opportunities are given to people with expertise who live in Africa, Asia or Latin America or who have their origins in those countries
- effective strategies for ensuring that the beneficial impact of their work is multiplied and sustained over time

How to apply

All applicants must complete the datasheet (available from the foundation) and send it to the foundation together with:

- a brief description of the current work and experience of the applicant organisation including details of staffing, organisational structure and use of volunteers (the information about staffing should include details of the gender and ethnicity of employees and of senior staff)
- an outline description (not exceeding 3 pages) of:
  - what is proposed and will be achieved with the grant
  - the need that will be tackled and how it was assessed
  - how long the activity will take to be completed
  - who will carry out the work

– who will benefit from the work, what numbers of people, in what ways and for how long

– why your organisation is equipped to carry out the work

– how the proposed activity will be documented, monitored and evaluated (a condition of any grant will be that a final report is made available to the foundation)

– what, if any, funding has been or might be attracted from elsewhere if the initiative is successful (the detailed brief, if funding is requested to pay for a consultancy

• a detailed budget for the activity for which the grant is requested

• the income/expenditure projection of the organisation for the current year

• the organisation's most recent audited accounts or financial report required by the Charities Act (if the year covered by these accounts ended more than 12 months previously, an income/expenditure report for the most recent complete financial year must also be included)

• the organisation's most recent annual report, if one is published.

This grants programme has no deadlines; applications can be sent to the foundation at any time. All will be acknowledged within two weeks of receipt. The foundation's staff or advisers may need to telephone or visit the applicant organisation. A decision will take at least two months and may take up to six. The applicant will be notified of the outcome by letter.

Applications will only be considered if all the supporting information listed above and the completed datasheet (available from the office above) are sent to the foundation.

Exclusions See the detailed lists in the Guidelines for the appropriate programme that are printed above.

Applications See the Guidelines above. Note that there is no provision for 'general' applications that lie outside the foundation's specific programmes.

The Barnabas Trust

£305,000 (1996/7)

Evangelical Christianity

63 Wolsey Drive, Walton-on-Thames, Surrey KT12 3BB
Tel: 01932-220622

Correspondent Mrs Doris Edwards, Secretary

Trustees S M Lennard; N Brown; K C Griffiths.

Beneficial area: UK and overseas.

Information available Full accounts are on file at the Charity Commission.

General By the year ending April 1997 the trust's assets amounted to £4 million and about 100 grants had been made in the year. These ranged between £100 and £30,000 but most were for under £1,000. The majority of funds and grants were gifted to organisations helped by the trust in prior years. The trust has a list of about 50 charities (which remains largely unchanged from year to year) to which they give regular support. After these recurrent grants have been disbursed, around £150,000 remains from which grants are made in response to unsolicited applications. The trust says it disburses about 85% of funds to evangelical groups (for missionary projects, students on theological training, provision of bibles etc.) and 15% to social causes.

Up to 1997 the trust had not classified grants in their report and accounts and the deed mentions only general charitable objects. However, from studying the names on the grants list it is apparent that nearly all beneficiaries are overtly evangelical Christian organisations. About 75% were Christian colleges or evangelical missions, four of which were overseas. The largest of these grants, and indeed the largest of all grants went to SGM International which received a total of £80,000 in three grants (24% of total charitable expenditure).

About 16 welfare organisations were assisted (including many care organisations such as the Princess Alice Hospice, £10,000), but the trust says that many of these were previously known to the trustees (for example, the Shaftesbury Society, £12,000). Furthermore, the trust has told us that the trustees are currently moving away from 'social' causes to concentrate more on the propagation of Christianity.

Applications In writing to the correspondent, giving as much detail as possible, and enclosing a copy of latest audited accounts, if applicable. The trust states: 'Much of the available funds generated by this trust are allocated to existing donees. The trustees are willing to consider new applications, providing they refer to a project which is overtly evangelical in nature. If in doubt about

whether to submit an application, please telephone the secretary to the trust for guidance'.

The trustees meet four times a year, or more often as required, and applications will be put before the next available meeting.

Lord Barnby's Foundation

£269,000 (1997/98)

General

Messrs. Payne Hicks Beach, 10 New Square, Lincoln's Inn, London WC2A 3QG
Tel: 0171-465 4300

Correspondent The Secretary

Trustees Sir John Lowther; Lord Newall; Sir Michael Farquhar; George Lopes; Countess Peel.

Beneficial area Unrestricted.

Information available Report and accounts, described as complying with the SORP. They contain neither an analysis and explanation of grants nor a narrative account of the work of the charity of the kind described in that document.

General 'The charity has established a permanent list of charities which they support every year'. Because the grants list is in apparently random order, it is difficult even to establish which charities have been supported in succeeding years. However the 'permanent list' appears to refer to a group of five charities for the benefit of the Polish community in Britain. Otherwise the beneficiary organisations, 75 of them in 1997/98, are extremely diverse. However a few groupings appear that are unlikely to be accidental:

Poland	*6 grants*	*£12,000*
Ex-service	*4 grants*	*£7,000*
Cathedrals	*4 grants*	*£6,000*
Northants	*2 grants*	*£2,000*

There is a clear interest in Ashtead, Surrey and possibly in Northamptonshire.

There was just one really substantial grant, that of £50,000 for an all-weather hockey pitch at Therfield school in Surrey, for use also by the local community. Beneficiaries of amounts from £10,000 to £12,000 included Motor Neurone Disease, the Royal Commonwealth Society for the Blind, Medical Emergency Relief International,

Anglo Romanian Education Trust, the Game Conservancy Trust, Atlantic College and the Countryside Foundation.

This foundation has high administrative costs. The £55,000 in 1997/98 was not typical, but even the £35,000 in the previous year was high in relation to grants of £126,000 (28%), or as a cost per grant (£625), especially when most of the grants were for amounts of £1,000 or less.

Unusually, some or all of the the trustees are themselves paid, to a total of £3,040, up from £2,250 in the previous year (and there was another £800 worth of personal expenses). In the view of these editors, the notion that trustees should not be remunerated is an excellent one, even where it is both legal and proper to do so. It is, they suggest, possible to find trustees, of the highest quality, who will not require payment for the interesting and charitable job of giving away someone else's money, especially on this relatively modest scale.

Exclusions No grants to individuals

Applications Applications will only be considered if received in writing accompanied with a set of the latest accounts.

The Barnwood House Trust

£1,104,000 (to organisations, 1997)

Disability charities in Gloucestershire, medical research

The Manor House, 162 Barnwood Road, Gloucester GL4 7JX
Tel: 01452-614429; 01452-372594

Correspondent Paul Guy

Trustees The trust is controlled by an elected governing council which appoints a chairman and board of trustees (total 12) which is responsible for the day to day running of the trust.

Beneficial area Gloucestershire.

Information available Excellent report and accounts. Four information leaflets are available: Grants to Organisations, Notes for Guidance; 'For Your Information'; Grants to Individuals, Notes for Guidance; Grants for Course Fees, Notes for Guidance.

Summary The trust helps people in Gloucestershire with serious mental and physical disabilities or disorders by its grants to both organisations and individuals. It also supports related medical research. There are three grant programmes for organisations:

- research budget: research into the causes and treatment of disability;
- strategic grants budget: '... the capacity to make very large grants for worthwhile capital projects and to support selected service organisations with revenue grants'. These grants can be either one-off or recurrent.
- grants budget: ... responds rapidly to small one-off appeals from organisations.

This entry gives a description of the grants made by the trust to organisations, and then reprints in full the relevant parts of the unusual and interesting annual report. The trust also makes grants for the benefit of individuals, work that is not covered by this book.

General This energetic trust shows exceptionally careful, active and enterprising grant making in a local setting. It is both a grant-giver and a service charity, running a day care home, sheltered housing and disability bungalows. It has a wide and active body of voluntary governors and their helpers, including two separate committees for the different grant programmes as well as an overall policy committee to look at the needs of disabled people in the county as a whole. This structure should be an interesting model for a number of other grant makers. Its 1997 narrative report is reprinted at the end of this entry.

The trust's disposable income is solely from its investments and properties. It has considered, but rejected, the idea of opening up its own fund raising programme (perhaps considering that it would then be in competition with the organisations it already supports in its fairly specialised field of work).

The trust states in its leaflet 'Grants to Organisations, Notes for Guidance' that it is interested in the following activities:

- Provision of day care and occupational therapies/activities;
- Provision of respite care, in its various forms;
- Provision of housing and residential care;
- Social and recreational activities;
- Transport needs;
- Adult education and training;
- Scientific and medical research.

During 1997 a total of £1,104,000 was disbursed to 200 organisations, either in Gloucestershire or to national medical research programmes (a further £398,000 was distributed in grants for individuals).

The grants to organisations were broken down as follows:

Strategic grants	*£470,000*
Smaller local grants	*£302,000*
Medical research	*£332,000*

Another way of looking at the same figures is as follows:

Physical disability	*64%*
Learning disability (mental handicap)	*15%*
Mental illness 2	*1%*

Such a formal breakdown is valuable, as this editor, for example, had formed an inaccurate impression just from looking through the grants list as a whole.

There were 15 grants of £15,000 or more (excluding those medical research), headed by £57,000 for the Gloucestershire Association for Mental health's Belsize House in Gloucester. Among the three grants of £50,000 was one for an unusual 'challenge fund' in the Forest of Dean. Both this and another similar size award to improve community transport in the area followed consultation and discussion with disability organisations in the Forest. Some of these awards were for capital purposes such as the £25,000 towards a new building for St Luke's Trust in Stroud or the £24,000 for adaptations to Gloucester's Resource Centre. However, project or revenue grants, even though usually on a one-off basis, were more common. They included £30,000 to the Yercombe Trust for 'the provision of residential care throughout the year' and £20,000 to MENCAP for a family advisor post.

The 150 grants of less than £5,000 accounted for just £14,000 and included many small Christmas donations of just £100.

The trust is a member of the Association of Medical Research Charities, and so all research projects are subject to a formal peer review process. Donations are mostly made to selected national medical research 'clearing house' charities. The trust does not normally accept applications direct from research bodies or individual researchers.

Six national medical research charities received grants of £20,000 or more. The largest was again to the British Neurological Research Trust for continued research into repair of the spinal cord by Dr Raisman (£100,000). £72,000 was given for three projects supported by the Mental Health Foundation, and £60,000 to the Brain Research Trust.

Annual Report 1997

'Barnwood House Trust, established in its original form in 1792, is Gloucestershire's largest charity aiming to assist people with disabilities, including those with mental disorders who live in the County. Its current endowment arises principally from the sale of the land upon which Barnwood House Hospital stood until 1966. From then it has developed as a provider of facilities for the disabled and of grants and loans to alleviate their problems.

'Grant making activity continues to grow and a number of new initiatives such as the Barnwood Challenge Fund will be implemented in 1998. Gerry Sherman-Ball retired as Chief Executive last July and his place, as Director, has been taken by Paul Guy. Christine Ellson and Peter Rumsey have been promoted to Assistant Director (Grants) and (Administration) respectively. Gail Rodway is now Grants Administrator.

Policy Sub-Committee

'The Policy Sub-Committee was created to seek information from all relevant sources in order to make recommendations about changes in policy, to keep client needs and the development of policy and priorities under continuous review, and to undertake monitoring and evaluation of the effectiveness of the trust's funding to other organisations.

'It ensured the complete review of the terms of reference for each of the sub-committees, expanding and clarifying their objectives. The grant-making committees' spending in 1996 was analysed which resulted in several new initiatives. Particular enthusiasm was shown for the Barnwood Bursary and the Challenge Fund, initially introduced into the Forest of Dean district. It will continue to encourage ways in which the trust can pro-actively spend its revenue income.

'As part of the trust's ongoing programme of keeping itself informed regarding changes in the statutory sector, excellent presentations were received from the County Director of Social Services, Andrew Cozens and subsequently from Jeff James, Chief Executive of the Health Authority.

'It commissioned research into the provision of Respite Care particularly in Gloucester City. This research forms the basis for our anticipated support for such a service in 1998.

'Monitoring and evaluation reports showed that the great majority of our grant expenditure is being well utilised by the recipients. In a few cases it was found that the beneficiary was unable to utilise the funds as intended and the grant returned.

'The trustees believe that we will continue to have greater influence both with the statutory and voluntary sectors if we remain a grant-making trust and perform no fund-raising activities.'

The Grant Committees Chairmen:
Sir Peter Miles (Strategic Grants)
Mrs Janet Kirkwood (Grants up to £25,000)
Mrs Heather Miles (Individual Grants)

Grants in 1997

'1997 saw the trust actively involving itself in examining needs among Gloucestershire people with disabilities and encouraging locally based solutions. Much has been achieved during this our 16th year of making grants – over 200 grants to organisations and over 1,500 grants to individuals have been approved. Apart from funding for medical research, almost all the grants have been for Gloucestershire people with physical or mental disabilities.

'Grants accounted for in 1997 (£1,503,102) and future commitments (£1,035,583) were an all time record of £2,538,685.

'In addition the trust made charitable loans to individuals totalling £11,294 for building adaptations and pledged a charitable loan of £100,000 to the National Star Centre for its proposed Brain Injury Rehabilitation Centre at Ullenwood near Cheltenham.

'These grants and loans are the outcome of much effort and activity made possible by all those associated with the trust. Our enormous thanks go to our committee members and volunteers who undertook visits, making reports and recommendations for the trust.

Current grant programmes

'The current grant programmes are :

- the research budget dedicated to medical research into the causes and treatment of disability
- the strategic grants budget which has the capacity to make very large grants for worthwhile capital projects and to support selected service organisations with revenue grants
- the grants budget which responds rapidly to small appeals from organisations and makes grants for a host of activities which complement and enhance the work of statutory and voluntary organisations
- the individual welfare fund which helps meet the special needs arising from individual disability.

'While it has never been the trustees' intention to set policy in tablets of stone, the need for clear and published priorities has been recognised by the trust. Our consultation with other grant-makers and key personnel in the voluntary and statutory sectors to help inform our policy decisions, has been both stimulating and helpful. We are indebted to all those outside the trust who assisted in this process.

'Several priority areas have been identified:

- transport
- housing
- day and respite care
- advice, support and advocacy
- training
- medical research
- needs of the mentally ill.

'The trust continues to adapt its grant programmes in response to changing needs among individuals and organisations; and to find new ways of reaching out to people and collaborating with other organisations.

'The groundwork for the £50,000 1998 Challenge Fund for the Forest of Dean was laid in 1997, following consultation and discussion with disability organisations in the Forest. (*Programme now closed. Ed.*)

'These discussions also highlighted for the trust the transport needs of people with disabilities in the Forest, particularly those in the central area who lack a good service. Money has been set aside to help resolve the problems.

'Barnwood's Strategic Grants Committee has also pledged to help trial a new volunteering concept called Fair Shares in the county – the first in the UK. This scheme should be operational in 1998.

'Local research has indicated the need for a new sitting service for carers and their disabled relatives in Gloucester City. Much of the work in determining how the trust could kick-start a new initiative took place in 1997 and the signs are hopeful that, with the trust's support, a service for people with Alzheimer's disease will be started in 1998.

'The Barnwood Bursary, enabling individuals with disabilities to undertake a personal challenge, was successfully launched in early 1997 and attracted a number of interesting applications.

'Our Individual Welfare Fund and Grants Committee between them make a very large number of smaller grants for individual needs and for projects and activities which improve the quality of life for people with disabilities. Grants included provision of respite care, clothing, holidays, disability and household equipment, arts, crafts, social and sports activities, advice and support services for people with disabilities, training and education, residential and day care and community transport.

'The trust continues to maintain its policy of accepting one-off applications from individuals referred or sponsored by their health or social work professional. This is judged to be a very effective way of targeting the trust's resources. The average individual grant remains at under £300.

'The following examples illustrate the range of activities supported by the trust. We are in no doubt that the trust's resources will continue to be in demand when State health and welfare services are unable to match the expectations of more and more people living longer with disabling conditions:

'Our grant of £7,500 to the Malcolm Sargent Cancer Fund for Children was an excellent instance of collaboration with other charitable trusts to meet a proven need. The social worker post at Gloucestershire Royal Hospital, dedicated to supporting children with cancer and their families and funded for a number of years by the Malcolm Sargent Fund, was under review because specialist treatment for Gloucestershire children with cancer had moved to Southmead Hospital in Bristol.

'As initial diagnosis and palliative care still remained a function of GRH, hospital staff and families were very concerned that withdrawal of the social worker would remove a vital plank of support at times of great need. In partnership with the Summerfield Charitable Trust and the Henry Smiths Charity, Barnwood's contribution has enabled this post to remain in place for three years, and has been wholeheartedly welcomed by the Consultant concerned.

'At the same time, a contribution was made to the Jack and Jill Appeal at Southmead NHS Hospital, which cares for patients from Gloucestershire, to improve their facilities for children.

'With the incidence of cancer increasing, our grant of £30,000 to the Cotswold Care Hospice at Minchinhampton serving Stroud and surrounding districts has contributed to a major refurbishment of the day centre, improving the quality of life for people with a terminal illness.

'MENCAP which champions the interests and needs of those with a learning disability started up its own

Family Adviser Service in Gloucestershire in response to changes within social work provision by GCC Social Services. This new service is funded jointly by Health and Social Services. The contribution of £20,000 in 1997 from Barnwood enabled the Family Adviser Service to expand its activities.

'During 1997 Barnwood continued to support the work of the Gloucestershire Association for Mental Health, following the purchase and refurbishment of Belsize House in Gloucester, with grants for rent, an arts and crafts organiser, client holidays and sports activities. The amenity of Belsize House is a tremendous asset to GAMH and has given fresh impetus to its charitable work.

'Further support has been given to Gloucester Clubhouse with a grant for an additional employee to expand the number of employment training places available. Milsom Street Day Centre in Cheltenham, which provides support for the mentally ill living in the community, sought funding to introduce a "Hearing Voices" support group for people with schizophrenia. The group needed skilled help to offer cognitive therapy, teaching people how to manage the problem of living with distressing voices.

'The trust continues to support medical research across the spectrum of disability with grants, for example, to the Mental Health Foundation, the Hearing Research Trust and Action Research. Dr Geoffrey Raisman (British Neurological Research Trust) has reported significant advances in his search for a way to repair damage to the spinal cord. This research is of international importance and our support is pledged for two more years.'

Exclusions Other than for selected clinical research projects, referred by co-ordinating organisations which have undertaken peer review, GRANTS ARE RESTRICTED TO GLOUCESTERSHIRE.

Applications On trust application forms obtainable from Mrs Christine Ellson, Assistant Director (Grants) or Mrs Gail Rodway, Grants Administrator, at the address above (Tel: 01452-611292). Applications from organisations are investigated by representatives of the trust who then make recommendations to the trustees. Trustees meet every other month. Grant-making committees meet quarterly.

For information about grants for individuals, contact the trust.

The BBC Children in Need Appeal

£17,711,000 (1996/97)
Child welfare

PO Box 7, London W12 8UD
Tel: 0181-735 5057

Beneficial area UK.

Information available Excellent annual reports, guidelines and application forms, all informative and accessible, are available from the four UK national offices (listed under 'Applications' below).

Summary Thousands of grants ranging from a few hundred pounds to £500,000 are made each year for specific projects which directly help disadvantaged children and young people (18 and under). The awards are made towards capital or revenue costs and may be one-off or repeated over two or three years. Most are for under £5,000 but the bulk of funds go to pay for a couple of hundred grants worth between £30,000 and £100,000 (usually payable over three years).

In 1996/97 the appeal raised nearly £17 million and so with a further £1.8 million earned from bank interest, income totalled £18.7 million.

The grants were allocated in four programmes as follows:
Children living in poverty and deprivation £7,963,000;
Children suffering through illness, abuse or neglect £4,850,000;
Children with mental or physical disabilities £3,991,000;
Children with behavioural problems £907,000.

The entry below starts with a general description of the four programmes from the 1996/97 annual report. This is followed by a reprint of the Appeal's excellent Grant Guidelines (except that a couple of the administrative sections will be found at the end of the entry, under the heading 'Applications'). Then we quote extensively from the

Trustees' Review of 1996/97. Finally we describe some of the larger grants (and just a few of the smaller) from that year.

General 'The BBC has been broadcasting a children's appeal since 1927. Initially a fairly minor radio broadcast, this is now a major event encompassing radio and television which has raised over £200 million over the years. Just about all of the charity's income comes from donations generated every November through the appeal itself and a myriad of associated fundraising activities. Their fundraising success is assisted by the fact that bank interest is used to pay for all fundraising and administration costs, enabling the charity to say, quite correctly, that every pound donated to it goes directly to the target causes.

'The four grant headings are described as follows in the annual report:

Poverty and deprivation

'Poverty can be disabling. Disabling in the sense that it excludes children from some of the normal activities of childhood. It is also known to affect their health.

'Poverty is growing up in a family where dad has never, or hardly ever worked, or in a family where there is no dad but only mum trying to cope against the odds. Poverty is living on run down housing estates where the only space to play is full of broken glass and rusting cars. It's not having a home at all or a space to call your own.

'Poverty is being left behind when your mum can't afford the pocket money. Poverty is never having a birthday party or, like 7 year old Michael, not able to go to your best friend's party because there is no money to buy a present. Poverty stops you joining in.

Illness, distress, abuse, neglect

'Some children suffer, quietly and stoically, in situations which would tax the spirit of adults. They may experience long-term illness; the loss of a parent; physical or mental abuse from adults in a position of trust and a lack of those vital ingredients for children everywhere – simple love and attention.

'We can't always stop the suffering but through the charities we fund we can reach out and show these children that we care.

'We give grants to help with children's hospices, for support groups for children with rare diseases, for work with children affected by HIV/Aids and for counselling to help with bereavement and other traumatic events.

Disability

'The word disability covers a wide range of conditions in varying degrees of severity – deafness, brain injury, cerebral palsy, muscular dystrophy – these are but a few of a very long list. Children are certainly not in need just because they are disabled. Were attitudes different, many of these children could lead full lives.

'Sarah, 13 years old, told us with a giggle "I was shopping with my mum and because I use a wheelchair I held all the bags outside a shop. As I was sitting there some people dropped money into the bags and walked away without a word. It was so embarrassing".

'There are children who do need that charities offer – maybe to improve their self confidence or to cope with the insensitivity of others. But some will never be able to look after themselves although, with sufficient support, their abilities might be enormously improved. We fund charities which can make an positive difference.

Behavioural and psychological difficulties

'Sadly there are children whose birth or background has been such that they have not learned how to behave. We can't afford to ignore them as many are desperately unhappy young people who lack guidance and have low self esteem. Many want to change but don't know how.

Young Wayne behaved so badly at primary school that his teacher couldn't cope with him. His parents couldn't cope either until they attended a project which helped them to learn new parenting skills. Wayne's behaviour is now becoming more acceptable.

We fund many charities which are skilled in helping with behavioural problems for children of all ages. Some work with parents, others offer older children and young people the chance to gain self respect through training and team work.'

Grant Guidelines

These read as follows:

'We welcome applications for good quality projects which show a clear focus on children and careful planning in order to bring a positive difference or change their lives.

The children we help are aged 18 years and under and in the United Kingdom. Their disadvantages include:

- mental, physical or sensory disabilities;
- behavioural or psychological problems;
- living in poverty or situations of deprivation;
- illness, distress, abuse or neglect.

'Please do not apply for a grant to benefit children who do not fall within the above categories. We appreciate the good work which is done for the average child or young person in average circumstances but we are unable to make a financial contribution.

'BBC Children in Need is a national grant-making trust which distributes between £10 and £20 million a year to help children in need in the UK. The trustees, appointed by the BBC's Board of Governors, are advised by regional committees whose members have knowledge of child welfare issues and the voluntary sector.

When to apply

(See under 'Applications' below)

How we work

'... We receive around 6,000 applications each year and most applicants are contacted by our freelance assessors who work from home.

'An assessor may phone you or your referee to clarify the information provided on your application or to ask you to send additional information. If they cannot reach you during normal working business hours they may phone in the evening. Assessors report to our advisory committees but have no decision making powers.

'We only have a small staff but we aim to give a friendly service. If you have a problem please contact one of our offices.

Who can apply

'We welcome applications from properly constituted not for profit groups. These may be:

- self help groups;
- voluntary organisations;
- registered charities.

'We give low priority to applications from statutory (public) bodies and local authorities for schools, hospitals, social services, etc.

'Such grants are rarely over a few thousand pounds and most are for much smaller amounts.

'We regret that we cannot accept applications from private individuals or parents, nor from social workers or to other welfare professionals on behalf of their clients.

'However, we do allocate funds to the Family Welfare Association to make grants to individual children on our behalf.

'Applications must be made by a qualified social worker or other welfare professional and forms can be obtained from the FWA at 501-505 Kingsland Road, Dalston, London E8 4AU.

One, two or three year funding?

'We give salary and revenue grants for one, two and three years except for the following, to which we give grants for one year only:

- capital projects;
- seasonal projects, eg: holiday playschemes;
- holidays and outings;
- equipment and welfare funds.

'It is unlikely that further applications will be considered during the duration of two or three year funding.

Salaries

'If you are applying for staff salaries we will be looking at your experience as an employer or your plans to acquire the management skills you need.

'In the interests of equal opportunities all new posts funded by BBC Children in Need should be publicly advertised, unless for short term or sessional staff.

'Please would you:

- state whether a salary is for a new post or for an existing one;
- make sure your costs include all the extras involved in employing staff (for example: recruitment costs, inflation, and increments, employers costs and any other on-costs)
- enclose a job description, person specification and a first year plan with your application form.

Monitoring and evaluation

'When we give grants to salaried staff we ask organisations to take responsibility for monitoring and evaluating their work. This is particularly important when organisations want us to fund their work for more than one year.

'Monitoring and evaluating is about measuring what you have achieved, and comparing it to what you hoped to achieve. So you need to set clear and realistic targets before you write your application.

'The kind of answers we are looking for here are to do with keeping records, doing surveys, getting feedback from your users, or anything else you think gives us an indication of your progress

'We ask for this information so we can spend our money as wisely as possible, but we do understand that progress isn't problem free, so please be as clear and honest as you can.

Child protection

As an organisation working with children, you have a responsibility to protect them from any harm, including the possibility of abuse, while they are in your care. We would ask you to think carefully and take any relevant action or advice.

Medical equipment or mobility/ communication aids

'When making an application for medical equipment or mobility communication aids please:

- enclose a professional assessment from a relevant consultant or therapist;
- confirm that your organisation will take responsibility for ensuring that the equipment meets safety regulation and will be suitably insured and maintained;
- if you operate a loan system, explain how it will be administered and what criteria will be used.

Transport

'If you are requiring a minibus please explain why you should not borrow, share or hire transport instead. It is expensive to run a minibus and you will need to show how you will meet these costs.

'We never fund "old bangers" and we rarely provide the total cost of, or a starter grant for, a new vehicle although we may consider a completion grant. If you cannot present a really good case for a vehicle, would it not make sense to apply for transport costs instead?

What we are looking for. A focus on children and quality

'We are looking for quality work and projects which show a clear focus on children.

- Your project should be about changing the lives of children for the better.
- It should be for children (rather than their parents or for the needs of your organisation).
- Where possible and appropriate it should take account of children's views and involve them in the decision making.

A properly completed form

(See under 'Applications' below)

A thoughtful and honest application

'A thoughtful and honest application always stands out in the crowd! Tell us clearly what the problem is, and how your project will do something about it. Give us relevant facts and figures, please don't use jargon, and don't be vague. You don't need to promise us the moon, just tell us what you can realistically achieve.

'Your budget should show that you've done your homework and know what things cost. A thoughtful and honest application isn't a hurried and last minute dash to meet our deadlines with something dreamed up overnight. It is a serious and sincere attempt by your organisation to use its experience and skill to make a positive difference where it is needed.'

Trustees' Review 1996/97

The Trustees' Review of 1996/97 included the following:

'This year the appeal raised income of £18,743,000, which was an increase of £1,918,000 on the previous year. This was encouraging, since the majority of the rise came from an increase in voluntary income.

'During the year, the trustees distributed £17,711,000 in grants to help children in need. This was higher than the £15,326,000 distributed during the previous year in line with increased income.

Grant expenditure

The charity received 5,015 applications for grant aid totalling £99.7 million (1996: 5,612 totalling nearly £92 million). 2,635 grants totalling £17.7 million (1996:2,2911 totalling £15.3 million) were awarded to benefit children in need through a wide range of organisations which included national children's charities and thousands of small local organisations. The charity aims to provide a service to the entire country and grants were allocated throughout the UK as shown below:

	Value	%
South East	£2.74 million	15%
Scotland	£2.34 million	13%
Midlands, East	£2.18 million	12%
North West	£1.58 million	9%
Northern Ireland	£1.52 million	9%
North West	£1.51 million	9%
South West	£1.36 million	8%
Wales	£1.34 million	8%
All England	£0.39 million	2%
All UK	£2.75 million	15%

In distributing grants the trustees are advised by one central and eight regional committees who are assisted in making their recommendations by freelance assessors with relevant expertise and local knowledge.

The charity distributes grants to a wide variety of projects and organisations helping children with many disadvantages. A summary of the type of grants is set out below:

- £400,000 went to schools, hospitals and social services for activities and equipment for children.

- £5,900,000 to children in care or living in women's refuges or other projects providing care and support.
- £2,100,000 to playgroups, nurseries and other services for disadvantaged children under 5.
- £1,300,000 to fund children's hospices, child abuse work, projects for children affected by AIDS/HIV and organisations giving emergency grants to individual children.
- £1,400,000 to help young people in trouble because of homelessness, drugs or solvent abuse, alcohol problems or eating disorders.
- £3,900,000 to involve children, may with physical and mental difficulties, in activities such as sport, drama, music and play.
- £1,200,000 to provide safe outdoor play facilities and holidays in the UK for children who need them.
- £1,500,000 to fund therapy for disabled children and advice and counselling services for children with special needs.

Size of grants

Range	Number	Totalling
£0 – £1,000	941	£621,000
£1,001 – £5,000	1,074	£2,761,000
£5001 – £10,000	247	£1,826,000
£10,001 – £25,000	190	£,089,000
£25,001 – £100,000	178	£8,400,000
Over £100,000	5	£1,015,000

'The above table shows that most of our grants were for under £5,000 – small grants to make a big difference. Most of the money – about £10 million – was spent on 515 grants ranging from £5,000 to £25,000 per annum. Our top 50 total £3.7 million and go to charities everywhere in the UK.

Grants in 1996/97

The largest grants in 1996/97 included the following:

- £500,000 to the Family Welfare Association to provide emergency help for individual children in need (see Guidelines above);
- £150,000 to NCH Action for Children to provide support to children who are caring for dependent relatives through a network of local projects;
- £143,000 over three years to The Independent Panel for Special Education Advice to provide advice to parents on the education of children with special needs;
- £105,000 over three years to the Dumfries and Galloway Befriending Project which provides adult friendship and support to youngsters with behavioural problems;

- £96,000 to the Medical Foundation for the Care of Victims of Torture towards work with refugee children who have been tortured or witnessed torture;
- £57,000 over three years to Nexus Institute in Northern Ireland to provide counselling to children and young people who have been traumatised by sexual abuse;
- £60,000 to the Child Accident Prevention Trust to develop a national support initiative for injured children.

Five £50,000 grants went to:

- Children's Trust in Tadworth, Surrey towards the cost of building a rehabilitation unit for children with severe brain injuries;
- Foundation for Conductive Education in Birmingham (for work with children with Cerebral Palsy);
- Joseph Patrick Memorial Trust (to provide wheelchairs and special beds to children with muscular dystrophy);
- Royal National College for the Blind (to help improve residential facilities for visually impaired teenagers).

'£45,000 went to Centrepoint for running costs in providing refuge for young homeless. £41,000 was gifted to the Butterwick Hospice in Stockton towards the cost of building a hydrotherapy pool in a hospice.'

The smallest grants included £150 gifts to the Beaumont Parent and Toddler Group in East London to take their toddlers for a trip to the seaside; Joint Openshaw Group in Manchester to buy play equipment for after schools clubs; Ruchaize Junior Club in Scotland for games and equipment; and West End Under 5s Playgroup in Rhyl, North Wales to buy toys.

The clear and open way in which BBC Children in Need performs and reports its work is an excellent example of the transparency that should follow for all grant-makers that accept the spirit as well as the letter of the Charity Commission's SORP requirements.

Exclusions The Appeal does not consider applications from private individuals or the friends or families of individual children. In addition, grants will not be given for:

- Trips and projects abroad;
- Medical treatment or medical research;
- Unspecified expenditure;
- Deficit funding or repayment of loans;
- Projects which take place before applications can be processed;
- This takes up to five months from the closing dates;

- Projects which are unable to start within 12 months;
- Distribution to another/other organisation(s);
- General appeals and endowment funds;
- The relief of statutory responsibilities.

Applications Admirably straightforward application forms and guidelines are available from the Appeal at the address above or from:

Scotland: Broadcasting House, Queen Street, Edinburgh EH2 IJF
Tel: 0131-248 4225

Wales: Broadcasting House, Llandaff, Cardiff CF5 2YQ, Tel: 01222-322 383

Northern Ireland: Broadcasting House, Ormeau Avenue, Belfast BT2 8HQ, Tel: 01232-338221.

When to apply

In 1997/98 there were two closing dates for applications – November 30 and March 30. Organisations could submit only one application and could apply to only one of these dates.

Applicants should allow up to five months from each closing date for notification of a decision. (For summer projects applications must be submitted by the November closing date or be rejected because they cannot be processed in time.)

The Beaverbrook Foundation

£200,000 (1995/96, but see below)

General

11 Old Queen Street,
London SW1H 9JA
Tel: 0171-222 7474

Correspondent Jane Ford, General Secretary

Trustees Lord Beaverbrook, Chairman; Lady Beaverbrook; Lady Aitken (Deputy Chairman); T M Aitken; Laura Levi; J E A Kidd.

Beneficial area UK and Canada.

Information available Out of date accounts on file at the Charity Commission, and then without a list of grants.

General After we sent the foundation a copy of the draft entry they sent us a more up-to-date set of accounts, 1996/97. Unfortunately it arrived too late for inclusion in this edition.

The foundation has seen a gradual rise in its income (£477,000 in 1992/93 to £777,000 in 1995/96) matched with a gradual decline in donations (from £332,000 in 1992/93 to £200,000 in 1995/96).

Assets have steadily risen and in 1995/96 amounted to £15.1 million. Management and administration costs were very high at £172,000 or 22% of income.

One reason for the decline in grant giving may be due to the costs of running Cherkley Court, Lord Beaverbrook's ancestral home. 1994/95 was the first year the foundation made a contribution, £20,000 towards adminstration costs, but by 1995/96 this had risen to £193,000 and now included maintenance, restoration, salaries, rates etc. Even so, there was an unspent surplus of £177,000

The foundation has produced no grants list since 1993 when, from an income of £477,000 in 1993, donations of £332,000 were made in 49 grants. Examples of the largest at that time included Beaverbrook Canadian Foundation (£100,000); National Association of Boys Clubs (£32,000); Reading University (£14,000); and six awards of £10,000 to the National Association for the League of Hospital Friends, Raleigh International, Cartoon Art Trust, Isle of Wight Youth Trust, St Thomas' Hospital- Tommy Campaign, and ReSolve.

Applications In writing to the correspondent, with an SAE. Trustees meet in May and November.

The Beckwith Charitable Trust

£497,000 (1995/96)

General

Pacific Investments Ltd, 9th Floor, 195 Knightsbridge, London SW7 1RE
Tel: 0171-917 1777

Correspondent J L Beckwith, Trustee

Trustees J L Beckwith; H M Beckwith; C M Meech.

Information available Accounts up to 1995/96 only on file at the Charity Commission in September 1998

General The trust says that it gives grants 'mainly to educational charities, the underprivileged, the royal marines heritage appeal and charities covering overseas aid, the blind and the young.'

In 1995/96 total grant giving was almost ten times the income, at £500,000. This was represented by 22 grants, 11 of them repeats from the previous year and 11 new. Just over 90% of the money was concentrated in grants to just two organisations: The Teenage Cancer Trust (£226,000) and the Youth Sports Trust, which was founded by John Beckwith to improve sporting provision for children in the UK (£188,000).

Examples of the remaining grants include: Downe House Education Scholarship (£30,000); Harrow School (£20,000); Royal Marines Heritage Appeal (£10,000), London West End British Olympic Appeal (£6,000); and Church School (£5,200).

Applications To the correspondent

The Bedford Charity (formerly known as the Harpur Trust)

£764,000 (to organisations 1996/97)

Education, welfare and recreation in and around Bedford

Princetown Court, Pilgrim Centre, Brickhill Drive, Bedford MK41 7PZ
Tel: 01234-342424; Fax: 01234-273174

Correspondent D Wigan, Clerk

Trustees The Governing Body consists of the Mayor of Bedford and the MPs for Bedford and Kempston and for North East Bedfordshire; four university nominations; the nominees of the teaching staff and parents of the trust's four schools; eight co-opted trustees; two representatives from Bedford Borough Council and four from Bedfordshire County Council. The Chairman is Professor C J Constable.

Beneficial area Bedford and its neighbourhood in Bedfordshire.

Information available Accounts are on file at the Charity Commission. The trust publishes a comprehensive report and accounts and an annual review. It also provides a useful note: 'What is the Harpur Trust?'.

General Established in 1566 by Sir William Harpur and his wife in the town of Bedford, the objectives of the trust are:

- the promotion of education;
- relief of the aged, sick and poor;
- provision of recreational facilities.

Although only the last two are specifically aimed at the 'area of Bedford and the neighbourhood thereof in the County of Bedfordshire', in practice all the grant giving is in this area.

Total assets of the trust amount to £144 million held mainly as school and almshouse property. The trust has written that 8/11ths of the endowment income is to be 'devoted to the welfare of pupils at its four main schools, primarily in the form of means tested Harpur Bursaries for the provision of means tested remission of school fees and, secondarily, a contribution to the cost of capital projects of the schools'.

The remaining 3/11ths are at 'the disposal of the grants committee for the maintenance of almshouses and financial grants to individuals and projects in North Bedfordshire'.

A total of £764,000 was given out to institutions during 1996/97. Almost a third of the grants were repeats, with the majority being for £10,000 or less. Every year the trust puts aside at least £100,000 to enable it to support one major project. For 1996/97 this was given to St Etheldra's Trust for its 16 Plus Individual Living Skills Project (£350,000).

Educational grants

About £590,000, including the project grant, was given out. Examples of awards include: £15,000 to Daubeny School (for CDT refurbishment); £10,000 to the Prince's Trust (for Study Club Project) and £7,400 to Grange School (for a senior school library).

Poor/sick

Grants totalling about £91,000 were given to local organisations such as: £7,500 to Mencap Bedford Appeal (for the Blue Sky Appeal), £5,000 to the MS Therapy Group (for a Hydrotherapy Pool); and £4,000 to Family Groups (for running costs).

Recreational

About £250,000 was given out to a variety of sports bodies, local councils, community projects, youth groups and arts. Examples include: £40,000 to Piazzi Smyth Observatory (for a community observatory); £35,000 to Bunyan Museum Appeal (for fitting out museums); £19,000 to Bedford Borough Council (for three part time workers for community centres); £15,000 to Community Arts (salary for a project worker); £1,500 to Bridge Studios (for recording equipment); £1,000 to Sounds Alive (for Music Festival 97); and £1,000 to Bedfordshire Fire Service (for a fire advice vehicle).

Exclusions No grants to organisations or individuals outside the borough of Bedford, unless the organisation supports a significant proportion of residents of the borough.

Applications In writing to the correspondent.

Benesco Charity Limited

£2,900,000 (1996/97)

See below

c/o Chantrey Vellacott, Russell Square House, 10-12 Russell Square, London WC1B 5LF

Correspondent Arthur Levin, Secretary

Trustees Directors: John Alexander Franks; Arthur Levin; Henry Prevezer.

Beneficial area UK.

Information available Report and accounts.

General 'The group is an investment group which passes its income to another charity, The Charles Wolfson Charitable Trust... a grant making charity which derives the bulk of its income from grants received from this group. Two of the directors of this group are also trustees of the Charles Wolfson Charitable Trust, and the Annual Report of that charity notes that this body has acted on its behalf in making investments in property.'

During the year (1996/97) the group made a contribution to a charity, as detailed above, of £2,900,000. In addition, the group continues to provide seven residential properties to operational charities on a rent-free basis for use as student hostels and for welfare purposes and has added an eighth property, on a similar rent-free basis, which is provided for use by a primary school.

During the year, services were provided to the group by Chethams Solicitors, of which J A Franks is a consultant, at a cost to the group of £120,000. The services provided were in respect of professional fees and were charged at commercial rates. No charge is made by the firm for the services of J A Franks.'

Though legal, the practice of paying fees to organisations with which trustees are connected, especially on such a large scale, is one which these editor's think undesirable, unless there are unusual and specific reasons why this is the only effective method of proceeding. Where such is the case, the reasons should be set out.

In 1996/97 Benesco generated an excellent income totalling £5.5 million from assets amounting to £42.5 million at the year's end.

Applications No applications: see the entry for the Charles Wolfson Charitable Trust.

Percy Bilton Charity Ltd

£796,000 (1997/98)

Young, old or disabled people, medicine

Bilton House, 54 Uxbridge Road, London W5 2TL
Tel: 0181-579 2829

Correspondent Mrs Wendy Fuller, Administrator

Trustees Directors: R W A Groom; A Fowler; Mrs M Loxton; M Bilton.

Beneficial area UK.

Information available Full annual reports and accounts are on file at the Charity Commission. Guidance notes for applicants are available from the trust, and largely reprinted below.

Summary The charity runs small grant (up to £500) and 'main' grant (up to £40,000) programmes which make awards towards the capital costs of charities and to individuals. Around two thirds of funds are awarded to youth or disability organisations, and other grants are made to support the elderly, individuals and a variety of causes. Awards are usually for capital costs and can be spread over several years.

General The trust was founded by its namesake in 1962. It continues to operate from the headquarters of Percy Bilton plc but otherwise is wholly separate from it.

In the year ending April 1998, income of £897,000 was generated from assets totalling £17 million. A huge number of applications was received, reflecting its well-established place in the social welfare world, – 9,380, of which about 1,200, or 13%, were successful. A total of 29 five figure grants were paid (varying between £10,000 and £25,000) amounting to £565,000, or 71% of total charitable expenditure. The grants are categorised in the table herewith. Although 85% of donations were for under £500, these only amounted to 36% of total funds donated.

A further £574,000 was lying in a reserve fund to pay for grants which have been awarded but not paid (as of April 1998), including a grant of £40,000 to the White Lodge.

'The largest grant of the year went to the Prince's Trust (£25,000) as the second of our donations towards the development of a national network of study support centres for 11–16 year olds. Donations of £20,000 were to Age Concern, Middlesex and Nottinghamshire (refurbishment, furnishing costs), Boys and Girls Welfare Society, Cheshire (school for disabled children), British Disabled Water-Ski association (for boats), Disabled Living Foundation (refurbishment), and Sea Cadets, Lincoln (building).'

A typical section of the admirably full grants list reads as follows:

- Coram's Fields and Harmsworth Memorial Playground, London WC1

Percy Bilton Charity Ltd

	1997/98		1996/97	
	Value	*%*	*Value*	*%*
Disabled	£234,000	29%	£376,000	48%
Youth – general	£191,000	24%	£74,000	9%
Elderly	£117,000	15%	£124,000	16%
Individuals in need	£84,000	11%	£60,000	8%
Christmas hampers	£80,000	10%	£76,000	10%
Youth – small grants	£43,000	5%	£36,000	5%
Miscellaneous	£36,000	5%	£33,000	4%
Medical	£11,000	1%	£10,000	1%
Total	**£796,000**	**100%**	**£790,000**	**100%**

to identify the services they need and want.

'Our new guidelines make explicit what we expect of applicants. There are no hidden agendas. We are convinced that it is in everyone's interest to be clear and open. To that end the Bridge House Grants Committee meetings are open to the public and, whilst transparency can at times be uncomfortable, it is always worthwhile.

'It is too early to gauge the impact of the trust's new approach. Our grant-making programme is evolving and, to ensure that it does so effectively, we are committed to a process of monitoring and evaluation not only in terms of grants awarded, but in terms of our own performance. We have a tiered approach to monitoring grants and our monitoring requirements are tailored appropriately to the size of the grant. All our grants over £100,000 are externally evaluated.

'This year our grant-making has largely been reactive, and we are gaining in experience and knowledge. We have commissioned an independent review of our funding in Tower Hamlets, where we have awarded most grants. This will also explore the funding needs of that borough's voluntary sector.'

The total net income of the trust in 1997/98 was £28 million, generated mainly from assets of £500 million. Grant giving was made up of £10.1 million through 283 grants.

Guidelines for Applicants

The rest of this entry comes from the Guidelines for Applicants and the grants list for 1997/98.

Access to transport, buildings and opportunities for older people and people with disabilities.

(Readers should not be deterred by the word 'transport' above: a wide range of projects offering opportunities for these groups are assisted under this heading. Ed.)

'This programme aims to:

- improve services and opportunities to older people and disabled people
- to encourage their active participation in the planning management of services.

'*Principles of good practice:* When the request is for vehicle purchase groups need to demonstrate:

- appropriate garaging and security arrangements
- evidence of planning for insurance and running costs
- commitment to safety and driver training

- that there is no existing community or specialist transport service which can provide the level or nature or the required service.'

Exclusion Not included is access to churches and large, national public buildings such as museums, galleries and arts venues. However local and community resources can be supported.

In 1997/98 107 grants totalled £3.5 million. The awards were made in three priority areas:

Access to opportunities
      62 grants/ £2.0 million
Access to buildings
      24 grants/ £0.9 million
Access to transport
      21 grants/ £0.6 million

Access to opportunities

'The trust welcomes applications from organisations providing:

- training, employment, arts, sports and leisure activities
- information, advocacy and community support
- training for independent living
- specialist aids, equipment or communication facilities signing
- disability equality training
- increased social participation and integration.'

Examples of grant giving included: Action for Dysphasic Adults (£66,000 over three years towards the cost of self-help groups for people with impaired use and understanding of language); Drake Music Project (£60,000 over two years towards training tutors and providing music workshops for people with severe physical disabilities); Kenya Community Relief Association (£6,000 towards the training expenses of volunteers supporting people from the Kenyan community affected by AIDS); Providence Row Night Refuge and Home (£210,000 over two years towards the capital costs of a wet shelter, the revenue costs of developing a project for young people and a volunteer programme); and the Royal National Institute for Deaf People (£20,000 towards the costs of two information workers providing information to deaf people hard of hearing).

Access to buildings:

'The trust wishes to encourage:

- projects improving access to buildings in the voluntary and community services
- schemes improving access to the built environment
- schemes increasing access awareness, information and design.'

Some of the larger grants given include those to:

Scope (£300,000 to improve the accessibility of a new London office for people with cerebral palsy and associated disabilities); The Positive Place (£65,000 towards the costs of a support centre for people affected with HIV/AIDS).

Access to transport

'The trust welcomes applications from:

- community transport schemes
- projects demonstrating maximum or shared usage of vehicles
- schemes improving transport services through better co-ordination.'

Beneficiaries in 1997/98 included Greater London Association of Disabled People (£70,000 over three years towards the cost of a transport policy officer to promote transport needs of disabled Londoners); Community Transport Wandsworth (£55,000 to purchase two accessible minibuses; and Heart 'n' Soul (£40,000 to purchase a touring truck for a learning disabled music and theatre company).

Environmental conservation

'The trust supports a diverse range of projects which protect, improve and sustain London's environment. The programme aims to help:

- maintain, protect and enhance the natural environment
- maintain London's biodiversity

'The trust welcomes applications from organisations which are working to:

- develop environmental education work
- protect and improve the natural environment
- maintain London's biodiversity or variety of life
- raise awareness and knowledge of environmental issues within the wider community
- ensure that resources are used in the least harmful and most efficient way.

'*Principles of good practice:* The trust particularly wishes to support projects which:

- enable other organisations to benefit and learn from successful initiatives
- encourage the involvement of all sections of the community, particularly marginalised or disadvantaged groups.
- demonstrate innovative approaches to address environmental issues
- show a commitment to 'sustainability' or minimising the drain on the world's resources
- encourage the involvement of volunteers

'*Areas of interest:* The trust is interested in supporting smaller organisations and organisations which do not have the environment as their main focus. The trust will therefore support:

- local development agencies and larger environmental organisations to provide help in kind, resources, staff time, and technical assistance to smaller organisations.
- consortium bids under which a number of of smaller groups could form partnerships with a well established charitable organisation when applying for funding.

'The trust will also allow community organisations which do not have environment as their main focus to make a separate application for an environmental project in addition to a proposal addressing another of the trust's categories.'

In 1997/98 23 grants totalling £1.1 million were made. All of the grants were for more than £10,000, with most of the grants for between £15,000 to £30,000. About half the grants were for multiple year funding, up to a maximum of three.

Examples of the larger grants include:

Forum for the Future (£315,000 over three years towards three inter-related environmental projects working with local economies, key players in the investment community and young people with leadership potential);

Common Ground (£110,000 over two years towards the staff costs of an educational initiative to create an awareness of protecting, valuing and conserving water and the river Thames);

Bioregional Development Group (£89,000 over two years towards the development of an initiative to reduce paper consumption in London and create 'local paper');

Global Action Plan UK (£50,000 over two years towards the running costs of work promoting environmental action in households and schools);

Tower Hamlets Environment Trust (£50,000 towards the continuation of a community involvement programme for Mile End Park);

Bat Conservation Trust (£23,000 towards the staff and running costs of a project to conserve bats in London).

Children and young people

'This programme has three aims:

- to support children and young people to develop their potential

- encourage the active involvement of young people in society
- support young people in crisis to reestablish their lives positively.

'*Principles of Good Practice:* The trust wishes to encourage:

- the principle of involving young people in the planning and delivery of services
- projects aiming to give young people the opportunity to participate actively in society.

'*Exclusions*: The trust does not usually fund under 5s work, play provision, playschemes or after school care.

'The trust has identified three main themes under which a total £2.7 million was awarded in 79 grants:

Preventative work with children and young people (aged 5-16):

'This includes work with families, individuals and groups, particularly

- work preventing homelessness or drug and alcohol misuse
- advice, counselling and information services
- life skills and personal development projects
- work breaking cycles of violence, abuse, crime and mental illness.'

Examples include:

Life Education Centres (£80,000 over three years towards Mobile Education Centres developing drugs prevention programmes);

London Youth Matters (£47,000 towards the initial year of a project to co-ordinated with children and young people's involvement in the Millennium celebrations);

Mediation for Families (£10,000 towards a co-ordinator to manage a mediation service for families).

Work promoting active involvement of young people (aged 11-18):

'Encourage work that will:

- enable young people to realise their potential
- encourage young people to take responsibility
- involve young people actively in their communities, including inter-generational work
- developing personal and emotional skills, especially in areas of parenting, life skills and relationships.'

Grants were given to organisations such as:

Changemakers (£24,000 over two years to develop young person led community schemes in schools);

Bromley Youth Agency (£40,000 over two years towards a youth worker salary and running costs for The Zone, an advice and information provision for young people);

Youth Action 2000 (£15,000 over two years to promote the Duke of Edinburgh's Award Scheme in deprived estates and provide access for young people to the sports facilities at Crystal Palace.

Young people in crisis (aged 16-21):

'Applications are welcome from:

- projects tackling drug and alcohol problems and homelessness.
- groups supporting young parents, young carers or those with mental health problems
- projects offering fresh opportunities to those who are living in poverty or deprivation.'

Grants were given in 1997/98 to;

Hammersmith & Fulham Partnership Against Crime (£20,000 towards a mentoring project to divert young offenders into education, training or employment);

Housing Services Agency (£24,000 over two years towards the staff costs of a new post to help resettle young single homeless people);

NSPCC (£263,000 towards the costs of two Child Support Workers assisting young witnesses involved in the justice system); and

TACADE (£188,000 to develop youth participation in drugs prevention work and evaluation and to publish good practice guidance).

Assistance to older people to stay within the community

'The trust supports a range of services which improve the lives of older people. Defined as those aged 60 and over). The trust's aims are to:

- support older people to remain in their own homes
- improve the care and support of older people
- promote the health and well-being of older people
- give older people greater choice and control over services they receive
- focus on those in greatest need particularly disadvantaged or marginalised groups.

'The trusts highlights the following priorities and welcomes applications from organisations that are working to:

- represent and empower older people without a strong or clear voice

- enable older people to make informed choices
- address the needs of older people affected by depression and other mental health problems
- enable older people in residential or nursing home care to maintain their involvement in the wider community.

'*Principles of good practice:* The trust wishes to support applications from organisations that demonstrate a commitment to:

- respect for privacy and dignity
- maintenance of self-esteem
- fostering independence
- choice and control (including the involvement of older people in the management and planning of services where possible)
- recognition of diversity (including ethnic, cultural, religious and social diversity) and individuality
- safety of older people who use services
- responsible risk taking
- citizens right
- sustaining relationships with friends and relatives
- opportunities for leisure activities.

'*Exclusions:* The trust does not usually support applications for the capital costs of sheltered housing schemes or residential care costs.'

In 1997/98 about £1.3 million was given out in 37 grants. Most of the grants were multi year awards; just 11 of the 37 were for only one year. Grants were rarely less than £10,000, with the average size around £30,000.

Examples of some of the larger grants include:

St Botolph's Project (£88,000 over three years towards floating support services to older ex-homeless people who need to remain housed);

Crossroads Lambeth (£75,000 over three years to provide holiday respite for carers of older people with dementia, disabilities or frailty);

Kensington & Chelsea Staying Put for the Elderly (£64,000 over three years towards small repairs service for older people living in the private housing sector);

Age Concern Newham (£51,000 over three year towards the support of older people from the Asian community leaving hospital);

Islington Chinese Association (£44,000 over two years towards the staff and running costs of a luncheon club for Chinese elders and to employ a specialist fundraising consultant).

Technical assistance to voluntary organisations:

'Technical assistance is defined by the trust as the provision of information, advice, training and consultancy to help voluntary organisations to develop. The programme aims to:

- strengthen the voluntary sector
- assist voluntary organisations in long term development and financial planning.

'The trust welcomes applications from groups which are working to:

- improve the delivery of services by second tier organisations to other voluntary organisations, especially smaller voluntary organisations
- assist voluntary organisations with their organisational development, for example, training for management committees or volunteer, advice on funding matter and legal advice
- provide specialist training and information to non-specialist organisations, for example, training and information on disability equality, HIV/AIDS or substance misuse
- develop councils for voluntary services in boroughs which lack co-ordinating bodies
- support organisations which promote volunteering.

'*Principles of good practice:* the foundation also wishes to encourage applications that will:

- encourage collaboration amongst organisations and better co-ordination of services
- promote the sharing of best practice
- minimise unnecessary duplication'

For 1997/98 about £1.4 million was awarded through 34 grants. Only four grants were for less than £15,000, and the largest was for £150,000 over three years to Community Links (towards First Steps organisational development programme for small voluntary organisations).

Grants went to a variety of other voluntary and community organisations. including:

Volunteer Bureau Wandsworth (£112,000 over three years towards the development of a standard for the management of volunteers by volunteer bureau in the boroughs of Wandsworth, Merton, Sutton, and Croydon);

Voluntary Service Council Hackney (£64,000 over two years towards staff and running costs of a project advising voluntary organisations on funding applications and fund-raising activities);

Southwark Community Care Forum (£50,000 over two years towards the salary and on-cost of a Fund-raising and Technical Assistance Officer to assist small organisations working with Community Care client groups);

Film and Media Training company (£20,000 towards the cost of a pilot multimedia and Internet project).

Exceptional grants

'Occasionally grants are made outside the above priority areas. Applications will be considered from organisations which demonstrate one of the following-

'That they are:

- demonstratively hard to find
- proposing innovative projects
- responding to new need and circumstances which may have arisen since the trust fixed its priorities (eg a major catastrophe impacting on London)
- requiring short-term assistance to cope with unforeseen circumstances enabling them to adapt to change and move forward (need arising from poor planning will not be considered).

'Only a small number of grants is likely to be made in this category.'

And indeed, for 1997/98 only three 'normal' grants were made totalling £147,000. These were made to Family Service Units (£90,000 over three years towards the cost of a dedicated post to support the London regional work); Nigel Clare Network Trust (£35,000 towards a Director of Family Services working with families who have a child with a life-threatening illness; and Newpin, Tower Hamlets (£21,000 towards the salary and running costs of a training programme for parents).

One wholly exceptional grant of no less than £815,000 was given to the Peabody Trust for a ground breaking development for elderly people in Southwark (Peabody is also a grant making body, but this project was not connected with that side of its work).

Exclusions The trust cannot fund:

- political parties
- political lobbying
- non-charitable activities
- statutory or corporate bodies where the body involved is under a statutory or legal duty to incur the expenditure in question
- grants which do not benefit the inhabitants of Greater London

The trust does not fund:

- individuals;
- other grant-making bodies;

- schools; universities or other educational establishments except where they are undertaking ancillary charitable activities specifically directed towards one of the agreed priority areas;
- medical or academic research;
- churches or other religious bodies where the monies will be used for the construction, maintenance and repair of religious buildings and for other religious purposes;
- hospitals.

Grants will not usually be given to:

- organisations seeking funding to replace cuts by statutory authorities
- organisations seeking funding to top up on under-priced contracts.

Applications

How to apply

Applications must be submitted on an application form with accompanying documentation. Applications sent by fax will not be considered. The form is a substantial eight page document. It includes a full page summary 'request for funding' which will be copied to trustees.

'Applications from unincorporated bodies, unless they are registered charities, will not be considered unless a registered charity has agreed to receive and account for any grant that may be awarded.

Timetable

'Trustees meet regularly and applications are accepted throughout the year. It takes about four months from receiving your application until a final decision is reached.

What type of grants do we give?

'We give grants for both running costs and capital costs. Grants for running costs are usually for projects rather than core costs and can be from one to three years.

When can you re-apply?

'Normally we would make only one grant to an organisation at a time. If you receive a grant then you can reapply for a different purpose at the end of the period of the grant when the work has been evaluated.

'In the case of capital grants a year must have elapsed since payment

How much do we give?

'We have no minimum amount but applications over £25,000 need to be accompanied by a detailed proposal. Large grants to small organisations are unlikely to be made.

'We expect organisations to have some other revenue funding before making a grant.'

Burdens Charitable Foundation

£377,000 (1996/97)

General

St George's House, 215-219 Chester Road, Manchester M15 4JE
Tel: 0161-832 4901; Fax: 0161-835 3668

Correspondent A J Burden

Trustees A J Burden; R D W Evans; G W Burden; Mrs H M Perkins; Mrs S A Schofield.

Beneficial area UK and overseas, with a special interest in Powys, Bristol, Midlands and the North West.

Information available Report and accounts with list of top 50 grants, without the required analysis of donations, but see below.

Summary Most grants are for £2,000 or less and these account for around half of charitable expenditure. The maximum grant is in the region of £20,000. Beneficiaries are said to be usually, but not exclusively, small, local, social welfare organisations working within deprived areas.

General This family trust was set up in 1977 by the late founder and chairman of W T Burden Ltd. In 1996/97 assets totalled £7.7 million from which £467,000 income was generated.

Management and administration costs were a notably low £7,000, or 2 pence per £1 donated, £21 per grant.

The foundation states its objectives thus:

- emphasis on the relief of human suffering and impairment, and of economic deprivation;
- preference is given to small local groups rather than to large or national and publicly well supported charities;
- emphasis is given to needs in the communities in which the individual trustees and W T Burden are active, particularly Powys, Bristol, Midlands and North West;
- relief and development in the world's most impoverished countries and through umbrella agencies;
- social outreach projects of local churches.

In 1996/97 a total of 378 awards were made (average donation £1,000). Although the grants list shows only the largest 50 grants, these accounted for

57% of charitable expenditure. Furthermore in 1997 the foundation reported an increased investment in data processing and so 'they expect that later reports may well be more informative in principle regarding the nature of the charities given preference'.

The largest grants went to CAB, Moss Side, Manchester (£22,000), Homefield Project, Prestatyn (£17,500), and Easton Christian Family Centre (£14,000). All other donations were under £5,001. The partial grants list shows a strong preference for Manchester, with a number of grants for charities in Africa, Wales and other parts of Northern and Western Britain. For once, London is largely absent from the list.

Applications In writing to the correspondent, accompanied by recent, audited accounts and statutory reports, coupled with at least outline business plans where relevant.

The R M Burton Charitable Trust

£290,000 (1997/98)

Jewish charities, social welfare, education, the arts, especially in Yorkshire

c/o Trustee Management Ltd, 27 East Parade, Leeds LS1 5SX

Correspondent Raymond M Burton

Trustees Raymond M Burton; Pamela Burton; Arnold Burton.

Beneficial area England, with a preference for Yorkshire, particularly Leeds, and Humberside; also Israel.

Information available Accounts on file at the Charity Commission, but without a narrative report.

Summary A very wide range of charities are assisted, around a half of which are for explicitly Jewish causes. Grants vary from £1,000 to £100,000 and many are made to organisations previously funded by the trust. Although there is a preference for Yorkshire and Humberside, about 70% of funds are awarded outside of this area.

General The trust was established in 1956 by Raymond Burton and for 50 years from that date its income may be used to make grants for charitable purposes. After this period the trust's assets will be given to the founder's descendants. At least half of grant-aid goes to Jewish organisations and remaining funds are disbursed to many different causes including housing, children, community, disabled, churches, education and particularly medical welfare, arts and culture.

The trust provided information on the grant total and major grants for 1998, but the information below is from the 1996/97 accounts. In 1997/98 grant giving totalled £290,000 with major awards going to an unnamed organisation in Israel (£100,000), Royal Opera House (£25,000) and £10,000 each to the Leeds Jewish Welfare Board and the Victoria and Albert Museum.

In 1996/97 income of £291,000 was generated from a capital base valued at £4.5 million by the end of the year. Over 50% of charitable expenditure was disbursed in the largest five awards to: Jewish Philanthropic Association of Israel (£100,000); Leeds Jewish Housing Associ-ation (£25,000); Reform Foundation Trust (£16,000); Leeds Jewish Welfare Board (£10,500); and the University of London (£10,000).

The trust's guidelines are as follows:

'Grants are made at the discretion of the trustees who will give favourable consideration only to registered charities. Jewish charities, education, arts, medicine and conservation are areas which will have priority.'

Apparently unaware of its legal obligations, the trust told us:

'We do not send copies of our reports, accounts and grants lists to anyone except to the Charity Commissioners and the Inland Revenue'.

Exclusions Local charities outside Yorkshire. "With limited resources the trustees have decided to restrict very closely the support given for individuals."

Applications In writing to the correspondent at any time. The trustees try to make a decision within a month. Negative decisions are not necessarily communicated.

The Audrey & Stanley Burton Charitable Trust

£380,000 (1996/97)

Health, Jewish charities, welfare and general

Trustee Management Ltd, 27 East Parade, Leeds LS1 5SX
Tel: 0113-243 6786

Correspondent The Secretary

Trustees Mrs A R Burton; Miss A C Burton; Mrs D M Hazan; P E Morris; D J Solomon.

Beneficial area Unrestricted, with a special interest in Yorkshire.

Information available Annual reports and accounts on file at the Charity Commission.

General This trust was established in 1960 by S.H. Burton who died in 1991. Members of the family remain as trustees.

Assets of the company amount to £1.6 million. The income, amounting to £390,000 for 1996/97, is mostly from additional donations made to the trust over the year.

Total grants for the year were £380,000, up by £70,000, with a variety of organisations being supported. Although the largest grant was for £78,000, most grants were for less than £5,000.

The trust seems to support the following broad categories;

- *Health/medical:* the largest group with about 43% of the donations given. Examples include £78,000 to the Mental Health Foundation, £2,000 to St Luke's Hospice and £2,000 to the National Deaf Children's Society.
- *Arts:* about 5% of the donations to organisations such as the Public Art Development Trust (£1,000) and the Leeds Grand Theatre & Opera House Ltd (two grants totalling £10,000).
- *Education:* about 8% of the donations by value, the only notable grant being to the University of Newcastle (£5,000), the remaining were small grants for educational purposes.
- *Social need:* accounting for about 10% of the donations given, examples include the Little Sisters for the Poor (£5,000), Save the Children (£5,000) and Craven RELATE (£200)

- *Jewish charities:* donations in this section represent about 32% of the total. Examples include JPAIME (£52,000), Jerusalem Foundation (£13,000), Jewish Blind and Physically Handicapped Society (£10,000), Leeds Jewish Welfare Board (£10,000), Jewish Deaf Association (£5,000) and Jewish Child's Day (£150).

Some grants are also given to overseas, conservation and environmental charities, but these amount to only about 1% of the total.

After the above was written from an analysis of the 1996/97 grant list at the Charity Commission, Mrs Burton suggested that the following list, perhaps from the 1997/98 list that these editors have not seen, would give a broader outline of the trust's present interests. It indicates a strong interest in overseas activities and an emphasis on children that was not previously evident.

Oxfam	*£103,000*
Save the Children	*£50,000*
ActionAid	*£61,000*
Children's Aid Direct	*£50,000*
Manic Depression Fellowship	*£9,000*
United World College of Atlanta	*£12,000*
Assoc. for Spina Bifida	*£10,000*
The Clockmakers Company	*£8,000*
Children in Crisis	*£10,000*
Whizz-Kidz	*£10,000*

Exclusions No grants to individuals

Applications In writing to the trust managers. Unsuccessful applicants will not necessarily be notified.

The Barrow Cadbury Trust, and the Barrow Cadbury Fund

£2,463,000, B C Trust; £236,000 B C Fund (1997/98)

Civil rights, community democracy, disability, gender, penal affairs, racial justice

2 College Walk, Selly Oak, Birmingham B29 6LQ
Tel: 0121-472 0417; Fax: 0121-471 3130

Correspondent Eric Adams, Director

Trustees Anna C Southall, Chairwoman; James Cadbury, Deputy

Chairman; Charles Cadbury; Catherine Hickinbotham; Philippa Southall; Roger Hickinbotham; Richard Cadbury; Erica Cadbury; Ruth Cadbury; Candia Compton; Thomas Cadbury; Helen Cadbury; Nicola Cadbury.

Beneficial area Unrestricted, but mainly UK.

Information available Excellent report and accounts with full grants list and narrative; guidelines for applicants.

Summary Support is largely offered to help marginalised, discriminated against, groups in society such as ethnic minorities, women, prisoners, refugees etc. A typical grant would be for £15,000 but awards vary from around £1,000 up to about £150,000. Most are given toward salaries and running costs. Both one-off and long-term assistance is available. Donations are made throughout the UK and, in rare instances, abroad. Grant-making is no longer focused on Birmingham and the West Midlands, although there are two programmes, described below, with a special interest in this area.

General What is now the Barrow Cadbury Trust was founded in 1920 as the Barrow and Geraldine S Cadbury Trust. Its name was changed in 1944 following a merger with the Paul S Cadbury Trust. The Barrow Cadbury Fund Ltd was set up in 1924 as a registered company with the primary purpose of supporting 'non-charitable projects which are considered important within the programme areas of the trust... any income not committed under this criterion will be devoted to issues of community democracy'. The directors of the fund are the trustees of the trust.

Guidelines

The guidelines read as follows:

Trustees and directors:

- '• seek to support projects of an innovatory nature and national significance which aim to realise a more just and democratic society. Grants may be for capital or revenue purposes.
- rarely respond to general appeals, or applications to local projects.
- do not acknowledge unsolicited approaches unrelated to published criteria.
- have no deadlines for relevant applications and no application form, in the belief that applicants can best express their needs in their own ways.
- like to receive copies of minutes, accounts, budgets and working papers which indicate the thinking which has gone into making the application.

- aim for a mutual trust and respect between the recipient and the trust so that there can be a sharing of the ideas and aspirations associated with the project.
- require adherence to a formal set of terms during the period grants are made and expect to receive regular copies of minutes, reports and accounts.
- are concerned that all sections of the population should benefit through the effective application of equal opportunities policies.

Programmes:

The trust makes grants totalling around £2 million a year in the following programmes:

Civil rights – support for the settlement needs of refugees and the rights of asylum seekers and immigrants.

Community democracy – the promotion of a just and peaceful society and support for education and training programmes in community organising.

Disability – national projects promoting inclusive education and the inclusive society for those with learning difficulties.

Gender – women-led initiatives enabling women to take a full part in creating a just, equal and democratic society.

Penal affairs – promotion of a humane and just prison and remand service and an equitable system of justice.

Racial justice – support for black and multi-racial projects fostering self advocacy and inter-ethnic and religious understanding.

Barrow Cadbury Fund

The Barrow Cadbury Fund Limited is a registered company and is not restricted to grant-making for charitable purposes. Its annual income after tax is about £300,000.

Grants are made in the same fields as the Trust if there are grounds for assuming that the activity would not be deemed charitable in the legal sense.

It is intended that any income not committed under the above criterion will be devoted to wider issues of community democracy.

Grants in 1996/97

In 1996/97 the trust's income was a little low in relation to its assets of over £51 million and administration costs a little higher than is usual for grant-making trusts: income totalled £2,096,000 and administration and support costs were £344,000 (16 pence per £1 granted).

The fund generated £400,000 income from assets totalling £12,620,000, and paid £50,000 for administration and £121,000 in tax.

Trust Grants in 1997/98

Community democracy	28	£552,000
Justice and peace	43	£420,000
Gender	45	£351,000
Racial justice	25	£328,000
Disability	21	£313,000
Civil rights	21	£238,000
Penal affairs	8	£165,000
TOTAL	191	£2,367,000

Fund Grants 1997/98

Community organising	25	£117,000
Justice and peace	6	£49,000
Disability	1	£3,500
Penal affairs	1	£8,000
Personal	49	£59,0000
TOTAL	82	£236,000

The Grants Report 1996/97

The excellent grants report is reproduced below (and further grant information has been added in brackets):

'We have consolidated some our programmes such as civil rights, community organising, disability and penal affairs, and continued to develop others such as gender and racial justice, while reviewing the direction of the justice and peace programme. We do not anticipate much variation in our programme of grant giving during the forthcoming twelve months but we do begin to grow conscious of the departure of our Director in three years' time.

Community Democracy

'This programme focuses on:

- the introduction into the UK of the concept of community organising;
- the promotion of a just and peaceful civil society, with a particular concern for Northern Ireland.

'The Citizen Organising Foundation (£165,000) offers education and training in citizenship through the UK's six broad based organisations in Bristol, Merseyside, North Wales, the Black Country, Sheffield and East London; our grants have been used for central administration and training

'We have continued our support for Women Acting in Today's Society (£70,000), which has inspired self help groups of women in often very distress-ing circumstance, and the Community Resource and Information Trust (£110,000) whose commitment and endeavour in this field continue to impress.

'The trust's other major grant in this programme is our support for the West Midlands Planning Aid Service

(£30,000) which has made a distinctive national contribution to the development of planning aid. We are pleased to see that there is at least some financial recognition of the importance of this work nationally through the Town and Country Planning Association.'

'(Grants in this category from the fund include: £34,000 to South Bristol Regeneration Force for running costs; £12,000 to Trillick Enterprise Group, Co. Tyrone £12,000 (for a salary); and six £10,000 awards for local organisation training to Impact, Sheffield; Citizens, the Black Country; Communities Organised for a Greater Bristol; Merseyside Broad Based Organisation; The East London Community Organisation; and Trefnu Cymunedol Cymru.)

Justice and Peace

'This portfolio reflects the specific commitment of the Barrow Cadbury Trust to justice, peace and reconciliation. We remain open to new projects, particularly those which are concerned with people participating in justice and peace in their community. We try to balance funding for experts or academics in this field with grass roots initiatives.

'Many of our smaller grants support individuals working in areas where people have not had the opportunity before to participate in activities which focus on democracy, peace, justice or reconciliation. In doing so we hope to foster the growth of local organisations which are able to carry the work forward. We recognise that such initiatives can come from all over the world and at present we fund some small scale innovative projects outside the United Kingdom. We are also willing to fund projects in this country which foster international understanding.

'Two major initiatives, the George Bell Institute (£50,000) and the Foundation for Civil Society continue to make significant impacts in their distinctive ways, the latter through our support for CENTRIS (£40,000).

'The Northern Ireland aspect of this portfolio is focused on three areas which effectively have their own budgets. These are in Fermanagh (£50,000), Omagh (£15,000) and Armagh (£10,000). We retain a modest commitment to cross-province community reconciliation programmes.'

(Other grants in the year included: £6,000 to Anti-Slavery International for a publication; £27,000 to Mediation UK towards running costs; £20,000 to Trust for Early Childhood, Family and

Community Education also for running costs; and £40,000 to the Department of Peace Studies, Bradford for salaries and bursaries. Fund grants went to: Committee on Administration of Justice £20,000; Fermanagh Prisoners Dependents Association £5,000; and International Democracy £21,000.)

Gender

'• Women led initiatives which enable women to take a full part in the creation of a more equal, just and democratic society. Priority is given to West Midlands based initiatives.
• Applications which can effect change in policy, practice attitudes and opinions on gender equality and women's rights at a national level.
• In Northern Ireland priority is given to women-led, rural based projects and trustees are keen to enable women to raise the profile of gender equality on the public and political agenda.

'The gender programme seeks to empower women to take a full part in the creation of a just and democratic society and cultivate different approaches towards their active participation in social change. Support is centred on local groups in the West Midlands and Northern Ireland.

'Following the successful pilot scheme, three years' funding was given for local grant-giving schemes in the West Midlands to allow small women's groups to address issues of local concern (examples are: Catalyst, Dudley, £5,000; Training for All Foundation, Sandwell £5,000; Walsall Council for Voluntary Service, £5,000). As a result of the pilot phase, it was established that applicants to the schemes require developmental advice and support and a regional network has been formed to raise funds to address these needs.

'Northern Ireland grants concentrate on women-led rural based groups to give women a platform to voice gender inequality and civil rights issues and influence the formulation of policy and practice. Support was provided to Fermanagh Women's Network (£7,000) for the development of local groups, and the Women's Support Network (£4,000) in the promotion of the Northern Ireland Office's recommendations on 'Policy Appraisal and Fair Treatment'.

Our few grants to national organisations focus on short-term projects which can demonstrate progressive impact on women's rights and gender inequality. These include the Women's Communication Centre (£11,000), for research on a fresh perspective to

improving gender equality; and co-funding the first phase of a major research project at the University of East London (£6,000), looking at women's organisations.

Racial Justice

'In seeking to create an inclusive society in which all peoples and groups participate, we have continued to support organisations empowering black and minority ethnic communities to address their needs, and secondly from those that address overt and institutional racism in improving the quality of life for their community.

'In recognising the double isolation of Bangladeshis from the wider society and from within their own community, we supported younger members to become more effective in improving the quality of life for their community (Bangladesh Centre, Sparbrook £16,000 salary grant; Bangladesh Youth Forum, Birmingham £22,000 for salary and running costs).

'A BREAD Youth Project in Bristol (£5,000) enables them to develop new approaches to work with disenfranchised young black men from a culturally appropriate perspective that can help them to reduce the extent of anti-social behaviour and build self-esteem; and funding of a regional development workers post with Sia (£47,000) recognises the importance of a regional presence for black-led groups in influencing change and fostering collaboration within the black-led voluntary sector.

(Awards for salary and running costs were also made to: Society of Black Lawyers, £30,000; Asian Resource Centre, Birmingham, £18,000; Black Employment Institute, £23,000.)

Disability

'• Trustees seek to foster inclusive education and the inclusive society for those with disability.

'The programme review for 1998 endorsed the aim of the trustees 'to sustain an articulate role in society for those with learning difficulties'.

'Several grants this year have been made to individuals, some of whom have group involvement, while others have not, to enable them to take a greater control in their lives. For example, Anne Rae and Martin Yates (Martin Yates Foundation, £5,000) have been supported to enable them to continue their proactive work in support of people with disabilities. Circles Network (£40,000) has promoted the ethos of helping individuals achieve ambitions that would not be possible without others around them. Similarly

Parents with Attitude (£6,500) offered Directors a very persuasive argument to back their publications.

'Trustees have wished to maintain a very modest overseas dimension to the programme. Action on Disability and Development (£20,000) has a long track record of enabling people with disabilities to make positive changes in their lives, often in very adverse circumstances, and our commitment has been extended. Additionally the programme has maintained support for a number of national projects involved in inclusive education and a new grant for Dr Andrew Grayson's research at Nottingham Trent University (£8,000) adds impetus to the pioneering work in the UK on facilitated communication at Ravenswood (£25,000). Thus fostering new and more appropriate environments the trust hopes to offer new opportunities for individuals to take greater control of their lives.'

(The fund also made a single grant of £3,500 to Action for Inclusion, Bolton, for bursaries.)

Civil Rights

'The programme encompasses the following main areas of concern.

- the rights of asylum seekers, refugees and immigrants;
- the settlement needs of refugees, where initiatives can effect change in policy and practice.

'The civil rights programme focuses on the needs and rights of refugees and asylum seekers in British society. Funds are particularly directed towards asylum and immigration rights and the resettlement needs of refugees through action research and casework which is concerned with policy and practice, bringing the experiences of refugees to the attention of policy makers. It is also vital to raise public awareness of the treatment of refugees and support has been provided to the UK for the United Nations High Commissioner for Refugees (£5,000).

'Following support for a study on alternative asylum procedures offering more positive models of practice, a further grant was made to Justice (£15,000) to service a joint working party to agree and seek to implement procedural reforms. Manchester Metropolitan University (£14,000) was supported in a study to highlight the incongruities between children's welfare policy and immigration policy and a grant was given to Immigration Law Practitioners' Association (£13,500) to identify good practice in the representation of asylum seekers and highlight the need for changes where asylum seekers are unfairly treated by the Immigration Service.

'Priority has been given to newly formed refugee led groups and established groups seeking to improve their management, organisational, legal representation and advocacy skills. In addition the Refugee Women's Legal Group and the Black Women's Rape Action Project (£16,500) have been helped to highlight the needs of women refugees who have experienced rape and sexual violence as a form of persecution as grounds for asylum.'

Penal affairs

'The trust has continued to give support to organisations that are working for better conditions for prisoners and detainees in Britain. Sadly, cost-cutting within the Prison Service has caused opportunities for personal development and pre-release training to be dramatically reduced. The long-term cost to society will be enormous.

'The Cropwood Fellowships and the Cropwood Conferences at the Institute of Criminology at Cambridge University (£30,000) were started by Paul Cadbury in 1968. Both these ideas have proved very productive and the Conferences in particular now carry great prestige in the penal field. We are delighted at the calibre of recent fellows and the imaginative and thorough organisation of the conferences.

'In association with the Institute a programme of master studies for senior police officers has been launched by Police Staff College at Bramshill. We are impressed by the joint endeavours which appear to have made a speedy and significant impact in the training of senior policemen and women destined to be our future Chief and Assistant Chief Constables. It is a heartening venture.

'Finally, the completion of the three year experiment of Cadbury Youth Justice Fellowships (£8,000) pioneered by the Trust for the Study of Adolescence should be acknowledged as a splendid success, with all credit to that trust's insight and commitment which should give new heart to staff in young offenders institutions – and to the public.

(Further grants in the year went to: Penal Affairs Consortium, £21,000; Prisoners Advice Service, £20,000, and the Prison Reform Trust £62,000 – all three were for running costs. The fund made a £3,500 gift towards administration costs to PROP, the National Prisoners Movement.)

Exclusions The trustees rarely respond to general appeals or applications from local projects except, as indicated, in the Racial Justice and Gender programmes.

Applications Informal enquiry by telephone is encouraged before formal application is made.

Applications relevant to the Community Democracy, Disability and Penal Affairs programmes of the trust should be discussed with the Director, Eric Adams.

Applications relevant to the Civil Rights, Gender and Racial Justice programmes of the trust should be discussed with the Assistant Director, Dipali Chandra.

Trustees meet in March, July and November. Applications have to be received at least two months before the meeting.

The Edward Cadbury Charitable Trust

£2,083,000 (1997/98)

Religion, general

Elm field, College Walk, Selly Oak, Birmingham B29 6LE
Tel: 0121-472 1838

Correspondent Mrs M Walton, Secretary

Trustees Charles Gillett, Chairman; Christopher Littleboy; Charles Gillett; Andrew Littleboy; Nigel Cadbury.

Beneficial area UK, with a special interest in West Midlands, overseas.

Information available Report and accounts with full grants list; information sheets.

Summary After major donations to the Quakers' Selly Oak complex of charities and buildings, with which the foundation has a close connection, about 150 further grants, worth about half a million pounds, are made ranging from £25 to around £60,000 but typically for between £1,000 and £5,000. Beneficiaries are varied but well supported causes include local (ie. West Midlands) charities involved in education or the church and small national organisations. A few grants are awarded to UK groups working overseas and overseas charities.

General In 1997/98 the trust generated income of £855,000 from assets totalling over £25 million by the end of the year.

152 charities received grants ranging from £25 to over £1 million. Nearly £2 million went to Selly Oak Colleges, an organisation with which the trust a has strong, on-going involvement. The trust describes the grants to this organisation in its annual report, which is reproduced below followed by our analysis of the other grants made in the year.

Guidelines

The trust's guidelines state:

Policy of trustees: 'To continue support, where appropriate the charitable interests of the founder and of the trustees. The voluntary sector in the West Midlands, including education, Christian mission, the ecumenical mission and inter-faith relations.

Type of grants: 'The size of grant varies, but most are between £250 and £2,500 and are usually one-off, for a specific purpose or part of a project. On-going funding commitments are rarely considered.

Type of beneficiary: 'Registered charities working within the areas outlined under policy. Preference to the newly established.'

Trustees' Report

The Trustees' Report 1997/98 reads as follows:

'Trust policy has remained unchanged. Two large projects have been identified for prospective funding.

'Our portfolio of investments has performed strongly, rising from £18,217,000 to £25,239,000, a 39% increase after funding of Selly Oak Colleges Endowment Trust for building costs of their Orchard Learning Resource Centre and their purchase of the former Kingsmead College site, referred to below.

Selly Oak Colleges Endowment Trust – Orchard Learning Resource Centre

The centre was completed on time and to budget, coming into use when students returned to the colleges in September. During the year we paid £670,000 against the £4 million promised, leaving £60,000 still to be paid.

Kingsmead College: As indicated in last year's report Selly Oak Colleges Endowment Trust did manage to secure the purchase of this important property for £1,250,000 which has been funded by this trust, and during the year this sum was given plus £116,000 for professional costs involved and most of the demolition costs.

Other grants

Excluding grants to Selly Oak Colleges projects, 148 grants were made totalling £549,000. £221,000 was disbursed in these six grants for over £20,000:

- Centre for Black and White (£37,000);
- DEBRA (£46,000);
- Elizabeth Fitzroy Homes (£25,000);
- Friends House (£30,000);
- Leighton Park School (£62,000);
- University of Birmingham (£21,000).

Ten Awards for £10,000 each went to:

Bernard Isaac's Memorial Fellowship Appeal;
Bootham School;
Jubilee 2000 Forum;
Move International;
MSA Midland People with Cerebral Palsy;
National Deaf Children's Society;
Prospect Hall Ltd;
Sibford School;
St Giles Medical Rehabilitation Centre;
Worcs Young Farmers' Clubs.

Smaller gifts included those to Warwickshire Association Boys' Club (£1,000); Royal National Mission to Deep Sea Fisherman, £400; Victim Support, £750; St Mary's Hospice, £5,000; Seedcorn Enterprises, £1,000; Plantlife, £5,000; Prison Fellowship £1,000; Birmingham Royal Ballet, £1,000; African Caribbean Community Initiative, £500; Christian Education Movement, £1,000; British Nutrition Foundation, £1,000; and Children Nationwide, £5,000.

Grants directed at causes overseas included the following: Book Aid International, £1,000; Global Care, £1,000; International Childcare, £3,000; International Voluntary Service, £1,200; Prisoners of Conscience £1,000; School of Mission and World Christianity, £750; World University Service £15,000; and the University of Cape Town, £5,000.

Exclusions Registered charities only. No student grants or support for individuals. The trust is unlikely to fund projects which have popular appeal or fund things which are normally publicly funded.

Applications At any time, but allow three months for a response. Applications that do not come within the trust's policy as stated above will not be considered or acknowledged.

The trust does not have an application form. Applications should be made in writing to the correspondent, they should clearly and concisely give relevant information concerning the project and its benefits, an outline budget and how the project is to be funded initially and in the future. Up to date accounts and the organisation's latest annual report are also required.

The William Adlington Cadbury Charitable Trust

£536,000 (1996/97)

Society of Friends, churches in the West Midlands, health, social welfare

2 College Walk, Selly Oak, Birmingham B29 6LQ
Tel: 0121-472 1464 (am only)

Correspondent Mrs Christine Stober

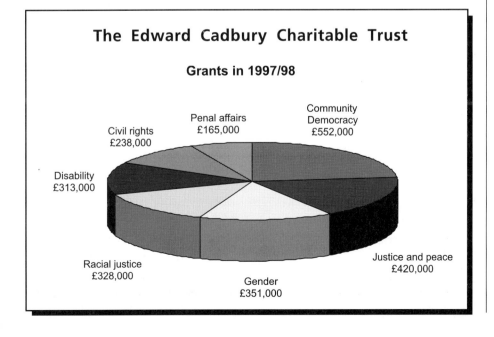

The Edward Cadbury Charitable Trust — Grants in 1997/98: Community Democracy £552,000; Justice and peace £420,000; Gender £351,000; Racial justice £328,000; Disability £313,000; Civil rights £238,000; Penal affairs £165,000.

Trustees Brandon Cadbury; Hannah Taylor; James Taylor; Rupert Cadbury; Katherine van Hagen Cadbury; Margaret Salmon; Sarah Stafford; Adrian Thomas; John Penny.

Beneficial area Mainly West Midlands; some UK (including Northern Ireland), and overseas.

Information available Full Report and Accounts. Guidelines for applicants.

Summary Awards, usually for amounts between £50 and £10,000, but occasionally up to £20,000, are made to organisations under 17 headings. About half of the grants go to first-time applicants and more than half of the beneficiaries are based in the West Midlands. Other grants in the UK are for national projects.

General The trust was established in 1923 to make grants for general purposes with preference to be given to charities in the West Midlands. Its guidelines read as follows:

Areas of benefit:

- organisations serving Birmingham and the West Midlands;
- organisations whose work has a national significance;
- organisations outside the West Midlands where the trust has well established links;
- organisations in Northern Ireland;
- UK based charities working overseas.

Types of grant: Trustees favour specific grant applications. They do not usually award grants on an annual basis, except to as small number of charities for revenue costs.

Applications are encouraged from ethnic minority groups and women led initiatives.

Grants, which are normally only made to, or through, registered charities, range from £100 to £5,000. Larger grants are seldom awarded. Major appeals are considered by trustees at meetings in May and November each year. Small grants of up to £500 are made on a continuing basis under the trust's small grants programme.

Grant programmes:

West Midlands

- Churches – the Religious Society of Friends (Quakers) and other churches.
- Medical – hospitals and nursing homes, health care projects.
- Social welfare – community groups, children and young people, the elderly, people with disabilities, the homeless, housing initiatives, counselling and mediation agencies.

- Education and training – schools and universities, adult literacy schemes, employment training.
- The environment and conservation work.
- Preservation – museums and art galleries.
- Arts – music, drama and visual arts.
- Penal affairs – work with offenders and ex-offenders, police projects.

United Kingdom

- The Religious Society of Friends.
- Medical research.
- Education projects which have a national significance.
- Environmental education schemes.
- Preservation of listed buildings and monuments.
- Penal affairs – penal reform, work with offenders, ex-offenders.
- Northern Ireland – cross community health and social welfare projects.

International

- UK charities working overseas on long-term development projects.

The trust's 1997/98 Report reads:

'In the year 1 April 1997 to 31 March 1998 the trust received 1020 applications for assistance, 336 fewer than in the previous accounting period. This year, there has been a significant increase in the number of charities requesting copies of the trust's grant-making policy statement and trustees believe that, as a result, charities are taking greater care to

ensure that applications fall within this policy.

'Although the number of applications fell within most of the trust's grant-making categories, in line with the total number of applications received, trustees saw a sharp decline in applications from churches and charities working on behalf of the homeless.

'However, the number of applications received from organisations working in Northern Ireland increased, and there were 102 applications from individuals, ten more than last year. Most of these were from people seeking to fund educational courses, or from students wishing to undertake voluntary assignments overseas.

'Of the 228 donations made this year (*22% of applications were successful, Ed.*), 108 were awarded to first time applicants. Once again, in line with the trust's policy, 132 grants were made to charities in the West Midlands.

'Trustees continue to encourage applications from ethnic minority groups and women-led initiatives. However, the level of applications received and grants made this year to these groups remained the same as those for the previous reporting period.

'Although trustees saw a decline in the number of applications received this year, they increased their levels of grant-making to charities working with children; the homeless; and to nurseries

The William Adlington Cadbury Charitable Trust

Grants made in 1997/98

Children: youth projects	23	£26,000
Churches: Christian projects	13	£11,000
Community services	32	£45,000
Disability groups	9	£22,000
Education: training	12	£9,000
Expeditions	1	£250
Health care: medical research	13	£57,000
Homelessness: housing projects	8	£25,000
International projects	31	£127,000
Mediation: counselling	15	£55,000
Northern Ireland	8	£34,000
Penal affairs: police projects	10	£27,000
Playgroups: nurseries	7	£1,700
Preservation	2	£4,000
Society of friends	15	£34,000
Arts	21	£46,000
Environment	8	£13,000
TOTAL	**227**	**£536,000**

and playgroups. Trustees awarded significantly higher donations to charities providing services in the community, to medical research groups, arts based projects and to charities working on long-term development projects overseas.

'The level of grant-making fell in the categories of education and training; the environment, preservation and the Society of Friends and other churches; people with disabilities; and penal affairs. However, grant-making was maintained at the same level as last year for organisations working in Northern Ireland. In the category of the elderly, 15 applications were considered, but no grants were awarded.'

Exclusions The trust does not fund:

- individuals (whether for research, expeditions, educational purposes etc.);
- projects concerned with travel or adventure;
- local projects or groups outside the West Midlands.

Applications In writing at any time to the correspondent. There is no formal application form, but applicants should include the charity's registration number, a brief description of the charity's activities, and details of the specific project for which a grant is being sought. A budget of the proposed work together with a copy of the charity's most recent accounts should also be included. Trustees will also wish to know what funds have already been raised for the project and how the shortfall is to be met.

Trustees meet in May and November. Applications are not acknowledged unless a stamped addressed envelope is provided.

The Campden Charities

£982,000 (to organisations, 1997/98)

Welfare and education in Kensington, London

27a Pembridge Villas, London W11 3EP
Tel: 0171-243 0551

Correspondent A E Cornick, Clerk

Trustees J R Madge, Chairman; M Heald (Chair, Finance and general purposes committee); Dr Hamilton (Chair, Case committee); Lady Astor (Chair, Education committee);

D C Banks (Chair, Organisations committee and Strategy Group); and 13 others.

Beneficial area The former parish of Kensington, London; a North/South corridor, roughly from Earls Court to the North of Ladbroke Grove. Map with the Guidelines.

Information available Admirable annual report and accounts, available from the charities, showing grants over £1,000, categorised and explained, reviewing grant-making and analysing trends. Guidelines for applicants.

Summary These charities support both organisations and individuals in educational endeavours and for the 'relief of need'. The benefit area is strictly defined – the guidelines contain a map. Grants vary from under £1,000 to around £50,000 and may be annual awards towards running costs or one off payments for specific projects. This entry focuses on the grants to organisations: assistance to individuals for welfare or educational purposes is covered by other Directory of Social Change publications.

The income of the charities is rising, and at the end of the 'general' section below we reprint their appeal for more, high quality, applications.

It is a pleasure for these editors to be able to leave most of the rest of this entry to the charities' own description of their work.

General The charities were formed during the first half of the seventeenth century with endowments totalling around £400 from the first Viscount and Viscountess Campden. The Charities' aims are 'to relieve poverty, hardship and distress among the residents of the old parish of Kensington and to promote the education and training of children and young persons in the parish in order that they achieve their full potential'.

By 1998 their net assets had climbed to over £52,000,000 and income of £2,218,000 was generated, making the organisation one of the richest local trusts in the UK.

Guidelines

The guidelines state:

'Grants are made to meet the needs of individuals and organisations serving those suffering deprivation but without replacing funding which statutory authorities are obliged to provide.

'A number of committees deal with specific aspects of the Charities' work. They are serviced by a Clerk and a small team of staff.

'The trustees provide grants for registered charities and other organisations usually, but not necessarily, based in Kensington, who devote a significant part of their effort to either relief of poverty, hardship or distress among Kensington residents or to promoting the education and training of children and young persons living in the area.

'The Charities welcome grant applications in the social welfare or education and training fields in their widest sense. Grants can be for one-off capital costs, projects and core funding.

'Each application is considered on its merits and provided funds are available, is measured against current criteria and priorities which are reviewed annually. Such factors as status, constitution and management and financial standing including availability of reserves are taken into account, as well as the efficacy of the project, the organisations ability to raise other funds and the degree of deprivation of the geographical area concerned.'

Grant allocations in 1997/98

	No of grants	Value
Education		
Organisations	66	£311,000
Individuals	143	£279,000
Relief of Need		
Organisations	136	£671,000
Pensioners	649	£278,000
Other individuals	639	£143,000
Total		
Organisations	202	£982,000
Individuals	1431	£732,000

About 60% of the organisations supported in the year were also assisted in 1996/97.

The Annual Report 1997/98

The annual report (1997/98) contains the following review of grants to organisations:

General

Grants made to organisations this year rose to almost £1 million. Education, older people and youth were the major beneficiaries. However, the number of grants reduced to 202. In line with Trustees' previously stated policy, there were fewer small grants for holidays and Christmas. The average grant size rose as a result to £4,860.

Relief of Need

Relief of need grants to organisations amounted to £671,000 (68% of total grants made). Disadvantaged groups such as ethnic minorities, the homeless and drug users, benefited in particular.

'Demand for community arts activities stimulated over the past five years by City Challenge seems to have contributed to a rise in both numbers and that total amount awards to arts projects. Trustees have also joined with other funders to improve the community facilities for deprived areas of North Kensington.

'Notable examples of grants in relief of need were:

- £56,000 for two grants to Action Disability (Kensington and Chelsea), for running costs and holidays for the disabled.
- £50,000 towards the Alexander and the Seventh Feathers' new youth club.
- £44,000 to improve the Look Ahead Housing Association's hostel for the homeless.
- £31,000 for two grants to the community centre for running costs and their summer playscheme.
- £30,000 to equip the rebuilt Tabernacle Community Arts Centre.
- £30,000 towards provision of a new resource centre for the Migrant and Refugee Community Forum.
- £30,000 towards a kitchen in the Pepper Pot Club's new premises.
- £20,000 providing security TV for the Wornington Estate.
- £20,000 to Staying Put for the Elderly, for running costs of two projects.

Advancement of Education

'The assistance provided to organisations and schools involved in education and training was considerably increased over the year both numerically and in total. £311,000 (31% of the total grants made) was awarded to 66 organisations, 5% more than last year. Most grants were relatively small in size, covering a wide variety of activities such as: supplementary schools, nurseries and playschools, homework classes, revision schemes, training courses for the unemployed and to provide for education in subjects such as music, theatre and the arts, for which only limited statutory funding is available. Major examples were:

- £17,000 for three grants to RBKC Youth Training Scheme.
- £15,000 for computers at St Clement and St James Primary School.
- £15,000 towards summer playscheme, rent and volunteer expenses at the Pimento Project supplementary school.
- £12,000 for an ESL project at St Clement and St James' Community Development Centre.
- £12,000 towards running costs for Nova Training for the unemployed.

- £10,000 for two grants for capital and running costs to North Kensington Video Drama project.

The future

'Trustees have agreed to increase grants to organisations for running costs by some £210,000 next year, to assist 27 groups who have lost City Challenge funding in 1998/99. Recurring grants for core funding need to be limited in order to achieve a sustainable level of funding for new projects in the future. As a result, in many cases grants were made for one year only, to provide stop gap funding whilst new sources of income can be found. The total grants budget for organisations has been increased to between £1.3 million and £1.5 million to allow for this, and to assist in a substantial way new and innovative projects in Kensington. This will involve considerable use of reserves, and beneficiaries should not expect continuing expenditure at this level after 1999.

'1997/98 was a year in which the trustees and staff were able to realise considerable capital from residential properties for the long term benefit of the Kensington community. This generated more income, but most was received too late to be fully utilised in the reporting year. At the same time, grant making committees have looked at new ways to help voluntary organisations cope with reduction in funding from other sources. Trustees have endeavoured to ensure that new recurring grants for core funding, or pensions, or for the education of individuals, are sustainable in the longer term, whilst retaining sufficient annual income for new projects and for major capital grants.

'The board has agreed that next year the total grant making budget will be increased substantially, dependent upon receipt of suitable applications. Trustees would therefore welcome requests for assistance, especially for one-off grants, for all areas of grant making which fall within the Charities stated objectives. Particular areas of interest are for original and imaginative projects aimed at improving the quality of life within deprived areas, inculcating skills for citizenship potential, or which reach the most disadvantaged groups in Kensington.'

Exclusions

- national charities or charities outside Kensington, unless they are of significant benefit to Kensington residents;
- schemes or activities which are generally regarded as the responsibility of the statutory authorities;

- national fundraising appeals;
- environmental projects unless connected with education or social need;
- medical research or equipment;
- animal welfare;
- advancement of religion or religious groups, unless they offer non-religious services to the community;
- commercial and business activities;
- endowment appeals;
- projects of a political nature;
- retrospective capital grants.

Applications

Organisations: Initial enquiries from organisations should be made in writing or by telephone to the Clerk or Organisations Assistant for advice and an application form which must be completed and returned with supporting information as required. Office visits are also encouraged to discuss complex applications or staff may visit organisations.

The organisations committee which meets 11 times a year, first considers applications and Trustees may decide to visit the organisation or invite them to present their request in person. The committee's recommendations are subsequently approved by the board of trustees. This process can take up to two months.

Trustees' decisions are imparted to the applicant by letter, which stipulates the nature and size of the grant, date of payment and follow up reports required from beneficiaries. Beneficiaries must ensure monies are spent only as intended. The Charities' staff monitors grants made by studying annual or follow up reports and by visits.

Individuals, welfare: Applications must be made through RBK&C social workers or local welfare organisations on an application form obtainable from the Assistant Clerk. Telephone enquiries can be made to establish eligibility.

Individuals, pensions: Applications may be made to the Assistant Clerk directly by individuals either by telephone or in writing. A visit will be made to them by a pensioner visitor and, if eligible, their name will be placed on the waiting list for eventual consideration for a pension.

Education grants to individuals: Applications should be submitted as early as possible in the calendar year and be addressed to the Education Assistant by telephone or in writing. After a preliminary interview by the Education Assistant, completion of an application form and submission of references, eligible applicants will be called for interview with the education committee which meets monthly.

Capital Radio – Help A London Child

£775,000 (1997)

Children in London

c/o Capital Radio, 29/30 Leicester Square, London WC2H 7LE
Tel: 0171-766 6203; Fax: 0171-766 6195

Correspondent Adam Findlay, Administrator

Trustees Richard Eyre; Richard Park; Alan Schaffer; Martina King.

Beneficial area Greater London.

Information available Annual report and accounts; an annual review with full grants list but limited narrative on grant-making; application form with guidelines.

Summary A few hundred grants are made each year to groups benefiting disadvantaged children. There are nine categories of beneficiaries. Awards are small – the average is £2,000 and the maximum grant is around £15,000. Donations are for capital or revenue costs and repeat grants are made.

General Help a London Child was formed in 1975 and launched as a charity by Capital Radio in order to raise funds for 'the relief of poverty or deprivation, or the promotion of the physical, mental and general welfare of children resident within the Greater London area'. The vast majority of their income comes from public donations arising out of a number of annual fundraising initiatives. Donations were categorised as follows:

Grants are allocated within the following categories:

- Play groups offering child care and play facilities for children under the age of 10.
- Youth Clubs and centres involved in issues facing children over the age of 10, including the scouts and guides.
- Refuge/homeless organisations addressing homelessness, including cases involving domestic violence.
- Cultural groups addressing the needs of local ethnic or religious communities.
- Health Projects offering care, rehabilitation and counselling for health issues including disability, drugs, alcohol and depression.
- Social/leisure – local groups organising music arts, drama and sporting activities for young people.
- Community groups – tenant's associations and community centres addressing deprivation and poverty issues at a very local level.
- Education groups addressing education for children and families, particularly those with special needs.
- Lone parents.

In 1996, income generated totalled £793,000 (£747,000 from donations) and grants amounting to £733,000 were made. Fundraising and publicity costs totalled £62,000; in other words 8 pence was spent to raise £1. Management and administration costs were £69,000, or £160 per grant.

In 1997 the largest grant was for £16,000 and went to the Children's Country Holiday Fund. All other grants were for less than £10,001 and the vast majority of the money was therefore disbursed in grants of under £5,000 (average: £2,000). Donations are categorised in the chart herewith.

Some examples are as follows::

	Asked	Given
Dalston Children's Center Community (Get Moving)	£1,104	£1,104
Greenwich Chinese Community Culture (Summer activity 1998)	£4,480	£2,000
Ealing Music Therapy Project Education (Workshop scheme)	£1,188	£1,188
Children with Aids Charity Health (Dippy Duck Appeal)	£5,000	£3,000
Holburn and Camden Gingerbread Lone Parents (Hostel weekend)	£1,380	£1,380
Elizabeth Lansbury Toy Library Play Groups (Provision of toys)	£800	£650
East Berkshire Women's Aid Refuge (Child welfare worker)	£8,000	£1,985

The Charity comments:

'Groups are encouraged to apply for grants from Help a London Child between January and May each year, and this year [1996] we received 624 applications (705 were successful. Ed.). These come from small groups and large; from new projects and from long established charities.

'Each of these applications is examined by our allocations panel, made up of independent assessors from the voluntary sector.

'Almost invariably there are more applications than can covered by the amount raised, however the panel endeavour to ensure that the money is used most efficiently.

'Sadly, some projects are not successful although they are encouraged to apply the following year. Roughly two thirds of applications are successful.

'The list of groups benefiting from Help a London Child grant illustrates the importance of the smaller charities to whom a grant of around £300 goes a very long way.'

The policies which guide the panel in their endeavour to 'ensure that the money is used most efficiently' are not

---

Capital Radio – Help a London Child

Donations in 1997

	Number of grants	%	total awarded	total requested
Community groups	68	15%	£120,000	(£204,000)
Cultural	34	7%	£58,000	(£150,000)
Education	34	9%	£71,000	(£98,000)
Health	69	23%	£180,000	(£305,000)
Lone Parents	6	1%	£9,000	(£14,000)
Play Groups	68	13%	£101,000	(£152,000)
Refuge/homeless	23	7%	£53,000	(£91,000)
Social/leisure	46	12%	£95,000	(£134,000)
Youth	37	9%	£68,000	(£125,000)
Total	**377**	**100%**	**£775,000**	**(£1,259,000)**

clear and it would be useful to see more information on grants and grant-making published in the annual review. In the 1996 edition there are four pages of narrative on fundraising but only two pages on grant-making procedure and categories (each category of grant described in a single sentence).

Exclusions Help a London Child will not fund:

- individual children or families;
- retrospective funding;
- statutory funding – funding for schools or health projects that would otherwise be covered by designated statutory funding from the local authority;
- salary posts for more than 12 months;
- deficit funding or repayment of loans;
- medical research;
- purchase of a minibus;
- trips abroad;
- distribution to other organisations.

Applications Application forms (including guidelines) are available from January to May and require an A4 SAE. Closing date for applications is the end of of May and is clearly marked on each application form. Successful applicants will receive grants by the end of November. The Allocations Panel sits throughout the Summer/Autumn.

Caritas (also known as Rothschild Foundation)

£638,000 (1997)

Heritage, Jewish charities, general

c/o Saffrey Champness, Fairfax House, Fulwood Place, Gray's Inn, London WC1V 6UB
Tel: 0171-405 2828

Correspondent Julie Christmas, Secretary

Trustees Lord Rothschild; Lady Rothschild; M E Hatch, S J P Trustee Company Ltd.

Beneficial area UK and overseas.

Information available Reports and accounts on file at the Charity Commission, but without the newly required narrative.

General From an asset base of £15.7 million in 1997, income was very low at

£388,000 (about 2% of the assets). Grant giving of £638,000 was concentrated in just one grant of £521,000 for Waddesdon Manor, the restoration of this former Rothschild family palace having been a priority for the present Lord Rothschild. The remaining £117,000 was given out in 65 grants, of which only about 25 were over £1,000.

Other grants were to Jewish charities, education and research organisations, conservation, medical and health charities.

Examples of some of the larger grants include those to; Wadham College, Oxford (£50,000); Natural History Museum Development Trust (£10,000); Museum of Jewish Heritage (£6,200); Mt. Sinai Medical Centre (£6,000); United Medical Schools of Guys and St Thomas' (£3,000); Anglo Israel Association (£2,800); Anglo Israel Trading Ltd (£1,000); Trinity Hospice (£1,000) and the Institute for Jewish Policy Research (£1,000).

Most of the grants over £1,000 were to charities that were also supported in the previous year.

The Carlton Television Trust

£506,000 (1997)

Young people

101 St Martin's Lane, London WC2N 4AZ
Tel: 0171-615 1641

Correspondent Liz Delbarre, Administrator

Trustees Nigel Walmsley, Chairman; Michael Green; Colin Stanbridge; Sara Morrison; Karen McHugh; Baroness Jay of Paddington.

Beneficial area Greater London, and part of the counties of Essex, Hertfordshire, Buckinghamshire, Bedfordshire, Oxfordshire, Berkshire, Surrey, East and West Sussex and Kent.

Information available Report and accounts; fully detailed grants list; guidelines and application forms; five year review magazine.

Summary Over a hundred grants are made each year to a variety of registered charities providing help to disadvantaged children in a broadly educational way. Grants vary from £200 to £30,000 (average £4,000) and are given towards capital or revenue costs. In exceptional

circumstances 2 or 3 year awards are possible and repeat grants resulting from reapplications are made.

General The trust was set up in 1993 with the purpose of benefiting the community within the Carlton Television transmission zone. Its particular mission is to provide educational opportunities for special needs or otherwise disadvantaged young people. The trust's sole source of income is a grant from Carlton Broadcasting Ltd who have pledged to commit £500,000 a year.

In 1997, 120 projects were supported with grants. The largest grant was for £30,000 and went to the Royal Academy of Dramatic Arts. The award was the first of four instalments towards rebuilding premises, establishing a trust fund to secure their financial position and an endowment fund to provide scholarships for talented but poor students. Together with 20 other donations of between £10,000 and £20,000, it accounted for a total of £159,000, 31% of grant expenditure. Nearly all other grants were for under £5,001. £20,000 donations went to the Sports Aid Foundation in Camden (to provide training grants), and to MENCAP in the City of London (towards the salary of a family advisor).

Summary of grants made in 1993 to 1997

Training and employment projects		
110	£583,000	26%
Educational establishments and projects		
137	£505,000	22%
Arts organisations and projects		
101	£413,000	18%
Young people's activities		
65	£258,000	11%
Play and minded care projects		
112	£245,000	11%
Support for families		
38	£232,000	10%
Miscellaneous		
15	£43,000	2%

The trust describes its policy:

'We will consider applications from properly constituted non-profit making voluntary organisations and organisations registered as charities in the UK. Grants are only paid to registered charities so non-registered groups must find a charity willing to endorse their application and receive any grant on their behalf. Lower priority is given to appeals from statutory services and local authorities. Although the trustees may consider support for individuals through charities which can speak for their families' social and economic circumstances, no such grants have yet been made.

'Capital or project grants are considered. Grants for 2 or 3 years may be made in exceptional circumstances only for salaries and running costs for registered charities. This type of grant should be to establish new ways of meeting need or to enable an organisation to move to a new level of effectiveness. No 2 or 3 year grants have yet been made (although posts in some charities have been supported for more than one year following repeat applications). All projects must be of educational benefit to children and young people who have special needs or are disadvantaged in other ways. We will only consider the provision of transport and transport costs for young people with physical and/or learning disabilities. There are no set minimum or maximum levels for grants which have ranged in size from £200 to £30,000 in any year.

'Grants have been awarded for such purposes as tutors' fees, salaries and costs for education/training posts, toys and books and play equipment, drugs education packs, IT courses, drama and dance workshops, and course on parenting skills.'

The following is a typical section of the trust's excellent grants list (1997), which describes the beneficiary and the specific purpose for the grant:

Mirage Children's Theatre Company, Kensington and Chelsea. 'Multicultural children's theatre company which aims to take high quality entertainment, especially theatre and puppetry, to children who would not normally get the opportunity to experience it. £4,950 towards production of dual language tapes of traditional stories used in most nursery and infant schools. Many refugee children can't understand the original material so restricting their ability to participate. The tapes will benefit six groups: Somalis, Kurds, Tamils, Bosnians, Vietnamese and Farsi speakers.

National Pyramid Trust, Ealing. Uses screening, inter agency co-operation and therapeutic activity groups (Pyramid Clubs) to promote resilience and self-esteem in vulnerable children.

New Assembly of Churches, Wandsworth. 'Group of black-led churches working with young offenders and those in danger of offending. Includes a pre-release course and post-release support for inmates at Feltham YOI. £5,000 towards the development of the pre-release course at Feltham to include more training in basic skills and greater

coverage of life and work skills. The grant will be used towards the salary of the principal tutor.

MENCAP, City of London. 'Provides services for people with learning disabilities including housing, employment and leisure opportunities. £20,000 towards the salary of a Family Advisor for Southwark, who will offer information, advice and direct support for young people with learning disabilities, aged 14-18. The primary concern will be education helping with the transitory period when a child leaves school.'

London Connection, Westminster. 'Day centre for young homeless people offering a wide range of services. £10,000 towards salary of the Playspace *Project Worker*, the parenting skills project providing education and support to around 300 young homeless families. Introduces then to constructive play, positive discipline techniques and child development issues.'

In the five year review, the Chairman wrote:

'The goals are to help those within the community who are disadvantaged through social and economic deprivation, homelessness, unemployment, disability or because they have special needs, including, for example, refugees or ex-offenders.

'In order to encourage the widest possible range of organisations to apply, we have sought to spread awareness of the trust through the national, local and voluntary sector press, local authorities and entries in funding directories, as well as through Carlton's regional programmes. Each year at least half the proposals came from first-time applicants.

'We review our criteria and policies each year to ensure that we take into account changes within the sector we support, and regularly exchange views with other funders. In some cases our grants provide pump-priming for new projects which have surpassed all expectations; in others they help maintain existing services which are examples of good practice. We usually arrange an opportunity every twelve months or so to meet with representatives of some of the organisations we have assisted.'

Exclusions Grants will NOT be given for:

- Trips abroad;
- Projects outside the Carlton Television transmission area. Please contact the trust if you are uncertain of the area covered;
- Unspecified expenditure;

- General appeals;
- Deficit funding and repayment of loans;
- Distribution to other organisations;
- Retrospective funding of projects which will take place before applications can be processed;
- The relief of statutory responsibilities;
- Conferences and seminars;
- Ongoing salaries and running costs (see note on grants for 2 or 3 years under 'Applications').

Applications Funds are disbursed once a year only. Application forms are available between April and early June ONLY and an A4 SAE (postage for 75 grammes) should be sent to:

Carlton Television Trust
PO Box 1
London W12 8UB

The closing date for receipt is shown on the form. Organisations may submit only one application per calendar year for projects due to take place from November onwards. Decisions will be made by 30th November.

Applications must come from properly constituted non profit making organisations in the Carlton transmission area. Grants will be made payable only to organisations registered as charities.

Each application must be endorsed by a management committee member, and an independent referee, or the registered charity supporting the request and acting as a conduit for the funds.

Very low priority will be given to applications from statutory services and local authorities.

Grants may be considered for individual children and young people if the applications come from organisations which apply on their behalf and which can speak about the family's financial circumstances. (Applications are not accepted from private individuals or parents, nor from teachers or other welfare professionals on behalf of their clients.)

Applications for educational equipment or mobility/communication aids must

- enclose a professional assessment from a relevant consultant or therapist;
- confirm that the organisation will take responsibility for matters relating to safety regulations, insurance and maintenance;
- explain any loan system and its criteria (if administered).

Grants for 2 to 3 years are exceptional. An organisation applying for salary costs for up to 3 years must be a registered charity in its own right. Such grants should establish new ways of meeting need or to enable new levels of effectiveness to be met.

The guidance leaflet provides more useful guidance about transport requests.

The trustees meet in September to shortlist applications and in November to decide the allocation for grants.

The Carnegie United Kingdom Trust

£1,126,000 (1997)

Community service, arts, heritage

Comely Park House, Dunfermline, Fife, KY12 7EJ
Tel: 01383-721445; Fax: 01383-620682

Correspondent John Naylor, Secretary

Trustees: Dame Gillian Wagner, Chair; Anthony Mould; George Atkinson; Linda Brown; George Adamson; The Countess of Albemarle; Sir Timothy Colman; Sheriff John Stuart Forbes; Lady Anthony Hamilton; Walter Hutchison; Prof David Ingram; Joy Kinna; Alexander Lawson; Janet Lewis-Jones; L E Linaker; Lord Murray; David Tudway Quilter; Arthur Robertson; Sandy Saddler; James Scott; Jessie Spittal; David Stobie; Sir Kenneth Stowe; William Thomson; C Roy Woodrow.

Beneficial area UK and Eire.

Information available Policy guidelines are available free on receipt of an A5 SAE. A copy of the Annual Report will be supplied for £6 including postage. The annual report (ISBN prefix 0 900259) is lodged in all main public and reference libraries and with major voluntary organisations. Intending applicants are advised to read a recent report to gain a better idea of the aims and work of the trust.

Summary The trust makes grants of usually between £1,000 and £50,000 for up to three years in a limited number of fields.

For the period 1996 to 2000 these cover the following fields (and are explained in full under 'Current grant programmes' below:

- *Arts*
  Young people
  Multi-Media
  Voluntary Arts
- *Heritage*
  Independent Museums
  Village halls
- *Community*
  Young people
  Parenting
  Third Age
- *Unusual initiatives*

General The Carnegie United Kingdom Trust was founded in 1913 with a $10 million endowment from the fabulously successful Scottish industrialist Andrew Carnegie. Though of only moderate size (grants have grown from around £0.8 million in 1993 to £1.1 million in 1997), the trust has for years carried an influence far beyond its apparent weight. This is due to its welcome but unfortunately most unusual practice of taking up particular limited causes and supporting them consistently over a number of years, with direct campaigning and by encouraging other funders to join in the enterprise, as well as by its own grant making. Past examples are its campaigns to make arts venues accessible to people with disabilities or to get the features of 'heritage' locations clearly explained to visitors.

Annual report for 1997

The report gives an admirable account of the work of the charity:

'The Trust Deed indicates that the income "shall be applied for the improvement of the well-being of the masses of the people of Great Britain and Ireland, by such means as are embraced within the meaning of the word 'charitable'... remembering that new needs are constantly arising as the masses advance". With such a broad remit the Trustees' Review and change policies every five years. The changes are evolutionary with about a third of the policies changing each quinquennium.

'New grant-giving policies in this quinquennium are multi-media in the arts; electronic information for the voluntary arts; two independent museum initiatives – volunteer development and innovation in the use of information technology; and unusual initiatives – an overarching policy to encourage creative partnerships and original thinking.

'As well as giving grants, the trustees also initiate their own research aimed at highlighting new developments and seeking practical solutions. This influences grant policies. In these guidelines, among the policies which

have emerged in this way are the third age, voluntary arts, volunteer development in independent museums, and young people and the arts post-school.

Strategic initiatives

The secretary's review of 1997 describes how these strategic initiatives work in practice:

'Although different initiatives require different approaches, experience shows that to be successful and meaningful each requires long-term commitment and investment. This is a key distinguishing factor for Carnegie with each major initiative taking ten years or so to complete.

'A pattern has emerged based on the pioneering Carnegie work on the third age. Firstly, to define the issues takes between one and two years. Secondly, detailed research with publication and public dissemination takes another three years. Thirdly, there is the follow up action to effect change, taking about three years. Finally, comes establishment of the issues among policy makers and opinion formers in the wider community.

'The Carnegie third age programme which the trust has helped to finance since the major inquiry was inaugurated in 1989, is now in its final stages with eight organisations taking forward not only the findings of the research but also the practical outcomes of the follow up programme.

'The more recently established Carnegie Young People Initiative is moving into its second stage, that is from defining the issues and initial research into active research at the grass roots. In this it will be collaborating with a large local authority and it is hoped this work will later be applied in a series of area programmes throughout the country.

'The Voluntary Arts Network (VAN), another Carnegie initiative began with a concept conference in 1987. Since then, the trust has contributed more than £205,000 to establish this widely recognised voice of the voluntary arts in the UK which received its last core grant from the trust in 1997.

'The Arts Council recognised that VAN was one of the first voluntary, as opposed to professional, arts bodies to receive its funding, a breakthrough which has led to other grants to other voluntary bodies. In keeping with its policy to retaining a commitment to its initiatives, the trust is giving support to the voluntary arts infrastructure through two grant policies.

'One is to establish electronic links between VAN and its constituent parts in partnership with the National Lottery and the other is assisting joint board and staff training.

'Volunteer Development in Independent Museums has been another long-term Trust interest which began with a conference on visitor care in 1991. After follow-up research, the focus moved from purely visitor care to volunteer development and visitor care.

'In 1995, a Carnegie conference explored the research and wider issues of volunteer management which has lead to a number of training initiatives for volunteers. The trust in 1997 gave funding to the British Association of Friends of Museums to assess the impact of present training and to identify what more needs to be done.'

Other grant making

On the trust's general grant giving the Secretary wrote:

'Every five years the trust reviews its priorities to provide a framework for its grant making. The 113 new grants made in 1997 reflect the trustees' policy of responding to a wide range of applications with a bias towards the small organisations who find funds hard to raise.

'As befits a pioneering trust, risks are taken; partnerships with other organisations are encouraged. Where appropriate, the applicant is linked with the trust's own strategic initiatives and the outcome is disseminated so that the impact of grants as a whole is greater than the sum of individual projects.

'The trust's policy for expanding information technology in independent museums illustrate these principles. The bias is towards smaller museums as the policy is only open to members of AIM (Association of Independent Museums).

'Many of the projects are pioneering the new use of IT. For example, at the Weald and Downland Open Air Museum in Sussex, sensors are being installed to show the impact of visitors and weather on the building. Responses of the sensors are then multiplied as if the impact was over a number of years and fed back to the visitor centre so that the potential long-term impact of the environment can be seen.

'The Association of Independent Museums and the Museum Documentation Association as partners comment on every application. Finally, as a condition of grant, each project – whether successful or not – is written up.

They will be brought together by the Museum Documentation Association and circulated to all independent museums to stimulate other museums to develop or even start creatively using information technology.'

'Within the headings set out below, preference is given to proposals which are innovative and developmental; have potential to influence policy and practice more widely; and are undertaken in partnership with others.' Probably as a consequence of its very specific fields of interest, few applications are accepted – in 1997 the trust received more than 2,500 applications but made only 113 grants.

Current grant programmes

The four current (1996-2000) grant making programmes are:

Arts

Young people: Open to local, regional and national voluntary arts bodies to help young people participate in the arts outside and beyond formal education. Priority will be given to projects which develop links between voluntary arts bodies and educational establishments to encourage a smooth transition for young people (aged 14-25) to enjoy continued development in the arts. Funding comes with stringent guidelines for expenditure.

Multi-Media: Open to national, regional and significant local groups which work with electronic multi-media and the arts for creative purposes, ie. not for management information. Priority will be given to initiatives outside the formal educational system for young people without other access to multimedia. Consideration will also be given to cross generational applications. Proposals with a wider community dimension or which link with libraries will be of particular interest.

Voluntary Arts – Electronic Information: Open to national and regional umbrella bodies for the voluntary arts. Hardware, software and training to electronically link with the Voluntary Arts Network information service, to access CD based reference material and to offer on-line information services to groups will be considered.

Voluntary Arts – Training: Open to national, regional and other major local voluntary arts organisations, eg. those with buildings or undergoing major developments. Training should be for key paid staff and volunteers and in co-operation to strengthen the management and administration of the arts organisation. Special consideration will be given to training which has a cascade

effect, ie. those who receive the initial training and will it on to others.

Heritage

Independent Museums: Open to members of AIM (Association of Independent Museums) and registered with the Museums and Galleries Commission. A) Innovation in the use of information technology. Special consideration will be given to those who are prepared to share their success or difficulties with others and indicate how they will do it. B) Volunteer Development. Limited funding is available to enable volunteers to undertake structured training, preferably leading to a recognised qualification and for initiatives which improve volunteer management.

Village Halls: Open to village hall committees where the population is below 5,000. Grants of up to £5,000 are available to develop a new activity for equipment and relevant building alterations but not for general repairs and access. Between 1930 and 1949, the trustees assisted with the early development of village halls. Now they wish to support halls' development and growth by encouraging their use as multi-purpose village centres. These grants are administered in conjunction with ACRE (England), WCVA (Wales), SCVO (Scotland) and Foras Eireann (Ireland).

Community

Young People: During this quinquennium (1996-2000) the Carnegie UK Trust, in collaboration with others, will be initiating a project to examine the social, economic and personal issues affecting young people, drawing mainly on existing knowledge but with some capacity for original research. Its purpose will be to improve the prospects for young people by influencing public policy, agency and professional practice, and adult attitudes, so as to secure the practical application of current and new knowledge.

An information leaflet giving more details about the project will be available.

The trust will await the conclusions before considering specific policies.

In the meantime, the trust retains its interest in young people from the previous quinquennium. It will consider exceptional proposals which broaden constructive experience by involving disadvantaged young people in the community in ways that develop responsibility and possibly leadership potential. Preference will be given to proposals involving young people in the management.

Parenting: For national and regional voluntary agencies which support local development. Priority is being offered to proposals focusing on fathers, couples, parents of teenage children and grandparents and which encourage the improvement of parental care through practical support services and informal education projects. Other parenting projects may be considered but lower priority will be given to applications which focus on mothers of young children as these were the main beneficiary in the previous quinquennium. Schemes mainly for counselling, crisis intervention, conciliation and child development are excluded.

Third Age: Open to national and regional organisations and those local organisations developing initiatives which could spread regionally or nationally. Designed to make the third age 'vastly more rewarding', this Carnegie driven initiative is now in its final stages. The trust will support selected proposals which have emerged from Carnegie Third Age Programme thinking and are focused on those who have completed their main career and child rearing. Priorities will include projects which introduce or re-introduce people after a long absence to volunteering.

Unusual Initiatives

Open to national, regional or local organisations. Creative initiatives which pioneer new ways forward across traditional boundaries will be considered by the trust. These may involve unusual collaborations, completely new ideas or the identification of gaps in provision which have emerged because they do not fit present institutional frameworks. The proposal should have significant ramifications, indicate what its wider impact might be and show how findings, approaches or ideas will be disseminated if the initiative is successful.

Grants in 1997

In 1997 grants from unrestricted funds totalled £1.44 million, with a further £173,000 in restricted funds (the Tomorrow Project received most of this).

Arts In 1997, £189,000 was distributed to 19 projects; typical grant £10,000.

Young people and Multi-media:

The largest grants were to ENO (£21,000 to fund a three year outreach programme to bring accessible vocal music to the Hackney community) and to the Easterhouse Arts Project (£20,000 towards the development of a Performance Art Youth Network).

In 1997, the Place in King's Cross received the highest award (£15,000) for the Cyber Challenge, a project linking dance technology and disadvantaged young people.

Voluntary Arts – Electronic Information: The bulk of funding in 1997, a grant of £25,000 out of a total £35,300, went to the Voluntary Arts Network in Cardiff.

Training: No grants were made in 1997.

Heritage Grants totalling £279,040 were made to 65 projects during 1997, £189,285 went to 25 independent museums and £89,755 to 40 village halls.

Independent Museums: £12,600 was granted to the Boat Trust to establish a common computerised group visitor booking and data retrieval system which could be used by other museums. The British Association of Friends of Museums were awarded £20,000 to research volunteer development needs, and provide a set of skills and standards which can be used throughout the sector.

Village Halls: In 1997, £89,755 was awarded to 40 halls in grants of between £250 and £5,000. Laughton Hall (East Sussex) and Polgooth Hall (Cornwall) were both awarded £5,000 for drama group equipment.

Community Within the three subdivisions of this programme 29 projects received grants totalling £657,250 in 1997. A total of £260,000 went to the trust's own initiatives, the Carnegie Third Age Programme and the Carnegie Young People Initiative.

Young People: In the past, the largest grant has gone to the Carnegie Young People Initiative (£215,000 in 1997). The main thrust of the initiative's work is to discover how the trust and others in the voluntary, corporate and public sectors can best use their limited resources to help young people through the transitions of youth. This is done by monitoring and analysing projects and policies designed to benefit young people, with the aim of producing a set of recommendations that can be applied at every level.

Ten external grants were paid, six of which were for sums of around £30,000. For example, a £30,000 revenue grant (to be paid over three years) went to YMCA Ireland in order to extend the work of 'Parents and Kids Together' (PAKT) throughout Northern Ireland.

Parenting: Eleven grants were made ranging between £1,750 and £30,000, the highest going to Children First for the development of a parent helpline and the National Council of YMCA's to evaluate and develop a parent education programme.

Third Age: The majority of funds (£45,000 of the total allocation of £87,000 in 1997) went directly to the Carnegie Third Age Programme, while remaining funds support proposals emerging from the Programme's thinking.

Unusual Initiatives: Only one grant was made in 1997; £5,000 for salary costs to Church Action on Poverty.

Exclusions Grants are not made in response to:

- general appeals;
- closed societies;
- endowment funds;
- debt clearance;
- individuals;
- replacement of statutory funding.

The following are specifically excluded during the quinquennium, 1996-2000:

- restoration, conversion, repair and purchase of buildings;
- formal education – schools, colleges and universities sports;
- research or publications, conferences and exhibitions (except in special circumstances where trustees wish to initiate certain work);
- community business initiatives;
- animal welfare;
- sports;
- medical or related health-care purposes;
- holidays, adventure centres and youth hostels;
- residential care, day-care centres and housing;
- conciliation and counselling services;
- care in the community;
- pre-school groups and play schemes;
- arts centres, professional arts; companies and festivals, including performances and workshops;
- pipe organs in churches and other buildings;
- environmental matters...including displays and trails;
- libraries.

The trust does not usually accept another application from the same organisation within 12 months from the date of the decision in the case of a rejection, or completion in the case of a grant receipt.

Applications

Application is usually by letter, except for proposals to the Voluntary Arts – information network, Independent Museums – Volunteer Development and Village Halls programmes. All applications should be directed to the secretary. Applicants should not approach individual trustees.

All applications need to include the information listed below:

- Brief description of the organisation – its history, work budget, management and staffing.
- Last annual report, audited accounts, the main part of the constitution, charity registration number and committee membership.
- Description of the project including its purpose; time scales incorporating any milestones during the programme; expected outcomes; number of people who will benefit; and how the project will be managed.
- Amount requested from the Carnegie UK Trust.
- Budget for the project, including details of funds already raised and other sources being approached.
- How the work will continue after the trust's grant has been completed – plans for monitoring and evaluating the project. The trust attaches great importance to this.
- How information about the project will be shared and what has been learnt from it with others in the field.
- Contact name, address, telephone and fax numbers. This should normally be the person directly responsible for the work, not the fund-raiser. The application letter should be signed by the senior person responsible, such as the chairman or the director.
- Deadlines for applications are 30 January for the March trustees' meeting, 30 April for the June meeting and 30 September for the November meeting. Applications can be submitted at any time. Early preliminary submissions are particularly welcome so that a comprehensive application can be presented to the trustees. The trust aims to inform applicants of trustees' decisions by the end of the month in which the meeting is held. However, the volume of applications received and the need for assessment may mean consideration is delayed.
- Applications are acknowledged on receipt.

Inquiries about trust policy and a possible application are invited by telephone to the secretary or administrator.

Applications within guidelines and being considered for a grant may be followed up with enquiries for further information and by a visit from a trust representative.

Sir John Cass's Foundation

£805,000 (to organisations, but see below, 1997/98)

Education in inner London

31 Jewry Street, London EC3N 2EY
Tel: 0171-480 5884

Correspondent Colin Wright, Clerk

Trustees 18 in all, of whom the following are members of the grants committee: M Venn; G C Lawson; K M Everett; Sir Peter Newsam.

Beneficial area The inner London boroughs – Kensington & Chelsea, Camden, City of London, Greenwich, Hackney, Hammersmith & Fulham, Islington, Lambeth, Lewisham, Newham, Southwark, Tower Hamlets, Wandsworth, Westminster.

Information available Report and accounts, with good details of grants but without the required narrative account of the foundation's charitable activities (financial matters are covered well). Guidelines for potential applicants.

Summary Grants, usually for amounts between £5,000 and £40,000 to organisations, be they schools, organisations working with schools, or those with educational programmes outside school, for educational work with children and young people in London.

General The foundation's Guidelines, in part, read as follows:

'The foundation was established to educate "poor but worthy" children in the Portsoken ward of the City of London. Since that time the foundation's beneficial area ... has been extended to include the City of London, the City of Westminster, the Royal Borough of Kensington & Chelsea, and the London Boroughs of Camden, Greenwich, Hackney, Hammersmith & Fulham, Islington, Lambeth, Lewisham, Newham, Southwark, Tower Hamlets, and Wandsworth. (According to a recently published history of the charity, there is also 'further provision for grants to outer London' but this option is unlikely to be exercised in the immediate future. Ed.)

'The foundation can only consider proposals from schools and organisations that will benefit young people under the age of 25, who are permanently residents of inner London.

'The foundation will consider applications for time-limited projects where it is clear for what purpose and activities grant assistance is being sought. In 1997/98 the foundation made grants totalling £1.1 million (some, to connected bodies, are not included in the total above. Ed.), the value of which ranged from £670 to £30,000 (but see details of individual grants below. Ed.).

'Foundation governors wish to encourage and, where appropriate, support applications which:

- incorporate structured educational content related, where appropriate, to the teaching and learning of the relevant key stage(s) of the national curriculum.
- demonstrate a realistic likelihood of continuing after the expiry of the foundation's grant
- are innovative, in the sense of identifying and meeting educational needs not met by other grant making bodies.

'Within these parameters, governors particularly favour applications which:

- promote the teaching of science, maths, engineering and technology.
- develop programmes that improve access to the curriculum and prepare beneficiaries for the world of work.
- develop curricula or activities outside the normal school day.

'Preference is given to original developments, not yet part of the regular activities of an organisation; to developments that are either strategic,

---

Sir John Cass's Foundation

Grants in 1997/98

Literacy and numeracy	15 grants	£229,000
Employment training	11 grants	£182,000
Arts activities	14 grants	£93,000
Youth activity	6 grants	£90,000
Environmental education	4 grants	£60,000
Health education	2 grants	£60,000
Science and technology	2 grants	£32,000
Miscellaneous	3 grants	£59,000

such as practical initiatives directed toward addressing the root causes of problems; or seminal, because they seek to influence policy and practice elsewhere.

'Due to the large number of applications in relation to the limited funds available, many good applications still have to be refused – even though they fit within the foundation's general guidelines. The foundation may also, from time to time, initiate new projects that do not fall into the priority areas for grants. In this fashion the governors explore potential areas for involvement in the future.'

In recent years the foundation has been in the unhappy position of having to refuse as many as nine out of ten of the applications it has received. To try to reduce this figure, as wasteful for applicants as for the foundation itself, there is now an increasing concentration on its local areas of Hackney and Tower Hamlets, and three of the 'priority areas' described in the previous edition of this book have been dropped:

- educational methods to divert young people from criminal activities
- work to enhance facilities for sports education
- youth activities.

Grants in 1997/98

The grants 1997/98 are categorised differently in the annual report and accounts to the headings given above. They are as shown in the table herewith.

The largest grant was of £45,000 for the Metropolitan Police's community programme. Two awards were listed at £40,000 each, for bursaries to enable children go on school journeys to the Margaret McMillen Field Studies Centre, and to the Seafood Training School Project. £34,000 was given to the National Literacy Trust for its work in London.

Grants of between £21,000 and £30,000 were given to London Youth Matters (for a support service for voluntary youth organisations), the YMCA (for a motor vehicle training project), Working Support St Peter's Centre and to Focus E15. But, as suggested above, such grants are unlikely to be repeated.

Few grants were for less than £5,000. Nor are supplementary schools as visible in the grants lists as in previous years.

Exclusions Other than in exceptional circumstances, the governors will not normally fund:

- basic equipment or salaries that are the responsibility of the education authorities
- the purchase, repair or furnishing of buildings

- performances, exhibitions or festivals
- independent schools
- local youth projects (though see above. Ed.)
- conferences or seminars
- university or medical research
- establishing funds for bursary or loan schemes
- mother tongue teaching
- retrospective grants to help pay off overdrafts or loans, nor will the foundation remedy the withdrawal or reduction of statutory funds
- the purchase of vehicles
- sporting equipment, or the sponsorship of sporting endeavour
- one-off music, drama, dance or similar productions, or the tours of such productions, nor does the foundation support ticket subsidy schemes
- school journeys, trips abroad or exchange visits
- general fund raising campaigns.

Applications 'There are several stages in the application process.

1. An initial letter outlining the application should be addressed to the Clerk to the Governors. It should include some basic costings of the project and background details of the organisation.
2. If the project falls within the foundation's current policy and its basic criteria are satisfied, you will be invited to submit an application under headings that the foundation will provide, together with an annual report and audited accounts.
3. Upon receipt of the completed application, foundation staff will discuss your proposal with you and may arrange to visit.
4. Completed applications are considered by governors (who meet quarterly).

'Applicants are notified in writing within seven days of a grants committee meeting.

'Throughout the application process, the foundation's staff will be happy to clear up any questions you might have and are available to receive initial telephone enquiries.'

The Charities Aid Foundation

£576,000 (1997/98)

Charity management and finance

Kings Hill, West Malling,
Kent, ME19 4TA
Tel: 01732-520031

Correspondent Judith McQuillan, Grants Administrator

Grants Council David Carrington (Chairman); Professor Naomi Sargant, (Vice Chairman and CAF Trustee); Revd Dr Gordon Barritt (children and young people); John Bateman (children and young people); Babu Bhattacherjee (voluntary action in general); Yogesh Chauhan (black & ethnic minorities); Gillian Crosby (elderly people); Anthony Hewson (people with mental disabilities); Andrew Kingman (aid to developing countries); Jane Lewis (science and education); Graham Marchant (cultural activities); Dorothy McGahan (people with physical disabilities); Professor Peter Quilliam (medicine and health): Ceridwen Roberts (family matters): Peter Woodward (environmental issues).

Beneficial area UK and overseas.

Information available Guidelines for applicants (largely reprinted below), annual report and accounts and exemplary further information about the charity's grant making is available from the foundation.

Summary The foundation's Guidelines describe its grant making as follows:

'The Charities Aid Foundation makes grants to enable charities to improve their management and effectiveness, in order to strengthen the UK charitable sector.

'Grants are made to assist a charity:

- to improve its effectiveness in meeting its objectives
- to improve its use of financial resources, facilities, members, staff or volunteers
- to improve its stability or effectiveness
- to move into new areas of need.

'Emergency grants may be given to meet an exceptional, unforeseen financial setback, or where a single injection of funds is required to restore the viability of the charity.

'Grants are normally made to small and medium sized charities with a proven track record. Applications are encouraged from black and ethnic minority groups.

'Funds are limited. Grants are normally one-off and should be used within 12 months of receipt. Only in quite exceptional circumstances may funding be awarded provisionally for a period of up to 3 years, subject to an annual review.

'Grants do not exceed £10,000. The average award is less than £4,000 and only two thirds of applications are successful. Grants are seldom for the full amount requested.'

This is an unusual and most welcome description. An activity has been identified, the development of financial stability, where a relatively modest injection of funds can make a big impact on a charity's future, and a suitably focused programme has been devised. As a result, a major impact is being achieved for a relatively modest outlay and with no grant being for more than £10,000.

General The Charities Aid Foundation's main activities lie in providing financial services, some them invaluable, to the voluntary sector. Grant making is a relatively minor part of its work, and is conducted by a separate Grants Council. This is now chaired by David Carrington, the Director of the new and huge PPP Healthcare Trust, described elsewhere in this book. He was previously the Director of the Baring Foundation, whose strikingly innovative new programmes were developed while he was there.

The Council's Grants Review contains the following: 'In 1997/98 the Grants Council made 144 grants totalling £576,300 using CAF's criteria from the Foundation's own funds, special donor funds and from funds distributed on behalf of trust or company clients. This compares with 156 grants made in the previous year (1996/97) when £576,800 was allocated.

'Twelve fewer grants were made in 1997/98 than in 1996/97. However, the average size of grant in 1997/98 was some £300 higher than in the previous year – £4,000 compared to £3,700 1996/97.

'The table below shows the range of grants awarded in the year 1997/98. As in 1996/97, the majority of grants made, 118 (82%) of the 144, were for £5,000 or less. Only four grants of less than £1,000 were made in 1997/98 – eight fewer than in 1996/97. There were five

grants over £8,000 in 1997/98 compared to four in the previous year but only one was at the maximum level of £10,000 compared to two in 1996/97.

Level of Grant	No. of Grants	Total
£3,000 or less	49	£110,000
£3,001 – £ 5,000	69	£290,600
£5,001 – £ 8,000	21	£131,400
£8,001 – £10,000	5	£44,300
Totals	144	£576,300

The purposes of grants

The figures for the four years 1994/98 are as follows:

Staff Fund raiser	£475,000
Fundraising consultant	£464,000
Fundraising material	£24,000
Organisational, planning and other consultancy	£593,000
Training	£211,000
Meeting financial setbacks	£201,000
Project funding	£244,000
Other	£111,000

The 1997/98 Review comments 'As in 1996/97, the largest proportion of grants was made to assist with fundraising, £231,500 (41%) followed by help with organisational reviews, business planning and other consultancy fees £204,900 (36%). The corresponding proportions in 1996/97 were, fundraising 38% and other consultancy fees 27%.' Geographical Spread of Grants

'The current year shows a continuing decline in the number of grants to national and international charities from 41% in 1994/95 to 27% in 1997/98.

'In 1997/98 both the highest number of grants and the largest proportion of grant aid were made to charities working in London and the South East – 56 grants (39%) totalling £209,100 (36%).

'Support for charities in the North West, the East Midlands and East Anglia all showed a decline.

'Although the number of grants – 21 – to charities in Wales, Scotland and Northern Ireland remained the same as in 1996/97, the value of grant aid has increased by 9%, from £86,200 to £94,200 in 1997/98, 16% of total grants awarded.'

The Annual Grants Review gives detailed figures covering a four year period. Because of this excellent reporting, it has been possible for these editors to calculate the total grant per 1,000 population over this period. As is usual when such a calculation is possible, the variations in the figures, which exclude grants to national or international charities, are remarkable:

Value of grants per 1,000 pop. 1994/98

London	£75.25
Northern Ireland	£48.45
Wales	£35.92
South West	£32.17
Scotland	£28.33
North East	£27.17
South East	£20.25
West Midlands	£17.90
East Midlands	£15.28
Yorkshire and Humberside	£12.80
East Anglia	£8.66
North West	£7.46

The foundation's success in getting a fair share of their money to Scotland, Wales and Northern Ireland is exemplary. However the figures show that even a national charity, one of the most widely known throughout the voluntary sector, and one clearly conscious of its responsibilities to attempt a fair geographical distribution of its monies, still faces great difficulties in achieving this throughout the country.

These editors have come to the view that, if it is desired to achieve a fair geographical distribution, it will usually be necessary for such grant makers to set provisional budgets down to at least regional level, and often lower still, and when necessary to advertise to the sector locally the fact that they are not receiving sufficient good applications to enable these budgets to be spent.

Field of activity

Although social welfare charities once again as in 1996/97 received the most support, 32 grants totalling £115,500 (20% of all grants made); this was £25.1 (18%) less than in 1996/97. Four fewer grants were made in 1997/98.

Special funds

There are 16 Special Funds which provide donors with an opportunity to support particular fields of charitable activity, including the environment, children and young people, overseas aid and health care. Thirteen of the Funds are distributed by the Grants Council within its criteria to charities working in these fields. During 1997/98 £115,000 was distributed from these Special Funds.

Youth Appeal For Eastern Europe

The small grants provided by this Fund (maximum £1,000) are intended to strengthen the development of organisations working with or for children and young people in Central and Eastern Europe and the Newly Independent States of the Former Soviet Union. Using the expertise of the Charity Know How Grants Committee, during 1997/98 ten grants totalling £9,300 were made to UK charities working in partnership with organisations in the region to assist their partner organisations. The administration for this appeal has been transferred to Charity Know How at CAF's London office, 114–118 Southampton Row, London WC1B 5AA.

Ethnic Minorities Fund

All but one of the 18 grants recommended by the Advisory Group in February 1997 were to provide training for management committee members, staff or volunteers of new organisations serving Black and ethnic minority communities in the UK, and grants totalling £4,800 were paid.

CAF Disasters Emergency Fund

The CAF Disasters Emergency Fund differs from other CAF Special Funds in that the Foundation holds the donations given, releasing them only when an emergency of significant proportions occurs. The funds are generally distributed through the organisation most appropriately placed to meet the needs of the disaster.

During 1998 a grant for £20,000 was made to the DEC in support of the Sudan Crisis Appeal. These funds were issued immediately when the decision was taken to launch the appeal, providing vital first stage funding.

Betard Bequest

Funds from this unique bequest are distributed through the Grants Council. Modest grants are made to adults and children suffering from rheumatism and arthritis, and to old and lonely Scottish and French people who are resident in the United Kingdom. Applications are usually made through a social worker or by welfare charities. In 1997/98 35 grants totalling £32,800 were made.

Patrick Berthoud Charitable Trust

Funds from the Patrick Berthoud Charitable Trust, which was set up from a substantial legacy left to CAF, are used to further medical research in neurological diseases and illnesses of the brain and central nervous system. Eight grants totalling £42,000 were awarded to medical charities to assist peer-reviewed innovative research projects in the field of neurological diseases.

Grants in 1997/98

The following short selection from the grants list may give a flavour of this remarkable programme:

Threshold Centre (£6,300 for a consultant to help develop a fundraising strategy)

Tindal School, and Community Association (£4,300 towards the salary and recruitment costs of a fundraising coordinator)

Tree-aid (£3,600 for a consultant to carry out an organisational review)

Ulster Guide Association (£5,000 for a consultant to help revise the strategic plan)

Waste Not Recycling (£4,800 emergency grant until a merger can be completed)

Waterloo Breakaway (£2,000 towards raining for staff, volunteers and management committee).

Exclusions The Grants Council does not consider applications

- to assist with Lottery bids
- for retrospective funding
- to clear debts or repay loans
- towards the regular, central core and administrative expenditure of the charity
- for training which is part of a charity core activity, for example organisations whose main function is to provide counselling services, or is part of a charity's regular training programme
- for the erection, repair or purchase of buildings, nor for the provision of furniture or office equipment (including computer hardware)
- for start-up costs of new charities
- for scientific, medical or educational research
- for the purchase of vehicles
- from individuals or for the direct benefit of individuals.

Grants are not provided in response to general appeals, no matter how worthwhile the cause.

Applications In writing to the correspondent. Grants are decided four times a year, in February, May, August and November, and applications should be received two months in advance.

Charity Association Manchester Ltd

About £500,000 annually

Jewish charities

134 Leicester Road, Salford, Manchester M7 0HB
Tel: 0161-740 6678

Correspondent P Koppenheim

Beneficial area UK and Israel.

Information available In the past the charity has supplied information for previous editions of this book. In September 1998 no accounts were on file at the Charity Commission since those for 1992/93, and even then without a list of grants.

General This charity has apparently still not submitted an up-to-date reports and accounts to the Charity Commission. The information below is reprinted from the previous edition:

'The most recent information about this charity is for 1992/93. This was given by Mr Koppenheim, its director, who has been contacted again for more up-to-date information. Whilst he confirmed that the charity gives out about £500,000 each year he had no time to supply more details of its work. He assured this editor that its work does not change greatly from year to year and that it is mainly concerned with Jewish charities in the UK and Israel working in education and for the relief of need.

'In 1992/93 it had assets of £2.8 million, consisting mainly of ten wholly owned subsidiary companies. The income for the year was £539,000 of which £339,000 was from income from investments and £225,000 the operating profit from the ten subsidiaries. £25,000 was received in bank interest.

'Total donations amounted to £636,000 in 1992/93. £445,000 was distributed in 46 grants of £2,000 or more, all of them going to charitable Jewish organisations. These included those given to the Academy for Rabbinical Research (£48,000), Emunah Education Centre (£27,000), the Zichron Yaakov Centre for Torah Education (£20,000), Talmud Torah Breslau (£10,000), Kahaz Chassidim Bobov (£5,000), and M H Synagogue (£3,800).

'The charity has stated that there were "many more donations given out in smaller amounts, this being a distribution charity in similarity to the Charities Aid Foundation. We estimate that there were anywhere between 1,500 and 2,000 donations during the course of the year". £192,000 was distributed in grants of this kind.'

Applications In writing to the correspondent.

Charity Know How

£415,000 (1997)

Central and Eastern Europe and the former Soviet Union

114/118 Southampton Row,
London WC1B 5AA
Tel: 0171-400 2315; Fax: 0171-404 1331

Correspondent Nev Jefferies, Director

Trustees Trustees of the Charities Aid Foundation. Grants Committee: Anne Engel (Prince's Trust – Action), Chair, and representatives from the fund contributors.

Beneficial area All of Central and Eastern Europe and the former Soviet Union, but with special programmes for Armenia, Azerbaijan, Bulgaria, Georgia, Romania, Russia (Archangelsk), Slovakia and Ukraine.

Information available The fund publishes a clear and informative annual report, applicant guidelines and an application form.

Summary Grants, seldom for more than £10,000, are made to pairs of organisations seeking to work in partnership for the development of NGO activity in these areas.

General Charity Know How is a joint initiative of a group of grant making trusts and of the Department for International Development. It is a grant making organisation established in 1991 to assist the revitalisation of the voluntary sector in Central and Eastern Europe and the republics of the former Soviet Union.

The aim of CKH funding is to enhance the transfer of skills and know how and to form productive and supportive links between NGOs in the region and the UK. 'During the past six years CKH grants have benefited more than 2,000 NGOs which have received in excess of £2.5 million in grant awards.'

CKH makes two kinds of grants in addition to new proactive programmes in the eight countries named above.

Project grants Applications for these grants must come from two partner organisations, either one in the beneficial area and one in the UK, or both from the area ('East-east' applications). Awards are seldom for more than £10,000 and usually for less than £5,000.

CKH funds skill-sharing partnership projects between UK charities and NGOs, or between NGOs from different countries in this region. All applications must be joint projects and involve a transfer of know how.

We are looking for projects which

- Enhance the capability of the NGO(s) in the country(ies) concerned to manage or organise their time, funds and activities.
- Have a relevance to, or are demonstrably part of, the development of the voluntary sector in general in the town, country or region concerned.
- Take into account all parties which may have an interest in, or could contribute to, the project.
- Demonstrate an awareness of the importance of developing NGOs in a way which allows them to operate free from the undue influence of, or dependence upon, State authorities, funders, or short-term foreign assistance.'

Exploratory grants: These are small grants made to enable potential partner organisations to meet face to face to decide whether their proposed partnership is appropriate.

The information and application forms available from the address above are particularly clear and well thought through.

Applicants should note that the trusts supporting CKH directlt are unlikely to make grants to organisations working in this field. They include

- Joseph Rowntree Charitable Foundation;
- Headley Trust;
- Charities Aid Foundation;
- John Ellerman Foundation;
- Wates Foundation;
- Baring Foundation;
- Polden-Puckham charitable Foundation;
- Dulverton Trust.

However, it is the experience of this editor that a number of other 'general purpose' trusts, even though they may have no expressed interest in this area, may be willing to give small amounts to a straightforward appeal. About £8,000 was raised for a truck for a Moscow welfare charity with a simple single page letter to 80 such trusts.

Exclusions

Grants are not normally available for the following:

- The teaching of English as a foreign language;
- The costs of offices, salaries or equipment (including fax machines and other communications equipment).

- Any building or capital cost;
- The costs of transporting humanitarian aid or medical equipment;
- Attendance at conferences where the benefit to NGO development is not clearly demonstrated;
- The administration of schemes for UK volunteers (eg. working holidays);
- Core funding in the region or the UK;
- Full professional fees for any consultancy (although some replacement costs may be considered);
- Activities considered by the Grants Committee to be for personal rather than institutional development;
- Youth, artistic or cultural exchanges;
- The promotion of a specific religion or sectarian belief;
- Applications from individuals;
- Student programmes or scholarships;
- Retrospective grants.

Applications There is a clear application form to which other material can be attached, together with comprehensive guidance notes for applicants. The Grants Committee meets four times a year, in March, June, September and December, and there is a published deadline for receipt of applications for Regular grants (more than £1,000) about six weeks in advance of these meetings. Potential applicants should first read the Guidelines for Applicants available from CKH.

Small grants (£1,000 or less) or exploratory grants can considered at any time except in the six weeks before committee meetings, and a decision is made within six weeks.

The Chase Charity

£207,000 (1997/98)

Social welfare, heritage, the arts

2 The Court, High Street, Harwell, Didcot, Oxfordshire OX11 0EY
Tel: 01235-820044

Correspondent Ailsa Hornsby

Trustees A Ramsay Hack (Chairman), Gordon Halcrow, Richard Mills, Elizabeth Moore, Alexander Robertson; Ann Stannard, Ninian Perry.

Beneficial area UK, with a special interest in rural areas and no grants to London.

Information available Full report and account available from the charity. Leaflets on 'How to apply for a grant' is available.

Summary This is a small charity that prefers to help small agencies and projects particularly in rural areas. Grants are usually made for specific purposes and very occasionally the charity will help with running costs or salaries to met shortfall. Though its resources would not normally justify inclusion in this book, its connection with the Lankelly Foundation, with which it shares administration and staff, means that readers may wish to read about the two together, even though their policies and operation are distinct. Lankelly has its own entry in this book.

Three main areas are funded:

Social Welfare

'The Trustees give away over 50% of the Charity's income on social welfare each year. They are aware that in times of hardship marginalised groups are the most vulnerable. With this in mind, therefore, the Trustees' aim is to help projects working with the following groups: frail elderly people, people with special needs wishing to live independent and fulfilling lives, young people who are in trouble or at risk of getting into trouble, fragile communities, particularly those outside urban areas, vulnerable families, homeless people, only in rural areas.

The Arts

'The trustees have their own schemes for young artists and musicians and these exhaust the funds available for this purpose; eg. the charity remains the main funder of the Kirkman Concert Society which the trustees established in 1963 to give young professional musicians platform opportunities.

'Another aim is to further the arts in outlying areas. Small touring dance, theatre and opera groups are helped, mainly with one-off needs. Grants are also made for theatre buildings and community arts centres outside London and other large cities. Help with production or running costs is rare.

'The trustees would like everyone to be able to enjoy, and where possible participate in the arts, particularly people who live in isolated areas or who are disabled. The Trustees recognise the therapeutic value of such involvement, but will only support programs which also pursue excellence.

Historic Buildings

a) Churches

'Grants are restricted to small rural parishes charged with the care of a national treasure. Local effort is a vital factor.

b) Almshouses

'Most of the charity's help is concentrated on historic buildings in rural areas.

c) Other buildings

'Small, interesting buildings, again in rural areas, are a priority; however, preference is given to historic buildings which are used for community purposes.

Annual Report 1997/98

'The small group of people who founded the Chase Charity anonymously in 1962 were much influenced by a philanthropist, also anonymous, with whom they were associated. The objects of the charity reflected his love of England's heritage, particularly churches, almshouses and other buildings of historic interest and beauty, and his appreciation of the arts. A general purpose clause also enables trustees to work in the social welfare field.

'Over the last year the charity has made some changes to its criteria; it has now increased its grant range from £500-£5000 to £1,000-£10,000; and the charity will now consider making grants over more than one year and for needs other than capital costs. The charity now have also removed penal affairs from their funding list, along with addiction in the previous year. The final change has been to focus grant giving to homelessness solely on projects working in rural areas.' We prefer to support smaller charities who, as a group, are less likely to have a sophisticated approach to fundraising.

'The charity had assets of just over £5 million, which generated an income of £314,000 in 1996/97. However, even though the charity's income has increased the total amount given out has declined. Grants totalling £207,000 were allocated to priority areas as follows:

Social Welfare	£121,000
The Arts	£45,000
Heritage	£41,000

'The number of applications we received rose from 1,300 in 1996/97 to 1,500 this year [*1997/98*]..we exclude from our calculations individuals asking for money as outside our guidelines. The number of grants and the total money given in grants were both slightly lower than in 1995/96.

'Monitoring was carried out for the first time this year to find out how we could improve the way we worked. We sent forms to 55 charities to which we had made grants and received 43 replies, a 78% response rate. Enquiring about our policy of visiting projects, we were pleased to find that applicants welcomed it; they also stated that the grant had helped than to lever money from other bodies. In a separate exercise we sought the views of 56 unsuccessful organisation in which 33 responded (59%); for the majority it was their first application to us and, significantly, they had not seen our guidelines beforehand; a number wanted tighter guidelines and one commented that in 11 years this was the first time they had ever received a monitoring form from a trust.

'As usual the council tried to distribute its funds widely, making grants from the Isle of Wight to the Orkneys. 17% of all applicants came from the South East which, with London, receives the highest proportion of charitable funds available nationally and over 17% of our funds went to that area. Since we no longer support projects in the capital, both the applications we received and the grants we made there fell. One of the two we did make was to the Family Welfare Association, which we have funded for the last 32 years. We have continuing confidence in the professional way in which the money is allocated by the Association's committee to individuals who are not only poor but may be ill, disabled or elderly; they have tried and failed to obtain help from the usual sources and have been directed to the FWA as a last resort.

Geographical Spread:

'We are conscious that the number of grants we make annually is small, so looking instead at the number given over the last five years (374), it is clear that, apart form Northern Ireland, the North West remains the area where the fewest grants are made, even though three other regions, East Anglia, the East Midlands and Wales, submitted fewer applications. The South West consistently generated the largest number of letters and netted the most grants outside London and the South East.

Subject Spread:

Almshouses	*7%*
Arts/Community Arts	*22%*
Children & Young People	*8%*
Community Welfare	*9%*
Conservations & Museums	*2%*
Disabilities & Special Needs	*14%*
Elderly	*8%*
Historic Buildings	*10%*
Homelessness	*12%*
Neighbourhood Work	*8%*

'The fluctuations in our geographical spread were echoed in our subject spread. As the chart shows, applications from arts projects remained high and those from the elderly remained low; grants to children and young people were up, those for disabilities and special needs were down. In respect of the latter grants were relatively evenly spread across the fields of physical and mental disability and mental ill health, implying that the voluntary sector is still playing a vital role in plugging the gaps in the provision of services to the mentally ill left by Care in the Community. Interestingly, only one grant was made in this category specifically for disabled access; it is a sign of a more creative and positive attitude towards the needs and abilities of the disabled and that the money was mainly spent on providing activities and improving independence.

'The charity continues to single out projects dealing with the problems of people living in rural areas, particularly those on low incomes, with major areas of grant giving in the Social Welfare sector being to Homelessness activities (£25,000) and to Disabilities and Special Needs (£28,000). Examples of grants given out in these areas include £4,000 to St Mark's Church Community Centre, Bradford (to help with the cost of purchasing a portakabin as a base for a local autistic society), £3,500 Lochaber Community Care Forum, Fort William, Scotland (towards the cost of establishing a 20 week pilot scheme involving people with visual impairments), £5,000 to the Bethany Project Stafford (towards the cost of re-ordering and improving premises to provide additional bed space), £1,400 to Kent Community Housing Trust Complex, Margate (towards the cost of equipping two crash pads for homeless young people).

Other grants include '£7,500 to Family Welfare Association, London (to support FWA's grants to individual needs), £5,000 to Turning Point Theatre Company, Topsham, Devon (to help with cost of purchasing office equipment), £2,000 to St Swithin's Church, Clunbury, Shropshire (towards the cost of major roof repairs), £4,000 to Voluntary Hostels Group, Norwich (to help establish a register of hostel workers as a one year pilot scheme, and £3,000 to The Abbey Centre Users Association, Northampton (towards the cost of extending the community centre).

The charity has found the Lottery a mixed blessing and comments: 'The Lottery continues to affect our work. Almost all applicants have been in contact with at least one of the boards apart from those with moral reservations; some assume our criteria are the same as those of the Lottery,

which is not the case; others ask if we will award a grant in anticipation of a Lottery grant, which we will not; other again ask us for a sum which they will also ask the lottery for, which is a waste of time. However we are aware that if it were not for the lottery, which is probably more of a household name than that of Hoover, there are many people who would not have believed it possible to start a charity or realise a dream.'

Exclusions The trustees do not contribute to large appeals or circular letters. Grants are not made to individuals, including students. Large national organisations and their branches fall outside the guidelines. Requests for revenue or salary support is only exceptionally given.

Applications 'When we receive your letter, if we think we can help, we may seek more information from you and ask you to write back at a stated time (we do not use application forms). If you reply, usually two or three months before the trustees meet one of the staff will arrange to visit you or meet you at our office. If you have applied to a Lottery Board for the same need, your request will not be considered until after you have heard from the Board.

'As soon as possible after the trustees' meeting the staff will write to you with the decision. If a grant is agreed, you will be informed of any conditions attached to it.

We reply to all letters we receive, except for circular letters, and the trustees see summaries of all the applications.

What we need from you:

- Your initial letter should describe briefly what you do and why you need our help.
- You should describe the origins and status of your organisations e.g. is it a company, charity or co-operative.
- You should enclose your Annual Report and accounts.

'You should answer the following questions:

- How much do you need to raise in total?
- How soon do you need to raise it?
- How much have you already raised?
- Who has given you that money?
- Are you waiting to hear from any other sources of funding.
- Have you applied to the Lottery? If so, which Board(s) and or how much?

Trustees' meetings are held in February, May, September and November.

The Childwick Trust

£3,000,000 (1995/96)

Education in South Africa, health, medical research

9 The Green, Childwick Bury,
St Albans, Herts AL3 6JJ
Tel: 01727-812486; Fax: 01727-844666

Correspondent Peter Doyle, Resident Trustee and Administrator

Trustees C A S Grimston, Chairman; P J Doyle; P G Glossop; P S Willett; J D Wood.

Beneficial area UK and South Africa, with a local interest in Hertfordshire/Bedfordshire.

Information available Full accounts with a list of the top 50 grant beneficiaries only. The grants are neither analysed nor explained (though the list is headed 'analysis'). There is a limited Trustees' Report.

Summary Massive support for the Jim Joel Education and Training Fund in South Africa (£1 million in 1998). Over 200 other grants a year, about 150 of them for £10,000 or less, but ranging above £100,000 or more, to mostly national institutions, or those local to the St Albans area. The large grants, and perhaps the small ones as well, go to a little changing list of regular beneficiaries.

General Little is known about the basis for the grant making of this trust. It is modestly run, with much of the administration being carried out by the unpaid trustees. There are three staff, some or all of them probably part time, earning a total of £25,000.

There was massive capital growth in 1997/98.

This was one of the first trusts to supply a list of just the top 50 grants, the minimum that may be permissible under the SORP (the requirement is to list all material grants, which must always include at least the largest 50; but more may be required). In this editors' view it is unreasonable to declare that 200 grants worth £800,000 are not 'material'. The consequence is that readers find it hard to get a full view of the work of a public institution.

The principal objects of the trust are given as the following:

- Elderly people in need
- UK charities connected with horse racing and breeding

- Jewish charities in the UK
- Charities for those connected with mining in South Africa
- Education in South Africa
- The promotion of health and assistance for people with disabilities in the UK.

The trust describes its 1995/96 grant making as follows:

'Biannually the Trustees' Review all written applications for funds from various institutions and charities. An assessment is made to ensure potential donees concur with the objects of the trust. To further this, throughout the year the trustees undertake visits to both potential and current beneficiaries.

'During the year under review the trustees have processed in the region of 730 applications for funds (*Down from 1,000 in each of the two previous years. Ed*). From these, 252 individual donations were made to 225 separate beneficiary bodies.'

In the 1997/98 list of the 50 largest grants, £1 million was given in a single award, probably to the associated Jim Joel Education and Training Fund in South Africa (£700,000 in 1996/97 and £500,000 in 1995/96). This grant is listed in the Annual Report as being for the 'JCI Education and Training Fund', but it is likely to be the same institution as the JJ Education and Training Fund of previous years. Though there is no indication of this in the report, the charity is believed to be South African and is probably concerned with the education of South Africans connected with the mining industry in that country. A massive transfer of money of this kind should undoubtedly be described and explained by the charity.

The Equine Fertility Unit (described unhelpfully in the accounts as 'EFU') is another regular beneficiary, receiving £125,000 in two grants. The other major beneficiaries in both 1997/98 and in the previous year were Northwick Park Institute for Medical Research (£145,000 and £112,000); RAFT (£105,000 and £180,000 for facial reconstruction), King Edward VII Hospital; Midhurst (£90,000, and £193,000); and the Animal Health Trust (£50,000 and £75,000).

It is hard to be sure because the same institution often seems to appear under slightly different names in different years, but there were probably only five new beneficiaries among the top 30 awards. They included Cassell Hospital Families Centre (£50,000); Langford Trust, Bristol (£30,000); Gray Laboratory Cancer Research Trust (£25,000) and the National Kidney Research Fund (£25,000).

In previous editions of this book we reported that the smaller grants showed a definite interest in the area around the trust's headquarters in Hertfordshire. This can no longer be identified, as the details of such grants are withheld, and there is no mention of such a (perfectly reputable) policy in the Report. However, among the larger awards that are disclosed there are two payments, for £10,000 each, to Hertfordshire charities, which is more than for any other county – to DEMAND and to Hertfordshire Community Trust. It is likely that the trust continues to be an important source of funds in its local area.

There continue to be a sprinkling of grants for specifically Jewish organisations, led by the New West End Synagogue (£35,000 and £75,000) and Jewish Relief (£40,000 and £15,000).

Overall, the concentration of the grants on medical research appears to be increasing. There is no indication of the basis on which such scientific funding decisions are taken. The trust is not a member of the Association of Medical Research Charities, for whom a systematic peer review process is a condition of membership, though this does not mean that such a system is not in place.

Exclusions 'Students requesting grants are **not** covered under the objects of the trust.'

Applications To the correspondent in writing, including most recent audited accounts. The trustees meet in May and October, and applications should be received by the end of previous month.

The Chippenham Borough Lands Charity

£291,000 (1997/98)

General in Chippenham

16 Market Place, Chippenham, Wiltshire SN15 3HW
Tel: 01249-658180

Correspondent B D Coombs, Clerk

Trustees Mrs. J M Wood; Mrs. R Angill; E Taylor; Mr. Dobson; Mrs. Woodman; Mrs. Lang, Mr. Poole; Mr. Grace; Mr. McGregor, Mrs. Lloyd; Mrs. Wood; Mr. Baun; Mr. Jenrich.

Beneficial area Chippenham Parish.

Information available Accounts are on file at the Charity Commission,

with a partial list of organisations supported, and those without the amount given.

Summary There is no longer satisfactory information about the beneficiaries of this charity.

General The history of this charity goes back to Queen Mary's reign when she gave assistance to Chippenham by means of a royal charter, and by the subsequent bestowal, in order to ingratiate herself to the Bailiff and Burgess of Chippenham, of what are now known as the Borough Lands. Charters amending the original one and confirming the gift of lands were issued by later monarchs. Several local government reviews changed the status of Chippenham and the ownership and administration of the lands was then transferred to the latest established governing body, culminating with the formation of the North Wiltshire District Council. A fortuitous detailed study of the charters and deeds, caused by a proposed new road, found that the various charters created a charitable trust. The District Council, acting as the trustee of the charity created a small committee to deal with charity matters until the new scheme came into force in April 1990, when the council handed over all deeds, documents and assets to the new trustees.

The objectives of the charities are to provide for:

(i) the aged, sick, disabled or poor inhabitants of the parish of Chippenham;
(ii) the inhabitants of the parish of Chippenham and its neighbourhood or any section of those inhabitants of facilities for recreative or leisure-time occupation;
(iii) education for the inhabitants of the parish of Chippenham;
(iv) other charitable purposes.

Total assets of this trust amounted to £6.2 million, generating an income of £230,000 for 1997/98. Grant giving has seen a rise of £50,000 from the previous year to almost £291,000. The annual report classifies the areas of expenditure as follows:

Education/Pre School	*£70,000*
Physically handicapped	*£62,000*
Community Centres	*£40,000*
Relief of Poverty	*£38,000*
Social/Medical Welfare	*£26,000*
Environment	*£20,000*
Youth Community Work	*£15,000*
Mentally Ill, Handicapped	*£10,000*
Care of Elderly	*£7,000*
Music & Arts	*£3,000*
Total	*£291,000*

Although the Trustees' Report states that 265 applications were considered, it did not specify the number of grants given, their individual value, the basis on which they were selected, nor what they were used for. The report does, however, include a few choice comments of thanks from grateful beneficiary institutions.

It is possible that some of the grants are for the benefit of individuals.

Exclusions Anyone outside Chippenham

Applications In writing to the correspondent.

CHK Charities Limited

£1,239,000 (1997/98)

General

PO Box 191, 10 Fenchurch Street, London EC3M 3LB
Tel: 0171-475 6246

Correspondent N R Kerr-Sheppard, Administrator

Trustees D A Peake, Chairman; D A Acland; Mrs S E Acland; Mrs K S Assheton; Mrs L H Morris; Mrs S Peake; Mrs J A S Prest; Mrs C S Heber Percy.

Beneficial area UK, Gloucestershire and Oxfordshire.

Information available Full accounts and schedules of grants, but with almost no description of the Charities' policy and no narrative report on the years activities.

Summary. Around £1.5 million in donations are made every year to charities working in a variety of fields. Normally grants are one-off and for revenue or capital costs. Occasionally, donations are paid over three to five years. Grant size is typically £5,000 but can vary from £1,000 to £100,000.

Because of its increased endowment, the income of the charities is likely to increase to several million pounds a year in the future.

General In 1963 the banker Cyril Kleinwort established the 'Sir Cyril Kleinwort Charitable Trust' for general charitable purposes and for the provision of 'homes for sick, infirm and elderly people in the UK (in all cases being poor)'. In 1996, the trust deed was terminated, and the whole of the trust fund and income (£12.4 million) was

transferred to CHK Charities Ltd, a new charitable company. Also during 1996, the charities received £28.5 million from other Kleinwort family resources following the takeover of Kleinwort Benson Group plc by Dresdner Bank AG.

In 1997/98 CHK had assets of a little over £55 million which generated the low income of £1.8 million. 170 donations totalling £1.2 million were paid. 44% of this sum was paid in a few grants of £50,000 and over, but normally grant size is in the £2,000 to £5,000 range. It is very difficult to discern any patterns in grant-making as the annual report fails to meet the Charity Commission requirements concerning these. The purpose of grants is not shown and there is no narrative exploration of the year's donations. Furthermore, there are no categories of giving and so what kinds of causes are receiving support is not known. However the trust does state that 'It is not possible to discern any patterns in grant-making because the trustees are reactionary (sic), and therefore there should be no patterns in their grant-making.' Kleinwort Benson Trustees Ltd manages and administers the charity and were paid £44,000 for this service in 1997/98.

The information that the trustees give is as follows:

'The trustees current policy is to consider all written appeals, but only successful applications are notified of the trustees' decision. During the year under review the trustees made a total of 162 donations, and showed particular interest in charities working in the fields of education, job creation, conservation, arts, population control, crime prevention and youth development. In approved cases the trustees will provide assistance towards start-up or capital costs and on-going expenses. This may take the form of a grant for say three to five years following which support may be withdrawn to enable the resources to be devoted to other projects. The trustees do not normally respond favourably to appeals from individuals, nor to those from small local charities, e.g. individual churches, village halls, etc., where there is no specific connection.'

'Type of Beneficiary. 'Charities known or local to the Trustees and substantial national charitable bodies (but not normally the local branches or offshoots of these).'

This last paragraph implies to these editors that applicants who do not know any of these trustees need to remedy this situation and would do well to make themselves known to trustees

individually, rather than just approach them through the correspondent. However the trust objects most strongly to this suggestion.

The largest grants of 1997/98 were paid to DGAA Homelife (£100,000; Durrell Institute of Conservation and Ecology (£91,031); Royal Shakespeare Theatre, Stratford upon Avon (£82,500) and; the British Museum £51,500. The Charities Aid Foundation were given £75,000, which will probably be used to make small grants.

Exclusions No grants to individuals nor to small local charities, eg individual churches, village halls, etc, where there is no special connection to the trust. Appeals from local branches or off-shoots of national charitable bodies are normally not considered.

Applications To the correspondent. CHK charities say:

'Appeals will usually be considered within three months, but may be referred for further consideration at board meetings which are held twice a year, normally in March and October.'

The Church Urban Fund

£2,713,000 (1997)

Welfare, Christian development in disadvantaged urban areas

2 Great Peter Street, London SW1P 3LX
Tel: 0171-222 7010;
Fax: 0171-799 1829;
E-mail:<first surname>@cuf.org.uk;
Website: www.cuf.org.uk

Correspondent Angela Sarkis, Chief Executive

Trustees The Archbishop of Canterbury (Chairman); Stephen O'Brien (Vice-Chairman); Mark Cornwall-Jones; Richard Farnell; Ven. G Gibson; Ruth McCurry; Michael Mockridge; Eileen Lake; Alan McLintock; Canon John Stanley; Elaine Appelbee.

Beneficial area Urban priority areas in England.

Information available Full information available from the offices of the fund about its work and future intentions. A general advice leaflet for applicants is available.

Summary Grants of up to £40,000 a year are made to grass roots projects working, through a variety of means, to improve life in impoverished urban areas. Most of the funds are disbursed in awards of less than £10,000. The fund offers one-off or continuing support for both capital and revenue costs. Beneficiaries are based in the community, and usually have ties with local churches.

General CUF was established in 1998 following the publication of the report 'Faith in the City', commissioned by the Church of England. The report suggested that the church should 'set up a fund to help churches work more closely with their local communities to help people tackle poor housing, poor education, unemployment and poverty'. The fund says that it aims to:

'• respond positively to the needs of urban priority areas (UPAs) by supporting, through grants and other resources, the development of targeted schemes which directly benefit local communities.

• encourage the Church to recognise and better understand the needs and gifts of people living in UPAs and in partnership with others, develop and implement a range of practical and sustainable responses, taking full account of local resources and potential.

• influence national and international regeneration policy through the systematic analysis of projects supported by CUF and, with appropriate partners, collate and publish information to inform the wider debate on urban regeneration.

• attract substantial new resources for the continuation and development of the fund's work.

• operate efficiently with a strong sense of accountability to stakeholders, upholding the principal of equal opportunity.'

In 1997 the fund generated income totalling £2,531,000, 57% of which came from investments (assets now amount to £26 million) and the remaining £1,046,000 was voluntary income. In its annual report, CUF lists only the largest grants (£10,000 and above) paid in the year (see below). These total £876,000 or just 32% of grant expenditure and therefore might not give an accurate representation of the fund's grant-making.

CUF says:

'Grants awarded were significantly higher than in previous years, at £3.5 million, signalling the fund's renewed commitment to maintaining grant awards at the originally designated level of £2.5 million plus increases in the retail prices index since 1987. However, as many of the funds revenue grants are spread over several years, this increase in the level of awards (from £3.1 million in 1996) will only gradually give rise to a higher level of grant payments. A total of £29 million has been awarded since the fund was established 10 years ago, of which £6.2 million is earmarked as payable in 1998 or later.

'In response to the recent policy review, the fund has clarified its criteria for local project grants and improved the application and assessment process. We believe we can make the most effective use of our limited resources by targeting funds to projects that:

• are based in a urban priority area as defined by the fund, which uses census data and other statistical evidence to determine levels of need;

• involve the local community in identifying needs, initiating responses and running the project;

• are part of the local Anglican church's outreach to the community, or are building working relationships with the church;

• have charitable purposes;

• are able to raise part of the required money from other sources.

'Projects that do not meet these minimum criteria are not eligible for funding.

'Local projects remain at the heart of the fund's work, and during 1997 we were pleased to support 193 projects with awards totalling £3.5 million. As always the range of activities funded was as diverse as the communities served.

'In addition, 110 projects benefited from our small grants programme. This scheme offers modest sums (under £2,000) to enable small specific initiatives, such as children's activities or credit union start-ups, or to provide project support such as feasibility studies, evaluations and management committee training.'

Types of grant

The fund gives the following examples of the three types of grant it makes:

Revenue grants: help to cover the costs of running a project, such as a worker's salary or general operating expenses – Taunton East Action, Somerset. In 1997, we made our first ever award in the diocese of Bath and Wells. A grant of £21,000 over three years will enable All Saints Church, located in the heart of one of the largest housing estates in Taunton, to employ a youth development officer.

The project is part of an ambitious community regeneration effort in an area that offers nowhere for young people to meet and nothing for them to do. The local council is providing space for a drop-in centre, and activities will be determined by the young people themselves. "I don't want to impose ideas", says youth worker James Levasier, "I want to make them part of the process of deciding what we'll set up".

Capital grants: support extensions or renovations that allow church buildings to be opened up for wider community use.

In Norfolk, the North Lynn Action Group – a grassroots association of tenants in local authority housing – is converting a redundant church into a base for community activities with the help of a £30,000 grant from the CUF. The derelict building had become a venue for "unsavoury activities" and was badly vandalised. Yet it retained a feeling of belonging to the people of the area, with many of the older residents having contributed a "shilling a brick" towards its construction in the 1960's.

The group hopes the new centre will bring a sense of community spirit and pride back to the neighbourhood and will be a place where the younger and older generations can come together.

Continuation funding: CUF offers time-limited additional support to projects whose achievements have been confirmed by independent evaluation – A grant in 1993 helped to establish The Kabin in Kingsmead, a high density estate in Hackney, East London. At the time, the estate was synonymous with drug dealing, mugging and burglary. Facing high levels of unemployment and neglected housing stock, residents often feel alienated and powerless.

Against this backdrop, members of a local church got together with tenants to provide a space which people on the estate could use as they wanted. Today The Kabin's shop-front room is regularly transformed from homework club to advice club to drop-in centre. Each Friday, Kidstuff sets up shop, offering clothing, toys and books at bargain prices, then recycling the proceeds into trips and outings for local families.

Continuation funding of £14,000 for two years will help the project to consolidate and strengthen this work, as well as explore new ways of responding to community needs.'

Grants in 1997

Opening up church buildings 13 grants £270,000;

St Stephen's Living Stones Project,

London £40,000 for church extension and improvements; Church Family Centre, Leyton £30,000 towards a new church and community centre; St Mary's Balderstone Reordering Project £25,000 for church and community facilities; St Matthias' Community Action Group, £25,000 towards a community hall.

Social Care 9 grants £168,000;

Manna Counselling, London £13,000; Black Women's Resource Centre, £14,000; The Roby, Manchester, holistic approach to social care, £12,000; Brent Care for Refugees, £12,000 for facilities.

Community work 13 grants £164,000;

St Bartholomew's Centre, Sheffield, £11,000 for a project manager; The Light of the World Gospel Church, Bradford, £20,000 towards a community centre; and £15,000 grants each to Eastmoor Estate Community Project (for a community artist) and Delph Hill Community Centre, Bradford (towards a community centre).

Education/young people 7 grants £89,000;

£16,000 to the New Hope Project, London for youth facilities and advice centre; £14,000 to Parkway Parent and Child Project, Bristol; £10,500 to Strategies to Elevate People for work in motivating young people; and £10,000 to Allen's Croft, Birmingham for a youth coordinator.

Racial justice 1 grant £80,000;

The money was disbursed to an undisclosed number of projects identified by the Churches Commission for Racial Justice.

Housing and homeless 3 grants £37,000;

Manchester Rent Guarantee Scheme (£15,000); Nightstop, Southampton (£12,000); Project John'93 (£11,500) for skills and employment training.

Urban regeneration 3 grants £36,000;

Syac Ltd, Sheffield, £15,000 for a community bakery enterprise; Brixwork; Christ Church North Brixton, £11,000 for developing life skills in young people; Roapp Hall, Darltston, a community-based employment agency, £10,000.

Poverty 1 grant £22,000;

Action Station, South Shields, £22,000 for community development, debt and unemployment counselling.

Interfaith 1 grant £10,000;

Wolverhampton Inter-Faith Group (£10,000)

Health. None; 3 grants

Although there were no grants in 1997,

the programme is still running. 1996 grants were to: SADACCA Day Centre, Sheffield – £40,000 for care in the Afro-Caribbean community; £12,000 to Unity Centre Balham for help with the mentally ill; and Focus on Mental Health, Nottingham received £15,000 towards care in the community work.

Broad based organising None; 4 grants

This programme is still open. Four 1996 grants totalled £57,000, all of which were made for 'community empowerment': £15,000 each went to IMPACT Community in Partnership for Action, Citizen's Black Country Organising, East London Community Organising; and Community organising in Greater Bristol received £12,000.

Annual Report 1997

'The Church Urban Fund adds a vital new dimension to the Church of England's ministry as it seeks to carry out our Lord's commandment to love our neighbours as ourselves and promote the value of God's Kingdom of love and justice. Through our partnership with the Church and its network of dioceses and parishes, the fund has established a solid track record over the past ten years for effectively channelling grant aid to local projects seeking to bring hope to disadvantaged communities. Our challenge now is not only to respond to the symptoms of urban poverty but also to confront its systemic causes.

'This past year has seen significant developments in the fund's work as we have begun to implement the strategic aims identified during our policy review in 1996/97. These goals were directed towards strengthening both our relationship with the Church and our broader role in public policy making, and we are pleased to report our progress as the fund aims to:

1. Respond positively to the needs of urban priority areas (UPAs) by supporting, through grants and other resources, the development of targeted schemes which directly benefit local communities:-

'In response to the policy review, our grants committee and staff have clarified the criteria for grants to local projects as well as improved the application and assessment process.

2 'Encourage the Church to recognise and better understand the needs and gifts of people living in UPAs and in partnership with others, develop and implement a range of practical and sustainable responses, taking full account

of local resources and potential:-

'Crucial to meeting identified need in disadvantaged communities is the effective targeting of resources to areas of greatest need and the active involvement of those directly affected in the development of services. Building on our experience, working in partner ship with the dioceses, the fund aims to identify and support the gifts and skills of local people, local agencies concerned with urban poverty and other potential local partners who are best placed to develop projects and initiatives which meet local needs.

3 'Influence national and international regeneration policy through the systematic analysis of projects supported by CUF and, with appropriate partners, collate and publish information to inform the wider debate on urban regeneration:-

'We have for some time recognised the need for the CUF to find more effective ways of collating, analysing and disseminating its accumulated experience to faith communities and beyond. The establishment of a development fund from which we hope to make the first awards in 1998 drawing on start-up monies transferred from our accumulated funds, and the convening of a new initiatives working party to assist trustees and staff in identifying, agreeing and setting priorities for the develop programme mark the beginning of progress in this direction. Our steps were the expansion of our City Lights newsletter to include an analytical component, and our response to an increasing number of invitations to present the work of the fund more widely, as interest among potential partners grows.

'A significant development was the invitation of our Chief Executive, Angela Sarkis, to take up a part-time secondment with the newly established Social Exclusion Unit.

4 'Attract substantial new resources for the continuation and development of the fund's work:-

'As we break new ground, however, it is acknowledged that we must widen our fundraising base, and much effort has gone into the identification of new resources to enable the fund to continue its work in future years. We have developed a new fundraising strategy, begun a renewed appeal to existing and new supporters, and plan a fresh covenant recruitment drive in 1998. In the longer term the strategy also envisages targeting new opportunities with business, other charitable sources and partnerships with government schemes that focus on urban poverty.

5 'Operate efficiently with a strong sense of accountability to stakeholders, upholding the principal of equal opportunity:-

'During the year staff have been engaged in an internal review of the fund's administrative systems. This has resulted in some restructuring of staff and responsibilities. This is already contributing to greater efficiency in the office and more accurate analysis of the impact of our grants.

'Whilst not increasing our overall staff complement, more staff are now available to become directly involved with the dioceses – through our development and grants assessment programmes – and are able to provide additional constancy support to them.

Chief Executive's Report, 1997

'This past year has seen significant developments in the fund's work as we have begun to implement the strategic aims identified during a wide-ranging policy review. These goals were directed towards strengthening both our relationship with the Church and our broader role in public policy-making.

'Through our relationship with the Church of England and its network of dioceses and parishes, the fund has established a track record over the past ten years for effectively channelling resources where they are needed the most, bringing hope – and the courage to act – to disadvantaged communities. Our 10th anniversary has offered an opportunity to evaluate and consolidate the fund's achievements and begin to build on these accomplishments.

'The challenge now is to start to move beyond responding to the symptoms of urban poverty and, learning from our experience, begin to confront the causes – a challenge I will also be facing in my part-time secondment to the Prime Minister's Social Exclusion Unit. This will be an opportunity for the fund to make a contribution at different levels, offering us the chance to influence thinking about the issues closest to our hearts and to have an even more effective presence in urban communities.

'The heart of that presence, however, is the hundreds of local projects and local congregations, staff and volunteers, who are working tirelessly to identify needs and find innovative ways of meeting them.

Chairman's message

'The great strength of the fund is that it is not a top down organisation, but seeks to enable renewal at the edges of society, building on the resilience and ingenuity of local people themselves. Through its grants to local projects it supports the outreach and social action that give the Church authenticity in many people's eyes. It helps the church to stand with young people, refugees, the elderly, lone parents, job seekers and those who have lost the hope to seek.

'But these projects, however important, cannot substitute for action at other levels. We must allow the insight from these projects, both spiritual and social. To fertilise the wider witness of the Church. Together with our partners in other churches and other faiths, we must continue to work to influence policies and assumptions in favour of the poor, trying to give a voice to the voiceless and include those who are so frequently forgotten.

'That's why I am particularly excited by the launch of the fund's new development programme. Working closely with the dioceses, it will support the Church in its prophetic role by encouraging theological reflection as well as sharing and building on good practice. It is designed very much to complement the local grants programme, helping to increase the impact and significance of these grants in urban priority areas.'

Exclusions Payments for stipendiary clergy; projects and activities for which full funding is normally available from the Church Commissioners, Dioceses, local authorities, statutory bodies or organisations for the conservation of historical buildings; charitable grants to individuals; direct support of other grant-making institutions. Capital support for voluntary aided schools eligible for statutory funding. Individuals.

Applications Check with the fund whether a project falls into one of the supported areas, and request a formal application form. All applications for grants are first of all sent to the diocesan bishop, who will help put forward applications . They must be approved by him before being sent to the trustees. The bishop is also requested to indicate the priority of projects in relation to the long-term plan for the diocese. Projects which survive this procedure will go to the trustees of the fund who may sanction assistance. Field officers also visit every applicant to help with applications.

The grants committee meets in March, June, September and December for which applications have to be sent over two months in advance. Contact the fund for details of exact dates.

The City Parochial Foundation (see also entry for Trust for London)

£5,124,000 (1997)

Social welfare in London

6 Middle Street, London EC1A 7PH
Tel: 0171-606 6145; Fax: 0171-600 1866

Correspondent Bharat Mehta, Clerk

Trustees 21 trustees nominated by

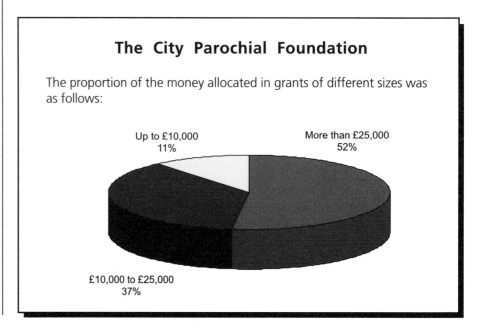

The City Parochial Foundation

The proportion of the money allocated in grants of different sizes was as follows:

Up to £10,000
11%

More than £25,000
52%

£10,000 to £25,000
37%

10 bodies including the Crown, the University of London, the Church Commissioners, the Bishopsgate Foundation and the Cripplegate Foundation. Chair, Professor Gerald Manners.

Beneficial area The Metropolitan Police District of London and the City of London.

Information available Leaflet on policies and procedures, annual report, a review of policy for the years 1997-2001 and an annual Grants Review, the whole being an example of good practice.

Summary The foundation makes nearly 250 grants a year, most often to fund specific salaries, to organisations working for the benefit of poor people within all 32 London boroughs and the City of London. They are usually over a period of three years but are often an extension of existing support. Amounts are seldom for more than £30,000 or for less than £5,000 (for small grants in similar fields, see the separate entry for the associated Trust for London).

The foundation has published detailed and interesting 'Policies and Priorities' for the years 1997-2001 which are largely reprinted below, after the foundation's Grant guidelines.

There are two priority concerns:
- the need to tackle social isolation, injustice and exclusion;
- the need to provide help for young people (aged 10 to 25 years) experiencing poverty.

The foundation, under its recently retired Clerk, Tim Cook, has been a pacemaker in the development of creative and effective grant making in Britain in recent years, and new initiatives continue in that tradition. Grants made in 1997 are categorised in the table herewith.

'During the period 1997-2001 a range of new ways of making funding available are being tried. These include working with local communities, working in alliance with other funders, and focussing on a particular section of the community (young people) and inviting applications from organisations working with them.'

The foundation, in recent years, has also been a standard setter in its relative accessibility to the kind of small community organisation that is often daunted by large grant making trusts.

Background and administration
The City Parochial Foundation was established in 1891 following the recommendations of a Royal Commission appointed to investigate the numerous parochial charities of the City of London (at that time there were 112 parishes within the City). The income of many of these charities had greatly increased with the growth of the City as a world financial centre, but the numbers of their potential beneficiaries had fallen. The City of London Parochial Charities Act provided that the largest five parishes should continue to manage their own endowments, but the bulk of the remainder of the charities should be administered by a new corporate body, to be known as the Trustees of the London Parochial Charities.

The trustees, who hold office for renewable periods of six years, manage two funds: the City Church Fund, and the Central Fund (with which this entry is concerned), which was endowed with all non-ecclesiastical funds of the City parishes. In 1986 the foundation also undertook the administration of the Trust for London, (see separate entry). As the Trust for London covers broadly similar fields, most readers who find this entry relevant to their interests should also look at the entry for the Trust for London.

In 1997 the foundation had an income of £4.9 million from an endowment held mainly in the form of property, and made grants to the value of £5.1 million. Administrative costs are a bit higher than for most trusts in this book, but the grant making is also considerably more sophisticated, as will appear from reading the rest of this entry, and excellent value appears to be being had from this expenditure. The names of the main grant making staff are listed under 'Applications' below.

The new Clerk, Bharat Mehta, was previously Chief Executive of the National Schizophrenia Fellowship; before that, he was the policy officer for the National Council of Voluntary Organisations (NCVO) and the Principal Officer for Voluntary Organisations with the London Borough of Waltham Forest.

Grant-making policy 1997-2001

In its new policy the foundation has chosen to focus more sharply on support to certain types of voluntary activity which help to combat poverty rather than on specific groups of disadvantaged

The City Parochial Foundation

The grants in total

1997 grants were classified as follows:

	No. of grants	Amount	%
Social isolation, injustice and exclusion	65	£1,415,120	27%
Young people experiencing poverty	34	£705,600	14%
Indirect and strategic work to alleviate poverty	35	£776,100	15%
Foundation's initiatives (youth)	3	£169,336	3%
Continuation grants	48	£1,526,334	30%
Other small grants	44	£345,055	7%
Grants under previous programmes	11	£187,083	4%
Total	**240**	**£5,124,628**	**100%**

The grants are analysed in the Review by total for each London borough. The table below gives the 'highs' and 'lows', ranked by the value per 1,000 population, a more useful form of presentation:

	No. of grants	Amount	Total per 1,000 pop.
Tower Hamlets	11	£242,936	£1.40
Kensington	11	£212,000	£1.38
Hammersmith	7	£182,000	£1.17
Lewisham	19	£273,800	£1.14
Southwark	10	£229,500	£0.99
Croydon	10	£194,000	£0.59

people. However, it continues to target young people. In addition it seeks to support the infrastructure of the voluntary sector and its advocacy work for policy change.

The size of the foundation's grants varies. It runs a special scheme for small one-off grants of up to £10,000 (see below) and the majority of its other grants, spread over a two and three year period are likely to be between £20,000 to £45,000.

Throughout its history the foundation has been guided by two major principles:

(i) An awareness of, and a need to guard against, the tendency for benefactions intended for the poor to fall into the hands of a somewhat higher income class.

(ii) A concern not to finance schemes which can be financed by local or central government so that charitable funds are, in effect, used to subsidise the statutory authorities.

The foundation's guidance is as follows (except for parts which will be found under 'Exclusions' and 'Applications':

Grant Guidelines
Basic Requirements

'The following will apply to all work funded during the Quinquennium:

- Applicants must demonstrate that their organisation is open to all wishing to join or make use of the services offered.
- All applicants seeking to work directly to alleviate poverty must show how the work to be funded will benefit the poor of London and how their active involvement will be achieved.
- The foundation requires that monitoring and reporting procedures are built into the funded work from the outset. Emphasis will be placed on recording the way work is undertaken, as well as its outcomes.

Grant-making Strategy: 1997 – 2001
Direct work to alleviate poverty

'During the preparations for the quinquennium the trustees were struck forcibly by the way in which poverty can lead to social isolation, injustice and exclusion in all sections of the community and by the effect of poverty on young people.

'In consequence the foundation has decided to focus a *significant part of its resources* upon what it regards as two priority concerns.

These are:

- the need to tackle social isolation, injustice and exclusion as they affect individuals in any section of the community.
- The need to provide help for young people (aged 10 to 25 years) experiencing poverty. *(A third priority, disability, is expected to follow within the next couple of years. See full Review below.)*

'The particular way in which these two concerns will be addressed is through grants to assist direct work *only* by means of:

i) the provision of advice, information and assistance with individual advocacy.
ii) Local initiatives to combat racial harassment and crime.
iii) Support for education and training initiatives and schemes.

Indirect and strategic work to alleviate poverty

'The trustees also appreciate the importance of back-up and development work for the voluntary sector and will be prepared to consider applications to assist work in the following areas;

i) Infrastructure support for the voluntary sector
'Experience has repeatedly shown that in the individuals boroughs and across London there is a need for infrastructure support for voluntary organisations, and that service providers need to have the best advice, information and training to develop high quality services for the poor of London.

ii) Advocacy for policy change
'Work in the voluntary sector can highlight the need for policy change, and arguments need to be constructed and presented to the appropriate authorities for improvements. This is a legitimate part of charitable activity, provided it falls within the Charity Commissioners' published *Guidelines on Campaigning by Charities*. Within these the trustees will consider applications which aim to bring about changes in policy or service provision for the benefit of the poor of London. Such proposals must clearly arise from the applicant's current work.

iii) Collaborative responses
'The trustees wish to encourage organisations within one borough or across several boroughs to work together to meet the needs of the poor.

Continuation grants, small grants and unexpected needs

'In addition the foundation will consider applications which are for:

i) *Continuation grants*
It is recognised that some work does not easily attract new funding and a continuation grant for work previously funded by the foundation may be appropriate for a limited period.

ii) *Small grants*
Any organisation working directly to benefit the poor of London, except those listed below as exclusions, may apply for a one-off grant of up to £10,000.

iii) *Unexpected needs*
The trustees are always ready to consider proposals to address new or emerging needs.

Dissemination

'In certain cases the foundation will consider with the beneficiary how best to disseminate the experience or the lessons learned from the work it has funded either through local workshops, individuals reports, seminars, or a foundation publication.'

Foundation's Initiatives

During the quinquennium the foundation will continue to take its own initiatives. These are likely to include:

- special funding programmes for which applications will be invited;
- local area based work;
- alliances with other funders to deal with certain complex issues.

Details of the above will be publicised as and when initiatives are launched.

(The 1997 Grants Review says that there are to be three of these special programmes during the quinquennium. The first of these, in 1998 was a Youth programme).

Grants Review 1997

In the introduction to Grants Review 1997 the chair of the foundation, Professor Gerald Manners wrote as follows:

'Some of the new priorities have rapidly attracted a large number of applications, for example, advice, information and advocacy; others, such as local initiatives and work to tackle racial harassment, will need more work to bring in appropriate applications. This review contains more details about the work initiated by the staff as part of our new priorities, some of which will no doubt take all of the next five years to bring to fruition.

Local area work

'During the quinquennial preparations in 1996 the foundation commissioned a review of needs in the London Boroughs. trustees were particularly interested in undertaking local area based work in areas which may not have benefited from large scale government initiatives. Local area based projects would work closely with the residents in areas of considerable need in order to develop long term benefits for the people and the community.

'Three local areas were identified:

Kilburn; with others, the foundation has commissioned an investigation into the needs of young people. The outcome is a proposal for a multi-agency youth information and advice project.

Greenford (Ealing); a detached youth work project in partnership with the Greenford Community Association.

St Peter's Ward, Tower Hamlets; a collaborative major five year project of community and economic regeneration, working with the Peabody Trust (which has its own entry in this book) and the local authority.

Youth programme

'During 1997-2001 it is the foundation's intention to run three special funding programmes. The first of these is the Youth Programme'. Nine organisations were selected in 1997 for funding in 1998, including the Who Cares? Trust in Islington, the Downside Settlement in Southwark and The 409 Project in Lambeth.

'In preparing for the programme, the foundation was urged to listen to what organisations felt they needed and not to impose funding priorities which might conflict with or detract from existing work. The trustees have funded ongoing good work rather than insisting on new specially established initiatives.

'It is intended that the work of the nine projects will be monitored throughout the programme and that examples of good practice will be widely disseminated.'

Alliances

'The trustees believe that several funders working in alliance can make a greater impact than one acting alone. The foundation's concern with school exclusion and the voluntary sector infrastructure is shared by others.

'During the year several trusts and London Boroughs grants met to discuss issues relating to voluntary sector infrastructure. This has proved to be a most successful forum for discussion.

'A mapping exercise of London based work on school exclusion was commissioned by a group of concerned trusts. The results ... are guiding this group of funders to explore ways of making an impact on what they feel is an important issue.

Refugee Education Unit

'The ... Unit is the clear result of a successful alliance between the Tudor Trust, Henry Smith's Charity, the Lloyds/TSB Foundation, the City Parochial Foundation and several voluntary organisations. The Unit exists to link refugees, principally young men, with educational opportunities ... .'

Examples of grants

The grants list is alphabetical, without any classification, but with a brief account of the purpose of each award. It is not usually clear, though, when the grant is for new activity or to continue existing work (about half of the grant total, as mentioned above).

Much the biggest grant, other than those for projects already mentioned, was that for £108,000 to the Bourne Trust for the cost, over two years, of running its remand counselling service. Other major grants were to Safe Ground (£30,000 for the post of Artistic Director) and Interchange Legal Advisory Service (£41,000 over two years for a Property Advisor). Awards of £30,000 usually for salary costs over two years went to, among others, Hounslow Law Centre, Barking and Dagenham Disablement Association, Leytonstone CAB and Richmond CVS.

To give a flavour of the grants, one page of the 1997 list starts as follows:

Pakistan Women's Welfare Assn. £5,000 for for fitting and installing emergency lights, a fire alarm system, intercom and security system.

Pan Project Ltd. £30,000 costs of employing a Community Officer for three days a week over three years.

Peabody Trust £84,336 to meet the salary costs of the community development worker in the St Peter's North Community Project over three years.

Pecan Ltd, Peckham £12,000 recruitment costs of Employment Preparation Course.

Peel Institute £20,000 to provide for extra provision for junior age children over three years.

Pepys Resource Centre £7,000 costs of additional education classes.

Plumstead Community Law Centre £26,820 costs of the post of the Thamesmead solicitor over two years.

Polyglot Theatre Company £7,500 to help meet the costs of the education programme over three years.

Exclusions No grants for community business initiatives; medical research and equipment; individuals; fee paying schools; trips abroad; general holiday playschemes; one-off events; publications; sports; major capital appeals; the direct replacement of public funds; endowment appeals

Applications There are no application forms. Prior to submitting a detailed application, it is advisable to discuss the proposed application with one of the staff.

It is required that all applicants adopt the following basic format:

- statement about the organisation: legal status, aims, brief history, staffing and management committee details, and current activities; reference to any previous grants from the foundation or Trust for London should be made;
- detailed financial position of the organisation listing main sources of income;
- statement on the particular need for which funding is being sought;
- full costing of the proposal;
- details of other funding sources, especially applications to other trusts;
- details of the monitoring to be carried out on the scheme for which funding is being requested.

The above should be accompanied (where available) by a copy of the constitution; most recent annual report; most recent audited accounts; budget for the current financial year; the job description, if application concerns a post; equal opportunities policy; list of names and addresses of office holders.

The application should not exceed three sides of A4 plus necessary appendices.

*All applications must be **finalised** by:*

- 31st January for April meeting
- 30th April for July meeting
- 15th August for October meeting
- 15th November for January meeting.

An application is only finalised when all documentation has been received, staff have no further questions to raise, and where necessary a meeting has taken place between the applicant and a member of the foundation's staff.

In 1998 there were three field officers helping the Clerk in the foundation's grant making work, as follows: Alison Harker (senior), Ann Curno and Helal Uddin Abbas.

The Elizabeth Clark Charitable Trust

£224,000 (approved, 1996/97)

Nursing – palliative care in the community

See entry for the 'Sainsbury Family Charitable Trusts'
Tel: 0171-410 0330

Correspondent Michael Pattison, Director

Trustees Lord Sainsbury of Turville; Miss J Portrait (HON & V Trustee Ltd); Dr Jane Davy; Dr Gillian Ford; (Miss Ethel Wix and Dame Cicely Saunders retired July 1997).

Beneficial area UK and overseas.

Information available Full report and accounts are available. The officers are listed as the director, P Spokes, finance director and M Williams, executive.

General This trust is one of the Sainsbury Family Charitable Trusts which share a joint administration.

'The trustees have for the time being adopted a policy that reflects the settlor's wish to bring about improvements in nursing.......and have decided to concentrate on developments in palliative care in the community, with the object of establishing standards of good practice that may be widely adopted.'

The trust's asset value was just over £1 million in April 1997 and its net income during the year was £50,500. Practically all its investments are held in J Sainsbury plc. The trust is making payments from both its capital and its income and appears to be winding down. It had outstanding commitments of £928,000 in April 1997.

In 1996/97 approved grants totalled £224,000 compared with £732,000 in 1995/96.

The major grant in 1996/97 was made to the National Council for Hospice and Specialist Palliative Care Services, towards core costs and for research and dissemination of papers on aspects of specialist palliative care (£158,000 over 4 years). The major grant in 1995/96 was made to South East London Cancer Support and Palliative Care Project, to support a co-ordinated approach to the delivery of palliative care services in South East London to demonstrate a model of interagency services (£680,000 over 5 years).

Exclusions 'The trust does not normally support capital or revenue appeals from hospices or make grants to individuals.'

Applications The trustees met twice during the year. 'The trust is proactive in its grant-making and unsolicited applications are unlikely to succceed.'

One application to a Sainsbury trust is said to be an application to all. See entry for the Sainsbury Family Charitable Trusts for the address and further information about the trusts.

Cleveland Community Foundation

£377,000 (1998)

General, in Cleveland

Cleveland Community Foundation, Southlands Business Centre, Ormesby Road, Middlesbrough TS3 0HB
Tel: 01642 314200; Fax: 01642 313700

Correspondent Kevin Ryan, Director

Trustees Dr. Tony Gillham, Chair; Michael Stewart; Robert Sale; John Bennett; John Bloom; John Foster; Chris Hope; Marjory Houseman; Alan Kitching; Jack Ord; Pat Sole; Simon Still; Bernard Storey; Kath Taylor.

Beneficial area The old county of Cleveland, being the local authority areas of Hartlepool; Middlesbrough; Redcar and Cleveland; and Stockton.

Information available Full information available from the foundation.

General Like other community foundations, but with exceptional success over the last two years, this charity is both building up an endowment, from it which it generates an income for grant making, and acting as an expert conduit for the charitable giving of others, both companies and individuals.

In 1997 there were five grant making programmes

Teesside Youth Development Programme
73 grants totalling £131,000, ranging from £250 to £7,000 (Action for Loftus Youth). 'TYDP allocates its grants in three ways:

a. Reactive – responding to requests.
b. Pro-active – researching areas of need and finding ways of meeting them.
c. Competitive – funding the winners of competitions for the best youth projects.

The Cleveland Fund
'A general fund, giving 50 grants to a value of £68,000, none of them for more than £2,500. A wide variety of groups were supported, from Victorian Asian Ladies (£1,300) to Teesside Witness Service (£2,000).

Teesside TEC Football Fund
'£76,000, mostly for the East Wing Community Initiative.

Teesside Power Fund
'£19,000 for groups in in the nine wards of the Teesside Tower Station region.

Prince's Trust / CCF Partnership Fund
'£13,000 in very small grants, through local organisations, for individuals who are suffering some form of disadvantage.

Voluntary Sector Management Training Fund
'£9,000 in 31 small grants.'

Applications Through the correspondent.

The Clore Foundation

£2,881,000 (1996)

Jewish charities, arts/museums, education, children, general

Unit 3, Chelsea Manor Studios, Flood Street, London SW3 5SR
Tel: 0171-351 6061

Correspondent Sally Bacon, Executive Director

Trustees Mrs Vivien Duffield, Chairman; David Harrel; Sir Mark Weinberg; Sir Martin Gilbert.

Beneficial area UK, but most money goes to London based institutions.

Information available Spartan accounts up to 1996 are on file at the Charity Commission, but a grants list for 1997 was supplied to help in preparing this entry.

Summary The filed accounts are old and incomplete, and there has been none of the required information about the work of the charity; the largest trust of which this can be said. However things are changing and the new Director has supplied much useful material for incorporation in this entry, as set out below.

In October 1998, this and its sister organisation, the Vivien Duffield Foundation, published a lavish and informative, though somewhat partial, account of their work since 1983. This was in association with the two foundations' joint announcement of major new funding programmes for museum and gallery education – 'Clore Centres for Education' – at the Tate Gallery, Bankside, and the British Museum (£2.5 million each), the Natural History Museum and the new Clore Small Grants Programme for regional museums and galleries (£1 million each).

At the same time a complete 1997 grants list was supplied to these editors

General The foundation was set up in 1964. It shares the same administration as the Vivien Duffield Foundation (see separate entry), and it also has Mrs Vivien Duffield, the daughter of Charles Clore, as the prime mover behind the activities of the foundation.

Assets in 1996 amounted to £28.5 million. This generated a high net income of £3.2 million. Donations for that year totalled £6.3 million for which no grants list or information is provided. However a £2 million interest free loan over three years to the Royal Opera House Development Land Trust, where Mrs. Duffield is also a board member, was reported.

The new and helpful executive director sent us the following information about the activities of the foundations:

'Education has remained a major concentration of the trustees of the foundation, and the other areas in which the foundation currently gives funding are:

- health;
- social welfare
- Jewish causes;
- education;
- museums and
- the arts.

These funding policies are reviewed periodically; however, the broad subject areas are unlikely to change.

'The trustees draw a balance between supporting large-scale national projects with long term effects and local community endeavours with a more spontaneous impact.

'The foundation's policy has been to respond where there are deserving projects in danger of failing or needing to help develop, rather than being bound by a rigid strategic approach or constricted by a long list of exclusions.

'The foundation maintains a balance between Jewish and secular causes.

'The foundation concentrates its funding in Great Britain (excluding Northern Ireland).

'The trustees of the foundation may be quite happy to consider working in partnership on charitable projects, and to try new approaches for the right projects. The foundation can make an extremely wide range of grants including both capital and revenue grants.'

New information for potential applicants has also been provided, and will be found in the 'Applications' section below.

Grants in 1997 were led by £1,345,000 in three grants to Birkbeck College for funding its Clore Management Centre. Other major beneficiaries included Nightingale House (£200,000 for redevelopment), the Royal Opera House (£135,000), and the Imperial War Museum (£100,000 towards its Holocaust Exhibition).

£120,000 was given to St Mary's Hospital, London , £84,000 to the Oxford Centre for Hebrew and Jewish Studies, £75,000 to the West London Synagogue, £64,000 to Simon Marks School (for a new technology wing) and £50,000 to the National Theatre to refurbish its foyer.

There were 34 grants in all, a number of them for less than £10,000. Beneficiaries included Elderly Accommodation Counsel (£10,000 towards staff costs) and Mencap (£35,000 for its work in Redbridge).

Exclusions No donations or grants to individuals, whether for education or any other purpose.

Applications Applications should be made in writing on no more than three sides of A4, and should be accompanied by an SAE. Following this, if the trustees are interested in the proposal, they are likely to request more detailed information, and organise a meeting with the applicants. Final decisions upon the awarding of grants are only made at the formal meetings of the trustees. These however are not on a fixed schedule; there is an ongoing process of assessment that allows the trustees to meet as and when there are sufficient applications.

The Clothworkers' Foundation and other Trusts

£3,202,000 (1997)

Clothworking, general

Clothworkers' Hall, Dunster Court, Mincing Lane, London EC3R 7AH
Tel: 0171-623 7041

Correspondent Michael Harris, Secretary

Trustees The Governors of the Foundation.

Beneficial area UK and overseas.

Information available Accounts; Annual Review with full grants list, analysis of grants/grant-making, policy and guidelines.

Summary Hundreds of grants varying from a few hundred pounds to a few hundred thousand pounds are made to an array of charities under nine categories. Some grants are annual, some paid over two or three years and others are one-off. They are most often made towards capital costs.

In 1998, to mark the Millennium, a special grant of £1,200,000 was offered to support the creation of St Ethelburga's Centre for Peace and Reconciliation, within the IRA bombed City church of that name.

General This foundation is the charitable arm of the Clothworkers' Company, one of the City of London's 'Great Twelve' livery companies. It was originally formed to protect its members and its craft (the 'finishing of woven woollen cloth'), but for centuries charity has been a main activity. Most grants (76% by value in 1997) are awarded from the foundation's own funds. The other donations are disbursed from 17 other trusts and total about £700,000 a year.

In 1997 the foundations' assets totalled over £40 million, income was £3,310,000 and it made grants amounting to £2,450,000. Management and administration costs are high, £409,000 or 13% of total charitable expenditure, including awards from the other trusts. However, these include substantial programmes of grants for individuals, a far more costly process than the awarding of grants to organisations.

The foundations' aims are:

- the evolution and development of clothworking in general;

• the enhancement of the quality of life for young and aged; the disabled and infirm; the disadvantaged, needy abused and underprivileged;

and also, but to a lesser extent:

• the work of the church;
• the promotion of the arts, so as to enrich the cultural climate of the UK;
• the well being of the natural heritage and its environment;
• the provision of aid to the underdeveloped world overseas;
• the support of those organisations providing relief following international disasters;

and further:

• the consideration of all areas of charitable giving.

Grants in 1997were categorised as follows:

	Grants	%
Clothworking	£608,000	19%
Relief in need/welfare	£538,000	17%
Medicine/health	£501,000	16%
Education/sciences	£443,000	14%
Overseas	£316,000	10%
Children/youth	£69,000	12%
The Church	£176,000	5%
Heritage/environment	£174,000	5%
Arts	78,000	2%
Total	£3,202,000	100%

18% of the trusts' charitable expenditure went in two grants of £53,000; 40% in nine awards between £20,000 and £50,000 and 26% in 14 donations of £10,000 to under £20,000. Many of the larger awards are made annually 'under the terms of the trust instrument'. Other non-permanent donations went to Henshaw's Society for the Blind (£45,000 contribution to an Art and Craft Centre); Birmingham Royal Institution for the Blind (£32,500) towards an information network system for the Queen Alexandra College; and the Restoration of Appearance and Function Trust (£25,000 for three years).

The annual review 1997

Distribution of funds 'During 1997 the governors disbursed a total sum of £3,202,000 in the payments of grants to no less than 201 charitable organisations and objects. Unfortunately, the number of applications, from registered charities, to which we were unable to respond in 1997 numbered 835. Each of these unsuccessful applications received full and careful consideration and each received a reply, even though we could not help them. The majority of these appeals did not fully comply with the foundation's current grant making policy.'

Grants from the Clothworkers'

Foundation. 114 grants were approved in 1997. A single grant of £350,000 accounted for 14% of charitable expenditure; nine awards between £50,000 and £100,000 for 26%; 35 between £20,000 and £45,000 for 36%; and those under £20,000 but over £10,000 for 20%.

The £350,000 grant was the second instalment of a three year grant totalling £1 million in order to establish the Clothworkers' Centre for World Textiles within the British Museum Study Centre. Grants of £100,000 went to St Mary's Hospital Special Trustees to meet the costs of a children's resuscitation room, and to the University of Surrey as the first instalment of a £300,000, three year, grant to establish the Biological Resource Unit for the Isolation and Exploitation of Organisms for Composting and Bioremediation Processes.

Grants from the Charitable Trusts 'During 1997 there were 17 charitable trusts administered by and under the trusteeship of the Clothworkers' Foundation.

'No charge is made by the Foundation to any of these trusts thereby enabling the whole of the income to be available for distribution in accordance with the objectives of each of the trusts.'

Grant Making Policy 'All appeals received from registered charities, if specifically addressed to the Clothworkers' Foundation are considered, and in so far as these are refused without direct reference to the trusts and grants committee, lists are circulated to the committee and the governors on a quarterly basis in case any governor may wish to request that an appeal be referred back for further consideration.

'The foundation takes great pride in the fact that it welcomes telephone discussions between the foundations' staff and appeal officers, when friendly, positive and helpful advice can be given as to what the foundation will and will not support, and as to how an application should be submitted to the foundation. Advice can also be given on the likely scale of competition for funds; how an application will be dealt with and approximately how long it will take for a decision to be reached. Experience has shown that providing help and guidance over the phone is highly cost effective, efficient and helpful service to our applicants. As a matter of policy, grant interviews are rarely given in connection with fundraising since there would be insufficient time for all such interviews during each working day.'

Exclusions No support is given from the foundation's own funds for:

• direct relief of state aid or in the reduction of financial support from public funds;
• organisations which are not registered charities;
• individuals;
• fund-raising activities on behalf of any charity;
• the general maintenace or restoration of ecclesiastical buildings unless they have a close connection with the Clothworkers' Company, or unless they are appealing for a specific purpose which is considered to be of outstanding importance in relation to the national heritage;
• schools and colleges unless they have close ties with the Clothworkers' Company;
• organisations or groups whose main objects are to fund or support other charitable bodies.

Assistance to individuals for educational purposes is limited; in London such grants are made through the associated Mary Datchelor Trust, details of which can be found in the companion Educational Grants Directory.

Applications The foundation does not issue application forms. However, all applicants must complete a Data Information Sheet, available from the ofice above, which should accompany the written application. The foundation provides the following general guidelines for potential applicants:

1a. Applications should be made in writing on the registered charity's official headed notepaper. Ideally, the appeal letter itself should be no longer than two and a half pages of A4.

b. Detailed costings or a budget for the project or projects referred to in the appeal letter should form a separate appendix or appendices and should provide the fullest possible detail.

c. The latest annual report of the applicant charity, together with the latest full audited accounts, including a full balance sheet, should also accompany the written application.

2. During the course of the application letter, applicants should endeavour to:

a. Introduce the work of the charity; state when it was established;describe its aims and objectives; and define precisely what the charity does and who benefits from its activities.

b. Comment on the applicants track record since its inception and refer to its notable achievements and successes to date. Endeavour to provide an interesting synopsis of the organisation.

c. Describe the project for which a grant is being sought fully, clearly and concisely and comment on the charity's plans for the future.

d. Provide full costings or a budget for the project/projects to include a detailed breakdown of the costs involved.

e. Give details of all other applications which the applicant charity has made to other sources of funding, and indicate precisely what funds have already been raised from other sources for the project.

f. All applicants are, of course, perfectly at liberty to request a precise sum of money by way of a grant. However it can be more beneficial for the applicant to concentrate on providing accurate and detailed costings of the project concerned thereby enabling the foundation to make its own judgment as to the level of financial support to be considered.

3. Applicants can greatly help their cause by concentrating on clarity of presentation and by providing detailed factual information.

Preliminary information required in support of any application must include the latest annual report and full audited accounts. Trustees meet regularly in January, March, May, July, October and November. The committees' recommendations are then placed before a subsequent meeting of the Governors. Accordingly there is a rolling programme of dealing with and processing applications and the foundation prides itself on flexibility.

All unsuccessful applicants receive a written refusal letter.

Richard Cloudesley's Charity

£700,000 (1998)

Medicine and welfare, churches,

Beaufort House, 15 St Botolph Street, London EC3A 7EE
Tel: 0171-247 6555; Fax; 0171-247 5091

Correspondent K Wallace, Clerk to the Trustees

Trustees Appointed by the local council, the local Church of England churches, and co-options by the trustees.

The Mayor of Islington and the Vicar of St Mary's, Upper Street are also trustees.

Beneficial area North Islington only – see below for details.

Information available

Comprehensive guidelines entitled 'Help for Islington Charities. How to apply for a block grant'. Annual Report and Accounts.

Summary Grants of between £1,000 and £30,000 are made to benefit the 'sick poor', ie; people in need of financial and medical help. Only charities benefiting, or individuals residing in, the 'Ancient Parish' of Islington will be helped. Donations come with no conditions and all are one-off. Regular support is possible albeit without commitment by the charity to continue funding in the next year.

General The guidelines tell us:

'Richard Cloudesley's Charity is Islington's oldest and largest endowed charity.

'It was founded in 1517 by the Will of a pious Islington resident, Richard Cloudesley. He left the rent from a 14 acre field in Islington to be used for the benefit of residents of Islington parish.

'The field was in Barnsbury and its centre was Cloudesley Square. During the Depression in the 1930's about two thirds of the land and buildings were sold, mostly to residents, and the proceeds were invested'

In 1996/97 the charity had net assets totalling £14,918,000 and low incoming resources of £487,000. 81 grants were made, including one of £82,545 to the charity's welfare fund which gives donations to individuals. The remaining 80 awards totalled £450,000, half of which was paid in grants to medical/welfare causes and half to churches. In the latter category, 21 churches received awards ranging from £1,000 to £23,000. 65% of the total £225,000 was paid out in grants of £10,000 or above.

Grants in the medical and welfare sector were more plentiful but smaller. 59 charities received donations ranging from £100 to £13,500. Nine of these (30% of expenditure in this category) were for £5,000 or more, the rest were typically around £1,000. Apart from its grant programme, the charity also assists the people of Islington by providing stable long-term housing on a managed estate.

The following description of the grant programme is taken from the guidelines:

Geographic Scope. 'Cloudesley money can only assist in activities in the

"Ancient Parish" of Islington. This is the Northern part of the modern London Borough of Islington – roughly everything North of Chapel Market and City Road.

'Obviously enough there are a few bodies that confine their work to a small area like the Ancient Parish of Islington. We are quite used to helping charities in Islington as a whole, or Islington and nearby London Boroughs. What we ask is that you give us an assessment of the proportion of what you do that can be said to be related to people living in the Ancient Parish of Islington.

'The geographic scope makes for difficulties in grant funds to nationally organised charities. Some of these have locally accounted branches – and others have locally identifiable projects – but without some restriction like this, we will be unable to assist.

Purpose/Scope. 'Grants can only be made to benefit the "sick poor". This means that both a medical and a financial need must be shown.

Medical Need. 'The Cloudesley trustees take a generous view on what is a medical need. As well as supporting bodies working with conventional medical conditions – strokes, arthritis, mental handicap, for example – grants have been made recently to charities dealing with -

- drugs
- alcohol abuse
- sex problems
- victim support
- bereavement counselling

Financial need: 'The Cloudesley charities take the view that charities working in the "medical field" – in its wider interpretation – are supporting those in financial need. Pure medical research, though, would be outside the permitted ambit.

'Can other causes be helped? Often charities whose work is outside the "medical" field may be able to identify some aspect of what they do which can be viewed as medical.

Example 1. 'Cloudesley money can't be used for prisoner's welfare but it is given for facilities in Pentonville Prison hospital wing. Inmates in the wing are seen as falling within the "sick poor" test.

Example 2. 'Charities helping the homeless are outside scope but any "medical" or health services made available to homeless people can be the subject of grant assistance.'

Despite the fact that the charity only makes one-off grants with no commitment to repeat funding, it often will repeat grants. For example, all but one of the churches assisted in 1997 were also helped in the previous three years and the great majority of the medical /welfare causes were likewise supported both years. 15 new awards were made in 1996/97, the largest went to The Church on the Corner (Holy Trinity Centre £6,000) and Islington Age Concern (£2,000).

Exclusions Applicants must fall within the geographic and purposes scopes of the charity.

Applications The guidelines say:

'If you think your charity is going to be able to qualify for consideration of a grant, write first to the Clerk to the Charity. You will than get an application form.

'Applications should be:
- timely
- in writing
- supported by accounts

'If you would like us to acknowledge your application, please send a self-addressed envelope. Otherwise, to save expense, we will not confirm safe receipt.

'Block grants are considered twice a year, around late April, and early November at a Grants Committee meeting.

'Recommendations are made by the Grants Committee at these meetings and are reviewed and authorised by the Cloudesley trustees as a whole two weeks later. The trustees normally adopt all the recommendations.

'We need to know what work your charity does, how it fits within geographical scope and purpose scope and the purpose for which you are seeking a grant. So long as this is clearly set out, we do not need a great deal of detail.

'We place a great deal of importance on receiving the accounts of the charities we fund so please be sure to send these each time you apply.

'We will give brief reasons with any application that is not successful.'

Clover Trust

£348,000 (1997)

Elderly, Young People

Messrs Herbert Pepper and Rudland (GFDW), 66-70 Baker Street, London W1M 1DH

Trustees N. C. Haydon, S. Woodhouse

Information available Accounts, but lacking both the required and narrative report, on file at the Charity Commission.

General In 1997 assets amounted to £5.3 million, generating an income of £383,000. After paying out management and administrative costs (£5,000) and portfolio management fees (£34,000, a high 0.6% of the value of the assets) about £348,000 was given out in 76 donations. The accounts note a £10,000 loan to the Parnham Trust.

The Trust supplied information on up-to-date grants, unfortunately it arrived too late for inclusion in this edition. The 1994 grants list is reprinted below.

For 1994 £218,000 was disbursed through about 50 grants. Grants were between £750 and £15,000. Examples include:

Children Charities: Action Research for Crippled Children (£15,000); NSPCC (£15,000); Friends of Orphans in Romania (£10,000), Barnardo's (£250).

Welfare and Health: Parkinson Disease Society (£2,000); Dorset Action for the Disabled (£5,000); Speech Language and Hearing Trust (£1,000).

Catholic: St Francis Leprosy Guild (£5,000); CAFOD (£10,000); Plymouth Diocesan Catholic Children's Charity (£6,000).

Clydepride Ltd

£134,000 (but see below, 1995/96)

Jewish charities, general

144 Bridge Lane, London NW11 9JS
Tel: 0171 405 2194

Correspondent L Faust, Secretary to the Trustees

Trustees L Faust; D Faust.

Information available Accounts up to 1995/96 only, and then without grants

lists, on file at the Charity Comission in September 1998.

General In 1995/96 income totalled £1 million, hence the entry here despite the low reported level of grant making. Management and administration costs were almost double the grant giving at £240,000.

Little information is available: 'It is not company policy to give any information.' and 'we give grants in too many areas to tell you; write in and we will consider it.' (which has already been done-Ed).

The objectives are to 'advance religion in accordance with the Jewish Orthodox faith; relief of poverty and general charitable causes.'

John Coates Charitable Trust

£260,000 (1996/97)

Health, community, environment, arts

Crockmore House, Fawley, Henley on Thames, Oxon RG9 6HY
Tel: 01491 573367; Fax: 01491 411641

Correspondent Mrs P L Youngman

Trustees Mrs McGregor; Mrs Kesley; Mrs Lawes; Mrs Youngman.

Beneficial area UK.

Information available Report and accounts available on file at the Charity Commission. Grants list but no narrative report.

General The trust gives grants to both large national organisation and small local charities 'which are of personal interest to one or more of the trustees'.

In 1996/97, from assets of £6.8 million, income was low at £223,000. Grants totalling £260,000 were given in 64 awards and went to a variety of health, community and environmental preservation charities. About half the grants were to organisations supported in the previous year.

The largest grant went to Lymington Museum (£15,000) and the next largest to Painshill Park Trust (£13,000). Nine grants of £10,000 were made. These went to Chichester Cathedral, Chichester Festival Hall, Jubilee Sailing Trust, International Spinal Research , Mary Rose Trust, Royal Botanic Gardens Kew, St Mungo's Association, and Shelter.

Smaller grants went mainly to local organisations: Wildfowls and Wetlands

Trust (£2,000); Pocklington Canal Amenity Society (£500); Hampshire County Youth Band (£500); and Daffodil Ball Appeal (£250).

Exclusions Grants are not given to individuals.

Applications To the correspondent.

The John S Cohen Foundation

£380,000 (1996/97)

Music and the arts, Jewish charities, general

85 Albany Street, London NW1 4BT
Tel: 0171-486 1117; Fax: 0171-486 1118

Correspondent Duncan Haldane, Administrator

Trustees Dr David Cohen, Chairman; Elizabeth Cohen; Richard Cohen.

Beneficial area UK and overseas.

Information available Full accounts are on file at the Charity Commission, accompanied by annual reports from the administrator.

General The foundation was established in 1965 with assets donated by John S Cohen, his wife and children. After his death he was succeeded as chairman by his son; fellow trustees are also brother and sister.

The trustees aim is to seek out projects which have an 'unusual and innovative nature whilst maintaining support for a number of regular beneficiaries. It has a particular interest in music and the arts, education, social and Jewish charities.'

Assets of the foundation total £6 million. With an income of only £490,00 administrative and management costs are high at £125,000.

Grants for 1996/97 totalled £380,000 through 113 grants. The top 57 grants accounted for £350,000. Grants ranged in size from £33,000 to £2,000, with many repeated.

Grants list for these top 57 grants are categorised as follows:

Music and the Arts	£158,000	45%
Education	£70,000	20%
Social	£47,000	13%
Medical	£35,000	10%
Jewish Charities	£30,000	9%
Environment	£10,000	3%
Total	£350,000	

Music and Arts: As the above table shows, this category takes by far the largest share of donations. Most of the charities funded are large national organisations, the only local charities that seem to attract funding are London based. Examples of beneficiaries include: the English National Opera (£33,000), Scottish Opera (£25,000), the National Gallery (£17,000), National History Museum (£10,000), London String Quartet (£5,500), Academy of Ancient Music (£5,000), Almeidia Opera ((£5,000), Dulwich Picture Gallery (£5,000) and the Handel House Trust (£5,000).

Education: Grants went mainly to larger established universities, with a preference for Oxford University, and to a number of smaller educational charities. Major grants in this category included: Oxford University (£15,000), Lincoln College, Oxford (£10,000), Kellogg College, Oxford (£5,000) and Book Aid International (£2,000).

Social: Taking £47,000 of the total grants made available, this category deals mainly with charities concerned with prison reform, population control and the family. Examples include Childline (£10,000), Parent Network (£10,000), Population Concern (£10,000) and the Howard League for Penal Reform (£2,000).

Medical: The only grant currently being given is a repeated grant of £35,000 to the Royal Free Hospital School of Medicine. This will be paid annually until 1998/99, when the trustees will decide on a new project to fund.

Jewish Charities: A variety of nationally based charities are supported, such as Jewish Care (£10,000), Jewish Museums (£5,000) and World Jewish Relief (£5,000).

Environment: Covering both the built and natural environment, the larger grants included: CPRE (£4,500), Society for the Protection of Ancient Buildings (£3,000), and Shape London (£2,000).

Exclusions Grants to registered charities only; no grants to individuals; no further medical support.

Applications No response is made to applications unless it is decided to make a grant. Applicants should state the purpose for which a donation is required briefly outlining related work and the financial circumstances. Trustees meet in March and October and applications should be received a month previously.

The Colchester Catalyst Charity

£353,000 (1996/97)

Health in north-east Essex

Lodge Lane, Langham, Colchester CO4 5NE

Correspondent P W Fitt

Trustees Director: C F Pertwee, Chairman; R W Whybrow; Dr R W Griffin; A H Frost; P W E Fitt; Dr E Hall; C Hayward.

Beneficial Area North-east Essex.

Information available Full accounts are on file at the Charity Commission.

Summary Grants and interest-free loans are given to organisations and individuals. There are 13 categories of giving, all of which could be subsumed under the broad heading of medical/special needs welfare. Awards vary from £200 to £25,000 and are usually one-off payments towards capital costs.

General The charity was set up in 1990 following the sale of the Colchester Oaks Hospital to Community Hospitals plc (on condition of building a new hospital).

In the year ending September 1997 it had assets of over £8 million (£1 million more than in 1996) and income of £410,000. Grants of £25,000 (accounting for 14% of the sum value of grants) were made to Macmillan Cancer Relief to employ a family support worker, and to Tendring CVS to help with repairs and refurbishment of a new HQ. Three further awards of over £10,000 and under £20,000 accounted for 10% of the total, and 12 of under £10,000 to £5,000 for 20%.

Applications in 1996/97:

	organisations	individuals
Received	110	75
Accepted	49	44
Declined	36	18
Awaiting decision	25	13

Within the 13 categories, charitable expenditure was disbursed as follows:

Learning difficulties	£68,000	19%
Cancer relief/ hospice care	£39,000	11%
Physical difficulties	£35,000	10%
Family support	£17,000	5%
Mental health	£10,000	3%

Sensory impairment	£12,500	3%
Information and services	£12,500	3%
Elderly	£9,000	2%
Children with disabilities	£8,000	2%
Medical	£1,600	0.5%
Total	£354,000	

The 1996/97 report reads:

'The charity again made significant contributions in most categories of care, where it could establish that help required would not be forthcoming from statutory organisations. Grants were up 19% over the previous year. Particular emphasis continues to be laid on the special needs of individuals – 40% of grants made were a direct contribution to those needs.

'The over-riding concern of the charity is to provide support where it will benefit the greatest number of people, principally by direct contributions to organisations or specific and well defined projects including therapeutic aids, equipment and buildings for medical or nursing care.

'The charity recognises the need of specialised equipment for some disabled people. Where it is established that such equipment is not available from statutory organisations a contribution may be made towards the cost involved.

'General funding or contributions to staff or other running costs are excluded but recognising the often overlooked needs of carers the charity will consider funding respite care provided the care period is well defined, carefully controlled and readily monitored.

'Where financial help is given the directors will satisfy themselves that satisfactory management and organisation exists to ensure that the money is properly used and in the case of equipment, that it can be efficiently operated and maintained.

'In appropriate cases a grant or loan may be offered for full or part-time funding of a project or equipment.'

Exclusions No support for general funding, staff or running costs (usually). Retrospective funding is not considered.

Applications In writing to the correspondent.

The Colt Foundation

£431,000 (1997)

Occupational and environmental health research

New Lane, Havant,
Hampshire, PO9 2LY
Tel: 01705-491400

Correspondent Miss Jacueline Riley

Trustees Jerome O'Hea, Chairman; Mrs Mary Ault; Timothy Ault; Mrs Clare Gilchrist; Mrs Patricia Lebus; Walter McD Morison; Christina Fitzsimons; Alan O'Hea; Peter O'Hea.
Professor D Denison and Prof D Coggon act as Scientific Advisers.

Beneficial area UK.

Information available Report and accounts with grants list and narrative explanation of grants and grant-making policy.

Summary Grants are made to support organisations and post-graduate students for research into occupational and environmental medicine. Donations to organisations vary from a few thousand pounds to £100,000 and may be repeated over two to five years. Beneficiaries are well established research institutes (awards to individuals are made through such), usually already well known to the foundation.

General The trust was established in 1978 by the O'Hea family with an initial gift of a 30% stake in the Colt Group ltd. Its original and current purpose is 'the promotion and encouragement of research into social, medical and environmental problems created by commerce and industry'.

In 1997/98 the foundation had assets totalling nearly £12 million from which £613,000 in income was generated. A total of 14 grants amounting to £366,000 were made to organisations and £65,000 was awarded to an unknown number of students. Of the organisations, all had been supported in the previous year and most have long-term funding relationships with the trust. The largest grants were to the National Heart and Lung Institute (£67,000), Hearing Research Trust (£53,000) and Napier University (£47,000). Of the remaining donations, four were between £20,000 and £30,000, five between £10,000 and £19,000 and two under £10,000

(smallest: £2,500 to the Royal Brompton Hospital).

The trust says:

'We are interested in research into the causes of illnesses resulting from conditions at the place of work and in the wider environment. Such conditions are rarely, if ever, the sole cause, but we are interested if these are a significant factor. We are only interested where the science is of the highest quality and the subject is relevant to human welfare.

'We prefer to be the sole source of finance in a project. We never contribute to the general funds of another charity and we do not support overseas projects simply because we have not got the resources to assess or supervise them. We aim to help not only with money, but from the experience of our scientific advisors, and of our trustees, to make a constructive input.

'We support students for higher degrees in related subjects. In the case of PhD's in a scheme with the Faculty of Occupational Medicine, which is advertised annually in January, and for MSc's through the medium of certain university departments. We do not make grants directly to students.

Exclusions
Grants are not made for:
- the general funds of another charity;
- projects overseas.

Applications

To the correspondent. Trustees meet in May and November and applications may be submitted at any time.

Sir James Colyer-Fergusson's Charitable Trust

£632,000 (1996/97)

Church buildings, general, in Kent and Suffolk

c/o Farrer & Co, 66 Lincoln's Inn Fields, London WC2A 3LH
Tel: 0171-242 2022

Correspondent Mrs Judith Hill

Trustees J A Porter;
Sir Matthew Farrer; Jonathan Monckton; Simon Noel-Buxton.

Beneficial area Kent and Suffolk.

Information available Accounts with only a spartan report. There is no comprehensive narrative report, nor are the grants adequately analysed and explained.

Summary The trust makes grants ranging from £500 up to around £20,000, with occasional exceptional awards for larger amounts. Usually donations are for Anglican churches' capital costs, but a variety of other causes are also supported.

General The trust was founded in 1969. After revaluation of its property investments in 1996/97, the trust reported assets of over £22 million – nearly £10 million more than in the previous year (£12.5 million in 1995/96). However, at £650,000 1996/97 income was £8,000 lower than in 1995/96. Such an income is very low given the revised size of the assets.

Grants to churches are typically for £2,000 but can be as high as £20,000. Other causes have recently received donations varying from £250 to £163,000.

In its 1996/97 report the trust says:

'The trustees receive numerous appeals for funds. The requests are considered on a quarterly basis usually in March, June, September and December. The trustees' policy is to consider appeals for charitable causes in Kent and Suffolk only. The trustees' preference is to support smaller charities. The trustees currently regard churches as their priority for funding but if there is a surplus income available will also consider donations for other purposes.

'In addition, the trustees also support the work of the Tureck Bach Foundation. The trustees have a research grant agreement with the trustees of the foundation which provides an annual grant of £45,000 to be paid to the foundation.

'The trustees continued to make grants in accordance with their policies. A total of 104 donations were made during the year of which 56 went to churches.

'During the year, the following payments were made to the University of Kent: £110,000 to the Musical Endowment Fund and £52,000 for Theatre Refurbishment.'

Other non-church causes to be supported in 1996/97 included the Canterbury Youth Project; the Kent Trust for Nature Conservation; Plantlife and the New Medway Steam Packet Company Ltd, who received £10,000 each.

Exclusions No grants to charities outside Kent or Suffolk, other than small grants made from covenanted donations. No grants to individuals.

Applications In writing to the correspondent. Application forms available but not necessary.

Comic Relief

£5,857,000 in Africa; £1,987,000 in UK (1996/97)

Community based UK charities, Africa (see below)

74 New Oxford Street,
London WC1A 1EF
Tel: 0171-436 1122; Fax: 0171-436 1541;
Minicom: 0171-631 1190;
E-mail: red@comicrelief.org.uk

Correspondent UK Grants Department; Africa Grants Department

Trustees Sir Tim Bell, President; Peter Benett-Jones, Chair; Richard Curtis, Vice-Chair; Colin Howes, Secretary; Mike Harris, Treasurer; Emma Freud; Lenny Henry; Nalini Varma; Laurence Newman.

Beneficial area UK and Africa.

Information available A full annual report and grant guidelines available from the charity. All information on its grant-making programme is also available in big print, audiotape and braille versions.

Summary Comic Relief runs two grants programmes, one aimed at the UK and the other towards Africa. About twice as many grants are made in the UK programme as in the Africa programme, but the latter accounts for two thirds of charitable expenditure. An African grant is on average £25,000 (varying from £1,000 to around £200,000), while a UK grant averages around £6,000 (ranging from £1,000 to £30,000). In both programmes awards are made towards capital or revenue costs and may be single payments or spread across a few years.

General Comic Relief/Charity Projects (its sister company) has developed a reputation for supporting organisations at grass roots level in which the disadvantaged group(s) targeted are themselves closely involved in the development and management of the initiative (a precedent it set for the later, bigger National Lottery Charities Board).

Current grant-making policies cover 1996-1999. While the programmes for Africa are likely to remain much the same after this period, the UK grants programmes and applications process are due to be reviewed in the run-up to Red Nose Day 1999 and may change significantly. The outcome of this review should be known by March/April 1999.

Comic Relief publishes eight page booklets for the UK and Africa grants programmes. These guidelines, which reveal sharply focused funding priorities and procedures, are essential reading for any potential applicant.

The charity's mission statement runs:

'Comic Relief exists to tackle poverty and social injustice by helping disadvantaged young people in the United Kingdom and Africa to realise their aspirations and potential. We do this by:

- raising money from the general public by actively involving them in events and projects that are innovative and fun;
- informing, educating, raising awareness and promoting social change;
- allocating the funds we raise in a responsible and effective way to a wide range of charities, which we select after careful research;
- ensuring that our red nose day fundraising costs are covered by sponsorship in cash or kind so that for every penny donated, a penny goes to charity.

UK Grants

In 1996/97 in excess of 400 awards totalling £1,987,000 were allocated (and a total of £2,987,000 disbursed) to organisations within four programmes:

Young people		
– disability	£490,000	25%
– homelessness	£412,000	21%
– alcohol/drugs	£344,000	17%
Older people	£608,000	30%
Cross programme	£133,000	7%
Total	£1,987,000	100%

Around £600,000 (30% of the total) was disbursed in 27 donations of £20,000 or more, but most of the money was allocated in awards of about £6,000. The largest grant was for £52,000 and went to the Refugee Council.

The UK programme

The charity gives the following description of the UK programme (though, as noted above, likely to be re-constituted in early 1999):

'Whether its helping women escaping domestic violence or giving a voice to young people, Comic Relief's grants actively involve people in finding their own solutions, because the evidence is that projects which draw on people's own skills and resources are the most likely to succeed.

'To make our grant-making as effective as possible, this year we decided to make fewer, larger grants. The aim is to help projects make a significant impact when they're tackling the burning issues we support. We have also introduced a new two-stage application process, so that we can help organisations wasting time, and make sure applications really meet the requirements of our three programme areas, which are:

- young people;
- older people;
- disabled people.

'We have recognised that we need to respond to the increasingly complex and inter-connecting problems faced by young people. That is why we have broadened this programme to cover new projects dealing with bullying, mental health or sexual abuse, for example – so that we can target the young people whose needs are most acute.

'Nearly £2 million in UK grants was paid out this year [nearly £3 million paid out according to the accounts, Ed.]. As a result of the changes in benefit legislation for asylum seekers, some of our money has helped literally destitute people in the UK for the first time. We have continued to support groups of disabled people and older people in their fight for equal rights and full participation in society.'

New focus: young people's voices.

'"Trouble-makers", "layabouts" – young people sometimes don't get a very good press. But then they rarely get consulted or asked for their views or feelings, still less involved in the organisations which control their lives. But we think that if you give young people the chance to participate in running projects, they can achieve remarkable things. Like in, for example, the peer education drugs project in Solihull which we've been funding, where young people are trained to educate people their own age about drugs.

'An important part of our new focus on young people is to listen to their needs and help them find a voice – especially if they face discrimination – and to make sure that voice is heard by decision-makers.'

Africa Grants

During the year 1996/97 a total of £5910,000 was allocated in around 140 donations by the Africa grants

programme. 46% of this money went in 18 grants of at least £100,000. A further 37% was disbursed in 33 donations of under £100,000 but over £50,000. The largest grants were to Save the Children Fund (£210,000 for community based rehabilitation in Tanzania); Actionaid (£206,000 for reducing poverty in Bwaise district, Uganda); and ACORD (two grants of £200,000 towards the Red Sea Hills programme, Sudan; and to pastoralists in the Gambos region of Angola).

Africa grants allocated in 1996/97

• women	£1,498,000	25%
• conflict	£1,364,000	23%
• pastoralists	£1,102,000	17%
• urban	£993,000	17%
• disability	£953,000	16%
Total	£5,910,000	100%

The Review 1996/97

In the 1996/97 review the foundation wrote:

'19 of the 20 poorest countries in the world are in Africa- which is why we devote two thirds of the money we raise to tackling the challenges people face there. Those challenges are huge – from grinding poverty to civil war – but everywhere, people are managing to find creative solutions to tackle problems and meet their needs.

'That's where the resources raised by Comic Relief come in. We pass on funds to UK registered charities working with local organisations across Africa. The projects we support help people to help themselves, and enable people who are marginalised and dispossessed to improve their chances in life. Every two years we look again at where to spend the money raised.'

These are our current priorities:

- people affected by conflict
- women
- disabled people
- pastoralists (who depend on animals for their livelihood)
- people living in poverty in towns and cities.

'Our resources are limited compared with the enormous needs, so we try to target where we can be most effective – rather than just fire fighting the symptoms , we can help people to address the underlying causes of injustice and poverty.

'Comic Relief has committed as much as £5.9 million over the past year, to 57 different agencies working in over 24 African countries. But giving money is just the start of our work. We look

carefully at all the grants proposals we receive, making sure we allocate the money in the most effective way.

'Then we keep in touch with the 400 or so "live" grants we have given, studying their reports to make sure lessons are learned and passed on. We are constantly building up relationships with many groups in Africa – as well as with the major aid offices in Brussels and Whitehall.

'We also aim to keep the people who support Comic Relief informed – organising trips to keep staff, celebrities and professionals appraised of the issues. And it means providing expertise and support for the film-makers who bring home our work – and inspire people to carry on giving.

New focus: a partnership approach.

'Comic Relief has always been committed to helping people tackle their own problems and to achieve long-term change. To reinforce this, we have launched the idea of 'partnership grants' to tackle the root causes of injustice and poverty.

'"Partnership" means that, instead of using a scatter gun approach to making grants- which can loose their impact amongst the enormous needs which have to be satisfied – we will be building deeper, long-term relationships with agencies working in Africa.

'This should mean we can begin to link people's basic needs to their basic rights – like helping dispossessed people in Elandskloof in South Africa to assert their rights over their own lands. It also means we have set ourselves the tough challenge of building more equal relationships with the organisations we fund – relationships which can survive the ups and downs of what may be a ten year programme to help poor people make lasting changes to their lives.'

Comic Relief continues to be a standard setter for grant makers both in the UK and overseas. In particular its concern to continually review and refine its programme is exemplary.

Exclusions The following exclusions apply for grant-making:

For UK Programme:

- academic research;
- general appeals;
- schools, colleges and hospitals;
- individuals;
- trips abroad;
- holidays and outings;
- promotion of religion;
- purchase of minibuses;
- services run by statutory/public authorities;

- medical research/equipment;
- bodies that are essentially fundraising organisations;
- minibuses;
- sporting activities;
- lunch clubs;
- general youth work.

For Africa Programme:

- general appeals;
- completed projects;
- agencies that aim to convert people to any kind of political or religious belief;
- academic or medical research;
- applications where the benefit goes to one person or where the cost to each person is too high;
- administration and costs based in the UK that are not directly related to the application, or that are too high in relation to overall costs;
- work where a large amount of funds will be spent outside Africa or on goods imported from outside Africa;
- constructing public buildings as a major part of the application;
- vehicles, unless you can prove that they are essential.

Applications Please send an SAE (39p) for an application pack for UK grants.

For Africa grants request a pack by phone or e-mail.

Association of Community Trusts and Foundations (ACTAF)

4 Bloomsbury Square,
London WC1A 2RL
Tel: 0171-831 0033

Correspondent Gaynor Humphreys, Director

General This is the national association for the relatively recent development of local community foundations in the UK. These bodies are independent charities but collectively represent an energetic movement. They seek, by calling on local loyalties, to build up a grant making capacity in their area, usually based on the accumulation of a permanent endowment.

A list of them follows, with their grant totals for 1997/98. Collectively they are growing fast and some may well become 'major' grant making charities during the currency of the present edition of this book. Five of the largest, marked with an asterisk in the list below, are already big enough to have their own entries in this book.

Berkshire Community Trust (£129,000)
Arlington Business Park
Theale
Reading RG7 4SA
(01189 303021)

The Birmingham Foundation (£15,300)
16 Westbourne Road
Edgbaston
Birmingham B15 3TR
(0121 456 3293)

Calderdale Community Foundation (£74,000)
Dean Clough Industrial Park
Halifax HX3 5AX
(01422 349700)

* *Cleveland Community Foundation* (£377,000)
Southlands Business Centre
Ormesby Road
Middlesbrough
Cleveland TS3 0HB
(01642 314200)

County Durham Foundation (£40,500)
Aykley Vale Chambers
Durham Road
Aykley Heads
Durham DH1 5NE
(0191 383 0055)

Dacorum Community Trust (£10,000)
48 High Street
Hemel Hempstead
Hertfordshire HP2 5HL
(01442 231396)

Derbyshire Community Foundation (£81,400)
The Arkwright Suite
University of Derby
Kedleston Road
Derby DE22 1GB
(01332 621348)

Essex Community Foundation (£85,500)
52A Moulsham Street
Chelmsford
Essex CM2 0JA
(01245 355947)

* *Greater Bristol Foundation* (£284,000)
PO Box 383
16 Clare street
Bristol BS99 5JG
(0117 921 1311)

Community Trust for Greater Manchester (£69,800)
PO Box 63
Beswick House
Beswick Row
Manchester M4 4JY
(0161 829 5542)

Hertfordshire Community Trust (£113,600)
(includes the area of Barnet)
2 Townsend Avenue
St Albans
Herts AL1 3SG
(01727 867906)

Isle of Dogs Community Foundation (£84,900)
PO Box 10449
London E14 8XT
(0171 531 1200)

* *Milton Keynes Community Trust* (£271,000)
Acorn House
381 Midsummer Boulevard
Central Milton Keynes MK9 3HP
(01908 690276)

* *Northern Ireland Voluntary Trust* (£8,500,000)
22 Mount Charles
Belfast BT7 1NZ
(01232 245927)

Oxfordshire Community Foundation (£21,200)
15-19 George Street
Oxford OX1 2AU
(01865 798666)

Royal Docks Trust, London (£80,000)
77/79 Rushey Green
Catford
London SE6 4AF
(0181 461 1500)

St Katherine & Shadwell Trust (£276,000)
1 Pennington Street
PO Box 1779
London E1 9BY
(0171 782 6962)

South East Wales Community Foundation (£454,600)
14-16 Merthyr Road
Whitchurch
Cardiff CF4 1DG
(0122 520250)

South Yorkshire Community Foundation (£62,200)
Heritage House
Heritage Park
55 Albert Terrace Road
Sheffield S6 3BR
(0114 273 1765)

Stevenage Community Trust (£33,100)
c/o MMS (Space Systems) Ltd
Gunnels Wood Road
Stevenage
Hertfordshire SG1 2AS
(1438 773368)

* *Tyne & Wear Foundation* (£1,244,000)
(includes the Northumberland Fund)
Cale Cross House
156 Pilgrim Street
Newcastle upon Tyne NE1 6SU
(0191 222 0945)

Wiltshire Community Foundation
   (£108,600)
48 New Park Street
Devizes
Wiltshire SN10 1DS
(01380 729284)

Exclusions Contact individual foundations

Applications Contact individual foundations

The Ernest Cook Trust

£563,000 (1997/98)

Rural environment, conservation techniques, general

Fairford Park, Fairford, Gloucestershire
GL7 4JH
Tel: 01285-713273; Fax: 01285 713417

Correspondent John G K Malleson, Agent and Secretary (Mrs J R Malleson, Grants Administrator)

Trustees Sir William Benyon, Chairman; Sir Jack Boles; C F Badcock; M C Tuely; A W M Christie-Miller.

Beneficial area UK, but with a special interest in Gloucestershire and in other areas where the trust owns land (see note below under 'General').

Information available Report and accounts with full grants list; policy and guidelines leaflet; annual review with an explanatory paragraph for each grant.

Summary Under 200 grants are made a year for amounts varying from £100 to £15,000. These are made as a contribution to capital or revenue costs and made be single payments or spread over up to three years. Beneficiaries are most often rural organisations running conservation or environmental projects with an educational/training angle. A substantial number of grants are awarded to groups outside this definition but usually possessing one of the attributes mentioned.

General The trust was founded as an educational charity by Ernest Cook in 1952 and endowed with 17,000 acres of land. This wealth arose from the family travel business, Thomas Cook & Sons, which he sold in the 1930's. Ernest Cook is known as one of the pioneers of the conservation movement and before establishing the trust he devoted much of his energy and money to preserving great houses, estates and works of art.

Today the main thrust of the trust's work continues to be support for educational organisations with a rural conservation theme (or vice-versa), although an 'other projects' category accounts for about 40% of charitable expenditure.

By the year ended March 1997, the trust's assets totalled over £37 million but income of only £997,000 was generated in the year. Such a low income is perhaps understandable given that much of the trust's investment is in land and farms and their mission is to conserve the rural environment rather than exploit it for maximum profit.

Some 177 grants were made totalling £487,000 and averaging £2,750. The largest award was for £15,000 (to the Elm Farm Research Centre). The following 12 organisations received £10,000 each, which together accounted for 25% of the grant expenditure.

- Farms for City Children;
- Soil Association; Landlife;
- Henry Doubleday Research Association;
- Amber Foundation;
- Cities in Schools;
- Comeback;
- Cotaswold Community;
- Farmington Institute;
- Robert Owen Foundation;
- British Federation of Young Choirs;
- Oxford Forestry Institute.

Most of the money went in awards of around £5,000, although a little under half of the grants were under £1,000. Donations in 1996/97 and 1997/98 are categorised in the table herewith.

Concerning these categories the trust says:

'*Educational schemes* which relate to rural conservation form the major part of the trusts' work, and the trustees' support for work in this field and for education and training in the arts, architecture and architectural crafts forms, as it were, an extension of their work in conservation. Also, but not least in importance, support is given to a few of the many projects submitted which have no rural bent, but which seem to the trustees to be particularly effective in their use of education as a catalyst to help alleviate hardship, handicap or social ills. It is a small way in which they feel that a country based organisation, which has many pressing concerns of its own, can look outside and give a little help to the towns and cities.

Countryside and Environment 'In view of the trust's association with land, emphasis is placed on the schemes which benefit rural areas. Grants in this category are made for educational work concerning conservation of the ecology of the countryside and for schemes which lead to a greater understanding of the countryside and rural life generally. Support is also given to responsible projects designed to increase an intelligent concern for the environment as a whole.

Other projects 'A number of projects which lie outside the immediate areas of ECT concern are supported simply upon their merits as outstanding schemes or because they show potential for small amounts of money to have maximum impact on worthwhile activities. Among these, consideration is given to particularly innovative schemes providing a combination of housing, education and training for homeless and unemployed young people. Exceptional grants are also made for educational projects which have a geographic connection or close link with the trust.

Arts, craft and architecture 'While it is not the policy of this trust to fund work connected with building or structural conservation, trustees encourage appreciation of architecture and support organisations providing training in

The Ernest Cook Trust				
	1997/98		**1996/97**	
Countryside and environment	£297,000	53%	£256,000	53%
Other projects	£173,000	31%	£150,000	31%
Arts, craft and architecture	£81,000	14%	£53,000	11%
Environmental research projects	£12,000	2%	£28,000	6%

practical conservation skills. Support is also given to rural craft training schemes. Funding is rarely given to community arts projects, concerts, festivals, theatre, dance and sculpture projects.

Environmental research 'Grants for research are made to universities or other relevant institutions. Projects supported reflect the trust's concern for the rural environment.'

Exclusions The trustees do not award grants for charitable purposes which are not educational or to organisations which do not hold charitable status. Projects allied to medicine and health are not supported nor are requests for general funding or from individuals. Building, restoration and conversion programmes, sport and recreational activities and overseas projects all lie outside the trust's usual field of interest. Because of the large number of Trusts for Nature Conservation and Farming & Wildlife Advisory Groups, support for these organisations is largely restricted to those based in counties in which ECT owns land. Awards are not made to agricultural colleges.

While exceptions are occasionally made to the above restrictions, these are confined to projects meriting special consideration.

Applications Proposals are welcome throughout the year. There is no set form for these but they should be submitted by the person directing the project and information should be given to a maximum of four sides of A4 paper. Applicants are advised to focus their request on a specific educational need.

Trustees meet in the Spring and Autumn to consider proposals and additional meetings are held at three monthly intervals to consider applications under £2,000. All applications accepted for submission to trustees will be acknowledged, but it is regretted that those not being put forward will be acknowledged only when a self-addressed envelope has been enclosed. Applicants are welcome to discuss a project on the telephone prior to submitting a request.

The majority of grants are paid within 2-4 months of commitment, small grants being paid more quickly. Recipients of traditional grants are usually given up to 12 months to meet the provisos. Reports are requested on all work supported by grants of over £5,000 and payment of annual grant instalments is dependent upon work undertaken in the previous year.

The Sidney & Elizabeth Corob Charitable Trust

£330,000 (1995/96)

Jewish charities, art, general

62 Grosvenor Street,
London W1X 9DA
Tel: 0171-499 4301

Correspondent Mrs S Berg

Trustees S Corob; E Corob; S Berg.

Beneficial area UK.

Information available In September 1998 the most recent report and accounts on file at the Charity Commission were those for 1995/96.

General The trust gives most of its largest grants for specifically Jewish causes, for scholarship more commonly than for welfare. The rest of the grants are more widely spread and there are a substantial number of awards of less than £1,000 whose beneficiaries are not given.

The 1995/96 grants list was headed by an unusually large grant for of £75,000 to 'University College' (probably, though not neccessarily, the London college of that name, and for undisclosed purposes). No other grants in either that or the previous year were for more than £25,000.

The 1995/96 list of grants was otherwise headed by the following awards:

Oxford Centre for Postgraduate Hebrew Studies	*(£25,000)*
Oxford Centre for Hebrew and Jewish Studies	*(£15,000)*
Jews College	*(£14,000)*
United Synagogues	*(£13,000)*
Jewish Care	*(£10,000)*

Amounts between £10,000 and £1,000 included grants to a number of arts charities, among others, including the Courtauld Gallery, English Touring Opera, Live Music Now and Glyndebourne Opera. there were also a few environmental grants including one to the Jerusalem Botanical Garden.

A further £51,000 was distributed in grants of less than £1,000.

Applications In writing to the correspondent.

Cripplegate Foundation

£701,000 (1997)

Social welfare in Cripplegate/Islington, London

76 Central Street, London EC1V 8AG
Tel: 0171-336 8062; Fax: 0171-336 8201

Correspondent David Green, Clerk

Governors Rev David Rhodes; Gavyn Arthur; Miss Stella Currie; Mr Roger Daily-Hunt; Mrs Barbara Riddell; Christopher Calnan; Pat Haynes; Mrs Maxine Roberts; Mrs Rosemary Boyes-Watson; Mr John Broadbent; Robert Cooper; Miss Caroline Phillips; Mr Willis Hunt; Mr Kweku de Graft-Johnson; Dr Bryan Green; Nicholas Nightingale; Jack Sheehan.

Beneficial area The ancient parish of St Giles, Cripplegate, London, the former parish of St Luke Old Street as constituted in 1732 (broadly speaking the southern part of Islington and the north of the City of London), and now extended to include the Islington Council Wards of Barnsbury, Bunhill,

Cripplegate Foundation

Grants in 1997

Physical & Mental Disabilities	£55,000	8%	8 grants
The Elderly	£41,000	6%	5 grants
The Young	£94,000	13%	18 grants
Education & Training	£181,000	26%	16 grants
Arts & Leisure	£41,000	6%	7 grants
Community Work	£24,000	3%	1 grant
Social Welfare	£132,000	19%	10 grants
Health	£25,000	4%	3 grants
Individuals	£107,000	15%	424 grants

Clerkenwell, Canonbury East, Canonbury West, St Mary, St Peter and Thornhill.

Information available Full reports and accounts are available from the foundation. Guidelines and application forms also available.

Summary After under spending their income for some years, the foundation has decided to extend its area of benefit into eight wards in Islington. The foundation is already accepting applications from this enlarged area but recommends that applicants first contact the grants officer.

In 1997 about £600,000 went in 70 grants to organisations. Grants are only given in the area of benefit and usually support groups involved in social welfare, health, community, arts and leisure, education and training, youth, elderly, and disabilities.

From 1997-2000 the needs of young people will be a high priority.

General Established in 1891, the foundation has recently enlarged its area of benefit, as above. The original area of benefit is the ancient parish of St Giles, Cripplegate and the ancient parish of St Luke's, Old Street, in modern times relating to an area that runs from the Barbican in the south nearly up to the Angel and Islington. Since 1998 this has been extended further into the London Borough of Islington, to now include the Islington Council Wards of Barnsbury, Bunhill, Clerkenwell, Canonbury East, Canonbury West, St Mary, St Peter and Thornhill. The population served has consequently increased, from 11,000 to 68,000;

The 1998/99 guidelines for applicants reads as follows

'Grants are made:

- for the relief of need, hardship and distress
- to provide facilities for recreation or leisure-time occupations that promote social welfare
- or for other charitable purposes which are for the general benefit of the inhabitants of the area.

'The governors are particularly looking for projects:

1. Addressing an identified need in the main area of benefit
2. Addressing a need not covered by other local projects
3. Which draw funds and resources from other sources
4. Which provide a benefit at a reasonable cost per head

'The governors have identified the needs of young people as a high priority in the coming three years. Applications are sought from schools and from organisations working with young people, whether within formal education or outside it. The foundation has adopted clear guidelines for the funding of the 30 schools in the extended area of benefit. The objective is to assist in raising the levels of achievement and to enrich the pupils experience of the curriculum, for example through projects in art or music. The foundation also provides grants to assist schools in addressing social issues such as bullying, racism or awareness of drugs. Projects which will work in more than one school will be especially welcome.'

The foundation has been interested in being pro-active in grant making and has commissioned a number of surveys and conferences to assess the needs of different groups in the area of benefit. In 1993 the foundation commissioned a survey of its area, and followed it up with a conference in 1994 for those working with young people. Another survey was commissioned in 1996 to report on the views of older people about the services in the area.

Grants in 1997

Grants in 1997 are categorised in the table herewith.

Major grants were as follows:

Physical and mental disabilities: Islington Mencap (£21,000 towards the cost of the salary for the new post of Director); and Federation of Artistic and Creative Therapy (£15,000 towards salary and running costs).

Elderly people: Cripplegate and St Luke's Holiday Scheme (£38,000 to provide seaside holidays for elderly people in 1997 and 1998)

Young people: Islington Boat Club (£30,000 towards salary and running costs of deputy leader post over two years); and grants of £10,000 each to LB of Islington Holiday Grants Committee (contribution to cost of five area of benefit summer play schemes), London City YMCA (towards running costs of their WHY projects and especially their detached youth work project in Braithwaite House) and Manor Garden's Youth Project (towards the cost of a year long video project for young people with disabilities).

Education and training: £50,000 each to City and Islington College (cost of refurbishing their premises) and Guildhall School of Music and Drama (bursary fund for post graduate students over two years); and £20,000 to Central Foundation Boys School (three grants for refurbishment, salary and running costs).

Arts and leisure: Little Angel Marionette Theatre (£20,000, contribution to the refurbishment of workshop and storage areas, and to develop an education centre).

Community work: Islington Voluntary Action Council (£24,000 towards salary and running costs)

Social welfare: Clerkenwell Citizens Advice Bureau (£62,000 towards salary and running costs); Bedford Institute Association (£34,000 in two grants towards rent and salary costs for New Life Electrics); and Salters City Foyer (£10,000 towards capital costs).

Health: Dr G Neaman's Practice (£11,000 towards the cost of the salary for their Practice Assistant).

Exclusions

- National charities and organisations, or organisations outside the area of benefit, unless they are carrying out a piece of work in the area of benefit
- Schemes or activities which would be regarded as relieving either central government or local authorities of their statutory responsibilities
- Grants to replace cuts in funding made by the local authority or others
- Medical research or equipment
- National fundraising appeals or appeals to provide an endowment
- Advancement of religion and religious groups, unless they offer non-religious services to the local community
- Animal welfare
- Retrospective grants
- Commercial or business activities
- Grants for concerts or other events held in the Church of St Giles-without-Cripplegate

Applications Application forms are available. The foundation welcomes a preliminary approach by telephone from charities, organisations or individuals who are unsure how to complete their application form or if they are eligible for a grant. The best people to speak to are Kristina Glenn, Grants Officer, or David Green, the Clerk to the Governors. Before an application goes to the governors an applicant will normally be visited and should allow time for this when applying

Applications for less than £12,000 are considered at grant committee meetings in February, June and October. Applications for £12,000 or more are considered by the full board in April, September and December. Application forms are required to be returned at least one month before the meetings.

The Cripps Foundation

£2,928,000 (1997/98)

Education, healthcare and churches in Northamptonshire, Cambridge University

Mellors Basden and Co,
8th Floor Aldwych House, 71/91
Aldwych, London WC2B 4HN
Tel: 0171-242 2444

Correspondent The Secretary

Trustees Sir Humphrey Cripps, Chairman; E J S Cripps.

Beneficial area Northamptonshire, Cambridge University.

Information available The trust did not send its accounts on request (as it is required to by law) and reports and accounts up to 1995/96 only were on file at the Charity Commission in the summer of 1998. On seeing a draft of this entry, a copy of more recent accounts was offered for an exorbitant £25.

Summary Almost all the money is given in a few very large awards, probably only to organisations already well known to the trustees. The foundation has a small capital base and most of its income comes from donations from the Chartwell Group of Companies. Income in 1995/96 totalled £430,000 (£401,000 gift and £29,000 from investments).

The foundation says that its major recent grants have been as follows:

£2,000,000, Northampton School for Boys (£2,000,000 also in the previous year)
£840,000, Magdalen College, Cambridge
£50,000 Peterborough Cathedral.

In addition there were seven grants in excess of £1,000, totalling £37,000.

The foundation says that some or all of these payments were for building works (with sums of this size, it would be nice to know what was being built).

The accounts list for 1995/96 gives the 'three principal grants' as £230,000 to the Northampton School for Boys (£10,000) and the Old Northamptonians Association (£220,000), £88,000 to Magdalen College Cambridge and £50,000 to the Peterborough Diocesan Board of Finance. However, a separate grants list reveals further donations to Queen's College Cambridge and Northampton School for Girls amounting

to £282,000. All other grants were for less than £6,000 and included £5,000 to the Northampton Choral Foundation, £5,500 to St Mary's Church, Roade and £5,000 to the Trust for Victoria County History of Northamptonshire.

The trust says:

'Support is generally concentrated on, and committed to major single projects which would not otherwise be undertaken. The foundation does not welcome applications generally because it has a long list of projects it would like to support already when funds are available, and as it concentrates on major projects it has few funds for minor purposes.'

Sir Humphrey Cripps, the founder and chairman is, or has been, a Governor of Northampton School for Boys (where he was schooled) and of Northampton School for Girls, a member of the trust for Peterborough Cathedral, and an honorary fellow of the following Cambridge Colleges; St John's, Selwyn, Queen's and Magdalen.

As the major grants in 1996/97 and previous years went to these organisations, it seems likely that applications for large grants are unlikely to succeed unless the organisation has a personal connection with Sir Humphrey.

The trust notes that previous entries in this book have been inaccurate; in the absence of verifiable and legally required information this, unfortunately was probably true. For this entry, some more information has been made available, for which we are grateful, but it should all have been on file, in up to date form, at the Charity Commission.

Exclusions No grants are made to individual applicants or to organisations based outside the beneficial area.

Applications To the correspondent in writing, but see above.

The Harry Crook Foundation

£243,000 (1996/97)

Education, general, in Bristol

Veale Wasbrough, Solicitors, Orchard Court, Bristol, BS1 5DS
Tel: 01179-252020

Correspondent Ms J Pierce

Trustees J O Gough (chair); T G Bickle; R G West; Mrs I Wollen; D J Bellew.

Beneficial area Bristol.

Information available Accounts on file at the Charity Commission. Grants list without narrative.

General Established in 1963 by Dr. Harry Crook, who endowed it with shares in his Kleen-E-Zee Brush Co. Ltd, famed for its door to door brush salesmen. The trustees 'consider it their duty to maintain and support those causes which were dear to Harry Crook's heart... by supporting charitable causes which serve the city of Bristol or its immediate environs, or which are personally known to the trustees'.

Assets for the foundation amount to £3.3 million, generating an income of £110,000. Grants and donations, however, were more than income at £243,132, a trend which has been mirrored in previous years. The average size of grant was for £2-3,000, with much the largest being to St Peter's Hospice (£150,000).

A large number of grants were given to youth organisations such as: the Bristol Boys Club £7,700), Boys Brigade (£5,000), Bristol Sea Cadets Corp (£2,500), Duke of Edinburgh (£2,000), Explorers (£1,600 in 16 grants) and the St. Paul's Holiday Camp Project (£400).

Many grants were also given for civic/ social organisations. Examples include: the Salvation Army (£5,000), NSPCC (£2,000), St. Johns Ambulance (£2,000), Addiction Recovery Agency (£1,000), Eastern Family Centre (£1,000) and Walingham House (£1,000).

A substantial number of grants were also given to charities concerned with the disabled or for health. Major grants include: the Multiple Sclerosis Society (£5,000), Bristol Area Stroke Foundation (£5,000) and £1,000 each to the National Listening Library and St. Mary's Hospital.

A few large grants were given to educational organisations, such as St. George's Musical Trust (£30,000) and Colsten Girls School (£8,000).

Other grants included Bristol Music Space (£4,500), Bristol Age Concern (£2,000) and Sandwells OAP (£1,000).

The grants are nearly all to the Bristol area. Grants to the Boys Brigade, Salvation Army and the St. Johns Ambulance were for the local branches in Bristol.

Applications In writing to the correspondent. The trustees meet twice a year in November and July, but applications can be sent at any time as there is a vetting process prior to the trustees meetings.

Itzchok Meyer Cymerman Trust Ltd

£819,000 (1995/96)

Jewish Orthodox education, other Jewish organisations

22 Overlea Road, London E5

Correspondent I M Cymerman

Trustees Governors: Mrs H L Bondi; I M Cymerman; M D Cymerman; Mrs R Cymerman; Mrs S Heitner.

Beneficial area UK and overseas.

Information available No accounts are on file at the Charity Commission later than 1995/96. They include a list of grants over £1,000.

General The objective of the trust is 'to advance religion in accordance with Orthodox Jewish faith and general charity'. In practice all funds are awarded to Jewish organisations, religious or otherwise.

In 1995/96 the trust's assets totalled £3 million and their income was £680,000. 45 grants were made for over £1,000 and an unknown number of awards were made for less than £1,000. However, the latter amounted to only £9,000, or 1% of total grant expenditure. The trust does not categorise beneficiaries and the cause they are involved in is usually not readily apparent from their name alone. Of the recipients whose mission was implicit within their title there were two schools, a ladies guild, immigrant aid charities and handicapped homes.

Five donations of over £50,000 amounted to £358,000 (44% of total charitable expenditure) and ten awards between £20,000 and £49,999 accounted for a further £295,000 (36%).

The largest award in the year went to Agudas Beis Haknesses D'Casidei Gur Beis Ovos for the Aged (£100,000) and other substantial gifts were to: Yeshivas Chidushei Harim (£34,000), Gur Trust Building Fund (£33,000), Yeshiva Lezerim Torah Etz Chaim (£30,000), and the Russian Immigrant Aid Fund (£26,000).

Applications In writing to the correspondent.

The Roald Dahl Foundation

£418,000 (1996/97)

Haematology, neurology, literacy

92 High Street, Great Missenden, Bucks HP16 0AN
Tel: 01494-890 465

Correspondent Julia Mayo

Trustees Felicity Dahl, Chairman; Quentin Blake; Ernest Cole; Martin Goodwin.

Beneficial area UK.

Information available Accounts; guidelines; grants list from 1992 to date; recent projects list.

Summary About 40 grants are made each year. These are usually between £1,000 and £60,000. Grants are predominantly aimed at young people. Within the medical care category, grant-making is strictly limited to the fields of neurology and haematology. A number of small grants are made to individuals and families to assist with medical care.

General The foundation was established in 1991 by Mrs F Dahl in honour of her late husband. The aims of the foundation reflect the history of the Dahl family: 'literacy because it was Roald's crusade, neurology, because brain damage has so often struck the Dahl family and haematology because leukaemia was the cause of Roald's death'.

The foundation's income comes from fundraising events, donations, royalties and investment, a welcome example of a trust doing more than rely on its endowment. 77% of income in 1996/97 was raised through the annual 'Readathon', a national sponsored reading event supported by the Arts Council. Fundraising, publicity, management and administration costs totalled £139,000 or 20% of income, £800 per grant. 154 grants were paid in the year and the average award was £2,700. 43% of the money was disbursed in nine grants for £20,000 or over and 18% in awards between £10,000 and £19,999. 122 small grants to individuals amounted to £40,000, 10% of charitable expenditure.

Breakdown of grants paid in 1996/97:

Haematology		
– organisations	£70,000	17%
– individuals	£19,000	5%
Neurology		
– organisations	£207,000	50%
– individuals	£21,000	5%
Literacy	£101,000	24%
Total	£417,525	100%

The foundations says

'The aims of the foundation are to provide help for problems for which Roald felt a particular concern. They include problems of literacy, neurology and haematology. Each year the foundation will raise an amount of money for chosen projects in these three fields. The projects will be chosen by the trustees with the help of an advisory board, either from outside applications or internal ideas.

'In general we aim to provide help to organisations to whom funds are not readily available, We prefer to help small or new organisations in favour of long-established, large or national organisations.

Neurology and haematology 'In these fields we are keen to help children and young people up to the age of 25 (and their families) who suffer from blood disorders which are not cancer related, from epilepsy and head injury. Specifically, grants may be made for:

- pump-prime funding of specialist paediatric nursing and other care, especially where there is an emphasis on community care, for a maximum of two years. We will require information about the source of permanent funding after the two year period.
- assistance to residential and day care centres for children and young people who come into the above medical categories. Such grants would normally be awarded on a project basis.
- small items of medical equipment that will allow the patient to be cared for in the home, with community care/hospital back-up;
- individual grants of £50 to £500 to the children in the above categories from families that are suffering financial hardship, for specified needs.'

Literacy 'Through its association with the Readathon, the national sponsored reading event, the foundation is already actively involved in promoting literacy throughout the UK. In the next few years we will be particularly interested in making grants for:

- after school clubs for children and their families who would like to improve their literacy skills;

- centres which offer or wish to initiate literacy programmes for young people (16-25) as part of their normal activities.
- computer/technological assistance for reading for the partially sighted, blind or head injured.'

Grant size The range is wide. At the moment, the individual grants vary from £50 to £500 and those to organisations from £1,000 to £25,000.

The nine grants over £20,000 were awarded to:

- Education Extra (£46,000);
- John Grooms Association (£32,000);
- Children's Hospital Manchester (£29,000);
- Primary Immunodeficiency Association (£26,000);
- Haemophilia Society (£25,000);
- University of Glasgow, Department of Neurosurgery (£25,000);
- Newcastle General Hospital (£22,000);
- National Society for Epilepsy (£20,000);
- Book Trust (£20,000).

Exclusions No support will be given for:

- general appeals from large, well established charities or national appeals for large building projects;
- research in any field;
- any organisations which do not have charitable status or exclusively charitable aims;
- statutory bodies;
- core funding;
- outside UK;
- school or higher education fees.

Applications

Organisations

By application form with a covering letter if you feel that any other information is relevant.

If you are writing from a hospital regarding a new post or small items of equipment, the application must be signed by the relevant consultant or head of department.

We endeavour to visit as many applicants as possible, but we may simply telephone for more information.

The trustees meet regularly throughout the year to discuss grants. You will be contacted shortly after your application haas been received and told, if your application is within the criteria, when it will be considered.'

Individuals

Applications should come to the small grants manager via a social worker or health care professional, using the attached form.

Our maximum payment is £500 in this category and only in very exceptional circumstances will we fund holidays.'

The Daiwa Anglo-Japanese Foundation

£251,000 (excluding scholarships, 1996/97)

Anglo-Japanese relations

Daiwa Foundation Japan House, 13/14 Cornwall Terrace, London NW1 4QP
Tel: 0171-486 4348;
Fax: 0171-486 2914; E-mail:
daiwafdn@clus1.ulcc.ad.uk

Correspondent Christopher Everett, Director General

Trustees Lord Roll of Ipsden; Y Chino; Lady Adrian; Professor Sir Alec Broers; Lord Carrington; Akio Morita; N P Clegg; H Fujii.

Beneficial area UK, Japan.

Information available An information leaflet is available from the foundation. Full report and accounts are on file at the Charity Commission.

General The foundation was set up in 1988 by Daiwa Securities Co Ltd on the initiative of its then chairman, Mr Yoshitoki Chimo.

It funds a number Anglo-Japanese cultural exhibitions, concerts, meetings and events. The foundation has three objectives:

- Advancement of UK and Japanese citizens understanding of each others peoples and culture
- Award of scholarships and maintenance allowances for UK or Japanese students to travel abroad to pursue education.
- Grants to institutions involved in promoting education in the UK or Japan, or research into cultural, historical, medical and scientific subjects and publication of such research.

In 1996/97 assets were £32 million, generating an income of £1.5 million. Donations totalled £629,000 and were subdivided as follows:

Grants	*£251,000*
Scholarships	*£324,000*
Awards	*£54,000*

Examples of the wide range of grant giving can be seen in awards of £2,000 to Place Theatre, London (towards the cost of including Japanese dance programme); £2,000 to Mugenkyo (as a contribution to the Taiko drumming group Mugenkyo taking their drumming group to students outside London); £1,000 to Campion School, Northampton (for the purchase of books in Japanese language for the resource centre); £1,000 to Durham Johnston School (towards the annual student exchange with schools in Fukushima, Oita, and Osaka in Japan); and £750 to Penny Underwood (as part of a contribution to study pruning tree training and maintenance techniques in Japan).

Applications Applicants are encouraged to write in their own style to explain their project, and should include the budget and information on any other sources of help available. Applicants are interviewed before recommendations are made to the trustees. Applications are considered quarterly.

Applications from Japan should be sent to Tomohiro Abe, Daiwa Anglo-Japanese Foundation, Nishigotanda 7-13-5, Shinagawa-ku, Tokyo 141.

Baron Davenport's Charity Trust

£535,000 (to institutions, 1996)

Children, almshouses/ residential homes, in the Midlands

Portman House, 5/7 Temple Row West, Birmingham B2 5NY
Tel: 0121-236 8004; Fax: 0121-233 2500

Correspondent J R Prichard, Secretary

Trustees G R Willcox; A C S Hordern; P A Gough; P Heath. There is also one ex-officio trustee, Mrs S Wood,the Director of Finance of the City of Birmingham.

Beneficial area Birmingham and the Midlands.

Information available Accounts, without the required narrative report or any details of grants: See below.

General The trust made 453 grants to institutions in 1997, worth £535,000. The money is required to have been divided equally between 'charities in Birmingham and the Midland Counties benefiting children' and 'almshouses or homes for the aged poor in or near Birmingham.

By conscious decision of the trustees there is no information whatsoever as the policies followed in allocating this money; the financial statements do not include details of material grants to institutions as required by the SORP. The trustees have said to the Charity Commission that such disclosure would prejudice the furtherance of the purposes of both recipient institutions and the trust. They also consider that such disclosure would be detrimental to their discretionary powers.

The trust has long been opaque, but this statement takes it to new levels of reticence; it most surprising that it has been agreed by an officer of the City of Birmingham, an authority with a good policy of transparency in its finances.

On the basis of past practice, the actual grants made have probably been far from contentious, and disclosure is unlikely to reveal anything more untoward than a taste for conservatism in grant making. However trustees in many foundations have long sought, through secrecy, to avoid the embarrassment of having to explain why they have favoured one application over another, and this is the most likely explanation for the course they have adopted.

The Charity Commission has absurdly accepted this situation, which nullifies its own years of supposed effort, through the SORP, for greater transparency in the grant making field. The list of material grants, which was sent to the Commission for their private use only, was in fact placed on the public file, but was specifically removed before these editors could see it.

In the previous edition of this book, the grants to organisations in 1995/96, the most recent year for which proper information is available, were described as follows:

Between 200 and 300 grants are given to children's organisations in each half year, none for more than £2,000 and most for amounts between £250 and £1,000. All kinds of groups are supported, from children's camps and boys' clubs to local branches of charities. About two thirds of the grants are recurrent, but this still means that many new awards are made each year.

Approximately 50 grants are given in each half year's distribution under the heading Almshouses, but the great majority of these are recurrent and only a handful of new beneficiaries appear each year. The grants are more widely spread than the heading would suggest and cover a variety of residential accommodation for elderly people in need. Grants are mostly from £1,000 to a maximum of £5,000.

Exclusions Areas outside the Midlands.

Applications In writing to the correspondent. The closing date for applications is March 15th and September 15th. Applications should contain details of the need, the cost, the expected shortfall in finances and a copy of the latest accounts. Unsuccessful applicants are notified of the trustees' decision. Widows, spinsters etc. should contact the secretary for an application form.

The Gwendoline & Margaret Davies Charity

£263,000 (1997/98)

Not known

Perthybu Offices, Sarn, Newtown, Powys SY16 4EP
Tel: 01686-670 404

Correspondent Mrs S Hamer

Trustees Hon I E E Davies; R D Davies; Hon J H Davies; Dr J A Davies; T A Owen.

Beneficial area Wales

Information available Accounts, without the required narrative report or list of grants.

General The only information available about grant making is set out under 'Applications' below, making this the briefest description in this book in the twelve years of its publication

Exclusions Grants to registered charities only.

Applications The trustees consider appeals on an individual basis ... There are no application forms as the trustees prefer to receive letters from applicants setting out the following information:

- Is the organisation a registered charity?
- Details of the reason for the application – the type of work etc.

- The cost.
- How much has been raised so far towards the cost?
- The source of the sums raised.
- A copy of the last audited accounts if available.
- Any other information that the applicant may consider would help the application.

Unsuccessful appeals are not informed unless a s.a.e is enclosed.

The Diana, Princess of Wales Memorial Fund

£4,500,000 (estimated for 1999)

Welfare, especially of children

The County Hall, Westminster Bridge Road, London SE1 7PB
Tel: 0171-902 5500
Fax. 0171-902 5511

Correspondent Dr Andrew Purkis

Trustees Lady Sarah McCorquodale, President; Anthony Julius, Chairman; Michael Gibbins, Treasurer; Earl Cairns; John Eversley; Baroness Pitkeathley; John Reizenstein; Christopher Spence; Nalini Varma.

Beneficial area UK, including UK organisations working overseas.

Information available Grant application pack and grant criteria. Information supplied by the fund for this entry.

Summary From early 1999 the fund will be making grants under the headings listed below. They may be for capital or revenue, and typically funding will be given for three to five years and for amounts between £15,000 and £100,000 a year. In addition, consideration will be given to one off grants for conferences, publications, evaluation and dissemination.

Details of a separate international funding programme were expected to be finalised in December 1998, too late for inclusion in this book.

The funding priority for 1999 is help for children and young people between the ages of 12 and 18 who have suffered personal loss. The fund will consider applications from organisations that support work in the following categories:

- Children/young people whose parent or prime carer has died
- Children/young people whose sibling had died
- Young carers who have lost the person for whom they cared
- Children/young people with a parent or prime carer in prison
- Refugee children alone
- Children/young people who have lost a family member as a result of extreme violence
- Children/young people in care

General In the terms of the present book, and despite media coverage of heroic extent, this new fund is not particularly unusual. Its grant making priorities for 1999 seem interesting and well chosen, but similar in kind to those of many other trusts. The proposed levels of grant are substantial, but not outside the usual range. The most unusual, and very welcome, feature is the trust's willingness to consider grants over a period of up to five years: the now conventional three year maximum is proving ever less satisfactory, in part because of its very universality.

The origins of the fund have been sufficiently public not to need rehearsal here. By the Autumn of 1998 the value of the endowment had reached about £65 million , which could generate an income for grant making of perhaps £4-5 million a year

'The trustees intend that annual grant giving should be a minimum of £4 million to £5 million with approximately 25% going to UK based organisations working in other countries.'

The first grants, made in March 1998, were to the charities with which the Princess was most closely connected, as follows (all grants in the region of £1 million):

- Centrepoint
- English National Ballet
- Great Ormond Street Hospital for Children
- The Leprosy Mission
- National Aids Trust
- Royal Marsden NHS Trust

A grant of £1 million has also been awarded to the Osteopathic Centre for Children in recognition of the 'Sweet Pea Appeal' that Diana, Princess of Wales was to have launched to raise money for a new centre in September 1997.

A further sum of £5 million was put aside for the 95 other charities with which the Princess was personally involved, but to a lesser extent. This money is separate from the programmes outlined above.

Future funding priorities will be based on the wider charitable objectives of the fund, 'to benefit and charity or any purposes which are charitable, with regard (but without fettering the trustees' discretion) to those charities and charitable causes with which Diana, Princess of Wales was associated during her life.'

'The main funding themes are:
- Displaced people; this would include children and adults made homeless, or deprived of rights for other reasons (e.g. young people living in residential care);
- People at the margins of society (this includes those who are jobless, homeless or excluded through public prejudice or through mental and physical disability, addiction and disease)
- Survivors of conflict and those requiring conflict mediation (this could include land mine survivors and those affected by family strife)
- Dying and bereaved people.'

Readers should note that 'grants are available ONLY for specific subjects within these themes, as selected by the trustees from time to time (*and as set out above for 1999. Ed.*)

Exclusion

What will not fund:

- Projects outside our funding priorities for 1999
- Individuals
- Services run by statutory or public authorities*
- Organisations that are principally fundraising bodies
- Arts and sporting activities which give little benefit in terms of social inclusion
- Academic research
- Schools, colleges and hospitals
- Repayment of loans
- Promotion of religious beliefs
- Rapid response to emergency situations
- Retrospective funding
- Debts
- Capital expenditure for religious institutions or buildings
- Party political organisations
- Fees for professional fundraisers

*While we will not fund activities which are the responsibilty of any statutory agency, for example a government department, Local Council or Health Authority and we will not fund projects that are direct replacements of statutory funding, we welcome applicants for collaborative projects and those involving both the voluntary and public sectors.

Applications Send a large 39p SAE tot he above address for the application pack.

The Dinwoodie Settlement

£122,000 (but see below, 1997)

Postgraduate medical education and research

5 East Pallant, Chichester, PO19 1TS
Tel: 01243-786 111

Corespondent The Clerk

Trustees W A Fairbairn; Dr J M Fowler; Miss C Webster.

Beneficial area UK.

Information available Good Report and Accounts available on file.

General The trustees set out to 'assist ... postgraduate medical education, primarily by improvements to the buildings of independently controlled Postgraduate Medical Centres (PMCs) and by enabling a limited number of postgraduates to widen their knowledge through medical research and by obtaining appropriate experience in hospitals overseas'. They also state that they will continue their 'policy of identifying and supporting significant projects in the field of medical education and research.'

The charity is larger than is suggested by the grant figure quoted above, though the actual levels depend on the demand for sand and gravel, the trust endowment being in the form of mineral rights. Income was £336,000 in 1996/7, but as the trustees may commit themselves to contribute up to a maximum of £1 million on any one PMC project, the total for grants may vary greatly from year to year – £0.5 million was given in 1995/96 for Stafford's PMC alone. Because of existing involvements, further grants for PMC building projects may only be on the basis of construction after 2000.

Grants in 1996/97 were as follows:

St George's Hospital Medical School	
- *Research fellowship grant*	£20,000
- *Travel fellowship grant*	£2,000
Mid Staffordshire Medical Education Centre	£50,000
Worthing PMC trust Ltd	£50,000

To date, up to two fellowships at a time have been awarded to postgraduates closely associated with St George's Hospital Medical School's Department of Surgery. The trustees have recently decided to consider applications from further afield, but funds earmarked for fellowships are fully committed until 2001.

Applications In writing to the correspondent.

The Djanogly Foundation

£599,000 (1996/97)
General, Jewish charities

Serck House, 60/61 Trafalgar Square, London WC2N 5DS

Correspondent The Secretary

Trustees Sir Harry Djanogly; M S Djanogly.

Beneficial area UK, with a special interest in Nottinghamshire and Israel.

Information available Accounts are on file at the Charity Commission, with grants list but without the required analysis or explanation.

Summary Grants vary from around £100 to £150,000. Most funds are disbursed in a few large grants. Awards of £10,000 or more are normally only made to organisations assisted by the foundation in previous years. Beneficiaries are varied, but there is preference for Nottingham, education, arts, Jewish charities and medicine.

General The foundation was established in 1980 by Harry and Michael Djanogly. In 1997 its assets totalled £21,262,000 and income generated in the year was £1,268,000. The 1996/97 annual report says simply that 'the trustees policy is to sponsor development in medicine, education, social welfare and the arts. To relieve distress and to promote the welfare of the aged and young'.

Around 70 grants were made in the year, the six largest of which amounted to £482,000 or 80% of all grant expenditure. They went to:

The Jerusalem Foundation £72,000 (£147,000 in 1995/96); Nottingham City Technical College £67,000 (£15,000);

Nottingham Trent University £125,000; Royal Academy of Arts £25,000 (£23,000 in 1994/95); University of Nottingham £153,000 (£157,000); Wordsworth Trust £40,000.

About half of the grants were for £500 or under and these went to a wide range of organisations, for example: Barbican Centre, £250; British Horological Foundation, £25; Crimestoppers Trust, £500; and World Jewish Relief, £200 (£80). Five mid-sized awards were made to: George Spencer School, Nottingham £12,500 (£46,000); Jewish Care £11,000 (£10,000); London Sympathy (sic) Orchestra £10,000; Mencap £15,000 (£10,000); and Weizmann Institute £10,000 (£11,000).

Applications In writing to the correspondent.

The Drapers' Charitable Fund

£2,222,000 (April 1996/July 1997–16 months)
General

Drapers' Hall, Throgmorton Street, London EC2N 2DQ
Tel: 0171-588 5001; Fax: 0171-628 1988

Correspondent Miss D J Thomas, Charities Administrator

Trustees The Drapers' Company

Beneficial area UK, with a special interest in the City and adjacent parts of London.

Information available Report and accounts with full grants list and narrative review of grant-making.

Summary 'Our strategy has been re-organised following a substantial contraction in funding and the need to reduce our administration costs. ... No unsolicited requests for funding are being considered. Energies are now being focused on a relatively few causes where there is a particularly strong relationship with the Company or its members.' The charity will 'select specific charitable activities, types of project and geographic areas on a regular basis for targeted funding. Particular charitable organisations or projects will be invited to submit an application for consideration. ... The areas initially selected for emphasis are appeals benefiting Northern Ireland or service charities.'

General The fund was set up by the Drapers' Company in 1959. It manages 24 charities: 4 general charities; 5 almshouse charities; 12 education charities; and 2 poor relief charities. In the past, grants have varied from less than a hundred pounds to over half a million pounds and there has been no typical amount. Beneficiaries have generally been national charities, and organisations where there has been a connection with the City or Mayor of London, with the Company or its members, or with the drapery or textile trades.

The charity's new practice of being wholly proactive, and not even considering unsolicited applications, is acceptable, even welcome to these editors, provided that the alternative process is thorough and informed, as should be visible in future annual reports. Unfortunately, too often in the past a 'particularly strong relationship' with Livery companies has been a reference to independent schools catering for the already most prosperous parts of society, and a similar relationship with their members has meant good connections with rich City folk – very difficult to achieve for organisations outside London and the Home Counties. It will be interesting to see to what extent this charity succeeds in rising above such precedents. Its initial emphasis on Northern Ireland is a good omen.

In the light of the policy changes active from April 1997, and noted in the summary above, information about past grants may not be a guide to future awards. It is nevertheless given here as a matter of record.

In 1996/97, over 250 donations were made. Management and administration costs were a high £304,000 -14 pence per £1 donated, £1,200 per grant to charities. However, the charity has since said that it plans to reduce administration costs. At least 75% of the total value of grants in the period was disbursed to schools and colleges – £1,283,000 (61% of the overall total) was paid in four grants to an independent school group in Wales (Howell's). Other causes supported included medical research, disability, care/welfare and homelessness. Only 17% of the total was spent in awards under £10,000.

Aside from the four large grants to Howell's Schools, large grants were awarded to Bancroft's School (£136,000), Queen Mary and Westfield College (£61,000), and Counsel and Care for the Elderly (£44,000).

Exclusions
The following will not generally be supported:

- unsolicited requests;
- running costs;
- statutorily funded organisations.

Applications 'No new unsolicited requests for funding to be considered unless there is a prior connection with the Drapers Company.'

Duchy of Lancaster Benevolent Fund

£273,000 (1997/98)

Welfare, churches, general

Duchy of Lancaster Office, Lancaster Place, Strand, London WC2E 7ED
Tel: 0171-836 8277

Correspondent N Davies, Secretary

Trustees Mr Justice Blackbourne; R G McCombe; Sir Michael Peat; M K Ridley; Lord Shuttleworth; J B Timmins; A W Waterworth; Mrs I Short.

Beneficial area Lancashire, Greater Manchester, Merseyside, but see below.

Information available Report and accounts.

General In 1997/98 the fund received a donation to the investment fund of £146,000 and investment income of £320,000.

Grants amounted to £273,000 representing 305 awards, mostly for amounts under £1,000, but including a grant of £20,000 to Invalids at Home and of £15,000 to the Prince's Youth Business Trust. In the previous year there had also been one £20,000 award, to the Manchester Emergency Fund (following the IRA bombing of that city).

The charity notes that it supports organisations in the above areas, but also in others 'where the Duchy has historical links (such as landed interests and the presentation of church livings)'. From the grants lists these appear to include Pontefract and Leicester.

The grants were were categorised as follows:

Community help	*£74,000*
Youth and education	*£77,000*
Handicapped elderly and infirm	*£68,000*
Religious causes	*£39,000*
Miscellaneous	*£14,000*

Grants under these headings can be described as follows:-

Community Help: £74,000 in 85 grants, 66 of which were for amounts of less than £1,000. Major beneficiaries, with £5,000 each, were Chethams Library, Foxton Youth and Community Centre, the Salvation Army, SHADO and The Way (North West).

Youth and Education: £77,000 in 62 grants, of which 17 were for £1,000 or more, representing nearly three quarters of the total. Beneficiaries receiving £5,000 grants were Bolton Lads and Girls Club, Lytham Youth Service Project, Northern College of Music, Lancaster Royal Grammar School and Lancaster University.

Handicapped Elderly and Infirm: £68,000 in 62 grants, of which 12 grants were for £1,000 or more. £5,000 awards went to Broughton House, Christie's Against Cancer, Royal Lancaster Infirmary Macmillan Appeal and Sue Ryder – Birchley Hall.

Religious Causes: £39,000 in 22 grants, of which 11 were for £1,000 or more. Two the three grants of £5,000 were made to Blackburn Cathedral Lantern Tower Appeal and Liverpool Metropolitan Cathedral Appeal.

Miscellaneous: £14,000 in 20 grants.

Applications To the correspondent, at any time.

The Vivien Duffield Foundation

£2,131,000 (1997)

The arts, heritage, children

Unit 3, Chelsea Manor Studios, Flood Street, London SW3 5SR
Tel: 0171-351 6061; Fax: 0171 351 5308

Correspondent Sally Bacon, Executive Director

Trustees Vivien Duffield; David Harrel; Sir Jocelyn Stevens; Caroline Deletra; Michael Trask.

Beneficial area UK, but most money goes to London based institutions.

Information available Accounts for years up to 1996 only were on file at the Charity Commission in the summer of 1998, and then without the

recommended list of grants or narrative report. However a grant list for 1997 was provided to help in preparing this entry.

Summary The charity makes grants, and is willing to receive applications, in the following fields:

- the arts and arts education;
- museum and gallery education;
- heritage
- social welfare, particularly of children and young people.

Though closely associated with the Clore Foundation (see separate entry), sharing the same administration and common trustees, it makes its grants separately and has slightly different priorities.

The trust appears, by her own account, to be run on personal lines by Mrs Duffield, and in many cases her personal interest may need to be engaged before a grant can be given.

General Until 1998 spartan accounts on file at the Charity Commission revealed little of the foundation's work, but there has been a recent and welcome surge of information, discussed in the box herewith.

As in the case of the Clore Foundation, the new executive director has been helpful in providing the following information on their activities and policies.

'There is a quite strong focus on the arts and related topics. The other areas in which the foundation currently gives funding are: arts education; museums and gallery education; heritage; and social welfare, with particular focus upon children and young people. These funding policies are reviewed periodically; however, the broad subject areas are unlikely to change.

'The trustees draw a balance between supporting large-scale national charities with long term effects and local community endeavours with a more spontaneous impact.

'The foundation's policy has been to respond where there are deserving projects in danger of failing or needing help to develop, rather than being bound by a rigid strategic approach or constricted by a long list of exclusions.

'The foundation concentrates its funding in Great Britain. The trustees of the foundation may be happy to consider working in partnership on charitable projects and to try new approaches for the right projects.'

Information for potential applicants has also been provided, and will be found in the 'Applications' section below.

In 1995/96, the most recent year for which full information is available, the foundation's assets totalled £21 million from which income of £1,476,000 was generated. The only information given then on the foundation's beneficiaries was as follows: In 1995 trustees agreed £4,000,000 to the Royal Opera House Development Appeal, with £2,000,000 to be reserved from income.'In past years the foundation has provided assistance chiefly to children and the arts.'

However a grants list for 1997 was provided to help in preparing this entry. The major beneficiary was again the Royal Opera House Development Appeal (£1.5 million). Awards of £155,000 were made to the MusicSpace Trust and grants of £100,000 each went to the Albert Memorial Trust and Whitechapel Art Gallery. Glyndebourne and the NSPCC received £50,000 each and grants of

between £10,000 and £25,000 went to, among others, Sir John Soane's Museum, the Ragged School Museum and the Victoria and George Cross Association.

Most though not all grants were towards capital or production costs, but there were grants for the Chicken Shed Theatre's general costs and for an education officer for the Royal Naval Museum.

This list should be read in association with that from the sister Clore Foundation.

Exclusions No grants or donations to individuals whether for education or any other purpose.

Applications Applications whose proposals fall clearly within the foundations defined areas of interest are advised to submit first-stage letters of

application, on no more than 3 sides of A4.

The Dulverton Trust

£2,704,000 (1997/98)

Youth and education, general welfare, conservation, Christian religion

5 St James' Place, London SW1A 1NP
Tel: 0171-629 9121

Correspondent Major General Sir Robert Corbett, Trust Secretary

---

Philanthropy and Mrs Duffield

In October 1998, the foundation, with its sister Clore Foundation, announced very loudly some major new funding programmes for museum education – 'Clore Centres for Education' at the Tate Gallery, Bankside, and the British Museum (£2.5 million each), the Natural History Museum and the new Clore Small Grants Programme for regional museums and galleries (£1 million each).

At the same time, the foundations published a lavish account of their work since 1983 and Mrs Duffield herself gave an extensive series of press interviews. These lauded the foundations' work and expressed Miss Duffield's dismay at the allegedly low respect in which public benefactors were held in this country, compared to the USA.

In the past, this editor has been dismayed in his turn by some of the ways in which these foundations have operated. In particular, it was annoying to have printed in good faith their suggestion that no applications would be considered 'unless accompanied by a request from someone known to the trustees' only to have Mrs Duffield, in a newspaper interview published soon after, describe the pleasure and interest she took in reading and responding to just such unsolicited applications.

Secondly the level of disclosure of information has fallen short of that called for both by the Charity Commission and by a decent respect for the taxpayer who is having to put up the money foregone to the public purse because of the tax exemptions of these charities.

In some ways the new 1998 report continues this pattern; for example, the Royal Opera House rates just five lines, after support for six other opera organisations has been extolled. Yet grants for Covent Garden have been more prominent in the grants list of both foundations for many years; and Mrs Duffield's continuing support has indeed been carried to the point where the brave seems to merge with the foolhardy (£1.5 million pounds in 1997 alone).

Again, the document refers to the foundations having 'kept their application procedures simple, flexible and sensitive to changing needs' and 'being concerned with the well-being of some of society's most vulnerable individuals', statements hard to reconcile with their formal refusal for years even to consider applications from anyone not already known to the trustees.

Finally, the suggestion, in an interview with the Times, that this country needs 'greater respect for the benefactors of the arts' and praising the 'social honour' that is available for purchase in the USA by this means, is not attractive to everyone.

Nevertheless Mrs Duffield may actually deserve most of the praise she says is due to benefactors such as herself. The grants made by these trusts stand out from those made by other, more reticent, donors. They are often accompanied by a high level of involvement from Mrs Duffield herself, and they are, where necessary, big enough, and where needed, risky enough, to make a significant impact in the field concerned. It is the view of this editor that the value of foundation grants is often directly related to the level of accompanying personal involvement and support, and to the level of funding being appropriate to what is needed to do the job properly – rather than just to what the applicants think they can raise.

The Eureka! project in Halifax set new standards in accessibility to children that have been enormously influential; the Clore Gallery at the Tate is an important addition to London's great institutions; and her new £6 million education projects at the British Museum, the Tate at Bankside and the Natural History Museum are majestic enterprises for private philanthropy, trumping the similar but less publicised scheme funded by the Sainsbury family at the National Gallery.

The support for the Royal Opera may, as it seemed at the time of writing, to have been gold down the drain. But it is the point of private foundations that they can take big risks, and therefore risk big setbacks. Most foundations described in this book can be fairly criticised for their lack of ambition. They could usefully learn from Mrs Duffield's example.

Trustees The Hon Robert Wills, Chairman; Lord Carrington; Lord Dulverton; Colonel D V Fanshawe; the Earl of Gowrie; John Kemp-Welch; Sir Ashley Ponsonby, Vice Chairman and Chairman of Finance Committee; Lord Taylor of Gryfe; J Watson; Colonel S J Watson; Dr Catherine Wills; C A H Wills; Sir David Wills.

Beneficial area UK but limited support to parts of Africa; see below. Few grants for work in London.

Information available Reports and accounts with analysed grants schedule; leaflet stating policy and practice.

Summary Grants vary between £1,000 and £125,000 (average: £10,000) and are made only to registered charities. A broad variety of organisations, usually with a national remit, are supported under 12 grant-making headings. Awards are towards capital or revenue costs, and are normally one-off payments.

The trust's areas of interest are set out in the table herewith.

General The trust was founded by the first Lord Dulverton in 1949. By the year ending March 1998 it's assets totalled £91 million (up from £74 million a year ago) and investment income of £3,088,000 was generated. The trust received 1,578 applications of which 278 (18%) were accepted. The smallest grant was for no more than £1,000 and the largest for £125,000. There were four awards between £50,000 and £100,000, totalling £252,000 (9% of the sum value of grants) and fifty-two between £20,000 and £45,000 amounting to £1,289,000 (48%). Grant size and spread was similar between the various categories.

The largest donations were to Farmington Trust (£125,000), University of Oxford Dulverton Scholarships (£100,000), the Jim Conway Foundation (£45,000) and World Wide Fund for Nature (£52,000). Overall, somewhere in the region of a third of funds went to organisations also supported in the previous year. Repeated annual grants made up 20% of the trusts overall grant making capacity in 1997/98.

Annual Review 1997/98

In the 1997/98 review the trust wrote:

'The first Lord Dulverton was determined that the trust should be wide ranging, flexible and enterprising in its grant making policy, and these principles are said to have been continued by its successors, adapted as necessary to suit changing circumstances. *(In practice, the opposite seems sometimes more true . Though there are indeed enterprising*

grants to be found, and though grants do cover a wide field, the money mostly goes to a conventional list of well-established charities. Ed.) Policy is normally reviewed by the trustees at 5 yearly intervals and this was last done in May 1994. The next review was started in the summer of 1998 and was expected to be confirmed by the close of the year.

'Current policy ... is to apply its funds for general charitable purposes with the main work of the trust being aimed at three areas of particular relevance: these are Youth and Education, Conservation and General Welfare. Other areas of priority are; Religion, in which the main emphasis is the promotion and development of religious education in schools, principally through the Farmington Institute in Oxford, followed by Industrial Relations, Peace and Security and Preservation. Other causes considered by the trustees to have special merit may also be supported, and grants are made, but on a limited basis, to old contacts and associations in East Africa; more recently some grants have been made in South Africa. Grants are only made to registered charities or to other exempt bodies.

'As a general rule the trust supports national projects, but regional and local organisations may be helped if trustees feel they are of significant merit. Annual policy grants represent a significant proportion of the trust's work. The number of these grants is restricted and the Trustees' Review them annually, with one years notice of cessation. Grants phased over a number of years are seldom made in order to allow the trustees greater flexibility.

Youth and education 'In the view of the trustees this is the most important area of

the trust's work; and this is reflected in the proportion of grant making capacity put towards it. Funding is split broadly between appeals for education and personal development. The trust, while unreservedly concerned for the disadvantaged, is also keen to reward excellence. The latter includes promoting the establishment of strong democratic roots in Central and Eastern Europe and Russia through support for graduate and post-graduate scholars at Oxford University and Atlantic College.

'The development of co-operation between the many similar agencies working for young people in the UK remains an objective.'

Major grants in the category included £40,000 to Outward Bound (Loch Eil); £30,000 to Refugees Studies Programme; £25,000 to Prince's Trust and £20,000 to Farms for City Children.

General welfare 'This has traditionally been a key area of grant giving by the trust, and remains so today. Inevitably the categories helped in this category cover a very wide spectrum, but in general the trustees particularly wish to direct their assistance to the young and old, both age groups who are unable to help themselves and who are vulnerable to circumstances outside of their control. Support for marriage and the provision of relief for those devoting much of their lives to the care of others are also considered important areas by the trustees.'

The beneficiaries also included many ex-services charities, perhaps reflecting the interests of the trustees and staff, a group which includes two Colonels – trustees – and a Major General – the Secretary. Large donations included those to the NSPCC (£50,000);

The Dulverton Trust

Summary of grants made in 1997/98 and 1996/97

Youth and education	£901,000	33%	£1,022,000	36%
General welfare	£690,000	26%	£682,000	24%
Conservation	£222,000	8%	£288,000	10%
Religion	£217,000	8%	£174,000	6%
Africa	£107,000	4%	£86,000	3%
Minor appeals	£100,000	4%	£100,000	4%
Peace and security	£88,000	3%	£85,000	3%
Industrial understanding	£50,000	2%	£70,000	2%
Preservation	£49,000	2%	£114,000	4%
Annual subscription	£25,000	1%	£25,000	1%
Local appeals	£20,000	1%	£20,000	1%
Miscellaneous	£235,000	9%	£86,000	3%
Total	**£2,704,000**	**100%**	**£2,825,000**	**100%**

Children's Society (£40,000); College of St Barnabas (£25,000); Family Mediation Scotland (£20,000)

Conservation 'The trust wishes to encourage greater recognition of the need for conservation of the environment, not only in the well publicised areas of wildlife and nature conservation, but also by supporting research in to the issues raised by industrial and commercial activities, and in ways in which environmental damage can be avoided.'

In 1997/98 the UK Centre for Economic and Environmental Development received £21,000, the Countryside Foundation £20,000 and the British Trust for Conservation Volunteers £15,000.

Religion 'Trustees continue to place great importance on support for religious education, with its implications for the moral and spiritual welfare and development of young people, especially the work done by the Farmington Institute and others in raising the standard of RE in schools and colleges throughout the country.'

Aside from the large award to the Farmington Trust covered earlier in this entry, other sizeable amounts went to Company of Seekers (£20,000); Christian Education Movement (£20,000) and Coventry Cathedral Development Trust (£20,000).

Africa 'The trust provides limited support for organisations working in East and South Africa, particularly those involved with education and personal development, small businesses and agriculture.'

Eight grants were made in 1997/98 to organisations such as Intermediate Technology (£20,000); CARE international UK (£19,000); Book Aid (£17,000); and FARM (£13,000).

Minor appeals 'Grants not exceeding £1,500 each are made to an annual total of £100,000. 103 such grants were given in this year to a wide spectrum of charitable works. Lord Dulverton has an allocation of £20,000 for local appeals in the Cotswolds, and 10 grants were made in the year totalling £20,000.

Peace and security 'Trustees place particular importance on the development of international research, analysis and education involving peace and security issues. The lack of stability around the world of which the continuing threat of conflict in South East Europe and in the Middle East, together with the financial and social turmoil in Asia, as examples, make clear the need for such work.'

The Royal United Services Institute for Defence Studies received a grant of £25,000 in 1997/98 and four other awards were made including £20,000 to the Airy Neave Trust and £18,000 to the Royal Institute of International Affairs.

Industrial understanding 'Trustees continue to fund the development of trade union research and education, largely through the Jim Conway Foundation, with the aim of furthering industrial understanding. Such work contributes to the overall improvement in relationships between employer and employee through the provision of information and education.'

Aside from the £45,000 donation to the Jim Conway Foundation mentioned already, only one other was made – £5,000 to the Industrial Society.

Preservation 'Grants are made for preservation projects in this relatively restricted area of the work of the trust. Small annual grants are made towards the preservation and restoration of churches.'

In the year under review three grants were made- £20,000 to College of Arms Trust; £15,000 to Historic Churches Preservation Trust and £9,000 to Scottish Churches Architectural Heritage Trust.

Miscellaneous 'This category includes charities which are on the margins of the trust's guidelines but which trustees consider to be of special merit. This is particularly so in the case of medical and surgical appeals which would otherwise be excluded from the trust's work.'

Examples include: Centre for Practical Ethics in Health Care (£50,000); Tate Gallery (£40,000); and RUC Disabled Police Officers Association (£20,000)

Trust staff are headed by Major General Sir Robert Corbett (The Secretary) and are: Colonel J G Crisp (Deputy and Financial Secretary) and Mrs J L Channon (Assistant Secretary)

Exclusions 'The trust does not operate within the broad fields of medicine and health, including drug addiction and projects concerning the mentally and physically handicapped. Also generally excluded are projects concerning museums, churches, cathedrals and other historic buildings.

'The whole field of the arts is excluded (*though see above, Ed*) together with projects for schools, colleges and universities. The trust very seldom operates within the Greater London area, or in Northern Ireland except for specific nominated charities.

'No grants to overseas charities, except for the limited activity on a reducing scale with old contacts and associations in Central and East Africa.

'Grants are not made to individuals or for expeditions.'

Applications Applications should be made in writing to the secretary. Trustee meetings are held four times a year – in January, May, July and October. There is no set format for applications, but it is helpful if they can include the background and a clear statement of the aims of the appeal together with the funding target and any progress made in reaching it. Applications should, if possible, be restricted to a letter and maximum of two sheets of paper. Initial applications should always include a summary of the previous year's accounts.

The Dunard Fund

£280,000

Not known

c/o Dunard Ltd, 4 Royal Terrace, Edinburgh EH7 5AB
Tel: 0131-556 4043

Correspondent Mr & Mrs Hogel

Trustees Mr & Mrs Hogel.

Beneficial area Probably Scotland.

Information available None. Despite the requirement to do so, the Fund has not supplied a copy of its most recent Report and Accounts.

General In response to a telephone call, we were told that 'unsolicited applications go 'straight into the bin'. The fund has been reported to give grants to 'a variety of local causes'.

Applications See above

The Dunhill Medical Trust

£3,650,000 (1996/97)

Medical research, integrated care and accommodation for the elderly

I Fairholt Street, London SW7 1EQ
Tel: 0171- 584 7411; Fax: 0171-581 5463

Correspondent The Secretary

Trustees Mrs Kay Glendinning, Senior Trustee and Administrator; Ronald E Perry; Timothy Sanderson; Dr Christopher Bateman; Professor M H Lessof.

Beneficial area UK, with some special interest in West Sussex.

Information available Annual report and accounts now includes a full grants list. There is a short document on donation policy and donation terms and conditions.

Summary Large grants for medical research projects and fellowships. Projects may be for hundreds of thousands of pounds and spread over as much as ten years. About one third of the money goes to institutions where the trustees are professionally connected.

The administration of the trust, as shown in the annual report for 1996/97, is startling. Among other things, the Senior Trustee is paid over £100,000 to act as the Administrator of the trust, two thirds of the high investment management fees are paid to a company of which another trustee is a Director, and the total cost of administration is £6,000 for each new grant or fellowship awarded.

General The trust was established in 1950 with an endowment from Herbert Dunhill. The money was derived from the tobacco company of that name, but the trust no longer has any specific connection with the tobacco business.

The trust lists four purposes, though not all them are necessarily pursued at any given time:

- the furtherance of medical knowledge and research;
- the provision of medical care and facilities;
- research into the care of the elderly;
- provision of accommodation and care of the elderly.

The grants list for 1996/97, reviewed below, suggests that work under the first heading pre-dominates, though there were substantial grants for a scanner (£210,000, being the second of an unknown number of payments to Hammersmith Hospital for this purpose), and for Toynbee Hall (a welfare charity in London, receiving £10,000 for its Service for the Elderly programme). There are a small number of usually quite modest grants in the area around Chichester, such as the £1,500 for Chichester Stroke Club. The trust was also funding 11 hospital fellowships in 1996/97.

Medical research grants are not necessarily subject to the process of formal peer review, and the trust is not a member of the Association of Medical Research Charities. There is an expert Medical Review Committee that sees some applications. It provides 'expert opinion in those cases where the trustees feel that their own expertise is inadequate'.

The annual report includes the following useful list of the largest new projects in 1996/97:

Guy's Hospital UMDS (£500,000 for a skills centre)

Northwick Park Institute for Medical Research* (£300,000 for the Department of Cardiology)

University College, London (£150,000 for Fetal Medicine Research, Professor Rodeck)

Professor Barker, Southampton (£138,000 for further work on maternal nutrition)

Lewisham Hospital (£100,000 for equipment for their new Academic Centre)

Hill Homes (£100,000 for a new nursing home)

King Edward VII Hospital, Midhurst* (£100,000 for new cardiology centre)

Frenchay Hospital, Bristol (£50,000 towards rebuilding the children's unit)

Guys Hospital (£40,000 for a study of inherited breast cancer)

(* Asterisks indicate 'those institutions where the trustees ... have an involvement.')

The accounts further note that 'where possible the trustees take an active part in donee institutions to ensure their monies are applied for their intended purpose.'

The Donation Policy document available in Summer 1988 makes the following comments about its medical research programme (there is no equivalent for the rest of its work): 'Research grants will primarily be given to enable new research to get under way and no grant will normally commit expenditure over more then three years. Grants may also be made for building work, and for equipment purchases. A number of small grants will be made each year to appropriate medical charities. The trustees will only support projects of which they have previous knowledge or association'.

These statements were amplified by a new and helpful, but short lasting Secretary: 'Yes, we only give money to people we know, but we get to know new people all the time. If we are interested in what an organisation wants to do, we will want to talk to them.' It is clear both from the information in the annual report and accounts and from conversations with the trust that personal relationships play a large part: 'Mrs Glendinning has extensive contacts in the medical research field'.

Note 10 to the 1996/97 accounts gives information about the role of trustees. It reads as follows:

'Transactions with Trustees and Connected Persons

a. Emoluments paid to Trustees and Connected Persons

Trustees

Mrs K Glendinning	*£103,369*
Mr T Sanderson	*£76*

Connected persons

Mr PJ Glendinning	*£24,256*
Mrs D Sanderson	*£7,638*

b. Other transactions

'Mr R Perry is a partner in Vizards, solicitors. Legal fees amounting to £14,399 were paid by the trust to Vizards during the year.

'Mrs D Sanderson purchased a vehicle from the trust for £14,000, its market value.

Mr T Sanderson is a Director of Delaware International Advisers Ltd. (This company) manage approximately £40 million of the trust's investments and they were paid £167,882 in fees ... .'

c. 'Three trustees claimed expenses from the trust amounting to £8,090. This was in respect of travel, entertainment and sundry items relating to trust business.'

Note 11 to the accounts further notes that £32,800 was paid in pension contributions for trustees. This is presumed to refer to Mrs Glendinning, the Senior Trustee, the only one paid directly by the trust. This will bring her total salary and pension costs for the year to £136,249.

The trust has given further information about some of these payments. Mrs Glendinning is regarded as the Senior Trustee and also acts as the Administrator of the trust, as is permitted by the Trust Deed. The payment to Mr PJ Glendinning was for help with the trusts property transactions and that to Mrs D Sanderson for administrative help.

There were an average of seven employees in 1996/97, including Mrs Glendinning. Although her salary and benefits are reported as £103,000 in note 10 of the accounts they later say that the highest paid employee had emoluments in the band £40,000 to £50,000 (Note 11).

The expenses of the trust included £83,000 in travel, hotel and various motoring costs, £17,000 for 'Entertaining and charitable events' and a further £14,000 expense is noted as 'Wimbledon debenture written off'.

The total investment management fees were £257,000 (there are two other investment advisers besides that connected with one of the trustees). The trust does not think £257,000 is high. We disagree. It is much more than is paid by far larger trusts such as, for example, Tudor or the Rowntree Charitable Trust. It represents no less than 0.35% of the trusts assets every year.

Unusually, the value of the very restricted portfolio did not rise significantly during 1996/97. The major unpooled investment was in the Vendome Luxury Group plc. There was also an unusual investment of £50,000 in debentures with the All England Lawn Tennis Group.

The trust has fixed assets, mainly unspecified property or properties, worth almost £2 million, for use in carrying out its grant making work. They may include the house in Knightsbridge and the farmhouse in West Sussex that are recorded as its 'Principal Offices'. The assets also include £60,000 worth of motor vehicles.

These editors regard the payment of over £100,000 to a trustee as regrettable. First, the principle that trustees should not benefit personally from their trusts is a good one. Secondly, the amount involved is far higher than is required to obtain the services of even the most highly qualified charity directors, experienced in running charities of this relatively modest size; seven staff in a body making less than two hundred grants a year.

Further, it is not normally necessary to employ trustees, or their relatives, or the companies with which they are connected, to carry out work for a charity. Even the most commonly found exception, of a legally qualified trustee carrying out occasional small transactions on a remunerated basis, is unusual. The situation here, where large payments are being made to an investment management company of which a trustee is one of the Directors, is most undesirable.

Exclusions The trustees will not normally approve the use of funds for

- providing clinical services that, in their opinion, should or could be provided by the National Health Service

- individuals or organisations outside the United Kingdom
- charities representing specific professions or trade associations
- institutional overheads
- travel/conference fees

Applications To the correspondent. Note that 'the trust will only support projects of which it has previous knowledge or association'. Trustees meet in March, May, September and November.

The E B M Charitable Trust

£761,000 (1996/97)

Children and young people, animals, general

St Paul's House, Warwick Lane, London EC4P 4BN
Tel: 0171-248 4499

Correspondent R Moore

Trustees R Moore; M Macfadyen; Harry Holgate; C Fitzgerald.

Beneficial area UK.

Information available Accounts, without analysis or explanation of grants, or narrative report.

General The trust reports that in 1996/97 its 'beneficiaries included charities involved in animal welfare and research, youth development and the relief of poverty.' It adds 'The trustees' funds are fully committed and therefore unsolicited applications are not requested'.

The purposes of the 1996/97 grants are not disclosed, but, from the names alone the following rough classification can be made:

Child health and welfare
	6 grants	£253,000
Youth	2 grants	£185,000
Animal welfare (mainly horse)		
	4 grants	£162,000
Medical research		
	2 grants	£60,000
Other/unknown		
	6 grants	£101,000

The major grants were to; Fairbridge (£150,000); Shaftesbury Homes (£125,000); Thoroughbred Breeders Assn Equine Fertility Unit (£112,000).

Grants of £50,000 were given to Treloar School and to the Lord Mayor's Cancer Research Appeal.

Beneficiaries outside the categories described included BBONT (Berks,

Bucks and Oxon Nature Trust, £27,000) and the Worshipful Company of Shipwrights (£30,000).

The Sir John Eastwood Foundation

£386,000 (1995/96)

Social welfare, health, in Nottinghamshire

Burns Lane, Warsop, Mansfield, Nottinghamshire NG20 0QG
Tel: 01623-842581

Correspondent Gordon Raymond

Trustees Mrs C B Mudford; Mrs D M Cottingham; Gordon Raymond; Mrs V A Hardingham; P M Spencer.

Beneficial area UK, but mainly Nottinghamshire in practice.

Information available Accounts up 1995/96 only on file at the Charity Commission in September 1998.

General This trust concentrates its grant giving in the Nottinghamshire region, supporting mainly local youth/community, health and education organisations and a few national medical charities.

In 1995/96 the foundation had a low income of £295,000 from assets of £7.8 million. Grant giving was up from £260,000 in the previous year and 142 grants were awarded. 54 were for less than £1,000 and only six were for more than £10,000. Much the largest went to Nottingham Community Housing Association (£100,000). A large number of the grants were to organisations also supported in the previous year.

Awards made to youth/community organisations included those to the Salvation Army (£15,000); Warsop Youth Club (£5,000); Lincolnshire Rural Activities (£5,000); CRYPT (£5,000); St John's Ambulance (£5,000) and the NSPCC (£500).

A number of grants were also given to local health and national medical charities such as Nottingham Hospice (£4,000 in two grants); Regional Society for Autistic Children and Adults (£3,000); Cancer Relief Macmillan Fund (£5,000); Winged Fellowship (£2,000); MIND (£2,500); Nottingham Resource Centre for Disabled (£5,000) and Imperial Cancer Research (£1,000).

Examples of the larger grants made to education institutes included those to Portland College (£25,000); Yeoman Park School (£5,000); and Stubborn Wood School (£1,500).

Exclusions No grants to individuals.

Applications In writing to the correspondent.

The Maud Elkington Charitable Trust

£447,000 (1996/97)

Social welfare, general

c/o Messrs Harvey Ingram Owston, 20 New Walk, Leicester LE1 6TX
Tel: 0116-254 5454

Correspondent The Clerk to the Trust

Trustees Roger Bowder; Allan Veasey; Mrs C A Macpherson.

Beneficial area Northamptonshire and Leicester (especially Desborough, Kettering).

Information available Accounts with grants list showing awards over £1,000 but no narrative report on grant-making policy or practice.

Summary Grants vary from under £1,000 to £100,000. Beneficiaries are registered charities from many fields, but in particular social welfare. In practice the only groups supported 'outside' the catchment area are national organisations but such grants may in fact be targeted for projects within the area.

General The trust was established in 1972 with a settlement from its namesake. The late Maud Elkington lived around Kettering and Desborough and the trustees focus grant-making on this area.

In 1996, the trust received a £5.5 million legacy from the settlor, boosting its assets to over £13 million. In 1996/97, the trust generated its highest ever investment income (£555,000). In the year, 156 charitable grants were made. 63% of grants were for below £1,000 but these only accounted for 14% of the money. 34 donations were between £1,000 and £3,000. A single award of £100,000 accounted for 22% of charitable expenditure and four grants in the region of £20,000 to £30,000 for 21%.

Of the grants listed (all over £1,000, 86% of all donations), the vast majority were for organisations based in Leicester or Northamptonshire and more specifically Kettering and Desborough.

The largest grant of 1996/97 (£100,000) went to Leicester Children's Holiday Centre. Other substantial awards were to Kettering General Hospital NHS Trust (£31,000); LOROS (£24,000); Northants Libraries and Information Services, Books on Tape Services (£20,000); Northamptonshire Social Services (£19,000); Leicester Grammar School Bursaries (£17,000); Desborough Town Cricket Club (£15,000); and British Red Cross, Northamptonshire (£13,000).

Exclusions Individuals.

Applications In writing to the correspondent. Trustees meet every eight or nine weeks.

The John Ellerman Foundation

£3,825,000 (1996/97)

Community development, social welfare, medical research and care, disability arts, conservation

Aria House, 23 Craven Street, London WC2N 5NT
Tel: 0171-930 8566; Fax: 0171-839 3654; email:postmaster@ellerman.prestel.co.uk; Website: www.ncvo-vol.org.uk/jef.html

Correspondent Eileen Terry, Appeals Manager

Trustees Dennis G Parry; Sir David A Scott; Dr. John Hemming; Peter Strutt; Angela Boschi; David D Martin-Jenkins; Peter C Pratt; Vice-Admiral Anthony R Revell.

Beneficial area UK and overseas, other than Central and South America.

Information available Guidelines for applicants. Excellent annual report with analysis of grant making including a full list of donations, but without information on the purposes of individual grants.

Summary Each year the foundation makes grants, normally for core or revenue funding, from a minimum of £10,000 up to £100,000 and either in single payments or spread over two or three years.

It has recently acquired a new Director, Chris Hanvey, and is developing an interesting and thoughtful approach to grant-making. One major change, in Autumn 1998, has been the foundation's complete withdrawal from the funding of purely local charities or initiatives. Such applications will no longer be considered by the foundation.

Other changes are described as follows: 'Two specific new funds have been introduced (*though there have not yet been enough suitable applications for these funds to have disbursed more than relatively modest sums. Ed.*). The first is aimed at encouraging two or more registered charities to work collaboratively on joint projects... in response to the belief that there is considerable duplication across the whole sector ... . A second fund aims at fostering that genuinely innovative work that has always been at the core of the UK voluntary sector but which is made more difficult by a culture which encourages charities to take on contracts for work previously done by, say, health or local authorities.

'Funding ... will continue to be made in the areas of medical research and medical care, disability, community development and social welfare, the arts, conservation and overseas aid.' There is a growing interest in community development and social welfare.

The foundation receives many applications and only 13% were successful in 1996/97.

General The foundation (which before 1992 was known as the Moorgate and New Moorgate Trust Funds) was established in 1972 by the late Sir John Reeves Ellerman, a shipping magnate. The foundation has recently instituted an interesting two stage application process to reduce the time wasted in preparing unsuccessful bids. See under 'applications' below.

In 1996/97 it made 348 grants totalling £3,825,000. Although grants in that period started at £1,000, a new policy sets a minimum grant level of £10,000, and it is intended that the average grant will be at a much higher figure.

Annual Report 1996/97

'The foundation aims to support a broad cross-section of charities doing work of national significance. It recognises that the running of charities has become a highly complex operation in a rapidly changing world. It is working towards making fewer but larger grants, and towards developing partnerships with funded charities.

'Trustees have a preference for working with headquarters organisations and umbrella bodies rather than local groups. While recognising the value of small amounts of funding to local organisations, the foundation's view is that smaller trusts often having local knowledge, are better placed to provide this (*Note that, as reported above, trustees have now decided that they will only fund national or umbrella organisations. Ed.*). Our resources, as one of the UK's top grant-making trusts, allow us to make larger grants which we hope will enable charities to make a difference to people they serve. For this reason our minimum grant is £10,000, and it is intended that the average grant will be a much higher figure.

New policies 'The last year has seen considerable change for the John Ellerman Foundation. A revised funding strategy has been approved by the trustees, a new staffing structure implemented and two other trustees recruited to the board. Additionally, a new computer system has been installed, the foundation has joined the growing number of internet users and it has simplified the review process, to ensure that all grant recipients are appropriately monitored. To a large extent, these changes reflect the rapidly shifting face of the voluntary sector itself.

'Two major factors have dominated the charitable sector in the last twelve months. As the number of registered charities continues to grow (by the end of 1995 there were 181,467 charities in England and Wales) so too do the demands made upon them. The contracting – in both senses of the word – of the welfare state means that many charities are being asked to take on work traditionally performed by, say, health authorities or social services departments. This inevitably leaves major grant making trusts, like the foundation, to question how far they should be assisting in what was formally regarded as statutory funding. Grant making trusts are providing over £1,850 million in total and this represents a considerable impact on the sector as a whole. As health authorities establish charitable arms, local authorities contract out more and more of their services and some voluntary organisations become multi-million pound providers, grant making trusts are involved in a growing debate about how they respond to these new market forces.

'Equally new is the pressure and impact of the National Lottery. In 1995 and 1996 the five National Lottery Boards gave away a combined total of £2.7 billion. Of this, the National Lottery Charities Board, alone, gave a combined total of £478.4 million to charities. These statistics help to illustrate how major grant making trusts are, again, having to think through their funding strategies, to decide how far, for example, they will provide matching funding or pick up the financial tab when Lottery grants expire.

'Both the Lottery and the new 'contract culture' are examples of a major sea change effecting grant-making trusts. They have, in turn, led the trustees of the foundation to look afresh at funding strategy and to think through those ways in which the maximum impact can be made with the available funds.

'In order to address some of these changes, funding policy has been both enriched and modified. Two new funds have been introduced. The first is aimed at encouraging two or more registered charities to work collaboratively on joint projects. This fund is very much in response to the belief that there is considerable duplication across the whole sector and that collaboration both assists in keeping infrastructure costs down and can widen the help available to good causes. A second fund aims at fostering that genuinely innovative work that has always been at the core of the UK voluntary sector but which is made more difficult by a culture which encourages charities to take on contracts for work previously done by, say, health or local authorities.

'At the same time, the trustees have tightened up other areas of their guidelines, favouring national and regional organisations, and giving to umbrella organisations where these exist, as in the case of the hospice movement. Funding will continue to be made in the areas of medical research and medical care, disability, community development and social welfare, the arts, conservation and overseas aid, but will exclude deficit funding and the direct replacement of former public services.

Grants in 1996/97

'The foundation awarded 348 grants in 1996/97, a slight increase (8%) on the number for the previous year. As a result of a rise in investment income, the trustees were also able to distribute a further £400,000 with average grants of £10,991. The foundation is gradually moving to a point of making larger grants, sometimes spread over a two or three year period and, where necessary, available for core funding. This is in recognition that, for many charities, it is the day to day running costs that prove the biggest fundraising challenge.

(About 2,500 applications were received in 1996/97 of which only 13% were accepted – Ed.)

'Medical and Disability remain the two largest categories. Medical includes both medical research and practice and the trustees recently reconfirmed an earlier decision to fund this on a 50/50 basis. Disability embraces both physical and learning difficulties, with additional grants also made in the area of mental illness.

'Finally, donations policy for overseas grants represent the intentions of the late Sir John Ellerman; grants are given, principally, to Central and Southern Africa.

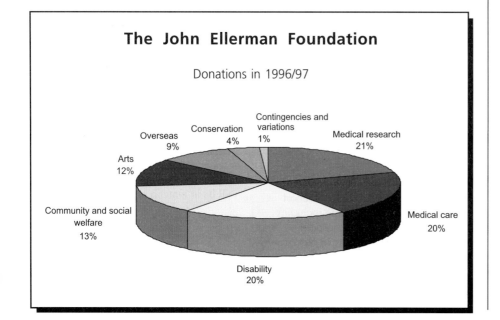

The John Ellerman Foundation

Donations in 1996/97

Contingencies and variations 1%
Conservation 4%
Overseas 9%
Arts 12%
Community and social welfare 13%
Medical research 21%
Medical care 20%
Disability 20%

'As the foundation matures and refines its donation policies, it is helpful to reflect upon the strategy over the last ten years. Significantly, medical work and disability have consistently attracted the greatest percentage of donations. At the other end of this spectrum, both religious charities and education no longer receive consideration by the charity.

'In the next ten years, it is likely that these patterns will change even more. The foundation is driven by a desire to provide assistance where it can be most effective and to be part of that wide redefinition which is affecting the whole of the voluntary sector.

Guidelines

'All appeals from registered charities are considered by the trustees who, apart from a few exceptional circumstances, increasingly prefer to support work of national importance rather than local causes (see section on local charities below). Normally, the minimum grant awarded is £10,000.

'An application will need to demonstrate:
- the necessity for the work
- the timescale and detailed costings
- arrangements for monitoring and detailed evaluation
- the long term viability of the organisation
- details of any other funding received towards this appeal

'The trustees meet regularly throughout the year but, because of the large number of appeals received, it may be some time before an appeal is considered. Receipt of appeals can only be acknowledged if a stamped-addressed envelope is enclosed.

'At present the foundation has a particular interest in supporting innovatory work or co-operation between two or more charities in any of the following categories:

Medical research and medical practice: 'Includes both medical research and practice and the trustees recently reconfirmed an earlier decision to fund this on a 50/50 basis. More specifically, grants are given for preventive medicine, treatment, rehabilitation, relief of suffering, care and support.

Disability: 'Physical and learning difficulties and mental health.

Community development and social welfare: 'Children, youth work, substance abuse, housing and homelessness, and disadvantaged people and communities.

The arts: 'Includes archaeology, historic buildings, museums.

Conservation: 'The environment.

Overseas Aid: 'Principally Central and Southern Africa. Support for Eastern Europe is given through a grant to Charity Know How.

'Local charities will be considered if they:
- are based in a deprived area;
- promote self help;
- aim to improve the skills, qualifications, employment prospects or quality of life of local residents;
- have at least a 50% representation of local residents on the management committee;
- are doing work of national significance.'

Grants in 1996/97

The three largest payments (all repeated from 1995/96) were for £100,000 and went to: Help the Hospices; Imperial Cancer Research Fund and the National Hospital for Neurology and Neurosurgery. The foundation, however, is a rapidly changing organisation and grants made in 1996/97 are not necessarily an indicator of present priorities. For example, the support for cancer charities represented a considerable commitment from the foundation's resources and is unlikely to be extended. Among the new grants are a number which demonstrate a growing interest in community development and social welfare: Cardinal Hume Centre (£10,000), Community Network (£5,000), Howard League (£10,000), Prisoners of Conscience (£10,000), YHP Community Projects (£5,000). Grants are normally made for core and project funding, rather than capital appeals.

New grants of £30,000 were to the National History Museum Down House appeal; Medical Foundation for the Care of Victims of Torture; Cookridge Cancer Centre and ELF Elimination of Leukaemia Fund. The purpose of the funds is not known.

Exclusions 'Grants are made only to registered charities, and are not made for the following purposes:
- for or on behalf of individuals
- individual hospices
- local branches of national organisations
- 'friends of' groups
- education or educational establishments
- religious causes
- conferences and seminars
- sports and leisure facilities, and local sports groups
- purchase of vehicles (except those used for aid transport)
- the direct replacement of public funding
- hospital radio stations
- deficit funding
- local arts, theatre, dance and music groups
- local youth groups
- local advice centres
- domestic animal welfare
- circulars (will not receive a reply)

Applications In common with many other foundations, we receive many more applications than we can possibly fund. Last year only 13% of all appeals within our guidelines were successful. We recognise that preparing good applications places heavy demands on the time and resources of charities, and diverts energies from their ultimate purpose. Accordingly, we ask potential applicants to write to us initially with a brief description of the charity and its current needs for funding. The letter should be no more than one or two pages of A4, and there is no need to send annual reports or background material at this stage. Trustees will decide from this letter whether they want to invite a formal application; if so an application form and further details will be sent. Whatever the decision, all letters will receive a reply.

We are happy to discuss potential applications by telephone; please ask for the appeals manager (Eileen Terry).

The trustees meet regularly throughout the year and there are no deadlines.

Elman Charitable Trust

£260,000 (1996/97)

Jewish charities

1 Chadwick Road, Westcliffe-on-Sea, Essex, SS0 8LS
Tel: 01702-431327

Correspondent C Elman, Trustee

Trustees Charles Elman; Kenneth Elman; Colin Elman.

Beneficial area UK and Israel

Information available Accounts for 1996/97 with grants list, but no narrative, on file at the Charity Commission in September 1998.

General This trust seems to be reducing its grant making. In 1996/97 grants totalled £260,000, a drop from £330,000 in 1995/96 and £438,000 in

1994/95. Assets dropped from £437,000 in 1994/95 to £138,000 in 1996/97

Income for the year amounted to £156,000.

Although 31 awards were made, all to Jewish charities, about 80% of total grant giving went to just four organisations: Emunah Women's Organisation in Israel (£96,000); Friends of Asraf Harofeh Medical Centre and Jewish Care (£50,000 each); and Nir Yisrael Educational Trust (£11,000).

Other grants went to Friends of OHR Samayach (£6,000); Our Future - the poor of Herzelia (£5,300); British Friends of Aleh and Ohel Moshe Synagouge (£5,000 each).

The Englefield Charitable Trust

£284,000 (1997/98)

General, in Berkshire

Englefield Estate Office, Theale, Reading RG7 5DU
Tel: 01734-302 504

Correspondent A S Reid, Secreatry to the Trustees

Trustees Sir William Benyon; James Shelley; Mrs Elizabeth Benyon; Richard H R Benyon; Mrs Catherine Haig.

Beneficial area UK, with a special interest in Berkshire.

Information available Report and accounts with full grants list but lacking the required explanation and analysis of grants.

Summary Around 100 grants are made to registered charities, most of them based in Berkshire. The amount donated varies from £250 up to around £40,000, with most near £1,000. The trustees say they do not have a preference for any particular charitable fields. Although a wide variety of causes are sponsored many are Christian.

General The trust was founded in 1968 by the settlor, and current trustee, Sir William Benyon (who is also the Chairman of the Ernest Cook Trust, which has its own entry in this book).

In addition to grant-making, the trust also provides low cost and retirement housing. The latter cost the trust £71,000 in 1997/98.

By April 1998 the trust's assets totalled £10 million and income of £398,000 had been generated in the financial year. The schedule below shows how most of the grants budget was disbursed:

No of grants	Value	%
1	£41,000	14%
7	£10,000	25%
11	£5,000	19%
16	£2,000-£3,000	12%
36	£1,000	13%

The largest grant went to St Mary the Virgin Church, Reading (£41,000) and the £10,000 awards were to Padworth Village Hall; Order of Christian Unity; St Mary the Virgin, Hampstead Norreys; St Peter de Beauvoir PCC; Theale Green School Trust; West Berks. Education Business Partnership and Douglas Martin Trust.

Exclusions Individual applications for study or travel.

Applications In writing to the correspondent stating the purpose for which the money is to be used and accompanied with the latest accounts.

All applicants should be registered charities.

Entindale Ltd

£526,000 (1996/97)

Orthodox Jewish charities

14 Mayfield Gardens,
London NW4 2QA
Tel: 0181-458 9266

Correspondent Mrs B L Bridgeman, Trustee

Trustees A C Becker; Mrs B A Sethill; Mrs B L Bridgeman; S J Goldberg.

Information available Reports and accounts on file at the Charity Commission.

General This trust aims 'to advance religion in accordance with the orthodox Jewish faith'.

In 1996/97 about 73 grants were made ranging from less than £1,000 to £85,000. Examples of the larger grants given include those to: MGS (£85,000); SOFOT (£30,000); British Friends of Ohr Someach (£26,000); Beer Avrohom UK Trust (£22,000); Telz Talmudical Academy Trust (£18,000); Guvurath Ari Torah Academy Trust (£18,000); North West London Communal Mikveh (£10,000); and Gateshead Talmudical college (£8,000).

ENTRUST

See below

Environmental improvement

Suite 2 5th Floor, Acre House, 2 Town Square, Sale, Cheshire M33 7WZ
Tel: 0161 972 0044

Correspondent Dr Richard Sills, Chief Executive

General Entrust is not itself a grant maker, but is the body organising the Landfill Tax system under which 20% of landfill proceeds are cycled by Landfill Operators to environmental bodies. The sums involved are large – over £100 million a year – but most of it goes to active environmental organisations that have established direct links with a a local landfill operator.

However a proportion is going to grant making organisations such as the Gloucestershire Environmental Trust Company which has its own entry in this book (and in income from this source of no less than £750,000 a year).

Any project to be funded in this way, whether directly or indirectly, must be approved by ENTRUST and the recipient organisation must be enrolled with that body, either directly or through the grant making body concerned

Those interested, should contact the number above for information on local landfill operators whom they can contact directly. Alternatively, information will usually be available from readers local Wildlife Trust.

The Equitable Charitable Trust

£3,000,000 (income in 1996/97)

Education of disabled or disadvantaged children

5 Chancery Lane, Clifford's Inn, London EC4A 1BU
Tel: 0171-242 1212

Correspondent B T McGeough, Managing Trustee

Trustees Brain McGeough; Roy Ranson; Peter Goddard.

Beneficial area UK.

Information available Full report and accounts.

Summary Grants, sometimes for six-figure sums, for both capital and revenue projects.

Background The trust was established as part of a commercial school fees prepayment scheme.

The annual surplus being applied for charitable purposes. The attraction to the contributors was the tax-exempt status of the operation. After some years of controversy and discussion, further sales of schemes of this nature were disallowed by the Inland Revenue and the Charity Commission, but it was agreed that schemes for existing contributors could be continued until completion. The effect of this is that the income from such contributions is now diminishing year by year and will end when the education of the last pupils is complete.

However, the trust has already begun accumulating a part of their income into a permanent endowment, so that the trust will continue to operate after its present source of funds comes to an end. By the end of 1996 this new capital fund stood at £1.5 million.

Grant making The trust is managed by Brian McGeough, one of its trustees and who is himself the full time Treasurer of the mighty Henry Smith Charities. His time is donated to this trust by the Smith Charities.

The trustees 'will continue to concentrate on the educational needs of disadvantaged children by making grants for specific projects to schools and other organisations catering for such needs. They will also fund interesting and innovative educational projects of all kinds wherever they can find them, especially if they are capable of being introduced into a large number of schools to supply needs not adequately met at present.'

In 1996, because of the uncertainty at that time surrounding the future of the charity, few grants were made, totalling only £141,000 (the potentially disposable surplus income of the trust was about £3 million). In future years the amount given in grants will be determined to a great extent by the amount put aside into the endowment for the future. However, this editor guesses that the total will probably lie between £1.5 and £2.5 million in the next few years.

The trustees say that 'they will continue to make grants available for the purchase of computer equipment for use by disabled young people in connection with their education. These will continue to be the only grants made to individuals'.

However the few awards that were made may indicate some of the particular interests of the trustees. The list is headed by £45,000 for Musicworks, a community music organisation, £36,000 for a special needs teacher in Cheddington County Combined School, and £29,000 to help with the relocation of The Pace Centre, a school for children with motor disorders, within the grounds of a mainstream school.

Exclusions No grants to individuals except for the purpose of purchasing computer equipment necessary for the education of disabled students.

Applications In writing to the correspondent.

The charity does not use application forms but offers the following guidelines to applicants for grants:

1. Applications should be no longer than four A4 sides (plus budget and accounts) and should incorporate a short (half page) summary.

2. Applications should:
   a. state clearly who the applicant is, what it does and whom it seeks to help.
   b. give the applicant's status (eg. registered charity).
   c. describe the project for which a grant is sought clearly and succinctly; explain the need for it; say what practical results it is expected to produce; state the number of people who will benefit from it; show how it will be cost effective and say what stage the project has so far reached.
   d. enclose a detailed budget for the project together with a copy of the applicant's most recent audited accounts. (If those accounts show a significant surplus or deficit of income, please explain how this has arisen).
   e. name the applicants's trustees/ patrons and describe the people who will actually be in charge of the project giving details of their qualifications for the job.
   f. describe the applicant's track record and, where possible, give the names and addresses of two independent referees to whom Henry Smith's Charity may apply for a recommendation if it wishes to do so.
   g. state what funds have already been raised for the project and name any other sources of funding to whom the applicant has applied.
   h. explain where the on-going funding (if required) will be obtained when the charity's grant has been used.
   i. state what plans have been made to monitor the project and wherever possible to evaluate it and, where appropriate, to make its results known to others.
   j. ask, where possible, for a specific amount.

3. Please keep the application as simple as possible and avoid the use of technical terms and jargon.

The trustees meet monthly.

The Eranda Foundation

£1,460,000 (1996/97)

The arts, general

New Court, St Swithin's Lane, London EC4P 4DU
Tel: 0171-280 5000

Correspondent Geraldine Harkins, Secretary

Trustees Sir Evelyn de Rothschild; Mrs Renée Robeson; Lady de Rothschild; Leopold de Rothschild; Graham Hearne.

Beneficial area UK.

Information available Report and accounts on file at the Charity Commission but now without the required grants list, but stating that such a list is available from the Foundation. No list, though, was supplied when requested by these editors.

Summary Most funds are disbursed in a few large grants between £25,000 and about £200,000. There seems to be a preference towards charities with a national remit or and/or those based in London.

General The foundation was established in 1967 by Evelyn Rothschild with the objects of 'the advancement of learning in the Arts and Sciences, in particular:

- health and the prevention/relief of sickness, in particular by medical research and teaching and by the organisation and development of medical and health services;
- social well-being, in particular by scientific research and scientific education including training or study and the provision of scholarships and prizes.'

During 1996/97 the foundation's endowment generated the rather low income of £1,272,000 (0.36%) from assets which totalled £35,000,000 at the end of the year. However the return increased to almost 5% in 1998.

The funds were disbursed as follows:

	1996/97	(1995/96)
Education	*£689,000*	*(£473,000)*
Health welfare and medical research		
	£396,000	*(£451,000)*
Arts	*£317,000*	*(£510,000)*

The foundation reports receiving over 10,000 applications a year, a scarcely credible figure, and one far above the figures reported by other general purpose trusts of similar size. A selection are chosen by Sir Evelyn de Rothschild and the Secretary to be put before the trustees collectively.

'Grants are mainly given ... for a specific project'. They may be for up to three years and may cover both capital and revenue costs.

The foundation has given details of three major grants in 1998:

NH Trust (sic)	*£225,000*
Global Cancer care	*£25,000*
Leo Baeck College	*£20,000*

There is no grants list for 1996/97 on file at the Charity Commission; however, there is such a list for 1995/96 when arts and environment grants included the following:

RSA (probably the Royal Society	
of Arts. Ed.)	*£170,000*
National Trust	*£125,000*
Buckingham City Museum	*£10,000*
St Peters, Tyringham	*£10,000*
World Monument Fund	*£5,000*
Chicken Shed Theatre Company	*£5,000*
Flora and Fauna International	*£5,000*

Awards within the health, welfare and medicine field included £125,000 to Caldecott, £52,000 to Norwood; £50,000 to St Mary's A & E; £27,000 to International Spinal Research, £25,000 to Research into Ageing; £15,000 each to Turning Point and Cancer Research; £10,000 awards to Tommy's Campaign and Willen Hospital; and £5,000 to the Anna Freud Centre.

Applications In writing to the correspondent.

The Eveson Charitable Trust

£2,058,000 (1996/97)

Health, Welfare.

45 Park Road, Gloucester GL1 1LP
Tel: 01452-501352; Fax: 01452-302195

Correspondent Alex D Gay, Administrator

Trustees Bruce Maughfling, Chair; Rt Revd John Oliver, Bishop of Hereford; Peter Temple-Morris MP; J Martin Davies; David Pearson.

Beneficial area West Midlands, Herefordshire and Worcestershire.

Information available Full report and accounts are on file at the Charity Commission. The trust also publishes a thorough and admirable grants list and guidance notes for applicants.

Summary The trust gives grants of up to £50,000 for both capital and running costs to organisations working with children, young people and those who are disabled, homeless or elderly. Most grants, though, are for amounts between £3,000 and £10,000. Note that at present the trust operates only in West Midlands, Herefordshire and Worcestershire.

General The trust was set up in 1994 with an endowment of nearly £50,000,000 from the will of Mrs Violet Eveson. Although grants are currently restricted to the geographical areas outlined above, this is not a specific requirement of the will and this limitation may be loosened in the future.

During 1996/97, 291 grants were made out of an investment income of £2,338,000. Support and administration costs accounted for a modest 3.4% of income, or £270 per grant. These figures are the more impressive given that the trust's representatives made over 80 visits to grant applicants and attended 50 other events.

The social care and development programme was the major interest of the charity accounting for 55% (£1,144,000) of the total grants expenditure in 1996/97. The funds went to 'organisations providing human and social services' to the target groups (children and young people, disabled, homeless, elderly).

Most grants were between £5,000 and £10,000, although many were more substantial and 62 were for £2,000 or less. Age Concerns fared well with eleven charities sharing £104,000 (almost twice

the sum given in 1995/96). Other generous grants went to Bromyard Community Transport Ltd (£29,000 to fund a minibus for the disabled) and to the Breakthrough Trust (£25,000 to cover capital costs of a training facility for the deaf).

Grants falling within the *health care* category totalled £640,000. The trust states that this class includes 'grants to organisations which focus on the prevention or treatment of specific diseases, the prevention or treatment of disease generally and/or health problems, the rehabilitation of disabled individuals, residential nursing homes for the frail, elderly, severely disabled and those offering terminal care.'

Although total funding was about half that of the social care programme, individual grants were larger. Only seven were for amounts of £2,000 or less and about half were for £10,000 or more. The trust's highest awards are also in this class, for example the Royal National College for the Blind (Hereford) was given £60,000 for remodelling of a Hall of Residence and St Mary's Hospice received a capital grant of £50,000.

The smallest programme – *accommodation* – paid out a total of £274,000. There is less focus here on disability and the elderly and more upon the homeless (£94,000 in 6 grants), refuges for abused women (£86,000, 8 grants) and holiday accommodation for disadvantaged children (£41,000, 5 grants).

The trust is saddened that increasingly large numbers of statutory bodies are having to approach them for 'what might have been considered essential funding'. However, unlike many other trusts Eveson does not necessarily refuse to make up the shortfall in public funding.

This trust is one of a number of energetic and enterprising foundations in its region, along with, among others, Barnwood and Summerfield.

Exclusions Grants are not made to individuals, even if a request for such is submitted by a charitable institution.

Applications The trustees meet quarterly, usually at the end of March and at the beginning of July, October and January.

Applications can only be considered if they are on the trust's standard, but very simple, Application for Support form which can be obtained from the administrator at the offices of the trust in Gloucester. The form must be completed and returned (together with a copy of the latest accounts and annual report of the organisation) to the trust's offices at least six weeks before the meeting of trustees at which the application is to be considered, in order to give time for necessary assessment procedures.

Before providing support to statutory bodies (such as hospitals and schools for people with learning difficulties), the trustees require written confirmation that no statutory funds are available to meet the need for which funds are being requested. In the case of larger grants to hospitals, the trustees ask the District Health Authority to confirm that no statutory funding is available.

Where applications are submitted that fall clearly outside the grant giving parameters of the trust, the applicant is advised that the application cannot be considered and reasons are given.

All applications that are going to be considered by the trustees are acknowledged in writing. The applicants are advised of the reference number of their application and the quarterly meeting at which their application is going to be considered. The decisions are advised to applicants in writing soon after these meetings.

The Esmée Fairbairn Charitable Trust

£11,589,000 (1997)

Social welfare, arts and heritage, education, environment, social and economic research

7 Cowley Street, London SW1P 3NB
Tel: 0171-227 5400

Correspondent Margaret Hyde, Director

Trustees John S Fairbairn, Chairman; Jeremy Hardie, Treasurer; Sir Antony Acland; Ashley G Down; Mrs Penelope Hughes-Hallet; Martin Lane-Fox; Baroness Linklater; Lord Rees-Mogg; Andrew Tuckey.

Beneficial area UK.

Information available Detailed Guidelines for Applicants (to be revised early in 1999). The fine Annual Report and Accounts have an excellent narrative review of the work of the trust, though relatively weak in their numerical analysis of the grants made.

Summary Now one of the largest and most interesting trusts in the country, Esmée Fairbairn is rapidly developing its grant making practice. It has extensive programmes under each of its main headings:

- Social welfare
- Arts and heritage
- Education
- Environment
- Social and economic research.

Major grants are typically for between £15,000 and £30,000 a year over two or three years, but much larger awards are possible – £750,000 was the largest in 1997. There are also numerous small grants for amounts of less than £10,000.

Until recent years this trust was one of the lightly staffed and 'distant' funders with which there was little personal contact except where the trustees developed specific interests. The trust has now decided to enlarge its administrative staff, including the appointment of five part time regional advisers, and with these extra resources it intends to 'enhance its contact with applicants', especially those seeking major funding. Already, it reports inviting short-listed applicants to its special environment fund of £1 million to make presentations directly to trustees (see under 'environment below). It has accepted that administrative costs will rise from about 3% to 6% of income. The trust is also developing its information systems with a view to becoming a much more pro-active grant maker. These changes are welcome, as in the view of these editors the value of many grants is greatly enhanced when they are accompanied by personal interest, enthusiasm and support. Money is well spent in achieving this.

Most grants are in response to the applications received but the trust also puts aside substantial sums for pro-active programmes in which, after consultation, it invites applications in specific fields. In 1998 the subject concerned was education at primary age and below.

This entry, after an introduction based on the Chair and the Director's comments in their 1997 Annual Report, reprints and reviews the trust's guidelines and the corresponding 1997 grant making under each of the headings above.

Background This trust is the owner of one third of the M & G finance group, which was founded by the uncle of the present chairman. The endowment is effectively undiversified and its value is prone to swings, having declined by £40 million in 1996 and then risen by £80 million in 1997 (though the Accounts correctly note the difficulty of putting a market value on such a holding). *(If permitted by the Trust Deed, these editors would prefer to see the investments diversified according to normal practice although they note that the Trust's investment policy has resulted in the trust becoming one of the largest in the country. Ed.)*

Like a number of others described in this book, the trust states that its policy is to dispense all of its income every year. However 'income' is not a 'given' but is a figure usually decided by the policy of the trustees on the realisation and treatment of capital gains. The concept of 'total return' is more appropriate. In practice the value of this endowment has been accumulating in real terms.

In his 1996/97 Chairman's Statement Mr Fairbairn notes his expectation that the government's abolition of the Advance

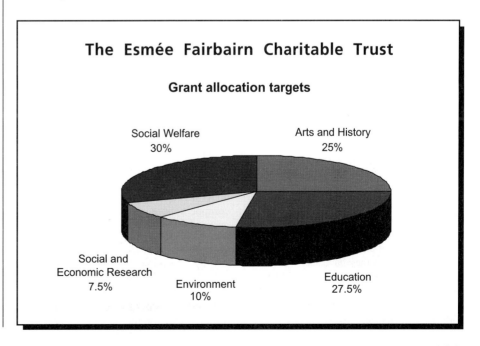

The Esmée Fairbairn Charitable Trust

Grant allocation targets

Social Welfare 30%
Arts and History 25%
Social and Economic Research 7.5%
Environment 10%
Education 27.5%

Corporation Tax credit will reduce the trust's income by no less than 18% after the end of transitional relief in 2004 (in 1997 terms, a loss of £2.3 million a year).

Grant making policy

The 1996/97 Chairman's Statement includes the following: '... grants to charities totalled £11.6 million compared with £11.4 million in 1995/96. The number of grants made was 866 compared with 1108, and during the year we received 3,872 applications. The average size of grant rose from £9,415 to £11,649.

'In the early part of last year the trustees decided that staffing levels should be increased somewhat and further use made of consultants to ensure high standards in the assessment of appeals and the monitoring of grants. When these decisions have been implemented in full the trust aims to contain its operational costs at around 6% of its income.

'It is the trustees aim to bring a sharper focus to bear in our grant making policies as set out in published guidelines for applicants, and in this context we are now in the process of reviewing our policy in the field of social welfare. We believe that a sharper focus helps to make our grants more effective and, in so far as we can publish clear guidelines for applicants, the latter should be spared from wasting time on submissions that are unlikely to meet with success.

'... I would like to dwell on one particular grant made in 1997, namely £500,000 to the Royal Opera House over four years. This was to some extent a controversial grant because we were not unaware of management problems at Covent Garden and a disturbing financial situation. Our grant reflected the need, which we have long recognised, for maintaining an international house in London that is capable of presenting opera to the highest standards with singers and artists of the top calibre drawn from all over the world and in a setting to match. Our grant was of course made some months before Gerald Kaufman's Culture, Media and Sport Committee criticised the board and management of the ROH in its well publicised report and the Secretary of State asked Sir Richard Eyre to make suggestions on the future of the Royal Opera House and English National Opera. Our Director subsequently wrote to Sir Richard arguing strongly that there is an important role for each of the two companies but that they have such different aims and styles that it would be a mistake to bring them together under one roof. The solution lies in ensuring that both companies have directors and senior

staff with requisite vision and expertise, including marketing and pricing expertise, and that new ways should be found to develop and tap private sources of funding, which will in turn need a tax regime wholly favourable to giving to the arts and other charitable causes.

'During the year Elwyn Owens completed an experimental period as the trust's representative in the North West, during which it became apparent that his knowledge of the area and assessment skills contributed very positively to our grant making and made the work of the trust better known in a part of the country which our staff can visit only occasionally. I am pleased to say that Elwyn Owens has now accepted a permanent appointment with the trust, and building on this experience we shall be aiming to make similar appointments in other regions.'

The Annual Report continues with the following introduction from the Director, Margaret Hyde:

'The trustees' policy meeting at Cumberland Lodge, Windsor Great Park in January 1997 looked ahead over the next five years to where the trust aims to be in 2002 and what it would wish to be known for. The trust's funding has enabled much to be achieved since it was set up in 1961. Income growth has been particularly marked in the 1990s and the average grant size has grown. Among the trust's desired aims as it looks ahead to 2002 are being better able to assess the results of the grants it has made across a given category or funding programme, as well as at the level of the individual recipient; and publishing and disseminating the results in a way that helps others to benefit. Some of the stronger foundations to enable this to happen began to be put in place in 1997, as the Chairman's Statement indicates.

'Better and more timely information to underpin decision-making is one. Implementation of the computerisation project began in the Autumn. The new database system which lies at the core of the project will greatly enhance the quality of the information available to management and the efficiency of its production. The trust will be able to track and analyse applications and grants under management more effectively, and compile a more accurate picture of demand from different areas of the country. Flexible word processing systems linked to the new database should also enable improvement in the quality of response to applicants.

'Towards the end of 1997, the trust also began to take the measured steps to

enhance the level of staffing as agreed by trustees at the Cumberland Lodge Meeting, while still maintaining a tight grip on administrative costs. A strengthened administrative and grants team will take total staffing to thirteen during 1998. Following a successful appointment in north west England, the trust also plans to appoint up to five more part time regional advisors who will represent the trust in other areas of the United Kingdom and enhance its contact with applicants. There can be something of a communications gap between fund-seeking charities and a charitable trust and trustees hope that the steps they are taking will address this.

'They will underpin another of the trust's aims to 2002 which is to meet more applicants, particularly those seeking major funding, as part of improving the grant assessment process.

'New applications to the trust in 1997 fell by some 10% from the peak figure of 4,314 in 1996 to 3,872, though still well up on the 1995 figure of 3,379. 1996 was the first full year for the trust's published guidelines and this may have accounted for the surge in that year. The trust now has two full years' experience of using the guidelines. Their general clarity has received favourable comment from applicants and there has been a perceptible improvement in the quality of applications accompanied by a reduction in ineligible ones. Learning from this experience, further improvements in the clarity of information to applicants will be introduced when the guidelines are revised during 1998. The major category of spending currently undergoing review is Social Welfare, following completion of a report by Janet Morgan on behalf of the trust towards the end of 1997. Some modifications to policy may occur in other categories, but the trust is unlikely to move away from its concentration on five areas of grant making.

'Trustees continued in 1997 to allocate a guideline percentage of the trust's available income, of over £12 million, to each category. These were:

Arts and History	*25%*
Education	*27.5%*
Environment	*10%*
Social and Economic Research	*7.5%*
Social Welfare	*30%.*

In practice, actual spending on social welfare exceeded its respective guideline figure with a corresponding reduction in other categories and particularly in education spending.'

This last remark is needed because, despite a guideline allocation of 30% to Social Welfare, the actual outcome was no less than 42%, presumably reflecting the pressure of demand from this part of the charitable sector. The actual amounts are given below when the 1997 grants are reviewed.

The trust, like a number of others, employs independent assessors and advisers, but unlike some others, names them in its Annual Report. At the end of 1997 these included:

Sir Christopher Ball
Hilary Bartlett (music, formerly with the British Council)
The Earl of Cranbrook
Elwyn Owens (North West England representative)
Catherine Graham-Harrison (formerly Director of the Hamlyn Foundation and currently a trustee of the Joseph Rowntree Foundation)
Barbara Riddell (who has also worked for the Baring Foundation)
Janet Morgan (social welfare, formerly with the staff of the Sainsbury Family Trusts).

Grant Making Guidelines

The trust's Guidelines give the following general information (guidance on each interest category is reprinted in the relevant section below).

General information

- The ... trust makes grants under five specific categories. These are
  - *Arts and heritage*
  - *Education*
  - *Environment*
  - *Social and economic research*
  - *Social welfare*
- The trust's grant fund currently exceeds £10 million and more than 3,000 applications are received each year.
- The smallest grant paid last year was £250 and the largest £250,000. There is no set pattern for making grants up to a specific percentage of the cost of a project. Grants of up to 100% may be considered in certain ircumstances.
- Grants may be awarded for one year or phased.
- Grants may be made towards revenue, capital or project expenditure.
- Retrospective grants are not made.
- The trust always receives more applications than it has funds to support. Even if a project fits the trust's policy priorities, it may not be possible to make a grant.
- The trust was formed in 1961 by Ian Fairbairn, a prominent City figure and pioneer of the unit trust industry, in memory of his wife. A large part of the trust's income derived from its share holding in M&G Group PLC.

- A copy of the trust's Annual Report is available on request.

Small grants scheme

'The trust operates a Small Grants Scheme covering grants of up to £5,000. Preference is given to projects that might be substantially enabled to happen with the trust's funding, rather than to projects where a grant would form part of a larger funding scheme. Local district and smaller national organisations are particularly encouraged to apply. (For details of how to apply under this scheme, see under 'Applications' at the end of this entry.)

The trust's guiding principles

- the purpose must be **charitable** and normally the trust will only consider applications from registered charities;
- the trust's area of interest is **UK-wide**. The trustees aim to give particular attention to less advantaged areas;
- in general the trust favours projects which will contribute to the preservation and development of a **free and stable society**;
- there is a preference for projects which are **innovative**, **developmental**, designed to make a **practical impact** on a particular problem and reflect the principles of **market forces**. Especially in the case of local projects preference is given to those which demonstrate **active local participation** and **support self-help**;
- the trust welcomes applications from **black and minority ethnic groups**.
- the trust will be alert to the needs of disabled people in all appropriate funding decisions;
- the trust looks favourably on projects undertaken in **partnership**, for example with another charitable trust;
- the trust attaches importance to the **assessment and dissemination** of the results of work it has funded, so that others might benefit.'

The sector Guidelines and the 1997 grants

These grants are tabulated as follows (with their indicative percentage allocations in brackets), but the figures include part payments following grant decisions made in earlier years

Allocation		No	Value
• Social welfare	(30%)	424	£4.3m
• Arts and heritage	(25%)	271	£2.7m
• Education	(27.5%)	80	£1.8m
• Environment	(10%)	68	£1.0m
• Social and economic research, other	(7.5%)	23	£0.5m
• Major grant programmes		N/A	£1.5m

The trust received 3,872 applications in the year, from which it follows that these have a 'success rate' of about one in five (though not always for the full amount requested). As noted below, the pressure of applications is greatest under the Social Welfare heading, so success rates are likely to be at their lowest there and to be rather higher for other categories.

The heading in the accounts for 'Major grants' refers to the fact that since 1994 the trustees have made annual provision for amounts of up £1.25 million to be utilised in a particular field where the beneficiaries have not yet been identified. In 1997 they completed an 'Environment' programme where £1.25 million was being divided between the country's Wildlife Trusts, including those in Scotland. They also launched a new primary education initiative described under 'Education' below.

The following sections look at each of the trust's funding areas in turn, starting with the relevant section from the trust's Guidelines, and continuing with the comments, often both interesting and valuable, that are made in the 1996/97 Annual Report. Where possible, these editors have added, in brackets, the amount involved in each of the specific grants that are mentioned. Finally in each section a few of the other large or interesting grants are listed, some of them carried on from the previous year.

Social welfare

The Guidelines read as follows:

'The trust prefers prevention to palliatives. It wishes to foster self-help and the participation of those intended to benefit; enable less advantaged people to be independent, gain useful skills and overcome handicaps; and encourage volunteer involvement. The trust supports practical initiatives embodying some or all of these characteristics in the following priority fields:

- Permanent physical and sensory disabilities;
- Mental health and learning difficulties (most funding is done through another grant-making body, the Mental Health Foundation. Consult the secretary before applying);
- Young people, especially those who are under-achieving or living in difficult circumstances;
- Parenting and family support;
- Carers, ie people caring for the sick, elderly or disabled people at home;
- Homelessness;
- Ageing, ie social aspects of elderly

people living in the community;
- Crime prevention and the rehabilitation of offenders and ex-offenders;
- Substance abuse;
- Regeneration and other schemes which support and develop community resourcefulness, particularly in less advantaged areas.'

The 1997 Annual Report gives the following description of this programme:

'Social welfare is the trust's largest spending category and is where the budgetary pressure is greatest. Along with Education, it is the category where the boundary between what is appropriate for the trust to fund and what should be left to the statutory authorities is at its most grey. This is not a straightforward matter of what is a statutory duty and what is merely a power to fund. The trust is often faced with applicants seeking to replace funding from a relatively short-term government programme whose ending is wrapped up in exit strategies, or from smaller national organisations dealing with a tapering core grant or a switch to project funding. The continuation of a programme of work or salaried post should not be seen as an end in itself, but the energy being expended often fruitlessly to secure alternative funding must often displace person power directed at benefiting clients or users who indirectly therefore bear the cost.

'In 1997 the trust approved 365 new and 59 continuing grants totalling £4.32 million. A number of potentially promising new initiatives have been supported. These include the Institute of Community Studies Social Entrepreneurs programme (£50,000); a pilot community information service using modern technology being set up under the aegis of Whitewater (£25,000); Project 2001, under the auspices of the Royal Society of Arts, which is developing an accreditation scheme for local volunteering (£25,000); and Charities Aid Foundation's Investors in Society fund which provided loan finance to charitable projects unable to raise finance in the commercial market .

'One of the themes in the trust's social welfare spending is that local people can be enabled to improve the quality of their lives and the conditions of their neighbourhoods and communities. The trust gave further funding to the Neighbourhood Initiatives Foundation's charitable fund addressing neighbourhood renewal (£60,000 over two years). Grants were also made to Herefordshire and Worcestershire Credit Union Development Agency for training

(£16,000), CADISPA for work with rural communities in the remoter regions of Scotland, and ACRE Suffolk for work with local people on local action plans (£7,500).

'Grants to support work and training opportunities for special needs groups were made to Edinburgh Community Trust, SMART Charitable Trust in South Liverpool (£48,000), Tranmere Methodist Church in Birkenhead (£60,000), and North Staffordshire Furniture Mine (£7,500). Of a different order but still supporting local initiatives, grants were made to Calderdale Community Foundation's endowment fund (£50,000), to South East London Community Foundation (£15,000), and to Community Links Trust for its 'Firsteps' programme of training support for embryonic or small local voluntary organisations and groups in East London (£13,000).

'Improving people's quality of life in later years and enabling them to lead independent lives was reflected in grants to the Workers Educational Association in Scotland (£23,000), Salford's Anti-Rust Project (£10,000), Bramley Elderly Action and Swarcliffe Good Neighbours Scheme in Leeds (£6,500). A feature of the Salford scheme is forging links between early retired people and the younger community, looking at experience and skills which can be shared between the generations.

'Enabling disabled people to lead as independent lives as possible was the subject of a grant to the Papworth Trust to establish a 'progression' centre in Suffolk for moving to independent living (£34,000). The Royal London Society for the Blind received funding for a work placement scheme and job search facility (£25,000), and the Percy Hedley Centre in Newcastle for development of its centre for those with cerebral palsy and speech and language difficulties.

'How parents and families can best be supported and nurtured is a subject of much current comment and debate. During the year the trust made grants to a number of initiatives. These included parenting courses run by Barnardo's on the Benchill estate in Manchester, an area with the highest number of households living on benefits and the proportion of single parent families in the city; support to ATD 4th World's Frimley programme for families experiencing difficulties (£48,000); Brent Welcare for its family support project (£60,000); and the Children First/Royal Scottish Society for the Prevention of Cruelty to Children's initiative to establish a national parent's helpline

(£41,000). Grants were also made to the National Association of Family Mediation and Conciliation Services (£60,000), and to Family Mediation in Scotland (£90,000).

'The trust supported several social welfare organisations in Northern Ireland during the year. A major grant was given to NIACRO, the Northern Ireland Association for the Care and Resettlement of Offenders, towards a programme to co-ordinate support services for offenders and their families across the province (£100,000). The Women Caring Trust was also supported in its work with children and their families living in the parts of Ireland most affected by community tension (£50,000).

'Many of the trust's applicants are youth organisations. This year the trust made a major grant to Fairbridge in Scotland for its programme to support young people in Edinburgh and Glasgow leaving care (£120,000). It also supported foyer schemes providing housing tied to training and employment opportunities by making grants to the The Foyer (Slough and Thames Valley) (£75,000), Salter's City Foyer in London, and St Vincent's Housing Association in Manchester (£15,000). Other projects with young people which gained grants included Longbenton Youth Programme in Newcastle (£45,000), the Laburnham Boat Club in London (£10,000), Wiltshire Young Carers, the London Brook Advisory Centres Brixton project (£50,000 for refurbishment) and Halton Young Citizens' Forum.'

In addition to the grants described above, the Mental Health Foundation received £100,000 for two multi-year programmes carried on from decisions in previous years; £60,000 was given to the Big Issue Foundation towards vendor support; Prisoners of Conscience received £25,000 to assist with emergency help for asylum seekers. Among the list of grants of £10,000 or less there are a number of local umbrella organisations, such as Whitby Volunteer Centre (£5,000), but few for the local branches of national charities. The £4,000 for Berkshire St John's Ambulance was unusual.

Arts and Heritage

The Guidelines read as follows:

'The trust wishes to help extend the artistic and business development of the performing and creative arts, and it is more likely to support organisations or projects less able to raise substantial funds from other sources. In this area, the trust's priorities are:

- The professional development of performers and other artists who have completed their formal training and are in the earlier stages of their careers. No grants are made to individuals;
- Initiatives which improve the management, artistic or business performance of arts organisations, or their financial independence;
- The public presentation or performance of contemporary work;
- Arts provision amongst groups or places less well-served;
- Audience development;
- Arts education work involving local communities, particularly those less well served.

In the heritage field, the trust additionally supports:

- Significant acquisitions by provincial public museums and galleries (only limited support since the trust channels most its funding in this area through another grant-giving body, the National Art Collections Fund. Please consult the trust's secretary before applying);
- The preservation of buildings of historic or architectural value where these are put to public use, and the conservation of artefacts.'

The 19997 Annual Report gives the following description of this programme:

'The trust's grant making in the arts and heritage field is largely responsive in character, guided by the trust's stated policy priorities. Trustees approved 238 new and 33 continuing grants totalling £2.71 million in 1997, reflecting the trust's wide range of interests in the performing and creative arts. A limited number of grants were to organisations in the heritage field.

'The trust believes that it can make the greatest impact, in this as in other categories, by concentrating the majority of its funding on project and revenue grants. Its support to capital projects generally is therefore limited but tends to arise more in this category than most others. Capital spending in the Arts and Heritage field has been driven in recent years predominantly by the availability of Lottery funds, although recent changes to the rules are introducing greater project and even revenue spending which is altering the pattern somewhat. The trust has been careful about its support to Lottery related projects on two main counts. First, trustees have preferred not to commit funds to projects too far in advance of likely start dates, so they have taken a cautious approach to projects which have yet to secure Lottery funding. Second, trustees have tried in the main to direct their support towards less high profile or nationally prestigious projects.

'Two exceptions to this are the trust's support to the capital redevelopment of The Royal Opera House (£500,000), on which the Chairman has commented in his Statement, and to the Royal National Theatre (£100,000). Other capital grants, not all Lottery related, approved during the year were to the Soho Theatre redevelopment (£100,000), Hestercombe Gardens Trust near Taunton (£40,000) for restoration of the historic gardens, Friends of the De La Warr Pavilion for the further restoration of this 1930s Grade I listed building, the new Poole Study Gallery for the twentieth century arts works, Northton Heritage Centre for its genealogical research centre on the Isle of arris, Stills Gallery in Edinburgh (£30,000), Chester Cathedral for its concert venue development, Beckford Tower Trust in Bath (£35,000), and Curwen Print Study Centre in Cambridge.

'A number of grants were made to support the further management or artistic development of arts organisations, London Sinfonietta (£37,000), Northern Stage, Drake Music Project (£12,000) and the Arvon Foundation (£90,000) were among those receiving help of this kind. A grant was made to Southern Sinfonia to help the transition from a largely volunteer run organisation to a small professional management team. Dance City's support service for young artists in the north of England, providing advice on career planning, artistic development and help with accounting and budgeting, was another beneficiary (£10,000).

'Arts education involving local communities is one of the trust's priorities. Among those receiving support were Warehouse Artists Studios in East Anglia (£10,000) for its outreach programme for schools, special needs groups and amateur artists; Highpeak Community Arts for its arts development programme (£50,000); the Horniman Museum (£25,000), 198 Gallery (£15,000) and Museum of East Asian Art for education work; and English National Opera towards its Baylis Programme (£90,000).

'ENO's Contemporary Opera Studio also benefited from the trust's grant. The 'Granula and Spect' project from Composers Desk Top (£16,000), World Music Days' New Music 98 (£36,000), Society for the Promotion of New Music (£7,000) and Huddersfield Contemporary Music Festival (£10,000) were among others benefiting under the contemporary work heading, while the City of Birmingham Symphony Orchestra received a further grant towards the final year of Judith Weir's Composer in Association term with the Orchestra (£15,000).

'Other interesting or unusual projects receiving support included research into how concert programme notes can be improved to make them clear, accessible and user friendly, especially for first-time and occasional concert goers (the Association of British Orchestras with the Royal Society of Arts, £10,000); a project for Large Saxophone Ensemble involving twenty players (Mass Producers); and the Brass Band Heritage Trust's work to enhance band culture particularly in places where it has diminished in recent years (£18,000).'

Education

The Guidelines read as follows:

'The trust is interested in supporting the projects which will contribute to the development of a better educated society. Projects falling in the following fields are given priority:

- early learning, covering the years 0-7;
- further education of 16-19 year olds, particularly the academically less able;
- the professional development and further training of teachers
- adult education, especially where this combats earlier under achievement or creates second chances.

(No grants are made to individuals).'

The 1997 Annual Report gives the following description of this programme:

'The trust's spend in the education field has been of two kinds: taking initiatives and responding to applications received. In 1997 it approved 59 new and 21 continuing grants to the value of £1.7 million. A number of the trust's past initiatives in the early learning field have greatly helped to increase the awareness of the central importance of this building block in a child's education, and have contributed to strategic developments at national and local level in early years education.

'Pre-school and early years education initiatives, a number of them having a social welfare dimension, have featured strongly in the trust's responsive grant making in 1997. Blackbird Leys Community Development Initiative (£37,000) received funding to provide pre-school education on this multi-ethnic housing estate on the periphery of Oxford. Pen Green Centre for Under 5s and Their Families received a grant

(£180,000) towards a research project into how parental involvement benefits children attending nurseries, while Barton Hill Settlement Bristol's Family Playcentre, which many parents have been involved in helping to build, was awarded a core grant (£50,000). The National Association of Toy and Leisure Libraries received funding (£25,000) for a development project to help achieve a higher profile for toy libraries in schools. The contribution that the arts can make to enabling learning to happen was recognised with a grant to West Yorkshire Playhouse for its work on arts and creative teaching in the primary classroom (£50,000). The Trust also supported Kent Children's University, an initiative to provide additional learning opportunities outside normal classroom hours across a wide range of academic and vocational subjects to primary school children (£50,000).

'Higher up the age range, an initiative by Community Service Volunteers and supported by the trust focuses on wider skills by helping young people in secondary schools to develop a greater sense of citizenship through community service (£150,000). In the adult education field, the trust has offered major support (£80,000) to the University of Exeter's proposed Research Centre for the Learning Society which will support the development of lifelong learning, and at the other end of the spectrum a small grant (£3,500) has been made to Housebound Learners, an initiative in Wandsworth to help housebound adults to take up education opportunities.

'A theme which has appeared in a number of applications received during the year has been that of children and young people excluded from school. At a policy level, the trust has taken part in discussions with other trust funders in London about this growing problem, exacerbated by the unplanned consequences of performance targets and school league tables. At a practical level the trust has agreed a number of grants to initiatives catering for those who have been excluded or are at risk, including Toxteth Tabernacle Baptist Church, a school for young people aged 14-16 excluded from mainstream schools in Liverpool (£45,000), and also to Elimu Study School in the same city (£5,000); The Children's Society for the SHINE project in two south London schools (£30,000); Second City Second Chance in Birmingham which uses peer tutors and mentors with young people at risk of exclusion (£40,000); and Ormiston Children and Families Trust for a project on behaviour and social skills for

children excluded from school in East Anglia (£3,000).

'An issue which has preoccupied the trust has been investigating where the trust might make the most effective intervention to improve educational attainment in schools at primary level and below. In recent years the trust has made a number of very large grants in some of its other categories, the last being in the environment field (see page 15). In 1997 trustees set aside the sum of £1 million towards a major initiative in the education field, and set out to explore the hypothesis that class size, expressed in terms of adult-child ratios, was a critical determinant of educational attainment and that a project centred on improving the ratio of adults to children could be designed both to satisfy the criteria of rigorous research and to make an impact on the education of several cohorts of children. The trust consulted a range of institutions and experts in the field. There was a widespread response in support of the case for rebalancing education budgets to enable more resources to be directed to primary education. There was less agreement that adult-child ratios was the critical variable in attainment, respondents pointing instead to other influential factors such as parental involvement and teacher education. The shape and development of the trust's intervention will take account of these views and the available evidence behind them.'

Environment

The Guidelines read as follows:

'The trust wishes to promote sustainable development principally through practical projects, research where this is geared to advancing practical solutions, and education:

- The preservation of countryside and wildlife, appropriately linked to public access;
- The reconciliation of the needs of the environment and the economy, ie projects which sustain the former and promote solutions to any adverse environmental effects associated with economic development;
- The development of alternative technologies that help attain these objectives.'

The 1997 Annual Report gives the following description of this programme:

'Promoting sustainable development is central to the trust's environment policy. In 1997 it approved 46 new and 22 continuing grants to the value of £1.05 million. The trust made a further grant to Forum for the Future (£26,000), which

aims to identify, develop and share practical solutions to environmental problems, and move forward the whole UK sustainable development agenda. Other grants included: Forest Stewardship Council, to define standards for sustainable forest management in the UK (£10,000); Sunderland University Ecology centre, to research the effects of insecticides on Britain's declining bird life (£36,000); and West Devon Environmental Network (£3,000).

'Care and protection of the countryside and wildlife provided the framework for grants to the Association for the Protection of Rural Scotland (£50,000); Scottish Native Woods (£60,000); the Campaign for the Protection of Rural Wales for the purpose of strengthening links with local communities, statutory agencies and local authorities, encouraging them to adopt a sustainable approach to environmental management (£105,000); and to Trees for Life towards the restoration of a large area of the Caledonian Forest in Glen Affric (£10,000). Grants were also made to British Butterfly Conservation Society towards its audit of national populations (£66,000), Bat Conservation Trust for the recruitment and training of volunteers to help implement conservation strategies and monitoring (£68,000), and to Froglife. Development grants were made to the newly established Landscape Foundation to help fund a core post (£60,000), and to the Garden History Society (£10,000).

'In 1997 the trust completed the allocation of a special fund of £1 million, set aside to spend on the "environment" category. Major environmental organisations were consulted on priority areas for funding and criteria for the Environment Large Grant Fund drawn up taking account of the consultation results. Applications were invited that fell into one or more of the following categories: projects aimed at reconciling the use of the environment with conservation; restoration and recreation of lost habitats and subsequent maintenance/management; education and awareness-raising schemes aimed at practitioners, decision makers and opinion formers who have a major impact on the environment but who may not appreciate the benefit of an environmentally sensitive approach to resource management. Thirty nine outline applications were received from which eight were invited to submit a full proposal. From this group four were selected to make presentations to trustees in March 1997. Trustees decided to exceed the original sum set aside by making two grants as follows: £750,000 to the Wildlife Trusts towards the development of local record centres which will hold detailed information about the state of wildlife locally and which collectively will provide a national picture of our environment; and £500,000 over four years to the Scottish Wildlife Trust towards a scheme to secure the long term conservation of wildlife sites in lowland Scotland.'

Social and economic research

The Guidelines read as follows:

'The trust wishes to encourage the application of new ideas (or the challenging of old ones) to contemporary socio-political and economic issues. It supports research to this end, especially that designed with practical applications in mind, principally through the medium of independent research institutions.'

The 1997 Annual Report gives the following description of this programme:

'Social and Economic Research is the trust's smallest category of spending. The trust has a marked preference towards supporting research designed with practical applications in mind. The greater part of the trust's grant making has traditionally been directed to independent think-thanks and research institutes and this continued in 1997. In all the trust approved 17 new and 6 continuing grants, totalling £0.5 million.

'The majority of major grants were to address social policy issues. Demos received funding (£61,000)for its social exclusion programme (ahead of the new Labour Government's decision to set up its own social exclusion unit in the Cabinet Office); the new International Centre for Prison Studies based at King's College London received support towards its running costs (£100,000); and a grant was made to enable the senior research fellowship at the City University's Rehabilitation Resource Centre, conducting work on disability issues, to continue for a further year. Grants touching more on economic issues were made to the Parenting Fiscal Reform Group to investigate the fiscal context of parenting (£30,000). The Charity Law Unit at Liverpool University received a grant to research issues around the so-called contract culture affecting charities (£30,000). In the more speculative category, a small grant (£7,000) was made to The Tomorrow Project for work on issues for policy makers likely to be emerging in the first two decades of the next century. Finally, it was also gratifying to note that the report on the policy choices facing the UK on European monetary union 'The Ostrich and the EMU',

stemming from an earlier grant made to the Centre for Economic Policy Research, has had some influence on Government thinking on this subject.'

Exclusions Grants are made to registered charities only.

The trust is unlikely to support the following:

- charities whose operational area is outside the UK;
- large national charities which enjoy wide support;
- branches of national charities;
- individuals;
- schools;
- medical (including research) or health care;
- expeditions;
- conferences or seminars;
- general appeals;
- sports;
- commercial publications;
- overseas travel;
- individual parish churches;
- animal welfare;
- sectarian religions;
- the direct replacement of statutory funding.

Retrospective grants are not made.

Applications All applicants should first obtain the trust's guidelines (send s.a.e.).

Applications for grants over £5,000 should be in the form of a letter with supporting information where necessary. The following information is required:

1. A brief description of your organisation, its work, management and staffing structure, and current budget.
2. Description of the purpose of the project for which funds are required, the amount sought from the trust, who will manage the project, the project start/finish dates and the results expected.
3. A budget for the project, details of funds already raised and other sources being approached.
4. How your organisation intends to monitor and evaluate the project.
5. Your plans for sharing information about the project and what you learn from it with others in the field.
6. The most recent annual report and audited accounts.
7. Your organisation's charitable status, mentioning the charity's registration number.
8. The contact name and address and telephone number.
9. In addition, please quote the code for the current guidelines (EFCT/G1 for the guidelines used for this entry in

the summer of 1996, Ed).

Applications for grants up to £5,000 (Small grants scheme) should be made on the trust's application form. Copies are available from the Secretary, Judith Dunworth, at the trust address (send s.a.e.).

Both kinds of application can be made at any time of the year, but allow good time for the processing, before their consideration at the trustees' meetings in February, May, July and November, since applications can take up to six months to process.

Once the application has been considered the trust does not usually accept another application from the same organisation within 12 months from the date of the decision.

The Fishmongers' Company's Charitable Trust

£534,000 (to organisations 1997)

Relief of hardship and disability, education

The Fishmongers' Company, Fishmongers' Hall, London Bridge, London EC4R 9EL
Tel: 0171-626 3531

Correspondent K S Waters, Clerk

Trustees The Wardens and Court of the Fishmongers' Company.

Beneficial area UK, with a special interest in the City of London and adjacent boroughs.

Information available Annual accounts, without the required listing, analysis and explanation of grants, and with no narrative report. The trust notes that they have been approved by the trustees and audited by a major firm of accountants. These editors remain unimpressed, fearing that where trustees wish to minimise disclosure about their work, their accountants may too often seek to assist their clients in doing so.

General Donations are said to be for the relief of hardship and disability, education, the environment, heritage and fishery related charities. They are reported to go to national organisations only, except for those local to the City of London or adjacent boroughs, but as there is none of the required information, this cannot be verified. There is no information whatsoever about the size, nature or purposes of the grants.

In the case of requests for help from cathedrals, abbeys, churches and other old buildings, 'priority will be given to St Paul's Cathedral and Westminster Abbey'.

Exclusions No grants are made to individual branches of national charities or to regional or local charities, other than those in the City of London and adjacent boroughs. No grants are awarded to individuals except for education. Educational grants are not awarded to applicants who are over 19 years old.

Applications In writing to the Clerk. Meetings take place three times a year in March, June, July and November and applications should be received a month in advance. Grants are made on a one-off basis. No applications are considered within three years of a previous grant application being successful.

Unsuccessful applications are not acknowledged.

The Donald Forrester Trust

£461,000 (1996/97)

Disability

231 Linen Hall, 156-170 Regent Street, London W1R 5TA
Tel: 0171-434 4021

Correspondent Ms Brenda Ward

Trustees Anthony Smee; Michael Jones; Gwyneth Forrester; Wendy Forrester.

Beneficial area UK and overseas.

Information available Accounts on file at the Charity Commission but without a narrative report.

General The trust appears to give mainly to well known national organisations that help people with disabilities. Some modest grants are also given to hospices and a few youth organisations.

The trust had assets of £9 million in 1996/97, held almost entirely as investments in Films and Equipments Ltd. Income generated from this amounted to £418,000, with total grant giving at £461,000. The trust made about

114 awards, but only about 25 were new grants to charities not also supported in the previous year. There were no very large awards, the biggest going to Guide Dogs for the Blind Association (£10,000).

The beneficiaries of £5,000 grants included the Alzheimers Disease Society, British Diabetic Association, National Deaf Children's Society, SCOPE, Cancer Relief Macmillan Fund; Cystic Fibrosis Trust, Leukemia Research Fund, Concern, and the Samaritans.

Applications The trust has written to say that applications are not considered and that all grants are "made at the discretion of the trustees". The trustees meet in February and September.

The Hugh Fraser Foundation

£1,385,000 (1995/96)

General

Turcan Connell, Saltire Court, 20 Castle Terrace, Edinburgh EH1 2EF
Tel: 0131-228 8111

Correspondent George Menzies

Trustees Dr K Chrystie, Chairman; Lady Fraser of Allander; Hon Ms A L Fraser; Ms P L Fraser; B Smith.

Beneficial area Principally West of Scotland and deprived areas of Scotland.

Information available Out of date accounts are available from the trust for the impressive charge of £10.

General The foundation was established by Lord Fraser of Allander and endowed by him with shares in House of Fraser and Scottish and Universal Investments (SUITS), the two West of Scotland based companies he directed.

The foundation supplied us with a copy of their most recent annual report and accounts, those for 1995/96. Readers should be aware of the dated nature of the information provided.

'The trustees' policy is to pay special regard to applications from the West of Scotland and applications from those parts of Scotland where the local economy makes it more difficult to raise funds for charitable purposes.

'The trustees consider that grants to large highly publicised national appeals are not likely to be as effective a use of funds as grants to smaller and more focused

charitable appeals.

'The trustees also consider that better use of funds can be made by making grants to charitable bodies to assist them with their work, than by making a large number of grants to individuals.

'The trustees are prepared to enter into commitments over a period of time by making grants in successive years, often to assist in new initiatives which can maintain their own momentum once they have been established for a few years.

'The foundation makes donations to charities working in many different sectors, principally hospitals, schools and universities, arts organisations and organisations working with the handicapped, the underprivileged and the aged. The trustees are nevertheless prepared to consider applications from charities working in other fields.'

From assets amounting to £24 million the foundation generated an income of £1.3 million. Management and administration costs were low at less than 2% of the income. The grants total for 1995/96 was £1.39 million in 108 awards.

Only the six organisations which received grants of 2% or more of the gross income are listed. These represent 55% of the grants total and were: Epilepsy Association of Scotland (£39,000); Cancer Research Campaign of Scotland (£123,000); Cancer Relief Macmillan Fund (£25,000); University of Aberdeen Development Trust (£600,000); Weipers Equine Trust (£72,000) and University of Glasgow, Wellcome Surgery Unit (£33,000).

Exclusions Grants are not awarded to individuals. Major highly publicised appeals are rarely supported.

Applications In writing to the correspondent. The trustees meet on a quarterly basis to consider applications.

The Joseph Strong Frazer Trust

£356,000 (1996/97)

General

Scottish Provident House, 31 Mosley Street, Newcastle Upon Tyne, NE1 1HX
Tel: 0191-232 8065

Correspondent The Secretary

Trustees Sir William A Reardon Smith, Chairman; Rita M Gibson; D A Cook; R H M Read.

Beneficial area England and Wales only.

Information available Report and accounts with grants list, but without the required analysis or explanation, on file at the Charity Commission.

General In 1996/97 income of £466,000 was generated from assets totalling £8 million. Management and administration costs amounting £145,000 were high; 40 pence per £ of grant, or about £2,000 per grant awarded.

Around 70 grants, varying from under £1,000 to £7,000, were awarded. About half of the funds were distributed in grants of less than £2,000. Twenty eight awards for £2,000, eight for £3,000 and nine between £5,000 and £7,000 totalled £168,000.

Recipients cover a wide variety of fields and are based all over England and Wales (the trust appears to be one of a very few in this book to have a specific interest in Wales). The awards were categorised as follows:

	1996/97 (1995/96)
Health and Medicine	*£98,000 (£70,000)*
Education	*£66,000 (£54,000)*
Culture, sport and recreation	*£57,000 (£46,000)*
Medical research	*£46,000 (£33,000)*
Welfare services and relief	*£25,000 (£15,000)*
Religion	*£17,000 (£15,000)*
Social services and relief	*£14,000 (£36,000)*

The largest grants were to Hill Homes and the Salvation Army (£7,000 each). Other beneficiaries included: Bearwood College (£6,000); Royal Theatrical Fund (£5,000). British Institute for Brain Injured Children, Stroke Association and the Merchant Navy School (£4,000 each).

Beneficiaries receiving £3,000 grants were: Welsh National Opera; King Alfred School; Alzheimer's Research Trust; Royal British Legion Poppy Appeal.

£2,000 gifts were made to: Cardiff YMCA; Barnet Bereavement Project; Barnardo's (Wales and the West); Trust for Sick Children; Hearing Dogs for the Deaf; Multiple Sclerosis Society; and the National Museum and Galleries of Wales.

Exclusions No grants to individuals.

Applications In writing to the correspondent. Trustees meet twice a year, usually in March and September. Application forms are not necessary but it is helpful if applicants are concise in their appeal letters which must include a SAE if acknowledgement is required.

The Gannochy Trust

£3,091,000 (1996/97)

General, in Scotland

Kincarrathie House Drive, Pitcullen Crescent, Perth PH2 7HX
Tel: 01738 – 620653

Correspondent Mrs Jean Gandhi, Secretary

Trustees Russell A Leather, Chairman; Stewart Montgomery; Mark Webster; James A McCowan; Neil MacCorkindale; Dr James Kynaston.

Beneficial area Scotland, with a preference for Perth and its environs.

Information available Annual report and accounts with grants list and narrative explanation of major grants.

Summary An unknown number of grants are made each year to charities working for various causes. About ten large grants (up to £1 million, typically £150,000) account for approximately half of the donations budget. Grants are normally one-off but each year three specific organisations receive around 10% of total charitable expenditure.

General 'The Gannochy Trust was founded in 1937 by Arthur Kinmond Bell, whisky distiller of Perth, who built the Gannochy Housing Estate in Perth consisting of 150 houses which was completed in 1932. This model scheme was a significant element in the foundation of the trust.'

The trust's charitable activities consist of the provision of subsidised housing for the elderly, and grant-making to charities. This entry will focus on the latter.

In 1996/97 the trust's assets totalled over £107 million and their income was £4.5 million. Administration costs were low – £121,000 or 3 pence per £1 of charitable expenditure.

Breakdown of grant-making 1996/97

Health	*25%*
Education	*23%*
Social Welfare	*22%*
Recreation	*17%*
Arts	*9%*

Environment	*4%*

These figures are largely in line with previous years.

The interests of youth were amply served under all headings.

The trust says:

Prime objects are the needs of youth and recreation, but the trustees are not restricted to these objects. The benefit of all donations must be confined to Scotland. There is an obligation to show a preference for Perth and its environs.'

The annual report only lists grants which, individually, account for more than about 2% of income. In 1996/97, nine such grants varying from £82,000 to £300,000 totalled £1,432,000 (46% of total grant expenditure). Several of them are described by the trust as follows:

Major donations (Organisations marked with an '*' are supported regularly.)

£400,000 was donated to Perth and Kinross Recreational Facilities Ltd*, of which £200,000 was applied mainly for the renovation and repair of community halls in the Perth area. A proportion of this sum was directed to sports coaching for youth. £200,000 was donated specifically towards the construction of to Strathearn Recreation Centre at Crieff, Perthshire.

£300,000 was donated to the National Museums of Scotland Charitable Trust towards the construction of the Museum of Scotland in Edinburgh.

£200,000 was donated to the Ayrshire Hospice for the provision of a new day care unit and palliative education facilities in Edinburgh.

£150,000 was donated to the University of Dundee for the Tayside Institute of Child Health at Ninewells Hospital.

Perth and Kinross Heritage Trust* received £100,000 for the general purposes of that trust.

£100,000 was donated to the Abbeyfield Perth Society towards the extension of Viewlands House, Perth, a home for the elderly.

£100,000 was donated to the Prince and Princess of Wales Hospice at Glasgow towards the extension and refurbishment of the day care unit.

£82,000 was donated to the Kincarrathie Trust for refurbishment and maintenance at Kincarrathie Home for the elderly, Perth.'

The smaller grants (under £82,000) accounted for 54% (£1,660,000) of the overall total. Three regularly supported organisations received grants amounting to £582,000 or 19% of the sum value. It is not known how many smaller grants are repeated.

Exclusions No grants to individuals. Donations are confined to organisations recognised by the Inland Revenue as charitable.

Applications In writing to the correspondent, confined to 2 pages of A4 including:

- a general statement on the objects of the applicant's charity;
- the specific nature of the application;
- the estimated coat and how this is arrived at;
- the contribution of the applicant's charity towards the cost;
- the contributions of others, actual and promised;
- estimated shortfall;
- details of previous appeals to the trust – whether accepted or rejected;
- a copy of the latest audited accounts.

Time rarely permits visits either to the trust office or to the charity concerned.

Garrick Club Charitable Trust

Perhaps £300,000 a year, but see below.

Probably arts, children in London

15 Garrick Street, London WC2E 9AY
Tel: 0171-395 4100

Correspondent The Secretary

Information available The trust was established by the members of the Garrick Club in London in 1998. It was expected to be endowed with about £8 million from the proceeds of selling the Winnie the Pooh copyright to the Disney organisation; however the deal had not been completed at the time of writing.

In November 1998 reported areas of future work were help for arts organisations and for disadvantaged children in the East End of London.

Applications The trust was not yet in operation as this book went to print.

The Gatsby Charitable Foundation

£28,591,000 (approved, 1997/98)

Technical education, mental/other health, economic and social research, children/young people, welfare, development in Africa, plant science, arts, general.

See the entry for the 'Sainsbury Family Charitable Trusts'
Tel: 0171-410 0330

Correspondent Michael Pattison, Director

Trustees A T Cahn; Miss J Portrait; C T S Stone, but see below.

Beneficial area UK and overseas.

Information available Report and accounts, including narrative comment on the main programmes and descriptions of individual projects approved. Both grants paid and approvals of new awards are listed in full. The foundation's principal officers include Michael Pattison, the director, Professor R C Baker, director – technical programmes, Paul Spokes, finance director, and M J Williams, executive.

Summary This huge foundation is one of the Sainsbury Family Charitable Trusts which share a joint administration. It makes awards over a number of years to carefully chosen organisations and is particularly interested in advancing policy and practice within its chosen areas (see above) usually by means of research which is practically oriented. In doing so Gatsby is proactive and rather than responding to individual applications from the charitable sector it decides according to its own strategies which organisations it may or may not support. It is not led by the application process and deters unsolicited applications.

In 1997/98 its predominant support was to Cognitive Neuroscience (over £10 million) followed by Technical Education (over £7 million), Third World Development (over £5 million) and Mental Health, Disadvantaged Children, and the Arts (over £1 million

each). In this year Economic and Social Research, Plant Science, and Social Development all received under £1 million.

There are considerable fluctuations annually in the size of its giving to different categories of work caused by the large advance funding commitments awarded by the foundation.

General The Gatsby Charitable Foundation is the fourth largest grant making trust in the UK. It was set up in 1967 by David Sainsbury, created life peer and Lord Sainsbury of Turville in 1997. He resigned as Chairman of Sainsbury plc in 1998 and has become a Labour minister as Parliamentary Under Secretary for Science with the Department of Trade and Industry. The asset value of the Gatsby Charitable Foundation increased by £225 million to £618 million in the year to April 1998. It had a net unrestricted income of over £18 million in 1997/98 with a total of £32.7 million available for distribution.

After the Wellcome Trust and the National Lottery Charities Board, which deal with about 10 times Gatsby's annual approvals, only the Foundation for Sport and the Arts dispenses more funds annually (just). The Garfield Weston Foundation, another family operation whose wealth and largesse is based within the food industry, follows it in size.

Its worth mentioning these other massive grant making trusts if only to emphasise Gatsby's difference. One idiosyncrasy is that Lord Sainsbury himself has never been a trustee of Gatsby. The trio of trustees includes Christopher Stone, director of Diatech Ltd, and financial adviser to David Sainsbury and Andrew T Cahn a recent 1996 appointee, who is a senior civil servant. However, the Great Gatsby in Scott Fitzgerald's novel also wielded power and influence with a light, shadowy touch. Perhaps this is why this is said to be David Sainsbury's favourite novel. It is also said that all the areas of giving which this foundation pursues represent his interests both business and personal. He seems to be a man in which the two would be intertwined since he was born into fortune and its responsibility, and served as Sainsbury's financial director long before he became its chairman.

The funding by Gatsby is strategically and astutely chosen. It aims to make an impact on the future and to do so by concentrating the major part of its funding upon carefully selected centres of excellence, in whatever the field of work and through considered co-operation with other forces. A recent example is the funding in 1997/98 of University Challenge, a joint initiative with the Wellcome Trust and the government to allow universities to set up their own University Seed Venture funds (£2 million over 2 years). The policies that inform the foundation's categories of giving also reflect long range interests related to Lord Sainsbury's former business interests: plant growth and food production, business management, technical education, to pick a few. One beneficiary over two decades, Social and Community Planning Research, may seem, by its size of grant, relatively insignificant compared with others but its annual research into British social attitudes, is highly valuable to all marketing people. Know your public.

So how does this foundation differ from the others named above? It has clearly articulated policies (made public during the past decade) which it works out with advisers of the highest calibre. Some are named in the extracts from the 1997/98

report below. The connections are powerful, close and intricate. Sir John Ashworth, for instance, who has in previous reports been named as general adviser to Gatsby is also a director of Sainsbury plc, current chairman of the British Library and former director of the London School of Economics. Gatsby uses its network of expert connections in whatever field, business, medical, social, education, to explore current and potential areas of concern. In doing so it is not different from many other well organised major trusts which take advice and have carefully selected interests often based on direct personal knowledge. But Gatsby ploughs its own furrow, is proactive and rather than responding to individual applications from the charitable sector decides according to its own strategies which organisations it may or may not support. It is not led by the application process. It deters unsolicited applications. It is individualistic, self-determining and has the stamp of a person.

It still retains, however, one area of 'old fashioned' charitable giving related to disadvantaged children. Here grants are made to some 40 local groups throughout the country and in addition 15 grants made to individual children in need via local authorities and organisation. These more modest allocations comprised some £220,000 in 1997/98 - a small sum for this trust but enough in itself to qualify, if run as a separate trust, for its own entry in this guide to the top 300-400 grant making trusts.

As a rule though, people are supported to help themselves. This is done often indirectly by the development of better educational processes particularly in the less glamorous but essential areas of maths, science and technical education, or by the development of better technical facilities for those disabled by communication problems. In Africa four separate Gatsby trusts run by Africans concentrate on providing microcredit for the small business person. In the UK a

The Gatsby Charitable Foundation

£'000 (Grants/no) %

	1997/98			1996/97			1995/96			1994/95	
Economic/ Social Research	765	(9)	3%	5,847	(12)	25%	945	(8)	6%	1,498	6%
Technical Education	7,571	(25)	26%	5,736	(23)	25%	4,533	(28)	27%	2,257	9%
Plant Science	250	(3)	1%	307	(10)	1%	1,431	(22)	8%	13,651	55%
Cognitive Neuroscience	10,406	(6)	36%	64	(2)	0.2%	171	(9)	1%	262	1%
Health Care/ Service Delivery	–			850	(12)	4%	1,116	(11)	7%	508	2%
Mental Health	1,423	(21)	5%	2,203	(14)	9%	3,033	(15)	18%	1,941	8%
Children/ Young People Disadvantaged Children	1,020	(64)	4%	1,319	(47)	6%	1,809	(59)	11%	682	3%
Social Development	248	(4)	1%	340	(7)	1%	1,744	(3)	10%	–	
Third World Development- Africa	5,108	(25)	18%	1,176	(9)	5%	214	(5)	1%	2,133	9%
Arts	1,573	(19)	6%	–			–			–	
Total	28,591	(193)	100%	23,372	(172)	100%	16,994	(194)	100%	24,800	100%

small Gatsby grant making fund is administered by the National Tenants Resource Centre to enable tenants to empower themselves to improve their own circumstances.

The following table gives an overview of the fluctuations in scale of different categories of grant approvals over a four year period. It can mislead. For instance under the Plant Science heading Gatsby has given massive support to the John Innes Foundation and the Sainsbury laboratory over the past decade yet the £250,000 in 1997/98 looks 'minimal' and could erroneously suggest a withdrawal from long-range support to this institute, both for its work in the UK and from co-operative work with related institutes in Africa. On the other hand the massive funding to Cognitive Neuroscience in 1997/98 compared with the funding in earlier years shows a classic Gatsby 'build-up' to give major, but not necessarily exclusive, funding to one chosen base (see account below).

A Note on Gatsby by a Trustee

It seems worth quoting from an article by Christopher Stone, a trustee, in the first issue of the excellent newsletter *Gatsby Inter Trust Newsletter- promoting Micro-Enterprise* published by and for the Gatsby trusts in Africa.

'Gatsby is administered by a small office in London and the trustees meet every six weeks to consider progress reports on existing projects and new project proposals. Although they are not trustees, Mr and Mrs Sainsbury (now Lord and Lady Sainsbury of Turville, editor) take a close personal interest in all of Gatsby's activities....I hope that an observer looking at Gatsby would see that:

- there is a close and productive relationship between trustees, who set general policy and approve grants and the executive staff, who advise the trustees and ensure that the programmes are effectively implemented;
- the aim of Gatsby's programmes is to bring about practical and measurable improvements in each area of activity, with clearly stated objectives whenever possible;
- Gatsby tends to begin its activities on a relatively small scale but is willing to persevere for long periods, gradually increasing the size of grants as the trustees become more confident in their understanding of the subject;
- Gatsby tries to be specific and consistent, yet flexible, in its approach and is willing to take risks;

- Gatsby nearly always works within the 'system' to bring about improvements, rather than trying to create new institutional structures;
- in each programme Gatsby works through and with people of integrity who are well respected within their communities and who share Gatsby's objectives.'

This is a helpful general overview. Even though it was written for the African context it appears to be equally relevant to all newcomers to Gatsby's work whether in the UK or overseas.

Just a couple of comments to illustrate, or slightly qualify, some of the generalities of the statement. The gradual build up of support is illustrated by the funding to cognitive neuroscience shown in the financial table above.

Gatsby works with governmental organisations, both central and local, and major institutes. The 1997/98 award to University Challenge with the Wellcome Trust and the government to enable universities to set up their own University Seed Venture Funds is one recent example. However Gatsby has also been noteworthy among the Sainsbury trusts, and grant making trusts generally, in setting up new organisations where it sees they could perform a necessary additional service or approach- the Sainsbury Mental Health Centre is the most longstanding, but Gatsby Technical Education Project (GTEP) and Science and Plants in Schools (SAPS) are other more recent initiatives.

The 1997 Annual Report

The account below is taken directly from the foundation's 1997/98 report. Where possible the actual grants are included by the editor in brackets within the text.

Economic and Social Research - £765,000 approved 1997/98

'The trustees continue to support economic and social studies through a selected group of research bodies. They also support management education with the objective of enhancing UK business performance through better equipped managers and employees.

'The trustees are providing funds for studies to identify the reason for regional success in fostering new business development, the potential for new areas of UK manufacturers and the manufacturing needs for industries of the future.

'The trustees' other major continuing commitments include the Professor of Agribusiness and Food Marketing at Wye College, and the chair in business studies at Birkbeck College, University of London.'

Approved grants in 1997/98 also

included those to the Social Market Foundation towards its core funding (£338,923) and the Wider Share Ownership Movement (£240,000 over 3 years towards a 3-year cycle of programmes). The foundation also continued its funding of Social and Community Planning Research for their British Social Attitudes series (£129,601 over 3 years). In 1996/97 the London Business School, of which Lord Sainsbury is the Chairman, received massive support for its building appeal (£5 million).

Technical Education - £7,571,000 approved in 1997/98

'The trustees' objectives are to ensure that able young people with appropriate high quality education and training apply technology in industry to the creation of wealth. The trustees' programmes which seek to achieve this are:

- to encourage technology transfer between universities and industry;
- to encourage the most able technologists to aspire to leadership in manufacturing industry both at professional and at technician level;
- to encourage good teaching and good materials in schools in maths, science and technology as an essential prerequisite to the health of the manufacturing base;
- to encourage appropriate IT development which will enhance maths, science and technology in schools;
- and to ensure that the courses and the awards are respected and valued by industry, parents and students.

The trustees are encouraging development in university/industry links. They wish to foster technology transfer in both product and production systems. They are supporting manufacturing education through the Advanced Course in Manufacture and Management and a course for Leaders in Manufacturing at Cambridge University. The trustees are also assisting Cambridge University Institute for Manufacturing to work with industry, particularly Small and Medium Sized Enterprises, and to develop collaboration between the university and instrumentation companies. This will form part of the industry/university network support which is being funded by the trustees to provide a mechanism for technology transfer. The trustees are assisting with other technology transfer schemes between universities and industry, which develop a range of models from which to demonstrate successful practice.

'The Engineering Education Continuum is administered by the Royal Academy of Engineering and encourages the most able students studying maths and science to aspire to a leadership role in the engineering industry and to assist them by providing early leadership and entrepreneurial opportunities. (Royal Academy of Engineering £1.5 million to roll forward the continuum to 1999/00 and £51,000 towards the Sainsbury Management Fellows in the Life Sciences scheme).

'The trustees have provided funding for the Action for Engineering's SETNET charitable company, and are providing additional funds for some regional SETPOINTS which encourage collaboration between education/industry schemes.

'The trustees have encouraged and funded DATA (the Design and Technology Association) to provide support for technology teachers.

'*GTEP (Gatsby Technical Education Project)* is a separate charity, established by trustees to enrich and enhance learning and teaching in schools through developing curriculum materials and offering training to teachers in science, maths and technology. Some of the programmes include:

- The Technology Enhancement Programme which aims to improve capability in technology and to link it with mathematics and science for the practically able by developing curriculum support materials for students is the 14-19 age range, so that they will provide a well trained and motivated foundation for industry;
- The Mathematics Enhancement Programmes for primary and secondary schools which emphasis application of good practice in schools and the provision of material required by teachers;
- Preliminary work being done on the establishment of a Science Enhancement Programme, which will build on the successful Teacher Scientist Network at Norwich and other current science initiatives funded by the trustees;
- the encouragement of greater coherence between A-levels and GNVQs.

'In addition GTEP is exploring methods to deliver A-level further maths using IT, and has commissioned a limited review of the A-level maths requirements by universities for various subjects.'

Funding to *Gatsby Technical Education Project (GTEP)* of £1.57 million in 1997/98 included £840,000 for core costs over three years. In the previous year the

project had been been awarded £2.6 million. Its trustees are Dr John Ashworth, Miss J S Portrait, C S T Stone. GTEP Head of Office is Dr John Williams.

'*SAPS (Science and Plants in Schools)* is a separate charity, supported by Gatsby aimed at stimulating an interest in plant science among secondary school age students through developing curriculum materials and offering training to teachers.'

The trustees from July 1998 are Professor John Gray, Professor John Parker, Stephen Tomkins and Miss J S Portrait. The director is Richard Price. Although Gatsby remains the principal core funder SAPS also attracts funding from other sources. Gatsby funding of SAPS in 1997/98 was relatively modest compared with other initiatives (£21,083 with £105,000 in the previous year).

The report lists 19 people who have advised the trustees in the area of technical education during 1997/98: Professor Diana Bowles; Andy Brecon; Professor David Burghes; Julian Critchley; Dr Bob Ditchfield; John English; Sir James Hamilton, Mike Ive; Dr Chris Martin; Dr Ray Peacock; Andrew Ramsey; Professor David Reynolds; Dr John Sellars, Geoff Stanton; Kate St John; Mike Tomlinson; Sir Peter Williams; Professor Alison Wolf; Dr John Westhead.

Other beneficiaries in 1997/98 included University Challenge, a joint initiative with the Wellcome Trust and the government to allow universities to set up their own University Seed Venture funds (£2 million over 2 years), the Cambridge Foundation (£570,000 plus £406,000 in the previous year) and Women's Education in Building (WEB) to develop a second centre in south-east London (£481,000 following grants in 1995/96 of £25,000 to upgrade their centre and £45,000 for a feasibility study of the proposed new centre).

Plant Science - £250,000 approved 1997/98

'The Gatsby plant science programme is aimed both at the development of basic research in the UK and also at encouraging more young people to develop and maintain an active interest in research.

'The main vehicle for the trustees' funding continues to be the Sainsbury Laboratory at the John Innes Centre in Norwich. The Laboratory carries out research in molecular plant pathology. The aims of the work are to drive new understanding about the fundamental processes of plant growth and development from an analysis of the

diseased and disease-resistant state of plants and genetically to engineer plants to resist viral, bacterial and fungal pathogens. The Laboratory is in its second five year research cycle (1994-1999), following an excellent formal peer review of its scientific outputs by a team of international experts.

'The trustees have funded a number of summer studentships for undergraduate students at leading research institutes. The trustees continue to encourage the most able young people to consider a career in plant science research by supporting up to three PhD students each year. The trustees also appointed their first post-doctoral fellow.

'To encourage students to keep in touch with each other and with the foundation, a network provides conference support, training and news interchange.'

The trustees were advised during 1997/98 by Dr John Ashworth; Professor Enrico Coen; Professor Ian Crute; Professor Dick Flavell; Dr Roger Freedman; Professor John Gray; Professor David Ingram; Richard Price.

Cognitive Neuroscience - £10,406,000 approved 1997/98

'The trustees emphasis in this relatively new category is on interdisciplinary development which bring together theory and experiment with fundamental techniques and measurements, rather than problem areas or specific illnesses. They are conscious of the need to avoid providing funds when these should be available from the Research Councils. Therefore:

a) Gatsby expects to fund projects for which government funding of basic facilities is already in place, allowing Gatsby to provide funds for specific and definable projects outside this normal funding and

b) Gatsby will contribute in ways which are qualitatively different from research council funding and allow interdisciplinary and speculative projects.

'This year the trustees have made a major commitment over ten years to set up a unit at University College, London, which will develop computational modelling under the direction of Professor Geoffrey Hinton FRS (£10 million over 10 years).'

'The trustees are advised by a committee comprising: Dr John Ashworth; Professor Richard Frackowiak; Professor Horace Barlow; Dr Roger Freedman.'

Mental Health - £1,423,000 approved 1997/98

'The trustees chose to revise their grant-making in the areas of health care and service development to concentrate on mental health, principally by continuing to fund the Sainsbury Centre for Mental Health. The trustees also supported a small number of health and social welfare charities (four grants).

'A fund of £430,000 has been set aside for palliative care projects as proposed by the trustees' advisers. Two grants were made from this fund to St Christopher's Hospice. The first was for £70,000 over two years towards developing an IT-assisted decision-making system. The second, also for £70,000, was towards a new education centre.

'The trustees continue to support work which will help improve the quality of life for people with long term and serious mental health problems. There remains a stigma attached to mental health problems while well-publicised tragic cases highlight gaps in provision which are damaging to people who are ill and potentially damaging to the wider community.'

Sainsbury Centre for Mental Health

This centre is the main vehicle for the trustees' mental health funding which is set up as a separate charity with Miss J S Portrait and C T S Stone as trustees and Dr Matt Muijen as director. The centre produces its own report with fuller details of its work.

A joint project, called the Sainsbury Initiative, led by the Sainsbury Centre and the Department of Health was launched in 1994. It has explored the impact of a range of service interventions and disseminated the findings. Eight sites were selected from over 300 applications. The evaluation of services funding under the Initiative will be completed in 1999.

'The lessons learnt will be made known with a vigorous dissemination programme. This has highlighted exemplary models of care, such as the crisis care developed in North Birmingham. To promote wider adoption of these, the Sainsbury Centre for Mental Health began a joint development programme with the King's Fund to reconfigure services for people with severe mental health problems in three inner London health authorities (£500,000 over 2 years).

'The centre published a number of studies and reports, including a review of best practice in crisis services. A system of locality profiling was established which will provide standardised information on mental health services on a national basis. An innovative postgraduate diploma course on effective

care for people with mental health problems was accredited by Middlesex University and rolled out on 12 sites.'

'A peer review by an eminent group of internationally recognised experts concluded that the Sainsbury Centre for Mental Health was performing very effectively.'

Fourteen separate grant awards for the centre totalling over £960,000 were approved by the foundation in 1997/98.

Disadvantaged Children - £1,020,000 approved 1997/98

'The trustees' aim in this area is to fund projects that develop and deliver better services to young people with mental and physical disabilities and/or subject to social disadvantage. The trustees are concerned that people who may face multiple disadvantages should have access to opportunities to help themselves and have access to the services they need.

'The trustees continued to fund projects in two areas of particular concern:

- communication skills for disabled/ disadvantaged children and young people;
- means of overcoming social disadvantage, particularly interventions to improve the mental health and well-being of children and young people.

'The trustees also reviewed their policy in this area, with the aim of establishing a more coherent grant-making programme and decided to concentrate on the following;

- the care and education of children with special educational needs, especially speech and language disorders
- children and young people at risk of homelessness, ending up in prison or unemployment because of a combination of difficult family circumstances and disengagement with school.

'The trustees continued their support for the ACE Centre Advisory Trust, which researches and develops communication aids for severely disabled children. This included a peer review of this charity's work, which confirmed its excellence and necessity (£340,000 towards relocation costs).'

In addition to this large grant five others between £50,000 and £180,000 were awarded. They included the Bibini Centre, towards this family crisis support service and evaluation of its pilot programmes (£180,000 over 3 years), the Care for the Carers Council towards the East Sussex Young Carers Project, on

condition the project is completed, and dissemination and replication built in so that any materials produced are available for wide distribution (£99,000) and Home-Start UK to enable it to consolidate developments in their training work with their local schemes (£80,000 over 2 years).

In addition 40 grants between £500 and £15,000 were awarded mainly to local projects and a number of schools. These included Write Away and Parents and Children's Support (£15,000 each), North Eastern Prison After Care Society and Lister Lane School Bradford (£10,000 each), Isleworth Explorers Club and the special Needs Activities and Play Provision in York (£3,000 each). A further 15 grants between £50 and £300 totalling £3,390 were given to local authorities and groups to assist particular disadvantaged children. This provision is in marked contrast to the rest of the foundation's work. It more closely resembles the work of many trusts which donate to direct relief and provision rather than policy. This part of its work appears to differ from the foundation's general assertion that unsolicited applications are rarely successful.

Social Development - £248,000 approved 1997/98

'The trustees wish to make a contribution towards practical development to improve the environment and well-being of people living in run-down urban areas.

'The trustees continue to fund a programme run by the National Tenants Resource Centre and the London School of Economics which provides small grants to local residents and self-help groups in urban areas subject to appropriate training being undertaken (£1,250,000 over 5 years was awarded in 1995/96). The trustees have also renewed their support for local credit union groups through the National Federation of Credit Unions (£54,000 over 2 years awarded in 1996/97).'

Grants in 1997/98 also included Emmaus UK to establish a community in Gloucestershire (£80,000) and the Foyer Federation towards financial advice for new local initiatives (£93,000 over 3 years).

Third World Development - £5,108,000 approved 1997/98

'The trustees have supported a range of projects in the Third World for over 20 years in the spheres of economic research and via direct programmes to help people in poverty. In the late 1980s the trustees decided that, in order to maximise the value of their support which in relative terms can only ever be a tiny contribution, they would concentrate their resources in Africa, in countries with reasonable stability and to support small-scale wealth creation in agriculture and manufacturing, and primary health care in support of women and small children. The trustees also decided to work through local people to develop sustainable projects and ensure any effort was genuinely responsive to local needs.

'In order to do this effectively, the trustees supported the establishment of local trusts, directed by local trustees, which now exist in Kenya, Tanzania, Uganda and Cameroon. These trusts direct and monitor funding in those countries as the most effective means both of ensuring the local relevance of projects and ensuring that the trustees' funds directly reach the areas they want to support. (Each of these four trusts was awarded some £420,000 over 4 years for their core costs in 1997/98).

'Mainly through the above structures, the trustees fund small-scale agriculture credit, manufacturing and handicraft developments in Kenya, Uganda, Tanzania and Cameroon. The local trusts are encouraged to share experience through occasional seminars and the joint production (published by the Tanzania Gatsby Trust) of an inter-trust newsletter. This process has been particularly helpful in areas such as regional and international marketing opportunities for local small-scale producers with whom the trust works.

'In Uganda the local trust encourages mutually beneficial links between small-scale enterprises and Makerere University. This, in turn, lead to staff and student collaborative projects with the enterprises. This initiative has led to a network of industry clubs bringing together local entrepreneurs in various areas of Uganda.

'The trustees also fund scientific research on staple food crops in Africa through recognised international food research institutes based in that continent. These are followed through into pilot schemes at farm level in several countries. (Beneficiaries included the International Institute for Tropical Agriculture awarded £675,000 over 3 years for a collaboration in Nigeria with the John Innes Centre.)

'In addition, the trustees have supported a family planning programme in Tanzania through Marie Stopes International (£600,000 over 4 years).

'In South Africa the trustees have initiated a major programme in the Western Cape to enhance the maths, science and technology education of the non-white races at all levels from pre-school to post-graduate and to identify a small number who would be encouraged to aspire to industrial leadership. The first cohort of engineers to go through the MBA course will graduate in December 1998. (Western Cape Tertiary Institutions Trust, Adamastor Trust, over £1 million in 3 awards.)

'The trustees are providing funds to support legal action to recover land which was lost by non-whites during the apartheid era (Legal Resources Centre, £120,000 over 3 years). They are supporting a project in the Karoo on land reform with the Surplus Peoples Project (£244,500). They are exploring the possible development of microloans in these areas and other funding mechanisms to help black farmers.

'The trustees have initiated a modest programme aimed at raising funds for housing for homeless people through inviting hotel guests visiting South Africa to donate to a local trust which in turn funds a rotating loan scheme.'

Laurence Cockcroft advises the trustees on their Africa programmes.

Arts - £1,573,000 approved in 1997/98

'The trustees grants under this category are focused on two major beneficiaries, the Sainsbury Centre for the Visual Arts at the University of East Anglia (£294,158), and the Royal Shakespeare Company (£850,000 mainly for preparatory work for the rebuilding of its Stratford complex). Beyond these, small grants are made pro-actively for specific theatre and musical projects.

'The trustees are not able to consider unsolicited applications.'

The foundation has made regular grants in recent years to the Robert and Lisa Sainsbury Trust, the trust of David Sainsbury's father and mother. In addition to the major grant noted above another was made to this trust for art purchases and catalogue expenses for the Sainsbury Centre for the Visual Arts at UEA (£297,850).

The trust had made a few arts grants in previous years, but these were categorised then as General. They had also included grants to the RSC and Gate Theatre.

General grants - £228,000 approved in 1997/98

The largest grant was made to St Paul's Girls' School towards a scholarship in honour of the retiring Headmistress (£125,000). Other grants included Second Chance (£20,000) and two awards to the village in Buckinghamshire from which Lord Sainsbury took his title - Turville School Trust (£5,000) and Turville Village Hall (£7,500).

Exclusions No grants to individuals, and no applications for building grants will be considered.

Applications The trustees met 10 times in 1997/98 and 11 times in 1996/97.

Grants are made for projects within the categories shown above which the trustees 'judge to have particular merit. Many of their grants are for projects which the foundation has helped to initiate. Therefore the trustees generally do not make grants in response to unsolicited applications.'

The previous edition noted that although unsolicited applications are rarely successful all that are received will be acknowledged. They can be submitted at any time in writing with the latest report and accounts. They should be concise (one to two pages), identifying aim, approach, justification and timeliness and the amount sought. Further communication will only take place if the appeal is being seriously considered.

It is said that an application to one of the Sainsbury family trusts is an application to all. See the entry for the Sainsbury Family Charitable Trusts for their address and further advice.

The Robert Gavron Charitable Trust

£572,000 (1996/97)

Arts, policy research, disability, general

44 Eagle Street, London WC1R 4FS
Tel: 0171-400 4301

Correspondent Dilys Ogilvie-Ward

Trustees Robert Gavron; Charles Corman; Katharine Gavron; Jessica Gavron; Sarah Gavron.

Beneficial area UK.

Information available Full report and accounts.

General This is a personal foundation, with an active founder and settlor. Much of the money follows Robert Gavron's own charitable involvements. The trust generally makes a small number of substantial grants, which account for most of the money, together with a larger number of more modest donations or subscriptions.

In 1996/97 there were 65 beneficiaries, but just five grants accounted for £397,000, or 70% of the grant total. They were as follows

Royal Opera House	*£205,000*
Open College of the Arts	*£65,000*
Institute for Public Policy	
Research	*£51,000*
Refresh	*£50,000*
St Peter's College, Oxford	*£25,000*

Other major beneficiaries were King Alfred School (£20,000), the Ashten Trust (£13,000), Adventure Unlimited and the London School of Economics (£10,000 each).

The remaining grants covered a wide field. Some were very small, such as the £25 to the Friends of the British Library but more substantial awards went to bodies as varied as the friends of CABx (£2,000), One World Action (£6,000), the Type Museum (£10,000) and the Holocaust Educational Trust (£1,000).

Applications In writing only to the correspondent. Please enclose a SAE and latest accounts. However the trust has said that its funds are committed for the next couple of years. There are no regular dates for trustees' meetings, but they take place about eight times a year.

J Paul Getty Charitable Trust

£1,567,000 (1997)

Social welfare, conservation

149 Harley Street, London W1N 2DH
Tel: 0171-486 1859

Correspondent Ms Bridget O'Brien Twohig, Administrator

Trustees Sir Paul Getty; Christopher Gibbs; Rt Hon James Ramsden; Vanni Treves.

Beneficial area UK, but see below.

Information available
Exceptionally full report and accounts. Application guidelines, Trustees' Report, grant conditions and a booklet 'The First Five Years' is available from the administrator.

Summary The trust looks to fund 'unpopular causes', ie. those which have little appeal to the general public. Donations, seldom for more than £10,000, are nearly always made as a

contribution towards revenue costs and may be paid as a single sum or over two or three years.

General The trust was founded and funded by J Paul Getty Jr (of the American oil dynasty), now living in London. Although Mr Getty also makes very considerable personal gifts to the arts and other causes in England (£50 million to the National Gallery, £1 million to enable the Canova Three Graces to remain in this country), these donations are separate from those of the trust. Furthermore, neither the trust nor J Paul Getty Jr are in any way connected to the Getty Foundation in the USA or to the J Paul Getty Museum in California (which tried to buy and export the Three Graces); both these organisations were endowed by J Paul Getty Senior.

Guidelines
In its guidelines the trust gives the following unusually full and interesting description of its grant-making strategy:

'The trust aims to fund projects to do with poverty and misery in general, and unpopular causes in particular, within the UK. The emphasis is on self-help, building esteem, enabling people to reach their potential. The trustees favour small local and community projects which make good use of volunteers. Both revenue and capital grants are made, but please read the categories not included section ['*Exclusions*' in this book – Ed.] below carefully, as it is possible that the particular aspect of your application rather that the general purpose of your organisation may be excluded.

'Priority is likely to be given to projects in the less prosperous parts of the country, particularly in the North of England, and to those which cover more than one beneficial area.

'Grants are usually in the £5-£10,000 range, capital and revenue, and those made for salaries or running costs are for a maximum of three years. Some small grants of up to £1,000 are also made.

1. Social welfare
'Mental health in a wide sense. This includes projects for:

- mentally ill adults
- mentally handicapped adults
- drug, alcohol and other addictions, and related problems;
- support groups for people under stress, eg; battered wives, victims of abuse, families in difficulty, etc;
- counselling, especially young people
- mediation.

'Offenders, both in and out of prison, men and women, young offenders, sexual offenders.

'Communities which are clearly disadvantaged, trying to improve their lot, particularly projects which help prevent people becoming homeless or resettle them.

'Homelessness, particularly projects which help prevent young people becoming homeless or resettle them.

'Job Creation projects or ones aimed at making long-term constructive use of enforced leisure time, particularly projects aimed at integration.

2. Arts
'Only the following will be considered:

- therapeutic use of the arts for the long-term benefits of groups under social welfare;
- projects which enable people in these groups to feel welcome in arts venues, and which enable them to make long-term constructive use of their leisure.

3. Conservation
'Conservation in the broadest sense, with emphasis on ensuring that fine buildings, landscapes and collections remain or become available to the general public or scholars. Training in conservation skills. Not general building repair work.

4. Environment
'Mainly gardens, historic landscape, wilderness.'

Annual report 1997
The trust produces excellent annual reports and accounts and the bulk of the narrative from those for 1997 is reproduced below:

General Comments
'The number of applications received by the trust went down the second year running in 1997, bringing the total almost exactly to 1993 levels. We should have found the reduction a positive help, as the trust receives more applications in relation to the funds available than some of the wealthier trusts, and can only support a small proportion of them. However, to our surprise we found it harder than ever to identify well-managed, small, entrepreneurial local organisations to fund. The proportion of applications which fell outside the criteria of the trust remained irritatingly high at the 35% to 40% mark. These applicants do not appear to have read the trust guidelines, and have assumed that the beneficial arts reflect, rather than counter-balance, Sir Paul Getty's personal interest in cricket and the arts.

'In addition, we have found it prudent to put on hold applicants who have been assessed by the Lottery, and are awaiting a decision. This is because some applicants in whom we had invested time investigating and visiting, and in one case funded, subsequently received ample funding from the National Lottery Charities Board, and did not need help from this trust after all. We have discussed these problems with the powers-that-be at the National Lottery Charities Board, and hope that a modus operandi will be found in 1998 for our proposal to set up an informal chain of communication between them and the charitable trust world.

'As we do not want to lower the standards we look for of energy, commitment and ability to manage, we plan to fill the gap by investing more time and funds in enabling organisations known to us to develop and extend their work to other parts of the country, and by seeking out new initiatives. We have also increased the number of small grants (up to £1,000) made.

'We do realise that fundraising is hard work, and have tried to help applicants this year by reducing the time taken to make decisions about funding. Applicants should hear whether their proposals are being taken forward or not within 4-6 weeks, and should have a decision within 2-4 months.

'However, the good news is that we have been able to keep up the level of grants made to fund salaries over 2 or 3 years. We take the view that we are backing the people behind the projects, and we are prepared both to give people setting up new initiatives a chance to put their ideas into practice, and to support those who have established a worthwhile project which deserves to continue. The longer period of contact also gives us the chance to monitor the effectiveness of our grant-giving.

Comments on Geographical Spread. 'The trustees continue to give priority to areas of greatest need, particularly to the inner cities and towns in the northern part of the country. Efforts are made to cover Scotland, Wales and Northern Ireland, but all applicants are short-listed on merit. We are doing less for Northern Ireland for the time being, as there are extra funds available there which are not available to other deprived parts of the UK. There is no target distribution set for any area. Most projects are visited by the administrator, Bridget O'Brien Twohig, before a proposal is considered for funding. Visits were made this year to Birmingham (three times), Northern Ireland, East Anglia, Yorkshire (three times), Merseyside (twice), Manchester, Sheffield, Nottingham, Newcastle and surrounds, and Devon.

Comments on Categories. 'The trustees continue to give priority to 'unpopular causes' which have little appeal for the general public (young offenders, mentally ill people, homeless people, addicts), and favour small, local organisations run efficiently by lively people. Most (90%) of the funds have been awarded to the Social Welfare categories. This year we have decided to highlight our continuing efforts to help families in difficulty to stay together by taking them out of the community category and identifying them separately. Recipients included the Ferries and Port Sunlight Family Groups (£24,000 over three years) in Merseyside who recognise that lots of people miss being part of a family for many different reasons, and lonely mums and older people with time on their hands have a great deal to give one another. Bentley Association for Supportive Help outside Doncaster (£30,000 over three years) is run from the parish church with people from an outlying estate of great deprivation. Depression Alliance, an excellent network of self help groups for people with depression which we have funded for a number of years, received a further grant of £5,000 towards a new office in Scotland. Full Potential Arts, set up by a group of young artists in Birmingham, was awarded £36,000 over three years to expand their imaginative work with mentally ill people.

J Paul Getty Charitable Trust

Categories of New Grants Authorised in 1997

Area 1997	No (1997)	£ Total (1997)	No (1996)	£ Total (1996)
Community Groups	25	£287,350	21	£306,500
Mental health	11	£139,200	15	£127,050
Family	8	£102,200	–	–
Youth	15	£223,000	17	£207,100
Offenders	10	£139,650	8	£88,300
Drugs and Alcohol	8	£126,100	4	£50,100
Homeless	14	£181,500	13	£166,400
Ethnic Minorities	6	£81,000	7	£87,000
Women	5	£32,950	4	£17,100
Physically Handicapped	6	£87,500	9	£82,500
Conservation/Heritage	19	£90,700	25	£227,050
Environment	4	£47,000	9	£114,000
Miscellaneous	7	£28,480	11	£77,260
Total	**138**	**£1,566,630**	**143**	**£1,550,360**

Geographical Spread of Grants Authorised in 1997 and 1996

	No (1997)	£ Total (1997)	No (1996)	£ Total (1996)
Birmingham	7	£171,000	7	£76,200
Cumbria	–	–	3	£35,500
Devon & South West	4	£36,250	5	£59,500
East Anglia	7	£85,00	6	£69,500
Headquarters/National	26	£317,730	28	£288,360
Ireland	2	£11,000	3	£31,500
London & Home Counties	11	£115,500	17	£147,000
Manchester and Lancashire	11	£108,500	–	–
Merseyside	9	£124,000	5	£47,500
Newcastle and the North East	10	£84,100	17	£235,400
Scotland	10	£29,400	10	£175,500
South	5	£89,000	5	£26,600
Wales and Bristol	7	£86,000	4	£60,500
Worcester and Hereford	2	£6,000	6	£56,300
Yorkshire	21	£260,450	21	£206,370
Other	6	£52,700	6	£34,630
Total	**138**	**£1,566,630**	**143**	**£1,550,360**

'The trust gives lower priority to physical disability, and this year decided to make one strategic award for this category by giving DIAL UK £45,000 over the three years to computerise their data dissemination process, as information on what is available where is crucial to disabled people. Lifeshare in Manchester (£36,000 over three years) comforts and finds homes for single homeless people and childless couples considered low priority by the Council. The Doncaster Open House, largely run by long standing volunteers who first noticed people sleeping rough in the City in the 80's, was awarded £7,000 for furniture. A large one-off further grant of £20,000 was made to the Stepping Stones Trust in London which has been quietly providing a home and support for several years for sexual offenders on release from prison.

'DISC Spennymoor Drug Project (£30,000 over 2 years) aims to tackle the increasing and depressing availability of drugs in a small county Durham town, as does project 6 in Keighley in Yorkshire (further grant of £10,000). Project Challenge in Halifax (£60,000 over three years), run by imaginative, determined local business people, takes on only the most hopeless young people for whom all else has failed and is proving remarkably successful with quite a number eventually coming off drugs, keeping out of trouble and even going back to finish their education. Grants were made to refugee projects which help all comers rather than specific ethnic groups, including £22,500 over three years to RETAS (education and training advice), and £100 to St Mungo's Asylum Seekers Project to provide travel and telephones cards.

'Grants in the small heritage/ conservation category were all one-off. The largest was £18,000 to SAVE Britain's Heritage, to provide a revolving loan fund for emergency action to halt the demolition of fine buildings under threat.

'There is another unofficial category worth mentioning: projects with problems. We back new, young organisations, and things can go wrong. We mean it when we say we like to hear the bad news as well as the good from our grant recipients, and in the past year the Administrator has put extra time into helping ten projects which developed management and other problems.'

This trust is laudable for its efforts to focus its support on the most neglected areas, both geographically and socially, and, for these editors, it represents a model of thoughtful and enterprising

grant-making, fully reported and clearly explained.

Exclusions

The trustees do not generally consider applications for the following:

- elderly
- children
- education
- research
- animals
- music or drama (except therapeutically)
- conferences and seminars
- medical care (including hospices) or health
- medical equipment
- churches and cathedrals
- holidays and expeditions
- sports or leisure facilities (including cricket pitches).

Residential projects or large building projects are unlikely to be considered.

The trustees do not support national appeals or grant giving trusts such as community trusts. Headquarters of national organisations and 'umbrella' organisations are unlikely to be considered, as are applications from abroad.

No applications from individuals are considered.

The project must be a registered charity or be under the auspices of one.

Applications Please request from the trust a copy of the guidelines before applying. The 1997 guidelines contain the following information:

'A letter no more than two pages long is all that is necessary at first, giving the outline of the project, a detailed costing, the existing sources of finance of the organisation, and what other applications, including those to statutory sources, have been made. Please also say if you have applied to or received a grant previously from this trust. Please do not send videos, tapes or bulky reports – they will not be returned. Annual accounts will be asked for if your application is going to be taken further.

'The project will also have to be visited before an application can be considered by the trustees. This may mean a delay, as it is only possible to visit a small part of the country between each quarterly trustee's meeting. Some small grants of up to £1,000 can be made without a visit, but only for specific purposes.

'Applications can be made at any time and all letters of appeal are answered – but please remember ONLY 2 PAGES in the first instance.'

The G C Gibson Charitable Trust

£488,000 (1997/98)

Churches, hospitals, medical research, general

Deloitte & Touche, Blenheim House, Fitzalan Court, Newport Road, Cardiff CF2 1TS
Tel: 01222-481111

Correspondent Karen Griffin

Trustees R D Taylor; Mrs J M Gibson; George S C Gibson.

Beneficial area UK, with interests in East Anglia and Wales.

Information available Report and accounts with full grants list but lacking narrative explanation.

Summary About of 150 grants are made a year to a broad selection of charitable causes. Grants are in the range of £1,000 to £10,000 with many around £2,000. Grants are usually repeated and a good proportion are made to organisations in Wales.

General The trust was founded by George Cock Gibson in 1969 and by the year ending February 1997 it had assets of over £10 million from which a high £629,000 in income was generated. The trust is manged by its accountants, Deloitte & Touche, Cardiff. Running costs in 1996/97 were a low £8,000, 2% of charitable expenditure or £50 per grant.

In 1996/97, 150 grants were made, around 80% of which were repeated from the previous year. The organisations supported work within a range of charitable fields, but as the trust does not categorise them it is difficult to discern trustees' preferences. Some of the better funded charitable fields are perhaps: churches, medical research, hospices/nursing homes, military welfare and youth/education. Beneficiaries are frequently well-established national charities – about 10% have 'royal' or 'national' in their titles.

The great majority of grants by number and value were for one, two or three thousand pounds. Six awards for over £5,000 accounted for 12% of charitable expenditure and 31 grants of £5,000 for 35%.

The four largest grants of that year were all for £10,000 and went to St Nicholas'

Hospice (Bury St Edmunds), St Michael's Hospice (Hereford), the Weston Spirit and Trinity College, Glenalmond.

A sample of other larger beneficiaries included: Wildfowl and Wetlands Trust, £7,000; The Dorset Respice and Hospice Trust, £5,000; Royal National College for the Blind Hereford, £5,000; Llandaff Cathedral Restoration Fund, £5,000; Multiple Sclerosis Society, £5,000; Nuffield Nursing Home, £5,000; and Marie Curie Foundation, £4,000.

Exclusions Only registered charities will be supported.

Applications To the correspondent in October/November each year. Trustees meet in December/January. Successful applicants will receive their cheques during January. 'Due to the volume of applications, it is not possible to ac-knowledge each application, nor is it possible to inform unsuccessful applicants.'

Simon Gibson Charitable Trust

£301,000 (1996/97)

General

Hill House, 1 Little New Street, London EC4A 3TR

Correspondent Bryan Marsh

Trustees Bryan Marsh; Angela Homfray; George Gibson.

Beneficial area UK, International with an interest in East Anglia, particularly the Newmarket area, and Wales.

Information available Report and accounts with full grants list but no analysis of grants and grant-making.

Summary Around 100 mostly small and repeated grants are made each year

to a broad variety of charities. Beneficiaries are often national charities, well established, and/or based in Wales.

General The trust was established in 1975 by George Simon Gibson, son of George Cock Gibson whose trust is examined in the preceding entry. By the year ending April 1997, its assets totalled £7.3 million and an income of £317,000 was generated. Running costs were a notably low £3,000, a penny per £1 donated. A little over 100 donations were made in the year, so the average grant was £3,000. Most awards were for £2,000 and the largest were for £15,000. Approximately three quarters of grants and funds went to organisations also supported in the previous two years. The largest awards – two of £15,000 (to Prince's Youth Business Trust and, Royal Academy of Music) and three others for £10,000 accounted for 20% of total charitable expenditure. Nearly all other grants were between £2,000 and £3,000.

Approximate breakdown of grants by category

Welfare	*26%*
Youth	*16%*
Medical	*14%*
Church	*10%*
Animal welfare	*7%*
Arts and culture	*7%*
International	*5%*
Miscellaneous	*15%*

Many of the recipients in the welfare group were 'profession' charities such as the Army Benevolent Fund (£2,000), Mission to Seamen (£2,000) and the Tinplate Workers Education Fund (£10,000).

A large number of both the medical and welfare grants went to organisations involved with mental or physical disability. Examples of these include awards to the Welsh Paraplegic and Tetraplegic Sports Association (£2,000), National Osteoporosis Society (£2,000) and Brain Injury Rehabilitation and Development (£2,000).

Although it is not clear from the trust's information, 'Youth' awards probably included a number of donations to schools (amonst these were £1,000 gifts to Harrow School and Cheltenham Ladies' College) and others to the National Playing Fields Association (£3,000), and Holiday Explorers (£2,000).

Exclusions No grants for individuals.

Applications In writing to the correspondent. Telephone calls should not be made. The trust has no application forms. It acknowledges all applications but does not enter into correspondence with applicants unless they are awarded a grant. The trustees meet in May and applications should be received in March.

The Glass-House Trust

£1,222,000 (approved 1996/97)

Parenting, family welfare, child development

See entry for the 'Sainsbury Family Charitable Trusts'
Tel: 0171-410 0330

Correspondent Michael Pattison, Director

Trustees A J Sainsbury; T J Sainsbury; Miss J M Sainsbury; Mrs C Woodward; Miss J S Portrait.

Beneficial area UK and overseas.

Information available The trust provides a full report and accounts. Its principal officers in 1996/97 are listed as Michael Pattison, the director, Paul Spokes, the finance director and Miss H Marriott, executive.

Summary This trust is one of the Sainsbury Family Charitable Trusts which share a joint administration. It is adventurous and has doubled its grant approvals between 1995/96 and 1996/97. Its major beneficiaries are chosen within a single policy area. Its key grant in 1996/97 was for research relating to the care of young children – a focal part of the government's evolving National Childcare Strategy. Its grant making in this respect appears to run in tandem with the Tedworth Trust, another Sainsbury Family Charitable Trust (see separate entry).

The Glass-House Trust

	1996/97			1995/96		
Parenting Family Welfare Child Development	£899,000	12	74%	£526,000	13	81%
General	£323,000	10	26%	£120,000	4	19%
Total	**£1,222,000**	**22**	**100%**	**£646,000**	**17**	**100%**

General Alexander Sainsbury is the settlor of this trust. Its net income amounted to £487,000, over £100,000 more than in the previous year, although its asset value had decreased by nearly £1 million during the year to £10.8 million at April 1997. About 88% of its investments, by market value as at April 1997, were in J Sainsbury plc.

The trust is advised by consultants 'as appropriate'.

Parenting, family welfare & child development

The allocations made under this broad category were listed within the following sub groups:

Childcare (one grant of £1,000 to Gingerbread for its Advice Line);

Mental health (two grants totalling £6,300, mainly to the Child Psychotherapy Trust – £6,000);

Parenting skills (3 grants totalling £11,500, largely to Parent Network towards its office relocation (£10,000);

School-based intervention & after-school provision (four grants totalling £135,000).

The school-based and after-school sub group was 'new' in 1996/97. Grants had been allocated under all the other sub-groups in the preceding year.

The largest grants in 1996/97 were to the Institute of Education Social Science Research Unit, University of London/ Borough of Hackney towards the establishment of a children's centre in Hackney to offer educational, recreational and health/welfare opportunities to children and young people aged 8-14 years (£60,000 over 2 years) and the Bow Family Centre to support intervention work with young people (and their families) and address problems which may prevent them making the most of school (£40,000 over 2 years).

Research/policy development (two grants totalling £745,000);

The major allocation of 1996/97 was made to the Royal Free Hospital School of Medicine/Institute of Education, Oxford University, for a research programme'Families Children & Childcare' to investigate the intereaction between aspects of children's relationships with their parents and various childcare experiences, including relationships between parents and carers (£700,000 over 7 years). This is a joint grant with the Tedworth Charitable Trust, the trust of Alexander Sainsbury's elder brother (see separate entry).

The National Children's Bureau was supported to build on and develop organisational networks to improve the quality of life for children and young people 'through the spread and replication of good practice'.

Other (one grant totalling £165,000)

A major one-off grant was made to Kaleidoscope to produce (with Icon Books) a practical guide for concerned parents on the use of illegal drugs (£165,200).

General grants

Apart from annual grants to the Headley and Jerusalem Trusts (£52,408 each in 1996/97 and £16,362 each in 1995/96), grants have been made mainly in those two years to environmental and arts activities. The Woodland Trust was supported for its 'Woods on your Doorstep' tree-planting programme in Northern Ireland (£25,000 over 5 years); Friends of the Earth was supported to establish an internet database on SSSIs in the UK and threats to them (£8,333). These grants are made jointly with the Tedworth and Staples trusts (see separate entries).

In 1995/96 grants had been made to the Rear Window Trust towards the costs of staging educational art exhibitions (£57,000 in 3 one-off grants) and to the Civic Trust for its Campaign for Liveable Places (£30,000 over 2 years).

Exclusions Direct grants to ndividuals.

Applications The trustees met three times during 1996/97 and in the preceding year. 'Proposals are generally invited by the trustees or initiated at their request. The trustees prefer to support innovative schemes that can be successfully replicated or become self-sustaining.'

It is also said that one application to a Sainsbury trust is an application to all. See the entry for the Sainsbury Family Charitable Trusts for the address and other advice.

The Glencore Foundation for Education & Welfare

£2,640,000 (1996)

Education, welfare, Jewish charities

c/o Glencore UK Ltd, 49 Wigmore St, London W1H OLU
Tel: 0171-412 3132

Correspondent J Boxer, Secretary

Trustees D Dreyfuss, M D Paisner; L M Weiss; J G Pattullo; J M J Boxer.

Beneficial area International, but mainly to Israel.

Information available Excellent, though elderly, reports and accounts on file at the Charity Commission

General The principal areas of activity of this trust are in education and social welfare, with particular reference to Israel.

In 1996 assets totalled just £780,000. Income for the foundation amounted to £3.3 million, made up almost entirely of donations, which funded £2.64 million of grant making activities.

A five page grants list of 133 grants is included with information on the purpose of each award. Grants range in size, with the lion's share of the grant total (almost 50%) going to three organisations: the Solon Foundation, Switzerland, for the Tiger Kloof Bursary (£1 million); School for Educational Leadership, for developing leadership courses (£125,000); and to Children of Chernobyl, for humanitarian and medical relief programmes (£120,000). The trust rarely gives out grants for less than £1,000, with sizes generally ranging from £2,000 to £50,000.

Apart from the grants mentioned above (and £30,000 to the North African Conference, developing a programme for Ethiopian pupils) most of the grant giving was concentrated on social, educational and community development work for Israeli and Jewish based charities. Examples of beneficiaries include; Haifa Arts Foundation (£50,000 for program enrichment); Ben Gurion University (£50,000 to the Doran Rich immigrant scholars funds); Al Sam Anti Drug Abuse (£25,000 to the prevention of drug addiction programmes); Jewish School at Minsk (£20,000 for educational activities for pupils); Zahani Association (£15,000 for a joint mini club for immigrant children); Ravenswood Foundation (£10,000 for horticultural training); Jewish Arab Community (£5,000 for Jewish Arab community informal education activities); and the Tel Aviv Rape Crisis Centre (£3,900 for projects in high schools in Tel Aviv).

The Gloucestershire Environmental Trust Company

£750,000 (income, 1998)

Environmental improvements

Moorend Cottage, Watery Lane, Upton St Leonards,
Gloucestershire GL4 8DW
Tel: 01452 615110 Fax: 01452 613817

Correspondent Lynne Garner

Trustees Jonathon Porritt, Chairman; David Ball; David Burton; Paul Holliday; Gordon McGlone; Jack Newell.

Beneficial area Gloucestershire only.

Information available Excellent leaflet 'Applying for a Grant', and application form with guidance notes

Summary The trust can make grants for

- the physical and natural environment
- education and research on better waste management
- open spaces, important buildings or public amenities near landfill sites.

General This trust

- is a body which exists to make grants for schemes that will benefit the environment and people of Gloucestershire.
- receives its income through a scheme set up by Cory Environmental under the Landfill Tax regulations.
- requires that schemes gaining its support shall satisfy one or more of its objects as described below.
- requires that schemes shall have gained approval from ENTRUST (qv).

'Preferential consideration may be given to projects which are close to the Hempsted, Stoke Orchard or Elmstone Hardwicke landfill operations.

'The objects of the trust are

1. The conservation, protection and improvement of the physical and natural environment within Gloucestershire.
2. The advancement of public education and research in encouraging more sustainable waste management practices and lessening environmental impacts.
3. The provision of open spaces in the vicinity of landfill sites for the recreation ... of the public.
4. The restoration, preservation and repair of buildings of historical importance or architectural value, which are in the vicinity of landfill sites.
5. The maintenance and repair of public amenities in the vicinity of landfill sites ... .'

The trust notes the following possible examples of fundable activities: repair or restoration of places of worship; canal restoration; purchase and development of nature reserves or public parks; research into sustainable waste management, etc.

Full or part funding is available. A maximum grant (or amount of grant in one year for a single organisation) has been set at £100,000. It is envisaged that a wide range of bodies, not all of them necessarily registered charities, could get grants. They include churches, community groups, wildlife trusts, village hall committees, historic buildings trusts and waste management research establishments

The largest grants to Sept 1998 were as follows:

The Natural Step (£96,000 over two years); Woodchester Mansion (£55,000) and the Farming and Wildlife Advisory Trust Group (£29,000).

The Goldsmiths' Company's Charities

£1,266,000 (1996/97)

General, London charities, the precious metals craft

Goldsmiths' Hall, Foster Lane,
London EC2V 6BN
Tel: 0171-606 7010; Fax: 0171-606 1511

Correspondent R D Buchanan-Dunlop, Clerk

Trustees The Goldsmiths' Company.

Beneficial area UK, with a special interest in London charities.

Information available Excellent report and accounts with full grants list and narrative exploration of grants and grant-making; guidelines; application form.

Summary Approximately 300 grants are made a year to support a broad array of causes, but to London-based or national charities only. Most grants are between £1,000 and £2,000 with a maximum of around £50,000. Half of the beneficiaries in any one year receive grants repeated over three years. Donations are usually for revenue but are sometimes given for capital costs.

General The Goldsmiths' Company can trace its origins back to the mediaeval trade guilds. Trust funds accumulated over the centuries and by the end of the 19th century there were 57 separate charities. The majority were amalgamated in the first half of the 20th century and currently there are three major and three minor trusts. This entry will look at the former three, namely: John Perryn's Charity; the General Charity; and Goldsmiths Charitable Donation Fund.

These are treated as a whole in the annual report and accounts.

In 1996/97 the charities had net assets of £51,500,000 and total incoming resources of £1.7 million. In the region of 280 grants were awarded, typically for £1,500. Three grants totalling £391,000 went to the Goldsmiths' Arts Trust Fund (for educational projects). 15% of charitable expenditure went to the following seven organisations:

- Wiltshire Community Foundation, two grants of £25,000 for further distribution;
- International String Quartet, £23,000 for competition expenses;
- BMA Educational Trust, £30,000 for second degree medical students;
- £25,000 for the provision of musical practice rooms at Goldsmiths' College;
- Science for Society Courses for Teachers, £28,000 for four residential courses;
- £33,000 for Teachers Mid Career Refreshment Grants.

Six gifts of between £10,000 and £18,000 accounted for a further 6% of grant expenditure: HACT (£10,000 and £15,000); London Borough of Islington (£10,000); Historic Churches Preservation Trust (£10,000 – the first of three annual grants); City Music Society (£18,000); Education of the Children of

London Clergy Scheme (£14,000).
Nearly all other grants were in the range
of £1,000 to £3,000.

Grants by category, 1996/97

Support for the craft	*£463,000*	*37%*
General welfare	*£280,000*	*22%*
Education	*£213,000*	*17%*
Medical Welfare and the disabled	*£96,000*	*8%*
Youth	*£116,000*	*9%*
Arts	*£81,000*	*6%*
Church	*£34,000*	*3%*
Heritage and conservation	*£13,000*	*1%*
Total	*£1,266,000*	*100%*

Annual Report 1996/97

Since 1996/97, the charities have been
publishing a more in-depth annual report
with about six pages of useful narrative
information on the charities and its
grant-making. The trustees' report is
reproduced below and where grant size
was not shown, we have added this
information:

'This is the first occasion that the
Goldsmiths' Company has published an
annual report on its charities. It follows
the Charities Act 1993 and its related
Statement of Recommended Practice –
but more importantly conforms to the
new spirit of openness now prevalent in
the charity sector – and although we do
not agree with all the requirements of the
SORP, the Goldsmith's Company is not
only happy to comply with them but to
support its thrust.

'The Goldsmiths' Company is one of the
twelve great companies of the City of
London with its origins in the mediaeval
trade guilds. Over the centuries charitable
trust funds have been built up through the
munificence of a variety of benefactors.
At the end of the 19th century 57 separate
charities were recorded. Today, following
the amalgamation of the majority of these
in the first half of this century there is
only a handful. This report covers the
three main charities: John Perryn's
Charity (the only one to retain the name
of its original benefactor), the General
Charity and the Goldsmiths' Charitable
Donation Fund, which the Charity
Commissioners have agreed may be
treated as an entity for the purpose of the
annual report and accounts.

'Although there are differences between
the operations of the charities –
principally the General Charity may be
used for grants in the London area only,
and the Goldsmiths' Charitable Donation
Fund's investment scheme does not
include land – the purposes of these
charities are closely allied and in terms
of the company's overall grant-making
policies are treated equally.

'The Goldsmiths' Company's grant-
making policies fall into three main
areas:

• 'Support of the goldsmiths' craft:
support is given to higher and further
educational establishments, to
students and apprentices, to promote
excellence in design and
craftsmanship, and to help young
people to develop their potential to
secure jobs in the precious metals
and jewellery industry. Exhibitions
are also mounted to further the
public's knowledge and enjoyment of
silverware and jewellery;
• General charitable support: the
largest areas of grant making is
toward general charitable needs,
ranging from the disadvantaged in
society and general welfare to
churches and the arts;
• Education: in addition to support for
the craft, the Goldsmiths' Company
sponsors a number of general
educational initiatives. These are
directed mainly towards primary and
secondary education. Grants are
made to individuals only where they
have a connection with the
Goldsmiths' Company or as part of
one of the company's schemes, grants
are not normally made to students
whose claims fall outside of these
schemes.

'Applications when received are screened
by three specialist committees: the charity
committee, the education committee and
the design and technology committee (for
support of the goldsmiths' craft). The
recommendations of these committees are
then reviewed by the Court of Assistants
acting as the trustee.

General Charitable Work

'The best indication of the thrust of the
company's giving is to read the grants list.
With a few specific exceptions the
company adopts a reactive policy.
Informal caps on certain areas of grant-
making may be determined throughout the
year but no quotas are established and the
pattern of grant making largely reflects
the quantity and type of applications
received and more importantly the critical
assessment of both the objects of the
charities concerned and the feasibility of
the purposes for which a grant is
requested. In principle grant-making is
confined to London-based and national
charities only.

'If the eight grants over £5,000 are
removed from the total of some 280
grants, the average grant, aside from
grants to individuals is approximately
£1,650. 50% of the grants paid are part
of three year recurrent grants, and
although the average size of the grant

may seem modest, the company attaches
considerable importance to helping with
revenue funding over a period of years.
This not only assists charities in an area
for which it is particularly difficult to
raise funds, but gives them a greater
degree of flexibility in their budgeting
and forward planning.

'Many of these grants have helped a
variety of community projects, and
amongst the ethnic minorities involved
two grants have been made to Kurdish
charities: the Greenwich Kurdish
Community Association [£2,500] and the
Kurdish Association [£1,000].

'The company makes no grants toward
medical research but nevertheless helps
with palliative care; grants to the
Hoxton Health Group for Shiatsu
massage for carers [£750 – *the third of
three grants*] and to the Special Needs
Sexuality Project [£2,000 – *third of
three*] amongst others give some idea of
the diversity of projects supported. The
company has received an increasing
number of applications from small
largely self-help medical groups, many
representing congenital defect medical
conditions. While the company has felt
unable to help the majority of these, in
the past year it has given grants to the
Brittle Bone Society [*£1,500, 2nd of
three grants*] and the Huntingdon's
Disease Association [*£1,500 – first of
three*].

'Grants to youth projects have included
help for homelessness such as the Alone
in London Service for Borderline and St
Mary Le Bow for its Young Homeless
Project [*£1,500 – 2nd of three
payments*]. A significant number of
applications have been received for a
variety of holiday schemes for the
disadvantaged in society. All are
worthwhile, but the company has found
it necessary to be selective and four
such charities only have been helped
this year. Hard on the heels of
children's holidays are adventure
playgrounds, and here again it is felt
necessary to be selective, a single grant
being made to the St John's Wood
Adventure Playground [*£1,500*].

'A wider area of youth support includes
those charities providing adventurous and
leadership pursuits, some in this country
including Fairbridge [*£1,800 – second of
three*], Weston Spirit [*£1,500 – second
of three*], Discovery Dockland [*£1,500*]
and the Shadwell Basin Activities Centre
for work with children with special
needs [*£1,000 – second of three*], others
operating further afield such as Raleigh
International [*£4,000*], GAP Activity
Projects [*£3,000*] and the Sail Training
Association [*£5,000*].

'Heritage grants this year have totalled under £12,500 and have acquired a Scottish flavour with grants to Scottish United Services Museum [*£2,500*] for assistance in purchasing the swords and medals of Lord Northesk who was third in command at the battle of Trafalgar, and to William McCann Trust for archive work on the City of Edinboro smack [*£500*].

'Heritage spills over into the company's support for the Church where grants have been made to the Historic Churches Preservation Trust (*£10,000 for the first tranche of a three year grant*) and the Historic Chapels Trust [*£6,000 over three years*), as well as to the Council for the Care of Churches specifically for the repair of a church silver plate. Some years ago the company was instrumental in initiating a scheme of diocesan treasuries where church plate from parishes could be preserved and exhibited, and this year a grant was made to fund a conference at Norwich Cathedral for those responsible for running these treasuries.

'In arts the lion's share of funding has gone to music. The company makes an annual grant (*this year £17,000*) to the City Music Society to assist it in mounting six evening concerts and a grant of £23,500 was made to the London International String Quartet Competition to assist it with its triennial competition. This competition, a week long event, has now been held at the Goldsmiths' Hall for the third consecutive time. By contrast grants have also been made to the Tate Gallery [*£5,000*] for its new Bankside Gallery and to the Dulwich Picture Gallery [*£3,000*] which operates a model educational project.

'Other major grants have been given for a variety of charitable needs. £25,000 representing part of a £45,000 grant was given to the Housing Associations' Charitable Trust. £50,000, the second instalment of a two-year grant, was given to the Wiltshire Community Foundation. This grant is one of a series given to emerging community foundations over the past decade. Having helped three foundations in the North-East, the company turned its attention to rural poverty and has been particularly impressed by the Wiltshire Community Foundation's grant-making expertise. We are now looking further west to Cornwall which as yet has no community foundation.

'The grant of £9,400 to the Binney Memorial Fund reflects a unique function of the Goldsmiths' Company. Each year the company is responsible for organising an awards ceremony and reunion for citizens who have carried out acts of bravery in support of law and order in London. The fund was established by friends of Captain Ralph Binney RN who was killed trying to thwart a robbery of a jewellery shop in the City of London in 1944, but it has insufficient funds to support what has become a major event. The 1996 awards were presented by the Lord Mayor of London.

'Finally there are two blocks of grants to individuals. One is for £10,000 to Islington Social Services Department for distribution, and the other (*£15,000*) is to a variety of Inner London social services departments for individual cases of hardship, and to a number of freemen and members of the goldsmiths' and silversmiths' trade. In making these grants the company is aware that it is only able to tackle the very small tip of an enormous iceberg of those whose often desperate circumstances cannot be adequately catered for by the State or local social services' budgets.

Education

'While the company maintains its open door policy towards grant applications for educational projects, the core of its educational policy comprises a number of pro-active schemes.

Mid-career refreshment grants (*£33,000*) 'This scheme began nearly forty years ago with the aim of providing secondary school teachers with a travelling scholarship to enable them to recharge their batteries at mid-career point and thus bring a renewed stimulus to their classroom teaching. An important ingredient has been to provide the parent school with additional funding for a replacement teacher where this is necessary. In 1997 the scheme was widened to include primary school teachers and teachers are now encouraged to undertake their travel mainly during the school holidays. A feature of the grants is that they should be for an area of interest outside the recipient's teaching speciality. In 1997 grants were made for such diverse purposes as photographing and drawing the marine culture and vernacular architecture of the coastline of Maine, New England; researching the manufacture of double basses in Cremona, Italy; and studying sustainable forms of agriculture in Eastern Uganda. One of the reports received from the previous year's grants covered research by the teacher into her father's war diary from D Day 1944 to February 1945, and has now been published as a book.

Science for society courses (*£28,000*) 'Another scheme with a similarly lengthy pedigree is a series of residential courses in the summer designed to provide science teachers with a wider experience of subjects in the A level syllabus, thereby bringing an extra dimension to the classroom. Originally initiated to introduce teachers to the peaceful benefits of nuclear energy during the cold war, the courses have been refined over the years. Four courses were run in 1997: Medical Physics at Sheffield University, Farm to Mouth (a topical review of the food chain) at Reading University, the communications industry at the Cable and Wireless College, Coventry, and the water industry based at Reading University and London. All courses, each catering for 20 plus teachers were oversubscribed.

Primary schools literacy project 'In an attempt to identify and subsequently disseminate models of best practice for assisting in the improvement of literacy in primary schools, a number of primary schools outside of London were invited to submit projects illustrating how they would use an initial grant of £5,000 to improve literacy in their school. Seven schools (three in Hertfordshire, two in Oxfordshire and two in Walsall) were subsequently selected and the results of their pilot schemes will be evaluated in Summer 1998.

'Outside these schemes a major grant of £30,000 (funding for two years) was given again to the British Medical Association Educational Trust, to provide bursaries for undergraduates who are studying medicine as a second degree and who are ineligible for the normal student grants. At a more modest level a continuing grant of £4,000 was made to the National Florence Nightingale Foundation to enable two nurses to study overseas.

'Goldsmiths' College has achieved an enviable reputation for its music department, and a grant of £25,000 to the College forms part of an overall grant of £100,000 to help with the refurbishment of its practice rooms. Another musical association has been maintained with the award of a bursary of £3,500 to St Paul's Cathedral Choir School.

Support of the craft

'Grants totalling £391,000 have been made by the three charities to the Goldsmiths' Arts Trust Fund which is responsible for administering projects and grants in support of the silverware and jewellery craft. A separate report and accounts has been prepared for this fund, but in view of the scale of the funding from the three charities the scope of its grant making is repeated here.

'The lion's share of the grants was once again used to fund two exhibitions. The main summer exhibition British Master Goldsmiths featured the work of 24 of the country's premier silversmiths and jewellers. The company also coordinates and helps to fund an annual exhibition "Passing Out" which provides a showcase for the cream of the work of graduating students from universities and art colleges teaching silversmithing and jewellery throughout the United Kingdom.'

Exclusions Medical research; memorials to individuals; overseas projects; animal welfare.

Applications Applications for all of the charities applying for general charitable support should be made on an application form and should be accompanied by the following information.

- an outline of the current work and experience of the applicant organisation including details of staffing, organisational structure and use of volunteers;
- the organisation's most recent annual report, if one is published;
- a detailed budget for the proposed activity;
- the organisation's most recent audited accounts (or financial report required by the Charities Act);
- the methods by which the success of the project will be evaluated;
- the income/expenditure projection for the organisation for the current year;
- other grant-making organisations appealed to for the same project and with what result;
- preference for a single or annual grant for up to three years.

Trustees meet monthly except during August and September.

The Gosling Foundation Ltd

£700,000 (1996/97)
Naval charities, general

21 Bryanston Street,
London W1A 4NH
Tel: 0171 499 7050

Correspondent A Yusof, Secretary

Trustees Sir Donald Gosling; Ronald Hobson.

Beneficial area UK.

Information available Accounts on file at the Charity Commission. The grants list for 1997 is absent.

General Sir Donald Gosling, founding director of the National Parking Corporation and also a trustee of the Bernard Sunley Foundation, established the foundation in 1985. Most of its assets are in shares in his company, whose value has fluctuated greatly in recent years. In 1996/97 assets were £42 million and generated an income of £1.2 million, down from £11.7 million in 1995/96.

Similar fluctuations can be seen in grant giving; from £1.2 million in 1993/94, down to £543,000 in 1994/95, up to £945,000 in 1995/96 and then down to £700,000 in 1996/97. The foundation underspent its income by about £0.5 million in 1996/97 and by about £10 million in 1995/96.

Unfortunately there is now no grants list on file at the Charity Commission, so the following information has to be based on the 1995/96 grants list, when a total of £945,000 was awarded in 145 grants. About 100 grants were for £1,000 or more, and only 12 were for £10,000 or more. Grants ranged in size from £383,000 to the Fleet Air Arm Museum Appeal, which also received the largest grants in previous years, to just £10 to the Ocean Youth Club. Most of the grants went to organisations that have been supported for number of years.

Nearly all the larger grants went to the welfare funds for naval vessels, a wide range of maritime organisation and various other military charities. Examples include; The White Ensign Association (£100,000); Chatham Historic Dockyard (£100,000); St Dunstans (£30,000); HMS London Welfare Fund (£10,000); King George's Fund for Sailors (£10,000); Imperial War Museum Duxford (£10,000); and the Royal Navy Benevolent Fund (£6,500).

A number of grants were given to royal causes including: the Duke of Edinburgh Award (£11,000); Royal Parks Tree Appeal (£10,000) and the RSPCA (£5000).

Grants were also given to a variety of social causes, such as the Macmillan Fund (£5,000); National Asthma Campaign (£3000); Save the Rhino (£2,000); Dyslexia Institute (£1,000), Save the Children (£1,000), and the Wiener Library Endowment Appeal (£500).

Applications To the correspondent in writing.

The Grand Charity of Freemasons

£1,083.000 (in non-masonic donations 1996/97)
Health, education and welfare

60 Great Queen Street,
London WC2B 5AZ
Tel: 0171-395 9293

Correspondent The Secretary

Trustees The Council, consisting of a president and 24 council members, listed in the annual reports.

Beneficial area England and Wales, with a special interest in London.

Information available Detailed annual report and biannual newsletters available from the charity; full accounts on file at the Charity Commission.

Summary The charity gives away around £3 million per annum in grants to individual Masons, Masonic Charities and non-Masonic charities. A little over a third of the grant budget goes to the latter, usually to groups involved in youth, or medical research and hospices. Grants typically vary from under £1,000 to £250,000.

General The Grand Charity is the central grant-making charity of the Freemasons in its 'English Constitution' which has provinces all over England and Wales and in several districts worldwide. It was established in 1980 as a replacement for the Board of Benevolence with the intention of extending the level of support given to non-Masonic causes. This entry concentrates on these.

Although most grants are to medical research charities, such awards are usually small and the bulk of funds are disbursed in a few large grants to youth causes. Aside from donations to hospices, most grants go to organisations based in London. However, most of these are national charities and so the money is not ultimately focused on Londoners.

Income in 1996/97 totalled £4.3 million (down from £6.5 million in the previous year). 50 grants to non-Masonic organisations were made or recommended hence the totals do not match.

The charity categorised these in this way:

Major grants	5	£840,000	52%
Intermediate grants	6	£199,000	12%
Hospices	170	£247,000	15%
Minor grants	317	£310,000	19%
Other small grants	4	£6,400	-%
Emergency grants	2	£10,000	1%
Total	504	£1,612,000	100%

Annual Report 1997

'Non-Masonic donations actually paid during the year amounted to £1,088,000. However, £577,000 was also placed in the Designated Fund for grant appropriated in 1997, but which will be paid over a number of years in the future. These sums reflect the council's continued dedication to this most important aspect of the Grand Charity's work. Three of the four major grants and most of the intermediate grants are directed at the youth of the country, to match the council's current strategy. I [*the President, Ed.*] believe that the grants to aid research into Parkinson's and Alzheimer's diseases will, however, strike a chord with most Masons.

Major grants

'Four new major grants were made in 1997. £250,000 was placed in the designated fund for primary prevention of drug abuse. Subject to approval at the AGM in March 1998, the money will be used to set up an annual freemasons' award for best practice in the area of primary prevention: that is conveying the message to children before they come under peer pressure to experiment with any sort of drug.

'£190,000 was given to Fairbridge, which works with disadvantaged, demotivated young people mostly from inner cities. The grant will provide 'Lifestart' bursaries for 190 of them to go through…progressive personal development and dynamic training.

'£175,000 was given to the Prince's Youth Business Trust which helps young people who would not otherwise have the opportunity, to contribute to the community through the medium of self-employment. The grant is being used to fund outreach workers and advisors over the next three years.

'£125,000 was place in the designated fund to cover a grant to the Alzheimer's Research Trust, subject to approval at the AGM. This grant will support a new research programme in to the fundamental causes of this dreadful disease. Specifically it will fund the salary of a post-doctoral research scientist.

'The last of five annual instalments of £100,000 each in respect of the 1993 major grant was paid to Macmillan Cancer Relief for its paediatric nursing services.

'In 1996, the council decided to mark the turn of the century by making a larger than normal grant (or grants). £1,000,000 was transferred to the designated fund for the "Millennium Fund" and the council is working to determine the area of charitable activity to which the fund will be devoted, before seeking applications from charities active in the selected area.

Intermediate grants

'Six new intermediate grants were made or recommended during 1997.

'£90,000 to the Parkinson's Disease Society Brain Research Centre in support of a project to establish a blood/brain bank. The grant will fund the salary of one state registered nurse and subject to the project going ahead satisfactorily will be paid over three years.'

The other grants were to: Centrepoint (£25,000); Diana Princess of Wales Memorial Fund (£25,000); the Royal Philanthropic Society (£25,000); the Orpheus Trust (£24,000) and; Divert Trust (£10,000).

Hospices

'Grants to hospices increased by 19% to meet the growing needs of the hospice movement. To date the Grand Charity has regularly helped 185 hospices all over England and Wales with annual grants ranging from £500 to £3,000. The major grant in 1997 was a commitment to donate £250,000 to the hospice movement, in tranches of £50,000 over the following five years. The idea clearly struck a chord with the membership and has therefore been continued ever since. Many hospices are now supported, not only by the Grand Charity but also by provinces and local lodges.

Minor grants

'These are generally given to smaller charities in England and Wales which do not enjoy such wide public support as the well known large national charities. Grants normally range from £500 to £2,000. On the principle that local charities should be looked after by local freemasons, the Grand Charity generally considers appeals from registered charities that operate nationally.'

National medical research/welfare groups are particularly prominent in the small grants list. 15% of the budget is reserved for London charities (but here nearly all beneficiaries are youth causes).

'Emergency grants of £5,000 went to Monserrat (towards portaloos for refugees from volcanic eruptions) and the city of Jabalpur in India which had suffered an earthquake.'

Though this has not been confirmed, it is possible that applications are more likely to succeed if they have the support of active Freemasons.

Exclusions No support for local charities outside London, or for individuals who are not connected with Freemasonry.

Applications To the correspondent.

The Great Britain Sasakawa Foundation

£556,000 (1997)

Links between Great Britain and Japan

43 North Audley Street,
London, W1Y 1WH
Tel: 0171-355 2229; Fax: 0171-355 2230;
E-mail gbsf@gbsf.demon.co.uk

Correspondent Peter Hand, Administrator

Council Prof Peter Mathias, Chair; The Hon. Yoshio Sakurauchi; Lord Butterfield; Michael French, Treasurer; Baroness Brigstocke; Jeremy Brown; Baroness Park of Monmouth; Earl of St Andrews; Kazuo Chiba; Professor Harumi Kimura; Yohei Sasakawa; Akira Iriyama; Professor Shoichi Watanabe.

Beneficial area United Kingdom, Japan.

Information available Accounts and report (separate documents) with full grants list showing the purpose of grants. A leaflet about the foundation, its aims and eligibility of applicants is available.

Summary Grants are awarded for initiatives which 'improve relations between the UK and Japan by furthering a better understanding between the peoples of both nations'. Fields supported include 'cultural, linguistic, sociological, educational, academic research, environmental, sport and youth exchange'. The grants vary from around £1,000 to £25,000 but are usually for less than £5,000. Beneficiaries are based either in the UK or in Japan.

General The foundation was established following a meeting in 1983 when the late Ryoichi Sasakawa, a shipbuilding tycoon, and the late Robert Maxwell met a number of senior British politicians to discuss Anglo-Japanese relations. The foundation was inaugurated two years later with a gift of £9.5 million from the Japan Shipbuilding Industry Foundation (now called The Nippon Foundation).

In 1997 the foundation's assets totalled nearly £17.5 million and income was £694,000. 110 grants were made within eight categories; examples of the grants are given below under the category headings and in the partially reprinted chairman's message.

Over the 12 year period, 1985–1997, grants were disbursed as follows:

- *Cultural £1,779,000 27%*

(Examples of 1997 awards are: £5,000 to Patrick Carey towards the publication of 'Rediscovering the Old Tokaido'; £3,000 to Gaudeamus, London, for the production of Yukio Misimha's play 'Madame de Sade'; £2,000 to the Museum of Modern Art, Oxford, towards an exhibition of Yoko Ono's work; £10,000 to the orchestra Royal Academy of Music for a performance in Japan.)

- *Anglo-Japanese Relations £1,249,000 19%*

(Grants included; £4,000 to the Martial Arts Development Commission for the course fees of two students; £2,500 to the British Film Institute in support of the Kenji Mizoguchi film season; £5,000 to Exeter University for a collaborative political science research project; £10,000 was given to the Refugee Studies Programme at Oxford to support a Japanese Fellowship.

- *Youth Exchange £975,000 15%*

(A total of £12,500 went to support GAP year visits to Japan – Kokoban Community Centre received £7,500 for this and four students from the Isle of Coll, Argyle received between £500 and £1,500; and the Guide Association, Anglia, was given £1,000 towards the visit of ten Brownies to Japan.)

- *Linguistics £759,000 12%*

(Grey Coat Hospital, Westminster, £5,000 for the expansion of a Japanese language programme; Tile Hill Wood School, Coventry, £2,500 to help it apply to the DfEE for language college status; and £3,000 to Gateway Japan Centre for a programme of Japanese language teaching.)

- *Science, industry, technology*

£645,000 10%

(No grants were awarded in 1997)

- *Medical and medical research £458,000 7%*

(One award was made – see below)

- *Japanese studies £411,000 6%*

(£5,000 was awarded to Roehampton Institute for a Anglo-Japanese research project into school bullying; £9,000 went to the Visual Learning Foundation, Islington for a teaching pack to promote Japanese Art and Culture in UK primary schools; and £3,000 was given to SOAS for a trip to the University of Tokyo by Dr John Breen.)

- *Sport £220,000 3%*

(Two grants were made: £5,000 each to JFK Goju-Kai, London for a karate seminar and examination board and to Tokei Martial Arts Centre, London, refurbishment costs.)

- *Religion, conservation, ecology and environmental £33,000 1%*

(There were two beneficiaries in 1997: Plymouth University, £1,000 support for a visit to Japan to present a environmental paper; and Scientists for Global Responsibility, £2,500 towards funding 40 scientists and NGO delegates to travel to the Kyoto conference in 1997.)

The guidelines read:

'The foundation aims to advance the education of the citizens of Great Britain and Japan in many fields to develop mutual appreciation and understanding of the institutions, people and history, language and culture of the two nations, to promote research and to publish the useful results of such research.

'The foundation has supported a wide range of projects including:

- visits between Japan and Great Britain by public servants, leading figures, writers and academics, students, teachers, journalists, artists, and former prisoners of war, their captors and others;
- work in the visual or performing arts, translation and publication of books serving foundation aims, and the teaching of the Japanese language in the United Kingdom;
- research in the fields of education, the arts, history, medicine and sociology and environmental studies.

'In addition the foundation may conduct seminars, meetings and lectures and undertake other activities to encourage understanding between the peoples of Japan and the United Kingdom.'

Annual Report 1997

The Chairman's Message for 1997 says:

'We continued our assistance to the Burma Campaign Fellowship Group but instead of our earlier support for exchange visits to and from Japan, this year we funded their establishment of a permanent Burma Campaign Memorial Library at SOAS, London, the cost of which will be spread over two years (£10,000 each year).

'We were once more able to assist with the visit to Japan by medical advisors from the Care and Action Trust for Children with Handicaps (CATCH!) in Swansea who have helped establish a centre in Isekai, Gunma ken, to give Japanese parents practical help with the care of children with disabilities (£4,000). We were delighted to learn that, in recognition of his services to the handicapped in Japan, Mr Trevor England, the founder of CATCH!, was awarded the Japan Society Cortazzi Award for 1998.

'In Japan we continued the JETRO: international Educators to Japan Programme which has been supported for the past five years, during which time 36 teachers from the United Kingdom have visited Japan to gain experience from teachers in similar posts in Japan and impart to them their own knowledge gained from teaching in the UK (£15,500).

'The foundation continued to note a further sharp increase in the number of applications for help with the teaching of the Japanese language from schools and colleges in the United Kingdom. Among the nine schools favoured were awards to the Ley School, Cambridge (£7,000), to which school a number of children of the Japanese Imperial Court were sent to study at the turn of the century, to Montgomery High School in North Blackpool (£10,000), a school of 1,087 pupils that offers exceptional linguistic teaching to young people and adults in the community and to Park View Community School in Chester-le-Street, County Durham (£10,000) an LEA community school of 1,300 pupils. The school is located between Sunderland and Newcastle and only four miles from Washington Tyne and Wear, the hub of Japanese manufacturing in the North of England.

'We helped fund the establishment of a Europe-Japan Social Science Research Centre at the University of Glasgow (£15,000 in two annual tranches) to be headed by Professor Robert Miles and at Southampton University (£5,000) we supported two medical research projects concerned with head injuries and amputee rehabilitation to be conducted by Dr Yuriko Watanabe who is attached Southampton General Hospital.

'We were pleased to be able to support again a joint initiative the Momji Venture (£9,000) between the Japanese Red Cross and the Red Cross in the United Kingdom involving the visit to the UK in 1997 by ten Japanese people with special needs.

'Another example of the increasing level of support which trustees sought to give to the growing numbers of youth exchange visits between the United Kingdom and Japan, was the funding of a joint visit to Japan by ten students from Northern Ireland – five from a Catholic School and five from a Protestant school (£7,500). As a result of this exchange the pupils involved have now developed strong inter-community friendships and all meet together on an on-going basis.

'1997 also saw the very impressive Hiroshigie Exhibition curated by Matthew Forrer at the Royal Academy of Arts, which was sponsored by our parent body, The Nippon Foundation.'

Exclusions Grants are not made to individuals applying on their own behalf. The foundation can, however, consider proposals from organisations which support the activities of individuals, provided these are citizens of the United Kingdom or Japan.

No grants can be made for the construction, conservation or maintenance of land and buildings.

The foundation will not support activities involving politics, legislation or election to public office.

Grants are not normally made for medical research.

Applications The Awards Committee meets twice a year, in mid May and mid November. Requests for grants should made by means of an application form which may be obtained from the Administrator at the London headquarters: requests in Japan should be sent to the Tokyo liaison office. Applications should contain the following information as appropriate:

A summary of the proposed project and its aims, making clear whether the request is for a single grant or some form of continuing commitment.

Total cost of the project and the amount of the desired grant, together with a note of other expected sources of funds. Estimated period for research projects, visits or study.

A description of the applicant's organisation and, where relevant, brief career details of the main participants in any project, and where appropriate the ages of those individuals who may be the recipients.

Applicants are expected to make careful calculation of all costs of a project before seeking a grant. Where a grant is approved no application for an increase will be accepted after approval except in very special circumstances.

The foundation will not consider making a further grant to an applicant until at least two years after a successful application. Organisations applying should be registered charities, recognised educational institutions, local or regional authorities, churches, media companies, publishers or such other bodies as the foundation may approve.

School applications are requested to first file an application with the Youth Exchange Centre, The British Council, 10 Spring Gardens, London SW1A 2BN (which is part of the British Council), whose Japanese Exchange Programme, to which the foundation alone grants external finance, is aimed at encouraging the exchanges (both ways) for schools in Great Britain and Japan.

All applicants are notified shortly after each Awards Committee meeting of the decisions of the trustees. Trustees meet in May and November.

Greater Bristol Foundation

£274,000 (1997/98)

Social welfare, health

PO Box 383, 16 Clare Street, Bristol BS99 5JG
Tel: 0117-921 1311

Correspondent Helen Moss, Director

Trustees A Morris (Chair); J J Burke; J N Tidmarsh; E H Webber; Rt Rev Barry Rogerson; D M Parkes; J Bryant – Pearson; G Camm; D M Claisse; G R Ferguson; M Jackson; J G Pontin; H W Pye; T P Stevenson; S Storvik; A R Thornhill; D M Wood; H Wheelhouse.

Beneficial area Greater Bristol.

Information available Guidelines and application forms, full report and accounts available from the foundation.

Summary This is one of the most successful of the new breed of

community foundations, raising capital locally to form an endowment, the income from which can be used to meet local needs.

Guidelines for applicants
The following is reprinted from the Grant Making Policy and Guidelines, June 1998:

General Criteria
'We aim in our grant making:

- to reflect the concerns and priorities of people living and working in our areas of concern.
- to support people's involvement in their local community
- to support small neighbourhood organisations as well as those working across a wider area
- to assist these organisations to increase the effectiveness of their work through discussion of their strategy and support for their development
- to target funds at those most disadvantaged in the community.

Geographical Area
'Our area of concern lies within a ten mile radius of Bristol city centre.

Main Concerns
Young People
'We offer support to organisations which give young people the chance to explore the wide range of opportunities for their personal and social development. We want to encourage applications where young people are fully involved in all aspects of the project. Areas of work might include:

- arts-based projects
- volunteering in the community
- recreational activities
- training
- projects developing self esteem through specific activities.

Disabled People
'Support for projects and organisations which work with disabled people to identify and provide the services and strategic support they need. We would like to encourage applications from organisations which demonstrate that disabled people are involved in the planning and management of the project. People with learning disabilities are included in this category. Areas of work might include:

- information services
- projects addressing issues of access.

Homeless People
'Support for projects which address their immediate needs and those which are helping them to break the cycle of 'no

home, no job'. We would hope that the views of the homeless people were taken into account when projects are being planned.

'Areas of work might include:

- helping the transition to supported, or own, accommodation
- first stage training to help people take advantage of mainstream training provision.

Isolation.

'We support projects which aim to relieve isolation amongst vulnerable people in the community. this isolation can take many forms and can be made worse by lack of knowledge about what services and activities are available. areas of work might include:

- information services and training
- elderly people's groups
- projects addressing discrimination
- support for carers
- projects addressing issues of access.

Safer Community Environments

'Support for projects aimed at encouraging people to feel safer in, and more involved in shaping, their community environments. We want to encourage applications that address local people's priorities for the area in which they live. Areas of work might include:

- supporting communities in making the best possible use of open spaces for day to day and recreational use
- diversionary activities for young people
- activities which aim to increase safety and reduce crime'

Grant programmes

The foundation runs four grant making programmes which are also detailed:

Express Grants: 'This programmes is intended to benefit smaller, locally based projects where a smaller amount of funding can make a significant difference.

- applications for up to a maximum of £1,500 can be submitted to the foundation at any time
- applications will normally be dealt with within a period of four to five weeks
- there are no deadlines for express grants.

Impact Programme: 'Grants under this programme will be made where organisations can show that the funding can make a significant impact on a particular need or issue over a maximum of three years.

- a grant of up to £20,000 a year for three years is available

- outline bids should satisfy the following criteria: sustainability; involvement of people; working in partnership; use/reuse of resources.
- bids should be no more than two pages long at this stage and should cover the following points: aims and objectives of the projects; what you hope to achieve in three years; how you intend to do this; what impact you aim to make.

Special Advised Funds: 'The foundation manages a number of special funds that have their own criteria and deadlines. These include:

- Churngold Environmental Fund-grants of up to £5,000 to support environmental and educational projects. One meeting per year, contact the foundation for deadlines.
- BYCA-Bristol Youth Community Action- grants of up to £1,000 for activities organised by and for young people, addressing issues around community safety, in Bristol City area only. Two meetings per year in June and October; contact 964 6006 for more details.
- Broadmead Collection Box Scheme-funds raised through the collection boxes placed in the main shopping centre in the city. Grants of up to £1,000 to meet basic needs of homeless people in the city. Four meetings per year; closing dates are the end of February, May, August and November.
- Bristol University Students Rag-grants up to £1,000 to support charities working with homeless people and disabled children. One meting per year.

'Please contact the foundation for the details of these funds and the appropriate application form.

Catalyst Programme: 'The foundation is in contact with many people and organisations who are interested in charitable activity within the Bristol area. they recognise that we have the contacts and networks within the voluntary and charity sector which can help them direct and charitable giving they may choose to do in the most effective way possible.

'From time to time the foundation may be able to offer large grants from these sources. Please contact us and let us know your needs and plans and we will help if we can.'

Grants in 1997/98 The 1997/98 annual report summarises the year's grant making activities:

'During the year, the foundation developed and broadened its range of support for voluntary organisations: under the new Express Programme, 99

grants of £1,500 or less were made using a simplified and streamlined application procedure. Through this programme, the foundation was able to direct relatively small amounts of money to make a real and timely difference at a very local level. A grant was made under the Impact Programme which offers £20,000 a year for up to three years, to the Southmead Project as seed corn for a community enterprise providing training and employment alongside relapse prevention for former drug users.

'A number of specially advised funds were established within the foundation, introducing new ways of decision-making while making use of the established administrative procedures. These included the management of the funds collected in the Broadmead shopping centre for people who are homeless in Bristol, the University Rag and the Churngold Fund, which distribute credit available under the Landfill Tax regulations to local community organisation for environmental projects.'

In 1997/98 the foundation's assets stood at £4 million. Income was £724,000, made up mainly of donations. Grant giving was £274,000. Only four grants were for £10,000 or more and the average grant size was between £1,000-£2,000.

Grants for over £1,000 are listed by the foundation and examples of beneficiaries include Hartcliffe Leisure Ltd (£19,000 in two grants); Southmead Project (£15,000); Drugs & Alcohol Specific Project (£10,000 in two grants); CAB (£3,000); Somali Refugee Rehabilitation Project (£2,000); Parkway Parent and Child project (£1,400); Yate Detached Youth Work (£1,000) and Filton Environment Action Group (£1,000).

Grants of £1,000 went to Community Action, Cruse, Easton Community Association, and Avon Scout and Guide Canoe Centre.

Exclusions The foundation will not normally fund the following through its own grant making programme:

- general appeals
- individuals
- overseas travel for individuals
- fee-paying schools
- direct replacement of statutory funding
- promotion of religious causes
- medical research and equipment
- organisations with no permanent base in the Greater Bristol area
- sports without an identifiable charitable element

It is unlikely that vehicles, conferences and exhibitions will be funded.

Applications You will need to show:

- that you are a registered charity
- that your project is well managed and holds up-to-date financial records which can be made available to the foundation's staff
- that the activity is well-planned, realistic and well organised
- that you have clear plans for the long term viability of your organisation and its role within the community
- how you plan to show what difference the work will make and its effects on the wider community
- how you involve and support volunteers where appropriate
- a commitment to equal opportunities
- where appropriate, we would hope that the users of services are involved in the design, planning and delivery of those services

The Constance Green Foundation

£438,000 (1997/98)

Medicine, health, social welfare, general

Corner Cottage, 1 Trimmingham Lane, Halifax, West Yorkshire HX2 7PT
Tel: 01422-380975 (also Fax)

Correspondent M Collinson

Trustees M Collinson; Col. H R Hall; N Hall; A G Collinson.

Beneficial area England, with some preference for Yorkshire.

Information available Accounts, but without the required narrative report or analysis and explanation of grants.

General The trust was established in 1976 by its namesake. Its stated policy follows:

'Some preference is given to charities operating in Yorkshire. In previous years, grants have been made mainly but not exclusively to national organisations in the fields of medicine and social welfare with special emphasis on the support of young people in need and both mentally and physically disabled persons.

'Preference is given to .. funding special projects being undertaken by charities rather than grants to supplement funds used for general purposes.'

In the year ending April 1998 assets totalled £8.8 million and income of £651,000 was generated. Grant giving amounted to £438,000 in 56 grants. The trust notes that 1,130 applications were received, giving the low success rate of about 1 in 20.

Over the two years to April 1998 the largest activity has been the award of £250,000 to 'St Aidan's Church of England High School'. Neither the location of the school nor the purpose of the grant are reported.

Examples of the other larger grants given in 1997/98 included those to Barnardo's (£80,000); Sense and Sign (£50,000 each); The Camphill Village Trust, Malton (£25,000) and five grants of £10,000 each to West Yorkshire Police, St George's Crypt; St Anne's Shelter and Housing Action, the Fund For Epilepsy, and the Paul Strickland Cancer Centre.

Administration costs in the year were high at £63,000; about £14,000 of grant giving or £1,100 per grant approved. The reasons for such overall cost levels for a trust with no other reported activities than making gifts to charities should be spelt out in the annual reports.

These costs included £19,000 remuneration for trustees, for professional charges, and nearly £11,000 for 'secretarial, hotel, travelling and entertainment' costs. While such costs are legal, these editors feel that there are plenty of competent people who would be willing, at no cost, to carry out the agreeable task of disbursing other people's money to worthy causes.

In all £46,000 was paid for financial or legal services to companies which employ, or employed, trustees of the charity, including £18,000 in commission on the sale or purchase of investments, £16,000 for investment advice, £5,000 for investment advice and £7,500 for legal charges.

The trust points out that these arrangements were envisaged and endorsed by the settlor. In these editors' view, that does not, in itself, make them desirable.

Exclusions Sponsorship of individuals is not supported.

Applications At any time in writing to the correspondent (no special form of application required). Applications should include clear details of the need the intended project is designed to meet plus an outline budget. Applications are not generally acknowledged unless a SAE is provided.

Greggs Trust

£499,000 (1997)

Poverty and social deprivation in the North East

Fernwood House, Clayton Road, Jesmond,
Newcastle upon Tyne NE2 1TL
Tel: 0191-281 1444

Correspondent Jenni Wagstaff, Trust Administrator

Trustees Ian Gregg; Jane Gregg; Fiona Nicholson; Felicity Deakin; Andrew Davidson.

Beneficial area North East of England.

Information available Annual reports and accounts. Policy guidelines, and guide for applicants available

General The trust has recently revised its policy for grant making.

'The main priority of the trust is supporting organisations that work to alleviate poverty and social deprivation. The area of benefit is principally those areas in which the Greggs business operates: Northumberland, Tyne and Wear, County Durham and the former county of Cleveland.

'The trustees will give priority to grants for local, or in certain cases regional, organisations and projects. They will also continue to allocate a proportion of the funds available for distribution, through a small number of approved agencies, in grants to individuals experiencing hardship.

'Major grants made during 1997 reflect the policy review undertaken in 1996 as well as the increased income of the trust. As intended the trustees have approved grants between £3,000 and £10,000, while still awarding a few grants between £1,000 and £3,000. Some projects are being supported for more than one year; but in order to retain the scope for annual distribution, the trustees will set a limit on such commitments. There is a strong preference for community-based and locally-managed activity, and for estate and neighbourhood-based projects. Recent grants have included support for work with homeless people, older people, young people, children and women, including the unemployed, and for people with disabilities.

'Applications from small community-led organisations and self-help groups are

157

more likely to be successful than those from larger and well staffed organisations and those which have greater fund-raising capacity. Exceptions may be made where innovative work is being developed by established agencies or where such agencies are providing services to smaller or local groups. Applicant organisations should be able to show that they are working in partnership with relevant statutory and voluntary agencies and that they are aware of, and are applying to, other sources of funds.'

As well as awarding a number of special grants each year, the trust administers money through three programmes:

- major grants: grants between £3,000 and £10,000 for two or three years, and a number of one-off grants for amounts between £1,000 and £3,000.
- small grants: usually up to £500 to local organisations, groups and projects, and a small number between £500 to £1,000. Small grants are also made through Divisional Charity Committees which support local projects that employees have an interest in.
- hardship payments to individuals: grants between £50 and £200, application made via welfare agencies, eg, Social Services, Probation Services and Citizens Advice Bureau.

In 1997 the trust's income was £583,000, of which about 60% was donations from Greggs plc and unnamed individuals. Assets stood at £5 million and grant giving totalled £499,000, subdivided as follows:

Special grants	£178,000
Major grants	£129,000
Small grants – head office	£50,000
– divisional	£86,000
Hardship payments	£52,000
Discretionary grants	£4,000

Special grants: This included a payment to the Bampton Trust, which shares three trustees with Greggs trust, of £151,000, and grants to the Tyne and Wear Foundation (£30,000 a year for three years for the South East Northumberland Project); the Diana, Princess of Wales Memorial Fund (£17,000) and the Woodlands Trust (£10,000 for the planting of trees in Longhirst, Northumberland, in memory of the late Neil Calvert, a former trustee).

Major grants: About 25 grants, mostly between £3,000 and £10,000, going mainly to health, community and social welfare organisations. Examples of the larger beneficiaries included The

People's Kitchen, Newcastle (£10,000 for refurbishment costs); Scotswood Area Strategy Youth Project, Newcastle (£10,000 towards the purchase and conversion of a shop premises to be run by young people); Northern Initiative on Women and Eating, Newcastle (£10,000 a year for two years for salary costs); St Simon's Community Project, Jobs, Education and Training, South Shields (£6,500 towards operating costs); and grants of £5,000 each for running and capital costs to Laurel Avenue Community Association, Durham; Shopmobility, South Shields; Willows Community Art & Education Project, Stocton-on-Tees (a year for two years); and Caring hands, Newcastle (a year for two years).

Small grants: 130 grants to local projects and groups in the north east of England. No grants list is provided for these; one assumes they are all for less than £1,000. The Divisional Committee distributed a further 230 grants to a variety of children's, health and medical organisations. Examples included Northern Counties School for the Deaf (£5,100); Children in Need (£4,000); Highfield School (£3,000); and Evelina Children's Hospital Appeal (£2,000).

Exclusions Grants will not be made to:

- individuals, other than for hardship grants;
- national appeals and, other than in exceptional circumstance, appeals of national organisation for work at regional or local level;
- activities which are primarily the responsibility of statutory agencies or which are likely to get funding from such agencies on a contractual basis;
- appeals of charities set up to support statutory agencies; fund raising organisations; general fund raising appeals; fund raising events and sponsorship;
- hospital, Health Service Trusts, medically related appeals and medical equipment;
- school appeals other than for projects at LEA schools in areas of greater social need, eg, after school clubs and activities promoting parental and community involvement;
- advancement of religion or religious buildings. Community aspects of church-based or religious projects may be considered if projects show outreach into the community or particularly to disadvantaged or at-risk groups;
- restoration and conservation of historic buildings and the purchase or conservation of furnishings, paintings, other artefacts or historic equipment;

- purchase, conversion and restoration of buildings other than community-based projects serving areas of greater social need and/or particularly disadvantaged or at-risk groups;
- capital appeals or running costs of fee charging residential homes, nurseries and other such care facilities;
- appeals from organisations associated with the armed services;
- minibuses and vehicles, other than community transport schemes which serve a combination of groups in a wide geographical area;
- foreign travel and expeditions. Holidays and outings, other than in exceptional circumstances for children, young people or adults from areas of greater social need, or other disadvantaged groups;
- sports buildings, equipment and sporting activities other than where disadvantaged groups are involved and the activity is ongoing rather than one-off;
- academic and medical research. Conferences, seminars, exhibitions, publications and events other than where they are closely related to the trust's main areas of interest;
- festivals, performances and other arts and entertainment activity, unless of specific educational value and involving groups from areas disadvantaged by low income, disability or other factors;
- appeals for projects or from organisations working abroad;
- animal welfare;
- loans, repayment of loans or retrospective funding.

Applications Application in writing to the correspondent.

Applicants for major grants are asked to set out their application briefly in a letter, giving full address, phone/fax number and a contact name, the purpose of the application, the amount requested, details of other applications for the same purposes. More information about the project may be provided in supporting documents.

The following should be included:

- Latest audited accounts or financial report required by the Charity Commission and, if a period of three months or more has passed since the end of the year of the accounts/report, a certified statement of income and expenditure for the period.
- Latest annual report or, if not available, summary of current work.
- The applications organisations's Equal Opportunities policy and practice.
- Details of constitutional status; charity registration number if

applicable; organisational structure; composition of managements arrangements for the project for which application has been made.

- If support for a salaried post or posts is requested, the job description for the post(s).
- Details of the organisation's policy and provision for training of management body, staff and volunteers.
- Details of how it is intended to evaluate the work for which the grant is requested.

The trustees meet twice a year to assess major grants applications, usually May and November. Applications should be be sent no later then mid-March or mid September.

The trust aims to respond to applications for small grants within approximately two months and to acknowledge applications for major grants in the same period. Applicants will be informed if their application has not been selected for further consideration.

The Grocers' Charity

£321,000 (1996/97)

General, independent schools

Grocers' Hall, Prince's Street, London EC2R 8AD
Tel: 0171-606 3113; Fax: 0171-600 3082

Correspondent Miss Anne Blanchard, Charity Administrator

Trustees Directors of The Grocers' Trust Company Ltd (about 30).

Beneficial area UK.

Information available Annual accounts; annual report with list of grants (for £600 or more), detailed narrative breakdown of grants/grant-making. Guidelines for applicants.

Summary Approximately 200 grants are made each year within a variety of categories. A little under half of the charitable budget is reserved each year to make awards to a few independent schools with which the charity has strong links. Excepting these, grants are made for between a few hundred pounds up to around £5,000 with most between £1,000 and £2,000.

General The charity says: 'The Grocers' Charity is the charitable arm of

the Grocers' Company, one of the senior livery companies of the City of London. Although the Grocers' Company has an historic tradition of dispensing monies to diverse charitable causes, it was not until 1968 that the charity itself was formally established. It is administered by the Grocers' Trust Company Ltd.

'The charity is funded by its own investments (current value £6.6 million) together with an annual grant from the Grocers' Company (£60,000) and the income from covenants and donations made by members of the Grocers' Company (£36,000).'

In 1996/97 nearly 200 grants were awarded. Aside from those regular annual donations to various schools, practically all grants were one-off and for less than £2,000. 15 grants for more than £2,000 accounted for only 16% of the total value of these 'one-off' awards. Although the charity does not specify any geographical boundaries for grant-making, in practice few donations are made outside of Southern England.

Allocation of funds in 1996/97:

Education	*25*	*£131,000*	*41%*
Disability	*63*	*£61,000*	*19%*
Relief of poverty			
(inc. youth)	*49*	*£47,000*	*15%*
Medicine	*14*	*£18,000*	*6%*
Churches	*9*	*£18,000*	*6%*
Heritage	*10*	*£17,000*	*5%*
Arts	*13*	*£13,000*	*4%*
Elderly	*7*	*£12,000*	*4%*
General	*6*	*£2,000*	*1%*
Total	*196*	*£321,000*	*100%*

The Charity has responded well to the recent Statement of Recommended Practice (SORP) for charities and it now publishes an exceptionally informative annual report. The following is taken from this report:

Annual Report 1996/97
'The charity has wide charitable aims. Each year the majority of its annual expenditure [*41% of total charitable expenditure in 1996/97, Ed.*] is committed on an on-going basis in the field of education, by way of internal scholarships and bursaries at schools and colleges with which the Grocers' Company has historic links.

'The balance [*£190,000 in 1996/97, Ed.*] is spread across several areas of interest, namely the relief of poverty (including youth), disability, medicine, arts, heritage, the church, the elderly, with emphasis currently being given to the first two categories.

'Of the 893 applications received during the year, 150 were successful [*17%, Ed.*]. The remainder received full

consideration and all were informed by letter that their application had been unsuccessful.

'The other donations [*about 21, Ed.*] made during 1996/97 were to organisations with which there is an historical link and to which support is given on a continuing basis.'

The largest new grants of the year (all for £5,000) went to: King's College Cambridge, Bursary Fund; Canine Partners for Independence; Cancer Research Campaign; Peterborough Cathedral Trust and; Canterbury Cathedral.

The report is too long to reprint in full, but includes the following:

'A new sub-committee has been formed to enable Members of the Livery of the Grocers' Company to participate and support the work of the charity. Called the Grocers' Initiative, its aim is to identify a charity or charities working in areas of current interest, and to organise paying events that will raise money to support the chosen project. This year the Initiative held a wine tasting at the Hall to support the work of the Samaritans, and in particular the Central London Branch's Youth Outreach Programme. The event was attended by ninety-two members and their guests, and a total of £1,686 was raised. Building on the success of this event, it is planned to hold a major fund raising event next year with the proceeds once again going to the Samaritans Youth Outreach Programme.

Education 'This category accounted for nearly half the Charity's total expenditure for the year, and the major proportion was distributed to educational establishments linked with the Grocers' Company.

'The Company's schools at Oundle in Northamptonshire received a total of £78,600 to fund internal scholarships and bursaries.

Relief of Poverty (inc. Youth) 'The largest donation made in this category was paid to Voluntary Service Overseas (VSO), to sponsor volunteers going overseas to work in under-developed countries. The Grocers' Company was one of the first organisations to support VSO when it started in the 1960's and, through the Charity, it has maintained that support over the intervening period.

Disability 'A greater proportion of the charity's budget was expended this year in this category. Donations were made to a wide variety of organisations which provide support and services to disabled people of all ages. A donation of £5,000 was made to Canine Partners for

Independence, a charity that trains dogs to assist severely disabled people by performing a large number of everyday tasks. The donation will be used to train a golden retriever puppy called Fergal, and it is anticipated that he will prove to be as successful as the first dog that was sponsored by the charity back in 1991. This dog, Alex, also a golden retriever, has not only been a much loved companion to his wheel-chair bound partner, Ian F., but also proved his worth on several occasions. On one such occasion Ian fell out of his wheelchair and was knocked unconscious. When he came to Alex was by his side. On Ian's command he fetched the mobile telephone, and Ian was able to summon assistance. Without Alex's help, Ian would have been on the floor for several hours before his human helper was due.

Once again, through the disability aid fund, we have given donations to enable the latest computer equipment to be purchased for individuals.

A capital grant of £3,000 was made to the Spring Lane Project, a voluntary organisation that has built and runs and equal play adventure facility in East Hackney. Priority is given to children who cannot use existing facilities because of the nature or extent of their disabilities.

Medicine '£5,000 was donated to the Lord Mayor's Annual Appeal in support of the Cancer Research Campaign.

'The charity continues its policy of not giving donations to appeals on behalf of hospices. However, exceptions are made when there is a company connection, and it was for this reason that a donation of £2,000 was made in support of the work of the St Nicholas Hospice in Bury St Edmunds.

Heritage 'Another category traditionally supported by the charity, and to a greater extent this year.

'Two donations of exceptional size were made in response to appeals from cathedrals, one in support of Peterborough Cathedral and the other to Canterbury Cathedral. Peterborough Cathedral has links with the Company's schools at Oundle in Northamptonshire.

'Other charities supported in this field include the Wildfowl and Wetlands Trust at Cambridge which received a donation of £1,000 for the Pond Explorer Station which is being constructed in the new Wetland Conservation Centre, and £1,500 was given to NADFAS (National Association of Decorative and Fine Arts Societies) to produce a revised edition of the Church Recorders manual.

Arts 'Notable were the donations of £2,000 each made to the Dulwich Picture Gallery, in support of the renowned work of the education department, and to Hackney Youth Orchestras Trust, which promotes and develops musical education for the borough's young people.

Churches 'All the donations made in this category were to churches with which there is an historic Grocer's Company connection, although there are some exceptions.

The Elderly This category received a larger proportion this year, the reason being the significant donation of £4,000 made to the Sussex Housing Association for the Aged in support of the anniversary appeal to build an extra care home in Crowborough for the frail elderly.

General 'Five donations totalling some £2,000 were made in this category, together with one donation of £1,000 made to the Charity Parents Against Injustice. This is a national charity that provides advice and support to those who have been mistakenly involved in allegations of child abuse.

Exclusions Organisations which are not registered charities. Support for churches, educational establishments, expeditions, hospices and research projects restricted to those having specific close and longstanding connections with the Grocers' Company. Donations to individuals are made through registered charities only.

Applications In writing to the correspondent on the charity's official headed notepaper (sic), accompanied by a copy of the latest accounts. Applications, which may be submitted at any time, are not acknowledged, but all are notified of outcome (this may take several months depending on the time of year when the application is submitted). The trustees meet four times a year, in January, April, June and November. Informal telephone enquiries to the Administrator are encouraged.

The Gulbenkian Foundation

£2,024,000 (1997)

Education, arts, welfare

98 Portland Place, London W1N 4ET
Tel: 0171-636 5313; Fax: 0171-637 3421

Correspondent Ben Whitaker, Director

Trustees The foundation's Board of Administration in Lisbon.

Beneficial area United Kingdom and the Republic of Ireland.

Information available As the foundation is not a charity registered in Britain there are no files at the Charity Commission. However it publishes superb annual reports with full details of its thinking, policies and grants. A free leaflet 'Advice to Applicants for Grants' is also available. This entry is quoted or summarised from these sources.

Summary Though one of the best known foundations in Britain, Gulbenkian is not one of the largest, and very few of its grants are for more than £10,000. Its fame rests more in its careful investigation of areas of possible intervention, and its early, if modest, support for new initiatives. Typically, a published report on a particular subject will lead to a corresponding funding programme, to get things moving in the way recommended (and perhaps in the hope that heavier funding guns may then come in behind).

Current examples of the process range from participatory music to work concerned with children and violence.

The foundation presently operates in four fields, as follows, with the 1997 grant totals. Note that Republic of Ireland grants are now handled within the other programmes.

Social Welfare	£717,000
Education	£495,000
Arts	£444,000
Anglo-Portuguese	
Cultural Relations	£197,000
Republic of Ireland	£171,000

This entry starts with the foundation's excellent 'Advice to Applicants' leaflet, and then reprints substantial sections of the 1997 Annual Report – these documents have a long history of clear and trenchant comment on the work of the foundation and on the problems that it addresses, as well as describing many of its specific grants.

Background

'Calouste Sarkis Gulbenkian was an Armenian born in 1869. He became a British citizen, conducted much of his work in Britain, and finally settled in Portugal. The Calouste Gulbenkian Foundation was established in 1956, a year after his death.

The headquarters of the Foundation are in Lisbon and consist of the administration, which deals with grant-giving throughout the world, together with a museum housing the founder's art collections, a research library, a centre for scientific research, concert halls, indoor and open-air theatres, exhibition galleries and conference halls, a centre for modern art, a children's pavilion, an orchestra, a choir and a ballet company. The Foundation also maintains a Portuguese Cultural Centre in Paris, and a grant-giving branch in London for the United Kingdom and the Republic of Ireland.'

The last activity mentioned is the subject of this entry. The UK branch (referred to here, for convenience, simply as the Gulbenkian Foundation, does not have its own endowment, but is funded directly from Lisbon. The foundation is substantially and expertly staffed, and, as well as making grants, organises its own projects and publications.

Advice to Applicants

The January 1998 edition read as follows:

ARTS

Assistant Director, Arts – Siân Ede

This programme deals with arts for adults and young people out of formal education settings.

Mainly for non-professional practitioners:

1. Participatory music: This priority is linked to the foundation's report, Joining In, (copies available from the foundation but it is not essential to read this book before applying), which makes a case for increased opportunities for non-professionals to participate in music-making.

The programme is designed to encourage new developments particularly from and for non-professional groups. Support may take the form of small one-off grants to help individual groups establish musical skills and activities which can be sustained over time, or undertake pioneering work from which others can learn.

For professional practitioners:

2. Two cultures – the Arts and Science: This programme is designed to encourage professional arts groups to produce practical projects which demonstrate a creative engagement with new thinking and practice in science and technology, especially those which involve some collaboration with scientists and technologists.

For professional practitioners:

3. Time to experiment Support is available for groups of professional artists to devise and experiment before they perfect a project. This is a popular

programme and priority is given to applications which demonstrate a genuine ground-breaking development for the art-form as a whole, as well as being challenging for the artists involved.

Activities would normally lead towards a particular production or work, although they should take place at an early stage of the project's development, well before the rehearsal or normal preparation phase. Consideration will also be given to applications for advanced creative training activities for groups of practitioners from particular art forms.

Support is for self-generated practical activity and not for academic research, visits, conferences or discussion.

If you have a project in mind within any priority area please write to the Assistant Director (arts) with an outline application for the potential project. Include a brief description of general future plans if you

have them. Please note that ideas for potential applications should be broached at least three months in advance of a projected starting date for the project applied for.

EDUCATION

Assistant Director, Education – Simon Richey

1. Educational innovations and developments

a. Education for relationships and parenthood
(i) projects in schools which promote self-esteem, communication skills and the ability to handle conflict; (ii) projects in schools, colleges or youth centres designed to help young people consider what it means to be a parent and, through programmes of work, to identify the choices, responsibilities and skills which parenting involves.

b. The ethos of the school

The Gulbenkian Foundation

Geographical distribution of 1997 grants

	No. of Grants		Amounts	
Arts				
National	27	(40%)	£223,408	(51%)
London	8	(12%)	£45,900	(10%)
Other regions	32	(48%)	£174,259	(39%)
	67		**£443,567**	
Education				
National	22	(32%)	£220,975	(45%)
London	7	(11%)	£40,340	(8%)
Other regions	39	(57%)	£233,505	(47%)
	68		**£494,820**	
Social Welfare				
National	50	(56%)	£415,439	(58%)
London	4	(5%)	£40,000	(6%)
Other regions	35	(39%)	£261,682	(36%)
	89		**£717,121**	
Republic of Ireland				
National	14	(56%)	£97,620	(57%)
Dublin	5	(20%)	£32,900	(19%)
Other regions	6	(24%)	£40,420	(24%)
	25		**£170,940**	
Anglo-Portuguese	22		**£197,450**	
Totals				
National	113	(42%)	£957,442	(47%)
London/Dublin	24	(9%)	£159,140	(8%)
Other regions/Portugal	134	(49%)	£907,316	(45%)
Grant Total	**271**		**£2,023,898**	

Projects in schools designed to
(i) improve the level of pastoral care;
(ii) remedy pupil disaffection;
(iii) combat bullying.

c. Under achieving pupils
Support for initiatives by schools, or by organisations that work with them, designed to combat the current under-achievement of certain categories of pupils in secondary schools, and for the evaluation and dissemination of such initiatives.

2. Arts for young people in schools

a. Support for the arts in schools
Grants of up to £5,000 will be offered for projects in the following categories:

- Self-help; arts initiatives by self-help groups of primary and secondary school teachers, including support for the establishment of such groups, formed in response to the reduction of LEA advisory services;
- Agencies: help with the establishment, or with the work of, arts education agencies (i.e. agencies that serve as intermediaries between artists and the education sector), designed to assist schools in promoting the arts;

b. Pupil referral units
Help with the costs of residencies by companies or artists, and with the costs of evaluating and disseminating the initiatives in question; priority will be given to especially original or enterprising developments.

Exceptional grants may be offered for Arts for Young People in Schools projects outside the above categories.

SOCIAL WELFARE

Deputy Director and in charge of Social Welfare – Paul Curno

1. Children and young people

a. Regional and national initiatives which aim to improve the status of children or young people up to age 18 in society, and encourage their participation in policy-making and practice at all levels.

These could include:

- schemes which develop or support the leadership of children and young people in ventures concerned with health, education, the environment, recreational and cultural activities;
- schemes which promote the introduction of democratic structures designed to encourage the participation of children and young people in settings such as schools, youth organisations, community facilities, etc.

b. Proposals which promote the

recommendations of the foundation's Commission on Children and Violence, and other initiatives designed to lead to the creation of safe, non-violent communities, especially those involving children and young people themselves.

c. New measures exploring policies and opportunities for greater parent-child contact for parents in employment, through job-sharing, teleworking, flexitime, parental leave, etc.

2. User involvement in the running of voluntary organisations

The foundation is interested in funding projects which promote the role of users as vital stakeholders in the voluntary sector. Initiatives will explore new models of user involvement in running organisations, especially those agencies offering services to people with mental and physical disabilities, addictions and mental health problems, and to ex-offenders.

3. Community-based regeneration organisations in urban and rural areas

Support for new initiatives which explore and help secure the long-term future of community-based regeneration organisations such as development trusts and in particular develop long-term financial self-reliance.

ANGLO-PORTUGUESE CULTURAL RELATIONS

Director – Ben Whitaker

This programme aims to help Portuguese cultural projects in the UK and Ireland. (British cultural projects in Portugal are the responsibility of the British Council.)

"Cultural relations" are taken to include social welfare, as well as activities in the arts, crafts and education.

The programme includes:

- activities in the UK and the Republic of Ireland concerned with Portugal – its language, culture, people – past and present;
- cultural and educational interaction between British or Irish and Portuguese people;
- the educational, cultural and social needs of the Portuguese immigrant communities (but not individual Portuguese immigrants or visitors) in the UK or the Republic of Ireland.

But grants are not normally given for projects focused upon:

- sporting activities, tourism, holidays
- full-time teaching or research posts or visiting fellowships
- the maintenance, salary or supervision costs of researchers
- attendance at conferences or similar

gatherings
- fees or expenses of individual students pursuing courses of education and training, or doing research
- UK cultural or other work in Portugal.

ANNUAL REPORT 1997
Grant summary for 1997

Arts	*£443,567.00*
Education	*£494,820.00*
Social Welfare	*£717,121.57*
Anglo-Portuguese Cultural Relations	*£197,450.00*
Republic of Ireland	*£170,940.00*
Total	***£2,023,898.57***

'Last year the high conversion rate of sterling resulted in our having slightly less to spend than in the previous year. We regret we had to say no to 1,669 written applications, a small increase on 1996. It is all the more important for a grant-giving foundation to use its inevitably limited opportunities in the most effective way.

'What might that be? Foundation employees almost by definition rarely hear criticisms of themselves. However Mr Craig McCoy recently contributed a salutary review of US foundations' grant-making, which he termed 'under-whelming', to the *American Foundation News and Commentary*:

'The three main roadblocks to foundation effectiveness are unlimited lifespans (why take risks? – we're here forever), staffing by college and university bureaucrats (replace them with entrepreneurs and invenstors), and a total lack of accountability (what's to penalize a foundation for mediocre grant-making or to reward one for being outstanding?)... To fund a proposal that would turn into a great one would require taking a chance on a project with less than 10 percent of success. I know of no foundation in the United States that would consider doing that.

'Nonprofit organizations learned a long time ago not to submit a proposal unless it had a very good chance of succeeding. With lower expectations, everyone loses. Despite having complete freedom to take chances and be creative and innovative, an arid climate has developed over the years that is conservative, boring, and with no sense of urgency to solve or eliminate problems. Foundations are no longer the nonprofit world's source of risk capital but merely an adjunct for federal and state funding. Let's hope the change comes sooner than later.'

'His view would have probably found a supporter a century ago in his compatriot Andrew Carnegie, who argued that charities are 'band-aids', whereas philanthropy should try to remove the causes which necessitate charities. No matter which government holds office, society in the UK has not changed so significantly that we can afford complacency. The 1997 United Nations Human Development Report stated that poverty is rising faster in Britain than in any other major industrialised country; that a higher proportion of old people live in poverty in Britain than anywhere else in the western world; and that Britain's child poverty rate is second only to that of the United States. Corroboration for this is offered by the European Union, which reported that the proportion of children living in poor households in the UK (32%) is significantly worse than the next two highest EU countries, Ireland (28%) and Portugal (27%).

Children in Poverty

Percentage of children living in poor households, 1993

Denmark	*5*
France	*12*
Germany	*13*
Belgium	*15*
Netherlands	*16*
Greece	*19*
EU AVERAGE	*20*
Luxembourg	*23*
Italy	*24*
Spain	*25*
Portugal	*27*
Ireland	*28*
UK	*32*

Source: Eurostat

'Meanwhile, however, public donations to charity in the UK are continuing to decline despite an anticipated increase following the death of Princess Diana. The National Council for Voluntary Organisations reported last October that total donations, including those made through the National Lottery, have fallen by 20% since 1993, with average monthly donations dropping from £11.86 in 1992 to £8.51 (at constant prices) in 1996. The Institute for Fiscal Studies confirmed that the number of households giving to charity has fallen by nearly 5 percent over the last 20 years but found no evidence that the National Lottery has had a significant effect on household giving.

'Analysts of the grants in this report will notice how firmly we now give priority to projects which include plans for an independent evaluation. This helps both the project and grant-making, although by dispensing with formal application forms we seek to avoid drowning busy charitable workers in unnecessary paperwork. Many such workers deserve

our sympathy. The Special EU Support Programme for Northern Ireland, for example, involves (in a contemporary variation of partridges in a pear-tree):

25 *main Funding Measures,*
12 *Sub-measures,*
9 *Intermediary Funding Bodies,*
5 *Second-tier Funding Bodies,*
15 *Government Departments,*
26 *Partnerships,*
6 *Local Authorities,*
4 *State Agencies,*
A *Monitoring Committee,*
A *Consultative Forum*

Several Local Task Forces, working in three currencies and in two jurisdictions.

'It is not difficult to see why we also thought it right to give carte blanche to David Thomas (the former Chief Executive of the Community Development Foundation) to make an independent review of all our social welfare grant-making. Since much of this took place before my own arrival, perhaps I might be allowed to cite one of the findings:

'The Gulbenkian Social Welfare staff saw themselves as active participants in a process of change; advising on giving money was only a part of their contribution. They saw themselves as partners, giving time, energy and commitment as well as the prospect of cash. They helped people develop their ideas, to find further sources of finance, and linked them up with others in the field to encourage cooperation and synergy in effort ... to extend the rights and power of the dispossessed ... "They treat us as colleagues, not people going with a begging bowl."'

'This human factor is undoubtedly the crucial ingredient in determining success, whether as regards applications, charities or projects (and, as will be seen later, it is also the reason why some modestly-resourced museums or galleries can be much more user-friendly than far wealthier ones). In this context, I'd like to pay warm tribute to the colleagues I am fortunate to work with at the UK Branch of the Foundation.

'Alan Pifer, the widely respected president of Carnegie Corporation for fifteen years until 1982, said, "The human qualities of its staff may in the end be far more important to what a foundation accomplishes than any other consideration."

'He warned however that some foundation officers "have fallen into the habit of pontificating rather than listening... and who are patronizing towards grant-seekers... genuinely

believe that simply being part of a profession as worthy as philanthropy automatically makes them worthy people too... To applicants who are not part of an inner circle of favoured grantees, they manage to convey a kind of... disguised hostility. 'Who are you?' they seem to suggest, 'to have the nerve to come here and try to get some of my money?' This, one need hardly add, does not endear them to the outsiders."

'Foundations do not as yet have any citizen's charter or mission statements. But perhaps we might, for example, aim to reply to applicants as quickly as possible (since, for many of them, delays can have serious consequences), and we should recognise it does applicants no favour to give them unsubstantiated optimism about their prospects of being funded. In return, every grant-seeker would be well advised to read a foundation's guidelines before sending a proposal, and should resist taking rejection personally.

'We here offer a free leaflet 'Advice to Applicants for Grants' to grant-seekers about what we are - and are not - currently able to consider funding, and how to apply. Most of all, we welcome applications to help useful, original projects: practical initiatives – preferably displaying imagination or courage – which aim to tackle the root causes of problems, and have more than a local value by demonstrating solutions that could be applied elsewhere. We generally offer to assist with comparatively limited grants of £5,000 to £10,000 or less, which might make a crucial difference to an admirable - but sometimes undeservedly unpopular – project. We are very reluctant to give funding to replace government cuts, lest doing so might only encourage the Treasury to cut further. We also strongly prefer projects away from the south-east of England. London has its obvious problems, but since the great majority of foundations and charitably-inclined companies have their headquarters there, fundraising is immeasurably easier for people in or near the London area than it is for those living, for example, in mid-Wales, Cornwall, Ballybeg in rural Ireland, or the Highlands and Islands of Scotland. In 1997 we gave 19 grants totalling £107,912 in Scotland; 11 totalling £90,300 in Northern Ireland and 7 totalling £57,000 in Wales – all proportionately fewer than we would have wished. We also gave 19 grants last year totalling £150,225 to ethnic minority groups' projects. We continue especially to welcome good projects which assist women, or which are focused on trying to help needs in rural areas. In both the UK and Ireland, rural job opportunities continue to disappear as fishing, traditional seaside tourism, defence establishments and the agricultural labour market (further seriously wounded by the BSE crisis) haemorrhage. The decline of rural transport, village shops and affordable housing is accelerating the departure of skilled and young people as well as causing homelessness to become an increasingly visible problem in country areas.

'Particular efforts during the year to improve parenting, to help participation in arts, and directed at how best to protect children and safeguard their rights and responsibilities are described later. Homelessness undeniably still demands to remain a special priority. Abused women and children were helped with six grants. Substantial grants assisted both ChildLine (£29,000) and the Missing Persons Helpline to extend their excellent work, as well as the invaluable Samaritans organisation to expand in both parts of Ireland (£10,000). Foyers (for those who recognise them as somewhere other than for buying ice-cream in a cinema) were helped by the commissioning and publication of Colin Ward's book *New Town, Home Town* as well as by two grants. Self-building projects were assisted with grants to Community Self-Build Scotland (£5,000) and Young Builders Trust (£9,000). Young people in care were helped with five grants and carers themselves with another five. Through the admirable organisation Live Music Now, whose young musicians give free performances in places such as hospices, three new pieces of music were commissioned respectively from Welsh, Irish and Scottish musicians and successfully performed before a large audience at the Barbican in June (£9,000).

'Support for developments in the arts, which only a handful of other foundations fund, is facing an increasingly difficult future, underlined by current public opinion in the UK.

'Some arts people too easily assume that they do not have to prove their right to subsidised expression, with an arrogance which is unappealing to the people patiently waiting for better hospitals and schools.

'Our public museums and galleries would be wise to heed a similar warning. A sharply declining number of the UK population (29%, cf. 43% in 1995) want lottery money to be spent on museums or on purchasing works of art, preferring priorities such as national and public parks. Unless museums and galleries

radically improve their efforts to make the public feel welcome (instead of seeming intruders, as in some cases), they cannot be surprised if they receive a declining share of scarce national resources.

'We are very grateful to the Secretary of State for Culture, Chris Smith, and to Professor Joseph Lee for presenting our respective British and Irish Museum Awards, which aim to help remedy this situation and give recognition to those who succeed in creating exceptional achievements, irrespective of resources. A recent Demos report quoted a British Tourist Authority survey published last year which showed that many foreigners view Britain as "being bogged down by tradition, riven by class and threatened by industrial disputes, the IRA and poverty-stricken inner cities", while the British people are seen as "insular, cold, arrogant and snobbish". Since 26 million people now visit Britain each year, there is much that museums as well as city-planners could be doing to help change such views – and not to mirror them – by the use of imagination, friendliness, creativity, intelligence and good design.

The Arts Programme

'The winds of change are stirring in the arts world at large. Indeed the climate may be altered for ever. This year the Foundation has drawn attention to two potentially radical movements – the arts in which the 'ordinary' non-professional can participate, and the increasing awareness of scientific discovery and its relevance to the ways in which we express our views and feelings through the arts.

'In the autumn the Foundation published its investigation into participatory music in the British Isles. *Joining In* was written with elegance and wit by Anthony Everitt after a year tirelessly visiting, interviewing and observing a hitherto invisible if not inaudible phenomenon – the great British public making music for sheer enjoyment. Here are the choirs, jazz combos, samba bands, orchestras, bell-ringers, steel pan bands, pop groups, folk singers, tabla players, madrigal ensembles – even karaoke gets a mention. Participatory music in Britain is a success story, although inevitably it would benefit from better support, especially to maintain instrumental tuition for young people, for training and the exchange of ideas. Consequently the book is not simply a celebration. It fixes a very determined gaze on the decision-makers and funders, not least those who administer the Lottery funds.

'The book's main recommendation is that there should be easy access to music-making for everyone in the country. Everyone knows where to go if they want to take up any kind of sport. The same should be true for music. But the book does not propose a network of new buildings. It recommends that decision-makers should build on what already exists and identify the gaps for new initiatives. There could be much more sharing of resources and, crucially, support of *people* – those unsung leaders, teachers and animateurs who singlehandedly do so much to make this a musical land.

'*Joining In* has been very well received and much thanks is due to Anthony Everitt and the spirited and distinguished Steering Group, chaired by poet Jo Shapcott, whose discussions were a privilege to hear. By the end of our series of meetings there resulted an extraordinary change of view – the world turned upside down, so that we were able to look at music-making from the ground first, not from the lofty heights of professionalism. We recommend this new perspective.

'Simultaneously the Foundation has run a programme called *Participatory Music* to encourage non-professional music-making all over the country. We have been able to support many excellent small music groups who are doing the groundwork for our ideal network. In the inner city the Hackney Music Development Trust aims to provide a central music resource for the whole of this richly multicultural borough. The Foundation supported a summer programme of introductory music-making for beginners on particular housing estates. This was so successful that further activities have been planned, including a pensioners' choir and electronic keyboard classes. In the remotest of rural areas the Lochaber Music Trust, based in Fort William, Scotland, is running residential orchestral weekends in village schools for young players who cannot travel over mountain and sea for regular classes. On the larger scale grants have been awarded for the development activities of three important participatory music umbrella organisations. These are the National Federation of Music Societies, whose membership includes every local choir, orchestra and music ensemble in the country; Sound Sense, which represents community musicians; and Contemporary Music for Amateurs, which commissions new music for non-professionals to play. In Ireland, Sound People will run a pilot scheme in Cork to develop music activities in many different community settings in the City and it is hoped this will eventually be replicated all over the country.

'The Foundation's next publication will look at the ways in which artists could, and arguably should, respond to the many astonishing discoveries in science. When Galileo, after Copernicus and Kepler, discovered that the earth was not the centre of the universe, when Darwin tentatively published *The Origin of Species* our view of the world changed for ever. Today concepts such as selfish genes, black holes, complexity theory, the edge of chaos and so on are becoming part of our metaphorical landscape. Is science replacing art in its ability to astound, frighten or move to contemplation? The Foundation's programme *Two Cultures – The Arts and Science* has attracted many artists and arts organisations. The Laboratory at the Ruskin School places artists with the various schools of science at Oxford University so that they can develop their creative ideas through examining scientific rationale. Artists Agency in County Durham has placed an artist to work with environmental scientists and villagers to create a wetland using the water from a disused mineshaft. The fashion designer Helen Storey has worked with her sister Kate Storey, an eminent biologist, to create a striking fashion collection – a work of art – using accurate research into the first 1000 hours of human life. The project also incorporates the latest in technology using lasers, ultra sound and fibre optics to create the materials.

'The third Arts programme, *Time to Experiment,* which supports the early, pre-rehearsal creative development of productions or exhibitions is very popular. We are interested only in supporting truly excellent work, although this is sometimes difficult to determine from a mere project description. Our faith is usually borne out when we see the final production. We were very glad to have helped the implementation of the outstandingly imaginative ideas of the dance artist Yolande Snaith for her work with set, costume and lighting design. We are also pleased to have been able to help with the development of two of the most acclaimed productions within the London International Festival of Theatre and Shared Experience's adventurous exploration of *Jane Eyre.*

The Education Programme

'Much of the work that the Education programme has supported in recent years - what in general terms might be described as helping young people to develop their emotional skills – stands a better chance of succeeding in schools where there is a clear commitment by the staff to Personal and Social Education, or PSE as it is commonly called. PSE provides a natural 'channel' for the work we support and helps guarantee that, once introduced, such work is likely to continue. The difficulty is that PSE provision in schools is notoriously uneven. This is not always because schools lack the necessary commitment: there is uncertainty as to how its different facets - health education (which may include education for relationships and parenting), citizenship education, drugs education and the rest - fit together and form a coherent, organic whole and this in turn can discourage teachers from developing effective practice.

'In order to address this problem in 1997 the Education programme initiated a project that will offer to schools a national framework for PSE. The purpose of the framework is to bring to PSE the necessary coherence and rigour and also to indicate to teachers how it might progress and develop across the Key Stages. At a time when a number of government-appointed Working Groups are beginning to look closely at the different components of PSE with a view to promoting them more energetically in schools, the need for coherence and a clear sense of direction is especially important.

'One component of PSE to which the Education programme has given particular attention is education for parenthood, or opportunities for older pupils to reflect on a reality that for many of them may not be too distant. In June of last year the Parliamentary Under Secretary of State, Estelle Morris, spoke at the launch conference of a Foundation report on this subject, entitled Tomorrow's Parents, and it was gratifying to note that the White Paper on education published the following month indicated the government's wish to see all secondary schools teach young people the skills of good parenting.

'A wide range of projects funded during the year reflected the Education programme's commitment to the emotional well-being of young people, including four grants to RELATE to enable it to develop further its work in schools (£29,000 in all), the Meridian Broadcasting Charitable Trust (£13,000), the Roehampton Institute (£13,000) and Antidote (£12,000). One grant in particular, however, deserves special mention. Bristol City Council is piloting in a selection of its primary schools what it describes as the 'Emotional Curriculum'. The aim of the project is to develop children's emotional literacy by providing a coherent programme of classroom activities which will introduce key skills in the early years of schooling and then re-visit them in age-appropriate ways as the children move on to secondary school. The range of skills in question includes self-awareness, the capacity to manage one's own feelings and respond appropriately to those of others, the development of empathy and the acquisition of communication skills. What makes this project significant is not only its content but also the fact that it was initiated – for the first time it should be added – by a local education authority. The Foundation was especially pleased to be able to support this development (£10,000).

'Two new priorities were introduced at the beginning of 1997. The first offered support to pupils who, as indicated by OFSTED and others, are seriously under-achieving in schools and a range of projects assisted during the year illustrated this new category of support. The second new priority, incorporated into the Education programme's support for the arts in schools, offered help with the costs of residencies by companies or artists who wished to work in Pupil Referral Units (PRUs) which many of the country's excluded pupils attend in place of school. The arts have a particularly valuable role to play in the lives of young people in PRUs since they can develop their self-esteem and their ability to communicate, attributes which these young people often conspicuously lack. It is encouraging to report that the number of applications made against this priority was particularly high, suggesting that the priority had been introduced at a timely moment. The range of projects funded, furthermore, indicates that the initiatives in question have been undertaken by an encouraging spread of agencies: by the PRUs themselves (The Park Education Support Centre, £5,000, and Sherborne Pupil Referral Unit, £1,600), by a local education authority (Brighton and Hove, £5,000) and by arts institutions (Four D Associates, £5,000, and The Place – Contemporary Dance Trust, £5,000).

The Social Welfare Programme

'For more than thirty years the majority of grants given by the Social Welfare Programme have been governed by two guidelines: first, initiatives funded should offer those excluded from mainstream social and political life and services a voice and opportunities to influence their situation; second, that projects should be seminal, and likely to have implications for policy and practice beyond the immediate work being supported.

'In addition, the Programme has always concentrated on a limited number of areas of need, usually those receiving little attention from society or government. The commitment to each area is sustained over several years and is comprehensive, involving perhaps the raising of public awareness of the issues, the provision of information and advice to those in need, training for professionals, support for new initiatives and organisations, and policy development through working parties, studies, seminars and publications. In past years those areas which have been the focus of attention have included community development, race relations, housing, social care, community arts and local economic development.

'The current three priorities of the Social Welfare Programme reflect these prerogatives. One of the priorities is support for user involvement in the running of voluntary organisations, an example of which is the grant given to ACENVO to produce guidance for its 900 Chief Executives on strategies and methods for achieving such participation (£15,000). Backing for community based regeneration organisations in urban and rural areas is the second priority. However the main attention of the Programme in recent years has been on the third priority, the human rights of children and young people up to age 18. The Programme has used the three main categories of the U.N. Convention on the Rights of the Child, ratified by the British Government in 1991, as a framework within which to work. They are:

provision - the rights of children and young people to adequate standards of living, minimum standards in education, health, physical care, family life, play and culture;

protection - the rights of children and young people to be safe from physical abuse, exploitation, discrimination and injustice;

participation - the rights of children and young people to information, freedom of speech and opinion, and to be consulted about issues of concern to them.

'The list which follows reflects grants in each of the Convention's categories but focuses especially on the third, participation, with help given to a number of organisations which assist children and young people to express their opinions on matters they consider important. Thus funds were provided to Action for Sick Children to establish Children's Forums in co-operation with NHS Trusts and hospitals to enable children's views to influence health

care (£5,000); to Play-Train for a national initiative to involve children and young people in planning and implementing arts, leisure and cultural activities (£10,000); to the Daycare Trust (£10,000) and Choices in Childcare (£5,000) to canvass children's own views and experience of childcare; and to A Voice for the Child in Care to enable children and young people in local authority care to tell of their experience of using complaints procedures (£6,000).

'A variety of publications – reports, packs, pamphlets, leaflets and sometimes videos – form an important strand of the Programme's implementation of the comprehensive commitment to an area of work, as mentioned above. They may be targeted at policy makers, users of services, professionals, children and young people, parents or the wider public. Examples published in 1997 include *Never Too Young*, a helpful booklet for parents on encouraging children under eight to take responsibility and make decisions, produced by the National Early Years Network (£1,500). The Institute of Education published and disseminated widely a short and lively summary of its report *Children's Services: Time For A New Approach* (£5,000), which complemented a report published by the Foundation in November 1996 intended for civil servants and politicians, *Effective Government Structures For Children*. Also with the Foundation's help Alcohol Concern produced two publications: a guide for teenagers *Enough bottle: Can You Handle Booze?* and *Under The Influence,* a report on the needs of children of problem drinkers which was aimed at professionals. The Mental Health Foundation published a booklet for parents and carers wanting to know more about anxiety in children and young people, *The Anxious Child.*

'Finally, UNICEF's International Child Development Centre in Florence, Italy, published *A Model For Action: The Children's Rights Development Unit. Promoting the Convention on the Rights of the Child in the United Kingdom,* written by Gerison Lansdown. The Foundation was instrumental in establishing the Children's Rights Development Unit in 1991 which was set up to assist voluntary and statutory agencies implement the Convention. The Foundation funded the analysis and publication of the report so that the lessons learnt could be shared with individuals and agencies in Britain and throughout the world.

The Anglo-Portuguese Cultural

Relations Programme

'The highlights of the year were two memorable exhibitions by female Portuguese artists. The first was the outstanding retrospective of Paula Rego's paintings at the Tate Gallery, Liverpool during February-April (£10,000); the second, the exhibition of the paintings of Josefa de Obidos at the European Academy for the Arts in London during October and November. Both exhibitions attracted extensive praise from visitors as well as the media. The latter's success owed a great deal to the skill of its presentation by Dr Angela Delaforce, who also arranged an interesting series of lectures to complement the exhibition (£20,000).

'Portugal 600, under the continuing chairmanship of Manuel Villas-Boas and direction of Michael Collins and Andy Wood, had a successful year with its virtually single-handed efforts to get Portuguese arts and culture better known in the UK and Ireland, with substantial help from the UK Branch (£50,000). It organised a special concert at Apsley House, partly to welcome a visit by the Portuguese Minister of Education and also the arrival of the new Portuguese Ambassador to London, H.E. José Gregório Faria, whose support for Portugal 600 is much appreciated. The Anglo-Portuguese group Quarteto Lacerda played the UK premieres of works by Luis de Freitas Branco and Alexandre Delgado (£10,000) before a large invited audience.

'In the field of Portuguese writing, the UK Branch assisted the publication of translations of José Hermano Saraiva's *Portugal - A Companion History* (which fills a long-felt gap in providing an accessible summary). Portugal 600 also provided support for the special focus on Portugal at the Frankfurt Book Fair, featured in special editions of the *Times Literary Supplement* and the *European Bookseller*, and it distributed to a wide range of British and Irish publishers a specially commissioned pack of information on recommended books by contemporary Portuguese and Luso-African writers. Issue no.15 of the magazine Cultura, focused on the Expo, was also published with the Branch's help.

'As a major contribution to the Southwark Festival, A Capella Portuguesa and the London Festival Orchestra both gave concerts featuring Portuguese music. There was also an exhibition of new works by the young Portuguese artists Teresa Furtado, Graciela Machado, Pedro Gomes, Sofia Leitão, Alexandre Fontoura and Pedro

Moitinho (£6,000).

'The 1997 European Discoveries Music Festival in Clerkenwell presented several evenings of music by Portuguese composers and performers. Atlantic Fusion was assisted with a multi-media arts event about the Azores (£5,000); the Grand Union Music Theatre was helped to make and distribute a CD recording of its original work *Por Mares do Imaginario* (£5,000); the Music Resource Centre of Brixton was funded for its Abandapa Portuguese music project for children (£2,500); and a poem by Pessoa was featured on the London Underground (£7,000).

'Outside London, an exhibition of photographs by Pedro Sena Nunes (£1,000) took place in Glasgow; Bristol hosted performances and workshops by Toque de Caixa (£3,000); the Caledonian Portuguese Association was funded to exhibit Portuguese books at the Edinburgh Book Festival (£1,500); Chipping Norton was assisted with its 'Everything Portuguese' Festival (£2,500); the enterprising Dublin publisher Mermaid Turbulence was given funds to translate Alberto Tavarez and Antero de Quental (£3,000); and the Tagus Theatre was funded to tour two Sampaio plays (£5,000).

'The Portuguese community in the UK was helped with grants to assist mentally and physically disabled people (£4,000), and for bilingual computer training for unemployed people (£5,000).

The Republic of Ireland Programme

'Although during 1997 we were glad to be able to give a slightly higher number of grants in Ireland, the scarcity of grant-giving foundations there still remains conspicuous in the face of the obvious charitable needs.

'As in the UK, good projects aiming to help vulnerable women and children are a particular concern for the Foundation, and earn a high priority for our assistance. We gave £15,000 over two years to the Ana Liffey Drug project which helps the children of drug-using parents in north inner-city Dublin, where heroin is tragically rife. The Line Projects were also helped with their work for young people in the same area (£7,000). Across the country in Donegal the Anti-Bullying Research and Resource Centre was assisted to pilot a project to train primary school teachers develop whole-school anti-bullying strategies (£7,500), and in Cavan workshops were funded to help teachers tackle bullying through drama (£2,000). A major grant

was given via Barnardo's Republic of Ireland to help the work of implementing in Ireland the UN Convention on the Rights of the Child (£20,000). A further substantial grant was given to the Irish Association of Pastoral Care in Education to help promote effective pastoral care in Ireland's schools (£13,000).

'Other grants sought to tackle differing manifestations of disadvantage. The Camphill Communities of Ireland were funded to train volunteers who work in their impressive communities in which disabled people live (£8,000). The excellent The Big Issues of Dublin was helped to develop its writers workshops for homeless and long-term unemployed people. Calypso Theatre Company was funded for a cross-border project for young people to tackle issues of discrimination, particularly against Travelling people (£4,000). The National Missing Persons Helpline was assisted to set up an office in Dublin. APIC – the National Arts and Disability Centre – was given funding over two years for a training programme led by professional arts practitioners for youth leaders who work with disabled young people (£10,000); and the National Gallery of Ireland was helped with its very enterprising educational work for deaf people and disadvantaged primary schoolchildren (£5,500).

'The Foundation's Arts programme has also stimulated enterprising activities in the Republic. The idea of promoting Participatory Music in Ireland seems to fall into the 'coals to Newcastle' category and our first impulse was to make use of the Irish experience to see what we could learn for the rest of the UK. We were very lucky to have on the Steering Group for our publication *Joining In* the knowledgeable Dermot McLaughlin, Music Officer at the Arts Council of Ireland, and himself an accomplished fiddle player. As a bonus he played his fiddle to accompany the book's launch. Within the Arts and Science programme we supported a project at Arthouse which gave a number of leading Irish artists, including Alice Mayer and Dorothy Cross, the opportunity to try out digital technology (£5,000). The medium is only as good as the message and in this case the high quality of the artists' work set a new standard. We were pleased that Opera Theatre Ireland had an opportunity through our Time to Experiment programme to work in greater depth on the development of My Love, My Umbrella, and that the new dance centre, the Firkin Crane in Cork, was able to run experimental dance activities (£10,000).

'Our Awards for the best Irish Museums and Galleries, given in conjunction with the Heritage Council, were presented by Professor Joseph Lee of the University of Cork (see page 58). Administered from Belfast, presented in Dublin, and judged by an unpaid panel of cross-border experts, these have long been a shining example of supra-national cooperation. (For those who know their history, the fact that 1996's main Awards went to museums in Kilmainham Gaol and Belfast's Upper Shankhill shows how intelligence and common-sense can bridge community divides. The all-Ireland Gulbenkian 'Environmental Endeavour' Awards and the Citizenship Foundation's Gulbenkian Youth Awards for Ireland both gave recognition to an unsung army of mainly young people in all parts of Ireland whose voluntary work helps their communities. The Foundation's Irish Civic Trust Awards for 1997 once again ably administered by Denis Leonard of Limerick, went to the Kilmore Flour Mill project in Cork (in the infrastructural category) with Derry's Georgian House restoration project commended; and to the Roundstone Beach Committee in Co. Galway as winner in the environmental category .

'As we regularly emphasise, the depth and breadth of the charitable needs in Ireland impel us to repeat our offer to give any help or advice which might be required by other grant-givers who are uncertain about how to assist projects in Ireland.'

Exclusions The foundation gives grants only for proposals of a charitable kind, usually from organisations, which should normally be registered charities or otherwise tax-exempt.

It does not give grants for:

- the education, training fees, maintenance or medical costs of individual applicants; science; medicine and related therapies;
- the purchase, construction, repair or furnishing of buildings;
- performances, exhibitions or festivals;
- conferences or seminars; university or similar research;
- science;
- medicine or related therapies;
- holidays of any sort;
- sectarian religion;
- establishing funds for scholarships or loans;
- projects concerning drug-abuse and alcoholism;
- animal welfare;
- sports; equipment, including vehicles or musical instruments;
- stage, film or television production costs;

- commercial publications;
- basic services (as opposed to imaginative new projects) for elderly or disabled people;
- overseas travel, conference attendance or exchanges, or housing.

It never makes loans or retrospective grants, nor help to pay off deficits or loans, nor can it remedy the withdrawal or reduction of statutory funding.

It does not give grants in response to any large capital, endowment or widely distributed appeal. If some specific item in such an appeal would constitute a suitable project, then that item should be proposed in its own right.

Applications Applicants are asked to bear in mind the size of grant the UK branch of the foundation is normally able to make. At present there is a notional limit of £10,000 to any one grant, seldom exceeded.

There is no application form or suggested length of submission. Applications should be made in writing. Essential information should include:

- the exact purpose for which the proposed grant is sought; the amount required, with details of how that amount has been arrived at;
- information about other sources of income, if any: those that are firm commitments as well as those being explored;
- most recent annual report and accounts;
- plans for monitoring and evaluating the work (this is regarded as very important and a report of work undertaken is always required);
- information about the aims and functions of the organisation and about its legal status. If a registered charity, send the registration number, or if your organisation has an official tax exemption number or letter, send the reference. The foundation sometimes makes a grant available to an organisation which does not yet have charitable status through an organisation which does, when there is a suitable association between them.

Preliminary work on an application involves consultation, modification or development, and often an on-site visit, all of which takes time. Fully prepared proposals are usually considered at trustee meetings held in February, April, July and November. Approximately the same amount is distributed in grants at each meeting.

The Paul Hamlyn Foundation

£2,806,000 (1997/98)

Arts, education, overseas, publishing

18 Queen Anne's Gate,
London SW1H 9AA
Tel: Tel: 0171-227 3500,
Fax: 0171-2322 0601,
e-mail: phf@globalnet.co.uk

Correspondent Patricia Lankester, Director

Trustees Lord Hamlyn; Lady Hamlyn; Michael Hamlyn; Jane Hamlyn; Robert Gavron; Mike Fitzgerald.

Adviser, Education: Sir Claus Moser.
Adviser, Publishing: Sue Thomson

Beneficial area UK and overseas (mainly India).

Information available Guidelines for applicants and full reports and accounts available from the foundation.

Summary Most grants are made in one of four areas:

- The arts: increasing awareness of arts; arts in education and support for individual artists.
- Education: schools and access to higher education.
- Book publishing: training and education; increasing access and awareness to books; provision of expertise and bursaries to selected institutions for postgraduate studies in publishing
- Overseas: mainly in India supporting development projects for women, local NGO's, children and the disabled.

Outside these priorities, something over 10% of grants by value go to a range of medical research programmes (usually concerned with Parkinson's Disease), and to other bodies, most often to support social campaigns.

Revised guidelines were being published in early 1999 and the foundation should be contacted for them.

Almost £3 million was given in 1997/98 in 460 grants. Grants averaged £7,000, with a few large awards in excess of £100,000. Grants are sometimes given for more than one year, but usually only for specific projects.

General The foundation's Guidelines were under revision in Autumn 1998 and were expected to be available in their new form in early 1999. Reprinted below

are those in force in 1998, together with sections of the Annual Report and Accounts for1997-98 which amplify some of the foundation's thinking.

Support is concentrated on arts, education, publishing and overseas projects, mainly in India.

The arts
Increasing awareness of the arts and art in education

'The foundation supports schemes which encourage new people to visit theatres, galleries, museums and other venues throughout the UK. Such projects usually include a programme of outreach work and discounted tickets so that they will genuinely attract people for whom the arts will be a new experience. The foundation is particularly interested in places where successful projects have not already been undertaken.

'Arts in education is an integral part of increasing awareness for the arts. A particular project may well fit both categories. In addition the foundation's priorities for supporting the encouragement of arts in school are:

- Out of school arts activities for children in places currently not well served.
- Partnerships between schools and other organisations which aim to promote the arts for pupils.

Support for individual artists

- A foundation award for individual artists was launched in 1993. From 1998-2000 the awards will be for the visual arts, with a strong emphasis on experiment, innovation and cross arts collaboration. Five awards will be made.
- The foundation provides bursaries to selected institutions for students on a small number of courses which are outstanding in their field. No other student bursaries are given.

Education
Schools

'The foundation looks to support innovation and experiment designed to help overcome barriers to learning in disadvantaged schools. Priority will be given to schemes which schools themselves have originated and which are likely to serve as pilots for other schools with similar problems and aspirations, and particularly those which address:

- General levels of attainment in such schools
- Problems of motivating pupils who may not achieve any formal qualification by the school leaving age.

Access to further and higher education

- Schemes to encourage pupils to stay on at schools and to enter further and higher education
- Schemes to promote access for mature students entrants, especially those from ethnic minorities.

Publishing

'Support for publishing is currently focused on the following areas:

- Training and education for publishing and book selling in the UK and, where appropriate, the transfer of British expertise overseas.
- Increasing access to and awareness of books and the British publishing industry.
- The provision of publishing expertise or financial assistance to organisations whose work is of direct interest to the foundation and whose principal activities do not include publishing and distribution
- Bursaries to selected institutions for students undertaking postgraduate courses in publishing.

Overseas

'The trustees have decided to limit the foundation's funding for the developing world to direct local projects in India, concentrating on the following areas:

- Development schemes for women.
- Programmes to strengthen NGO's generally through training, information exchange and networking.
- The development and dissemination of simple technology for the disabled, particularly the Jaipur Foot, a lower limb prosthesis developed in India.'

Annual Report 1997-98

The following paragraphs have been taken from the annual report for 1997-98:

'Four years ago the foundation's trustees and staff watched the advent of the National Lottery with interest, curiosity and some concern about the likely impact of such large players as the five Lottery boards on our own operations. We took the view that the Paul Hamlyn foundation must continue to seek out innovation and talent, to support pilot projects which might then become blue prints for large Lottery funded schemes, and that our flexibility and ability to respond quickly to applications for small grants should remain the cornerstone of our approach to grant making.

'The trustees agreed a grant of £1 million to the Tate Gallery of Modern Art at Bankside for the redevelopment of educational facilities. The grant was part capital and part revenue and is already enabling the TGMA to work with local communities to make connections between personal experience, creative processes and the work of living artists. In the same vein, we revised our Awards for Artists scheme, established in 1992, so that new awards will have a greater impact on the creative process by being offered over a longer period. The new scheme was launched in March, 1998 with a commitment of £450,000 from the foundation over the next three years.

The arts

'The foundation particularly supports projects which increase awareness of the arts, or which extend new opportunities to large numbers of people. It is also concerned to support talented individuals practising in a specific area, and to help ensure the centrality of the arts in education.

Education

'The foundation's concern is to improve access to education and to enable greater participation at all levels. It gives support to practical innovations and projects which work to combat educational disadvantage. It has a strong interest in arts education and in after-school activities.

Publishing and bookselling

'The foundation's support for publishing and bookselling concentrates on training and education. It is designed to encourage the raising of standards in the UK and to make skills training available to those working in the industry who might not otherwise be offered training opportunities.

Overseas

'The foundation's funding is concentrated on direct support for local projects in India. The priority areas are for support for the disabled and for the development of local NGO's.

'Grants of up to £3,000. In addition to the major grants awarded, the foundation makes a number of smaller awards to support local schemes and initiatives within its main areas of interest. 203 such grants were made in 1997-98.'

Grants in 1997/98

In 1997/98 the foundation had assets of £105.3 million and a rather low income of £3.8 million. Grant giving stood at £2.8 million in 464 grants. Management and administrative costs were relatively high at £564,000, 15% of the grant total or about £1,200 per grant approved. This is not surprising considering the foundations involvement in developing and supprting a wide range of specialist programmes. The trust received 1,985 applications, making the success rate of applications 23%, though this is increased to about 50% when ineligible applications are removed.

Examples of beneficiaries were as follows:
Arts

- General; £364,000 total: Tate Gallery (£250,000 towards educational facilities at the Tate Gallery of Modern Art); Trinity College of Music (£15,000 for a music education scheme in East Anglia Schools); Brouhaha (£10,000 for an outreach worker for a street theatre festival 1997) and the Drake Music Project (£5,000 for an after-school music workshop for children with disabilities).
- Increasing awareness; £503,000 total: Royal National Theatre (£157,000 for the Hamlyn Festival 1998); London Philharmonic Orchestra (£44,000 towards a family access scheme); Irish Museum of Modern Art (£25,000 for a regional access programme); and Tricycle Theatre Company (£4,000 towards a youth arts card).
- Arts in education; £171,000 total:

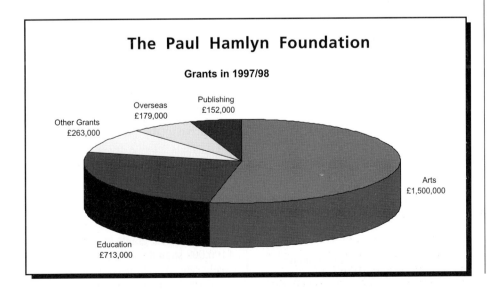

The Paul Hamlyn Foundation

Grants in 1997/98

Overseas £179,000
Publishing £152,000
Other Grants £263,000
Arts £1,500,000
Education £713,000

169

London Musica (£20,000 towards a residency at Thames Valley University); Theatre Royal (Norwich) Trust (£20,000 for a Norwich school project); and Spitalfields Festival (£5,000 for education and community work).
- Individual artists; £220,000 total: Five awards to poets (£121,000).
- Other grants up to £3,000: £242,000

Education
- General; £468,000 total: University of the First Age (£108,000, for a teacher fellowship scheme); Education Extra (£55,000 for after school and holiday activities); Kidscape (£5,000, training guide on bullying); and Total Learning Challenge (£4,000, for an arts based group for disaffected children).
- Literacy; £83,000 total: Norfolk County Council Education (£20,000 for a family literacy project); Pecan (£5,000 for an ESOL class for refugees); and Prisoners of Conscience (£4,000 towards the cost of running English classes).
- Training (£39,000): Kids Club Network (£29,000 for a training development programme)
- Access to Higher and Further Education; £65,000 total: University of Humberside (£40,000 for an access to higher education project); and University of Dundee (£5,000, meetings for co-ordinators of access programmes).
- Other grants up to £3,000: £57,000

Publishing
- General; £14,000 total: Schools Publishing Awards 1997 (£8,000); and Oxford Brookes University (£6,000 for a special collection on publishing in Africa).
- Training and Education; £103,000 total: Bookseller Association (£20,000 towards training grants for small booksellers); London College of Printing (£10,000 for a postgraduate publishing bursary) and AN Publications (£3,000 for an editorial traineeship).
- Access and awareness; £21,000 total: Federation of Children's Book Groups (£12,000 for a children's book award).
- Other grants up to £3,000: £13,000

Overseas
- General; £59,000 total: FUNDECI (£18,000, for emergency self-help housing and health education programmes in Mangura, Nicaragua); and the Institute of Neurology, India (£10,000 towards the transfer of technology).
- Women's development programmes

in India; £30,000 total: Mobile Crèches (£11,000 towards salaries); and Community Action for Rural Development (£4,000, towards coir rope making for women).
- Support for local NGO's; £18,000 total: Rathambhore Foundation, India (£9,000 for maternal health and family planning).
- Support for disabled in India; £66,000 total: Bhagwan Mahaveer Viklang Sahayta Samiti (£30,000 for a limb fitting centre in Jaipur); and Rotarian Community Service Foundation (£15,000 towards research and development of Jaipur Foot).
- Other grants up to £3,000: £6,000.

Other grants
- General; £125,000 total: Runnymede Trust (£56,000 for the commission on the future of multi-ethnic Britain); Refugee Support Centre (£10,000, towards refugee counselling services) and Redress Trust (£5,000 production of a handbook for clients).
- Medical; £122,000 total: St Mary's Hospital Medical School (£50,000 Parkinson Disease Nurse Project); and Imperial College (£30,000, for funding of a community base PDNS Project).
- Other grants up to £3,000: £16,000.

Exclusions The foundation is flexible but will only exceptionally consider applications which fall outside its declared areas of interest and priority.

It will not support:
- general appeals or endowments;
- buying, maintaining or refurbishing property
- individuals, except where a special scheme has been established;
- general support for individual schools, theatre companies or productions;
- education projects relating to specific issues e.g. environmental problems, health awareness etc.

Applications If you still want to make an application:
- talk to us first
- complete the cover sheet
- write not more than five single sides of A4, with a further page for the budget. Supporting information may be supplied in appendices, but the main statement should be self contained and provide the essential information required by the trustees.

This should include:
- what sort of organisation you are; what is the general aim of the project

and its specific objectives
- how it is to be done and by whom
- what problems you anticipate in doing it
- whom it is intended to benefit and how many
- when it will start and how long it will take
- how much money you need and for what purposes – salaries, rent, administration and so forth
- how other interested parties will be informed of the outcome
- how you will know whether or not it has succeeded
- which other funders you have approached and with what success
- if you will need funding beyond the period of the grant, where it is to come from.

Please enclose with your application a copy of your most recent accounts.

Procedures
Applications will be acknowledged when received, but it may take some time to assess them. This may involve correspondence and meetings between staff and applicants and will involve consultation with the trustees, advisers and independent referees.

Applications for sums of £3,000 or less are handled by a committee which meets monthly. These applications should be for specific projects rather than revenue or deficit funding and the grant requested should represent a substantial part of the funding required. Grants will be made for one year only. Applications in consecutive years from the same organisation will not normally be considered. Applications received by the first Friday of each month, except August, will be dealt with in the same month, otherwise the following month.

Applications for sums from £3,000 to £25,000 are dealt with by a second committee which meets every second month. These meetings usually take place in February, April, June, September and November. Applications should reach the foundation in the first week of the preceding month.

Applications for larger sums will be considered by the quarterly meetings of the trustees, which generally take place in January, April, June and October. The closing date for applications is six weeks before each meeting. the exact dates are available from the administrator at the foundation.

Applications for grants in excess of £100,000 should also be submitted six weeks before each meeting. They will be considered in two stages: trustees will decide whether or not they are prepared to consider an application at a first meeting and if so will consider the application proper at the next quarterly meeting.

The Hampstead Wells and Campden Trust

£267,000 (to organisations 1996/97)

Welfare in Hampstead

62 Rosslyn Hill, London NW3 1ND
Tel: 0171-435 1570; Fax: 0171-435 1571

Correspondent Mrs Sheila A Taylor, Director and Clerk to the trustees

Trustees Up to 20 trustees including the Vicar of Hampstead Parish Church and five trustees appointed by the London Borough of Camden. J A Lemkin, Chair.

Beneficial area The former Metropolitan Borough of Hampstead; organisations covering a wider area but whose activities benefit Hampstead residents among others may also apply.

Information available Guidelines from the trust, with details of the streets falling in the beneficial area. Excellent reports and accounts.

General The trust makes grants to organisations 'providing services or facilities which afford relief of need or distress' for residents in Hampstead. Grants range from under £500 up to £60,000. It also makes grants for the benefit of individuals in need.

About 100 grants to organisations are made each year, ranging from a few hundred pounds up to an exceptional £30,000 or more. Unusually they are divided into awards for £500 or less or £1,000 or more. More than half the awards of £1,000 or more are to groups that were also supported in the previous year, but the amount usually vary, rather than being regular subventions. They fell within the following range:

£0 – £500	£19,000	(51 grants)
£501 – £999	£900	(1 grant)
£1,000 – £60,000	£245,000	(41 grants)

The largest grant, of £31,000, was to the Royal Free Hospital. There were two of £15,000, to Camden Crossroads, the Central and Cecil Housing Trust. £10,000 each was given to Camden

Family Service Unit, Hampstead Community Counselling, London Marriage Guidance Council, Swiss Cottage Community Association and Three Acres Community Play Project.

The charity has taken advantage of the skills of its local residents, and has recruited as trustees at least two people already well known in the trust world – Gaynor Humphries, the Director of the Association of Community Foundations, and Alan Goodison, former Director of the Wates Foundation.

The trust also makes grants for the benefit of individuals, an activity not covered by this book. However, it is agreeable to read that this includes an original and unusual activity, the provision of 'kitchen starter packs', assembled at the trust's offices, for young people on state benefits who are setting up home for the first time.

Applications At any time. The trustees meet eight times a year and in addition requests for smaller grants are considered at more frequent intervals. There is no application form (for organisations), but 'it is imperative to show, preferably with statistical information, how many people in the former Metropolitan of Hampstead have been or will be helped by the project. Applications may be discussed with the staff of the trust prior to their submission.'

The Hampton Fuel Allotment Charity

£1,042,000 (for organisations 1996/97)

General, in Twickenham and Richmond

15 Hurst Mount, High Street, Hampton, Middlesex TW12 2SA
Tel: 0181-941 7866

Correspondent M J Ryder, Clerk

Trustees J A Webb, Chairman; A G Cavan; Mrs. M J M Woodriff; H E Severn; Dr. D Lister; Mrs. M T Martin; P W Simon; A D Smith; Rev W D F Vanstone; H A Wood, Rev. D Winterburn.

Beneficial area Hampton, the former borough of Twickenham, and the borough of Richmond.

Information available Full report

and accounts meeting most but not all of the SORP requirements; the narrative report does not cover all of the prescribed headings. Unusually and usefully the full grants lists cover separately both grant approvals and actual payments, but there is no indication of the purposes of even the larger awards.

Summary Grants for most kinds of health, welfare and educational organisations, many of them recurrent. For capital projects, they may be for sums up to at least £300,000, but most grants are in the £1,000 to £20,000 range.

General This is one of the largest 'local' trusts in the country, its wealth deriving from a concession under the local enclosure act of 1811 whereby 10 acres was put aside to produce wood fuel for the inhabitants of the parish of Hampton. The land, having become immensely valuable, was sold for a supermarket in 1988, and the area of benefit widened appropriately in line with the huge income now available.

There is a large programme of help for individuals in need, not covered by this book, and which takes about about a third of the income of the charity. The balance is distributed to organisations on the following basis (1996/97 figures):

Community work	*£429,000*
Housing	*£199,000*
Schools and council	
related matters	*£183,000*
Mentally ill and handicapped	*£111,000*
Social and medical welfare	*£39,000*
Recreation	*£35,000*
Youth work	*£25,000*
Pre- and after-school	
care groups	*£22,000*

115 grants were made in all from an unknown number of applications. An analysis of two of these headings suggests that about two thirds of the organisations supported had also been helped in the previous year, and that about one third had also received help in 1993/94, three years earlier. There is no indication of the basis on which trustees decide relative merit between applications, or of their average success rate.

The largest grants in 1996/97 were to St Stephen's Church, East Twickenham (£300,000 for a new community building), to a Hampton Scout group for new premises and to Welcare and West Middlesex Hospital (£100,000 each).

Administrative and investment management costs were £210,000, 12% of grant expenditure, which is reasonable given the extensive programme of grants for individuals.

171

Exclusions

The charity is unlikely to support

- grants to individuals for private and post-compulsory education;
- adaptations or building alterations for individuals;
- holidays, except in cases of severe medical need;
- decoration, carpeting or central heating;
- anything which is the responsibility of a statutory body;
- national general charitable appeals
- animal welfare;
- religious groups, unless offering a non-religious service to the community;
- commercial and business activities;
- endowment appeals;
- political projects;
- retrospective capital grants.

The trustees are also reluctant to support on-going revenue costs of organisations unless they can show clearly that within the area of benefit a substantial number of people are being charitably assisted. They also expect organisations to show that other support will be forthcoming and that the organisation will become self reliant over an identified period of years.

Applications Application forms are available from the correspondent (on disk if required). Trustees meet quarterly but there is a separate grants panel that meets every two months. Larger awards will be considered by both bodies.

The W A Handley Charitable Trust

£243,000 (1996/97)

General, in Northumberland and Tyneside

c/o Ryecroft Glenton, 27 Portland Terrace, Newcastle upon Tyne NE2 1QP

Correspondent The Secretaries to the Trustees

Trustees Anthony Glenton; David Miligan; Douglas Erington.

Beneficial area Northumberland and Tyneside.

Information available Report and accounts.

Summary About 75 one-off grants, most for £1,000 or less, but occasionally

up to £10,000 or more. Numerous regular annual grants.

General The list of one-off grants in 1996/97 totalled £130,000, and was headed by £25,000 for Newcastle Preparatory School, with awards of £10,000 going to Kings School, Tynemouth, Lindisfarne Church Heating Appeal and La Sagesse High School. £5,000 was given to Northumbria Coalition Against Crime, Newburn District Sea Cadet and Save the Children in Newcastle.

Grants of between £300 and £1,500 are made on a regular annual basis to over 100 local charities, to a total of £113,000 in 1996/97. The only exceptions to this size limit in were SSAFA (Tyne and Wear) (£5,000 for emergency cases), Disability North (£2,500) and St Oswalds Hospice (£2,000).

The trust's policy statement reads as follows:

'Grants will be in response to applications from within the Northumberland and Tyneside areas and from national charities either operating within or where work may be expected to be of benefit to this area.

'Grants will commonly be in response to appeals directed towards

Crisis funding
Pump priming finance
Operating expenses
Alleviation of distress

'Grants to youth and uniformed groups will be made to the local umbrella group where possible, rather than to individual clubs and associations.'

Total administrative and support costs of £43,000 in 1996/97 were high, at 18% of charitable expenditure of £243,000. They included £37,000 paid to the professional firms of which the trustees are all partners, and which undertake the administration of the charity.

In these editors' view, it is better for trustees not to be remunerated, directly or indirectly, for their services to a charity, unless there are unusual and specific reasons why this should be done in the interests of the charity's beneficiaries.

Exclusions No grants to individuals

Applications In writing to the correspondent. Grants to registered charities only.

William Harding's Charity

£224,000 (1996)

Education, welfare in Aylesbury

c/o Parrott & Coales (Solicitors), 14 Bourbon Street, Aylesbury, Buckinghamshire HP20 2RS
Tel: 01296 82244

Correspondent J Leggett

Trustees Albert Roblin, Chairman; Mrs Zena Williams; Richard Pearce; Vincent Robinson; William Chapple; Gerrett Ravens; Mrs Freda Roberts; Bernard Griffin.

Beneficial area Aylesbury in Buckinghamshire, only.

Information available Accounts up to 1996 only were on file at the Charity Commission in September 1998, but they did not include a grants list nor a narrative report.

General After we sent a copy of this draft entry to the trust they kindly sent us a copy of their report and accounts with an invoice for copying charges. Unfortunately it arrived to late for inclusion in this edition.

The revised objectives of the trust are stated as for 'the benefit of residents accommodated in the almshouses of the charity; relief in need; providing special benefits of any kind not normally provided by the Local Education Authority or any other institution of further education substantially serving the town of Aylesbury; providing exhibitions tenable at any school or institution of higher education to be awarded to persons under the age of 25 years resident in the town of Aylesbury; awarding maintenance allowances tenable at any school, university or college of education.'

In 1996 assets of the trust amount to £13.4 million, made up of property and investments. This generates an income of nearly £560,000. Since only less than half of this (£224,000) is being given out as grants, the charity may possibly be saving for a major capital investment. This accumulated 'cash in bank' now stands at £1.3 million.

Grants in 1996 were given out to unknown beneficiaries under the following categories:

Equipment and tools	£11,700	5%

Travel	*£13,400*	*6%*
Pupil support	*£16,300*	*7%*
Youth groups	*£26,000*	*12%*
Schools/education	*£92,000*	*41%*
General grants	*£37,000*	*17%*
Alms	*£27,500*	*12%*

Exclusions 'All persons and organisations not based in Aylesbury Town.'

Applications In writing to the correspondent.

The Philip and Pauline Harris Charitable Trust

£525,000 (but see below, 1996/97)

General

Harris Ventures Ltd, Central Court, 1b Knoll Rise, Orpington, Kent BR6 0JA

Correspondent Donald G Bompas, Managing Executive

Trustees Malcolm Barton; Lord Harris of Peckham; Sir Ridley Sykes.

Beneficial area UK and overseas.

Information available Accounts, but without a narrative report.

General This trust appears to be winding down. All investments have been disposed of and two thirds of remaining assets have been designated for ongoing projects. The trust has no other income and seems unlikely to continue substantial grant making unless further donations are made to it.

This was foreshadowed by the trust in 1994/95.

Applications In 1998 the trust stated: 'The trust is fully committed.'

The Hayward Foundation

£1,241,000 (1997)

Welfare, medical research, elderly, special needs, general

Hayward House, 45 Harrington Gardens, London SW7 4JU
Tel: 0171-370 7063

Correspondent Mark T Schnebli

Trustees I F Donald, Chairman; Sir Jack Hayward; G J Hearne; Mrs S J Heath; Dr J C Houston; C W Taylor; J N van Leuven.

Beneficial area UK.

Information available Full report and accounts, with grants list and analysis, are on file at the Charity Commission.

Summary Grants vary from around £1,000 to £100,000. They are made within six categories of interest and are normally only given for capital costs. About half of the funds are disbursed to charities working with special needs. Grants are categorised in the table herewith.

General In 1997 the foundation generated £1,708,000 income from assets which totalled £29 million at the end of the year. Seventy five grants were paid; half of the money went in thirteen grants of more than £20,000 each (see below). The foundation's concise but informative Report and Accounts for the year includes the following information:

'The foundations grant making policy concentrates on the following six areas:

- special needs;
- youth and community;
- medical (including research);
- arts, education, preservation and the environment;
- elderly;
- general welfare.

'Projects usually of a capital nature, have been selected which demonstrate a tangible voluntary input and the delivery of services to those in need.

'Revenue applications succeed occasionally where it is felt that the excellent work of a organisation can best be assisted with a revenue grant and where there is little need for capital.

'The foundation aims to help funding organisations and projects which make available additional services and benefits rather than those for which there is already a statutory duty of provision.

'The foundation continues to receive many applications which are outside its grant-making scope or are badly prepared.'

The Hayward Foundation

		% of total	number of grants
National organisations	£182,000	17%	15
England	£814,000	75%	53
Wales	£53,000	5%	3
Scotland	£9,000	1%	1
Northern Ireland	£26,000	2%	2
TOTAL	**£1,084,000**	**100%**	**75**

The grants were further categorised as follows

		% of value	number of grants
Special needs	£513,000	47%	33
Youth and community	£205,000	19%	17
Medical (including research)	£182,000	17%	11
Arts, education, preservation and the environment	£97,000	9%	7
Elderly	£57,000	5%	2
General welfare	£16,000	1%	3
Hospices	£13,000	1%	2

At the beginning of the year the trustees decided to pay special attention to 'youth at risk' as they regard an early investment in this area of prevention as being meaningful and effective.

Grants in 1997

722 applications were received and 51 offers made, totalling £1,262,000, to organisations representing a wide range of urban and rural needs.

Special needs

The largest grants in the year were to:

Enham Village Centre, Andover (£100,000 for refurbishment costs);

Pace Centre, Aylesbury (£31,000 towards equipping three bathrooms);

The Royal Hospital for Neurodisability, Putney (£50,000);

Glebe House, Cambridge (£25,000 towards family therapy and arts development);

British Stammering Association (£18,000 for the production of a teachers education pack).

Youth and community

Awards went to:

Fairbridge, London (£32,000);

Joint Educational Trust (£15,000 for boarding fees of children at risk);

Newbridge III, London (£10,000 towards family matters courses in prisons);

Cities in Schools (£25,000 for Yorkshire operations management).

Medical (including research)

Substantial grants included those to:

Imperial College of Science and Technology (£50,000);

Muscular Dystrophy Group (£22,000 for third year of research at Charing Cross);

Parkinson's Disease Society (£20,000 for research at Kings into L-dopa;

The Royal Victoria Infirmary, Newcastle-upon-Tyne (£15,000 to pay for a research technician).

Arts, education, preservation and the environment

The Royal Academy of Arts (£18,000 for the restoration of books);

Oriel College, Oxford (£25,000 toward the Hayward Fellowship; third annual payment of five);

National History Museum (£50,000 towards renovation costs);

Chichester Festival Theatre (£1,000 for its general funds).

Elderly

The Griffin Community Trust, London (£50,000 for construction)

Relationships Foundation, Cambridge (£7,000 for a relational audit for elderly care homes).

General welfare

St Boltoph's Project (£10,000 for phase II of the renovation of a crypt centre)

Changing Faces, London (£3,800 for office equipment).

Hospices

The Marie Curie Cancer Centre Fund (£12,000 for research and training into the alleviation of Lymphoedema)

St David's Hospital Newport (£1,000 towards general funds).

Exclusions The trustees do not make grants to individuals nor for revenue, holidays, travel, churches, expeditions, vehicles, general appeals, deficit funding and what is properly the responsibility of a statutory body.

Applications Applications should contain a description of the current work, such as annual report, and a full set of recent annual accounts; also a description of the project, the need, and the benefits that will be achieved. There should be a full cost breakdown of the project, and details of funds raised so far with donors identified where possible. Any of the organisation's own resources being used should be noted, as well as applications pending with other funders. Finally, a timetable for the project should be included.

Applications may take several months top process, as there is usually a waiting list. Trustees meet three or four times a year.

Foundation staff are willing to advise telephone callers on the suitability of projects, prior to a formal application being made.

An associated trust, the Charles Hayward Trust, based at the same offices, concentrates its funding programme towards smaller and local charities and voluntary organisations.

The Charles Hayward Trust

£521,000 (1996/97)

Welfare, health

45 Harrington Gardens, London SW7 4JU
Tel: 0171-370 7067

Correspondent Mark T Schnebli, Administrator

Trustees I F Donald, Chairman; A D Owen; Miss A T Rogers; Miss J Streather; B D Insch; Mrs J Chamberlain

Beneficial area UK.

Information available Full report and accounts are on file at the Charity Commission. Guidelines available from foundation

Summary The trust share the same address, trustees and similar policies as the Hayward Foundation, the main difference being that it deals with smaller locally based organisations and does not fund medical research. The trust notes that it often receives applications that have been passed on from the foundation due to their greater suitability for this body.

The trust says that its current policy is in five main areas of work:

- care of the elderly, including day-care and respite care
- general welfare
- community and youth, including offenders and youth at risk
- a lesser interest in art, preservation and the environment
- special needs, including drug and alcohol dependency, mental, physical and learning disabilities.

The trust notes that it normally likes to fund the 'capital cost of buildings, adaptation, equipment, furnishings and fittings. Revenue funding is sometimes granted for start-up or development activities where this is not yet part of the on-going requirement of the organisation.

'Grants are typically £2,000 to £10,000, or larger if the project is considered to be exceptionally worthy.'

General In 1996/97 income was £620,000, generated from assets of £9.7 million. This funded grant giving of £521,000 in 130 grants, 83 new and 47 repeats. Grant giving was subdivided in the table herewith.

Grants averaged about £6,000, with many small grants of £750 or less. The trust reports that it received 764 applications for their 130 grants, a success rate of one in six. Most of the grants were for capital costs.

Examples of grants included the following:

Community and Youth: CRACA, Salford (£10,000 for a child minder service); Abbey Community Centre, London (£3,000 for toys, learning equipment and lighting); Champion house, Sheffield (£5,000 for the extension of the adventure centre); and St Matthew's Church (£13,000 for a roof replacement).

Special Needs: Warley Leisure Project, West Midlands (£8,000 refurbishment of RGMC for project use); TEDDA, Scotland (£5,000 for building refurbishment); and Tools and Self Reliance, Milton Keynes (£2,000 for equipping and fitting out a new workshop).

General Welfare: Northern Ireland Voluntary Trust (£15,000 for distribution among local projects); Colchester Baptist Church (£10,000 for running a health care clinic); and Southport Hospital Radio (£3,000 for studio equipment).

Elderly: Penzance and West Penwith Old People's Welfare Trust (£10,000); Rotary Club of Wolverhampton (£8,000 for energy subsidies and outings for elderly); and Tile Cross and Fordbridge Community Projects (£3,000 for a porch and ramp).

Hospices: Demelza House Children's Hospice (£15,000 for construction work); and Wheatfields Hospice (£10,000 for refurbishment of the coach house).

Arts, Education, preservation and Environment: Longbenton community garden project, Newcastle (£3,000 for building a community garden).

Exclusions Specific exclusions:

- Grants are not made when funding could be considered to be the responsibility of others, such as the local authority or government.
- Grants are not made to individuals, to pay off loans, or for transport, travel, bursarships, general repairs, or endowment funds
- Grants are not given for medical or social research, computers, expeditions or vehicles.

Grants for national appeals should be directed to the Hayward Foundation.

Applications There is no application form. Applicants should write to Mark Schnebli, the Administrator and include the following details:

1. A brief description of your present work and the priorities you are addressing. This may be in the form of an annual report.
2. Two recent sets of your full audited accounts. If there are connected organisations, include their accounts also.
3. A description of the project you are undertaking, detailing the number of people and groups who will benefit and how. Demonstrate the need for the project and describe any increased activities that will be achieve.
4. The timetable for the project, when it will start and be finished.
5. A full cost breakdown for the project, separating capital from revenue expenditure where applicable.
6. A list of the funds raised to date towards your target with donors identified where possible. Specify the amount of any of your reserves going into the project. If you have bids outstanding with other funders, list them, the amount anticipated and the date they will be considered.
7. An explanation of how you are going to evaluate the success of the project, and how you might report this back

to us.
If relevant you may also enclose:

- references, recommendations or letters of support.
- floor plans, drawings or pictures (no larger than A3)
- a budget for the on-going running costs of your project, and details on how this will be funded.

The trust welcomes applicants to contact them directly and discuss their project prior to making a formal approach. mark Schnebli or David Brown can be contacted on 0171 730 7063.

The trustees meet between three and four times each year to consider applications, which can be made at any time. As there is often a waiting list it may take several months for applicants to hear the results of their bid.

The Headley Trust

£3,135,000 (approved 1997)

Arts, environment, education, health and social care, medicine, overseas development

See entry for the 'Sainsbury Family Charitable Trusts'
Tel: 0171-410 0330

Correspondent Michael Pattison, Director

Trustees Sir Timothy Sainsbury; Lady Susan Sainsbury; T J Sainsbury; J R Benson; Miss J Portrait.

Beneficial area UK and overseas, with a possible local interest in north Hampshire.

Information available Full accounts with exemplary report are available. In addition to the director (noted above) the trust's officers are listed as Paul Spokes, finance director, and Hester Marriott, executive.

Summary This trust is one of the Sainsbury Family Charitable Trusts which share a joint administration. It has a particular interest in the arts and arts education and has made substantial grants in partnership with major Arts Council lottery grants, particularly for museums, galleries, libraries and theatres. In addition it supports a wide range of social welfare issues and like other Sainsbury Family Charitable Trusts supports work concerned with parenting

---

The Charles Hayward Trust

Grants in 1996/1997

Community and youth	40	£194,000	37%
Special needs	20	£100,000	9%
General welfare	12	£90,000	17%
Elderly	13	£74,000	14%
Hospices	5	£43,000	8%
Small grants	39	£18,000	4%
Arts, etc.	1	£3,000	1%

and literacy. Its support to activities in developing countries is focused on sub-Saharan anglophone countries, central and eastern Europe and the former Soviet Union.

General The settlor of this trust is Sir Timothy Sainsbury. His co-trustees include his wife, eldest son and legal advisors. The asset value of the trust increased from £64.4 million in December 1996 to £80.2 in December 1997. The major part of the trust's investments (82%) were held in J Sainsbury plc in December 1997.

The trust has supported the development of a community centre at Ma'a lot in Israel from a restricted fund over the past decade. In 1997 the balance of this fund (£117,000) was transferred to the now registered charity.

During the two years, 1996 and 1997, a lower proportion was given under the Health & Social Welfare category than in the years 1991-1995 when between 30% and 43% had been allocated.

The trust's 1997 report was exemplary and, in compliance with SORP, with far more detailed information than in previous years. Then only the names of beneficiaries were listed under a heading with the category total. Now a short policy outline describes each category, followed by a list of beneficiaries, their grant and a short descriptive sentence about each. The names of the beneficiaries of grants of £5,000 and less were listed beneath an overall total.

Grants are summarised in the table herewith.

Arts and the Environment (home) – £1,376,000 (approved 1997)

'The trustees support a wide variety of conservation projects, as well as arts projects with an educational element. Trustees have also made substantial

grants towards partnership funding for major National Lottery grants, particularly for museums, galleries, libraries and theatres.'

The two largest grants in 1997 were made to:

Victoria & Albert Museum, towards the display of ceramics in the redeveloped British Galleries (£500,000);

Sadlers' Wells, towards its redevelopment project (£250,000).

All other grants were under £50,000. They included Southern Sinfonia for its core costs (£10,000 over two years) and the National Museums & Galleries of Wales for the St Teilo's reconstruction projects and Space Studios towards the salary of the Friends of Space co-ordinator (£45,000 each over three years).

Cathedrals budget

'Substantial grants are available for restoration or repair work to the fabric of cathedrals and large churches of exceptional architectural merit. Trustees do not normally provide funding for modern amenities, organ repair/ restoration, or choral scholarships.'

Six grants were given in 1997. The largest was to St Alban's Cathedral Trust towards the restoration and renewal of the presbytery vault (£40,000) and the smallest to Sherborne Abbey (£5,000).

Parish churches budget

Funding for fabric repair and restoration is considered for mediaeval parish churches (or pre-16th century churches of exceptional architectural merit) in rural, sparsely populated, less prosperous villages, through a process of review diocese by diocese. Urban churches are not eligible, and funding is available for fabric only (including windows) rather than refurbishment or construction of church halls or other modern amenities.

Arts and the Environment (Overseas) – £220,000 (approved 1997)

'Trustees support art conservation projects of outstanding artistic or architectural importance; particularly the restoration of buildings, statuary or painting, principally in the countries of Central and Eastern Europe. Grants are channelled through especially reputable conservation organisations in the countries concerned.'

The largest grant in 1997 was made to the International Trust for Croatian Monuments for the restoration of St Lawrence Cathedral (£40,000). The smallest grant was made to the UK Antarctic Heritage Trust towards a publication (£10,000). ICOSMOS UK was funded to give two conservation scholarships each year to Central and Eastern European scholars (£28,000 over three years).

Health and Social Welfare – £663,000 (approved 1997)

'Trustees contribute to a broad range of health and social welfare projects, particularly charities supporting carers of an ill or disabled relative, and those that support elderly people of limited means.'

In 1997 grants ranged from an after school club in Hackney to horticultural therapy and to the provision of alarms for old people. Grants in 1997 seemed to show a particular interest in issues relating to children and the family. Such beneficiaries included Family Links, programmes for parents and children in Oxfordshire schools (£30,000 over 2 years), Release for outreach work with young people (£20,000) and Sheffield University for research and evaluating of family group conferences (£50,000 over 2 years),

£19,000 was given in small grants via 32 organisations in both the voluntary and local authority sectors to assist people with physical disabilities.

Developing Countries – £394,000 (approved 1997)

'Priority is given to applications from countries in sub-Saharan anglophone Africa, and Central and Eastern Europe and the former Soviet Union. Focus areas include

- water projects (eg. which give disadvantaged communities access to safe water, preserve ecologically or culturally important wetland areas, improve sanitary conditions or promote better use of water);
- forestry projects (eg. which preserve areas of natural woodland or encourage environmentally or socially sustainable methods of forestry);

The Headley Trust

	1996 Grants Approved			1997 Grants Approved		
Arts & Environment (Home)	£2,475	31	63%	£1,376	61	47%
Arts & Environment (Overseas)	£105	6	3%	£220	11	7%
Health & Social Welfare	£753	88	19%	£633	81	20%
Developing Countries	£193	6	5%	£394	12	11%
Education	£282	10	7%	3345	16	10%
Medical	£93	3	2%	£67	5	5%
Total	**£3,901**	**144**	**100%**	**£3,135**	**186**	**100%**

- education and literacy projects (eg. which improve quality of education and literacy standards for underprivileged people through supply of materials, construction, training support etc);
- health projects (particularly those which support blind or partially sighted people).

Trustees look for projects where income generation is an integral element.'

The largest grant in 1997 was to BookAid International towards the Intra-Africa Book support scheme (£52,000 over three years). Grants also included Project North East towards the micro loan fund in Hungary (£20,000 over two years).

Education – £345,000 (approved 1997)

'The trustees' main focus is the provision of bursary support, particularly for artistic or technical skills training. They have also helped to encourage high standards of literacy in children and young people.'

The largest grants in 1997 were given to Understanding Industry, for a new programme for 14-16 year olds (£48,564 over 3 years), the Courtauld Institute of Art Fund for the salary of a librarian for the proposed Courtauld Institute Research Library (£36,000 over 2 years) and to both the Guildhall School of Music and Drama and the Royal Northern College of Music for bursaries to talented music students from Central and Eastern Europe (£39,000 to each college over 3 years). Other grants included Volunteer Reading Help (£24,000 over 2 years) and the North Kensington Video/Drama Project for vocational skills training/support for disabled young people (£22,500 over 3 years).

Medical – £67,000 (approved 1997)

'Trustees are particularly interested in research into ageing and osteoporosis.'

Two large grants were given to University College London Hospitals for clinical research into osteoporosis (£90,000 over two years) and Research into Ageing, for research into Alzheimer's disease (£60,000 over three years).

Exclusions No grants direct to individuals.

Applications The trustees met five times in 1997. It is said that an application to one of the Sainsbury family trusts is an application to all. See the entry for the Sainsbury Family Charitable Trusts for the address and further advice. However, the trust says,

like all the other trust, that it is proactive in its choice of beneficiaries and that 'unsolicited applications are rarely successful'.

The Hedley Foundation Ltd

£899.000 (1997/98)

Health, welfare

9 Dowgate Hill, London EC4R 2SU
Tel: 0171 489 8076

Correspondent P T Dunkerley, Secretary

Trustees P H Byam-Cook, President; C H W Parish, Chairman; Sir Christopher Airy; D V Fanshawe; P Holcroft; J F M Rodwell; C R S Broke.

Beneficial area UK.

Information available Accounts and brief report.

General The foundation describes its current funding priorities as:

- Young people: their education, training, health and welfare (currently about half the foundation's budget);
- Churches and local community centres: construction, adaptation or improvement for community use;
- Disabled people: provision of specialist equipment and assistance with access;
- Seriously ill: the construction or extension of hospices and the setting up of specialist nursing schemes;
- Hospitals: the provision of specialist medical equipment and the support of medical research.

'Grants are for specific projects only, mostly one-off but a limited number of recurring grants for three to five years. The average grant is £5,000. National and very large appeals will not be considered.'

Assets, held mainly as land and investments, were £23 million in 1997/98. Income was £1.3 million (£1.3 million in 1996/97), and came from covenants with trading companies, rental income and dividends. Grant giving was down to £899,000 in 244 grants from £979,000 in 236 grants in 1996/97. Management and administration costs were high at £161,000, or 18% of the grant total.

A long grants list was included, with awards 'for a wide range of health and welfare activities with an emphasis on youth.'

Grants ranged in size from £15,000 to £500. The largest grants went to Weston Spirit (£15,000), Action on Addiction and Drive for Youth (£12,500 each), Cumbria Association of Youth Clubs, GAP Activity Projects (GAP) Ltd, Help the Hospices, Raleigh International and United World Colleges (£10,000 each).

The following is an example of the spread of grant making in each of the priority areas, as far as we can determine from organisation name:

Young people: Youth Clubs UK (£7,500); Merchant Taylor's School (£5,000); Brunswick Boy's Club (£5,000); Kirkham Grammar Centre (£3,000), London's Children Camp (£1,500); and a number of Girl Guide and Scout groups (7).

Churches and local community centres: Hereford Cathedral (£5,000); Camphill Village Trust (£5,000); Tregadillet Church/Community Centre (£5,000); St Albans Cathedral (£4,000); Holy Trinity Hounslow (£3,000); and St John's Church Community Centre (£3,000).

Disabled: Queen Elizabeth's Foundation for Disabled People (£5,000); Royal School for the Blind (£3,000); East Midlands Riding Association for the Handicapped (£3,000); Gardening for Disabled Trust (£1,500) and the Disabled Christian Fellowship (£1,000).

Seriously ill: Mental Health Foundation (£6,000); Hospice in the Weald (£5,000); Down's Syndrome Association (£4,000); and the Little Sisters of the Poor (£3,500).

Hospitals: Royal Marsden Hospital Cancer Fund (£5,000); Cancer Relief Macmillan Fund (£5,000); African Medical Research Foundation (£3,900); Kidney Research Aid Fund (£3,000); and Research into Ageing (£3,000).

Exclusions Grants made only to registered charities.

No grants to:

- overseas charities
- individuals, under any circumstances
- national and very large appeals

Applications The trustees meet about every six weeks, so applications receive promp attention. They should be accompanied by the latest available accounts, a note of the present state of the appeal and its future prospects and, in the case of buildings, outline plans and details of planning status. For community schemes it would be helpful to have a brief description of the community, its history, present make-up and aspirations, what is going for and against it and so on to put flesh on the application.

Help the Aged

Probably about £10 million in UK, but not disclosed

Day centres, hospices, general, for the elderly

St James's Walk, Clerkenwell Green,
London EC1R 0BE
Tel: 0171-253 0253; Fax: 0171-250 4474

Correspondent Michael Lake,
Director General

Trustees John D Mather, Chairman;
Philip Ashfield; Henry Bowrey; Peter
Bowring; Priscilla Campbell Allen;
Beverley Castleton; Jo Connell; Vera
Harley; Anne Harris; William Hastings;
Professor Kay-Tee Khaw; Trevor Larman;
Ian Macleod; Lady Jean Macpherson;
William Menzies-Wilson; Hugh Peppiatt;
Kevin Williams; Christopher Woodbridge;
Angus Young.

Beneficial area UK and overseas.

Information available Inadequate
1997/98 Report and Accounts.
Application form for smaller grants.

Summary Help the Aged has two
programmes by which its funds are
transferred to other charities working in
their field in the UK:

- Project fundraising (perhaps £10
  million in 1997/98).
  Help the Aged fund raisers run major
  appeals in its own name, to raise
  money for the projects of other
  charities. This is not a grant
  programme to which other charities
  can apply but a system of fundraising
  partnerships. Nevertheless the
  payments qualify as grants as defined
  by the Charity Commission's SORP
  and should be, but are not, disclosed.
  The charity offers these valuable
  services to its partners free of charge
  as a major part of its charitable
  activities.
- Grants programme (£1.1 million in
  1997/98).

In addition to the programmes above, the
charity also has its own direct
programmes, where grants are provided
in response to applications received,
mostly for small capital expenditures.
There is also an extensive programme of
assistance for organisations working
overseas, operated mainly through an
associated charity, Help Age
International (£6 million in 1997/98),
which is not covered by this entry.

General It is not possible to give a
proper account of the money that this

major fundraising charity transfers to
other organisations in its field, as its
accounts do not distinguish between its
own charitable expenditures and money
given to others to use. The estimate
above of £10 million in 1997/98 is made
by this editor but may be wrong by up to
a couple of million pounds either way.

The Charity Commission's SORP
(paragraph 138) requires all material
grants (very broadly defined as 'any
application of property in favour of .. an
institution, in furtherance of the objects
of the grant maker') to be disclosed each
year, with the name of the recipient
organisation and the amount of the grant
or grants. There is no such information
available in the charity's accounts. It did
provide a list of institutions where
appeals were in progress and to which
such grants payments might at some time
be expected, but there was no indication
of the timing or of the amounts involved.

The previous edition of this book
criticised the way in which money raised
by this charity was appearing as
fundraised income both in its own
accounts and in those of the charities that
Help the Aged was assisting. This
practice has happily now been ended,
following specific management action.

There was further criticism of the high
level of apparent fund raising costs,
reported as 31% of Incoming Resources
Available. By 1997/98 this had been
reduced to a much more acceptable 24%.
However when both the costs and the
income from selling donated goods are
removed from the figures, fundraising
costs as a proportion of donations,
incoming grants and legacies are still a
challenging 31%.

This high figure may be the result in part
of an inappropriate allocation of costs.
As mentioned above, the fund raising
staff of Help the Aged work for the
appeals of other charities. A proportion
of the resulting income goes directly to
those charities, without passing through
Help the Aged's accounts, yet all the
costs of the fund raising concerned do
appear in those accounts. Such costs are,
in fact, a donation in kind to the charity
in whose name the appeal is being run,
and should be accounted for as such (as
was recommended in the previous
edition of this book).

Total UK expenditures in 1997/98 were
categorised as follows (the asterisked
programmes are believed to be those
mainly carried out by Help the Aged
itself rather than through payments to
other charities):

Day Centres	£5,967,000
Health and Medical (believed to be mainly hospices)	£2,920,000
Minibuses	£2,064,000
Heating grants	£1,147,000*
Home safety	£699,000*
Community Projects	£427,000
Isolation	£289,000
Elderly homelessness	£163,000
SeniorLink telephones	£149,000*
Housing and care projects	£84,000
Other	£659,000

Project Fundraising 'The Project
Fundraising Department aims to to assist
other registered charities with all aspects
of their fundraising'. There is no charge
for the service, often one of a
particularly valuable sort. The service is
comprehensive, can cover both capital
and revenue needs and includes the
training and support needed to leave the
benefiting charity in a sound financial
position for the future. In the Summer of
1998 there were 75 such appeals in
progress, though many were quite small
minibus projects. A list of the names of
the partner organisations showed projects
in all parts of the country except Wales.

In the previous edition of this book we
were able to describe three selected
examples of such appeals, but there was
no such information available in 1998
(and in any event these editors find such
selected examples sometimes give only a
partial indication of the nature of the full
list). However, it is clear from the
headings given above that most of the
money must be accounted for by appeals
for day-centres.

Help the Aged also works as a partner in
projects to be funded by the National
Lottery Charities Board, helping charities
prepare their applications and taking part
in the NLCB's assessment visits.

The level of support offered varies, and
may sometimes involve experienced Help
the Aged fund raisers being seconded
virtually full time. The charity being
helped will provide its own input to the
appeal in addition. There is sometimes a
difference of emphasis between the two
partners as to the proportions of the
overall effort contributed by each, but the
kind of expertise available from Help the
Aged would be very difficult for most
local charities to provide in any other
way.

There is no specific procedure for
admission to this programme other than
through contacting the department. The
criteria by which partner organisations
are chosen are not known.

The Grants Programme This is a very
much smaller affair, in which Help the

Aged transfers only about £1 million to other charities, as opposed to perhaps ten times that amount from the Project Fundraising activity. However, unlike the latter, full and helpful details are available from Help the Aged (although still not disclosed in the accounts). In 1997/98, 309 grants, totalling £1.2 million, were paid out, covering all fields of the charity's work in the UK, but over half the awards were in Yorkshire (by number, but not by value; many of them were small). There were 11 grants for £20,000 or more, though perhaps half of these grants were for less than £1,000.

The list was headed by Crowthorne C.O.A.T.S. (£30,000 to refurbish the kitchen); The Nutmeg Partnership in Ludlow (£28,000 as a final instalment towards a mobile outreach service); the Indian Senior Citizens centre in Manchester (26,000) to refurbish the centre; and Wai Yin Chines Womens' centre, also in Manchester (£26,000 for posts for a development worker and a cook). There were many small amounts for specific items of equipment such as the £250 for a fridge/freezer for Button Hill Senior Citizens in Leeds.

Applications There is a three page application form for the grants programme, but for most organisations it might be sensible to approach, in the first instance, the Project Fundraising Department at the above address, through which contact with regional or local Help the Aged staff can be arranged.

The Grants Committee meets monthly.

Alan Edward Higgs Charity

£382,000 (1996/97)

Child welfare, general, in or near Coventry

5 Queen Victoria Road,
Coventry, CV1 3JL
Tel: 01203-221311

Correspondent Mr A J Wall, Clerk

Trustees Mrs M F Knatchbull-Hugesson; D A Higgs; W H D Jenson.

Beneficial area Within 25 miles of the centre of Coventry only.

Information available Accounts on file at the Charity Commission but without a grants list or narrative report; information sheet.

Summary The charity's policy limits grants to the Coventry area and focuses on disadvantaged children.

General The charity was established to benefit 'wholly or mainly the inhabitants of the area within 25 miles of the centre of Coventry...preferably child welfare, and particularly under-privileged children'. National charities may be supported if they can 'show that any grant would be used to benefit persons in the geographic area'.

The charity is one of the few grant making trusts not to publish the required list of grants in their report and accounts, an omission. Very little is therefore known formally about the grants made. Nor is the charity well known locally – a Coventry fundraiser told us 'we have to rely on books like yours'. The sparse information revealed in the report and accounts is as follows.

In 1996/97 the charity had total funds of £15 million and made 96 grants amounting to over £380,000 (120 grants totalled £414,000 in 1995/96). Of these 37 (39%) were new, as opposed to 66 (55%) in the previous year. The average amount donated was £4,000 (£3,500). Concerning their grant making, the trustees said that 'the increasing range and diversity of donations continue to be welcomed'.

The charity says:

'It is the aim of the trustees to reach as wide a selection of the community as possible within the geographical limitations. They are happy to receive applications for grants from local bodies or associations and from national organisations which can show that any grant from the charity would be used to benefit persons resident within the geographical area.'

Exclusions Applications from indviduals are not normally entertained.

Applications In writing to the Clerk to the Trustees, along with:

- a copy of the latest audited accounts;
- charity number (if registered);
- a detailed description of the local activities for the benefit of which the grant would be applied;
- the specific purpose for which the grant is sought.

The Hilden Charitable Fund

£412,000 (1997/98)

Minorities, third world, penal, homelessness, general

34 North End Road, London W14 0SH
Tel: 0171-603 1525

Correspondent Rodney Hedley, Secretary

Trustees Mrs M G Duncan; Mrs A M A Rampton; Dr D S Rampton; Mrs G J S Rampton; Mrs H M C Rampton; J R A Rampton; J Rampton; CSLR Rampton; Dr M B H Rampton; Professor C H Rodeck; Mrs E K Rodeck; C H Younger; Ms M E Baxter.

Beneficial area UK, and overseas.

Information available Report and accounts with full grants list and considerable narrative analysis of grants; guidelines; 'summary of funding request' form.

Summary In any one year, around 90 grants are made benefiting a variety of charitable causes, in particular minorities and the third world. Donations are usually one-off and for revenue or capital costs (but not salaries). Most are between £3,000 and £5,000, but donations dip to £1,000 and peak at £15,000.

General In 1996/97, the fund held assets close to £10 million and generated an income of £456,000. Grants for £10,000 and over accounted for 19% of total charitable expenditure with the majority by value and number being close to £4,000. The trust is one of a small but growing number of trusts that have a two stage application process.

In 1996/96 over a thousand funding enquiries were received by the fund, about 9% resulted in awards. Grants continued to be made within five categories of giving.

The fund says:

'The trustees main interests are:

- homelessness;
- minorities and race relations;
- penal affairs;
- third world countries (to a limited extent).

'Overseas grants concentrate on development aid generally made only to UK registered charities retaining supervision of grant expenditure.

'Grants are rarely given to well established national charities or to individuals. Fund policy is directed largely at supporting work at a community level within the categories above.

'Priorities given to different types of work within the main categories may change from time to time, as dictated by circumstances. It should not be assumed that an application, even though it may generally qualify, will necessarily be considered. Grants for capital or revenue rarely exceed £5,000 and are not often made for salaries.

'Minorities grants were made to the Runneymede Trust for work on anti-discrimination and good practice in race relations and the Tower Hamlets Summer University. The needs of asylum seekers and refugees were met through grants to the Migrants' Resource Centre, London, for employment training; the Immigrants Aid Trust; and Asylum Aid, for advice and information; and to Richmond Refugee Support Network, and the West African Welfare Association, for help with housing and social support.

'Self-help initiatives were supported for the African Caribbean Community [3 grants, Ed.], the Asian community [5]. The Eritrean Community in Lambeth, Somali Community Centre, Islington, the Iraqi Community Association and the Afghan Association of London, Harrow received grants.

'Grants were made to develop minority initiatives: training on housing issues for refugees; services to ethnic minorities with mental illness; an Asia careers initiative and; cricket opportunities to under represented groups.

Third world 'Libraries in Sierra Leone were supported and grants were given to support what are currently called micro-enterprise schemes in the Caribbean,

Ghana, Uganda, Peru, Zambia, and Zimbabwe. A grant aided a small initiatives aid programme with the South African agency, Interfund. Health projects were supported in Palestine, Brazil, India, and Sudan. The University of Cape Town received a grant for the training of black student doctors. Childcare and education for under 7s was supported in St Lucia. Tools for self reliance and the Tanzania Development Trust both received grants for their core work. Interights was grant aided to work on human rights issues; and a grant was allocated to the individual ad community rights forum to establish a research foundation on forestry in Papua New Guinea.'

In June 1998, the trust said that 'policy on third world development is being discussed and may change'.

Penal Affairs 'The fund continued to support work on reform and good practice in the penal system with grants to the Prison Reform Trust, and the Howard League for Penal Reform, the latter receiving a grant to develop the League in Scotland. Other grant aid was for what might be called 'hands-on' projects to enable people from being diverted or rehabilitated from offending.

Homelessness 'Most of the grant aid on homelessness projects was for the provision of services in hostels and day care centres. Rent deposit schemes were supported; a return scheme for Manchester young people living in London and a landlord scheme were both supported. A grant was given to the Wandsworth Money Advice Service to advise people facing house re-possessions.

Other grants 'A number of grants were made outside the priority areas, although dovetailing with them. The following allied projects were given grants: Donald Chesworth Educational Trust; the Guild of Psychotherapists; Kaleidoscope

(services for drug addicts ad refugees). Reflecting the trustees long-standing interest in Richmond, the Star and Garter Home (for ex-servicemen and women) and the Richmond Boat Project received grants. The remaining grants reflect special interests of the trustees.

Grant aid in Scotland 'A grant was given to the Scottish Council for Voluntary Organisations to administer a grants programme on behalf of the fund to "voluntary organisations, community groups and ethnic minority groups which are unlikely to find money elsewhere through national appeals.

Playschemes 'In 1996/97 the fund allocated £10,000 to support summer playschemes and groups from refugee and immigrant communities were given priority. Twenty small grants averaging £500 were made.

Grant aid in Northern Ireland and Wales 'No grants were made to projects in Northern Ireland with receipt of only a handful of applications. only one project was supported in Wales (Newport Mind), again in response to only a tiny number of applications.

In 1996/97 1,125 enquiries were received concerning grant aid. Of these, 463, resulted in applications for consideration by the fund. 105 grants were made. Crudely speaking, this means that applications had a 25% success rate.

The grants are categorised in the table herewith.

Nearly all the applications met the Hilden broad guidelines in some way. Discounting agencies which have a third world or a national brief, around 40% of the project supported were agencies in the London area; the vast majority of playschemes were in greater London.'

The largest grants in the year went to Interfund (£15,000) and Individual and Community Rights Advocacy Forum (£14,000).

Exclusions No grants to individuals.

Applications All applicants are required to complete a very brief summary form outlining their request before they are considered. Otherwise all applicants will be regarded as enquiries. Potential applicants should contact the office for guidelines and forms.

Applications should include:

- most recent audited accounts;
- most recent annual report;
- projected income and expenditure for the current financial year;
- explanation of how your reserves stand;

The Hilden Charitable Fund

Grants in 1996/97 and 1995/96

		1996/97			1995/96	
Minorities	27	£134,650	30%		24	35%
Third world	18	£108,000	24%		15	24%
Penal	14	£64,000	14%		14	12%
Homelessness	15	£58,000	13%		14	13%
Special	10	£51,000	11%		6	6%
SCVO	1	£26,250	6%		1	7%
Play schemes	20	£10,000	2%		18	3%
Total	105	£452,000	100%		92	100%

- particular features of your costs, eg high transport costs in rural areas;
- details of other funders approached;
- any significant achievements and/or problems or difficulties;
- how you approach equal opportunities;
- any 'matching grant' arrangements.

For projects working in the Third World

- ensure there is a short briefing note on the political and economic situation on the country in which you intend to work (a sketch map be helpful);
- details of Department for International Development involvement;
- details of currency exchange;
- details of local management and control of project.

Distribution meetings take place at three to four-monthly intervals.

Evidence of separately registered charitable status is required.

Historic Churches Preservation Trust (with the Incorporated Church Building Society)

£475,000 in grants (and £204,000 in loans 1996/97)

Historic churches

Fulham Palace, London SW6 6EA
Tel: 0171-736 3054; Fax: 0171-736 3880

Correspondent Michael Tippen, Secretary

Trustees Joint Presidents: The Archbishops of Canterbury and York. Chairman: Lord Nicholas Gordon Lennox.

Beneficial area England and Wales.

Information available Annual report and accounts with full grants list and review of the years activities; guidelines; quarterly 'Review' magazine.

Summary Around 300 grants and loans are made each year towards the upkeep of fine Christian churches in England and Wales. They start at a few hundred pounds and peak at £6,000.

General The trust was set up in 1953 after a report commissioned by the

Church of England found that the nation's churches were in a state of decline. As these problems were not confined to the established Church, the trust was conceived as a non-denominational charity to help finance church repairs in England and Wales.

The trust also administers the smaller Incorporated Church Building Society (ICBS, established 1818). Both the trust and the society make interest-free loans and grants. The trust's money comes solely from voluntary donations, some of which has been used to create a capital base from which investment income can be generated. The trust runs a number of fundraising initiatives involving the general public, private companies and other grant-making trusts. It currently has a membership of 2,000 'friends'.

In 1996/97 the trust's income totalled £781,000 (ICBS's income was £43,000). Management and administration costs were a fairly hefty £139,000, or £500 per grant/loan (average £2,400). The trust made 213 grants and 64 loans varying between £250 and £6,000 with most around £2,000. 23 churches received the maximum loan of £6,000.

There are a number of conditions which must be met before assistance is given. For example the church must be over 100 years old, Christian and located in England (including the Isle of Man and Channel Islands) or Wales. Money is only donated or loaned toward fabric repairs on conservation standard churches where the PCC has insufficient funds. Work should not have started before the specification has been renewed.

Interest-free loans are repayable in four equal annual instalments starting 1 year after the date on the loan cheque.

Exclusions The HCPT and ICBS will not fund new amenities; re-ordering; church clocks; heating & lighting; stained glass; furniture and fittings; organ repair; murals; monuments; decoration (except after repairs); re-wiring; churchyards & walls; work that has already been started or completed.

Applications A written approach should be made in the first instance to seek a preliminary assessment. The case is then referred to a Diocesan Advisory Committee. With its recommendation secured, an application form is sent with which full specifications etc. are required. Trustees meet nine times a year to assess grants.

The Jane Hodge Foundation

£1,337,000 (1996/97)

Medicine, education, religion, mainly in Wales

Ty-Gwyn, Lisvane, Cardiff CF4 5SG
Tel: 01222-766521

Correspondent Mrs Margaret Cason, Secretary

Trustees Sir Julian Hodge; Lady Moira Hodge; Teresa Hodge; Robert Hodge; Julian J Hodge; Joyce Harrison; Derrek Jones; Ian Davies.

Beneficial area Unrestricted, but a preference for Wales.

Information available Excellent report and accounts available from the trust.

Summary This energetic trust, the largest in Wales, concentrates its grant giving in three areas: medical research, education, and religion. The foundation supports a number of long term capital projects, for which funding is usually ongoing, as well as a number of pound for pound appeals. One-off grants are usually for less than £10,000. There are over 300 awards a year.

General The foundation deals with a number of long term programmes as well as an annual one-off grants programme. An excellent and enlightening description of the programmes that the foundation supports is included in the Trustees' Report for 1996/97, which is reprinted as follows:

The Trustees' Report 1996/97

The Wallich Clifford Community (Homes for the Homeless)

'£1,000,000 has been reserved for this and other projects to help the homeless. As part of this commitment, £75,000 was paid in September 1996, £75,000 in March 1997, £75,000 in July 1997 and a further £50,000 paid in October 1997 specifically for providing accommodation for heavy drinkers. Revised commitments in August 1997 allows £190,000 for each of 2 hostels for heavy drinkers- making £380,000.

'A further commitment of £350,000 has been made to Cardiff Universities Social Service Emergency Accommodation Service to help those released from long term hospital care. The first tranche of £50,000 was paid in August 1997, and the second £50,000 in January 1998

Hospice – The Little Company of Mary

'The trustees have retained £1 million for the construction of a purpose-built hospice to be run by The Little Company of Mary, if a suitable site can be found.

Archbishop Murphy Memorial Fund

'The £250,000 pound for pound scheme set up by the trustees to help raise £1 million to secure funding for the future training of priests, was completed successfully and thus the foundation paid £250,000 to the Archbishop Murphy Memorial Fund.

Prince's Youth Business Trust

'The annual payment of £5,000 was made as usual in 1997. A balance of £10,000 remains to be paid by the foundation in respect of their commitment to donate £50,000 over a period of ten years in support of this charity.

Multi-Faith Centre, Pontprennau, Pentwyn, Cardiff

'The trustees confirm their commitment to contribute £250,000 capital to help provide a Multi-Faith Centre in Pontprennau, Pentwyn, the fast growing residential development in the North of Cardiff. The estate will have a population of 6,000 and this will be the only church presence.

Bobath Cymru

'As mentioned in last year's report, the anticipated second pound for pound scheme up to £50,000 has now been launched. It is hoped to raise £50,000 as part of Bobath Cymru's 5th Birthday Capital Appeal to raise funds for the purchase of their centre at 19 Park Road Whitchurch. To help them in the meantime, £15,000 was donated in January 1997.

Trust for Sick Children in Wales

'The parents accommodation block has now been completed, and was officially opened by Viscount Tonypandy in June 1997.

Diocese of Menevia – St Mary's Convent Swansea

'Between March 1997 and January 1998, £107,000 was paid by the foundation to finance the conversion of St Mary's Convent in Swansea. The work has now been completed, to the satisfaction of those involved.

University of Wales College of Cardiff- establishment of new chairs

'£25,000 has been paid this year as part of the £125,000 reserved for the establishment of two new chairs at the Cardiff Business School, University of

Wales, Cardiff: The Sir Julian Hodge Chair in Marketing & Strategy and the Sir Julian Hodge Chair in Marketing and International Business.

Red Dragon Radio Trust

'A pound for pound scheme up to a maximum of £30,000 was agreed by the trustees for the 'Help a South Wales Child' appeal. It was completed successfully and this amount was paid in November 1997.

New Thornhill Church

'£25,000 was donated in May 1997 in support of this new community church.

Archdiocese of Cardiff- Finance Office- general requirements

'The trustees are giving active consideration to the needs of the Archdiocese, particularly in respect of their upgrading of certain schools and other capital projects.

New Cathedral

'It is confirmed that £3 million is still reserved for this (Cardiff) project.

Weizmann Institute

'The trustees reaffirm their commitment to support the work of the Institute in their search for a cure for AIDS.

Third World Applications

'Applications from the third world continue to receive a sympathetic response from the trustees, especially in respect of charities working abroad with the very poor and disadvantaged eg One World Action, The Salesian Sisters of St John Bosco and their work in India, and also the Sacred Heart Sisters Missionaries in El Salvador. In addition, this year a couple based in Rwanda working with the children orphaned as a result of AIDS or the war, have received substantial help via Echoes of Service.

'Father Greenway, an old friend of the foundation, has asked for the trustees to help launch a scholarship fund for the education of severely disadvantaged children in Kerala, Southern India. The scheme will run for three years. The first payment of £15,000 was duly paid in August 1997.

Sir Geraint Evan Wales Heart Research Institute

'The pound for pound scheme mentioned in last years report was successfully concluded, and thus £100,000 was donated to this charity in May 1997.

Diocese of Portsmouth

'£50,000 pound for pound appeal was agreed by the trustees to raise funds to

protect the future of one of three churches in the parish, under threat of closure. The appeal closed in December 1997, and £43,000 was duly paid by the foundation in January to match the amount raised by the Parish.

LATCH

'Sponsorship of a concert to raise funds for this charity based at Llandough Hospital in Cardiff, was agreed at a cost of £10,000. This took place in December 1997.

Father Finbarr O'Leary (Ecuador)

'The trustees have agreed to support a pound for pound appeal up to a maximum of £15,000 to help raise funds for Father O'Leary's work in Ecuador. The date of commencement has yet to be agreed, but thought to be likely during Lent 1999 with the full support of the Archbishop of Cardiff.

Hamlin Churchill Childbirth Injuries fund

'Although recent publicity has helped to raise the profile of this charity, and consequently more financial support, the trustees have again donated £5,000 to help with the very valuable work undertaken in Addis Ababa.

CADMAD

'To help with the celebrations in respect of their 50th Anniversary of Independence, the trustees agreed a donation of £8,000 to CADMAD.'

In 1996/97 the trust had an income of £1.27 million, derived mainly from interest on £26 million in assets. Charitable donations amounted to £1.34 million, subdivided as follows:

Medical	£220,000
Educational	£207,000
Religious	£515,000
Other	£396,000

A comprehensive grants list details about 304 grants. About half the grant total went to 20 organisations, most of which are mentioned above, in grants ranging from £15,000 to £250,000. Most of the remaining grants averaged between £1,000 and £5,000, and about 100 were for less than £1,000.

Examples of other beneficiaries include: Age Concern, Wales (£10,000 in 2 grants); One World Action (£7,500); Worth Abbey School (£5,000); Royal Society for the Encouragement of Arts (£5,000); Hamlin Churchill Childbirth Injuries Fund (£5,000); Shelter Cymru (£5,000); CAFOD, Catholic Fund for Overseas Development (£1,000); Owl Fund (£5,000 in 3 grants); Great Ormond

Street Hospital (£3,000); NCH Action for Children (£2,500); Church Army (£1,000); James McDonald Cancer Trust (£1,000) and the Welsh Heritage Schools Initiative (£1,000).

Exclusions The foundation makes grants to registered charities or exempt only. No grants to individuals.

Applications To the correspondent.

The Horne Foundation

£218,000 (1996/97, but see below)

Education, arts, youth, in or near Northampton

The Gnomes, Church Street, Boughton, Northampton NN2 8FG
Tel: 01604-821515; Fax: 01604-846987

Correspondent Mrs R M Harwood

Trustees E J Davenport; R M Harwood; C A Horne.

Beneficial area Mainly Northamptonshire.

Information available Accounts, but without the required list of grants or narrative report.

General In 1996/97 the foundation had the high income of £631,000 from an endowment valued at £6.3 million – exactly 10%. Part of this comes from a shareholding in the unlisted family company Kenneth Horne Family Holdings. Grants totalled only £218,000 so unspent income is being accumulated. This should be for some particular charitable purpose as, unless there is a specific provision to the contrary in the trust deed, such accumulation is not otherwise permitted; but the subject is not discussed in the report.

The foundation says that it makes predominantly large grants towards educational and welfare building projects to which it is the major contributor. It has a preference for local (causes) with occasional grants to national and international organisations dealing with the areas mentioned above. There is a preference for organisations without religious affiliation. It also says that, 'with rare exceptions, it does not respond to appeals from other charities'.

The only information about the 1996/97 grants is as follows:

Education grants, building and student

support £52,000 (£235,000 in 1995/96)

Special project housing £73,000 (£10,000)

National/international charities, crisis appeals £5,000 (£28,000)

Exceptional one-off donations £88,000 (£390,000)

Such a listing, without explanation, is not enough to enable the reader to form a true and fair view of what the charity is doing.

In the previous edition of this book, when disclosure was not compulsory, the charity nevertheless offered further information which enabled the following to be written:

'The foundation gives about 30 grants a year, some of them recurrent, for capital or project work. Grants normally range from a few hundred pounds to £10,000, but the foundation has said that its funding priorities are 'predominantly large grants towards building projects (education, welfare) in which the foundation is the major contributor. The foundation does not respond to appeals from other charities or individuals.'

'The foundation has a 'preference for local charities in the Northampton area, with occasional grants to national and international organisations dealing with the foundation's areas of interest.'

At that time the foundation cited the following sample grants (1994/95): NBC Sixfields Athletics Club (£100,000 for new club house and track), Young People's Hostel in Kettering (£75,000), Young Mothers Education (£11,000), Central Opera Trust (£10,000), and Moulton Football Club (£5,000).

Exclusions The foundation 'does not respond to appeals from charities providing local services in communities located outside Northamptonshire'. It prefers organisations without religious affiliation.

Applications In writing to the correspondent, at any time.

The Housing Associations Charitable Trust (HACT)

£971,000 (1997/98)

Housing and related social need

78 Quaker Street, London E1 6SW
Tel: 0171-336 78777

Correspondent Jane Minter

Trustees June McKerrow, Chair; Margaret Bennett; Matthew Bennett; Rosalind Brooke; Pat Chown; Rosemary Crawley; Aman Dalvi; Barbara Dennis; Christine Forrester; Viscount Nicholas Gage; John Hanlon; Trevor Hendy; Peter Molyneaux; Elahi Panahi; Philip Richardson; Professor Bert Rima; Paul Tennant; Ian Timmins; Janis Wong.

Beneficial area UK.

Information available Very full information, including detailed guidelines and advice sheets for applicants, available from the trust.

Summary Grants and loans are made, for amounts usually between £500 and £20,000, to help provide good quality housing and related services for four kinds of beneficiary:

- people with special needs
- older people
- refugee-led groups
- black and minority ethnic communities.

Besides providing grants and loans, HACT also gives fundraising information and advice and promotes housing issues to other donors.

General This trust acts as a non-endowed specialist grant maker in the difficult field of housing need, funded not only by housing associations but also by other trusts, many of which are themselves featured in this book, such as Comic Relief, Esmée Fairbairn Charitable Trust, the Baring Foundation or the Goldsmith's Company.

HACT is important not only for its own excellent grant making but also as a model for other trusts seeking to bring help to those in greatest need.

After some years of tight finances, 1997/98 saw the trust once again on an upwards trend with grants, among other things, rising from £899,000 to £971,000.

The trust produces an excellent booklet, 'Grant Guidelines' the text of which follows immediately. The entry ends with a brief account of HACT's grants in 1997/98.

Grant Guidelines

What is HACT?

'HACT was set up in 1960 to raise and distribute charitable money to improve the quality of life for the homeless people and people with housing and support needs.

'HACT is now one of the largest

specialist grant-making charities in the United Kingdom. Through financial support and specialist advice we have helped to establish and support hundreds of projects and organisations to meet the housing needs of communities all around the country.

How do we help?

- We raise and distribute £1 million a year in grants and loans to voluntary organisations throughout the United kingdom;
- We provide advice and support for local, under-resourced groups to access funding and to develop into variable and stable organisations;
- We advise other charitable funders on the most effective ways they can support voluntary housing projects;
- We identify gaps in housing provision and encourage both funders and providers to consider ways they can meet these needs;

Who do we help?

'HACT will consider applications from organisations which provide housing or housing related services for:

- older people
- people with support needs
- black, minority ethnic and refugee communities.

Who can apply?

'HACT makes grants and loans to the following types of organisations in the United Kingdom:

- voluntary organisations and community groups, (including groups in the process of formation), with housing related aims;
- housing associations.

'HACT focuses its support on organisations with limited financial resources.

About HACT's grant-making

What are our aims?

'HACT aims to encourage housing solutions which:

- break new ground in housing provision and services
- extend user involvement, choice and participation
- improve the quality of life for users
- promote equality of opportunity
- develop provision to meet new needs
- strengthen the voluntary housing sector through training and consultancy
- encourage the sharing of new ideas by supporting guidance material of national benefit.

What will we pay for?

'HACT will consider applications under the following three grants programmes:

- housing for older people
- housing for people with support needs
- housing for black, minority ethnic and refugee communities.

'Applications for the following purposes will be considered:

- small grants to meet the costs of establishing a new voluntary organisation aiming to provide for an unmet need; eg. funding for items such as registration costs, information leaflets, basic training etc.
- grants for training or consultancies for small organisations to tackle a specific problem
- the cost of work to provide evidence of need in order to negotiate for statutory funding
- the salary and related costs of employing a development worker to carry out the necessary groundwork to establish a new service within a limited time period
- the costs of undertaking a piece of work which will promote good practice and new housing solutions, the results of which will be of wider value to the voluntary housing sector
- loans towards the capital costs of some housing related services which do not qualify for statutory funding.

'Further details of specific funding available under the three different programmes can be found below.

What will we not pay for?

'HACT will not make funds available for:

- purposes which are eligible for statutory funding, including furniture and building costs of housing schemes
- ongoing revenue funding, including items which would normally be included in an organisation's annual budget
- individuals
- well-resourced organisations.

How much do we give?

'As a general guideline, grants of between £500 and £20,000 can be made. HACT can sometimes provide grants for up three years – years two and three funding is agreed in principal and subject to progress reports. The amount of funds to be made available will be discussed as part of the assessment process where advice on other funding options will be provided.

'All applications are carefully considered by staff and trustees but it should be remembered that HACT has limited funding and not all requests will be successful.

How often can you apply?

'In general a maximum of one application will be considered by the grant-making committee each year and one further application per year can go through the delegated authority process (ie under £3,000).

Will you qualify for a grant or a loan?

'Loans are offered whenever repayment is a possibility. They can normally be interest free and repayment can be deferred for a period of three or five years.

'Loans will always be made available for capital projects, unless there are exceptional circumstances.

How many applications are successful?

'HACT deals with approximately 500 applications per year with around 200 receiving financial support from the trust.

'In many cases advice is provided on other sources of financial help.

Housing for older people

What are our aims?

'HACT considers applications which will help all older people in housing need and encourages a range of housing options and solutions for older people

'HACT particularly welcomes applications which meet the housing and support needs of:

- older people from black and minority ethnic communities
- homeless older people
- older people with dementia and other mental health problems.

What will we pay for?

'The following examples are not exhaustive but give an idea of the types of projects HACT funds under this programme:

- feasibility studies or needs assessment surveys to produce information which will help projects to receive statutory or other charitable funding, eg for older people from particular minority ethnic communities or for older people with dementia
- new initiatives which enable older people to remain safe and secure in their own homes, eg the setting up in Care and Repair schemes of new services such as Handyperson schemes or the employment of workers to meet the needs of minority ethnic communities
- the development of specialist housing advice services which inform older people of their housing rights/benefits etc
- the production of good practice

guidance material which highlights a new approach to housing provision and service for older people such as in sheltered housing provision or Care and Repair

- extra provision in housing schemes which develop community services, eg lunch clubs, day care facilities, outreach services
- loans to upgrade facilities or to provide specialist equipment for older people in residential or sheltered accommodation which enhances their quality of life

'Who to contact for further information?

Jane Minter, Assistant Director, Policy and Grants Tel: 0171-336 7877.

Housing for black, minority ethnic and refugee communities

What are our aims?

'HACT's aim is to strengthen the development of housing provision and the choice for black and minority ethnic and refugee communities. HACT only considers applications from black and minority ethnic led housing organisation and refugee-led groups.

What will we pay for?

'The following examples are not exhaustive but give an idea of the types of projects HACT funds under this programme

- small grants to meet the initial expenses of new voluntary housing committees meeting clearly identified needs which are not being met, eg for a particular minority ethnic minority;
- training for staff and committee members in order to improve the level of service provided to their communities such as housing finance or housing management training;
- consultancies to produce business plans to enable organisations to grow and develop;
- bursaries to enable staff and committee members to attend conferences on issues relevant to the communities they serve;
- feasibility studies or needs assessment surveys in order to help projects receive funding from statutory authorities and other charitable funders;
- supporting the development of organisations through early staff costs, eg. a grant to employ a member of staff to set up a new service
- promotional costs such as the production of information leaflets which allow organisations to reach the people good they aim to help
- good practice initiatives particularly

relevant to small black and minority ethnic or refugee community groups such as stock condition surveys, studies of rent levels, management issues etc

- the establishment of emergency provision for asylum seekers made homeless as a result of the Asylum and Immigration Act 1996

'Who to contact for further information?

Reena Mukherji, Grants and Advice Manager, Minority ethnic communities Tel: 0171-336 7877.

Housing for people with support needs

What are our aims?

'HACT's aims in funding supported housing projects are to promote good practice in delivery of services, to identify and provide for unmet need, to combat discrimination and promote the active involvement of users in services

What are our priorities?

'HACT is focusing its funds for supported housing on five priority areas.

'Applications can only be accepted if they specifically relate to one of the following:

- the development of supported housing services in rural areas;
- the development of supported housing services for single homeless people with mental health problems;
- the development of supported housing services for people from black, minority ethnic or refugee communities;
- the development of supported housing services for women with disabilities, drug or alcohol problems, who have been in or with HIV/AIDS;
- the involvement of users in the development and management of supported housing services.

What will we pay for?

'The following examples are not exhaustive but give an idea of the types of projects HACT funds under this programme:

- small grants to meet the initial expenses of new voluntary housing committees meeting clearly identified needs which are not being met, eg young homelessness in a rural area;
- training or consultancy work to strengthen a small voluntary housing organisation or to tackle a specific problem, such as a staffing or financial review or equal opportunities training;
- feasibility studies or needs assessment surveys to provide evidence of supported housing needs

in order to negotiate statutory or charitable funding, eg for people from black and minority ethnic or refugee communities;

- the salary and related costs of employing a person for a limited period to establish appropriate supported housing provision, including the development of 'floating support' services, eg the development of specialist supported housing for people from a minority ethnic community or the development of a new service providing housing support in a rural area;
- the development of housing advice services for people with support needs in rural areas;
- the cost of work which will promote good practice in existing or new supported housing services, eg. the development of user participation in management and advocacy schemes;
- loans to meet the shortfall in the capital costs, (excluding furniture), of day care or similar facilities linked to supported housing schemes , eg a new day care facility for single homeless people with mental health problems.

'Please remember that every application must be linked to one of the priority areas listed on the previous page.

'Who to contact for further information?

Ginny Castle, Grants and Advice Manager, Supported Housing Tel: 0171-336 7877.

Applying to HACT

Encouraging enquiries

'HACT welcomes and encourages initial enquiries about potential applications. Discussion with a member of our Policy, Grants and Advice Team will help you decide whether or not your application meets HACT's current criteria, and provide you with advice on other funding options. Applications should phone or write with an outline proposal to the relevant member of the Policy, Grants and Advice Team for further information and guidance. If the project falls within HACT's criteria, an application form will be sent.

About the application form

'Although the application form must be completed in as much detail as possible, the itself is only the first part of the application process and a decision will not be based on the form alone.

About the assessment process

'A combination of telephone discussion, requests for further details and a visit, where arranged, form part of the assessment process.

The assessment will include:

- Details of the organisation seeking funds: aims and objectives, services and plans, strengths, management abilities, operational issues, financial situations, equal opportunities and user involvement;
- Details of the proposed project: the background, how the need has been identified, support from other agencies, its aims and objectives, services and plans, staffing and monitoring arrangements and future prospects;
- How the project meets HACT's criteria;
- What funds are required.

'Discussion will take place regarding the extent of HACT's likely support, plus advice will also be provided on other funding sources, where appropriate, and other organisations that can help.

The decision-making process

Grants up to £3,000

'Decision on grants and loans up to £2,000 are taken internally by HACT's Policy, Grants and Advice Team and can usually be made within two weeks of relieving all the details requested by HACT.

'Decisions on grants and loans between £2,000 and £3,000 will be made by the Chair/Vice Chair of the Grant-Making Committee and therefore take a little longer.

Grants and loans over £3,000

'Applications for grants and loans over £3,000 must be submitted to a committee meeting for a decision. The Grant-Making Committee meets six times a year. Normally it is necessary for completed application forms to be received at least two months prior to a committee meeting to allow time for staff to visit organisations and prepare reports as necessary.

How we inform you of the outcome

'All applicants will be notified in writing of the outcome of their application. The decision of the trustees is final.'

Grants in 1997/98

The grants and loans were categorised as follows:

Older people's housing: 42 grants totalling £470,000.

The largest awards were to Help the Aged in Northern Ireland (£35,000 for two handyperson projects) and Care and Repair in Pembrokeshire (£30,000).

£25,000 was given to AIMS to help develop a national conciliation service covering supported housing. Other major beneficiaries included Abbeyfield nationally and the local Abbeyfield in Seascale (£20,000 each). More typical were small grants such as the £3,000 to Age Concern Leominster for a preventative support service or the £5,000 for Glasgow Jewish HA to identify housing needs in that community.

Refugee housing: 37 grants totalling £143,000.

Most of these grants were for £5000 or less and were given to refugee community groups specifically towards the travel costs of asylum seekers who had been denied benefits. There were 13 larger awards of between £5,000 and £14,000 for the salary costs of housing workers. Beneficiaries included the Iranian Community Centre in Islington, the Welsh Refugee Council and the Refugee Advice Centre in Waltham Forest.

Single homeless people: 16 grants totalling £92,000.

There were three grants of more than £10,000, to Bibini Centre for Young People, Manchester (£15,000), East Bristol Youth HA (£17,000) and the National Homeless Alliance (£12,000).

Supported housing: 24 grants totalling £152,000.

Most grants were for £5,000 or less. Exceptions included St Anne's Shelter in Leeds (£30,000) and PUSH in Perth and Kinross (£14,000).

Black and ethnic minority housing: 18 grants totalling £122,000.

Only one grant was for more than £10,000, the £20,000 for Scotland's Positive Action in Housing. Mote typical were the grants to Millat Asian HA in Merton (£5,000 for salary costs) or the £3,000 for SADAAHA in Sandwell and Dudley to train committee members.

Exclusions No grants to individual applicants. Only work covered by the specific criteria of the trust can be considered.

Applications Potential applicants should first contact the trust to obtain copies of their Grant Guidelines (those reprinted above may be out of date by the time this entry is being read) and to discuss their application. The contact people concerned are:

Jane Minter: Assistant Director: Housing for older people, and all other enquiries.

Ginny Castle: Grants manager: Supported Housing.

Reena Mukherji: Grants manager: Housing for black, ethnic minority and refugee groups.

The grant-making committee meets in February, April, June, September, October and December.

The HSA Charitable Trust

£295,000 (to institutions 1996/97)

Health care

Hambleden House, Waterloo Court, Andover, Hants SP10 1LQ
Tel: 01264-353211

Correspondent Mrs Hancock

Trustees P S Howard (Chairman); I D Adam; P Benner; R H Crawford; J A Elliott; Mrs C Lemon.

Beneficial area UK.

Information available Annual Report and Accounts. Information brochure available.

Summary Grants are made to hospitals and health charities, and also to help fund secondary education for NHS Nurses. About 180 grants were made in 1997, the largest being £10,000 and most between £1,000-£2,000.

General The HSA Charitable Trust was first established in 1972 by the HSA, a non-profit healthcare assurance organisation. Each year the trust is covenanted a large donation from the HSA.

The trust states that: 'Although the trust is committed to providing financial help to a wide range of deserving causes, it is particularly concerned to support those charities and charitable organisations that are likely to benefit a substantial number of HSA contributors. The principle for distribution of funds is that all charities with medical research, after care and welfare aims and ambitions are considered.

'We tend to be more sympathetic towards smaller and lesser known organisations – particularly those that might benefit HSA members. In addition, we do make substantial donations to the larger charities from time to time.

'The objectives of the trust are :

- to provide monetary grants to members of The Hospital Saving Association (HSA) suffering exceptional financial hardship as a result of ill health but who are not entitled to normal benefits under the association's rules;

• financially to support persons and institutions to enhance their ability to care for HSA members and their family when ill;

• to provide and award scholarships and prizes for nurses, health visitors and others engaged in or undergoing a course of education, training, or preparation for the treatment or prevention of illness.'

In 1996/97, the Hospital Savings Association donated £820,000 to the trust. This was distributed in '164 grants to HSA members suffering exceptional financial hardship, donations to the non-public funds of 705 hospitals, donations to 178 institutions and the award of 95 new scholarships to nurses, midwives and professional therapists.'

Grants for 1996/97 are categorised as follows:

Donations to free funds of hospitals
£97,000   (£96,000)
HSA Scholarship Awards
£194,000   (£157,000)
Grants to individuals
£27,000   (£22,000)
Grants to institutions
£295,000   (£545,000)

The grants to institutions are listed (about 178), with money going to a variety of health and medical related charities. They seem to be well spread between local and national charities. Examples of charities supported include Lord Mayor Trelor (£10,000); St Barts Royal London School of Medicine (£6,000); Chailey Heritage £5,000); Mencap (£5,000); The Samaritans (£5,000); Avert (£2,000); Beechwood Donation (£2,000); Countess Mountbatten House Campaign (£2,000); Glasgow Council on Alcohol (£2,000); Kent Air Ambulance (£2,000); Northern Counties Kidney Research (£2,000); Praxis (£2,000); St Helen's Hospice (£2,000); Waverley Care (£2,000); Wessex Multiple Sclerosis (£2,000) and Young Minds (£2,000). Over half the grants are for less than £1,000, but these constitute only a third by value.

Applications In writing to the correspondent, including a copy of the most recent audited accounts. Trustees meet four times a year.

The Isle of Anglesey Charitable Trust

£481,000 (1997/98)

General in Anglesey

Isle of Anglesey County Council, County Offices, Llangefni, LL77 7TW
Tel: 01248-750057

Correspondent The Treasurer

Trustees The County Council.

Beneficial area The Isle of Anglesey.

Information available Report and accounts.

General The trust was formed in 1990 by the then Isle of Anglesey Borough Council 'to administer investments purchased from monies received from Shell (UK) Limited when the company ceased operating an oil terminal on Anglesey'. This compensation money from the company was part of the agreement in the original 1972 private Act of Parliament which had enabled the terminal to be set up in the first place.

The objectives of the trust are 'to provide amenities and facilities for the general public benefit of persons resident in ... the Isle of Anglesey'. The county council is the sole trustee.

The accounts for 1996/97 showed assets of £10.7 million which generated a net income of £663,000. Grants totalling £469,000 were allocated as follows:

Ynys Mon Borough Council, for Oriel Ynys Mon £205,000
Leisure and heritage
Village halls running costs
£20,000   39 grants
Capital grants, community and sport
£92,000   15 grants
Voluntary Organisations
£12,000   15 grants
Eisteddfod Mon £3,500
Social services
CAB £78,000
Voluntary organisations
£9,000   18 grants
Education
Voluntary organisations
£9,000   10 grants
Capital grants, churches and chapels £40,000   16 grants.

The largest grants, other than those noted above, were to Clwb Rygbi Porthaethwy (£30,000) and Clwb Peldroed Pentraeth (£12,000).

Applications In writing to the correspondent, following advertisements in the local press.

The J J Charitable Trust

£264,000 (approved, 1996/97)

Environment, literacy, general

See entry for the 'Sainsbury Family Charitable Trusts'
Tel: 0171-410 0330

Correspondent Michael Pattison

Trustees J J Sainsbury; M L Sainsbury; Miss J S Portrait.

Beneficial area UK and overseas.

Information available The trust provides a full report and accounts. Its principal officers in 1996/97 were Michael Pattison, the director, Paul Spokes, the finance director and Miss J Shepherd, executive.

Summary: This trust is one of the Sainsbury Family Charitable Trusts which share a joint administration. It gives its major support to environmentally sustainable work overseas. It also funds environmental education activities which help young people track major contemporary problems such as air pollution, energy conservation or transport. In addition the trust shows a particular interest in dyslexia and other problems affecting literacy particularly amongst young people at risk.

General Julian Sainsbury is the settlor of this trust. In April 1997 it had assets of over £8 million. During the year the trust received another donation of £1.8 million from its settlor following £1.7 million in the preceding year. Both these sums were included as expendable endowment. A total of £384,000 was available for distribution in 1996/97- its net income, plus over £100,000 brought forward from the previous year.

The trust gives useful policy information and a helpful and interesting outline of the purpose of each grant. The grants seem, at a first quick glance of the report copy, to be only for a single year. However this is a mistaken view and several projects are supported over a number of years.

Literacy Support

'Grants are made to improve the effectiveness of literacy teaching in the primary education sector of children with general or specific learning difficulties, including dyslexia, and to do the same through the agencies working with ex-offenders or those at risk of offending.'

In 1996/97 the largest grant in this category was to the New Assembly of Churches, The Foundation Centre, Battersea, to 'provide literacy support to young people at risk of offending. In particular those people who have very fundamental problems and basic needs and who cannot otherwise be helped at this time.' (£20,600). Another major grant was to Youth at Risk in Knowsley, to 'support a special needs teacher and assistants in the design and implementation of a pilot literacy and education project as part of the wider Youth at Risk project. It is hoped this could be replicated in the future if successful' (£18,000).

Environment – UK

'The trustees are interested in environmental education, particularly supporting projects displaying practical ways of involving children and young adults. The trustees are also interested in the potential for energy efficiency and renewable energy in the wider society. The trustees have made grants to projects which seek to develop alternative transport schemes.'

The largest grant in 1996/97 was made over a three year period to the Children's Play Council: Home Zones 'to develop safe residential areas through new traffic management measures. This project works with local people and groups wishing to establish Home Zones and seeks to encourage the development of a related legislation and policy framework' (£14,885). Two grants of £10,000 were made to Sustrans, towards the initial

costs of a 10 mile stretch of Millennium Cycle Route and to the Schools Network on Air Pollution (SNAP) Project run by the Institute of Education in which 20 schools collect and analyse air samples; the grant enabled the project to continue for a third year (£10,000). In the previous year it had received £32,516 from the trust.

Environment – Overseas

'The trustees continue to support community based agriculture projects which aim to help people to help themselves in an environmentally sustainable way. The projects supported may be long term. This year one project in particular is expected to be supported for five years.'

The largest grant by the trust of the whole year (£117,229) was made to SOS Sahel in Kenya 'towards the Meru Dryland Farming Project working with farmers in three low-income communities in a semi-arid region of northern Kenya, to help improve farming methods and livelihoods without damaging the natural resource base. The project will also strengthen local community groups'. The second grant, over two years, was also made in Kenya to the Rural Outreach Programme of Professor Ruth Oniango towards a project in Buture to increase the security of traditional vegetable production amongst the whole community with particular support to women's groups to market these vegetables throughout the country.

In the previous year the major project supported overseas had been FARM Africa for an afforestation programme at Babati in Northern Tanzania (£35,000).

General

In 1996/97 this catchall category included the trust's small regular grant to the Save the Rhino Trust (£500) and

another to Oxfam for its emergency work in Central Africa (£5,000).

Exclusions Individuals.

Applications The trustees met six times in the year (five times in the preceding year). 'Proposals are generally invited by the trustees or initiated at their request.' See entry for Sainsbury Family Charitable Trusts.

The Dawn James Charitable Foundation

£447,000 (1996/97)

Education and other charitable purposes in Bristol

7 Clyde Road, Redland, Bristol BS6 6RG
Tel: 01179-239444

Correspondent Mrs J Norton Administrator

Trustees David Johnson; Joan Johnson; Thomas Webley; Elizabeth Chamabers; Jacqueline Marsh; Michael Cansdale; John Evans; Gloria Powney.

Beneficial area UK, mainly Bristol.

Information available Full accounts but without the required narrative report.

General 'The foundation was established in 1979 to provide charitable donations for the relief of poverty and sickness, and the advancement of education in Bristol.

'The foundation's donation policy remains unchanged with assistance given to medical, educational and other local charities. £447,000 was donated during the year and a review of longer term commitments led to a revision of the terms of the Enrichment Fund Scheme for State Secondary Schools who had participated in the original scheme. The end result of the review is that long term commitments now stand at £2 million over the next five years. This commitment will be met with future income.'

Total assets of the foundation are currently £10 million, generating an income of £560,000. The grant giving of £447,000 was a small drop from the previous year's £553,000.

Grants for 1996/97 were listed under the following headings:

The J J Charitable Trust

	1996/97			1995/96		
Literacy support	£67,000	5	26%	£37,000	3	18%
Environment UK	£50,000	9	20%			
Environment – Overseas	£142,000	2	56%	£151,000	9	76%
General	£6,000	2	2%	£13,000	4	6%
Total	£254,000	18	100%	£200,000	16	100%

Bristol's Independent Schools Scholarship Fund (£280,000). Eight awards for £30,000 (including Bristol Grammar School, Red Maids School and Queen Elizabeth Hospital) and two grants for £20,000.

Bristol Schools Special Prizes (£60,000). Mainly awards of £2,000 to various Bristol schools

Bristol Comprehensive Schools Enrichment Fund (£26,000). A number of grants including Brislington School (£9,000), St Bernadette's School (£10,000), St. George's School (£2,000), and Lockleaze School (£4,000).

General Donations (£81,000). Although a large number of grants went to Bristol based charities they were usually for small amounts. There seems to be support for youth, children and health charities. Support is also noted for the elderly and the arts. Examples include: Jessie Mary Trust (£10,000), Barton Hill Settlement (£15,000 in two grants), Pensioners Welfare Fund (£5,000), Bristol Care and Repair (£2,000), Handicapped Children's Pilgrimage Trust (£2,000), British Polio Fellowship, 133rd Bristol Disabled Scouts (£1,500), Bristol Amateur Operatic Society (£1,000).

Applications In writing to the correspondent. The trustees meet regularly throughout the year to consider policy objectives and to approve donations.

John James Bristol Foundation

£1,009,000 (1996/97)

Education, general in Bristol

7 Clyde Road, Redland,
Bristol BS6 6RG
Tel: 0117-923 9444;
Fax: 0117 923 9470

Correspondent Julia Norton, Administrator

Trustees Joan Johnson; Thomas Webley; David Johnson; Elizabeth Chambers; Jacqueline Marsh; Michael Cansdale; John Evans; Gloria Powney.

Beneficial area UK, mainly Bristol.

Information available Report and accounts with grants policy and list (reprinted below) are on file at the

Charity Commission or available from the foundation for the fee of £5.

General The foundation was set up by John James in 1983. Each year the great majority of funds are disbursed in one or two very large grants made according to the following objects set out in its deeds:

- The relief of poverty and sickness or the advancement of education among the inhabitants of Bristol.
- General – at the discretion of the trustees.

In 1996/97 assets totalling £27 million at the end of the year (an increase of over £4 million from the previous year) generated £1,168,000 income.

The Trustees' Report says: 'The foundation's donation policy remains unchanged with assistance being given to medical, education and other local charities. £1,009,000 was donated during the year with the trustees taking into account the wishes of the recipients as to the timing of large donations so as to maximise their potential in the charity receiving them. The trustees accept that this can result in appreciable fluctuations in annual totals for accounting purposes.'

The grants in the year went to: St Peter's Hospice, Bristol (£750,000); Windmill Hill City Farm (£250,000); Victim Support Bristol (£6,000 – the fourth of four similar annual payments); and the Salvation Army, Bristol (£3,000 – repeated from 1995/96)

Applications In writing to the correspondent.

The James Pantyfedwen Foundation

£321,000 (1998)

Religion, education, general, in Wales

Pantyfedwen, 9 Market Street,
Aberystwyth SY23 1DL
Tel and Fax: 01970-612806

Correspondent Richard H Morgan, Executive Secretary

Trustees There are 24 trustees in all. A full list is available in the annual report. It includes Professor G L Rees (Chairman).

Beneficial area Wales.

Information available Accounts and separate annual report with most grants listed and some narrative analysis.

Summary Gifts ranging between £10 and the current maximum of £8,000 are given for church buildings, Eisteddfodau (Welsh arts events), students and general charities in Wales.

General The James Pantyfedwen Foundation is the new name for the 'John and Rhys Thomas James' and the 'Catherine and Lady Grace James' Foundations which were amalgamated in April 1998. The original foundations were set-up by Sir D J James who established the first 'super' cinema in London (the Palladium in Palmers Green) and owned 13 other pre-war cinemas.

The foundation says 'the purposes of the new foundation are, more or less, identical to those of the previous foundation'. These purposes are fairly rare for trusts in that they exclusively target grant-making at Welsh charities – these generally get little attention from trusts, even those claiming a UK-wide area of interest (it is also true that Wales spontaneously generates less than its proper share of good applications, but this is a problem for the trusts to overcome, as much as it is one for Welsh charities). Although this entry is based on the report and accounts of the two pre-merged foundations it attempts to treat them as one.

In the year ending March1998 the foundations' assets totalled £6,909,000 and income of £402,000 had been generated.

Allocation of grants 1997/98

Religious buildings	44	£67,000:
- Church in Wales		(£16,000)
- Methodist		(£13,000)
- Presbyterian Church of Wales		(£8,000)
- Baptist Churches		(£7,000)
- Welsh Congregational Churches		(£3,000)
- Other churches		(£20,000)
Educational grants (individuals)	38	£53,000
Eisteddfodau	72	£44,000
Religious purposes	—	£43,000
- Sunday schools	31	(£2,900)
- other	—	(£40,000)
General	—	£56,000

The annual report for the Catherine and Lady Grace James Foundation (from which most awards by value and number were made) said:

Religious purposes grants

'The sum of £17,000 was contributed towards the various denominational stipend and pension funds. The following grants were paid to charities under the religious purposes section of the trust deed: St Michael's Church, Aberystwyth £1,000; Lightship 2000 Project, Cardiff Bay £2,000; Llanover Trust, Abergavenny £1,000; Welsh Sunday Schools Council £1,000; Llanfair Penrhys Uniting Church, Rhondda £500. A grant of £350 was paid to St Michael's Theological College, Cardiff to aid in meeting the cost of publishing "Essays in Canon Law."

Nine theological students received grants amounting to £8,000 towards their expenses in pursuing their training. Thirty-four retired ministers of religion and minister's widows whose names had been submitted by the various denominational secretaries, received a total of £11,000.

Educational grants

'Seven bursaries of £4,000 were paid to students undertaking post-graduate study. A total of 31 students in further and higher education received a total of £53,000 to aid them in their studies during the year. This total includes eleven male students (£17,000) and 20 female students (£36,000).

General grants

The foundations' general grants during the year included those to: Waunfawr Community Association, Aberystwyth £1,000; Unitarian Churches (in-service training) £1,500; Raven House Trust, Newport £500; St Illog Hirnant Community, Rhayader £2,000; 1st Tredegar Guides, Brownies and Rainbows £200; and Action Centres UK £500.'

Exclusions Applications are considered from (a) students following approved courses mainly of a postgraduate nature (b) churches for the repair of the fabric (c) registered charities for capital expenditure only. Registered charities only.

Applications A form for applications is available from the correspondent. Applications from churches and registered charities can be submitted at any time (trustees meet about five times a year in March, May, July, September and December); student applications should be submitted before July 31st in the academic year for which the application is being made. All unsuccessful applicants receive a reply.

Rees Jeffreys Road Fund

£450,000 (planned for 1998)

Road and transport research and education

13 The Avenue, Chichester, West Sussex, PO19 4PX
Tel: 01243-787013

Correspondent B Fieldhouse, Secretary

Trustees P W Bryant, Chairman; D Bayliss; Dr S Glaister; M N T Cottell; Mrs June Bridgeman; Sir James Duncan; W H P Davison; M J Kendrick.

Beneficial area UK.

Information available Report and accounts with full grants list, exploration of grants, and descriptions of the trust's history and objects.

Summary The fund gives financial support to research and other projects designed to improve the safety and beauty of public highways. Grants vary from £1,000 to over £100,000, spread over a few years, and are mostly made for research and/or academic study (though the fund says that the maximum is now £70,000).

General The fund was established in 1950 by the sole settlor, the late William Rees Jeffreys. Mr Rees Jeffreys was a 'road enthusiast' and was described by Lloyd George as 'the greatest authority on roads in the United Kingdom and one of the greatest in the world'. The fund is just one legacy of a life-time dedicated to the improvement of roads; Rees Jeffreys was the author of an historical and autobiographical record of sixty years of road improvement (The King's Highway, published 1949) which is introduced with the words "I early knew my mission in life". Ironically, given the conquering of the road by the petrol engine and bicycling's shift off-road, he was also a very keen cyclist.

At the close of 1997 the fund totalled £6.7 million and generated income of £252,000 (there were unrealised gains of £749,000).

The fund 'gives financial support for research to improve the quality and efficiency of roads and their use by vehicular traffic, cyclists, pedestrians and public transport. Grants for individual projects range from £1,000 to £70,000 and include academic study and

improving the roadside environment.

Its activities embrace:

- Contributing to the costs of university teaching in disciplines directly concerned with roads and transportation.
- Providing bursaries or other help for postgraduate study in those disciplines.
- Encouraging the creation of roadside rests for motorists and the improvement of the immediate roadside environment.
- Stimulating research into the challenge of emerging transportation issues and al aspects of road usage and road traffic and their economic and environmental implications.
- Supporting transportation research, including recently issues of congestion, ravel modes, the deployment of resources, road use by pedestrians and cyclists, and road safety.'

In 1997, 15 projects received support amounting to £199,000 and a number of academic posts and studentships were sponsored with funds totalling £146,000. Project grants varied from £1,000 to £133,000, but no single organisation received more than £30,350 in the year.

The fund's objects include:

- to sponsor lectures, studies and scholarships to improve public highways and adjoining lands;
- to promote schemes for the provision of roadside parks and open spaces designed to enhance the beauty and attractiveness of the highways;
- to encourage the improvement of public highways (including bridges, tunnels, footpaths, verges and cycle tracks) to maximise their safety and beauty;
- to buy or assist in the purchase of property adjacent to roads so as to conserve amenities – preserve a view, park, resting and recreation grounds.

'The fund's principle project 'explores what the transport reality might be which could follow the recognition of the realism that emerged from (the fund's) earlier studies into current transport policy'. The project, entitled Realism to Reality, is the fund's largest to date and is expected to cost £300,000 by the time of its completion in December 1998. In 1997 five universities received grants between £20,000 and £30,000 to further the project's aims.

'Other interesting awards included: £9,800 to the Cleveland Wildlife Trust to provide a 'Wildlife Stop' for motorists and £4,000 to the Pedestrian Association as a 'contribution towards a survey exploring local authority policies on walking as a mode of transport'.

Applications There is no set form of application for grants. Brief details should be submitted initially. Replies are sent to all applicants.

The Jerusalem Trust

£2,345,000 (approved, 1997)

The promotion of Christianity

See entry for the 'Sainsbury Family Charitable Trusts'

Correspondent Michael Pattison

Trustees Lady Susan Sainsbury; Sir Timothy Sainsbury; V E Hartley Booth; Rt Rev Timothy Dudley-Smith; Mrs Diana Wainman.

Beneficial area UK and overseas.

Information available The trust provides a full report and accounts. Its principal officers in 1996/97 included Michael Pattison, the director, Paul Spokes, finance director, and Miss J Lunn, executive.

Summary This trust is one of the Sainsbury Family Charitable Trusts which share a joint administration. It concentrates its giving entirely on Christian evangelical activities of many kinds and in many contexts at home and abroad: social welfare work and Christian education in the UK and relief work overseas as well as media work and art activities.

General In 1997 the net income of this trust devoted to the advancement of

Christianity was £2.87 million. Its asset value had risen during the year by £15 million to £76.8 million in December 1997.

The trustees are advised by consultants (the annual report does not name them).

Christian Evangelism and Relief Work Overseas

'Trustees are particularly interested in proposals for indigenous training and support and production of appropriate literature and resource materials for Christians in Central and Eastern Europe, the former Soviet Union and Africa.'

Grants ranged between £50,000 each to the Tear Fund and World Vision UK to support their relief and development work during 1997, to £30,000 over three years to the Nairobi Evangelical Graduate School of Theology for bursaries. The Peter Deyneka Russian Ministries were funded with £40,000 over two years for the development of a Christian Resource Centre in Moscow. Ten grants were for £5,000, or less.

Christian Media

'Trustees are particularly interested in supporting training and networking projects for Christians working professionally in all areas of the media and for those considering media careers.'

Major grants were given in 1997 to Jerusalem Productions Limited, co-production funding of *God's Army,* three Channel 4 programmes about the Salvation Army (£81,000) and the Television Training Bursary Fund (£56,527 over 3 years).

Christian Education

'Trustees are particularly interested in the development of Christian school curriculum resource materials for RE and other subjects, support and training

for Christian teachers of all subjects and lay training.'

The major grant in 1997 was awarded to Stapleford Centre for its curriculum resources work (£438,260 over 3 years). Culham College Institute received two grants, one towards a series of five short programmes on 'Christianity in the early years' to be broadcast on Channel 4. (£168,000 over 2 years), the other to produce and distribute a colour leaflet of selected Christian resource materials for primary schools (£29,700).

Christian Art

'Trustees mainly focus on a small number of pro-active commission of works of art for places of worship'.

In 1997 the Art Christian Enquiry Trust received two grants totalling £14,550 towards the funding of a part time director and a leaflet on contemporary Christian art.

Christian Evangelism and Social Responsibility at Home

'Trustees are particularly interested in Christian projects which develop new ways of working with children and young people and projects which promote Christian marriage and family life. They are also interested in church planting and evangelistic projects which undertake Christian work with prisoners, ex-prisoners and their families.'

In 1997 a major grant was awarded to the National Biblical Heritage Centre towards *BC/AD, The Living Bible Adventure* (£150,000 over 3 years). Other grants included Positive Parenting Publications for a national co-ordinator of the One Stop Parenting Project (£54,000 over 3 years), Radstock Ministries for editorial support and marketing of the *Ichthus File* (£49,500) and Visible Communications, for a full-time director of this organisations for Christian work with deaf people (£38,250). As many as 18 grants in this category were for £5,000 or less.

Exclusions No grants direct to individuals.

Applications The trustees met five times in 1997. 'Proposals are generally invited by the trustees or initiated at their request. Unsolicited applications are discouraged and are unlikely to be successful, even if they fall within an area in which the trustees are interested.'

However it is also said that an application to one Sainsbury trust is an application to all. See the entry for the Sainsbury Family Charitable Trusts for the address and further advice.

The Jerusalem Trust

	1996/97			1995/96		
Evangelism/ Relief work overseas	£444,000	24	19%	£449,000	28	19%
Media	£246,000	11	10%	£266,000	11	11%
Education	£764,000	16	33%	£574,000	12	23%
Art	£30,000	5	1%	£54,000	3	2%
Evangelism/ Social responsibility Work at Home	£860,000	49	37%	£1,037,000	43	43%
Total	**£2,345,000**	**105**	**100%**	**£2,419,000**	**97**	**100%**

The Jerwood Foundation

Perhaps £3,000,000 for capital projects in 1999

Education, arts, general

22 Fitzroy Square, London W1P 5HJ
Tel: 0171 388 6287

Correspondent Roanne Dods

Council Alan Grieve, Chairman; Dr Peter Marxer; Dr Walter Kieber; Barbara Kalman.

UK Advisory Board Viscount Chilston; Lady Harlech; Dr Kerry Parton; Edward Paul; Julia Wharton.

Beneficial area Unrestricted.

Information available Guidelines for Applicants (reprinted below, as of November 1998); Annual reports, but with no financial information (as this is not yet a British registered charity, it has had no obligation to supply accounts)

Summary This is a Liechtenstein registered foundation, but in the process of registering a new UK charitable foundation with the Charity Commission. It was established by John Jerwood, an Englishman who lived most of his life in Japan, making his fortune from the marketing of cultured pearls, before his death in 1991.

The foundation is best known in the UK for supporting young people of exceptional promise in education and the arts, particularly the performing arts, by means of sponsorship and awards programmes (activities not covered in this book). It has also established the Jerwood Space, a drama and dance rehearsal complex with an art gallery in South London.

In November 1998 the foundation announced that it had begun funding capital projects, with a commitment of £7.2 million for this purpose; £4.2 million of this was committed; and was discussing detailed proposals for the remainder.

The foundation also sponsors and supports occasional activities in other fields, including medicine and overseas development, with a special interest in Nepal.

Generally, the foundation is highly pro-active, seeking out organisations with which to work. However the new UK charitable foundation will receive unsolicited applications, but these should be in tune with the nature of the foundation, as described in its own words below, from its Guidelines for Applicants and from its 1997 Annual Report.

The major new capital projects announced in 1998 were as follows:

- Natural History Museum, London: £900,000 for the Jerwood Gallery
- Trinity Hall, Cambridge: £1.4 million for the Jerwood Library.
- Witley Court, Worcester: Jerwood Sculpture Park.
- The Jerwood Space, Southwark, London.

The foundation is run by its Chairman, Alan Grieve, who was a personal business associate of John Jerwood and also his legal advisor.

The trust is expected to be registered by 31 December 1998 and will then have an independent board of trustees. The meeting dates and procedures will then be established. The foundation will also issue updated guidelines.

As this book was going to press, the foundation was reported to have offered £3 million to complete the funding for rebuilding the Royal Court Theatre in London. However a request that the new building should include the Jerwood name was causing resistance to the proposal.

General The Guidelines available in 1998 read as follows:

'The Jerwood foundation is a private foundation established in 1977 by the late John Jerwood. It is dedicated to imaginative and responsible funding and sponsorship of the arts, education, medicine, science, engineering and other fields of human endeavour, achievement and excellence.

'The foundation places particular emphasis on projects which assist the cultural and vocational education of young people between the ages of eighteen and thirty, and which will foster the development and recognition of their talents.

Funding policy

'In every case the foundation seeks to secure tangible and visible results from its grants and sponsorships. Influence and effect beyond the immediate recipient of a grant is encouraged. We aim to monitor the chosen projects closely and sympathetically, and are keen to see recognition of the foundation's support.

'The strategy is to support outstanding national institutions while at the same time being prepared to provide seed corn finance and financial support at the early stages of an initiative when other grant-making bodies might not be able or willing to act. The foundation may wish to be sole sponsor (subject to financial considerations) or to provide partnership funding.

'Although the foundation normally funds projects based within the United Kingdom, it will also consider applications from UK organisations working overseas.

'The foundation council believes that the foundation should not be merely the passive recipient of requests for grants but should identify areas to support and develop projects with potential beneficiaries.

Areas of special interest

'The Jerwood foundation has certain primary fields of interest, although these are constantly being reviewed and developed.

'In the performing arts the foundation has developed a particular role; the support and reward of young people who have demonstrated achievement and excellence, and who will benefit from a final lift to their careers. This special role is intended to open the way forward for young achievers and give them the opportunity to flourish.

The arts and heritage

'The foundation is a major sponsor of all areas of the arts. We are particularly interested in projects which involve rewards for excellence and the encouragement and recognition of outstanding talent and high standards, or which enable an organisation to become viable and self financing. In the visual arts, the Jerwood Painting Prize and the Jerwood Prizes for the Applied Arts draw attention to and reward the outstanding work being achieved by artists and makers in the United Kingdom.

'We rarely sponsor single performances or art events, such as festivals, nor do we make grants towards running costs of established arts organisations.

'The foundation is active in support for conservation of the artistic and architectural heritage. However, we do not make grants towards building restoration projects.

Education

'The foundation aims to support projects which are educational in the widest sense, and it has in the past sponsored educational projects and awards in many fields. Currently, preference is given to initiatives benefiting young people who have left school but are continuing their vocational educational development.

'We regret that we are unable to make grants to cover course fees for individuals. We do not contribute to fundraising appeals by individual schools or colleges, nor except in very rare instances will the foundation fund bursaries.

• *Medicine*

'Medicine is not a primary area for the foundation. However, support has been given to projects involving preventative medicine, health education for the young, international medical relief, and the development of specialist techniques for training in the identification and assessment of orthotic problems. In every case, the foundation requires to be assured that funding will result in tangible and visible benefits.

'We do not support pure medical research nor do we contribute to general appeals from hospital trusts, patient support groups, and local hospices.

• *Environment*

'The foundation is interested in supporting projects in the area of environmental conservation and education to increase environmental awareness.

Types of grants

'The foundation makes both revenue grants and capital donations on a 'one off' basis. There is a strong element of challenge funding whereby the foundation will make a grant provided the recipient can match it. The foundation will rarely commit to funding over a fixed number of years, yet will in many cases be prepared to maintain support if consistency and partnership will secure better results.

'Applications are made and assessed throughout the year. They are normally assessed by the foundation's staff, with the help of expert advisors where appropriate.

'Applications will be acknowledged. Decisions can normally be expected within four to six weeks and will be notified immediately. In view of the number of appeals we receive, detailed reasons for the rejection of an application are not generally given.'

In the Annual Report for 1997 the Chairman, Alan Grieve, wrote as follows:

'During 1997 the Jerwood foundation has continued to direct its resources to benefit exceptional young people in forming their lives and enabling them to

contribute their talents, energies and aspirations as an essential element in the fabric of our society. For the foundation I see this as realism rather than élitism, however difficult we find the selection of whom or what we support.

'The fulfilment of our concept to create The Jerwood Space as a unique centre for rehearsal and production facilities for young drama, dance and media groups, together with three galleries for emerging artists, is now well under way.

'Other major initiatives in 1997 have been: the Jerwood Painting Prize, which has continued to grow in stature; the Jerwood Prize for Applied Art which was awarded for textiles; and another highly successful Jerwood Season for New Playwrights with the Royal Court Theatre. New initiatives included sponsorship of the Britton-Pears Orchestra and of young composers working with the London Sinfonietta.

'I believe our ability to be innovative is demonstrated by the award scheme we have developed for bringing contemporary art into Anglican cathedrals. No statement from me at this juncture would be complete without reference to the hanging of our painting by Craigie Aitchison, Crucifixion 1994, in the Whichcote Chapel of King's College Chapel, which has made a profound contribution to this heritage location. Also in Cambridge, we have initiated a scheme with Kettle's Yard arts centre to restore the collection of paintings and prints which are loaned to students.

'Our special mission to Nepal has widened. Not only are we continuing to educate forty-six children of former Gurkha soldiers and build or rebuild schools in partnership with the Gurkha Welfare Trust, we have also, through the UK charity IMPACT, funded five ear nose and throat surgical camps in Nepal. We have entered into partnership with Student Partnership Worldwide to bring together British volunteers with young Nepalis to work at preserving the environment.

'We have promoted the National Association of Air Ambulance Services. With the Department of the Environment and David Wilson Homes Limited as co-sponsors, we have commissioned research into the public's attitude to new housing through the Popular Housing Forum, a Jerwood initiative. I believe these activities exemplify our willingness to promote important, but sometimes difficult or elusive issues.

'There is much talk of change, technological or otherwise, and dark

hints about the new millennium. I believe the Jerwood foundation must achieve a balance between enlightened support and sponsorship, and ensure good use of our money and resources. I feel this should be achieved with an understanding of the particular fields in which we operate and by placing confidence in the individuals and institutions with whom we work. Committees are usually the body corporate of the middle rather than the high ground and encourage layers of over-correct paperwork. Commentary and criticism, however clever, is a poor substitute for activity and action. I would wish the Jerwood foundation to be open-minded but decisive, staunch and prepared to lead as the late John Jerwood was in his role as soldier, merchant and benefactor.'

Examples of the foundation's work in 1997 include donations to:

Music: London Sinfonietta (part of the Sinfonietta's thirteenth anniversary concert); Dante Quartet (for underwriting the costs of the groups first CD); and Performing Arts Lab (support for PAL's Opera and Music Theatre Lab).

Art: Royal Botanic Gardens and the Royal College of Art (sponsorship of 'Hot House', a sculpture exhibition by graduates of the RCA) and the Jerwood Award for Art and Crafts in Cathedrals (allocation of £10,000 a year to commission works of art to beautify cathedrals).

Conservation: The Jerwood/MGC Conservation Award, winners in 1997 included the Science Museum, London and the Conservation Centre of the National Museums and Galleries of Merseyside.

Museums: The Jerwood/MGC Cataloguing Project (three year initiative to help museums catalogue their collection).

Dance: Royal Academy of Dancing, London (various student awards).

Drama: Motley Theatre Design Course (underwriting the costs of a dictionary of theatrical terminology).

Education: Oakham School, Rutland(scholarships and bursaries) and Sunningwell School of Art, Oxfordshire (grants for artists material).

International Initiatives: Gurkha Welfare Trust, Nepal (supported since 1993); Student Partnership Worldwide, Nepal (two year grant to bring young people from the UK to work as peer educators in poor communities) and IMPACT (grants to support surgical camps in Nepal).

Film and Television: National Film and Television School, Ealing (graduates of the documentary film makers' course received grants for their final films).

Literature: A grant to the Arvon Foundation (to enable it to run an important pilot project for talented young writers).

Science and Engineering: Salters' Jerwood Awards (prizes for chemistry and chemical engineering graduates) and the Royal Academy of Engineering (encourage outstanding men and women to choose engineering as a career).

UK Medical Charities: National Air Ambulance Association (support for an integrated organisation for air ambulances) and Medical Emergency Relief International, MERLIN (funding a director's post).

Social Welfare: Guardian Jerwood Awards, (awards to recognise excellence achieved by individuals within social or welfare charity).

Small Awards: No Frontiers; Oswestry Choral Society and the Pushkin Society (prizes for creative writing by Scottish children).

Exclusions Unless there are exceptional circumstances, the foundation will not consider applications on behalf of:

- individuals;
- buildings or capital costs (including purchase of equipment);
- projects in the field of religion or sport;
- animal rights or welfare;
- general fundraising appeals which are likely to have wide public appeal;
- appeals to establish endowment funds for charities;
- appeals for matching funding from National Lottery applications;
- grants for the running and core costs of voluntary bodies;
- projects which are of mainly local appeal;
- medical research without current clinical applications and benefits;
- social welfare, particularly where it may be considered a government or local authority responsibility.

Applications Applications should be by letter, outlining the aims and objectives of the organisation and the specific project for which assistance is sought. With the application we need:

- a detailed budget for the project, identifying administrative, management and central costs;
- details of funding already in place for the project, including any other trusts or sources which are or have been approached for funds;

- details of the management and staffing structure, including trustees;
- the most recent annual report and audited accounts of the organistion, together with current management accounts if relevant to the project.

As the foundation receives a large number of applications, we regret that it is not possible to have preliminary meetings to discuss possible support before a written application is made.

The application should be addressed to the secretary to the Foundation Council at the address above.

J G Joffe Charitable Trust

£421,000 (1996/97)

Overseas causes

Liddington Manor, The Street, Liddington, Swindon SN4 0HD

Correspondent Joel Joffe

Trustees Mrs V L Joffe; J G Joffe.

Beneficial area Almost exclusively the Third World.

Information available Very basic report and accounts with grants list showing only names of recipients and amounts received.

Summary The trust gives a small number of mid-size grants (typically £15,000) to registered charities almost always working for the development of Third World nations.

General The charity was set up by the settlor, Joel Joffe, the co-founder of Allied Dunbar and Chairman of OXFAM, along with fellow trustee Mrs Vanetta Joffe.

In 1996/97 the trust held assets of over £9 million which generated income of £360,000. Total donations in that year amounted to £421,000 and trust expenses to a further £28,000 (7% of donations or £1,000 per grant). In the charity's review the Trustees' Reported:

'Although the income of the charity declined from £433,965 to £359,826 the grants increased from £265,000 to £421,000 in accordance with a policy decision by the trustees to increase grants to a level of approximately £500,000 per annum.

'The main focus of the charity is upon the developing world, and in deciding upon grants the trustees are particularly

influenced by the quality of leadership of the organisations applying to the trust. Grants made are nearly always for development type activities.'

27 donations were made in 1996/97 (about twice as many as previous years), all but one to registered charities (Legal Aid Bureau, Johannesburg). Grant size ranged from £1,000 to £50,000 with 15 awards of between £10,000 and £20,000. The largest grant of £50,000 went to the Institute of Community Studies. The next highest were for £30,000 (OXFAM) and £26,000 (Saferworld). These last two groups and three others had also been supported in 1994-96.

Applications No applications will be considered or acknowledged.

The Elton John Aids Foundation

£641,000 (1997)

HIV/AIDS welfare and research

7 Kings Street Cloisters, Clifton Walk, London W6 0GY
Tel: 0181-846 9944

Correspondent Robert Key, Director

Trustees E H John; J Reid; A M Haydon; R J Key; J Scott; D Furnish; L Jackson.

Information available Accounts and reports, but no grants list, up to 1996/97 on file at the Charity Commission.

General The foundation was established in 1985 by Elton John, who remains a trustee. Its objectives are for 'supporting men, women, young adults, children, infants and entire families living with AIDS.' The foundation notes that it will also fund research and assist in the provision of medical care, drugs, equipment, facilities and services for the afore mentioned,

Income for 1996/97 was £618,000, made up mainly from donations. This funded grant making of £641,000. No grants list is supplied, despite the SORP requirement to the contrary, but a brief narrative states that major donations went to: 'a new out patient centre at Brighton Hospital, and for collaborating with a number of hospitals to increase the quality of hospital food so that patients can met the dietary requirements of new combination drugs.'

The Jones 1986 Charitable Trust

£1,049,000 (1996/97)

General, especially in Nottinghamshire

Eversheds, 1 Royal Standard Place,
Nottingham NG1 6FZ
Tel: 0115-950 7000

Correspondent Messrs Eversheds

Trustees J O Knight; R B Stringfellow.

Beneficial area UK, especially Nottinghamshire.

Information available Report and accounts with full grants list but with no further analysis of grants and grant-making.

Summary Currently around 50 grants are awarded in the year for a minimum of £1,000 and a maximum of about £200,000. The average grant is for just over £20,000. Most of the grants by value and number go to charities also supported in the previous year. Nearly all, or perhaps all, are based in Nottinghamshire. Beneficiaries come from most sectors of the charity world but there seems to be a preference for schools for the disabled, for other children's charities and for medical research.

General The trust was set up by Philip Locke Jones in 1986 without any endowment and receives most of its income from five family settlements.

Total income in 1996/97 was just under £1 million. Management and administration costs are very low.

Many local charities are 'well known to the trustees' and they will 'ignore' unsolicited applications. In light of this, charities seeking funding had better get themselves known to the trustees rather than appeal directly to the correspondent.

In 1996/97, 6 awards of £50,000 or more accounted for 43% of charitable expenditure and 13 ranging from £20,000 to £40,000 for 36%. 46% of the organisations supported in the year were also supported in both of the two previous years and 62% in just the previous year. The 20 new grants totalled £263,500. Of these, at least half went to children's charities or schools for the disabled.

The largest grant of the year was to Nottingham Health Authority (£187,000, £55,000 in 1995/96, £51,000 in 1994/

95). The biggest new donations were awarded to Portland College (£50,000), Long Eaton Sea Cadets (£35,000) and Nottingham High School (£30,000).

Other major grants in 1996/97 included £50,000 to Bluecoat School; £32,000 each to Nottingham Leukaemia Appeal and University of Nottingham Cancer Research; £25,000 to Yeoman Park School; and £22,000 to Nottinghamshire Probation Services Charity.

Exclusions No grants to individuals.

Applications The trustees identify their own target charities and do not wish to receive applications.

The Judge Charitable Foundation

£65,000 (1996/97, but see below)

General

Grange Farm, Elmbridge, Droitwich,
Worcestershire WR9 0DA
Tel: 01527-861204

Correspondent Sir Paul Judge

Trustees Sir Paul Judge; Lady Judge.

Beneficial area UK, with a local interest in Worcestershire.

Information available Accounts, without the required list of grants.

Summary Across the foundation's lifetime most charitable expenditure has been in grants made toward the Institute of Management Studies at Cambridge University but a variety of other organisations have received grants of up to £60,000.

General The foundation was established in 1992 by Sir Paul Judge who, by 1997, had gifted around £8 million to it. Most of these funds have been donated on to other charities rather than used to build up a capital base. However this may be changing – in 1996/97 the foundation received a donation of £985,000 but resources expended in the year totalled £65,000 (£64,000 in donations). This had the effect of increasing funds from £1.8 million (1995/96) to £2.8 million (1996/97).

The 1996/97 accounts have no grants list or narrative analysis of policy or grant making and the following chart 'analysing' charitable expenditure is the only light shed on the foundation's work:

	1997	1996
Education	£50,000	£1,146,000
Others	£14,000	£19,000

Before 1996/97, the great majority of funds went towards the development of the Institute of Management Studies at Cambridge University. Other grants have been to Worcester Cathedral Trust (£60,000 and £30,000), the Prince's Trust (two awards of £10,000) and Worcestershire Nature Conservation Trust (£12,000).

Exclusions No grants to individuals or medical causes.

Applications In writing to the correspondent.

The Anton Jurgens Charitable Trust

£304,000 (1996/97)

Welfare, general

c/o Saffery Champness, Fairfax House;
Fulwood Place, Grays Inn,
London WC1V 6UB
Tel: 0171-248 9898

Correspondent Ernest W Jowett

Trustees C V Jurgens (Chairman and Secretary); A H Jurgens (Treasurer); Miss B W Jurgens; E Deckers; M J Jurgens; F Jurgens.

Beneficial area UK.

Information available Accounts are on file at the Charity Commission, but without a narrative report.

General In 1996/97 the trust had assets of £6.5 million, generating an income of £299,000. Grant giving was £304,000 in over 50 grants and went to a variety of disability and social welfare groups. Grants ranged from £50,000 to £500 and averaged between £2,000 and £5,000. Just under half the grant giving was concentrated on three beneficiaries: Prince's Trust (£50,000); Fairbridge Mission (£50,000); St John, Berkshire – care in the community (£25,000).

Other beneficiaries included Woodland Trust (£15,000); Combat Stress (£12,500); Aidiss Trust (£10,000); The Treloar Trust (£10,000); Carpaid Trust (£5,000); Hope Nursery (£2,000); The Quaker Opportunity Group (£2,000); Handicapped Adventure Playground Association (£2,000.

Applications In writing to the correspondent.

The Stanley Kalms Foundation (formerly the Kalms Family Charitable Trust)

£291,000 (1996)

Jewish charities, general

c/o Titmuss Sainer Decheot, 2 Sarjeants Inn, London EC4Y 1LT

Correspondent Miss O Morgan

Trustees Stanley Kalms; Pamela Kalms; Stephen Kalms.

Beneficial area UK and overseas.

Information available Accounts up to 1996 were on file at the Charity Commission in September 1998. A list of grants is included but without a narrative report.

General Established in 1989, this charity states its objectives as the encouragement of Jewish education in the UK and Israel,. Other activities include support for the arts and media and other programmes, secular and religious.

Total assets of the charity amounted to £1.8 million in 1996, with incoming resources at £68,000. The annual report and accounts shows that 56 grants were given in 1996, totalling £291,000.

Grants were mainly to Jewish organisations (social and educational) with grants also going to the arts, education and health. Most of the grants were for less than £5,000, with the largest being for over £100,000 and the smallest for £1,000. About a quarter of the grants are repeated from previous years.

Examples of the larger beneficiaries include: Immanual College (£102,000), Institute for Policy Research (£25,000), Shalom Hartman Institute (£21,000), Ravenswood Foundation (£17,000), Community Security Trust (£12,500), Nightingale House (£12,500), Royal Opera House (£12,000), Institute for Jewish Policy Research (£11,000), Economic Education Trust (£10,000), and the Mencap Challenge Fund (£10,000).

Other smaller examples include British Friends of Art Museums in Israel (£4,000), Jewish Care (£2,000), Jewish

Marriage Council (£2,000), National Opera Studio (£1,000), Kings Diabetic Fund (£1,000) and the Kings Appeal (£1,000).

Applications In writing to the correspondent, but note that most of the trust's funds are committed to projects supported for a number of years.

The Karten Charitable Trust

£951,000 (1996/97)

Technology centres for disabled people, post-graduate scholarships

The Mill House, Newark Lane, Ripley, Surrey GU23 6DP
Tel: 01483-225 420; Fax: 01483 222420

Correspondent I H Karten

Trustees Ian H Karten; Mrs M E Karten; T M Simon.

Beneficial area Great Britain and Israel, with some special interest in the area local to its address, given above.

Information available Otherwise detailed and clear reports and accounts do not meet the Charity Commission requirements, as there are no lists of grants made. Usefully they clearly report the 'total return' on their endowment, as opposed simply to dividend income.

Summary This unusual and interesting trust, described in this book for the first time, runs three grants programmes, the chief among which is the funding of a network of adaptive computer technology centres (within established charities) for people with disabilities (£503,000). In addition it runs a general programme which donates to a range of 'qualifying institutions and charities' (£186,000). Finally, grants are also given for postgraduate students, a field not covered by this book (£262,000).

General The trust was founded in 1980 by the original donor, Ian Karten, who is still contributing towards its increasing endowment and dedicates his working week to managing the trust's operations. In 1996/97 it had a total return on its endowment of £2.6 million, mostly in the form of capital gains.

The trust has recently developed an exciting programme of creating, with partner organisations, a network of 'CTEC Centres'. To carry out this mission the trust has established a sister

organisation, the Karten Alpha CTEC Trust. The programme is described as follows in the 1996/97 report:

'A year ago the trustees decided to devote in future a substantial part of the trust's resources to the rehabilitation of severely disabled people by encouraging and providing funding for the establishment of special centres equipped with "adaptive computers". Specialist staff ... would, together with the client, produce an individual development plan for him or her. The Centres are to be known as CTEC Centres – Computer-aided vocational Training, Education and Communication.

'... the first Centre has been established and ... is located in the grounds of Ravenswood Village, Crowthorne.

'This first centre serves both the residents of Ravenswood, itself a residential unit for young people with learning disabilities, and clients from the local area who are referred to it by the social services or the NHS. Another two Centres were under construction, one in North London and one in Jerusalem.'

Later, in Summer 1998 the trust released further information:

'In order to make reasonably rapid progress in establishing a network of such centres, the policy of the trust after the first one has been to work in partnership with other charities concerned with people with disabilities. The trust identifies suitable charities and offers them generous funding for the establishment of a CTEC centre including initial costs, the total cost of the equipment and software programmes, and substantial contributions to the operating costs in the first two years. In return it requires an undertaking that the charity will continue to operate the centre for at least four more years, and that it will participate with the trust and other CTEC centres in an on-going exchange of experience and expertise. The trust also expects to fund research into novel ways to use adaptive computer technology to assist disabled people, and to make the results of this research available to all CTEC centres.'

Within the general programme, the trust made 251 donations totalling £186,000 to charities under the three headings:

Education	*(£92,000),*
Medical/rehabilitation	*(£41,000),*
Other	*(£28,000).*

The largest awards were made in the education category and went to Surrey University (£40,000 towards technology bursaries) and Southampton University (£30,000 for fellowships). There were ten medical/rehabilitation grants and these varied between £1,000 and £12,000 (the latter amount was to the Disability Aid Fund). At least 90% of 'Other' grant beneficiaries were Jewish organisations such as the Jewish National Fund (£15,000) and the Israel Free Loan Association (£3,000).

Potential applicants for general funds should take note of the following information given by the trust in 1998:

'Those interested in the CTEC programme should contact Mr Karten. During the next two years the trust's resources will be heavily committed to this programme and to its scholarship scheme. Appeals for endowments and other substantial grants are therefore unlikely to be successful. Appeals for smaller donations will be considered from charities already being supported by the trust and from other UK registered national and international charities, and from charities operating in London and Surrey.'

The present editor has long been urging trusts to take a more direct and proactive approach to the uses of their resources, so it is very welcome to find another trust developing an enterprising new programme of its own.

Exclusions The trust does not provide grants to individuals except within the framework of its scholarship programme. For details of eligibility criteria for scholarships apply to the trust.

Applications Those interested in the CTEC programme should contact Mr Karten. Applications for general grants should be sent in July or August only.

The Mendel Kaufman Charitable Trust

£444,000 (1993/94)

Jewish charities

c/o Cohen Arnold & Co, 13-17 New Burlington Place, Regent Street, London W1X 2JP
Tel: 0171-734 1362

Correspondent Cohen Arnold & Co

Trustees Z M Kaufman; I I Kaufman; J Kaufman.

Beneficial area UK, especially the North East of England.

Information available Accounts up to 1993/94 only were on file at the Charity Commission in September 1998 and even then without a list of grants.

General The last set of accounts available for this trust are those for 1993/94 which were audited only in April 1996. As usual, they are skeletal, with no notes nor a list of grants. The following is reprinted from the previous edition:

'The trust supports Jewish organisations, with a preference for the North East of England, especially the Gateshead area. In 1993/94 the trust had assets of nearly £3 million, but this value includes all its investments at cost instead of at market value. One of the liabilities of the trust is a loan for over £1 million, but with no explanation in the accounts about its purpose. This loan accounts in part for the high administration expenses (19% of income) which included £111,000 for bank charges and interest.

'The trust had an income of £604,000 in 1993/94 generated mainly from property revenue (£401,000) and donations received (£122,000). A total of £444,000 was distributed in grants, lower than the total in 1992/93 (£509,000). There is no known reason why this trust should not disclose any information about its charitable activities.'

Applications In writing to the correspondent.

The Kay Kendall Leukaemia Fund

£1,601,000 (approved, 1997/98)

Research into Leukaemia

See entry for the 'Sainsbury Family Charitable Trusts'
Tel: 0171-410 0330

Correspondent Michael Pattison

Trustees Simon Sainsbury; Miss J Portrait; A O B Riviere.

Beneficial area Primarily UK.

Information available Report and accounts on file at the Charity Commission. The principal officers are Michael Pattison, the director, Paul Spokes, the finance director and Miss E Storer, trust secretary.

General This trust is one of the Sainsbury Family Charitable Trusts

which share a joint administration.

The trust only funds research into Leukaemia. Its net income for 1997/98 was £1.8 million and a total of £2.34 million was available for distribution. The asset value of the trust rose by nearly £16 million to £58.24 million during the year to April 1998.

In 1997/98 the fund approved a total of £1.6 million in grants (compared with over £3 million the previous year).

The trustees' advisers are: Professor John Goldman, Chairman, Professor Mel Greaves and Dr Tony Green.

The fund outlines its policy and guidelines for awarding grants with its accounts. These may be obtained in full from the fund. It is prepared to consider proposals from both UK and non-UK based organisations but those from the latter must involve some degree of collaboration with UK colleagues. Capital requests and large single items of equipment are considered. Research grants are normally awarded for five years with initial support for three years and support for the final period subject to a progress review.

Eight institutions – hospitals, medical schools, universities and research institutes – were supported in 1997/98 with a total of 14 awards. Major allocations were made to Christie Hospital Manchester (£634,000 in 2 awards), St Mary's Hospital Manchester (£337,819 in 2 awards) and the Royal Free Hospital London (£324,529 in 5 awards). This compares with total of 16 institutions supported in 1996/97 with a total of 32 awards. The major allocations in 1996/97 were made to the Royal Free Hospital, London (£424,330 in 6 awards), MRC Laboratory, Cambridge (£291,000 over 3 years) and the University of Sussex (£212,400 over 3 years).

In 1996/97 the special fellowship fund set up by the trust, the KKLF Research Fellowships, was allocated £1.2 million (£400,000 over 3 years) to maintain its support.

Exclusions Clinical trials, project grant proposals and other small requests are not normally eligible, neither are circular appeals.

Applications The trustees met twice during the year to consider applications. See the entry for the Sainsbury Family Charitable Trusts for the address and further advice.

The Peter Kershaw Trust

£357,000 (1997/98)

Medical research, education, general.

Higher Town Farmhouse, 4 Warwick Close, Knutsford, Cheshire WA16 8NA

Correspondent Mr G J Wallwork, Secretary

Trustees P Kershaw; H F Kershaw; B B Pugh; M L Rushbrooke; R P Kershaw; H W Thompson

Beneficial area Manchester and the surrounding district only

Information available Report and accounts on file at the Charity Commission.

General 'The principal activities of the trust continue to be those of funding medical research, grants to medical and other institutions and to schools in respect of bursaries.'

In 1997/98 assets with a market value £7.5 million generated an income of £329,000. Grant giving of £357,000 was awarded in 27 grants.

Donations were distributed as follows:

Medical institutions	£59,584
Other donations	£236,501
Medical research	£28,795
School fees	£32,350

The largest grants were given to Wrightington Hospital (£48,000 in two grants); David Lewis Appeal (£35,000); The Big Step (£30,000); Lifeshare (£25,000); and £20,000 each to the Booth Drop-In Centre and the George House Trust (£20,000); Withington Girls School (£16,000) and the Family Welfare Association (£15,000).

Exclusions No grants to individuals.

Applications In writing to the correspondent.

King George's Fund for Sailors

£2,910,000 (1997)

The welfare of seafarers

8 Hatherley Street, London SW1P 2YY
Tel: 0171-932 0000;
Fax: 0171-932 0095

Correspondent Captain Martin Appleton, Director-General

Trustees The General Council. Admiral Sir Brian Brown, Chairman; Captain A D Braithwaite, Deputy Chairman.

Beneficial area UK and Commonwealth.

Information available Good annual report and accounts available from the fund and on file at the Charity Commission.

Summary Grants, often recurrent, for a very wide but little changing range of charities for the benefit of seafarers. Grants range from a few hundred pounds to several hundred thousand.

General The fund was set up in 1917 as a central fundraising organisation to support other institutions for the benefit of seafarers. It has a large fund-raising operation, with a network of area committees, though most of its income now comes from the interest and dividends on its investments.

Grant making in 1997

While about nine out of ten organisations appear regularly in the grants lists from year to year, amounts can vary substantially, and it seems likely that the fund will make special awards to help with major capital programmes, in addition to its more regular subventions.

The funds grants were categorised as follows (with 1996 awards in brackets):

Hospitals, rest homes, rehabilitation centres, homes for the aged etc: £648,000 in 31 grants.

The largest grant, £100,000 (£20,000), was to the Erskine Hospital in Renfrewshire. Other major beneficiaries were St Dunstans, £50,000 (£60,000), and the Royal Alfred Seafarers' Society, Banstead and Eastbourne, hospital and homes for seafarers, £45,000 (£45,000).

Children's Homes, training ships, schools, scholarships and bursaries: £607,000 in 20 grants ranging from £1,000 to £340,000.

The outstanding grant was given to the RN and RM Children's Trust, for seafarers dependents, £340,000 (£310,000) followed by the Royal Merchant Navy School Foundation £70,000 (£70,000), ANED the Sea Cadet Corps £56,000 (£45,000).

Funds supporting needy seafarers or their dependents: £1,423,000 in 28 grants.

The major beneficiary is the Shipwrecked Fishermen & Mariners'

Royal Benevolent Society, £466,000 in two grants (£494,000), followed by the Royal Navy Benevolent Trust, £310,000 (£308,000).

Missions, clubs, societies and associations: £219,000 in 10 grants.

The largest grants were given to the Royal National Mission to Deep Sea Fishermen, £78,000, and to the Seamen's Mission, London: Queen Victoria Seamen's Rest, £52,000.

Fund raising costs

Previous editions of this book have commented with dismay on the very high fund raising costs of the charity. However only a minor part of its income comes from these activities. There was an endowment worth £42 million in 1997 which generated an income of £1.7 million. There were also a further £7.4 million of unrealised capital gains. If the charity chose to base its expenditure on the value of the total return on its endowment, over time, (as is the practice of many trusts in this book) it could probably maintain indefinitely its present level of charitable expenditure in real terms, without any of the present fund raising activity.

1996 was another disastrous fundraising year, with the charity spending £700,000 to raise just £668,000 in voluntary income, plus a further £346,000 in legacies. Even including the latter, this means that of every pound raised, 69p was spent on fund raising costs. Fortunately there was a substantial improvement in 1997. Voluntary income rose to £1,243,000 with a special one-off 'YOTS' appeal, and there was a surge in legacies to £875,000. The net result was that fundraising costs came down to 31p for every pound raised. Hopefully this downwards trend can be continued in the future.

Nevertheless the fact remains that, over a three year period, fundraising costs have averaged 46p for every pound raised. It is the view of these editors that unless this figure can be permanently reduced by a very substantial amount, say half, the charity should close down its fundraising activities and rely solely on the income from its substantial endowment and from the legacies that would doubtless continue to arrive, if on a reduced scale.

Such a policy would only reduce the net income of the charity by about 15% to 20%, even without the realisation of any capital growth, and it would become a more seemly operation.

The charity correctly points out that its traditional support base is declining because of the major run down in the numbers serving at sea, and that meanwhile the very large numbers of those who served at sea in the last war are getting much older and need more and more support. Nevertheless these editors feel that the fund's creditable efforts to increase income from its existing constituency have now been sufficiently tested, but without enough reward to justify their continuation.

Exclusions The fund does not make any grants direct to individuals but rather helps other organisations which do this. However the fund may be able to advise in particular cases about a suitable organisation to approach. Full details of such organisations are to be found in the Guide to Grants for Individuals in Need.

Applications Applications from organisations should be addressed to the Director Finance and Grants. Trustees meet in July and November.

The King's Fund (King Edward's Hospital Fund for London)

£1,844,000 (1998)

Health and health care

11-13 Cavendish Square,
London W1M 0AN
Tel: 0171-307 2495; Fax: 0171-307 2801;
E-mail: grants@kehf.org.uk

Correspondent Susan Elizabeth, Grants Director

Trustees The Management Committee under the authority of the President and General Council, including Sir Graham Hart, Chairman.

Beneficial area London.

Information available Annual report and accounts with full grants list and narrative analysis; clear and detailed guidelines for applicants (reprinted below).

Summary The fund makes about 120 grants a year ranging from £300 to £80,000. Both voluntary and statutory sector organisations are supported under three programmes:

- 'Programme' (major) grants;
- 'Development' (main) grants;
- 'Stimulus' (small) grants.

'Although the funding priorities within programmes change over time, they are

all aimed at improving public health care, with a general emphasis on innovative and potentially influential projects. Awards are also are given to support individual health care professionals for specific endeavours related to their work.'

General The fund was established in 1897 by King Edward VII (who was Prince of Wales at the time) to support the improvement of health care in London. Today it fulfils this mission not only via grantmaking (accounting for just 10% of the overall budget) but also through running various other operations. In 1997 these were: a Management College (30% of total expenditure), a Development Centre (25%); Organisational audit (15%); Policy Institute (8%); London Commission (1%); and Centenary project (2%). This entry concentrates solely on the grants programme.

The fund produces detailed and informative guidelines for applicants and those for 1998-2000 are reproduced below. The great bulk of the information is about the development grants programme, from which most grant expenditure (more than 80%) is disbursed (where relevant, we have added further information about 1997 grants in brackets):

'At present our grants committee gives about £2 million each year in grants. Grants are made to a wide variety of organisations in the health sector, both statutory and voluntary. In all cases grant applications must show how the work will affect either the provision or the commissioning of health services in London.

Programme grants (£500,000): 'Each year the grants committee makes a substantial investment in a grant programme which addresses a particular theme identified by the fund. In addition to grant monies, we will usually provide educational development support throughout the programme, and commission an independent evaluation of the work. Programme themes are advertised each year, inviting bids to join the programme. Unsolicited applications will not be considered.' (The grant in 1997 and 1998 went for Mental Health in London (£1,000,000).

Development grants (40 grants totalling £1,580,000): 'Most of these are given for work in priority areas identified below by our grants committee.'

Guidelines for development grants

'What we look for when we judge an application:

- Will it improve London's healthcare? Applications must show that their project will either improve either the health of Londoners or the development of London's health services.
- Is it promoting fairness in health care? We are keen to support vulnerable or disadvantaged groups that need our help, including minority ethnic communities.
- Will it involve health service users? Applications must show that they have the interests of health service users at heart. They must be able to describe how they will involve or consult people who will benefit from the work.
- Will it be clear whether it works? Applications must show plans to monitor the results of the work against their aims and objectives, and demonstrate how the work will be evaluated.
- Will others be able to learn from this work. Applications must show how learning from the project will be shared.
- Does it support equal opportunities? We are committed to equal opportunities for everyone. We expect organisations to show the same commitment in their employment practices and in how they run their services.

'Within these criteria preference will generally be given to projects which:

- demonstrate a new approach, or a new way of thinking;
- seem likely to influence policy and practice elsewhere;
- are of more than local significance.'

Projects that encourage equal access to health care (13 grants, £448,000)

'London has a very mixed population and a high concentration of vulnerable or disadvantaged people who need health care. London has more elderly people, more one-parent families, more refugees and more homeless people than any other part of the country. There are also large minority ethnic communities who do not get the health care they should. Health services find it difficult to overcome barriers caused by cultural and language differences, and to identify new ways to help people who have special needs.

'We look for applications that:

- will make it possible for minority ethnic communities to express what their health needs are, and set up new services to meet those needs. Within this priority the committee has a specific interest in the health needs of refugee communities, particularly those that have been settled in the UK for less than ten

years. We will give preference to applications from organisations which:
- are user run;
- can show how they have assessed the need for a health project;
- can demonstrate that they have established contact with mainstream health services.
- address the health needs of homeless people, including refugees and asylum seekers;
- will work to open up existing health service to patients from a range of disadvantaged groups, including minority ethnic communities, homeless people and people with disabilities.' (Examples of 1997 grants are: Afiya, £50,000; Beckton Community Health Project, £53,000; Centre for Armenian Information and Advice, £26,000; Foundation for the Study of Infant Deaths, £43,000; HM Prison Service, £50,000; SANE, £46,000; Uplift Ltd, £25,000.)

Projects that will strengthen the voice of the user (7 grants £313,000)

'The fund believes that the people who use London's health services must be involved in decisions about the future of those services. It is important that:

- users and patients are consulted and listened to;
- groups who are experienced or disadvantaged in relation to the statutory health service are included in consultations in an effective way;
- genuine agreement is built up between the different groups of patients, the health and local authorities who manage the resources, and the GPs, hospital and social work staff who provide service costs.

'We look for applications that:

- will help service users to express their priorities and to take part in local planning services. We are looking for examples of good practice, which can be used by others for a guide. For this reason, we prefer applications with a strong emphasis on assessing how effective they have been;
- will strengthen the voluntary health sector by:
  - setting up new organisations that will offer information, self-help or advocacy support to users of health services, usually where no similar organisation exists; or
  - helping existing voluntary organisations to express users' views more effectively.' (Bloomsbury Community Health Council, £46,000; British Lung Foundation £52,000;

Carers National Association, £29,000; Hackney Patients Council, £40,000; Women in Special Hospitals, £15,000.)

Projects that link the arts and health (2 grants, £41,000)

'In recent years there has been a growing interest in holistic approach to health. While the traditional approach to health looks at the individual and their illness, the holistic approach looks at the whole person and at their relationships within the family, the community and the environment. Within the holistic approach, there is growing evidence that the arts can improve health, both in individuals and in the wider community.

'We have limited sums available for applications that want to show the impact of arts on better health.

'We look for applications that:

- will explore, or show, how art and design can create positive surroundings for effective health care;
- will use the creative arts to improve the health of individuals or communities.'

(Art in Hospitals Forum, £16,000; Public Art Development Trust, £25,000)

Improving the patients' experience: easing the transition across service boundaries (new programme)

'People with long-term illness or disability do not fit neatly into health and social care categories. To maintain a good quality of life they are likely to need support from different parts of the health care system (GPs, hospitals, community services); from local authority services such as housing, day care and domiciliary services; and from voluntary sector organisations providing advice, support or direct services. However, despite the hard work and good intentions of many people in many agencies, "the system" often fails to function as well as the parts. Efforts to create flexible and individually appropriate "packages of care" have been dogged by a range of organisational problems:

- the different funding regimes of health care and social services;
- funding patterns lagging behind the changing patterns of hospital use and growing emphasis on community based services;
- difficulties of establishing effective methods of inter-agency collaboration;
- entrenched professional divisions or rivalries;
- the complexity of managing chronic

illness or disability.

'Our concern is to develop responsive, flexible services which allow people with long-term illness or disability to move through the social and health care systems with the minimum of difficulty and to receive the services which ensure the best possible quality of life.

'Our emphasis is on supporting processes of change, rather than one-off projects. We believe that this has the most likelihood of achieving lasting improvement in existing services. Support from the fund will be offered in the form of the grant, plus constancy help to support the process of change. The exact nature of this support will be agreed with applicants, following discussion.

'We invite bids for funds to support the process of achieving change across traditional service, or sector, boundaries. Examples might include pilot studies of new ways of working between existing services, joint appointments across services or the creation of new, integrated services. Applications need to show:

- a commitment to practical improvements in the delivery, or commissioning of services for people with a long-term disability or illness;
- a clear statement of the difficulties to be overcome;
- an appreciation of the role which organisational development support could have in achieving change;
- evidence of a senior level commitment from a partnership, or consortium of agencies or professional groupings;
- involvement of service users in the process of change;
- willingness to share learning from the process with other agencies or professional groups.

Open Category

'We are always aware that we must be ready to support projects that will deal with new or unexpected health needs as they arise. We will look at applications that do not come under one of the above headings, but they must meet our general conditions for grants and the following conditions:

- the project must be work new to the UK;
- the application must be able to show that it will have practical results for either the provision of the commissioning of health services;
- the application must prove that the work cannot take place without our support.'

(Breast Cancer Care, £11,000; Enuresis Resource and Information Centre, £27,000; Health Service Journal, £23,000; National Food Alliance, £25,000; Nigel Clare Network Trust, £16,000; Post-adoption Centre, £53,000; She UK, £5,500.)

How to apply for a development grant

'Please read all the following notes carefully. We have written them to help you with your application, and to make sure you have included all the information we need.

'It is important that you ask for what you need. Do not assume that an under-budgeted application is more likely to be successful. However, the largest development grant awarded in the past three years was £80,000. If you are applying for a large and expensive project, you will probably need to find partner funders, and give details of who you have approached or intend to approach for this.

'We are willing to give grants to both voluntary and statutory organisations.

'Statutory organisations applying for a grant must show that the work cannot take place without our support. They must also explain why they cannot get money from statutory sources or, if they can, show that it would not be enough to pay for the work. In some cases, statutory organisations can improve their chances of success if they can show that they are working in partnership with a voluntary organisation.

'In general, very new or small voluntary organisations (such as those with no paid staff and income under £10,000) are unlikely to be awarded development grants. These organisations may want to apply for a stimulus grant. From our point of view, this is a good way for us to begin to get to know new organisations.

'We do not support clinical research. We will look at research projects that are in our priority areas as long as they can show how the results of the research will be shared with other organisations, and can be used to improve health services. In general we are keen to support projects that will:

- evaluate new approaches to, and new types of, health care;
- share their research findings to bring about change;
- use the results of research to develop new health services.

'We will only consider small research projects, or small contributions to large research projects. We are unlikely to give more than £25,000. We will not pay for

overhead costs of academic institutions or for the purchase of computer hardware. We will not consider applications unless they include a clear plan for how the work will be used to influence health service provision.

Stimulus grants (65 awards amounting to £131,000).

'These are small grants, given to support the setting-up of new health projects targeting disadvantaged groups or to encourage the exploration and sharing of new ideas in the health field, via publications, conferences and networking. The biggest grant under this scheme is £5,000, but most grants are for much less than the maximum.'

(1997 awards included the following: Action for Irish Youth, £2,000; The Befriending Network, £750; Cancer Black Care, £2,000; Ealing Travellers Project, £2,500; Female Prisoners Welfare Project, £4,800; Health Action for Homeless People, £5,000; Medicinema, £3,400; National Back Pain Association, £1,000; The Patient's Association, £3,000; Refugee Support Centre, £3,000; St John's Hospice, £1,500; Transcultural Psychiatry Association, £1,000; YTouring, £5,000.)

Educational bursaries (£52,000)

'These bursaries are for qualified nurses or professionals allied to medicine who work in the London area bounded by the M25.

Travelling fellowships (£39,000)

'The King's Fund offers a limited number of fellowships to medical practitioners seeking to widen their professional post-graduate experience at a centre of specialist medical practice overseas. Applicants should currently be engaged in, and intend to return to, medical practice within the London area bounded by the M25 motorway.

Director's Report 1997

'In many respects, 1997 can be looked back on as the year in which the fund's grant making since 1993 came to maturity.

'Two major grants programmes (*now called Programme grants, Ed.*) were in operation during the year. Our investigation of citizens' juries in health authorities (£50,000) went "live" at the start of the year and fieldwork in the three selected health authorities continued until Easter. The summer was spent in active reflection on the work among the project team and the autumn in preparing a book *Ordinary Wisdom: reflections on an experiment in citizenship and health*. The independent

evaluation commissioned from the Health Services Management Centre at the University of Birmingham continued throughout the year, with both publications due to come out in spring 1998. Our major grant programme on health and homelessness completed its development phase and the project "Under one roof", an innovative one-stop approach to the needs of homeless people in South London, was chosen to receive a grant for implementation, over a period of two years. By the end of the year a project coordinator had been appointed, operational preparations were under way and an official launch at the end of February 1998 was being prepared.

'At the same time that these two programmes were active, discussions were on-going about how to shape the committee's 1997 major grant programme on Mental Health in London (£450,000), within the context of a wider programme of work on mental health across the fund.

'Within our main grants programme (renamed "development grants") we completed a review of the five priority themes. This led to the replacement of two earlier themes (Developments in primary and community care, and Improving the quality of London's acute health services) with a new theme, Improving the Patient's Experience: easing the transitions across service boundaries, which recognises that really entrenched difficulties lie at the interfaces between services, sectors and professional groupings.

The key trends to note are:

- Equal access to health care accounted for the largest proportion of the main grants programme, for the further year running. At 41% of the total (of development grants), it had increased substantially from 1996, when it had accounted for 28% of the total, but did not match the 1995 peak of 48%.
- Strengthening the voice of the user remained a strong theme, accounting for 21% of the grants allocated. This has been a broadly consistent level of activity since 1994.
- Arts in health grants accounted for only 4% of the total this year, a decline from the previous year's peak of 10%
- Developments in primary and community care, and Improving the quality of London's acute health services together received only 13% of funds allocated. This reflects that 1997 was a year of transition in which we were seeking to close our commitment to these two themes and

bring a new priority theme on stream in their place.

- The open category remained buoyant, accounting for 21% of the sums allocated, a small rise on the previous year (19%).

'The small grants programme (now called "stimulus grants") came under increasing pressure for funds as the year progressed, evidence that it is becoming better known among its target audience – a fact which is borne out by the 70% increase in applications received since the scheme was reviewed and revised in 1995. Our two educational grants programmes, Travelling Fellowships and Educational Bursaries, consolidated after changes in their operation in the proceeding two years. The Travelling Fellowships panel held their first evening forum, providing an opportunity for past and aspiring fellowship holders to meet and share their experiences.

'The Educational Bursaries panel held their first advisory seminar for applicants for the five larger bursaries which are offered each year and which have a research focus. It was generally agreed that the offer of one-to-one advice had substantially improved the quality of applications which eventually came before the panel.

'An important new initiative for the department in 1997 was our collaboration with SmithKline Beecham, to develop, launch and manage the Community Health IMPACT Awards, a national scheme recognising excellence on the part of small to medium sized voluntary organisations working in health.

Exclusions

- Medical or clinical research;
- General appeals;
- Long term funding (our maximum length of funding is three years);
- Capital projects (buildings and equipment, including medical equipment);
- Holidays and outings;
- Individuals;
- Local projects based outside London;
- Projects were the work has already started;
- Projects that are seeking on-going funding after a statutory grant has run out;
- Vehicles.

Applications Applications need to be received at least three months before the meeting at which they will be considered.

The fund's guidelines read as follows:

'We give here a general guide to help you with your application. If your application does not cover all of these points properly, we will have to contact you for more information. This will delay the decision on your application.

'Please make your application clear and to the point. Try not to use jargon because the committee members may not be experts in your field. All applications must meet our general conditions, and your work must fall within one of our priorities.

'Put your case using no more than six sides of A4 paper. Please also send a budget, a work plan and a job description for any job you are asking us to fund.

'We cannot accept faxed or e-mailed applications.

'Please give a brief description of your organisation including:

- its aims, legal status, charity number (if you have one), size and history;
- how it funds its work;
- whether you have applied to us before.

'The background to the problem you want to tackle:

- Why is your project needed?
- What are the causes of the problem?
- Are you building on earlier work, done by your organisations or others?
- How will you avoid overlap with other organisations?

The Project:

- What are the aims of the project?
- What are your objectives and targets (i.e. how will you achieve your aims)?
- How will the work be supervised and managed?
- What is your organisation's track record in this field, and why are you the right organisation to undertake this project?

The cost:

- How much are you asking for from the King's Fund?
- What is it for? (is it for a salary, a publication, an event?)

The timescales:

'You must tell us when you want the project to start, and how long it will run (remember to apply at least four months before you plan to start the project).

Monitoring and Evaluation

'We believe monitoring the project and evaluating its success are extremely important and you should tell us what plans you have for monitoring and evaluation. The following summary may

help you:

'Monitoring means collecting information to see what progress you are making. It may include:

- keeping a record of the facts and figures about your work;
- asking users what they think of your work;
- getting progress reports from the people managing, or working in the project;
- organising meetings of the project team to discuss the work, and any problems, successes or new developments, and:
- checking that you are getting and giving value for money.

'Evaluation means using the information you have collected from your monitoring to see what you can learn from the work so far. For instance:

- Have your methods been successful in doing what you set out to do?
- How does your approach compare with other ways of tackling the problem?
- What have you learnt about how to develop this kind of work, in relation to your staff, clients, or other organisations?
- Have you learnt anything that might help future projects?

Sharing the lessons you learn

'We believe that if you learn important lessons in the course of your work, it is very important that you share this information with other people working in the same field. You should include in your application your plans for sharing what you learn from the work. This is especially important if you are applying for a grant for a research project.

Job description

'If you are asking us to fund the salary for a post, you should include a full job description, which shows salary scale and details of who will oversee the post.

Work Plan

'It is helpful for us to see an outline work plan for at least the first year of the project, showing what you hope to achieve by certain points in time. This need not be more than one side of A4.

Your budget and accounts

'Please read this section carefully.

'Your budget should be on a separate page at the end of the application.

'It must include:

- the full cost of the project;
- the exact amount you are asking for;
- details of how you arrive at that figure.

'We will also need to know:

- What other income you will have from this work, if any. Please tell us about firm commitments of money as well as those that you are exploring. If you are not asking for the full cost of the project, please tell us how you intend to raise the rest.
- How you expect to pay for the future work once the grant is finished.
- What money you are likely to raise from any work that will be paid for by the grant. This is particularly important if you are asking for a grant towards a publication or event.
- If you are applying from a statutory organisation, we need to know what statutory sources of funds you have applied to, and what the results were.
- If you are applying for a salary, you can also include recruitment costs, and inflation costs, if you are asking for a salary of more that one year.
- You can also include suitable overheads in your calculations. In general, the maximum amount we will consider for overheads is 25% of any salary. This figure would include all employer's contributions, management costs and running costs (i.e. heat, light, telephone and rent). This figure would not have to include direct project costs (the additional funds needed to run the project, such as producing literature and running events). In all cases you must show how you have worked out all the costs shown in the budget.

'We cannot consider your application unless you send it with a copy of your most recent audited accounts.

'If your organisation has a gross income under £100,000, then we will accept an independent examination of the accounts, but this examination must be undertaken by a qualified accountant who is a member of one of the five main recognised supervisory bodies in the UK. However, we reserve the right to request audited accounts in certain circumstances. Please contact the grants department if you need to discuss this further. If no accounts are available because your organisation has been formed recently please explain this in your application letter, and send a budget for the organisation.

Extra literature

'Please do not send any any extra literature, such as brochures or press articles, unless we ask for them. If you think there is something important in the literature tell us about it in your applica-

tion.

Checklist

'Before you send in your application, please make sure that you have included:

- your written application, with a covering letter on your organisation's headed paper. Please make sure that this letter is signed, and gives the grant applicants contact details, and a direct dial telephone number if one is available;
- a budget;
- a work plan;
- a job description, if you are asking us to fund a post;
- your organisation's most recent accounts and annual report.

How we will deal with your application.

'If the kind of work that you want to do is not what we normally make grants for, we will write to you as soon as possible to tell you that we cannot help – usually within four weeks. If we do normally make grants for the kind of work that you want to do, our staff will look into your application more closely. This may involve meeting with you, and asking for confidential external advice. This helps the grants committee to learn more about your work, but it does not guarantee that a grant will be made.

'Applications for the development grants programme are considered five times a year, in February, May, July, September and November, but they need to be submitted at least three months before the meeting concerned, and at least four months before the project starts. Usually you can apply only once a year, but you can apply more than once if your applications are for different projects.

'Applications for the stimulus grants programme are considered at the end of each month with the exception of August and December. Applications need to be received at least six weeks before the meeting concerned.

'*Educational Bursaries and Travelling Fellowships:* The travelling fellowships panel meets in May and November, and the scheme is advertised in the Lancet and the BMJ in March and September. Details of the educational bursaries scheme are advertised in March in the Nursing Times and Health Service Journal and the bursary panel meets in June.

'For further information on these please send an A4 stamped envelope marked 'Educational Bursaries' or 'Travelling Fellowships' to the grants department.'

The fund says 'Before you send in your application, you may want to contact our grants department if:

- you are not sure if your work fits into one of our priority areas; or
- you need help to put your application together.'

This is followed by a plea, which would probably be echoed by many trusts in this book, not to ring after the application has been submitted to ask how it is getting on!

The Mary Kinross Charitable Trust

£1,212,000 (1998/99) but see below

Mental health

36 Grove Avenue, Moseley, Birmingham B13 9RY

Correspondent: Fiona Adams

Trustees Elizabeth Shields, Chairwoman; Fiona Adams; H Jon Foulds; Robert McDougall; John Walker-Haworth; Peter Wreford.

Beneficial area UK.

Information available Reports and accounts with full grants list and narrative exploring large grants.

Summary The trust makes about 30 grants a year, usually between £300 and £50,000, although they can be as high as £1 million or more. A wide range of charities are supported but the great majority of funds go to those working in mental health or penal matters. Donations may be given on a one-off basis or over several years towards capital or revenue costs. Beneficiaries are usually based in London/South East or Birmingham/West Midlands.

General In 1996/97 the trust's assets totalled more than £18 million and income was £578,000. Charitable expenditure changes dramatically from year to year. For example it went from £213,000 (1994/95) to £1,373,000 (1995/96), then down to £686,000 (1996/97) and £275,000 (1997/98). At the time of writing the trust had future commitments totalling £1,212,000 in 1998/99 and £94,000 in 1999/2000.

Although the trust gives awards of all sizes, most of the money is disbursed in a few large grants to carefully selected charities. In 1995/96 a single grant of

£1 million accounted for 82% of the total grants value and 50% of the remaining funds were used for 4 awards of £20,000 or more.

The trust has made two outstanding grants of £1,144,000 (1996) and £1,000,000 (1998/99) to the Brain Research Trust. Together, these awards accounted for 60% of charitable expenditure from 1995/96 to 1998/99.

Breakdown of grants in 1997/98:

Penal affairs	12	£88,000	32%
Youth	4	£80,000	29%
Mental health	5	£67,000	24%
Miscellaneous	11	£35,000	13%
Medical research	1	£5,000	2%
Total	33	£275,000	100%

Annual Report 1996/97

The trustees' report of 1996/97 says:

Policy 'Trustees wish to continue the policy of the founder – to use the trust income to support a few carefully researched projects rather than make many small grants. At least one trustee takes responsibility for ensuring the trust's close involvement with organisations to which major grants are made.

'During the year trustees have concentrated grants in the areas of mental health and penal affairs and are considering further projects which aim to prevent young people from entering or continuing a life of crime and delinquency.

'For the organisations we support we are able to pay core office costs which often enable staff to apply to other sources of funding. Unfortunately we have to disappoint the great majority of applicants who nevertheless continue to send appeal letters. Trustees do not welcome telephone calls from applicants soliciting funds.

The report continues with details of some of its grants:

Mental Health 'National Schizophrenia Fellowship (£36,250). We made a further donation of £35,000 towards the core running costs of the London and South East Region (LASER).

'£1,250 represents the first payment to an independent consultant who is researching and writing a report on the development of LASER from 1992 to 1997. The trust has made a major contribution to LASER's work and we wanted to record and evaluate the multiple benefits that have resulted from making a substantial investment in this small development team.

Penal Affairs 'NACRO (£82,561). This grant has been made to support a pilot victim/offender mediation and conferencing project which NACRO is setting up in Hackney with backing from the Inner London Probation Service and Hackney Social Services.

'Prison Reform Trust (£16,000 p,a. for each of two years). Having made a grant last year to assist with a special fundraising effort, Trustees decided to offer a continuation of this funding for a further two years.

Safe Ground (£5,000 p.a. for each of three years). This grant is to support Safe Ground's theatrical work in prisons and schools co-ordinating interchange between the two different types of institution after groups from each one have worked on the same material. Recent work had involved drugs awareness and truancy projects.

'Society Of Voluntary Associates (£7,000 p.a. for each of two years) We are one of the trusts contributing to a basic education project at Feltham YOI. The project employs two coordinators to recruit and train volunteers who teach basic literacy and numeracy on a one to one basis to some sentenced prisoners as well as to some who are on remand.

'Urban Adventure Support Group (£23,000) This grant supported the work of the West Midlands Police officers who have set up a charity to enable them to help young people deemed at risk of being drawn into antisocial or offending behaviour, or at risk of being victims of crime. They run a constructive, confidence building programme of positive intervention through structured outdoor activities under the instruction and guidance of fully trained and qualified police officers. Our grant supported the purchase of equipment and the costs of running activities.'

Medical Research 'St Bartholomew's and the Royal London School of Medicine (£5,000 p.a. for each of three years). The Mary Kinross trustees have also had responsibility for the Vaughan Hudson Clinic Research Trust which was wound up during the year. The proceeds (£4,534) will be used to fund undergraduate elective bursaries for medical students interested in the field of immunology. We have made this grant of up to £5,000 and have agreed to give the same amount for the following two years.

'St Mark's Research Trust (£45,000). This grant represents our continuing support for the development of a endoscopy simulator. John Bladen writes: "Despite proving to be an immensely challenging and complex task, the endoscopy simulator is making excellent progress. We have developed our own multi-dimensional force feedback system – a world first, and essential for colonoscopy – and have also made good progress with the modelling of the endoscope and colon behaviour, and endoscopic view graphs. There are many parts to this project and we are in the process of drawing together all the component parts in order to produce our first version of the system to be used at St Mark's teaching centre.

On-going grants 'HARP (Helping the Homeless with Alcohol and Related Problems) (£17,500). This grant represents a contribution to salary costs. HARP provides a befriending and counselling service to people in Birmingham who are homeless and have an alcohol problem.

'Warstock and Billesley Detached Youthwork Project, now known as Youthwise (£22,000 + £14,000 being the cost of the feasibility work for the building project). This grant represents an on-going commitment for the payment of salaries of youth workers who contact and assist "at risk" young people in an outer ring housing estate area of Birmingham. The trust has made a considerable investment of time and funds to try to resolve the accommodation needs of this project. Having, together with Birmingham City Council, been major funders of the work since its inception, trustees wish to find a way for the detached youth workers to have a safe base from which to work which will not result in them running a youth centre, or spending much time raising funds to pay the rent and other costs of a building.

'As elsewhere the problems caused by large groups of disaffected youth – whose main source of pleasure seems to be the consumption of cheap, strong cider – continue to affect the community.'

Exclusions No grants to individuals.

Applications By letter to the correspondent. However, the trust states (and its grant-making confirms this) that it hardly ever responds to unsolicited appeals. Furthermore, the majority of funds up to the year 2000 have already been committed. Trustees meet quarterly.

The Graham Kirkham Foundation Ltd

£361,000 (1996/97)

Ex-services, general

Bentley Moor Lane, Adwick Le Street, Nr Doncaster, South Yorks DN6 7BD

Correspondent G Kirkham.

Trustees Directors: G Kirkham; P Kirkham.

Beneficial area UK.

Information available Accounts are on file at the Charity Commission but without the grants list, analysis and explanation of grants, and narrative report that are now required.

General The foundation was established in 1981. It has no endowment and relies upon the receipt of donations to make grants. The amount of money it receives in donations and the level of funds disbursed fluctuates dramatically from year to year. In the past few years income has varied between £31,000 (1996/97) and £1 million (1995/96) and grant expenditure has ranged from £54,000 (1993/94) to £837,000 (1994/95).

No grants lists since 1994/95 are on file at the Charity Commission and the accounts do not analyse grant making. The only grants information disclosed in 1996/97 is the grant total, £361,000, and the largest grant, £100,000 to the Gurkha Brigade Association Trust.

In 1994/95, the most recent year for which the proper information is available, fifteen grants were made including: Prince's Youth Business Trust (£500,000), Animal Health Trust (£104,000); Age Concern (£112,000); Cities in School (£25,000); and £20,000 each to Children's Hospice Appeal, Malcolm Sargent Cancer Fund and Friends for the Elderly.

The following purposes are set out in the foundation's memorandum of association (though the charity is bound to stay within these fields, it need not be active in more than one of them):

i) The development, study and appreciation of literature, art, music or science, in particular by providing accommodation, and the purchase of works of art, other objects of aesthetic merit or educational scientific value.

ii) Education, including vocational training (any age) and physical education of young people in full time education through scholarships allowances or lump sums for attending school, university or other educational establishments.

iii) The relief of poverty and hardship by providing financial assistance and accommodation for people and their dependents.

iv) Relief of illness and disease by providing treatment. The company also supports research into the treatment and prevention of illness.

v) The relief of suffering of animals and birds.

vi) The relief of poverty and hardship and the promotion of well being of people connected with the armed services

vii) Support and protection to those dependent on or in danger of becoming dependent on drugs.

viii) To provide facilities for public recreation.

ix) To preserve buildings of architectural interest and sites of historic interest or natural beauty.

Applications In writing to the correspondent.

Kleinwort Benson Charitable Trust

£247,000 (1997)

General

Kleinwort Benson Ltd, 20 Fenchurch St, London EC3P 3DB

Correspondent Miss J A Emptage

Trustees Kleinwort Benson Trustees Ltd

Beneficial area UK

Information available Report and accounts on file at the Charity Commission.

General The trust supports organisations concerned with medical, welfare, youth, conservation, inner cities and the arts.

The 1997 report states that 'support was again given to national rather than local charities, and sympathetic consideration was given to charities with which staff members of the Dresdner Kleinwort Benson Group had an active involvement. Three special donations of £12,500 each were made to charities selected via ballot by employees of the Dresdner Kleinwort Benson Group.'

In the year ended 1997 income was £263,000, made up mainly from gift aid from the Kleinwort Benson Group Ltd, and donations amounted to £247,000 in 161 grants. Seventy-three grants (about 45%) were for less than £1,000, and seven were for £10,000 or more.

The three special donations for £12,500 went to the Alzheimer's Disease Society, ME Association and Childline.

Other large grants went to Atlantic College (£11,900); Treloar Trust (£11,000); Hackney Music Development Trust (£10,500); Water Aid (£10,000); and grants of £5,000 each to Glyndebourne Festival Opera, Business in the Community and the Imperial War Museum.

Ernest Kleinwort Charitable Trust

£2,696,000 (1996/97)

Health, environment/ conservation, overseas, general

PO. Box 191, 10 Fenchurch Street, London EC3M 3LB
Tel: 0171-956 6600; Fax: 0171-956 6059

Correspondent The Secretary

Trustees Kleinwort Benson Trustees Ltd; Madeleine, Lady Kleinwort; the Earl of Limerick; Sir Richard Kleinwort; Miss M R Kleinwort; R M Ewing; Sir Christopher Lever.

Beneficial area UK and overseas, with a special interest in Sussex.

Information available Full accounts on file at the Charity Commission, but without the required narrative report or analysis and explanation of grants.

Summary Grants vary from around £1,000 to over £100,000. Larger grants are made to a variety of causes as listed below. Either the large grants represent part payment of even larger total awards, or about half of such recipients are supported again from one year to the next. there is also an extensive programme of undisclosed smaller awards, probably but not certainly concentrated in the fields described below.

General The charity was established in 1963 by Ernest and Joan Kleinwort and their son Kenneth with an endowment of shares in the merchant bank, Kleinwort Benson. The trustees' only stated policy, for what it is worth, 'is to consider all written appeals'.

In 1996/97 the settlement generated income of £1,743,000 (£2,037,000 in 1995/96) from assets of £39 million (£37 million). 322 grants were made 'principally in the fields of the environment and conservation; disabled; medical research; elderly and youth welfare, and preference was given to charities in Sussex'.

The settlement does not categorise grants or analyse them, but from the names of beneficiaries receiving £10,000 or over (accounting for 82% of grant expenditure) a rough analysis is shown in the table herewith.

In the following lists of beneficiaries in 1996/97, an asterisk indicates that the charity was also supported in the previous year.

Most of the largest awards went to hospitals and hospices: St Catherine's Hospice* (£109,000); Crowborough Hospital (£100,000); Hospice in the Weald (£100,000);). Other health charities supported included Cancer Relief Macmillan Fund* (£50,000) and Dr Jan de Winter Clinic for Cancer Prevention Advice (£50,000).

Beneficiaries in the environment category included many groups working overseas such as: Tusk Trust (£115,000); Diane Fossey Gorilla Fund* (£60,000); and Born Free (£50,000). More local organisations included the River Trust* (£85,000) and WWF UK* (£50,000).

Overseas development is the only well funded cause which is not identified by the charity as one of its areas of preference. Most grants and most of the money in this category went to the following family planning organisations: Population Concern (£90,000); Marie Stopes International* (£80,000); International Planned Parenthood (£40,000); and the Jamaican Family Planning Association (£10,000). Other awards were to: Intermediate Technology* (£90,000); Water Aid (£30,000); and VSO (£11,000).

There were a number of grants for independent schools; for example the following each received £50,000: Ardingly College Sports Hall; and Ovingdean Hall School.

Exclusions Local charities outside Sussex are normally excluded.

Applications To the correspondent. International grants are for conservation and planned parenthood. Trustees meet in March and October.

The Sir James Knott Trust

£1,171,000 (1997/98)

General, in the North-East

16-18 Hood Street,
Newcastle-upon-Tyne NE1 6JQ
Tel: 0191-230 4016

Correspondent Brigadier J F F Sharland, Secretary

Trustees Viscount Ridley; Mark Cornwall-Jones; Oliver James; Charles Baker-Cresswell.

Beneficial area Tyne and Wear, Durham and Northumberland.

Information available Report and accounts with list showing all grants of more than £1,000 but without explanation or analysis.

Summary Over 300 grants a year are made to registered charities in a variety of fields but with a preference for community welfare and youth/children's causes. Awards are in the range of a few hundred pounds to £50,000 with most for £5,000 or less. Most are one-off, but substantial on-going support is given for projects of particular interest to the trustees.

General The trust was founded in 1990 with a settlement from its namesake. It takes much interest in its grant-making policy and in the organisations supported. For example, an independent assessor visits a random selection of beneficiaries in an attempt to ensure that grants are being well targeted and well employed. Other initiatives include the fostering of co-operation between local trusts (through active membership in the North-East Trust Secretaries Group) and funding research into the options for change in trusts' grant-making in light of the impact of the National Lottery Charities Board.

In 1996/97 the trust held assets of nearly £25 million and generated income of £1,132,000. 337 grants were made amounting to a little more than the year's income as shown in the table herewith. These allocations have remained largely stable in the last few years.

189 grants of £1,000 or less amounted to £107,000 or 9% of the sum total.

Nearly half of charitable expenditure (47%) was disbursed in numerous grants between £1,000 to £8,000. Examples of such awards are: £3,000 to Hexham Abbey Festival; £5,000 to the Natural History Society of Northumbria; £2,000 to the Newcastle Children's Adventure Group; £2,000 to the Northumberland Playing Fields Association; £4,000 to the Royal National Mission to Seamen; and £3,000 to Samaritans of Tyneside.

19 awards from £10,000 to £20,000 accounted for 19% of grant expenditure and a further 25% of the money went in the following 8 grants for £25,000 – £50,000:

Ernest Kleinwort Charitable Trust

grants in 1997

Health/disability	£637,000	20	(28%)
Environment	£554,000	14	(25%)
Overseas development	£311,000	7	(14%)
Youth (mainly independent schools)	£310,000	11	(14%)
Elderly	£260,000	4	(12%)
Other/cause not known	£159,000	7	(7%)
Total disclosed	**£2,231,000**	**63**	**(100%)**

The size of awards was as follows:

Range	Number	totalling	% of grant total
£50,000 – £115,000	17	£1,244,000	(46%)
£20,000 – £49,999	25	£737,000	(27%)
£10,000 – £19,999	21	£250,000	(9%)
£1,000 – £9,999	259	£464,000	(17%)

Citizen's Advice Bureau NE £25,000;

Community Council of N'bld, Coalfield Project £50,000;

Institute of Health for the Elderly £25,000 and £50,000;

North of England Cadet Forces Trust £50,000;

Northern Counties School for the Deaf £30,000;

St Oswald's Hospice Newcastle £25,000;

Stanegate Inheritance Project N'bld (Town Hall) £30,000.

The trust says:

'Grants are normally only made to registered charities, in response to applications from within the North-East of England and from national charities either operating within, or where the work may be expected to be of benefit to, the North East of England. Grants will not normally be made outside of this area.

'Grants will commonly be made in response to appeals to support education, training, medical care, historic buildings, environment and the arts; as well as the welfare of the young, the elderly, seaman's and services charities, the disabled and the disadvantaged. Grants are made out of income and not normally out of capital.

'We do not issue specific guidelines for applicants but discuss the requirements of potential applicants with them as and when necessary. Rather than issue strict guidelines/pro formas on what we want, we find it helpful to listen to what the applicant thinks is important first: we than ask supplementary questions as necessary.'

This enterprising trust shows a real concern for how its (and other trusts') money can be best used to achieve charitable aims. The independent assessment of beneficiaries' achievements is laudable as are the trust's efforts to react to changes brought about by the National Lottery.

Exclusions The original trust deed excludes Roman Catholic charities. No applications considered from individuals or from non-registered charities. Grants are only made to charities from within the North East of England, and from national charities either operating within, or where work may be expected to be of benefit to the North East of England.

Applications In writing to the correspondent. 'Please be brief. Do not, for example, explain at great length why it is that a blind, starving, bankrupt, one-legged man from Jupiter, needs help'.

Despite the plea for brevity, the trust requests that applicants should address the following questions, although 'not all the questions necessarily apply to you, but they give an idea of the kind of questions that the trustees may ask when your application is being considered:

- Who are you? How are you organised/managed?
- What is your **aim**? What co-ordination do you have with other organisations with similar aims?
- What do you do and how does it benefit the community? How many people "in need' actually use or take advantage of your facilities?
- How have you been funded in the past, how will you be funded in the future? Enclose summary of last year's balance sheet.

- How much do you need, what for and when? Have you thought about depreciation/running costs/replacement? If your project is not funded in full, what do you propose to do with the money you have raised?
- What is the overall cost, what is the deficit and how are you planning to cover the deficit? Is it an open-ended commitment, or when will you become self-supporting?
- If you will never be self-supporting, what is your long-term fundraising strategy? Have you even thought about it?
- Who else have you asked for money, and how have they responded? What are you doing yourselves to raise money?
- Have you applied to the National Lottery? When will you get the result? If you have not applied, are you eligible and when will you apply?
- What is your registered charity number, or which registered charity is prepared to administer funds on your behalf? How can you be contacted by telephone?'

Trustees normally meet in February, June and October. Applications need to be submitted up to two months in advance.

The Kobler Trust

£268,000 (1994/95)

Arts, Jewish charities

BDO Stoy Hayward, 8 Baker Street, London W1M 1DA
Tel: 0171-486 5888

Correspondent Alfred A Davis

Trustees Alfred A Davis; A Xuereb; A H Stone.

Beneficial area UK

Information available Accounts and reports up to 1995 only on file at the Charity Commision in September 1998

General The trust has not updated their files at the charity commission since 1995, so the information below is dated.

The trust shares the same correspondent and address as the Adint Trust (see seperate entry). In 1995 it had an income of £216,000, generated from assets of £3 million. Donations totalled £268,000 and went to 23 institutions. The trust gives a small number of large grants to a variety of Jewish welfare and arts charities. The

The Sir James Knott Trust			
grants in 1996/97			
Community welfare	103	£359,000	31%
Youth/children	87	£246,000	21%
Medical: care and research	24	£156,000	14%
Handicapped	36	£87,000	7%
Heritage/museums	9	£75,000	6%
Elderly	10	£49,000	4%
Service charities	12	£43,000	4%
Conservation/horticultural	11	£40,000	4%
Education/expeditions	18	£38,000	3%
Arts	12	£34,000	3%
Maritime	4	£18,000	2%
Housing/homeless	11	£8,000	1%
Total	**337**	**£1,153,000**	**100%**

largest grants went to Adventures in Motion Picture (£60,000) and Four Seasons, Jewish Care and Imperial College (£50,000 each).

Other large grants include those to Beit Issie Shapiro (£35,000); Chicken Shed Theatre (£20,000); Federation of Jewish Relief (£16,000 in two grants) and the Royal Academy of Music (£10,000).

Exclusions Grant are given to individuals only in exceptional circumstances.

Applications In writing to the correspondent.

The Kreitman Foundation

£300,000 (1996/97)

Jewish charities, the arts, general

Citroen Wells (Chartered accountants), 1 Devonshire Street, London W1N 2DR
Tel: 0171-637 2841

Correspondent Eric Charles, Trustee

Trustees Hyman Kreitman; Mrs Irene Kreitman; Eric Charles.

Beneficial area UK and Israel.

Information available Full accounts on file at the Charity Commission, but without a narrative report.

General The trust was established in 1970 by Sybil Kreitman. In the year ending April 1997, its assets totalled £26 million and £1,105,000 income was generated. Administration cost £75,000 or 25 pence per £1 granted.

The report accounts list 15 grants of £1,000 or over, and which account for 97% of the foundation's giving, but do not say for what purpose they were given, nor is there any indication of the trustees charitable policies.

Of the listed grants, ten were specifically Jewish causes, and five were involved in the arts. Nine of the recipients had also received grant-aid the year before. The largest four grants, totalling £268,000, or 89% of grant expenditure, were to: Royal National Theatre (£106,000); Ben Gurion University (£59,000); Tate Gallery Foundation (£53,000); and the Joint Jewish Charitable Trust (£50,000). This last organisation appears not to have been helped by the foundation in previous years, and other 'new'

beneficiaries included: British Emunah Child Resettlement Fund (£1,000); Institute for Jewish Policy Research (£6,000); and the London Symphony Orchestra (£1,000). An unknown number of donations, totalling £10,000, was made for under £1,000.

In 1997, the foundation had future commitments of over £3.8 million, most of which (nearly £3 million) has been earmarked for the Kreitman School of Advanced Graduate Studies at Ben Gurion University. Other commitments are to the Tate Gallery (£450,000 over three years for the Bankside Gallery and £200,000 over four years for acquisitions) and Beit Shirene Immigrant Home for the Aged (£162,000).

Exclusions No grants to individuals.

Applications The trust does not seek applications.

The Neil Kreitman Foundation

£298,000 (1996/97)

Jewish charities, arts

Citroen Wells (Chartered accountants), 1 Devonshire Street, London W1N 2DR.
Tel: 0171-637 2841

Correspondent Eric Charles, Trustee

Trustees Roger Kreitman; H Kreitman; Mrs. S I Kreitman; Eric Charles.

Beneficial area UK and Israel.

Information available Full accounts on file at the Charity Commission, but without a narrative report.

Summary About 15 grants are made a year. Practically all funds go to charities previously assisted by the foundation. The beneficiaries come from a variety of charitable fields, but the large grants (which account for most of grant expenditure) are usually made to cultural institutions.

General The foundation was set-up in 1974 by Neil Kreitman. It's practices, stated in the 1996/97 report are as follows:

'The foundation generally supports projects in the fields of culture, education, health and welfare. The foundation makes grants to registered charities only and to organisations which are exempt...and

which are based in the UK.

'The foundation's day to day activities are administered by its accountants as it employs no staff. Its trustees are solely responsible for the consideration and authorisation of the donations made. It is the usual policy of the trustees to make awards from the accumulated fund only.'

In 1996/97 £294,000 income was generated from assets totalling £5.8 million. Fourteen organisations received grants, thirteen of which had also been assisted in 1995/96 or the year before. As in the previous two years the largest donation went to the Ashmolean Museum (£180,000 in 1996/97, £152,000 in 1995/96). Along with the two next largest grants to Ancient India and Iran Trust (£30,000, and £13,000 in 1995/96) and the British Library (£25,000, £9,000) it accounted for 81% of grant expenditure. The remaining eleven grants were as follows: Corpus Inscriptionum Iranicum, £13,000 (£13,000 in 1995/96); The Onaway Trust, £11,000 (£11,000); and RELEASE, £10,000 (£10,000).

£2,000 awards (in both years) went to the Multiple Sclerosis Society, British Heart Foundation, Malcolm Sargent Cancer Fund for Children; and the NSPCC. Other beneficiaries included the Queen Elizabeth Fund for the Disabled (£2,750, both years); and International PEN Foundation (£5,000 both years). The only new beneficiary was the Henry Spink Foundation (£1,000).

Exclusions No grants to individuals.

Applications To the correspondent in writing.

Laing's Charitable Trust

£683,000 for organisations (1997)

General

PO Box 33, 133 Page Street, London NW7 2ER

Correspondent D W Featherstone

Trustees Sir Kirby Laing; Sir Maurice Laing; R A Wood; Sir Martin Laing; D C Madden.

Beneficial area UK.

Information available In August 1998 the most recent accounts on file at the Charity Commission were those for 1996; there is an information sheet, incorporated in the entry below.

Summary The trust states that grants are 'mainly one-off' and that the beneficial area is 'mainly national'. In practice many grants are repeated from year to year. Around a third of funds go to UK charities and the remaining two thirds are disbursed to present or retired employees of the John Laing group of companies. Awards to organisations range from around £100 to £30,000.

General The trust was established in 1962 by the building company John Laing and Son Ltd. Individual members of the Laing family, including some of these trustees, have endowed their own foundations, with adjacent entries in this book, and collectively they form an example of the remarkable philanthropy of many families whose fortunes were made in this industry – Tudor (Wimpey), Wates, Bilton and Sunley are other examples.

Accounts for 1997 showed that the income for the year was £1,760,000, generated from assets totalling £41 million. £684,000 was distributed to organisations and £715,000 to individuals.

The grants list shows the largest grants to institutions (£2,000 and over) which amount to £502,000, or 73% of the total funds awarded.

The trust does not categorise beneficiaries, but from looking at the names of the disclosed recipients of 51 grants in 1996 (the most recent year for which such information was available to these editors) the following rough analysis can be made:

- *Youth 9 grants, £121,000.*
Grants included £31,000 to Young Entrepreneurs; £30,000 for Drive for Youth; £20,000 to the Children's Society; and £5,000 to the Prince's Youth Business Trust.

- *Community 5 grants, £95,000.*
Examples are: £30,000 each to the Civic Trust (repeated from 1994/95) and Business in the Community (£62,000 over the two previous years); £15,000 to the Community Development Fund; £10,000 to Hertfordshire Community.

- *Education 8 grants, £94,000*
A selection of the awards: United World College of the Atlantic (£23,000, and a total of £57,000 over the two preceding years); Tyneside City Technical College (£20,000 repeated from the year before); Cities in Schools (£20,000); University of London (£10,000); and University of

Cambridge (£6,000).

- *Medical 7 grants, £29,000*
Including £6,000 to the Progressive Supranuclear Palsy Europe Association; £4,000 to Cryotherapy Research, Harefield Hospital; and £3,000 each to Cancer Relief Macmillan Fund and the Medical Committee on Accident Prevention.

- *General/unknown 22 grants, £108,000*
These grants included a few to homeless groups (Banbury Homeless £3,000, Big Issue £3,000) and others to the WWF (£10,000 and £25,000 in 1994/95)); the John Laing Band (£10,000); the National Museum of Scotland (£6,000) and the Samaritans (£6,000).

Exclusions No grants to individuals (other than to Laing employees and/or their dependents).

Applications In writing to the correspondent. No particular application form is required. Receipt of applications is not acknowledged unless successful – or unless a reply paid envelope is sent with the application. The trust does not encourage exploratory telephone calls on how best to approach the trust.

The Beatrice Laing Trust

£718,000 (1994/95)

General

Box 1, 133 Page Street, Mill Hill, London NW7 2ER
Tel: 0181-238 8890

Correspondent Miss Elizabeth Harley

Trustees Sir Kirby Laing; Sir Maurice Laing; Sir Martin Laing; David E Laing; Christopher M Laing; John H Laing.

Beneficial area UK and overseas.

Information available Report and accounts with full grants list and brief review of the year's grants.

Summary Nearly all grants and are made in awards of £2,000 or less. Causes supported are wide ranging and many are supported on a regular basis. The largest donations are typically for about £30,000 and are given very rarely.

General The Beatrice Laing Trust is one of several trusts founded and endowed by members of the Laing family. It is closely allied with the Maurice Kirby and Hilda Laing Foundations; so much so that an

application to any one of them is an application to them all. They run similar grant making programmes, the chief differences being the size of grants and of categories. In the case of the Beatrice Laing Trust awards are many and small (averaging, and typically for, about £1,500).

The trust had an income of £910,000 in 1996/97 and held assets of over £21 million. 24 grants of £5,000 and over accounted for 22% of total giving. In all 457 grants were awarded in the following categories:

• Social welfare	£201,000	28%
• Disabled	£122,000	17%
• Child and youth	£73,000	10%
• Religious		
– building	£5,500	
– home	£38,000	
– individuals	£18,000	
– overseas	£7,000	
– total	£68,000	10%
• Overseas aid	£66,000	9%
• Mental health	£62,000	9%
• Medical welfare	£53,000	7%
• Old people	£41,000	6%
• Education	£20,000	3%
• Armed services	£6,800	1%
• Trades and professions	£2,600	—

The above percentages are not necessarily indicative of future ratios as the categories tend to vary from year to year.

In the 1997 report the trustees said:

'It is the policy of the trustees to give a very large number of modest sized gifts to smaller charities who might otherwise find difficulty in attracting funds from the larger grant-making trusts. A total of 457 grants were made during the year, the largest being for £27,000 and the smallest for £150. Gifts were made across a wide range of charities operating in the fields of social and medical welfare and evangelical work, including a few gifts to individuals engaged in evangelical mission.

Major gifts included:

£27,250 to SENSE for running costs and their new building project in Exmouth;

£26,500 to Echoes of Service for evangelical work;

£10,000 to Anchor Trust for running costs and building costs and Hackney Hospital Discharge Project;

£10,000 to APT Design and Development to enable production of an up-to-date manual on paper technology for third world countries.'

A selection of smaller grants is as follows: Carers National Association

£1,000; Bow Self Help Alcoholic Recovery Programme £1,000; Edinburgh Furniture Initiative £1,000; Homeless North £2,500; Lambeth Drugline £2,000; Shelter Cymru £1,000; Surrey Care Trust £500; Refugee Support Centre £1,250.

Exclusions No grants to individuals; no travel grants; no educational grants.

Applications One application only is needed to apply to this or the Maurice, Hilda or Kirby Laing trusts. Multiple applications will still only elicit a single reply; even then applicants are asked to accept non-response as a negative reply on behalf of all three trusts, unless an SAE is enclosed. Applications are considered monthly.

These trusts make strenuous efforts to keep their overhead costs to a minimum. As they also make a very large number of grants each year, in proportion to their income the staff must rely almost entirely on the written applications submitted in selecting appeals to go forward to the trustees. Each application should contain all the information needed to allow such a decision to be reached, in as short and straightforward a way as possible. Specifically, each application should say: what the money is for; how much is needed; how much has already been found; where the rest is to come from. Unless there is reasonable assurance on the last point the grant is unlikely to be recommended.

This Editor would add that, in the light of the very large number of grants being made by a small staff, the plea above for simple, straightforward applications is even more appropriate than for other funders.

Hilda Laing Charitable Trust

About £1,000,000
Christianity, poverty

Box 1, 133 Page Street, Mill Hill, London NW7 2ER
Tel: 0181-238 8890

Correspondent Miss Elizabeth Harley

Trustees Sir Maurice Laing; Lady Hilda Laing; Peter J Harper; Robert M Harley; Thomas D Parr.

Beneficial Area UK and overseas

Information available A new foundation, so no Report and Accounts

are yet prepared. The trust has provided the helpful information below.

General The trust was established in 1996. During the first sixteen months three main areas of interest have emerged:

- *the advancement of the Christian religion* through evangelistic activities and the promotion of high quality religious education and projects designed to promote Christian ethics, especially among young people;
- *relief of poverty within the UK* with particular emphasis on projects in which the Christian faith is being manifested through practical action to help those in need.
- *relief of poverty overseas,* where priorities include work with children, especially those living on the street, projects addressing population issues, including work to improve the basic education of women and the quality of reproductive and primary health care, and small scale development projects, especially those run by Christian organisations.

In the first sixteen months, despite the fact that the Trust is still relatively young and not yet widely known, the trustees distributed £1.4 million. This represents 105 gifts, 43 of which were between £200 and £4,000, and made from funds deposited with the Charities Aid Foundation. Gifts of £250,000 were made to the Lambeth Fund, the second instalment of a four year commitment, and £100,000 to the Salvation Army towards the development of Greig House detoxification unit.

Exclusions No grants to groups or individuals for the purpose of education, travel, attendance at conferences or participation in overseas exchange programmes.

Applications The trust is administered alongside the Beatrice Laing Trust and the Maurice and Kirby Laing Foundations. None of the trusts issue application forms and an application to one is seen as an application to all. In general the trusts rarely make grants towards the running costs of local organisations, which they feel have to be raised from within the local community. Applications for grants towards specific capital projects should be in the form of a short letter giving details of the project, its total cost, the amount raised and some indication of how it is to be financed.

A copy of the organisation's latest annual report and accounts, together with a stamped addressed envelope should be enclosed. Unless a S.A.E. is enclosed

applicants are asked to accept non-response as a negative reply.

Trustees meet quarterly to consider applications for larger grants (above £10,000). Applications for smaller amounts are considered on an on-going basis.

The J W Laing Trust

£4,182,000 (1996/97)
Christian evangelism, general

PO Box 133, Bath BA1 2YU
Tel: 01225-310893

Correspondent B J Chapman, Secretary

Trustees The Stewards' Company.

Beneficial area UK and overseas.

Information available Accounts on file at the Charity Commission.

General This trust is administered alongside the J. W. Laing Biblical Scholarship Trust (see separate entry) by the Stewards' Company Ltd. The trust benefits Christian work in the UK and overseas with particular reference to the Christian Brethren Assemblies. A portion of the gifts made are nominated by the Beatrice Laing Trust.

Assets for 1996/97 amounted to £95 million, generating an income of about £4.3 million. About £4.2 million was given out in grants in three broad categories; 'overseas' (49%), 'home' (43%) and 'charitable organisations and objects' (8%).

- *Overseas (£2,044,000).* Fifteen grants were given, all of them repeated from the previous year. Grants ranged up to £480,000 and all were involved in Christian teaching. Examples include: Echoes of Service (£480,000); Echoes of Service Medical fund (£275,000); Building Projects and Vehicles (£169,000); Miscellaneous (£427,000); Scriptures and Literature (£168,000); Missionary Project (£35,000) and Interlink (£110,000).
- *Home (£1,798,000).* Grants were given under the following headings: Places of Worship (£562,000); Scriptures and Literature (£430,000); Evangelistic Outreach (£375,000); Youth and Children's Organisations (£193,000); Colleges and Schools

(£49,000); Evangelists and Teachers (£42,000) and Miscellaneous (£147,000).

• *Charitable organisations and objects (£340,000).* None were specified. The top 50 grants were listed under their specific names. Examples of the larger ones include those to Interhealth (£110,000); Scripture Gift Mission (£325,000); Stewards Association in India (£50,000); Wycliffe Bible Translators (£95,000); Counties Evangelistic Work (£68,000); CYC Camp Trust (£50,000) and Medical Missionary News (£60,000).

Examples of the smaller grants given include those to Ahorey Gospel Hall (£10,000), Ebenezer Church, Weymouth (£12,000); Mbabane Chapel, Swaziland (£10,000); the Open Air Mission (£15,000) and the Scottish Christian Counselling Trust (£12,000).

Applications The trust states that it does not accept applications from those outside its own particular circles.

The J W Laing Biblical Scholarship Trust

£1,055,000 (1996/97)

Christian evangelism

PO Box 133, Bath BA1 2YU
Tel: 01225-310893

Correspondent B J Chapman, Secretary

Trustees The Stewards' Company.

Beneficial area UK and overseas.

Information available Full accounts are on file at the Charity Commission.

General The trust was established in 1947 and is administered by the Steward's Company, as is the J. W. Laing Trust (see separate entry).

The trust is concerned with matters covering bible studies generally, and also benefits work connected with students and undergraduates who are specifically mentioned by the original donors.

In 1996/97 the trust had assets of £23 million, which generated the low income of £1.1 million. Donations totalled £1.06 million, which was distributed to 23 organisations dealing mainly with

Christian teaching organisations. Eighteen grants were repeated grants from the previous year.

The largest grants were to The Universities and Colleges Christian Fellowship (£525,000), Stapleford House Religious Education Projects (£130,000), and the London Bible College (£45,000).

Examples of the new grants made were those to Myrtlefield Trust (£15,000), University of Cambridge Scholarships (£17,000), Bible Society (£10,000) and John Rylands University Library (£800).

Exclusions No grants to individuals.

Applications In writing to the correspondent.

The Kirby Laing Foundation

£1,174,000 (1997)

General

Box 1, 133 Page Street, Mill Hill, London NW7 2ER
Tel: 0181-238 8890

Correspondent Miss Elizabeth Harley

Trustees Sir Kirby Laing; Lady Isobel Laing; David E Laing; Simon Webley.

Beneficial area UK and overseas.

Information available Report and accounts showing all grants of £5,000 and over and with brief narrative report on the year's grant-making.

Summary More than 200 grants are made a year to a wide variety of causes in over ten categories. Most awards are under £4,000 but the majority of the money is spent in grants of £10,000 and above. The highest grant given in 1997 was for £45,000 but in previous years they have been for as much as £250,000.

General The foundation is one of at least seven Laing family trusts. It is administered alongside the Maurice Laing Foundation and the Beatrice and Hilda Laing Trusts.

In 1997 gross income was £1,457,000 (including a donation from Eskmuir Ltd of £187,000). The following 14 grants for £20,000 or more accounted for 39% of charitable expenditure:

NSPCC £20,000;
British Trust for Conservation Volunteers £37,000;
Parnham Trust £25,000;

Royal Botanic Gardens, Kew £20,000;
Calvert Trust £25,000;
Cheltenham and Gloucester College of Higher Education £30,000;
St Lawrence College £50,000;
Restoration of Appearance and Function Trust £25,000;
Armonia (sic) UK Trust £26,000;
University of Cape Town £40,000;
Tyndale House £45,000;
Youth with a Mission £25,000;
Leprosy Mission £25,000;
SAT-7 £25,000.

A further 19 grants between £10,000 and £19,999 totalled 19% of grant expenditure, awards between £4,000 and £9,999 for 20% and those under £4,000 for 22%.

The categories of giving in 1997 were:

• Religious organisations
  – (building £15,000) 1%
  – home £148,000 13%
  – overseas £141,000 12%
• Charities Aid Foundation £250,000 22%
• Education £123,000 10%
• Overseas aid £110,000 9%
• Cultural and environmental £109,000 9%
• Medical welfare £75,500 6%
• Disabled £63,000 5%
• Child and youth £56,000 5%
• Social welfare £43,000 4%
• Mental health £20,000 2%
• Old people £18,000 2%
• Armed Services £5,000 —
• Miscellaneous £1,200 —

The amount of money donated within a category is not stable year to year.

The 1997 report said:

'During the year under review the trustees continued their policy of making a large number of small to moderate sized gifts to a wide range of charities. The trustees approved a total of 215 gifts, 138 of which were made from funds deposited with the Charities Aid Foundation and were for amounts ranging between £50 and £4,000. A large proportion of these represented annual donations to the core funding of national organisations working in a variety of different fields. Unfortunately despite a continual stream of requests, the trustees are rarely able to make similar contributions to the running costs of local organisations and indeed it is a matter of regret that the total number of gifts made represents only a very small proportion of the ever increasing number of appeals received.

'All gifts of £5,000 and above are listed in....the accounts. The trustees are interested in the advancement of the Christian faith and its manifestation through practical action to help those in need. This was reflected in the number of gifts for £5,000 and above made to 'religious organisations' working both in the UK and overseas. The largest of these, a grant of £44,690 to Tyndale House, Cambridge, was for various projects of biblical research, and this was also the purpose of various gifts of £30,000 and £15,000 made to Cheltenham and Gloucester College of Education and the University of Oxford respectively in the field of education. Also in this field a gift of £50,000 was made to the St Lawrence College Sports Appeal, although the trustees would be unlikely to give to similar projects where there is no direct relationship with the trustees.

Other major gifts included: £40,000 to the University of Capetown, to be split between the work of the Writing Centre in helping educationally disadvantaged students to complete their course and the Department of Primary Healthcare and; £40,000 to Rocklands Campsite Trust, also in South Africa, for the completion of the road leading to the trust's Simonstown site. However, the trustee's overseas interests were not confined to South Africa. The gifts to UK aid agencies also represent support for projects in Kenya, Tanzania, Zimbabwe, Bangladesh and Mexico.'

Exclusions No grants to individuals; no travel grants; no educational grants.

Applications One application only is needed to apply to this or the Maurice Laing Foundation or Beatrice or Hilda Laing Trusts. Multiple applications will still only elicit a single reply. These trusts make strenuous efforts to keep their overhead costs to a minimum. As they also make a very large number of grants each year, in proportion to their income, the staff must rely almost entirely on the written applications submitted in selecting appeals to go forward to the trustees.

Each application should contain all the information needed to allow such a decision to be reached, in as short and straightforward a way as possible. Specifically, each application should say: what the money is for; how much is needed; how much has already been found; where the rest is to come from. Unless there is reasonable assurance on the last point the grant is unlikely to be recommended. The trusts ask applicants, in the interest of reducing costs, to accept a non-response as a negative reply; if more is sought, a stamped addressed envelope must be sent with the application. Decisions are made on an on-going basis.

212

The Maurice Laing Foundation

£2,411,000 (1997)

Medicine (including complementary medicine), welfare (especially of the young), general

Box 1, 133 Page Street, Mill Hill, London NW7 2ER
Tel: 0181-238 8890

Correspondent Miss E A Harley

Trustees David Edwards, Chairman; Sir Maurice Laing; Thomas D Parr; John H Laing; Peter J Harper; Andrea Gavazzi.

Beneficial area Unrestricted.

Information available Report and accounts with grants list showing all grants of £5,000 and above, a short review explains only the largest grants.

Summary In past years grants have varied between £125 and £888,000. Although most are for amounts less than £10,000 the majority of charitable expenditure is represented by a few larger awards. A wide range of causes are supported, some over several years and others with one-off donations.

General The foundation is one of many grant making Laing family trusts. It is operated in conjunction with the Beatrice and Hilda Laing Trusts and the Kirby Laing Foundation. These three organisations have similar categories of giving and indeed if you apply to one you apply to them all. There are differences between grant making policy; Maurice Laing Foundation grants are the most substantial and its highest awards are about as large as those of any UK trust.

In 1996/97 six grants of £50,000 or more accounted for 42% of the total money given in grants and 10 donations between £20,000 and £49,999 absorbed 17% of the pot. The grants are categorised in the table herewith.

The trustees 1997 report says:

'All gifts of £5,000 and above are listed... in the accounts. The trustee's interest in environmental and botanical issues was reflected in a grant of £125,000 to the Royal Botanic Gardens Kew in support of the Millennium Seed Bank Appeal, a gift which will be repeated next year, and in awards totalling £305,000 to the World Wide Fund for Nature in support of the PSD21 Initiative, the Marine Stewardship Council and the Forests for Life Campaign.

Research into the efficacy of complementary health treatments and their integration into general practice also remains a focus for the trustees and the gift of £888,861 made to the

The Maurice Laing Foundation

Grants in 1997

• **Cultural and environmental**	8	£557,000	37%
– cultural and environmental	7	£497,000	
– animals and birds	1	£60,000	
• **Health and medicine**	19	£256,000	17%
– complementary	5	£131,000	
– disabled	7	£60,000	
– medical welfare	7	£65,000	
– mental health	0	£0	
• **Small grants via Charities Aid Foundation**	157	£240,000	16%
• **Child and youth**	12	£154,000	10%
– child and youth	8	£105,000	
– education	4	£49,000	
• **Social welfare**	12	£143,000	9%
– old people	3	£33,000	
– social welfare	9	£110,000	
• **Overseas aid**	7	£112,000	7%
• **Religion**		£1 43,000	3%
– home	1	£43,000	
– overseas	0	£0	
Total	**206**	**£1,506,000**	**100%**

University of Maryland in the previous year was followed by a grant of £50,000 to the Dove Healing Trust to support research work at the University of Southampton and gifts totalling £55,000 offering further support to the Laing Chair in Complementary, Medicine at the University of Exeter.

Other major gifts included an award of £50,000 towards Actionaid's work in Ghana.

146 gifts ranging from £125 to £4,000 were made from funds deposited with the Charities Aid Foundation [*for details on policy concerning such grants see the Kirby Laing entry Ed.*].'

Exclusions No grants to individuals for education or travel.

Applications One application only is needed to apply to this or the Kirby Laing Foundation or the Beatrice Laing Trust. Multiple applications will only receive a single reply. The trusts ask applicants, in the interest of reducing costs, to accept a non-response as a negative reply; if more is sought, a stamped addressed envelope must be sent with the application.

Each application should contain all the information needed to allow a decision to be reached, in as short and straightforward a way as possible. Specifically, they should cover:

- what the money is for;
- how much is needed;
- how much has already been found;
- where the rest is to come from (Unless there is reasonable assurance on this point the grant is unlikely to be recommended).

Applications for smaller amounts are considered on an on-going basis; larger grants are considered quarterly; the exact dates of meetings vary from year to year.

Lambeth Endowed Charities

About £500,000 (for organisations, 1996)

Education, general social needs in Lambeth

127 Kennington Road, London SE11 6SF
Tel: 0171-735 1925; Fax: 0171-735 7048

Correspondent Robert Dewar, Director and Clerk

Trustees 15 co-optative trustees and governors, and two representative trustees and two representative governors appointed by Lambeth Borough Council.

Beneficial area London Borough of Lambeth.

Information available Exemplary report and accounts and information leaflet.

Summary These excellent charities make grants, on a one-off or recurrent basis, to educational, welfare and health organisations and individuals in the borough of Lambeth. They range from a few pounds to over £30,000.

General Lambeth Endowed Charities is a collective title for three different trusts, some dating back to the seventeenth century, which are administered from the same office: the Walcot Educational Foundation, the Hayle's Charity, and the Walcot Non-Educational Charity.

The 1996 report notes that the grants to organisations 'reflect the diversity of community life and activity in the borough. A grant of £14,000, the largest grant made during the year, was to fund a Youth Crime Audit. It is hoped that the findings of this study will generate new approaches to crime prevention from individuals, community groups, statutory and voluntary organisations and local government.

'It is in the response to initiatives which provide new services or bridge gaps in existing ones that the impact of the charities is best measured. Some look to to charitable trusts as an alternative source of funding from local and regional governments. The Charities themselves are not empowered to make grants where funding should be provided by statutory bodies.'

Grants to organisations in 1996 were categorised as follows:

Support for voluntary aided schools	*20 grants*	*£46,000*
Other schools and colleges	*28 grants*	*£53,000*
Small educational projects	*69 grants*	*£31,000*
Larger educational projects	*61 grants*	*£187,000*
Arts and welfare projects	*65 grants*	*£108,000*

There are also extensive programmes of support for individuals in educational or other need in the borough.

The largest grants were to Lambeth Partnership Policing Strategy Group (£14,000 as mentioned above), Archbishop Tenison's School (£10,000

for a library management system) and St Luke's West Norwood Primary School (£10,000 for building improvements).

Exclusions Beneficiaries must be residents of the London Borough of Lambeth.

Applications All applications must be made on an application form available on request from the office. The trustees meet quarterly, usually in March, June, October and December and applications must be received at least 6 weeks before the date of the meeting. Please ring the office to check deadlines for applications.

Once your application has been received you will be contacted by the director or the fieldworker who will usually arrange to visit your project to discuss your application in more detail.

Successful applicants will be asked to give a report about how a grant has been used within 12 months of receiving it.

The Allen Lane Foundation

£542,000 (1997/98)

Disadvantaged minorities, unpopular causes

6a Winchester House, 11 Cranmer Road, London SW9 6EJ
Tel: 0171-793 1899

Correspondent Heather Swailes, Executive Secretary

Trustees Charles Medawar; Clare Morpurgo; Christine Teale; Zo' Teale; Ben Whitaker.

Beneficial area UK, with a separate programme for the Republic of Ireland.

Information available Probably the best annual report seen by these editors with full grants list and detailed analysis of grant-making and grants; accounts; guidelines.

Summary Grants generally range from about £250 to £10,000 for one-off grants, and from £1,000 a year to £5,000 a year (up to three years) for revenue grants. About a third of grants are repeated over two or three years. Beneficiaries are organisations supporting disadvantaged people – particularly those on the margins of society. Although a variety of projects are assisted, the foundation has fairly specific preferences and it seems unlikely that assistance will be given where a proposal does not fall within these tight guidelines.

General The foundation was established in 1966 by the late Sir Allen Lane, founder of Penguin Books. Apart from this historical link there is no other connection between the foundation and the publisher, although three of the trustees are relatives of the founder.

In the year ending April 1998 the foundation's assets totalled £16 million and income was a modest £556,000 (including a donation of £51,000 but not including £4.9 million in unrealised gains). 119 new grants amounting to £342,000 were awarded, a further £119,000 paid in previously agreed grants and £78,000 (IR£87,000) donated within the Irish programme.

Guidelines for Applicants

The Guidelines for Applicants describes the trusts policies as follows:

'The broad areas of work which are priorities for the trustees include:

- the provision of advice, information and advocacy;
- community development;
- employment and training;
- mediation, conflict resolution and alternatives to violence;
- research and education aimed at changing public attitudes or policy;
- social welfare.

'The trustees make grants to organisations whose work the trustees believe to be unpopular. Priority groups for the foundation include refugees and asylum seekers, black and ethnic minority communities, those experiencing mental health problems, those experiencing violence or abuse, offenders and ex-offenders, and travellers amongst others.

'The foundation covers the whole of the United Kingdom. Currently trustees wish to give priority to work outside London and only make grants for work in London in very exceptional circumstances. The foundation targets about 80% of its grant-making on national or regional organisations.

'Grants generally range from about £250 to £5,000. Grant to local projects are usually less than £1,000. Grants are normally single payments but may sometimes be for up to three consecutive years. The trustees wish to make grants which will make a significant impact and, as the grants are relatively small, priority is given to organisations of a modest size. The foundation only very rarely makes grants to national organisations with an income of more than £500,000 or to local ones with an income of more than £100,000.'

Annual Report 1997/98

The foundation also produces an exemplary annual report. Aside from generously fulfilling the Charity Commission's reporting requirements, it includes further unusual but useful information such as a breakdown of the reasons for refusals, and short biographies of the trustees. A 'downside' of such a thorough review is that it is too long to reproduce here in its entirety. However, as it would be of use not only to potential grant applicants but also to other grant-making trusts seeking to improve their own reports (and these editors feel the vast majority of them should be doing this), the great bulk of it has been included in this entry. Where relevant, we have interspersed the foundation's report with examples of grants made during the year:

Policy priorities

The foundation went to considerable lengths to publish its new policy on refugees and this seems to have got the message across reasonably successfully.

'The decision taken last year not to fund in Greater London is one which has only been communicated through the Guidance for Applicants leaflets, and the directories of grant making trusts therefore contained out of date information for much of the year. It is perhaps not surprising therefore that so many applications are still received from London.'

'Some examples of grants made to refugees' organisations include £5,000 to Asylum Aid to raise their profile and income, and £9,000 to Refugee Education and Training Advisory Service towards the publishing of a good practice guide (both funds were to be spread over two years).

Funding in the Republic of Ireland

'The foundation has had a grant making programme in the Republic of Ireland for a number of years targeting women's groups. The last of these ended in 1997. From 1998 the programme will focus on penal reform and work with offenders and ex-offenders.

Categories of work

'The foundation has chosen these areas of work because it wishes to fund work which will make a longer term difference to people's lives and the problems they experience. Although in the past the foundation made a considerable proportion of its grants in the area of social welfare, and direct service provision, the trend away from that area (6% this year compared with 24% last year) and towards advice, information and advocacy, and policy oriented research

reflects the desire to use funds to do more than alleviate day to day problems.

'Donations in these latter, currently more favoured categories include £10,000 over two years to the Public Law Project for work on travellers and the planning system and £15,000 (over three years) to the Women's Aid Federation England to help with the costs of a helpline.

Grants analysed by category 1996/97

Advice, information and advocacy	33%	(22%)
Policy oriented research and public education	21%	(12%)
Mediation, conflict resolution and alternatives to violence	15%	(13%)
Community development	15%	(13%)
Employment and training	10%	(12%)
Social welfare	6%	(24%)

Beneficiary groups

'Last year saw the publication of the new guidelines for applicants which are more explicit about the beneficiary groups the foundation wishes to target, although it has for many years spoken of funding 'unpopular work or groups'. Much work will, naturally, apply to everyone in the community – for example general advice services – but it is encouraging to see the higher proportion of grants going to particularly marginalised groups such as travellers, refugees and people with mental heath problems.'

'In the year such beneficiaries included the Cardiff Gypsy Sites Group (£7,500 over two years for work on racial discrimination) and Alternatives to Violence (£2,200 for training workshops in prisons).

'The figures show a decrease in the amount going to work with the specific beneficiary groups (for example, children and young people, or people with disabilities) which are not among the current priorities. Such priorities always seem hard hearted and it is not an easy message to give an applicant – it can sound as though we do not think their work is valuable. But we try to make it clear that priorities are chosen simply to enable us to focus our resources and use them effectively.

Grants analysed by beneficiary group –

	1997/98	(1996/97)
Everyone/open to all	34%	(30%)
Refugees and asylum seekers	17%	(10%)
Black and ethnic minority communities	13%	(10%)
Women	10%	(12%)
Offenders and ex-offenders	7%	(8%)

Travellers	6%	(2%)
People with mental health problems	5%	(6%)
Single parents	1%	(1%)
Lesbians and gay men	1%	(0%)
Other specific groups (eg. children)	6%	(21%)

Grant highlights

The foundation wishes to fund work which is innovative, where a relatively small grant may make a significant impact or where the issue is unpopular and less likely to attract funding elsewhere. The trustees believe that all the grants made this year were potentially valuable and stood out as exceptional among the many applications received. Two themes are particularly illustrated...the wish to make a permanent difference and the willingness to fund work which benefits groups who are the object of dislike, discrimination and even hatred.

'Trustees also believe that an effective way of using the foundation's resources is to help provide people with information or skills so that they can help themselves, whether by claiming benefits or other rights, finding out about educational opportunities, improving their skills or participating in the processes that affect their lives. The grants for employment and training are made for similar reasons.

'The grants are presented within the categories of work, but the descriptions of the work often show how hard it is to categorise an organisation or its projects. Many are providing advice, and at the same time delivering a service of some kind of social welfare, and well as influencing policy or public opinion about a particular issue. Indeed this multiplicity of functions is often one of the strengths of the organisations funded by the foundation and enables them to achieve the maximum effectiveness because they operate on several levels or in several different modes simultaneously.'

An example of a grant made for these reasons is that to the Neighbourhood Initiatives Foundation (£5,000 per annum for two years), a 'national organisation working with local communities in innovative ways to enable people to be involved in shaping the future of their own communities'.

Refusals

The foundation gives applicants broad indications of why their application has been turned down. The reasons for refusal are:

'• Outside policy (18%) – as listed in the foundation's guidelines. Two of the specific exclusions – individuals (6%) and work in London (9%) are identified separately.
- Not a priority area (35%) – that is to say that, although the kind of work or the beneficiary group is not explicitly excluded in the guidelines, it is not one which we have identified as one which we wish to focus on at present.
- Too big – because the foundation's average grants are comparatively small, we try to make grants where they will make a significant difference. We look at the size of an organisation in terms of its income and the number of staff it employs as rough guidelines, and each case is looked at on its merits. The foundation only very rarely makes grants to national organisations with an income of more than £500,000 or to local ones with an income of more than £100,000.
- Too soon – the foundation will not normally consider an application within a year of an earlier refusal.
- Not exceptional (32%) – this is the shorthand for those applications which are within our remit, but which fail simply because of the strength of competition. The pressure on resources is such that only the most exceptional applications are successful and many good ones are turned down because there are simply not enough funds for everyone who meets our criteria.

'A significant minority of applications refused were outside the stated focus of the foundation. Perhaps the applicants has not seen the guidelines, or were relying on out of date directory entries – or were hoping that their application would be an exception. When the foundation turns down 27% of applications which were within its remit it becomes clear that there are unlikely to be any exceptions to the stated exclusions.

Size of grants

'Trustees made a decision to try moving towards fewer but larger grants this year and, as the figures show, this has begun to happen. They will also be considering whether it would be appropriate to increase their current guideline of £5,000 as the usual upper limit of single grants.

Number of grants analysed by size

Less than £1,000	30%
£1,000 to £2,999	39%
£3,000 to £4,000	12%
£5,000 to £9,999	11%
Over £10,000	8%

Geographical distribution

'The trustees wished to focus more on national or regional grants and less on purely local work. The relatively high grants for Yorkshire and Humberside and for the North East mainly reflect a handful of grants relating to regional work, such as the North of England Refugee Service, and a grant to the Catholic Housing Aid Society in York for an innovative research project on the provision of advice in rural areas.

'However, it is fair to say that the foundation's record on geographical spread is also strongly affected by the reactive nature of our work and the power of the grapevine. However much our policy is publicised, it is still true that making one grant in a particular town or country is much more effective in generating more applications from that area than any attempts at formal publicity. Foundations who complain that they do not get enough applications from, for example, Wales or the North West might try making a single grants in one such area and then wait for the grapevine to do the publicity.'

Grant distribution in the UK 1997/98

UK wide	52%	(48%)
England outside London	29%	(27%)
Scotland	7%	(6%)
Wales	6%	(4%)
Northern Ireland	5%	(2%)

Grant distribution in England excluding London

Yorkshire and Humberside	25%	(13%)
South Central	18%	(19%)
North East	17%	(13%)
North West	8%	(15%)
West Midlands	8%	(4%)
East Anglia	7%	(14%)
East Midlands	7%	(3%)
South East	5%	(10%)
South West	5%	(9%)

Executive Secretary's report

The foundation had a busy year as can be seen from the following table. Only the targeted use of information technology enables the staff of one full time and one part-time person to handle this volume and ensure that every applicant receives a prompt response.

	1997/98	(1996/97)
Enquiries	732	(492)
Applications	1414	(1540)
New grants committed	119	(159)
Refusals	1295	(1351)

'These figures may suggest that at least some potential applicants were taking note of the guidelines and not submitting inappropriate applications, although as an analysis of refusals indicates, many applicants had not seen the guidelines first. The chances of success dropped from 10% to 8%, but those grants made were rather larger. The programme of funding in Ireland showed the biggest increase in applications and together with the evaluation of the programme absorbed a good deal of time.

'The foundation has continued to clarify its policy and to publicise it as widely as possible in order to save applicants' disappointment. In addition to entries in the various directories of grant-making trusts, and distributing its own guidelines for applicants, the Executive Secretary spends a considerable amount of time talking to potential applicants on the phone.

'The foundation has also supported various training events run by voluntary sector agencies and by the Association of Charitable Foundations, aimed at helping organisations to prepare good applications and target them effectively.'

Trustees' report

'This has been a year of consolidation after one which saw considerable changes. As always the demand for grants outstrips the resources available. The foundation's actual income was slightly reduced from £666,000 last year to £556,000. The foundation received slightly fewer applications than last year, and made 119 new grants in the UK (compared with 159 last year). In addition to £342,000 committed in these new grants, a further £119,000 was paid out in instalments on previously agreed grants, and £78,000 (IR£87,000)in the Irish programme.

'Trustees agreed a more detailed policy relating to refugees and asylum seekers. This is one group of beneficiaries which we were particularly keen to support, recognising the considerable deprivation and disadvantage they suffer. However with limited resources of both administration and money, we needed to decide how to target our money effectively. We decided that we would not fund local community groups, mainly because of the difficulty of assessing or monitoring them. Equally, at the other end of the scale, we felt that it was not a wise use of our resources to make grants to very large organisations to whom our relatively small grants would be unlikely to make a significant difference. We therefore decided to focus on groups of a moderate size, with either a regional or a national area of interest. The new policy was widely publicised and while it has not yet made a significant impact in reducing unsuitable applications, we are gratified by the number of excellent proposals we have received and for which we have made grants.

'Our major piece of work this year has been the evaluation of our funding programme for women's groups in the Republic of Ireland. Trustees were pleased that the foundations funding had helped so much good work to be done. The foundation has been funding in Ireland for nine years. When the programme began, women's groups there were finding it extremely difficult to raise funds, but that position has now changed and although demand always outstrips resources, there is now European and state funding available – indeed probably rather more per capita than in the UK. Trustee have therefore decided not to start a further programme for women's groups, but will be exploring other possibilities for funding in Ireland.'

The trust finishes their annual review with in depth exploration of 20 grants, which have been chosen 'to demonstrate and celebrate the variety of work funded'. They include awards of £5,000 per annum for three years to: the Scottish Refugee Council towards core costs; 'Respond' who are establishing a project aimed at breaking the cycle of sexual abuse; and Runneymede Trust, 'an independent research and policy agency concerned with issues of racial equality, social justice and cultural diversity'.

Exclusions The foundation does not generally make grants to:

- academic research;
- addiction, alcohol or drug abuse;
- animal welfare or rights;
- arts or cultural or language projects or festivals;
- holidays or playschemes, sports or recreation;
- housing;
- individuals;
- large general appeals from charities which enjoy widespread public support;
- medical care, hospices or medical research;
- museums or galleries;
- overseas travel;
- private and/or mainstream education;
- promotion of sectarian religion;
- publications;
- purchase of property, building or refurbishment;
- restoration or conservation of historic buildings or sites;
- vehicle purchase;
- work which the trustees believe is rightly the responsibility of the state;
- work outside the United Kindom (except the Republic of Ireland);
- work which will already have taken place before a grant is agreed.

Applications In writing to the correspondent (not the trustees). Grants are made only to or through registered charities. There is no application form. An application should be no more than 4 sides of A4 (but the budget may be an extra page) and should be accompanied by the last annual report and accounts. It should answer the following questions:

- What are the aims of your organisations as a whole?
- How do you try to achieve these aims?
- What do you want our grant to help you do and how will you do it?
- How much will it cost? (Please submit a budget showing how the total figure is calculated)
- Are you asking the foundation to meet the whole cost? – What other sources of funding are you approaching?
- How will you know if your work has been successful?
- How will the work, and the way it is done, promote equal opportunities? If you do not think equal opportunities are relevant please state why.

If further information is needed this will be requested by the Secretary and a visit may be arranged when the application can be discussed in more detail.

In order to give as many applicants a chance of funding we do not accept applications from the same organisation more frequently than once a year.

Applicants should plan well ahead to allow sufficient time for applications to be assessed. If we are unable to help we will try to give you a decision within a few weeks, but grants are allocated at meetings of the trustees which are held three times a year so it may be as long as four months before a decision is made.

The Lankelly Foundation

£3,020,000 (1997/98, but see below)

Social welfare, disability

2 The Court, High Street, Harwell, Oxfordshire OX11 0EY
Tel: 01235 820044

Correspondent Peter Kilgarriff

Trustees Cecil Heather (Chairman); Leo Fraser-Mackenzie; W.J. Mackenzie; Georgina Linton; Lady Merlyn-Rees; A Ramsay Hack; Shirley Turner.

Beneficial area UK, except London.

Information available Full report and accounts. Information leaflet is available.

Summary 'Grants, seldom for less than £5,000, are given for the areas of work mentioned above. The broad priorities are 'the support of communities and families who are striving to create an environment in which they can flourish; the support of those people whose mental or physical disabilities require special resources; and the support of groups marginalised because of poverty, unemployment or crime, including domestic violence.'

'There is no fixed value for grants. They have ranged from as much as £75,000 over three years to just £4,000. Grants are rarely for less than £5,000 and may cover capital or revenue needs. Last year 125 grants were given out. Trustees will be reviewing their policies in November 1998, for April 1999 onwards.'

An early outcome of that review was a decision that the foundation would not make grants to replace time-expired National Lottery Charities Board grants.

The foundations income is set to rise sharply in coming years.

General 'The Lankelly Foundation's original brief was for general charitable purposes but over the years the trustees have refined their grant making policies. We continue to help in wide areas of social need and, deliberately, they remain active, responding to needs identified by those directly involved in the provision of services. Nevertheless, the foundation's detailed and personal response involves considerable dialogue and visits by members of staff.

'From its beginnings, the administration of the foundation has been linked to that of the Chase Charity. This has proved beneficial for a number of reasons. It gives staff a broader contact with voluntary organisations, it helps us respond more flexibly and it cuts administration costs. Nevertheless, the Lankelly Foundation and the Chase Charity remain two quite distinct trusts to which separate applications have to be made.

'The priorities of the foundation from 1996 to 1998 *(which are being reviewed in early 1999 Ed)* are:

- the support of communities and families who are striving to create an environment in which they can flourish;
- the support of people whose mental or physical disabilities require special resources;
- the support of groups who are marginalised because of poverty, unemployment or crime, including domestic violence.

'These broad priority areas will include elderly people, homelessness, alcohol and drugs, penal affairs, ethnic minorities and young people.

'We shall be expecting to support community initiatives to meet local needs. We shall look for user involvement as well as the proper use and support of volunteers and you will have to provide evidence of sound management and a culture which fosters equal opportunities. We intend to concentrate upon smaller charities, many of whom will have only a local or regional remit. Grants to large national charities are likely to be rare.'

The foundation no longer makes grants in the heritage and conservation field (though see the entry for the associated Chase Foundation).

Trustees' Report 1997/98

The report of the trustees for 1997/98 includes the following:

'The Settlor, who wished to remain anonymous, died on 17th October last year and his death will prove to be the watershed for the foundation. His generosity has already established the Lankelly foundation as one of the larger charitable trusts in the United Kingdom but his legacy will almost quadruple the Foundations capital and give us the potential to do considerably more in future years.

'Staff have responsibility for day-to-day management and, as far as applications are concerned, have a dual role of investigation and then advocacy. The first part rests upon a detailed exchange of information and personal visits; the second on first hand information about the work and the people who are seeking our support. This involves staff visiting all applications which are able to be considered in detail by the Trustees. We know that this is still unusual but this contact is mutually beneficial. Last year we began an evaluation of past grants and it is clear from this that our visits are highly valued.

'This evaluation, carried out by means of a questionnaire which had an 82% response rate, gave weight to our conviction that grants are indeed used for the purpose agreed and that they achieve that purpose. Of the schemes we had funded, two-thirds believed that our grant had helped to attract funding from other sources. they were complimentary also about our procedures and administration although this, perhaps, is to be expected. However a little later in the year we carried out a monitoring survey of organisations which we had turned down

(in one particular month). Here we had a smaller but still encouraging response rate of 63% and the results showed interesting pointers. Most of the respondents had not seen our guidelines before they applied to us; almost half felt that our response had been satisfactory, albeit disappointing, (although it is clear that too swift a response makes people feel that their case has not been properly considered); most significantly, only 13 of the 69 respondents had managed to raise the funds they needed from other sources.

The Grants Programme

'The trustees remain committed to those who are working directly with people in need and we try hard to make it as easy as possible for those people to contact us. We base our decisions upon what people are doing rather than who they know (although people seem to expect that this is how things work) which means paying attention to detail and spending time investigating applications. We also want to be convinced that our intervention is appropriate, for our understanding of partnership may be very different from what others understand by the word; it does not automatically absolve government from its responsibility to fund essential services.

'The past year has seen our total grants topping £3m for the first time and we have visited and made grants to more charities than ever before. However, we are conscious of our size relative to need, especially in poor communities and amongst unpopular groups, and the number of applicants we get is rising – although last year over a quarter fell outside our published guidelines. We know that even with our increased resources we shall still be able to meet only a fraction of the appropriate requests which come our way.

'When we reviewed our grant-making policies in the autumn of 1995 we decided to withdraw from funding in the areas of Greater London and Northern Ireland in order to concentrate on regions which appear to find it more difficult to attract trust funding. As a result, when we measure the distribution of our funds over a three or four year period, we hope to be able to show a greater parity between our work in the various regions.

'Numbers, though, are not as important as quality, and size and wealth are relative. The list of grants which follows shows that we can make a real impact on small or medium sized organisations and we actively seek to do this. This has a number of effects. In general terms we are making larger grants over longer periods, thereby responding to the often expressed need for revenue or core funding. Nevertheless, we do not want our work programme to silt up with organisations who are depending on us for long term support, and it is pleasing to note that 77% of those who received grants from the foundation last year had never had a grant from us before. This makes it even more important that our grants are well researched, targeting work which comes within our guidelines, which is well planned and whose need is proven.

'The trustees are keen that the staff should maintain the existing strong link between investigation and advocacy.

Breakdown of grants by category

Alcohol and drugs	*1%*
Arts/community arts	*5%*
Children and young people	*13%*
Community welfare	*11%*
Disability & special needs	*26%*
Domestic violence	*5%*
Elderly	*7%*
Heritage & conservation	*2%*
Homelessness	*7%*
Neighbourhood work	*13%*
Penal affairs	*9%*

'Once again the general field of disability and special needs took the largest percentage of our funds (26% – £804,000) but children and young people (£401,000), community welfare (£342,000) and neighbourhood work (£394,000) each claimed more than 11%. These last two categories include the grants we make in support of communities, although we use the latter to define local community initiatives. Between 5% and 10% of our funds went to organisations working with elderly people (£210,000) and in the fields of homelessness (£228,000), domestic violence (£151,000) and penal fairs (£283,000). Heritage and the arts continued to take a lower profile.

'As in previous years, we do not have a special category for ethnic minority projects but these are well represented in the grants list under the various categories of work. The foundation welcomes applications from ethnic minority groups and monitors its involvement carefully. Last year we made grants totalling £216,000 to eight different projects.

'The foundation`s annual income rose by over 23% on the previous year to £2,657,000. This comes from three principal sources: from dividends and interest of investments, from bank interest and from the Northwood Trust, an associated non-charitable trust whose unspent income comes to the foundation.

'Total direct charitable expenditure amounted to £3,141,000. This includes grants agreed of £3,020,000 and associated support costs of £121,000, which is in line with the Charity Commission`s Statement of Recommended Practice.'

'Last year 2,077 applications were received and 125 grants were made. Grants range in size from £75,000 to the Family Welfare Association, London (to support FWA's grants to individuals in need) to £3,000 to Prisoners' Wives & Family Society (to extend support to the centre and help with general running costs).

'We want our grants to be effective, to achieve something which otherwise would not happen, or sustain something which otherwise might fail, but we do not make grants to replace funds that have been withdrawn from other sources. Grants are rarely less than £5,000 and are always made for specific purposes but they may cover capital or revenue needs. We have extended the possible term of our revenue support to a maximum of five years. We shall monitor the effectiveness of all grants but those made over a number of years will involve more detailed evaluation.'

Examples of grants include the following:

£48,000 over three years to Women In Secure Hospitals (WISH), Ashworth, Liverpool (to employ a second worker to be based at Ashworth Special Hospital, over three years).

£10,000 to Wood End Advice and Information Centre, Coventry (towards the cost of converting and equipping an adjacent flat).

£5,000 to Deckham Community Care, Gateshead (towards the cost of completing repairs to the roof).

£30,000 to Young Homeless Project, Leamington Spa, Warwickshire ('to extend our existing funding to underpin the work of the project for a further two years').

£25,000 to The Shared Earth Trust, Lampeter, Wales (towards the cost of purchasing Denmark Farm and equipping a residential/education centre).

£7,200 to Age Concern Romney Marsh, Kent (towards the cost of purchasing a new minibus.

£38,600 over two years to Women Acting in Today's Society Trust (WAITS), Birmingham (towards the cost of employing a counsellor over three years to work with women who have suffered from domestic violence).

£30,000 to The Hall for Cornwall Trust, Truro, Cornwall (to help complete a major capital projects and ensure access

for people with disabilities).

Exclusions The foundation does not contribute to large, widely circulated appeals. More particularly, grants are not made in support of:

- the advancement of religion
- conferences or seminars
- festivals or theatre productions
- publications
- films or video
- research and feasibility studies
- sport; individual youth clubs
- travel, expeditions or holidays
- medical research
- hospital trusts
- formal education
- individual needs
- endowment funds
- animal welfare
- other grant-making bodies

Applications from the Greater London area are not considered.

Applications The foundation receives many more applications than it can help, and less than one in fourteen applicants are successful. This inevitably means that we have to disappoint good schemes which meet our criteria.

There are no application forms, except for the Summer Playscheme programme. The trustees meet in January, April, July and October.

Applications may be submitted at any time, but you should be aware that agendas are planned well ahead and you should expect the process to take some months. If we think we may be able to help, we will talk to you to clarify issues, give time for your plans to mature and for other funders to give an initial response.

Two or three months before the trustees consider a formal submission one of the staff will arrange to visit you or meet you at our office.

You will be notified of the trustees' decision as soon as possible and, if a grant is agreed, of any conditions that may have been attached to its release.

Applicants should include the following information with the initial letter:

- what you do and why you are seeking the foundation's help
- brief information about the origins and current company/charitable status of your organisation
- annual report and accounts
- answer to the following questions:
  how much do you need to raise?
  how soon do you need to raise it?
  what support have you already attracted?
  who else have you asked to help?

All applications receive a written answer

and we try to act as quickly as we can. The length of this process depends to some extent upon the size of the appeal but more upon your readiness to keep us informed.

A separate application needs to be made to the Chase Charity which shares the same administration.

The Leathersellers' Company Charitable Fund

£1,000,000 to institutions (1996/97)

General. See below.

15 St Helen's Place,
London EC3A 6DQ
Tel: 0171-330 1444

Correspondent Capt. J G F Cooke
The Clerk to the Trustees

Trustees The Warden and Society of the Mystery and Art of the Leathersellers of the City of London

Beneficial area UK.

Information available Reports and accounts up to 1996/97 on file at the Charity Commission.

General The 1996/97 annual report says 'The policy of the trustees is to provide support to registered charities associated with the Leathersellers' Company, the leather and hide trades, education in leather technology and for the welfare of poor and sick former workers in the industry and their dependents. Thereafter financial support is provided to registered charities associated with the City of London and its environs. Support is provided to the charitable objectives of education and sciences, relief of those in need, welfare, disabled, children and youth, medicine and health, the arts, the advancement of religion and the environment.' The trustees have further written that it is their policy to give at least £1 million a year.

Income for 1996/97 amounting to £1.37 million was generated from assets of £27 million. Investments and property are shown at cost rather than market value as specified in the Charities Regulation Act 1995, the trustees believing that market value is an inappropriate measure for these assets.

Grant giving stood at £1.02 million

(down from £1.45 million in 1995/96) disbursed in 250 grants; 195 to institutions (£1 million) and 55 to individuals (£22,000). Three types of grants are given:

- Single Grants;
- Guaranteed Annual Grants; a fixed sum paid for a period of four years;
- Recurrent Grants; fixed or variable annual payments made for an indefinite period or for variable annual sums paid for a fixed period.

Grants to institutions are classified into following categories:

Education and Sciences	£315,00	(31%)
Relief in need, Welfare	£200,000	(20%)
Disabled	£78,000	(8%)
Children and Youth	£206,000	(20%)
Medicine and Health	£124,000	(12%)
Advance Religion	£33,000	(4%)
Environment	£22,000	(2%)

The largest grant was to the Leathersellers' University Exhibition (£105,000), which has been a beneficiary for a number of years. About 87% of the grants were for £5,000 or more.

Examples of beneficiaries of some of the other larger grant giving include: Colfe's Educational Foundation (£59,000); Pendergas School for Girls, Lewisham (£50,000); British School of Leather Technology, Neve College (£44,000); Centrepoint (£39,000); Rainbow Trust (£37,000); National Listening Library (£32,000); Woodlands Centre Trust (£32,000); London Connection (£30,000); Childline (£25,000); Leather Conservation Centre (21,000); Royal Hospital of Neurodisability (£20,000) Whizzkidz (£20,000).

A large number of grants for £10,000 were given with beneficiaries such as: KIDS; Fitzwilliam College, Cambridge; St. Catherine's College, Oxford; Whitechapel Mission and the Queen Elizabeth Foundation for the Disabled.

Examples of organisations receiving £5,000 include: Barnardo's, Eating Disorders Association, Greater London Central Scout Council, London Sailing Project and Trinity Hospice.

Applications To the correspondent in writing. "It should, however, be noted that before an award is made, the charity is thoroughly investigated and visited which, of necessity, limits the number of appeals capable of being processed in any one year."

The William Leech Charity

£468,000 (1996/97)

Health and welfare in the North East

4 St James Street,
Newcastle-upon-Tyne, NE1 4NG
Tel: 0191-232 7940

Correspondent Mrs K M Smith, Secretary

Trustees R E Leech (Chairman); K G Alberti; C J Davies; J Miller; N Sherlock; B W Spark; A Reed.

Beneficial area Northumberland, Tyne and Wear, Durham.

Information available Full accounts are on file at the Charity Commission. Guidelines for applicants available from the trust.

Summary The charity's mission is 'to encourage local and community spirited people to create and sustain interest in voluntary charitable work'. Supported organisations are usually in Northumberland, Tyne and Wear, and Durham, 'with only occasional extensions into Cleveland and Cumbria'. However, 'grants for other areas are sometimes made if there is a substantial connection with the settlor or a local organisation'. Grants are usually one-off capital grants. The charity also makes crisis loans (often to churches) and 'challenge grants' which match other funding £1 for £1.

General The charity was established by property developer Sir William Leech in 1972 with an initial gift of property worth £550,000. Later donations of £450,000 and £120,000 (also originating from the founder), have helped the charity's assets grow to £10,663,000 (1997). Income generated that year amounted to £572,000, of which £468,000 was paid out in 208 grants. Running costs for the charity were remarkably low; a mere £11,352, 2% of income.

In the original guidelines, Sir William wrote:

'I would avoid clubs, etc who receive substantial grants or donations from local councils or the Government. I do not regard them as charities because they are subsidised.

'It is not my intention to subsidise social services even if grants by the Government or Council have been reduced. It is my intention to do what the social services do not support or do.

'I would fully support independent boys' and girls' clubs, YMCA, YWCA, Scouts, Guides (Boys Brigade) and Christian youth clubs and Christian teaching colleges'.

Although the removal of local authority support to some social services 'continues to trouble the trustees', preference is still given to causes not traditionally supported by public funds.

The University of Newcastle Medical School receives annual awards amounting to 'one third' of the income (43% of total donations in 1997). Beyond this annual fund, payments are made to:

1. Organisations in which a high proportion [at least two thirds] of the work is undertaken by voluntary unpaid workers. The trustees have set up a voluntary support programme and are 'actively seeking ways of reaching such..groups'.
2. Organisations with a close connection to the settlor, or with districts in which William Leech (Builders) Ltd, built houses during the time when the settlor was active in business.
3. Organisations with an active Christian involvement.
4. Organisations working in deprived areas for the benefit of local people, especially those which encourage people to help themselves. [In response to the occasional need for 'qualified and necessarily paid work' an inner city grants programme has been developed to 'favour three or four charities and give them larger annual donations towards running costs and salaries.']
5. Organisations doing practical new work and putting new ideas into action.

In 1997, excluding grants to the University of Newcastle, 83% (27% of funding) were for less than £1,000 and 12% (25%) for between £5,000 and £10,000. Grants in excess of £10,000 went to the Royal Victoria Infirmary Children's Fund (£30,000), St Oswald's Day Hospice (£25,000), the Salvation Army Foyer Project (£20,000), and St John's College (£11,000). Unfortunately, the specific purpose of payments is not mentioned in the report and accounts.

The charity appears to be energetic and thoughtful. Running costs are exceptionally lean and the accounts and guidelines explicit. However, more information on the purpose and effectiveness of donations would be useful.

Exclusions The Chairman and the Secretary are instructed to reject applications from the following:

- Community centres and similar (exceptionally, those in remote country areas may be supported);
- Running expenses for youth clubs (as opposed to capital projects);
- Running expenses of churches. This includes normal repairs. But churches engaged in social work, or using their buildings largely for 'outside' purposes may be supported;
- Sport;
- The Arts;
- Applications from individuals;
- Organisations which have been supported in the last 12 months. It would be exceptional to support an organisation in two successive years, unless we had promised such support in advance;
- Holidays, travel, outings;
- Minibuses (unless over 10,000 miles a year is expected);
- Schools;
- Housing associations.

Applications A full written application is required. Appeals are considered at bi-monthly meetings.

The Leeds Hospital Fund Charitable Trust

£711,000 (1997)

Hospitals in Yorkshire, charities in Leeds

41 St Paul's Street, Leeds LS1 2JL
Tel: 0133-245 0813

Correspondent Angela Romaine, Secretary

Trustees V Barker; C S Bell; Mrs P J Dobson; T Hardy; R T Strudwick.

Beneficial area Yorkshire.

Information available Full report and accounts on file at the Charity Commission

Summary The great bulk of donations, by number and value are awarded to hospital, hospices and convalescent homes, Grants are typically for £10,000 but unusual grants have gone as low as £50 and as high as £275,000. Only rarely are grants made to organisations without a medical connection – in a broad sense.

General The Leeds Fund was formed in 1887 as a non-profit health care insurance scheme. It was one of the many 'Healthcare Cash Benefit Schemes' nationwide which were common before the days of the National Health Service in 1948. In that year a new 'contributory benefit scheme' was drawn up offering financial help to contributors and convalescent service to help in recuperation. As the fund is non-profit, it uses its surplus income (about 3% of total contributions from its members) to make grants to health/welfare organisations in the Leeds area, through the charitable trust described in this entry.

In 1997 the trust received £788,000 in covenanted income from the company fund. Donations totalled £711,000 and distributed in three grants programmes with the self-explanatory titles: Hospitals and Hospices; Other Donations; Christmas Gifts. In addition, a considerable annual donation is made to the fund's Convalescent Homes Charity. In 1997 they were funded in these proportions:

Hospitals and hospices	22	£367,000
Other	32	£49,000
Christmas gifts	5	£18,000
Convalescent homes charity		£275,000

In the hospitals category most grants were for capital costs. Nearly all awards were for around £12,000 with the notable exceptions of grants to St James & Seacroft University Hospitals (for new equipment) and United Leeds Teaching Hospitals (refurbishment) who received £72,000 each.

Hospices received £10,000 each except St Gemma's (£20,000) and Wheatfields (£15,000). All hospice grants were made towards running costs. Almost exactly the same institutions benefited from this programme in both 1996 and 1997, though each grant was for a specific purpose.

The 'Other donations' and 'Christmas gifts' programmes make much smaller awards (capital or revenue, usually £1,000) and the recipients vary from year to year with only a 30% overlap between 1996 and 1997. The largest went to Leeds Children's Holiday Camps for updating facilities and Little Sisters of the Poor for new beds (£10,000 each). Other new 1997 awards were to Barnardos (£1,000 for local projects); Leeds Autism Group (£1,000); and TOCH (£100 for 20 cameras for disabled children).

The Convalescent Homes Charity supports the Springfield Convalescent Home at Bridlington which provides short periods of convalescence for patients.

Exclusions Individuals

Applications The trustees meet in February, May, July and November to consider applications.

The Kennedy Leigh Charitable Trust

£722,000 (1996/97)

Israel, Jewish charities, general

6 Arlington Street, St James's, London SW1A 1RE
Tel: 0171-491 4190; Fax: 0171-495 1306

Correspondent M J W Lunt, Administrator

Trustees G W Leigh; Mrs A Kennedy Leigh; Mrs L D Berman; Mrs L I Foux; G Goldkorn; Mrs C Berman Sujo; Mrs A Sorkin; Mrs M Foux.

Beneficial area UK and Israel.

Information available Report and accounts with outline of grant-making policy, partial grants list.

General The trust's deeds require that a quarter of its income should be disbursed to UK (or outside of UK) charities and the remainder to organisations based in Israel.

In 1996/97 income of £1,022,000 was generated from assets totalling £15,800,000. £772,000 was paid out in an undisclosed number of grants to largely unknown groups (the accounts show only four grants amounting to £255,000; 33% of grant expenditure).

The trust says:

'During the year the trustees made a number of new major commitments to Israeli charities. These included:

'The funding of a new residential units at the children's settlement at Yemin Orde (the accounts say that £656,000 is being held for the Yad Yemin Orde and will shortly be transferred to their control, Ed.).

'Various research projects connected with the Hebrew University of Jerusalem (£69,000 for three years).

'The cost of a nursing sister at St John's Ophthalmic Hospital in Jerusalem for three years.

'New facilities at Ofakim Tennis Centre.

'The work in support of immigrants from distressed countries, particularly Ethiopia and the former Soviet Union.

'A report by the Institute for Jewish Research was commissioned on the subject of the problems of immigrant communities in Israel and how they might be helped.

'In the UK the purchase and refurbishment of the new residential home for Ravenswood was completed.

'The construction of a new academic and research facility for endoscopy at St Mark's Hospital in Harrow will shortly be completed (£80,000).'

The accounts refer to two other grants: University of Cambridge, £100,000 (£150,000 the year before); British Technion Society, £6,500 (£65,000).

In 1996/97 the trust had committed itself to future grants totalling £1,313,000.

Exclusions Private individuals

Applications 'None considered. Funds fully committed.'

The Leverhulme Trade Charities Trust

£465,000 (1997)

Charities benefiting commercial travellers, grocers' or chemists

1 Pemberton Row, London, EC4A 3BG
Tel: 0171-822 6915

Correspondent The Secretary

Trustees Sir Kenneth Durham (Chairman); Viscount Leverhulme; Sir Michael Angus; Sir Michael Perry; N W Fitzgerald

Beneficial area UK.

Information available Report and accounts available.

General The Leverhulme Trade Charities Trust derives from the will of the First Viscount Leverhulme, who died in 1925. He left a proportion of his shares in Lever Brothers Ltd upon trust and specified the income beneficiaries to included certain trade charities. In 1983, the Leverhulme Trade Charities Trust itself was established, with its own share holding in Unilever, and with grant-making to be restricted to charities connected with commercial travellers, grocers' or chemists, their wives, widows or children. The trust has no full time employees, but the day to day administration is carried out by the director of finance of the Leverhulme Trust (see separate entry).

The trust has close links with Unilever with three trustees who are former chairmen, Sir Kenneth Durham, Sir Michael Angus, now chairman of Whitbread, and Sir Michael Perry. Mr N Fitzgerald is the current chairman of Unilever.

In 1997 the trust had assets with a market value of £26 million which generated a very low income of £544,000. The trust seems to receive very few eligible applications, and anyone working in these areas would be well advised to apply for funding.

The Trustees' Report notes that 'steps were taken to explore a scheme to help support the education of the children of the eligible occupations'. Further information is expected and applicants are advised to contact the trust directly.

Eleven grants, totalling £465,000, were made over the year. Only two of these grants went to organisations that had not received funds from the trust in the previous year. Unless otherwise noted all the organisations received an equal amount in 1996.

Over half the donations were given to benevolent funds, and these included a massive grant to the Commercial Travellers Benevolent Institution (£150,000).

Five other benevolent funds, four regular beneficiaries and one new, were supported. These were the Confectioners' Benevolent Fund (£40,000, new grant), the UCTA Samaritan Fund (£35,000), Royal Pharmaceutical Society of Great Britain Benevolent Fund (£25,000), the Provision Trade Benevolent Institution (£15,000), and the Commercial Travellers of Scotland Benevolent Fund (£10,000).

A series of educational grants were given to the Royal Pinner School Foundation (£70,000), the Girls' Public Day School Trust (£81,000, with 53,000 in the previous year), United Reform Church Schools (£14,000), Research Fellowships with the Royal Pharmaceutical Society (£12,000), Royal Wolverhampton School Orphan Foundation (£13,000, new grant).

Exclusions No grants to individuals.

Applications By letter to the correspondent. All correspondence is acknowledged. The trustees meet in February and applications need to be received by the preceding October.

The Leverhulme Trust

£15,240,000 (1997)

Research and education

1 Pemberton Row, London EC4A 3BG
Tel: 0171-822 6938; Fax: 0171-822 5084;
e-mail policies@leverhulme.org.uk;
Website http://www.leverhulme.org.uk

Correspondent Professor Barry Supple, Director

Trustees Sir Kenneth Durham, Chairman; Viscount Leverhulme; N W A Fitzgerald; Sir Michael Angus; Sir Michael Perry.

Beneficial area UK and developing countries.

Information available Detailed annual booklet on policies and procedures, and an annual report are available from the trust. Information also on the web site above.

Summary In 1997 179 grants were made to institutes for research, principally for academic research, but also for education. About 90% of funds are awarded to organisations (universities, charities etc.) and the remainder goes to individuals. Grants vary from a few thousand pounds to £1 million (given over five years). The trust's support covers the range of academia.

General The trust was established after the death of the first Viscount Leverhulme, in 1925. His legacy endowed the trust with shares in Lever Brothers Ltd (now Unilever plc) which the trust still retains.

In 1996/97 the value of this holding (which accounts for over 90% of the trust's assets) increased by 47%, or £284 million, to a total of £888 million. In all the trust's assets totalled £943,000,000 and income amounting to £20 million was generated, a low figure for an endowment of this value.

Guidelines for Applicants

The trust produces excellent guidelines and reports, too extensive to reprint here in full, and although this entry attempts to give a full account of what the trust does, it is insufficient as guidance for applications. Those interested in making an application should obtain a copy of the trust's full guidelines.

The following passages are reprinted from the guidelines along with additional information on the grants made in 1997:

'Social and educational conditions have changed radically since 1925. Correspondingly, the principle governing the direction of the trust's grant-giving efforts have evolved. That evolution has entailed variation of emphases as well as huge expansion. At present the trustees award grants mainly for original research but also, to a very limited extent, for the support of students and instruction in areas of distinctive educational activity (mostly in the performing arts).

'The trust has a total staff of twelve. We try to deal with each potential applicant individually, and our computer systems help us to do this. However, we have up to 1,000 grants current at any time, and up to a similar number of applications at peak times. Please remember this when contacting us.'

Grants to institutions for research (£11,646,000 disbursed in 1997)

'To enable established scholars occupying posts in eligible institutions to employ a research assistant or assistants and to meet modest direct support costs for a specific piece of novel and significant research rather than to create a post for a person otherwise without one. In rare circumstances, the trustees offer replacement teaching costs for the applicant. Students may not be employed on these grants.

'In addition to standard project grants (up to three years), applicants for pilot projects and, in exceptional circumstances, very large-scale projects (up to five years) will be considered.

'*Priorities:*
- to fund excellence, novelty, and significance;
- in appropriate fields, to favour projects directed to the creation and/or use of wealth, and the promotion of increased efficiency when those objectives are too remote, to attract commercial or public support, in other fields, to favour projects making significant contributions to basic and cultural knowledge;
- to give preference to projects which are interdisciplinary or which fall between research councils or outside their terms of reference;
- in pure and applied sciences, to support only projects of exceptional originality and importance of method

The Leverhulme Trust

Payments to institutions:	1997	1996
Research and education		
- **economics, business studies, industrial relations**	£921,000	£647,000
- **law, politics, international relations**	£369,000	£389,000
- **social sciences (inc. anthropology, geography and social psychology)**	£480,000	£530,000
- **education**	£364,000	£491,000
- **medicine, health**	£127,000	£325,000
- **basic sciences**	£5,486,000	£4,121,000
- **applied sciences**	£837,000	£584,000
- **humanities (inc. architecture)**	£1,895,000	£1,726,000
- **fine arts**	£576,000	£624,000
- **regional studies**	£32,000	£80,000
- **libraries, archives, museums**	£395,000	£343,000
- **combined studies**	£82,000	£144,000
- **environmental resources**	£82,000	£205,000
Academic interchange	£301,000	£391,000
Major initiatives	£956,000	£156,000
Personal research Professorships	£401,000	£256,000
Payments to individuals via RAAC:		
Fellowships and grants	£878,000	£667,000
Emeritus fellowships	£305,000	£282,000
Study abroad studentships	£384,000	£482,000
Special research fellowships	£369,000	£189,000

or potential conclusions.'

'Eligible institutions:
Universities and other institutions of higher and further education in the UK;

- registered charities in the UK;
- institutions or organisations of similar status in countries of limited provision for private and or public research funding.
'NB; Joint applications from more than one institution and applicant, up to a maximum of four, are eligible. One institution and applicant must be designated as the lead, and must undertake to be responsible for administering the grant if awarded.

'The trustees support research in any field *except:*

- social policy and welfare (especially action research);
- medicine;
- school education (in very rare circumstances, the Director may use his discretion to accept an application of particular significance, breadth and originality);
- archival or cataloguing work unless it directly involved or leads to important and original research;
- archaeological digs unless the project concentrates on technical experiment and innovation.

'Eligible applicants:
Research programmes must be undertaken in the institution in which the applicant is employed or with which he or she is regularly affiliated. Applicants must have experience of and be directly responsible for research and take prime and direct responsibility for its writing up and dissemination.

(a) If applying for the salary costs of research assistance, applicants must be:

- staff employed in existing posts in the applying institution;
- or occupants of established and unfunded posts to which they have been appointed by the applying institution:
- or retired academics who have maintained close links with their institutions.

(b) If applying for their own salaries, applicants must be in posts with established status or posts funded on renewable but short-term contracts at applying eligible institutions, for a starting date after their current funding ceases. The principal purpose of the application must be to pursue a research project rather than fund a particular individual or particular post(s).

(c) If applying for replacement teaching costs, applicants must be people employed full-time on a continuing basis by an eligible institution when, exceptionally, they need to devote a substantial amount of time continuously to a specific piece of research. An applicant's study leave entitlement and recent periods of leave will be taken into consideration.

'Ineligible:

- the employment as a researcher of anybody registered for a higher degree;
- applicants permanently employed by eligible institutions requesting their own salaries;
- applicants who are unpaid visiting or honorary research fellows of the applying institution seeking a salary for themselves;
- applicants who are eligible for postdoctoral or junior research fellowships offered by other bodies or for the trust's special research fellowships scheme;
- applicants who are students;
- applications aimed at providing employment for a named person rather that at the undertaking and completion of a specific piece of research;
- the resubmission of an application substantially the same as one already rejected by the trustees;
- applications of which the principal object is the production of electronic editions and CD-ROMs. However, a special case may be made where the original contribution to knowledge is immediate and exceptionally significant.

'Eligible duration:

- from 6 months full-time in a year to three years.
- Different rules apply to pilot projects and large projects:

'Pilot projects:
The trust invites applications from individuals for research grants of up to £15,000 for pilot projects to be administered by institutions. Such grants are intended to enable a principal investigator to assess and demonstrate the feasibility of a project and would, typically, be for a duration not exceeding six months. The criteria and procedures governing these applications for grants are similar to those described above. An extended application will only be accepted when the results of the pilot project are available for appraisal by referees.

'Large project grants:
The trustees are prepared to consider proposals for a limited number of research grants of between £250,000 and £500,000 for up to five years as part of their institutional grants scheme. The criteria governing these grants and eligibility of proposals and costs will be generally identical to those described above, except as to duration. Proposals may relate to a single project or a small number of closely linked projects. Core funding is not eligible.

'The procedures used to assess such large applications will be more elaborate than is normally the case, involving not merely a preliminary short-listing on the basis of outline applications and the composition of detailed applications by those on the short-list, but subsequent site visits and discussions with applicants. Consequently, final decisions may take up to five months or more, from the date of the initial application.

Grants to institutions for education
'To offer a limited amount of support for education in a restricted range of fields – mostly confined to leading institutions in the performing and fine arts, although the trustees are willing to consider exceptional proposals in other areas of education. Support is normally offered in the form of bursaries or scholarships, designed to be made for the maintenance of students to be selected by the institution. However, in exceptional circumstances, grants can also be made to support distinctive teaching activity.

'Eligible institutions:

- institutions of higher and further education in the UK:
- registered charities in the UK in similar circumstances;
- institutions in developing countries of similar status.

'Eligible applicants: staff employed by eligible institutions, with approval from their employing institution. The selection of bursary holders is normally at the discretion of the applying institution's staff.

'Eligible fields: most grants are offered in the fine arts or performing arts. However, distinctive applications in other fields may be considered.

'Eligible duration: normally up to three years maximum. Some schemes may be eligible for renewal; in considering the renewal, the trustees have regard to changing circumstances, the record of past achievement, and efforts made to secure alternative funding.

'Eligible costs:

- contributions to maintenance for students chosen by the institution and engaged in programmes which are

available every year.
- support for a distinctive teaching activity.

'Ineligible: applications:
- from individuals;
- for university studentships in the UK and other developed countries;
- for university teaching fellowships.'

Grants to institutions for academic interchange (£301,000 in 1997)

'The trustees believe that international understanding and the spread of knowledge can benefit from interchange between academics. They have, therefore, from early days, approved a small number of schemes of varying dimensions to provide for visits involving scholars from groups or institutions to and from the UK. They are open to suggestions from national or international bodies for new schemes for which the need can be established. Such proposals should be designed to benefit all the research communities involved. The trustees periodically initiate their own schemes.

'Eligible institutions:
- groups of universities;
- other institutions of higher and further education;
- registered charities in the UK;
- similar bodies in developing countries.

'Eligible applicants: staff employed in an eligible institution. The selection of visitors is normally at the discretion of the staff of the applying institution.

'All fields are eligible. Eligible duration is normally up to three years in the first instance. Thereafter, schemes may be renewed at the trustees' discretion, depending upon the success of the scheme so far and the evidence of a continuing need which would not otherwise be met.

'Eligible costs: travel and subsistence at realistic level. For subsistence, the following are the maximum Leverhulme Trust levels per month:

United Kingdom, Asia and Australasia	*£1,750*
Europe and North America	*£1,495*
Middle East, North Africa and South America	*£1,390*
Rest of Africa	*£1,030*

'Ineligible:
- individuals seeking funding for visits abroad or to this country;
- applications intended to facilitate visit by a specific individual;
- students at all levels.'

Annual Report 1997

The trustees' Report gives details on all grants, for example who the grant went to, the purpose for which it was awarded and the period of the grant. It contains especially detailed accounts of 35 grants to institutions totalling £2,817,000; a few examples of these are:

'A residency by the Sorrel String Quartet. University of Liverpool (Professor Orledge). £83,000, 36 months. In the period of this residency, the Sorrel Quartet gave a series of 18 concerts which reflected the history of music lectures and seminars in the University Department. Masterclasses and workshops took place frequently, and often involved the participation of a member of staff as commentator on the music. It was hoped that interest in chamber music in Liverpool would be stimulated, and this did appear to be achieved, although audience numbers were not as high as they might have been. Unfortunately illness struck the leader of the quartet in the second year of the residency, and the considerable adaptation made necessary by the appointment of a new leader disrupted plans for orchestral coaching. The new leader turned out to be an excellent choice and the quartet goes from strength to strength.

'A greater Tibetan-English dictionary. School of African and Oriental Studies (Dr Skorupski). £243,000, 48 months. The basis for this work was a Tibetan-English-Chinese dictionary produced in Tibet and containing over 53,000 entries. For this new dictionary translation work of all Tibetan definitions of individual terms into English began in 1992, and these were supplemented with Sanskrit and Chinese equivalents for Buddhist and other technical terms. The Romanised Tibetan text was converted in to Tibetan fonts. By the time the grant period came to an end, a complete translation had been finished, the entire dictionary was on a computer in Tibetan and Roman fonts and printed on A4 paper, and proof reading had also been completed. Much of the editorial work was also finished. Publication is expected soon. A gratifying result.

'The peculiarities of information perversion under a totalitarian regime. Siberian Independent University, Novosibirsk (Dr V Leutin). £10,000, 36 months. The researchers investigated the effect of a totalitarian regime on people's reactions to certain positive and negative words. They found that people's reactions were often inverted to those normally expected – with the suppression of negative reactions and aggressive reaction to positive stimuli. The continuance of these reactions after a change of regime prompts questions about the passing on of attitudes to children, and indeed the possible rebirth of a totalitarian regime. Some research was also conducted on the left and right hemispheres of the brain and how they are affected. This small grant gave a valuable opportunity to researchers in Siberia, and its results were conclusive and well documented. Several publications have resulted.'

A selection of grants to institutions from the normal list is as follows:

University of Warwick (Professors Waddams and Waterson); Consumer producer and regulatory responses in new markets: domestic energy; £198,000, 48 months.

University of Oxford, Queen Elizabeth House (Dr E FitzGerald). Trends in the manufacturing terms of trade and the developing countries. £28,000, extension.

The Anna Freud Centre (Dr G Gergely, Professor P Fonagy). Causal versus teleological interpretations of behaviour in infancy £68,000 12 months.

University of Aberdeen (Dr C Secombes), University of York (Dr P Grabowski) The role of cytokines in the expression of nitric oxide synthase in fish £53,000, 24 months.

University of East Anglia (Professor Church). Product innovation, competition and the marketing of consumer goods 1840-1960. £52,000 34 months.

Occasional special schemes

'The trustees occasionally invite applications for programmes in specific areas.'

Awards to individuals (£1,936,000 in 1997)

A. *'Research fellowships and grants:* For those research expenses over and above normal living costs and/or a contribution towards replacement teaching or loss of earnings. Approximately 120 awards offered annually.

B. *'Emeritus fellowships:* For incidental research costs to assist recently retired scholars.

C. *'Study abroad studentships:* For holders of UK first degrees or equivalent UK qualifications normally under age 30 to enable them to study or research abroad for one or two calendar years.

D. *'Special research fellowships:* For experienced post-doctoral researchers normally under age 35: 50/50 salary costs shared between the trust and the employing university.'

The 1997 report on the trust's Research Awards Advisory Committee (RAAC) included the following:

'Approximately half of the trust's income is distributed in individual awards under schemes approved by the trustees. Selection is delegated to the RAAC, set up in 1933 and consisting of seven senior academics. In 1997 awards were made under four schemes as follows:

'Emeritus fellowships (tenable for between 3 and 24 months) to support academics in the UK aged 59 or above at retirement who wished to complete a piece of research for publication.

'Research fellowships and grants (tenable for between 12 to 24 months) to assist experienced researchers who were prevented by their routine duties from completing a piece of original research. Applicants had to be UK residents and have to have been educated in the UK or Commonwealth or able to demonstrate they were members of the UK scholarly community.

'Study abroad studentships (tenable for 12 or 24 months) to support graduates of UK institutions in a period of advanced study or research overseas (not in the USA).

'Special research fellowships (tenable for 24 months) to enable those without an established UK academic post to undertake a significant piece of research for publication. The scheme was based on a "pound for pound" system, whereby the trust paid 50% of each fellow's salary costs and the host institutions contributed the other 50%.'

Expenditure in 1997 (1996)

Grants to institutions £13,304,000 (83%)
Grants to individuals
  (via RAAC)   £1,936,000 (12%)
Administration   £810,000 (5%)

The Chairman wrote the following in the trust's 1997 Report:

'We continue to be concerned that in our grants to institutions the proportion of science grants continues to increase, but this situation is somewhat mitigated by the award of professorships in humanities and social sciences, by the higher proportion of humanities awards in the grants to individuals category, and by our decision to award four major programme grants in education and the social sciences. In the course of our review, we decided to hold a further competition for personal research professorships. Six professors appointed in 1997 is extremely encouraging too. In coming months, we will be announcing other initiatives resulting from our review.

'We try to ensure that news of such initiatives and indeed of our regular schemes reach academics throughout the country. The director and other members of staff are sometimes able to visit universities in order to describe, in more detail than is possible in our literature, the programmes that we run, and the thinking behind them. Nevertheless, we know that many universities, particularly those with only relatively recent experience of research, feel somewhat out on a limb. With this in mind, we held a briefing meeting for academic and administrative staff of new universities only on 15th October. The director, chairman of our research awards advisory committee, and members of staff gave presentations covering all aspects of the trust's work. The original response form those invited was very enthusiastic; seventy participants were expected. Reality was disappointing , in that only some forty people attended. We were surprised that so many delegates decided, at the last minute, that it was not worth attending or sending a substitute. Nevertheless, the day went well, with lively question and answer sessions and animated discussion during the breaks. I was encouraged that not only had we given university staff an opportunity to learn about our awards but that this was an occasion for people with similar aims and concerns to talk of them amongst themselves.'

Director's report, 1997:

'In last year's report I emphasised the commitments and what seemed to be the academic and administrative productivity which had characterised the activity of the trust in the course of 1996. The same points can certainly be made about our work in 1997 - the more so because a number of schemes came to maturity and because the year culminated in a major policy review by the trustees.

'Even so, and as has been beneficially the case for some time, the broad features of the trust's work continued to be characterised by the 'routine', but nevertheless never complacent or unthinking tasks, of responding to grant applications generated solely by the aspirations of academics researchers and, to a lesser extent, by educational institutions. In its stewardship of the various schemes for a large number of relatively modest individual grants, the research awards advisory committee continued to allocate some 10% of total grant expenditure - although in the November policy review the trustees acknowledged the importance and rapid growth of applications for research fellowships and grants to individual scholars by augmenting by 50% the proportion of the RAAC's budget devoted to that category with effect from 1998. The work of the committee is discussed later in the Annual Report from its chairman. As in earlier years, the section of the Report is concerned with the balance of grant committees, of varying sizes, categorised as 'institutional grants' and directly allocated by the trustees. The number of applications in 1997 (589) was virtually the same as in 1996 (590), although there was a slight decrease in the number of project grants made (179 as against 185).

'As already implied, and following the precedents of the last few years, the great bulk of such institutional grants were for specific and discrete research projects proposed on the initiative of individual scholars, which therefore continued to embody the activity for which the trust is perhaps best known and which represents its major contribution to scholarship. As I said last year, we are proud to be able to maintain such an abundant flow of funds to support research in almost the complete range of disciplines, unrestricted by any pre-determined assumptions about the priority to be attached to particular problems or fields of research. In continued contrast to most public funding bodies, therefore, the criteria adopted by the trustees in arriving at their decisions about research grants remained the originality, excellence and significance of the projects or uses to which grants would be put.

'In addition to this core of activity, the trustees continue to support study leave for academics through schemes administered by the British Academy and the Royal Society; research professorships in the humanities and social sciences; large-scale research programmes incorporating linked projects in specific fields; international exchange programmes and visiting fellowships; and a limited range of student bursaries and instruction, mostly in the performance and creative arts. The result is, we hope, a substantial contribution to the richness and variety of scholarship and education in further and higher education.

'For two years now, I have drawn attention to the uncomfortably disproportionate percentage of applications and grants accounted for by the natural sciences. And it says much for the quality of scientific research in British universities that this issue is still very much alive - in spite of the trustee's decision to apply particularly demanding criteria of originality and significance in these areas. Meanwhile, the healthy alternative of attempting to attract more and better applications on other fields continues. More generally, in awarding grants in general, the trustees focus solely on the quality of the applications, favouring or handicapping no category of institution. The proportion of institutional research grants going to Oxford, Cambridge and London Universities was 28.7% of the total, compared with 28.1% in 1996 and 19.5% in 1995.

'In line with stability of the number of applications and the relative stability in the number of grants, there was only a small change in the success rate. Having been about 40% in the 1980s and 34% in 1992-4, it had fallen to 30% in 1995, and risen slightly to 31% in 1996. Last year it was 30%. It is certainly true that these figures compare reasonably favourably with most funding agencies, but they are certainly too low in the context of effort and commitment needed to make or process fully detailed applications. This undoubtedly had a deterrent effect for many potential applicants, who are understandably reluctant to spend a good deal of time in compiling detailed proposals when the statistical chance of success was relatively low. For this reason, as anticipated in last year's Annual Report, the trust has introduced a system of outline applications, involving much less effort, on the basis of which the more promising proposals can be identified and their authors invited to submit detailed proposals. This system was introduced on a voluntary basis in September 1997 (and appeared to be quite popular even then), and obligatorily form January 1998. The change seems to be very popular, and is certainly economical of the time of applicants' and the trust's staff. So far, about 40-50% of those submitting outlines have been invited to make more elaborate applications. On the other hand, for the first time for some years, the trust advertised the existence of institutional research grants, which led to a dramatic leap in inquiries. Moreover, although it is too early to be certain, the greater facility of application at the initial stage also appears to have stimulated an enhanced flow of proposals. If this is sustained, and if the greater publicity also generates more proposals, then the success rate for detailed applications may begin to rise towards the former levels, albeit on the basis of a larger number of initial approaches!

'Returning to the outcome of the applications for project grants in 1997, the diversity of grants made is reflected in the summaries of a relatively small selection of completed grants provided in Item 5, although a fuller impression can be gained form a list of new grants agreed by the trustees and reproduced in Item 6. from the statistical and financial view points, all this should be considered in the context of the following table of statistics herewith.

'Although responsive grants are the core of the trust's 'regular' activity (they will continue to account for at least 95% of institutional grant expenditure over the next five years), and involve the processing of hundreds of applications and communications with thousands of applicants and referees, the trustee's initiatives have become an increasingly critical aspect of the trust's contribution to advanced research and education. Following their decision in 1996, the trustees once again awarded a number of Leverhulme Research Professorships in the humanities and the social sciences. In response to a huge number of applications, and in the light of the very high quality of applicants, nine new chairs were created, making 15 in all. The scheme to fund visiting fellows from overseas was renewed and another 30 universities were allocated such posts. In addition, as indicated in last year's Report, having noted the attractions and benefits of the decision in 1996 to fund two very substantial research programmes on unemployment and technical and structural change, the trustees decided to extend this policy. As a result, and after an extensive progress of application and consideration, four major grants, of some grants, of some £1 million each were made for a programme research into low educational achievement; the state, regulation and the market; the family, household and welfare; and business and industrial structures and performance. The trustees also decided too make three large project grants, of some £200,000 each, to proposals which had been short-listed for the programme competition. They were to the ESRC Centre for Business Research and the Department of Applied Economics at the University of Cambridge, for research into learning theory and literacy; and to the Warwick Business School for research into regular and public policy.

'The positive experience of new schemes in 1996 and 1997 was also taken into consideration when the trustees came to their policy review in November. While the future of the schemes for research professorships and research programmes is for future discussion, it was decided to encourage applications for both large(£250-£500, 000) and small pilot (under £15,000) grants in the normal course of the competitions for project funding. This is already resulting in a reassuring flow of new types of proposals. In addition, the trustees confirmed the broad balance of grants between research and education, as well as the principal focus of educational grants on the creative and performing arts. However, they decided to extend the range of type of the latter by inviting applications form selected institutions for innovative schemes in arts education.

'I pointed out last year that the growth and proliferation of activity in recent years, together with the heightened pressures on university research and teaching, have produced an intensification of the complexity with which the trust's rules have to be interpreted and applied. As a result it appeared desirable to undertake a major revision of the content and presentation of the trust's policies and procedures brochure. We hope that this clarified our procedures and rules, and that the amendments made have worked to the benefit of academic research. We are always open to comments and suggestions about our procedures, but meanwhile urge all potential applicants to read the brochure extremely carefully: at least 50% of the need to communicate with applicants before the trustees can consider proposals is generated by failures to take careful note of explicit material in our policies and procedures.

'In this respect, potential applicants should note that only holders of regular and established posts are eligible to apply: there is no intention of grants to institutions being used to fund posts for people wishing to undertake research but who have not yet obtained full-time paid employment.

'Potential applicants who are in doubt about their eligibility should contact me before going to the trouble of compiling an application. It is also necessary to re-emphasise the importance of grant-holders submitting within 6 months of the completion of the project and conform to the specifications embodied in the trust's terms and conditions. This is essential for the smooth running of the trust, relevant to the reputation of the grant-holder, and a vital aspect of the responsible use of the trust's funds.

'On a somewhat more generous note, it is also worth repeating that although retired researchers are still not eligible to apply for salaries for themselves under other grants to institutions scheme, they are now eligible to apply for institutional research grants to pay for research assistance even though they do not occupy a regular university post. The only condition is that they should have retained a continuing link with their former employing institution and that the latter should be willing to provide general facilities and accommodation for the relevant project.'

Exclusions See above within each category for relevant exclusions.

Applications The trust has detailed and specific requirements and procedures which applicants must meet, both as to timing and to content. All applicants should first ask for the trust's current 'Policies and Procedures' brochure before attempting to submit an application. The web site may also be consulted.

Lord Leverhulme's Charitable Trust

£759,000 (1994/95)

Education, general

Price-Waterhouse-Coopers,
1 Embankment Place,
London WC2N 6NN
Tel: 0171-583 5000

Correspondent The Trustees

Trustees A E H Heber-Percy; A H S Hannay.

Beneficial area UK, especially Cheshire and Merseyside.

Information available In September 1998 the most recent accounts on file at the Charity Commission were those for 1994/95. It is surprising that Price-Waterhouse-Cooper continue to act for a charity for which timely accounts cannot be produced.

General The trust is administered by the firm of accountants given above, who told these editors (in September 1998), that although most funds are already committed, there is money available for unsolicited grants. There are no guidelines for such grants, but all applications are said to be reviewed by Viscount Leverhulme and the trustees. Preference is given to the Cheshire and Merseyside areas where Viscount Leverhulme has been resident all his life.

As we have been unable to obtain any further information (from the Charity Commission or the trust), the rest of this entry is based on that in the previous edition of this book:

The trust was set up in 1957 by the 3rd Viscount Leverhulme for general charitable purposes. In 1995 it had assets of £13 million which generated the very low income of £450,000.

There are two restricted funds within the trust. One generates £30,000 a year which is paid to the Merseyside County Council for the trustees of the Lady Lever Art Gallery. The second is the Lord Leverhulme's Youth Enterprise Scheme; the income from this sponsors young people in the Wirral and Cheshire areas who receive support from the Prince's Youth Business Trust (£23,000 was given in 1994/95 in grants of £2,000 to £5,000 to seven enterprises managed by young people).

£705,000 was distributed in 1994/95 in 111 other grants. Eleven of them were large, ranging between £20,000 and £166,000, and 31 grants were between £1,000 and £17,000. More than half the grants were for less than £1,000, 48 of them for less than £100, including five for £5 (perhaps the smallest grants in this guide).

Although some of the larger grants showed continuing relationships, several were given to organisations not supported before. The larger grants were given to Liverpool University Student Community Action (£166,000), Hammond School (£117,000 with £5,000 in the previous year), Cheshire Cathedral Development Trust, St George's Church in Thornton Hough (£50,000 each), Royal College of Surgeons (£50,000, also the year before), Animal Health Trust (£30,000 with £28,000 the previous year. Lord Leverhulme is Chairman of the executive committee of this trust), Cambridge Foundation, Charter Educational Trust (£25,000 each), Parochial Church Council of Altcar Parish Council, the 22nd Cheshire Regiment, and Wirral Grammar School Activities Fund (£20,000 each)

The commitment to the Cheshire and Merseyside area was strongly evident with three quarters of grants given there. In addition to those mentioned above, grants were given to Camm Street Centre, Merseyside Society for the Deaf (£5,000 each), Birkenhead School (£3,700), Montessori St Nicholas Centre (£1,100), Wirral Dyslexia Association (£1,000), and Toxteth Community Council (£500).

Grants were also made to national organisations:

British Wheelchair Sports Foundation	*(£5,000)*
National Garden's Scheme	*(£3,900)*
Spinal Injuries Association	*(£2,000)*
National Asthma Campaign	*(£1,000)*

Exclusions Non-charitable organisations.

Applications By letter addressed to the trustees setting out details of the appeal including brochures.

The Joseph Levy Charitable Foundation

£1,037,000 (1996/97)

Young people, health, medical research, Jewish charities

37-43 Sackville Street, Piccadilly,
London W1X 2DL
Tel: 0171-333 8111; Fax: 0171-333 0660

Correspondent Dr Sidney Brichto, Director

Trustees Mrs N F Levy; Mrs Jane Jason; Peter L Levy; Silas Krendel; Neil W Benson.

Beneficial area UK and overseas.

Information available Full accounts and grants list, but without a narrative report, on file at the Charity Commission.

General The trust generated a high income of £826,000 from an asset base of £10.8 million in 1996/97. One million pounds went to about 90 organisations in grants of varying sizes. Administrative expenditure was also high at £251,000.

Grants appeared to be given in four main areas, with an apparent policy of giving one major grant in each category and then a number of smaller grants. Estimated category totals were as follows:

Youth/social	*£240,000*
Health/care	*£365,000*
Medical research	*£168,000*
Jewish charities	*£233,000*

Youth/social £240,000: Half the money in this category was made up of one grant to the London Federation of Boys Club (£145,000). Other beneficiaries included Romford Trumpet Corps. (£2,000), Bolton Lads and Girls Club (£5,000), Community Security Trust (£10,000), and the Drive for Youth Programs Limited (£15,000).

Health/care (£365,000): 70% of this grants total was given in just one grant to the Dementia Relief Trust (£257,000).

Other smaller grants included those to Belinson Medical Centre (£10,000), RELATE (£2,500), National Asthma Campaign (£2,800) and the North London Hospice (£6,000).

Medical Research (£168,000): Nearly all the money in this category went in one grant to the Cystic Fibrosis Research Trust (£119,000). Other grants included those to the National Hospital for Neurology and Neurosis (£22,000) and Quest Cancer Research (£1,000).

Jewish Charities (£233,000): The largest grant in this category went to the Ashkelen Foundation (£95,000). Other grants went to a variety of educational, social and medical organisations: Jewish Policy Research (£36,000), Sarah Hezog Hospital, Jerusalem (£20,000), Friends of Israel Education Trust (£12,500), Jewish Care (£10,000), West London Synagogue Charitable Fund (£5,000) and Ravenswood (£3,000).

Exclusions No grants to individuals, under any circumstances.

Applications In writing to the director at any time.

Lewis Family Charitable Trust

£585,000 (1996/97)

General, Jewish charities

Chelsea House, West Gate,
London, W5 1DR
Tel: 0181-998 8822

Correspondent David Lewis

Trustees David Lewis; Bernard Lewis.

Beneficial area UK and overseas.

Information available Accounts are on file at the Charity Commission; no narrative report or analysis of grants, despite the new requirements.

Summary Grants range from under £1,000 to £100,000. Most charitable expenditure goes to charities previously assisted by the trust. Perhaps up to half of funds are gifted to Jewish causes.

General The trust was established in 1969 to make grants for general charitable purposes and for 'the relief of poor persons', though the first purpose receives the great majority of funds.

In 1996/97 the trust's income was £670,000 (£205,000 in 1995/96) which consisted of £517,000 in new donations and £153,000 from investments (assets total £3.4 million). The 28 grants listed in the accounts for £1,000 or more accounted for 86% of grant expenditure. Five repeated grants totalled £208,000 (35% of the total). The trust does not say how funds were divided between the categories or classify grants by type of beneficiary. A crude analysis, however, can be made using the titles of the recipient organisations:

Medical	*£300,000*	*51%*
Education	*£122,000*	*21%*
General Jewish	*£78,000*	*13%*
Other	*£85,000*	*14%*

The medical grouping comprises largely of national associations for various conditions, hospitals and medical schools and there is particular emphasis on brain injury rehabilitation. Overall, 30% of grant expenditure went to Jewish charities, this is lower than in previous years when such groups shared about 50% of the grants budget. However, the accuracy of these figures is compromised by the fact that only charities with obviously Jewish names (ie. the Jewish National Fund for Israel) could be identified as such – therefore the actual percentages are likely to be higher.

The largest awards went to Lewis National Rehabilitation Institute (£100,000), Birth Defects Association (£61,000), the University of Miami School of Medicine. and the Joint Jewish Charitable Trust (£50,000).

Apparently the trust is not aware of its legal obligation to provide its report and accounts on request, for a reasonable fee if necessary, as it has stated that 'we do not issue copies of our accounts'.

Exclusions No grants to individuals.

Applications To the correspondent in writing. Grants are normally made once a year. Grants are not made on the basis of applications received'.

The Linbury Trust

£12,821,000 (approved, 1997/98)

Major capital projects, chronic fatigue syndrome, arts/art education, drug abuse, education

See entry for the 'Sainsbury Family Charitable Trusts'
Tel: 0171-410 0330

Correspondent Michael Pattison

Trustees Lord Sainsbury of Preston Candover; Lady Sainsbury; Miss J S Portrait.

Beneficial area UK and overseas, particularly South Africa.

Information available Accounts are available with an exemplary report. The principal officers for the trust are Michael Pattison, the director, D Brown, assistant director and P Spokes, financial controller.

Summary This trust is one of the Sainsbury Family Charitable Trusts which share a joint administration. In 1997/98 most of the trust's support (80%) was to capital projects in the arts and education. It has funded the Oxford University Business School and given generous support to many of the major national arts institutions as well as museums and galleries. It also supports colleges of arts education and has a particular interest in dance and dance education. The trust has pioneered research funding of Chronic Fatigue Syndrome. It is also concerned with major social welfare issues such as drug abuse, homelessness and the problems of young people at risk.

General After a long period of only supplying scant information, the trust now produces interesting accounts of its policies and grants in its narrative reports. The report for 1997/98 is exemplary in its compliance with SORP and far more detailed than that of the previous year. It goes further than many other trusts by carefully distinguishing between capital and revenue grants. Policy information about each of its categories of giving is accompanied by a short descriptive note of each grant over £5,000. Beneficiaries of smaller grants are listed with the amount given.

New Grants Approved – 1997/98

	Revenue £'000	Capital £'000
Arts & Art Education	*312*	*3,250*
Chronic Fatigue Syndrome	*584*	*-*
Drug Abuse	*173*	*-*
Education	*136*	*4,000*
Environment & Heritage	*51*	*-*
Medical	*1*	
Social Welfare (+ older people)	*767*	
Third World Education/ Social Welfare	*547*	
Others	*-*	*3,000*
Total	*2,571*	*10,250*

The only remaining mystery now is the "Other" – the large capital award/s totalling no less than £3 million (of which £2.57 million was paid out during the year) which is not listed under any named category. Perhaps this includes support to the ill-fated (and apparently ill-managed) Royal Opera House. In accordance with paragraph 138 of the Statement of Recommended Practice Accounting by Charities details of this grant or grants have been provided to the Charity Commission, but are withheld from the public file.

The trust's investments are predominantly in J Sainsbury plc and in April 1998 were worth £215 million (£136 million in the previous year).

In 1997/98 the trust approved 114 grants totalling £12.82 million compared with 121 grants totalling £7.42 million in the preceding year. The trust's net income after the costs of consultancy and administration was over £7 million which, with over £9 million brought forward from the previous year, gave a total of £16.5 million for distribution.

The descriptive statements within the report of the policy informing each category are quoted in full. The size of the grant/s are noted by the editor in brackets where not given in the text. (No statement was given in the trust report about its policy for support to Environment and Heritage.)

Education – £4,136,000 approved in 1997/98

'Trustees have from time to time made major capital grants to centres of excellence in the world of British education. In 1997/98 trustees decided to approve a major grant of £4 million for the Oxford University Business Management School. This grant is for the new building and to go towards the costs of the school's library.

'Trustees have also continued to support charities that help children with special needs, particularly those who have problems with literacy. Trustees help charities that enable teachers to be trained in the diagnosis of dyslexia and in how to help the children with such needs, especially those who do not receive the appropriate attention early enough (Dyslexia Institute, £8,500 for teachers' courses; Helen Arkell Dyslexia Centre, £12,000 for bursaries for teachers). General education appeals on behalf of schools or individuals or help with fees are not normally supported.'

Other grants approved in 1997/98 included Changemakers (£30,000), Education Extra for three after school clubs (£16,680) and Everyman's Millennium Library a project to place 250 classic titles in the nation's schools (£50,000).

Arts and Arts Education – £3,362,000 approved in 1997/98

'Trustees have continued to give significant support to major national institutions in the visual and performing arts, including Sadler's Wells (£100,000 paid for new dance studio in 1997/98), the Royal National Theatre (£250,000 approved for redevelopment appeal) and Dulwich Picture Gallery (no grant identified in report or in report of previous year). A major capital grant of £3 million was approved for the Tate Gallery on Millbank for new Exhibition Galleries.

'Art and Ballet Schools have also been supported in a number of ways, including student bursaries at the City and Guilds of London Art School (£12,400 paid 1997/98), a teaching Fellowship in Life Drawing at Wimbledon School of Art (£50,000 approved, £13,250 paid in 1997/98), the Summer School at the Royal Ballet School and bursaries at Rambert School within Brunel University for up to four young South African dancers each year (£44,059 paid in 1997/98).

'The Linbury Prize in Theatre Design, now in its tenth year, is unique in its field in encouraging the art of theatre design and in creating opportunities for four graduating designers to work in middle-sized or small theatres (£143,000 approved for 1997/98 competition, £118,000 paid).'

Sixteen small grants of £23,000 were also made, nine of these clearly to leading dance companies eg Mark Morris. (Lady Sainsbury is the former prima ballerina, Anya Linden.)

Social Welfare (including Older People) – £767,000 approved in 1997/98

'Trustees have continued to support charities that help young people who are homeless or in care and particularly those organisations that give young people an opportunity to change their lives. Trustees are of the view that if a young person has suffered disadvantage through deprivation, through family break-up or is at risk from drug misuse, he or she can benefit from a fresh start. Indeed, many who become involved in minor crime can also change their ways through schemes that include a closely monitored mentoring component young people can be diverted from the path of crime to one of relative success. Literacy is crucial in all this and ex-offenders who cannot read or write are even more likely to fail to get a job and to re-offend. Linbury supports charities which offer one to one literacy support to young offenders both in prison and before such extreme measures as prison

are necessary.

'Trustees also seek to support initiatives that improve directly the quality of life of older people and through which they are helped to continue their life in their own home. Whilst this is not a major category or priority for Linbury, good ideas will be considered.'

Grants in 1997/98 included those to Fairbridge for young people at risk (£200,000 over 2 years), Youth at Risk to divert young people from crime (£150,000 over 3 years) and Centrepoint Soho to improve service for the young homeless (£50,000).

Other projects included arts activities serving social welfare and health: the Age Exchange Reminiscence Theatre to support exhibitions and productions (£45,000 over 3 years); London Connection Charing Cross for a volunteer arts co-ordinator (£45,000 over 3 years) and Dementia Services Development Centre to research and publish art schemes in residential homes (£16,000 over 2 years).

Chronic Fatigue Syndrome Research – £584,000 approved in 1997/98

'Linbury's portfolio of research into the causes of Chronic Fatigue Syndrome continues to be the most sustained, broad-based body of research in this field in the country, comprising a coherent and balanced programme in many UK universities and hospitals. The trustees are advised by the following panel of distinguished doctors:

Professor A M McGregor (Chair) Professor of Medicine at King's College, London;

Professor L Borysiewicz, Professor of Medicine at University of Wales College of Medicine, Cardiff;

Professor T K J Craig, Professor of Community Psychiatry at United Medical Schools of Guy's and St Thomas', London;

Professor R S J Frackowiack, Professor of Neurology, Institute of Neuroscience, London.

'The Linbury trustees and the members of the advisory panel, whilst helping to fund a serious programme of scientific work on CFS, continue to recommend to the Department of Health that patients' needs should be properly met and to encourage NHS research and development and the Research Councils to offer more support for work in this field. Linbury has primed the pump and it is time for other funding bodies to add their support.

'Just after the year end Linbury published a book edited by Dr Robin

Fox of its portfolio in CFS research. On the same day the Chief Medical Officer, Sir Kenneth Calman, announced that he is to set up a working party to look at the clinical practice and management of CFS.

'At the moment, other medical causes are only supported in exceptional circumstances.'

Six new research grants were approved in 1997/98 over one, two or three years. The largest grant was for Professor P Cowan, Oxford University, to study abnormalities in serotonin function (£116,000+ over 2 years).

Drug Abuse – £173,000 approved in 1997/98

'Trustees have maintained the dual strategy of helping major providers of therapy and care, notably Turning Point (£20,000 for both their Hungerford Project and their Leeds Education project) and Phoenix House (£30,000 for a pilot vocational training project), whilst at the same time helping charities and agencies explore various avenues of education about drugs for the young and very young. Peer education works well in certain schemes and Turning Point are comparing various peer and young people programmes to ascertain what works best. The trustees have helped to finance the Standing Committee on Drug Abuse (SCODA) post of Head of Education and Prevention (£30,000 over 2 years) because all schools will need effective drugs education programmes taught by skilled, well informed and confident teachers and these will need a timetable slot in the working week for all pupils.'

Six organisations were awarded grants ranging between £20,000 and £33,000 in 1997/98.

Third World Education and Social Welfare – £547,000 approved in 1997/98

'Trustees during the year have intervened at short notice with grants for the emergencies in the Lebanon and in Albania. Trustees have continued to fund bursaries for undergraduates at the University of Cape Town to enable more black students to attend UCT. In 1998 trustees started a programme at UCT to fund PhD students in their three-year course, with their third year to be spent at Bristol, Oxford or Sheffield Universities in the UK.'

In 1997/98 the University of Cape Town was awarded £403,000 over 3 years.

Environment and Heritage – £51,000 approved in 1997/98

No further information.

Exclusions No grants direct to individuals.

Applications The trustees met 11 times in 1997/98.

'Trustees give priority to charities in which they have a particular interest and personal knowledge or experience, for the areas where they do not have such inters, knowledge of experience they seek expert advice from those who are highly qualified to give such advice. because of the trustees' proactive approach in their categories of priority, unsolicited applications are only successful occasionally. All applications are considered on their merits wiht the intention of distributing grants especially in the fields listed above. Applicants are always required to provide a detailed budget for their proposal and up to date audited accounts with a copy of the most recently published annual report.'

An application to one of the Sainsbury family trusts is an application to all; see the entry under 'Sainsbury Family Trusts, for address and application procedure.

Enid Linder Foundation

£487,000 (1997/98)

Health, welfare

35 Tranquil Vale, Blackheath, London SE3 0DB
Tel: 0181-297 9884

Correspondent B Billingham, Secretary

Trustees Jack Ladeveze; Audrey Ladeveze; C S Huntly, Geoffrey Jackson.

Beneficial area Unrestricted.

Information available Accounts on file at the Charity Commission for years up to 1995/96 only, in September 1998, but 1997/98 accounts made available for use in this entry. They state that they comply with the SORP but they do not, in that there is no narrative report of the kind required by Paragraph 28 of that document, nor are the grants analysed and explained.

Summary A relatively large number of generally small grants for a wide range of health and disability charities, preponderantly in London or the south of England.

General The foundation did not respond to a written request for a copy

of its accounts, nor were any up to date accounts to be found on file at the Charity Commission, though the file there noted that two exceptional requests for this information has been sent to the charity. The foundation says that information had been sent regularly to the Commission.

On receipt of a draft entry pointing out this situation, accounts for 1997/98 were sent to these editors, and the present entry is based on these.

In 1997/98 the trust had an income of £623,000, part from investment income on its assets of £7.7 million, and part from a subsidiary property investment company, Industrial Partners Ltd. Grant giving of £487,000 is listed but there was a further £99,000 of direct charitable expenditure on 'Teaching hospitals and universities'. This is explicitly separated from the 'Donations' heading, but there is no further explanation of what kind of activity this represents.

121 grants are listed, plus a further £17,000 as 'Donations to beneficiaries'. This may be for small grants, but the main list already includes grants as low as £269.

Most grants were for health or disability charities such as Macmillan Nurses (£8,000) or Seeability (£2,000). Only eight awards were for £10,000 or more, with the largest going to the Royal College of Surgeons (£35,000). Other major beneficiaries were Médecins sans Frontieres (£25,000), the Victoria and Albert Museum (£15,000) and 'Cancer Research' (£12,000, perhaps to the Cancer Research Campaign). Grants of £10,000 each went to Stoke Fund (sic), Mandent, MENCAP, and Brighton Society for the Blind.

Perhaps half of the grants were to national charities. Of the 17 local grants whose location was easily identifiable, 13 were in the southern half of England (seven of them in London) and four were in the Northern half of England. There was one grant in Scotland but Wales and Northern Ireland could not be seen in the grants list.

Applications In writing to the correspondent.

The George John Livanos Charitable Trust

£846,000 (1996)

Medical research, hospitals, general

c/o Jeffrey Green Russell, Apollo House, 56 New Bond Street, London W1Y 0SX
Tel: 0171-499 7020

Correspondent P N Harris, Secretary

Trustees Mrs S D Livanos; P N Harris; A S Holmes; P D Powell.

Beneficial area UK.

Information available Accounts up to 1996 only were on file at the Charity Commission in September 1998.

General This trust seems to concentrate its grant giving on medical and educational organisations. In 1996 the trust had assets of £7 million, which generated an income of £654,000. A total of £846,000 was given out in grants to 25 organisations. The largest, as in previous years, going to St Mary's Hospital, Paddington Department of Child Health (£316,000), and the smallest going to Whitechapel Mission (£1,000). Nearly half the grants were repeats, and most grants were for £20,000 or more.

A large number of medical institutions and hospitals were supported including:

Bedford Hospital	
Fort William	(£138,000)
Royal Surrey County Hospital, St	
Luke's Cancer Appeal	(£50,000)
Great Ormond Street	(£46,000)
Friends of Royal Marsden	(£20,000)
Lord Mayor's Appeal for Cancer	
Research Campaign	(£25,000)

Three large grants were also given to universities:

Glasgow University	(£33,000)
University of Nottingham	(£24,000)
University of Dundee	(£19,000)

A number of smaller grants were given to a variety of social causes including:

CARE	(£5,000)
Barnardo's	(£1,000)
Sheltered Work Group Project	(£1,000)

Applications Unsolicited applications are not requested

Lloyds TSB Foundation for England and Wales

£9,036,000 in 1997, but rising rapidly

Social and community needs, education and training

PO Box 140, St Mary's Court, 20 St Mary at Hill, London EC3R 8NA
Tel: 0171- 204 5276; Fax: 0171 – 204 5275; web site
www.lloydstsbfoundations.org.uk

Correspondent Kathleen Duncan, Director General

Trustees Joanna Foster, Chair; Revd. Rachel Benson; Jacqueline Carr (London); Howard Phillips (Eastern and East Midlands); J Peter Holt (Yorkshire and North East); Dr Christine Kenrick, West Midlands; Paddy Linaker; Virginia Burton (South East); Dr Pauleen Lane (North West); Linda Quinn (Wales); Professor Murray Stewart (South West); John Penny.

Beneficial area England and Wales. See separate entry for the Lloyds TSB Foundations for Scotland and Northern Ireland.

Information available Very good annual Report and Accounts. Guidelines for applicants. Extensive internal research reports and other papers made available to help in writing this entry. The graph herewith illustrates the grants given to areas of special interest in 1997.

Summary This foundation is growing dramatically and may soon be able to double the present amount to give out in grants each year. Correspondingly, it is developing active and interesting new policies and practices.

The foundation supports almost all kinds of community and social needs, but more than half of its grants by value, including most of those for larger amounts, fall within a list of 'areas of special interest'. Each of these areas is usually supported for a number of years, though not indefinitely, and minor revisions are made annually.

The 1999 list of the 'areas of special interest' is, in summary, as follows (the foundation's full text is given in the main part of this entry)

- advocacy
- opportunities for disabled people
- crime prevention
- family support
- homelessness
- prevention of substance misuse
- independent living for elderly people
- the needs of carers.

Most of the larger grants, say those from £15,000 to £150,000, are for salary or project costs, often spread over three or even four years (though often on a tapering basis). Smaller grants are also commonly made to help meet salary costs, but numerous grants are also made for equipment and other minor costs. They may be for amounts as low as £200.

The grant making is regionalised, with local budgets based on population but substantially weighted for the relative 'disadvantage' of the region concerned. There are Regional Coordinators, listed at the end of this entry under 'Applications', and applicants are encouraged to talk to the foundation before submitting their applications.

Over 2,500 grants were made in 1997, from 7,200 applications, a success rate of 38% (though the amount given may often be less than that which was requested). 'In 1998 the foundation was able to meet the requests of about 45% of eligible applicants, either in part or in full', so an application here will be high priority for many readers of this book.

After an introductory section, this entry has the foundation's 1999 Guidelines and then reprints much of the extensive and interesting Chair's Statement and Director General's Report for 1997, followed by details of the grants made during that year and, in some cases, in the first half of 1998.

Background

The Lloyds TSB Foundations are a result of the merger of Lloyds Bank and TSB Group. The four original TSB Foundations were formed at the time of TSB Group flotation in 1986, covering England and Wales, Scotland and Northern Ireland (see adjacent entries) and the Channel Islands, in part to answer critics of the flotation at the time.

The Lloyds TSB Foundations now own 1.5% of the enlarged Group's share capital (though in the form of limited-voting shares) and receive 1% of the Lloyds TSB Group's pre-tax profits averaged over three years. The shares cannot be sold. On the basis of the Group's current profitability, allowing nothing for further progress, the Lloyds TSB Foundations' annual income by 2000 could exceed £30 million. However this income must be dependent on the commercial success or otherwise of the banking group.

The foundations are operationally independent of the Lloyds TSB Group and their policies are determined by independent boards of trustees. Nevertheless the connections with the bank remain close, as described below.

The banks and the foundation

Although this foundation has happily established complete operational independence from Lloyds TSB Bank group, there is still a close relationship. In many ways the foundation is treated as the charitable arm of the bank, and in its Annual Report it refers to the creation of the Lloyds TSB Foundations from 1st January 1997, 'to handle all requests made to any of the companies within the enlarged Lloyds TSB Group'. Furthermore it is understood by foundation trustees that the bank group may, by publicising the work of the foundations, seek to gain credit with the public.

However the funding of the foundation is not an act of choice by the bank group. It has followed as a legal necessity from the Act of Parliament authorising the flotation of the Trustee Savings Banks, whose original purposes had a public benefit element which these arrangements were put in place to recognise. When Lloyds merged with the TSB, the legal status of the foundations' position as privileged shareholders had to be maintained.

It is therefore to be hoped that the Lloyds TSB Group will be developing and financing its own community involvement programmes, independently of the work of the foundations.

The main practical connections are as follows:

- All requests for charitable donations made to companies within the Lloyds TSB Group are referred on to the appropriate foundation.
- 5% of the foundation's expenditure is set aside for a Matched Giving Scheme in which staff who raise money for charities within the foundation's guidelines have the total raised matched by the foundation, up to a maximum of £500 per person per year.
- The bank features the work of the foundations in its advertising, notably in 1998 in the Daily Telegraph and on Classic FM.
- The bank assists with useful administrative facilities for the foundation.

How the foundation works

The foundation is expanding rapidly. As is apparent from the annual report for 1997, reproduced below, it is taking an increasingly pro-active approach to its job.

There is a system of regional trustees, admirably appointed after open advertisement, backed up by the work of regional coordinators whose names, addresses and telephone numbers (as in October 1998) are listed at the end of this entry under 'applications'.

Local applications for amounts of £10,000 or less are assessed by the regional coordinator and decided by the regional trustee. For amounts of £10,000 to £25,000, the decision is made by two regional trustees working together. Projects asking for £25,000 or more are considered individually by the full board. There are budgets for the different regions and these are substantially weighted for disadvantage on the basis so desirably pioneered by the National Lottery Charities Board.

There is a head office staff of about ten, including a development officer. This latter appointment means that trustees and staff are better informed by professional advice on the factual and research background to the decisions they are making than is usual for 'general purpose' trusts (in more specialised trusts there may well be formidably expert trustees and staff). Formal papers are presented analysing the needs of organisations working in the 'Areas of Special Interest', and comparing these with the pattern of the foundation's awards. Kathleen Duncan, the Director-General, says that this appointment 'has made an enormous difference, especially in enabling regional coordinators to identify gaps and encourage suitable applications with which to fill them'.

There is a formal evaluation process, concentrating on the larger awards, but also including a telephone or personal review of a 3% sample of all smaller grants.

Total administrative costs are low, despite – or perhaps because of? – the foundation's encouragement of preliminary telephone calls and discussions by applicants.

Apart from the Matched Giving Scheme, described below, the evidence is that grant making will not be influenced by lobbying from staff of the banking group.

Guidelines for applicants 1999
Introduction

The foundation primarily allocated its funds to support local communities, helping people to improve their quality of life.

The majority of the foundation's income is allocated to ten regional budgets, which mirror the government's standard statistical regions (About 65%. Ed). These budgets are determined on the basis of population, weighted for deprivation. A proportion of the foundation's funds is, however, allocated to appeals which cannot be considered on a regional basis.

The trustees' approach to grant-giving

The majority of donations are made on a one-off basis although commitments over two or more years are also considered.

The trustees prefer to make donations towards specific items and not to make contributions to large appeals for eg, building costs. It is, however, recognised that core funding is often a priority requirement for charities, and the trustees will consider contributing to these costs.

Lloyds TSB Foundation for England and Wales

Regional Coodinators

In October 1998 the coordinators were as follows

North West	David Kay	01925 444652
North East	Peter Ellis	0191-262 9021
Yorkshire/Humberside	Tony Hall	01904 628200
Eastern	Mark Ereira	01284 750168
East Midlands	Sue Denning	0115-958 8745
West Midlands	Karen Halfpenny	01785 247488
Greater London	John Aldridge	01245 347156
South East	John Paton	01705 652791
South West	Rodney Thorne	01278 444743
Wales	Mike Lewis	01222 728870

Applications are welcomed for projects which demonstrate collaboration between groups, for projects disseminating good practice, and for projects which support the activities of umbrella organisations.

The trustees also wish to support the infrastructure of the voluntary sector. Applications for initiatives which enable organisations to work more efficiently are encouraged.

General advice to applicants

In 1998 the foundation was able to meet the requests of approximately 45% of eligible applicants either in part or full. The most frequent reasons for the trustees not being able to make a donation include:

- the level of demand always exceeds the funds available
- requests being made for sums in excess of the ranges stated in the guidelines
- application forms not being fully completed
- applications not falling within the guidelines.

As a general guide, the trustees make donations in the range £300 – £5,000 when one-off local projects do not fall within the Areas of Special Interest as listed below. For local projects which do fall within these Areas, the range is generally £300 – £10,000. The trustees will also consider two or three year funding for such projects (ie. up to a total of £30,000. Ed).

Applicants are strongly advised to seek advice from the foundation before applying for sums in excess of these ranges, or for funding over two or more years.

A proportion of the foundation's income is available for projects where the benefit covers England and Wales as a whole, and an additional sum is set aside for pilot projects where there is potential for dissemination on a national basis. Donations within these national programmes are generally in the region of £10,000 – £30,000, and two or three year funding is often appropriate (ie. up to a total of £90,000. Ed).

Applicants are strongly advised to seek advice before submitting an application for support on a national basis.

Timing

The trustees will only consider applications which are submitted on the foundation's application form. Forms are available from the foundation's office (or from regional coordinators, as listed below) and can be returned at any time. Applications are reviewed on a continual basis. The board of trustees meets quarterly to approve donations. Decision making processes can therefore take up to three months but all applicants are informed of the outcome of their applications. (*If the application was not eligible for a grant, the applicant is so informed.*)

Successful applicants are advised to leave two years before applying for further support. Unsuccessful applicants should leave at least one year before re-applying.

What are the foundation's guidelines?

The overall policy of the trustees is to support underfunded charities which enable people, especially disadvantaged or disabled people, to play a fuller role in the community.

The foundation has three main objectives to which it allocates funds (*note that these are not the same as the Areas of Special Interest which are listed below. Ed*)

Social and community needs

A wide range of activities is supported, and the following are meant as a guide only

- *advice services*
addictions, bereavement, counselling, emergency and rescue services, help lines, hopelessness, housing, parenting.

- *community relations*
crime prevention, mediation, promotion of volunteering, rehabilitation of offenders, victim support, vulnerable young people.

- *community services*
after school clubs, community centres, elderly people's clubs, family centres, play schemes, youth clubs.

- *cultural enrichment*
improving participation in and access to the arts and national heritage.

activities with an educational focus for all ages.

improvements to buildings of historic or architectural value which increase their benefit to the community.

projects which have a strong focus on benefit to people and the social environment.

- *disabled people*
carers, day centres, information and advice, sheltered accommodation, transport.

- *promotion of health*
day care, information and advice, mental health, holistic medicine, home nursing, hospices.

Education and training

The objective is to enhance learning opportunities for disabled and disadvantaged people of all ages. The following examples are meant as a guide only:

- lifelong learning
- literacy skills.
- pre-school education.
- promotion of life skills and independent living skills.
- skills training for disabled people, including pre-vocational training.
- skills training for disadvantaged people, to enhance their potential to secure employment.

Medical research

A small proportion of the foundation's funds are allocated to medical research, and the trustees' objective is to support

Lloyds TSB Foundation for England and Wales
Grants to areas of special interest 1997

underfunded fields of research.

Current areas of support are mental health, substance abuse and ageing research projects. A pro-active approach is adopted, and unsolicited appeals are unlikely to be successful.

Areas of special interest for 1999

• *advocacy*
helping people to be involved in decisions that affect their lives, particularly for people with learning disabilities, people with physical disabilities, people with mental health problems, and older people.

• *creating positive opportunities for disabled people*
enabling people with either mental or physical disabilities to live independently.

• *crime prevention*
particularly activities involving young people, including opportunities for the development of self-esteem and motivation.

• *family support*
including the development of relationship skills for young people. and encouraging good relationships between generations.

• *homelessness*
in particular, helping homeless people back into mainstream society. including support after temporary or permanent accommodation has been secured.

• *prevention of substance misuse*
including both education and rehabilitation.

• *supporting independent living for elderly people*
enabling older people to live independently and to participate in the life of their community.

• *the needs of carers*
for example, information and advice services, and the provision of respite care.

1997 ANNUAL REPORT

Chair's Statement (Excerpts. Ed)

Trustees

'Three new trustees joined the Board during the year. Professor Murray Stewart works in the Faculty of the Built Environment at the University of the West of England, and has undertaken a wide range of research work in local government issues, including projects for the Joseph Rowntree Foundation. Jacqueline Carr has been involved with the development of the National Association of Citizens' Advice Bureaux equal opportunities policy and practice,

and Revd. Rachel Benson has a special interest in penal affairs, having chaired the Griffins Society for Women Offenders. Each has already made a valuable contribution to the strategic thinking of the foundation.

'For 1998 it has been decided to divide the South East region into two: Greater London, and the rest of South East, in line with the government's standard statistical regions. I am delighted that Jacqueline Carr has agreed to take on the role of regional Trustee for Greater London.

'The foundation has recently opened up the trustee appointment process through a series of public advertisements encouraging applicants.

Areas of special interest

'It has continued to be the policy of the trustees to allocate the majority of the funds to regional and local projects, and in 1997 65% of the income was allocated to the eight regional budgets. From those budgets it was further decided to set a target of 50% of the funds to support charitable work in the Areas of Special Interest identified for the year: carers, crime prevention, elderly people, employment training (for disabled and disadvantaged people), homelessness (in particular helping homeless people back into mainstream society), parenting, prevention of substance abuse, the promotion of volunteering, rural communities, and young people.

'A full breakdown and illustration of donations made to these areas is given (below), but the headline totals are 56% of donations, totalling £5.1 million. This compares with 42% of donations, totalling £1.3 million, in 1996.

National funding

'In last year's report, the Director General referred to the three-tier strategy which was to be pursued during 1997 - the continuing strong focus on local donations (65% of the income, or £6.8 million), a small proportion of the funds to social policy research for the first time, and an increase in the level of support for projects with benefit across the whole of England and Wales (increased to 15% of the income, or £1.4 million).

'For this budget it was decided to set a target of 75% of the available budget for projects falling within the Areas of Special Interest. ... The overall effect has been that the significantly increased level of funding has enabled the foundation to take a pro-active approach in certain areas such as the prevention of

substance abuse, and to commit to two- or three year funding for core costs.

'In respect of the proposed social policy research, other funders of research, including the Joseph Rowntree Foundation and the Leverhulme Trust, were approached for advice and to identify possible gaps. The trustees took the decision in September to undertake a project in the area of citizenship, with a closer focus on ways to enhance the prospects of young people in the care system, and also to explore links between good citizenship and crime prevention. We look forward to the development of a specific research project during 1998.

The national pool

'During the year, a small number of donations were made in collaboration with other Lloyds TSB Foundations. These included medical research projects in the fields of Mental Health (the Impact of Psychotherapy on the Lifetime Cost of Childhood Conduct Disorder, through the Mental Health Foundation), Ageing (a vision research project on age-related macular degeneration, and screening for osteoporosis, both through Research into Ageing), and on Substance Abuse (a study of the development of alcohol misuse among young people, through Alcohol Concern).

'A donation was also approved towards the 25th anniversary programme of events planned by Home-Start UK, involving a series of seminars in all parts of the UK to raise awareness of the charity's preventative work with young families under stress amongst potential volunteers, funders, and local authority staff in a position to refer clients to the service.

Staff Matched Giving Scheme

'A new scheme was launched in January, to cover all members of staff within the Lloyds TSB Group in the UK. 1,500 members of staff participated in the scheme, which matches fundraising efforts up to £500 per person per year for charities which fall within the foundation's guidelines. £424,671 was paid out under the scheme, which compares with 819 donations totalling £237,431 in 1996.

'For 1998, each of the foundations will run its own scheme, within common guidelines.

Strategic review

'A series of strategy meetings were held during the year in preparation for revision of the guidelines for 1998. These culminated in July with a combined meeting of the full Board of Trustees, the Regional Coordinators and head office staff.'

The Director General's Report 1997

Printed in the 1997 Report and Accounts, this admirably full report included the following:

'1997 has been a challenging and stimulating year of rapid growth and development in the operation of the foundation.

'7,200 applications were received, to which we have been able to respond with 2,700 donations (38%). This compares with 1,400 donations form 4,000 applications received in 1996 (being 35%). It is encouraging to note that the proportion of ineligible applications has continued to drop, from 18% in 1996 to 5% this year despite an increase in the foundation's income. However, demand still far outstrips the funds available and the trustees sadly have to turn down many good applications.

'The increased demand had been anticipated and planned for during 1996, as both the foundation and Lloyds Bank Charitable Trust informed charities of the creation of the Lloyds TSB Foundations from 1st January 1997, to handle all requests made to any of the companies within the enlarged Lloyds TSB Group.

Regional assessment

'The increased number of applications and assessments resulted in a 75% increase in workload for the nine full-time Regional Coordinators. Quarterly team meetings continue to be held to provide essential forums for the coordinators to discuss any issues arising form their work out and about visiting charities, and also smaller gatherings to discuss strategic issues arising from the analysis of social conditions being carried out by the newly appointed development officer, whose work is described below.

'It is a pleasure to report that the foundation has been able to offer, firstly, three-month work placement opportunities for young people on employment training schemes, to be followed, all being well, by the offer of a full-time position as administration assistants in the regional coordinators offices. By the end of December two trainees had successfully completed the three-month placement and have accepted the jobs offered. Having administrative support in the office to handle the day-to-day paperwork is enabling the coordinators to return to

spending a higher proportion of their time visiting and advising applicants, and also carrying out follow-up evaluation visits.

Head office staff

'In January the head office team expanded from four to eight, primarily to extend the capacity to develop the foundation's funding of projects benefiting people across England and Wales. This work has included assessment and subsequent funding of a number of innovative schemes to which we have been able to commit two-or three-year support. Examples are described in the Areas of Special interest section below.

'During the year the Trustees' Reviewed the ways donations are evaluated, and a great deal of preparatory work has been carried out to establish enhanced procedures, including the development of formal evaluation forms. We were delighted to accommodate a TSB Bank Graduate Management Trainee for six months of the year, who undertook much of this task. The role of Development Officer has now been established on a permanent basis to continue this work and also to provide much greater capacity for analysis and assessment of the foundations grant-giving. This will include analysis of how the foundation's patterns of giving at both regional and national level reflect social need as evidenced by publicly available statistics, and to inform discussions to which areas of social need the foundation should most urgently be devoting funds at its disposal.

'In August an Administration Assistant was recruited to handle the many enquiries for general information about the foundation.

Areas of special interest

'The chairman refers (above) to the decision to target 50% of the Regional budgets (£3.5 million) and 75% of the budget for England and Wales-wide donations (£1.6 million) to the Areas of Special Interest.'

'The following tables illustrate how the funds were allocated. (The heading 'general' covers everything outside the areas of special interest for the year.)

Total foundation spending, £9 million

General	*46%*
Employment Training	*7%*
Homelessness	*5%*
Crime prevention	*3%*
Carers	*5%*
Promotion of volunteering	*5%*

Parenting	*2%*
Young people	*10%*
Rural communities	*5%*
Elderly people	*7%*
Prevention of substance abuse	*5%*

Grants to areas of special interest

	National	*Regional*
Employment training	*6%*	*8%*
Homelessness	*7%*	*11%*
Crime prevention	*6%*	*5%*
Carers	*13%*	*8%*
Promotion of volunteering	*18%*	*5%*
Parenting	*8%*	*2%*
Young people	*20%*	*18%*
Rural communities	*7%*	*9%*
Elderly people	*5%*	*16%*
Prevention of substance abuse	*10%*	*8%*

Total spending in 1997:
Geographical breakdown

North West	*301*	*£1,093,000*	*12%*
North East	*199*	*£597,000*	*7%*
South East (inc London)	*672*	*£1,641,000*	*18%*
South West	*253*	*£550,000*	*6%*
Wales	*203*	*£477,000*	*5%*
Eastern	*327*	*£824,000*	*9%*
West Midlands	*308*	*£848,000*	*9%*
Yorkshire	*268*	*£747,000*	*8%*
England and Wales wide	*149*	*£2,258,000*	*26%*
National	*13*	*£346,000*	

The regions used for this analysis are not all fully identifiable – where are the East Midlands, for example – though the foundation notes that it is now moving to the standard government regional definitions. However on the assumption that London and the South East, Wales and the North East follow the usual boundaries, the value of grants per head (the proper measure of geographical distribution), the values were as follows:

Value of grants per 1,000 population

London/South East	*£110*
North East	*£158*
Wales	*£156*

It is most unusual, and very welcome, to see Wales appearing in its proper place in such a list.

The size of donations

The report continues with a breakdown of the size of donations. Unfortunately it is not possible to deduce how much of the money was given in the different size brackets.

Approximate number of donations by size

		1996	*1997*
£0	*– £2,499*	*1,100*	*1,400*
£2,500	*– £4,999*	*180*	*780*

| £5,000 – £9,999 | 65 | 390 |
| £10,000 + | 55 | 130 |

In areas with smaller budgets for the population concerned, the response of the foundation is often to reduce the size rather than the number of grants. In the first half of 1998, for example, the average grant in the North East was £4,700 but in the South East was only £2,400. However success rates of applications are also lower in the South East, 23% as against 36% in the North East (and no less than 47% in the West Midlands).

The report then has the following examples of larger grants made in its areas of special interest, with a national followed by a regional award in each case:

Carers:

£78,342 spread over three years will fund a senior post to develop Contact a Family's network of support and advice services for families caring for children with any type of disability. £1,000 towards the Trinity Church Sitting Service in Porthcawl, to give respite to carers.

Crime Prevention:

£45,000 spread over three years will fund a programme of Crime and Citizenship courses for young people. £3,600 towards the satellite Car Crime Project run by Trax: the Oxfordshire Motor Project, on the Blackbird Leys estate.

Elderly people

£150,000 spread over three years will enable Age Concern England to establish the Trans-Age Action Project, developing links between generations through a foster-grandparent scheme for children of lone parents. £1,389 towards a new telephone system for Age Concern, Lindsey, Lincolnshire.

Employment training:

£56,000 spread over three years will enable Workable to offer a mentoring scheme to the disabled graduates who are helped to find work experience, training and employment opportunities. £7,897 towards the computerised tuition club for young people from minority ethnic communities run by QED, Quest for Education and Development, Bradford.

Homelessness:

£157,745 spread over three years will fund two strategic posts in the newly relaunched National Homeless Alliance (formerly CHAR, the National Campaign for Single Homeless). The Alliance seeks to support and coordinate the work of grass-roots based homelessness organisations. This donation at national level complements the support given by the Foundation at local level to many of the Alliance's members. £5,000 towards the education project for homeless young people run by the Cardinal Hume Centre in London.

Parenting:

£40,000 spread over two years will enable RPS Rainer to pilot an Early Parenthood project identifying appropriate support for teenage mothers on the New Addington estate in Croydon. £7,500 spread over three years core funding for Ashfield parents Centre in Newcastle.

Prevention of substance abuse:

£65,000 spread over three years will enable the South London Drugs Referral Project to pilot a collaborative project helping young drug offenders who come into contact with either the police, courts, probation or prison and are not in contact with any treatment services. The project is unique in that it involves all the appropriate agencies in South London and aims to offer a complete treatment package to individuals.£5,000 towards volunteer training for the drug education programme run by Cascade, Solihull.

Promotion of volunteering:

£175,000 spread over three years will establish the Institute for Volunteering Research, based at the National Centre for Volunteering and managed in partnership with the University of East London Centre for Institutional Studies. The Institute will provide a focal point for research into volunteering, and enhance the information base on which decisions on policy an practice can be founded - by statutory and voluntary organisations alike. £1,000 towards equipment for the Dorchester Volunteer Bureau, Dorset.

Rural communities:

A one-off donation of £17,875 will fund the Development Officer for MIND's Rural Minds Project, based in the West Midlands. The project's aims is to study an identify ways to improve the provision of mental health services to people living in rural areas. £5,000 towards the Lancaster Rural Community Development Project.

Young people:

£100,000 spread over three years will support the work of St Christopher's Hospice in Croydon in the development of services for children who have been bereaved. The hospice continues its tradition of working at the forefront of good practice in hospice care, and it is anticipated that the lessons learnt from the project will be able to be disseminated throughout England and Wales. £2,000 towards furniture for the hostel for vulnerable young people run by Stonham Housing Association in Redditch.

The report continues:

Communication

'During 1997 we have continued to ensure that staff across the whole Group have been aware of the Foundation's activities, including the staff Matched Giving Scheme through a regular feature in the group's in-house magazine, and also by quarterly distribution of the lists of donations approved, to senior management.

'Awareness of the foundation's work has also been spread to a wider external audience through the Group's partnerships with the Daily Telegraph and Classic FM, which have provided charities with an opportunity to describe their work.

Training for voluntary sector managers

'It has once again been made possible for managers from the voluntary sector to attend, free of charge, appropriate in-house management training courses held at the Group's Management Centre in Solihull, through a scheme administered by the foundation. This year three managers attended courses, including Managing Pressure and Leading Effective Teams, and this brings the overall total to 140 managers since the scheme started in TSB Group in 1992.

'The places this year were offered to managers working, predominantly , in the field of the prevention of substance abuse, reflecting one of the Trustee's areas of special interest.'

The grants – general

The reports above concentrate on the grants for the Areas of Special Interest, which covered about 57% of grants by value. Further information was made available for use in this entry. One interesting statistic is that core funding in the first half of 1998 represented 44% of regional spending and 33% of national funding.

The regional donations

These are generally but not exclusively small. Many of the larger grants are spread over up to four years, and are often contributions to a part of a person's salary - for example the £3,000 a year for three years to Sharing and Caring, Bristol for salary costs.

In the south west for example, one of the smallest regions, there were 203 awards, totalling £477,000, an average of about £3,000 (it is hard to be precise because the lists available note just payments in the year, rather than the value of the award when it is staged). There were just two really large grant (£75,000 over four years to Cornwall Community Council's parish based millennium project, and £70,000 over two years to set up and pay the initial running costs of the Princess Royal Trust for Carers centre in Gloucester). There were four grants of £15,000 to £18,000, to the Industrial Therapy Organisation, Bristol; Devon Care Trust, Plymouth; Gloucestershire MIND;and SPLASH, Wiltshire. All of these were contributions to salary costs. The two £10,000 grants included the first for capital expenses; to Bristol Foyer to fit out their training room.

However awards ranged upwards from £200 and much more typical were, say, the £500 grants to Barnstaple's Parent Link, to Blockley village hall (for an accessible toilet) or to Budleigh Hospicare (for a flotation mattress).

England and Wales wide awards

There were 149 of these worth £2.3 million in 1997, with an average grant size of about £22,000. Grants are also classified under this heading if they are pilot projects expected to have national implications in the long term, even though the work itself may be carried out locally, or if the benefit covers the whole country; for example, the £65,000 for the South London Drugs Referral Project.

Three awards were for £100,000 or more; £157,000 to the National Homeless Alliance (formerly CHAR) over three years for two salaries; £150,00 to Age Concern England to pilot its Trans-Age Action programme of support for lone parents; and £100,000 for a pilot child bereavement Service at St Christopher's Hospice in Croydon. Other large awards were to the Princess Royal Trust for Carers (again) for a training programme; Victoria and Albert Museum's Mughal tent programme and a community arts post; and YMCA for a pilot parent education programme.

The national grants pool

All the TSB foundations contribute to a 'National Pool', from which grants are made over three years to UK-wide programmes. There were 13 such donations in 1997, totalling £346,000.

The list is headed by £157,000 to the Housing Associations Charitable Trust for the development of supported housing in rural areas, followed by £105,000 over three years to support Arthritis Care's Millennium Awards Scheme (largely funded by the Millennium Commission). Other large awards went to Research into Ageing (£88,000 over three years) and the Leonard Cheshire Foundation (£60,000 over three years for a Disabled People's Forum.

Exclusions

- Organisations which are not recognised charities;
- Activities which are primarily the responsibility of central or local government or some other responsible body;
- Activities which collect funds for subsequent redistribution to other charities or to individuals;
- Animal welfare;
- Corporate affiliation of membership of a charity;
- Endowment funds;
- Environment – conservation and protection of flora and fauna, geographic and scenic;
- Expeditions or overseas travel;
- Fundraising events or activities;
- Fabric appeals for places of worship;
- Hospitals and medical centres (except for projects which are clearly additional to statutory responsibilities);
- Individuals, including students;
- Loans or business finance;
- Overseas appeals;
- Promotion of religion;
- Schools, universities and colleges (except for projects specifically to benefit disabled students or which are clearly additional to statutory responsibilities);
- Sponsorship or marketing appeals.

Applications Application forms are available from the foundation's office or the regional coordinators and can be returned at any time. Information requested on the form includes:

- registered charity number or evidence of an organisation's tax exempt status;
- brief description of the activities of the charity;
- details of the project for which a grant is sought;
- details of the overall cost of the project and a breakdown;
- what funds have already been raise towards the overall cost and how the remaining funds are being raised;
- an outline of plans for evaluation;
- Trustee's Report and full edited or

independently examined accounts.

All applications are reviewed on a continual basis and the Board of Trustees meets quarterly to approve donations. Decision making processes can therefore take up to three months but all applicants are informed of the outcome of their applications.

In case of difficulty, up to date information can be had from the office of the foundation given above at the start of this entry.

Lloyds TSB Foundation for Northern Ireland

£1,130,000 (1998)

Social and community need, education and training, scientific and medical research

PO Box 4, 4 Queens Square,
Belfast BT1 3DJ
Tel: 01232 325599; Fax: 01232 231010

Correspondent Mervyn Bishop, Secretary

Trustees James Grew (chairman); Roy MacDougall; Mrs Brenda Callaghan; Ian Doherty; Mrs Breidge Gadd; Mrs Dawn Livingstone; Lady McCollum; David Magill; Mrs Anne Shaw; Dennis Wilson.

Beneficial area Northern Ireland

Information available Annual report and accounts available. no grant list. Guidelines:

Summary A large number of small grants are made, across virtually the whole field of health and welfare, with a very high success rate for applications.

General The smallest of the three Lloyds TSB Foundations described in this book, this charity follows the others in supporting local communities and helping people improve their quality of life. Most donations are made on a one-off basis, with a small number of commitments made over two or more years. The trustees state that they prefer to make donations towards specific items and not make contributions to large appeals, though the trust will consider core funding for small local charities.

Applications which help to develop voluntary sector infrastructure are encouraged.

Donations are generally between £2,500 and £5,000 but there is no minimum amount set by the trustees. Applications for larger amounts will be considered where there is wider benefit.

The trust has three main objectives:

1. Social and Community Needs: A wide range of activities for which the following is only meant as a guide

Community services: family centres, youth clubs, elderly people's clubs, after school clubs, playschemes, help groups, childcare provision.

Advice centres: homelessness, addictions, bereavement, parenting, helplines, counselling, housing, emergency and rescue services.

Disabled people: sheltered accommodation, day centres, transport, carers, information and advice, mental and physical disabilities.

Promotion of health: information and advice, mental health, hospices, day care, holistic medicine, home nursing, AIDS.

Community relations: youth at risk, crime prevention, promotion of volunteering, victim support, rehabilitation of offenders, mediation.

Cultural enrichment: improving participation in and access to the arts and national heritage for disabled people; activities in the fields of the arts and national heritage which have educational focus for all ages; improvements to buildings of historic or architectural value which increase their benefit to the community.

2. Education and Training: Cover projects which help people develop their potential and secure employment; employment training (for disabled and disadvantaged people); promotion of life skills for disabled people; enhancing education, for disabled young people, pre school education and literacy skills.

3. Scientific and Medical Research: Current areas of support are mental health, substance abuse and ageing research projects. A pro-active approach is adopted, and unsolicited appeals are unlikely to be successful.

Current priority areas are:

- cross community development
- carers
- crime prevention
- elderly people
- employment training (for disabled and disadvantaged people)
- homeless (in particular helping homeless people back into

mainstream society)
- parenting
- prevention of substance abuse
- promotion of volunteering

Particular emphasis is also given to the needs of young people and rural communities.

The foundation's funding has been dramatically increased as result of the Lloyds and TSB merger in 1996:

1994	£53,500
1995	£150,900
1996	£380,600
1997	£725,500

For 1998 it was expected that funding would exceed £1 million.

In 1997 a total of £773,000 was given out in 236 grants, making the average grant around £3,000. The foundation notes that it received 263 applications, making an extremely high success rate (90% of applicants receiving grants). Administrative costs were very low at only £8,000, about £34 per grant approved, and about 1% of total grant expenditure.

Unfortunately no grants list was produced.

Exclusions Areas of concern outside the guidelines:

- organisations which are not charities
- individuals including students
- animal welfare
- Environment- geographic and scenic, conservation and protection of flora and fauna
- overseas appeals
- activities that are the primary responsibility of central or local government or some other responsible body
- schools, universities and colleges
- hospitals and medical centres
- sponsorship or marketing appeals
- fabric appeals for places of worship
- promotion of religion
- activities which collect funds for subsequent redistribution to other charities or individuals
- endowment funds
- fundraising events or activities
- corporate affiliation or membership of a charity
- loans or business finance
- expeditions or overseas travel.

Applications Application forms available.

Information requested includes:

- registered charity number, evidence of tax exempt status
- brief description of the activities of the charity
- details of the project for which the grant is sought

- details of overall cost of the project, including breakdown
- what funds already raised
- how the remaining will be raised
- Trustees' Report and full audited or independently examined accounts.

Trustees meet quarterly to review applications.

The Lloyds TSB Foundation for Scotland

£2,618,000 (1996/97)

Social welfare, education and training, medical research

Henry Duncan House, 120 George Street, Edinburgh EH2 4LH
Tel: 0131-225 4555; Fax: 0131-260 0381

Correspondent Andrew Muirhead

Trustees J. D. M. Robertson, Chairman; Mrs E. A. Denholm; C. D. Donald; Professor Niall Lothian; P C Paisley; R G E Peggie; Mrs A J M Yerburgh; A. Robb; A. D. F. Findlay; J. G. Mathieson.

Beneficial area Scotland.

Information available Annual review and application packs, available from the correspondent.

Summary Funded by the LLoyds TSB Group plc., the foundation is operationally independent. Large numbers of grants are given, primarily to meet social and community needs. 70% of the awards, representing about a third of the money, go in grants of £5,000 or less. About 40% of the money is in multi-year awards.

The success rate for eligible applications, at 45%, is high, although many applicants may not receive the full amount requested (20% of applications are ineligible).

The foundation is energetic and accessible, something that may not be apparent from its pedestrian published materials. It has relatively a more extensive outreach programme relative to its size than any other large funder described in this book; staff of the foundation operate a major series of local 'surgeries' and also visit more than three-quarters of the eligible applicants. There is also an enterprising and, for once, genuinely innovative pilot programme for developing the capacity of the voluntary sector in Scotland (described below).

The foundation also supports a 'matched giving' programme for staff of the Lloyds TSB group in Scotland.

Background The Lloyds TSB Foundation for Scotland, formerly known as TSB Foundation for Scotland, was formed in 1986 as one of four independent charitable trusts established as part of the flotation of the TSB Group (which had always had an element of 'public benefit' in its otherwise commercial structure). Collectively these foundations distribute 1% of the bank groups's profits. Since the merger between Lloyds Bank and TSB Group, funding has been increasing rapidly. However, it does not represent a voluntary act of community support by the bank group, which can be expected to address this issue, in Scotland as elsewhere, independently of the work of this foundation.

Funding policies 'The foundation allocates its funds in support of the Scottish community, to enable people, primarily those in need, to be active members of society and to improve their quality of life.

'We are committed to operating in an open way and to be supportive to all groups eligible to apply for funds.

'The trustee's interests are primarily directed at local communities; however, larger appeals which provide benefit across Scotland have become a part of the foundation's activities.

'The average grant is currently approximately £7,000 and applicants should bear this in mind when submitting their appeal. The majority of donations are made on a 'one off' basis.

However the trustees will consider commitments over two or three years.'

From 1997 to the end of 1999 over 90% of all funding is said to be falling within one of the following priority areas:

* young people;
* rural deprivation;
* alleviation of homelessness;
* positive opportunities for those; mentally or physically disadvantaged;
* drug or alcohol abuse;
* support for minority groups;
* elderly people;
* improving the voluntary sector infrastructure.

Extensive and detailed consultation was taking place in 1998 about the priorities for 2000 and after. A different breakdown for the year 1997, however, shows that these categories cover, in practice, a very wide field:

Social and community needs	*(76%)*
Crisis and advice centres	26%
Community centres	19%
Health	19%
Civic responsibilities	15%
Disabled people	14%
Access to arts and culture	7%
Education and training	*(19%)*
Employment	34%
Life skills	28%
Enhancing education	23%
Training for disabled	15%
Scientific and medical research	*5%*

The foundations interests under these headings are set out as follows:

Social and Community Needs

* Community centres for all ages playgroups/nurseries benefiting children within Areas of Priority Treatment (designated by the Scottish Office), family centres, youth clubs, elderly people's clubs.
* crisis and advice projects homelessness, addictions, family guidance, bereavement, money advice.
* support for disabled people residences, day centres, transport, carers, advice and help.
* health issues information and advice, mental health, home nursing, hospices, elderly people.
* civic responsibility juveniles at risk, offenders and their families, crime prevention.
* cultural enrichment access to the arts and national heritage specifically for disadvantaged and disabled people.

Education and Training

* motivation and training projects which help individuals to get and keep a job, with particular emphasis on helping young people develop their potential and secure employment.
* employment training providing disadvantaged and disable people with employment opportunities.
* promotion of life-skills and independent living particularly for young people and those mentally or physically disadvantaged.

Science and medical research

'Given that only 2% of our spending found its way into scientific and medical research in 1995, the 5% in 1997 represents significant progress. We do not subdivide this category, however, we do tend to focus on the less fashionable, and hence less fundable areas of research.'

However, many of the organisations funded (as opposed, perhaps to the actual piece of work), seem to these editors to be fairly mainstream; for example the lists include charities such as Imperial Cancer Research Fund, Epilepsy Association of Scotland or the National Deaf Children's Society.

Voluntary sector infrastructure

'The trustees are also particularly aware of the need to support projects which improve the voluntary sector infrastructure in Scotland. Initiatives which enhance management skills, create operational efficiencies or improve access to funding for charitable organisations will be of great interest to the trustees.'

Reasons for the failure of applications

'The trustees regret that demands made on the Foundation's funds always outstrip the funds available and this means that many good applications, whilst meeting criteria,

---

The Lloyds TSB Foundation for Scotland

Major grants in 1997 (over two to four years)

Children First	£168,000
YCSA Training and Development Agency	£160,000
Royal Hospital for Sick Children	£120,000
Rural Forum Scotland	£90,000
Volunteer Development Scotland	£80,000
Imperial Cancer Research Fund	£75,000
Quarriers Homes	£68,000
St Ninian's, Ferguslie Park	£65,000
Fairbridge in Scotland	£60,000
Epilepsy Association	£60,000
Penumbra	£60,000
Caledonian Foundation	£60,000
Prince and Princess of Wales Hospice	£60,000

cannot be supported.

'Due to the high quality of applications in general, there is often a narrow margin between success and failure. Amongst applications assessed during the period of this review (1997), there were some recurring features in those which were unsuccessful:

- Lack of clear plans for other fund-raising where we might only be able to part-fund work.
- Insufficient detail on potential benefits a project would create and the way in which it would impact on people's lives.
- 'All or nothing' requests for large appeals (The foundation would prefer to see a shopping list of options).
- Where support was sought for recurring costs, insufficient thought had been given to planning for funding beyond the period for which support was being sought.

'We consider it vital that challenging objectives are established each year by projects seeking revenue support. Occasionally submissions contained vague objectives, lacking in measurement or deadlines for achievement.'

The work of the foundation

Outreach

A particular characteristic of the foundation is its efforts to establish direct and personal contact with as many potential applicants as possible – 'The Board is committed to removing barriers between the foundation and applicants'. In 1998, 60 local surgeries were being run, reaching over 1,000 organisations, many of which had never made an application to this or to any other funding body.

The advice given often covers other sources of possible funding, and discussion may well cover a wider review of the options open to the group concerned. It is the view of these editors that a programme such as this benefits both the funder, who will receive better, more appropriate applications, and the applicant, organisations who have the chance to discuss their needs with people who have a wide experience of the needs of other organisations. Compared to simply sending in a speculative written application, such a process is greatly preferable.

It is striking that this programme, together with personal visits to 75% of all eligible applicants, can be achieved within total administrative costs that represented only 7% of the value of grants made or an average of £290 per grant.

Capacity building

In 1998/99 the foundation was running a most interesting pilot programme in which organisations providing support and services to other groups were invited to identify their most pressing organisational needs, and then enabled to get expert advice in putting together plans for how these needs could best be addressed, plans which then became the basis of funding applications.

By enabling the organisations to become the foundation's 'customers', setting out their needs rather than addressing those already identified by the funder, the foundation is hoping to achieve a more effective use of its funds. The scheme has met with a most enthusiastic initial response, with eventual funding being agreed to meet the priorities of 39 out of the 49 original participating organisations.

Grants in 1997

The grants lists do not explain the purposes of even the largest awards, so there is no way of knowing whether they are for capital or revenue purposes. The largest single awards, new or carried forward from previous years, are shown in the table herewith.

Exclusions Grants to recognised charities only. No grants to:

- Individuals, including students;
- Animal welfare;
- Environment –
  Geographic and scenic;
  Conservation and protection of flora and fauna;
- Mainstream schools, universities and colleges;
- Hospitals and medical centres;
- Activities which collect funds for redistribution to others;
- Sponsorship or marketing appeals;
- Endowment funds;
- Expeditions or overseas travel;
- Fabric appeals for places of worship, other than where such buildings provide accommodation to community groups;
- Historic restoration.

Applications Rather narrowly worded application forms available, with useful guidance notes on the information required. As an example of the tone of the document, it refers throughout to the applicants 'appeal'. This terminology would not be that used by many community groups.

The suggestion that the foundation may be able to help applicants who find themselves in difficulties with their applications, apparent from the text above, can not be found in either of these documents.

In 1999 six trustee meetings will be held

in February, April, June, August, October, December. Closing dates for applications are normally 10-12 weeks prior to the meeting concerned. Specific details are available on request.

All applicants are required to leave at least one year between applications.

The Lolev Charitable Trust

£677,000 (1994/95)

see below

14A Gilda Crescent, London N16 6JP
Tel: 0181-806 3547

Correspondent A Tager, Trustee

Trustees A Tager.

Information available Only occasional reports and accounts, and those without grants lists, on file at the Charity Commission in September 1998, the most recent for 1995 and then 1992.

General The most recent accounts available are those for 1995, a bare unaudited two pages. There was no endowment, income coming entirely from donations to the trust during the year. Grants to unknown recipients amounted to £680,000. It is possible, though by no means certain, that the trust is no longer in operation.

Applications See above.

The Lord's Taverners

£1,361,000 (1997)

Minibuses for people with disabilities, cricket

22 Queen Anne's Gate,
London SW1H 9AA
Tel: 0171-222 0707

Correspondent David Stickels, Director

Trustees The Council of The Lord's Taverners comprising John Bromley OBE, Chairman and 17 others.

Beneficial area UK.

Information available Report and accounts with narrative analysis of grants; policy and guidelines; application forms.

Summary About 50% of funds are disbursed to youth cricket organisations, 40% is used to supply 'New Horizons' minibuses for disabled people and the final 10% to promote sports for the young and disabled.

General 'Founded in 1950 at the Old Tavern at Lord's by a group of actors, the charity has raised £19 million in 48 years – from £15,000 in one year to £1.59 million in 1997.'

In 1996/97 income of £3.7 million was generated. £2,883,000 (78%) was raised through fundraising events and the remainder came from donations, subscriptions and investments. £1,782,000 was spent on fundraising, so the charity had to spend 62 pence to raise £1. The reason for this is that much of the fundraising is done through fundraising 'events' where ticket buyers expect a good (and expensive) 'do'. The SORP does not allow charities operating in this way to 'net off' these operations and just show the income generated after the costs of the events have been paid. It might therefore be better for these operations to be run by a separate non-charitable organisation that would covenant its profits to the parent charity.

Administration costs were a further £343,000 (£286,000 on salaries including a £50,000 'termination payment'), or 25 pence per £1 of grant-aid.

Grant aid as 1997

National Playing Fields Association	*£25,000*	*2%*
National Cricket Association	*£274,000*	*20%*
English School's Cricket Association	*£95,000*	*7%*
Direct Cricket Grants	*£218,000*	*16%*
Kwik Cricket	*£20,000*	*1%*
Total Cricket	*£607,000*	*45%*
New Horizons Minibuses	*£649,000*	*48%*
Sports for disabled people	*£80,000*	*6%*

The annual report does not have a full grants list and so we are largely unable to report on the location of beneficiaries, size of grants, the specific purposes for which funds were awarded etc.

The following is taken from the guidelines and annual report (1996/97):

'The Lord's Taverners is accredited by the England and Wales Cricket Board (ECB)as the official national charity for recreational cricket. Grants are distributed on the recommendation of the ECB. An annual grant is also made to the English Schools' Cricket Association.

'There are 26 regions throughout the UK and 17 Lady Taverners Regions. They are run on an entirely voluntary basis and play an increasingly important role in our fundraising activities.'

'The Lord's Taverners and the ECB have adopted a common approach for the grant aiding of the game. ECB will support schemes organised at county level by its county cricket boards through the cricket foundation. The Lord's Taverners will concentrate their resources available for cricket at the grassroots of the game targeting young people at clubs and schools. Lord's Taverners grant aid will, in the main, be used to support Kwik Cricket; the provision of youth cricket equipment; grants towards the installation of non-turf pitches and practice areas; and support for schemes at local level. The overall aim is to encourage the participation of young people.

'The principle activities and charitable mission continues to be "to give young people, particularly those with special needs, a sporting chance" by:

- providing incentives to play cricket and other team games in schools and clubs;
- creating recreational facilities in conjunction with the National Playing Fields Association;
- encouraging those with disabilities to participate in sporting activities;
- giving mobility with New Horizons minibuses.

'The company allocates grants in line with the following guidelines:

- 50% cricket;
- 40% New Horizons minibuses;
- 10% sport for disabled people.

'To ensure that we retain firm links with the original aims of our founder members, the council maintains a policy that 50% of our disbursements are directly cricket related, including grants for disabled youngsters to play the game at grass roots level.

'We actively support the Cricketer Colts Trophy for schools, the Wrigley softball schools competition, the Sun Life of Canada under 15 and the Subaru under 13 championships. These are the largest competitions of their kind in the world. We also run the annual Lord's Taverners Britvic under 16 inner cities cricket cup with the finals at Arundel in August.

Youth Cricket

Equipment The Lord's Taverners will make two types of bags of cricket equipment available to schools and clubs where there is an active youth section. The red "junior" bag is for teams of

cricketers under the age of 13 and the blue "youth" bag is for those over 13 but under 16.

Non-turf pitches and practice areas: 'Grant available up to a maximum of £1,000 for a non-turf match pitch, £500 for a non-turf practice end and £300 for netting. Priority will be given where active links are established between a club and school(s) or where, by installation, such links will be established.

'In 1997 we made direct cricket grants to the English Schools Cricket Association, Arundel Castle Cricket Foundation, the London Playing Fields Association (Peter May Memorial), the Sir Leonard Hutton Foundation and the MCC indoor school. We made 901 grants through the ECB by providing funding towards 38 projects for coaching and competitions, help towards the installation of 63 non-turf pitches and distributing 800 of our Lord's Taverners bags of equipment to schools and colts sections of cricket clubs. Our grant of £20,000 to Kwik Cricket, focused by the Young Lord's Taverners, financed the supply of some 500 kits, mostly to primary schools and needy youth organisations.

'We are proud that our annual funding is now encouraging over 100,000 youngsters (boys and girls) to enjoy the benefits of cricket at both schools and cricket clubs.

New Horizons Minibuses

'The Lord's Taverners give new horizons minibuses to provide mobility for disabled young people and young people with special needs. Each minibus is custom designed and costs in the region of £28,000. Strict policy guidelines apply regarding the application and award of a new horizons minibus. Applicants must provide a donation of a minimum of £8,000 to the charity.

'Since 1980 we have donated 440 New Horizons minibuses. By the year 2000, the club's 50th anniversary, the target is to have 500 on the road. Each minibus, including its conversion, cost between £22,000 and £29,000. The Lady Taverners focus especially on fundraising for minibuses. In 1997 the 50th minibus bearing their distinctive pink bow was presented.

Sport for young people

'To encourage those youngsters with physical or mental disabilities to participate in sporting and recreational activities within a group environment. To help those youngsters achieve goals which may otherwise by beyond their reach.

'Essential elements for a successful application:

- sport or recreation activity within a group;
- youth participation;
- provision of equipment.

'From more than 1,000 applications received last year, the foundation awarded 33 grants totalling £99,000 to such wide-ranging projects as hydrotherapy pools and a narrow boat, sailing and canoeing, equipment for gymnastic clubs, sports and wheelchairs and specialised play equipment.'

These grants should be listed in the accounts.

National Playing Fields Association

'Close links are maintained with NPFA and we give an annual grant of £25,000 to help build multigames walls.'

Exclusions

Youth cricket: The following is not normally grant aided:

- building or renovation of pavilions;
- site screens;
- bowling machines;
- mowers/rollers;
- overseas tours.

Sport for young people with disability; The following will not normally be considered for a grant:

- capital costs;
- medical costs;
- running costs including salaries;
- individuals;
- holidays.

Minibuses: Homes, schools and organisations are entitled to only one minibus per location. Those who already have a (roadworthy) New Horizons minibus should not apply for another.

Applications *Youth cricket grants:*
Applications will be handled by the ECB through its County Cricket Boards from whom the necessary application forms are available

New Horizon's Minibuses: By application form along with a copy of your latest annual accounts.

Sport for young people with disability: By application form. Applications will be scrutinised by the Local Taverners Regional Chairman whose recommendation is essential before consideration is given by the foundation.

The Lord's Taverners Foundation normally meets quarterly to disburse the funds available and applicants will be informed as soon as possible on the outcome of the request.

Application forms are available from the Foundation Secretary.

John Lyon's Charity

£1,445,000 (1996/97)

Children and young people in North and West London

45 Pont Street, London SW1X 0BX
Tel: 0171-589 1114

Correspondent The Grants Officer

Trustees The Governors of John Lyon's School. The members of the Grant's Committee are: Prof M M Edwards, Chairman; H V Reid; Prof D M P Mingos.

Beneficial area Barnet, Brent, Camden, Ealing, Hammersmith and Fulham, Harrow, Kensington and Chelsea, the Cities of London and Westminster.

Information available Accounts are on file at the Charity Commission. The charity publishes an excellent annual report and guidelines for applicants.

Summary: John Lyon's Charity is a third branch of John Lyon's Foundation, a primarily educational charity. Its mission is 'to enhance the conditions of life and improve the life chances, of children and young adults' from specified London boroughs.

General The charity's history began in the late 16th century when John Lyon donated a 48 acre farm as an endowment for the upkeep of two roads from London to Harrow. In 1991, the charity was given discretion to use the revenue from the endowment to benefit the inhabitants of certain London boroughs. Today the site of the original farm is better known as Maida Vale. Following a revaluation of investments in 1996/97, the charity's assets more than doubled to a hefty £64,038,252, but it does not say in the published accounts whether or not this still includes some or all of the original 48 acres.

In 1996/97 £1.4 million was disbursed to 104 organisations subsumed under nine broad categories. Management and administration costs absorbed 12% of income or, put another way, represent £1,800 per grant.

Youth clubs/services	*£411,602*	*28%*
Education & training	*£311,525*	*21%*
The arts	*£193,675*	*14%*
Sport	*£161,116*	*11%*
Counselling	*£111,300*	*8%*
Childcare & parental support		
	89,430	*6%*
Housing & homeless	*63,900*	*5%*
Handicap & disability	*57,262*	*4%*
Youth/other		
	45,100	*3%*

Grants were substantial with many around £5,000-£10,000. Large grants went to the Nottingdale Partnership (£100,000 towards capital costs), the Brent Adolescent Centre (£25,000 a year for three years) and North Kensington Sports Scholarships (£40,000 for two years). At the other end of the scale, approximately 45 small grants of £1,000 or less were awarded.

Overall the charity provides an array of grants, small to large, capital and revenue, one-off and repeated. In addition, 'Support has not been limited to the disadvantaged, There has been an equal concern to encourage talent and 'enable the enabled'. This stance may be reflected in bursarial support at Harrow school.

Exclusions The following exclusions are specified in the guidelines:

- individuals
- research, unless it is action research designed to lead directly to the advancement of practical activities in the community
- medical care and resources
- response to general charitable appeals, unless they can be shown to be of specific benefit to children and young people in one or more of the geographical areas listed
- direct replacements for the withdrawals of funds by statutory authorities for activities which are primarily the responsibility of central or local government
- umbrella organisations to distribute to projects which are already in receipt of funds from the charity
- the promotion of religion or politics
- telephone helplines

Applications The following excerpt is take from the charity's guidelines:

'Please put in a letter the following information:

- a summary of the main purpose of the project
- details of the overall amount requested
- over what time-scale
- some indication of how funds from the charity would be allocated.

'If your first proposal is assessed positively, you will be sent an application form. This must be completed and returned by the deadline date in order for your project to be considered for funding.'

The grants committee meets three times a year. The closing dates for formal applications are; 17 April 1998; 16 October 1998; 8 January 1998; 9 April 1999. Proposals are considered at the meeting in the month following the deadline date.

The Mackintosh Foundation

£1,155,000 (1996/97)

Arts, education, young people, the homeless, AIDS, S E Asian refugees, general

1 Bedford Square, London WC1B 3RA
Tel: 0171-637 8866

Correspondent The Appeals Secretary

Trustees Sir Cameron Mackintosh, Chairman; Martin McCallum; Nicholas Allott; D Michael Rose; Patricia Macnaughton; Alain Boublil.

Beneficial area UK and overseas.

Information available Excellent annual reports; the required list of grants is not filed at the Charity Commission but is available on request to the foundation. Detailed and excellent information note available from the foundation, extensively reprinted below.

Summary Around 200 donations totalling £1,000,000 are made each year. The bulk of the foundation's income is given in donations to organisations working in the performing arts. A variety of other causes are supported, in particular refugees, for whom the foundation has set up a specific fund. Donations start from £50 and can occasionally climb as high as £1 million. The very large grants, and also accredited drama course bursaries, are often spread over up to 10 years.

General The foundation was established in 1988 by Sir Cameron Mackintosh, the internationally famed theatrical producer. By January 1998, the foundation had received over £14 million from Mackintosh's companies. Although most of this money has been disbursed to other charities, the foundation is building a capital endowment base (worth nearly £6 million in 1997) 'against the time when Sir Cameron's patronage will inevitably come to an end and the foundation will be obliged to rely on its own investment income and contributions from other donors, in order to continue its operations on approximately the present scale'. The foundation incorporates the 'Bui Doi Fund' which receives the profits from the musical 'Miss Saigon' and uses them to help refugees from Vietnam and other South-East Asian countries.

Although the information provided is otherwise excellent, the foundation was reluctant to provide the list of its major grants required by the Charity Commission's SORP. A request to supply 'a copy of your reports, accounts and grants lists ...' was not complied with on the ground that only a list of the top 50 grants was available, and the request did not specify this number – a reason this editor finds specious. Only a critical initial draft of this entry was able to extract this.

The reason for this reluctance was explained by the trust, and probably represents the feelings of a good number of the trusts described in this book: there will inevitably be disappointed applicants who see grants going to organisations that are, at least superficially, similar to their own, and they will feel resentful, and will blame these trustees.

These editors accept the force of this argument, but in turn argue that without disclosure of their awards, and the resulting open scrutiny of their work, trusts can become completely unaccountable to the public on whose tolerance of their tax exemptions they depend.

The foundation gives the following detailed account of its often unusual and interesting activities:

'As a matter of policy, the trustees of the foundation have tended to concentrate on charitable objects relating to:

- theatre and the arts;
- children and education;
- AIDS;
- the homeless;
- refugees from and the 'dust of life' in war-stricken or oppressed territories.

Distributions by the foundation

'During the ten years since it was set up the foundation has made over 2,000 separate grants (including repeats) totalling over £11 million to over 900 charities or charitable objects. It has endowed Oxford University with well over £1 million with a fund known as the 'Cameron Mackintosh Fund for Contemporary Theatre', part of which has been used to set up a visiting professorship of contemporary theatre. It has also agreed to provide a fund of £1 million over ten years (now partly paid up) to the Royal National Theatre, for revivals of classical stage musical productions under the auspices of the RNT.

'The foundation has also set up a drama school bursary award scheme to provide financial assistance for needy and deserving students on UK accredited drama school courses. 19 students to date have received awards under the scheme since it was set up in 1992.

'The foundation has pledged £500,000 over 5 years in respect of selected applications for 'partnership funding' under the Arts Councils Arts 4 Everyone scheme of National Lottery funding. Funded from National Lottery money, the larger Arts 4 Everyone Scheme offers grants from £5,000 to £500,000 for a wide variety of creative projects including the performing arts. Each project is expected to raise between 10% and 15% partnership support, depending on the size of the award, of which between 5% or 10% respectively (as the case may be) has to be in cash. Under arrangements made between the Foundation and the Arts Councils the latter will be referring suitable applicants for partnership funding to the foundation for consideration as to those which the foundation in its discretion may decide to support.

'Other major donations during the year were £250,000 to Prior Park College, £70,000 to Jefferies Research Wing Trust for medical equipment, £30,000 to Centrepoint Soho; £25,000 to Charity Projects Limited and £20,000 to the American Foundation for Aids Research.

'During the year the foundation made grants of £154,000 from the Bui Doi fund, the largest of which were £16,000 to Deaconess Hospital, £16,000 to Operation USA, £16,000 to Song Saigon Children's Charity and £15,000 to the Ockendon Venture for specific projects within the fund's terms of reference.

'The foundation has provided financial support to a number of projects in the United States and also donated $500,000 over 5 years to Sydney Theatre Company of Australia.'

Numerous grants are also made in the range of £500 to £10,000.

Donations in 1996/97 by value and number:

£150,000 – £199,000	*2*
£20,000 – £49,000	*3*
£10,000 – £19,000	*23*
£5,000 – £9,999	*48*
£1,000 – £4,999	*92*
Less than £1,000	*82*

Major grants in 1997/98

Tricycle Theatre	*£60,000*
Sydney Theatre	*£33,000*
Charity Projects	*£25,000*
Glasgow Homeopathic Hospital	*£25,000*
Kings Head Theatre	*£25,000*
Motivation Trust	*£25,000*
Variety Club	*£25,000*
Actors' Charitable Trust	*£24,000*
Forum for the Future	*£22,000*
Cancer relief Macmillan	*£20,000*
Capital Housing Project	*£20,000*

Over the years, though not represented by any major awards in 1997/98, the foundation has had an interest in welfare and the environment in the Western Highlands of Scotland, Sir Cameron's homeland.

Project administration The foundation has to date tended not to be involved very much in any hands-on administration of any charitable projects but has concentrated on providing funds to others for that purpose. The main reason for this is that the trustees of the foundation are all very busily engaged in other activities with little time to become more directly involved in the way its funds are used although there are some instances where help has been provided to needy individuals. Administration costs are kept to a minimum (in each of the years ending March 1991 to March 1997 amounting to less than 6.6% of income) since the foundation has no office establishment of its own and has comparatively few overhead expenses.

'Because of the foundation's limited monitoring resources, it has tended to concentrate its funding on other registered charities who are supervised in the conduct of their affairs by the Charity Commissioners, but the foundation not infrequently makes exceptions, particularly where overseas applicants and individuals are concerned.'

The foundation's weekly meetings to consider applications for small grants set a most desirable example of good practice for many other trusts described in this book.

Exclusions Religious or political activities.

Applications To the correspondent in writing. The trustees meet in May and November in plenary session, but a small grants committee meets weekly.

The MacRobert Trusts

£839,000 (1997/98)

General, mainly in Scotland

Balmuir, Tarland, Aboyne, Aberdeenshire AB34 4UA
Tel: 013398-81444; Fax: 013398-81676

Correspondent Major General J A Barr, Administrator

Trustees Air Vice-Marshal G A Chesworth; Mrs C J Cuthbert; I G Booth; D M Heughan; J Mackie; Dr J Paterson-Brown; R M Sherriff; A M Summers; A M Scrimgeour; Cromar Nominees Ltd.

Beneficial area UK, mainly Scotland.

Information available Guidelines for Applicants leaflet and detailed Reports and Accounts, but see below.

Summary There are two grant programmes, one for recurring annual donations, and the other for non-recurring grants. The split by value varies, but is generally about one third for the former and two thirds for the latter. A broad range of charities are supported. They are overwhelmingly Scottish, or for the Scottish activities of national charities. Most non-recurring awards are for amounts between £2,000 and £10,000 and may be spread over a period of up to three years. About a third of the donations by number have in the past appeared to be 'recurring', perhaps as small annual payments to national Scottish bodies or to local Aberdeen or Perthshire organisations.

The trusts have further non-grant making activities, running a large estate, a holiday home for serving or ex-service military officers and a small horticultural training scheme.

General

Finance and administration

Annual reports and accounts are available from this group of trusts, but only on the payment of £25. This is an unreasonable charge for an organisation with an income of less than £2 million a year (charities in Scotland, as elsewhere,

are under a legal obligation to provide these reports to any member of the public, for which they may make a reasonable charge, though very few do so). The accounts, though, are indeed complex and extensive, to an extent that it is hard to get any overall view of the work of the charities.

There are no less than seven organisations in the group, including an in-house Investment Trust, with overlapping trustees, purposes and activities, and with substantial inter-trust transfers. This structure is over the top for such a modestly sized outfit and the group might well apply through the Scottish Charities Office to reorganise on a more conventional basis, separating just the grant making role from the maintenance of the estate (it is not clear from the Reports and Accounts why this is a charitable activity), and of Douneside House as a subsidised holiday home for serving or retired military officers (doubtless those suffering from poverty).

In 1996/97 direct charitable expenditure was £944,000 and administration costs were £314,000, most of it spent in running the estate owned by the trusts. The direct charitable expenditure on one of the group's buildings included a further £106,000 in non-operational support and administration costs. Efforts are noted to reduce the costs of the unremunerative forestry activities of the group.

Grant policy and practice In 1996/97 about one third of the group's grants by value went to ex-service charities, particularly hospitals. From 19 grants in total, the largest were to Erskine Hospital (£50,000), the Royal Air Force Association (£25,000 for its Sussexdown Convalescent Home) and the Ex-Service Fellowship Centres (£20,000).

'Education' grants totalling £106,000 went to a varied group of organisations headed by Aberdeen University (£50,000) and including The Museum of Scotland (£12,500), Devon Guild of Craftsmen (£2,000) and Books Abroad (£200). There were also five grants under the heading 'Science and Technology', with £5,000 each for Demand, Floating Point Science Theatre and Stratosphere.

Between £20,000 and £40,000 each went to 'Medical Care', 'Disabled and Handicapped', 'Youth' and 'Community Welfare', but with no individual grants being for more than £5,000.

Music and the Arts received £34,000 in 12 grants headed by £5,000 each for the British Federation of Young Choirs, Glasgow School of Art and Haddo Arts Trust.

A separate heading for local Tarland and Deeside grants lists 12 awards, most for less than £1,000. There was also a small programme of grants for agricultural and horticultural charities, totalling £10,000.

As the grants lists give only the name of the recipient institution it is not clear either what the purposes of the grants may have been, nor how many of them are for activities in Scotland, though these are probably in the majority. The smaller grants, typically for £2,000 or less, tend to have specifically Aberdonian connections.

The Guidelines read as follow:

'The trusts are reactive so, with very few exceptions, only applications that are made to the trusts are considered by the trustees.

'The trustees consider their policy and practice of grant giving every five years, most revently in 1997. However it did not lead to any substantial changes in the information available. The beneficial area is UK wide but preference is given to organisations in Scotland. Grants are made normally only to a 'recognised' Scottish charity or a registered charity outside Scotland.

'Currently the major categories under which the trustees consider support are:

Science and technology
Youth
Services and sea
Disabled and handicapped
Ex-service hospitals and homes
Education
Community welfare

'The minor categories are:

Agriculture and horticulture
Arts and music
Medical care
Tarland and Deeside

'The trustees recognise the need to assist voluntary organisations which need funds to complement those already received from central government and local authority sources. However this is not to say that the trusts make a grant where statutory bodies fail to provide.

'The trusts are prepared to make core/revenue grants where appropriate, but favour projects.

'The trustees recognise that, at present, experiment and innovation are much more difficult to fund and the trusts' role in funding them the more significant'.

'The trusts ask organisations that make unsuccessful applications to wait at least one year from the date of decision before applying again. Successful organisations should wait at least two years.

Exclusions Grants are not normally provided for:

- religious organisations (but not including youth/community services provided by them, or projects of general benefit to the whole community, or local churches);
- organisations based outside the UK;
- individuals;
- endowment or memorial funds;
- general appeals or 'mail shots';
- political organisations;
- student bodies (as opposed to universities);
- fee-paying schools (apart from an Educational Grants Scheme for children who are at, or need to attend, a Scottish independent secondary school and for which a grant application is made through the Head Teacher);
- expeditions;
- retrospective grants;
- departments within a university (unless the appeal gains the support of, and is channelled through, the Principal).

Applications There is no application form. Note that in addition to the requirements set out below and which are taken from the printed Guidelines, the trust also asks that applications should be clearly and concisely set out on no more than two sides of A4. They should include:

- the charity title and description of the organisation's activities
- registered charity number or evidence of tax exempt status
- list of the charity's key people
- details of the project for which a grant is sought including costings, funds raised in relation to the target and funds promised (if any)
- the latest fully audited accounts and annual report.
- details of any application made, or intended, for funding from any National Lottery source.

The trustees look for clear, realistic and attainable aims.

Unsuccessful organisations should wait at least one year from the date of applying before re-applying.

Successful organisations should wait at least two years from receipt of a donations before re-applying.

In most cases the application undergoes scrutiny which may include a visit from the administrator.

The trusts no longer undertake to acknowledge all applications.

The trustees meet in March and October each year. Applications for the March meeting need to reach the trusts by late October, and for the October meeting by early June. Applicants are informed of the trustees' decision within one week of the meeting.

The Manifold Trust

£1,200,000 (1997, but see below)

Historic buildings, environmental conservation

Shottesbrooke House,
Maidenhead SL6 3SW
Tel: 01628-825660

Correspondent Miss C C Gilbertson

Trustees Sir John Smith; Lady Smith.

Beneficial area UK.

Information available Report and accounts.

Summary The trust supports the preservation of buildings especially parish churches; education, including museums; the environment; the arts; and other social causes. Most of the grants are between £400 and £5,000, although a number of grants up to £50,000 have been given.

General The trust was founded in 1962 and receives most of its income from rental properties. Grant giving has fluctuated over the years, in 1993 at £850,000, 1994 at £474,000, 1995 at £1.5 million, 1996 at £16 million (mostly to the Landmark Trust), and in 1997 at £1.2 million. The annual accounts comments on this. 'For many years the payments made by the trust have exceeded its income, the trustee believing that it is better to meet the present need of other charities than to reserve money for the future. Consequently, the trust's ability to make grants is declining'. In the previous year no less than £15.3 million was transferred to the Landmark Trust, thereby more than halving this foundation's capital base.

Current net assets amount to almost £12 million generating an income of about £750,000 (1997). A total of £1.2 million was given out in donations, but £500,000 of this went to the Landmark Trust as a special donation. The table herewith summarises total grants made in 1997.

In 1997 £681,00 was given out in 272 grants ranging from £100 to £50,000. Most of the grants (84%) were for £2,000 or less.

Examples of larger grants include £50,000 each to the Natural History Museum, Down House and the Amber Foundation (a Swindon based organisation training young unemployed people for jobs). Horsham, St Mary PCC received £25,000, and the Great Torrington & District Development Trust received £20,000. Two grants were given to Oxbridge colleges, £16,500 to New College, Oxford, and £15,000 to Magdalene College, Cambridge. The RIAS also received £15,000 and £12,000 was given to the Oxford Archaeological Unit. Only 13 grants were for £10,000 or more.

The trust has a special interest in parish churches with grants ranging from £100 to £7,000 (with one exception, £25,000 to Horsham, St Mary PCC) being given to 229 Parish Church Councils.

Other grants were given to Friends of the Textile Conservation Centre (£7,500), Society for the Protection of Ancient Buildings (£5,000), Hernhill Bell Fund (£2,500), The British School in Rome (£2,000), Thorney Island Society (£1,500), Winchester Cathedral (£1,000), Elisha Smith Institute 1794 (£750), Two Gates Ragged School, Cradley (£600), Tommy's Campaign (£500), Bubwith Village Trust (£500), and the the Little Ouseburn Mausoleum(£500).

Applications Applications can be made at any time (only registered charities can be considered) preferably on a single piece of paper, with details of the project, the amount needed and the amount already raised or promised. If the application is for funds to preserve a building, then a note on its history and a photograph should be sent as well. The trust points out that it is unable to reply to all unsuccesful applicants.

The trustees meet twice a month.

The Manifold Trust

Grants in 1997

Churches and other historic buildings (excluding a special donation to the Landmark Trust)	£383,000	56%
Arts and Education, including museums	£160,000	24%
Environment	£57,000	8%
Social Causes	£81,000	12%
Sub total	£681,000	100%
Special Donation to the Landmark Trust	£500,000	
Total	**£1,181,000**	

The Jim Marshall Charitable Trust

£594,000 (1997)

General

c/o Marshall Amplification plc, Denbigh Road, Bletchley, Milton Keynes MK1 1DQ

Correspondent Julie Lancaster

Trustees J Marshall; L Smith; K W J Saunders; B Charlton; S B Marshall.

Beneficial area UK, with a particular interest in the Milton Keynes area.

Information available Accounts are on file at the Charity Commission but without a narrative report or list of grants.

Summary Under its deed the trust was set up to benefit five named charities and 'others'. In practice it is operated by Mr Marshall on a personal basis and its grants, most of which are probably for health and welfare charities, may be better regarded as his personal benefactions and not as part of any institutional programme.

General The trust was founded in 1989 by its namesake who is also the founder of Marshall Amplification plc, sound equipment suppliers to many a rock n' roll legend (but reported in 1998, perhaps wrongly, to be facing financial difficulties). Essentially the trust has no assets (£310,000 in 1996/97) and its income comes from annual donations from Mr Marshall. Management and administration costs are extremely low. Up until 1985, grant making at least doubled every year – initially £12,000 in 1989, it reached £516,000 in 1985. The charities 'expressly...to benefit' according to the deeds are:

- Variety Club Children's Charity;
- London Federation of Boy's Clubs;
- Wavedon All Music Plan;
- MacIntyre Homes;
- Buckinghamshire Association of Boys Clubs
- Other charities.

The 1997 report notes that grants are for children, young people, families the sick and disabled. However as the annual report and accounts contain no grants list, no mention of any grant and no policy or guidelines regarding other donations, it is not known what 'outside' charities are helped, if any.

While Mr Marshall's philanthropic motives are not in doubt, charitable trusts are public institutions, not private ones. It is open to Mr Marshall to give personal donations anonymously (and tax effectively), but those given by a trust must be publicly listed and the Charity Commission should insist on this.

Exclusions Probably no grants to individuals.

Applications Unsolicited applications have not in the past been welcomed.

Marshall's Charity

£741,000 (1997)

Parsonage and church improvements

Marshall House, 66 Newcomen Street, London SE1 1YT
Tel: 0171-407 2979

Correspondent R Goatcher, Clerk to the Trustees

Trustees M J Dudding; P R Thompson, and others.

Beneficial area England and Wales.

Information available Full Report and Accounts.

General The charity is established to support parsonages throughout England and Wales, to help with the upkeep of churches in Kent, Surrey or Lincolnshire, to build new churches and to support in particular the Parish of Christ Church, Southwark.

In 1997 the charity spent £741,000 on these purposes, in 43 dioceses, including 212 grants for parsonage schemes, of which 113 included payment for security measures. 68 churches were assisted, with 'special consideration being given to parishes in Urban Priority Areas'.

No grant appears to have been for more than £9,000 for a parsonage or £5,000 for a church, and indeed the latter figure is probably the usual maximum in both cases.

Exclusions No grants to churches outside the counties of Kent, Surrey and Lincolnshire, as defined in 1855.

Applications To the correspondent in writing. Trustees meet in January, April, July and October. Applications need to be sent by the end of January, April, July and October for consideration at the next meeting.

Sir George Martin Trust

£252,000 (1997/98)

General, especially in Yorkshire

Netherwood House, Ilkley,
Yorkshire LS29 9RP
Tel: 01943-831019

Correspondent Peter Marshall, Secretary

Trustees T D Coates, Chairman; M Bethel; R F D Marshall; P D Taylor.

Beneficial area Largely Yorkshire with particular emphasis on Leeds and Bradford. Some grants are made in other parts of the North of England, and occasionally major national appeals are considered.

Information available Report and Accounts with full grants list and excellent narrative analysis; Guidelines.

Summary Grants between £50 and £15,000 are made under several specified programmes. Beneficiaries are registered charities in the geographical area of interest. Aside from several organisations well known to the late founder, continuing assistance is not normally offered. There is a stated preference to help with capital costs and to avoid paying for running costs.

The trust is now in the process of redefining its policy to concentrate grant-giving to a more confined area.

General The trust was formed from the assets of the late Sir George Martin.

In addition to running grant making programmes, the trust also supports the United Kingdom Charitable Trust

Initiative, a movement to persuade wealthy people to found new trusts in the United Kingdom.

The trust says:

'The trustees all knew Sir George Martin and generally approach the making of grants in the spirit of giving effect to what, they believe, would have been his wishes. They have adopted the guidelines which follow in this broad basis. The trustees will, in general, follow these guidelines although they may depart from them if they consider that a particular cause is of special merit.

'The trust prefers to make grants available for capital rather than revenue projects, and is reluctant to give grants for general running costs, or areas previously supported by state funds.

'The trust does not normally repeat grants to any charity in any one year, and the maximum number of consecutive grants is usually three. The trust prefers to adopt a one-off policy in terms of its giving.

Beneficial area: 'Largely Yorkshire, with particular emphasis on Leeds, Bradford and the old West Riding. Occasionally, grants are made in other parts of Yorkshire and Cumbria. The trustees will consider grants from the old Yorkshire coalfield area and, occasionally grants are made in Humberside. Grants are not normally made in the Sheffield or Cleveland areas.'

Guidelines for giving in various areas:

- *Church appeals:* 'The trust will in future only normally give money to church appeals which have a definite outreach factor. Request for restoration schemes of roofs, spires, etc. will not be supported.
- *Music and the arts:* 'The trust is getting so many requests in this area that it has decided to restrict the giving to areas which are known to have been of definite interest to Sir George Martin in his lifetime. These include the Leeds Pianoforte Competition, the Bradford Subscription Concerts, the Harrogate Festival, the Harrogate Choral Society; the Leeds Philharmonic Society, and the Wharfedale Festival. Only on rare occasions will the trust give to other charities outside this sector.

'The trust will consider appeals for the capital needs of theatre in the geographical areas of interest.

'The trust does not support individuals, sponsorship of productions, touring companies etc.

- *'Old age:* 'The trust will continue to support the elderly, and future grants will be given to such needs as Meals on Wheels, old people's holidays and outings, Abbeyfield projects. The trust is unable to support appeals for individuals' needs.
- *Schools, education, universities:* 'The trust will not support education in areas funded by the state. The trust will occasionally support educational projects in schools not funded by the state.

  'The trust will not support university or college appeals, and will not support appeals from individuals seeking grants for university fees, post-graduate courses, or other courses etc..

  'The trust will not support such areas as overseas seminars or exchange visits by individuals or groups.
- *Medical:* 'Sir George Martin was the chairman of the Leeds Royal Infirmary for several years, and the trust will consider capital appeals from the old Leeds General Infirmary, but intend to restrict itself in future to grants to that hospital. The trust does not support medical research.

'The trust will take a special interest in the work of the hospices in its geographical area of giving.

- *Museums:* 'The trustees have, in the past, supported important Yorkshire museums, such as the Eureka Children's Museum in Halifax, the Captain Cook Memorial Museum, the Yorkshire Dales Museum. They will continue to look at the capital needs of museums in their geographical area of giving.
- *Countryside, environment, green issues:* 'The trust will consider applications from these areas, provided they fit into the geographical area of giving.'

In 1997/98, the trust's assets totalled £6.5 million from which £367,000 income was generated. Administration cost £104,000, but this includes £65,000 (63% of the total) spent on the trust's United Kingdom Charitable Trust Initiative.

'Last year's donations averaged £1,250. For the future, it is intended to try to increase the average value of our donations and, at the same time, narrow the type of charity we support.

'The trust made a grant of £3,000 to an Alms House Association at Arksey, near Doncaster. The trust made an exception in the medical area by making a grant of

£5,000 for a scanner at Bradford Royal Infirmary, in view of their association with out late Chairman, Mr Robert Martin, who was a senior surgeon there.

'Headingly Methodist Church, which was Sir George Martin's local church, received a grant of £2,500 for restructuring their voluntary work at the church. A grant of £15,000 was made to the new Arboretum, which is to be run at Castle Howard by Kew Gardens.

'Meanwood Valley Farm received a grant of £8,500 to help match a lottery grant to build a new centre at this important Leeds urban farm. Scarborough Parish Church received a grant of £3,000 to help rehabilitate their church and encourage outreach work. St George's Crypt, Leeds received a grant of £5,000 to help then on their way to their £1 million appeal to renovate this important Leeds Charity. Batley Grammar School received a grant of £5,000 to help with their appeal for a new music centre, which hopefully, will attract lottery money from the National Lottery Arts Board.

'The donations policy for the year ending April 1998 was much in the same terms of where we gave our grants in the previous year. In total £252,000 was donated in over 193 charitable donations. Analysing our grants by sector, the following enjoyed grants as a percentage of the total:

Youth Projects 26%
- play groups, scouting, Yorkshire Schools Exploring Society (£4,250), toy libraries – this sector includes the Roses Project (£1,700), a charity which we have sponsored for many years taking young people from inner cities to outward bound experiences in Scotland.

The environment 15%
- National Trust (NT, Halifax £250; NT Yorkshire Dales £2,500), Woodland Trust, Inner City Farms.

Medical schemes 12%
- Hospice support, a major capital appeal for Leeds Infirmary (£8,250).

Education 11%
- One or two small appeals from non-state schools. Education schemes with mentally handicapped people, education schemes including Yorkshire Ballet Seminar (£4,000), Yorkshire Farming Museum (£2,000) etc..

Arts projects 7%
- support for Harrogate Festival (£3,000), Yorkshire Choral Society, Ilkley Music Festival, Sir George Martin Memorial Concerts.

The aged 6%
- Methodist centres for the aged, old people's outings; Christmas lunches, church schemes for the aged etc.

Church restoration schemes 6%
- for all types and denominations (i.e. Methodist, Anglican, Yorkshire cathedrals)

Church outreach projects 5%
- from all denominations (Methodist, Catholic, Muslim).

Medical research 2%
- This area mainly concerns small donations to local research campaigns in Leeds, cancer research, research into ageing, Autistic Society, etc..

General 9%
- This concerns such area as the Craven Community Foundation (Craven Trust £350), Calderdale Community Foundation (£2,500) and some support for a local CVS.

'The trust gave free advice to many people who visited our offices in Addingham. To include but half a dozen: these were the Mikron Theatre Company, Addingham Parish and Methodist Churches; Abbeyfield Ilkley, Marie Curie Nursing in Bradford, and the Ilkley Playhouse. We strongly believe that running a charitable trust is not just a matter of grant giving, but giving helpful advice where appropriate.'

United Kingdom Charitable Trust Initiative:

'The trust completed an exercise under its United Kingdom Charitable Trust Initiative during the year in which we finally completed some 70 seminars attended by 2,500 people.

'This had resulted in over 100 new trusts, with a value of £85 million being established. These figures are conservative estimates as the result of our work, the creation of a charitable trust, does not immediately happen in practice. We sow the seed of the idea of a trust with many people.

'The Initiative will now major its efforts in the corporate area where there is a dramatic need for more charitable giving. It is estimated that UK companies give about 0.2% of pre-tax profits to charity, whereas in America the figure is 1.8%. The Initiative has started by approaching companies in Yorkshire on the subject of new charitable trusts, and we have persuaded two large companies to set-up foundations.

'Future approaches will be made nation-wide to plcs and privatised companies. We will also approach the privatised utilities and building societies.

'A great-niece of the founder, Sir George Martin, has been invited to join the trustees'.

Exclusions See the exclusions under the various programmes described in the guidelines above.

Applications The trust meets in December and June each year to consider applications. These should be made in writing to the secretary in good time for the meetings which take place in the middle of the month. Applications which are not within the guidelines cannot be answered due to substantial increase in costs. Applications that are relevant will be acknowledged and, following meetings, successful applicants will be told of the grants they are to receive. Unsuccessful applicants will not be informed.

The trust is unable to consider applications from organisations without charitable status. Telephone calls are not encouraged as the office is not always staffed – it is better to write or fax.

Mayfair Charities Ltd

£2,500,000 (1995/96)

Orthodox Judaism

Freshwater House, 158-162 Shaftesbury Avenue, London, WC2H 8HR Tel: 0171-836 1555

Correspondent Mr C. Morse, Secretary

Trustees B S E Freshwater (chairman); D Davis.

Beneficial area UK and overseas.

Information available In September 1998 no reports and accounts later than those to April 1996 were on file at the Charity Commission.

General About 200 grants were made in 1995/96, with nearly all going to various Jewish educational institutions, schools and synagogues, in the UK, USA and Israel.

Income for the year totalled £3 million, generated from assets of £57.2 million. Grants of about £2.5 million were made, with values ranging from £500 to nearly £500,000. The largest grant, also made in the previous years of similar value, was to the Beth Jacob Grammar School Ltd (£490,000).

Examples of some of the larger grants in 1995/96 include those to: the Mar Kaz Lechinuch Kolel (£154,000), Society of Friends of the Torah (£103,000), Beth Jacob Grammar School expenses (£28,000), Horomo Yeshiva (£25,000), Kedushat Zion Yeshiva (£25,000), Emuno Educational Trust (£24,000), Rabinous Divrei Shiv Kolel (£20,000), Yasheva Brei Zion, London (£19,000), Heiden Trust Beth Harnedrad (£14,000), London Academy of Jewish Studies (£14,000), Academy Rabbanical Research (£11,000), Ahavat Shahan Yeshiva (£6,000), Cosman Belz ltd (£5,000), and Hebron Yeshiva (£3,000).

The trustees' report states that the trustees have decided to 'support certain major projects which have received substantial financial grants from the company. At the present time the governors have entered into commitments for financial support of colleges and institutions which would absorb approximately £5 million over the next five years.' This is reflected in the annual reports where assets include £1 million held in 'property for charitable purposes.' The annual report specifies that this is made up of 'the cost of land and buildings intended to be used for the purpose of constituting a girls grammar school as part of the Special Projects Fund.'

Applications In writing to the correspondent.

The Medlock Charitable Trust

£1,162,000 (1997)

Education, general

Newark House, Cheltenham Street, Bath BA2 3EX
Tel: 01225-338 616

Correspondent David Medlock, Trustee

Trustees Leonard Medlock; Brenda Medlock; David Medlock; P H Carr.

Beneficial area UK especially Bath, Boston

Information available Report and accounts with full grants list and a narrative review of grant-making.

Summary Around a hundred grants are made a year ranging from £150 to £200,000. Beneficiaries are most often educational establishments in the Boston or Bath areas, but various causes

working in England (in practice the South) are also supported. About 20% of awards are repeated in the following year.

General The trust was established in 1985 and presently has an income of at least £1 million a year from its investments, most of which was gifted by the settlor Leonard Medlock and the Hebron and Medlock group of companies.

In the year ending July 1997, £1,256,000 was generated from investments totalling £18 million and a donation of £190,000 boosted total income to nearly £1.5 million. At £9,000, management and administration costs were very low – less than one pence per £1 donated or about £90 per grant.

The trustees' brief but good report says:

'The charity will continue to be proactive in the areas of Bath and Boston, to support and fund desirable and needed educational, social and medical projects which will fulfil a need not catered for by public funds. The charity will also consider all applications for grants made to it, which will be referred to the trustees on a quarterly basis for consideration.

'During the year the trust has continued with its policy of giving small unencumbered grants to schools in the Boston and Bath areas, supported mini-buses at Colston's [£12,000] and Summerfield Schools [£18,000], and responded to specific school appeals, the largest contribution being to King Edward School Bath [£100,000].

'Education has also been represented at university level by the final contribution to the Chair of Design and the first contribution towards the Dean of Engineering and Design, both at Bath University [£100,000].

'Medical charities have been supported by various grants and on-going support has gone to research for the elderly at St Martin's Hospital, Bath [£10,000] and BLISS [£50,000]. An exciting new medical research project at Southampton has been supported for this year and the next three years whereby the use of aortic balloons for the benefit of neurosurgery is being explored.

'Large capital projects continue to be supported with grants to Holly Cottage, Boston [£85,000] Grammar School [£100,000] and Boston High School [£200,000]. The major frustration of the year has been the lack of progress with the Boston Volunteer centre. This project is still anticipated and the trust is committed to support the project up to an

anticipated £750,000 over the 18 months build period.

'Various other grants have been made and the trustees consider all applications on their merits. There has been a total of 302 applicants to whom we have replied, 99 received donations and 19 have been from individuals who are not considered for grants.

'The trustees are currently receiving an increasing number of applications. We endeavour to send a reply in due course and the trustees are still actively pursuing new opportunities as well as supporting established links.'

Large grants outside Boston and Bath not already mentioned include £50,000 to the Cambridge Project, £20,000 to the Somerset Provincial Benevolent Fund and £15,000 to Age Concern.

Exclusions Individuals.

Applications In writing to the correspondent.

The Mercers' Charitable Foundation (and the Earl of Northampton's Charity)

£1,102,000 (1996/97)

Independent schools, education, general

Mercers' Hall, Ironmonger Lane, London EC2V 8ME
Tel: 0171-726 4991

Correspondent H W Truelove, Educational and Charities' Administrator

Trustees The Mercers' Company.

Beneficial area UK.

Information available Report and accounts with full grants list but lacking the required analysis and explanation of grants.

Summary In the region of three hundred grants are made a year to various UK charities although the majority of funds go specifically to support education organisations. Grants are for either capital or revenue costs and go as high as £150,000, but at least half of charitable expenditure is disbursed in numerous smaller awards of £1,000 to

£3,000. Awards are usually one-off though support over periods of up to three years is possible.

General The foundation was established in 1983 with the principal object to make grants for the benefit of a wide range of charitable purposes including welfare, education, arts, heritage and religion. It shares collective management with the six other charities of the Mercers' Company and applying to more than one of these would be a unecessary duplication of effort.

In 1996/97 assets totalled £10.5 million and income was £1.5 million – only £473,000 of which was generated from investments (the remaining £1,041,000 was donated).

Although the foundation does not break down grants by location, study of the grants list shows that while donations are made all over Britain there is a strong preference for the South of England. The trust says this is partly because, as a City of London Livery Company, they have stronger links in London and the South, and partly because they receive any more applications from these areas.

In 1996/97 over 300 grants were disbursed within the five categories below:

Arts	£63,000	6%
Education	£707,000	64%
Heritage	£102,000	9%
Welfare	£144,000	13%
Church	£85,000	8%
Total	£1,101,000	100%

Most grants were between £1,000 and £2,000 but four education awards between £50,000 and £150,000 went to independent schools and accounted for 35% of total grant expenditure.

Large non-education donations went to English National Opera (£20,000, Arts), St Bartholomew's Hospital (£40,000 towards the Chair of Radiology, Welfare), Sail Training Association (£25,000, Welfare), the Historic Churches Preservation Trust (£16,000, Church) and the National Manuscripts Conservation Trust (£5,000).

Exclusions The company does not respond to circular (mail shot) appeals. Unsolicited general appeals are considered but not encouraged. Grants are only made to individuals in the form of educational support – see the companion volume 'The Educational Grants Directory'.

Applications Initial applications should fill about 2 sides of A4 and be sent to the corespondent. The charitable trustees meet every month; the educational trustees every quarter.

The Metropolitan Hospital-Sunday Fund

£381,000 (1997)

Sick and disabled people in the London area

45 Westminster Bridge Road,
London SE1 7JB
Tel: 0171-922 0200

Correspondent Howard Doe, Secretary

Trustees The board of the fund, which is divided between clerical and lay members.

Beneficial area Greater London, within the M25.

Information available Detailed annual reports and appeal leaflets available from the fund.

Summary The fund makes grants to independent hospitals and homes, and to other health organisations. They are usually but not exclusively for modest capital items, and seldom for more than a few thousand pounds.

General The fund is financed by interest on the balances built up over the years and, to a much lesser extent, by an annual appeal in places of worship on Hospital-Sunday. The administration of the charity is now undertaken by the Peabody Trust. Besides the on-going grant making described below, it is also raising money for a specific 125th anniversary project, the Sundial Centre, a multi-faith day centre for elderly people in Bethnal Green – over £1 million has been raised towards a target of £1.7 million.

The main programmes are to give grants, usually for specific items of equipment to two types of charitable organisations, independent hospitals and homes, and then to other health charities.

There were 44 grants to independent homes and hospitals in 1997, totalling £189,000. The largest were both for passenger lifts, to Homesdale in Woodford (£25,000) and to the Shaftesbury Society's Coney Hill School in Bromley (£18,000). Much more typical were the £2,800 for 15 dining chairs for Abbeyfield's Morriss House in London N8 or the £4,000 for

refurbishing two kitchens at Haverstock Hill Group Home.

The 41 grants to other health charities were worth £162,000 and were remarkably widely spread. The largest was for £10,000, to Whizz Kids for mobility aids. Grants for £8,000 each was given to the British Disabled Water-Ski Association for a boat and to The Food Chain for hot food wrappers for the distribution of hot meals for housebound people with HIV aids. Unusually, £7,000 was given towards funding a nurse's post at the Elizabeth Baxter Centre. Other beneficiaries included Crossroads Pregnancy Crisis Centre (£2,400), Brent Bereavement Centre (£3,000 for counselling work) and the City of London Sinfonia (£2,500 towards a music for children project).

The fund also enables hospital social workers to help meet the immediate needs of patients which cannot be met from statutory funds, to 'relieve worry and distress. It can also make some larger grants to help patients on low incomes to meet, for example, household bills due to a long hospital stay....'

Exclusions No grants to individuals, except through NHS hospital social workers. Organisation grants to registered charities only.

Applications Independent hospitals, homes and other medical charities should write to the correspondent in January of each year for a Specific Purpose grant application form. Application forms must be returned by the end of March 9 for new applications) or June (for existing applicants). Awards are made annually in December. There is no restriction on the number of successive years that the same charity may submit an application, or on the number of years that an applicant may be awarded a grant.

Hospital social workers may apply at any time for Samaritan Fund grants.

Milton Keynes Community Trust

£271,000 (1997/98)

Welfare, arts

Acorn House, 381 Midsummer Boulevard, Central Milton Keynes, MK9 3HP
Tel: 01908 690276
Fax: 01908 233635

Correspondent Tim Hill, Chief Executive

Trustees Dorothy Cooper; Philippa Eccles; Naomi Eisenstadt; Rob Gifford; Richard Hall; Brian Hocken; Chris Hopkinson; Simon Ingram; Andrew Jones; Peter Kara; Juliet Murray; Michael Murray; Stephen Norrish; Francesca Skelton; Lady Tudor Price; Tony Walton.

Beneficial area Milton Keynes.

Information available Full information available from the trust.

Summary One of the most successful of the new 'community foundations', this charity raises money locally, mostly for its permanent endowment, and also makes grants for a wide range of purposes in Milton Keynes.

General The trust gives grants in the Milton Keynes Council area. It states its aims as:

- supporting initiatives that combat disadvantage
- supporting arts, sports and leisure initiatives
- creating resources needed for these initiatives and
- involving local people in the work of the trust.

The trust distributes grants through a number of funds, and requests that applicants contact the trust to discuss which fund they are eligible for. General applications are made through the Community Fund, and more specific ones through the Arts Fund.

Community Fund: Projects working with poverty, ill health, disability and other disadvantaged groups receive priority. Applications from other fields that benefit the Milton Keynes Council area will also be considered. As long as the organisation is undertaking charitable work, it does not need to be a registered charity to apply.

Four types of grants are made:

- Small grants for sums up to £1,000 are made monthly. The deadline for the receipt of completed application forms is noon on the last Friday of each month. Applications are considered during the following month
- General grants of up to £5,000 are made quarterly. The deadlines for receipt of completed applications forms are noon on the first Friday in February, May, August and November. For this type of grant the trust will not normally consider applications for ongoing running costs, except for project funding

where a percentage towards running costs may be considered. Typical grants made include the buying of equipment, small building works, short-term projects and one-off training courses.

- Development grants are typically for amounts between £7,000 and £18,000 and this type of grant can be made available for up to three years. Core costs may be included but an application will need to show what will happen to the project at the end of the term, i.e. It will have completed its work, become self-funding, etc. Applications for these grants are considered annually and the closing date is mid November. The office should be phoned to confirm the deadline.
- Umbrella grants: the trust also makes grants to a number of organisations for them to pass on as small grants to groups within their area of activity. These grants are for groups which are starting up, embarking on a new initiative or taking on a new area of work.
- Margaret Powell (Grants) Fund: This fund is held by the Community Trust specifically for making grants to benefit elderly people and disabled people of all ages, and also for groups who want to improve access or facilities for people with disabilities. Applications are made through the relevant small, general or development grants procedure.

Arts Fund: Grants are given to projects, events and activities which are innovative, imaginative and of high artistic quality. Current priorities are as follows:

- Innovative arts projects of high artistic quality from any source with impact and significance for the whole community of Milton Keynes.
- Projects which significantly benefit and/or take account of the needs of young, elderly and disabled people.
- Grass-roots community arts projects (these are normally channelled through the Milton Keynes Arts Association).
- In exceptional circumstances, awards may occasionally be made to individuals.

Grants start at £1,000 up to a maximum of £5,000. Projects under £1,000 should be addressed to the Milton Keynes Arts Association.

In 1997/98 the trust's income was £446,000, made up of donations and investment income. Assets totalled £3.3 million, while grant giving for the year stood at £271,000 made through 105 awards. Grants were split in the following general areas:

Health/disability	*21 grants*	*20%*
Social/ community	*47 grants*	*45%*
Arts	*20 grants*	*34%*
Education	*1 grant*	*1%*

Grants ranged from £150 to almost £23,000, with the average around £2,500. Examples of beneficiaries included: CVO Milton Keynes (£23,000, in an accumulation of several grants); Interaction (MK) Limited (£19,000); NCH Action for Children (£17,000); Drugs and Alcohol Support MK (£17,000); Arts Association MK (£9,000); Brook Advisory Centre MK (£5,000); Midsummer Art Show (£5,000); Family Mediation Service (£4,000); Shelter Housing Aid Centre (£4,000); Sports Council MK (£3,000); Volunteer Bureau MK (£3,000); Pre-School Learning Alliance MK (£2,000); Racial Equality Council MK (£1,000).

Exclusions Grants are normally not given to proposals chiefly focused upon the following:

- musical instruments;
- travel expenses;
- commercial publications;
- conferences or seminars;
- university or similar research, formal education or training;
- retrospective grants or are not made, nor grants to pay off deficits;
- projects connected with promoting a religious message of any kind will not be funded.

Applications Application forms and guidelines are available, but the trust advises applicants to phone them to discuss the proposal with a relevant grants co-ordinator.

The Monument Trust

£4,428,000 (approved, 1997/98)

Health & community care, HIV/AIDS, environment, arts, social development, general

See entry for the 'Sainsbury Family Charitable Trusts'
Tel: 0171-410 0330

Correspondent Michael Pattison, Director

Trustees S Grimshaw; Linda Heathcoat-Amory; R H Gurney; Sir Anthony Tennant.

Beneficial area UK and overseas, with a probable special interest in Sussex.

Information available Accounts with a full report are on file at the Charity Commission. The principal officers of the trust in 1997/98 were the director; P Spokes, finance director; Professor R Baker, assistant director; M Williams, executive.

Summary This trust is one of the Sainsbury Family Charitable Trusts which share a joint administration. It continues to be a consistent supporter of AIDS/HIV related work although only a small proportion of its giving is now directed there. Its funding spans a wide range of charitable activities, from health and community care to the arts and the environment. The trust makes major capital grants as well as revenue grants.

General This trust was endowed by Simon Sainsbury and registered as a charity in 1965 but he has never been a trustee. Its net income in 1997/98 was £4.79 million. The trust's report notes that its asset value increased to £143.3 million in April 1998 compared with £99.6 million at April 1997. Most of the trust's investments (70%) continue to be held in J Sainsbury plc.

Since most of the trust's grants are made over a number of years forward commitments are considerable. As a result annual approvals may vary considerably from year to year eg. £4 million in 1997/98 compared with £6 million in the previous year. However total annual approvals have increased substantially since the previous edition of this guide (£2 million, 1994/95).

Unlike other Sainsbury Family Charitable Trusts, the Monument Trust, at this point in time does not provide a narrative report of its policy for grant making of the kind recommended by the SORP, although the information given

about individual grants helps to fill this gap. Beneficiaries are listed in alphabetical order with their grant size and a very brief descriptive note of their purpose, sometimes only of their duration. The total of grants of less than £5,000 is given and the beneficiaries simply listed. The trust has a consistent approach to its grant making and has been funding projects within the above areas of work for at least a decade.

Health & Community Care – £983,000 (approved 1997/98)

The largest grant accounted for over half the total within this category in 1997/98 and was given to the Institute of Cancer Research towards the building of a new male cancer research centre in Sutton (£500,000 over 2 years). Two large grants over £100,000 each were made to the Papworth Trust, for a programme to help institutional care providers develop models for community living (£128,595 over 3 years) and to the Dementia Relief Trust to provide a seed fund to develop a specialist nurse service (£120,000). Four grants were given to hospices, the largest to St Christopher's Hospice towards a new child bereavement service (£40,000 over 2 years). (Fifteen grants were less than £5,000 each in 1997/98.)

In the previous year the three largest grants had been made to the Kings Fund for their Intermediate Care project (£200,000 over 2 years), CHAR towards the resettlement and training initiative (£100,000 over 2 years) and Phoenix House, St Mungo's and London Connection to help develop joint services for homeless people with multiple needs (£150,000 over 3 years).

AIDS – £446,000 (approved 1997/98)

This trust has been a valued supporter of work in this area for many years. In 1997/98 major grants included those to the UK Coalition of People Living with

HIV and AIDS for a new information technology system to improve production of a treatments information magazine and the salary of a p/t specialist editor (£67,005 over 2 years) and the Leith Drug Prevention Group for the employment of a coordinator (£81,570 over 3 years).

In 1996/97 two major grants were given to support work for children infected by AIDS – Positively Women to fund a specialist children's worker (£50,000 over 2 years) and the Waverley Care Trust to develop children's services (£66,088 over 3 years).

The Environment – £1,202,000 (approved 1997/98)

This category demonstrates a particular interest in the architectural heritage (from historic churches to theatres), horticulture and historic gardens.

In 1997/98 the largest grant in this category was given to the Royal Horticultural Society for the development of its educational facilities at Wisley (£500,000) with an associated smaller grant to the National Council for the Conservation of Plants and Gardens for its medium-term accommodation at Wisley (£20,000). Another major grant was made to Hackney Empire for theatre development (£200,000 over 2 years).

In the previous year the largest grant was awarded to British Trust for Conservation Volunteers towards its core costs (£166,500 over 3 years) and another theatre had received support – the Winchester Theatre Appeal (£15,000).

The Arts – £942,000 (approved 1997/98)

The major grant in 1997/98 was to the National Gallery, towards a new schools' education centre (£700,000 over 3 years). In the previous year the much larger allocation in this category arose from two major grants – to the Royal Opera House Trust for 'supplementary grants' covering redevelopment and current costs (over £1 million) and to the Royal National Theatre for redevelopment (£1 million). In the same year both the Wallace Collection and Friends of Pallant House received grants of over £250,000.

Social development – £798,000 (approved 1997/98)

In 1997/98 the largest grants were made to Centrepoint for rehabilitation and training for homeless people with multiple needs (£178,500 in 2 grants), Education Extra to develop a family sports initiative (£110,600 over 3 years) and the Empty Homes Agency to help

The Monument Trust						
	1996/97			**1995/96**		
Health & **Community Care**	£983,000	27	22%	£898,000	29	15%
AIDS	£446,000	15	10%	£325,000	11	5%
Environment	£1,202,000	22	27%	£437,000	20	7%
Arts	£942,000	17	21%	£3,116,000	26	51%
Social Development	£789,000	18	18%	£891,000	17	15%
General	£67,000	4	2%	£420,000	7	7%
Total	**£4,428,000**	**103**	**100%**	**£6,086,000**	**110**	**100%**

local community groups bring empty public buildings back into use for housing (£81,200).

In the previous year a grant was given Bootstrap Enterprises Ltd for their volunteer programme (£124,400 over 3 years).

Several arts projects with social aims (or vice versa) receive support: Clean Break Theatre Company, Half Moon Young People's Theatre, Ragged School Museum Trust, and Spitalfields Market Opera.

Activities relating to homelessness are supported under both 'Health and Community Care' and 'Social Development'.

General – £67,000 (approved 1997/98)

As the trust's name suggests there is a keen interest in historic buildings and monuments. In 1997/98 a grant was made to the Buildings Books Trust towards new editions of Pevsner's *Buildings of England* (£30,000 over 3 years).

In 1996/97 a major grant was made to Cambridge University for bursaries to enable UK public and charitable sector people to undertake MBA courses at Judge Institute (£375,000 over 3 years). This is the business institute housed in former Addenbrookes Hospital renovated and restored by the Monument Historic Buildings Trust of which Simon Sainsbury and Sir Paul Judge are both trustees.

Exclusions No grants directly to individuals.

Applications The trustees met five times in 1997/98. 'Proposals are generally invited by the trustees or initiated at their request. Unsolicited applications are discouraged and are unlikely to be successful, even if they fall within an area in which the trustees are interested. The trustees prefer to support innovative schemes that can be successfully replicated or become self-sustaining.'

However it is also said that an application to one of the Sainsbury trusts is an application to all. See the entry for the Sainsbury Family Charitable Trusts for the address and further advice.

The Henry Moore

Foundation

£863,000 (1996/97)

Art, particularly sculpture

Dane Tree House, Perry Green, Much Hadham, Herts. SG10 6EE
Tel: 01279-843333; Fax: 01279-843647; e-mail: curator@henry-moore-fdn.co.uk; Website: http://www.henry-moore-fdn.co.uk/hmf

Correspondent Timothy Llewellyn, Director

Trustees Sir Rex Richards, Chairman; Sir Alan Bowness; Margaret McLeod; Lord Rayne; Joanna Drew; Patrick Gaynor; Henry Wrong; Prof Andrew Causey; David Sylvester.

Beneficial area Europe, mainly UK.

Information available Review magazine with a list of donations without figures. Separate guidelines are available.

Summary The primary aim of the foundation is to promote the artworks of its namesake and the visual arts in general. Exhibitions, conferences and publications are supported and grants are made to institutions for teaching and research. Donations are usually one-off, though support over two or three years is possible.

General With an income of £6 million in 1997/98, the foundation is one of the largest arts trusts in the country. In that period, £3.1 million went into charitable expenditure, £529,000 into the foundation's running costs and the remaining £2.5 million remained unspent. Of the charitable expenditure, £2.3 million was paid in donations to the foundation's own causes: the Henry Moore Projects and the Henry Moore Institute. This left a minority, though substantial, fund of £863,000 for outside organisations and this money is the focus for this entry.

The foundation's advice to applicants describes the grants programme:

'The foundation was established in 1977 to advance the education of the public by the promotion of their appreciation of the fine arts and in particular the works of Henry Moore. It concentrates its support on sculpture, drawing and printmaking.

'The functions of the foundation are achieved through specific projects initiated within the foundation and the Henry Moore Sculpture Trust,

particularly exhibitions and publications, and by giving grant aid to other suitable enterprises. Grants are usually restricted to support for undertakings in the following categories:

- exhibitions (established galleries only);
- conferences, workshops and symposiums;
- fellowships and bursaries for artists and art historians at appropriate institutions;
- museum and gallery acquisitions of sculpture;
- conservation work and research;
- minor capital projects, primarily those designed to provide improved facilities for the exhibition of sculpture.'

In 1997/98 the foundation agreed to assist 36 exhibitions with grants ranging from £500 to £78,000 (totalling £287,550). 44% of the sum value went on two grants to the Yorkshire Sculpture Park for £78,000 and £50,000, and most other awards were for around £4,000. Other large grants were awarded to the Victoria and Albert Museum (£22,184); the British Library, £20,000 for public sculpture; and £21,500 (for three years) to the Henry Moore Study Centre. 18 fellowships or bursaries were also supported, to a total value of £148,000.

Exclusions The foundation does not give grants to individual applicants and cannot fund on a regular basis the revenue expenditure of galleries and other publicly supported institutions.

Applications In writing to the Director. The guidelines state that all applicants should cover the following.

- the aims and functions of the organisation;
- the precise purpose for which a grant is sought;
- the amount required and details of how that figure is arrived at;
- details of efforts made to find other sources of income, whether any firm commitments have been received, and what others are hoped for;
- details of the budget for the scheme and how the scheme will be monitored.

Applications are usually considered at quarterly meetings of the donations sub-committee which makes recommendations to the management committee of the trustees.

George A Moore

Foundation

£184,000 (1997/98), but an average of £264,000 since 1994/95

General, mostly in Yorkshire

Follifoot Hall, Pannal Road, Follifoot, Harrogate, North Yorkshire HG3 1DP

Correspondent Miss L P Oldham

Trustees Directors: George A Moore; Mrs E Moore; J R Moore; Mrs A L James.

Beneficial area Principally Yorkshire and the Isle of Man but also some major national appeals.

Information available Report and accounts with grants list but without narrative analysis of grants; Policy outline sheet (fully reprinted below).

Summary Grants are generally for £1,000 or less, but most of grant expenditure goes in a few large grants of up to £100,000. Awards are usually one-off payments, but many, including the large donations, go to organisations previously funded. Beneficiaries are charities working in a variety of fields, but particularly for the young, old or disabled.

General In 1997/98 the trust's assets totalled £6.7 million, income of £453,000 was generated and administration costs were £71,000, or 39 pence for each £1 granted – over £1,000 per grant (the average grant was for £2,900).

The foundation's policy outline is as follows:

'The trustees select causes and projects from the applications received during the year and also independently research and identify specific objectives where they wish to direct assistance. The types of grant can vary quite widely from one year to another and care is take to maintain a rough parity among the various fields covered so that one sphere of activity does not benefit unduly at the expense of another. Areas which are not or cannot be covered by official sources are favoured.

'The beneficial area is principally Yorkshire and the Isle of Man but consideration is given to some major national charities under certain circumstances.

'Grants are normally non-recurrent and the foundation is reluctant to contribute to contribute to revenue appeals. Approximately 75% of the grants made are £500 or below.

'Only registered charities are considered and the foundation rarely contributes seedcorn finance to newly established organisations. Projects for young people (teenagers/young adults) are favoured, as are community care projects.'

About 60 grants were made in 1997/98. Most were for £500 or under, but the two largest grants amounted to £150,000, or 82% of grant expenditure. These two awards were to the York Minster Fund (£100,000) and Prince's Youth Business Trust (£50,000). About 30% of beneficiaries were national charities and in two cases the grant was given for a specific area: Age Concern, Knaresborough, £15; Mencap Northern Division, £750. Although only five grants were repeated from the previous year these included the two large grants and therefore most of the funds were awarded to organisations previously supported. Remaining beneficiaries were a varied mix of charities, including:

- 14 medically-related charities (for example: British Polio Fellowship, £500; Yorkshire Spinal Injury Centre Appeal, £1,000; Primary Immunodeficiency Association, £500; Macmillan Cancer Relief, £25; Down's Syndrome Association, £100, National Asthma Campaign, £500);
- 14 organisations supporting disabled, and old people (Leeds and District Social Club for the Blind, £100; Support Dogs, £250; Methodist Homes for the Aged, £1,000; Yorkshire and Humberside Special Olympics, £700);
- 13 youth causes (Whizzkidz, £1,000; Follifoot primary school, £500; Children Safety Books UK, £150; 1st Copmanthorpe Scout Group, £1,000);
- and others (Coltman Area Community Fellowships, £250; Grassington Festival, £500; Ramsey Rugby Football Club, £100; St John's Parish Church, £200).

Exclusions No assistance will be given to individuals, courses of study, expeditions, overseas travel, holidays, or for purposes outside the UK. Local appeals for national charities will only be considered if in the area of interest. Because of present long-term commitments, the foundation is not prepared to consider appeals for religious property or institutions, or for educational purposes.

Applications In writing to the correspondent. No guidelines or application forms are issued. The trustees meet approximately four times a year, on variable dates, and an appropriate response is sent out after the relevant meeting.

The Moores Family Charity Foundation

£840,000 (1996/97)

General, especially in Merseyside

PO Box 28, Crosby, Liverpool, L23 0XJ
Tel: 0151-949 0117

Correspondent Mrs Patricia Caton

Trustees John Moores; Peter Moores; Lady Grantchester; James Suenson-Taylor; Mrs Janatha Stubbs.

Beneficial area UK, with a preference for Merseyside.

Information available Annual report and accounts.

General The foundation was set up in 1968 by John Moores of Littlewoods Stores. It does not own substantial assets (£317,000 in April 1997) and most of its income comes from annual donations from the Moores family and their businesses. About 80% of this income has been paid out in grants to other foundations including the Peter Moores Foundation (£147,000 in 1996/97), the Nigel Moores Family Foundation (£80,000), and the John Moores Foundation (£289,000); these three foundations have their own entries in this book. The remaining funds have been used to make numerous small grants in the Liverpool area. However, all this seems set to change; in 1998 the foundation said:

'The foundation no longer welcomes unsolicited applications and will not respond to them. The trustees have chosen to respond to some specific projects which are of particular interest to them. Consequently, the office is not staffed and will be closed before the end of 1998.'

Although these editors sometimes cast a sceptical eye over such pronouncements, they are confident that in this case uninvited applicants will be unsuccessful and all remaining charitable expenditure will indeed be made in a few, large donations to organisations well known to the trustees.

In 1998 Cottage Homes (the national charity of the fashion and stores trade) received £3.5 million from the foundation. £1.5 million of this money went towards the building of a sheltered housing complex, £500,000 to support UK-wide regional offices (in support of the employees and retirees from the fashion and stores trade), and the remaining £1.5 million was used to establish a trust fund, to be managed by Cottage Homes, which will assist Littlewoods' employees and pensioners.

Exclusions Projects not of particular interest to the trustees.

Applications The foundation does not welcome unsolicited applications.

John Moores Foundation

£792,000 (1996/97)

Social welfare in Merseyside and Northern Ireland

Neighbourhood Resource Centre,
79 Gorsey Lane, Wallasey,
Merseyside L44 4HF
Tel: 0151-637 0924; Fax: 0151-637 0925

Correspondent Tara Parveen, Grants Director

Trustees Mrs Jane Moores; Barnaby Moores; Ms M McAleese.

Beneficial area UK, but at present only in Merseyside, plus Skelmersdale, Ellesmere Port and Halton, and Northern Ireland.

Information available Report and accounts with categorised grants list and short narrative analysis of grants.

Summary Most grants are for £1,000 or less but these account for only around 15% of grant expenditure. Around half of the funds go in awards of £10,000 or above. A variety of causes, clearly specified by area and field, are supported (see below). About 10% of total value of grants is disbursed to charities in Northern Ireland.

General The foundation was established in 1963 and generates its income largely from investments, it also receives an annual donation from the Moores Family Foundation but this is diminishing and will soon cease.

In 1996/97 the foundation's assets

totalled over £8 million and its income was £813,000 (including a donation of £237,000 from the Moores Family Foundation). Beyond the £792,000 in grants paid the foundation committed to a further £134,000 in future payments. Twenty-one grants for £10,000 or over amounted to £437,000 (55% of charitable expenditure). Gifts between £2,001 and £9,999 totalled £261,000, or 33% of the total value of grants. 92% of grants expenditure was disbursed within Merseyside and other selected areas nearby (outlined below), and the remaining 8% went to Northern Irish organisations.

Grants made in 1996/97 are categorised in the table herewith.

The trust says:

'Policy (*see below*) is currently under review though no major changes are anticipated. For up-to-date information, applicants are advised to telephone the foundation's office.

'Grant making is mainly directed towards new and/or small organisations in the area of Merseyside (including Skelmersdale, Ellesmere Port and Halton) and in Northern Ireland, who work with disadvantaged or marginalised people who find it more than usually difficult to raise money from other sources. Preference is given to organisations seeking funds for projects which fall within the foundation's target areas for giving which are:

- women including girls;
- black and ethnic minority organisations;
- race gender and disability awareness;
- advice and information to alleviate poverty;
- tranquilliser users;
- second chance learning;
- grass roots community groups;
- people with HIV/AIDS, their partners and families;
  and in Merseyside only:
- people with disabilities;
- carers;
- support and training for voluntary organisations;
- homeless people;
- unemployed people;
- childcare
- small grants to a wide range of charitable organisations which do not fall within the above target areas.

'During the year the foundation received 440 written applications (450 in 1995/96), of which 351 were from Merseyside and Northern Ireland. A total of 165 grants (125 in 1995/96) were made, of which 126 were in Merseyside, 34 in Northern Ireland and five elsewhere.'

'Within the grants list are grants to a handful of projects which have been supported for a number of years including Merseyside Information and Advice Project (£83,000) and Bronte

John Moores Foundation

	Number of grants in 1996/97	Total
Merseyside and other local areas	131	£730,000
Advice	12	£130,000
Women	17	£99,000
Second chance learning/training for community groups	9	£61,000
Youth	8	£59,000
Black and ethnic minority organisations	7	£58,000
Childcare	15	£51,000
Disabled	16	£48,000
Homeless	11	£42,000
Social Welfare	16	£33,000
Carers	6	£22,000
Community organisations	10	£18,000
Other	4	£111,000
Northern Ireland	34	£63,000
Women	19	£37,000
Black organisations	2	£8,000
Advice	2	£2,500
Community	1	£2,000
Second chance learning	3	£1,500

Neighbourhood Centre (*Bronte Youth and Community Project received two grants amounting to £38,000*).

'The pattern of giving remained broadly consistent with the previous year, in that over 75% of grants were for £5,000 or less, and almost a third of grants were for £1,000 or less.

'One new grant was given for revenue funding for more than one year.

'The largest grant was made to Merseyside Information and Advice Project (*£83,000*), which has been supported by the foundation since its inception and of which the settlor and the first named trustee are also trustees. Two exceptional grants were made by trustees, both of £50,000. One grants was to Crisis for work with homeless people countrywide, and the other to British Red Cross Crisis in Africa Appeal.

'15 grants were made to support childcare, a new area of giving in 1995/96, – funded by the trustees to enable parents, particularly women to return to education, training or employment. Grants were made to after school clubs, play groups, crèches and for child care development work.'

(*They included: West Everton Community Council, £10,000; SMART Charitable Trust, Liverpool, £2,000; Lee Manor High School, Liverpool £325; Strand Crèche, Sefton, two £5,000 grants; and Mersey Park Playgroup, Wirral, £250.*)

'Four grants were made to make premises accessible to disabled people.'

(*Grants for disabled people included the following: Wirral Inroads, £550; Greenbank Project, Liverpool, £5,000; Liverpool Family Service Unit £16,000; Merseyside Autistic Children's Society, £750; and People First, Liverpool, £1,000.*)

'It is the policy of trustees to monitor all grants made, whenever possible through visits as well as written reports. Trustees have discussed during the year the employment of additional staff top enable more projects to be visited.

'The trustees have responsibility for the administration and grant making of South Moss Foundation, a small trust which makes grants to individual children and young people who are in care or at risk.'

Aside from those already mentioned, other large grants included the following:

Anfield Citizens Advice Bureau,	£10,000
Churches Action for Racial Equality,	£15,000°
West Everton Community	

Council,	£10,000
Whitechapel Centre, Liverpool,	£10,000
Byrom Education and Training Trust, Liverpool,	£10,000
Sheila Kay Fund, Liverpool,	£20,000
Supportive Help and Development Organisation,	£10,000
St Helen's and District Women's Aid, St Helens,	£10,000
Women's Educational Training Trust,	£15,000

No such big grants were made in Northern Ireland, where the largest awards were as follows:

Northern Ireland Council for Ethnic Minorities,	£5,000
Magherafelt Women's Group, Derry	£5,000
Lower Ormeau Residents Action Group,	£4,000
Women's Resources and Development Agency, Belfast	£4,000
Family Centre, Gobnascale,	£3,000
Footprints Women's Centre, Belfast,	£3,000
Forum for Community Work Education	£3,000

Exclusions *Unsolicited applications for projects which fall outside current policy will not be considered.* The foundation does not give grants for:

- Academic or medical research;
- Animal charities;
- Arts;
- New buildings;
- Churches for church based or church run activities. (although community groups running activities in church premises which come within the foundation's policy guidelines will be considered);
- Conservation and the environment;
- Employment creation schemes;
- Holidays and expeditions;
- Individuals;
- Medicine or health;
- National organisations;
- Parties and outings;
- Schools, universities or colleges;
- Statutory bodies;
- Vehicles.

Applications Applications should be in writing and accompanied by an application form, copies of which are obtainable from the grants director. Before submitting an application, please make sure that your project does not fall into one of the excluded areas (see exclusions). If you are unsure and you would like to discuss your application, telephone the grants director.

'Applications are expected to contain the following information:

- A description of your organisation,

its work and existing sources of funding.
- A description of the project for which you are applying for funds.
- Detailed costings of the project, including details of funds already raised or applied for, if any.
- Details of how the projects will benefit people within the foundation's target groups.

'Applicants should also send if possible:

1. Their constitution.
2. Latest accounts.
3. Latest annual report.
4. List of management committee members.
5. Equal opportunities policy.

'Unsolicited applications which fall outside current policy will NOT be considered.

'Most groups who apply for funding are visited, but we may simply telephone for more information. Trustees meet every six weeks although organisations are advised to allow up to three months for a decision to be made.'

The Peter Moores Foundation

£4,980,000 (1996/97)

The arts, particularly opera, social welfare

Wallwork Nelson and Johnson, Ref M139/MJ/IGG, Derby House Lytham Road, Fulwood PR2 4JF

Correspondent Peter Saunders

Trustees Mrs Barbara Johnstone; Trevor Conway; Peter Egerton-Warburton; Donatella Moores; Alan Swerdlow.

Beneficial area UK and Barbados.

Information available Reports and accounts, with grants list but no narrative, are on file at the Charity Commission.

Summary Most of this trust's resources are dedicated at present to the great Compton Verney opera project, which received almost £4 million in 1996/97. However there are other varied, interesting and unusual grant programmes in addition to this.

General The trust was established in 1964 by Peter Moores, who remains a patron of the foundation. It primarily supports the arts, the particular regard for opera reflecting Mr. Moores personal involvement.

For 1996/97 income totalled £3.21 million, received through donations and gains on investments. There is little permanent endowment, although assets of over £3 million were held in in the form of a variety of artworks. Grant giving for the year amounted to £4.98 million (up from £2.71 million the previous year), with grants going into four areas, categorised by the trust as follows (with the previous year's figures in brackets):

	1996/97	(1995/96)
Creative	£4.47m.	(£2.18m.)
Sociological	£190,000	(£216,000)
Barbados	£296,000	(£315,000)
Various one-offs	£24,000	(£3,000)

Grant size varied from £500 to almost £4 million. The grants list was further subdivided as follows:

Music: (£476,000), under the following headings:

- Performance (£174,000): Examples of beneficiaries include: the Almeida Theatre (£50,000); Rossini's Opera Festival (£50,000) and the Scottish Opera Irish Cross Border Project (£8,000).
- Recording (£168,000): Examples include grants given to the 3 Rossini Tenors (£59,000) and to Ricardo e Zorande (£5,300)
- Training (£134,000): Made up mainly of grants to the Royal Northern School of Music Scholarships (£37,000) and 52 individual awards (£89,000).

Fine Art (£3,970,000): The principal grant was to the Compton Verney Opera House Trust, where both Peter Moores and his sister Mrs. Stubbs are trustees (£3,953,000). The Royal College of Art received £9,000.

Heritage (£15,000): Made up mainly of two grants, one to the National Maritime Museum (£10,000) and one to the Textile Conservation Centre (£3,500).

Youth (£59,000): Examples include Millfield School (£15,000), Christ Church, Oxford ((£13,000), and the London Institute of HEC (£6,000).

Race Relations (£55,000): Grants include those given to the National Museum and Galleries on Merseyside, and the Lord Pitt Foundation (£9,800).

Social (£8,000): Made up almost entirely of a grant to Dark Horse Venture, education for the elderly, (£6,000).

Health (£68,000): Three main grants were made in this category: the Immune Development Trust (£15,000), International Rescue Committee (£10,000) and to Blackliners, AIDS (£10,000).

Environment (£500): Only one grant given, to Farm Africa (£500).

Barbados (£296,000): Major grants to the Peter Moores Barbados Trust (£245,000) and the University of the West Indies (£48,000).

One-offs: made up entirely by one grant to the Donatella Moores Charitable Trust (£24,000).

Applications In writing to the correspondent but applicants should be aware that its 1995 report states that the foundation 'will normally support projects which come to the attention of its patron or trustees through their interests or special knowledge. General applications for sponsorship are not encouraged and are unlikely to succeed.'

The Mulberry Trust

£284,000 (1995/96)

General

Messrs Farrer & Co, 66 Lincoln's Inn Fields, London, WC2A 3LH
Tel: 0171-242 2022

Correspondent Charles Woodhouse, Trustee

Trustees J G Marks; Ms A M Marks; C F Woodhouse.

Beneficial area UK, probably with a special interest in North East London and surrounding areas.

Information available In September 1998, the most recent accounts on file at the Charity Commission were those for 1995/96 (this was still the case in November as this book went to press, though more recent accounts were said by the trust to be then in transit). These were unaudited and apparently incomplete. Binder Hamlyn, accountants, had prepared, but not audited, 12 pages of these, but only five of the pages were on file and these were without any list of grants.

General We cannot report the grants made by this trust for any year since 1991. At that time the bulk of the grants by value were bring spent in the area

described above, with awards in Havering, Waltham Forest, Harlow and Chelmsford. Among wide interests, there appeared then to be an interest in specifically Christian charities and in money advice.

After the paragraph above had gone to press, the Christian and money advice interests were confirmed by the correspondent and an 'education' interest was added.

The trust has said that it 'will not, as a matter of policy, consider favourably applications which are unsolicited'. Consequently, the trust did not wish to be described in this book; however it is the policy of the Directory of Social Change to include all grant making trusts, as the book constitutes a review of that sector as a whole, as well as being a guide for potential applicants.

It is surprising that up to date, audited accounts were not on file at the Charity Commission, and that the trust did not accede to a written request for a copy of its most recent accounts, as the correspondent and one of the trustees, Charles Woodhouse, is a partner in Farrers, a law practice prominent in the world of charitable foundations.

Applications See above.

The National Art Collections Fund

£2,407,000 (1997)

Acquisition of works of art by museums and galleries

Millais House, 7 Cromwell Place, London SW7 2JN
Tel: 0171-225 4800; Fax: 0171-225 4848

Correspondent Mary Yule, Assistant Director and Head of Grants.

Trustees Committee: Sir Nicholas Goodison, Chairman; David Barrie, Director and 18 others.

Beneficial area UK.

Information available Weighty annual review with accounts gives a full illustrated record of all works assisted. Leaflet - Information for grant applicants.

General 'The National Arts Collections Fund is Britain's largest arts charity. It receives no Government or National Lottery funding and relies on the support of over 102,000 members and on legacies and donations from private individuals, corporations and charitable trusts.

'Since its launch in 1903, the fund has helped hundreds of galleries, museums and historic houses to acquire over 100,000 works of art. The fund supports the purchase of art of all types and ages, from ancient civilisations to the contemporary world. It supports not only great national museums but also smaller museums and historic properties across the country.

'In 1997 the fund offered £3 million to collections throughout the UK. The fund also campaigns to prevent public collections from being dispersed or downgraded.'

Fundraising for the arts is an expensive business. One third of the fund's income (other than from investments) was spent on fundraising and administrative costs. Several trusts described elsewhere in this book were major supporters of the fund in 1997, including Wolfson Foundation (£100,000), Esmée Fairbairn, Garfield Weston (£50,000 each), 29th May Charitable Trust, John Ellerman Foundation and Rayne Foundation (£10,000 each).

Of the 52 museums and galleries supported in 1997 (to the sum of £2,026,000), the best funded were the Fitzwilliam Museum, Cambridge (£245,000 towards six works), Newhailes in Musselburgh (£245,000) and the Tate Gallery in London (£234,000 towards six works). 13 awards of £50,000 or more accounted for 75% of the total value of grants paid.

Exclusions Grants are restricted to establishments which are constantly open to the public.

Applications To Mary Yule, Assistant Director and Head of Grants. A basic information leaflet is available for applicants and an application form. The trustees meet monthly except for August.

The National Lottery

General The National Lottery Charities Board has a brief adjacent entry. The other lottery distributors also make grants to organisations. Details can be obtained as follows:

Arts Councils

England	0171	973	6517
Scotland	0131	240	2444
Wales	01222	388288	
Northern Ireland	01232	385200	

Heritage Lottery Fund

0171 591 6000

Millennium Commission

0870 600 1999

New Opportunities Fund

0171 222 3084

Sports Councils

England	0345	649649	
Scotland	0131	339	9000
Wales	01222	300500	
Northern Ireland	01232	382222	

The National Lottery Charities Board

About £285,000,000 (from 1999)

Those at greatest disadvantage in society

St Vincent House, 16 Suffolk Street, London SW1Y 4NL
Tel: 0171-747 5300
Web site www.nlcb.org.uk

Correspondent Timothy Hornsby, Chief Executive

Board Members David Sieff, Chairman; Sir Adam Ridley; Tessa Baring; Amir Bhatia; June Churchman; Stella Clarke (Chair, England Committee); Tom Jones (Chair, Wales Committee); Amanda Jordan (Chair, UK Committee); Monica McWilliams; Garth Morrison (Chair, Scotland Committee); John Simpson (Chair, Northern Ireland Committee); Noel Stewart; Professor Sir Eric Stroud; Steven Burkeman; Anne Clark; Kay Hampton; Barbara Lowndes; William Osborne; Ron Partington; Elisabeth Watkins.

Beneficial area UK and UK charities working overseas.

Information available Full information available. For current application packs and information, ring 0345-919191 or 0345-778878 (overseas). For other information contact the relevant regional or national office, as listed under 'Applications' at the end of this entry.

General This is not an independent charity, but a government appointed committee responsible for spending public money. However, as it is a member of the Association of Charitable Foundations, it has been given a brief entry.

Note that it it is only one of six bodies making grants from the proceeds of the lottery. For contact details for the Arts and Sports Councils, the Heritage Lottery Fund, the Millennium Commission and the New Opportunities Fund, see the adjacent entry for the National Lottery

The full, and fine, purposes of the Charities Board (NLCB) are 'to help meet the needs of those at greatest disadvantage in society and to improve the quality of life in the community'. It has tackled the job with energy and enterprise, and in doing so has set new grant making standards for many of the other trusts whose work is described in this book.

The NLCB had five funding programmes at the end of 1998. They were as follows (with approximate values for 1999):

Community involvement: continuous open application (£100 million)

Poverty and disadvantage: continuous open application (£100 million)

International: an annual cycle, with autumn application (£25 million)

Health and social research: an annual cycle, with autumn application (£20 million)

Small grants: for bodies with an income of less than £15,000 (£40 million).

Grants, except under the small grants scheme, are generally for any amount between £5,000 and an only seldom exceeded £500,000; can be for capital or project funding, and for up to three years (five years, and sometimes larger sums, for International grants). Only a handful of grants have been for amounts between £500,000 and the highest yet awarded of £1.1 million. There is no requirement for matching funding.

In a major change since the previous edition of this book, organisations can now hold separate and simultaneous grants, if they and their projects qualify, from each of the programmes and, for each of the two main programmes, from each country or regional committee – one for each of England, Scotland, Wales and Northern Ireland, and one for each England region (or a single application to the UK committee can be made in place of applications to all of the country committees). The jackpot for a national charity also working overseas would be 27 grants (and if their local branches or affiliates qualified as applicants in their own right, many more).

Grants are made following a formal, scored assessment against published criteria. These cover both the competence of the organisation to carry out effectively the work concerned, and the extent to which this work meets NLCB policies – which are weighted towards the 'empowerment' of disadvantaged communities through the maximum practicable user or beneficiary participation in the activities supported.

Success rates have been running at about one in four applications. About a quarter of applications are still being ruled ineligible, either in law or for being outside stated NLCB policies (most often because of a perceived danger of replacing statutory funding). A further quarter or so do not meet the minimum organisational requirements; for those who pass these two hurdles the success rate is nearer 50%. However this varies from area to area, partly because of the varying number and quality of applications, but also because country and regional budgets are heavily, and most desirably, weighted for the relative disadvantage of the region (and because similar weightings are less formally, but nevertheless vigorously applied within countries and regions).

So far, funding has been largely 'project' based. The impact of the NLCB's work will be defined to a large extent by the scale on which grants, originally for three year funding, are in practice renewed. This was not yet apparent in Autumn 1998 but will become clearer during 1999.

The introduction of the Small Grants programme at last and belatedly rectifies in part the situation in which charities with paid staff got most of the money while the wholly voluntary part of the sector, which carries out most of the charitable activity, was relatively neglected.

Readers who have noticed the high administrative costs of some other large grant makers described in this book may be interested to note that administrative costs of the NLCB represent less than 6% of the value of grants committed. This is despite by far the most elaborate grant assessment and policy development procedures of of any grant maker.

The loudest complaint against the NLCB, the complete lack of feed back to unsuccessful applicants on the reasons for their lack of success, was partially rectified in in 1998. For those applications deemed ineligible, an explanation was at least being given. For the rest of the unsuccessful applicants there was still little feedback except for

two trial areas, Scotland (with telephone feedback) and the North East of England (a written summary of the assessment).

There are Development Officers in all the Board's offices whose responsibility includes assisting potential applicants. Though this cannot always be done on an individual basis, all have information programmes locally.

All applications must be made on the appropriate application form. The telephone numbers from which these can be obtained are set out under 'Applications' below – or copies can be downloaded from the NLCB's website, as above.

National and Regional Offices

UK Office
St Vincent House
16 Suffolk Street
London SW1Y 4NL
Tel: 0171-747 5299
Fax: 0171-747 5214
Head of UK and Overseas grants:
  Gerald Oppenheim

Scotland Office

Norloch House
36 King's Stables Road
Edinburgh EH1 2EJ
Tel: 0131-221 7100
Fax: 0131-221 7120
Director: John Rafferty

Office for Northern Ireland

2nd Floor, Hildon House
30-34 Hill Street
Belfast BT1 2LB
Tel: 01232-551455
Fax: 01232-551444
Director: Ann McLoughlin

Wales Office

Ladywell House
Newtown
Powys, Wales SY16 1JB
Tel: 01686-621644
Fax: 01686-621534
Director: Roy Norris

England Office

Readson House
96-98 Regent Road
Leicester LE1 7DZ
Tel: 0116-258 7000
Fax: 0116-255 7398/9
Director: Janet Paraskeva

Regional Offices
East Midlands Region

3rd Floor, 33 Park Road
Nottingham NG1 6NL
Tel: 0115 934 9300
Fax: 0115 948 4435
Regional Manager: Vacant

Eastern Region

Great Eastern House
Tenison Road
Cambridge CB1 2TT
Tel: 01223-449000
Fax: 01223-312628
Regional Manager: Janette Grazette

London Region

3rd Floor, Whittington House
19-30 Alfred Place
London WC1E 7EZ
Tel: 0171-291 8500
Fax: 0171 291 8503
Regional Manager: Janice Needham

North East Region

Ground Floor, Bede House
All Saints Business Centre
Broad Chare
Newcastle upon Tyne NE1 2NL
Tel: 0191 255 1100
Fax: 0191 233 1997
Regional Manager: Peter Deans

North West Region

Dallam Court
Dallam Lane
Warrington WA2 7LU
Tel: 01925 626800
Fax: 01925 234041
Regional Manager: Andrew Freeny

South East Region

3rd Floor, Dominion House
Woodbridge Road
Guildford
Surrey GU1 4BN
Tel: 01483 462900
Fax: 01483 568764
Regional Manager: Dorothy Buckrell

South West Region

Pembroke House
Southernhay Gardens
Exeter EX1 1UL
Tel: 01392-849700
Fax: 01392-491134
Regional Managers: John de la Cour &
Pipa Warin

West Midlands Region

Edmund House
4th Floor, 12-22 Newhall Street
Birmingham B3 3NL
Tel: 0121 200 3500
Fax: 0121 212 3081
Regional Manager: Fran Jones

Yorkshire & the Humber Region

3rd Floor, Carlton Tower
34 St Pauls Street
Leeds LS1 2AT
Tel: 0113-224 5300
Fax: 0113-244 0363
Acting Regional Manager: Helen
  Woollaston

Applications Application lines

In all cases, applications can only be made on the appropriate application forms, which are available from the following numbers;

Community Development Poverty and Disadvantage Health and Social Research	0345 919191
Small grants, England and Northern Ireland	0345 458458
Scotland (Awards for All)	0645 700777
Wales	0345 273273
International	0345 778878

The Needham Cooper Charitable Trust

£270,000 (1996/97)

Medical, general

Home Farm, Yate Rocks, Yate,
Nr Bristol BS37 7BS

Correspondent Mrs E J B Cooper

Trustees Mrs E J B Cooper;
S T F Cox; Mrs J L V Penson;
R C Baxter.

Beneficial area Bristol and district.

Information available Report and Accounts, including grants list but with no analysis of grant making or policy.

Summary Grants vary from under £1,000 to around £50,000 and are made to registered charities in the area of interest. Most funds are awarded to the same charities from year to year.

General The trust was established in 1988 and the settlor is Wilfred Needham Cooper who bequeathed a 44% holding in Engineering and Allied Holdings along with 20 acres of his farm near Bristol.

In 1996/97 the trusts assets totalled £2,721,000 from which a high income amounting to £239,000 was generated. The pattern of donations was largely unchanged from recent years and most of the major awards were repeated. For example St John's Ambulance received £25,000 (£25,000 also in 1995/96 and in 1994/95), Bristol 2000 £20,000 (£20,000 in both years) and Bristol University Department of Surgery £20,000 (£20,000 in 1995/96). Other large grants went to Bristol Ace Care (£53,000), Greater Bristol Foundation £10,000 and Unity Fund £10,000.

In 1996/97, the foundation had made future grants commitments totalling £56,000 in 1998/99 and £50,000 in 1999/

2000. In Summer 1998 it stated 'we are not taking on any new charities for the next two years'.

Exclusions Support is given only to registered charities; no grants to individuals.

Applications In writing to the correspondent. If the trust considers supporting an organisation they will first want to see the accounts for the last year.

The trust has stated that it will not be accepting any more applications until 2000.

The trustees meet in March and August.

The Network Foundation

£526,000 (1996)

Environment, human rights, peace, arts

BM Box 2063, London WC1 3XX

Correspondent Vanessa Adams, Administrator

Trustees Patrick Boase, Chair; John S Broad; Ingrid Broad; Samuel P Clark; Oliver Gillie; Hugh MacPherson; Sara Robin; Dr. F Mulder, P Hadwick; C Carolan.

Beneficial area UK and overseas.

Information available In September 1998 no reports and accounts later than those for 1996 were on file at the Charity Commission.

General The 1996 accounts show an income of £665,000 for the foundation, made up mostly from donations. Grant expenditure is noted at £526,000 and is split under three categories:

- *Funding Cycle (£304,000):* Members of the foundation assess small projects under the following headings: Human Rights and Solidarity; Health and Wholeness; Peace and Preservation of the Earth; Arts and Media. For 1995/96 about 30 projects were funded, examples include: Christian Aid (£30,000); Gaia Foundation (£20,000); Ashoka (£18,000); Results Education (£15,000); Refuge Council (£14,600); Responding to Conflict (£13,000); Homeopathy for a Change (£11,000); Permaculture Association (£10,000); Research Foundation for Science and Technology (£9,000); Aspect Theatre Production (£6,000); Genetics Forum (£6,000); and the Triangle Arts Centre (£6,000).

- *Informal Funding (£78,000):* For individual members to bring forward projects they intend to fund personally and which they want to invite others to join them in funding.
- *Major Projects (£145,000):* This category is for projects that the foundation wants to fund significantly over several years. Currently areas of funding named are in Third World Debt and Homelessness.

The description of this unusual foundation given in the previous edition of this book may still be of interest. No more recent information is available. It reads in part as follows:

The income of this unusual foundation, which does not seek applications, comes from donations by members of the associated company, the Network for Social Change Ltd, 'a community of wealthy individuals seeking to realise their visions in ways that enable others'.

It is understood from a 'recruitment bulletin' of the company that in 1993 grants of an average size of about £3,000 were given to about 80 projects/ organisations. There is little more recent information. This bulletin explained how the foundation worked, at least at that time:

"The Network as a whole has no expressed policy on the types of organisation or projects it will back. The responsibility for bringing forward applications lies with the members. Because they are such a diverse group, so are the applications. However, ...Network members' interests tend to lie in smaller projects and organisations, in backing the inspired project or individual who is in a good position to create wide ripples, and exclude relief work....Because the sponsorship ...is in the hands of the members, rather than lying open to public application, the relationship...can be more of a partnership than is normal in a funder-funded situation."

1) The Network 'Funding Cycle' takes place once a year and takes six months. Small groups of members assess the projects under one of four headings:

> *Peace and Preservation of the Earth;*
> *Human Rights and Solidarity;*
> *Health and Wholeness;*
> *Arts and Media.*

Once this is done a "package of projects" is presented to the membership. The members then allocate the funds they are donating under the four headings. They cannot allocate to individual projects.

2) The Network 'Informal Funding' process allows individual members to bring forward projects they intend to fund personally and which they want to invite others to join them in funding. These meetings are usually run four times a year with a quick turnaround of cash.

3) Network Major Projects, currently four of them, are ones in which the Network plays a significant funding role over several years. Most relate to development issues or economics.

Two three-day conferences are held in late Winter and early Autumn. Other meetings and smaller events are also arranged. Prospective new members are introduced either by meeting an existing member or attending a group introductory session held from time to time in London. They are then invited to a conference.

Applications The Network chooses the projects it wishes to support and does not solicit applications. Unsolicited applications cannot expect to receive a reply.

The Frances and Augustus Newman Foundation

£527,000 (1997/98)

Medical research and equipment

c/o Kidsons Impey, 33 Wine Street, Bristol BS1 2BQ
Tel: 01179-252255

Correspondent Miss E Yeo, Secretary

Trustees Mrs Frances Moody Newman; Spencer Seligman; Sir Rodney Sweetnam FRCS; John Ll. Williams FRCS.

Beneficial area UK (mainly London and Bristol) and overseas.

Information available Full accounts on file at the Charity Commission.

General The trust supports projects in the field of medical research, mainly in London and Bristol. In a very few instances grants have also been made towards the cost of purchasing equipment.

In 1998 assets of the foundation amounted to £10.7 million, with an

income of £612,000. About £527,000 was given out in donations, up from £473,000 the previous year, with grants ranging from £9-£51,000, usually to well established hospitals, research centres and national organisations.

Grants are categorised as follows (with 1996/97 figures in brackets):

UK Ongoing Research
	£134,000	(£280,000)
UK 'One-Off'	£366,000	(£226,000)
Overseas	£27,000	(£28,000)

Ongoing research grants: UCL; £51,000 for a study by Prof. J. O. Riordan into the genetic factors in the development of osteoporosis: Bristol University; £26,000 for hip, replacement research: : Royal Nat. Hospital for Rheumatic Diseases; £14,000 for osteoporosis research: Lancaster University; £23,000 for skin cancer research: Elizabeth Garret Anderson Hospital; £20,000 for research into pelvic injuries.

'One-Off' grants: There were twelve of these awards, headed by £50,000 to the Royal College of Surgeons (of which two trustees are members). Other large awards went to Birmingham University (£37,000 the work of Mr A D Lander) and Bristol University (£30,000 for research on cell signalling)

Overseas: There was just one award, of $44,000 for the Paracare Association of Palm Beach.

Applications To the correspondent.

The Northern Ireland Voluntary Trust

£6,465,000 including European funding (1996/97)

Social welfare

22 Mount Charles, Belfast, BT7 1NZ
Tel: 01232-245927; Fax: 01232-329839

Correspondent Avila Kilmurray, Director

Trustees David Cook, Chairman; Vivienne Anderson; Mary Black; Mark Conway; Eamonn Deane; Sammy Douglas; Mari Fitzduff; Sheelagh Flanagan; Jim Flynn; Philip McDonagh; Aideen McGinley; Angela Paisley; Ben Wilson.

Beneficial area Northern Ireland.

Information available 'Guidelines for Grant Seekers'; separate guidelines

for each of the specific schemes outlined below; detailed annual report; Strategic Plan 1995-1999.

Summary This is an independent charitable trust, though largely supported by public funding, which supports and encourages the efforts of voluntary and community groups to tackle the worst effects of Northern Ireland's social, economic and community problems. Over 2,500 applications were received and dealt with under the EU Special Support Program, with 1,000 grants being awarded. Grants are of various size; specific programs should be examined for their criteria.

General The NIVT has benefited from a substantial injection of funds from the European Union to allocate as revenue grants to small and medium-sized community projects across Northern Ireland. This quadrupled its amount of funding (in 1994/95 NIVT gave grants of about £1.5 million, compared to 1996/97 where £6.5 million was disbursed). Of the £6.5 million only about £1million comes from other sources of incomes, donations and dividends. However the EU funding program is only for 1995-1999 and unfortunately NIVT has no idea as to whether there will be any further investment after 1999. This may mean that after the present funding has stopped, the level of grant giving may return to the previous level of about £1 million.

The trust is assisted by an Advisory Grant Committee of 107 members, who assist the trust in making decisions about the allocation of funding.

General priorities: The following information is taken from the trust's *'Guidelines for Grantseekers'.*

'The trust targets its resources on supporting community development responses to the social, economic and cultural problems and opportunities in the areas of greatest need throughout Northern Ireland. The trust is particularly keen to receive applications from rural self-help groups.

'Preference is given to projects which:

* involve the active participation of local people in the design and management of the project;
* help community groups in areas of need to acquire skills, knowledge and confidence;
* improve understanding and communication within and between communities;
* encourage co-operation within the community sector and with other relevant agencies and sectors;

- try out new approaches to social needs and in so doing have the potential to influence social policy.

'The trust also feels that is is important for groups to work to achieve a fairer and more equitable society in Ireland. To this end it will prioritise both community and issue-based work which seeks to promote initiatives that either:

- work for the active participation of groups in society that are disadvantaged and/or marginalised;
- develop new strategies to achieve equality of opportunity;
- initiate advocacy work with marginalised groups; and/or
- value ethnic and cultural diversity.

Current Priorities

'During 1995-1999 the trustees have decided to support initiatives that:

- help local communities to work together for social and economic development in both urban and rural areas;
- support the setting up and development of both local women's groups and women's networks;
- stimulate creativity and self-expression through community arts;
- support initiatives which progress social rights and civil liberties;
- encourage community-based responses to health issues;
- support work with the disadvantaged ethnic and racial minorities;
- promote new approaches to work with, and by, disadvantaged young people;
- offer new approaches and ideas in relation to community action;
- address issues of poverty, low income and various aspects of deprivation;
- encourage a developmental approach by the community and voluntary sector to community care;
- develop the confidence and skills of community activists and groups in areas of greatest need.

'The trustees will also consider support for:

- modest targeted research proposals which seek to address issues related to community development and social policy;
- evaluation of community development and social action initiatives;
- the publication of reports and findings related to community development issues;
- modest targeted research proposal which seek to provide disadvantaged and/or excluded groups with a voice on issues of social policy and social

rights.

'In recognition of the specific problems of Northern Ireland, and the resulting political and community divisions, applications which promote a more pluralist and open society are encouraged.

'Applications are invited for projects which:

- provide new methods of community organisation which help achieve community participation;
- seek common ground on issues related to justice, civil liberties and social inequalities;
- allow the expression of the hopes, aspirations and fears of local communities.'

Directly Funded Grant Program

Grants administered in 1996/97:

Telecommunity: This was set up in 1989 through donations from British Telecom and the Trade Union BTUC. The award scheme targets people of all ages with disabilities in disadvantaged areas in Northern Ireland. The award specifies that it accepts applications of those involved in: community education and training opportunities, communication and leadership skills, local ininiatives to improve resources and community facilities, creativity and self expression through drama, music or arts activities, and out of school projects for young people.

Grants are from a fund of £50,000 per annum, of which grants are given that do not normally exceed £5,000, but can be more for exceptional cases. In 1996/97 a total of £52,650 was given in 14 grants, of which £8,500 was given to the Downe Residential Project.

Belfast & Regional Community Development Demonstration Programme: The trust set up this project in 1995, with the financial support from the Targeting Social Needs and Community Infrastructure Measure of the EU PSEP, Making Belfast Work and private monies. The project targeted eight areas to research future policies, and work on community based initiatives has already commenced. The areas targeted were Regional Programmes- Strabane, Gilford, Larne, Ballymaguigan & Creagh; Belfast Programme- Greencastle/Bawnmore, Albertbridge, The Bone and Taughmonagh.

EUROPEAN UNION FUNDED PROGRAMMES

The bulk of trust's funding at present comes from administering the European Union related funding programme; the Regional Community Support

Programme and the Special Support Programme for Peace & Reconciliation. A grant total of £27 million will be available between 1996 and 1998.

Grants are awarded in the following areas:

Community Arts: 'For the last 12 years the NIVT has supported Community Arts through its work and in particular through its Community Arts Award Scheme'. This program is now funded through the EU fund for Special Support Programme for Peace & Reconciliation.

The aim of the programme is 'to reinforce progress towards a peaceful and stable society and to promote reconciliation by increasing economic development and employment, promoting urban and rural regeneration, developing cross-border cooperation and extending social inclusion.'

Two types of grants are available; *Seeding Grants,* £100-£1,500 for small new or innovative local projects, and *Project Grants,* £1,500-£30,000 a year for projects that attempt a longer lasting impact in their community. A total of £181,230 was disbursed through 53 grants, ranging from £52,000 to Northern Visions to fund a Community Media Development Worker over two years, to £600 for the Kilkeel Community Association. Applications for grants from this program need to be through the special EU application form available on request.

Community Development & Inclusion of Women Project: Through this project the NIVT utilises the money made available through 'Community Action and Inclusion of Women Measure 4.1'. The project recognises '...the importance of community development and capacity-building at local community and neighbourhood level. The Measure also acknowledges the key role of women in both community development and in initiating local groups and centres.'

Two types of grants have been available: grants for discrete work or to offer risk funding for new or pilot projects of up to £3,000; Main Grants were also offered of up to £30,000 a year, and in the case of a small number of innovatory projects a maximum of £50,000 was given.

In 1996/7 a total of £8 million was awarded through 490 grants, ranging from £2000 to the Ann Cran/The Tree Project to £37,000 for the Owenkillew Community Development Project.

At the time of writing (Autumn 1998) there was no further funding available for this project. It was unclear as to whether there will be money available in the future as no definite commitment has been made. Interested applicants should contact NIVT to check.

Promoting the Inclusion of Vulnerable Groups: This project was developed under the 'Supporting Marginalised/ Disadvantaged Groups Measure 4.4' of the EU special support program. The programmes looks to target those that are particularly vulnerable to social exclusion: victims of violence, homeless people, people with disabilities, those with, or at risk from, drug dependency problems, politically motivated prisoners and ex-prisoners, travellers and other minority ethnic groups, and young people at risk from offending.

In 1996/97 a total of £5,620,000 was distributed to 224 organisations, with grants ranging from £2,800 for PANDA, to £152,000 over three years to LINC Resource Centre.

Cross Border Programme: This project has been developed through a co-operative approach between NIVT and the southern based Combat Poverty Agency (CPA) and the Area Development Management (ADM) to enact 'Cross-Border Community Development and Reconciliation Measure 3.4.' The programme seeks to foster cross border links between grass roots community organisation around themes of common interest.

A total of 118 awards have been made since the programmes inception giving an expenditure of £2,742,000, of these 53 awards have been of under £3,000.

Applications for the above four programmes can apply for funding from the NIVT under the Special Support Programme for Peace and Reconciliation.

Belfast Community Support Programmes: This programme is a partnership between the European Union and Making Belfast Work to fund locally based community projects in Belfast. The general aim is to improve the social and economic conditions of the most disadvantaged areas and people through enhancing employment opportunities.

For 1996/97 £690,300 was given through 29 grants. Two types of grants are available- Small Grants of up to £1,500 and Main Grants of up to £20,000 per annum. A large number of the grants being made are as annual salary grants, for example £60,000 over 3 years to Gingerbread to pay for the cost of employing a Group Support Worker.

Regional Community Support Programme 1994-1999: This project is conducted in collaboration with the Community Development Unit of the Department of Health & Social Service and the European Union. The program is open to community and voluntary groups for projects directed towards meeting the needs of people living in disadvantaged communities outside the Belfast area. The project does not need to be new or particularly innovative, but it must be clearly thought out and should involve the local community and/or user groups. An emphasis is placed on supporting community based self-help initiatives, and recognises that in many cases communities lack the basic facilities to make an effective contribution to programmes aimed at overcoming social exclusion.

For the year 1996/97 £76,600 was awarded through 6 grants. As with the Belfast Community Support Program two types of grants are available. See above for detail.

Exclusions The trust will not fund:

- Individuals;
  on-going running costs of
- organisations;
- major capital building programmes;
- travel;
- vehicles;
- holiday schemes;
- play-groups;
- sports activities;
- housing associations;
- promotion of religion;
- pay off debts;
- retrospective grants;
- general appeals.

Neither will the trust fund projects where there is a statutory responsibility or respond to cutbacks in statutory funding.

Applications Since the EU funding program is nearing completion we suggest that you inquire as to whether the specific pograms have any funding remaining.

There are no formal application forms so groups should write to the trust and include the following:

1. A description of your group – its aims and activities.
2. A description of the proposed project, its origins, purpose and cost.
3. A copy of your group's constitution and latest annual report, if available.
4. A recent statement of accounts.
5. Information on other possible sources of funding.
6. An outline of the measurable goals by which you intend to access the progress of your project.
7. A contact address and telephone number.

Upon receipt of an application, which falls within the trust's broad remit, a member of the trust's staff and/or a trustee will contact the applicant with a view to appraising the application on behalf of the trustees (who meet six times a year) to consider requests for grants above £1,500. Requests for grants below £1,500 can be considered outside of full trustees' meetings, so decisions on grants, when full information is available, can usually be made within a period not exceeding two months. Due to existing financial commitments to development posts the trust is unlikely to respond positively to requests for salaries of development workers in the foreseeable future.

Trustees meet in February, April, June, September, October and December.

The Northern Rock Foundation

£8,000,000 (estimate for 1999)

People with disabilities and their carers

21 Lansdowne Terrace, Gosforth, Newcastle upon Tyne NE3 1HP
Tel: 0191-284 8412,
Fax: 0191-284 8413

Correspondent Fiona Ellis, Director

Trustees W R Atkinson, Chairman; Lady Bonfield; R H Dickinson; L P Finn; P R M Harbottle; Lord Howick of Glendale; A E Kilburn; J A Logan; Lady Russell; Miss E E Slattery; J P Wainwright.

Beneficial area Mainly the North East of England, but applications also considered from Scotland, Cumbria and the North West of England.

Information available Guidelines and application forms. Those available in 1998 reprinted below.

Summary This exciting new foundation for the north east of England has launched two major programmes for 1999 on:

- help for disabled people and their carers (£3 million)
- small grants, up to £10,000, for welfare and community groups (£1 million).

There are also three pilot programmes (with initial budgets up to £200,000) and operating to begin with only in Tyne and

Wear, Northumberland, Durham and Teeside. During 1999 they may be prolonged or extended, either financially or geographically. They cover:

- promotion of good parenting
- development of literacy
- community self-help.

The Director says 'The foundation intends to be both "responsive", offering grants to applicants under published guidelines, and also an inventive, risk-taking grant-maker, identifying and promoting ideas, creating one-off schemes and backing unusual projects which do not fit current programmes.'

'Our policy in responding to applications is to visit or meet with applicants before making a grant of £30,000 or more. Occasionally staff will visit for smaller requests. We also want to be as transparent as possible so we will give reasons for declining applications where we think they can be helpful to the applicant. Alas sometimes the reason is honestly that we just ran out of money; in the cut and thrust of final decision, there is justice but it is rough.'

General This new trust was established as an independent grant making body in 1997 when Northern Rock Building Society was converted to a public limited company. The main objective of the foundation is: 'to help improve the conditions of those disadvantaged by age, infirmity, poverty or other circumstances. It will support causes mainly, but not exclusively, in the North East of England.'

The foundation is completely independent of the building society. Its Director, Fiona Ellis, was previously responsible for the well known arts funding programme of the Gulbenkian Foundation(UK).

Main programmes
Initially, the foundation will run two main programmes:

1. Programme for disabled people and carers (funding available: £3 million in 1999, estimated)

'The aim of the program is to improve the quality of life of people with disabilities and carers by promoting independence, raising disability awareness and enabling disabled people to play a full and active role in society. The foundation is keen to hear from self managed and self-help organisations, particularly those which involve members of the beneficiary group'.

'Projects will be considered in the following areas:

- independent living;
- physical access improvements;
- improved services in rural communities;
- improving information;
- removing barriers from social/leisure opportunities;
- adult education and training;
- personal development programmes;
- employment opportunities.

'Applications are also invited from carer groups for programmes to assist carers in maintaining their own health, skills and access to social and cultural opportunities. These may include support for respite care. Basic costs of care – eg. residential services which should be met by statutory funders – will not be supported.'

Grants may be for limited capital, core or project funding and for varying periods of time.

2. Small organisations and projects (funding available: £1 million in 1999, estimated)

'Small grants, for amounts between £1,000 and £10,000, can be used for: projects with limited lifespan; core funding lasting up to four years where the total amount does not exceed £10,000; capital or equipment purchase.

'We particularly welcome applications from organisations working in the fields of:

- disability
- caring: provision of respite care and support
- homelessness: prevention, support and access to housing
- young people at risk, especially initiatives offering alternatives to crime
- improvements to the quality of life for older people
- money management schemes
- self help schemes to enable communities to improve their living environment.'

The guidelines note that for small grants the applicant should have an annual income of less than £25,000. They do not have to be registered charities, but they must, however, show that they are: an organisation with a legal framework; be established for public benefit; and have purposes recognised by law as charitable.

Pilot programmes

At the end of 1998 there were three programmes for which 'the trustees invite applications, initially on a pilot basis, in order for the foundation to test priorities for further development'. These policy areas may be developed or withdrawn in the light of experience'

Note that during these schemes the foundation will only accept applications from Tyne and Wear, Northumberland, Durham and Teeside, that the schemes are cash limited, and that the Exclusions and Guidelines below apply just as with the main programmes.

Promotion of good parenting
'The foundation wishes to promote parenting skills among existing and prospective parents. We therefore welcome applications from organisations or initiatives that:

- help parents in difficulty through stress, unemployment, family break-up or other causes to develop or improve their parenting skills
- support parents in dealing with difficult or challenging behaviour of their children
- help prepare young people for parenthood – with preference given to initiatives outside the formal, education system
- promote better parenting by fathers including those living apart from their children
- help new partners, parents, or step parents, find an appropriate parenting role in a new family
- advocate conditions that nurture good parenting e.g. the promotion of policies in buildings, work and leisure opportunities etc. designed to recognise and support parental responsibility.

'In all cases, the aim must be to help parents reach a state where they are confident in their own abilities to bring up their children.

'The programme is not intended for initiatives helping parents of children with disabilities; proposers of such schemes are directed to the Disability and Caring programme.

Development of literacy
'The ability to read and write is critical to employment and often to full participation in citizenship. The trustees wish to assist projects that help those who have emerged from the education system without literacy skills. Projects addressing the needs of adults, either employed or not, and young adults and recent school leavers will be welcomed.

'In addition to accepting applications from agencies or organisations specialising in the promotion of literacy, we will also consider approaches from other non-specialists who have innovative ideas or proposals to tackle this subject. In such cases, we would prefer partnerships that include experts in the field.

'The programme is not designed to support either mainstream educational needs or the special needs of school age children with disabilities and/or communication problems.

Community self-help

'The trustees would like to support voluntary groups in creating local solutions to local problems. Applications are invited from groups intending to tackle, for example, poverty, social exclusion, vandalism, local crime, the absence of basic amenities, or other sources of disadvantage from which they suffer themselves. Groups may have been created specifically to address the problem or may already exist but, in both cases, they are likely to be small and not have paid workers.

Grants may be provided for equipment or running costs. Salaries are unlikely to met. Projects begun by the beneficiaries themselves will be strongly favoured over those initiated by outside agencies.

'Applicants should:

- explain what is the problem they are trying to solve
- outline what their proposed solution is
- describe how they arrived at the scheme they propose
- describe how they will go about their activities including the timetable they propose
- provide some evidence to show that they are the right people to take on the task or describe who will help them
- explain how much money they need and show what it will be spent on
- tell us how they will know whether or not they have succeeded.

'Groups must show that their purposes are charitable and should provide two referees who can vouch for them. Since our grant must be made to or through a registered charity, groups may need to seek advice or help from their Council for Voluntary Service or Voluntary Organisations Development Agency.'

Exclusions Applications for local project outside the North East of England, Cumbria, Yorkshire and the North East of England and Scotland will not be considered, nor:

- organisations which are not registered charities
- charities which trade, have substantial reserves or are in serious deficit
- national charities which do not have strong significance in the North East and North
- open ended funding agreements
- general appeals, sponsorship and marketing appeals
- retrospective grants
- endowment funds
- replacement of statutory funding
- activities primarily the responsibility of central or local government
- individuals including students
- animal welfare
- mainstream educational activity
- medical research, hospitals (other than hospices) and medical centres
- environmental projects which do not accord with the main objectives of the foundation
- buildings other than charitable schemes for housing individuals
- promotion of religion
- fabric appeals for places of worship
- corporate applications for founder membership of a charity
- loans or business finance
- expeditions or overseas travel.

Applications Application will consist of:

- completed application form
- two page supporting statement (what need the organisation is trying to meet; how it will meet this; what you plan to do and a timetable; budget and full costing; how much raised from other sources and how you propose to raise the other funds; and how you will evaluate the success of your work)
- your most recent annual report
- copy of your Memorandum and Articles or Constitution with reference to your objectives
- current budget for the year and most recent treasurer's report, management accounts, or regular financial report
- a small sample of illustrating material if you wish; this can only be returned if a stamped addressed envelope is included.

The Norwich Town Close Estate Charity

£284,000 to organisations (1997/98)

Education in and near Norwich

10 Golden Dog Lane, Magdalen Street, Norwich NR3 1BP
Tel: 01603-621023; Fax: 01603-767025

Correspondent Mrs S A Franklin, Administrator

Trustees M G Quinton, Chairman; N B Q Back; P J Colby; T C Eaton; R E T Gurney; A P Hansell; J S Livock; F G Self; H E Boreham; Mrs A Brown; Mrs R Frostick; Mrs S James; R H Pearson; A B Shaw; D H Pardey; R G Round.

Beneficial area Within a 20 mile radius of the Guildhall of the city of Norwich.

Information available Report and accounts, but without analysis or explanation of grants.

General Though the main purpose of this charity is to support individuals in need, educational and otherwise, it can also make grants to for educational purposes to charities that operate within 20 miles of Norwich.

£284,000 was spent on such grants in 1997/98, much of it in four grants each of £50,000. The beneficiaries were the Horstead Centre; the Memorial Trust of 2nd Air Division USAAF; Norwich School; and the Centre of East Anglian Studies at the University of East Anglia.

Other significant beneficiaries were Eaton Vale Scout and Guide Association (£25,000); Hethersett Old Hall and Norwich High School Minerva Appeal (£15,000 each; the Care for Clare Appeal (£14,000); Inspire (£10,000); Taverham Hall Educational Trust and Quidenham Children's Hospice (£6,000 each); St John Ambulance (£5,000).

The charity says 'Because of financial constraints, the trustees ... have to suspend making such grants from time to time. A telephone enquiry may be made ... to establish whether the trustees are considering such grant applications at the present time'. But feast may follow famine, as the 1997/98 annual report also notes that 'trustees continue to examine opportunities to utilise the unrestricted funds of the charity'.

There are two other charities, sharing the same administration, which may also give grants to organisations, the Norwich Consolidated Charities and Anguish's Educational Foundation.

Exclusions No grants to individuals who are not Freemen of the city of Norwich; charities more than 20 miles from Norwich; charities which are not educational.

Applications After a preliminary enquiry, as noted above, in writing to the clerk.

'When submitting an application the following points should be borne in mind:

- Brevity is a virtue. If too much written material is submitted there is

a risk that it may not all be assimilated.
- The trustees like to have details of any other financial support secured.
- An indication should be given of the amount that is being sought and also how that figure is arrived at.
- The trustees will not reimburse expenditure already incurred.
- Nor, generally speaking will the trustees pay running costs, e.g. salaries.'

The Nuffield Foundation

£6,399,000 (1997)

Education, child protection, family law and justice, access to justice, mental health, older people and their families.

28 Bedford Square,
London WC1B 3EG
Tel: 0181-346 2600

Correspondent Anthony Tomei, Director

Trustees Lord Flowers (Chairman); Professor Anthony Atkinson; Sir John Banham; Dame Brenda Hale; Professor Sir Robert May; Professor Sir Michael Rutter; Mrs Anne Sofer.

Beneficial area UK and Commonwealth.

Information available Excellent annual report; detailed guidelines for applicants (summarised below, but all potential applicants should obtain a copy).

Summary This foundation supports research and development, rather than on-going activity, mostly in the fields stated above
- education
- child protection
- family law and justice
- access to justice
- mental health
- older people and their families

There are also grants in a number of other areas for which there are usually specific schemes.

In 1998 an investigation was in hand into a further area – the UK's language capability – which may lead to a funding programme in the future.

Grants are of two kinds:

Project grants. These are larger grants, in the range £5,000 to over £100,000. They support research, developmental or experimental projects that meet a practical or policy need and are made only to institutions or organisations. They can be spread over two or three years.

Award schemes. There are several 'award schemes', often for work by individual researchers. They are described below under this heading.

The foundation also runs two of its own projects, the Nuffield Curriculum Projects Centre and the Nuffield Council on Bioethics.

The foundation has an academic flavour. One mark of this is that all applications are subject to independent expert review. The foundation also has a substantial and experienced staff of its own.

This entry, after a background introduction, reprints most of the very full 1998 Guide for Applicants. This is followed by some of the text of the excellent annual report for 1997. The final 'Applications' section contains further material from the Guide for Applicants.

Background The Nuffield Foundation was founded by Lord Nuffield in 1943 with a then enormous endowment of £10 million consisting of shares in Morris Motors Ltd. The shares were finally sold in 1975, by which time their relative value was sorely diminished. The foundation now has a diversified portfolio of investments, worth £203 million by the end of 1997, and generating an income of £8.4 million.

Very creditably, and in a manner that should be emulated by other trusts in this book, the annual accounts show investment performance over five years against the WM Index for charity investments generally. The performance, by Schroders, assisted by two independent investment advisers, has been excellent, at an average total return of 14.4% against the index figure of 13.9%. As is normal, the return is unfortunately shown before investment management costs are taken into account, but these too were modest, at £226,000 or 0.11% of the value of the portfolio.

The foundation has a strong and expert professional staff of 17 people (with a further seven managing its own projects). As a result its grant programme administrative costs are high, at 17% of grant expenditure. These costs, which include some of those incurred in disseminating the results of the research paid for by the fund, appear to this editor to be justified by the range, sophistication and complexity of the work being undertaken, but readers of this entry can form their own opinion.

Guide for Applicants

(Note that this Guide is revised annually)

Criteria

'The foundation seeks to fund self-contained practical or research projects which are:

- innovative:
the trustees are keen to fund work that has a clear element of originality. They will not fund routine research, nor the mere repetition of existing work;

- practical:
the trustees look for outcomes that will either influence practice directly or that

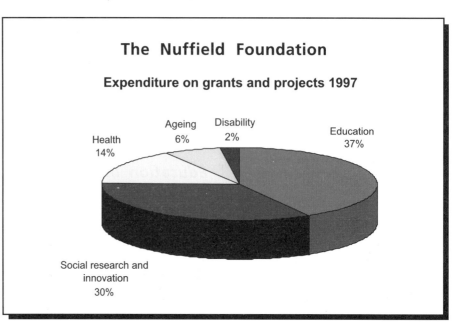

The Nuffield Foundation

Expenditure on grants and projects 1997

Education 37%
Disability 2%
Ageing 6%
Health 14%
Social research and innovation 30%

can be translated into policy or practice in the short or medium term.

• generalisable:
the trustees will not consider proposals of purely local interest but seek to fund work that will be widely applicable;

• reflective:
trustees look for evidence that applicants have thought carefully about how to evaluate the work undertaken and judge whether it is successful or not.

'Not all projects that receive foundation money meet all these criteria, but the great majority meet most of them.

'Applicants must be able to convince the trustees that proposals are especially suited to the foundation, and could not as easily be considered by a government department, research council or a more appropriate charity.

'The trustees do not give project grants for routine academic research, nor do they support projects that involve simply the doing of good works or the continuing provision of a service, however worthwhile.

Types of project

'Most of the projects supported by the foundation involve one or more of three kinds of activity: research, experiment or practical development.

'*Research* projects must be intended to have a practical or policy outcome in the short or medium term. The trustees will not normally support research that simply advances knowledge, which is properly the domain of the research councils.

'*Experimental* projects involve trying something new and evaluating the outcome. Such projects must be of more than local interest. They must have the potential to be widely applied, either directly or as a model that others can follow. Evaluation must be carefully considered, as must the dissemination of the findings.

'*Practical development* projects involve the development of some facility that will be of practical value. The range of possible projects is wide and could include, for example, written materials, a new way of providing advice or some other service, a physical device, or eve setting up a new organisation. Again, such developments should be of general rather than local interest and the trustees will look for evidence that applicants have carefully considered how the information can be disseminated. Some element of evaluation is also desirable.

'The trustees currently have five declared **areas of special interest:**

• Child protection, family law and justice
• Educational research and innovation
• Access to justice
• Mental health
• older people and their families

'These are described in more detail below. Grants in these areas account for around half our project grant funding.

'The trustees are, however, interested to hear of projects of exceptional merit that lie outside these areas of special interest. The foundation therefore keeps an 'open door' to projects that lie within our general areas of activity, and meet the criteria outlined above. Such projects must lead in some way to the advancement of education or social welfare; projects relating to disability or to the care of the elderly are of special interest. In science and medicine, trustees are interested in supporting innovation and development, but by means other than the direct support of scientific or medical research.

'The trustees are willing to consider funding research that objectively examines and evaluates current statutory arrangements. Applications may examine arrangements in any area, but our particular concerns are education policy-making and the effects of policies on disadvantaged sections of society. Proposals to study health care will be considered only if they are demonstrably unsuitable for consideration under the programmes of the King's Fund, the Department of Health or the Medical Research Council. Projects to study housing will similarly be considered only if they are unsuitable for funding by the Joseph Rowntree Foundation or one of the statutory agencies concerned with housing.

Child protection, family law and justice
(Contact, Sharon Witherspoon)

'This programme supports work to help ensure that the legal and institutional framework is best adapted to meet the needs of children and families. It is interested in a broad range of topics going beyond child protection in a narrow sense, and in practical developments as well as research. The programme funds projects on:

• the rights and responsibilities of children and families, for example in contact after separation or divorce and following adoption (special guidelines are available in this latter area);
• children in the legal system, for

example, child witnesses;
• children at risk or in need;
• the development of an integrated system of family justice, drawing attention to the anomalies and obstructions in the present system;
• the training needs of professionals in the system, and the setting up of appropriate training programmes;
• the development of family mediation and support services for the family jurisdictions;
• interdisciplinary work in the family law and the family justice systems, including aspects of practice that may be affected by the implementation of the Family Law Act.

Educational research and innovation
(Contact, Helen Quigley)

'The foundation is a major independent funder of research and innovation in education. The trustees wish to support work of high quality which will either improve practice or inform policy making in the pre-school, compulsory school age and FE sectors. Particular areas of interest are:

• Science, mathematics and technology teaching:
Early learning of mathematics;
Mathematics, science and technology teaching in primary and secondary schools;
Factors influencing differences in attainment in mathematics, science and technology.
• Education for 16-19 year olds:
Mathematics, science and technology teaching in vocational courses;
Comparisons with overseas practice;
Developing the whole curriculum for ages 16-19.
• Children with special needs:
Raising the achievement of lower attaining pupils;
Provision for the education of children with emotional and behavioural difficulties, including those excluded from mainstream schooling;
Provision for the education of children with learning difficulties (including language delay and specific language impairment);
Provision for children whose needs differ from those of the majority, EG.refugee children, travellers' children;

Critical studies of the implementation of the legislation and statutory arrangements for dealing with the education of children with special needs.

• Organisation and effectiveness of the

education system
Critical studies of the impact of recent changes in the education system:
The changing role of LEAs, government agencies, governors, parents and teachers in promoting effective education.

- The curriculum:
Projects which will complement, or further, the work of The Nuffield Curriculum Projects Centre;
Projects to promote, or develop, the concept of citizenship;
Development of the whole curriculum in the primary school;
Projects to examine the use of IT in encouraging effective teaching and learning across the curriculum.

Access to Justice (Contact, Sharon Witherspoon)

'The foundation has long had an interest in the area of access to justice. Its current objectives in this area are:

- to promote developments in the legal system that will improve its accessibility to all people;
- to fund research and promote developments in alternative dispute resolution;
- to promote wider access to legal services and advice and a better understanding of the obstacles to access justice;
- to help promote a greater public understanding of the role of law in society and of the legal system;
- to help promote a greater knowledge of the rights and duties of the individual, including those of the European citizen.

'Replacement or core funding of existing services (such as law centres) will not be considered. Projects on penal policy, drugs, policing, crime prevention or environmental law will not normally be supported under the Access to justice area of special interest unless they fulfil one of the objectives set out above.

Mental health (Contact, Anthony Tomei)

'The trustees are interested in funding projects of high quality which have as their objective the development or improvement of educational or social provision that meets the needs of those with learning disabilities or mental health problems. The following areas are of particular interest:

- children and young people, particularly in the context of families and schools;
- ethical and legal issues arising from mental incapacity;
- employment, in particular transition from school to work for young

people with mental disorders or disabilities (work therapy is not a priority area);
- specific language impairment, in particular implications for for schooling and work. (Purely linguistic or clinical projects are excluded.).

'Projects in the following areas will not generally be funded:

- community care (including normal service provision; development of new services; evaluation of services; research; training);
- mental health and old age;
- counselling;
- clinical research into mental illness or learning disability;
- basic studies of normal or abnormal mental processes.'

Older People and their Families

'As with all the foundation's areas of special interest, trustees are interested in funding both research and practical development projects. Research projects must have a bearing on policy or practice in the short or medium term. Practical projects may, for instance, be experiments or pilots of new methods of service delivery, or the development of good practice guides, or other projects that will improve the lives of older people and their families.

'The foundation wishes to fund work that starts from the perspectives, needs and interests of the older person and his or her family, rather than those of service providers. It is interested in projects that will enhance individual autonomy and choice and that recognise variation in preferences and provision.

'The foundation is keen to support work that brings an international comparitive perspective to bear and is particularly interested in fostering work that considers European as well as other countries' perspectives.

'As with all its areas of grant making, the foundation is interested in a wide range of topics. Issues that might be of interest include:

- The financial circumstances of elderly people and economic planning for later life. This might include pensions and insurance (including private as well as state provision), pension splitting on divorce, intergenerational transfers and so on. It is particularly interested in projects that recognise the complex relationship between state, private and family provision.
- Family solidarity and family

obligations, including projects focussing on caring responsibilities between generations; their implications for the labour market; legal and social obligations; changing relationships as a result of family change; and ways of supporting family ties.

- Autonomy and decision-making in later life, including socio-legal matters such as competance, powers of attorny, conflicts of interest, advance directives and so on. The foundation wishes to foster work that improves autonomy as well as social responsibilities of older people.
- Retirement work and citzenship, including the diverse positions of older people in employment; retirement and employment rights; and activities that promote active citzenship for older people.
- The interface of health and social care, including innovative schemes to support interaction between professionals, informal carers and health care workers, social workers and so on. there may be particular scope for European comparisons here.

Award schemes

'Each of these schemes has its own procedures and closing date. There is an explanatory leaflet (and usually an application form) for each. If you are interested in applying, you should first contact the administrator concerned and ask for the relevant information. (Note that there are further schemes solely for the support of individual researchers and students that are not covered by this book)

Social sciences: small grants scheme (Contact, Ms Louie Burghes or Ann Weber)

'This scheme gives small grants to support social science research expenses. Awards are normally up to £5,000 but in exceptional cases grants of up to £10,000 may be made.

'Following a recent review, trustees have identified three priorities for funding:

- projects that develop social science research capacity particularly by supporting the work of those new to social science research;
- self-contained or pilot or preliminary projects that address the wider objects of the foundation, namely a broad concern with the 'advancement of social well-being'.
- outstanding small projects in the social sciences.

'Detailed Guidelines, Notes for

Applicants and Application forms are available.'

The scheme for Social Science Research Fellowships was being reviewed in 1998.

'The Oliver Bird Fund (Contact, Vicki Hughes or Caterina Carrozza) is a separate fund, with its own endowment and trust deed. Grants are made to support research into the basic causes and processes of rheumatism and arthritis. Preference is given to younger researchers. The fund has an annual income of around £420,000 and eight grants were made in 1997.

'The Phoenix Fund (Contact, Ann Weber) Grants are made to support practical projects that help older people. Unlike most of the foundation's funding, there is no emphasis on innovation. The fund has an annual budget of £220,000 and eight grants were made in 1997.

'The Viscount Nuffield Auxiliary Fund (Contact, Sarah Lock) Grants are concentrated in the fields of communication aids and mobility aids for disabled people. The intention is to make existing technology work better for people with disabilities by research, development and the provision of training. The fund has an annual budget of £130,000 and 11 grants were made in 1997.

'Commonwealth programme (Contact, Sarah Lock) The aim of the programme is to support the development of service provision or policy making in developing Commonwealth countries and to promote links between the UK and those countries. The programme funds projects which develop the expertise and experience of practitioners and policy-makers, working on well defined practical initiatives or policy developments in their own countries. The programme's £500,000 annual budget is jointly funded by the foundation and the Commonwealth Relations Trust.'

The Annual Report 1997

This report includes a number of 'case histories' to illuminate the descriptive text. These have been omitted here, because of shortage of space.

Overview

'Around 80% of the foundation's expenditure is in the form of grants to institutions in the United Kingdom. Since its earliest days the foundation has focused on the support of research and innovation, and this is the common thread in much of the work it funds. Around two-thirds of the foundation's

expenditure is on grants in support of experimental or development projects which advance education or social welfare. Within this there are areas of special interest which change form time to time. Present areas of special interest include curriculum development, particularly science and mathematics education; child protection and family law and justice; access to justice; and mental health.

'The remainder of the foundation's expenditure goes to support academic research through schemes of small grants and fellowships for scientists and social scientists in British universities. There is also a scheme to support developments in the Commonwealth by means of advanced training or research. this scheme is funded jointly with the Commonwealth Relations Trust.

'The foundation also administers a number of special funds. These are: the Oliver Bird Fund for research into arthritis and rheumatism; the Elizabeth Nuffield Educational Fund, which provides financial assistance for the education of women; and the Commonwealth Relations Trust.

Expenditure on grants and projects 1997 (£6,399,000)

Education	*37%*
Social research and innovation	*30%*
Health	*14%*
Ageing	*6%*
Disability	*2%*

These totals were broken down further as follows:

Education
Grants	*£994,000*
Science award schemes	*£621,000*
Grants to individual women	*£228,000*
Managed curriculum projects	*£635,000*

Social research and innovation
Grants: child protection and family law	*£561,000*
Grants : access to Justice	*£450,000*
Grants: other	*£455,000*
Social science award schemes	*£488,000*

Health
Grants: mental health	*£95,000*
Grants: other	*£118,000*
Rheumatism research grants	*£469,000*
Managed projects: bioethics	*£181,000*
Managed projects: Rheumatology	*£70,000*

Ageing
Project grants	*£234,000*
Phoenix fund	*£184,000*

Disability
Grants	*£140,000*

Commonwealth
Grants	*£476,000*

Trustees Report – Policy

'Having issued new and detailed guidance to applicants early in 1997, the trustees implemented no major policy changes during the year. The foundation's overall pattern of expenditure was similar to that of the previous year, with around 10% of expenditure going to support in-house activities (principally the Curriculum Centre and the Bioethics Council) and the balance being divided equally between project grants and award schemes.

'Project grants are the larger grants made by the foundation, typically in the range £500 to £150,000. The new guidance and procedures implemented at the beginning of the year seem to be having an effect. We now require potential applicants to submit a short summary of their project before proceeding with a full application. While this additional stage means that it may take a little longer to reach a final decision, in the long run it saves time and effort both for applicants and for the office. Feedback from applicants suggests that this new procedure is greatly appreciated.

'The foundation has five Areas of Special Interest. These are child protection and family law and justice; access to justice; education and mental health; older people and their families.

'Another major initiative, announced early in 1998, was an 'Inquiry into the UK's capacity on Languages'. The Inquiry will set out to estimate the UK's needs in terms of capability in languages over the next twenty years, and to assess whether the present situation represents a firm foundation for the future. The Inquiry began its work in the Spring of 1998, and plans to issue an interim report later in the year.

Social research and innovation

'Social research and innovation' is not of course a theme for grant-making. Many of the grants in other areas of working involve social research, and all, we hope, involve some innovation.

'Within our larger 'social research' project grants, the foundation currently has two declared areas of special interest: Child protection and family law and justice and access to justice. In these areas we hold regular meetings with policy-makers, academics and practitioners, and fund substantial programmes of work involving both research and practical developments.

'But outside our areas of special interest, the foundation also keeps and 'open door' to ideas which span disciplinary boundaries or examine statutory provision of public services,

269

and we are particularly interested in projects that focus on the disadvantaged (or, in more fashionable language, the 'socially-excluded'). This is particularly so where social problems require thinking across different departments or functions of provision. In 1997, even before the autumn financial statements and the 1998 Budget, some of the grants made in both these areas of special interest and under our 'open door' were for projects relating to child-care: how it was shared between parents, what legal rights were, and what it cost.

Child protection and family law and justice

'The foundation's funding in this area largely falls into distinct clusters including adoption, fostering and child placement; child support policy; and the efforts of divorce and family breakdown. We are also interested in work that brings together research results to help professionals and policy-makers improve practice.

'In 1997 we convened a seminar on minority ethnic issues in child protection and family law. This illuminated many issues where research might improve practice and we hope gradually to make a cluster of grants in this area. In the meantime, a grant was made to Ms Sonia Shah-Kazemi of the University of Westminster for a study on mediation carried out by the Muslim Law Shari'ah Council.

Access to justice

'In 1997 we made almost twice as many grants in this his area as we had originally planned. This is perhaps unsurprising at a time when the Woolf legal reforms remain on the agenda, and when there is increasing interest in alternative or appropriate dispute resolution – including mediation and ombudsman schemes – and in using the courts only in the last instance. Certainly the foundation's grant-making in this area has long started from the premise that the legal system is only one means of achieving access to justice. Next year we hope to be able to report findings from the Access to Justice surveys carried out by Professor Hazel Genn of University College London and SCPR about the variety of ways people handle issues which might potentially be disputed in civil law.

Other project grants

'Outside our areas of special interest, the foundation remains interested in projects that will help the disadvantaged, that cross professional and disciplinary boundaries, and that involve practical research or reflective practice. For

example, a research grant relevant to welfare issues and one practical project that may help improve prospects for women in prison.

Education

'The advancement of education' is specified in our Trust Deed as one of the main objectives of the foundation and has always been one of its more important activities. The current education programme has three aspects:

- project grants are awarded for research and innovation in education. The focus of these grants varies form time to time to reflect the needs and interests of those concerned with education. In 1997 trustees supported projects to advance the teaching and learning of science, mathematics and technology; projects to develop, or examine, provision for children with special educational needs or students aged 16-19, and projects that examined the organisation and effectiveness of the education system.
- The Nuffield Curriculum Projects Centre, now based in the main foundation building in Bedford Square, produces innovative curriculum material for schools and college.
- The foundation also administers the Elizabeth Nuffield Educational Fund, which provides grants to enable women to further their education.

Nuffield Curriculum Projects Centre

'The Centre supports curriculum projects across all the National Curriculum key stages and for post-16 courses. Projects work in partnership with publishers, awarding bodies and industry to share the best of current thinking from schools and colleges. Project teams offer a high level of user support by working closely with teachers, advisers, trainers and researchers. Projects have networks to keep in touch with pioneering centres, to disseminate ideas and to train teachers in new approaches.

Science schemes

'The trustees believe that one way of ensuring the health of the scientific community is by encouraging and supporting young scientists at key points in their careers. To this end the foundation has a variety of award schemes targeted, currently, at senior school students who are considering a career in science; science undergraduates; newly appointed lecturers; and promising researchers. The nature, content and purpose of the schemes are regularly reviewed.'

Exclusions 'The foundation is a charity and makes grants only to other charitable or non-profit organisations. We normally make grants only to UK organisations, and support work that will be mainly based in the UK, although the trustees welcome proposals for collaborative projects involving partners in European or Commonwealth countries.

'The trustees will not consider the following:

- general appeals;
- buildings or capital costs;
- projects which are mainly of local interest;
- research that is of mainly of theoretical interest;
- day to day running costs or accommodation needs;
- the provision of health or social services;
- grants to replace statutory funding;
- health care (outside mental health);
- the arts, religion;
- museums, exhibitions, performances;
- sports and recreation;
- conservation, heritage or environmental projects;
- animal rights or welfare;
- attendances at conferences;
- expeditions, travel, adventure/holiday projects;
- business or job creation projects;
- academic journals;
- medical research (other than in rheumatism and arthritis).

Grants are not made for the following purposes except when the activity is part of a project which is otherwise acceptable:

- work for degrees or other qualifications;
- organisation of conferences or seminars;
- production of films, videos or television programmes;
- purchase of equipment, including computers.

Applications The foundation updates its guidelines annually and applicants should ensure that they are using the current version before making an application.

'If you are thinking of making an application, you must first send a written outline proposal. A member of staff will then advise you whether the proposal comes within the trustees terms of reference and whether there are any particular questions or issues you should consider. The outline should describe:

- the issue or problem you wish to address;

- the expected outcomes(s);
- what will happen in the course of the project;
- (for research projects) an outline of the methods to be employed;
- an outline of the budget and timetable.

'The outline must not exceed three sides of A4, but you are welcome to include additional supporting information about yourself and your organisation.

'If the decision is to proceed with a full application, the staff member dealing with your application (*probably the contact person named under the relevant programme in the text above. Ed.*) may suggest a meeting or, if matters are straightforward, may advise you to proceed straight to a full application.'

The foundation does not use application forms and there is no standard format. However the Guide to Applicants includes several pages of the most detailed guidance (too extensive to be reproduced here) as to what is required in a full application.

The trustees meet in February, April, July and October. Outlines applications should reach the foundation by dates published annually, generally about six weeks before the deadlines for full applications. Final applications are sent by the foundation for comment to independent referees. 'We need time for this, and to deal with any questions that may arise, so deadlines for final applications are some two months before trustees' meetings. Closing dates for receipt of completed applications in their final form are approximately eight weeks before these meetings.

The Nuffield Trust (formerly the Nuffield Provincial Hospitals Trust)

£709,000 (1997/98)

Research and policy studies in health

59 New Cavendish Street,
London W1M 7RD
Tel: 0171-631 6632; Fax: 0171-631 8451
e-mail: mail@nuffieldtrust.org.uk
Web site: www.nuffieldtrust.org.uk

Correspondent John Wyn Owen, Secretary

Trustees Sir Maurice Shock, Chairman; J Burnett-Stuart; Professor J Ledingham; Professor D Pereira Gray; Sir Keith Peters; Dame Fiona Caldicott; Sir Christopher France; Alexander Carlile.

Beneficial area UK, except London.

Information available Full accounts on file at the Charity Commission. The trust produces annual reports and guidelines for applicants, copies of which are available on request.

Summary This trust sees itself, in an interesting phrase, as a 'philanthropic venture capitalist'. It makes substantial, often on-going grants in its specified fields of research and policy studies in health. Many of these arise out of the programmes that the trust itself has instigated, but is also interested in unsolicited applications, especially in its priority areas, as specified below.

General The trust, formerly known as the Nuffield Provincial Hospitals Trust, has no connection with the Nuffield Foundation (described in the preceding entry) beyond a common founder. It has acted in the past as 'an independent commentator on the UK health scene and the NHS, and in particular of hospital and other medical services. It has set out to illuminate current issues through informed debate, meetings and publications; and has also commissioned research and policy studies aimed at the development of policy and the improvement of health services.'

In 1997 it agreed 'a direction ... focusing on health research, new knowledge and insight, policy development and practice, the intention being to encourage exchange and dissemination of ideas ... exploring issues rather than disciplines ...

'The year has seen a greater coordination of the trust's various activities – grants, publications, fellowships, alliances and partnerships. The trustees have aimed to operate as a philanthropic venture capitalist, willing to take a risk with ideas and people. ... The trust takes a medium to long term perspective – five to ten years – on the return from investments. It will take a risk, but this is minimised by sound staff work. ... It is not the trustees intention to be the main financiers of projects; rather they provide a measure of working capital to enable ideas to be brought to the point at which they can be taken to established funders; the trust will always plan an exit strategy for the activities and projects that it supports as they become mainstream.'

The trust has set eight ambitious priorities for the immediate future, though some of these may be pursued by means of the trust's own internal activities rather than through grant making.

Priorities

- Policy futures – a group that will produce an annual health futures review and assessment.
- Globalisation, devolution and national health policy – the trust has unusually strong international interests, even if devolution must take immediate prominence.
- Public health – extensive internal work is planned.
- Quality – work has been commissioned on the coordination of quality initiatives.
- Health of the NHS workforce – an established concern of the trust.
- Humanities in medicine – the trust organised the meeting which resulted in the welcome Windsor Declaration on this subject, and is organising Windsor II for 1999.
- How well is the NHS? – There is a programme of internal work, as also in ...
- The NHS of the future.

The grant programme

'The grant programme has contributed and continues to contribute significantly to the UK health service research programme. The trust is open to grant applications that contribute to health gain, people centred services and sound stewardship of resources. The trust will continue to support research that:

- promotes health policy and practice
- fosters appropriate settings for care
- promotes an appropriate balance of investment in health promotion, disease prevention, diagnosis, treatment, care and rehabilitation.
- supports investment in the development of the workforce and managerial and professional leadership.
- encourages effective, efficient and financially sustainable delivery of health care.
- promotes a learning culture founded on well-validated knowledge based research and development.'

It is not clear quite how the two list of priorities listed above interact with each other when grants come to be made. It seems likely that a significant proportion of grants, probably much more than half by value, arise out of work on the first list of priorities, but that there is also some room for applications that qualify under the second more general list.

The ambitious initial aspirations are indeed clearly reflected in a number of the 1997 grants that are described in the report. There was a grant (£35,000) to Robert Hazell's constitution unit it at University College, London to examine Devolution and Health, an issue which has indeed been neglected. £93,000 over two years went to Sheffield's Institute of Work Psychology for a study of the impact of mental health on job performance on the NHS, continuing a well established interest in the health of the huge NHS workforce. A clearly risky grant was the £14,000 extra to an existing study on whether TV series can influence medicine in the real world. Not surprisingly, the work has been found to be more complex than had been anticipated.

Not all grants were to academic or specifically policy focused institutions. Arthritis Care and the Children's Chronic Arthritis Association, admittedly working with Coventry University, received £40,000 for piloting and evaluating a workshop for parents of arthritic children, while the Maternity Alliance was given one of the few small grants, £2,000 towards a conference on the effects of poverty on pregnant women.

About a third of the money is given to work in three units set up in specific universities by the trust, two of them for Community Care (Glasgow and Leicester) and for Policy in Nursing Research in London.

Exclusions Grants are not awarded to individuals for personal studies, nor to meet the core costs of other organisations.

Applications Potential applicants are strongly advised to obtain up-to-date Guidelines for Applicants before approaching the trust. These are available, in some detail, from the site listed above.

Applicants for grants are normally expected to write to the secretary initially, giving a brief outline of the study for which they seek funding; if appropriate the secretary then advises on the requirements for submitting a formal application to the trustees. The trustees meet in March, July and November.

The P F Charitable Trust

£1,195,000 (1994/95)

General charitable purposes

25 Copthall Avenue,
London EC2R 7DR
Tel: 0171-638 5858

Correspondent The Secretary

Trustees Robert Fleming; Valentine P Fleming; Philip Fleming; R D Fleming.

Beneficial area UK, with apparent special interests in Oxfordshire and Scotland.

Information available Report and accounts listing the 50 largest grants; full grants list; basic grant information sheet.

Summary Several hundred grants are made to various registered charities across the UK. Grants average, and are typically for, £2,000, although awards of £500 or less are frequent. The largest and rarest grants go as high as around £30,000. Both one-off and recurrent awards are made.

General The trust was set up in 1951 by its settlor and namesake, the banker Philip Fleming. Its grant-making ability was enhanced considerably in 1983 when the settlor's son, Robert Fleming made substantial donations to the trust.

In 1996/97 assets totalled £38.5 million and income accrued in the year was £1,473,000. Awards totalling £1,195,000 (according to the accounts – the grants list totals £1,183,000) were made and a further £723,000 in future grants had been promised. About 600 awards were made, all to registered charities within 15 categories. The size of the awards within the various categories was very much the same – the vast majority were between £500 and £2,000. The eleven largest grants ranged from £20,000 to £34,000 and amounted to £282,000 (24% of the total). Beneficiaries were most often national charities and/or those based in the South of England and Scotland.

Schedule of grants, 1996/97:

Welfare

– old folks	£51,000	4%
– youth	£70,000	6%
– rehabilitation	£86,000	7%
– settlements	£2,500	-%
– housing associations	£6,000	-%
– miscellaneous	£74,000	6%

Medical research	£191,000	16%
Hospitals and associated organisations	£198,000	17%
Music, theatre, art	£148,000	12%
Conservation	£141,000	12%
Universities, schools	£76,000	6%
Blind and deaf	£48,000	4%
Youth clubs and associations	£28,000	2%
Animals	£17,000	1%
Miscellaneous	£46,000	4%
Total	£1,183,000	100%

The trust no longer gives to:

- individual hospices but instead grants to Help the Hospices.
- individual churches but, instead, grants to the Historic Churches Preservation Trust, Scottish Churches Architectural Heritage Trust and to the Baptist Union Home Missions and Methodist Church Home Missions.

The largest grants went to Cancer Research Campaign (£28,000), St Mary's Church Steeple Barton (£34,000) and Guidepost Trust (£30,000). £25,000 awards were to Royal Hospital Neurosurgical Research Fund, St Thomas' Charitable Trust, Children's Trust, Help the Hospices, Almshouse Association and the Tate Gallery.

Small grants were awarded to national charities or local organisations all across the UK but typically within London, Oxfordshire or Scotland. Examples of these are awards to the Royal National Institute for the Blind (£5,000), Tower Hamlets Old People's Welfare Trust (£5,000), Oxfordshire Probation Service (£1,600) and Scottish Conservation Projects Trust (£5,500).

Exclusions No grants to individuals or non-registered charities. Individual churches and hospices are now excluded.

Applications To the correspondent at any time, in writing with full information. Replies will be sent to unsuccessful applications if a SAE is enclosed. Trustees meet monthly.

The Rudolph Palumbo Charitable Foundation

£434,000 (1992/93)

Education, relief of poverty, conservation, general

37a Walbrook, London EC4N 8BS

Correspondent T H Tharby

Trustees Lord Mishcon; Sir Matthew Farrer; Lady Palumbo; T H Tharby; J G Underwood.

Beneficial area UK and overseas.

Information available 1992/93 accounts were the latest on file at the Charity Commission.

General The foundation refused our request for an annual report and accounts and also appears to be neglecting to send these to the Charity Commission. It is still a registered charity (but see below) and is therefore legally obliged to send the report and accounts to the Commission and to make them available to the public.

In June 1998 the foundation wrote:

'There is a major reorganisation due in this trust. It is also fully committed for at least the next two years.

'I would therefore suggest that reference to it is omitted for the time being from your Directory so as to prevent the frustration of applicants whom we cannot respond to.'

While all this may be true, it is not an excuse for the foundation's neglect of its statutory obligations.

The charity later told these editors

'There is a legal question over the charitable status of the foundation and for the time being no grants are being made; watch this space.'

Applications In writing to the correspondent.

The Parthenon Trust

£4,473,000 (1997)

Medical research, emergency relief, Third World, social welfare, education, disabled

La Maison de Huite, St Saviour, Guernsey GY7 9XR, Channel Islands
Tel: 01481-65177

Correspondent John E E Whittaker, Secretary

Trustees Dr J M Darmady; Prof C N Hales; Mrs Y G Whittaker.

Beneficial area UK and overseas

Information available Reports and accounts avaialable.

Summary The trust makes a small number of large grants each year, 60 awards typically between £50,000 and £100,000 and sometimes over £1 million. A large number of grants are given to overseas organisation.

General The trustees' report states the policy of the trust as placing 'primary emphasis on the relief of hardship and the advancement of health. Trustees are particularly interested in helping war and famine victims (including refugees). They are also interested in helping the aged and the long term unemployed; in supporting long term development in the third world; and in supporting medical research in areas which appear to be underfunded in relation to the likelihood of achieving progress. They are also interested in supporting hospices and rehabilitation and in helping the disabled (including the blind, the deaf and the mentally and physically handicapped).'

Income for 1997 amounted to £4.7 million, made up almost entirely of donations and gifts to the trust. The report notes that substantial support was received from a foundation based overseas.

About £4.5 million was given out in over 60 charitable grants in 1997:

- 39% went to charitable organisations providing emergency relief (often to war and famine victims)and/or undertaking development projects in the Third World;
- 25% went to medically related purposes (mostly research);
- 36% of grants went to a wide variety of organisation including hospices,

assistance to the mentally-handicapped and the underprivileged, the provision of a meeting place for young people, a residential home for the physically disabled and assistance to mine victims.

A grants list of the top 30 odd grants, provided to us by the trust for this entry, shows that over 60% of total grant giving went to 11 organisations. The largest grant, of £1.25 million, went to Medecins sans Frontiers (UK).

Grants for over £100,000 went to a number of overseas and international organisation:

Catholic University of Louvain (£240,000),
Save the Children (£180,000),
Cambridge University (£172,000 for the work of Professor C N Hales, who is also a trustee),
OXFAM (£150,000),
Fondation ATD Quart Monde Belgique a.s.b.l. (£150,000),
European Organization for Research and Treatment of Cancer Foundation (£125,000);,
L'Institute Medico-Pedagogique 'La Providence' a.s.b.l. (£120,000),
Les Amis de l'Institute Bordet a.s.b.l. (£100,000).

Grants totalling almost £500,000 are listed under Miscellaneous Grants and no information is available on these.

Exclusions No grants for individuals or scientific/geographical expeditions.

Applications Unsolicited applications are not normally acknowledged

The Peabody Community Fund

£802,000 (1998/99)

Social welfare in London

45 Westminster Bridge Road, London SE1 7JB
Tel: 0171-928 7811

Correspondent Everton Counsell, Peabody Community Fund manager.

Trustees Sir John Cubitt, Chairman; James Hambro; Professor Valerie Karn; Albemarle Bowes Lyon; Micheal Haines, Sir Idris Pearce; Anne Chan; Tim Cook; Ken A Olisa; Shamit Saggar; Geoffrey Wilson.

• Peabody

Beneficial area London.

Information available Full reports and accounts available from the Peabody Trust. Application form and information pack available.

Summary The grant making arm of the Peabody Trust, this fund concentrates funding in four main areas:

- employment initiatives;
- community support;
- disabled;
- urban regeneration.

In 1996/97 about £720,000 was given out in 80 projects. The trust says that it is now concentrating a larger percentage of its resources on proactive schemes which target economic and urban regeneration.

The following two important criteria apply in all cases:

- most of those who benefit from the grant must be Londoners; either born in Greater London or currently living in the capital.
- the scheme must be targeted at those in lower income groups.

General This is the grant-making arm of the Peabody Trust, an independent charity and housing association formed in 1862 by American philanthropist and banker George Peabody. It was established in 1981 to provide financial aid in areas not concerned directly with housing provision and concentrating on social and economic deprivation.

The fund wishes to concentrate its resources in the following priority areas:

- Employment initiatives focused on vocational training/education and creating job opportunities for those from deprived backgrounds.
- Community support among London's deprived groups including education, training, developing non-dependency and helping those for whom housing cannot be provided.
- Projects designed to open up facilities for the mentally/physically disadvantaged and in particular, aim at ensuring that those with such disabilities and who are poor, are not deprived of access to help and support.
- Economic and urban regeneration proposals which tackle the problems of deprivation in a comprehensive way and focus on some of London's poorest and run down areas.

The fund now also distributes grants to individuals under the Peabody Trust Millennium Awards 'Leaders for London' scheme. £1.2 million is available over three years for individuals who live or work in the London boroughs of Hackney, Islington,

Lambeth, Newham, Southwark and Tower Hamlets. Individuals from these boroughs may apply for a maximum of £3,500 to run projects that will benefit themselves and the communities in which they live. Projects must fit within the themes of health, education, culture or race. Priority is given to projects that benefit young people.

'As well as its grant making work the PCF continues to promote a selected number of pioneering initiatives. These include the "gift in kind and time" scheme, which includes offering organisations redundant office equipment, as well as consultancy advice on areas such as finance, housing and economic development.'

In 1996/97 the fund awarded £720,000 to 80 projects across the capital. The fund concentrated its funding into the following priority areas:

Investing in Community	
Support	*£396,000*
Employment Initiatives	*£171,000*
Overcoming Handicaps	*£124,000*
Regeneration	*£30,000.*

Most of the grants given in each of these areas were for refurbishment and equipment costs, with some going towards running costs, and a few grants were for purchasing vehicles.

Investing in Community Support: This is concentrated in areas of education, training, and helping those for whom housing cannot be provided. There is a preference for deprived groups.

By far the largest area for grant giving, this heading covered almost £396,000 to 50 organisations. Grants ranged from £600 to £33,000. Most of the grants (31) were for less than £8,000. Examples of the larger grants include £33,000 to the Mobile Warden Project for two Peabody Estates (for salaries and administrative costs associated with the post); £30,000 over two years to Community Service Volunteers (administrative costs for their literacy programme); £25,000 to the Notting Dale Partnership (for extensive refurbishment of the community resource centre); £20,000 to PRAXIS (to pay for the extension of a community centre); and £13,000 to the Refugee Council (for roof repairs and camping equipment).

Employment Initiatives: These focused on vocational training/ education, and funding organisations that seek to promote job opportunities.

Grant giving in this area accounted for £171,000 in 13 grants. Grants ranged from £1,500 to the African Churches Council for Immigration and Social Justice (for the purchase of the

computer) to £32,000 to the Finsbury Park Community Trust (for equipping an IT training suite). Most grants were between £8,000 and £15,000. Examples include: £24,000 to Custom House and Canning Town Community Renewal Project, PITSTOP (for the extension of a workshop for training schemes); £15,000 to Streets Ahead (for funding a 'job readiness programme); £11,000 to Prince's Youth Business Trust (for administrative costs for an outreach manager); £9,500 to Hackney Employment Link Project (to purchase computer equipment).

Overcoming Handicaps: This was mainly for providing facilities for the mentally and physically handicapped, and access and support for those who are disabled and poor.

In 1996/97 about £124,000 was given to 15 charities. Grants ranged from £3,000 to £15,000, with the majority of grants (10) for £10,000 or less. Examples of grants include: £15,000 to Kensington & Chelsea Mencap (for a new resource centre), £10,000 to CCP Housing Ltd (to refurbish the tenants' resource/meeting room), £9,000 to APFT -Lisson Grove Social Education Centre (towards the purchase of a caravan for the disabled), and £4,000 to St James' House (towards the administrative costs of its advocacy service).

Regeneration: Only one grant was given in this area: £30,000 to the Open Age Project (to refurbish the centre on Peabody's Dalgarno Estate).

Exclusions See above for specific project exclusion.

No grants for the benefit of anyone other than Londoners, nor for

- political or religious purposes;
- the direct provision of housing accommodation;
- to support ordinary ongoing revenue activity;
- purposes already catered for by statutory bodies, unless the project aims to promote further action by central and local authorities, rather than to relieve them of their responsibilities;
- general appeals;
- individuals (note- 'Leaders for London' scheme);
- the arts;
- medical charities unless projects overcome handicaps;
- intermediate bodies for redistribution to other organisations.

Applications All applications must be made using the application form available from the trust. The trust requests that all questions are answered in as much detail as possible, and that replies such as 'see attached' are not used as far as possible. This will help us get an idea of your organisation's ethos and ways of working, as well as finding out specific information about your project. Please ensure that the documentation asked for is provided, as application cannot be considered until all necessary paperwork is received.

Completed forms should be returned to the Peabody Community Fund Manager. If you have any queries, please discuss them with that officer (direct telephone 0171-922 0201).

For a 'Leaders for London' application form, contact 0171-928 7811.

You will be notified of a decision made by the governors as soon as is reasonably possible. Governors have decided that they will consider applications three times a year (usually June, October and February).

Note: organisations seeking funds from several sources can usually enhance their success rate where they can show existing commitments from grant-making bodies. The PCF is, therefore, particularly interested in making such 'partnership' grants, where it will generate at least equivalent funding from other sources.

The Peacock Charitable Trust

£2,095,000 (1997/98)

Medical research, disability, general

P.O. Box 902, London SW20 0XJ

Correspondent Mrs Janet Gilbert

Trustees W M Peacock; Mrs S Peacock; C H Peacock.

Beneficial area UK.

Information available Accounts are available, including a full list of grants but without a narrative report.

Summary This is a family trust, concentrating mainly on medical research, disability and some youth work. Most of the money goes to organisations supported over a number of years. Only a third of the grants given out in 1997/98 were to new organisations, and almost 70% of these were for less than £10,000.

General The trust was established in 1968 by the Peacock family who are the current trustees. In 1998 the assets of the trust were £42 million, which included £7 million worth of shares in Brooker Plc. Consent is required from Mr Peacock for any change in investments. From the trusts income of £3 million, about £2.1 million was given out as grants. There were very low administrative costs of £16,000. It seems that the trustees do most of the work themselves.

In 1996/97 the charity gave out 1.7 million in 160 grants ranging from £100 to £110,000, with most of the grants (110) being for amounts between £1,000 and £10,000. Nearly 70% of the beneficiaries also received support in the previous year.

The top 15 grants (£30,000 or more) accounted for nearly half the total grant aid; of these only two had not been supported in the previous year. Three major cancer organisations received large grants and have also been long term beneficiaries: the Cancer Research Campaign (£110,000), Marie Curie Cancer Care (£70,000) and Macmillan Cancer Relief Fund (£43,000, which includes £3,000 for marathon runners). Other recipients of large grants include the Mental Health Foundation (£50,000) and the Iris Fund for the Prevention of Blindness (£40,000).

Organisations working in medical research and disability predominate among the major grants, although large grants were also made to youth work charities such as the National Council of YMCAs (£50,000), National Federation of City Farms (£50,000), Jubilee Sailing Trust (£50,000), Youth at Risk UK (£40,000), and the Prince's Youth Business Trust (£30,000). In 1997 only about 4% of the trusts grant-aid went to conservation whether for the built heritage or the natural environment. Few grants were given to local groups. These were mainly in the Merton and Wimbledon areas

Applications Only registered charities should apply in writing, preferably early in the year and accompanied by full accounts. Applications should include clear details of the need the intended project is designed to meet plus any outline budget.

No donations are made to individuals and only in rare cases are additions made to charities already being supported.

To maximise the use of funds, only applications being considered will receive replies.

The Dowager Countess Eleanor Peel Trust

£364,000 (1994/95)

Medical research, health, general

6 New Square, Lincoln's Inn, London WC2A 3RP
Tel: 0171-831 6292

Correspondent Anthony G Trower

Trustees R S Parkinson; Anthony G Trower; R G Swainson; J W Parkinson; R L Rothwell Jackson; L M Valner.

Beneficial area UK.

Information available In September 1998 the most recent accounts on file at the Charity Commission were those for 1994/95. There is a history, now intensifying, of the late filing of accounts.

Summary Around 80 grants are made a year varying from £500 to about £60,000; most are for £1,000 to £2,000. Beneficiaries were usually grant-assisted in the previous year, but a handful of awards are made to charities never previously assisted. A few, often larger, grants are made up to three years.

General The trust was established in 1951 from the legacy of Eleanor Peel. The following charities are targeted in the deed:

- Medical charities, including medical research.
- Charities in association with old people.
- Charities assisting those who have fallen on evil days through no fault of their own.
- Charities specified in the schedule of the deed.

'Grants shall not be made to charities primarily devoted to children. They (the trustees) are prohibited from giving money to charitable bodies substantially under the control of central or local government.'

In 1994/95 the trust generated £448,000 income from assets totalling £6,339,000 at the year's end. In all £375,000 was disbursed in grants – £11,000 to the charities specifically named in the deed and £364,000 to others. High administration costs of £51,000 included £14,000 in trustees' expenses. These editors believe that excellent trustees can be recruited to a grant making trust who will be less expensive than this.

The grants list is unusual in that it lists all 540 charities that have ever received a donation from the trust and so a full grasp of the trustees interests can be ascertained.

Eighty donations were made in 1994/95; ten were new grants and 70 went to organisations also helped by the trust in previous years.

The new beneficiaries were: Abbeyfield Bramhall Society (£2,000); Barrow and District Spastic and Handicapped Society (£3,000); Coronary Artery Disease in Women (£25,000); Lilian and Faithful Homes (£2,000); Lune Valley Transport (£2,000); Scottish Gospel Outreach (£3,000); St Helen's Knowsley Hospice (£3,000); Teeside Hospice Cancer Care Appeal (£3,000); Trinity United Reform Charity (£2,000); and Yehudi Menuhin School (£500).

Six 'annual grants' (spread over two or three years to charities selected by the trustees – not those specified in the deeds) included those to: Coronary Artery Disease in Women (£25,000 a year until 1997); Institute for the Care of the Elderly (£35,000 up to 1997); and the Royal Free Hospital School of Medicine (£40,000 until 1997).

The largest beneficiaries included: Cheshire Homes for the Sick (£22,000 in 1994/95, £60,000 in total); Disabled Living Foundation (£57,000, £978,000); Jefferiss Research Wing Trust at St Mary's Hospital, London (£21,000, £149,000); and the Research Institute for the Elderly (£35,000, £75,000).

Charities to whom the trust has historically given the most funds include: the Church of England Clergy Stipend Fund (£10,000 in 1994/95, £232,000 overall); Guys and Lewisham Hospitals, Dr Graham Jackson (Nil, £200,000); Institute of Psychiatry, Eleanor Peel Lectureship in Psycho-Geriatrics (Nil, £300,000); Peel Studentship Trust, University of Lancaster (£20,000, £288,000).

Exclusions No grants to children's charities, individuals.

Applications To the correspondent. The trustees meet on at least three occasions each year. All applications for grants are vetted by the Secretary or the Chairman and the Secretary. Any application rejected at this stage are listed in the agenda for the next trustees meeting with the reason for rejection. Applications for consideration by the trustees are presented with a report and summary of the financial statements for the complete year.

The Pilgrim Trust

£2,378,000 (1997)

Social welfare, art and learning, preservation

Fielden House, Little College Street, London SW1P 3SH
Tel: 0171-222 4723; Fax: 0171-976 0461

Correspondent Georgina Nayler, Director

Trustees Mary Moore, Chairman; Neil MacGregor; Nicolas Barker; Lady Anglesey; Sir Claus Moser; Lord Armstrong; Lord Bingham; Eugenie Turton; Lord Cobbold; Chris Patten..

Beneficial area UK, but not the Channel Islands and the Isle of Man

Information available Guidelines for applicants and excellent annual report and accounts.

Summary Grants are usually for capital expenditure and may be offered for more than one year, but not for more than three years. Except for some 'block grants' in the preservation field, very few awards (just one in 1997) are for more than £30,000.

The areas of interest are a curious mixture; projects, often unusual and interesting, in specific fields of social welfare; and art and preservation, usually of a sophisticated kind.

General This trust was a pioneer of imaginative grant making in the years before and after the war – including being one of the originators of the three year 'project' grant that is now all too standard practice for many trusts described in this book, but which in its time was a big step forward for the sector.

Following a policy review, the 1997 report sets out a number of changed or more closely defined policies. These can be read in the text of the report below, but they include the following general points:

'We will not normally make grants that will make a negligible contribution to the overall scheme. Largely for this reason, we shall not normally in future give grants towards the purchase of works of art and other museum objects.

'In the field of social welfare we have decided to concentrate on three main areas:

- projects that will help divert people from crime, drug and alcohol abuse and into employment and training;
- the support of people who suffer from mental health problems and learning disabilities
- the rehabilitation of people who have experienced long term homelessness.

'We are particularly wary of applications from voluntary organisations seeking to win contracts from a statutory authority as local service providers. We prefer not to offer grants towards an organisation's ongoing running costs. We can, however, be flexible about contributing to salary and other administrative costs where a specific project has a defined time limit and clear objectives.'

In 1997 there were 1,233 applications, of which 241 led to grants being made. This represents a success rate of one in five applications.

This is a national charity. The distribution of 1997 grants, expressed as a value per thousand population, was as follows:

England	*£1.02*
Scotland	*£0.28*
Wales	*£0.21*
Northern Ireland	*£0.17*

The social welfare projects are concentrated in London and the south of England. Those for art or preservation are much more widely spread, with an unusual and welcome interest for a London based foundation in projects outside England.

Guidelines for Applicants

Guidelines and priorities of the trust in Autumn 1998 were as follows:

Social Welfare

- projects that encourage people to be active members of society and of their local communities. Trustees will, in particular, look favourably upon projects that help young people into education training and employment away from crime and drug and alcohol misuse. Projects concerned with people who are particularly disadvantaged will be a priority.
- projects concerned with the employment, support or housing of those with mental illness or severe learning difficulties, especially those living as part of their local communities.
- projects that aim to rehabilitate and assist people who experience long-term homelessness.

Art and Learning

- the promotion of scholarship, research, cataloguing and conservation within museums, galleries, libraries and archives.
- support for the pre-publication costs of learned works in areas of interest to the Pilgrim Trust. This may include research costs, but not salary or substitution payments. Grants may not be given direct to individuals but must be made to a charitable organisation.
- projects that seek to widen access of theatre, music, museums and the other arts, particularly for young people.

Preservation

- preservation of particular architectural or historical features on historic buildings or the conservation of individual monuments or structures that are of importance to the surrounding environment. Trustees will not normally contribute to major restoration s or repairs unless a discreet element of the project can be clearly identified as appropriate for the trust to support.
- projects that seek to give a new use to obsolete buildings which are of outstanding architectural or historic interest.
- dissemination of information about historic buildings and documents and their importance to the community.

The trust will also consider the cataloguing and conservation of records associated with archaeology, marine archaeology, historic buildings and landscapes.

Places of worship

The trust supports the conservation of both the fabric and the contents of churches, but it does this indirectly through block grants to the Historic Churches Preservation Trust, its Scottish equivalent, and the Council for the Care of Churches. Applications for work not covered by these bodies can be made directly to the trust.

The Annual Report for 1997

'Last year, in our Annual Report for 1996, we said that during 1997 we would be undertaking a review of The Pilgrim Trust's policies. This review has now taken place and our new guidelines for applicants were published in September *(See above. Ed.)*. These set out the trustees' priorities for the next few years and specify the information we need in order to consider projects submitted to us. We hope that applicants will find this information helpful; the Director and other members of our staff are always ready to provide further help if needed.

'We will continue to consider applications in our traditional fields of Social Welfare, Art and Learning and Preservation. Within these areas, however, we have tried to define more clearly the type of projects that we feel to be important, and in which our grants can make most impact. We continue to seek to support projects that find it difficult to raise funds from other sources.

'During consideration of our future policy we thought carefully about our role in relation to major capital

developments. We have decided that we will not normally make grants that will make a negligible contribution to the overall scheme. Largely for this reason, we shall not normally in future give grants towards the purchase of works of art and other museum objects. We hope, however, to find other ways of helping non national museums. For example, during 1997 we made a grant to the Buckinghamshire County Museum for the purchase of a secure showcase for the Tucker-Dayrell Cup, an outstandingly important piece of the silver bought from abroad with funds from, among others, the Heritage Lottery Fund and the National Art Collections Fund.

'The public increasingly expects museum collections to be made more accessible through the use of modern technology. However, making collections available on the Internet and providing interactive displays for visitors can be successfully achieved only after a considerable amount of staff time has been spent in research, cataloguing and conservation. The Pilgrim Trust will continue to encourage museums and galleries to catalogue and conserve their collections, and to promote scholarship and research. Since we also believe that access to a collection via computer technology is no substitute for visiting a museum and seeing the objects themselves, we shall also encourage projects designed to encourage such visits.

'We have continued to assist universities, libraries and record offices to purchase significant manuscripts, as well as helping them with cataloguing and conservation; during 1997 we helped the University of Leicester to buy Joe Orton's papers and Kent County Council, through the Centre for Kentish Studies, to buy the Amherst archive.

'We say in our new guidelines that we particularly welcome collaboration between organisations to achieve shared goals. The Pilgrim Trust itself follows this policy wherever practical, maximising the effect of our grants while keeping our administrative costs low. The National Manuscripts Conservation Trust, which gives grants towards the conservation of important manuscripts, is administered from the British Library and can thus draw freely on the Library's expertise. We have agreed to work closely with the NMCT and now encourage applicants to apply to them in the first instance. The NMCT then evaluates the application and makes a recommendation to The Pilgrim Trust. This year we made three grants through NMCT, to the Universities of Durham and Glasgow and to the College of Arms.

The Pilgrim Trust

Grant making was categorised as follows for 1997 (with 1996 figures in brackets)

Social welfare	**£1,210,000**	**(£741,000)**
Homelessness	£363,000	
Support of mentally ill in the community	£107,000	
Youth projects	£208,000	
Penal affairs	£227,000	
Unemployment	£111,000	
Drug and alcohol abuse	£176,000	
Miscellaneous	£25,000	
Preservation	**£479,000**	**(£546,000)**
Ecclesiastical buildings	£342,000	(£278,000)
Secular buildings	£116,000	(£203,000)
Countryside	£21,000	(£65,000)
Art and learning	**£690,000**	**(£384,000)**

We shall review the arrangement at the end of 1998, but at the moment it seems to us sensible for The Pilgrim Trust to make maximum use, wherever possible, of expertise available in other organisations.

'Another example of the trust's drawing on expertise available in other organisations is our long standing practice of giving an annual 'block grant' to each of the Council for the Care of Churches, the Historic Churches Preservation Trust and the Scottish Churches Architectural Heritage Trust. These three organisations make a large number of relatively small grants towards the repairs and conservation work required by historic and architecturally significant places of worship, and all applicants to The Pilgrim Trust for such grants are referred to one or other of these organisations. However, as the first two of these cannot by their own terms of reference give grants for repairs or conservation in churchyards, we have decided to accept applications direct for this type of project. Such work can be particularly useful as well-kept churchyards greatly improve the setting of their churches and often provide pleasant green and open spaces, particularly in urban areas.

'In this field of church maintenance we have yet to see the full impact of the 'Joint Scheme for Places of Worship', run jointly by English Heritage and the Heritage Lottery Fund under which £20 million per annum will be made available. We shall watch with interest the development of the scheme and shall be ready if necessary to adjust our priorities in this field. We also look to the recipients of our grants to keep their own priorities under review.

'The Pilgrim Trust seeks to encourage young people to enjoy music, the theatre, ballet and opera; and the general widening of access to the arts is another of our priorities. During the year, we made a grant of £5,000 to the Performing Arts Lab for a course to stimulate new work for younger audiences, and £9,000 to the Early Music Network for music workshops in primary schools and for work with youth orchestras.

In the field of social welfare we have decided to concentrate on three main areas: projects that will help divert people from crime, drug and alcohol abuse and into employment and training; the support of people who suffer from mental health problems and learning disabilities and the rehabilitation of people who have experienced long term homelessness. Last year we committed a large proportion of our total expenditure on social welfare projects. While we accept the importance of this area of our work we wish, over time, to maintain a balance between our three spheres of interest.

'Like many other charitable grant giving bodies, we are increasingly concerned at the blurring of the lines between statutory responsibilities and those of the voluntary sector. We are still, therefore, reluctant to take over the funding of areas that have in the past been the responsibility of government, either local and national; and we are particularly wary of applications from voluntary organisations seeking to win contracts from a statutory authority as local service providers.

'It is difficult for people who have been homeless for many years to integrate themselves back into society, even when they find somewhere to live. We were pleased to offer one of our largest grants of the year, £50,000, to St Mungo's for a pilot project aimed at supporting people who have in the past experienced long term homelessness when they enter new employment. The project will not only offer support to the employees, but will also advise and assist employers. We look forward to learning more about the results of this project.

'We prefer not to offer grants towards an organisation's ongoing running costs. We can, however, be flexible about contributing to salary and other administrative costs where a specific project has a defined time limit and clear objectives. We will also consider applications for core administrative costs if applicants can demonstrate that Pilgrim Trust funding is essential as part of a strategic development and that plans are in place for other support to take over when our grant ceases.

'During 1997 a drugs co-ordinator was appointed by the new Government. We hope that his future strategies and plans for fighting drug abuse in the UK will help to inform and guide our grant giving in this area. During the year we have been approached by several organisations seeking funds for drug education projects in schools. We have been, and remain, concerned about the lack of analysis and evaluation into the results of such projects. It is difficult for us, as funders, to know which type of project we should support when there is so little information available about the relative success or otherwise of such schemes. There are many organisations active in the drugs education field but there appears at present to be little exchange of information between them.

'During the year we received 1,233 applications for grants. Of these, 241 were successful and commitments were made totalling £2,463,069 at our four meetings. Some £90,000 of grant offers were cancelled or returned due to the applicants' changed circumstances. The Pilgrim Trust's grant commitments during 1997 represent a significant increase on the sums offered in previous years and the Trust has also offered a number of larger grants than in the past. We hope to see this trend continue in 1998. However, we will also be operating a small grants programme, since we are well aware that a modest contribution from the Pilgrim Trust can often make a significant difference.

Grants in 1997
Preservation

Ecclesiastical

Kilmore Non-subscribing Presbyterian Church, Northern Ireland. Towards the complete repair of the east wing of the church. (£6,000)

Liverpool Cathedral. Towards the cost of repairing the roof of one of the perimeter chapels. (£20,000)

Secular

Ampthill Feoffee Estate Charity. Towards the repair of the almshouses in Ampthill, Bedfordshire. (£10,000)

Hestercombe Gardens Trust. Towards the restoration of two garden buildings, situated in the outstanding landscape park at Hestercombe, near Taunton in Somerset. (£10,000)

Scottish Lime Centre. Towards the acquisition of a traditional roller pan mortar mill. (£1,713)

Countryside and landscape

Landscape Foundation. Towards the investigation of disused viaducts in Southwark for development as public open space. (£5,000)

Lincolnshire and Humberside Trust for Nature Conservation. Towards the Trust's data work which would involve inputting information on species and habitats in Lincolnshire on to a computer as part of a wider county and national initiative, payable over three years. (£15,000)

Art and Learning

Museums and Galleries

Bethlem and Maudsley NHS Charitable Trust Funds. Towards the conservation of the portrait of Henry VIII attributed to the circle of Holbein. (£5,000)

Charleston Trust. Towards the purchase of a painting by Duncan Grant. (£5,000)

Museum of the History of Science, Oxford. Towards the cost of new showcases for the top gallery in the Museum. (£37,075)

West London Museums Group. Towards the cost of "Tudor Resources", replica Tudor costumes and objects for use with schools as part of an educational project. (£2,000)

Libraries, archives and publications

Bedfordshire County Record Office. Towards the completion of the catalogue of the Wrest Park (Lucas) Archive payable over two years. (£10,000)

Commonweal Collection. Towards the reclassification and cataloguing of the collection. (£3,000)

University of Leicester. Towards the purchase of the Joe Orton Papers. (£8,000)

Music, Ballet and Opera

Early Music Network. Towards the costs of a series of early music workshops in primary schools and a series of baroque string workshops with youth orchestras. (£9,000)

Wren Trust. Towards the microfilming and cataloguing of the Baring-Gould Collection of folk songs to allow greater public access. (£1,770)

Theatre projects

Garrick Theatre, Altrincham. Towards essential backstage refurbishment. (£8,550)

Parasol Theatre. Towards a catalogue and conservation assessment of the Lanchester collection of puppets. (£8,750)

Social Welfare

Homelessness

Burnley, Pendle and Rossendale CVS. Towards the renovation and refurbishment of three houses in Burnley and Padiham to provide six bed spaces for young single people. (£10,426)

Mission in Hounslow. Towards the costs of furnishing move-on accommodation for homeless young people. (£10,000)

Support of the mentally ill in the community

Cellar Project. Towards the cost of purchasing the 'Old School', Shipley to continue providing employment opportunities for people with mental health problems, in the Bradford Metropolitan area. (£20,000)

National Missing Persons Helpline. Towards the salary costs of a case manager to specialise in the field of

mental health, payable over 3 years. (£24,750)

Youth Projects

Friends United Network. Towards the cost of a pilot project to extend a befriending scheme for young people at risk, payable over three years. (£36,000)

Gulbenkian/ Who Cares? Trust. Towards a study and national strategic development to equip local authorities to meet the educational needs of children in care. (£10,000)

Penal Affairs

International Centre for Prison Studies (King's College, London). Towards the establishment of the Centre. (£30,000)

New Assembly of Churches. Towards the purchase of a computer training system for the Career Workshop at Feltham Young Offenders Institution (£29,500)

Sinfonietta Productions. Towards the costs of a series of workshops to be given by members of the London Sinfonietta in Bullingdon Prison, payable over three years. (£20,000)

WISH. Towards the salary costs for a branch manager for the WISH (Women in Special Hospitals), Rampton Branch, payable over three years. (£30,000)

Unemployment

CVS (Springboard Hackney). Towards the establishment of Springboard Hackney, a training scheme for disadvantaged young people in a new training centre. (£10,000)

Wandsworth Youth Enterprise Centre. Towards the Youth Enterprise Accredited Business Skills and Planning Course. The grant to be paid over three years. (£30,000)

Drug and alcohol abuse

Broadreach House. Towards refurbishment of a cottage as an extension to Longreach House, a treatment centre for women. (£15,000)

Greater Manchester and Lancashire Regional Council on Alcohol. Towards the cost furniture for St Luke's Hostel, Preston. (£2,800)

Police Foundation. Towards an independent, multi-disciplinary review of the Misuse of Drugs Act 1971, payable over 2 years. (£30,000)

Miscellaneous

University of East Anglia Towards the cost of 'The Tracking Project' to track the progress of the homeless, mentally ill, addicts and prisoners through various agencies in Norfolk. (£10,000)

Exclusions No grants are made to individuals, or for projects outside the UK.

Grants are not made for:

- major capital projects and major appeals, particularly where 'partnership' funding is required and where any contribution from the Pilgrim Trust would not make a significant difference
- acquisition of works of art and other museum objects although the acquisition of material for special collections in libraries and record offices will be considered where the Pilgrim Trust's contribution can make a significant impact
- activities that the trustees consider to be primarily the responsibility of central or local government
- medical research, hospices, residential homes for the elderly and scheme specifically to give access to public buildings for people with physical disabilities
- youth or sports clubs, travel or adventure projects, community centres or children's playgroups
- re-ordering of churches or places of worship for wider community use
- education, assistance to individuals for degree or post degree work, school, university and college development programmes
- trips abroad
- one-off events such as exhibitions, festivals, seminars and theatrical and musical productions
- commissioning of new works of art
- general appeals.

Applications An Application Form and the following supporting information is required:

Your organisation:

- latest audited annual accounts and report
- organisation's aims and objectives
- track record and the support it enjoys from other organisations working in the same field.

The Project:

- full description of the project including a budget and, if relevant, a projected income and expenditure account for the organisation as a whole
- the problem you are seeking to tackle, its urgency, and how your project will solve it.
- for projects involving salary costs, relevant job descriptions with the proposed salaries and the proposed management structure
- * how you will monitor and evaluate the project

- list of other organisations you have approached for funding and any offers you have received
- where you are requesting grants for less than £5,000 you should send two references from organisations with which you work
- for historic building repairs you should include details of the repair scheme costs
- for cataloguing and conservation projects you should demonstrate how you should demonstrate how you have chosen the people who will do the work and give details of their relevant expertise
- photographs should be sent where appropriate.

The Pilkington Charities Fund

£450,000 (1996/97)

General

Chartered Accountants, PO Box 4, Liverpool L37 1YJ
Tel: 01704-834490

Correspondent Roberts Legge & Co, Chartered Accountants

Trustees Dr L H A Pilkington; Mrs J M Jones; A P Pilkington.

Beneficial area Worldwide with a preference for Merseyside.

Information available Report and accounts with full grants list but no analysis.

Summary Grants support a variety of causes but the bulk of funding is to well established medical and/or welfare charities. Usually recipients are based in Merseyside and the North West of England although awards are made throughout the UK, particularly to national institutions. Grants vary from one to fifty thousand pounds and the great majority are repeated annually.

General The fund was established in 1950 and its full title is the late Colonel W W Pilkington Will Trusts. In 1996/97 it held assets totalling over £16 million from which a low income of £495,000 was generated. At £12,000 (3 pence per £1 donated), management and administration costs were very low.

The largest grant in any one year, accounting for about a quarter of total charitable expenditure, is normally made to the C & A Pilkington Trust Fund (which has a similar grant making

policy). The other beneficiaries are predominantly major local or national charities (MENCAP £1,000, NSPCC St Helens £5,000, Samaritans £1,000, Liverpool Royal School for the Blind £3,500 etc.). Most grants are made twice a year (November and April). 90% of them are to the same organisations and usually for the same amount of money. In 1996/97, 210 such grants were made to 70 charities. On average an organisation were given £3,800, although some got as little as £500 and one got £50,000.

The largest awards in 1996/97 went to: Barnardos (£50,000); Intermediate Technology (£30,000); and Jefferiss Research Trust (£20,000).

Exclusions Individuals.

Applications In writing to the correspondent.

The Austin & Hope Pilkington Trust

£328,000 (1996/97)

General, see below

Church House, Bisley, Stroud, Gloucestershire GL6 7AD

Correspondent Penny Shankar

Trustees Dr L H A Pilkington; Mrs J M Jones; Mrs P S Shankar.

Beneficial area UK.

Information available Full accounts on file at the Charity Commission.

General The trust has decided to focus its wide-ranging funding in specific and changing areas each year:

1997 *Community, poverty and religion.*
1998 *Youth and children, elderly, medical.*
1999 *Music and the arts, famine/overseas*
2000 *Community, poverty and religion.*

In 1996/97 assets of £8 million generated an income of £314,000. A total of £328,000 was distributed amongst 72 organisations, with most grants being between £2,000 and £4,000. The largest grant, of £20,000, went to the Mental Health Foundation.

- Housing/welfare: Taking about 45% of the total grant giving, examples of grants included those to Centrepoint and London Connection (£15,000

each); Single Homeless Project (£10,000); Char and Penrose Housing Association (£5,000 each); and Caring for Life (£1,000).
- Health and medical: 16% of grant giving with beneficiaries such as the Mental Health Foundation (£20,000), the Hope Trust (£2,000); and the National Autistic Society (£5,000).

A grant of £47,000 was made to Purcell School.

Exclusions Grants only to registered charities.

No grants to individuals.

Grants for purely local organisations.

Applications In writing to the correspondent. Please note the selected areas for each year as given above. Applications should include full budgets and annual accounts where appropriate.

The Polden-Puckham Charitable Foundation

£293,000 (1996/97)

Peace and security, ecological issues, social change

PO Box 951, Bristol BS99 5QH

Correspondent Bevis Gillett, Secretary

Trustees Carol Freeman; Candia Carolan; David Gillett; Harriet Gillett; Jenepher Gordon; Heather Swailes; Anthony Wilson.

Beneficial area UK and overseas.

Information available Full accounts on file at the Charity Commission, although without a narrative report.

Summary One of the few consistently radical funders, whose primary aim is 'to support projects that change values and attitudes, promote equality and justice, and that develop radical alternatives to current economic and social structures.'

General 'The foundation's policy is to support work in the following areas with grants usually in the £500 to £5,000 range:

- Peace – development of ways of resolving international and internal conflicts peacefully, and of removing the causes of conflict.

- Ecological issues – work which tackles the underlying pressures and conditions leading towards global environmental breakdown; particularly initiatives which promote sustainable living.'
- Other – PPCF also supports work on women's issues, human rights and social change. It has a long standing link with the Society of Friends.

In its work the foundation ... gives particular consideration to small pioneering headquarters organisations.'

The 84 grants in 1997 were headed by £20,000 for Quaker Peace and Service, £15,000 for the New Economics Foundation and £10,000 each for the Fawcett Trust and Saferworld.

Grants of £5,000 or more went to the Centre for Conflict Resolution in South Africa; the Centre for Defence Studies, King's College; Climate Action Network; the Environmental Law Foundation; Friends World Committee for Consultation; the Ecological Foundation, Oxfam; Oxford Research Group; Powerful Information; the Social Investment Forum; SOS Sahel; Transport 2000; UNA Trust; Womankind; Women's Environmental Network; and VERTIC.

About half the grants go to organisations that were also supported in preceding years (which is almost inevitable in such specialist fields of interest).

Exclusions Grants to individuals; travel bursaries; study; academic research; capital projects; community or local projects (except innovative prototypes for widespread application); general appeals.

Applications The trustees meet twice a year in late March/early April, and October. The foundation will not send replies to applications outside its area of interest.

Up to date guidelines will be sent on receipt of a stamped addressed envelope.

Applications should be no longer than two pages and should include the following:

- a short outline of the project, its aims and methods to be used.
- the amount requested (normally between £500 and £5,000 over one to three years), the names of other funders and possible funders, and expected sources of funding after termination of PPCF funding.
- information on how the project is to be monitored, evaluated, and publicised.
- background details of the key persons

in the organisation.

Please also supply:

- latest set of audited accounts;
- a detailed budget of the project;
- annual budget if available;
- list of trustees or board of management;
- names of two referees not involved in the organisation;
- charity registration number, or name and number of a charity which can accept funds on your behalf.

The Porter Foundation

£456,000 (1996/97)

Jewish charities, general

PO Box 229, Winchester,
Hants SO23 7WF

Correspondent Paul Williams, Director

Trustees Dame Shirley Porter; Sir Leslie Porter; Steven Porter; David Brecher.

Beneficial area UK and Israel.

Information available Full report and accounts.

General The trust says that it 'supports projects in the field of education, culture, the environment and environment and health and welfare which encourage excellence, efficiency and innovation and enhance the quality of peoples lives'.

In 1996/97 the trust's endowment of £26 million generated the low income of £1.1 million. About £456,000, less than half the income, was given out in grants. The foundation has been reducing grant giving and accumulating income for some time possibly in preparation for major future projects. The foundation is not connected with Dame Shirley's personal assets, the subject of on-going dispute.

Major grants were given to a number of Jewish organisations that have been supported for number of years, including Tel Aviv University (£123,000, part of an annual donation for the next seven years); JPAIME (£79,000, part of a commitment of £768,0000 over two years); Oxford Centre for Hebrew and Jewish Studies (£65,000, annual donations for two years); British Friends of the Council for a Beautiful Israel (£37,000); Jewish Continuity (£25,000); New Israel Fund (£12,000); and Jewish

Care (£10,000).

Large non-Jewish organisations that received funding included the National Portrait Gallery (£25,000); Tidy Britain Group (£4.000); Age Concern Westminster (£2,000); and Chicken Shed Theatre (£1,000).

Exclusions 'The foundation funds only charitable organisations and does not make grants to individual applicants or respond to circular appeals.'

Applications In writing to the correspondent.

The J E Posnansky Charitable Trust

£276,000 (1996/97)

Jewish charities, health, welfare

c/o: Baker Tilly, 2 Bloomsbury Street, London WC1B 3ST
Tel: 0171-413 5100

Correspondent P A Cohen

Trustees Lord Mischon; Philip A Cohen; Beryl Inglis; Gillian Raffles; Anthony Victor Posnansky.

Beneficial area UK and overseas.

Information available Accounts are on file at the Charity Commission.

General This trust gives mainly to Jewish charities, which account for over 60% of total grant giving. Grants are also made to social welfare and health charities.

In 1996/97 the trust had an income of £271,000 generated from assets of £5 million. Grant giving of £276,000 was through 122 awards.

Most of the larger grants went Jewish charities, such as JPAIME (£25,000); Society of Friends of the Federation of Women Zionists (£15,000); Jewish Care (£14,000); Friends of Hebrew University for Jerusalem (£13,000); General Jewish Hospital and Ravenswood (£10,000 each); World Jewish Relief (£7,000); Ben Gurion University, Friends of Neve Shalan and Tel Aviv University Trust (£5,000 each).

Other grants went to social welfare and health organisations such as Save the Children (£10,000); CARE (£5,000); Marie Curie Cancer Fund and Terrence

Higgins Trust (£3,000 each); Sue Ryder Foundation and Amnesty (£2,000 each) British Home and Hospital for the Incurable and Age Concern (£1,000 each).

Applications To the correspondent. The trustees meetings are held in May.

PPP Healthcare Medical Trust

£17,000,000 (anticipated disposable income)

Healthcare

13 Cavendish Square,
London W1M 9DA
Tel: 0171-307 2622 Fax 0171-307 2623

Correspondent David Carrington, Chief Executive

Trustees Sir Peter Gadsden, Chairman; P H Lord; Sir Richard Bayliss; Dr. R H McNeilly; Dr. L T Newman; Professor B L Pentecost; B H Asher; D H Probert; M Sheldon; Sir Keith Peters; Lord Renfrew; R B Blaxland; Sir Anthony Grabham; M B Sayers; Professor Mary Marshall; Professor Sir Michael Peckham; Sir Peter Morris.

Beneficial area UK.

Information available See below.

General This charity was the sole beneficial owner of the PPP healthcare private health insurance company, the second biggest of its kind (after BUPA). When the business was sold to Guardian Royal Exchange, the proceeds became an endowment for the charity. An initial £450 million may rise to a final total of over £500 million.

The purposes of the charity, all of which will be addressed from the start of grant making operations in 1999, are to promote:

- medical research and the publication of the useful results of such research;
- medical education and training, including the education and training of nurses;
- others involved in the provision of healthcare;
- others involved in the management and administration of healthcare providers;
- the relief of sickness and disability and the preservation and protection of public health;
- the relief of the aged.

Up to 2% of income may be spent on other charitable activities.

Full Guidelines will be available from the address above by the time this book is published, but had not been finally agreed at the time of going to press.

The Director of the charity, David Carrington, was previously with the Baring Foundation, whose imaginative new programmes, largely developed under his management there, are described elsewhere in this book.

While wishing nothing but well to this exciting new enterprise, the membership of its 'augmented' board of governors is dissapointing. Given that most healthcare, formal or informal, is delivered by women, it is sad to find only two female trustees among 15 men. If this is a relic of the trust's past history as a primarily scientific body, it should be remedied.

Applications See above.

The Prince's Trust

£1,370,000 (to organisations 1997/98)

Disadvantaged young people

18 Park Square East,
London NW1 4LH
Tel: To contact local committees, 0800-842842. Otherwise 0171-543 1234; Fax: 0171-543 1200

Correspondent Tom Shebbeare, Director

Trustees William Castell, Chairman; Sir Angus Ogilvy; Sir Christopher Harding; John Jarvis; Kate Thomas; Stephen Lamport; Peter Mimpriss; Mike Woodhouse; John Rose.

Beneficial area UK and Commonwealth.

Information available Full information from the charity.

Summary As well as running the Youth Business Trust, the Volunteers personal development programme and the Bro environmental project in Wales, the Prince's Trust has three grant making programmes, for both individuals and to organisations working with disadvantaged young people, through its subsidiary Prince's Trust – Action. Grants are made locally, and are relatively small.

General All grants are made through the 60 or more voluntary local committees of Prince's Trust– Action, an exemplary example of low-cost but effective grant-making. Details of how to contact these committees (frequently changing information) can be had through a 24-hour helpline on 0800 842 842.

Small grants of up to £2,500 can be awarded, through a simple application to the local Prince's Trust committee, as one-off grants to local organisations working with groups of young people. The total awarded in 1997/98 was £1,160,000 in 600 grants.

Local Initiative grants of up to £10,000 can be awarded to organisations working, in association with their local Prince's Trust Committee, with groups of young people that have been identified as particularly disadvantaged. The approach for these is more formalised and is described below. The total awarded in 1997/98 was £210,000 in 25 grants.

The pioneering programme for centres for out-of-school learning is now under review following the government's decision to allocate lottery funds for 'after school clubs' from its New Opportunities Fund.

Applications under the Local Initiatives programme must meet the following criteria:

1. The local Prince's Trust committee must have taken a leading role in the origination and development of the initiative.
2. The initiative must be innovative and clearly be breaking new ground in the locality.
3. The proposal must have attracted other funding partners – statutory, voluntary or private. 'Our role is to pump prime only'.
4. The initiative must be unlikely to go ahead without the trust's involvement.
5. The local committee's contribution should be significant – £2,500 or 10% of its annual allocation, whichever is the lower.
6. Initiatives should normally meet the needs of at least one of the following groups of disadvantaged young people:
   - Under achieving in education. Each year, over 33,000 young people in England and Wales will leave school with no GCSEs and research suggests that school underachievers become disaffected.
   - Excluded from education. Boys, particularly those from Afro-Carribean origins and those who are in the care of a local authority are most vulnerable to school exclusion. It has

proved very difficult to return those excluded to mainstream education.

- Being discriminated against. Care leavers, the disabled and those young people from ethnic minorities are frequently victims of discrimination. Unemployment rates are far higher for these young people.
- Leaving care. Over half of care leavers are unemployed and more than 75% have no qualifications. Over 33% of young single homeless people have been in care and about a third of young offenders have a care background.
- Endangering their health. Areas of concern include experimentation and drug dependency (including alcohol), sexually transmitted diseases, self-harm, teenage pregnancy and homelessness.
- Unemployed. Officially there are an estimated 600,000 unemployed 16-24 year olds. However the actual figure is likely to be much higher since many young people operate outside the system. There is concern that the New Deal will not tackle the most disadvantaged and this is a problem the trust should attempt to address.
- Committing crime. Among 14-25 year olds, one in two males and one in three females admit to having committed an offence. Crime has been correlated with social disadvantage and poverty. People living in deprived circumstances are at greater risk of being perpetrators, and victims, of crime.
- Suffering from abuse. Sexual, physical, emotional and institutional abuse can be equally damaging. Victims of abuse have low expectations of themselves.
- In rural isolation. Young people living in rural isolation lack the opportunities to gain social skills, education and employment.

Millennium awards

The Millennium Commission is funding a programme in which grants averaging £10,000 will be awarded to groups of young people to develop projects of benefit to the lives of people in their community.

Applications Call the local Prince's Trust Committee (numbers from 0800-842 842) . For Local Initiative grants they have copies of a full application form.

Mr and Mrs J A Pye's Charitable Settlement

£368,000 (1997/98)

Environment, mental health, general

c/o Sharp Parsons Tallon,
167 Fleet Street, London EC4A 2EA
Correspondent The Secretary

Trustees G C Pye; J S Stubbings; D S Tallon.

Beneficial area UK, with a special interest in the Oxford area, and, to lesser extent, in Reading, Cheltenham and Bristol.

Information available Full accounts, but without any analysis or explanation of grants and with only a limited narrative report. Good Guidelines for applicants.

Summary The charity has wide-ranging interests, but these do not generally include social welfare. It makes about 12 large grants a year which account for about two thirds of all the money. There is a further programme of small grants of £2,000 or less, and indeed mostly for less than £1,000. The number of these small grants, however, decreased sharply between 1997 and 1998.

General 'The overall policy of the trustees is to support under-funded charities in their fields of interest ... . Unfortunately, due to the demands made it is not possible to support all applications even though they may meet the charity's criteria. However the trustees particularly recognise the difficulty many smaller charities experience in obtaining core funding ... .'

The trust sets out the following areas of interest in its Guidelines for Applicants, but points out that it is not exhaustive and 'is given for guidance only'.

- Environmental – this subject particularly deals with organic farming matters, conservation generally and health related matters such as pollution research.
- Health – especially causes supporting the following; post-natal depression, schizophrenia, mental health, alternative or holistic medicine.
- Youth – particularly projects encouraging self reliance.
- Regional causes around Oxford, Reading, Cheltenham and Bristol – under this category the trustees will consider academic and arts projects as well as those listed above.'

The grants lists confirm these interests. A noticeable characteristic is the general absence of awards in the field of social welfare that dominates the giving of most trusts described in this book. To speculate, the lists have the air of following the personal charitable interests of some or all of the trustees, rather than being the result more concrete policies.

The major grants in 1998 were as follows (with the 1997 values in brackets where relevant);

Elm Farm Research Centre, £121,000 for organic farming development and £35,000 for diesel emission research (£80,000 in 1997);

Parnham Trust, £35,000 for Hooke Park College (£5,000);

British Trust for Conservation Volunteers, £23,000 (£7,500);

The Association for Post Natal Illness, £22,000 (£22,000);

Radcliffe Medical Foundation, Oxford, £15,000;

London Immunotherapy Cancer Trust (£15,000);

Magdalene College School (£14,000);

Harris Manchester College, £12,000 (£12,000);

Music at Oxford, £10,000 (£10,000).

The charity has also made substantial loans to charities, including £100,000 to the Parnham Trust and £30,000 to Music at Oxford.

As the new accounting standards require, but as this editor doubts to be the universal practice, the accounts note that two of the trustees are the Chairs of recipient charities (Music for Oxford and the Children With Aids charity) and that the partnership of trustee D S Tallon was paid £10,000 for its work in administering the grant making routine (this charge is modest, at 3% of the total value of grants), and the company of another, J S Stubbings, was paid £1,550.

Exclusions

- Organisations that are not recognised charities;
- Activities which are primarily the responsibility of government or some other responsible body;
- Activities which collect fund for subsequent re-distribution to other charities;
- Corporate affiliation or membership of charities;
- Endowment funds;
- Expeditions or overseas charities;

• Fabric appeals for places of worship, other than in geographical locations indicated above;
• Fundraising events or activities;
• Hospitals or medical centres (except for projects that are clearly additional to statutory responsibilities);
• Individual, including students;
• Overseas appeals;
• Promotion of religion.

Applications There are no application forms but the following information is essential:

• Registered charity number or evidence of an organisation's tax exempt status;
• Brief description of the activities of the charity;
• Details of the project for which a grant is sought;
• Details of the overall cost of the project and a breakdown, where appropriate;
• Details of the funds already raised and the proposals for how remaining funds are to be raised;
• The latest trustees report and full audited or independently examined accounts (which **must** comply with Charity Commission guidelines and requirements).

Trustees meet quarterly to take decisions. Any decision can therefore take up to three months before it is finally taken. However, all applicants are informed of the outcome of their applications and all applications are acknowledged.

Queen Mary's Roehampton Trust

£615,000 (1997/98)

War disabled ex-service people and their dependents

13 St George's Road, Wallington, Surrey SM6 OAS
Tel: 0181-395 9980

Correspondent Alan H Baker, Clerk to the Trustees

Trustees J J Gunning, Chair; H L Payne, Vice Chair; J J Macnamara, Hon. Treasurer; Colonel S D Brewis; Colonel A W Davis; Brigadier A K Dixon; Col J L Franklin; Col J T Keating.; Brigadier J O E Moriarty; Dr E Nelson; Major General T A Richardson; M H Wainwright; B Walmsley; Dr J Watkinson.

Beneficial area UK.

Information available Good report and accounts.

General The trust makes grants to organisations helping ex-service men and women. Forty three grants were made in 1997/98, eight of which, totalling about £45,000, were to new applicants. The largest grants to existing beneficiaries were to the Royal Patriotic Fund (£78,000 for its TV scheme for war widows), the 'Not Forgotten' Association (£32,000), and to the Army Benevolent Fund (£30,000),

The trust continued to support the modernisation of nursing and residential homes for ex-service disabled people. Fifteen organisations received grants totalling £263,000 under the 'building schemes' section. Among those supported were the Chasely Trust and the Erskine Hospital (£50,000 each) and the Ex-services Mental Welfare Society (£40,000).

The largest of the awards to new beneficiaries went to the Lord Kitchener Memorial Holiday Centre (£20,000).

Applications In writing to the correspondent (six copies), to be submitted in April and September annually. Details must be given of the number of war disablement pensioners assisted during a recent period of twelve months. In the case of nursing/residential homes, information concerning occupancy will be required under a number of headings (complement, residents, respite holidays, waiting list). Three copies of latest annual reports and any appeal leaflets should be enclosed.

The Joseph Rank Benevolent Trust

£3,365,000 (1997)

The Methodist Church, Christian-based social work

11a Station Road West, Oxted, Surrey
Tel: 01883-717919 Fax: 01883-717411

Correspondent John A Wheeler

Trustees J D Hutchison, Chairman; Rev D Cruise; Rev Dr D English; Rev P Hulme; Mrs A J Moon; Ms Gay Moon; C R Rank; J A Reddall; Rev Dr R J Tudor; Mrs Sue Warner.

Beneficial area UK and Ireland.

Information available Full and clear accounts and grants lists with a well laid out and succinct but limited narrative report.

Summary Over half of the trust's grants are for improving Methodist churches and properties, and its extensive grant programmes for youth and for community service projects also support many activities connected with that church. There is, though, substantial support for projects that have no obvious Methodist affiliation, but are in sympathy with the trust's Christian aspirations. Most non-church grants are to help with revenue costs and may be spread over as long as five years.

General The trust is an amalgamation of two separate foundations established in the 1930s by Joseph Rank, and hence it has two separate income streams, one of which, representing over quarter of total revenues is restricted to the support of specifically Methodist activities. The rest, the trust's general fund, can be spent more widely, but in practice about 60% of all grants are for the costs of improving or adapting Methodist church properties to improve their facilities to meet current needs.

The trustees describe their policies for their General Fund as follows:

'The trust represents a continuing practical expression of the Founder's desire to stimulate and support initiatives which promote the Christian faith and Christian principles.

'The General Fund of the trust is available to support any charitable object although the trustees are particularly interested in those which have been established by committed Christians, and others, to address social needs and which represent a practical expression of Christian principles.'

In 1997 103 such General Fund grants were made, totalling £2,099,000, an average of £20,000, though there were grants of as much as £78,000 and as small as £1,000.

The remaining grants in 1997 and in the previous year were categorised as follows:

	1997	1996
Youth projects	£519,231	£398,000
Community service	£358,000	£259,000
Religion – education	£236,000	£443,000
Elderly	£110,000	£181,000
Disabled	£10,000	£17,000
Health and healing	£20,000	£60,000
Health care	£13,000	£3,000
Religion – fabric	£0	£10,000

The major youth grants were in support of specific Methodist initiatives, partly in association with the Pastoral care and Education Division of that church, and partly as five year funding for 12 projects under the Rank charities' 'Youth or Adult' programme.

£73,000 was spent on other youth projects including the Toxteth Centre 63 Church of England Youth Centre (£29,000) and Centrepoint (£2,000).

The larger community service grants were typically being paid over three years, with annual payments of up to £50,000 (to AIDS Care Education and Training), but few others were for more than £20,000 a year. New three year programmes in 1997 included annual payments to Langley House Trust (£30,000 for a Housing Development Officer for ex-offenders) and RELATE (£15,000 for support for young people suffering from the effects of their parent's divorce).

Some of the new grants for religious education were for evangelical institutions such as Holy Trinity, Brompton (£150,000), or Premier (£50,000 towards the operating costs of this Christian radio station) but included support for the Inter Faith Network and for Luton's inter faith Grassroots programme (£60,000 over three years).

There were seven new grants under the Elderly heading, led by £18,000 a year for three years for the Alzheimer's Disease Society towards support for sufferers on North Tyneside. £20,000 was given for Christmas bonuses for the widows of Methodist Ministers, probably a regular commitment.

The trust spent £77,000 on administration in 1977, being just over 2% of the value of its grants.

Exclusions No grants to individuals.

Applications Unsolicited appeals are considered although the chance of a grant being made is small. General appeals should be addressed to the correspondent and include full details of the appeal and a copy of the most recent audited accounts.

Appeals from within Methodism should only be put forward after consultation with the relevant division of the church.

The Rank

Foundation

£7,530,000 (1996/97)

Christian communication, youth, education, general

11A, Station Road West, Oxted, Surrey, RH8 9EE
Tel: 01883-717 919; Fax: 01883-717 411

Correspondent John A Wheeler, Director

Trustees R F Cowen, Chairman; M D Abrahams; Lord Charteris; Mrs S M Cowen; M E Davies; Mrs L G Fox; J R Newton; F A Packard; D R Peppiatt; V A Powell; Sir Michael Richardson; Lord Shuttleworth; D R Silk; M J Thompson.

Beneficial area UK.

Information available Excellent reports and accounts.

Summary The foundation assists around 800 charities a year with grants from £500 to about £200,000 (average £12,000).

A categorisation, with grant totals for 1996/97, is as follows:

The promotion of education £3.2 million

Education	£301.000
Youth	£2,910,000
Youth or adult?	£1,474,000
Inventing success	£643,000
People and work unit	£81,000
Gap scheme	£235,000

Promotion of general charitable Objects £23 million

Elderley	£764,000
Disabled	£530,000
Community service	£507,000
Medical/healthcare	£440,000
Animal conservation/welfare	£55,000
Cultural	£32,000

Promotion of Christian religion £2.0 million

Most awards are one-off but the foundation also has its own longer-term initiatives with funding given over three or more years. The foundation claims to make grants all across the UK and, unlike many other trusts proclaiming a similar policy, it actually does. However nearly half of grant expenditure is disbursed to charities that the foundation identifies as national.

General In 1996/97 the foundation's assets totalled £182 million (£164 million in 1995/96) and generated income of £8,479,000 (£9,123,000).

Administration expenses for the year came to £500,000, most of which was accounted for by the five staff salaries. The foundation paid three members of staff around £45,000, one about £75,000 and another £85,000.

Annual Report 1996/97

The following is reprinted from the foundation's exceptionally full annual report and where a grant is mentioned we have added in brackets (the amount of money) given in 1996/97.

'The company was founded in 1953 by the late Lord and Lady Rank. It was one of a number of companies and charities established by the founders at that time and to which they gifted their controlling interest in the Rank Group plc.

'The company has three main objectives which are the promotion of:

- The Christian religion, Christian principles, Christian religious education and the study of the history of the Christian faith by the exhibition of religious films or any other lawful means.
- Education.
- Any other objects which are exclusively charitable.

'Grant funding decisions are made by two committees which meet three or four times a year: (i) Appeals and community care, (ii) Education and youth.

Administration

'The directors (trustees) continue to take an active part in all areas of the work of the foundation, including the identification of appropriate initiatives for support and the monitoring of their progress.

'Three committees of directors (i) Appeals and community care, (ii) Education and youth, (iii) Finance, oversee the day to day administration of the foundation. All committee meetings are attended by members of the executive staff, who are charged with implementing the policy which has been agreed by the directors and monitored by the committees.

Appeals and community care committee

'During the year the committee met formally on four occasions. The function of the committee is to consider all unsolicited appeals which are received in addition to initiatives brought to its attention by the executive staff.

'The committee has limited discretionary powers under which it makes grants. Grants in excess of these powers, together with recommended deadlines, are put forward in recommendations to the main board of directors. This process seeks to ensure that all directors are aware of appeals which have been received.

Education and youth committee

'The committee met formally on three occasions to consider recommendations put forward by the executive staff on initiatives which fall within guidelines agreed by the directors.

'Whilst individual projects cover a wide spectrum of work, the overall objective is, in the case of education, to provide bursary support at selected schools and, in the case of youth work, to encourage leadership by involving young people and making them responsible for their decisions.

Promotion of education

(£3,210,000)

'In interpreting this objective, the directors take a broad view and include work with young people which is designed to involve them in decisions which affect their future and to cultivate them in attitudes which will make them useful members of society.

'There are substantial commitments in the field of education, in which the directors include youth work, and projects in this are are mainly identified by staff who have considerable experience and contacts within the field.

'Education (£301,000)

'The foundation has continued to support in a number of independent schools of boys and girls who are thought to have leadership potential and where there is financial need which, but for the help of the foundation, would result in a change of school at a critical time (£278,000 was disbursed in bursaries to 42 private schools around the UK. No reason is given why such support is conferred to independent schools – scholars in state scools often have pressing financial problems that hinder their development).

As part of its more general work, the foundation is currently supporting a number of projects involving work with young people who have fallen on the wrong side of the law. These include an education initiative in Feltham Young Offenders Institution (*£25,000 to New Assembly of Churches*), mentoring schemes with the Humberside Probation Service (and with the Airborne Initiative (Scotland) (*£10,000*), work with young teenagers excluded from school in South West England through Cities in Schools (*£20,000 in 1995/96*) and the Hampton Trust's pilot scheme in Hampshire involving family conferencing as an

alternative to a Court appearance.(Other large awards in 1996/97 were to:East Durham Groundwork Trust (*£3,000 towards costs of an additional worker* helping young people to gain a wide variety of technical skills in sports and outdoor pursuits; and Learning Through Action (*£10,000 for core costs of helping schools tackle behavioural problems*)).

Youth (£2,910,000)

'The directors subscribe wholeheartedly to the views of the founders that young people are the seedcorn for the future wellbeing of our society and that they should be encouraged to develop to the full extent of their potential.

'The directors decided that the funds available to them would best be used in firstly identifying worthy projects and then funding them on a meaningful basis over a number of years. It was also agreed that an integral part of the process should be careful monitoring and these have been the bases on which funding has been committed.

'The work of the foundation falls into three main programmes which are the "Youth or adult initiative?", "Investing in Success" and its "Gap scheme".

Youth or Adult? (£1,474,000)

'The scheme, under which projects are supported over five years, embodies two key aspects which are the training of local youth leaders who are experienced by unqualified and involving young people in the design and implementation of an active programme which reflects real responsibility and commitment by them. The trainees are all enrolled on a part-time distance learning course with the YMCA George Williams College (£189,000) but continue to be involved with local community life during their training, successful completion of which results in a professional qualification in the form of an ordinary degree in Formal and Community Education from the University of Kent. Fourty-four trainees are currently registered with the support of the foundation.

'A wide variety of fields of work are supported. In homelessness the St Anne's Day Centre in Leeds was able to help 377 new young homeless people (£61,000). The Gateway Award in Sutton Coldfield (National Federation of Gateway Clubs received £24,000) involved 80 special needs young people in adventure and survive in the community. Multi-racial work was developed by the King's Cross and Brunswick Neighbourhood Association (£68,000) and won awards from the British Urban Regeneration Association

and the Football Association for helping promote good community relations. For William Youth Cafe £27,000) is an initiative tackling rural isolation in the Highlands and includes a community arts programme and international exchanges. Inner city Belfast's Challenge for Youth (£27,000) links young people into a volunteer programme of training and community leadership projects (other substantial gifts were to: Scotquest £4,000; Youth Projects, £52,000 for assessment conferences; Townhill detached youth work project, £63,000; and £33,000 to Corrymeela Community, Northern Ireland).

Investing in Success (£643,000)

'This initiative builds upon the effective partnerships which have been developed over the years with a number of established organisations. It involves a five year commitment to provide funds to enable these organisations to develop their services to young people in the light of current needs and the likely requirements of the next century.

'There are currently eleven of these initiatives in the UK including one at Centre 63 Church of England Youth Centre in Kirkby, Merseyside (£56,000), whose ten apprentice leaders are gaining qualifications in fields such as youth work, sports leadership and health education.

'The People and Work Unit (£81,000) in partnership with the Prince's Youth Business Trust (£40,000) is working with 600 young people in the field of employment and training in Ebbw Vale and in a number of Welsh valleys.

'A national initiative is underway with Youth Link Scotland (£78,000) to train and qualify apprentices across Scotland in fields such as health education, ethnic groups, crime prevention and practical conservation (further grants went to Dundee Drugs and Aids Project, £72,000; Devon Youth Association £49,000; and Cheshire and Wirral Federation of Youth Clubs, £81,000)

Keyworkers posts

'A number of keyworkers posts are supported with in organisations with which the foundation had worked for some time where qualified workers are needed in dealing with such matters as homelessness, the outdoors, informal education and conservation. One such example is the Urban Adventure Project at the Salmon Centre, Bermondsy, (£8,000) which enables groups of young people from the streets to realise their own potential and self esteem through adventure training while at the same time training and developing voluntary staff. Another example is the Double Take Project (£23,000) which together with the Warwickshire Careers Service re-engages young people between the ages of sixteen and twenty-five who have dropped out or who have missed out on education, training or employment. In Glasgow Royston Youth Action (£25,000) draws together older and younger volunteers to work alongside young people thereby creating the relationships which fuel greater co-operation and mutual support. In Belfast a keyworker heads an initiative which seeks to engage young people as leaders through the use of drama, music, retreats, residentials and summer festivals (Youth Initiatives Northern Ireland £20,000).

Gap Scheme (£235,000)

'This scheme which encourages full-time volunteering in organisations with which the foundation is already working, either during the period between school and higher education or during a period of unemployment, continued to be successful and provides a valuable experience for those involved (£225,000 went to the foundation operated scheme, Gappers, and £10,000 was spent to increase awareness of opportunities available in Gap years).

'During 1997 more than forty full-time volunteers were supported and those involved came both from schools and from within host agencies. Sixty young people are registered on a one year foundation studies course with the YMCA George Williams College including young apprentices on the investing in success initiative, young volunteers and many on the Gap scheme.

'The programme, which works by exploring people's experiences as volunteers, introduces key ways of thinking about and undertaking work covering five main units, Induction, informal and community education, Designing and creating learning opportunities, Managing and working together and Reflecting on practice. The programme leads to the award of a Certificate in Foundation Studies in informal and community education which has been accredited and is equivalent to 1.5 'A' levels.

'The programme has also been designed to meet the requirements in Scotland for the pre-qualifying award for community education and with a qualification for part-time youth work in England, Wales and Northern Ireland. The result is that the certificate can help to gain access to higher education training programmes.

'The directors have been much encouraged by the development of confidence and awareness in those young people who have attended the scheme, many of which have made major contributions to raising awareness, both at national and local levels, of the needs and capabilities of young people.

Other projects

'In the course of considering unsolicited appeals, the directors see many examples of imaginative work at a local level; some of which can be greatly encouraged by modest financial help from sources outside the local community. The directors take into account the level of support which can be realistically expected from the local people and the likelihood of a small grant from the foundation in bringing an initiative to a successful conclusion is an important factor.

'Information on youth projects specifically initiated by the foundation can be obtained from the Hebden Bridge Office (for England and Wales) (28 Bridgegate, Hebden Bridge, West Yorks, HX7 8EX, Tel: 01422 845 172) or the Penrith Office (for Scotland and Northern Ireland) (Sunnyside, Great Strickland, Penrith, Cumbria, CA10 3DF, Tel: 01931 712 320).

General (£2,330,000)

'Appeals are considered from any registered charity but the directors are now taking a more active role in identifying areas and projects for support.

'The wide powers given under this objective can be restricting and liberating. The restriction is occasioned by the fact that the directors consider that they should acknowledge and consider all appeals, with the consequent administrative burden which that entails, whilst the liberating factor is the possibility of responding to changing needs which could not have been envisaged when the foundation was established.

'The fact that directors and staff are located around the country assists in balancing the needs and allocation of resources in addition to providing local knowledge or contact in identifying example of good practice which may be supported in the hope of encouraging similar development elsewhere.

'Within the wider area of the foundations work, the directors have singled out work benefiting the elderly and disabled members of society as being particularly worthy of support and have taken active

steps to identify and support examples of good practice.

Elderly (£764,000, 10% of total grant expenditure)'

'The foundation has taken one major new initiative in its work with older people by developing strategic partnerships with three leading organisations with which the foundation has already been working. To counter the problems voluntary organisations face with the growth of short-term funding and consequent difficulties in developing long-term strategy, the foundation has agreed to provide substantial funds over a long period to three voluntary organisations. This long term security allows major changes to be made.

'Otherwise the emphasis has remained broadly similar to that adopted in previous years: help for people in rural areas (there are now fifteen rural development posts) and for carers (two new posts for Crossroads Caring for Carers (£44,000), for example, in addition to other posts described below).

'The foundation's support has been strengthened in Scotland with the appointment of a development officer with Crossroads Scotland (£29,000) in the West of Scotland and an additional post for Carers National Association (£137,000) to support and extend the carers' network in Scotland. Also a post to help older people in Glasgow from black and ethnic minority backgrounds.

'Age Concern Northern Ireland is being enabled to seek joint funding from the local Health and Social Service Boards for the appointment of community development workers in two of the four Board areas.

'The foundation has worked with Age Concern Northern Ireland previously to establish daycare services for dementia sufferers, pump priming work that was subsequently taken up by Health Trusts. Similarly some pioneering work using music therapy as a treatment for dementia will now be funded by the foundation. Music therapy will be provided at Age Concern Northern Ireland's day care services for one day a week for three months in each of three years. The experience gained from this work is to be monitored closely for possible use throughout the United Kingdom. (*According to the grants list 14 branches of Age Concern, none of them in Northern Ireland, received grants of between £4,000 and £78,000. The foundation says that 'the Age Concern projects are mostly in rural areas to support work at at local level to develop initiatives benefiting the elderly'. Ed.)*

'The foundation continues to work closely with Carers National Association and has now formed a five year strategic partnership wishing to "invest in success" and to enable the organisation to provide more support of the Chief Executive at a time of significant growth in the workload and influence of the organisation.

'A similar partnership with Alzheimers Disease Society (£110,000 in four grants to the main office (£41,000), East Anglia (£18,000), Lincolnshire (£28,000), Shropshire (£14,000)) has enabled it to continue its rural development work and make significant changes to its information and advice service for carers and professionals, which would have been more difficult without the confidence of a longer term partnership. A similar strategic partnership has been developed with Alzheimer Scotland – Action on Dementia (£110,000).

Disabled (£530,000)

'In addition to continuing its promised support for 14 of the projects described last year, 11 fresh applications were successful in 1997. Of these two are concerned with residential centres in Northern Ireland, three to help young people of 19+ with multiple difficulties, four support key members at the centre of national organisations, three are more local, and one seeks to influence the nursing profession. This report concentrates on a small sample.

'A grant to PHAB Northern Ireland (£77,000) will enable it to appoint a project coordinator of an "inclusion network", this is designed to help integrate young people in society, to increase the number of areas where PHAB clubs are established, to improve the training of PHAB leaders and to influence the leaders of traditional youth clubs to make their clubs accessible to people with disabilities. It also seeks to encourage Statutory Education Authorities to make more of their courses and buildings accessible.

'The problems of young people with multiple disabilities when they reach the age of 18/19 is not readily understood by society. A group of parents in Surrey has been exploring the difficulties which their children, who have a variety of learning difficulties, are going to face when they reach that age. A project worker under the umbrella of MENCAP (£2,000) will provide partial information, advice and support to parents of people with learning difficulties in the area; the worker will also seek to influence planners, employers and those who offer

services such as further education and training.

'Funding for three years for the Chief Executives of National Information Forum and DIAL UK (*not apparent in the grants list*) and for an influential member of Spinal Injuries Association (£25,000) and a Senior Development Officer of Contact a Family (£28,000) is in each case designed to provide some stability to the organisations concerned.

'Further grants included the following: Blind in Business, £30,000 'towards core costs of initiatives helping to reduce the unemployment levels among blind people – 2nd of 3 years'; Winged Fellowship, £20,000 'to help with the expansion of the volunteer recruitment programme'; and RADAR, £25,000 'towards the core costs of this organisation seeking to improve quality of life'.

Further programmes

Six further programmes, all 'general charitable projects' not explored in the director's report are:

Community Service (£507,000)

Around 200 grants were made mostly for around £1,000 to a variety of charities, perhaps a quarter of which were Churches. Large awards went to: Retired and Senior Volunteer Programme (£25,000 'towards the core costs of a development programme to increase the number of volunteers over 50' – second of three payments; Painswick Inn Project £20,000 'towards costs of supporting a worker at a training centre for young, single homeless'; and £15,000 to Barnardos for a parenting initiative in Birmingham. Example of smaller grants include: Breakout Children's Holidays (£500); Christian Aid (£2,300); Darnall Joblink Projects (£1,000); Live Music Now, Ireland (£1,000; Oasis Christian Centre £1,000; Mountain Rescue (Central Beacons £2,000, Patterdale £2,500, Oldham £2,000); YMCA, Norwich (£500); and Sandes Soldiers and Airmen's Centres (£2,000).

Medicine/healthcare (£440,000)

27 grants including: £159,000 to Glasgow University; £121,000 to Queen Mary and Westfield College (both for a joint initiative with the Rank Prize Funds in providing core funding over ten years for Rank Departments for Human Nutrition); £25,000 to Rose Road Association for core costs of centre for people with severe and multiple disability; £12,000 to Helen House, Oxford towards rebuilding a whirlpool at a children's hospice; and £10,000 to Lincoln County Hospital for a body

scanner. At least eleven hospices were assisted with funds totalling £77,000.

Animal conservation and welfare (£55,000)

Four grants were made in the year: £50,000 to the Game Conservancy Trust 'towards the cost of employing a head of Wildlife Disease Research'; £3,500 to the RSPB; and £1,000 each to People's Dispensary for Sick Animals and Ada Cole Rescue Stables.

Cultural (£32,000)

A total of five gifts went to: National Youth Orchestra of Great Britain (£20,000 towards establishment of endowment fund – second of three payments); Foundation for Young Musicians, National Associations of Youth Orchestras (£5,000 each); Buildings Books Trust, National Youth Wind Association (£1,000 each).

Research (NIL)

Awards from this category amounted to £50,000 in 1995/96.

Religion – fabric (NIL)

Although no grants were made in 1996/97, £9,000 was disbursed in 1995/96).

Promotion of Christian religion

(£1,990,000, 26% of total grant expenditure)

'The directors have a substantial and continuing commitment to the Foundation for Christian Communication Ltd (FCCL) which, through its Christian based training courses and audiovisual production facilities, is involved with the promotion of Christianity.

'FCCL has continued to be involved in a full schedule of productions, both on its own account and on a co-production basis with commercial undertakings.

'The foundation's commitment to the work of FCCL means that it is unlikely that the directors would be able to fund other projects in that are of work.

Geographical distribution

Geographical analysis of grants:

National	£3,342,000	44%
Scotland	£849,000	11%
North East	£567,000	8%
South West	£350,000	5%
South Central	£358,000	5%
London	£407,000	5%
Midlands	£294,000	4%
Northern Ireland	£227,000	3%
South East	£172,000	2%
Anglia	£144,000	2%
Wales	£182,000	2%

The foundation's excellent report seems to reveal the care and attention to grant making often characteristic of trusts with religious influences. Its grant-aiding of groups in the more deprived areas of the country (which are also frequently under-represented in trusts' grant making) such as Northern Ireland, Northern England, Wales and Scotland is one indication of this.

Exclusions Grants to registered charities only. Appeals from individuals or appeals from registered charities on behalf of named individuals will not be considered, neither will appeals from overseas or from UK based organisations where the object of the appeal is overseas.

Applications Applications should be addressed to the general appeals office at *4/5 North Bar, Banbury, Oxfordshire OX16 0TB* (Tel: 01295-272337; Fax: 01295-272336).

There is no formal application form but for administrative purposes it is helpful if the actual appeal letter can be kept to one or two sides of A4, which can be supported by reports etc. General appeals, including unsolicited appeals relating to youth projects, should include: charity registration number, full details of project and funding sought, amount already raised, and the most recent audited set of accounts.

Preliminary enquiries are welcomed.

Unsolicited appeals are considered quarterly (see below). All appeals are acknowledged and applicants advised as to when a decision can be expected.

The trustees meet quarterly, in March, June, September and December.

The Rayne Foundation

£1,730,000 (1996)

Higher education, medicine, social welfare, the arts, general

33 Robert Adam Street,
London W1M 5AH
Tel: 0171-935 3555

Correspondent R D Lindsay-Rea

Trustees Lord Rayne (chairman); Lady Rayne; R A Rayne; Lord Bridges; Lord Greenhill of Harrow; Sir Claus Moser; E L George.

Beneficial area UK and overseas.

Information available 1996 accounts were the latest on file at the Charity Commission in September 1998. They lacked the required narrative report, analysis and explanation of grants.

General The annual report and accounts state the objectives as: 'to sponsor development in medicine, education and social welfare and the arts, and to relieve distress and to promote the welfare of the aged and young.'

Assets in 1996 amounted to £27.9 million, generating an income of £1.74 million. Grants totalled £1.73 million. Policy seems to be give both a small number of substantial grants, and a large number of small grants. A total of £1.67 million was given in grants for £5,000 or more, the only ones listed. This money could be appropriately categorised under the following headings:

Education	*£544,000*
Social	*£432,000*
Arts	*£214,000*
Medicine	*£211,000*
General	*£165,000*
Jewish	*£100,000*

Education The lion's share of the donations given were educational. The major awards went to well established Universities including the largest grant of £200,000 to Darwin College, Cambridge, although one grant was given to Childeric Primary School (£10,000). Other large beneficiaries include Birkbeck College (£50,000), University of Wales (£50,000), and LSE (£10,000).

Social A number of grants were given out with the majority being for less than £10,000. Examples of the larger ones include those to Refuge (£35,000) and Dementia Relief Trust (£10,000).

Medicine Substantial medical grants included those to the Cancerkin Development Fund (£25,000) and the Royal College of Physicians (£25,000). It is not possible to tell if any of the educational grants are being used for medical purposes.

Arts Most of the grants given were for less than £10,000. Money was mainly given to the larger charities, but local organisations in London did manage to attract money. Examples include The Chicken Shed Theatre (£15,000), Islington Inter Festival French Theatre (£15,000) and the Royal National Theatre (£5,200).

Jewish charities Three large grants were given to Jewish organisations that have all been funded in previous years; the Jerusalem Foundation (£52,000 in two grants), Ravenswood (£30,000) and

Norwood Childcare (£12,500).

Other grants include those to Rayne Trust (£150,000 in six grants), Charities Aid Foundation (£7,500, probably to be used for small awards from this foundation) and the Alpine Club (£5,500).

Although a large number of grants were made, very few were made outside England, the only one of note was to the University of Wales (£50,000)

Exclusions No grants to individuals.

Applications In writing to the correspondent at any time.

The Sir James Reckitt Charity

£484,000 (1996/97)

Society of Friends, general

233 Carr Lane, Willerby,
East Yorkshire HU10 6JF
Tel: 01482-652 363

Correspondent I Gillespie, Administrator

Trustees Miss C Pollock, Chairman and twelve others, mainly descendants of the founder.

Beneficial area Hull and the East Riding of Yorkshire, UK.

Information available Report and accounts with a list of grants but lacking narrative analysis; guidelines for applicants.

Summary Grants are made in support of a broad variety of causes in the local area. Both organisations and individuals are supported, although grants to the latter account for a minimal proportion of expenditure. Awards are usually one-off, typically for about £2,000 and peak at £20,000.

General The charity was established in 1921 by Sir James Reckitt (as in Reckitt and Colman plc), a Quaker with business interests in Hull. Today, the trustees continue to follow the original intentions of the settlor, and in making grants give priority to charitable work in-line with Quaker beliefs. There are eight programmes of grants and within each, the variety of causes supported is broad, with the exception of the religious classification which tends to make donations only to Quaker groups.

In 1996/97, the charity's assets totalled

£14,342,000, and investment income of £515,000 was generated. A total of 333 grants were awarded including 55 to individuals (amounting to £11,000). The largest grant was for £29,000 (towards the Quakers' Britain Yearly Meeting). The eight next largest awards (all those between £10,000 and £20,000) accounted for 21% of the money paid in grants (£101,000). Nearly all of the other donations were under £3,000.

The charity's guidelines state:

'The trustees support general charitable causes, but in accordance with the wishes of the founder give priority to:

- purposes in all localities connected with the Society of Friends (Quakers);
- purposes connected with Hull and the East Riding of Yorkshire.

'Other areas of support are charities, both national and regional, particularly those concerned with current social issues, and whose work extends to the Hull area.

'International causes are considered in exceptional circumstances, such as major disasters, with support usually being channelled through the Society of Friends or the British Red Cross Society.

'Grants are normally made only to registered charities. Support for new projects without such status, is usually channelled through an existing registered charity.

'Appeals from individual Quakers need the support of their local monthly meeting. Appeals from other individuals are usually only considered from residents of Hull and the East Riding of Yorkshire.'

Summary of grants in 1996/97

Social work	180	£174,000	36%
Education	16	£84,000	17%
Medical	32	£62,000	13%
Religion	21	£58,000	12%
Youth	48	£42,000	7%
Children	15	£23,000	5%
Elderly	14	£22,000	5%
Environment	7	£19,000	4%
Total	333	£484,000	100%

The proportions above are very similar to those of past years with the exception of the environment category which had previously accounted for only 1% of charitable expenditure.

Examples of social work grants include donations for £10,000 to the Elizabeth Fry Young Offenders Trust and the Humberside Police – Action Against Drugs, £6,000 to the Sobriety Project, and £5,000 to the British Red Cross –

African Emergency Appeal.

The largest awards in other categories were: £20,000 to Quaker Social Responsibility and Education; £12,700 to North Humberside Hospice Project; £4,300 to Hull Boys Club; £3,700 to the Pre-School Learning Alliance and £3,200 to Swarthmore Housing Society Ltd.

In its 1996/97 the trustees reported the following interesting new initiative:

'In order to recognise the 75th anniversary of the trust in 1996, the trustees encouraged the formation of a consortium of grant-making trusts in Hull and the East Riding of Yorkshire to improve assistance to individuals in need. The consortium responds sympathetically to a an increasing number of applications for local individuals from a wide range of charitable organisations. The consortium aims to improve co-operation between local grant giving trusts.'

Exclusions Local organisations outside the Hull area, unless their work has regional implications.

Support is not given to causes of a political or warlike nature and trustees will not normally consider a further appeal if a grant has been paid in the previous two years.

Grants are not normally made to individuals other than Quakers and residents of Hull and the East Riding of Yorkshire.

Applications In writing to the correspondent at any time. Applications need to arrive a month before the trustees' meetings, in May and November, to be considered.

The Richmond Parish Lands Charity

£699,000 (1997/98)

General, in Richmond

The Vestry House, 21 Paradise Road, Richmond, Surrey TW9 1SA
Tel: 0181-948 5701

Correspondent Andrew Ayling, Clerk

Trustees The mayor ex-officio of Richmond; three nominated by the borough of Richmond (not necessarily councillors or officials); five nominated by local voluntary organisations; up to five co-opted.

Beneficial area Richmond, Kew, North Sheen, Ham and Petersham. Also, for small grants, education fund and heating vouchers, East Sheen and Palewell.

Information available Guidelines for applicants, reprinted below, and good annual report.

Summary The charity makes grants, many of them recurrent and all but about 15% for revenue costs, to a wide range of Richmond charities.

Most funds are directed at organisations, but about a third go to individuals.

General The charity was established in its current form in 1968. The original 'lands' were a gift from King George III in 1786 to be used for the benefit of the poor.

In 1997/98 the trust held assets worth £33 million, £15 million of it in the form of property. Income was £1.3 million from which £699,000 was paid out in grants –

The charity publishes the following guidance for applicants:

'Every year the trustees make grants of about £400,000 (excluding grants to individuals for Education and for financial hardship) to organisations which cater to the needs of the people of Richmond, Kew and North Sheen in the following spheres covered by the charity's object:

1. The relief of the aged, impotent and poor.
2. The relief of distress and sickness.
3. The provision and support of facilities for recreation or other leisure time occupation.

'Even if your organisation is located outside our benefit area it may still qualify for a grant if a significant part of its work covers the area or if a number of its members are resident there.

'The amount of money sought in grant applications every year exceeds the available resources of the charity and therefore it may not always be possible to make a grant even if the application conforms with the criteria of the trustees.

'Most grants are in the region of £500-£5,000.

'Some grants recur annually but, except in some rare instances, the trustees are not prepared to make firm commitments to provide ongoing funding for organisations although they may indicate a willingness to continue to give help if their resources permit.

'The trustees have made a policy

decision to allocate their income resources to the provision of revenue grants. There is, however, a limited sum of accumulated reserves which is available as contribution towards funding capital projects including new building and major repair works. As a general rule, £15,000 is the maximum grant given in this category.'

In 1995/96 the charity decided to adopt, as its main objective for the year, 'a review of our policies and priorities for grant making'. In 1996/97 it reported the results – a decision to carry on pretty much as before, following an unsurprising endorsement of its present practices from 'organisations receiving grants from us'.

The trust made the following payments in 1997/98 in its various fields of interest:

Education	£129,000	(11%)
Social and Medical Welfare	£109,000	(9%)
Community Centres and Organisations	£108,000	(9%)
The Relief of Poverty	£106,000	(9%)
Mentally Ill and Handicapped	£65,000	(8%)
Care of the Elderly and Heating Vouchers	£83,000	(2%)
Youth and Community Work	£31,000	(2%)
Physically Handicapped	£24,000	(2%)
Music and the Arts	£15,000	(1%)

Unfortunately the 1997/98 Report arrived too late for complete re-drafting of the entry. The following grants information relates to 1996/97.

Typically, about 90% of the revenue grants are to organisations that were also supported in the previous year.

Education

£19,000 was allocated to the Education Projects Fund which provided 12 organisations with grants of between £500 and £6,000 to support their work in local schools. The rest of the expenditure under this heading was for programmes of grants for the education of individuals.

Social and Medical Welfare

90% of the grants were made to groups previously supported, though four 'newcomers' shared a total £11,000. There were 22 grants in all, ranging from £125 to £16,000 (typically £3,000). Organisations providing counselling services fared well; RELATE received £6,600 and Off the Record (youth counselling) nearly won the record grant with £8,250. That distinction, however, went to the Princess Alice Hospice which received an exceptional £16,000.

Community Centres and Organisations

There was just one new support grant of £3,000 to Richmond and Kingston Accessible Transport. The Cambrian Centre received £35,000 (£34,000 in 1995/96) and ten other 'regulars' also received continuing support.

The Relief of Poverty

Most of the funds were given out in the form of small grants to help individuals in need of urgent assistance.

Mentally Ill and Handicapped

Support was almost identical to past years. 10 organisations received funds totalling £55,650. A total of £33,600 of this went to RABMIND and a further £11,750 to MENCAP.

Capital grants

£86,000 was committed in nine one-off grants, the largest being to Richmond Homes for Life Trust (£25,000) and £15,000 each Richmond CAB (for moving costs) and WELCARE (for new premises).

Exclusions The following exclusions are outlined in the charity's Notes to Guide Organisations Seeking Grants:

Projects and organisations located outside the Benefit Area unless it can be demonstrated that a substantial number of residents from the benefit from their work.

National Charities (even if based in the Benefit Area) except for that part of their work which caters specifically for the Area.

Applications The charity publishes the following advice:

'If you would like some clarification on whether you organisation would qualify for a grant, please contact the Clerk to the Trustees (0181 948 5701) who will be able to give you guidance. You will also be given an application form.

'When you send in your application form be sure that you have filled in all sections and that you have enclosed all the documents requested.

'If your organisation or project is new you will probably need to write a covering letter giving relevant background and explanation.

'On receipt of you application the Clerk to the trustees will evaluate it and may wish to ask further questions before submitting it to the trustees for their consideration. You may be assured that all eligible applications will be put before the trustees.

'Trustees' meetings are held every five weeks at which eligible applications received 14 days before are considered by the trustees. They may decide that they need further information before they can make a decision regarding a grant.

'You will be advised by letter within 10 days of the meeting whether or not your application has been successful. If you wish to know before that you may of course telephone the Clerk.

'If your organisation or project is new to the charity you will be asked to sign a brief document in which the terms and conditions of the grant are set out. On receipt of the signed agreement a cheque will be sent for the appropriate amount.'

The Robertson Trust

£4,569,000 (1997/98)

General, mainly in Scotland

PO box 15330 Glasgow GI 2YL
Tel: 0141-352 6620 Fax 0141 352 6617

Correspondent Sir Lachlan Maclean, Secretary.

Trustees J A R Macphail, Chairman; J J G Good; K D M Cameron; B McNeil; T M Lawrie.

Beneficial area UK, especially Scotland

Information available Annual accounts are available, with details of eight major grants only.

General The trust describes its grant making as benefiting 'education in universities and schools, care of the elderly, the young and the infirm, medical research, the arts, disability, drugs preventions, public service and national heritage.

In 1997/98 the trust received the low income of £4.6 million from assets of £182.5 million. Donations of £4.6 million went to 280 charities. The trust received over 1,000 applications, making the success rate about 1 in 4. The annual report notes that '24 grants were for £1,000 or less, 76 for £10,000 or more and the majority being in the £4,000 £10,000 bracket. Education received the largest amount of funding which included grants for capital projects at several Scottish Universities including Edinburgh, Heriot Watt, Strathclyde and Paisley.'

Only the nine grants in excess of 2% of gross income are listed, the minimum required by Scottish Law; these represent about 56% of total grant making.

They were as follows:

Herriot Watt University	*£700,000*
University of Strathclyde	*£500,000*
University of Paisley	*£300,000*
University of Edinburgh- Royal (Dick) School of Veterinary Studies	*£277,000*
Royal College of Surgeons	*£250,000*
Calton Athletic Recovery Group	*£176,000*
The Piping Trust	*£150,000*
The Robertson Scholarship Trust	*£115,000*
The Medical Council on Alcoholism	*£93,000*

With one exception, the purpose of these grants is not disclosed.

The annual report notes that its donations 'help some of the most needy and deprived members of our society'. There is little information available about how this is done, presumably mainly through the 272 undisclosed grants. Indeed, if the statement is accepted, the report and accounts do not seem to give a true and fair view of what the charity is doing. As the report also contains a complaint about the increased tax burden the trust will soon bear, and bases this on its help for these 'needy and deprived' people, it seems that it must itself bear part of the blame for this tax change being introduced with so little public complaint. Why should the public seek to support charitable activities of which they are allowed to know so little?

The one exception to this is a single short reference to a seemingly interesting project: 'The trustees continued with their support for Carlton Athletic Recovery Group with an increased donation of £176,000 to fund their Drug Awareness Programme that is now running in both secondary and primary schools in Scotland. The trustees welcome the emphasis being put on the prevention of young people being involved in drugs, but see little evidence of increased financial support coming to the providers of this service.'

In practice it is believed in Scotland that most of the trust's grants are quite widely spread, and that the few, exceptionally large, that are listed above, are not representative of the spread of smaller grants. But any estimate of the extent to which this may so is speculation.

The financial situation of the trust is unusual. Its endowment is held mainly in the form of shares in Edrington investments, which it isn't free to sell. These showed strong capital growth in 1997/98, of £12 million, which the trust could not realise, even if the trustees so wished. As a result the trust is accumulating as much as using its wealth. Its income was just £4.6 million while its net worth was £182 million, a sum which might normally be expected to generate a return of over £9 million a year.

Applications Applications in writing to the correspondent

Applications should include the applicant's charity number and a copy of their latest set of accounts.

Trustees meet six times a year in January, March, May, July, September and November

Mrs L D Rope Third Charitable Settlement

£440,000 (1996/97)

Religion, education, relief of poverty, general

Crag Farm, Boyton, Near Woodbridge, Suffolk IP12 3LH
Tel: 01473-288987; Fax: 01473-217182

Correspondent Crispin M Rope

Trustees Mrs Lucy D Rope, Jeremy P W Heal; Crispin M Rope.

Beneficial area UK and overseas, but mostly in south-east Suffolk.

Information available Exemplary report and accounts. Model 'Guidelines for Grant Seekers'.

Summary This is a modest but engaging trust, the great majority of whose funds are already committed to projects it has initiated itself or to on-going relationships. Nevertheless this entry may be worth reading, if only to see a model of good practice. Its written materials are exceptional both in giving the impression that the charity would very much like to help, if it possibly could, and in describing a wholly personal range of charitable interests. The 'guidelines' are reprinted below. Other trusts may also be interested in obtaining a copy of the narrative annual report, if only to see how the demanding requirements of the SORP can be effectively met.

However, except for charities in south east Suffolk, the amount of money available for responding to unsolicited applications is so slight as to make application here a low priority for most organisations.

The major on-going programme for some years has been the Science and Human Dimension Project based at Jesus College, Cambridge

Guidelines for applicants
Background information

'Our charitable trust was founded in 1984. We are based near Ipswich, in Suffolk, and take a keen interest in helping people from our local area, although we do also help other charities and individuals throughout the UK and overseas.

'Roughly 75% of our grants are used to develop our own projects each year but there are funds left over for people who write in to us. The figures that follow will give you some idea of the size of our trust.

'For the year to April 1997:

'Our income was £461,773 and we spent £437,237 on charitable work whilst our assets totalled £14,849,000.

'We have written these guidelines to help you understand what sort of applications may be likely to appeal to our trustees. We don't like disappointing you and we don't particularly like having to tell you that your application was unsuitable. Having only a small staff, we would much rather spend time making better grants to the most deserving cases. This makes our work worthwhile. So, we would ask that you take some time to read through the following pages carefully.

'Finally, please bear in mind that we receive many more applications than we could possibly help. Whilst you may believe that your request can seem well fitted to a single one or perhaps two of our categories, it is often those applications that meet a combination of requirements that are most successful.

Our priorities

'The ... charity ... may give to a variety of charitable causes. Our trust deed gives the following descriptions:

Relief of poverty

'Support for a number of causes and individuals where the trustees have longer term knowledge and experience, particularly those both in the UK and in the Third World who are little catered for by other charities or by grant or benefits from governments or other authorities or are in particularly deprived areas.

Advancement of education

'Support for a proposed airship museum; support for Catholic schools in the general area of Ipswich; and projects relating to the interaction of mathematics and physical science with philosophy.

Advancement of religion

'Support for the Roman Catholic religion and ecumenical work, both generally, and for specific institutions connected historically with the families of William Oliver and Alice Jolly and their descendants.

General charitable purposes

'Public and other charitable purposes in the general region of south east Suffolk and in particular the parish of Kesgrave and the areas surrounding it, including Ipswich.

'In considering many applications since 1984, our trustees have forged policies to help them stay close to the wishes of the founder (Still happily with the trust. Ed). Their judgement is based on a desire to help where it is most needed, particularly those charities and individuals who find it hard to find funding from other sources or who come from the most deprived areas of the UK and overseas.

Your application may be considered if ...

'Successful unsolicited applications usually display some or all of the following features:

1. Size. We very much prefer to encourage charities who work at 'grassroots' level within their community. Such charities are unlikely to have benefited greatly from grant funding from local, national (including funds from the national lottery) or European authorities. They are also less likely to be as wealthy in comparison with other charities who attract popular support on a national basis. The charities we assist usually cannot afford to pay for the professional help other charities may use to raise funds.
2. Volunteers. Our trustees welcome applications from charities that are able to show they have a committed and proportionately large volunteer force.
3. Administration. Related to point 2. above, the less a charity spends on paying for its own administration, particularly as far as staff salaries are concerned, the more likely it is to be considered by us.
4. Charities qualifying under 1. 2. and

3. above that work in any of the following areas of interest:
   a. Helping people who struggle to live on very little income, including the homeless.
   b. Helping people who live in deprived inner city and rural areas of the UK, particularly young people who lack the opportunities that may be available elsewhere.
   c. Helping charities in our immediate local area of south east Suffolk.
   d. Helping to support family life.
   e. Helping disabled people.
   f. Helping Roman Catholic charities and ecumenical projects.
5. How we can help. Grants made to charities outside our local area are usually one-off and small (in the range £100 to £750).
6. Unlike many trusts, we can consider helping people on a personal basis. We give priority, as we do with charities, to people struggling to live on little income, with an emphasis on those from our local area.'

Exclusions The following are the main categories of exclusion for unsolicited applications; they are spelt out in more detail in the guidelines than is possible here:

Overseas projects (the trust uses CAFOD to offer most of its overseas help)

National charities

Replacement of statutory funding

Requests for core funding

Buildings

Medical research, health care, palliative care, except perhaps in the local area

Students, except for a few foreign post graduate science students in the last stages of their studies.

Schools, except in the local area.

Environmental charities and animal welfare

The arts

Matched funding

Individuals – repayment of debts.

Applications 'Please send us a concise letter (preferably one side of A4) explaining the main details of your request. Please always send your most recent accounts and a budgeted breakdown of the sum you are looking to raise. We shall also need to know whether you have applied to other funding sources and whether you have been successful elsewhere. Your application should tell us who your trustees are and include a daytime telephone number.

'Individuals should write a concise letter including details of household income and expenses, daytime telephone number

and the name of at least one personal referee.'

The Rose Foundation

£659,000 (1996/97)

General

28 Crawford Street, London W1H 1PL
Tel: 0171-262 1155;
Fax: 0171- 724 2044

Correspondent The Trustees

Trustees John Rose; Paul Rose; Martin Rose; Alan Rose.

Beneficial area UK, mainly Greater London.

Information available Full Accounts with comprehensive narrative report.

Summary: This family foundation gives grants almost exclusively for capital projects to charities in the greater London area. Aside from financial donations it also gives professional advice to charities planning building work.

General The foundation's charitable expenditure has been rising steadily over the past few years. In 1996/97 it made total donations of £659,250 (from an income of £927,573), an increase of 176% over those made in 1993/94. The very high management and administration costs of £210,000, or 31% of the value of grants, may be misreported in the accounts, as the annual report refers to a member of staff offering professional services to a beneficiary charity. Such costs should be shown as Charitable Expenditure. Investment management fees of £70,000 were also high at 0.6% of the value of investments.

In response to a trustee continuing to live in the US (Alan Rose), the Foundation established the New Amsterdam Charitable Foundation in 1996/97. NACF receives funds from the Rose Foundation and makes grants within the States ($113,000 in 1996/97).

The Rose Foundation outlines its policy thus:

'Notwithstanding that monetary donations are occasionally made, the main emphasis of our work is to undertake building projects for other charities. A policy of seeking small self contained projects of between £5,000 and £20,000 has now been adopted. These will usually be located in London or the Home Counties, in order that the trustees can effectively monitor their progress. The trustees' policy is to offer assistance where needed with the design and construction process, ensuring wherever possible that costs are minimised and that the participation of other contributing bodies can be utilised to maximum benefit of the scheme.'

In addition the trustees have offered their time and property experience to other charities with administrative problems.

During 1996/97 the foundation committed funds to an eclectic array of causes including an arts gallery, schools, the NHS and a theatre company. A total of £629,750 was paid out in capital grants with a further £29,500 in small donations. The Royal Academy of Arts was awarded £125,000 for the restoration of Gallery No.IX and the trustees hope that this will act as a catalyst for other donations. The second highest payment (£15,000) was to an independent school in Hendon to pay for a playground rebuilding scheme.

The foundation receives written and telephone applications. Decisions are taken by the trustees who meet informally virtually every day and formally by regular arrangement. Commitments to small building projects (£5,000 to £20,000) to be undertaken in the following year are made in a meeting usually in May. Other meetings are concerned with the progress of existing and future (ie: further than a year away) projects. The foundation monitors the progress of the projects to which they contribute funds and summarises this in their annual report.

The Rose Foundation is very much a family enterprise which clearly takes a strong interest in the outcomes of their professional and financial assistance.

Exclusions Income support, contributions to running expenses, and viability studies.

Applications In writing to the correspondent. Commitments to small building projects are considered in a meeting which takes place around May.

The Jacob

Rothschild GAM Charitable Trust

£1,608,000 (1995/96)

Heritage

14 St James' Place,
London, SW1A 1NP
Tel: 0171-493 8111

Correspondent Miss S A Gallagher, Secretary

Trustees Lord Rothschild; Lady Rothschild; Hannah Brookfield; Beth Tomassini; Nils Taube; M E Hatch; S J P Trustee Company Ltd.

Beneficial area UK.

Information available Accounts up to 1995/96 only on file at the Charity Commission in September 1998.

General Most of the £1.82 million income for 1995/96 was generated through donations from an overseas charitable trust, the Waltus Trust. Assets were £1.97 million and grant giving totalled £1.61 million. The accounts were unaudited.

As in the case of another Rothschild family trust, Caritas, total grant giving was concentrated on a single activity, with £1.6 million being given for the restoration of Waddesdon Manor. Most of the grant giving in previous years has also gone to the same cause (in 1994/95 Waddesdon Manor received a grant of £2.9 million from total donations of £2.93 million).

The remaining three grants went to the Butrint Foundation (£31,000); Portobello Trust (£2,000); and the Whitechapel Art Gallery (£5,000).

Applications To the correspondent, but with only four grants in the year the chances of success for unsolicited applications seem slight.

The Rowan Trust

£505,000 (1995/96)

Third world development, social welfare

c/o Coopers and Lybrand, 9 Greyfriars Road, Reading RG1 1JG
Tel: 0118 959 7111

Correspondent The Secretary

Trustees H Russell; C Jones.

Beneficial area UK, especially Merseyside, and overseas.

Information available In the summer of 1998 the most recent report and accounts available were those for the year to October 1996. Good Guidelines for applicants are available from the trust.

Summary The trust gives two thirds of its money to overseas projects and one third to social welfare projects in the UK. Most grants are for amounts between £1,000 and £10,000, though they can be for as much as £50,000. However the larger grants usually go to charities with which the trust has an existing connection.

The trust is open to radical projects and organisations.

General The trust 'gives a mix of one-off grants and recurrent ones. It has regularly given grants to a limited number of large national organisations and development agencies, but also gives smaller grants to much smaller organisations and locally based projects.

'The trust will support advocacy and challenges to powerful economic forces, on behalf of the poor, the powerless or the left out, especially if they themselves are enabled to participate in articulating a vision of economic justice.'

For the UK grants programme, 'the trust focuses on projects which will benefit disadvantaged groups and neighbourhoods in such spheres as:

- housing and homelessness
- social and community care
- education
- employment/unemployment
- after-care
- welfare rights
- community development
- environmental improvement.

'The trustees are interested in projects which are concerned with self-help or advocacy as well as service provision. They also look for:

- user and community involvement in the planning and delivery of the project
- a multi-disciplinary approach
- emphasis on empowerment.'

For the overseas projects, the trust focuses on projects 'which will benefit disadvantaged groups and communities in such spheres as:

- agriculture – especially crop and livestock production and settlement schemes
- community development – especially

appropriate technology and village industries

- health – especially preventative medicine, water supplies, blindness
- education – especially adult education and materials
- environmental – especially protecting and sustaining ecological systems at risk
- human rights – especially of women, children and disabled
- fair trade – especially relating to primary producers and workers.

'The trustees are interested in projects which

- involve the local community in the planning and implementation
- invest in people through training and enabling
- have a holistic concern for all aspects of life ... .'

In 1995/96 the trust made 41 grants totalling £325,000 for work overseas and 34 grants worth £180,000 to UK organisations.

In the overseas grants the long-standing relationship continued with Christian Aid (£50,000) and Intermediate Technology (£52,000). UNICEF received £20,000, Tools for Self Reliance, £12,500, and grants for £10,000 each went to ADD, the Fair Trade Foundation, Kaloko Trust, Lepra, Leprosy Mission, Motivation, Rainforest Foundation, and the UK Foundation for the South Pacific.

In Britain there were only four grants of £10,000 or more, to Barnardo's, Family Service Units and the Children's Society, all longstanding beneficiaries, but the largest grant was to the PSS in Liverpool (£20,000). About one third of all these grants appeared to have a Merseyside connection, such as those for Liverpool Spastics Fellowship or Wirral Music project (£1,000 each).

Exclusions The trust does not give grants for

- individuals
- buildings or building work
- academic research.

Applications In writing to the correspondent. No application forms are issued.

Applications should include: a brief description (two sides of A4) of, and a budget for, the work for which the grant is sought; the organisation's annual report and accounts; and an indication of the core costs of the organisation.

The applications need to provide the trustees with information about

- the aims and objectives of the

organisation

- its structure and organisational capacity
- what the funds are being requested for and how much is being requested
- how progress of the work will be monitored and evaluated.

Unfortunately the volume of applications received precludes acknowledgement on receipt or notifying unsuccessful applicants. The trust is unable to make donations to applicants who are not, or do not have links with a UK registered charity.

Trustees meet in January and July.

The Joseph Rowntree Charitable Trust

£3,631,000 (1997)

Poverty, economic and racial justice, handling conflict, Ireland, South Africa, democratic process and the abuse of power, corporate responsibility

The Garden House, Water End, York YO30 6WQ
Tel: 01904-627810; Fax: 01904-651990;
e-mail: jrct@jrct.org.uk;
Website: http://www.jrct.org.uk

Correspondent Steven Burkeman, Secretary

Trustees Andrew Gunn, Chair; Ruth McCarthy, Vice-Chair; Margaret Bryan; Christine Davies; Beverley Meeson; Marion McNaughton; Roger Morton; Vas Shend'ge; David Shutt; Peter Stark.

Beneficial area UK, Republic of Ireland and Southern (mainly South) Africa.

Information available Full accounts are filed with the Charity Commission. The trust also publishes a triennial report (latest 1994/96) plus a basic guidance leaflet for applicants and a note on grant/loan conditions. In addition, sheets are available on each of the programme areas. Updated information on grants' priorities and application deadlines are available on the JRCT web site.

Summary Grants, usually for core or

project costs, only in the fields of work shown above (and described in more detail below). Support may be for three or more years, but is seldom for more than £50,000 a year and is usually for much less. Many of the voluntary organisations in these specialised areas are quite heavily dependent on the trust's support, but new bodies are also frequently funded. The trust is much more approachable than the very extensive guidance material below may suggest, but it is plagued by applications that fall outside the very specific remits it has set for itself.

General This unusual trust decides fairly precisely what kinds of work it wants to see carried out, and sets this out in the considerable detail to be found below. Typically only about one in seven applications is successful, but this is a misleading figure. Most of these refusals are for applications that fall clearly outside the trust's extremely specific guidelines. For projects within the guidelines, something between a third and a half will typically be supported.

The very lengthy guidance to applicants, re-printed below in the main text and under the heading 'Applications', makes an exceedingly daunting read for those unused to making formal funding applications and, in these editors' view, risks deterring applicants from whom the trust would like to hear. Organisations which are sure they are working in the trust's specific fields of interest, having read the Guidelines, are recommended to write briefly to the trust at an early stage. The people concerned are interested and helpful – 'the difficulties began to fall away when we talked to them' .

The following 'programme by programme' notes, taken from the application pack, describes the trust's various programmes. For each programme we have given the total amount paid out in 1997 and in the previous year, and have added a paragraph identifying some of the more significant or interesting grants made in 1997.

The Racial Justice Programme

(1997, £586,000; 1996 £486,000)

'The trust seeks to create within the UK, a harmonious multi-racial and multi-cultural society based on the principles of justice and equality of opportunity. The trust seeks to work towards this aim through all its grant-making fields, in addition to its specialist racial justice programme. Currently this programme supports projects and individuals working to:

- promote issues of racial justice with

policy shapers, decision makers and opinion formers;

- empower black and ethnic minority people to contribute to policy development on the basis of their experience in meeting needs; and to participate at planning and decision making levels;
- monitor and challenge racism and racial injustice whether relating to colour or culture;
- explore ways to eliminate racial violence and harassment;
- promote the rights of black and ethnic minority people to equal opportunities;
- promote communication and co-operation between different racial groups.

'The trust seeks to encourage work aimed at furthering its objectives in the European Union. The trust expects that work undertaken on a EU wide basis will attract funds from sources in several EU member states. In particular the trust has supported projects working to:

- promote awareness amongst policy makers and within the European institutions of the need to protect the human rights of minority communities, asylum seekers and migrants;
- research and disseminate information concerning current EU policies and their impact on minority communities;
- provide a forum for NGOs from all EU countries to share experiences on matters relating to race and immigration and to build alliances on shared interests;
- work for a more accountable and open process for developing EU policy in relation to race and immigration.

'A small fund is available to support work on asylum and refugee issues. Grants have been made for work to:

- research and disseminate information on the impact of current policies on refugees and asylum seekers
- research into the likely future direction of asylum policy in the UK and the EU and into how this might be influenced to create a rationale and humane policy
- safeguard the rights of refugees through advice and advocacy services relating to legal protection in the North of England and in Scotland.

'The trust welcomes applications from black and ethnic minority groups and from multi-racial groups working in these areas. The trust encourages and looks for involvement of black and ethnic minority people at all levels of the projects and organisations it supports.'

The trust works at a local level in West Yorkshire, covered by a separate leaflet available from the office above.

Grants approved in 1997 included £75,000 for the core costs over three years of the Society of Black Lawyers, £46,000 to enable Cardiff University Law School to research traveller law reform, and £15,000 for a coordinator for West Yorkshire Black Governors Support Service. Small grants included £4,000 for the Green Alliance and £1,000 for the Living Heritage Centre in Leeds.

Handling conflict and promoting peaceful alternatives

(1997, £775,000; 1996 £781,000)

'Joseph Rowntree expressed the hope that the trusts he founded in 1904 should *sound a clear note with regard to the great scourges of humanity, especially with regard to war* ... Even if such guidance had not been bequeathed to them, it would be surprising if the trustees of JRCT, as Quakers, did not see this as an issue to which a significant part of trust resources should be devoted.

'The trust's Quaker heritage predisposes trustees to support a nonviolent approach to the management and resolution of conflict, and to the creation of just and peaceful alternatives. Trustees recognise that progress towards this ideal is likely to be made in small steps within the framework of an overall vision of a just society. This has led them to support work which demonstrates

- how mediation and other processes can help to reduce interpersonal, intergroup, and international conflict;
- how individuals can learn to handle potentially violent situations in transforming ways;
- how the degree of violence can at least be reduced in the handling of disputes.

'More specifically, in recent times, the trust has supported projects which have focused on the following issues:

- training and support for people involved in dealing with conflict and oppression, in a variety of settings: in the home, in the community, and at national and international level;
- demonstrating peaceful alternatives in relation to conflict at a local level;
- policy work on the social problem of violence as experienced by individuals, eg. children at the hand of carers or women at the hand of men known to them;
- the generation of balanced

information for UK and European legislators and policy shapers on constructive ways to achieve international security;

- work on the role of the UN in handling international disputes;
- the use of sophisticated information technology to improve the flow of information about international disputes for people working for peace;
- work on controlling or eliminating specific forms of warfare, such as the threat or use of chemical and biological weapons; nuclear weapons; and land mines;
- in certain cases, work on specific major conflicts (the trust has a major programme of work on the conflict on the island of Ireland, about which details are available separately; and has funded work on violence in South Africa).

'While the trust sometimes supports university-based research in these areas, it always looks for a firm and precise link to influencing policy and ultimately practice; Trustees are not interested in supporting purely academic research.'

Grants in 1997 included three awards totalling £126,000 for the Department of Peace Studies at Bradford University, £180,000 for the core costs of Saferworld over three years, and £5,000 to enable Felicity Arbuthnot to research depleted uranium weapons.

South Africa

(1997, £331,000; 1996 £334,000)

'Joseph Rowntree created the charitable trust at a time when much attention was focused on South Africa and the Boer revolt against British rule in the region. The Rowntree family incurred much public displeasure at the time (the Rowntree café in Scarborough was stoned by rioters) because of its support of the Boers rather than the British. ... A full grant-making programme began in 1964 and has continued since then.

'The main thrust of current trust funding is the support of work on conflict management and on the building of a human rights culture in the new South Africa. The trust support work in both urban and rural settings. In its conflict resolution work, the trust prioritises support to projects in Kwa-Zulu/Natal. The trust considers applications from South Africa and does not generally fund work in South Africa originating in the UK.

'In recent times, trust grants have focused on the following issues:

- conflict management in urban and rural settings;
- the use of paralegal training and legal

mechanisms to empower farm-workers and other marginalised communities;
- policy research on South Africa's security and defence arrangements;
- industrial and community mediation;
- work which focuses on the Truth and Reconciliation commission;
- the promotion of the constitutional rights of lesbians and gays;
- work to combat the abuse of women and sexual harassment.

'The trust is an associate member of Interfund, an international donor consortium with a staffed office in Johannesburg. Interfund provides investigative and monitoring services to the trust.

'While the trust works almost exclusively in South Africa, on occasion it is willing to fund work elsewhere in Southern Africa, provided that this fits other trust criteria.'

Grants in 1997 included about £100,000 over four years for the core costs of Cape Town's Centre for Conflict Resolution and about £60,000 for the Association for Rural Advancement in Pietermaritzburg.

Democratic process and the abuse of power

(1997, £537,000; 1996 £609,000)

'... The trust's current work on democracy is rooted in Joseph Rowntree's concern that his philanthropy should 'change the face of England'.

'Change remains the keynote of our approach to democracy today: change to bring about a greater understanding of democratic culture and the (mutual) responsibilities of democratic process throughout the United Kingdom; change to counter abuses of power. Our funding has focused on work in the following areas:

- the nuts and bolts of a new constitutional settlement, to tackle the weaknesses which result from our unwritten constitution;
- legal provision for freedom of information;
- the argument for a Bill of Rights and discussion of its content;
- the importance of local democracy as a counter to centralisation of power;
- ways to tackle the politicisation of the civil service;
- independent scrutiny of proposed legislation;
- the right relationship between the Executive and the Judiciary;
- alternatives to the present 'first past the post' electoral system;
- the need to protect and enhance civil

liberties and human rights;
- how to rectify the perception that people are subjects, rather than citizens with concomitant rights and obligations.

'In the recent past the trust has been able to support many of the major research and educational initiatives aimed at addressing these issues. The trust recognises that these central provisions are necessary but not sufficient pre-conditions for a fully democratic culture. It is also necessary that people should take seriously their democratic rights and obligations, exercising them so that they become real rather than merely theoretical. This may be achieved through educational work, or other kinds of 'bottom up' initiatives.

'The trust's major – and long-term – project in its Democracy Programme is the Democratic Audit of the UK, a programme commissioned by the trust from the University of Essex and the Scarman Trust, working jointly. The Democratic Audit has published the first of two major reports on the quality of democracy and political freedom in the UK, as well as a number of small reports on specific aspects of democracy in the UK.

'Applications to the trust should demonstrate clearly how the work is likely to make an impact. The trust is unlikely to support purely academic work in this area.'

Grants in 1997 included £62,000 for the Office for Standards in Inspection to commission an independent review of the OFSTED school inspection system and £50,000 over two years for the Fawcett Society.

Quaker and other religious concerns

(1997, £335,000; 1996, £396,000)

'The trustees are Quakers. Decision-making and practice are based on Quaker values ... The trust seeks to foster the development of ... a "powerful Quaker ministry", offered as inclusively as possible. This may include helping people to understand spiritual experiences, or working out Quaker-based responses to problems of our time.

'Grants are made to Quakers and to others in Britain. Trustees may find it easier to judge applications from Quakers, but wish to encourage others to apply. Work being done by those who are not Quakers is more likely to be considered when it reflects Quaker values, and when the applicant feels that their work is marginal to their own religious group.

'The programme supports individuals

and small groups.

'This programme is not intended to support individual Quakers who wish to spend some time 'travelling in the ministry' or otherwise strengthening the life of Britain Yearly Meeting. A special fund is available for this purpose.'

Grants in 1997 included £240,000 over three years for the Quaker Woodbrooke College, £52,000 for the Inter Faith Network, and £60,000 to provide the Britain Yearly Meeting of the Quakers with a Parliamentary Liaison Assistant.

The Ireland programmes

Northern Ireland (1997, £349,000; 1996 £361,000)

'For more than twenty years the trust has operated a specialist programme in Northern Ireland in support of work for peace, justice and reconciliation.

'Over the years the trust's programme has tended to focus on longer term community initiatives. More recently it has engaged more directly with the political conflict. Currently the trust's programme supports projects and individuals working to:

- promote new ideas to sustain the democratic process and democratic accountability;
- encourage accountability, openness and responsiveness in government, government agencies and the civil service;
- build new community structures to enable citizens to participate in the democratic process;
- protect and enhance civil liberties and human rights;
- promote dialogue, understanding and cooperation across political and religious divides;
- challenge sectarianism;
- promote nonviolence and creative ways to handle conflict;
- celebrate difference and value pluralism;
- tackle poverty, inequality and social exclusion;
- address contentious issues and develop new thinking on how to resolve these;
- explore new ideas about the future social, economic and political relationships within the island of Ireland, between Britain and Ireland, and within the European Union.

'The trust is interested in supporting work which addresses the root causes of the conflict in Northern Ireland and which is aimed at influencing policy. Much of the trust's work has been directed towards providing infrastructure, technical assistance and support for those working at a local level. A strong focus of the trust's programme has been on women's initiatives working in the areas outline above. The trust will need to be convinced that other funds, such as those from statutory agencies and the European Union, are not available for work which it funds.'

Grants in 1997 included £62,000 for the Kairos Project and £20,000 to enable the Deramore Group to compile a database of all the deaths caused by political violence in Northern Ireland.

Ireland (Republic) (1997, £90,000; 1996 £92,000)

'This programme supports projects and individuals working to:

- promote the concept of citizenship, the ability of all citizens to participate in the democratic process, and the freedom and rights of the individual;
- encourage accountability, openness and responsiveness in government, government agencies and the civil service;
- promote new ideas to sustain the democratic process;
- promote dialogue, understanding and cooperation across religious and political divides;
- explore new ideas about the future social, economic and political development of the island, north and south.

'The trust spends about UK£100,000 per annum in the Republic. Grants are restricted to those programmes that the trust believes will make a difference. Two types of grant are offered:

Strategic Grants

'A small number of strategic grants are offered to encourage organisational development and to raise the effectiveness and profile of key organisations. These grants are likely to fall within a range of UK£6,000 to UK£15,000 per annum and will be offered for a maximum of three years.

Project Grants

'A number of projects grants are offered for work such as – action research; the dissemination of research findings; conferences, seminars, and networking events; and publications. These are one-off grants and are likely to fall within the range of UK£500 and UK£6,000.'

Grants in 1997 included 352,000 for a Traveller Mediation Service, £40,000 for the core costs of the Irish Penal Reform Trust and £20,000 for the Irish Council for Civil Liberties.

Poverty and economic justice (1997, £275,000; 1996, £270,000)

'The trust is committed to the pursuit of a more just society in which significant sections of the population are no longer marginalised or excluded by poverty. While recognising that any significant change will only come about through the actions of government, the trust believes there is nevertheless a role for an independent charitable trust.

'The work in which the trust is interested may be concerned with current practice, or with developing new thinking and policy. The trust wishes to balance work which is primarily reactive to contemporary events, with work of a more visionary, radical or long-term nature.

'The trust wishes to make grants which tackle the causes of poverty, rather than making poverty easier to live with. It recognises that the causes of poverty vary and it is therefore appropriate to look at a variety of responses.

'The trust supports legally charitable programmes in the United Kingdom through the provision of core and project funding for organisations and individuals working in the following fields:

- raising the profile of issues of poverty and economic justice on the public agenda; pursuing ways of increasing public commitment to a more equitable society, with less extreme differentials in income and wealth;
- work focused on influencing the policy debate. This may include setting out the intellectual case for economic justice; providing independent, authoritative and reliable data; examining the forces and processes which impoverish and exclude; developing alternative policy options; suggesting how the results of research can be translated into policy and practice;
- enabling the experience of those who live in poverty to influence public opinion, policy and practice;
- promoting contact and mutual support between different groups of people who are more liable than others to experience poverty (including women, black and ethnic minorities, the elderly, and people with disabilities) – which are more liable than other to experience deprivation and poverty, to strengthen their position by recognising their common experience and by co-operating;
- promoting contact and mutual support between local, national and European initiatives;

- bringing test cases in order to clarify the law and publicise its consequences.

'Most grants will be made for work which is being done nationally, or which is of national importance. The trust particularly wishes to support work which is innovative and which challenges current assumptions that poverty is inevitable and acceptable.'

Grants in 1997 included £120,000 over two years for the Citizens' Income Trust, £90,000 over three years for Church Action on Poverty and £22,000 for the PR work of the New Economics Foundation.

Corporate responsibility (1997, £232,000; 1996, £201,000)

'For some years now the trust has responded to those who have sought to do work on the interaction of private and public organisations, their employees, their owners and those whom they exist to serve with the aim of improving their utility to society in both the short and the long term. This cannot simply be left to the market, where there is often an unequal balance of power and the knowledge necessary to take optimum decisions is not available to all.

'The trust's funding under this heading has encompassed issues such as the rights of whistle-blowers; the responsibilities of public companies to their various stake-holders – shareholders, customers, employees, and the communities in which they operate; and work on ethical investment.

'A number of projects funded by the trust under this heading (and some under other headings, such as Democratic Process/Abuse of Power) have been concerned to gather and disseminate information about the activities of companies and government agencies, while also encouraging those organisations to make such information more readily accessible themselves.

'This is a relatively small programme for the trust (spending on grants in 1995 amounted to less than £100,000) and in view of other claims on trust resources, this is unlikely to change in the near future.'

Two big awards accounted for most of the 1997 expenditure in this category; £172,000 for Oikos and £110,000 the work on whistle blowing of Public Concern at Work.

Exclusions Generally the trust does not support:

- work in larger, older national charities which have an established constituency of supporters;
- general appeals;
- local work (except in Northern Ireland and parts of Yorkshire);
- building, buying or repairing buildings;
- providing care for elderly people, children, people with learning difficulties, people with physical disabilities, or people using mental health services;
- work in mainstream education, including schools and academic or medical research;
- work on housing and homelessness;
- travel or adventure projects;
- business development and job creation;
- paying off debts;
- work which is not legally charitable;
- work which we believe should be funded by the State, or has been in the recent past;
- work which has already been done;
- work which tries to make a problem easier to live with, rather than getting to the root of it;
- the personal support of individuals in need;
- the arts, except where they are used in the context of the kinds of work which the trust does support.

Refer also to the relevant policy sheets reprinted above which explain more about what the trust may or may not make grants for.

Applications The trust supplies detailed guidelines (new edition September 1996) about how to apply for a grants. Those available in 1998 are largely reprinted above but up to date versions should be obtained and read thoroughly, with the relevant policy sheet/s, before attempting to make an application. You also must complete a registration form, on which you have the task of summarising your project in 50 words.

Write to us, saying what you want to do, and how you will do it.

'This should be no more than four pages, though the budget can be an extra page. You can present your application in whatever form you wish. It helps if the application is easy to read, and if the key points are clear.

Your application should answer the following questions:

The work

- What you want to do, how and why?
- What do you hope will be the results of your work – what difference might it make?

- Where will the work be done?
- How long will the work take?
- Are you or others already doing the work?
- How will you avoid overlap with other organisations?
- How sure are you that this work will produce the results you hope for? What risks are you taking? What might stop the work being effective?
- How do you think your proposal fits in with the relevant JRCT policy guidelines?
- How will the work and the way it is done promote equal opportunities? In particular, how far will the work, directly or indirectly, affect the status or role of women and of men; and of people from different ethnic backgrounds?
- If you don't think equal opportunities are relevant to your work, please say why.

The people involved

- Who will do the work?
- Why are you the right person or organisation to do this work?
- What skills and experience are needed?
- How will the work be supervised or managed?
- Do you have a Management Committee? Who is on it, what is the structure and how does it recruit new members?
- If the work is to be done by a group, how is the organisation structured, and how will this work fit in?
- How does it relate to any parent, subsidiary or associated organisations?
- If you are working on your own, how will you be supported and your work monitored?

Money

- How much will this work cost?
- Are you asking for core funding or a project grant?
- What will you spend the money on?
- If the application involves salary costs, how has the rate been fixed? What is the ratio between the highest and lowest rates of pay in you organisation?
- How much are you asking us for?
- If we are not being asked for, or are not able to give the full amount, how do you hope to raise the rest of the money?
- Are you applying to other funders?
- Will the work need to go on after any grant from us finishes? If so, how will you raise the money?

Evaluation

'How will the work be documented and monitored?

Getting the message across

'How will you ensure that the lessons to be learned from your work will become known by others?

Equal opportunities

'We wish to promote equal opportunities through our grant-making. We want to ensure that grants are used in such a way that work funded includes people regardless of race, colour, gender, sexual orientation, religious affiliation, national origin, age or disability. This applies to the planning and implementation, management and staffing, and benefit or outcome of the work.

The environment

'Have you thought about the effect of your work on the world's finite resources?

Who is responsible for the application?

'Ensure that the application is signed by its author(s) and any others who take primary responsibility for it, indicating in what capacity they do so.

About the budget

'You don't need to detail every item, but you should put costs under clear headings. Show us the actual costs of doing the work in the way that t needs to be done, over the time that it is likely to take. If you want funding for more than one year, please don't include inflation after the first year; if a grant is made it can be adjusted for inflation year by year. The trust does not generally fund work for more than three years at any one time. Please include brief notes to explain how you have calculated the figures. Include details of funds already raised and other sources being approached.

'For organisations, we want to see figures relating to the work you are asking us to fund and for the finances of your organisation as a whole. This applies also to associated organisations.

'For individuals, please include a figure for salary or reimbursement – we do not need a breakdown of your living expenses.'

If an application does not fit within the trust's areas of interest, a letter refusing a grant will be sent, usually within four weeks. Other applications may involve meeting the trustees, taking up references, or asking for confidential external advice. Final decisions are made at quarterly trust meetings. It can take up to six months before a final decision is reached.

Applications need to be sent at least ten weeks before a trust meeting.

The Joseph Rowntree Foundation

£6,770,000 (1998 planned)

Research and development in social policy

The Homestead, 40 Water End,
York YO30 6WP
Tel: 01904-629241; Fax: 01904-620072;
Website: www.jrf.org.uk1

Correspondent Richard Best, Director

Trustees Sir Peter M Barclay; Dame Margaret Booth; Kenneth Dixon; Robert Maxwell; J Nigel Naish; Sir William Utting; Catherine Graham-Harrison.

Beneficial area UK.

Information available Full and exemplary information available from the foundation, including a pack on its research and development programme with extensive guidance notes for applicants. It also publishes 'Search', a magazine of its research activities, and 'Findings', four-page summaries of the results of its projects.

Summary

The charity is the largest independent funder of social science research whose resources do not derive from public funds.

The foundation identifies areas where it believes pioneering development or research of high quality are needed and where the outcome may be of value in fulfilling its founder's famous concern: 'to search out the underlying causes of weakness or evil in the community, rather than remedying their more superficial manifestations,' thus contributing to 'the right measures of human advancement' which, 'over a period of time, could change the face of England'.

The foundation's interests are now UK-wide and cover the fields of housing, social care and and social policy, but within these fields it has specific priorities at any one time. The foundation often takes active steps to find the most appropriate partners with whom to take forward its programmes, but in other cases it considers unsolicited applications. Guidance is given on this in the regularly updated 'Current Priorities' leaflet.

Grants may be of almost any size.

Programmes change, and up-to-date information should be obtained before considering an application (most easily from the web site noted above; one of the few in the trust sector that these editors have found readily accessible), but the current priorities in 1998 were as follows (fuller descriptions of the programmes can be found below):

- *Housing research* Reforming house building; area regeneration; housing and community care; reconciling environmental and community concerns; house condition: repair and maintenance.
- *Social care and disability* Independent living; choices and voices, for people who tend to be excluded from decisions about their own lives; disabled children and young people; race equality; shaping futures, work towards a new vision of rights, entitlements and services.
- *Work, income and social policy* Work and opportunity; work and family life; welfare provision and social security.
- *Young people and families* Prevention and support; family conflict; young people in transition; hearing the voices of children and young people.

The foundation is widely regarded as a model of influential research funding (though the Directory of Social Change and this editor must declare an interest as grant holders themselves, for work on the national lottery). In particular, its extensive and expensive programme of dissemination of the findings of the resesarch that it funds is generally thought to add greatly to the impact of the work itself.

This entry re-prints, without further editorial comment, much of the material available from the foundation in October 1998.

INFORMATION FOR APPLICANTS

How are new projects selected?

Experience has convinced us that we are more likely to have greater impact on changing policy and practice through supporting programmes of work, rather than individual, free-standing projects. The majority of the projects supported by the foundation are part of a broader programme or are follow-on work and there are few opportunities for unsolicited proposals for work outside these programmes to be supported. The form(s) of the programmes vary. There is usually a responsive element within them but this depends in part on how clearly the key issues have been identified. Programmes are likely to follow these forms:

- most commonly, proposals will be invited under a number of themes within which specific topics and approaches are identified. This will often be part of a competitive process with proposals on specific topics requested by a particular date and choices made between them;
- some programmes will contain a number of themes and sub-theme covering a broad canvas within which proposals are sought over a period of time.

As a general rule, the foundation aims to provide full financial support rather than being one of a number of funders. However, where the involvement of another organisation would help the project achieve its aims, joint funding may be considered.

The Joseph Rowntree Foundation

Research & Development Financial Allocations

Research category:	1998 plan	(1997 estimate)
Housing research (inc regeneration)	£1,650,000	(£2,000,000)
Social care and disability	£1,100,000	(£1,120,000)
Young people and families	£1,000,000	(£910,000)
Work, income and social policy	£850,000	(£830,000)
Housing/care development	£670,000	(£590,000)
Support for voluntary charitable sector	£100,000	(£120,000)
Other commitments	£600,000	(£520,000)
Trustee direct commitments	£800,000	(funded separately in 1997)
Total	**£6,770,000**	**(£6,090,000)**

In the context of promoting knowledge-based change, the foundation is keen to fund a variety of different kinds of projects, depending on the state of knowledge about the particular topic. Thus if it is a new area of work we would expect to support some conventional research projects, which might help to define or redefine problems or issues. If these are already clear, we would expect to fund projects concerned to assess 'what works'. This could encompass evaluations of existing services or demonstration projects concerned with testing new ideas and would be expected to incorporate a strong monitoring and evaluation component. If there is evidence, from these projects or elsewhere, of the success of particular interventions, the foundation would wish to support work aimed at developing and extending this good practice to a larger number of organisations or settings.

How does the foundation inform policy and practice?

The foundation expects the reports of project findings to be written in an accessible style, usually telling the 'story' of what has been found out rather than a descriptive account of what the project has done. This report would normally be considerably shorter than the conventional academic report. A note on the Outputs we expect from projects and on Writing for different purposes is in the leaflet 'Publication & Dissemination – A Short Guide', enclosed in this Information Pack. Proposers should note that producing these outputs can be a demanding task. You should allow sufficient time to achieve these outputs, when finalising your timetable.

Dissemination activities vary according to the nature of the individual project and are usually discussed at the point when the project is coming to an end. Project workers are expected to take an active part in dissemination activities and additional funds may be made available for any time spent on this work outside the agreed timetable.

How do I make a proposal?

The Current Priorities leaflet (May 1998 edition reprinted below) will assist you in deciding whether your idea falls within the foundation's Current Priorities. If it does you should submit a proposal to one of the staff working with the relevant Committee. (see 'applications' below)

A number of interests run through the foundation's work regardless of the particular subject area. Proposers are expected to take account of these wherever relevant:

The importance of service users' perspectives and of involving users in the decisions that affect them. The foundation has a commitment to exploring ways of ensuring that people central to the research are involved in, and empowered by, the experience.

International comparative work, provided that lessons can be learnt for the UK from such work. (The foundation is restricted by its Trust Deed to work for the benefit of citizens of the UK and the Commonwealth, so studies focusing on other countries, without a comparative element, are outside its remit. The foundation is not currently funding work in other Commonwealth countries.)

Race, racism and the issues confronting minority ethnic communities. All proposals are expected to incorporate this dimension wherever appropriate. But the foundation also welcomes proposals that focus on issues which are of specific concern to minority ethnic communities.

The rural dimension. A small programme of work entitled 'Action in Rural Areas' is going ahead. It is expected that one or two projects with a rural focus will be supported within each of the major programmes of the different Committees. Projects relating to housing, area regeneration, work and opportunity, and

---

1997 ANNUAL REVIEW

(From the Chairman's Report)

Social Policy Research

This review of work, completed in 1997 (and our priorities for 1998) concentrates on those aspects of our work most directly impacting on this central theme [building communities, combating exclusion]. Nevertheless the past year has also seen the results of a wide range of work feeding into appropriate discussions and decisions. In relation to the general social policy , this includes, for example, work on the limits to private insurance as a mechanism for social welfare, and the conclusions from a large project, which examined for the first time in many decades the costs of children- with implications for social security benefit structures and many areas of policy. We have also published work relating to local authorities, such as the impact of charging for local authority services, the introduction of direct payments to disabled people, and allocation policies in social housing. A report examining drugs and youth culture was published and we have begun an Inquiry into Drug Use with the Royal College of Physicians and Psychiatrists. We also reported on the extent to which health inequalities (in terms of death rates) have widened since the 1950s.

It is not possible to review in short all the individual projects that have produced important findings during the year. We have now about 350 "live" research projects, with about 150 finishing each year. The four-page summary Findings that have been published in 1997 give a flavour of the range and depth of our work. The Findings are published in full on our website, as are details of work currently in progress.

We continue to put great emphasis on disseminating the results of our work widely through our four-page summary, Findings, our magazine, Search, our short, accessible project reports and increasingly- via videos and our Internet Web site. We have also awarded two journalist fellowships to allow journalists the time to write and publish what we hope will be seminal books, one on childcare and one on the phenomenon of the economically independent leaving our cities.

The variety of activities that bring us into more direct contact with individuals and organisation- which we refer to 'consensus building' and 'mediating activities'- are receiving more attention. These range from close involvement with particular local authorities, as in our 'Partnership Initiative for Communities' and in our involvement with the York Regeneration Partnership, to presentations to civic leaders in cities and towns around Britain, and meetings with ministers and policy review bodies. In all cases we learn from these exchanges about the issues of concern to policy-makers and practitioners as well as impart the conclusions from our research.

1998 will be an exciting year in taking forward this change in emphasis and we are appointing a new Director of Policy and Practice Development. We should also be gaining the first insights as a result of the chair we endowed at Goldsmith's College, where Professor Tim Newburn will be looking particularly at how more effective evaluation can indicate the directions that policy and practice should take.'

young people have already been funded or are under consideration. A review paper on rural issues relating to social care has been commissioned and decisions about any projects to support will be taken after the report is received in early 1998. Rural dimensions to all proposals submitted to the foundation would also be welcome.

Supporting and strengthening local communities. The trustees have agreed that ways of strengthening communities should be an overarching theme for the foundation's work. They are interested in changes to policies and practice which are likely to lead to greater cohesiveness within neighbourhoods – in contrast to the trend toward social exclusion' particularly in areas of concentrated deprivation. They would like to see this perspective as an ingredient within current programmes of work and Committee interests.

Common weaknesses of research proposals

1. Proposals which describe the background to the project at some length but give very few details about aims and methods.
2. The aims of the project are very vague or are couched in terms of the process, e.g., it is insufficient if the aim of the project is 'to carry out a descriptive study of X or a survey of Y'.
3. The design of the study lacks clarity or robustness so that there is a mismatch between the issues being addressed and the approach adopted, or what is planned is over ambitious.
4. Information about data collection are insufficiently detailed. If interviews are going to be carried out, it is important to give information about the number of interviews; how the sample would be selected; and the form in which the data would be collected. (Any proposal which talks in terms of 'some people will be interviewed' is unlikely to be funded).
5. Details of the way the data will be recorded and analysed are lacking. This is particularly the case where focus groups are are proposed.
6. 'Information about the knowledge and skills that the proposer brings to the project is lacking. In addition to the standard information provided on a CV, it is helpful to have a short summary – two or three sentences – of the experience that members of the research team carrying out research using the methods of data collection or analysis being proposed.
7. Timescales and staff resources are unrealistic or inappropriate. This includes too much work being

planned for the time available, or too much of the field work and analysis being left to inexperienced research assistants.

8. Outputs are proposed, such as a Training Pack, where it is unclear how these could be derived from the material that is being collected.'

CURRENT RESEARCH PRIORITIES (as at October 1998)

This section covers the current priorities (1998) of the:

- Housing Research Committee
- Social Care and Disability Research Committee
- Work, Income and Social Policy Research Committee
- Young People and Families Research Committee
- New Research Briefs.

Housing Research

1. Reforming House Building

The foundation is following up some of the ideas to emerge from the successful conference in 1997. Ken Bartlett will be leading on this work and is contacting potential collaborators.

2. Area Regeneration

In contrast to the reactive mode adopted during the early rounds of this programme, new proposals will be developed through a much more pro-active approach by JRF. Evaluation and employment issues will be pursued in more depth and it is hoped to engage in some development projects. Further details will appear as they become available.

3. Housing and Community Care

Any further work will result from a review of current projects and again the foundation will be identifying topics for further support. This work is likely to fall in the fourth quarter of 1998.

Reconciling environmental and social concerns

This is a new priority topic for the Housing Research Committee for 1998. We intend to open up the topic by directly commissioning a series of think pieces and briefs may be issued on particular topics to seek proposals for the fourth quarter of the year.

4. House Condition; repair and maintenance

Projects from the second phase of this programme are now concluding. While the foundation will retain an interest in this field there are no plans at this stage for a third phase of work.

Social Care and Disability Research Committee

The Social Care and Disability Committee supports research and development work into issues concerning people:

- who have their quality of life compromised by a condition of ill-health, frailty or impairment;
- are disabled by the loss or limitation of opportunity to take part in the life of the community on an equal level with others due to physical and social barriers.

An important criterion in judging all proposals is the extent to which those whom projects are intending to benefit (or research) are involved in identifying the issues to be addressed by the project and in its planning and execution. We also expect all proposals submitted to recognise and take account of the fact that the disabled people come from a variety of cultures and ethnic backgrounds (see paragraph on Race Equality).

There are five programmes

1. Independent Living

We continue to have an interest in supporting the development of independent living and the implementation of direct payments legislation. During 1988 we will be issuing briefs for specific pieces of work in the following areas:

- People with learning difficulties – supported decision making and consent
- Direct payments for people over 65
- Disability and employment
- Supported living
- Disabled parents

Please contact the Alex O'Neil or Linda Ward or add yourself to the R&D Notification List for news of developments in this programme.

2. Choices and Voices

This programme is about promoting choices for people who tend to be particularly excluded from taking decisions about their own lives and enabling them to have more say in choices which affect them. Some of the groups of people that might be included under this heading would be: people with autism; people with dementia; people with profound and multiple impairments; people with dual sensory impairments; people with mental health needs and people who use other ways of communicating.

The foundation would be interested to receive proposals on:-

- Ways of enabling people to be involved in decisions about their lives, eg decisions about where they live, what type of support they receive, their education and employment etc
- People's full participation in all aspects of life in the community (ways of listening to people's 'voices' and acting on their wishes).

Proposals focusing primarily on particular technological developments, therapies or service led training programmes are unlikely to be funded. If you are considering submitting a proposal in this area please phone Alex O'Neil at the foundation.

3. Disabled Children and Young People

The primary focus of this Programme is empowering disabled children and young people; those with profound and multiple impairments are of particular concern.

A number of projects concerned with disabled children and young people living away from their families have already been funded and are now nearing completion. Key messages from these projects will be disseminated in a variety of ways, including a conference, during 1998.

Priorities for the Programme in 1998 are:

- Disabled children with complex health and support needs (including those who may be technologically dependent)
- Transition: what makes for a more positive transition from child to adulthood, from school to post school, from family or residential home to more independent living?

The delivery and co-ordination of services to disabled children and young people and their families (including the implementation of the Children Act and issues around inter-agency working) continue to be of interest to us and is likely to be an important theme and context for proposals on the topics above. We would also welcome proposals focused on promoting the 'voices and choices' of disabled children (see section above) including projects on 'listening to' disabled children and promoting and sharing their coping strategies. If you are thinking of submitting a proposal under this programme please contact Linda Ward (at Norah Fry Research Centre).

4. Race Equality

The Social Care and Disability Committee of the Joseph Rowntree Foundation is working with the REU (Race Equality Unit) in developing a programme of work on Race Equality in Social Care and Disability.

Priorities for 1998

- How do services (or the lack of services) affect black and minority disabled people? Are there also good examples of service provision from which we can learn general lessons of good practice. (Social Care and Disability does not usually fund research about health services).
- The experience of disability. We need to recognise both the shared and different experiences of black and minority ethnic disabled people. We need to understand these in terms of communities in which they live as well as within wider society as a whole.
- Are there good examples of involving black and minority ethnic disabled people in the planning, development and delivery of social support? Can we develop and promote such good examples more generally?

If you wish to know more about any of the above, please contact Ratna Dutt at REU (Tel: 0171 278 2331) or Alex O'Neil at JRF.

5. Shaping Futures

The foundation is taking forward a new programme of work during 1998 called Shaping Futures. This is about helping to define a new vision of rights, entitlements and services, and about how such a vision might be achieved.

In 1998 briefs will be issued for work on topics including:

- consultation about ideas for improving rights, entitlements and services
- exploration of the social model of disability as it relates to different groups
- promotion of disability equality and the social model
- bringing about change in practice.

Please contact Alex O'Neil or add yourself to the R&D Notification List for news of developments in this programme.

Work, Income and Social Policy Research Committee

This section spells out the current priorities of the foundation's Work, Income and Social Policy Committee. This is one of the Committees which replaces the Social Policy Research Committee which was wound up at the end of 1996.

There are two Programmes

1. Work and Opportunity

This research programme is investigating the link between employment and social welfare. Projects in the first two phases of the programme have already been approved, under four main themes:

- Bridges and barriers: achieving a better understanding of the obstacles to entering the labour market and exploring the opportunities for entering and progressing within it;
- The distribution of work; identifying the factors underlying shifts the patterns of employment, their implications and exploring whether they can be altered with advantage;
- Real initiatives; looking at the impact and wider lessons of community employment/training schemes;
- Corporate behaviour; understanding the way companies take key decisions about jobs, terms of employment and plant location and the wider impact of these decisions.

The foundation's Advisor on Work and Opportunity is Pam Meadows. You should get further details from Derek Williams before considering a proposal for further phases. Priorities may change from the ones listed above, though the broad framework is likely to remain.

2. Work and Family Life

A new programme on Work and Family Life has begun in 1998. If you would like to be added to our mailing list to automatically receive information about this programme please, please add yourself to the R&D Notification List .

Other Priorities

- The future development of welfare provision, particularly alternative ways of meeting individual needs at different stages of the life cycle.
- Monitoring and evaluating changes taking place in the social security system.

Unsolicited proposals are welcome within these topic areas. Proposals may be sent to either Barbara Ballard or Derek Williams.

Young People & Families Research Committee

The Young People and Families Committee is currently supporting work in four main areas:

- Prevention and support for children and families;
- Family conflict and dispute resolution;
- Young people in transition;
- Hearing the voices of children and young people.

SOME 1997 PROJECTS

reported in 'Findings' in 1997

Housing Findings. 'The changing population in social housing in England', Roger Burrows; 'The market for a new private rented sector', Caroline Oakes and Eleanor McKee; 'The redevelopment of contaminated land for housing use', Paul Syms; 'Living in bed and breakfast in the 1990s', Mary Carter.

Social Policy Findings. 'Expenditure on children in Great Britain', Sue Middleton, Karl Ashworth and Ian Braithwaite; 'Long term unemployment and the threat of social exclusion', Jochen Clasen et al, 'National Lottery: current trends and future concerns', Luke FitzHerbert and Lucy Rhoades.

Social Care Findings. 'Living well into old age', Ann Bowling et al; 'Dealing with language impairment', Susie Parr et al; 'Parents living with children in old age', Judith Healy and Stella Yarrow.

Local and Central Government Relations Findings. 'The governance of local public spending bodies', Alan Greer and Paul Hoggett; 'The new government of London', Tony Travers and George Jones.

Foundations. 'Building lifetime homes', David Darton and Julie Brewerton; 'Partnership between government and voluntary organisations', Marilyn Taylor.

Exclusions

With the exception of funds for particular projects in York and the surrounding area, the foundation does not generally support:

- projects outside the topics within our Current Priorities;
- development projects which are not innovative;
- development projects from which no general lessons can be drawn;
- general appeals, for example, from national charities;
- core or revenue funding, including grants for buildings or equipment;
- conferences and other events or publications unless they are linked with work which the foundation is already supporting;
- grants to replace withdrawn or expired statutory funding, or to make up deficits already incurred;
- work relating solely to medicine, education and training courses or travel/adventure projects;
- educational bursaries or sponsorship for individuals for research or further education and training courses;
- grants or sponsorship for individuals in need;
- work that falls within the responsibility of statutory bodies.

Applications The detailed guidelines from the foundation are quoted extensively below as a general guide to good practice for these kind of applications.

Initial enquiries The foundation's staff are happy to give advice to those uncertain about the relevance of a proposal for the foundation, or the form in which it should be presented. Proposers are advised to obtain a copy of the most recent Research and Development booklet before making a proposal (call 01904-629241). A draft proposal or short outline covering the main headings identified below, received early is welcome and usually better than a telephone call. These should be sent to:

Dr Janet Lewis, Research Director, Joseph Rowntree Foundation, The Homestead, 40 Water End, York YO30 6WP (Telephone: 0904-629241) or the relevant Committee Secretary, as follows:

Housing: Theresa McDonagh.
Social Policy and Social Care: Barbara Ballard.
Disability and Community Care: Alex O'Neill.
Voluntary Action: Pat Kneen.

The form of the proposal: The foundation does not have an application form for proposals but does require them to follow a standard format. You should provide two unbound copies of the proposal presented as follows:

- a succinct but clear proposal of a maximum 3,000 words
- a summary of the proposal of not more than 600 words
- completed copies of the foundation's project budget forms, with supporting details
- a CV for the project proposer (and worker/s if known).

Any proposal not submitted in this way may be returned for revision and thus delayed for consideration by the relevant committee.

The required structure of proposals is the same whether you are making an unsolicited proposal or responding to a particular programme of work.

What should the proposal cover?

Title Give the project a short, explanatory title.

Background This section should explain the reasons for undertaking the project. You must place the proposed piece of work in the context of existing knowledge and practice, demonstrating a familiarity with the field and the relationship of your proposal to relevant recent or current work being carried out by others.

You should also explain the extent to which the new project will relate to or build upon previous work. Demonstration projects must give details about the innovative nature of the work and the evidence that such a development is likely to be beneficial. Projects concerned to transfer good practice from one setting to another must also provide evidence that the practice is based on a sound assessment of 'what works'. Research proposals should indicate what gaps in knowledge the proposed project seeks to fill.

Aims You must clearly state the aims of the proposal.

Policy relevance You must draw out the policy or practice implications of the proposed work. Be as explicit as possible about the scale and nature of the policy or practice questions your project will address and also the timeliness of the proposal.

Methods You must state clearly the methods to be adopted and why they are appropriate. This principle applies to both practice- and research-based work. Those proposing research projects should include details of the approach to be adopted; the way in which the work would be pursued (eg how samples for either qualitative or quantitative work would be chosen, numbers involved, methods of analysis etc). Demonstration and other development projects need to provide details of the work to be carried out and show how the activities would be monitored and evaluated.

Timetable You must provide a schedule setting out the elements of the work to be done. This should cover what activities will be carried out, when they will occur, how they relate to other activities and how long will they take. You must allow time within your schedule to complete the required outputs (usually a Findings and an accessible report). The Foundation gives close attention to ensuring that projects are completed on time (elements of funding may be withheld in the event of delays).

Staffing Those submitting the proposal should include a curriculum vitae detailing their qualifications, experience and any relevant publications. Similar details should be included for other key workers, where known. You should also provide information about the current and likely future commitments of staff who will be working on the project and the ways in which they would fit the additional work in with existing commitments. Any known or possible additional facilitation expenses for disabled people on the team should be included in the budget. (If facilitation expenses arise after the approval of a project the Foundation is willing, in principle, to meet the extra costs incurred in addition to the agreed budget. However, details should be discussed with Foundation staff before any commitments are made.)

Dissemination You should give details of the audiences who are likely to have an interest in the outcomes of the work, and which aspects of the findings are likely to be of particular interest to whom.

Other support You must include details of any other support which the project may have received or is seeking. (This may be in the form of other grants or in the provision of accommodation, office facilities, staff time, equipment, etc.)

Budget You must complete the Foundation's standard budget forms. You should provide staff cost breakdowns and supporting notes as requested in the guidance on the budget form.

The Foundation does not set a limit on the budgets for individual proposals but each Committee has an annual allocation of funding and 'value-for-money' is a prime concern.

Summary In addition to two copies of the detailed proposal, two copies of a summary of not more than 600 words are also required. following the guidelines for the general proposal, you should provide one or two paragraphs under each of the following headings: Background, Aims, Methods, The proposer, Costs, Expected outputs.

Project funding agreement: The foundation has introduced a Project Funding Agreement with those it supports. Its main intention is to clarify beyond doubt the obligations on both sides, in order to ensure that worthwhile results emerge from projects and that the resources of the foundation are spent in the most productive way. (A copy is available from the foundation, on request). A cornerstone of the agreement is the acceptance of a proposal by the foundation, including the expected outputs and completion date. Proposers should bear this in mind when developing the proposal.

Timetable for submissions: A final version of a proposal should reach the foundation in time for submission to the relevant committees, which meet about six weeks before each meeting of

trustees. The deadlines vary from year to year, and the dates should therefore be checked with the relevant committee secretary. The final date for the receipt of a proposal in its polished form is usually:

March trustees' meeting: mid-December
June trustees' meeting: mid-March
September trustees' meeting: mid-June
December trustees' meeting: mid-September.

Experience confirms that proposals benefit from early submission of an outline proposal and of the final version, to allow time for discussion between the foundation's staff and the proposers.

Joseph Rowntree Reform Trust Limited

About £750,000 (1998)

Innovative and reforming work, ineligible for charitable status

The Garden House, Water End, York YO30 6WQ
Tel: 01904-625744; Fax: 01904-651502

Correspondent Lois Jefferson, Secretary

Trustees Directors: Professor Lord (Trevor) Smith of Clifton, Chairman; Professor Lord David Currie; Christine Day; Christopher Greenfield; Archy Kirkwood MP; Diana Scott; David Shutt.

Beneficial area Mainly UK.

Information available An excellent leaflet including applications procedures and grant details, largely reprinted below; also a brief history of the trust entitled 'Trusting in Change, A Story of Reform', published 1998.

Summary Grants for non-charitable political campaigning, overwhelmingly in Britain.

General The trust was established in 1904 as the Joseph Rowntree Social Service Trust. It is one of three trusts set up by Joseph Rowntree, a Quaker businessman with a lifelong concern for the alleviation of poverty and other great social ills of his and future days. The three trusts are all entirely independent of each other and each has its own adjacent entry in this Guide.

Though the trust is probably best known for its continuing support, in the name of political diversity, of the Liberal Democrat party and its predecessors, it has supported liberal thought and activity in almost every political party in Britain (including, for example, paying for professional research assistance for David Trimble after his election as leader of the Ulster Unionist Party). The trust's work goes beyond parliamentary politics. It played an important part in the great development of British pressure groups in the 1970s – it was an early and major supporter of Amnesty, for example – and in recent years it has been the biggest supporter, in financial terms, of the movement for constitutional change that is now in hand.

Where next? Perhaps a greater interest in local diversity (it has already given some support to the North East Convention in this area)? Or more attention to Europe wide developments in citizenship? However, it is the strength of this trust in recent years that it has been willing, as well as able, to address big questions such as these without being much influenced by the immediate pressures or fashions of the day.

The trust's information leaflet explains that it differs from almost every other trust in this book in one crucial respect; it is not a charity (the other similar is the Barrow Cadbury Trust). It pays tax on its income and is therefore free to give grants for political purposes; to promote political reform and constitutional change as well as the interests of social justice. It does so by funding campaigning organisations and individuals who have reform as their objective, and since it remains one of the very few sources of funds of any significance in the UK which can do this, it reserves its support for projects which are ineligible for charitable funding.

From its assets, approaching £30 million in value (held mainly in major investment trusts and properties), the trustees allocate a potential grant budget of around £750,000 each year.

The trust's guidance notes go on to state: 'The trust's principal concern is the continuity of reform within the democratic system. It seeks to foster creative intervention by anticipating and brokering change within the body politic, and by identifying the points where the minimum amount of thrust will have the maximum effect when directed as accurately and efficiently as possible.

'Always aiming for good value from the projects its supports, the trust looks for those ideas whose time has come, or is about to come, and offers small amounts of money (as well as sometimes quite large amounts) at the moment when it judges that the most positive results can be achieved.

'The trust aims to correct imbalances of power; strengthening the hand of individuals, groups and organisations who are striving for reform. It rarely funds projects outside the UK, directing most of its resources towards campaigning activity in this country, and will not fund research or any other charitable activity.'

As a rule, the trust provides either funding for specific projects or seed corn grants to enable campaigns to get off the ground and attract alternative funding.

Political grants 'The trust is not committed to the policies of any one political party, and has supported individual politicians or groups promoting new ideas and policies from all the major parties in the UK. Grants are not normally given towards the administrative or other costs of party organisations. Direct party support has, however, been given when trustees have judged that particular political developments should be fostered, especially those central to a healthy democratic process such as constitutional and electoral reform.

'The trust's political grants aim to encourage the exchange of views and ideas among people involved in the political process, redress the balance of inequality between the parties and stimulate radical change.

'Political groups which have received grants include: Labour Campaign for Electoral Reform, the Association of Liberal Democrat Councillors, Campaign for a Scottish Assembly, Charter 88, Electoral Reform Society, Tory Reform Group, Labour Co-ordinating Committee, Labour Initiative on Co-operation, the Three Hundred Group and Conservative Mainstream.

Social Justice: 'The trust has helped a large number of non-party pressure groups and other organisations which are ineligible for charitable funding, but which need assistance for particular purposes in the short term (the trust will not normally provide long-term funding). Such groups need not be national organisations, but the national relevance of local campaigns is a crucial factor that trustees will consider.'

Some examples of groups helped are Amnesty International, Friends of the Earth, Plain English Campaign, Campaign for Press and Broadcasting Freedom, WaterWatch, Genetics Forum, and Inquest.

Personal awards: The trust occasionally gives personal awards to effective individuals.

Exclusions The trust will not fund research or any other charitable activity. It rarely funds projects outside the UK.

Applications The process of applying for a grant is straightforward and unbureaucratic. There are no application forms. Applicants should simply write to the trust's secretary, succinctly outlining the nature of the project and what it hopes to achieve, and enclosing a budget and any other supporting documents where appropriate.

Proposals are judged on their merits within the prevailing social, political and economic climate, so beyond the broad aims outlined above there cannot be any advance guidance about which areas of activity the trust is likely to support, the amount of funding which might be available or for how long.'

Trust staff make an initial assessment and can reject inappropriate applications. Those which pass this first stage are considered in greater detail but may still be rejected by the trust's office. All staff rejections are reported to the trustees at their next meeting, when those applications which have survived the preliminary vetting are submitted to the trustees for decision.

The meetings take place in March, June, September and December. Applications must be submitted at least one month in advance of the meeting dates. A system of small grants, up to £3,000, also operates between quarterly meetings. Such grants must be agreed by three trustees, including the Chairman, and applications can be considered at any time. In exceptional circumstances, larger grants may also be agreed at any time, but only by the unanimous postal decision of the trustees.

The J B Rubens Charitable Foundation

£453,000 (1995/96)

Mainly Jewish causes

Berkeley Square House, Berkeley Square, London W1X 5LE
Tel: 0171-491 3763

Correspondent Michael Phillips.

Trustees Michael Phillips; J B Rubens Charity Trustees Limited.

Beneficial area UK and Israel.

Information available Accounts are on file at the Charity Commission up to 1995/96. Grants list but no narative.

General In 1995/96 the trust had assets of £6.5 million, which generated an income of £351,000. Donations amounted to £453,000, partly funded through the trusts capital reserves, for just 4 grants. Consequently management and administrative costs seem high at £108,000, or about £25,000 per grant awarded.

Total grant giving was concentrated one award to the Jerusalem Foundation (£382,000). Other grants were Ruth and Michael Phillip Charitable Trust (£70,000), Cystic Fibrosis Research Trust (£1,000), and Holocaust Education Trust (£500).

Exclusions No grants are made to individuals.

Applications In writing to the correspondent.

The Rubin Foundation

£396,000 (1995/96)

Jewish charities, general

The Pentland Centre, Squires Lane, Finchley, London N3 2QL
Tel: 0171-631 0566

Correspondent A McMillan

Trustees Alison Rubin; Angela S Rubin; R Stephen Rubin; Carolyn Kubetz; Andrew K Rubin.

Beneficial area UK and overseas.

Information available Report and accounts to April 1996.

Summary In 1995/96 a few large grants were made to a slowly changing list of major beneficiaries, but this may be changing (see below). Small grants, mostly for a few hundred pounds went to a wide varity of charities. The foundation's grants probably represent the personal charitable concerns of the trustees, rather than being the outcome of any overall policy.

General From small organisations, great things may come; the 1995 annual report notes that no less than £1 million has been put aside for the eventual and overdue construction of the British Holocaust Museum at the Imperial War War Museum. At the same time, the foundation, previously funded by annual covenants, was also given a further £4 million, to be used 'for major projects'.

The 1995/96 annual report says 'We continued with the general charitable endeavours. A number of these are to provide continuous funding for projects'. Three of the organisations are named, where actual commitments had been made for future years. They were Save the Children (for work with Palestinian refugees), the Lancaster Acute Hospitals NHS Trust (£10,000 a year) and Oxford University (for a 'Research Director', £100,000 over four years).

Other major beneficiaries were the Foundation for Education (£200,000, with £80,000 in the previous year), The Prince's Youth Business Trust (£52,0000 and £50,000), Jewish Care (£20,000 and £10,000) and Community Security Trust (£20,000).

The remaining grants are spread over a wide range of charities, Jewish and otherwise, and are rarely for more than £1,000. Examples include arts organisations such as the Royal National Theatre (£700), and welfare groups such as the Fund for Refugees in Slovenia (£300). There are no identifiable local charities, other, perhaps, than some serving London generally.

Applications The trust has committed its funds for the next few years, and it uses the remainder for chosen charities known to members of the family, and those associated with the Pentland Group plc. Unsolicited applications are not welcomed, and individuals should not apply.

The Rufford Foundation

£2,085,000 (1996/97)

Conservation, environment, general

Old Chelsea House, 15a Old Church Street, London SW3 5DL
Tel: 0171 376 5534
Web site: http://www.rufford.org

Correspondent Terry Kenny, Trust Director

Trustees J H Laing; A Gavazzi; C R F Barbour; A J Johnson; K W Scott; M I Smailes; V Lees.

Beneficial area Developing countries, UK.

Information available Accounts with details of grants above £10,000 only. In future all grants will be listed and, for larger grants, explained. Further information supplied to help with this entry.

General The foundation was established in 1982 by J H Laing, still happily a trustee. 'There is a strong interest in conservation and the environment, with perhaps two thirds of the foundation's funding going to these areas. Many other causes are supported, especially in the field of social welfare. However gifts tend to be in the £250 – £5,000 bracket for these causes.

The trustees try to help organisations where they feel that their intercession will make a positive difference. The foundation tends to concentrate upon conservation in non-first world or 'developing' countries where funds are more scarce and there is much greater difficulty in raising the the required funding, rather than projects within the UK.'

253 grants were made in 1996/97

£250 – £5,000	198
£5,001 – £10,000	7
£10,0001 – £49,999	40
£50,000 or more.	8

The major grants are categorised in the box herewith.

The huge grant to the World Wildlife Fund is not unprecedented for the foundation. In 1995 it gave £500,000 to the World Humanity Action Trust, in a joint project with the London School of Economics.

The other disclosed overseas grants continue the rich variety seen in the list above, and include awards for Medicins San Frontieres (£20,000), the Dian Fossey Gorilla Fund (£19,000) and the United Mission to Nepal.

The medium sized grants show a greater proportion of charities that are probably working in the UK. They include the London Studio Centre (£18,000), Quidenham Children's Hospice (£20,000), Nottinghamshire Royal Society for the Blind (£11,000)and Jersey Wildlife Preservation Trust

---

The Rufford Foundation

Major grants

The major grants (those for more than £20,000) were as follows (with underneath the purpose of the 1996/97 award):

	1996/97	1995/96
World Wildlife Fund (to fund various overseas projects)	£553,000	£178,000
EIA Charitable Trust (for projects concerning illegal trade in wildlife)	£125,000	
Compassion in World Farming (for European exhibition 'Making Animals Matter')	£90,000	
Health Unlimited (Care programmes in Somaliland and Namibia)	£85,000	
The Salvation Army (HIV/Aids project in India, drug rehabilitation centre in former USSR)	£79,000	
Charities Aid Foundation (For further small donations)	£60,000	
Royal Botanic Gardens, Kew (Millennium Seed Bank appeal)	£50,000	£155,000
World Development Movement (Campaign for justice for the world's poor)	£50,000	
Conservation International	£47,000	
VSO	£45,000	£44,000
CRUSAID	£31,000	£21,000
The Samaritans	£25,000	
Abbotsholme School	£24,000	£44,000.

(£15,000). Though the foundation's interest in conservation is a repeated theme, it does not appear to exclude grants to charities with no such connection.

No less than 205 grants of less than £10,000, and worth in total £322,000, are not disclosed in the accounts – a programme that would on its own be large enough to justify its own entry in this book. There is no way of knowing whether the pattern that can be seen when going down the list of 48 larger grants is continued with this majority of the awards. It is very possible that the foundation is an even more major funder of UK charities than this entry has suggested.

Exclusions Only registered charities are supported. No grants to individuals. The foundation tends not to give grants for building costs.

Applications In writing to the correspondent, including budgets, accounts and an annual report if available. Please also see the foundation's web site (as above) for latest information.

The Raymond & Beverley Sackler Foundation

£1,487,000 (1995/96)

Probably art, science, medical research

15 North Audley Street, London W1Y 1WE

Correspondent C B Mitchell, Solicitor

Trustees Dr R R Sackler; Dr R S Sackler; J D Sackler; C B Mitchell; Dr R B Miller; Paul Manners; R M Smith.

Beneficial area UK.

Information available In Summer 1998, no more recent accounts on file at the Charity Commission than those for 1995/96, and those without a list of grants.

General The foundation was established in 1988 to make grants for 'the education of the public in the UK and elsewhere in the fields of art, science and medical research'. Little is known about the foundation's work as it does not file grants lists. Most income is derived from donations rather than

endowment and much of this may be granted on to a few regularly assisted organisations (see below).

In Summer 1988 the latest report and accounts on file at the Charity Commission were for 1995/96 (too early to be subject to the Commission's recent SORP requiring fuller disclosure).

The report states that grants 'included gifts to the British Museum (a four year commitment according to the 1989/90 report), the Institute of Astronomy, and the University of Cambridge (the 1989/90 report says that the foundation has made a five year commitment to establish the Institute of Medical Sciences there).

Future grant commitments over the next year (1996/97) totalled £250,000 and another £250,000 had also been committed over the next two to five years.

This is one of the larger trusts not to have filed the up-to-date information now required by the Charity Commission (and the law).

Applications In writing to the correspondent.

The Saddlers' Company Charitable Fund

£297,000 (1997/98)

General

Saddlers' Hall, 40 Gutter Lane, London EC2V 6BR
Tel: 0171-726 8661

Correspondent Group Captain W S Brereton-Martin

Trustees The Saddlers' Company: W Price, Master; E J Pearson; D S Snowden; M R Quirk and 24 other men.

Beneficial area UK, but mainly England in practice.

Information available Annual report and accounts. Sparse grant lists supplied for this entry.

General Most of the fund's income is committed in advance and new applicants will have potential access to only about £80,000 of the total given above.

In 1997/98, as in previous years, grants to just five organisations, all with long

standing connections to the Company, accounted for over 60% of the grant total:

Alleyns School, for scholarships)	*£92,000*
Riding for the Disabled Association, for running costs)	*£28,000*
British Horse Society, training and education)	*£22,000*
Royal Veterinary College , for equine research)	*£16,000*
Lord Mayor's Appeal,	*£10,000*
Leather Conservation Society	*£10,000*

There is then an extensive programme of small grants, none for more than £3,000 and most for less than £1,000. Some, to national charities, or to bodies connected with horses or leather, are generally repeated from year to year. In what seems to be a separate programme, perhaps half of the small grants are concentrated on the field of disability. An unusual and welcome characteristic of this programme is that locally resident members of the Company are asked to visit such applicants and make a written report to the fund.

These disability grants are well spread around the southern half of England, but the fund says that it would be interested to receive more applications from the North and the North West.

There is no immediate apparent evidence on the grant lists of any grants in Scotland, Wales or Northern Ireland. Of the nine 1998 grants of any kind where a local beneficiary can be identified, five were to London organisations (and three to Walsall, where there is a leather museum).

Breakdown of grants by category:

City of London	*£12,000*
The equestrian world	*£43,000*
Education	*£97,000*
Charities for disabled people	*£69,000*
General charitable activities	*£74,000*

Exclusions Appeals by individuals for educational grants cannot be considered.

Applications By letter, with supporting background information. Trustees meet in January and July.

The Alan and Babette Sainsbury Charitable Fund

£460,000 (1996/97)

Civil and minority rights, general

See entry for the Sainsbury Family Charitable Trusts
Tel: 0171-410 0330

Correspondent Michael Pattison

Trustees Simon Sainsbury; Miss J S Portrait.

Beneficial area UK and overseas.

Information available A report and accounts are available with a grants list.

General Simon Sainsbury now leads this trust after the death of his father, Lord Sainsbury of Drury Lane, in October 1998. The administration has transferred to the Red Lion Square offices of the other 'Sainsbury Family Charitable Trusts'.

In 1996/97 the trust had an income of £432,000 generated from assets of £8.9 million. A total of £460,000 was allocated in 64 grants ranging between £500 and £125,000. Most of the grants (42) were between £1,000 and £6,000.

Grants were catalogued in the 1996/97 accounts under the following headings. A variety of Jewish causes were supported in each category.

Overseas	*£184,000*	*10 grants*
Health and social		
welfare	*£159,000*	*33 grants*
Scientific and medical		
research	*£52,000*	*8 grants*
Education	*£33,000*	*5 grants*
Arts	*£24,000*	*5 grants*
Religion	*£8,000*	*3 grants*

The largest grant continues to be given to the Pestalozzi Children's Village Trust (£125,000) of which Lord Sainsbury was the President for many years. Other large grants were given to United Medical and Dental School (£29,000); Oxford University Diabetes Research Laboratories (£25,000); Imperial War Museum (£25,000). Grants of £10,000 were awarded to Caesek Hospital Families Centre, International Committee for Andean Aid and International Voluntary Service.

The trust is noteworthy for the consistency with which it has supported certain radical causes over a long period of time. Over the years these have included (1996/97 awards in brackets): Runnymede Trust (£15,000); Matthew Trust (£10,000); Minority Rights Group (£6,000); Child Poverty Action Group (£6,000).

Exclusions No grants to individuals.

Applications See entry for the Sainsbury Family Charitable Trusts but bear in mind the trust has only recently transferred to the joint administration at Red Lion Square. No mention was made by the previous administrators that unsolicited applications were discouraged.

The Robert and Lisa Sainsbury Charitable Trust

£466,000 (1996/97)

Education in the arts, general

c/o Horwarth Clark Whitehill, 25 New Street Square, London EC4A 3LN
Tel: 0171-353 1577; Fax: 0171-583 1720;
Website: www.horwathcw.com

Correspondent D J Walker

Trustees Sir Robert Sainsbury; Lady Lisa Sainsbury; C T S Stone; H O N & V Trustee Ltd (Judith Portrait).

Beneficial area Unrestricted.

Information available Accounts, with a brief report.

General The trust's erratic grant giving in recent years, from £1.5 million in 1989/90, £3 million in 1994/95 to £466,000 in 1996/97, can be attributed to its increasing reliance on donations as it disposes of its assets.

The trust has been continuing its two key interests; support for the medical care of people with terminal illness and for the University of East Anglia, Sainsbury Centre for the Visual Arts. This is also the home of Sir Robert and Lisa Sainsbury's magnificent personal collection of art which they donated to the university and which forms the hub of a public display in the building designed by Sir Norman Foster, which they also funded.

In 1996/97 the trust had an income of £440,000, made up mainly of grants and donations. Assets of £1.17 million have been steadily declining. Total grant giving was £466,000, of which about 96% went in three major awards to the University of East Anglia (£190,000), Hammersmith Hospital (£163,000) and Northwick Park and St Mark's NHS Trust (£96,000) with future commitments of £671,000 and £44,000 respectively to the two hospitals.

Of the remaining grants two were for £5,000, to Operation Hannibal and the Scottish National Gallery of Modern Art, and the rest for less.

The trust has also been supporting University of East Anglia Sainsbury Research Unit for the Arts of Africa, Oceania and the Americas with the annual income of a restricted fund since 1992. In August 1997 (a 'post balance sheet event') the assets of this fund (nearly £995,000) were donated outright to the Research Unit.

The trust also handles the expenditure related to the catalogue for the Sainsbury Collection at the Sainsbury Centre for Visual Arts at the University of East Anglia (£95,880). Over the past decade the trust has been receiving annual donations for this purpose from the Gatsby Charitable Trust (see separate entry.)

Exclusions No grants to individuals.

Applications To the correspondent.

The Sainsbury Family Charitable Trusts

See separate entries for each trust

9 Red Lion Court, London EC4A 3EB
Tel: 0171-410 0330

Correspondent Michael Pattison, Director

General The Sainsbury Family Charitable Trusts are unique among grant making trusts in this country: 18 separate charitable trusts covering three generations of the Sainsbury family share a common administration. Another unusual feature is that in most cases the settlor who endowed the trust is also an active trustee. This means that the policies and practices of these trusts are led by the settlors and reflect their interests in a close and intimate way. In most cases other near relatives also serve as trustees.

However each trust is independent of the others and has a clear and separate identity in its grant making. This needs to be emphasised. Each trust is as distinct as its own individual name despite the fact that there are areas where its interests may be mirrored by, or sometimes overlap with others.

Fourteen of these 18 trusts are large enough to have a detailed entry in this guide. The following list ranks the trusts covered in this guide according to size of their grant approvals in the most recent year for which information is available. These totalled over £58 million with the Gatsby Charitable Foundation contributing more than half. Total annual grant payments, as opposed to approvals, were probably about £44 million.

Gatsby Charitable Foundation	*£28.6 million*
Linbury Trust	*£12.8 million*
Monument Trust	*£4.4 million*
Headley Trust	*£3.1 million*
Jerusalem Trust	*£2.3 million*
Kay Kendall Leukaemia Fund	*£1.6 million*
Tedworth Charitable Trust	*£1.5 million*
Glass-House Trust	*£1.2 million*
Woodward Trust	*£0.6 million*
Ashden Charitable Trust	*£0.6 million*
Staples Trust	*£0.6 million*
Alan & Babette Sainsbury Charitable Fund	*£0.5 million*
J J Charitable Trust	*£0.3 million*
Elizabeth Clark Charitable Trust	*£0.2 million*

Additions and exclusions

The Alan and Babette Sainsbury Charitable Fund joined the joint administration in 1998 after the death of Lord Sainsbury of Drury Lane. The Woodward Trust joined in 1997, having chosen until then to use their accountants to handle the fund's administration. Two trusts seem to be winding down their particular, precisely defined operations – Lisa Sainsbury Foundation (nursing) and the Monument Historic Buildings Trust (restoration of specific buildings). Another two trusts are too small for Volume One of this book, the Mark Leonard Trust and the Three Guineas Trust.

The Sainsbury Fortune

Most of the investments of the Sainsbury Family Charitable Trusts are held in J Sainsbury plc. Lord Sainsbury of Turville (David Sainsbury) resigned as Chairman of the company in 1998 so that no member of the Sainsbury family has an executive role in the company. A few years before several members had been on the board of the company. The family is thought collectively to have a stake of between 33% to 40% in the former family business, itself worth about £10 billion in all. Only a small proportion of their holding in the company is via the charitable trusts.

Capital grants – the physical legacy

Major capital grants of many millions are given by the senior members of the family from their older, far larger trusts. These family members hold or have held honorary posts with a wide variety of national institutions particularly in the arts and business.

The trusts are best known for their generous support to major national arts institutions. Most famous is the spacious and elegant Sainsbury Wing of the National Gallery. The older trusts have more recently gone into partnership with many new developments amongst national arts institutions generated by the National Lottery Arts Councils' capital schemes. These include new galleries at the Bankside Tate, redevelopment of the National Theatre, Sadlers Wells, etc. Many of the older trusts, with the exception of the Gatsby, reflect a passion for opera.

These arts grants have a higher media profile but the major capital grants to science and medicine are more significant in cash terms and perhaps in changing the fabric of our future lives. The family has assisted pioneering work in palliative medicine. The Gatsby funded Sainsbury Laboratory at the John Innes Centre in Norwich leads research into plant genetics and now the Cognitive Neuroscience Unit at University College London is at the forefront of research mapping the brain. In addition, and not unsurprisingly from the trusts of former business leaders, business schools in London, Oxford and Cambridge have also been generously supported by the Gatsby, Linbury and Monument trusts.

Generalisations about their funding

Each of the trusts is distinctive. However all, in their different ways, are movers and shakers and co-operate with others in positions of power and influence, whether in central or local government, research institutions or the voluntary sector. They also employ their own chosen specialist advisors. A few of these are listed in the trusts' reports (see the separate entries) but this is only indicative. Many key advisers are not named and the trusts work by a process of continual consultation. For instance special gatherings may be arranged with a number of organisations to examine a subject and help direct policy formulation. (The Gatsby apparently brings together about two dozen people over 24 hours about six times a year to brainstorm on a subject.)

It is appropriate to repeat the general funding principles outlined by Christopher Stone, a Gatsby trustee.

The Sainsbury Family Charitable Trusts

The breakdown of the total funding

This is shown in the table herewith for the most recent years for which accounts are available.

Scientific, medical research (£10m cognitive neuroscience)	£15.0 million	26%
Education (£4m Oxford business school (£2m University Challenge)	£12.9 million	22%
Arts (£3m Tate Gallery)	£7.9 million	14%
Overseas	£7.1 million	14 %
Health & social welfare (£1.4m mental health, £3.2m children/parenting)	£5.9 million	10%
Environmental (£1.2m historic buildings)	£2.5 million	4%
Capital, unidentified	£3.0 million	5%
General	£3.6 million	6%

These are relevant to all the Sainsbury trusts small and large.

A trust seeks

- to bring about practical and measurable improvements in each area of activity, with clearly stated objectives whenever possible;
- to begin its activities on a relatively small scale but to be willing to persevere for long periods, gradually increasing the size of grants as the trustees become more confident in their understanding of the subject;
- to be specific and consistent, yet flexible, in its approach and willing to take risks;
- nearly always to work within the 'system' to bring about improvements, rather than trying to create new institutional structures.

Increasingly the trusts are publishing the results of their funding where this can promote work which needs wider dissemination. This has included a bibliography of CFS research (Linbury), the control of cassava disease in Africa (Gatsby), and company car taxation (Ashden).

Another characteristic of the trusts as a group is their disinclination to support the activities of well-established charitable organisations with strong balance sheets and a firm base for public support. 'Where an organisation has got to the point to employ a full-time fund raiser it has probably got to the point to look for people other than us.'

Independence and co-operation

Occasionally the trusts have joined together to support projects but this is apparently not as frequent as an outsider might expect. Six trusts supported palliative care at St Thomas' Hospital and more recently eight have supported the Woodland Trust Woodlands on your Doorstep campaign. Readers will note in the current entries £1.7 million from the Tedworth and Glass-House trusts for research into families, children and childcare. There has also been overlapping support to UK environmental organisations, particularly between the smaller trusts.

The smaller trusts are interesting in being amongst the few grant making trusts in the UK which support work connected with key environmental issues – transport, alternative energy, environmental taxation and recycling.

Support in Africa

Gatsby has set up four independent trusts run by Africans in sub-Saharan Africa – Uganda, Tanzania, Kenya and Cameroon. Four other Sainsbury trusts (Headley,

Ashden, Staples and J J) also support work mainly in these countries and also in South Africa. The international officer has written – 'The priorities of each trust tend to reflect to some extent the issues that the UK public is becoming increasingly aware of and concerned about. There is a noticeably strong environmental theme which is often combined with income generation, health or food security for low income groups.'

Unsolicited applications

It is important for all would-be applicants to realise that all the trusts, except Woodward, declare firmly that they are proactive and do not solicit applications. On the other hand the door is not completely shut. The common denominator for the general public is the joint administration, a staff of 22 led by their director, Michael Pattison. This administration fields about 20,000 applications a year. All these approaches are read and acknowledged. They are told that if their approach is of interest they will hear within six weeks, but that if no follow through occurs, to accept that the trusts will not be able to help. About 1,000 grants are made each year and only a very small proportion of these result from 'cold' applications.

Internally taken initiatives are the mainspring of their operations. To quote the director: 'The job of my staff, sometimes very much in partnership with the trustees, sometimes with delegated instructions to go and work something up, is to engage with organisations which may be able to work with the trusts in the territory the trustees identify.'

The exceptions to this rule are the small programmes of grants for disabled people run by the Headley and Gatsby trusts. All social welfare applicants are urged to read the policy outlines in this guide very carefully and then confirm the current details by telephone with the trust offices. The trusts have tried, unsuccessfully, to deter the hundreds of inappropriate and painstaking approaches from staff of social services departments for families in need.

Can new organisations get recognised?

It's worth looking at other common features of the way the trusts work. It's then for organisations outside the Sainsbury nexus to use their imagination (and cunning) try to work out ways of making their activities and plans known to the trusts in appropriate and effective ways. Keep the Sainsbury administration fully informed, both directly and indirectly through the usual promotional activities. You may hook into the network through other supporters

whether in the voluntary sector, business, or government.

Staffing Structure – 22 officers 1998

Trust officers – all the trusts are served by the director, Michael Pattison and the finance director, Paul Spokes.

Gatsby – Professor R C Baker, director technical programmes, M Williams

Kay Kendall – Miss E Storer

Elizabeth Clark – M Williams

Monument – Professor R C Baker, assistant director, M Williams

Linbury – D Brown, assistant director

Ashden – Jane Shepherd

J J – Jane Shepherd

Mark Leonard – Jane Sheperd

Headley – Miss H Marriott

Jerusalem – Miss J Lunn

Tedworth – Miss H Marriott

Glass-House – Miss H Marriott

Staples – Miss H Marriott

Woodward – Karen McLeod

Sarah Nichols – administers Headley budget for people with disabilities

Specialist officers

Third World – Michael Darby

Environment – Jane Shepherd

Exclusions No grants for individuals. In the past some of the trusts have had such programmes but it looks as if this is now channelled through other charities specialising in this kind of assistance. There is a slight and specialised exception in the Headley Trust, which has its own entry in this book.

Applications It used to be the general refrain from the administration that 'an application to one of the Sainsbury family trusts is an application to all' and a warning for a number of the trusts, though not all, that *unsolicited applications are unlikely to be successful.* (Certainly all the trusts are proactive in their approach to their grant making.)

This warning is now reinforced more emphatically in the majority the individual annual reports; 'Proposals are generally invited by the trustees or initiated at their request. *Unsolicited applications are discouraged* and are unlikely to be successful, even if they fall within an area in which the trustees are interested. Eight of the trusts use this wording, whilst the Headley, Monument, Glasshouse, JJ, Staples, Tedworth add this further rider: 'The trustees prefer to support innovative schemes that can be successfully replicated or become self-sustaining.'

However the office is generally approachable, and a telephone call may well establish whether there is any point in submitting a formal application. In making this approach it is only sensible to have done your homework and be able to refer to the programme/s of which trust/s cover the kind of activities in which you are involved.

If the basic advice from the trusts is ignored and a number of separate applications are sent to different trusts you will do yourself a disservice, and send out a strong warning about your lack of preparation and the likely thoroughness of your activities generally.

More importantly, how does an organisation get to be solicited by these trusts?

This editor's advice to potential applicants with suitable development activities is to keep the office above fully informed of what they are trying to do, both directly but also indirectly through the usual dissemination and promotion of a charity's activities. Many of the trustees and all of the staff are actively involved in the sectors they fund, and can be assumed to be on the look-out for interesting or important work of which they had not previously known. But if it is not actively promoted in the right quarters it may be missed.

Basil Samuel Charitable Trust

£383,000 (1996/97)

General

c/o Great Portland Estates Plc, Knighton House, 56 Mortimore Street, London, W1N 8BD
Tel: 0171-580 3040

Correspondent George Howkins

Trustees Coral Samuel; Richard Peskin.

Beneficial area UK and overseas

Information available Accounts, but without a narrative report, on file at the Charity Commission.

General The policy of this trust appears to be to make a number of substantial grants of £10,000 or more to organisations concerned with health,

educational and cultural activities, and a number of smaller donations to other charities.

From assets of £7.5 million, the trust generated an income of £475,000 in 1996/97. Grant giving amounted to £383,000 going to 26 organisations, of which 11 were supported in the previous year.

Grants to health and medical charities included: Jewish Care (£50,000); National Hospital for Neurology and Neurosurgery (£50,000); Cancer Relief MacMillan (£30,000); Service to the Aged (£25,000); and Home for Aged Jews (£10,000).

Grants also went to education: St Pauls School Foundation (£50,000); Queen Mary and Westfield College (£10,000).

Grants for culture and the arts included those to The Victoria and Albert Museum (£25,000); Royal Academy of Arts (£25,000); Natural History Museum (£25,000) and Jewish Philanthropic Association for Israel and the Middle East (£20,000).

Other grants were split amongst welfare organisations, of which the largest were to the Prince's Business Trust (£25,000) and the Police Foundation (£10,000).

Applications In writing to the correspondent.

The Save & Prosper Educational Trust

£1,001,000 (1996/97)

Education

Finsbury Dials, 20 Finsbury Street, London EC2Y 9AY
Tel: 0171-417 2332; Fax: 0171-417 2300

Correspondent Duncan Grant, Director

Trustees The trustee is the Save and Prosper Group Ltd., who have appointed the following Managing Committee: C J Rye, Chairman; A G Williams; M L Bassett; D Grant.

Beneficial area UK, with a special interest in the London Borough of Havering and in Edinburgh, and their surrounding areas.

Information available Report and accounts, which fall short of the SORP requirements in that the grants, though listed, are not analysed and explained.

The narrative report is modest. A good guidance leaflet for applicants.

Summary The trust makes grants to educational establishments, education and training in community projects particularly within inner cities, arts education, education for the disadvantaged, and to programmes of scholarships and bursaries. It is interested in supporting 'new and innovative ways of advancing education in the UK'. Grants generally range from £100 to £20,000 with a handful of larger grants. Support is provided for up to two years. The resources of the fund are in gentle but inexorable decline.

General The trust was established in 1974 in conjunction with the launch of a school fees planning service run by Save and Prosper Group Ltd. (itself a wholly owned subsidiary of the private Robert Fleming Group). The trust gets its income from this scheme but is managed as a separate entity with its own staff. Further recruitment of parents into the scheme has now been stopped by the Inland Revenue and the corresponding income for this trust will diminish to zero by the year 2014.

However, another charity, the Save and Prosper Foundation, is being built up as the old one declines. At present its grant making capacity is below the level needed for an entry in this book, and as most of its grants cover the same fields as the present trust, and are administered in common, applicants can generally regard an application to one as an application to both. In 1996/97, as in previous years, £125,000 was transferred from this trust to the new foundation.

The trust's Guidelines read as follows:

'We support educational projects which generally fit into one of the following categories:

- Support to primary and secondary schools, tertiary educational establishments such as universities as well as research bodies and museums;
- Community projects, particularly those relating to children and young people in inner-cities. We aim to improve the education and training of these people and to widen the opportunities open to them, giving them prospects of a more rewarding adult life;
- Arts education, with the emphasis on helping more people gain access to the arts and to better appreciate them. Support for performing, fine and decorative arts is usually directed at school-age children and students;
- Education for the disadvantaged. This covers special needs, inner cities,

ethnic minorities, rural disadvantage and youngsters in trouble or at risk.
- Scholarships and bursaries to organisations for educational fees and maintenance (Generally, *direct support is NOT given to individuals.*);
- New and innovative ways of advancing education in the UK.

'In recent years, we have provided educational grants which have ranged in size from £100 to £10,000. Usually, we fund a project for no more than two years. This means that we can support a variety of different projects and that we do not face long term commitments. In a few cases, however, we agree to review funding annually .... We find it useful to have regular reviews of projects that we support. For example, we sometimes ask for written reports or for a questionnaire to be completed, and for larger projects we arrange review visits.'

In 1996/97 the trust made 237 donations totalling £1 million (as against figures for two years earlier of 251 grants totalling £1,155,000). The largest payment was the annual transfer grant to the associated Save and Prosper Foundation (£125,000).

There were eight further grants that were for more than the usual maximum of £10,000. £33,000 was given to the Museum of Scotland; £22,000 to King's College, London; £20,000 to Young Enterprise; and amounts of between £12,000 ad £15,000 to Gatehouse Publishing Charity, the Borough of Havering, the Prince's Trust, St Bartholomew's Hospital and the Wildside Trust. However, most grants were for amounts of between £500 and £5,000.

As there is no explanation of the purpose of the awards, it is no longer possible to see the priority the trust is giving to different kinds of educational activity.

The range of the beneficiaries can be seen from the following short list of some 1996/97 beneficiaries: African Caribbean Network, £2,000; Air Training Corps GP Fund, £5,000; Aldeburgh Poetry Trust, £500; Ashingdon Primary School, £350; Association of Wheelchair Children, £4,000; Birkbeck College, £5,000; Chelsea Physic Garden, £5,000.

In the previous edition of this book, when rather more information was available, we estimated that about 21% of the grants by value were in the fields of art, craft and heritage, about 8% to schools, commonly in small awards to primary schools, and something less than 5% to institutions for higher education. The rest of the grants could not be categorised for lack of information.

Exclusions The trust does not support:
- open appeals from national charities;
- building appeals;
- charity gala nights and similar events;
- anniversary appeals;
- appeals by individuals for study; grants, travel scholarships or charity sponsorships.

Applications The initial approach should be addressed in writing to the director. It should preferably be in the form of a brief letter (not exceeding two A4 sides) setting out the reason for the application and enclosing any relevant publicity material and accounts.

Applications are always acknowledged. If the application is unsuccessful, applicants should wait at least a year before re-applying. Trustees meet in March, May, July, September and December. Applications need to arrive at least a month before the meeting.

The Francis C Scott Charitable Trust

£1,018,000 (1996/97)

Disadvantaged people

Sand Aire House, Kendal, Cumbria LA9 4BE
Tel: 01539-723415

Correspondent Donald Harding, Director

Trustees R W Sykes, Chair; W A Willink; Miss M M Scott; F A Scott; Mrs S E Bagot; W Dobie; I H Pirnie; F J R Boddy; C C Spedding.

Beneficial area North England.

Information available Full accounts with grants list; substantial report analysing the past three years activities; guidelines.

Summary Well over 100 grants are made each year towards capital or revenue costs. They vary from under £500 to around £100,000 and are typically for a few thousand pounds. Recipients are charities benefiting socially and economically disadvantaged people in Cumbria and Lancashire.

General The trust was created in 1963 by Peter Scott, the then Chairman of the Provincial Insurance Company. Together with other members of his family he endowed the trust with Provincial shares.

It was named in honour of Francis C Scott who was the previous chairman of the same company and son of its founder.

Assets totalled nearly £30 million in 1996/97 and from this base an income of £1,664,000 was generated. Approximately 130 grants averaging £9,000 were awarded that year. Three grants for £50,000 or more accounted for 22% of expenditure, 12 grants between £20,000 and £49,999 for 36%, and 12 grants between £10,000 and £19,999 for 19%.

The trust says:

'Following a policy review in 1995, the priorities have now been narrowed down to:

1. Cumbria and North Lancashire as far South as Lancaster and Heysham
2. The rest of the administrative county of Lancashire

'The trustees are seeking to identify existing charitable initiatives or to stimulate new ones in Cumbria, with a view to making substantial grants and achieving a significant impact in the selected areas.

'Our first concern is socially and economically disadvantaged people and communities. Examples of projects include:
- work with children and young people, family support, youth clubs, social education, child care;
- help with special problems, eg. disability, counselling and advice schemes involving eg. drug or alcohol abuse;
- self help projects to provide play faciities in deprived urban situations
- schemes to help housebound elderly people on low incomes
- services aimed at groups which are under-represnted or disadvantaged in their fundraising efforts because of gender, colour, age or lack of English skills;
- community development including community arts and theatre for eg. "special needs" clients.

'We currently analyse grants, for statistical purposes under the following headings:
- Youth
- Community development
- Families and children
- Disabled
- Elderly and sick
- Counselling
- Alcohol and drug abuse
- Homelessness
- Education training
- Councils for voluntary service

'We normally fund only registered

charities. While we do occasionally give grants to national charities these are usually only to fund a local service or appeal.

'We tend not to provide substitute funding for services provided by the State as a statutory responsibility but we may look favourably upon partnership funding with the private and/or public sector in providing additional services to the disadvantaged.'

The trust has disengaged from Arts and Museums funding.

Examples of grants:

Youth 'Cumbria County Council – Whitehaven Breakout Project, Whitehaven, Cumbria – £70,000 in 1994/95 and in 1995/96. The project aims to provide young people in the 13-17 age range who are low-achievers, offenders or are otherwise thought to be at risk with an educational experience aimed at improving their active involvement in the community, raising their self-esteem and confidence, enhancing their life-chance after school and enabling them to exercise greater control over their lives. Three 16 week courses were offered during 1994/95 accommodating a total of 55 young people.

Community development 'Strickland House Trust Ltd, Kendal – £20,000 in 1993/94, £5,000 in 1994/95 £10,000 in 1995/96 and £24,000 in 1996/97. Strickland House Trust is a registered charity seeking to provide accommodation and technical support to local charities and offering a one-stop service to users who may have a multiplicity of needs. The trust gave £15,000 for capital refurbishment and £5,000 pa for three years towards revenue costs. The trustees have agreed to donate a further £5,000 pa for two years to provide part-time administrative support for the manager.

Families and children 'Ewanrigg Family Support Services Project, Maryport, West Cumbria – £55,000 in 1994/95. £57,000 in 1995/96 and £57,000 in 1996/97). This initiative developed from proposals made by the Howgill Family Centre in Whitehaven in response to a request from the trust to identify a significant project to help families with young children in an area of high social stress. Initially four main support activities were offered by the service: a playgroup; training for parents; a training course in playgroup practise for volunteers and; family support and counselling.'

Other substantial donations of 1996/97 went to the Lake District Art Gallery and

Museum Trust (£10,000 for revenue and £14,000 for appraisal); Workington Youth Bureau £70,000 and; Howgill Family Centre (£57,000 and £6,000 for Ewanrigg Family Support Scheme) and: Brathay Hall Trust (£40,000 and £20,000).

Exclusions The trust does not support:

- unregistered charities;
- individuals;
- organisations suffering expired or withdrawn statutory funding;
- Church restoration;
- medical appeals;
- expeditions;
- scholarships and applications from schools.

Applications An application form is available from the correspondent and should be returned with the latest set of audited accounts. You are welcome to telephone the Director or his assistant for an informal discussion prior to submitting an application.

The trustees meet three times a year usually in March, July and November. Applications need to arrive one month before each meeting. The whole process of application to receipt of a grant may take up to four months.

The Frieda Scott Charitable Trust

£254,000 (1997/98)

Welfare, church restoration, village halls, general

Sand Aire House, Kendal, Cumbria LA9 4BE
Tel: 01539-723415

Correspondent Donald Harding, Director

Trustees Mrs C E Brockbank, Chair; Mrs O Clarke; R A Hunter; P R Hensman; Miss C R Scott; Mrs M G Wilson; Mrs J H Barker.

Beneficial area Old county of Westmorland and the area of South Lakeland District Council.

Information available Full reports and accounts.

General In 1997/98 the trust gave 87 grants totalling £254,000 (27 of them to organisations also supported in the previous year when £200,000 was given).

The largest single grant, of £60,000, was

given to the Brewery Arts Centre in Kendal (which had received a similar amount in the previous year). However this support will now end as capital has been earmarked to set up the Brewery Arts Centre Endowment Fund.

Other large donations included the following: The Gateway Exchange (£20,000) and about £10,000 each for The Bendrigg Trust, Cancer Relief Macmillan Fund, South Lakeland Council for Voluntary Action, Kendal and District CAB, Patterdale Mountain Rescue Association, and St. Martins Church, Windermere.

There were 37 grants for amounts between £1,000 and £8,000, mainly to churches for restoration, village halls and community centres, and welfare organisations in South Lakeland. Recipients included Westmorland Music Council and Alzheimers Disease Society (£7,000 each) and Kendal Lads and Girls Club (£1,000).

The remaining grants were generally for around £250 to £750 and included those to Animal Concern, Kendal Family Drop In Centre, Ambleside Oral History Group and a number of scout groups, parish halls and community centres.

Exclusions Applications are not considered if they are from outside the beneficial area.

Applications An application form is available from the correspondent and should be returned with the latest set of audited accounts. Potential applicants are welcome to ring for an informal discussion before submitting an application.

The Samuel Sebba Charitable Trust

£1,032,000 (1990/91)

Jewish charities in Israel and Britain

44a Cavendish Street, London W1M 7LG

Correspondent Clive Marks

Trustees M Sebba; L Sebba; S Sebba; L D Sebba; V Klein.

Beneficial area UK and overseas.

Information available Report and accounts with grants list and policy outline are on file at the Charity

Commission.

General The trust, established in 1967, makes grants usually between £5,000 and about £50,000. Beneficiaries are almost exclusively Jewish organisations and the trust states that its funds are already heavily committed to certain organisations and unsolicited applications will probably fail.

In 1996/97 the trust's income was £852,000 and its assets totalled £16.5 million. 78 grants were made, 58 of which were for £5,000. At least 90% of grant expenditure was disbursed to Jewish causes.

The trust outlines its policy as follows:

'The principal aims are to support a wide range of registered charities and to encompass many areas of the Jewish Community, particularly those involved in learning and teaching of the Jewish faith and history, as well as the training of Rabbis, teachers, lay-teachers and counsellors.

'The trust will from time to time fund a small number of specialist consultants to advise charities on their internal structure, budgeting, staff training, as well as future planning and efficiency.

'The trust constantly reviews the work of many of the organisations funded. Monitoring can be carried out when recommended by a small research team who are available to attend site visits, this facility enables the trust to support efficient and effective charities, giving them the support for on-going support.

'Future developments: The trustees will be concentrating principally on four areas:

- general communal matters including youth clubs and community centres;
- Jewish education, Jewish schools and training of future Rabbis;
- hospices and aged;
- medical aid and hospitals.

In 1996/97, the largest awards (accounting for 40% of grant expenditure) were to: Friends of Bar Ilan University (£210,000); Beth Jacob Grammar School (£50,000); Sage (£50,000); Israel Institute for Talmudic Publications (£43,000); British Council of Shaare Zedek Medical Centre (£35,000); and Amos Horev Appeal (£34,000).

Examples of the common £5,000 grants included: Sunderland Talmudical College; Yesodey Hatorah Nursery; Jewish Outreach Network; Lewis Hammerson Home for the Elderly; Friends of Ladach Hospital, Jerusalem. Non-Jewish beneficiaries were: Royal Opera House (£14,000); and the World Monument Fund in the UK (£5,000).

Applications Organisations applying must provide proof of need, they must forward the most recent audited accounts, a registered charity number, and most importantly a cash flow statement for the next 12 months. All applications should have a SAE attached. It is also important that the actual request for funds must be concise and preferably summarised on one side of A4.

Because of on-going support to so many organisations already known to the trust, it is likely that unsolicited applications will, for the foreseeable future be unsuccessful.

The Sheepdrove Trust

£294,000 (1997), but see below

General in North Lambeth, environment, education and care for the elderly

2 Methley Street, London, SE11 4AJ
Tel: 0171-735 5285

Correspondent Sarah Manasseh

Trustees Mrs J E Kindersley; P D Kindersley; Miss H R Kindersley; B G Kindersley.

Beneficial area UK, but especially North Lambeth, London.

Information available In the Autumn of 1998 there were no Report and Accounts on file at the Charity Commission later than those for 1994/95. Up to date filing, hopefully to SORP standards, was expected by the end of 1998.

General Little information is as yet available about this relatively new foundation. In 1994/95 there were assets of £22 million, which might be expected to generate an annual income of over £1,000,000, and it has made interesting donations such as £15,000 towards the expenses of a concert pianist and £20,000 to Spiritual Care for the Living and Dying.

Exclusions No grants to students or other individuals.

Applications To the correspondent.

The Sherburn House Charity

£494,000 (see below)

Residential care, welfare in the North East

Estate Office, Sherburn House, Durham DH1 2SE
Tel: 0191-372 2551

Correspondent Stephen Hallett, Chief Officer

Trustees Anne Beeton; Venerable Michael Bowering; Margaret Bozic; William Brooks; Maurice Crathorne; Charles Dickinson; Louise Farthing; William Firby; Doreen Gibson; Dorothy Hale; Mary Hawgood; James Mackintosh; John Marsden; Lindsay Perks; Graham Rodmell; Leslie B Smith; Venerable Trevor Willmott; Ron Wilson.

Beneficial area The ancient Diocese of Durham, effectively the land bounded by the Tyne, the Tees, the Pennines and the North Sea.

Information available See below.

General This is a new grant maker, formed from a reorganisation of Christ's Hospital in Sherburn, itself an active charity since 1181. It started making grants in the summer of 1998, on a tentative basis. Funding must be to 'relieve need, hardship or distress'.

Policy is still being developed, but areas of need already identified include the following:

- health (including mental health)
- learning disabilities
- physical disabilities
- substance abuse
- community needs
- homelessness
- special needs
- community environment
- effects of long tern unemployment.

The charity has decided that it will not commit itself to regular renewal of its grants.

Applications On the application forms available from the office listed above.

The Archie Sherman Charitable Trust

£1,589,000 (1996/97)

Jewish charities, arts

27 Berkeley House, Hay Hill,
London W1 7LG
Tel: 0171-493 1904

Correspondent M J Gee

Trustees M J Gee; A H S Morgenthau; E Charles.

Beneficial area UK and overseas.

Information available Report and accounts with grants list and limited analysis of grant activity.

Summary Nearly all beneficiaries are Jewish charities in the health or education sectors. Most funds are disbursed in grants of over £50,000 for projects towards which the trust has a long term commitment. A limited number of smaller grants are made to various organisations outside the main areas of interest.

General The trust was founded in 1967 by the late settlor, Archie Sherman (1911-1986). Most of its investments are in property and most income comes from shop rents.

Grants are made 'almost exclusively to benefit health and educational purposes, therefore hospitals, medical research, schools, universities, help for the aged and handicapped are principal recipients'. The following geographical boundaries for grant making are set out in the deeds:

1) UK
2) Canada, Australia, New Zealand, South Africa, Pakistan, Ceylon
3) India
4) Any other British Commonwealth country
5) Israel
6) United States of America

In 1996/97, assets totalled £16 million and £1.2 million income was generated. About 110 donations were made in the year. Although grants averaged £14,000, 68% of funds were disbursed in ten grants of over £50,000, and so typical grant size was lower – around £5,000. The vast majority of giving by both the number of grants and their value was directed at Jewish organisations. All of the ten large awards were examples of these and included £334,000 to Friends of the Hebrew University of Jerusalem, £132,000 to the Joint Jewish Charitable Trust and £129,000 to British Friends of the Assai Harofeh Medical Centre. Non-Jewish beneficiaries included the Royal Academy Trust (£36,000), the Ear Foundation (£45,000) and the Royal Opera House (£16,000).

The trust says:

'Archie Sherman Charitable Trust is committed to 24 long term projects with the payments spread over more than one year up to six. Regular progress reports are sent to the trustees and on site visits are also made.

'The trustees review all commitments on a forward, five year basis, so that new projects can be undertaken and income made available.

'Long term projects being assisted include a new building at University, a new home for neglected kids, medical equipment and a new operating theatre block.'

Applications In writing to the correspondent. Trustees meet every month except August and December.

The Shetland Islands Council Charitable Trust

£4,909,000 (1996/97)

General, in Shetland

Breiwick House, 15 South Road,
Lerwick, Shetland ZE1 0RB
Tel: 01595- 744681

Correspondent John Barnbrook, The Finance Department

Trustees 28 trustees, being the elected Shetland councillors (acting as individuals), the Lord Lieutenant and the Headmaster of the Anderson High School.

Beneficial area Shetland

Information available Model reports and accounts, available from the trust for £2.

Summary A wide variety of local initiatives are supported with grants or loans from £300 to about £300,000. Assistance is given, for example, to education, the elderly, disabled, local industry, recreational facilities, the environment, the arts etc. The common denominator between projects is that they all benefit 'Shetland and its inhabitants'. Most grants are recurrent – the trust has committed to fund most of its present beneficiaries up until 2001.

General The trust was established with 'disturbance receipts' from the operators of the Sullom Voe oil terminal. It continues to receive these payments but they are now almost insignificant (1% of total income) compared with investment income.

The trust is run by the Shetland Islands Council which receives around £700,000 a year for this service. Officers from the Islands' various council committees make funding recommendations to the trustees who do not consider 'applications from the general public'.

In 1996/97 the trust's assets amounted to £226,804,000 and income of £10,102,000 was generated.

Charitable expenditure 1996/97:

Social work	39%	£3,098,000
Community Services	38%	£3,067,000
Policy and resources	10%	£830,000
Planning	7%	£585,000
Education	2%	£124,000
Housing	2%	£130,000
Environmental services	1%	£73,000
Development	1%	£62,000

In its 1997 annual report the trust says:

'Certain principles have guided the trustees decisions over the years, but the main principle has always been to seek benefit for Shetland and its inhabitants. In particular the trustees set out to :

- improve the quality of life for the inhabitants of Shetland, especially in the areas of:
  – social need
  – leisure
  – environment
  – education
- build on the energy and initiatives of local self-help groups, and assist them to achieve their objectives, without destroying the independence and enterprise which brought them into being;
- utilise the funds in order to provide large scale facilities which would be of long term benefit to the inhabitants of Shetland;
- support traditional industries and assist in the introduction of new ones, in ways where a charity and a trust might usefully assist, particularly:
  – agriculture
  – fishing
  – knitwear
  – aquaculture

'The trustees regularly seek the opinions of the Shetland Islands Council, asking it to suggest how funds available for expenditure might be allocated. The council, through its committees and departments, provides a democratic structure through which the trustees may hear the views of the Shetland community.

'In practice the thorough discussions at Council level mean that most applications have been well prepared with likely problems and solutions fully considered before an individual project even reaches the trustees.'

The following is a summary of the trust's annual review:

Quality of Life 'During the year the trust has continued to assist with social need throughout the islands. This has been achieved partly through established grant schemes, and partly via local groups.

'Approximately £450,000 was allocated to the independence at home scheme to assist the infirm and/or elderly to remain in their own homes. Some £46,000 was provided for grants under the social assistance scheme, set up to make immediate payment of small sums to alleviate need. A further £140,000 was provided for the purchase of specialist aids, all of which form a library of equipment for use in the community.

"There are many local action and self-help groups formed and run by members of the public for a specific purpose, often to support a particular group of vulnerable or disabled people or to provide a service such as marriage counselling. These groups were allocated £230,000 during the year following recommendations from the council to the trust on individual and group needs.

'The trust also supports leisure and recreational, environmental and educational facilities.

'The trust supports the Shetland Arts Trust, in the field of artistic and cultural activities. Through the Shetland Amenity

Trust, the trust has funded the development of local museums, the employment of a full time archaeologist for Shetland and various environmental initiatives such as the anti-litter campaign.

'In the area of education the trust supports the Shetland Field Studies Trust in its development of an environmental education service to Shetland's primary schools. Funding was also given to the Shetland Islands CAB.'

Specialist Council-created trusts and local charities

'Whilst the trust does support some projects directly, for the most part it uses local charities and specialist council created trusts as intermediaries. By grant aiding such bodies the trust has managed to devolve the day to day management of smaller projects to skilled personnel with specialist knowledge.'

Large scale facilities

'Because of its substantial resources, the trust has been able to fund large projects. An example of this is the construction of four care centres in rural areas to provide residential and day care services to vulnerable people. The trust funds the net running costs of the centre's facilities and their management through the Shetland Welfare Trust.'

Traditional and other industries

'Crofters and farmers have continued to benefit from the trust's agricultural ten year loans scheme. The trust also continues to operate an agricultural bridging loan scheme to assist with projects which are grant aided by the Scottish Office Agriculture and Fisheries Department. During the year a total of 12 Agricultural loans totalling £162,800 were approved and 20 agricultural bridging loans to the value of £92,000 were advanced.'

'The trust has in the past provided assistance to local fishing, fish processing and salmon farming, knitwear and other businesses, but now provides this indirectly via the vehicle of its SLAP group of companies. SLAP Trading Ltd provided approximately £228,000 of equipment for local industry through hire purchase finance.'

Exclusions Funds can only be used to benefit the inhabitants of Shetland

Applications Applications from the general public are not considered. Projects are recommended by the various committees of Shetland Islands Council.

Henry Smith Charity (Kensington Estate)

£21,000,000 (planned for 1998)

Social welfare, disability, health, medical research

5 Chancery Lane, Clifford's Inn, London EC4A 1BU
Tel: 0171-242 1212

Correspondent Brian McGeough, Treasurer

Trustees Julian Sheffield, Chairman; Mrs. A E Allen; Lord Egremont; Lady Euston; Lord Gage; J D Hambro; Lord Hamilton of Dalzell; T D Holland-Martin; Sir John James; Lord Kingsdown; G E Lee-Steere; Major E J de Lisle; Ronnie Norman; P W Urquhart.

The two distribution committees are both chaired by Mr Sheffield.

Beneficial area UK. Local programmes in East and West Sussex, Hampshire, Kent, Gloucestershire, Leicestershire, Suffolk and Surrey.

Information available Long and most elegantly presented report and accounts, with good narrative reports on financial matters, but little discussion of the charity's grant making policies. An excellent list of grants, the purpose of each being briefly explained, but only the most limited overall analysis.

Summary Over 450 grants a year are made in the main grant programmes, usually for amounts of between £10,000 and £100,000 and averaging over

---

The Shetland Islands Council Charitable Trust

Details of significant grants paid in the years 1996/97 and 1995/96 are summarised below:

	1996/97	1995/96
Shetland Recreational Trust	£664,000	£2,306,000
Shetland Amenity Trust	£586,000	£561,000
Care Centres	£1,480,000	£1,469,000
Christmas grants to pensioners	£561,000	£581,000
Other grants paid	£1,618,000	£1,406,000
Total	**£4,909,000**	**£6,323,000**

£40,000 (though there is a programme of smaller awards for child and youth activities). Grants are divided almost equally between one-off capital or project costs and grants for two or three years, usually towards specific budget items or projects.

There are two further programmes. The first is the annually chosen 'major grant', usually worth over £1.5 million and for funding a specific geographical area or field of work over the subsequent three years; and the second is a long standing programme, worth about £1 million a year, for local grants in each of eight particular counties with which there is an historical connection.

Where possible, the trustees 'like to make grants to moderate sized projects to get them off the ground or to allocate a grant specifically towards a particular item within the budget of a larger project which they decide to support (eg. towards the cost of construction of a particular facility or the payment of a particular project worker's salary for a specific period).' Payments for running costs are limited to three years and are only renewed at the end of the period on consideration of a new application.

There is an unusual system for considering eligible applications for the main programme. Summaries, prepared by the charity's staff, are circulated to members of one of the two Distribution Committees, who indicate their support, if any, for further consideration. If sufficient support is forthcoming, the applicant is usually visited by the charity's staff Visitor, Virginia Graham, or her assistant, or by one of a panel of voluntary visitors, who then prepare a report for the distribution committee concerned. There is no information available about how many eligible applications are received or about the proportion which survive the first round of the process.

Applicants are asked, in the excellent guidance supplied by the charity and printed below under the 'Applications' heading, to include a half page summary of this report. It seems likely that in many cases this will be the text that is circulated to trustees, for a possible 'sudden death' decision based on this alone, and so particular care should be taken with its preparation.

General As this huge 17th century charity, with a 'national' remit, has grown in recent years it has slowly developed interesting proactive policies represented by its exciting major grants programmes. However, it has also kept in place some of the sector's most old-fashioned grant making, with its geographically biased main programme and its regrettable 'county' lists for the most prosperous shires in England – apparently continued on solely sentimental grounds rather than on any assessment of need. There is to be a policy review in 1999 at which it would be possible for such issues to be addressed.

Having sold to the Wellcome Trust the enormously valuable Kensington estate after which the charity is named, there is now a diversified endowment worth more than £550 million from which it is generating an excellent income of well over £20 million a year.

There are three grant programmes, each very different from the other. Applicants should note that the charity does not cover education, and that it has a longstanding and unusual interest in complementary medicine.

Main grants programme

The charity makes grants for amounts usually between £10,000 and £100,000, both one-off and staged, the latter for a maximum of three years. These are categorised as Special, for one-off awards, and General grants for those that are staged, descriptions that appear to date from an earlier part of the charity's history. In 1997 the one-off grants accounted for about 30% of these awards by value. There is no information about the number of grants in each category.

As has been criticised for years in succeeding editions of this book, the awards continue to be biased very strongly towards the South of England generally, and to London and Kent in particular. However, some changes have been made, though in an idiosyncratic way as is usual with this charity. First, the grants lists continue to reflect the welcome influence of the major grants schemes for the North East and, more recently, for South Wales and the Black Country (work has also begun on a proposed major grant for South Yorkshire).

Secondly a single geographical heading has appeared in the charity's list of grants, alongside headings such as 'Physical Disability' or 'Medical Research'; there now also appears a heading 'Grants made in the North East'. At £561,000 in 1997, this represents £20 per hundred people in that region, compared with an average available for the country as a whole of £23. When 'national' grants are taken into account, people in the North East are probably now getting a fair share of awards. This is an excellent programme, run in co-operation with the Tyne and Wear Foundation. But why just the North East? and why does it have to be a special programme?

The extent of the unfairness for other parts of the country is shown by a sample of 64 grants, covering three of the charity's subject headings, and excluding 'national' grants to mostly London based organisations. The amount given per head in the South of England was more than three times higher than for people living in other parts of the the North and Midlands. The approximate figures per hundred population were as follows:

London	£9.86
South of England	£5.26
North of England excluding the North East	£1.93

The charity points out that it cannot meet all needs throughout the country, a fair point. But if it is to concentrate on particular areas, it should choose those where need is greater, rather than where it has merely historical connections.

There were not enough grants in the sample to justify firm conclusions about the amount of money going to the other countries of Britain. A general reading of the lists suggests that it is slight (though perhaps less so for South Wales than for elsewhere).

The trustees repeat that they are interested in applications from all parts of the country, and they have previously told these editors that 'they wish to see more applications from the areas at present lightly represented in their lists'. Nevertheless these disparities continue generally unchanged and it seems likely that they are due more to the structure of the charity than to a shortage of suitable applicants.

The system of asking trustees to indicate their interest in particular applications is itself likely to lead to abuse if these trustees come pre-dominantly from one part of the country – and that is very much the case with these trustees coming overwhelmingly from London or the Southern counties of England. It will be natural, if wrong, for them to be most interested in applications from areas with which they are personally familiar. It is possible that there are substantial but undisclosed efforts to avoid this happening, but if so, they are not being effective.

Either the present system should be scrapped by the present trustees, and proper budgets set to achieve a fair distribution, or the Lord Chancellor and Archbishop of Canterbury (in whose hands these appointments lie) should appoint new trustees in the future who will give assurances that they will right the situation. The work of the National Lottery Charities Board, making very similar grants, has demonstrated that there are ample worthwhile causes to support in all parts of the country.

After this entry had been drafted and shown to the charity, it offered the following information 'A policy review will take place during the course of next year and, no doubt, geographical distribution will be on the agenda. The policy so far has been one of gradual expansion during which the charity has become familiar with particular areas of the country in which it wishes to work and hopes to continue to work once the major grant is completed'.

All of this is welcome news. However at the rate of what seems to be about one new area every two or three years, it looks like a 20 or 30 year programme before equity could be achieved.

Despite the presently unfair distribution, the grants made are often enterprising and much useful work is being supported. One problem it faces, though, is that its particular type of funding, generally the one-off capital appeal or the three year revenue grant, is now being duplicated on ten times the scale by the National Lottery Charities Board. It would be timely for this charity, as for others in a similar position, to review its practices and to try and develop forms of grant that would meet needs not already being addressed on so large a scale.

There is no information about actual grant making policies other than that described in the 'Summary' above. The charity says that it has no pre-set budgets; nevertheless the regularity from year to year of the breakdown under different headings (given below) suggests at least an informal understanding among trustees of how the funds should be allocated. One of the more common prejudices is obviously absent; the grants lists demonstrate that the charity is willing to fund core and salary costs, where a good case is made, and does not insist on a specific and often artificially created 'project'.

Grants in 1997

Payments (as opposed to new grant approvals) were classified as follows for 1997

Total	*£11,866,000*
Social welfare	£6,227,000 (52%)
Young people	*£1,372,000*
Community service	*£1,155,000*
Elderly	*£1,125,000*
Drugs and alcohol	*£569,000*
Homelessness	*£526,000*
Family advice	*£391,000*
General	*£526,000*
Disability	£2,858,000 (24%)
Mental	*£1,272,000*
Physical	*£859,000*
Multiple disability	*£777,000*
Medical	£2,731,000 (23%)
Medical research	*£1,606,000*
Hospitals	*£685,000*
Hospices	*£439,000*

These headings are not all mutually exclusive, but despite extensive overlaps they provide a useful structure for looking at the actual work of the charity.

Social welfare

Young people: 56 new grants. In addition to grants of the normal type for this charity, there appears to be a 'small grant' programme specifically for London for amounts of less than £5,000, and usually for Summer or holiday programmes. Typical recipients were Hackney's Centre Youth Project (£482 for a camping trip to France for young people with disabilities) or John Perryn Primary School (£1,500 for a school trip). Major new grants went to the YMCA (£90,000 for its Partnership in Prisons project and to Merseyside Accommodation Project £30,000).

Awards for capital projects included £50,000 for furnishing the Manchester Foyer and 36,000 to the Pedro Club in London to upgrade its computers.

Community service: 26 new grants. This is an ill-defined heading covering community centres and advice services but a number of other activities that might well come under others of the available headings. Recipients of major awards included the 999 Club in London (£225,000, an exceptionally large award for this charity), Brecknock Carers Centre in Wales and Sheffield Women's Aid (£102,000 each). More typical were the grant to Fulham Good Neighbour Service (£66,000 for a volunteer organiser) or the £60,000 to the Family Welfare Association for a development manager. This last may represent an investment in increasing the fundraising capacity of a beneficiary, a once rare kind of grant, but of great potential value.

Homeless: 10 new grants. Much the largest award (other than the 'major grant' programme for the elderly homeless which is described below) was of £150,000 to Centrepoint for the running costs of its Bufy House in Hammersmith. There were three one-off grants, led by £30,000 for the St

Mathew Society for a new group home in Bury St Edmunds.

Elderly: 13 new grants. The policy, exceptional for this charity, of giving a large grant for onwards grant making by HACT (the Housing Associations Charitable Trust) was continued: £400,000 in this year, towards housing projects for the elderly. HACT is a much respected specialist grant maker in this field. Two large capital grants of £100,000 were given to the Sussex Association for the Aged for a new Home and to Calvert Trust in Keswick, and an unusually small £9,000 to Windlesham United Charities for building works. Three year awards included £45,000 for Kensington Staying Put (for its small repairs service) and £30,000 to Camden House Bound Link Service for its core costs.

Drug and alcohol: 12 new grants, led by £100,000 for the capital costs of Phoenix House in London. £66,000 over three years was given to the Addiction Recovery Agency, in the former county of Avon, towards the salary of a counsellor. Both the amount and the proportion of funding in this sector has declined greatly in recent years.

Counselling and family advice: 8 new grants. The two largest awards, of about £75,000 over three years, went to the St Marylebone Healing and Counselling Centre, for its core costs (oddly not classified as 'medical') and to Cruse bereavement care. £60,000 was given to the Women's Therapy centre for a psychotherapy service to black, Asian and ethnic minority women.

Disability

Physical: 23 new grants, led by £90,000 for Canine Partners for Independence in Berkshire. Other big awards went to the National Library for the Blind (£75,000 for the production costs of material in Braille) and Vision Aid (£66,000 for salary costs of an outreach service).

Mental: 27 new grants. Two large capital grants dominate the list, an exceptional £150,000 for Scotts project in Kent (toward a residential home) and £100,000 for St Elizabeth's Home in Hertfordshire. The British Wheelchair Sports Foundation received £60,000 towards the salary costs of a Sports Development Officer.

Multiple disability: 21 new grants, including a rare and welcome grant of 330,000 in Northern Ireland, for the Mitchell House Special School. £100,000 was given towards the Inspire

Foundation in Wiltshire and there were two grants to the Bobath Centre in London, which has been supported by the charity in earlier years. Complementary medicine appears again, though this time with an exceptionally small grant of £2,000 to the Centre for the Study of Complementary Medicine.

Medical

Hospitals: 12 new grants, led by an exceptional £150,000 for the Bristol Cancer Help Centre (a major proponent of alternative approaches to the treatment of cancer). Given that the charity chooses to use this heading, a surprising characteristic of these grants is that only one of them was actually made to a hospital. There is a good reason for this as the charity does not normally support NHS hospitals – it is the heading which is odd. Although there is a separate heading for Medical Research below, £100,00 was classified here for research equipment for Imperial College and to the Blackthorn Trust in Kent received £10,000 towards a research project on treatment options. Other non-hospital grants were to the St John Ambulance, Surrey (towards a new headquarters building) and to Minchinhampton Centre for the Elderly in Gloucestershire (£35,000 to extend a Centre for the Elderly). The one exception to the no hospital characteristic was an award of £100,000 to the National Hospital for Neurology, for a Neuro-rehabilitation Centre.

Hospices: 12 new grants. The awards cover both capital, running and project costs, with awards for the salaries of home-care nurses and for general costs. There were eight capital grants of £50,000 each, to Ayrshire Hospice, Demelza House Children's Hospice in Kent, the Highland Hospice, Hospice in the Weald, Hospice of the Marches in Herefordshire, St Catherine's in Lancashire and St Peter's in Avon.

Medical research: 24 new grants. The charity says that 'the trustees seek advice from experts when making grants in areas such as medical research or treatment where they feel that specialist advice is required'. The charity is not a member of the Association of Medical Research Charities (where full peer review processes are a condition of membership) but most grants are made through established research centres or charities which have their own systems of project evaluation.

The size of the grants is similar to that under other headings. They include the deeply scientific, such as the £53,000 to the Dystrophic Epidermolysis Bullosa

Research Association for Dr Hovnanian to to develop gene therapy for this condition, to the more accessible £20,000 for Nuffield Orthopaedic Centre in Oxford to develop an 'intelligent' artificial hand.

The Major Grants programme

'The trustees select each year a special area which will be the subject of a Major Grant consisting of a programme of grants paid over a period of three years, with the aim of making a significant impact in the chosen field'. There is no information from the charity about how these programmes are selected, nor about the processes by which charities involved in the areas or fields concerned come to get involved. However, in the first example, the programme in the North West, the charity worked with the Tyne and Wear Foundation which advertised the programme locally.

To date, the fields chosen have been as follows:

1993 and 1994 The North East of England

1994 and 1995 Elderly homeless

Working with St Mungo's, this was a pilot project in London to assess the needs of of the elderly homeless and to discover why they are not gaining access to permanent housing. The 1997 Report suggests that the project has faced some difficulties, perhaps necessarily if its aims are to be achieved. A report on the project is presumably to be expected in due course. £363,000 was spent on the work in 1997.

1996, 1997 and 1998 The Valleys of Mid Glamorgan

This major grant is aimed to combat social deprivation in the valleys of Mid-Glamorgan. The programme was assembled with the help of South East Wales Community Foundation, among others. By its third year, six employment and welfare projects had been supported, though the amounts involved are not reported. 1997 expenditure was £454,000.

1997, 1998 and 1999 Persistent Young Offenders

Two projects are being funded, one in conjunction with Surrey Probation Service and the other, it is thought, with the London Action Trust. The Home Office is evaluating the effectiveness of the projects. £500,000 was spent in 1997.

1998, 1999 and 2000 Black Country Initiative

Grants totalling £2 million will be made during the three year period. A consultant, Maureen Stallard, has 'sought

out and assessed' projects. Though payments had not started by the end of 1997, the projects had been selected. These are listed in the 1997 Report and, for the first time, the amounts of grant are also given.

There will be 19 awards, closely resembling those given under the main grant programme described below, mostly being for three year's project or running costs, although Sandwell Young Carers will receive £105,000 towards the cost of new premises. Welcome though it must be to the beneficiaries involved, this programme seems the least likely of the series to meet the charity's objective of 'making a significant impact'. The National Lottery Charities Board is now allocating about £8 million a year to just the same kind of projects in this specific area, so a further £1 million a year for three years can make only a modest difference. It would seem more sensible for the charity to choose activities for which funding would otherwise be less likely, to be available.

The County grants

There are separate budgets, increasing in real terms from year to year to a total of £1.2 million in 1997, for local grants in each of the counties named below. This is because of their 'traditional connection' with the charity, though this does easily fit with its obligation to apply the charity's money where it is most needed.

Each county list is the responsibility of an individual trustee or other person who is normally resident in the county concerned. Applications are made both through the offices of the charity and direct to the trustees concerned. It is not known whether there is any formal assessment process for these applications or whether they are simply in the gift of the trustee concerned.

The counties concerned, the value of grants in 1995, and the appointed trustees are as follows:

Gloucestershire £137,000
T D Holland-Martin.

Hampshire £133,000
Julian Sheffield, Spring Pond, Laverstoke Lane, Whitchurch, Hampshire.

Kent £265,000
Ronnie Norman, St. Clere Estates, St. Clere, Kemsing, Sevenoaks, Kent.

Leicestershire £112,000
Major E J R M D de Lisle, Stockerston Hall, Uppingham, Leicestershire.

Suffolk £84,000
The Countess of Euston, The Racing Stables, Euston, Thetford, Suffolk.

Surrey £221000
G E Lee-Steere, Jayes Park, Ockley, Surrey.

East Sussex £144,000
Lord Gage.

West Sussex £99,000
Lord Egremount.

The grants are normally of a few hundred to two or three thousand pounds, though they can be as high as £10,000. They may be effectively in the gift of the trustee concerned.

The grants lists are relatively unchanging, with a strong concentration on youth clubs, scouts and local service charities like the Samaritans, the local branch of MENCAP or the Red Cross, but all kinds of charities are supported that fall within the remit of the charity generally. Typically there will be a dozen or so grants of more than £1,000 but hardly any of more than £10,000, with many small awards of £500 or less in most though not all of the counties.

Exclusions The charity cannot make grants for private education, for the care or restoration of buildings, or for individuals. Grants for the latter, except in the case of Henry Smith's poor kindred, are made through local parish charities only, as detailed in the companion Guide to Grants for Individuals in Need.

Applications In writing to the correspondent. The Chief Visitor is Virginia Graham. The trustees, and another, responsible for the 'county' allocations are identified in the section of the entry above dealing with these eight counties. The charity does not use application forms but offers the following guidelines to applicants for grants:

1. Applications should be no longer than four A4 sides (plus budget and accounts) and should incorporate a short (half page) summary.
2. Applications should:
   a. state clearly who the applicant is, what it does and whom it seeks to help.
   b. give the applicant's status (eg. registered charity).
   c. describe the project for which a grant is sought clearly and succinctly; explain the need for it; say what practical results it is expected to produce; state the number of people who will benefit from it; show how it will be cost effective and say what stage the project has so far reached.

d. enclose a detailed budget for the project together with a copy of the applicant's most recent audited accounts. (If those accounts show a significant surplus or deficit of income, please explain how this has arisen).
e. name the applicants's trustees/patrons and describe the people who will actually be in charge of the project giving details of their qualifications for the job.
f. describe the applicant's track record and, where possible, give the names and addresses of two independent referees to whom Henry Smith's Charity may apply for a recommendation if it wishes to do so.
g. state what funds have already been raised for the project and name any other sources of funding to whom the applicant has applied.
h. explain where the on-going funding (if required) will be obtained when the charity's grant has been used.
i. state what plans have been made to monitor the project and wherever possible to evaluate it and, where appropriate, to make its results known to others.
j. ask, where possible, for a specific amount.
3. Please keep the application as simple as possible and avoid the use of technical terms and jargon.

Trustees meet in March, June, September and December, and applications must be received at least two months before these meetings.

The Sobell Foundation

£3,663,000 (1996/97)

Jewish charities, health and welfare

P O Box 2137, Shepton Mallet, Somerset BA4 6YA
Tel: 0171 49813135 / Fax: 0171 49813136

Correspondent Mrs P J Newton

Trustees Mrs Susan LaCroix; Roger K Lewis; Mrs Gaie Scouller.

Beneficial area UK and Israel.

Information available Report and accounts for 1996/97, with only a partial list of grants (future accounts will be complete in this respect).

Summary A few very large grants, mostly but not exclusively to Jewish organisations. An extensive further grant making programme, involving a large number of quite small grants.

The amount awarded in grants in 1996/97 was exceptional, due to further distributions of assets and income from the estate of Sir Michael Sobell. An annual figure of around £1.5 million to £2 million a year seems more likely in the immediate future.

General This entry first describes the information that is available from the 1996/97 report and accounts and then repeats what was said in the previous edition of this book, when a full grants list was to hand.

During 1996/97 there were substantial further receipts from the estate of Michael Sobell and these were used to make a number of substantial grants on a scale that will probably not be sustainable.

The statement of policy in the 1996/97 report is that the founder, Sir Michael Sobell, now dead, 'was interested in causes benefiting children, the sick, elderly, needy and disabled, and that the present trustees tend to follow the founder's wishes. The trustees aim to achieve a balance between Jewish charities (in the UK and Israel) and non-Jewish charities in the UK.'

The list of interests above seems to cover almost the whole of the fields of health and welfare, leaving as the main exclusions art, heritage, environment and education other than that of children. Grants such as that described below for the University of Jerusalem may well be for activities in those institutions that fall within the interests of the founder as set out above.

The full list of grants given in the 1996/97 accounts (with figures in brackets for the amount given in the previous year) is set out in the box herewith.

Hebrew University of Jerusalem
£700,000 (£10,000)
Jerusalem Foundation £523,000
Jewish Care £500,000 (£26,000)
British Technion Society
£350,000 (£1,000)
Ravenswood Foundation
£300,000
Leonard Cheshire Foundation
£185,000 (£398,000)
Joint Jewish Charitable Trust
£177,000 (£25,000)
Oxford International Centre
for Palliative Care
£125,000 (£125,000)
The Weinstock Fund
£45,000 (£125,000)
Other donations £758,000 (£339,000)

The final figure in the boxed listing of £758,000 for 'other donations', would be more than enough in itself to justify a separate entry in this book. We therefore reprint below the description of the trust's grant making, from the previous edition of this book, when a full grants list (for 1994/95) was available.

Grants in 1994/95

The foundation made one exceptionally large grant of £180,000 to the Leonard Cheshire Foundation (42% of grant-aid). This is far larger than its major grants in previous years which have generally been for around £75,000 or £50,000. As a whole the foundation makes few large grants, but more should be expected in the future. In 1994/95 only eight organisations received grants totalling £10,000 or more. Another 40 grants were between £1,000 and £9,999 and practically all of these were in the lower range between £1,000 and £2,500. It is the habit of this foundation to spread the remainder of its funds widely in a very large number (500) of small grants of a only few hundred pounds. The trustees have recently decided that their minimum grant will be £250.

Grants to Jewish charities absorbed a lower proportion (about a third) of grant-aid than in previous years. Around 50 Jewish organisations covering all kinds of charitable activity received support, with the emphasis on the interests noted above, the needy, the elderly, the sick and disabled, especially children. The largest grant of the year was given to Jewish Care (£25,000) followed by Friends of the Hebrew University of Jerusalem (£20,000 in two grants), the Synagogue of Woburn House (£10,000) and Nightingale House, which accommodates elderly Jewish people (£10,000 in two grants) and the Children's Town Charity (£10,000).

Apart from the generous support to the Leonard Cheshire Foundation noted above, there were few large grants for health care and/or medical research and no substantial grants to medical institutions and hospitals in 1994/95 compared with previous years. The largest grant in this field of work was given to the Heart & Lung Institute (£12,000, also given in preceding years) followed by the Cancer Relief Macmillan Fund (£6,520) and the British Association of Cancer United Patients (£5,000).

The foundation's interest in education, shown in previous years by large grants to Jewish educational charities, was also not so apparent during this year. The foundation has an acknowledged interest in special care and schools for young disabled people, again not so apparent.

The small grants were given widely with disability organisations predominating. The following random sample gives a flavour of the range: the National Council on Ageing, the Association for Research into Stammering in Childhood, BLISS, the Derby Mountain Rescue Team and the International Relief Friendship Foundation.'

Exclusions No grants to individuals. Only registered charities or organisations registered with the Inland Revenue should apply.

Applications In writing to the correspondent.

Solev Co Ltd

£313,000 (1996/97)

Jewish charities

81/82 Roman Way, London N7 8UN
Tel: 0171-607 4470

Correspondent M Grosskopf, Governor

Trustees M Grosskopf; A E Perelman; R Tager.

Beneficial area UK

Information available Accounts on file at the Charity Commission. No grants list.

General In 1996/97 the trust had assets of £1.6 million and an income of £489,000. Grant giving was £313,000 and managament and administrative costs were £10,000.

Only two donations are mentioned in the annual report: '£100,000 to the Dina Perelmam Trust Ltd, a charitable company of which Mr Perelman and Mr Grosskopf are governors; and £40,000 to Songdale Ltd, a charity of which Mr M Grosskopf is an governor.

No grants list has been included in the accounts since 1972/73, when £13,500 was given to 52 Jewish charities. Examples then included Society of Friends of the Torah (£3,900); Finchley Road Synagogue (£2,300); NW London Talmudical College (£1,500); Yesodey Hatorah School (£700) and Gateshead Talmudical College (£400).

The Souter Foundation

£761,000 (1997)

Christianity, third world, social welfare

21 Auld House Wynd, Perth PH1 1RG
Tel: 01738-634745; Fax: 01738-440275

Correspondent Linda Scott, Secretary

Trustees Brian Souter; Elizabeth Souter; Linda Scott.

Beneficial area UK, but with a strong preference for Scotland; overseas.

Information available Annual report and accounts, (£5), and information sheet are available from the correspondent.

Summary The foundation makes an unknown number of donations each year to organisations. About 80% of the money is disbursed in about 20 donations for amounts of £10,000 or more. Grants are usually for revenue costs, vary from £200 to £50,000 and are occasionally repeated. A very small programme of grants for individuals accounts for 0.7% of charitable expenditure.

General The foundation was established in 1991 with an endowment from Brian Souter, who continues to make substantial donations. By the end of 1997 it had net assets approaching £8 million and an income of £1.7 million (including a donation of £1,360,000). A feature of this organisation is their low administration costs – £247 for the year.

The foundation does not say why grants are given, where the beneficiaries are based, or what they do. From studying the names of the recipients it appears that funds usually go to Scottish Christian charities working in a variety of fields.

The bulk of the foundation's information sheet is reproduced below:

'In the year ended 31 December 1997, charitable donations totalled £761,000 and ranged from £50,000 to an organisation working with the homeless to £200 to a local youth club.

'Most of the grants we make are in the region of £200-£500 (204 out of 285 in 1997). Our stated policy is to assist "projects engaged in the relief of human suffering in the UK or overseas, particularly those with a Christian emphasis". We tend not to get involved with research or capital funding, but would be more likely to assist with revenue costs of a project, for example, supporting a community worker. There is inevitably also a certain bias towards Scotland.'

The largest grants of 1997 were awarded to Church of the Nazarene (£125,000) and Strathclyde House Development Trust (£114,000; £171,000 in 1996). The third largest grant, for £50,000, was to Turning Point, – perhaps the 'organisation working with the homeless' mentioned in the foundation's information sheet. 46 individuals received donations totalling £6,000 (average £130).

Exclusions Building projects, personal education grants, expeditions.

Applications Applicants should apply in writing, setting out a brief outline of the project for which funding is sought. Trustees meet every two months or so, and all applications will be acknowledged in due course, whether or not successful.

Subsequent applications should be made no more frequently than annually.

The Southover Manor General Education Trust

£392,000 (1996/97)

Education, youth

Old Vicarage Cottage, Newhaven Road, Iford, Lewes, Sussex BN7 3PL

Correspondent The Secretary

Trustees B J Hanbury; Mrs R C Teacher; Miss S Aird; Brig J B Birkett; P E Cooper; Mrs M R Forrest; G R Furse; Mrs M Postgate; D W Usherwood.

Beneficial area Sussex.

Information available Report and accounts, without any of the required information about grant making, on file at the Charity Commission.

General The principal object of the trust is the 'education of boys and girls under 25 by providing books and equipment, supporting provision of recreational and educational facilities, scholarships and awards'. Grants are given to 'schools and individuals in Sussex'.

In 1996/97 the trust's income was £158,000 – less than half of grant expenditure. Nevertheless, due to

unrealised gains in investments, its assets still increased slightly to a total of £3,064,000.

There was no grants list for the year on file at the Charity Commission and the report and accounts gave no information about grants at all (beyond their total). However, the 1995/96 report and accounts are more revealing. In that year, the trust made 55 grants ranging from £100 to £50,000 (£277,000 in total). Four, accounting for a tiny percentage of total grants expenditure, were repeated from the previous year. The largest seven grants accounted for about 60% of the total. Most beneficiaries were state schools, but funds also went to private schools, individuals (amounts between £100 and £5,000), and other youth organisations (scouts, guides, the YMCA).

Exclusions Over 25 years of age. Organisations and individuals outside Sussex.

Applications In writing to the correspondent.

The Spitalfields Market Community Trust

£955,000 (1996/97)

Education, employment, welfare in Tower Hamlets

Attlee House, 28 Commercial Street, London E1 6LR
Tel: 0171-247 6689; Fax: 0171-247 8748

Correspondent Tim Budgen, Secretary; Sandra Davidson, Grants Administrator

Trustees Nigel Smith, Chairman; Mohammed Ali; Sunahwar Ali; Stella Currie; Ghulam Mortuza.

Beneficial area The London Borough of Tower Hamlets, Bethnal Green.

Information available Accounts. Director's Report with full grants list and abundant analyses of grants and grant-making.

Summary Around 100 grants a year are awarded to organisations benefiting the Tower Hamlets community in a variety of ways. Most of the money is given for revenue costs (about 60%) but capital projects also receive substantial

funding. Donations start at a few hundred pounds and peak at around £200,000. The trust expects to cease making grants in two to three years time (from 1998).

General The trust was established to benefit the members of Tower Hamlets with a particular emphasis on Bethnal Green. Founded in 1991 as a limited company (then called Startaid ltd), the trust was established as part of the 'planning gain' arrangements accompanying the development of what had been Spitalfields fruit and vegetable market, The trust received £3,750,000 from Spitalfields Development Ltd (the developers of the site) and £1,250,000 from the City of London Corporation (freeholders of the site). All directors of the trust have local connections.

Each year charitable expenditure exceeds income and therefore grant-making capacity is diminishing (total assets in 1996/97 were £4,797,000, and in 1992/93 £6.2 million). In 1998 the trust said that it expects to make fewer donations each year in the future, but it will also work in an advisory role only, giving information on fundraising and other charity matters.

The 1996/97 Director's Report says:
Funding Priorities 'The objects for which the trust was established are set out as follows:

- the advancement of education and relief of poverty in the London Borough of Tower Hamlets;
- to promote any other charitable purposes for the benefit of the community or of an appreciably important class of the community consisting of the inhabitants of Tower Hamlets.

'The trust continued to give priority to projects which meet it's objectives and which have the following features:

- impact;
- leverage;
- partnership;
- sustainability;
- equal opportunities.

In 1996/97, three grants of £50,000 or more accounted for 35% of charitable expenditure (including a single grant of £200,000), and 70% of grants were for £10,000 or less.

'To some extent this reflects the fact that the trust works to support a lot of small community groups in its area of benefit. These smaller amounts can help a group to establish their services, fund essential core costs or buy essential equipment. Some of the smaller amounts also represent the final year of funding that has been tapered over 2/3 years, smaller amounts may also be used to lever in or match funding received from other bodies.

'The trust has funded a broad range of activities. Again, the majority of funding was spent on environmental improvement. However, a large number of education, training and youth and community projects were funded in the year as illustrated.

'The trust has placed a high priority on supporting projects working with women and those working for the benefit of young people in Tower Hamlets through social education, supplementary schooling and youth activities. Capacity building and support for local community groups is also a priority; this is reflected through the trust's support of a major capacity building project in partnership with Cityside Regeneration. The trust also aims to be more proactive and set up specific projects in conjunction with other funding partners.

'Some of the work that is supported does not easily attract new funding and continuation grants may be approved for a limited period. Groups may come to rely on income from the trust; however, the trust's funds will be largely run down in two to three years time. The trust will therefore be giving more consideration to tapered funding and the provision of advice and support to groups to assist them to raise resources from elsewhere.'

The top of the grants list, (grants are listed sequentially according to size) reads as follows:

LBTH Allen Gardens, £200,000 towards the development and refurbishment of a public space.

JET Project, £82,000 towards a major 5 year vocational training initiative.

Toynbee Hall, £50,000 towards core running costs.

Bethnal Green High School, £44,000 to sponsor the school's application for technology college status.

St Hilda's East Community Centre, £35,000 towards the rebuilding of the Centre.

Christ Church Spitalfields, £25,000 towards the building project to extend and modernise the Hanbury Community Hall.

Some of the smaller gifts include:

Golden Moon Youth Club, £2,000 to purchase youth club equipment.

Udichi Shilpi Gosthi, £500 towards organising victory day celebration.

Drug-n-sport Don't Mix Initiative, £370 towards a visit to the United States for 5 young people from Tower Hamlets.

Exclusions No grants to organisations outside the London Borough of Tower Hamlets.

Applications To the grants administrator. Prior to submitting a detailed application, applicants are asked to submit an outline application.

All applicants are required to provide the following basic details:

- legal status and aims;
- a statement about the organisation, brief history, staffing and management committee details, current activities and reference to any previous grants from the trust;
- outline of the current financial position of the organisation;
- a statement on the particular need for which funding is being sought and who will benefit;
- full costing of the proposal;
- details of other funding sources for the project.

Applicants are also asked to enclose a budget for the current financial year, job description (if the application concerns a post) and a list of the names and addresses of the office holders of the management body. If an outline application is approved, applicants are asked to complete the trust's application form.

The directors of the trust usually meet monthly except in August and December.

Foundation for Sport and the Arts

£39,999,000 (1996/97), but see below

Sports, the arts

PO Box 20, Liverpool L13 1HB
Tel: 0151-259 5505; Fax: 0151-230 0664

Correspondent Grattan Endicott, Secretary

Trustees Sir Tim Rice (Chairman); Lord Brabazon (Deputy Chairman); Lord (Richard) Attenborough; Nicholas Allott; Dame Janet Baker; Sir Christopher Chataway; Robert Upsdell; Clive Lloyd; Lord Grantchester; Geoffrey Russell; Gary Speakman.

Beneficial area United Kingdom.

Information available Full information from the foundation. Monthly grants lists, containing a short informative note on the purposes of each grant. An application pack is available.

Summary The foundation is one of the largest funders of both sport and the arts, though its income, derived from the football pools, is now declining.

It usually gives one-off grants for buildings and equipment, but is now considering some revenue funding, as described below, together with interest-free loans. The maximum grant is now £75,000 although most grants are between £1,000 and £50,000. The foundation's aim has always been to support 'a lot with a little' and looks to encourage wide participation in sport and

The Spitalfields Market Community Trust

	No of grants	Capital	Revenue	Total
Housing	2	£5,000	£10,000	£15,000
Environmental improvements/ Building refurbishment	3	£239,000	£0	£240,000
Advice and information	7	£0	£73,000	£73,000
Arts/cultural/heritage	7	£20,000	£40,000	£60,000
Community development/support	13	£43,000	£101,000	£144,000
Education	16	£43,000	£113,000	£156,000
Community safety	1	£0	£3,000	£3,000
Social care	8	£3,000	£38,000	£41,000
Training	12	£49,000	£120,000	£169,000
Transport	3	£20,000	£10,000	£30,000
Under eights	3	£3,000	£6,000	£9,000
Youth services	14	£10,000	£47,000	£57,000
Totals	**89**	**£433,000**	**£561,000**	**£995,000**

the arts rather than élite performers and the development of excellence.

The money is divided into two thirds for sport and one third for art.

The foundation has always waged war on bureaucracy and retains an open and informal style. Decisions are made as quickly as possible by the trustees, although the funding arrangements of the foundation (see below) may often lead to delays between agreeing an application and the cheque being sent out.

General The foundation is an independent discretionary trust founded by and funded by way of the football pools. Support is directed to every level of sports and the arts, but the foundation is driven by a desire to put money back into those areas and communities where pools punters can see and enjoy the benefits. Grass roots activities with community benefit are warmly supported by the trustees.

The bulk of the sporting commitments are for 'athletic' activities. There is a smaller allowance for 'non-athletic sports' or recreational pursuits which nevertheless enhance or promote physical fitness.

The foundation's income

Income is entirely responsive to the fortunes of the football pools. There have been dramatic changes over the last four years, and regular readers of this guide will see a marked reduction from the £52.1 million reported in 1995/96. In its infancy after its creation in 1991, the foundation was giving away large grants, sometimes up to the giddy heights of £2 million for a single project. Grant totals peaked at around £70 million, with income of £1.4 million arriving weekly at the foundation, but are now in decline.

The decline is almost entirely the result of the arrival of the National Lottery in 1994. The Lottery has a not dissimilar programme of support for sports and the arts to that of the FSA. The FSA trustees feel keenly the double-whammy of reduced income and stolen funding clothes.

The likelihood is that income will continue to decline and may settle at around £10 million a year. This remains a very substantial annual investment in sport and the arts.

The grants: sports

The foundation has continued with its policy of giving awards mainly for capital and equipment. The desire to give pools customers something to see for their money informs trustees' decisions in every area of the foundation, including

the ongoing debate over revenue funding (see below). Grants are given for individuals' expenses, but usually where competitors face disadvantage or have a disability. A few grants are given to support team costs (travel and participation, but no longer for those going abroad) and events, or sports programme development.

The majority of the awards are directed towards small voluntary sports clubs representing an impressive array of sporting activity and taking in a large number of small communities throughout the country. Over 130 different sports have been supported from aikido to yachting. A tiny handful of sports are not supported by the foundation. These are: angling, croquet, fishing, horse racing, motorised sport. Shooting applications are considered on a case by case basis.

The FSA is keen to support all geographical areas. The enterprise is Liverpool based, and uses local advisers throughout the country. In 1996/97 money was given away throughout the four countries in the following amounts:

England	*£12,575,200*
Wales	*£1,178,500*
Scotland	*£1,884,252*
Northern Ireland	*£1,586,000*

There is an even distribution throughout the country, and unusually for a national foundation, there is no noticeable bias towards London and the south east.

The FSA does not allocate budgets to particular sports or geographical regions. The amount given to each activity or area is likely by and large to reflect the number of applications coming in. Where the FSA feels that a particular geographical area has been under-represented in recent grant giving, it gives preference to schemes from that area to maintain a rough balance. The distribution is totally in response to

applications, and the foundation makes no pretence at being proactive in its giving.

The FSA only supports individuals in exceptional circumstances. Recent grants have included £300 towards the equipment costs for a martial arts competitor, £500 for a cyclist's travel, equipment and training, and £1,900 for a triathlete's bike and wet suit. 'In such cases it is essential that the exceptional nature of the application is attested to in unqualified terms by an organisation of substance. In cases where the foundation finds it possible to help it is almost always because trustees fear real potential may be blighted by the difficult financial background of the persons concerned.' Much more often the grant is for a small group of sportsmen or women, to take part in an event in their field.

The FSA is not particularly interested in elite performers. These are the preserve of the Sports Council. It mainly gives grants to facilities which will encourage everyone to participate and enjoy sport, rather than for sporting excellence.

Revenue grants

The FSA has always supported capital costs. However, with the National Lottery funding similar items, the FSA has had to consider supporting running costs. In an interview in early 1996, Grattan Endicott considered: 'We have to be accountable to people who do the pools, and obviously it's easier to monitor a capital grant and say, "That's where your money went", than it is to point to salaries. But in the long-term, this may be part of what the FSA does'.

Later that year, in September, the FSA issued the following guidelines on revenue support: 'In the past we have avoided commitments to core funding and, in general, to payment of wages.

Foundation for Sport and the Arts

Grants for the arts, March 1998

Music (including opera)	Total: £109,846	(41 grants)
Museums and galleries	Total: £85,000	(2 grants)
Festivals	Total: £84,150	(12 grants)
Theatres	Total: £45,380	(3 grants)
Multidisciplinary	Total: £37,434	(8 grants)
Drama	Total: £27,200	(5 grants)
Visual arts (including sculpture)	Total: £20,829	(4 grants)
Film and Television	Total: £8,000	(2 grants)
Dance	Total: £3,770	(2 grants)
Crafts	Total: £2,000	(1 grant)

Where we can deal with cases on a two-year or three-year basis with no prospect of further funding subsequently, we have now made exceptions. Trustees are now prepared to look with interest at further applications coming forward.

'In preparing an application for revenue funding the following should be noted:

1. It is expected that a Business Plan will be required with closely detailed assessments of the revenue expenditure envisaged. Specify staff to be employed and why. The application should incorporate a plan in outline showing key figures or alternatively the full plan accompanied by a summary of key proposals.
2. Trustees will look for lean administration, economic and essential in its structure and practices.
3. Trustees should be given detail of the other revenue funding anticipated with information as to the extent to which it has been structured. Bodies that should evidently contribute to be designated and their position statements attached to the plan. (Local authorities in particular please note.)
4. Our reporting accountants will be asked at some stage to explore the proposals in the business plan.
5. To require prominent ongoing acknowledgement of any substantial grant-aid accepted from the foundation.

When discussing the subject, trustees indicated that revenue funding bids should be for schemes with a duration of not more that three years with no implication that the foundation would provide further funding beyond that. They have some particular anxieties about the 'ground level' management of facilities and resources already existing. They see the foundation's best use of revenue funding directed to the wider enjoyment of facilities and the more effective management of resources. However, there could also be scope in selected cases for start-up revenue funding in the first two or three years of a project.

Capital support and the National Lottery

The FSA is not curtailing its capital funding, and this is likely to remain the main element of the FSA's support. The FSA prefers projects where it is the lead funder, but will in some selected cases be involved in partnership funding where the Lottery is also supporting. 'In particular the foundation may be prepared to take on the principal funding of a discrete

segment of a project where this can be distinguished as a significant, self-contained 'foundation' exercise.' Liverpool Cricket Club are upgrading their facilities following amalgamation with a rugby and hockey club. They submitted an application to the FSA in parallel with a Sports Council lottery application. The FSA granted their application to refurbish ground floor changing facilities as this would be a discrete element of the overall development.

Loans

In December 1996, the foundation announced that it was considering making interest-free loans where appropriate. The potential borrower would have to show how the lease or purchase of land or property would make enough income available to repay the loan. Bristol Lawn Tennis Club Ltd has recently been offered a loan of £35,000 towards the cost of buying clubhouse buildings and a car park.

Examples of grants

In March 1998, £867,000 was given in 141 grants. 58 grants were for amounts up to £1,000; 55 were for amounts between £1,001 and £10,000; 24 were between £10,001 and £30,000; and 4 were between £30,001 and £50,000.

The following grants from the March 1998 list are typical of the projects the FSA supports:

£2,500 to Bowmen of Bosworth Archery Club for a new building;
£35,000 to Seckford Golf Club for upgrade of clubhouse;
£6,100 to Wyborn Youth Trust for fitness equipment;
£1,000 to Wishford C of E School for play equipment;
£500 to Collaton St Mary C of E Primary school for playground markings;
£675 to Halewood U3A for waterproof clothing for a walking group;
£25,000 to Cove Cricket Club for a new cricket square;
£12,500 to UOB Sailing Club for three Lark dinghies;
£20,000 to Toddington Tennis Club for resurfacing three tennis courts;
£4,200 to ADKC Action Disability, Kensington and Chelsea for basketballs and five lightweight wheelchairs;
£2,000 for Sport for Youth, Glasgow towards organising Glasgow Youth Games;
£5,000 to Rother District Council for skateboard and rollerblade park;
£11,900 to Uig Community Association for sports equipment in new community centre;

£33,000 to Craigcefnparc Welfare Association for refurbishment of community hall;
£750 to Tramways FC for kit and football equipment;
£550 to Cromarty Primary School for soccer sevens starter kit;
£1,500 to Matthew Sykes for canoe slalom championships;
£1,500 to Alresford Bowling club for a new mower;
£6,700 to Cynon Valley Cardinals Skater Hockey Team for kit and equipment;
£15,500 to Walton Rowing Club for three rowing boats and sculling oars;
£5,700 to Rosconnor Gaels GAC Hurling Club to establish under 10 hurling club for one year.

The grants: arts

These make up a third of the overall total. £12,692,000 was awarded overall in 1996/97, compared to the total of £17,159,000 in 1995/96. As in previous years, the awards were modest, with just a few 'flagship' projects peppering the grants lists. Larger beneficiaries included:

Glyndebourne Touring Opera	*(£75,000)*
Blackpool Grand Theatre	*(£70,000)*
Harrogate International Centre	*(£60,000)*
Almeida Theatre	*(£50,000)*
Edinburgh International Festival	*(£46,600)*
Dance UK	*(£45,800)*

As with sports, the days of £1 million or £2 million grants are a fading memory.

The FSA supports both amateur and professional activities and gives grants to most art forms. Literature is perhaps the least represented art form in the grants lists. Individuals as well as organisations can be supported, albeit with small grants. (£400 to each Foundation for Sport and the Arts scholar at the University of York's music department for instance and a more substantial £8,850 to a FSA scholar on a three year course at the Guildford School of Acting.) Church organs can be refurbished, but the trustees look closely at the extent to which the organ will be used for the wider public through recitals and concerts. Grants are not currently given for uniforms or instruments for brass, silver or marching bands.

An example: arts grants in March 1998

In this selection of grants the largest by some distance was £50,000 towards the development of the Handel House Museum. £35,000 was given to provide exhibition and performance space at the Theatre Museum in London, and £30,000 went to Cookstown District Council in

Northern Ireland towards installing seating in the new Arts Centre Theatre. Under 'multi-disciplinary', £19,800 was given to the Textile Conservation Centre at Hampton Court Palace. Grants for festivals revealed the FSA's eclectic approach with awards to celebrations of jazz, Haydn's, alternative, choral, early, and Elgar's music. £3,000 was given to the Hay Children's Festival of Arts and £6,600 to support the costs of the Scottish Symphony Orchestra at the St Magnus Festival on Lindisfarne.

These grants are categorised in the table herewith.

Other grants from the March list include:

£700 to a student for materials on a design course;

£18,700 to New Contemporaries 1998 Ltd (Manchester) for conversion of a tea factory for temporary exhibition space;

£11,800 to Stray Theatre Company (Argyll) to stage Romeo and Juliet at Dunstaffnage Castle;

£300 to Comic Fusion for production expenses and travel;

£1,300 to Lowender Peran (Cornwall) for a portable dance floor;

£5,000 to Hereford Arts in Action to produce a community play;

£1,000 to St Luke's C of E Primary School (Cambridge) for an expressive arts week to include poetry, dance, music and art;

£2,000 to Eyam Mechanics Institute for stage curtains;

£750 to Blantyre Youth Job Shop (Glasgow) to set up record label for local bands;

£2,400 to Edinburgh University Music Society for professional soloists for a performance of Carmen;

£3,000 to Kingsbridge Barbershop Harmony Club (Devon) for amplification and recording equipment;

£3,000 to an individual performer to buy a piano;

£11,600 to Opera North for a young people's workshop programme;

£2,000 to Junction Farm Primary School (Stockton-on-Tees) for an artist in residency scheme to create tapestries for the school hall.

As with sports, there is a fairly even spread of grants across the country. There is perhaps a slight preponderance of grants in Greater London and the South East.

Arts grants by region in 1996/97

Scotland	*£727,000*
Northern Ireland	*£371,000*
Wales	*£997,000*
North East	*£1,260,000*
North West	*£1,270,000*
Midlands	*£1,043,000*
South West	*£1,301,000*
South East	*£2,547,000*
Greater London	*£4,208,000*

Exclusions No grants outside the foundation's chosen fields, as described above.

Applications Full applications packs are available from the telephone number above. Grants are considered on a rolling basis.

Where applicants are considering revenue funding or interest-free loans, they also should read the notes above.

The following information should be included in the application:

- The latest financial statements of the enterprise to be assisted.
- A description of the purpose for which a grant is sought. Where applicable this should be backed up with the reports of consultants and professional advisers.
- The total cost of the project. The amount of the grant desired from the Foundation.
- A statement of the way in which it is proposed to fund the project, with information on other money which will, or may, be committed alongside that of the Foundation.
- A special point should be made of telling us (where applicable) such information as:

How many people will benefit form the proposal?

What numbers of people can be accommodated in the auditorium or spectator accommodation?

The precise nature of the ownership of the club, society, premises, trustees, members' committee or the like.

- Information as to the persons who will be involved in the realisation of the plan. Where available and applicable, facts as to suppliers and contractors who will be, invited to give effect to the proposals.
- A completed questionnaire. This is important: cases are delayed if there is no completed questionnaire.
- In the case of a club or organisation a potted history of its founding, development and future aims.

The trustees would prefer that a detailed application should be accompanied by a *synopsis of the key elements set out on a single sheet of A4 size paper.* Videos and books are not encouraged. A photograph or two may be helpful in some cases.'

When assessing an application, the trustees have two main considerations:

(i) *The project should benefit the general community:* 'The money comes out of the pockets of pools punters: we would like to plough it back largely into things that the general community will experience and enjoy'.
(ii) Therefore, the foundation is particularly keen to support the 'little clubs' – ie. regional and local clubs.

In recent years, the FSA has particularly look for how much self-help the application contains. It is keen to see other fund-raising initiatives as well as other supporters involved in the project.

An application's progress

1. The organisation sends an outline application to the FSA.
2. If the application seems relevant the FSA will send a questionnaire which asks for more detailed information. If it is not relevant, it will be rejected at this stage and the applicant will be told.
3. The organisation fills out the questionnaire and encloses the other information asked for.
4. The FSA tells the organisation that the application has been received.
5. Applications are passed to assessors for external comment.
6. If appropriate, the FSA asks for the views of umbrella bodies and others.
7. Applications are returned to the FSA with comments.
8. Applications are ordered into FSA priorities.
9. Approved applications are passed to the trustees.
10. If agreed, a Letter of Intent is sent to the organisation. If not, a rejection letter is sent.
11. Agreed applications wait for the necessary money to come in.
12. Once money has come in, the grant is sent to the organisation. The time lag from acceptance to payment can vary from days to months. There is a plea from the FSA for applicants not to telephone staff to find out how the application is doing.

Owing to the way the foundation is funded there may be time lags between agreeing a grant and the cheque being sent. The FSA empties the funding barrel whenever pools income is received. Successful applications have therefore to wait their turn. It can be four to six months or more depending on the size of the application. 'When a case is approved and put in the queue of potential grant offers waiting funds, we will send to the applicant a letter of intent. This is carefully worded so that it does not commit the trustees to a grant and the applicant is warned not to go too far in acting upon the content of the letter for this reason. Until a letter of intent is issued it remains the case that the final decision may be to refuse the application. No applicant should make an assumption that prolonged consideration implies an eventual decision to offer a grant.'

Pam Bennett leads the Sports Team; Carole McGiveron, the Arts, and Lila Thomas is in charge of Non-Athletic Sports.

The Staples Trust

£603,000 (approved, 1996/97)

Overseas development, environment, women's issues, general

See entry for the 'Sainsbury Family Charitable Trusts'
Tel: 0171-410 0330

Correspondent Michael Pattison

Trustees Miss Jessica Sainsbury; Alexander J Sainsbury; T J Sainsbury; P Frankopan; Miss J S Portrait.

Beneficial area UK and overseas.

Information available The trust provides a full report and accounts. Its principal officers in 1996/97 are listed as Michael Pattison, the director, Paul Spokes, the finance director and Miss H Marriott, Executive.

Summary This trust is one of the Sainsbury Family Charitable Trusts which share a joint administration. It gives most of its support to development/ environmental work overseas. It also supports UK-based environmental

activities. It is rare amongst trusts in naming women's issues as a particular concern.

General Jessica Sainsbury is the settlor of this trust. The trustees include her two older brothers who lead the Tedworth and Glass-House trusts (see separate entries) and her husband.

In 1996/97 the trust had a net income of over £479,000 and a total of £801,000 available for distribution. Whilst the net income of the trust increased by over £100,000 in 1996/97, its asset value decreased by over £1million to £10.6 million in April 1997.

Overseas Development – £270,000 approved 1996/97

'Support tends to be focused in East and South Africa, South and South East Asia and South America, although projects from other areas are considered on their merits.

'Trustees are interested in a range of activities, including income-generation projects, with a particular emphasis on the role of women in communities, shelter and housing, sustainable agriculture and forestry, and the rights of indigenous people.

Trustees are particularly interested to support development projects which take account of environmental sustainability and, in many cases, the environmental and developmental benefits of the project are of equal importance.'

The largest single grant in 1996/97 was made to CARE for a sanitation and family resource project to support local Bangladeshi NGOs to implement high-quality hygiene education programmes (£34,654). Other grants included the African Medical and Research Foundation for an income-generation, health and family planning project in Kitui district, Eastern Province, Kenya (£46,067 over 3 years), Medica mondiale e.V. for medical and psychological services to women victims of war in

Bosnia-Herczegovina (£25,000) and Drukpa Kargyad Trust towards the Ladakh school project (£10,000).

Environment – £133,000 approved 1996/97

'Projects are supported in developing countries, Central and Eastern Europe and the UK. Grants are approved for renewable energy technology, training and skills upgrading and, occasionally, research. In Central and Eastern Europe, trustees are interested in providing training opportunities for community/ business leaders and policy makers and in contributing to the process of skill-sharing and information exchange. In the UK, trustees aim to help communities protect, maintain and improve areas of land and to support work aimed at informing rural conservation policy.'

The largest grant in 1996/97 was given to WWF-UK for work gazetting and protecting the sacred coastal forests in Kwale and Kilifi, Kenya by developing workable programmes to prevent over-exploitation (£40,000). Support was given to IIED to produce and distribute a policy briefing and research methodology as part of its 'Hidden Harvest' project to encourage agricultural policy makers to take greater account of the importance of wild resources for rural livelihoods in developing countries (£18,555). Other beneficiaries were Friends of the Earth, the Field Studies Council, OXFAM, Plantlife and TUSK.

Women's Issues – £95,000 approved 1996/97

'Trustees remain interested in domestic violence issues, in particular the promotion of interagency co-operation. Trusts have also made a number of small grants to local refuge services and women's self-help groups to help with core costs. Trustees also support organisations working with women offenders or ex-offenders with specific problems (including mental illness).'

In 1996/97 three major grants were given to the Women in Special Hospitals and Female Prisoners Welfare Projects, both for core costs (£30,000 over 3 years) and London Action Trust to employ a London co-ordinator for domestic violence issues (£25,000).

General – £105,000 approved 1996/97

Grants of £52,408 each were made to the Headley and Jerusalem Trusts (see separate entries).

Applications The trustees met three times in 1996/97. The trust is proactive in its work and does not encourage applications. 'Unsolicited applications are unlikely to be successful.'

The Staples Trust

| | 1996/97 | | | 1995/96 | | |
	No of grants			No of grants		
Overseas						
Development	£270,000	14	45%	£357,000	11	73%
Environmental	£133,000	8	22%	£137,000	8	28%
Women's Issues	£95,000	8	16%	£121,000	4	25%
General	£105,000	2	17%	£57,000	3	12%
Total	**£603,000**	**32**	**100%**	**£487,000**	**37**	**100%**

However it is also said that one application to a Sainsbury family trust is an application to all. See the entry for the Sainsbury Family Charitable Trusts for the address and further advice.

The Steel Charitable Trust

£799,000 (1997/98)

Social welfare, health, medical research, general

3 Boutport Street, Barnstaple EX31 1QY

Correspondent The Secretary, Bullimores Chartered Accountants

Trustees N E W Wright, Chair; A W Hawkins; J A Childs; J A Maddox.

Beneficial area UK, with some preference for Bedfordshire.

Information available Report and accounts with full grants list for two years but lacking the required analysis and explanation of grant making. Guidelines for applicants.

Summary The trust supports a wide variety of causes but in particular focuses on social welfare which accounts for about 50% of grant expenditure. Typically grants are for £5,000 and vary from under £1,000 to £75,000 (although the guidelines give a maximum of £25,000). Although information on the location of beneficiaries is scant, most appear to be either national organisations or based in Bedfordshire.

General The trustees' policy is to make grants 'to a wide range of charitable bodies'.

In the year ending January 1998 it had assets of £23.6 million from which an income of £926,000 was generated.

About 90 grants were awarded in that period, more than half of them for £5,000. The grants are categorised in the table herewith.

15 organisations supported in 1996/97 were also supported in 1997/98 and these repeat grants amounted to £230,000 (28% of the total). Approximately a quarter of the total £799,000 in grants went in 12 donations of £20,000 to the following organisations: Imperial Cancer Research Fund; National Deaf Children's Society; PDSA; International League for the Protection of Horses; Donkey Sanctuary; Salvation Army; Friends of St Mary's Church, Luton; Gray Laboratories Research Trust; Roy Kinnear Foundation; Royal Academy of Music; National Institute for Conductive Education.

The largest grant of the year was a repeat grant of £50,000 to Luton and South Bedfordshire Hospice. Of the £20,000 grants, new beneficiaries were Gray Laboratories Cancer Research Trust and Roy Kinnear Foundation. The same amount was given to organisations that had previously benefited from the trust, including the Royal Academy of Arts Trust; Royal Academy of Music and the National Institute for Conductive Education.

Exclusions Individuals, students, expeditions.

Applications In writing to the correspondent including:

- statement of purpose for which the grant is required;
- full latest accounts showing all other sources of funding;
- statement of existing funding for the purpose of the grant application.

Meetings are held in January, April, July and October.

Applications are not acknowledged.

The Cyril & Betty Stein Charitable Trust

£256,000 (1996/97)

Jewish causes

Messrs Clayton Stark & Co, 18 St George Street, Hanover Square, London W1R 0LL
Tel: 0171-493 1205

Correspondent D Clayton

Trustees Cyril Stein; Betty Stein; David Clayton.

Beneficial area UK and Israel.

Information available Report and accounts on file at the Charity Commission.

General The trust makes a small number of substantial grants each year, all usually to Jewish charities in either Britain or Israel.

In 1996/97 there were nine grants in all, as against ten in the previous year, led by awards to the Jaffa Institute for the Advancement of Education (£67,000) and the Friends of the Hebrew University of Jerusalem (£44,000), both of which were also supported in the previous year.

Examples of the recipients of the smaller awards were the Lubavitch and Da'ath foundations, each receiving £5,000.

Applications In writing to the correspondent.

The Sir Halley Stewart Trust

£702,000 (1996/97)

Medical, social and religious research

88 Long Lane, Willingham, Cambridge CB4 5LD
Tel: 01954-260707; Fax: 01954-261623

Correspondent Mrs Polly Fawcitt, Secretary

Trustees Professor Lennard Jones (Chairman); Professor Harold C Stewart; Dr Duncan Stewart; Sir Charles Carter; William P Kirkman; Lord Stewartby; George Russell; Professor Phyllida Parsloe; Miss Barbara Clapham; Professor W Jacobson; Michael Ross Collins; Brian Allpress; Professor Philip Whitfield; Professor C Hallett.

The Steel Charitable Trust				
	1997/98		**1996/97**	
Culture and Recreation	£102,000	12%	£80,000	10%
Medical research	£93,000	12%	£101,000	12%
Health	£79,000	10%	£156,000	19%
Social services	£399,000	50%	£337,000	42%
Environment and preservation	£105,000	13%	£102,000	13%
International aid and activity	£21,000	2%	£34,000	4%

Beneficial area Unrestricted, but mainly UK and South and West Africa in practice.

Information available Accounts are on file at the Charity Commission, at last with a minimal list of grants, but still without the narrative report on the work of the trust that is required by law. Leaflet – 'Notes for those seeking grants'.

Summary At present, mainly medical research grants to universities and hospitals for work in Southern Africa, but the trust also supports small scale research in social, educational and religious fields, and these are likely to receive greater emphasis from trustees in future. There is an active interest in helping young researchers with innovative agendas.

General The trust was established between the wars in the splendid hope that it would, among other things, 'express the mind of Christ in the realisation of the Kingdom of God upon Earth'.

The trust's grant making is categorised in the table herewith

Some of the trust's policies are unusually interesting but also, in many cases, particularly difficult to implement. The preference for supporting 'a young person with whom they can develop a direct relationship' is relatively easy, but finding 'innovative research activities or developments with a view to making such work self-supporting' is usually more difficult. Unfortunately, there is no information from the trust to suggest the degree to which such policies are achieved in practice, or stay mainly as aspirations.

The accounts show the recipients of the larger donations but give no indication of the purposes the payments are intended to receive – for example, the list is headed by a baldly stated 'Oxford University, £66,000'.

The trust is keen to emphasise its religious, social and educational activities. In recent years most of the trust's money has been spent on medical research and the trust has specialist medical trustees and specific research priorities selected from within its main aims. However, such research is but a part of the trust's remit and there is likely to be increasing emphasis on the social and religious aspects in future.

The trust's leaflet advises applicants as follows:

Objects of the trust 'The trust has a Christian basis and is concerned with the development of body, mind and spirit, a just environment, and international goodwill. To this end it supports projects in religious, social, educational and medical fields. The trust aims to promote and assist innovative research activities or developments with a view to making such work self-supporting. It emphasises prevention rather than alleviation of human suffering.

Types of grant given 'Grants are usually in the form of a salary, and the trustees prefer to support a young person with whom they can develop a direct relationship. Sometimes a contribution towards the expenses of the project is given. Grants are normally limited to two or three years, but are sometimes extended. In general, the trustees do not favour grant giving to enable completion of a project initiated by other bodies.

Current priority areas:

Religious 'The trust is committed to advancing Christian religion. The trustees generally support religious projects which they have specifically sought out rather than those arising from speculative approaches for grants. Their particular interests are:

- Theological training in cases where there is a special and specific need (eg. in Eastern Europe or Africa);
- Teaching in the UK about Christianity, outside the formal education system.
- Encouragement of specific groups of people (for example, the elderly, people with disability, students in higher education, those from multi-ethnic communities…) to explore their spiritual needs and strengths.

Anyone contemplating approaching the trust for support in this field is strongly advised to make a preliminary enquiry before submitting an application.

Social and Educational 'Applications are welcomed for research and development projects which will have a direct impact on the conditions of a particular group of people, as well as having wider implications.

The trustees are particularly interested in

- Projects which attempt to resolve conflicts and increase understanding across racial, cultural, class, religious and professional barriers;
- Child neglect;
- Older people and their carers;
- Social problems of imprisonment;
- Small scale projects in South Africa and parts of West Africa, particularly those which contain a training element.

Medical 'Projects should be simple, not too molecular, not too far from clinical application, and they may include a

---

The Sir Halley Stewart Trust

1997/98 and 1996/97 grants were categorised as follows:

	1997/98		1996/97	
Medical	£432,000	62%	£435,000	59%
Social and educational	£197,000	28%	£255,000	35%
Religious	£72,000	10%	£47,000	6%

Breakdown of grants by size:

Size	Number of grants		total	
Less than £1,000	15	£6,000	16	£4,000
£1,000 – £4,999	23	£42,000	27	£60,000
£5,000 or more	34	£654,000	43	£673,000

The grants list only specifies those of £5,000 or more, however these account for about 90% of the money. From the names of the recipients, the major types of beneficiary seem to be:

	grants	total	
Universities	19	£397,000	58%
Hospitals	7	£87,000	13%
Southern Africa	6	£79,000	11%
Other charities	11	£126,000	18%
Total	43	£689,000	93%

social element. Non-medical trustees should be able to understand the application and appreciate the value of the work. Projects may be of a type unlikely to receive support from research councils or large research-funding charities.

Applications are particularly welcomed from within the following fields:

- Problems associated with the elderly such as Alzheimer's Disease, nutrition, osteoporosis and incontinence;
- The prevention of handicap in children;
- The prevention of topical infective and parasitic diseases;
- Crohn's Disease.'

Most grants are probably for experimental research to some degree though it is not clear how such a phrase relates to 'religious' – but perhaps this just represents ignorance of the field. There is a definite interest in Southern Africa (including countries such as Mozambique as well as South Africa itself).

Exclusions

- general appeals of any kind;
- the purchase, erection or conversion of buildings;
- costs of equipment and other capital costs;
- running costs of established organisations;
- personal education, including educational and travel projects for young people.

Applications Preliminary enquiries welcome, whether by telephone or in writing. No application forms. Research proposals to the secretary. The application should come, in the first instance, from the individual concerned, rather than the 'host' organisation.

'Applicants should first write to the Secretary with a short description of the proposed work. We need to know exactly what you plan to do with the grant, where you will be doing the work, how much funding you will need and approximately how long the work should take. We will also require a brief CV. The trust may wish to know where you hope to obtain future funding after the trust's support has ended.

'If we cannot help you we will let you know as soon as possible, probably within two weeks. It is worth pointing out that we receive many applications for support, and although your work may fit the objects of the trust, we may not necessarily be able to help you.

'If it is decided to take your application further, it will be seen by those trustees who are most interested in that particular field. They may ask for more details of the work at this stage. If they are enthusiastic they might then suggest that the application should be considered at a full trustees' meeting.

'The trustees' meetings are held three times a year in February, June and October. Applications need to be received at least two months before a meeting for consideration at the next one. Applications from outside the UK are considered if they are within our current priority areas.

The Stobart Newlands Charitable Trust

£490,000 (1996)
Christian causes

Newlands Mill, Hesket Newmarket, Wigton, Cumbria CA7 8HP
Tel: 01697-478 261

Correspondent Mrs M Stobart, Trustee

Trustees R J Stobart; M Stobart; R A Stobart; P J Stobart; L E Rigg.

Beneficial area Unrestricted.

Information available Accounts, but no report or grants list, up to 1996 available on file at the Charity Commission in September 1998.

General Thin two page accounts for 1996 showed assets of £2 million but a higher income than would be expected from these alone, of £730,000, derived from the profits of an associated animal feeds company.

There is no information about the 1996 grants, totalling £490,000, other than that 'it's a local trust that deals with the local area, and it is a family trust.'

The SORP requirements will require more detailed information in the future.

Exclusions No grants for individuals.

Applications Unsolicited applications are unlikely to be successful.

The W O Street Charitable Foundation

£426,000 (1997)
Education, disability, young people, welfare

c/o Barclays Bank Trust Company Ltd, Osborne Court Gadbrook Park, Rudheath, Northwich CW9 7UE
Tel: 01606-313213; Fax: 01606 313005/6

Correspondent Miss M Bertenshaw, Administrator

Trustees Barclays Bank Trust Co. Ltd; A Paines.

Beneficial area UK, Jersey.

Information available Report and accounts with grants list but lacking the required narrative explanation and analysis of grants.

Summary The foundation makes around 50 grants a year ranging from £500 to £50,000 (typically £2,500) to charities. There is a special interest in the North-West of England and Jersey.

General The foundation was set up in 1973 by a settlement deed of William Openshaw Street. In 1997 it had assets totalling over £16 million from which £655,000 income was generated.

Management fees from Barclays Bank were remarkably high at £164,000 or 25% of income or 38 pence per £1 donated out. Such fees do not include further costs such as 'trustees and other fees' (£10,690). There may be exceptional reasons for such a high level of administrative costs, but if there are they need to be explained in detail in the annual report. On seeing the previous sentences, the foundation noted that management fees are based on the capital value of the trust. 'Barclays' management fees for acting as a trustee are authorised by the trust deed in accordance with a published scale and are charged as a percentage of the trust's capital value'. This does not seem satisfactory; they might be better based on the work to be done.

As a trustee the bank, like any other trustee, has an obligation to secure the most effective and economical administration that is possible. Its own 'scale' of charges does not necessarily achieve this.

Despite the new statutorily based requirements of the SORP, the annual report does not say for what purpose donations were made nor does it give the nature or location of the beneficiaries; it is surprising that reports in conformity with the SORP are not one of the services provided under Barclay's 'scale'.

The foundation says:

'In considering grants the trustees pay close regard to the wishes of the late Mr Street who had particular interests in education, relief of poverty, the relief of persons with financial difficulties (particularly the aged, blind and disabled) and the relief of ill health or sickness and social welfare generally. Special support is given to the North-West of England and to Jersey. £69,951 was paid to the W O Street Jersey Charitable Trust – the trustees of which apply the income (and were appropriate the capital) for charitable purposes within Jersey. £64,800 was spent on education bursaries and a further £291,000 in grants for charitable purposes.

'The trustees have selected a limited number of educational projects to which significant grants are being given over a shortish period (usually no more than three years) to enable the projects to find their feet. The trustees are keeping this policy under review but it is likely that a programme of supporting projects of this nature will be sustained (at least for the foreseeable future). As a result the trustees will not be able to devote so much of their resources as they have in the past to smaller 'one-off' grants.'

The largest grants of 1997 were to Foyer Federation (£50,000), Home Start UK (£40,000), Education 2000 Trust (£38,000), and Life Education Centres (£12,000). All other grants were for £5,000 or less. Charities receiving £5,000 included: The Rose Road Children's Appeal; Perth College Development Trust; Action for Blind People; Status Employment; and Gloucester Association for Mental Health.

Exclusions No grants to individuals, hospices, medical research.

Applications To the correspondent in writing, with supporting balance sheet, details of capital projects and sums raised towards the project. The trustees meet four times a year, in January, April, July and October.

The Alan Sugar Foundation

£711,000 (1996/97)

Jewish charities, general

Brentwood House, 169 Kings Road, Brentwood, Essex CM14 4EF
Tel: 01277-228888

Correspondent Colin Sandy

Trustees Alan Sugar; Colin Sandy.

Beneficial area UK, overseas.

Information available Full accounts are on file at the Charity Commission with grants list but with no narrative report.

General This trust was established by the well-known chairman of Tottenham FC, and gives a small number of substantial grants each year.

Income for 1996/97 was £240,000 but a total of £711,000 was given out in grants to just seven organisations. Over 70% of the money went in one large grant to King Solomon School Redbridge (£510,000), which also received the largest grant in the previous year. The remaining grants went to Great Ormond Street Hospital (£100,000), Sinclair House (£50,000). Ravenswood (£30,000), NSPCC (£10,000), Imperial War Museum (£10,000) and to Public Concern (£1,000).

Exclusions No grants for individuals.

Applications In writing to the correspondent.

The Summerfield Charitable Trust

£295,000 (1997)

The arts, welfare general, mainly in the Gloucestershire area

PO Box 4, Winchcombe, Cheltenham, Gloucs. GL54 5ZD
Tel: 01242-676774; Fax: 01242-677120;
E-Mail:admin@summerfield.org.uk;
Website; http://www.summerfield.org.uk

Correspondent Mrs Lavinia Sidgwick, Administrator

Trustees Earl Fortescue; Martin Davis; Dr. The Hon. Gilbert Greenall; Mrs Rosaleen Kaye; Mrs Rachael Managhan.

Beneficial area Gloucestershire and surrounding counties.

Information available Full annual report and accounts on file at the Charity Commission: A very professional booklet 'Grants paid 1997' describes and analyses its work in text, tables and graphics; guidelines.

Summary This busy and conscientious trust is firmly rooted in Gloucestershire with a small and shrinking interest in the neighbouring counties. Each year it gives out nearly £300,000 to a variety of causes benefiting the community in general and the disadvantaged in particular. Most support is given in one-off, non revenue grants, typically for £1,000 and peaking at £16,000.

General The trust is named in honour of its founder, Ronald Summerfield, a local antiques dealer who died shortly after he established it in 1989.

The trust views especially favourably:
- projects which serve the needs of those living in rural areas;
- ventures which make a point of using volunteers (and which train volunteers);
- applicants who show clear indications that they have assessed the impact of their projects upon the environment;
- joint appeals from groups working in similar areas, who wish to develop a partnership, and interestingly;
- those who have a conscientious objection to applying for National Lottery funding.

The trustees particularly welcome innovative ideas from small voluntary groups.

A full page of guidelines sets out the trust's environmental policy, which encourages good practice in the organisations it supports and within the trust's own administration and investments .

Support in 1997 fell within one of eleven categories:

	Number of grants	Total
Arts	17	£44,250
Churches	14	£26,900
Conservation/ environment	10	£39,500
Counselling	5	£13,200
Disabled, chronically sick	23	£47,200
Education	23	£48,325
Elderly	8	£9,595
Homeless	4	£19,500
Museums	4	£2,800
Recreation	19	£34,150
Youth	7	£9,000

During 1997, £294,745 was distributed in 134 grants, mostly between £500 and £5,000. Applications had a 18% chance of success (a total of 734 were received). The pattern of giving has remained largely stable over the last six years. However, grants to the disabled and chronically sick have increased from 10% of the total grants expenditure in 1996 to 16% in 1997. This was balanced by a decrease in funding to the elderly from 10% to 3%, which the trust says was due to a fall in the number of applications rather than a shift in grant-making preferences.

Since 1993 the proportion of funds allocated to the Gloucestershire region has grown from 70% of grants to around 90%. In 1997 an increased number of grants went to projects involving volunteers (51% of funds) and to rural groups (21%). These trends are clearly not random, as they are in line with the trust's stated preferences.

Particularly sizeable awards were made to Forum for the Future (£16,000) for work 'to identify, develop and share solutions to today's environmental problems', and to the Gloucestershire Dance Project (£11,000) to develop dance opportunities for a range of community groups (the elderly, disabled, children etc.).

Within the churches programme, the trust looks to make grants to umbrella preservation groups rather than to specific churches, an example of this in 1997 was the £15,000 award paid to Gloucestershire Historic Churches Trust as the final payment of a £45,000, three year grant.

The trust's Annual Report is very informative and useful reading for anyone interested in its activities or other trusts wishing to improve their own reports.

Exclusions

Donations are rarely given to:

- medical research;
- national charities (unless a local branch);
- private education;
- animal welfare appeals;
- individuals (especially if not sponsored by a charity);
- London based charities.

Applications The trustees meet quarterly usually in January, April, July and October, when they consider all applications received by the end of the preceding month.

'Applicants should write to me [Lavinia Sidgwick] stating in their own words

what is required, the purpose of the application, a brief history, a financial summary and (where relevant) registered charity number. Further, please say if and when you have previously applied to the trust for a grant.

'It also helps if grant seekers say which other trusts they are approaching: we may consult them (or members of our informal panel of advisors), unless applicants specifically write to request us not to.'

If, having studied the guidelines, you are still unsure of whether or not your project falls within the trust's policy, telephone discussions are welcomed to prevent wasted effort all round.

New applications are acknowledged and all applicants informed of the trustees' decisions. SAEs are welcomed.

The Bernard Sunley Charitable Foundation

£2,772,000 (1997/98)

General

53 Grosvenor Street,
London W1X 9FH
Tel: 0171-409 1199 Fax; 0171-409 7373

Correspondent Duncan Macdiarmid, Director

Trustees John B Sunley; Mrs. Joan M Tice; Mrs. Bella Sunley; Sir Donald Gosling.

Beneficial area Unrestricted, but mainly Great Britain, especially London and the South East. Local interests in Ealing, Kent, Northamptonshire and Madrid.

Information available Report and accounts, the latter unusually clear and informative on financial matters, but there is no narrative report on policies and activities. List of grants paid, but with little indication of their nature or purpose other than for the 17 largest. The whole falls somewhat short of Charity Commission requirements, but useful further information was made available for use in this entry.

Summary Over 200 new grants are approved each year, 10-15% of them to organisations regularly supported, and covering most fields of charity. Most grants are for £3,000 or less, but they

can be for £200,000 or more, and may be spread over a number of years. The awards for £100,000 or more typically account for about one third of the money allocated, and are overwhelmingly for new buildings or for the refurbishment of existing buildings. Smaller grants are for a wider spread of purposes.

Nearly one third of the money goes to national charities. The rest is very heavily concentrated in London and the South East of England. Only the slightest amounts go to Scotland, Wales or Ireland, other than via grants to national charities.

General With its unrestricted 'general' interests, this foundation received over 2,000 appeals in 1997/98, of which 300 were successful, but most of these grants were for amounts of £1,000 or less.

The foundation now appears old-fashioned (though this is not necessarily a criticism), concentrating its money as it does overwhelmingly on buildings, giving a large number of low value awards to other charities, disclosing no information about the kind of activities it seeks to support, and having little personal presence in the voluntary sector. To some extent the foundation is probably still reflecting the influence of its former chairman for 21 years, Sir William Shapland, who took over in 1964 and remained a trustee until his death in 1997, and of a group of other long standing trustees. It may now be changing, but there is much to be said for its presently unfashionable investment in buildings for charities, if these are located within seriously under-capitalised parts of the country; a building there can represent a welcome long term endowment for such a community.

All applications are 'considered on their merits' but there is no indication as to how these are assessed. Policies or values must be in place to enable the trustees to choose between the applications they receive, but they may be unconsciously held.

Grant making practice The information available includes a table, reproduced herewith, showing the proportion of the total disbursed under a number of headings, a listing generally consistent over many years, though changing slowly over time. Unfortunately, as explained below, some of this categorisation is odd. A useful new listing of the breakdown of grants by UK region has been provided for use in this entry, and is also reproduced. Finally the accounts list 17 of the largest grants (out of a total of 300), including a note of the purpose of the award. These 17 cover nearly half of the total amount distributed, and they are analysed below.

What the foundation calls 'guidelines' for applicants (reprinted in the Applications section below) are in fact about how applications are to be presented and are not concerned with the kind of activities that the foundation is interested in supporting.

Though these figures are much affected in any one year by the particular distribution of just a few large grants, it does seem that the share going to 'Community aid and recreation (probably more or less equivalent to the more common heading of social welfare) has been rising, while that for universities, colleges hospitals and medical research has apparently been reducing.

The geographical breakdown of the 1997/98 local grants is uneven. Though the area of benefit of the foundation is unrestricted, in practice its work is very heavily concentrated in one part of England, London and the surrounding Southern counties, with little going to other parts of England and virtually nothing to the the other three countries of Britain.

To demonstrate the extent of this preference, the value of grants per 100 people in 1998 was as follows

London	*£6.50,*
North West	*£2.46*
North East	*£0.46*
Scotland	*£0.25*
Wales	*£0.03*
Northern Ireland	*£0.04*

Total grants were subdivided by region as follows:

	1997/98	*1996/97*
UK	*33%*	*38%*
London	*17%*	*20%*
South East	*11%*	*7%*
East Midlands	*10%*	*12%*
West Midlands	*7%*	*4%*
Central Southern	*7%*	*11%*
Overseas	*6%*	*4%*
North West	*6%*	**%*
East Anglia	*2%*	*1%*
South West	*1%*	*1%*
North East	**%*	*1%*
Scotland	**%*	*1%*
Wales	**%*	**%*
Northern Ireland	**%*	**%*

(*all for less than 1%)

The foundation has suggested in the past that the geographical distribution reflects the applications received and that the

foundations grants are equally open to all. It would be interesting to see the actual figures, because these disparities are greater than those those usually resulting from such a cause.

The East Midlands stands high in the list of favoured areas because of a strong and long standing special interest in Northamptonshire, which received at least 20 grants totalling £150,000. It may, perhaps, be centred close to the villages of East Haddon and Guilsborough, where grants seem to cluster most thickly. The previously noted Kent connection still exists, to the extent of about 15 grants in 1997/98, due to connections in that area with the Sunley family.

The connection with Madrid also continues, and there are some grants for New York and elsewhere overseas. The foundation points out that these are all to organisations with which trustees have personal connections and that otherwise the foundation confines its grant making principally to the UK and Northern Ireland.

Grants in 1997/98

The grants list for 1997/98 shows a reduction in both the number of awards – down to 300 from 312 in 1996/97– and in the total value of grants – down to £2.77 million from £3.12 million in the previous year.

The section of the 1997/98 Report describing the purposes of the 17 largest payments (just over 50% of the grant total) shows that almost all was for building or refurbishment projects.

The largest awards went as follows:

Purcell School (£200,000 as the second instalment of three for its relocation to a new site).

National Association of YMCA's (£125,000 as the second and final instalment given as part of 150th Anniversary Homeless Appeal).

Macintyre Housing Association Hereford (£115,000 for purchasing and outfitting property at Cherrymead).

Five grants for building and refurbishment and totalling £500,000 (about one fifth of the total grant making) went to Netherhall Educational Association, London (second of three); Barnardo's South City Project, Liverpool; Caldecott Community, Kent (second of two); The Almshouse Association (final instalment of a grant given as part of the Golden Jubilee appeal); and Extra Care Charitable Trust, Coventry (first of two instalments).

The Bernard Sunley Charitable Foundation

Grants

		1997 /98	1996 /97	1995 /96	1994 /95	1993 /94	1960 /97
Universities, colleges and schools	£380,000	14%	16%	8%	8%	11%	21%
Hospitals, medical schools and research institutes	£386,000	14%	8%	13%	10%	14 %	18%
Community aid and recreation	£774,000	28%	24%	24%	15%	11%	13%
Youth clubs, youth training, sports organisations	£238,000	9%	8%	12%	7%	19%	10%
Provision for the elderly, including housing	£278,000	10%	4%	3%	37%	5%	9%
General medicine	£106,000	4%	9%	12%	4%	12%	7%
The arts, museums, etc.	£105,000	4%	17%	10%	7%	7%	7%
Churches and chapels	£106,000	4%	3%	8%	4%	14%	5%
Overseas	£179,000	6%	4%	4%	3%	2%	4%
Professional and public bodies and miscellaneous	£62,000	2%	2%	2%	1%	2%	3%
Wildlife and the environment	£82,000	3%	4%	2%	3%	4%	2%
Service charities	£78,000	3%	1%	2%	1%	2%	2%

The National Gallery received £60,000 to fund a series of exhibitions in the Bernard and Mary Sunley Room. Eight grants of £50,000 each, mainly for capital costs, were made to the Royal National College for the Blind (strangely categorised as general medicine), Merseyside Youth Association, Macmillan Cancer Relief, Guildford, Liver Research Fund, London; National Hospital for Neurology and Neurosurgery (towards the cost of relocating the rehabilitation in-patient unit at Queens Sqare), London; National Heart and Lung Institute, London; Friends of the Elderly, Oxfordshire; and Save the Children in Zimbabwe, as a grant towards a clean water project in the Zambezi.

There continues to be an unusually strong presence in the grants lists of charities with uniformed/military, saintly or royal names (38, 22 and 8 examples respectively). The uniformed heading covers extensive support for scout and cadet units of various kinds, as well as for ex-service charities.

However these generally long established charities are accompanied in the grant lists by awards to newer organisations, such as the Sixteen Choir and Orchestra (£10,000) and the British Helsinki Human Rights Group.

The list overall, though a simple record of organisational names, may suggest an increasing emphasis on health and welfare projects (about 40 grants), but the evidence is too sparse for any firm conclusion about this.

The proportion of repeat grants to organisations is now slight, except when they represent staged payments of larger awards.

The foundation has commented pungently on the applications that it receives. 'Many of the applications fail to include even the most basic information, such as the amount to be raised or the purpose of the application. There is also a curious reluctance to include a copy of the accounts, or to send accounts that are several years out of date. Surprisingly, this criticism of the standard of applications applies equally to the larger organisations and to those employing a professional fund raiser. In this context, it is most striking that, when we write back to a charity requesting normal, simple but missing information, it is quite usual never to hear from that charity again.'

Exclusions No grants for individuals. 'We would re-iterate that we do not make grants to individuals; we still receive several such applications each week. This bar on individuals applies equally to those people taking part in a project sponsored by a charity such as VSO, Duke of Edinburgh Award Scheme, Trekforce, Scouts and Girl Guides, etc, or in the case of the latter two to specific units of these youth movements.

Applications In writing to the Director. 'The letter should include clear succinct details as to:

- What project the grant is required for.
- How much will it cost? Also sources of expected funding and how much has been raised or pledged to date.
- If it is for a building, some backup is required. ie. costings and drawings.
- The last set of audited or independently examined accounts as the case may be should be enclosed plus any Annual Report or Review prepared by the charity.
- Any appeal documentation.'

Trustees normally meet in January, May and October.

The Sutton Coldfield Municipal Charities

£966,000 (to organisations 1996/97)

Relief of need, education, general in Sutton Coldfield

Lingard House, Fox Hollies Road, Sutton Coldfield, West Midlands B76 2RJ Tel: 0121-351 2262

Correspondent D J E Field, Clerk to the Trustees

Trustees John Gray, Chair; Brian Fitton; Jean Millington; Col. Anthony Fender; Cllr. David Roy; John Slater; Alfred David Owen; Frank Hooley; Dr Nigel Cooper; Cllr. Alan York; Cllr. J Whorwood; Sue Bailey.

Beneficial area The former borough of Sutton Coldfield, comprising three electoral wards: New Hall, Vesey, and Four Oaks.

Information available Full accounts are on file at the Charity Commission. Annual report with plenty of information including a full grants list showing the purposes of the awards.

These are available at local libraries, or sold by the charity.

Summary About 60 grants are awarded each year for sums between £200 and £200,000 to assist groups in the former borough of Sutton Coldfield. Donations are usually made for capital expenditure but occasionally for running costs.

General The charity, which is one of the largest and oldest local trusts in the country, was set up by Royal Charter in 1528. In 1997 it held assets of over £23 million from which £1,228,000 in income was generated. In the 1996/97 financial year, 90% of the £1,086,628 paid in grants went to organisations and the remaining 10% (£120,000) was given in numerous small grants to individuals. 65 grants were awarded to organisations amounting to £966,000 (average grant £14,900). 62% of that total was disbursed in 7 grants of £50,000 or more, and 27% in grants of £10,000 and above.

The objectives of the charity are:

- to help the aged, the sick, those with disabilities and the poor;
- to support facilities for recreation and leisure occupations;
- to promote the arts and advance religion;
- the repair of historic buildings;
- the advancement of education through grants to schools, and individuals for fees, maintenance, clothing and equipment.

These objectives are achieved through the provision of almshouses (owned by the charity), school clothing vouchers and grant-making.

The annual report gives the following in-depth description of the grants programme (excluding school clothing grants which are administered through local schools):

'Applications are received from individuals and organisations, and total in excess of 200 per year. Except for those which cannot be considered because the applicants are from outside the area of benefit, each request is investigated thoroughly by the staff who then present a case to the Grants Committee which meets nine times a year. After considering each application in detail, the committee decides whether an award should be made and if so how much money should be granted.

'If the proposed grant exceeds £20,000 it is referred to the full board for a final decision, Staff keep detailed records and monitor decisions so that trustees have up to date information and comparisons with other grants made. No reasons are given to applicants for decisions taken by the trustees.

'Normally, payments are made directly to the suppliers or contractors and not to the applicants. In the few cases where this is not appropriate applicants receive a cheque, but proof of payment or, in the case of students, academic reports are required.'

The largest grants of 1996/97 were: Sutton Coldfield's Girl's School – £111,000 for the refurbishment of a library; Arthur Terry School – £106,000 for the renovation and extension of the library; Holy Trinity RC Church – £100,000 for a community centre; and Sutton Arts Theatre – £82,000 for improvements to the auditorium.

Grants are divided into the following categories:

Grants to groups 'The largest grants made each year are to local groups and organisations representing a wide variety of interests. Some are charities which aim to meet the needs of people with medical social and other problems. Others are groups providing for young people or those with disabilities or the elderly. Grants are also made to sports clubs, churches, drama and music groups and schools.

'Anyone considering making an application is invited to telephone the office to seek informal advice. There are no forms but an information sheet sets out the requirements. One of the officers usually meets the applicant representative, often on site, before the application is finalised in order to discuss the nature of the project and the content and timing of the application.'

School clothing grants Personal grants; Educational grants; Sponsorship These schemes are open to parents, individuals in need, students and voluntary workers respectively. In 1996/97, the average school clothing grant was £53 and the highest grant in the other categories were £4,189 (personal grant), £1,800 (educational), £1,500 (sponsorship). For those interested in these individual grant schemes, the editors recommend reading the annual report which describes them fully.

Exclusions No awards are given to individuals or organisations based outside the area of benefit.

Applications In writing to the correspondent. The following applies to applications from groups and organisations.

There are no forms, so applicants may provide information in a format which is most convenient for them but applications must include the following:

- A brief description of the organisation, its objects and its history.
- The number of members/users, their age range and any membership fees paid.
- A full account of the purpose of the project for which a grant is requested.
- Accurate costs, including VAT if payable. No additional sums will be granted if estimates prove to be inaccurate.
- 12 copies of the latest audited accounts or, for very small organisations, copies of bank statements. Notes of explanation may be included, eg. if accounts show a balance set aside for a particular project applicants may wish to point this out.

The clerk will be happy to discuss applications informally at an early stage and to comment on draft submissions. In some cases a visit is helpful.

Receipt of applications is not normally acknowledged unless a stamped addressed envelope is sent with the application.

There are application forms for individuals whom must obtain them from the charity.

The grants committee meet 8 or 9 times a year. Requests for grants over £20,000 must be approved by the trustees, who meet four times a year. Staff will advise applicants about the dates by which requests must be received.

The Sutton Trust

£700,000 (anticipated for 1998)

Education

5 Lower Belgrave Street, London SW1W 0NR
Tel: 0171-730 5600

Correspondent Laura Barbour, Administrator

Trustees Peter Lampl; Karen Lampl.

Beneficial area Unrestricted.

Information available A new foundation. The information below was supplied for this entry.

Summary The trust has three interests:

1. Educational opportunities for young people in the state sector with a particular emphasis on recognising the special needs of academically able young people from non-privileged backgrounds.
2. Projects which address the issue of widening access to universities.
3. Experimental schemes addressed to problems of early learning in the under-three age group and including the involvement of parents in stimulating their children's early mental development.

General This trust was in the headlines in October 1998, with its founder Peter Lampl, a successful entrepreneur who ran his own investment firm, offering to put up substantial funds, through this trust, to provide 'needs blind' access to one or more top independent day schools.

In October 1998 the trust said that it 'is currently looking at the practicalities involved. A number of issues such as recruitment, method of selection, means testing, etc. are being resolved so that a school is able to take any child based on ability, irrespective of parental income, up to 100% of its capacity. The aim is to establish pilot schools to provide working examples that can be used as a basis for wider implementation.

'Contrary to what was implied in some of the press reports this is not an Assisted Places replacement scheme and the trust will not consider requests for such purposes.'

The trust describes as follows the three projects it has already funded:

University Summer Schools at Bristol, Cambridge, Nottingham and Oxford Universities. These were week-long programmes for VIth Form students from the maintained sector, offering an opportunity for them to sample university life, realise that they could fit in and consider their 'A' level subjects in a wider context.

Teachers INSET week at Oxford. The Summer School provided a personal training opportunity for teachers from the maintained sector and at the same time introduced them to what the university has to offer their students and demystifying the process of applying to Oxford.

DfEE Independent/State school partnerships. The trust contributed £250,000 towards a scheme jointly funded by the government to develop partnerships between state and independent schools. The trust is funding additional projects independently, which were not selected for the scheme.

These Editors are delighted to find a new trust performing exactly one of the functions for which independent foundations are best suited, but which is too seldom seen – the support of what is, at least for the moment, politically and intellectually unfashionable.

Exclusions

- Scholarships
- Assisted Places replacement schemes
- Sports and arts projects
- Individuals
- Capital costs (equipment and buildings)

Applications There is no application form, but there are basic Guidelines that the trust will provide for applicants who are invited to apply.

To avoid applicants wasting their time, they are encouraged to understand that unsolicited applications are not generally considered. However they welcome applicants to write in with a brief outline of a project or to make an exploratory call to discuss their project.

The Charles and Elsie Sykes Trust

£327,000 (1997)

General

6 North Park Road, Harrogate, Yorkshire HG1 5PA

Correspondent David J Reah, Secretary

Trustees John Horrocks, Chairman; Harold T Bartrop; Mrs Anne E Barker; Mrs G Mary Dance; Dr Michael D Moore; Michael G H Garnett; Dr. Michael W McEvoy; John Ward.

Beneficial area UK and overseas, with a preference for the North of the UK.

Information available Full accounts, but with only a limited narrative report.

Summary Grants are made to a broad variety of causes – most charities could fit into one of the 17 categories of donations. However, the best funded are; medical research (19% of the 1997 grant budget); disability (14%); social and moral welfare (13%); and children and youth (11%).

About half the grants are repeated annually, the others being 'special'(ie. one-off). Successful applicants are often well established national or regional charities such as the British Heart Foundation or Barnardo's.

General The trust states a preference towards applications 'from the northern part of the United Kingdom'. Most grants are in fact made for projects in the north of England and the recent grants lists reveal very few donations to Scottish, Welsh or Northern Irish charities. However, as the trust reports only the title of the charities and the amount they received, their location is often a mystery.

In 1997, the two largest donations were to the Harrogate Community House Trust, a charity providing mainly office accommodation for small local charities(£31,500) and the University of Cambridge School of Clinical Medicine for research into AIDS (£11,000). No other five-figure grants were paid, although the Children's Liver Disease Foundation received £9,500 towards research costs and the British Red Cross £5,000 for disaster preparedness programme in Bangladesh.

The trust maintains a reserve approximate to an average year's income to enable a steady income for themselves and, therefore, their annual charities, while retaining the ability to give 'very large donations at what could be disadvantageous times'.

Exclusions 'Applications from individuals are (very) unlikely to be successful.'

Applications Applications from registered charities may be made with full details and stamped addressed envelope to the above address. Recently established charities are rarely assisted. Applications without up to date audited or examined accounts will not be considered. The trust regrets that it cannot conduct correspondence with applicants.

The Talbot Village Trust

£371,000 (1996/97)

General

Dickinson Manser, 5 Parkstone Road, Poole, Dorset BH15 2NL
Tel: 01202 673071

Correspondent G S Cox, Clerk

Trustees Sir Thomas Edward Lees; Henry Ernle Erle Drax; Sir George Meyrick; Sir Thomas Salt; James Fleming; Christopher Lees.

Beneficial area East Dorset

Information available Report and accounts on file at the Charity Commission.

General This is a large local charity with invested assets of £17 million in 1996/97 and able to give perhaps £0.75 million in grants each year. In terms of cost per grant, management and administrative costs were high at £226,000, or £6,500 per grant awarded.

Thirty five grants were made in 1996/97, all to local social and community organisations and activities, with grants being given mainly for equipment and capital costs. Examples of the larger beneficiaries included Victorian School Appeal (£50,000 for the Camel House Project); East Holton Charity (£58,000, part of Phase III assistance); Alder Road Baptist Church (£20,000 for development and extension work); St Edwards School, Poole (£40,000 for building a chaplaincy centre); Boscombe Family Drop In (£9,500 for garden room improvements); Winton Steel Band (£5,000 for equipment).

A number of loans were also made to various churches, parishes and community groups ranging from £5,000 to £150,000.

Exclusions No grants for individuals.

Applications In writing to the correspondent.

The Tedworth Trust

£1,556,000 (approved, 1996/97)

Parenting, family welfare, child development, environment

See entry for the 'Sainsbury Family Charitable Trusts'
Tel: 0171-410 0330

Correspondent Michael Pattison

Trustees T J Sainsbury; Mrs M Sainsbury; A J Sainsbury; Miss Jessica Sainsbury; Miss Judith Portrait.

Beneficial area UK and overseas.

Information available The trust provides a full report and accounts. Its principal officers in 1996/97 are listed as the Michael Pattison, the director, Paul Spokes, the finance director and Miss H Marriott, Executive.

Summary This trust is one of the Sainsbury Family Charitable Trusts which share a joint administration. It is adventurous and growing. It has quadrupled its grant approvals between 1995/96 and 1996/97. Its major beneficiaries have been chosen within a limited number of policy areas. Its key grant in 1996/97 was for research relating to the care of young children – a focal part of the government's evolving National Childcare Strategy. In this the trust has been working in tandem with another Sainsbury Family Charitable Trust – the *Glass-House Trust* (see separate entry).

General The settlor of this trust is (Timothy) James Sainsbury. Its asset value decreased by over £1 million to £10.8 million in April 1997. Its net income in 1996/97 was £370,000 making a total of £801,000 available for distribution. Its outstanding commitments in April 1997 amounted to some £1.9 million (including grants made in 1996/97).

Parenting, Family Welfare & Child Development

'The trustees remain interested in child mental health and development. During the year, support was continued for the Winnicott Research Unit (based at Reading University) which is looking at the development of infants and children in order to determine how environmental influences and interpersonal relationships influence individual characteristics and personality and vulnerability to physical and psychiatric disorder throughout childhood, adolescence and adult life.'

In 1996/97 support was agreed for a major programme of research at the Royal Free Hospital School of Medicine and Institute of Education, University of Oxford to look at the implications and impact of various forms of day-care (£1,038,000 over 7 years). This is a joint grant in conjunction with another Sainsbury trust, the Glass-House Trust which 'belongs' to his younger brother (see separate entry). Another large grant was awarded to DEMOS for research into employment and family issues (£250,000 over 5 years).

Environment

'In the UK, trustees aim mainly to help communities protect, maintain and improve areas of land and to support work aimed at informing rural conservation policy.'

The beneficiaries of two grants were also supported by the Tedworth and Staples trusts, also Sainsbury trusts (see separate entries). These were Plantlife for its 'Back from the Brink' project on rare plants (£15,000 over 3 years) and Friends of the Earth to establish an internet database on SSSIs in the UK (£8,333)

General grants

Two grants were made to the Headley and Jerusalem trusts (£52,408).

This trust lists all its grants whatever their size. Other grants included the arts and architecture, emergency relief and an appeal for medical equipment.

Exclusions Grants directly to individuals

Applications The trustees met three times in 1996/97. The trust is proactive in its work and does not encourage applications. 'Unsolicited applications are unlikely to be successful.'

However it is also said that one application to a Sainsbury family trust is an application to all. See the entry for the Sainsbury Family Charitable Trusts for the address and further advice.

The Thompson Family Charitable Trust

£183,000 (1996/97, but see below)

General

Hillsdown, 15 Totteridge Common
London N20 8LR
Tel: 0181-445 4343

Correspondent Mrs P Thompson

Trustees D B Thompson; Mrs P Thompson.

Beneficial area UK.

Information available Reports and accounts up to 1996/97 on file at the Charity Commission. Grants list but no narrative report.

General This charity has been underspending its income by a considerable amount, possibly saving for some huge project. In 1994/95 the trust pledged a total of £1.5 million towards the Vivat Appeal, spread over a number of years, for educational and sporting facilities at Haileybury School.

Income for 1996/97 was £2.5 million, a high figure for assets amounting to £20 million (of which nearly £12.5 million was cash-at-bank). 90% of the relatively tiny grant total went in just eight grants.

Much the largest was to Save the Children (£100,000). Other beneficiaries included Vivat Appeal (Haileybury independent school, £24,000); St Michael's Hospice (£11,000); Gredley Charitable Trust (£10,000); King Edward VI Aston Appeal (£!0,000); Alcohol Helpline (£5,000); One to One Project (£5,000); and the Equine Fertility Unit (£5,000).

Applicants should note the change of address above.

Applications To the correspondent.

The Sir Jules Thorn Charitable Trust

£4,102,000 (1997)

Medical research, medicine, humanitarian purposes

24 Manchester Square,
London W1M 5AP
Tel: 0171-487 5851; Fax: 0171-224 3976;
e-mail:julesthorntrust@compuserve.com

Correspondent David H Richings, Director

Trustees Ann Rylands, Chairman; Christopher Sporborg; Frederick Flynn;

The Tedworth Trust						
	1996/97			**1995/96**		
		No of grants			*No of grants*	
Parenting, Family Welfare Child Development	£1,159,000	8	74%	£248,000	6	75%
Environment	£23,000	2	2%	£52,000	4	15%
General	£374,000	9	24%	£33,000	2	10%
Total	£1,556,000	19	100%	£332,000	12	100%

Sir Bruce McPhail; Nicholas Wilson.

Beneficial area UK, but see 'Exclusions'.

Information available Report and accounts with grants list and some narrative analysis of grant-making. Guidelines.

Summary The lion's share of the donations are awarded to medical causes. Mostly these are medical research projects but medical education and hospitals also receive substantial support in some years. Limited assistance is given to non medical causes.

In total about 600 grants are made each year, though only about are substantial, and they range from a few thousand pounds to over £200,000. As a member of the Association of Medical Research Charities, the trust ensures that all its grants made in this field are subjected to a full peer review process.

General The trust was established in 1964 with an endowment from Sir Jules Thorn. His primary wish was to support medical research to alleviate the sufferings of patients and help with diagnosis. He was keen to find new projects which could achieve a major advance. Outside the field of medicine, he wanted to help worthy causes of a humanitarian nature.

In 1997 the trust had a weighty asset base of over £77 million from which income of £3.6 million was generated.

The grants in 1996/97 are categorised in the table herewith.

Medical research projects Around £2 million is awarded to such projects each year. Grants are nearly all for amounts over £50,000 and are typically £100,000. Occasionally, additional money will be awarded as an extension to an existing project. Research projects are normally funded for up to three years, to holders of established posts in a university, other institution of higher education, or a hospital. Priority is given to projects with clinical relevance, where the patient will benefit in the short to medium term. Projects

are selected by peer review and recommendations made by a medical advisory committee for approval by the trustees.

29 grants were made in 1997, 26 of which were for new projects (accounting for 96% of the programme's funds). These included £131,000 to Royal Free Academic Unit of Rheumatology; £95,000 to the University of Newcastle, £108,000 to the Institute of Psychiatry, £47,000 to University of Edinburgh Medical School and £8,400 to UCL Medical School.

Medically related projects In 1997 a total of £1.5 million (£120,000 in 1996) was donated under this banner, mostly to universities. The most substantial grant, accounting for more than half of the money, was for the Cruciform project at University College London (£838,000). Nine awards were for intercalated BSc degrees (all for £15,000) were made to the following universities: Bristol; Leeds; Leicester; UCL; Manchester; Newcastle; Southampton; Liverpool; and Birmingham. Gifts for fellowships and scholarships totalling £345,000 were made to the Royal College of Surgeons of Edinburgh (£150,000) and UCL (£195,000). Single donations went to St Mary's Hospital (£100,000), Royal Hospital for Neuro Disability (£100,000) and the Hospital for Tropical Diseases (£45,000).

Three remaining categories exist called 'special charitable project', 'non medical projects', and 'single donations'. The size of grants from each category falls respectively. Target beneficiaries are registered charities working within the area of 'humanitarian causes', but see the exclusions below.

Special charitable project Each year around £500,000 is given (to a single organisation or to several groups) for a specific cause, which is different every year. The trustees decide the cause to be funded about two years in advance and publicise their intentions through relevant channels. For example, for its special project on museums (1997), the trust reached potential donees through an umbrella group. The trust does not invite

unsolicited applications to this fund – the trust is proactive in these programmes. In past years special charitable projects have also included youth at risk and a community sports scheme.

Non medical projects Grants are typically around £15,000 and may be spread over a few years. Although the fund disbursed over £100,000 in 1996, no such grants were awarded in 1997.

Single donations This programme might be called 'small donations'. The trust considers contributions towards core funding but prefers specific appeals. In 1997 nearly 600 grants of £1,000 or less were made to various, unnamed, charities.

Annual Review 1997

In 1997 the trust made the following review of the year's activities:

Medical research grants and medically related projects (29 grants totalling £2,007,000). 1997 was a very busy year for the trust. Demands for grants and donations continued at a high level. The medical research community appeared to experience increasing difficulty in securing funding, and the trust was carrying a long waiting list of potential applicants for much of the year. A total of 26 new research grants was awarded, and three previous grants were increased. At any one time during the year, over 70 projects were receiving funding.

The research areas for which grants were approved in 1997 included: wound healing; hip fracture; lung fibrosis; preservation and reperfusion injury in lung transplantation; movement recovery after stroke; Psoriasis, Hepatitis G; Alzheimer's; respiratory syncytial disease.

The trustees' overriding concern in committing funds for research is to ensure that the science is of the highest quality. The trustees are pro-active in seeking appropriate opportunities for distributing income and last year the trust was able to make a substantial grant to the Cruciform project at University College London [£838,000].

Other significant donations went to:

- St Mary's Hospital London in support of their appeal for their new Children's Accident and Emergency Centre [£100,000].
- The Royal Hospital for Neurodisability at Putney, towards their new unit for patients suffering from Huntingdon's disease, and with behaviour disorders [£100,000].
- The Hospital for Tropical Diseases, London, towards the upgrade of

The Sir Jules Thorn Charitable Trust		
Grants and Donations	*1997*	*1996*
Medical research projects	£1,886,471	£1,581,635
Medically related projects	£1,529,917	£120,251
Special projects	£471,617	£2,564
Non medical projects	—	£103,525

accommodation, and to move to new premises [£45,000].

Sir Jules Thorn Fellowships and Scholarships (two organisations received a total of £345,000) The trustees are concerned about the future of academic medicine in the UK, and about the importance of young researchers being able to gain the necessary experience.

The fellowship programme enabled the trust to make several awards to University College London. These will support two gifted medical students for a three year programme of research leading to a PhD thesis, and will also fund four travelling fellowships to enable postgraduate medical researchers to undertake a highly specific year overseas to enhance their skills, thus enabling their skills to flourish on return to the UK.

Training and research fellowships were provided at the Royal College of Surgeons, Edinburgh, to enable surgeons to take time out to acquire advanced technological skills or to pursue a special research project at institutions within the UK.

'Sir Jules Thorn scholarships have been funded at nine top medical schools to assist students to take intercalated BSc degrees, for which Local Authority funding is not always available.

Special Charitable Projects (£617,000 was disbursed to four projects) It is the trust's practice to identify, each year, one special charitable project to receive a major allocation of funding. In 1997 the initiative focused on museum education, and resulted in four awards being awarded to projects submitted by the Tank Museum, Bovington (£225,000); Bruce Castle Museum, Haringey (£73,000); the Discovery Museum, Newcastle (£180,000); and a new mobile museum to be developed by the Shropshire Museum Service and other neighbouring museum services (£139,000). The awards were made in response to competitive bids, and will result in imaginative new educational facilities for the benefit of the communities served by each museum.

Charitable Appeals (several hundred awards amounting to £214,000) 'During the year the trustees approved approaching 600 donations of amounts of up to £1,000 each in response to charitable appeals. Most were contributions to core funding to support continuing operations but some were for capital raising projects.'

Exclusions

Medically related grants

Funds are not allocated to:

- cancer or AIDS research for the sole

reason that these fields are relatively well funded elsewhere;
- individuals, except in the context of a project undertaken by an approved institution;
- third parties who themselves fund research;
- joint projects with other organisations or 'top up' funding for on-going projects;
- projects or data collection overseas.

Single donations (non medical small grants)

The trust does not make donations to:

- overseas organisations or organisations based in the UK who use their funds for charitable purposes overseas;
- to denominational beneficiaries;
- to organisations undertaking research;
- for the purchase of raffle tickets;
- church restoration/repairs;
- where support has been given within the previous twelve months or for several consecutive years.[sic-Ed]

Applications Each applicant for support for medical research is asked to make enquiries from the Director to ascertain whether the project falls within the trust's areas of interests and its funding ability. A waiting list may apply before guidelines and a preliminary application form can be sent. Briefly, the preliminary application calls for not more than two sides of A4 covering:

1. Some tabulated information covering title, objective and clinical relevance.
2. Project outline, including background and methodology.
3. Direction, approval and supervision. Has ethical approval and/or a Home Office Licence (if relevant) been sought or granted?
4. Duration and approximate cost, preferably showing the likely split between salaries, consumables and equipment.
5. Other sources of funding for this project either received or expected.

Successful preliminary applicants are invited to send fully detailed applications. Applicants for funding for purposes other than medical research should submit brief applications to the correspondent in the normal way.

Trustees meet in April and November. All applications for medical research are subject to peer review by a medical advisory committee, which meets four times annually, usually in January, April, June and November, and makes recommendations to the trustees. Following receipt, applications are considered on the first available agenda

of the medical advisory committee. The Director will advise likely timescales.

Single donations

There is no special application form. Applicants should submit their appeal to the Director and ensure that they cover the following briefly:

a) nature and objectives of the charity;
b) the reason for the appeal;
c) how much is being raised in total and from what sources, including the charities' own resources, fund-raising and funding from local authorities/ statutory bodies;
d) the gap to be bridged;
e) a short financial budget (one side) plus a copy of the last audited accounts.

Items (a) through (d) in total should not extend to more than two sides of A4 paper. A brochure about the charity may be included.

The Tompkins Foundation

£546,000 (1996/97)
Health, welfare

31 St John's Square, London EC1M 4DN Tel: 0171-608 1369

Correspondent The Secretary

Trustees Elizabeth Tompkins, Patron; John Sharp; Colin Warburton.

Beneficial area UK.

Information available Report and accounts, without the required narrative report but with a grants list. The grants are not analysed or explained.

Summary About 30 grants are made each year from less than £1,000 to as much as £60,000 in support of a variety of causes. The trust has no paid administration and does not seek applications.

General The foundation was established in 1980 by the late Granville Tompkins, former director of GFRT Holdings (and founder of the Green Shield Trading Stamp Company) and his wife Elizabeth. The objects of the foundation are:

- The advancement of education, learning and religion.
- The provision of facilities for recreation and other purposes beneficial to the community in the parishes of Hampstead Norreys in Berkshire and of West Grinstead in

Sussex and any other parishes with which the patron may have a connection with from time to time. The relation of the above policy with the donations that the foundation makes are not always obvious. However, as the trust does not give information on the location of beneficiaries or the purposes of grants, analysis is difficult.

In 1996/97 the foundations income totalled £533,000 and it owned assets amounting to £8 million. Management and administration costs were minimal, at just £61. Twenty eight grants were made ranging from £650 to £61,000. The largest six of them accounted for 58% of grant expenditure: Variety Club (£55,000); Order of St John (£50,000); Foundation of Nursing Studies (£50,000); Royal Association in Aid of Deaf People (£50,000); Joseph Levy Foundation (£50,000); St Mary's Hospital (£61,000).

Other beneficiaries included the following: Forces Help Society (£23,000); Children in Crisis (£19,000); Isabel Hospice (£3,000); Chicken Shed Theatre (£20,000); Anna Freud Centre (£20,000; City of London Migraine Clinic (£10,000).

Applications The trust does not encourage applications and has written: 'As a small private Foundation I have to say that our funds are fully committed for the foreseeable future and in these circumstances we would much prefer that our name is not publicly recorded as it is obviously time-consuming in having to reply to prospective applicants and of course equally disappointing to them that we are unable to assist with funds'.

The Trades House of Glasgow

£417,000 (1994/95)

Social welfare, general, Scotland

310 St Vincent Street,
Glasgow G2 5QR
Tel: 0141-228 8000

Correspondent Mr Gordon Wyllie, Clerk

Beneficial area Scotland, particularly Glasgow.

Information available A booklet about the various trusts comprising this charity, its report and accounts are available. These do not include lists of grants.

Summary Grants are made to a range of charitable causes varying from a few hundred pounds up to £18,000, but more typically for £2,000 to £3,000. Awards are also made to individuals in the range of a few pounds to £3,000. All grants are one-off and the vast majority of funds are donated within Glasgow.

General The Trades House of Glasgow was first established in 1605. It manages a number of trust funds, each bound to their separate trust deeds. Fourteen of these are very old and the Scottish equivalent of the craft guilds and livery companies which developed in European cities in the middle ages. They include the Hammermen, Barbers and Masons whose members now cover such diverse professions as electronic engineering, surgery, surveying and civil engineering. Most of the trusts are tied to specific causes and locations. The majority are concerned with various aspects of social welfare and individual need, particularly in Glasgow. The charity employs two full time social workers.

By the year ending May 1997, assets totalled £10.5 million and income generated in the year was £616,000.

Grants were categorised as follows:

Grants in 1996/97

Organisations	£248,000	59%
Individuals	£166,000	40%
Bursaries and education	£3,000	1%
Total	£417,000	100%

The Trades House says:

'The assistance of needy pensioners, the encouragement of youth and the fostering of industrial initiative are now its chief objects. It concerns itself not just with the maintenance of tradition but the disbursement of substantial funds for numerous good causes; helping those in need, encouraging promising youngsters at college or in industry, and many other worthwhile projects. In addition when particular causes are put forward the Trades House seeks to respond by raising new funds to support them.

'The Trades House has always been concerned with the welfare of its least well-off members. It has provided hospitals for the sick, pensions for the elderly, succour for the needy. Over the years it has been concerned with the support of almshouses, schools, hospitals, asylums and even the raising of a battalion to fight in the Napoleonic Wars.

'In addition to administering its own funds the Trades House is responsible for a number of other funds some of which are of considerable size. This responsibility is discharged by committees with the assistance of a small staff including two qualified social workers who ensure the fair and efficient utilisation of funds.

'The Trades House operates under the chairmanship of the Deacon Convenor who is elected annually by its members, the representatives of the fourteen crafts and he plays a prominent role in the affairs of the city, including having a seat on the District Council.'

The note above, that the charity seeks to raise new funds when needed for particular causes, is most welcome, and a precedent that might well be followed by other 'ancient' welfare charities which tend to limit their response to modern needs to the funds that have been handed down from the past.

Exclusions The funds are held primarily for the benefit of Glasgow and her citizens and if you fall out with those parameters you should not submit an application. Political, municipal, and ecclesiastical appeals cannot be entertained. Charities duplicating rather than complementing existing services and those with national purposes and/or large running surpluses normally cannot be helped.

Applicants receiving help one year will normally be refused the next.

Applications There is no set form of application for organisations seeking help. You should write a summary in your own words extending to not more than a single A4 sheet, backed as necessary by schedules and accompanied by your latest accounts and/or business plan. Evidence of need must be produced, as should evidence that client groups participate in decision taking and that their quality of life and choice is enhanced. Where possible, costs and financial needs should be broken down, evidence of the difference which a grant would make be produced, and details given, with results, of other grants applied for.

Applications should include evidence of charitable status, current funding and the use you are making of that. Projects should be demonstrated to be practical and business-like. It is a condition of any grant that a report be made as to how the funds have been used. Grants not used for the purposes stated must be returned.

The Triangle Trust

£430,000 (1996/97)

General

Glaxo Wellcome House, Berkeley Avenue, Greenford, Middlesex UB6 0NN

Correspondent The Secretary

Trustees J C Maisey, Chairman, M Pearce; J Seres; Mrs J Turner; Rev D Urquhart; Dr Marjorie Walker; Mrs D Ware; Miss L Wilson.

Beneficial area UK.

Information available Basic annual report and accounts with grants list. Guidelines with some exploration of recent grants.

Summary Grants are made to organisations (about 35 such grants account for 80% of total charitable giving) and to individuals with a connection to the pharmaceutical industry (about 200 individual grants share the remaining 20% of the money).

Donations are made for education, the relief of poverty and general charitable purposes and may be one-off or on-going (usually over three years).

General The trust was established in the 1930's with private endowments. In 1997 it held assets of nearly £11 million from which investment income of £423,000 was generated. Management and administration expenses were £57,000 or 13p per £1 donated.

The trust's objectives are:

- 'the education and alleviation from poverty of past or present employees, and their dependents, of the pharmaceutical industry;
- promoting a good standard of health in the community, including recreational facilities and medical welfare;
- wide general charitable objects.'

Currently preference is given to projects supporting elderly, homeless and disabled people.

Grants to individuals are given for general hardship, or for education (third year of a degree, vocational courses and extra-curricular activities for school

children). The charity actively seeks applicants through industry contacts and advertisements. Applications must be submitted by a professional third party such as a GP, probation officer, teacher etc. The Family Welfare Association administers these grants on its behalf.

Grants to organisations account for the bulk of the trusts giving and are awarded for most charitable causes but see the exclusions below. In 1996/97 the trust was supporting 19 charities in the long-term (from two years up to five years) and made 17 one-off grants ranging from £500 to £5,000.

The annual report 1996/97 says:

'The trustees have developed a policy of selecting third party organisations to whom they make the majority of their grants in each of the broad categories of identified need.

'Under the wide ranging general charitable projects, long-term collaborative projects with charities and organisations which help disabled, elderly, homeless and disadvantaged people, and towards educational costs to give those who would otherwise be unemployed a chance of entering the workplace, continued. In addition emphasis has remained on the provision of money advice and debt counselling.'

The largest long-term grants in 1996/97 were probably to Depaul Trust (£34,000; a three year grant for employment of a resettlement worker and a volunteer coordinator, to work with homeless people in London), Sheffield City Council (£27,000 for the employment for five years of a volunteer coordinator at a Furniture recycling store), and Coventry Citizen's Advice Bureau (£24,000).

Sizeable single awards were to The Hoxton Trust (£34,000), CAB Haddington (£20,000) and Trafford Women's Refuge (£19,000).

Exclusions Environmental, wildlife or heritage appeals; medical electives; grants for further study in relation to employment; private medicine or education; loans; holidays or educational trips; nursing, convalescent or residential home fees.

Applications Organisations should write to the correspondent.

The trust's guidelines state:

'Applications will be considered when made by organisations that are approached by the trust. Trustees do not normally respond to unsolicited applications.

'Individuals, in the pharmaceutical

industry only by application form, available from the secretary. Applications on behalf of individuals for one-off grants are considered when submitted by social workers, CAB officers, health visitors, GPs, probation officers, employers etc., or (for educational grants) teachers.'

The Trust for London (see also the entry for the City Parochial Foundation)

£863,000 (1997)

Small community-based organisations in London

6 Middle Street, London EC1A 7PH
Tel: 0171-606 6145; Fax: 0171-600 1866

Correspondent Bharat Mehta, Secretary

Trustees The trustees of the City Parochial Foundation (see separate entry).

Beneficial area London.

Information available Excellent Guidelines for Applicants, Review of its policy for the quinquennium, 1997–2001, and annual Grants Review, are available from the trust.

Summary Grants of up to a maximum of £10,000 a year for small community groups, with not more than two staff, especially those working with women and black and ethnic minority organisations. The trust receives applications but also initiates its own programmes.

General The Trust for London was formed in 1986 and endowed with funds arising from the abolition of the Greater London Council and the re-distribution of its assets. It is managed by the City Parochial Foundation, but the foundation is legally distinct, has separate priorities, policies and procedures, and therefore a separate entry in this book. The endowment normally yields a grant income of about £600,000 a year. The grants committee of the trust comprises both trustees of the foundation and independent members with particular knowledge of the voluntary sector in London. Advisory groups are established from time to time to assist the trust's grant-giving.

Grant Guidelines for 1997-2001

General Policy and Approach

'The trust targets small locally based community organisations with charitable purposes, which are independent of larger bodies. "Small" is defined as being entirely volunteer or membership based, or with no more than the equivalent of two full-time paid staff.

'The trust particularly welcomes proposals from women's groups, black and minority ethnic women's groups and black and minority ethnic organisations.

'The trust seeks:

- to have an initiating and pro-active role, rather than to wait for applications
- to ensure that its grants have a distinctive and particular impact
- to be accessible to small groups.

Funding Priorities

'The trust will not make grants above £10,000 a year for capital costs or revenue costs. Revenue costs may be given over a two or three year period though normally with a reducing level of grant.

'Applications will be considered from small groups in any London borough as follows:

- any self-help group particularly women's groups and young and elderly people's groups
- supplementary and mother tongue schools
- organisations working with people with disabilities
- refugee and migrant groups.

'In addition

- any small charitable group can apply for a start-up grants of no more than £500
- any small charitable group can apply for a grant of up to £1,500 for training costs.

Continuation grants

'The trustees will consider applications from some of the organisations previously grant-aided for revenue costs by the trust. Further grants will not be given automatically but field officers will discuss with organisations what they require to continue effective work.'

The trust's quinquennial review, published in 1997, included the following:

Funding Policies and Priorities for the Trust for London 1997-2001

General Principles for Grant-making during the Quinquennium 1997-2001

'... the Trust for London should continue to focus upon small, locally based community groups with charitable objects which have no more than the equivalent of two full-time members of staff.

'The Trust has also, from the outset emphasised its particular interest in women's groups, black and minority ethnic groups and black and minority ethnic women's groups. Traditionally these groups find it hard to access funding and the Trust is an important potential source of funds for them. ... the Trust's commitment to these groups remains.

'... grants should continue to be made over a two or three year period and the maximum grant should remain at a level of £10,000 per annum.

Grant-making Priorities 1997-2001

- Small grants for start-up costs
- Small grants for training costs. The proposed training should be discussed with the Field Officer
- Grants for self-help groups with particular emphasis on the elderly and young people
- Grants for supplementary and mother-tongue schools

- Grants for refugee and migrant groups
- Grants for disability groups
- Continuation grants

'The proposal to include grants towards training costs is a new one. The need for such a fund to be made available has arisen during the field work carried out in the current quinquennium and is important in the context of the trust's traditional interest in providing infrastructure support to small groups. The finding of the Small Groups Workers revealed the effectiveness of in-house training for small groups and it is therefore intended to establish, as a priority, grants for in-house training costs.

'Supplementary and mother-tongue schools in London are well aware that the Trust for London is one of the few funders they can approach. Between 1993 and 1995, 41 grants were made to 33 schools. These covered 15 communities and 18 boroughs and the total made available was £352,500.

'New and emerging refugee and migrant groups have benefited from one-off grants from the trust since 1995 thanks to a sum of £75,000 being made available by the Baring Foundation on a one-off basis. Many of those who benefited are likely to return for continuation grants. Having assisted them to start up it is important to enable such organisations to continue.

'Continuation grants amounted to £1,008,882 between 1992 and 1995. The number of grants made was 118, that is less than 30 grants a year. The demand is important but not heavy. In only 17 cases had funding been made available for more than three years. It is not intended that the trust would normally make a continuation grant for longer than a two-year period.

In summary

'The grant-making priorities of the Trust for London for the Quinquennium 1997-2001 will be:

- *Small grants for start-up costs* – Applications will be considered for up to £500 per annum.
- *Grants for in-house training costs* – Applications will be considered for up to £1,500 per annum.
- *Self-help groups*, with particular emphasis on the elderly, and young people between 16-25 years of age – Applications will be considered for up to £10,000 per annum.
- *Supplementary and mother-tongue schools* – Applications will be

The Trust for London

Grants in 1997

	No. of grants	Amount	% of total
Refugee and migrant groups	28	£271,000	31%
Supplementary, mother tongue schools	33	£230,000	27%
People with disabilities	23	£212,000	25%
Self help groups	15	£79,000	9%
Continuation grants	7	£65,000	7%
Training grants	4	£6,000	1%
Total	**110**	**£863,000**	**100%**

considered for up to £10,000 per annum.

- *Refugee and migrant organisations* – Applications will be considered for up to £10,000 per annum.
- *Disability organisations* – Applications will be considered for up to £10,000 per annum.
- *Continuation funding* – Applications will be considered for up to £10,000 per annum.

Developmental Initiatives

'The trust has already made a commitment to establish a Resource Unit for Supplementary and Mother-Tongue Schools (operational from 1997. Ed.).

'The Trust for London has become known in recent years for its funding of the Small Groups Worker Scheme in nine London Boroughs. The Scheme has now drawn to a close insofar as other funders have begun to provide grant-aid, nevertheless, the trust is still interested in the concept and work of Small Groups Workers.

'Accordingly, the Policy and Monitoring Officer has been asked to maintain some contact with the Small Groups Workers, particularly in the two or three boroughs where the trust has made bridging grants to enable the continuation of the workers in post pending alternative long-term funding being made available from other sources.

'The trust will give consideration to a further initiative based upon the Small Groups Worker model.'

Grants in 1997

The purpose of the grants are summarised in the table herewith.

Nearly 30% of the awards were to organisations in just five boroughs:

Newham
Hackney
Brent
Merton
Southwark.

Four of these might be expected to appear in such a list, but the appearance of Merton is welcome. It is the impression of our editors that those welcome trusts that actively seek to help the most disadvantaged parts of the country often concentrate excessively on inner city areas, to the comparative neglect of the serious problems of many 'outer' areas of the larger cities.

The Resource Unit for Supplementary and Mother Tongue Schools, launched in 1997, is a welcome initiative by the trust, supported also by other funders, including BBC Children in Need. It is

already fielding requests for help from other parts of Britain. An earlier initiative, the Small Groups Worker scheme has now led to such appointments being permanently established and funded by individual London boroughs.

To give a taste of the work being supported, one section of the grants list reads as follows:

Corali Dance Company: £10,000 for part-time artistic director

Croydon Childminding Association: £5,000 for running costs

Enfield Caribbean Association: £10,000 for rent and running costs

Ethiopian Welfare Action Group: £8,000 over two years for rent, heating etc.

Greenford Neighbourhood Care Services: £1,760 for running costs

Greenwich Chinese Association: £8,000 for expenses of teachers.

Exclusions Grants will not be given for major capital schemes; in response to general appeals; to individuals; for research; as part of a full-time salary; to replace cuts by statutory authorities; to umbrella bodies to distribute; to organisations which have received grants from the City Parochial Foundation.

Applications As part of the applications procedure, organisations are required to fill in an application form and provide the documents requested on it. Application forms are not issued on request. Organisations are encouraged to discuss a potential application with the relevant field officer as a first step. If eligible to apply, the field officer will arrange a meeting. Only when the field officer regards the process as complete will the application be eligible to be considered. All applicants must indicate what monitoring they will carry out of the work funded. Successful applicants will be required to cooperate with the trust's monitoring procedures.

The trust requires accounts for the previous year and the year in which the grant is provided. A period of at least 12 months must elapse between the trust making a grant and any fresh application. The decision of the grants committee is final.

The grants committee meets four times a year, in March, June, September and December. Deadlines for completed applications are:

31 January for March meeting
30th April for June meeting
31st July for September meeting
15th October for December meeting.

'Completed' means that all documentation has been received, staff have no further questions to raise, and a meeting has taken place between the applicant and a member of the staff.

The Trusthouse Charitable Foundation

Probably about £2,000,000

General

Hambro's Trust Co. Ltd, 41 Tower Hill, London EC3N 4HA
Tel: 0171-480 5000

Correspondent Derek Harris, Administrator

Trustees Hugh Astor, Chairman, Alex Bernstein, Lord Boyd-Carpenter, Lord Callaghan, the Earl of Gainsborough, the Duke of Marlborough, Lord Peyton, Olga Polizzi, Sir Hugh Rossi, Sir Paul Wright.

Beneficial area Unrestricted.

Information available As a newly formed charity, no Report and Accounts had been produced at the time of going to press.

Summary The foundation will be giving one-off grants for specific purposes, to headquarters organisations and not normally to local branches of national charities, and it will have the following six priority areas for its funding:

- relief of hardship and disability
- education
- environment
- heritage
- the arts
- sporting activities.

General The foundation derives from a tranche of Trust House Hotels shares, which were held for the public benefit (though not for causes that were necessarily charitable). Trust House became a part of the Forte group, and the income from the shares was then distributed by the Council of Forte. When the Forte companies in their turn were taken over by the Granada group, the shares were realised for £50 million, placed as permanent endowment in this new, charitable, and welcome foundation.

In 1998 the foundation said that it was working towards the production of new policies and the outcome is the information given under the 'summary' heading above. One of these headings is unusual: sport is not in itself a charitable activity, and grants will need to be for educational or welfare activities, with a sporting connection.

These very general policies will probably need to to be developed further when the foundation comes under the day to day pressure of making major funding decisions.

The foundation supplies a general guidance note with its application form which includes the following terse but admirable summary of what these, and most other trustees, need to know from their applicants:

- Who are you?
- What do you do?
- How much do you want, and for what?
- Who will benefit?

Exclusions

- No grants to individuals.
- Appeals received directly from local branches will not normally be considered (see below)
- The foundation does not give grants to other grant-making bodies.

Applications On brief application forms available from the correspondent (one side of an A4 sheet). Applicants are invited, if necessary, to supply such supporting documentation as is required.

The accompanying guidance note says (in addition to the section quoted in the main text):

- The foundation does not normally commit itself to give grants for more than one year.
- Local branches of national charities are encouraged to channel appeals through their headquarters giving details, where appropriate, of particular projects and their costs.
- It would be helpful to the trustees if applicants could indicate a specific sum required when applying for a grant.

The trustees meet quarterly.

The Tudor Trust

£22,717,000 (1997/98)

Social welfare, general

7 Ladbroke Grove, London W11 3BD
Tel: 0171-727 8522

Correspondent Jill Powell, Grants Administrator

Trustees Grove Charity Management Ltd., of which the Directors are: Mrs M K Graves*; Mrs H M Dunwell*; Dr. D J T Graves*; Mrs P J Buckler; Christopher Graves* (also the present Director of the trust); R W Anstice; Sir James Swaffield; Mrs C M Antcliff; Mrs L K Collins; Mrs E H Crawshaw; M S Dunwell*; James Long*; B H Dunwell. Company Secretary: Roger Northcott* (Asterisks show membership of the grant making Trustee Committee).

Beneficial area UK and overseas.

Information available Good annual report and guidelines for applicants (reprinted below) are available from the trust.

Summary The trust's funding is now concentrated almost entirely on social welfare, though in a wide sense that includes educational and health promotion activities for people whose welfare is at risk. There are more detailed Guidelines for Applicants than before, especially full and useful in spelling out what will not be considered for funding (see under Exclusions below).

There was a policy review in 1997. Following this, two new priorities were adopted; work with young people who are in danger of being alienated from society and work for people who need support in family life.

Three new funding committees have been established, covering:

- Addictions
- The promotion of local communities
- The alienation of young people (now renamed as the Retracking committee).

The work of these committees is described in the excerpts from the 1997/98 annual report that are reprinted below.

The other priority funding areas are:

- Elderly mentally infirm and/or very frail
- Homeless
- Mentally ill or have a history of mental illness
- Offenders/ex-offenders/people at risk of offending.

Grants are still made on a large scale in the trust's other fields of work fields of work, and it is not clear whether applications in the 'priority areas' have a substantially greater chance of success.

Despite its very wide range of work, there some are substantial areas that are outside the trust's current priorities; for example, work with people with learning disabilities, who are physically disabled

or ill, or who are victims (see the full list in the following 'Guidelines' and under 'Exclusions' at the end of this entry). The trust stopped funding mainstream education some years ago and has recently dropped 'Arts' and 'Leisure' except where these are ancillary to welfare activities.

The trust makes grants of all kinds and sizes (and occasional loans) and sometimes gives sustained support over long periods to charities with which it has established a close relationship. It accepts about one in five of the applications that it receives (though not necessarily for the full amount requested). More often than not, refusal is simply due to shortage of funds.

In 1997/98 the divide between revenue and capital grants was as follows:

Revenue 743 grants £12.8 million 57%
Capital 277 grants £7.1 million 31%
Mixed 166 grants £2.8 million 12%

The trust continues to set the standard for its sector in a number of ways. One is the very fast response to most applications; normally a reply is received within eight weeks. Another is the large number of visits and face to face discussions that take place with applicants, over 450 in 1997/98, in a year when 1,200 grants were made and administrative costs were less than 4% of the value of grant commitments made. Less factually, and though these editors do not normally report hearsay, the extent of apparent 'customer satisfaction' with this trust is so high that it justifies recording here.

Overall, the work of this trust has a markedly individual flavour; it operates very close to the ground, quietly, flexibly and without much open participation in the public affairs of the sector as whole.

Guidelines for Applicants

The grant making programme is best described in the trust's own Guidelines for Applicants for 1997 to 2000:

'The trust makes grants to charities and to organisations with charitable objectives. Support is given both for capital and revenue costs. ... Priorities in grant making are constantly evolving and a full policy review is undertaken every three years.

'The trust is fairly selective in what it supports within relatively broad areas of activity. These guidelines give an overview of the trust's current interests. This is not a comprehensive list; however it offers applicants a firm indication of the trust's priorities and what organisations and activities are unlikely to receive a grant. Demand for funding greatly exceeds availability of funds and not all applications meeting the current criteria will be successful.

'The trust targets its funding almost entirely within the UK. The trustees recognise that there is considerable need and unrealised potential in both urban and rural communities. The trust is therefore particularly receptive to applications from organisations working directly in localities which

- are under resourced
- where there are high levels of social disadvantage
- projects encouraging people to play a part in their community.

'The trust supports projects which value people. In particular, it seeks to improve the quality of life of those people who are:

- Drug and alcohol abusers
- Elderly mentally infirm and/or very frail
- Homeless
- Mentally ill or have a history of mental illness
- Needing support in family life
- Offenders/ex-offenders/people at risk of offending
- Young and in danger of becoming alienated from society.

'The following areas of work will normally fall within the the trust's policies:

Advice and counselling

'Advice services delivered locally or meeting particular needs; family and other mediation; marriage counselling (training or premises); some counselling by accredited counsellors.

Education, training and employment

'Work with excluded and truanting, home/school links, education in citizenship, supplementary schools teaching core curriculum, literacy; employment schemes for mentally ill (emphasis on preparation for open employment), employment training for ex-offenders.

Elderly

'Day centres for frail elderly, befriending, practical help, enhancing quality of life; care and accommodation schemes for dementia sufferers.

Families

'Family work including some centres, parenting skills and preventative work with families on the verge of crisis, contact centres, accommodation with training/support for young people.

Health

'Accommodation, self help groups, centres, clubhouses and crisis services for mentally ill; community based projects for substance abusers and residential rehabilitation centres with special focus (particularly families); local day care and model residential schemes for head injured and people with autism, respite schemes for mentally ill; work

with carers.

Housing and homelessness

'Street homelessness, day provision, emergency accommodation, rent deposit/ guarantee schemes, care and repair, refuges, supported accommodation for mentally ill, ex-offenders and substance abusers.

Penal affairs

'Alternatives to custody, bail support, pre-release education and training, offenders with specific problems (including mentally disordered offenders); support for families.

Resources for local community

'Community buildings and support workers, especially those contributing to groups/needs identified elsewhere in this guidance note; charitable/not-for-profit schemes stimulating the local economy; local projects engaging people in their environment.

Young people

'Advice, counselling, detached work in especially difficult areas, some centres; residential care; support on coming out of care.

Areas unlikely to receive funding

- Advocacy
- After school clubs
- Arts in general (theatres, performances, musicals etc.)
- Camps, outdoor activity and confidence/skill-building courses

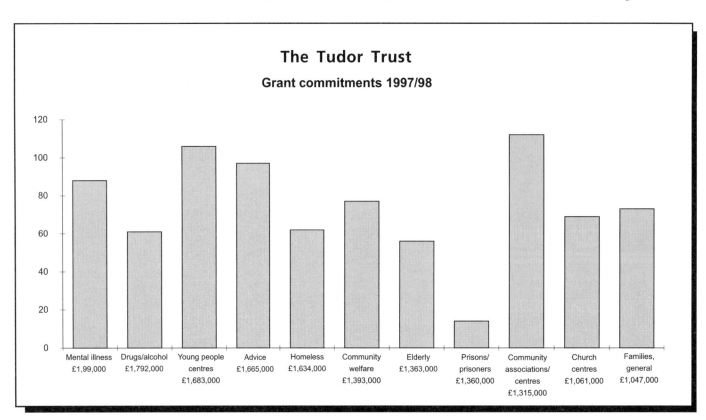

- Charities whose operational area is outside the UK *(but see under 'overseas' heading below. Ed)*
- Credit Union development
- Housing advice
- Large national charities enjoying wide support
- Minibuses
- Organisations working with people with learning disabilities
- Organisations working with people who are physically disabled
- Organisations working with people who are physically ill
- Research
- Schools (including playgrounds)
- Training and employment schemes
- Victims (of crime, sexual abuse, war, etc.)'

Areas that cannot be considered for funding

See the extensive list under 'Exclusions' at the end of this entry.

Background The 1997/98 Report notes that 'in the year the market value of the Tudor Trust's investments rose from £324 million to £385 million. The trustees' investment policy continues to be to optimise the total return. The Trustees' policy on reserves is to establish levels of annual expenditure so that over a period of years the value of the General Fund, which comprises expendable capital and accumulated income, is protected in real terms thus maintaining grant-giving capacity for the future.' This policy of seeking to optimise the total return is in contrast to the policy of some other comparable trusts, the Weston Foundation for example, where only the income from dividends and interest is regarded as available for charitable use, and capital growth is simply accumulated. These editors regard Tudor's practice as more desirable.

'The cost of administration and invest-ment management in 1997/98 was £854,000, compared with £787,000 in the previous year. This represented 3.8% of grant commitments made during the year.' This is a low figure, especially as it includes £198,00 for investment manage-ment. One reason for this must be the substantial unpaid time put in by the trustees. For example, the grant making Trustee Committee's six members (who include Christopher Graves, the Director, and Roger Northcott, Company Secre-tary) meet fortnightly; there are further subcommittees described below; and applicants from all over the country report visits from trustees as well as from staff.

The Report continues 'As the voluntary sector becomes more specialised we are committed to remaining a general fund, able to respond flexibly to requests large or small from charitable organisations which can demonstrate a real need and the potential to address it. We are fortunate to have a high-calibre team of officers who share our enthusiasm.' There are about ten staff regularly involved in the assessment and administration of applications.

Grant making policy and practice

In the past the trust has noted that it is willing to consider a wide range of grants, including support for the the core operational costs of organisations, as well as (sometimes substantial) grants for capital projects. It has talked too of 'the creation of effective funding relationships where dialogue can be sustained over a number of years'.

In its 1996/97 annual report, the trust noted that it 'is able to work closely with some applicants and to offer them legal, financial and architectural advice and support. This internal expertise is sometimes used to stimulate new activity such as, this year, the development of visitors centres for prisons and of voluntary sector offices', though it goes on note that such work is time consuming and therefore has to be carefully limited.

More generally, that report noted that the trust 'looks out for projects which address needs with vision, dedication and energy. Our job is to support those projects in the most effective and imaginative way we can. Grant making mixes detailed assessment with intuition. Calculated risks sometimes have to be taken. This is a proper role for an endowed charitable trust and we strive to make grants which are both pragmatic and creative.' While these editors welcome such an approach, they still await a report from a big trust in which the evidence of risk taking, which is occasional failure, will be reported. Perhaps some day the Tudor Trust may lead in this.

A year later the annual report for 1997/8 includes the following:

'The year 1 April 1997 to 31 March 1998 was the Tudor Trust's first with a new remit, the result of a policy review in January 1997, which will be in place until the year 2000. New guidelines for applicants *(reproduced above. Ed.)* were produced to reflect changes in the remit and also to make clearer what is unlikely to interest the trust. Potential applicants are now better informed about what projects might fall within the trust's current priorities.

'During the year the trust received 5,050 applications for funding and made 1,186 grant commitments *(a roughly one in five success rate. Ed.)* with a total value of £22,717,000. While the number of commitments was about the same as the previous year the total value was over a third (34%) more, and the average amount awarded was £19,155 compared with £14,273 in 1996/7. However almost 44% of commitments were for less than £10,000 and the range was from £200 to £800,000. The trustees remain committed to achieving a broad spread of grants whose size is appropriate to the scale of each project and its needs.

'While the volume of applications we receive makes it impossible to have the personal contact with applicants that we would like, trustees and staff visited 248 projects and held a further 208 meetings with applicants in 1997/8.

'A list of all grant commitments made in the year is given in the annual report. It may be noted that the headings of Arts and Leisure have been dropped: the trust has funded very few projects under these headings in recent years and now only does so on rare occasions when the project is aimed squarely at one of our specific interests such as mental illness or substance abuse (such projects are listed under Health).

'Applications for funding are administered by staff of the Tudor Trust. Each eligible application is considered by trustees. Their recommendations are submitted for decision to committees of the board including the trustee committee which meets fortnightly. The full board meets three times a year when the committees' grant decisions are ratified and large commitments and policy decisions are made.

Targeted funding committees

'The three Targeted Funding Committees which were established at the end of last year have been able to focus in detail on particular areas of need, something a UK-wide trust with a broad remit seldom has the opportunity to do. The committees, whose membership includes staff as well as trustees, have completed their initial investigations and begun to make grants with an emphasis on long-term support and increased dialogue between the grant recipient and the trust. This complements the trust's established, continuing work.

Addictions Committee

'The first focus of the Addictions Committee was on problems associated with crack cocaine use and it explored a number of projects in this specialist field.

Work to establish a rapid-access residential crisis centre for crack users unfortunately has not come to fruition due to lack of financial support from statutory authorities, but the project may yet be revived and the initial research has contributed greatly to the trust's understanding of addiction issues. The Committee made seven grants, mainly for treatment projects for drug misusers. It is now beginning to develop ideas focusing on help for alcohol abusers and their families.

Community Committee

'Community development is at the heart of the Tudor's Trust's work. The Community Committee has sought ways of encouraging voluntary activity, empowerment and regeneration in communities which might otherwise be marginalised. Members visited a number of dynamic projects and considered how to help replicate or adapt their successes in other locations. The Committee made a total of 15 grant commitments including areas of Wales, Leeds and Nottinghamshire, but its main focus is now on a central band of Lancashire where the trust has funded few projects before. It will be building close links with organisations there.

Retracking Committee

'The starting point of this Committee was the trust's concern about social exclusion, particularly among young people. The Committee focused on critical points in a young person's life where timely intervention, at the first signs of unusual behaviour or slow development, may lessen the chance of exclusion from school and society. The Committee listened to various practitioners and experts in this field. The move from primary to secondary school is a particularly vulnerable time and, together with East London Schools Fund, the trust is developing a major five-year programme of support, with home-school links, for a secondary school in Walthamstow and four of its 'feeder' primary schools. The Committee was also involved in making nine other grant commitments.'

Grant commitments in 1997/98

Grants are all listed within categories, such as Mental Illness or Employment, but within general headings such as Welfare or Health. There are therefore no totals, for, say, Mental Health as it appears repeatedly under separate headings. Some of the major fields of work have therefore been totalled up for this entry, but the list is far from complete, and major fields may have been missed.

Size of grants in 1997/98

The table below shows the value of new grant commitments in various size bands. 1997/98 saw a substantial swing towards larger grants. While the total amount given has increased, both the amount and even more the proportion going to grants in the smaller sizes has noticeably decreased. Meanwhile the number of grants of £50,000 or more rose from 47 in 1996/97 to 87 in 1997/98.

Grant size	No. of grants	Value of grants
£100,000+	19	£4.3 million
£50,000 - £99,999	68	£4.3 million
£20,000 - £49,999	328	£9.2 million
£5,000 - £19,999	407	£4.0 million
<£5,000	364	£0.9 million

The geographical distribution

Figures are given on a regional basis, but as they include awards to national charities (often London based), and no note is taken of the relative population differences of the regions concerned, no firm conclusions can be reached. However it is clear that grants are reaching all parts of the country in substantial numbers.

About 2% of the trust's grant total in 1997/98 was given to UK charities working for third world development.

1997/98 grant commitments

These are summarised as follows:

ACCOMMODATION

	No.	Amount £
Activity Centre	1	2,200
Advice	19	372,000
Elderly	1	800,000
Employment	1	42,000
Homeless	57	1,393,250
Homes	2	90,000
Hostel	16	763,500
Housing	17	433,500
Influencing/ Campaigning	3	145,000
Mental Illness	1	15,000
Offenders/Probation	1	20,000
Supported Housing	1	1,500
Women's Organisations /Refuges	13	283,500
Young People	5	95,000
TOTAL	138	£4,456,450

CRIME

	No.	Amount £
Advice	5	79,000
Arts	2	12,000
Counselling	1	39,000
Crime	1	2,000
Influencing/ Campaigning	1	75,000
Mental Illness	1	105,000
Offenders/Probation	17	273,000
Physical Illness	1	5,000
Prisons/Prisoners	14	1,360,000
Women's Organisations /Refuges	1	30,000
Young People	3	65,000
TOTAL	47	£2,045,000

EDUCATION

	No.	Amount £
City Farm	2	2,000
Education	29	651,200
Environment	2	8,000
TOTAL	33	£661,200

EMPLOYMENT/TRAINING

	No.	Amount £
Advice	1	24,000
Employment	1	5,000
Mental Disability/ Handicap	2	15,000
Mental Illness	6	240,000
Training	3	57,950
TOTAL	13	£341,950

ENVIRONMENT

	No.	Amount £
Environment	4	54,000
TOTAL	4	£54,000

HEALTH

	No.	Amount £
Advice	1	105,000
Alcoholism	22	566,600
Arts	2	11,500
Counselling	2	23,000
Day Care	2	6,500
Drop In	1	4,400
Drugs	39	1,225,000
Elderly	1	20,000
Hospital	1	15,000
Influencing/Campaigning	2	5,000
Medical Services	1	1,500
Mental Disability/ Handicap	8	91,700
Mental Illness	78	1,578,800
Physical Disability/ Handicap	9	221,500
Physical Illness	1	15,000
Psychotherapy	1	20,000
Refugees/Immigrants	1	1,500
Young People	1	30,000
TOTAL	173	£3,942,000

OVERSEAS

	No.	Amount £
Community Associations/ Centres	1	40,000
Community Welfare	7	110,350
Conservation	4	66,000
Education	1	2,500
Employment	1	15,000

	No.	Amount £
Environment	1	40,000
Homeless	1	29,000
Medical Services	1	40,000
Mental Illness	2	53,000
Physical Disability/		
Handicap	1	20,000
Regeneration	1	50,000
Statutory/Health/		
Local Authorities	1	5,000
Training	1	5,500
TOTAL	23	£476,350

WELFARE

	No.	Amount £
Activity Centre	1	20,000
Advice	71	1,108,820
Alcoholism	1	5,000
Arts	2	5,000
Children	8	140,050
Church Centre	69	1,061,000
Community Associations/		
Centres	112	1,313,550
Community Welfare	70	1,282,050
Conciliation	23	216,000
Counselling	60	573,250
Day Care	22	225,300
Drop In	3	70,000
Education	2	56,500
Elderly	54	542,700
Environment	3	53,500
Ethnic Minorities	1	3,000
Families General	73	1,047,450
Homeless	4	211,500
Influencing/Campaigning	6	158,750
Mental Disability/		
Handicap	1	2,000
Nursery	1	1,000
Offenders/Probation	1	20,000
One-Parent Single/		
Lone Families	2	21,500
Playgrounds, Parks,		
Gardens	2	21,000
Playgroup/Playscheme	3	7,500
Refugees/Immigrants	12	214,500
Regeneration	11	289,500
Well-Being	27	323,500
Women's Organisations/		
Refuges	13	253,500
Young People	61	1,204,500
Youth Centre	36	288,500
TOTAL	755	£10,740,420

Total grant commitments

1186 £22,717,370

Typical Tudor Trust grants

The following examples of grant commitments in 1997/98, given in the Annual Report, can be taken as exemplifying the kind of work that the trust likes to fund.

Abbeyfield Ballachulish Society (£800,000)

Abbeyfield, a national provider of housing and care for older people, is developing a new concept to provide a full range of care on one site. Five exemplar schemes are being established around the UK to demonstrate how this Integrated Care concept can work in any community. The Trust is contributing capital funding for one of these pilot projects, in the remote rural location of Ballachulish, Scotland. The proposed building will incorporate day care facilities for fifteen people from the wider community with residential provision for thirty including respite care, and will have the capacity to extend the level of care up to that required by dementia sufferers.

Bolton Young People's Advice and Support Service (£30,000 over three years)

BYPASS is a young people-led project providing drop-in advice and help on a range of issues including drugs, housing and sexual health, all under one roof. The Trust's funding is towards the provision of a counselling service.

Bradford Curry Project (£5,000 over two years)

This multi-racial, multi-faith, multi-cultural project (to use its own description) provides meals and other practical help for people who are homeless. Anglican, Catholic, Hindu, Muslim, Sikh and student organisations are all involved, making it a very positive example of diverse traditions and cultures working together to offer a service to the community. The Trust is helping to fund the employment of a Volunteer Development Worker.

Charities Aid Foundation (loan of £500,000)

The Charities Aid Foundation has established the Investors in Society Fund to provide low-interest loans to charitable projects. While the Tudor Trust normally prefers to deal with projects directly and rarely offers

loans, we recognise the value of a charitable loan fund which benefits from CAF's expertise and involves a number of trusts and banks as well as private individuals. Charities seeking loans will be expected to show that they are developing a sustainable approach to funding and have identified sources of income to repay a loan over a limited period. The Trust's contribution to the Fund will be used to support projects which are within our remit and will be reviewed after three years.

Crisis (£200,000 over three years)

Crisis is supporting the development of Open Houses to help people sleeping rough in areas where there have been few or no previous services. These areas are often rural and are not covered by the government's Rough Sleepers Initiative. Run by independent local charities, Open Houses aim to provide direct access accommodation and to help individuals finding a sustainable route out of homelessness. At the time of writing there are seven in operation and a further four are planned to open in the next few months. The Trust's grant builds on a previous commitment to the scheme and will be used for the capital costs of new Open Houses.

Damascus Road Association (£120,000 over three years)

The Damascus Road Association in Manchester provides a drop-in centre, counselling and a day treatment programme for people with alcohol problems. Working alongside a residential treatment unit, a community café and a nursery, the Association is able to help all sorts of people affected by alcohol abuse including women with children. Three separate organisations have been involved in providing these facilities and part of the Trust's funding will help with the development of a unified management structure.

David Gray House (£20,000)

The Salvation Army runs this probation and bail hostel on the Isle of Man. The Trust's grant is towards a new resettlement and training centre for offenders to be established alongside the hostel. It may be used for either capital or revenue costs.

Eastleigh Interface (£3,000)

This project in Hampshire is for people with drug and alcohol problems, their families and friends. It provides advice, support and counselling, drug screening, needle exchange, training, educational sessions in schools and outreach to rural areas. The hours of operation include two evenings a week. The Trust's grant is for core costs.

Enfield Parents Centre (£60,000 over three years)

This centre in north London supports families with children who have been excluded from school, have special educational needs or have difficulties gaining access to education for other reasons. It trains volunteers to give advice and support, for example in negotiations with schools, provides a mediation service and encourages the development of self-help groups. The Trust's funding is for operational costs including the employment of an Exclusions Project worker.

Kairos APAC Trust (£55,000 over three years)

The Kairos APAC Trust is introducing a model of therapeutic communities in prisons to the UK. APAC prison communities in other countries have been successful in increasing offenders' self-respect, encouraging mutual support and fostering a sense of responsibility towards families and communities and have shown a reduction in re-offending. The Trust's funding is for the development of the original UK project at HMP The Verne, Dorset, and the start-up of one at HMP Swaleside in Kent.

Kings Cross Homelessness Project (£25,000)

Changes in housing benefit regulations and in the local economy are resulting in evictions from 'bed and breakfast' accommodation in the Kings Cross area of central London. Recognising that this may lead to vulnerable people sleeping on the streets, the Trust is funding an advice and resettlement worker for a year to make contact with those affected and help them take up other options. The project will be written up so that organisations responding to similar problems elsewhere can learn from its experience.

Llanelli Centre Project (total of £29,000 over three years)

This busy centre for young people is open seven days a week and offers a range of activities including woodwork and other crafts, as well as a source of advice and drugs education. The Trust's funding is mainly for a youth worker post.

NEWPIN Derry (£20,000)

NEWPIN works with young families in difficulties, providing local centres where parents (mainly lone mothers) can find mutual support and follow a programme of personal development. Childcare is provided and parents learn play as well as parenting skills. Derry NEWPIN is the first in Northern Ireland, the Trust helped with initial capital costs.

Off the Record (£22,500 over three years)

This counselling and drop-in information service for under-25s in Bristol is developing work in schools and youth clubs, enabling it to reach more young people with problems. The Trust is helping to fund volunteer co-ordinator and outreach worker posts.

Pravasi Mandal (£40,000)

Currently running a lunch club for Asian elders from cramped and unsuitable premises, this Wellingborough group plans to build a new day care centre with catering, bathing facilities and a medical consultation room. The new centre will take up to 100 people a day and involve volunteer helpers. The Trust's grant is towards the construction costs.

Scottish Association for Mental Health: Core Club, Dunfermline (total of £59,000 over three years)

Established in 1992, the SAMH Core Club was Scotland's first Clubhouse project. Clubhouses are centres run by and for people with mental health problems to provide them with social, personal development and training opportunities. An important component of Clubhouses is a Transitional Employment Programme which helps members back into paid work through supported placements with local employers; the Trust's funding for the Core Club is towards a TEP co-ordinator post.

Tulip (£60,000)

Tulip provides accommodation and outreach support for people with severe long-term mental distress in Haringey, north London. Many of its users are from black and ethnic minority communities and many have other problems such as homelessness or substance misuse. The charity is developing a new resource centre, The Bridge, to be run along Clubhouse lines (see SAMH above) and the Trust is providing a grant to help link this building to Tulip's existing premises, creating the right environment for an integrated service to users.

West Harton Churches Together (total of £97,500 over three years)

This coalition of churches in Newcastle plans to convert a former bank into a community building. Linked to an existing advice centre next door, "Action Station" will provide a drop-in/coffee shop, debt counselling, training facilities and space for community groups. The Trust is providing £30,000 a year for revenue costs including a debt/advice worker post, and £7,500 for furniture and equipment.

Women in Special Hospitals and Secure Units (£45,000 over three years)

WISH works for and on behalf of women during and after psychiatric detention in high security hospitals and medium secure units. The Trust has supported WISH since its inception in 1990. Our current funding is for the North West branch which will be covering Ashworth Hospital, medium secure units/high dependency units, a prison psychiatric unit and a proposed women-only unit. It is enabling the branch to employ a second worker.

Exclusions 'These areas cannot be considered for funding:

Activity centres
Animals
Bereavement counselling
Commercial organisations
Community Foundations
Community transport
Conferences or seminars
Conservation/protection of buildings
Conservation/protection of flora or fauna
Endowment appeals
Expeditions/overseas travel
Fabric appeals for places of worship
Fundraising events/salaries of fund raisers
Health centres/well person's clinics
Holidays and holiday centres
Hospitals and hospices
Individuals
Medical care
Medical research and equivalents
Mother tongue classes/cultural activities
Museums/places of entertainment
Nurseries
Playschemes and groups, Mother and Toddler
Religion
Scouts, guides, other uniformed youth groups
Sponsorship/marketing appeals
Sports
Universities and colleges
Village halls
Women's centres.

Applications Applications can only be made in writing, at any time. We do not use an application form. Information needed includes:

- a summary of the current work of the organisation, with the latest annual report;
- a description of the project/proposals/ area of work for which funding is required;
- an indication of the numbers involved/likely to be involved and how they will benefit;
- a breakdown of costs (for capital works, these might be building costs, VAT, fees, furniture and equipment; for revenue they might be salaries, premises, training, publicity, expenses etc);
- details of funding raised or committed to date and steps being taken to raise the balance other than the approach to the Tudor Trust;
- any other relevant information such as catchment area served, numbers attending existing activities per month or per annum, how revenue implications of capital proposals will be met. For new buildings or major refurbishment schemes, drawings/ plans and possibly a photo are helpful;

- the latest annual accounts (or a copy of a recent financial/bank statement if the organisation is too new to have annual accounts).

Grants are given for amounts from £500 upwards. Loans are offered occasionally. Applications may be sent at any time to the Grants Administrator, Mrs Jill Powell.

Each application will be assessed taking account of current priorities and the funding available. Some applicants will be told almost immediately that the trust cannot help. For the remainder, there is a continuous process of assessment, and applicants will usually be told of the outcome eight weeks after all the information has been received by the trust. Please do not telephone for news of progress during this period.

A letter will be sent giving the trustees' decision. If a grant has been approved, conditions relating to the release of the grant will be included in the letter. A visit may be made to the project, but this will be initiated by the trust and will not necessarily result in a grant being approved.

Organisations are requested not to approach the trust again for at least twelve months after a grant has been paid or notification of an unsuccessful application has been given.

The Douglas Turner Trust

£322,000 (1996/97)

General

1 The Yew Trees, High Street, Henley-in-Arden, Solihull B95 5BN
Tel: 01564-793085

Correspondent J E Dyke, Trust Administrator

Trustees Roger D Turner; W S Ellis; J R Clemishaw; D P Pearson; T J Lunt.

Beneficial area West Midlands, particularly Birmingham; UK.

Information available Report and accounts, with grants list but no narrative report, are available from the trust for a fee of £5.

Summary Grants are made to a variety of charities most of which are local social welfare organisations. Awards are typically in the range of £1,000 to £5,000 but go as high as £40,000. Most are made on an annual basis and around

85% of charitable expenditure goes to regularly supported charities.

General In 1996/97 the trust's assets amounted to nearly £10 million and a total of 90 grants were awarded (average £3,600). Beneficiaries are not analysed by location in the report and accounts but the trust says that 'about 80%' of funds are awarded to groups in the Birmingham and West Midlands area. The largest grant in the year was for £40,000 and went to Age Concern Birmingham TV Fund (regularly supported). Other 'new' donations went to Malvern Festival Theatre Trust (£25,000), Theatre Ashram Community Service (£1,500), and the Children's National Medical Research Fund (£5,000).

Exclusions No grants to individuals.

Applications Registered charities only may apply. Telephone enquiries before formal applications are welcomed. Applications must include the latest annual report and accounts.

The Tyne & Wear Foundation

£1,350,000 (1997/98)

Social welfare, general

Cale Cross House, 156 Pilgrim Street, Newcastle upon Tyne NE1 6SU
Tel: 0191-222 0945;
Fax: 0191-230 0689
Email: TWF@onyxnet.co.uk Website: www.northeast-online.co.uk/TWF

Correspondent Maureen High

Board Members John Squires, David Francis, Sir Tom Cowie, the Duke of Northumberland, Derek Walker, John Hamilton, W. G. McClelland, Clare Dodgeson, Joy Higgins, Michael Worthington, Margaret Barbour, Brian Roycroft, Alan Share, Brian Latham, Derek Smail, Nigel Smith, Barbara Dennis, Alan Wardropper, Guy Readman.

Beneficial area Tyne & Wear and Northumberland.

Information available Excellent Annual Review and Grant Guidelines available from the foundation.

Summary This is one of the most successful of the new Community Trusts set up in Britain. Grants range from under £1,000 to over £70,000, with the possibility of multi year awards. There is a strong general interest in local community development, but grant giving is dealt with through a variety of funds that often have their own specific criteria.

General Now celebrating its 10th year, the foundation continues to support and promote charitable purposes in the area of Tyne and Wear, and, since 1993, in Northumberland. In the words of their President they aim, among other things, to 'provide a personal but professional service to anyone wanting to support their local community by managing charitable funds in their name and on their behalf.'

Total assets of the foundation in 1997/98 stood at £16.8 million. Income for 1997/98 amounted to £1.5 million; of this £1.35 million was awarded as grants to nearly 500 groups.

Grant Guidelines 1998

'Tyne and Wear Foundation is a local grant maker. Set up as a community foundation in 1988 to help people in Tyne and Wear and Northumberland, we bring together individuals and projects with people "who want to put something back into their community."

'We currently manage over 65 funds totalling £18 million which have been built by interested individuals and companies. Our work involves helping our supporters make grants in their fields of interest.

'In 1998 we expect to distribute well over £1 million in grants ranging from under £100 to longer term grants of over £10,000 a year. We also make a number of larger grants each year through our links with a national charity.

'We support a wide range of organisations and individuals with grants ranging from a few hundred pounds to several thousand pounds. In 1997 we distributed £1.7 million in grants.

'Three new developments last year were the launch of the Kellett Fund for the third age, the first full year of grants from the Readman Foundation to help young people and the Millennium Awards for community leaders.

'We are now able to consider requests for most activities which clearly benefit local people whilst still always interested to hear from new and small projects that have difficulty in finding funding.

'Our support includes grants for individuals as well as community groups. We can also consider requests for equipment and trips as well as for project

running costs.

'We welcome applications from all sections of the community and hope that we can help you meet the needs of local people in the region. Please contact us if you need further help when applying for a grant.

Examples of funds

'Some of our larger funds for specific purposes:

The Readman Foundation – supports work with young people.

Sir Tom Cowie Fund – has an interest in grants which help people on Wearside.

The Kellett Fund – benefits older people in the region in their third age.

The Chapman Fund – following the transfer of assets from the former Chapman Foundation, to provide equipment and help maintain buildings for youth projects in Tyne and Wear.

Procter & Gamble – starting this year, the foundation will be assessing grants on P&G's behalf.

'You do not need to identify a Fund when applying, as we will match your request to the most appropriate fund we manage.

Equality of opportunity

'We are keen to ensure that all sections of the community benefit from our grants and like to know that services are accessible to disabled people, and that facilities such as creches and signing, interpretation or translating services are provided where necessary.

Who do we support?

'We make grants to both large and small organisations working in local communities. Our support generally falls under the broad heading of social welfare and we particularly like to help grassroots projects run by local residents.

'Our grants also provide support for individuals under certain circumstances. The list below shows the spectrum of support we offer to meet the needs of local people.

How to apply

(See under 'Applications' below)

Making a lasting difference

'We make grants to support a wide variety of activities and circumstances. Our grants have supported many areas of work including:

• *Young people*

£7,300 to Mobex North East to train

young people as community leaders through the Readman Foundation.

£250 to help towards the education of a young girl leaving care through the Brian Roycroft Fund.

• *Children*

£400 for equipment for a playgroup in Shillbottle, Northumberland from the Northumberland Fund.

£12,000 to the Pre-School Learning Alliance in Gateshead to support training and work with local playschemes.

• *Elderly people*

£250 to Greens Pensioners Group managing a community bungalow.

£6,000 to Age Concern, North Tyneside for a volunteering programme in the borough.

• *Equipment*

£150 for computer software to record case details at North Tyneside Disability Advice Centre.

£1,000 for a wheelchair for a young disabled girl through the Sunshine Fund.

• *Rural Areas*

£400 for a village appraisal through the Bellingham Fund

£1,000 to Catton Village Hall, Northumberland for refurbishment cost through the Joseph Borough Charitable Trust.

£11,000 over 2 years to Castle Morpeth Disability Association to develop self help groups for the disabled in Northumberland.

£25,000 over 2 years to Children North East to work with families in Tynedale from the Henry Smith's Charity.

• *Advice & information*

£30,000 over 3 years to Northumberland CAB for money advice work.

£75,000 over 3 years to St. Simon's Community Project, South Tyneside for work with unemployed people through the Henry Smith's Charity.

• *Ethnic minorities*

£10,000 to the Rights Project in west Newcastle for welfare rights work in community centre's and people's homes through the Willan Charitable Trust.

£4,000 to Asian Voices for youth work with ethnic minority young people in Sunderland.

£15,000 to South Tyneside for advice work with ethnic minorities in the borough through the Joseph Rowntree

Charitable Trust.

• *Housing*

£48,000 to LINKS over 6 years for work with homeless people through the Homeless Young Peoples's Fund.

£12,000 to Wearside Women in Need over 3 years to support young people in their first tenancies.

• *Community Initiatives*

£500 to Glebe Community Association in Washington for the running costs of a centre run by local residents.

£5,000 to CHANCE to support local residents in Sunderland through the Sir Tom Cowie Fund.

• *Community Arts*

£4,000 to Headway Theatre for work with isolated young people.

£590 to Disability Action North East (DANE) for running costs.

• *People with Special Needs*

£500 to Speaking Up in Gateshead, volunteer run self help group providing training and support for members.

£90,000 over 3 years to Skill for People to develop a stronger funding base through Henry Smith's Charity

Developments in 1997

'Some major developments in the foundation in 1997 included:

- Managing a £300,000 programme to work with "hard to reach" young people in Ashington over the next three years. The funding is provided by three charitable trusts and Northumberland TEC.' The money has been awarded to a consortium of Endeavour Training, Mobex, North East and Trident.
- We are also administering an awards scheme for the Millennium Commission as one of their awards partners. Our scheme provides training and bursaries to community leaders and is worth £600,000 over the next three years.
- The foundation has just been asked to administer Procter & Gamble's charitable giving which will involve making awards of £50,000 a year, dealing with all P & G's charity correspondence and eventually building a fund with £1 million endowment.'

'On the recommendation of the foundation, Henry Smith's Charity gave out £622,000 in 21 grants in 1997/98. Most of the grants given are multi year awards and in projects that deal with the

community work, social and welfare work and children. Grants ranged from £65,000 to St Chad's Community Project (now in the second or third year of funding) to £7,500 to Grange Road Methodist Church (also in its second or third year of funding).

'The Readman Foundation was established in 1996 by businessman Guy Readman after he sold his company the previous year. The foundation's aim is to improve the prospects for young people in the North East. Mr. Readman will personally select projects to be funded and will consider multi year awards. In 1997/98 the foundation gave out £176,000 in 80 grants. Examples of grants given include £15,000 to the Endeavour Training Consortium, part of a multi year award, £4,800 to Streetwise, Newcastle, £2,000 to the Route 26 Music Collective, and two grants of £1,000 to individuals for their personal development.

The Kellett Fund was recently set up with a legacy from Douglas Kellett. The fund will primarily benefit people in the 'Third Age'- 'the period of active life following retirement when older people all too often lack opportunities to take up new activities, broaden their experience and contribute to civic life.' The fund gave out £100,000 in 16 grants, examples of which include £45,000 over three years to Equal Arts ('to provide opportunities for older people to develop their skills and participate in a range of arts activities including film, sculpture, mosaics, and photography throughout Tyne & Wear'), £6,500 to Age Concern Sunderland (to fund a 'pilot project for older volunteers to support carers in Washington who are housebound'), and £6,000 over three years to Roshni Asian Women's Centre, Newcastle ('to support a weekly elder women's group, Mahila Mandal, for ethnic minority women in the west end of Newcastle').

The Joseph Borough Charitable Trust, administered £32,000 through 24 grants in 1997/98. The trust seems to give one-off grants to social work and to disability. Only two grants were for £1,000 or more, the largest being £20,000 to the Borough Benevolent Association. Examples of other grants include £1,000 to Teeside Lions Wheelchair Basketball Club and £584 to South Tyneside Multicultural Project. The Tom Cowie Fund was set up by Sir Tom Cowie for projects in Sunderland. In 1996/97 a total of £27,800 was given out in 16 grants to a variety of projects dealing social work, youth projects, disability and schools. Examples include £4,000 to Sunderland Women's

Centre, £3,500 to Barbara Priestman School, £3,000 to Sunderland MIND, £2,000 to Pennywell Youth Project and £1,000 to Radio Sunderland.'

Exclusions Large capital projects.

Applications Your application will be registered with one fund at a time and an advisory panel will consider your request.

There are no closing dates for applications and within three months you should hear from us regarding a decision. However, the majority of requests will be considered within three months. Those taking longer will be considered by more than one fund.

We register applications and send an acknowledgement within 10 working days. Please get in touch if you do not hear from us.

Information we need from you:

- How the planned work meets the need of the project or individual
- Background information to set the request in context
- A clear budget
- The size of the grant requested
- Other funding secured
- The latest set of accounts for the organisation
- Other relevant information including an annual review, articles or reports
- Details of who a cheque should be made payable to.

The Ulverscroft Foundation

£307,000 (1996/97)

Sick and visually impaired people, ophthalmic research

1 The Green, Bradgate Road, Anstey, Leicester LE7 7FU
Tel: 0116-236 4325

Correspondent Joyce Sumner

Trustees David Thorpe; P H Carr; Michael Rich; Allan Leach; Michael Down.

Beneficial area UK, with a special interest in the Leicester area, plus other English speaking countries, particularly Australia, New Zealand, Canada and the USA.

Information available Report and accounts, but without narrative analysis and explanation.

Summary Recently in difficulties, the foundation happily appears to have recovered and was able to make new grant commitments in 1996/97 totalling £468,000. The main activity in the past has been the funding of professorial chairs of ophthalmological research at colleges and hospitals.

General The foundation is the owner of the Ulverscroft Large Print Books business, a commercial organisation that also benefits millions of partially sighted people. The foundation further distributes in grants the profits from the company.

The business has lately needed substantial reorganisation and reinvestment, but has now returned to profitability, with a net income of £147,000 in 1996/97 and £662,000 in 1995/96 (on turnover of about £11 million). During the period of change, in 1994, the then treasurer of the foundation made an unauthorised loan of £1 million to the company. This has now been formalised and will be paid back in full in the year 2000.

Meanwhile proper interest is being paid to the foundation.

Extra information provided by the trust reveals that a number of grants were for salaries to support Chairs of Research into eye diseases, Research fellows and Research Assistants at universities and hospitals in Great Britain and Austrailia. An interest free loan was also given to the Partially Sighted Society. 'Grants have been given to institutions who supply computers for the blind and talking books and music services. Art exhibitions and theatres have received grants to enable the visually impaired to partake fully.' The trust has also donated large print book and talking books to a variety of clubs, societies, hospital and homes for the visually impaired both in the UK and Abroad.

There were 20 grant payments made in 1996/97, some or all of them representing on-going payments. The largest payments were to Great Ormond Street Ophthalmology Unit (£73,000, the first of five instalments towards a £400,000 pledge for construction work on the Ulverscroft Children's Eye Unit); St Mary's Chair of Opthalmology (£66,000); St Mary's Chair of Ophthalmology (£66,000); the Institute of Ophthalmology (£25,000); the Lions Eye Institute (£23,000); and the University of New South Wales (£20,000).

Recipients of smaller grants included Electronic Aids for the Blind (£2,500); the Dyslexia Institute (£2,000) and the Pacific Islands Council for the Blind (£1,000).

Exclusions Applications from individuals are not encouraged.

Applications In writing to the correspondent. The trustees meet about three times a year to consider applications.

The Underwood Trust

£512,000 (1996/97)

General

32 Haymarket, London SW1Y 4TP

Correspondent Antony Cox, Manager

Trustees C Clark; R Clark; Mrs P A H Clark.

Beneficial area UK.

Information available Report and accounts with categorised grants list are on file at the Charity Commission or available from the trust for an expensive fee of £11.

Summary Donations are made to a range of registered charities. The sum given is usually £5,000 but has been as high as £100,000.

General The trust was established in 1973 by Robert and Mary Clark. Grants are made only to organisations within the four broad categories shown below (along with grants statistics for 1996/97 and 1995/96).

Generally, beneficiaries are well established, national, 'royal' or high profile charities and many receive regular support from the trust. Around 70% of grants were for £5,000 with a few smaller grants going down to £1,000 and a handful of larger donations (up to £100,000).

Within the medicine and health category the most substantial grants were to Frenchay Hospital (£100,000), the Royal Hospital for Children, Bristol (£50,000) and the National Eye Research Centre (£25,000).

Welfare grants included £25,000 to Centrepoint, and £10,000 gifts to the Wiltshire Community Foundation and Windmill Hill City Farm. Support given in the education field included £25,000 each to Farms for City Children and Trinity Hall Cambridge.

Exclusions No grants to individuals under any circumstances. Grants are not made for expeditions, nor to overseas projects.

Applications 'The trust's income is committed to long term projects, therefore new applications are very unlikely to be considered'. Applications are not normally acknowledged unless accompanied by a SAE.

Trustees normally meet quarterly.

John and Lucille van Geest Foundation

£711,000 (1996/97)

Medical research and welfare

42 Pinchbeck Road, Spalding, Lincolnshire

Correspondent S R Coltman.

Trustees Lucille van Geest; Hilary P Marlowe; Stuart R Coltman; Toni Gibson MBE.

The Underwood Trust			
	Number of grants	**Total 1996/97**	**(Total 1995/96)**
• **Medicine and health**	25	275,000	(£292,000)
• **General welfare**	20	£120,000	(£153,000)
• **Education, science, humanities and religion**	9	£81,000	(£72,000)
• **Environmental resources**	8	£36,000	(£50,000)
Total	**62**	**£512,000**	**(£569,000)**

Beneficial area UK and overseas, with a special interest in South Lincolnshire and adjoining areas.

Information available Accounts with a thin report which does not analyse or explain the year's grants.

Summary About thirty grants of between £1,000 and £100,000 are made each year. Most of the donations by value are awarded to large institutions and national charities for medical research and treatment purposes.

General The foundation dates from 1990 when it was established with the assets of the John Van Geest Charitable Fund. Most of the Geest shares comprising the original endowment have now been sold and investment diversified.

In 1996/97, the foundation had assets totalling nearly £20 million and an income of £750,000. 32 donations were made totalling £711,000. The trust does not say what donations were given for, but it appears that most of the money is awarded to medical research groups. Larger grants (£20,000 and above) were nearly always made to research institutions, while smaller grants (£1,500 to £10,000) were for medical welfare charities. For example the University of Cambridge (department unknown but probably a medical one) was awarded £100,000 and Children's Nationwide Medical Research, Nottingham Trent University and Queen Mary & Westfield College were each given £50,000. Meanwhile, causes such as the NSPCC, Spalding Spastics Society, and British Blind Sports were awarded sums of £10,000 or less.

The little narrative information that is given in the annual report includes the following:

In exercising their discretion the trustees in the main:-

- assist charities operating in South Lincolnshire and adjoining areas concerned with the welfare of the elderly and the young in need through illness or poverty;
- assist charities concerned with medical research.

The foundation has said that it does not seek applications, but the process by which it does make grants is not known.

While the trust says that their 'accounts have been prepared in accordance with the requirements of the Statement of Recommended Practice', a similar conscientiousness cannot be claimed for their annual report which fails to deliver a reasonable amount of narrative information.

The foundation says that it does not seek applications, but it appears to respond to at least some of those that it does receive.

Exclusions Individuals.

Applications 'The trust does not seek applications.

Bernard Van Leer Foundation

£395,000 (in the UK 1996/97)

Childhood development

The Royal Bank of Scotland plc, Private Trust and Taxation, 2 Festival Square, Edinburgh EH3 9SU
Tel: 0131-523 2657; Fax: 0131-228 9889

Correspondent David Macdonald

Trustees I Samren (Chair); M Craig Benton; J L Brentjens, R Freudenberg; J Kremers; H B van Liemt; A Mar-Haim; J K Pearlman; P J Rich.

Beneficial area International.

Information available 1995/96 report and accounts are on file at the Charity Commission; guidelines.

Summary This the UK branch of a Dutch based foundation. Support, usually through multiple grants, is given to governmental and non-governmental projects seeking to improve the lives and opportunities for young children. The foundation's area of interest covers 40 countries including the UK and Ireland. Grants made within the UK account for around 15% of the foundation's total charitable expenditure and vary from £1,000 to £75,000. The foundation does not normally consider unsolicited applications.

General The foundation was established by Bernard van Leer (1883-1958), a Dutch industrialist and philanthropist and founder of what is now Royal Packaging Industries Van Leer NV. Though this book does not normally include overseas grant makers, Van Leer has a charitable subsidiary registered with the CC, and has an apparently continuing commitment to this country. The trust deed outlines that special preference for grant assistance should be given to benefit 'education and youth...especially...projects aimed at enabling children and youth impeded by the social and cultural inadequacy of their background to achieve the greatest possible realisation of their innate intellectual potential'.

The foundation says that the vast majority of grants are made to organisations which it itself approached. More specifically it told these editors that 'in order to avoid the users of your guide needlessly approaching the foundation for funding, we would appreciate it if you would highlight that the foundation does not usually consider unsolicited appeals'. However, the foundation's guidelines for applicants (reprinted in full below) seem to give a more encouraging message.

In 1995/96 the foundation's income totalled £3.4 million and it made an unknown number of grants internationally amounting to £2,857,000. Within the UK 17 organisations received a total of 24 grants including: Glasgow Caledonian University – Scottish network family policy resource unit (£75,000); Save the Children Fund UK, Cynon Valley (£51,000); University of London, Quality in Diversity (£43,000); and the Scottish Early Years and Family Network (£36,000). In addition four health boards each received sums of around £30,000.

The foundation's guidelines say:

'Our mission is to enhance opportunities for children 0-7 years, growing up in circumstances of social and economic disadvantage, with the objective of developing their innate potential to the greatest extent possible. We concentrate on children 0-7 years because scientific findings have demonstrated that interventions in the early years of childhood are most effective in yielding lasting benefits to children and society.

'We accomplish this through two interconnected strategies:

1) a grant making programme in 40 countries aimed at developing contextually appropriate approaches to early childhood and development; and
2) the sharing of knowledge and know-how in the domain of early childhood development that primarily draws on the experiences generated by the projects that the foundation supports, with the aim of informing and influencing policy and practice.

'We make grants to about 140 major projects at any one time and these operate in a variety of contexts:

- some are in developing countries, others in industrialised countries;
- they may be situated in urban slums, shanty towns and remote rural areas;
- they may focus on children living in violent settings, children of ethnic and cultural minorities, children of single or teenage parents, children of refugees and migrants;

- they often work to improve quality in daycare centres, pre-schools, health or other services;
- they may develop community based services;
- they may improve the quality of home environment by working with parents and other family members and caregivers.

The foundation:

- is concerned with young children's overall development and therefore promotes a holistic approach including education, health and nutrition;
- believes that children's development is the primary responsibility of parents and therefore actively promotes the enhancement of parents' capacity to support their children's development;
- attaches great importance to the involvement of the community as a major factor in children's development and therefore promotes a development strategy that is rooted in the community and is culturally, socially and economically appropriate;
- has adopted a contextual approach which builds on people's strengths as a guiding principal and therefore encourages building of local capacity, local ownership and working in partnership.

'As well as our major focus, grant making is guided by thematic and programmatic priorities, geographic criteria, and budget limitations. Grants are made to governmental and non-governmental organisations.

'We encourage projects to document their experiences, and we collect and systemise materials, publications and videos that they produce. We also support projects in producing their own publications and videos for their principal audiences.

'The foundation's publications are available free of charge in single copies to organisations and individuals working in the area of early childhood development and related fields anywhere in the world. A list is available on request.

'*The foundation rarely considers unsolicited proposals* (Editors emphasis). The vast majority of the projects supported result from a process of consultation with organisations that have been identified by the foundation itself.'

Exclusions Grants are not made to individuals nor for the general support of organisations. The foundation does not provide study, research or travel grants. No grants are made in response to general appeals.

Applications Applications can only be made in writing. The trust does not use an application form. Information that you should include is as follows:

- charity title or a description of your organisations activities;
- registered charity number or evidence of tax-exempt status;
- list of the charities key people;
- a contact name, address and telephone number;
- summary of the current work of the organisation – with latest annual report;
- description of the project/proposals/ area of work for which funding is requested, including costs, funds raised in relation to the target and details of any promised;
- indication of the numbers of beneficiaries likely to benefit and how they will benefit;
- how you intend to monitor and evaluate the project.

The foundation gives preference to countries in which the Van Leer Group of Companies is established.

The trust will acknowledge receipt of your application and may contact you for further information prior to consideration. There is a continuous process of assessment and you will be advised of any decision and, if successful, of any conditions attached to it.

For further information on the trust please either write to the correspondent or you are welcome to call direct on the above number.

The Variety Club Children's Charity

£5,078,000 (1996/97)

Children's charities, 'Sunshine Coaches'

The Variety Club of Great Britain, St Martin's House, 139 Tottenham Court Road, London W1P 9LN
Tel: 0171-387 3311 Fax: 0171 387 3311

Trustees H Amaya-Torres; J Astaire; H-J Babini; L Barr; P Burley; S Crown; R Curtis; T Frame; R Freeman; N Garrod; G Huniford; T Langton; E Morely; J Morley; C Murray; R Nathan; J Ratcliff; M R Ratcliff; I Riches; A Rippon; N Sinclair; J Webber; J Whittell; P Zabludowicz.

Beneficial area UK.

Information available Report and accounts on file at the Charity Commission, with terse exploration of the grants programme and a list showing the largest 50 grants.

Summary The charity aims to help disadvantaged children by making grants to individuals and groups for coaches, wheelchairs, medical and social purposes. Donations have been as high as £3 million but most grants are for less than £5,000. Also a variety of entertainment for children is sponsored or donated free of charge.

General The British club was founded in 1949 (1928 in the USA) and has 47 branches worldwide. In 1999 the Variety Club of Great Britain celebrates its 50th Anniversary. Within Britain there are ten 'Variety regions' each with their own chairman and committee. The regions are: London; Merseyside and North Wales; South West; Midlands; Northern; North West; Scotland; South Wales; Sussex; Yorkshire & Wessex. The charity receives its income from the Variety Club of Great Britain whose members (recruited from entertainment, sport and business) raise funds through a number of activities and events. About half of charitable expenditure is on 'Sunshine Coaches', 10% on wheelchairs and the remainder goes to support a variety of projects which improve the quality of life of disadvantaged children.

Most of the charity's income (nearly £5.5 million in 1996/97) is generated by a trading subsidiary that organises fundraising events. The rest of their income (£3 million) comes from donations, legacies and interest. In 1996/97 the charity spent £1.3 million on fundraising and £0.5 million on administration (22 employees).

The charity says that its purposes are:

- 'to promote and provide for the care and upbringing of children suffering from physical or mental illness or injury or other physical or mental handicap or affliction and those deprived of parental care or of a stable home environment;
- 'the relief of poverty and the advancement of education of children of any race colour or creed;
- 'the relief of sickness and physical and mental handicap or affliction among children;
- 'the provision of facilities for recreation and other leisure time occupation for children in the interests of their social welfare;
- 'the support of associations,

organisations, institutions or other bodies (whether incorporated or not) whose objects shall be solely of a charitable nature.'

These aims are carried out through the provision of wheelchairs to individuals and coaches to organisations (for which purposes the charity runs specific programmes) and by making grants to both individuals and organisations for:

- projects and institutions and individual disadvantaged children;
- hospital development;
- specific equipment for hospitals, special schools and children's homes
- Christmas toy appeal.

Additionally, non-financial assistance is provided by the Variety at Work Committee which entertains children with programmed events which are either sponsored or donated free of charge. Such 'gifts in kind' were estimated to total £1.4 million in 1996/97.

The report and accounts do not show the sizes or nature of grants to individuals. The largest 50 grants to institutions are listed but these only account for about 30% of the total value of such awards (for 1996/97, the beneficiaries of over £3 million in grants are not disclosed). The purpose of the grants is not shown and it is not known how many applications were received. The geographical distribution of funds is not shown and so it is difficult to see whether certain areas of the country are better funded than others.

Seven awards of £60,000 or more accounted for 17% of the sum total of donations to institutions. There were six grants of between £20,000 and £36,000, and 10 grants between £10,000 and £20,000.

The annual report says:

'Variety Club has seen a growth in corporate sponsorship and this support has helped to provide 93 Sunshine Coaches to those in need. A further 42 sunshine coaches were also provided by the Variety Club Golfing Society which had another successful year. Through the Easy Rider Wheelchairs programme, Variety Club was able to provide nearly 200 children with customised electric wheelchairs, opening them up to a whole new way of life. Many of these wheelchairs were provided by individual sponsors, particularly at events such as the annual dinner and ball, the property lunch and party night.

'Also during the year, nearly 90,000 children benefited from outings organised by Variety at Work which

includes visits to zoos, theme parks, theatres and museums. Variety Club is particularly indebted to the Armed Services who have entertained many children at their various establishments.

'During the year the Variety Club received hundreds of appeals to help children throughout Great Britain. As always, each appeal was investigated and carefully considered before any payment of grant could be recommended. Sums ranging from £100 to many thousands of pounds were distributed.

'The last official engagement of Diana, Princess of Wales, was a visit to Northwick Park Hospital where she received a cheque on behalf of the hospital's Children's Centre Appeal from Variety Club for £100,000. Many other hospitals received substantial support from Variety Club for care of children.'

Other large grants of 1996/97 were to St George's Hospital Appeal (£250,000), London Federation of Clubs for Young People (£119,000), and the Children's Trust Tadworth Court (£100,000).

This charity is noteworthy for the impressive voluntary contributions of time and money it inspires. A proper analysis of the grant-making programme and its efficacy would be useful to the charity, to the organisations seeking support and ultimately the children who stand to be helped.

Exclusions No grants are made towards administration costs.

Applications In writing at any time to the Head of Appeals.

Sir Siegmund Warburg's Voluntary Settlement

£673,000 (1996/97)

Medicine and education

33 King William Street,
London EC4R 9AS
Tel: 0171-567 8000

Correspondent Hugh A Stevenson

Trustees: Doris E Wasserman; Hugh A Stevenson; Dr Michael J Harding; Christopher Purvis.

Beneficial area UK, London.

Information available Accounts with report lacking the required grant-making analysis beyond giving the beneficiaries name and the size of grant.

Summary About 15 grants, recurrent and single, of between £1,000 and £170,000 are made each year. The great majority of the money is awarded to well established institutions. No unsolicited appeals said to be considered.

General Six organisations that were supported in 1995/96 (to the sum of £257,000) were awarded further, usually more substantial, grants in 1996/97 (totalling £490,000 or 73% of total donation expenditure). Ten grants were made to new groups in 1996/97,

Sir Siegmund Warburg's Voluntary Settlement

Grants were as follows:

University of Birmingham	£167,455	(£64,000 in 1995/96)
Imperial College	£148,386	(£119,000 in 1995/96)
Institute of Child Health	£162,513	(£60,000 in 1995/96)
National Hospital Development Foundation	£50,000	
AIR Trust	£38,500	
Queen Mary and Westfield College	£30,000	
Ovingdean Hall School	£20,115	
St Mary's Hospital	£13,444	
Families at Risk	£12,500	
Bobath Centre	£10,000	
British Lung Foundation	£6,488	(£8,000 in 1995/96)
Juniper Trust	£5,000	
King Edward's School – Witley	£5,000	(£5,000 in 1995/96)
North England Faculty of RCGP	£2,137	
Horticultural Therapy	£1,000	
St Paul's Girls School	£1,000	(£1,000 in 1995/96)

although these only accounted for 27% of the total value of donations. The charity is administered by an independent consultant, P R Jessel. Administration costs were £48,849 in 1996/97, or £3,000 per grant.

The major grants are listed in the table herewith.

The charity has told these editors:

'As the charity's funds are required to support purposes chosen by the trustees, no unsolicited applications can be considered.'

Applications

In writing to the correspondent, but see above.

Mrs Waterhouse Charitable Trust

£291,000 (1996/97)

Health, social welfare and countryside preservation

25 Clitheroe Road, Whalley, Clitheroe, BB7 9AD

Correspondent D H Dunn, Trustee

Trustees D H Dunn; I Dunn.

Beneficial area UK, with an interest in Lancashire.

Information available Full accounts are on file at the Charity Commission, but without any narrative report on policy or analysis of grants.

Summary The trust mainly makes small recurrent grants towards core costs to charities in the Lancashire area. A limited number of more substantial awards are given also usually for capital projects. Grants range from £1,000 to £50,000.

General In 1996/97 the trust's assets totalled £5 million and nearly £300,000 was disbursed to 66 charities. The trust does not analyse their grants and the following information has been gleaned through study of the raw grants list.

Six five-figure grants were paid (accounting for a third of grants expenditure); all others were in the range of £1,000 to £6,000 (typically for £2,000). An eclectic array of causes were assisted: welfare; youth; elderly; education; church; animals etc., and in particular there seemed to be a modest preference for medical care and research charities.

It is particularly difficult to say what proportion of funds were allocated within the Lancashire area. However, it appears that the great majority of recipients were based in, or benefiting, Lancashire.

The two largest awards were to BHRV Healthcare Trust (£50,000) and the National Trust Lake District Appeal (£25,000).

Exclusions No grants to individuals

Applications In writing to the correspondent. There is no set time for consideration of applications, but donations are normally made in March each year.

The Wates Foundation

£1,333,000 (1997/98)

Social welfare

1260 London Road, Norbury, London SW16 4EG
Tel: 0181-764 5000

Correspondent Sir Martin Berthoud, Director

Trustees John Wates (Chair); Ann Ritchie; Andrew Wates; David Wates; Jane Wates; Rev Jonathan Edwards (The grants committee of the foundation also includes other members of the Wates family).

Beneficial area Unrestricted, but mainly London

Information available Exemplary reports and accounts, including details of the voluntary sector interests of individual trustees.

Summary The main emphasis is on help for the disadvantaged in the London area. There is particular attention to citizenship, urban regeneration, penal affairs and school exclusion. Since 1994, addiction and criminality have been an area of special focus (with a target of 20% of all funding). However grants are quite widely spread, as will be apparent from the text below. The foundation says that it is becoming more 'outcomes and impact orientated' in its grant making.

Grants are normally to a maximum of £25,000 and projects can be funded for up to three years. About 450 grants were made in 1997/98. There is a strong preference

for funding activities in London.

General The foundation says 'There is emphasis on the physical, mental and spiritual welfare of the young and disadvantaged aged 8-25. The problems of unemployment, homelessness, substance abuse and offending are of particular concern. Post-school education and training, particularly in good citizenship, are also supported. From 1994 there has been a concentration on the field of addiction and criminality. Racial equality is stressed throughout.'

The 1997/98 Annual Report elaborates: 'The directors have published various restrictions which range from grants not normally being made to general appeals from large well established charities to grants not being made to individuals. The directors have continued with their area of special interest in addiction and criminality. They have also expressed a particular concern for the broad areas of "citizenship" and "urban regeneration". Their desire to become more pro-active and to make fewer but larger grants will continue to lead to an increase in the rejection of unsolicited appeals.'

The trust notes the recent addition to the trustees of Reverend Jonathan Edwards, who is encouraging the trust to look at some of the problems of rural West Dorset.

In 1997/98 assets stood at £35 million and generated an income of £1.5 million. 1,707 applications were received and 248 grants made, a low success rate of about 1 in 7. However the foundation points out that two out of three applications turned down are from outside their preferred area of Greater London. Within London, success rates will therefore have been much higher, perhaps about one in two or three.

Total grant giving in 1997/98 was over £1.3 million, with an average grant size of £5,000 to £6,000. About 30 grants were for £500 or less. The guidelines point out that the normal limit to grants is £25,000 and the maximum length of support is for three years.

The trust's interest in penal affairs is shown by about 23 grants worth £160,000 (12% of total grant giving) going to various education, art, and community projects involving prisons and prisoners.

Analysis of grants disbursed by location reveals that three out of four of grants are to the London region (these figures cover only the major categories).

London and nearby	*155 grants*	*£823,000*
Northern Ireland	*10 grants*	*£41,000*
Rest of England	*27 grants*	*£83,000*

National organisation 4 grants £29,000
Overseas 7 grants £48,000

The reported interest in South London in particular is not apparent from the 1997/98 figures, which show as follows:

South London: 34%
Rest of London: 47%

This reflects the lack of enough good quality applicants, rather than showing any reduction in the foundation's desire to give help in this area.

Examples of organisations receiving large grants include the following:

Community projects and disadvantaged: Replay Trust (£20,000 to help this group to establish supportive homes for women on release from prison, with their children); Frontline Housing Advice and Referral (£16,000 to part fund a Housing Advisor post in this black housing agency in the Kings Cross area); Katherine Low Settlement, Battersea (£15,000 contribution to staff salaries and other costs); and International Centre for Prison Studies (£13,000 to set up a new centre which would act as a clearing house for thinking about prisons).

Area of special focus: Youth at Risk (£30,000 to help this group build up their training capability and expand their operations throughout the UK; and £15,000 for their programme in Sutton, taking former offenders through an intensive week of instruction and re-orientation): and Prison Resource Service (£20,000 for the support of staff costs of this service working within Holloway Prison).

Arts: Sound Arts (£13,000 for a one step musical education facility for young people); Clean Break Theatre Company (£10,000; vocational and educational

skills through theatre for women prisoners and ex-prisoners); and Geese Theatre Company of Great Britain (£7,000 towards the cost of a show that focuses on issues of re-offending, violence and drug abuse).

Education and science: Changemakers (£25,000, administration costs for this initiative promoting active citizenship among young people); and Place To Be (£20,000; counselling projects to give emotional support to primary school children).

Health: St Mark's Hospital, Harrow (£10,000; salaries); and Sesame Institute UK (£8,000; relief of people with a physical or mental health problem through the therapeutic use of drama).

Northern Ireland: Integrated Education Fund for Northern Ireland (£10,000, Chatterboxes Playgroup for children of pre-school age, benefiting both sides of the community).

Miscellaneous: Grants for £10,000 each to South East London Community Foundation(towards core costs), and Thames Community Foundation (also for core costs).

Overseas: Charity Know How (£15,000, towards supporting the voluntary sector in Central and Eastern Europe).

Church and religious: grants for £8,000 to Historic Churches Preservation Trust (annual grant), and Inter Faith Network (promoting good inter-faith relations through its information service).

Heritage, conservation and the environment: £5,000 each to Buildings Brooks Trust (to help with work on the Westminster volume of their new London series), and Thornham Field Centre, Suffolk (to help bring children to

make uses of the facilities of this centre).

Exclusions Grants are not usually made to general appeals from large well established charities, to umbrella organisations or national associations or in response to national appeals or for large building projects.

Grants are not usually made to other grant-making bodies or in response to medical appeals, nor are they made for sporting, social, or other fund-raising events.

Foreign travel, including expeditions, and conferences are not normally supported.

Grants are not generally made to schools (other than special schools) or to projects for children under 8 not suffering from special handicaps.

Appeals for the repair of churches and church halls are seldom approved.

A few grants for overseas projects are made to UK organisations working in Eastern Europe and the third world.

No grants in the Republic of Ireland.

Recipients must have charitable status.

No grants are made to individuals.

Applications Applications can be made at any time, by letter to the director, with a description of the project and the latest accounts of the organisation. If the foundation wishes to proceed further with an application, a proposal form is sent. Recipients of grants running longer than one year are required to send in a two-page interim report. Grant allocation meetings are held three times a year, in Spring, Summer, and Christmas.

The majority of grants are made in the London area, particularly in South London and nearby. A few are made in Northern Ireland. Applicants outside these areas should consider carefully whether their project is exceptional enough to justify a departure from the foundation's normal practice.

The Wates Foundation

In 1997/98 grant giving was categorised as follows:

Community projects and the disadvantaged	162 grants	£777,000
Area of special focus (addiction and criminality)	18 grants	£196,000
Arts	18 grants	£91,000
Education and Science	10 grants	£80,000
Health	10 grants	£47,000
Northern Ireland	9 grants	£41,000
Miscellaneous	5 grants	£38,000
Overseas	6 grants	£35,000
Church and religious projects	9 grants	£23,000
Heritage, conservation and the environment	3 grants	£11,000

The Wates Foundation 1997/98 Annual Report

In this box we reprint substantial sections of the excellent Annual Report; it may serve as one example of good practice to those trusts who believe that there is nothing useful or interesting to say about their work.

From the Chairman's Report

This year has seen the Wates foundation move slowly towards being pro-active and to making fewer grants but larger grants. I believe that a medium sized foundation such as ours has an important role to play as a "niche player". At the the one extreme there is the National Charities Lottery Board doing excellent work with very large grants. At the other end of the spectrum we work with two very good local Community Trusts- The South East London Community Foundation and the Thames Community Foundation- giving small grants. We have been delighted to have been able to provide support for these local organisation in their formative years to help them get "up and running". The Director also has a small grants allocation of up to £500; he reports that we sometimes get more heartfelt thanks following a grant of £150 than we do from one of £15,000!

But the justification of our existence will come from an imaginative use of our funds in making grants in the range of £5,000 to £25,000 if necessary for three years when we are funding salaries. To get the biggest "bang for our buck" I believe that we will do best if we stick close to home and be clear from the outset precisely what it is that the organisation we are funding is trying to achieve. To do this we are initiating the search for grantees ourselves and we are becoming "Outcomes" and "Impact" orientated.

Our contact with Croydon Health Authority and Council are examples of how we are putting our new approach into practice. We know that we would normally put something like £200,000 into our immediate area of Croydon over the next two or three years. We are also aware that Croydon Health Authority and the Council have been taking a strategic look at the needs of the area. Whilst there is no remit for the Wates foundation to take on the statutory obligations of the appropriate authorities, they have identified areas of need which included activities that the foundation would normally have been involved with. In fact, for reasons which were never clear to us, our talks with Croydon Health Authority produced no results. On the other hand, at our request, we met some excellent people from Croydon Youth Service and were able to identify three projects that were absolutely right for us. One these is likely to get local authority funding once the need can be demonstrated.

All of these "pro-active" grants will help to liberate the foundation from the "prison of the Director's post-bag" where our grants can only be as interesting as the applications that we receive. It does however limit the amount that is available in response to unsolicited appeals.

Another area that has exercised our minds over the last year has been our increasing insistence that organisations think clearly about what it is they are seeking to achieve the outcomes of their activities. So for example, the foundation has in the past funded a variety of arts activities in prison. These have been well received and we have had appreciative letters from prisoners. In future, we will only fund such activities if they are quite clearly being evaluated against defined and agreed outcomes. This could be measured by e.g. an absence of those concerned from Governor's Adjudications in the short term and, in the longer term, an increased ability to get jobs etc. and have lower levels of recidivism than the average.

So often the response to the question in our Proposal Form "How will you measure the success and impact of your project?" is "We will have a chat at the end of the activity and see if everyone is happy". Such replies are unlikely to elicit a grant from us in the future! With our limited resources we want to ensure that we get the maximum impact. It is likely that we will be making supplementary grants to ensure that appropriate grants have independent evaluation so that we can tell whether they have made a difference or not.

'As we look forward to the Millennium, I anticipate that the Wates foundation will be nudging applicants towards some degree of Quality Assurance. In the past we have requested evidence of Equal Opportunities policies. I hope the battle is now won. In future, we can expect that more small charities will have "Investors in People", ISO9000 or PQASSO or other appropriate accreditation. This gives assurance that the charity is conscious of the need to work in close consultation with its beneficiaries and has good management systems in place.

As well as evaluating others, the foundation needs to look at its own performance. Because trustees like to visit projects in which they have a specialist knowledge and are not always easily available, it can take an unacceptably long time to bring an application before the Grants Committee. This is an area, along with others, where we can set ourselves performance indicators. But, more importantly, we can start to think of ways of measuring "impact" that our grant making activities are having in our areas of interest. It is hard to know if this is capable of scientific analysis. I would think that, historically, our very substantial grant to the St Mary's Primary Health Care Research Projects under Dr. Patrick Pietroni gave a significant impulse in getting such therapies into the mainstream of medicine. More recently, our funding of the Addictive Disease Trust (now RAPt) in a local prison at Downview helped the move from total denial of a drugs problem in our prison to the current requirement that every prison should have a drug treatment programme. It may also be that some of the work that we are funding in schools will help produce practical solutions to the problems of boredom, absenteeism and exclusions with all their attendant ills. Whilst we cannot say that we have discovered the "silver bullet" for the social ills of South London, independent evaluation might be able to substantiate that we have, in some instances, made a measurable contribution to their alleviation.

From the Director's Report

Grant giving meetings have in effect been cut down to 3 a year, instead of 4. The questions on our Proposal Form, which needs to be completed by all applicants we have not rejected, have been refined and virtually all successful applicants for grants of over a year need to fill in an Interim Report Form before the next installment can be paid. This helps us to monitor performance. Where the report is inadequate, follow-up action is needed before next tranche can be sent. As the Chairman has explained, our approach has become more rigorous and we need to be convinced that there has been a positive outcome from our grant before renewing it.

Grant Making

Looking at individual sectors of our grant making, the trustees decided to continue with our Area of Special Focus, Addiction and Criminality, the period of which had initially been confined to 3 years from 1994. We did rather better in this area than in the previous year (nearly £200,000 this time), but still fell short of our target of 20% of grants. The reason was a lack of suitable applications. This in turn could owe something to strong Governmental focus on and thus funds for action against drugs. Straying unusually far from London, we gave £10,000 to a pioneering drug related arrest referral scheme in Brighton, rejoicing in the name Get it While You Can. The central feature of this is a visit to every prisoner in his cell on the day of his arrest to increase their chances of rehabilitation. In a similar area, we gave £30,000 to Youth at Risk to help them build up their operations, based on team programmes for former offenders, throughout the UK.

Social welfare is probably the best description for the totality of our work and it is therefore unsurprising that by far our biggest category, the bread and butter of our grants, continued to fall under the Community heading (58% of grants). Into this ultra-broad category fall some of our traditional preoccupations such as the homeless and unemployed. On the first, we gave £10,000 to the Empty House Agency, the imaginative group bringing back empty property into use. For the second a grant of £12,000 to Comeback helped both towards the employment and the longer-term rehabilitation of former prisoners.

There was also progress along less well trodden paths. A greater emphasis on citizenship qualities among the young has been a recent feature; hence a grant of £25,000 to the Citizenship Foundation to bolster work among schools. On the same sort of front, we were able to combine enthusiasm for our own locality (Croydon) and for education through our grant of £5,000 to the African & Caribbean People's Advisory Group, who have done pioneering work in reducing school expulsion of black pupils. Similarly, mentoring (as well as befriending) has entered our vocabulary as another potential way forward for the young drop-outs of society; here, we gave £10,000 to the Friends United Network operating in Islington.

There was, as usual, no shortage of arts projects catering for the disadvantaged. A good example is our grant of over £6,000 to the Greenwich Young People's Theatre to help their programme aimed at disseminating the anti-racist message among local schools.

A sombre feature of the year was the continuing plight of asylum-seekers and refugees in the country. Trustees had particular sympathy with the desperate circumstances of the hundreds of them held in detention centres; hence our continued support of the Refugee Council with a grant of £15,000 to help fund a Post Detention Support Worker. Actually abroad, as usual we did comparatively little outside our present subvention (£15,000) to the Charity Know How Fund.

To sum the year up, I think we made at least modest progress in our aim to concentrate more in our chosen fields, such as addiction/criminality, citizenship and school exclusions; also towards greater proactivity and larger grants. Further efforts will however need to be made in these areas as well as in applying the litmus-test of "outcomes" to many projects we examine.

The Weinstock Fund

£504,000 (1996/97)

Jewish charities, arts, medical and social

1 Bruton Street, London W1X 8AQ
Tel: 0171-493 8484

Correspondent Miss Jacqueline Elstone

Trustees Simon Weinstock; Michael Lester; Hon Susan Gina Lacroix

Beneficial area UK.

Information available Accounts are filed at the Charity Commission but without a narrative report.

General The trust was established by Lord Weinstock with an endowment of shares in the General Electric Company. Income in 1996/97 amounted to £425,000, which funded grant giving of £504,000. 219 grants were awarded, with the largest single grant going to the British Museum (£100,000); the remaining grants averaged around £2,000. Awards were mainly to Jewish charities, arts, welfare, children's and medical organisations.

Examples of other larger beneficiaries included:

Arts Royal Opera House (£26,000); Friends of Ravenna Festival (£36,000); French Theatre Season (£5,000); Constable Education Trust (£10,000); National Arts Collection Fund (£2,000); English Concert (£2,000); and Chicken Shed Theatre (£2,000).

Jewish charities Jewish Philanthropic Association for Israel and the Middle East (£20,000); Macarti Organisation of Synagogues (£10,000); Jewish Care (£5,000); Institute of Jewish Policy Research (£5,000); New London Synagogue (£5,000); Jewish World Relief (£5,000); Ravenswood (£2,500) and Association for Jewish Ex Service Men And Women (£1,500).

Medical British Heart Foundation (£5,000); British Red Cross (£2,000); Epilepsy Research Federation (£1,000); Global Cancer Concern (£1,000); Kings Medical Research Trust (£2,000); Moorfields Hospitals (£5,000); Prostate Research UK (£5,000); and the Royal Free Hospital (£5,000).

Social Welfare North London Hospice (£7,000); Volunteer Reading Help (£5,000); Community Security Trust

(£3,000); and King George's Fund for Sailors (£3,000).

Children Action for Sick Children (£1,000); Barnardo's (£1,500); International Centre for Child Studies (£1,000); British ORT (£5,000).

The largest grants to elderly and disabled groups were: Contact the Elderly, Hearing Research Trust and the Royal National Institute of Deaf People (£1,000 each).

Exclusions No grants to individuals or unregistered organisations.

Applications In writing to the correspondent. There are no printed details or applications forms. 'Where nationwide charities are concerned, the trustees prefer to make donations centrally'. Donations can only be made to registered charities, and details of the registration number are required before any payment can be made.

The Wellcome Trust

£227,000,000 (1996/97)

Biomedical research, history of medicine, public understanding of science

Wellcome Building, 183 Euston Road, London NW1 2BE
Tel: 0171-611 8888

Correspondent Dr Michael Dexter, Director

Governors Sir Roger Gibbs, Chairman; Professor Julian B Jack, Deputy Chairman; Professor Sir David Weatherall; Professor R M Anderson; Professor C R W Edwards; Professor Sir John Gurdon; Sir David Cooksey; Professor Sir Michael Rutter; Professor Martin Bobrow.

Beneficial area UK and overseas.

Information available Booklets Grants and Support for Biomedical Research and Grants and Support for Research in the History of Medicine are available from the trust, as are the Annual Report and Accounts.

Summary This trust is the main charitable funder of scientific biomedical research in Britain, with spending on a par with the government's Medical Research Council. In financial terms, it is one of the largest charitable

foundations in the world. Its programmes are so various and specialised that it is not possible to give a full description in this book, nor do these editors have the expertise to comment on their quality or effectiveness.

General Endowed originally with ownership of the Wellcome pharmaceutical company, the trust still held 40% of this company's shares until 1995, when it accepted an offer of £3.6 billion for them from the Glaxo company. As a result the trust now has a diversified portfolio of investment assets valued at £10 billion in October 1997 (this may be compared with the £2 billion of the next largest UK trust, the Weston Foundation). The endowment might be expected to generate a return of over £400 million a year in future, while still leaving room for some growth over the longer term.

In any event, however, the trust is accumulating and reinvesting some of the return on its investments. 'It continues to be the trust's policy to seek to achieve growth, in real terms ... over the long term'. In accordance with this policy, the grants programme has not expanded at the rate that might otherwise have been expected, given the growth in the charity's resources. However, the commitment, announced in 1998, of a further £300 million over three years, for the government's Joint Infrastructure Fund for the expansion of Britain's scientific research facilities, brings spending up closer to such levels. After the three years are up, though, there should be scope for replacement programmes on a similar scale. Over the long term major endowed foundations seem to be able to distribute 6% of their net worth every year while still leaving room for some long term growth (though the trust disputes this).

The Wellcome Trust

Grants in 1996/97

These are listed below by topic and this is followed by a listing of the main recipient institutions.

Career support	£40 million
Neurosciences	£33 million
Molecular and cell biology	£28 million
Building grants	£22 million
Equipment grants	£17 million
Infection and immunity	£17 million
Physiology and pharmacology	£17 million
International	£13 million
Tropical medicine and infectious diseases	£12 million
History of medicine	£5 million
Population studies	£4 million
Genetics	£3 million
Veterinary	£2 million
Understanding of science	£1 million
Other schemes	£7 million
Supplementation of grants	£7 million

The major recipient organisations were as follows:

Oxford University	£29 million
Cambridge University	£27 million
University College, London	£20 million
Daresbury laboratory	£12 million
Kew Gardens	£9 million
Edinburgh University	£7 million
Manchester University	£6 million
Bristol University	£5 million
Imperial College	£5 million
Dundee University	£5 million

The trust is managed by a compact board of governors (as its trustees are termed). The constitution allows them to receive salaries for their work (£50,000 each in 1996/97), a reasonable provision for an operation of this size. On the other hand some of them are also in paid employment elsewhere, and rather than a flat rate, it might be more appropriate for remuneration to be tied to the time spent on the affairs of the trust.

Objectives and policy

The objectives of the trust are to support research in the biomedical sciences for the benefit of humankind, and to support the history of medicine and the public understanding of biomedical science. The trust supports the research work of academic staff in universities, medical and veterinary schools and other institutions of higher education. Research funded ranges from the basic sciences related to medicine to the clinical aspects of medicine and veterinary medicine.

The trust aims to support and maintain the strength of biomedical and historical research by providing individual researchers of the highest quality with the resources they need to pursue their subject. In recent years the trust has made a firm commitment to increase its longer-term support for research and has redefined its policy of personal support for individuals through a fellowship scheme which spans every stage of their careers.

The governors review their policy regularly in response to proposals from their advisory panels and professional staff. At these reviews the governors decide how much will be available to each subject and policy area during the following year. In addition, the governors meet monthly to implement policy and to consider special cases.

Support is provided in these general categories:

- short-term and longer-term awards (project and programme grants) usually for three to five years;
- research training and career development: support is provided for individuals at all stages of their careers;
- funds for travel abroad for collaborative research, meetings and symposia;
- awards for equipment;
- capital grants for buildings.

In addition to grant funding, the trust also undertakes directly a number of activities designed to assist those researching into medical science and history, or to promote public understanding of the importance of biomedical research. Grants are given in 1996/97 are categorised in the table herewith.

The governors have a well-established system of of expert panels and interest groups to advise them on which applications to fund and on policy issues in various fields. Grants are awarded in competition with other applications and are assessed by peer review.

'During the year, 3,000 new applications were considered, of which 1,171 were approved, 39% of those requested.'

Exclusions The trust does not normally support cancer research, the extension of education and professional experience, or patient care. Contributions are not made towards overheads or office expenses. The trust does not accept applications from medical and veterinary students for support during their elective periods. The trust does not donate funds for other charities to use, nor does it respond to general appeals.

Applications Applicants are advised, in the first instance, to contact the grants section by telephone for further relevant information or to make a preliminary enquiry in writing, which should include brief details of the proposed research and cost. All grant applications must be submitted on the appropriate form, which can be obtained from the grants section of the trust.

A preliminary application form for a project grant is available via the trust's web site.

Applications can be received and considered at any time other than those for special schemes and initiatives with advertised closing dates.

The Welton Foundation

£769,000 (1996/97)

Hospitals, medical research, general

33 St Mary Axe
London EC3A 8LL
Tel: 0171-280 2800 (For Secretary)

Correspondent Robin R Jessel, Secretary

Trustees D B Vaughan; H A Stevenson; Prof J Newsom-Davis.

Beneficial area UK.

Information available Trustees' report and accounts with a thin description of the foundation's grant-making policy and no narrative exploration of the grant programme.

Summary Around 40 grants are made each year for sums in the range of £2,000 to £250,000. At least three quarters of the total value of donations is given to hospitals and medical research or training establishments.

General The charity is administered by an independent consultant, P R Jessel. Management and administration costs amounted to £62,000 in 1996/97, or about £1,500 per grant and 8% of charitable expenditure.

A little over 40 grants were made, 15 of which (65% by value) were to organisations also supported in the previous years. The largest grants went to well established, often national, organisations such as the Royal College of Physicians (£200,000), National Hospital for Neurology and Neurosurgery (£68,052) and the Royal College Post Graduate Medical School (£65,000), all of which have received grants from the foundation before. Large grants to organisations not recently supported by the foundation included £30,000 to St Mary's 150th Anniversary Appeal, and £16,700 to the Royal Free Hospital Medical School.

The foundation says:

'Grants are principally to approved or medically related appeals, but the trustees have discretionary powers to approve donations for other purposes.'

Although it is not always clear what sector beneficiaries are serving, it appears that at least ten non-medical causes were awarded grants in 1996/97. The largest of these were the Young Concert Artists Trust (£27,500), the Lord Mayor Treloar School (£20,000) and the Royal Academy Trust (£10,000).

The foundation does not say for what purpose grants were given nor does it report whether or not such purposes were successfully met.

Exclusions Grants only to registered charities, and not in response to general appeals.

Applications In writing to the Secretary, stating

- what the charity does;
- what specific project the money needed is for, giving as much detail as possible;
- how much money is needed;
- the source of any other funding.

Due to the number of appeals received, the foundation only replies to those that are successful.

The Westminster Foundation

£1,084,000 (1997)

General

53 Davies Street, London W1Y 1FH
Tel: 01252 722 557

Correspondent J E Hok, Secretary

Trustees The Duke of Westminster, Chairman; J H M Newsum; B A J Radcliffe.

Beneficial area UK, mainly the North-West of England and Westminster.

Information available Accounts are filed at the Charity Commission, with a basic list of grants but no narrative report on the work of the charity.

Summary: The foundation runs seven programmes of donations, the largest of which are Social and Welfare, Conservation, and Education. Funds are only awarded to registered charities, usually based in Westminster and North-West England. Grants range from £100 to £80,000 and are for capital or revenue costs.

General The foundation was established in 1974 by the fifth Duke of Westminster. For many years its assets were tied up in a private company, Grosvenor Estate Holdings, which failed to deliver a good level of income. Since the foundation realised these assets a few years ago both capital and income have increased dramatically and in 1997 assets stood at £31.8 million (£26.1 million in 1996) and income reached £1,436,000.

The 1997 accounts report that:
'It is probable, but in no way fixed, that the trustees will tend towards fewer but larger grants in the future. However, they will still assist the smaller charities in areas of local interest to them, specifically in rural Lancashire, Chester and its surrounding area, and central London. The trustees also anticipate becoming more active in addressing some of the needs which are rapidly becoming apparent in rural areas.'

During 1997, 159 grants totalling £1.08 million were made. About a third were made to organisations also funded in the previous year. Most were for between £100 and £5,000 though about 40 were for £10,00 or above. Management and administration costs were low, amounting to £0.04 per £1 donated (£271/grant). The chart below shows how charitable donations were distributed among the foundations seven programmes:

Social and Welfare	£452,395	42%
Conservation	£224,300	21%
Education	£203,275	19%
Church	£69,500	6%
Youth	£67,660	6%
Medical	£35,880	3%
Arts	£30,600	3%

These figures are explored further in the report and accounts:

The levels were roughly the same as 1996, except in the case of Conservation (increased from 13% to 21% of total grants for 1997) and Youth (decreased from 17% to 6%). The most significant grant in the Church sector was £50,000 to Chester Cathedral Development Trust. Other large donations made were to the Soil Association, which received support totalling £80,000; £50,000 and £55,000 respectively to Parnham House Trust , and the Royal United Services for Defence Studies, both being part of three year commitments towards major education projects; and £57,000 to the Trealor Trust (Social and Welfare).

A total of £100,000 towards the alleviation of homelessness was shared between Cardinal Hume Centre, Centrepoint Soho, Passage Day Centre, Chester Aid to the Homeless and CRISIS. The major part of this sum was annual support to the first three.

Exclusions Only registered charities will be considered, charitable status alone is not sufficient. No grants to individuals. 'holiday' charities, student expeditions, nor research projects. The arts and arts/education budget is fully committed until at least 2004.

Applications In writing to the secretary, enclosing an up to date set of accounts, together with a brief history of the project to date, and the current need.

The Westminster Foundation for Democracy

£3,000,000 (1998/99)

Strengthening democracy overseas

Clutha House, 10 Storey's Gate, London SW1P 3AY
Tel: 0171-976 7565; Fax 0171-976 7464

Correspondent Alexandra Jones

Trustees Ernie Ross MP, Chairman; Archie Kirkwood MP; Gary Streeter MP; Sir Archie Hamilton MP; Ieuan Wyn Jones MP; Mary Kaldor; Richard Page MP; Tim Garton Ash; Nik Gowing; Elizabeth Smith; Georgina Ashworth; Prof. Peter Frank.

Beneficial area Outside the UK.

Information available Annual report and accounts, information leaflets and details of projects supported available from the foundation.

Summary The foundation gives grants, seldom for more than £25,000, for projects to support democracy anywhere in the world, but its work is concentrated in Central and Eastern Europe, the former Soviet Union and in anglophone Africa.

General The foundation receives almost all its money from the government, but makes its own decisions about the projects to be supported. It describes its policies as follows:

'The ... Foundation may support any project which is aimed at building pluralist democratic institutions abroad. These may include:

- *election systems or administration;*
- *parliaments or other representative institutions;*
- *political parties;*
- *independent media;*
- *legal reform;*
- *trades unions;*
- *human rights groups;*
- *women's organisations;*
- *other political non-governmental institutions.*

'It will give preference to projects which contain clear action plans, designed to achieve concrete results; those whose effects will be lasting; and to building up organisations which can be self-sustaining, rather than encouraging continuing dependence on outside assistance.

'The foundation concentrates its funding on three priority areas: Central and Eastern Europe, the former Soviet Union and anglophone Africa. It will consider sympathetically applications from or for projects elsewhere in the world.

'The foundation seeks to avoid duplication of effort with other governmental and non-governmental agencies and to reinforce their commitment to enhancing participatory democracy. Where possible, it will carry out projects in cooperation with other organisation and foundations.

'Support for individual political parties is provided through that part of the foundation's budget which is channelled through the UK political parties [50%, Ed.] Individual parties from overseas seeking ... funding for their programmes must therefore apply to the individual UK party with which they have links.

'Alternatively, the foundation may carry out cross-party projects, where a range of political parties from a country are involved, and these projects are funded directly from the foundation's general resources.'

The foundation does not seek to foster any particular model of democracy. It seeks to keep administrative costs to a minimum, and will not support the administrative costs of it recipients beyond what is absolutely necessary, nor provide equipment beyond reasonable need.

In 1996/97 278 projects were funded, from 439 proposals submitted, a 63% success rate. Nearly one third were for amounts of less than £6,000, and less than one in ten for more than £21,000. The main areas of work were as follows:

Party training	*126 projects*
Building civil society	*81 projects*
Media	*39 projects*
Trades unions	*13 projects.*

The location of the projects was as follows:

Central Europe	*142 projects*
Former Soviet Union	*50 projects*
Anglophone Africa	*57 projects*
Other countries	*29 projects.*

The largest project (£50,000) was to enable the Conservative Party to support the centre-right opposition with polling station rooms, offices, telephones and faxes in the primary elections for the Bulgarian presidency (the first of their kind in Eastern Europe). £47,000 was spent through the Labour Party to help in the election campaign of the Czech SDP. Towards the other end of the scale, and more typical, was the £5,000 to help

with the establishment of the first independent daily newspaper in Macedonia, or the £3,000 for a local government training seminar in Katowice, Poland.

Exclusions The foundation does not fund conferences, research, educational scholarships, cultural, health or social projects.

Applications In writing to the correspondent. Applicants are advised first to obtain its pamphlet 'Overview' which includes some guidelines for applications. Project evaluations are part of the conditions of assistance from the foundation. Trustees meet in January, April, July and October.

The Garfield Weston Foundation

£22,430,000 (1996/97)

Arts, education, health, general

Weston Centre, Bowater House, 68 Knightsbridge, London SW1X 7LR
Tel: 0171-589 6363;
Fax: 0171-584 5921

Correspondent Fiona M Foster, Administrator

Trustees Garfield Weston, Chairman; Guy Weston; Galen Weston; Miriam Burnett; Barbara Mitchell; Nancy Baron; Camilla Dalglish; Jana R Khayat; Anna C Hobhouse; George G Weston.

Beneficial area UK.

Information available The foundation now produces an informative annual report and accounts with narrative report, grants analysis and a full list of grants (but charges an exorbitant £15 for it). There is a separate brief sheet outlining grant making practice.

Summary This mighty foundation makes about a thousand grants each year, normally single payments range anywhere from a hundred pounds up to several million. Over half the money is given in grants of £500,000 or more, spread across all fields of charity, usually going to major institutions, and for both capital and revenue projects. The typical size of grants varies for the different categories of giving; for example in 'health' it is around £100,000 while for 'youth' the figure drops to about £2,000. In general, the foundation concentrates

its large grants on art, education, environment and health, while grants are generally smaller, but more numerous, for all kinds of welfare and community organisations.

In 1996/97 no less than 40% of applications resulted in a grant, though not necessarily for the full amount requested.

General With an endowment valued at nearly £2.1 billion, this trust is second in wealth only to Wellcome. The total capital growth of its investments in 1996/97 was approaching £500 million, almost all of it unrealised. £23 million was available for grant making.

The foundation was established in 1958 with endowments in the family food business from the late Garfield Weston and members of his family. This endowment is still held almost entirely in the form of an 80% stake in Wittington Investments Ltd, which in turn holds the majority stake of Associated British Foods plc (and Fortnum and Mason plc.).

The foundation's financial review of 1996/97 said: 'The main source of income to the foundation throughout the year has been its investment in Wittington Investments Ltd. The income received by the trustees increased by 22.2% over the previous year. This enhanced level of dividend has enabled the foundation to increase the level of its charitable grants.'

While the interests underlying Whittington Investments are themselves diversified, the charitable endowment as a whole is relatively narrowly held and no matter how successful it is for the time being, it is therefore potentially at risk. Readers of earlier editions of this book may have noticed for example, the complete disappearance of the once very large Ronson foundations, caused by the failure of their trustees to diversify in time. In practice a planned programme of gradual disinvestment over time is often the most sensible route forwards.

If and when the trustees decide to seek, whether by diversification of their holdings or by realising a proportion of their capital growth, a higher level of return on their investments, the income of the foundation may soar, as has happened in recent years, for example, with the Wellcome Trust and the Henry Smith Charity. In such circumstances, income here might rise to as much as £100 million a year.

At the moment, 'the trustees keep the value of their investment and the fortunes of the underlying companies constantly under review'. In the light of this, they have said that they 'have no current intention of disposing of the interest in Wittington'. Let us hope that this decision turns out successfully. Meanwhile we can but celebrate this foundation's remarkable recent financial success.

Overview

In the 1996/97 report and accounts, the foundation published the following information concerning grant making policy:

'The objects of the charity are widely drawn and the trustees have maintained their well established policy of supporting a broad range of activities in the fields of education, the environment, the arts, health (including research), religion, welfare and other areas of general benefit to the community in the

UK. It gives the trustees as much pleasure to support requests from small charitable organisations where a grant from the foundation can make all the difference as it does to respond to large appeals of national importance.

'The foundation has continued its policy of considering appeals from UK registered charities only. It does not entertain applications from individuals. It is the foundation's policy not to spread donations forward but to make a single grant payment to the causes supported. All donations approved were paid during the year and at 5 April 1997 the foundation had no material forward commitments.

'A committee of trustees consider each application within broad policy guidelines with a view to spreading money widely.' The extremely low

administrative costs, just £137,000 in 1996/97, represent 0.6% of the value of donations or £135 a grant. 'The trustees see no reason at present to increase these costs by setting more stringent policy guidelines or by taking a more active role in the development of policy or practice in the voluntary sector.

Experience of other large foundations, both in Britain and in the USA, suggests that this hands-off and admirably low cost approach to grant making is seldom sustainable in the long term. It will be interesting to see the directions in which the foundation develops in future years.

The foundation's grants

These are categorised in the table herewith.

Just nine or ten grants of a half of a million pounds or more accounted for 65% of the foundation's grants in 1996/97 and for 54% in 1995/96.

Donations are made to charities lying within one of the ten categories in the table. In 1996/97, the foundation received 2,350 appeals, and from these 1,018 grants (43% of appeals) were made totalling £22.4 million. About 90% of grants lay between the range of £1,000 to £10,000, however 44% of the total value of grants was paid in a single grant of £10 million and 38% of the remaining £12.4 million was given in grants for £500,000 and over.

Grant Activity

This is described by the trust as follows:

The arts 'The trustees made one exceptional donation during the year which it is appropriate to mention specifically. The British Museum Great Court project is vital to the future of our national museum – the greatest museum of world culture. The great Court is a two acre site in the heart of the museum. This will be enclosed with a glass roof and will house new exhibition space, catering facilities and retail outlets, plus a centre for education which will include two auditoria, seminar rooms and computing facilities. The Great Court project has been made possible by the relocation of the British Library to St Pancras and will provide a unique educational resource and centre of excellence as we move towards the 21st century. The trustees have made a capital grant of £10 million. The trustees will be taking a continuing interest in the project as it moves forward.

'The foundation provided support for a total of 59 arts projects in 1996/97, covering in some cases capital costs and in some revenue funding. Showing its

The Garfield Weston Foundation

Grants

	1996/97	1995/96
British Museum	£10,010,000	£1,750,000
Bristol 2000	£1,000,000	
Forget-me-not Cancer Appeal	——	£600,000
London Playing Fields Society	——	£500,000
MENCAP	£500,000	
Methodist Homes for the Aged	——	£1,000,000
National Council of YMCAs	——	£500,000
National Hospital for Neurology	£500,000	
National Theatre	£505,000	
NSPCC	——	£1,000,000
Royal Hospital for Children, Bristol	£500,000	
Peterborough Cathedral Trust	£500,000	
Scout Association	——	£500,000
St Mary's Paddington Children's Appeal	£500,000	
Tate Gallery	——	£3,000,000
Technology Colleges Trust	£775,000	
Thrombosis Research Institute	——	£1,000,000
UMIST	——	£500,000

Grants in 1996/97

Category	Over £20K	No.	Under £20K	No.	Total amount	No.
Arts	£1,358,964	10	£174,500	49	£1,533,464	59
Community	£50,000	1	£401,750	157	£451,750	158
Education	£12,860,000	14	£305,750	74	£13,165,750	88
Environment	£252,500	4	£86,500	31	£339,000	35
Health	£2,830,000	15	£312,500	86	£3,142,500	101
Mental health/ Handicap	£575,000	3	£64,025	29	£639,025	32
Other	£250,000	3	£177,250	60	£427,250	63
Religion	£550,000	2	£411,000	154	£961,000	156
Welfare	£658,000	11	£518,450	159	£1,176,450	170
Youth	£250,000	4	£343,500	152	£593,500	156
TOTALS	**£19,634,464**	**67**	**£2,795,225**	**951**	**£22,429,689**	**1,018**

commitment to education in the arts, it has also provided endowment grants for scholarships in the fields of ballet, dance, music and drama.

'The Royal National Theatre's development appeal to restore, modernise, refurbish and re-equip the South Bank building was supported with a donation of £500,000. This will help to safeguard the fabric and quality of the theatre for future generations.

'The Welsh College of Music and Drama's development appeal received £200,000 towards the renovation of the Cardiff Castle Mews building for advanced teaching and performance space. One of the foremost educational establishments for drama and music, the College is particularly noted for high quality stage management, stage design and directing courses. The expansion into Cardiff Castle Mews will enable the College to continue to flourish and nurture the talent amongst young musicians, actors and designers.

'Grants of £50,000 to Welsh National Opera and £10,000 to English Touring Opera demonstrate the foundation's interest in helping quality productions to reach a wide variety of audiences around the UK. Regional organisations to benefit also included the Poole Study Gallery at Bournemouth and Poole College, the Haymarket Theatre in Leicester, the Theatre Royal in Winchester and the Balnain Trust in Inverness.

Community Projects 'The foundation provides a large number of small donations in this category, enabling local projects to achieve improved facilities for a wide variety of sectors in the community. Of the 158 grants made in this category, only 24 were in London postal districts. Scotland, Wales and Northern Ireland all benefited from donations.

'The largest donation of £50,000 to Withington Methodist Church supported a partnership with the Manchester Health Authority, the Citizen's Advice Bureau, Age Concern and ASSIST (a neighbourhood care group) for the modernisation and expansion of the church premises for social and community needs.

Education 'The £10 million grant to the British Library has already been covered above. A donation of £1 million to Bristol 2000, the landmark Millennium project on Bristol's harbourside, is being dedicated to an education centre at Science World. The centre will include laboratories and classrooms where schoolchildren and community groups will be able to devise their own

experiments. The latest equipment will be available for people to explore the world of science, bringing the subject to life through hands on experiences. This is part of a development which will also include Wildscreen World and a Centre for the performing arts.

'The Government sponsored scheme administered by Technology Colleges' Trust continued to receive funding from the Foundation in 1996/97. This initiative is open to voluntary aided, LEA county and grant maintained schools and has been supported by the foundation for a number of years. Colleges with technology and/or language status enhance the acquisition of practical, scientific, technological, mathematical and communication skills. Of the total grant of £775,000 provided by the foundation, £275,000 has been allocated to developing and creating an electronic link between 250 colleges and schools affiliated to the Technology Colleges' Trust network.

'The Universities of Edinburgh and Nottingham received grants of £300,000 and £250,000 respectively. The former is for an electronic library and the latter will provide an endowment for four postgraduate scholarships.

Environment 'The foundation responded to an appeal from the National Trust for Scotland with a donation of £100,000 to help rescue Newhailes, in East Lothian. Built in 1686, this outstanding house has been in the family since 1707 and the decoration and its contents remain more or less intact since that period. In desperate need of restoration, the house has been gifted to the nation but a large appeal was launched to save the contents and to provide for the necessary restoration and future upkeep.

'The Royal Botanic Gardens, Kew, received a further £100,000, to enable it to play an important and continuing role in the Convention on Biological Diversity.

'A £25,000 donation to Population Concern will be directed at its UK education programme. It will broaden the range of services available for schools through the publication and distribution of datasheets.

Health 'This category received grants totalling over £3 million, the second largest after education. Capital grants to children's hospitals accounted for £1,653,000 of this total. These included the Royal Hospital for Children in Bristol, the Children's Trust in Tadworth, Birmingham Children's Hospital, Northwick Park Children's Centre and St Mary's Paddington Children's Accident and Emergency development. £500,000

was donated to the National Hospital for Neurology and Neurosurgery and £250,000 to the Hospital for Tropical diseases.

'Medical research activities to benefit included RAFT (the Restoration of Appearance and Function Trust), the Dr Jan de Winter Cancer Prevention Foundation, Action Research and the Arthritis and Rheumatism Council for Research.

'Funding was also put into equipment rehabilitation, hospices and nursing homes.

Mental Health and Mental Handicap
'The largest donation in this category was given to MENCAP. £250,000 is being allocated to their Blue Sky appeal, which aims to develop new family support schemes throughout the UK. A further £250,000 will be used for existing projects in Avon, Worcester, the West Midlands, Derbyshire, South Wales and other areas. Included is a profound intellectual and multiple disability project in Manchester, which provides training and information for parents of profoundly disabled children.

'A total of seven branches of MIND around the country received funding.

'A capital grant to Scotts project in Tonbridge will go towards providing a new communal residential home for mentally handicapped adults.

Other 'The donation of £100,000 to the English speaking Union is to be used partly towards their educational work and partly towards the renovation of Dartmouth House, their headquarters in London.

'The Vivat trust acquires and preserves buildings of historical and architectural interest, some of which are subsequently used for holiday lets. A grant of £50,000 will enable them to continue to rescue parts of Britain's heritage at risk of falling into decay.

'A total of 63 applications were supported in this category, mainly with small grants.

Religion 'The foundation continues to support the nation's heritage through its help with the upkeep of churches. Almost £1 million was distributed to a total 156 local parishes, mostly in donations of £5,000 or less.

'An unusually large grant was given to Peterborough Cathedral Trust. A major restoration of this Norman Cathedral and some of the ancient buildings in the precincts is being undertaken and the trustees have donated £500,000 towards renovating the Nave ceiling.

367

Welfare 'Welfare projects continue to have a high priority for the foundation, with 170 appeals being supported. These benefited the elderly, disabled, disadvantaged and their carers.

'The largest donation was £250,000 to Methodist Homes for the Aged. This charity is dedicating considerable resources and expertise to specialist homes for dementia care and it has already received significant support from the Foundation in previous years for this purpose. Part of this year's grant will be used for their Live at Home Schemes, which provide one to one volunteer befriending for elderly people living in their own homes. This includes taking them out on trips or for appointments and helping them to regain their places within their local communities.

'A £100,000 capital grant was given to Winged Fellowship, an organisation which provides short-term respite care for chairbound disabled people, for the upgrade of their Skylarks holiday centre in Nottingham.

'£50,000 was donated to SCOPE and £50,000 to Adapt (Alcohol and Drug Addiction Prevention and Treatment). A number of homeless projects received support.

Youth 'The Youth Sport Trust was provided with a donation of £150,000. This organisation aims to develop and implement quality sports programmes for all young people, including those who are disabled. They have been appointed by the Government to provide support for a specialist sports college programme in secondary schools, which aims to improve the sporting education and facilities available for all standards. Also in the sporting arena, the National Playing Fields Association received a grant of £350,000.

'A £50,000 grant to Fairbridge will provide three Lifestart bursaries, enabling 50 young people in Glasgow, Cardiff and Tyne and Wear to participate in the Fairbridge programme. This programme provides personal development courses, addressing problems of long-term unemployment, crime, drugs, abuse and anti-social behaviour. It offers basic life and work skills, knowledge and experience to enable disaffected young people to return to education and training or to find employment.

'Raleigh International received a donation of £100,000 towards its Youth Development Programme, which takes young people at risk and provides them with opportunities to participate in community and environmental expeditions around the world.

'Other projects to receive support included a play support centre for disabled children, Guide and Scouting groups, youth drop-in centres, pre-school clubs, youth housing programmes, holiday clubs and church youth clubs.

Small grants 'Most grants are for less than £5,000. A reading of the 'Community' list for 1996/97 showed 44 organisations that could be geographically identified by this (London based) editor. Of these 37 were in the Southern half of England, 13 in the Northern half and only a handful in Scotland, Wales or Northern Ireland. This may well reflect the applications received, though it is these editors view that large national trusts have a moral obligation to achieve a fair distribution across all parts of the country, according to need – and that this can be achieved if the will to do so exists.

Exclusions The following excerpt is taken from the foundation's grant making policy:

'Support cannot be considered for organisations or groups which are not UK registered charities. Applications from individuals or for individual research or study or from organisations outside the United Kingdom cannot be considered. Animal welfare charities are also excluded.'

Charities are asked not to apply within a twelve month period of an appeal to the Foundation, whether they have received a grant or not.

Applications To the Administrator, including the following information:

1. The charity's registration number.
2. A copy of the most recent report and audited accounts.
3. An outline description of the charity's activities.
4. A synopsis of the project requiring funding, with details of who will benefit.
5. A financial plan.
6. Details of current and proposed fundraising.

'All applications are considered on an individual basis by a committee of trustees. From time to time, more information about a charity or a visit to the project might be requested. There is no deadline for applications, which are normally processed within three months of receipt. All applicants will be notified of the outcome by letter.'

A H and B C Whiteley Charitable Trust

£371,000 (1996/97)

Art, environment, general

Marchant and Co., Regent Chambers, Regent Street, Mansfield, Nottinghamshire NG18 1SW
Tel: 01623-655111

Correspondent Edward Aspley

Trustees Mrs B C Whiteley; E G Aspley; K E Clayton.

Beneficial area UK, with a special interest in Nottinghamshire.

Information available Accounts are on file at the Charity Commission.

General The trust was established in 1990 and derives most of its income from continuing donations. The trust deed requires the trustees to make donations to to registered charities in England, Scotland, and Wales but with particular emphasis on charities based in Nottinghamshire. Beneficiaries are varied, but the largest grant (which typically accounts for around 50% of the funds) usually, perhaps always, goes to the Victoria and Albert Museum.

In the year ending March 1997 the trust's income totalled £303,000; £242,000 came from donations and £62,000 was generated from its assets of £1.4 million.

Twenty two charities were grant-assisted. The largest five grants accounted for 74% of grant expenditure:

Victoria and Albert Museum,	*£150,000*
Chethams School of Music,	*£50,000*
National Trust,	*£31,000*
Mansfield Cat Protection League,	
	£23,000
Portland College,	*£20,000.*

A selection of the other awards is as follows: North West Cancer Fund (£2,000); Spinal Injury Association (£5,000); Samaritans (£10,000); Ashfield Group for the Mentally Handicapped (£4,000); Jerry Green Foundation (£4,000); Skylark Winged Fellowship (£2,000); Home Farm (£5,000).

When the above rather brief entry was sent in draft to the trust so that it could, if it wished, check its accuracy, the reply, from Marchants solicitors firm of which trustee E G Apsley is a partner, asked first 'for written confirmation that you will pay for the costs of providing you with the information that you have required'. Caution about accepting such potentially open-ended legal charges means that the entry remains unchecked.

Applications None are invited. The trust does not seek applications.

Sir Richard Whittington's Charity

£1,843,000 (1996/97)
Social welfare

Mercers' Hall, Ironmonger Lane, London EC2V 8HE
Tel: 0171-726 4991

Correspondent H W Truelove, The Charities Administrator

Trustees Mercers' Company

Beneficial area UK, London.

Information available Report and accounts with grants list but without the required narrative review of grant-making.

Summary Although around half of charitable expenditure goes in grants to closely allied organisations, a few hundred donations are made each year to various welfare charities and individuals. Beneficiaries are most often based in Greater London but grants are made throughout the UK. Awards are typically for £3,000 but vary from £1,000 to £15,000.

General The charity was endowed by London's most famous mayor, Dick Whittington, who arrived in London in the 17th century with allegedly only a cat and a knapsack. Today, it assists charitable causes through maintaining an almshouse complex called Whittington College and making grants to a broad array of welfare groups. The charity is managed by the Mercer's Company in conjunction with seven other charities including the Mercers' Company Trust Funds and the Earl of Northampton's Charity. When the Mercer's Company receives an application it is forwarded to the most appropriate trust fund (if any). An application to one charity is therefore an application to them all and there is no point in making more than one application to the Mercer's Company. If an application is unsuccessful, the Mercers' Company will not consider a re-application until three years have passed.

In 1996/97 the Whittington's Charity's assets totalled £31,461,000, nearly double the amount in 1994/95. Income amounted to more than £4 million, and £341,000 was spent on the almshouses' running costs. Although grants made in the year totalled £1,843,000, £830,000 of this went to the Mercers' Company Housing Association and a further £75,000 to Lady Mico's Almshouses (Mercers' also manages Lady Mico's Charity which maintains these almshouses).

Grants were divided into the following categories:

Almshouses	£75,000	4%
Housing Associations	£830,000	45%
Welfare	£575,000	31%
Individuals	£362,000	20%
Total	£1,843,000	100%

Of the welfare grants, the vast majority were for £5,000 or under with 12 grants over this amount accounting for 19% of welfare expenditure. Around 30 grants were for £5,000, 7 for £4,000, 45 for £3,000, 45 for £2,000 and 25 for £1,000. The trust does not further categorise the charities in the welfare programme but they appear to be work for a variety of causes including homelessness, education, medical care, and community projects. In a similar vein, although the trust does not analyse beneficiaries by location, most appear to be based in London (though many of these have a national remit), but funds are awarded elsewhere in the UK – South England and Scotland in particular.

The largest grants were to Thomas Telford School (£15,000 for needy children – clothing etc.) and the Bromley by Bow Centre (£15,000). Donations of £10,000 were made to Christ's Hospital (for needy children), Across Trust, Cancer Research Campaign, and London Playing Fields Society.

Typical smaller grants were local or national charities involved in care (in a wide sense) such as Highland Hospice (£3,000); the British Sports Association for the Disabled (£3,000); and the Princess Royal Trust for Carers (£5,000).

Applications In writing to the correspondent. Only one application is needed to apply to all and any of the grant-making trusts managed by the Mercers' Company.

The Will Charitable Trust

£1,471,000 (1996/97)
Environment/ conservation, cancer care, blindness, mental handicap

Farrer & Co Solicitors, 66 Lincoln's Inn Fields, London WC2A 3LH
Tel: 0171-242 2022

Correspondent Vanessa Reburn

Trustees H Henshaw; P Andras; A McDonald.

Beneficial area UK and overseas.

Information available Report and accounts on file at the Charity Commission.

General The trust, which is associated with the Will Woodland Trust, describes its policy as to support 'organisations whose activities fall within the following categories:

a) Conservation of the countryside in Britain, including its flora and fauna,

b) Care of blind people and the prevention and cure of blindness,

c) Care of and services for people suffering from cancer and their families

d) The provision of residential care for mentally handicapped people in communities making a lifelong commitment to provide a family environment and the maximum choice of activities and lifestyles.

'A proportion of the trust's income is devoted to assistance in other fields, but this is reserved for causes which have come to the attention of individual trustees. It is only in exceptional circumstances that the trustees will respond favourably to to requests from organisation whose activities fall outside the categories listed above.

'It is unlikely that applications relating to academic research projects will be successful. The trustees recognise the importance of research, but lack the expertise required to judge its relevance and value.'

In 1996/97 the trust had an income of £7.67 million. However £6 million of this came from a legacy from the founder and no further monies are expected from her. In 1996/97 assets of the trust stood at £26.2 million. However the trust informs us that during 1997/98 a substantial capital grant has reduced this by about £6–8 million. 'Future grant making is expected to be around 1995/96 levels, about £800.000.'

Grants for the year totalled £1.47 million, almost double the previous year (£810,000 in 1995/96) attributable to the legacy mentioned above.Fortynine grants were made and were subdivided as follows (amounts in brackets are for 1995/96):

Woodland development, improvement or management £655,000 5 grants (£20,000)

Other countryside conservation £155,000 10 grants (£185,000)

Care of mentally handicapped £196,000 10 grants (£165,000)

Care of the blind, prevention or cure of blindness £199,000 10 grants (£198,000)

Care of cancer patients £180,000 8 grants (£160,000)

Other awards £86,000 6 grants (£74,000)

Grants for *conservation* include those to the Will Woodland Trust (£220,000), Thomas Phillips Prince Trust, £100,000; CPRE, £30,000; and the Royal Society for Nature Conservation, £25,000.

Mentally handicapped: grants of £25,000 to L'Arche, Home Farm Trust and the Camphill Village Trust Ltd.

A number of grants were also given to *blind causes:* Royal National Institute for Care of the Blind (£35,000); grants of £25,000 to Birmingham Royal Institution for the Blind, Iris Fund and Sight Savers International.

Cancer: Cancer Relief MacMillan (£50,000) and Marie Curie Cancer Care (£40,000).

Grants were also made to a variety of social and community organisations. Examples of the larger ones include Royal UK Beneficent Fund, £30,000; Almshouse Association, £20,000; Benevolent Association, £30,000; and the Cambridge University Botanic Gardens, £16,000.

Exclusions See above.

Grants are only given to registered charities

Applications To the correspondent in writing. There are no application forms. The trust normally distributes income twice yearly. Grants are made in March to organisations whose activities fall within categories (b) and (d) above and applications should be received by 31st January at the latest. Grants are made in

October to organisations operating within categories (a) and (c) and applications should be received by 31st August at the latest.

The H D H Wills 1965 Charitable Trust

£915,000

General, environment

12 Tokenhouse Yard,
London EC2R 7AN
Tel: 0171-588 2828 Fax 0171-606 9205

Correspondent Mrs I R Wootton

Trustees John Kemp-Welch; John Carson; Lord Killearn; Lady Wills; Dr Catherine Wills.

Beneficial area UK.

Information available Report and accounts.

Summary The trust runs three separate funds with a combined income of around £1 million. About £900,000 a year is disbursed in grants but in some years about 85% of this money must be donated to certain named charities. Unrestricted grants start at £50, are usually under £1,000 and peak at around £125,000. However, most of the large grants are to charities with a strong family connection.

General The trust has been endowed by the family of Sir David Wills and has assets of more than £28 million. The three funds it operates are the Martin Wills Fund (partially restricted), the General Fund (unrestricted), and the Knockando Church Fund (restricted solely for the upkeep of that church).

Donations from the General Fund are made for general charitable purposes, which have recently included substantial amounts to the Ditchley Foundation and the Sandford St Martin Trust, the latter having been formed by Sir David Wills to promote high standards in Christian religious broadcasting. 90% of grants made from this fund are for amounts of £500 or less, but most of the money is given in only one or two repeated large awards.

The income of the Martin Wills Fund is donated to the following institutions in seven year cycles (started April 1992):

1st Year Magdalen College, Oxford (92/93), a college at which many family members have been educated.

2nd Year Rendcomb College, Gloucestershire (93/94), set up by Sir David Wills' father, Noel Wills in 1920 as a college for underprivileged Gloucestershire boys.

3rd and 4th Years Any registered charity dedicated or primarily dedicated to the preservation of wildlife (94/95 & 95/96), which was of particular interest to the late Martin Wills.

5th Year Ditchley Foundation (96/97), which was set up by Sir David Wills in 1965 as a conference centre to discuss topics of mutual Anglo/American interest.

6th and 7th Years Charities at the trustees' discretion (97/98 & 98/99).

The 95/96 donations from the Martin Wills fund totalled £555,000 (£253,000 in 1994/95). A total of 23 donations to wildlife and environmental causes were made (averaging £23,000). The three largest grants accounted for 63% of the money and were to the Martin Wills Wildlife Maintenance Trust (£200,000), Spey Research Trust (£125,000) and Farm Africa (£25,000). Eleven grants were for amounts between £10,000 and £20,000 and nine for under £10,000.

During the year the General Fund disbursed £360,000 in 72 grants. Three quarters of this money went in a single grant of £277,000 to the Ditchley Foundation. Apart from six other grants, including £50,000 to the Church of England (Sandford St Martin Trust) and £11,000 to the Ditchley Park Conference Centre, the remaining 65 donations were for £500 or less. Beneficiaries were a variety of causes from around the country and many had been supported in previous years.

Exclusions Individuals, national charities. Grants to registered or 'recognised' charities only.

Applications In writing to the correspondent. The trust considers small appeals monthly and large ones bi-annually. Only one application from a given charity will be considered in any one year.

The Francis Winham Foundation

£296,000 (1995/96)

The welfare of elderly people

35 Pembroke Gardens,
London W8 6HU
Tel: 0171-602 1261

Correspondent The Secretary

Trustees Francine Winham; Dr John Norcliffe Roberts; Gwendoline Winham.

Beneficial area England.

Information available In September 1998 the most recent Report and Accounts on file at the Charity Commission were those for 1995/96.

General The foundation had relatively modest assets of about £2 million in 1996, but its income was relatively high because of the excellent dividends received from two unquoted investments, in F.W.E.P. Ltd. and the Francine Trust.

Over 130 grants were made in 1995/96, spread throughout England. The list was headed by the following major awards:

SSAFA	*£27,000*
Universal Beneficent Society	*£26,000*
Camden Housebound Link	*£12,000*
St Catherine's House	*£12,000*
The Society for Complementary Medicine	*£10,000*
Help the Hospices	*£10,000*

There is no analysis of grant making in the annual report, but the list of awards include two grants in each of Hartlepool and Coventry, cities whose names do not feature as often as they might in the grants lists of 'country wide' trusts in this book.

Applications In writing to the correspondent. The trust regrets it cannot send replies to applications outside its specific field of help for old people. Applications through registered charities or social services departments only.

The Charles Wolfson Charitable Trust

£3,179,000 (1996/97)

Medical research, health, education, Jewish charities, general

c/o 129 Battenhall Road, Worcester
WR5 2BU

Correspondent Mrs Cynthia Crawford

Trustees Lord Wolfson of Sunningdale; Hon Simon Wolfson; Dr Arthur Levin; J A Franks.

Beneficial area UK, Israel.

Information available Report and accounts with full grants list but limited analysis and explanation of grants; information sheet.

Summary Around 40 grants are made a year between £3,000 and £700,000, but a single project may receive well over £1 million spread over a few years. A wide range of causes are supported, with the focus on medicine, education and general welfare. Somewhere around 30% of funds are allocated to Jewish charities and about 20% is awarded to organisations also supported the year before. The trust says that it only makes annually recurrent grants for medically related research projects and does not fund running costs.

The trust does not say what the grants are for. However, from studying the names of the beneficiaries the following tentative analysis can be made:

	No of grants	Total value	% of total
Medical	9	£1,064,000	(33%)
Education	7	£832,000	(26%)
General Welfare	10	£466,000	(15%)
Museums	3	£61,000	(2%)

General 'This is a private funded trust set up by the late Charles Wolfson and his son (now Lord Wolfson of Sunningdale) jointly in 1960 with an endowment of shares in the family business of the public quoted company, Great Universal Stores Plc.

'In later years, it was decided to invest funds in commercial property. This investment was carried out through the trust's associated charity Benesco Charity Ltd, which has been responsible for the management of the property

portfolio. The combined income of the Charles Wolfson Charitable Trust and Benesco Charity Ltd has grown over the years and is now of the order of £4.5 to £5 million per annum.'

This last sentence clears up a mystery that has puzzled the editors of previous editions of this book; the nature and role of Benesco Ltd (which has its own entry). It appears that this trust lent money to Benesco, itself a charity, for the purposes of property investment (in which it has been highly successful).

The trust employs no staff but, one of the trustees, Dr Levin, is paid for his services, receiving £7,500 in 1996/97 for advertising and recommendingon medical related grants. The trustees expenses, which 'represent reimbursement of expenses which arise because there are no staff, were £8,000 or on average of £2,000 a head. Total adminstrative expenditure was modest, at £56,000, for this reason.

Grant policy
The next section of this entry quotes from the 1996/97 trustees' report, and adds in brackets details of some of the grants referred; an asterisk indicates that the charity concerned was also supported in the previous year:

'The trust is a grant-making charity which derives the bulk of its income from grants received from another charity, Benesco Charity Ltd. Benesco Charity Ltd is an investment company whose income is passed to this trust for distribution. Two of the trustees of this trust are also directors of Benesco Charity Ltd.

'In making their selections the trust are to apply both capital and income to such charitable purposes as the trustees shall select. In making their selections the trustees are required to have special regard for:

i) Encouragement of medical and surgeries study and research.
ii) Advancement of medical and surgical science.
iii) Advancement of education or child welfare.
iv) Advancement of religion.

'The policies that have been adopted to further the trust's objectives include the making of direct grants, interest-free loans and rent free premises. Direct grants of money constitute the major part of the charitable application of funds.

'In the year to 5 April 1997, £3.2 million has been distributed by way of grants to operative charities. Major ongoing projects include substantial support towards the costs of building a day surgery centre at Kings Lynn and

Wisbech Hospitals [£26,000].

'At the balance sheet date, the trustees were continuing to support a number of community, medical and educational projects by means of annual grants for periods of two to three years in such fields as helping young families under stress (Homestart) [£50,000*] and SAFTA (support around termination for abnormality), for which grants have yet to be made.

The trustees also customarily make annual but uncommitted grants to major providers in the educational and religious fields and for scientific and medical research, including matters related to ecology. Future instalments of committed and uncommitted grants are expected to amount to approximately £3 million over the next three years.

The trustees have continued to support the development of a computerised Hospital Information System at the Royal Wessex Trust [£667,000], which is estimated to need a further £900,000 to complete, but the timescale of payment remains uncertain.

'Finally, the trustees propose to support the costs of a research project relating to the medical procedures of day surgery generally, using Kings Lynn as an example, during both construction and operation, but no grants had been made or commited by the balance sheet date.'

The information sheet amplifies this:

'The general programme of grants has been directed towards medical research, education and social projects on a one-off basis, although in the case of medical and similar research projects, grants may be made on an annual basis over a number of years, subject to regular reports being received.'

Grants in 1996/97

A total of 39 grants were made and the average amount was £82,000. There were six very large payments:

Royal West Sussex Trust (£667,000);

Beth Jacob Grammar School (£250,000); Jewish Care (£250,000);

Pardes House Grammar School (£250,000);

Parsha Ltd (£250,000);

Elimination of Leukaemia Fund (£200,000).

Thirteen donations amounting to £656,000 (20% of total grant expenditure) went to charities also supported in the previous year.

£760,000 went to 11 charities whose work cannot be discerned from their names alone.

At least 16 grants totalling £553,000 (17%) were to a variety of specifically Jewish organisations such as: Ben Gurion University Foundation* (£164,000); Weizmann Institute* (£97,000); Oxford Centre for Hebrew and Jewish Studies (£50,000); B'Nai B'rith Hillel Foundation (£5,000); World Jewish Relief and Norwood Ravenswood (£10,000 each).

In addition to those medical beneficiaries mentioned already, other awards were to: Scanner Centre Research (£55,000); St Mary's Hospital Medical School* (£30,000); Royal Free Hospital* (£29,000); Eastman Dental Institute (£28,000); and King's College Hospital* Special Trustees (£3,000). The trust is not a member of the Association of Medical Research Charities; membership of which entails a peer review system to evaluate research work. This function has been the responsibility of Dr. Levin.

Education gifts beyond those outlined above included £40,000 to Yesodey Hatorah Schools and £58,000 to Friends of Hebrew University*.

The three museum grants were to: Dyson Perrins Museum Trust, £10,000; Imperial War Museum, £50,000; Jewish Museum, £1,000.

Within the area of general welfare grants were to: Child Bereavement Trust* (£17,000); Community Service Volunteers (£60,000); Community Security Trust (£50,000); Lady Forester Nursing Home Appeal (£5,000); Sue Ryder Fund (£5,000); and Benevolent Aid Fund* (£30,000).

Exclusions It is not the policy of the trust to make grants to individuals or to charities for running costs.

Applications In writing to the correspondent. Grants are made in response to applications, and while all applications will be considered, the trustees cannot undertake to notify all unsuccessful applicants, because of the volume of appeals received.

The Wolfson Family Charitable Trust

£2,884,000 (1996/97)

Jewish charities, medicine, arts, education

8 Queen Anne Street,
London W1M 9LD
Tel: 0171-3235730

Correspondent Dr Victoria Harrison

Trustees Lord Wolfson; Lady Wolfson; Janet Wolfson de Botton; Laura Wolfson Townsley; Martin D Paisner; Sir Martin Gilbert; Professor Barrie Jay; Professor Sir Eric Ash; Sir Bernard Rix.

Beneficial area UK and Israel.

Information available Annual reports and accounts on file at the Charity Commission.

Summary This trust gives a relatively small number of large grants to a group of organisations that are generally supported over a number of years. About half the money goes to organisations based in Israel. The trust shares offices and administration with the Wolfson Foundation, and an application to one may be considered by the other.

Grants to universities for research and scholarship are normally made under the umbrella of designated competitive programmes.

General The trust notes its concerns as:

- encouragement of medical and surgical studies and research
- advancement of medical and surgical sciences
- advancement of education, arts and religion

In 1996/97 the trust had assets of about £40 million, which generated the high income of £3.7 million. Grant giving for the year stood at £2.9 million. There were very low administrative costs, £17,000 in 1996/97.

Grants in that year were allocated as follows:

Science and technology	*£1,643,000*	*57%*
Medical and welfare	*£875,000*	*30%*
Education	*£329,000*	*11%*
Arts and humanities	*£37,000*	*1%.*

About half the total grant giving went to organisations in Israel.

The 1996/97 payments were as follows:

Science and technology:

Birmingham University (Arthritis Research, £4,000); Cambridge University (Brain Imaging Centre, £140,000); Edinburgh University (Cell and Molecular Biology Centre, £320,000; Molecular Medical Centre, £200,000); Hebrew University (Ein Karen Campus, £150,000); Imperial College (Organic Chemistry Centre, £119,000); Technion Institute of Technology (Wolfson Centre of Research, £250,000); Tel Aviv University (Biology, £250,000; Electrical Engineering, £66,000; Life Sciences, £17,000; Wolfson Building Renovations, £85,000); Weizmann Institute (Biology, £26,000 Functional brain imaging, £125,000 Physics, £33,000; Physics, £12,000).

Education

Ben Gurion University (Biotechnology, £35,000; Russian PhD students, £31,000; Jewish Day School, £50,000); Technion Institute of Technology (Russian Phd students, £37,000; Biology research, £34,000; Wallenberg Appeal, £3,000); Weizmann Institute (Russian PhD students, £38,000; Biophysics research, £35,000; Molecular genetic research, £34,000; Plant genetic research, (£32,000).

Medical and welfare

Hadassah Hospital (Mother and Child Centre, £875,000).

Arts and humanities

Ashmolean Museum, Oxford (gallery restoration, £6,000); Cathcart Hebrew Cemetery, Glasgow (Prayer Hall renovation, £15,000); Israel Chamber Orchestra and Risha Zion Symphony Orchestra (£8,000 each for instrument purchases).

Exclusions The trustees do not normally make grants for:

- research or other projects which are considered to be the proper responsibility of another funding body (such as a Research Council or the National Health Service);
- costs of running or attending concerts, conferences, exhibitions, lectures, expeditions etc.;
- non-specific appeals (including circulars) and requests for contributions to endowment funds;
- the making of films; funding deficits;
- funding the running costs or overheads of organisations;
- requests from charities whose role is the redistribution of funds to other charities.

Applications The trust shares its application procedure with the Wolfson Foundation. A brief explanatory letter, with organisation and project details, including costs and current shortfalls, will cause an up to date set of guidelines to be sent, if the charity is able to consider the project concerned.

The Guidelines themselves are demanding, not surprisingly given the scale on which the charity often operates. In Autumn 1998 they stood as follows:

Guidelines

Before embarking on a detailed proposal, prospective applicants are advised to explore its eligibility by submitting in writing a brief outline of the project with one copy of the organisation's most recent audited accounts.

There is no application form but detailed proposals (preferably no longer than 1000 words excluding appendices) should be in the following format:

1) In lay terms a brief summary of the immediate and longer term objectives of the project.

For historic buildings, please specify category of building (grade, listed building), date of current building and enclose a recent photograph.

2) The proposal describing in non-specialist language the need or the problem, and justifying the approach proposed to satisfy this need or to solve the problem.

3) An illustration of the benefits which could accrue to individuals, organisations, commerce or society at large from a successful project.

4) Detailed proposals involving research or scholarship should be included in an appendix for assessment by independent referees, with the chief investigator's curriculum vitae and a list of, say, up to ten key publications.

5) Two independent, professional referees should be nominated for all applications, with full names, addresses and telephone numbers (e.g. senior members of relevant local or health authority).

6) A financial section giving a detailed breakdown of the grant requested and any other relevant financial information such as:

(a) For capital projects: architects' or surveyors' costings of the planned building work, together with explanatory sketch and floor plans (size A4 only).

(b) For student accommodation, please specify:

Cost per room
Detailed breakdown of the building costs in the following format:

Building costs	££
Fixtures & fittings	££
	TOTAL
Professional fees	££
VAT	££
	TOTAL

(c) Proposals for funding the entire project.

(d) Estimates of the subsequent running and maintenance costs of the complete new development and how these costs will be met. (NB. The foundation will not normally meet the costs of professional fees, VAT or maintenance).

7) The application must come from the vice-chancellor, chairman or equivalent person of the applying organisation.

Thirteen copies of each application are requested.

Grants to universities for research and scholarship are normally made under the umbrella of designated competitive programmes. These evolve from time to time and those seeking support are advised to contact the Executive Secretary before making a full application. The same appeal cannot be considered by both this trust and by its sister body, the Wolfson Family Charitable Trust. An application to one may, however, be referred to the other at the discretion of the trustees.

Unsuccessful applications cannot normally be reconsidered. Nor, usually, can further applications from the same body be considered until one year has elapsed, in the case of unsuccessful applicants, or five years if a grant has been awarded.

The Wolfson Foundation

£18,336,000 (1996/97)

Hospitals and university medical departments, health

8 Queen Anne Street, London W1M 9LD
Tel: 0171-323 5730

Correspondent Dr Victoria Harrison, Director and Secretary

Trustees Lord Wolfson; Lady Wolfson; Lord Quirk; Lord Quinton; Sir Eric Ash; Lord Phillips; Lord McColl; Professor

Sir Leslie Turnberg; Mrs Janet Wolfson de Botton; Mrs Laura Wolfson Townsley.

Beneficial area Mainly UK and Israel.

Information available Annual report and accounts with grants list and limited analysis; guidelines for applicants.

Summary Around 200 grants (varying from £2,000 to £10,000,000) are made each year to charitable organisations working in education, medicine, care or the arts (in 1996/97, there were 18 specific subcategories). The majority of funds are awarded in a few large grants to hospitals and university medical departments. Awards are usually for capital projects (frequently for equipment) and occasionally for revenue costs (especially for medical training). Recurrent grants are rarely made, although an organisation may receive many grants over the years for various projects.

General The foundation was established in 1955 by the late Sir Isaac Wolfson with the objects of advancing 'the progress of health, education, arts and humanities'. The Wolfson family continue to a play a substantial, perhaps dominant, role in the foundation and, as with many family charities, only limited information is disclosed about the thinking behind its grants. The trustee body consists of unpaid family trustees and paid academic trustees (fees totalling £24,000 were paid to them to 1996 and again in 1997).

By the year ending April 1997, the foundation's assets totalled £506 million and an income of £21,287,000 had been generated. The low administration costs amounted to £198,000 – a penny for every £1 awarded or about £1,100 per grant paid (the average grant amount was £107,000).

The foundation's guidelines state:
'Grants are made only to registered charities or to exempt charities such as universities. Areas supported by the trustees are:

- Medicine and health care – including the prevention of disease and the care and treatment of the sick, disadvantaged and disabled.
- Research, science, technology and education – particularly where the benefits may accrue to the development of industry or commerce in the United Kingdom.
- Arts and the humanities – including libraries, museums, galleries, theatres, academies and historic

buildings.

'Eligible applications from registered charities for contributions to appeals will normally be considered only when at least 50% of that appeal has already been raised.

'Grants to universities for research and scholarship are normally made under the umbrella of designated competitive programmes in which vice-chancellors and principals are invited to participate from time to time.

'Applications from university researchers are not usually considered outside these programmes

'The trustees make several types of grants which are not necessarily independent of each other:

- Capital projects: grants may contribute towards the cost of erecting a new building or' extension, or of renovating and refurbishing existing buildings.
- Equipment grants: the supply of equipment for specific purposes and/ or furnishing and fittings
- Recurrent costs: grants in this category are not normally provided unless they form part of a designated programme.

'Priorities, which are described in this report, include the renovation of historic buildings and libraries, support for preventative medicine, welfare programmes for people with special needs and education. Grants are made to universities both for student accommodation and equipment for research. Awards for the latter are now normally made under the umbrella of designated competitive programmes in which vice-chancellors and principals are invited periodically to participate.'

The 1996/97 report states:
'The Wolfson Foundation is a charitable foundation set up in 1955, whose aims were then stated by the founder to be to advance the progress of health, education, arts and humanities. These remain the aims of the trustees today. As a general policy, grants are given to act as a catalyst, to back excellence and talent and to provide support for promising future projects which may be currently underfunded, particularly for renovation and equipment. There is a continued emphasis on science and technology, research and education, and health. Trustees meet twice a year and are advised by panels comprising trustees and specialists which meet before the main board meetings.'

Grants in 1996/97

173 awards totalling £18,581,000 were agreed in the year and 262 amounting to £12,356,000 were paid. At April 1997 the foundation had committed to £27,767,000 in future gifts. This entry looks at the 173 grants that were agreed.

Around 70% of the total value of these awards went to university medical departments and hospitals. The grants are categorised in the pie chart herewith. Although the foundation does not analyse grants by geography it appears that the vast majority of funds were disbursed for capital projects. Grants were made all across Britain but with 86% of funds going to organisations in Southern England.

Health and welfare
– *Preventive medicine and clinical research:* Six grants amounted to £12 million. £10.8 million of this money went in two grants to University College London (the details of which are given

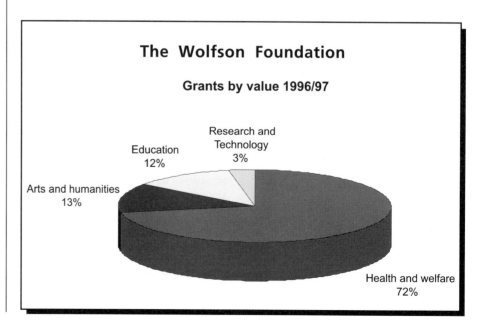

The Wolfson Foundation

Grants by value 1996/97

Education 12%

Research and Technology 3%

Arts and humanities 13%

Health and welfare 72%

below in the trust's words). Other awards were to the University of Glasgow (£250,000 towards equipment for the Department of Molecular Medicine) and to the National Hospital for Neurology and Neurosurgery (£220,000 towards out-patient equipment for the Neurorehabilitation Centre).

– *Hospitals:* In the year under review the Edith Wolfson Medical Centre, Israel received £250,000 from the foundation and Sarah Herzog Memorial Hospital £20,000. Both awards were for equipment.

– *Hospices:* A total of £114,000 went to six hospices: in Lanarkshire, Gwynedd, Merseyside, Essex, Kent and East Sussex. Four grants were for £25,000, one for £11,000 and another for £3,000.

– *People with special needs:* Eleven organisations benefited from awards amounting to £650,000. Included among these were gifts to: Ravenswood Foundation (£250,000 for five flats); Jewish Care (£100,000 for two rooms); Royal Hospital for Neuro-Disability, London (£100,000 for equipment); and Treloar Trust (£57,000 capital grant).

Arts and humanities

– *Heritage:* Nineteen grants between £10,000 and £700,000 were made for capital projects (totalling £1,685,000).

Most of this money was awarded to the following organisations: National Maritime Museum, Greenwich (£600,000 to £700,000 over three years); Royal Botanic Gardens, Kew (£250,000 over two years); Dulwich Picture Gallery (£125,000); and Scottish United Services Museum (£100,000). The National Art Collections Fund received £100,000 for buying works of art.

– *Music and dance:* Grants went to Sadler's Wells Theatre (£75,000) and City of Birmingham Symphony (£25,000).

– *Historic buildings:* Nineteen churches and one synagogue were awarded funds totalling £54,000. They were located all over Britain – Exeter, Folkestone, Oxfordshire, Powys, Norfolk, Yorkshire, Kilmarnock, Keith etc... and typically received about £2,000 each.

– *Libraries:* Eleven donations were made. All except two (for the Central School of Speech and Drama, £15,000 and the University of Manchester £87,000) were £50,000 gifts to Wolfson Technology Resource Centres based in nine major universities.

– *Literary award for history:* This year the £15,000 award went to Professor H G Matthew for the biography "Gladstone 1875-1898" (OUP)'

Education

– *Higher education:* Three grants totalled £240,000: Lucy Cavendish College Cambridge was awarded £115,000 for renovation; Magdalen College Oxford was given £100,000 towards a gallery for manuscripts and treasures; and Henley Management College received £25,000.

– *Medical education:* £174,000 was disbursed in 22 donations including: £25,000 to the University of Liverpool; £19,000 to Charing Cross and Westminster Medical School; £13,000 to St Bartholomew's and Royal London Medical College; £12,000 to University of Wales College of Medicine and £11,000 to the University of Bristol.

– *Student accommodation:* There were two grants awarded in the year to Wolfson College, Cambridge (£250,000) and Oatridge Agricultural College, West Lothian (£50,000).

– *Learned societies:* A total of £325,000 was paid out in four gifts to The British Academy (£100,000 towards the refurbishment of a lecture room); The Royal Society (£100,000 for renovation work); Royal Society of Edinburgh (£100,000 for renovation); and Royal Society for Arts, Manufacturing and Commerce (£25,000)

– *Secondary education:* Most funds were distributed for equipment (£880,000 – 89% of the total in this subcategory). Such grants varied from £35,000 to £5,000 but most (24) were for £20,000. Schools which received grants of £20,000 included: Great Yarmouth High School; Sunderland High School; London Oratory School; Watford Grammar School for Boys; Wolverhampton Girl's High School; and Ninestiles Community School, Birmingham. Two grants were made for building work to John Cabot City Technology College, Bristol (£75,000) and Royal Grammar School, Newcastle-upon-Tyne (£30,000).

– *Primary education:* A single gift of £5,000 went to Volunteer Reading Help.

– *Music:* £53,000 was disbursed in six donations, the largest of which were: £25,000 to the Yehudi Menuhin School; and £6,000 each to the Royal Academy of Music and the Royal Northern College of Music. The latter two awards were made from the Wolfson Instrument Fund.'

Research and Technology

Four grants totalling £509,000 were made to:

Cranfield University – Wolfson Laboratory for Microsystems Engineering (£250,000)

Cranfield Biotechnology Centre (£70,000 towards equipment for the extended Wolfson Centre);

University of Sheffield, Krebs Institute (£95,000 for the renovation of electron microscopy suite);

The Institute of Psychiatry (£94,000 towards equipment for molecular genetics unit).

The foundation is not a member of the Association of Medical Research Charities and it does not say whether the funded projects are subject to a peer review process. However, the foundation is believed to operate such a process.

The foundation's own description of a few selected grants are printed as follows in the 1996/97 Report under the heading 'New Developments':

University College London, Wolfson Institute: -The foundation has made a grant of £10 million for a new Wolfson Institute, under the direction of Professor Salvador Moncad, which has been established at UCL. The Institute's objective is to undertake research aimed at the prevention of major causes of death and illness and it is the intention to form national and international partnerships with industry to develop more commercial links to generate income for investment in these areas of strategic medical research.

The Wolfson Foundation

Summary of grants	1995 to 1996		1996 to 1997	
Health and welfare	£36,100,000	18%	£13,400,000	72%
Arts and humanities	£25,000,000	12%	£2,500,000	13%
Education	£47,700,000	24%	£2,200,000	12%
Research and Technology	£92,300,000	46%	£500,000	3%
Total	£201,100,000	100%	£18,600,000	100%

University Library Programme: 'The trustees decided to establish Wolfson Technology Resources Centres attached to the libraries of selected universities. Nine grants were made totalling £450,000 to facilitate students' access to IT databases for science, technology and medicine.

Health and preventative medicine: 'The trustees have continued to fund improvements in preventative medicine and have made a grant of £1,000,000 to the Institute of Child Health in Bristol to assist its relocation.

'Advances in the treatment of breast cancer and prostate cancer have been helped with a grant of £800,000 for Professor S Bown's work at the National Medical Laser Centre, UCL, where a unit has been set up with the aim of revolutionising the minimally invasive management of localised cancers. The foundation's grant has been used towards a second generation magnetic resonance scanner.

People with Special Needs: 'Grants totalling more than £600,000 have been made in the year for people with special needs and learning difficulties these include a grant of £250,000 for Ravenswood Village, Berkshire, to provide independent living facilities for some residents.

Heritage Programme: 'The foundation has entered in to partnership with the Heritage Lottery Fund whereby applicants may apply to both bodies, with a shared assessment process. nineteen awards were offered, totalling £1,685,000, including £250,000 to the Royal Botanic Gardens, Kew and £600,000 – £700,000 over three years to the National Maritime Museum, Greenwich.

Medical Training: 'The Wolfson Intercalated Awards, totalling about £150,000 a year are made for selected medical students who wish to spend a year between their pre-clinical and clinical studies on a research project. The purpose of the awards is to support outstanding students who are unlikely to pursue a clinical research career. The awards are or tuition fees, subsistence and project costs. Nominations are made by the medical faculties.'

Exclusions Grants are not made to individuals.

The trustees do not normally make grants for:

- Research or other projects which are considered to be the proper responsibility of another funding body (such as a Research Council or the National Health Service);
- Costs of running or attending meetings, conferences, lectures, exhibitions, concerts, expeditions, etc.;
- Non-specific appeals (including circulars) and requests for contributions to endowment funds;
- Making of films or videos;
- Overheads, running or administrative costs, VAT or professional fees;
- Charities which redistribute funds to other charitable bodies;
- Research involving live animals;
- The purchase of buildings.

Applications Before embarking on a detailed proposal, prospective applicants are encouraged to explore its eligibility by submitting in writing a brief outline of the project with one copy of the organisation's most recent audited accounts.

There is no application form but detailed proposals (preferably no longer than 1000 words excluding appendices) should be in the following format:

1) In lay terms a brief summary of the immediate and longer term objectives of the project.
   For historic buildings, please specify category of building (grade, listed building), date of current building and enclose a recent photograph.
2) The proposal describing in non-specialist language the need or the problem, and justifying the approach proposed to satisfy this need or to solve the problem.
3) An illustration of the benefits which could accrue to individuals, organisations, commerce or society at large from a successful project.
4) Detailed proposals involving research or scholarship should be included in an appendix for assessment by independent referees, with the chief investigator's curriculum vitae and a list of, say, up to ten key publications.
5) Two independent, professional referees should be nominated for all applications, with full names and addresses (eg. senior members of relevant local or health authority).
6) A financial section giving a detailed breakdown of the grant requested and any other relevant financial information such as:
   (a) For capital projects: architects' or surveyors' costings of the planned building work, together with explanatory sketch and floor plans (size A4 only).
   (b) For student accommodation, please specify:

cost per room
detailed breakdown of the building costs in the following format:

Building costs	££
Fixtures & fittings	££
TOTAL	
Professional fees	££
VAT	££
TOTAL	

(c) Proposals for funding the entire project.
(d) Estimates of the subsequent running and maintenance costs of the complete new development and how these costs will be met. (NB. The foundation will not normally the costs of professional fees, VAT or maintenance).
7) The application must come from the vice-chancellor, chairman or equivalent person of the applying organisation.

Thirteen copies of each application are requested with **one** copy of the audited accounts for the most recent two years.

Applications from organisations can be considered if they come within an active umbrella programme. These evolve from time to time and those seeking support are advised to contact the director before making a full application. The same appeal cannot be considered by both this trust and by its sister body, the Wolfson Family Charitable Trust. An application to one may, however, be referred to the other at the discretion of the trustees. Unsuccessful applications cannot normally be reconsidered. Nor, usually, can further applications from the same body be considered until one year has elapsed, in the case of unsuccessful applicants, or five years if a grant has been awarded.

Trustees meet in June and December and applications have to be made by 15th March and 15th September.

The Geoffrey Woods Charitable Foundation

£350,000 (1996/97)

Young people, education, disability, health

The Girdlers Company, Girdlers Hall, Basinghall Avenue, London EC2V 5DD
Tel: 0171-638 0488

Correspondent The Clerk

Trustees The Girdlers Company; N K Maitland; A J R Fairclough.

Beneficial area UK and overseas

Information available Accounts on file at the Charity Commission.

General The foundation is administered by the Girdlers Company. The grants list shows that the foundation supports a number of education, social, health, and youth charities.

The foundation administers funding through three funds:

1. Benefactors Fund (£214,000): by far the largest of the funds, it supports the general charitable aims of the foundation.

2. New Zealand Scholarship Fund: usually supports 3-4 New Zealand Scholars to Corpus Christi College, Cambridge (£13,000), a specific grant to Corpus Christi (£40,000), and another item of about £40,000 for 'college and other fees'.

3. General Court Charity Fund : Usually to support donations by anyone in the Girdlers Committee who makes a covenant with any charity. The foundation will match the covenant by up to double its value.

In 1996/97 the foundation received, through donations from the Girdlers Company, an income of £528,000. Total grant giving amounted to £350,000

By far the largest grant went to the London Federation of Clubs for Young People (£30,000). Other youth organisations supported included Crown and Manor Boys Club (£5,000, the second of three); Surrey County Cricket Board, youth section (£3,000); Surrey County Cricket Board, LCCA initiative (£6,000); and the Anna Scher Children's Theatre (£2,500, the third of three).

Several grants were also made for education: Cordwainers College (£5,600); Garden School (£10,000, the third of three); Chelsea Physics Garden (£1,500); and Kings College Cambridge (£5,000). A number of grants went to a variety of religious organisations including some overseas: Westminster Abbey Choir School (£10,000); All Saints Cathedral, Nairobi (£5,000); Sudan Church Association (£4,000); and St Pauls Church, Durban (£1,000).

Other grants went to health, medical and social organisations, the largest of which were the Almshouse Association (£10,000); Queen Elizabeth Foundation for the Disabled (£5,000, the second of three); and the National Spinal Injuries Unit (£5,000, the fourth of five).

Exclusions No grants to individuals for education.

Applications In writing to the correspondent. Deadlines for applications are the end of September and end of February.

The Woodward Trust

£1,045,000 (approved 1997)

The arts (particularly opera), children, disability, welfare, general

See entry for the 'Sainsbury Family Charitable Trusts'
Tel: 0171-410 0330

Correspondent Michael Pattison

Trustees Mrs Camilla D Woodward; Shaun A Woodward MP; Miss J S Portrait.

Beneficial area UK and overseas.

Information available A report and accounts are available. The principal officers of the trust are Michael Pattison, director, Paul Spokes, financial director and Miss K MacLeod, administrator.

Summary This trust is one of the Sainsbury Family Charitable Trusts which share a joint administration. Each year a small number of large, often capital, grants are made, mainly to opera. The trust also gives a large number of small grants under £10,000 to organisations working in a wide range of activities including health, disability, community and social welfare. It shows a particular interest in activities of all kinds that relate to children and young people.

General This is the trust of Camilla, née Sainsbury, and of her husband, Shaun Woodward, Conservative MP for Witney in Oxfordshire. The trust joined the Sainsbury Family Charitable Trust joint administration in 1997. Prior to this it was administered by its accountants and its registered office was the Woodward's home in Oxfordshire.

The trust had a net income in 1997 of £468,000 and a total of over £545,000 available for distribution. Its asset value was £14.8 m.

Grants paid		
1997	*1996*	*1995*
£554,000	*£554,000*	*£200,000*

The change in the trust's administration has coincided with a change in the presentation of its grant making in its accounts. The annual report in 1997 has divided the trust's giving into categories, within which the grants of £1,000 and more are listed. (Four anonymous grants totalling over £26,000 were paid and reported in confidence to the Charity Commission.) However there is, as yet, no narrative description of its grant making policy or decisions.

A total of 143 grants was approved in 1997 totalling over £1 million. The table herewith analyses the grants paid.

In 1997 out of a total of 142 grants, only 11 (12 in 1996) were for £10,000 or more. All but one of these was listed under 'Capital appeals anThe trust supplies an application sheet backed by a table of its grants over three years according to their category and scale. Most importantly it notes that 'grants of £10,000 or more tend to be through personal contacts or are areas in which the trustees have a particular interest'.

Capital appeals and special applications

This category is revealing – to a certain extent. What is meant by 'special

The Woodward Trust

	£	grants	repeat grants
Capital appeals/ special applications	393,00	34	8
Education	6,000	2	0
Community/Social Welfare	79,000	51	10
Overseas	8,000	8	3
Disability/health	56,000	40	11
Arts	7,000	3	0
Environment	5,000	4	0
TOTAL	**554,000**	**142**	**32**

applications' and why aren't certain grants classified under a specific category? Many of these larger grants run over a three year period, at least. A high proportion of the total funding in this category (44%) was devoted to major national arts organisations. Opera stands out as the main beneficiary of this trust. The largest grant in 1997 was £150,000 to the Royal Opera House Redevelopment Appeal (with £16,000 to the Royal Opera House Trust which had also received £24,000 in both 1996 and 1995). In addition a further £350,000 was approved for the Royal Opera HOther larger grants were made to ChildLine, founded by Esther Rantzen (£42,000 paid, £33,000 committed, plus £33,000 given in the previous year), Working for a Charity (£12,000 paid, £12,000 committed, plus £12,000 given in the previous year); Understanding Industry (£12,000 paid, £10,000 committed, plus an additional £5,000 under the Education category); Jesus College, Cambridge Shaun Woodward's alma mater (£10,000 paid, £10,000 committed, and also given in the previous year).

Also under this category were grants of £38,583 (£57,688 in 1996) donated to the Headley and Jerusalem trusts.

Community and Social Welfare

In 1997 the Who Cares? Trust which works with and for children in care (£10,289) received the only grant of over £10,000 which was outside the Capital appeals aThe long list of grants with the 1996 report which were not categorised seemed to show a particular interest in organisations working with children and young people. This interest is still apparent in 1997. About a quarter of the grants listed in the 1997 report (20 out of 84) are to such organisations: Save a Child; Barnardos; Child Psychotherapy Trust; Children 1st; Fair Play for Children; National Playbus Association; Parentline UK; Pestalozzi Children's Village Appeal; Youth at Risk; Youthreach Greenwich; Children's Heart Foundation; BLISS (Baby Life Support Systems); Osteopathic Centre for Children; Royal School for Deaf Children; Little Haven Children's Hospice; Merseyside Youth Association Ltd; Jewels for Children. They are listed under the Community and Social Welfare and the Disability and Health categories.

Very particular personal interest and involvement also shows with the small grant to the Ben Hardwick Fund (£Most of the listed grants in 1997 fell between £1,000 and £5,000. However the number of small grants under £1,000 dropped

considerably in 1997 compared with the previous year. Although they still comprised a third of all grants paid (47 out of 142), in the previous year as high a proportion as two thirds of the grants (113 out of 180 grants) were for less than £1,000. The trust then had a 'scattergun' style of charitable giving very unlike the approach of the other Sainsbury Family Charitable Trusts which give within the framework of stated policies and categories of giving, and where fewer and larger grants are made, which may be more likely to effect beneficial change. It seems probable that the change of administration has started to affect the manner of this trust's giving, but, as yet, not radically.

Exclusions Individuals, students, expedition costs or fees for courses.

Applications 'The trustees give priority to charities where they have a particular interest and/or personal knowledge. Unsolicited appeals are only considered once the applicant has completed an application form and submitted its annual report and audited accounts. Applications are considered twice a year, generally in January and July. Repeat grants are considered.'

The trust states that it considers applications within the categories listed in the table above. In addition it lists 'Religion' which does not feature in the categorisation for 1997 (although the grant to the Jerusalem Trust could be listed under this head).

The Zochonis Charitable Trust

£927,000 (1996/97)

General, especially Greater Manchester

Cussons House, Bird Hall Lane, Stockport, SK3 OXN

Correspondent The Secretary

Trustees John Zochonis, Richard B James; Alan Whittaker.

Beneficial area UK, particularly Manchester and its surrounding areas.

Information available Full accounts are on file at the Charity Commission, but without the required narrative report.

General The trust was established by John Basil Zochonis in 1977, who remains as a trustee. The trust gives grant to international and national organisations, with a preference for the

Manchester region.

Assets amounted to £21.5 million in 1997. This generated an income of £924,000, which included a donation of £40,000 from Miss C Zochonis.

For 1996/97 72 grants were granted, with the top 39 accounting for £710,000 of the total. Grants ranged in size from £100,000 to £2,000. Most of the grants were between £5,000 and £10,000.

Examples of the larger grants included those to: Lord Mayor of Manchester (£100,000), Voluntary Service Overseas (£70,000), CRISIS (£60,000), BESO (£31,000), Henshaws Society for the Blind (£30,000), NSPCC (£25,000), Peter May Memorial Appeal (£25,000), Royal Exchange Theatre (£25,000) and the Greater Manchester Shrievalty Police Trust (£25,000).

Grants to the Manchester area take nearly half the total grants and seem to support general causes. Examples include Manchester and Family Self Service Unit (£7,500), Manchester Cathedral (£5,000), Manchester Initiative (£5,000), Northern Chambers Orchestra (£10,000), Relate Manchester (£5,000) and Victim Support Manchester (£10,000).

A number of grants were given to various national organisation, though since a narrative is not included on what the grant is for, one cannot tell if they are supporting local the local Manchester branch or not. Grants were given to various health and social organisation such as Action Research (£5,000), Child Victim Support (£5,000), Family Welfare Association (£5,000), National Missing Persons Helpline (£10,000), and the Red Cross (£3,500).

Grants were also given to international charities with a variety of themes including Africa Now (£5,000), Book Aid International (£5,000), Sight Savers International (£5,000) and International Spinal Research (£10,000).

Happily Manchester, which is often starved of grants and donations is seen to be taking a large part of the grants list.

Exclusions No grants for individuals.

Applications In writing to the secretary by registered charities only. The trustees had not wished for an entry in the previous edition of this guide because of the large number of appeals they were unable to satisfy and the way in which such entries generate further appeals which cannot be helped.

Index